BUSINESS IN A CHANGING WORLD

Third Edition

WILLIAM H. CUNNINGHAM
Chancellor of the University of Texas System
Austin, Texas

RAMON J. ALDAG
Professor of Management
University of Wisconsin-Madison
Madison, Wisconsin

STANLEY B. BLOCK
Professor of Finance
Texas Christian University
Fort Worth, Texas

COLLEGE DIVISION South-Western Publishing Co.

Cincinnati Ohio

The cover illustration for *Business in a Changing World* is representative of several elements in today's changing business world. Symbolized by the globe, circuit board, gears, robotic arm, and human figure are the international environment, technology, manufacturing, management, social and ethical considerations, and human resources.

Acquisitions Editor: Randy G. Haubner
Developmental Editor: Cinci Stowell
Production Editor: Sharon L. Smith
Production House: GTS Graphics
Cover Designer: Ron Chan
Interior Designer: Joseph M. Devine
Marketing Manager: Scott D. Person

Cunningham, William Hughes.
    Business in a changing world / William H. Cunningham, Ramon J.
  Aldag, Stanley B. Block. — 3rd ed.
      p.   cm.
    Rev. ed. of: Introduction to business. 2nd ed. c1989.
    Includes index.
    ISBN 0-538-81391-1
    1. Business enterprises—United States.   I. Aldag, Ramon J.,
  II. Block, Stanley B.   III. Cunningham, William Hughes.
  Introduction to business. IV. Title.
  HD31.C844   1993
  650—dc20   92-16799
                                                                        CIP

2 3 4 5 6 7 KI 8 7 6 5 4 3

Printed in the United States of America

To my wife Isabella, son John, and parents Earl and Ann.

—Bill Cunningham

To my wife Holly, daughters Elizabeth and Katherine, and parents Melvin and Joyce.

—Ray Aldag

To my wife Cathy, children Michelle and Randy, and mother Mary.

—Stan Block

TO THE INSTRUCTOR

If there is one thing for certain in the world of business, it is change. New technologies, new discoveries, new needs, and new competition precipitate and drive change in all facets of business. While change itself is not new, the changes in today's business world seem to be greater and to occur more rapidly than ever before. And, like dominoes, change in one area of business affects another and another. Sooner or later, everyone and everything—including you, your students, and your course—are affected. The challenge is to keep up with change. This is precisely why *Business in a Changing World*, Third Edition, was developed—to meet your changing needs as an instructor and your students' changing needs as they prepare for careers in today's world.

Even in the short three years since the second edition of this text was published, there have been dramatic changes in our world that have impacted and will continue to impact the course of business: The fall of the Soviet economy. The emergence of global markets. Our recent economic swings. A continuing rise in dual-income households and the effect on the workforce as well as on the traditional family structure. Politics and public policy initiatives. The federal deficit. The immense changes in the banking and savings and loan industries. Challenges to America's role as world leader. Racial unrest. The AIDS problem. The aging American population. The ever-increasing importance of women and minorities in the workplace. FAX machines and cellular phones. These are but a few of the changes that affect the world of business.

Teaching students in a world so complex and ever changing is a challenge no one understands better than you. That very challenge is met in this third edition—a text changed so significantly from its predecessor that we even changed its name—from *Introduction to Business* to **Business in a Changing World**.

A TEXT AND SUPPLEMENT PACKAGE CHANGED TO MEET YOUR CHANGING NEEDS

Business in a Changing World is a single-source, introductory business text that provides comprehensive business basics in the context of our world as your students know it. The book has every feature and supplement currently available in introductory business texts. But that's not why you should choose it. *You should choose it because it takes you beyond the expected.* For example, it emphasizes critical thinking skills for students. Our cases will challenge students to think analytically. Read more about this topic on page vii of this preface. The book also emphasizes potential careers. In fact, it clearly stands in first place on this topic, thoroughly covering this very large concern of your students.

The text's material is fresh, relevant, accurate and as current as the Los Angeles riots and Barcelona Olympics. It is written in a quick-reading style and highlighted with abundant real-world terms, cases, profiles, and meaningful, relevant examples. We've purposely avoided speaking in abstracts or academic terminology. As experienced educators, we know the importance of "taking the students with us" on every page of the book.

The text and supplementary materials also have been developed in response to another change you face—the ever-increasing constraints and demands on your time. You can rely on *Business in a Changing World* to be the text package that lets you enter the classroom prepared and ready to teach. And you can trust it to be valid, current, and accurate from its content to the test bank, transparencies, annotations, and study guide.

Making the text unique among competitive texts is its *authors' expertise*. There are more than 50 years of combined classroom experience among the three authors. Each of us represents expertise in one of the three major areas of business—marketing, management, and finance. No other business introductory text can make this claim. While other texts are often written by professional textbook authors, *Business in a Changing World* comes from experienced educators and business practitioners. We think our real-world backgrounds and first-hand experiences with the material add a dimension to the text that educators like yourselves will appreciate.

THE EASY WAY TO MEET THE CHALLENGE OF CHANGE

Business in a Changing World meets the challenge of change. It covers all of the basic material and principles, but goes a step further to integrate those principles with today's business environment. The text is truly mainstream—real world in its wording, topics, and examples. Examples cover the full scope of business, from Gonzalez's Garage (extended example throughout Chapter 5) to General Motors. We wrote the text specifically to make it easy for you to keep your course up-to-date with today's changing world of business without making any dramatic changes to your teaching style. In fact, it eases your teaching with what we feel are the most helpful textbook features and tips, and the most complete assortment of support materials available.

The goal of the text was two-fold: (1) to equip you with a complete, accurate, and current text package that lets you easily adapt your course to the changing world of business and (2) to help students learn the basics of business as they relate to today's business climate, the first step to successful career preparation. We hope you'll agree that *Business in a Changing World* achieves these goals.

FEATURES OF *BUSINESS IN A CHANGING WORLD*

Critical to developing this Third Edition was that it quickly catch the interest of students with features that speak about a changing world of business—the world your students know. The text accomplishes this with special features including:

Current Topics/New Concepts

Current topics and new concepts in business can be found in all 25 chapters. Among those discussed are fetal protection policies, world class manufacturing, electronic bulletin boards, downfall of the Communist party and the new economic order in the former Soviet Union, competitive changes in the airline industry, slow growth of the U.S. economy, the savings and loan crisis and changing practices in banking, characteristics of entrepreneurs with a special profile of Ross Perot, the goal of stockholder wealth maximization (a text exclusive), the new European Community, and the use of insurance to help defray the costs of the Los Angeles riots.

A Major Focus on Careers

In response to your students' pressing concerns over landing a job and developing a career, *Business in a Changing World* provides students the most comprehensive look at career possibilities of any business introductory text. The text offers:

- A full chapter on careers.
- A careers appendix that highlights growing career fields.
- "Business Career" annotations throughout the text that provide a brief description and average salary of career options.
- A *Business Career Planning Guide*, by James D. Porterfield of The Pennsylvania State University (sold separately). This guide systematically leads students to assess their abilities and interests, match these characteristics to business career possibilities, and conduct a successful job search.
- Five regional and numerous city supplements accompany the guide. These outline economic conditions, quality of life, present and future employment prospects, and growing career fields in each region or city. These supplements are written by local experts who accurately provide the local flavor, attitudes, and business climate. The supplements let you customize the guide to your area or the area of interest to your students.

Learning Objectives Integrated among Text and Support Materials

At the beginning of each chapter is a list of learning objectives covering all key concepts. Next to each is a numbered icon: **1** . We have employed these icons to integrate the learning objectives throughout the text and all support materials. You'll see that the icons reappear in the margins of the chapter next to the related materials and again in the summaries and review questions, identifying where that learning objective is fulfilled. The icons also appear in the *Instructor's Resource Guide*, *Test Bank*, and *Study Guide*. This concept helps you and your students use the text's wealth of material to meet all learning goals. When students need further review to meet a certain objective, you and they can quickly identify the material covering that objective by simply looking for the icon.

Critical Thinking Cases To Help Teach Decision-Making Skills

Our society has an enormous capacity for generating data, but our ability to use the data to make good decisions has lagged behind. Experts contend that this is because too often we accept the data presented to us at face value, rather than evaluating it critically and making the effort to understand and interpret it. In the hope of better preparing the next generation of business leaders, many educators are beginning to place greater emphasis on developing critical thinking skills in students.

Business in a Changing World does so with an integrative "Critical Thinking Case" at the end of each of the text's six major parts. In the cases, the student is exposed to bias, propaganda, inadequate evidence, and poor decision making. Because you are dealing with an introductory course, we have specially designed the cases to be short, yet provocative. The cases cover topics from buying a company to the business side of intercollegiate sports. They challenge students to "dig" to get at the true issues; to not only find the solution, but sometimes also identify the problem; to identify cause and effect relationships, and to reconsider their original thinking once a new piece of information is introduced.

Real-Life End-of-Chapter Cases

Nothing teaches like example. That's why we have included so many examples from actual companies. Fifty end-of-chapter cases are featured throughout the text, relating chapter material to reality. Your students will read about such companies as R.J. Reynolds, Beech-Nut, GM Saturn, Disney, Citicorp, Union Carbide, Hewlett-Packard, Philip Morris, Carnival Cruise Lines, Blockbuster Video, IBM, Frito-Lay, McDonalds, and more.

Boxed Features

Students learn material best when it is presented visually. Therefore, we have highlighted in colored boxes issues and examples students will find both interesting and particularly relevant to today's business world:

C O N T R O V E R S I A L   I S S U E

The text addresses many of the most controversial topics in business today. Among them ... Are unions dying? Should whistleblowers be protected? Is there a glass ceiling? Do stock prices move in a random fashion? Should health insurance be nationalized? Should accounting data be reported on the basis of current values rather than historical costs?

E T H I C A L   I S S U E

Ethics are a growing concern in business today. Students need to understand that there is often no clear right and wrong to many ethical issues. The text helps students think through some ethical dilemmas with features like "Genetic Testing," "Clean Manufacturing," "To Go Along To Get Along Or Not," and "A Verdict on Greed: The Michael Milken Case."

I N T E R N A T I O N A L   E X A M P L E

More and more the world is becoming the marketplace. Multinational firms are breaking down traditional national boundaries to produce and sell internationally. Students are given a taste of the trend toward internationalization with features like "Decision Support for the 1992 Barcelona Olympics," "McDonald's Franchise in Russia," "The Pirating of U.S. Intellectual Property," and "Nestle, Coke and South Korea."

Students are intrigued by business leaders and their stories of success or failure. The text profiles 25 business leaders representing a wide variety of industries. Some of those included are: Ross Perot, the "Billionaire Boy Scout" businessman whose independent candidacy for President shook U.S. politics; Rear Admiral Grace Hopper, the driving force behind the development of COBOL; Edwin Gray, who presided over the S&L industry and whose warnings of impending crisis fell on deaf ears; Sam Walton, founder of Wal-Mart and the wealthiest person in the U.S. prior to his death in April, 1992; Ben Cohen, the off-beat CEO of Ben & Jerry's Homemade Inc.; Liz Claiborne, founder and Chairwoman of the Board for Liz Claiborne, Inc.; Myra McDaniel, distinguished attorney; Erroll Davis, President and CEO of WPL Holdings; and others.

Our Lighter Side features provide students with a look at the humorous side of business, with boxes such as "How To Succeed in Business the Unusual Way," "Leakers," and others.

Pedagogy Designed to Aid Comprehension

Learning Objectives The text and supplements are organized around goals for student learning.

Chapter Opening Vignettes To grab students' attention, we open each chapter with a brief business scenario that pulls students into the chapter's material.

Margin Definitions These bold definitions highlight and define key words where they are first introduced. Terms and definitions are compiled in a glossary at the end of the book for quick reference.

End-Of-Chapter Features

• *Summary Points* The main points of the chapter are succinctly summarized and related back to the learning objectives at the beginning of the chapter, via numbered icons.

- *Key Terms*   Important terms are listed with the page number where they are introduced.
- *Review Questions*   These questions are designed for students to check their understanding of chapter material, and also are integrated with the learning objectives through the numbered icons.
- *Discussion Questions*   Written to provoke lively classroom discussion, these questions challenge students to "think" about the material presented.
- *Experiential Exercises*   These exercises get students out of the classroom and into the business world to interview local business people, research current topics, or observe people at work.

ABUNDANT ANNOTATIONS PUNCTUATE INSTRUCTOR'S EDITION

In this Third Edition, we have gone to great lengths to include in the *Instructor's Edition* all of the margin information you want most—the tips, asides, and teaching aids that enrich your course, ease your preparation, and encourage classroom discussion.

- *Example*   Usually from business publications, these interesting examples can be used in your lectures to further illustrate text concepts.
- *For Discussion*   These provocative questions can help you spark lively classroom discussion.
- *Transparencies*   Cues in the margin indicate the appropriate point in the lecture to show the corresponding transparency and provide key points to emphasize or questions to ask.
- *Class Activity*   These are ideas for instructive group activities that can be done during class time or as outside projects.
- *Teaching Tip*   These tips mark places where students often have difficulty, and provide hints and points to stress to help them understand.
- *Additional Information*   To enhance your lectures, these notes provide information that goes beyond the text presentation.

VIDEODISC TECHNOLOGY MAKES LECTURES COME ALIVE

Laser videodisc technology is a new addition to the instructor package. The *Business in a Changing World* videodisc contains over 90 minutes of text-related video, as well as over 1,000 definitions, transparencies, and text illustrations for classroom projection. The videos and illustrations can be viewed in any order you choose, and, with an optional computer and South-Western software, you can prepare a complete video "script" of your classroom presentation ahead of time. An accompanying *Videodisc Guide* describes how to integrate this technology in your classroom. A compatible "CAV-type" videodisc player is required to use this ancillary.

A CRATE FULL OF SUPPLEMENTARY MATERIALS EQUIP YOU FOR SUCCESSFUL TEACHING

The text package for *Business in a Changing World* is flexibly designed to adapt to any teaching style. It includes all of the support materials you told us you need most. The support materials are organized to shorten your preparation time and ease your teaching load. Specifically, supplementary materials are bound, but perforated, so that you can remove all materials relating to a chapter and place them together in the preprinted manila chapter folder (included). This enables you to carry to class only the materials you need. For your convenience, many of the support materials are packed in a crate that accommodates hanging file folders. The crate is easy to handle and store. Every item in the text package provides an opportunity to further enhance your course and enlighten your students to the changing world of business.

Included in the crate:

- Manila folders, printed with the 25 chapter titles, plus "front matter" and "back matter."
- *Annotated Instructor's Edition* of the text, which is 3-hole punched and looseleaf.
- *Instructor's Resource Guide.* Along with learning objectives, chapter summaries, and complete solutions to text questions and cases, this comprehensive guide contains a course organizer for easy planning plus lecture outlines you can really use—not just a list of headings. At the end of the guide are additional discussion topics and activities to supplement your lectures.
- 150 multicolor acetate *Transparencies,* accompanied by *Transparency Lecture Notes.*
- *Test Bank.* More than 3,700 questions, each with a page reference indicating where the concept is covered in the text, a level-of-difficulty rating, and a numbered icon referencing it to the learning objective.
- *Business Documents* for handouts or overhead display.
- "*The Great Crate*" - a unique departure from conventional handling and storage methods.

Additional items not in the crate:

- *Annotated Instructor's Edition* (hardbound version).
- *Study Guide,* integrated with the learning objectives in the text and containing an abundance of questions that will help your students prepare for tests.
- *Business Career Planning Guide.* With this text-workbook you may choose from among five regional supplements and numerous city supplements to suit your students' needs.
- 25 custom-produced *videos* enhancing key topics covered in the text.
- *Video Instructor's Manual,* which includes descriptions, discussion questions, suggested uses, teaching objectives, chapter integration, and multiple-choice questions for each video.
- *Videodisc* and *Videodisc Guide* (discussed on p. x of this preface).
- *Lecture Presentation Manager,* a dynamic presentation software with graphics capabilities for customizing and delivering your lectures.
- *Computerized Test Bank* (MicroSWAT III). This software contains all test questions from the printed test bank, with a pull-down menu that allows you to edit, add, delete, or randomly mix questions for customized tests. The grade book feature affords easy grade calculation and recordkeeping.
- *Lecture Outline Software.* This software contains all the lecture outlines from the *Instructor's Resource Guide,* so you can easily adapt them to your needs.

A SPECIAL THANKS

Of all those whose efforts made *Business in a Changing World* possible, we would like to extend our special thanks to Chris Rogers, Professor of Business Administration at Miami-Dade Community College, and Joe Andrew for their help in preparing support materials. Chris also served as a consultant on the text. We would particularly like to thank Dr. Cathy Block, Professor of Education at Texas

Christian University, for her help and guidance in the development of material in the area of critical thinking, and Cinci Stowell for her exceptional work as the developmental editor for this book. For their research assistance, valuable suggestions, and support, we extend our appreciation to Nora Freed, Kim Parrell, Monica Tobin, Glen Allen, Connie Saathoff, Anita Mote, and Joyce Moos.

In addition, we owe our personal thanks to the reviewers whose comments and suggestions helped us work out the bugs. They are:

John F. Chisholm, Jr.
Allegheny Community College

Monico L. Cisneros
Austin Community College (Texas)

Rex R. Cutshall
Vincennes University

Helen Davis
Jefferson Community College (Kentucky)

Michael Dougherty
Milwaukee Area Technical College

Barbara Goza
South Florida Community College

Thomas E. Heslin
Indiana University

Robert Johnson
Jefferson College

Gary Key
Grayson County College

Lawrence M. Lesser
The University of Maryland

Justin G. Longenecker
Baylor University

Ann Maddox
Angelo State University

Patricia Manninen
North Shore Community College

James N. McGowen
Belleville Area College

Glynna E. Morse
Memphis State University

David G. Oliver
Edison Community College

Christopher W. Rogers
Miami-Dade Community College

James K. Seeck
William Rainey Harper College

Carolyn Painter Spangler
Blue Ridge Community College

Lynn H. Suksdorf
Salt Lake Community College

William M. Taylor
Oakton Community College

Shafi Ullah
Broward Community College

Jim H. Wells
Daytona Beach Community College

William H. Cunningham
Ramon J. Aldag
Stanley B. Block

TO THE STUDENT

What a world it is you live in, and how very different the business environment is today from that of past generations as they prepared to enter the working world. While some prefer to look at today's business climate pessimistically, we as authors, instructors, and real-world practitioners encourage you to look at it as a challenge—a challenge that is exciting and surmountable through understanding and adapting to the changes around you. We hope this text will help you view business as an intriguing area of study, and see the ever-changing business world as a place that offers opportunities for future business leaders like yourself.

This book is for every student. No matter where your future interests lie, a solid grounding in business will help you reach your goals. All of us interact with business through products we buy, advertisements we see, and money we invest in savings, stocks, bonds, and other securities. Knowledge of business and how it operates empowers us to make better decisions and be less vulnerable to bad investments, business mistakes, and other threats to our financial well being.

In writing an introductory business text, we had to make many choices about what to include and what not to include. Certain basics must be covered, and they are. Beyond the basics, however, we wanted this text to address the issues that concern you most and those that will best equip you for a successful future. We know that many of you are greatly concerned about how to land a job and build a career . . . how to live as well or better than your parents . . . and how to achieve personal success in our unpredictable economy.

Our goal in this text is to respond to those concerns and help you see your goals within reach. How? First, with a comprehensive overview of the business world and business basics as they relate to you today. You'll find coverage of all of the many dimensions of business—its organization, management, marketing, and financial operations. You'll find a special emphasis on reasons for today's changing business environment and how and why the changes affect business. The topics used to illustrate these points are as current as the Los Angeles riots, Barcelona Olympics, changing practices in banking, competitive changes in the airline industry, the recent recession, and dozens more.

Second, we provide a special focus on *careers*. Displayed in the margins of each chapter are descriptions of one or more career options for your consideration. Also, Chapter 25 and the Appendix are devoted to helping you evaluate your career options and get the job you want. If you want an even more in-depth, systematic approach to deciding on a career that is right for you and a plan to land a job in that field, you can purchase the accompanying *Business Career Planning Guide.* This guide helps you assess your abilities and interests, match these to career choices, and conduct a successful job search. This is not just another lesson in how to write a resume or dress for an interview. The guide offers a national outlook on labor market trends, as well as five regional and numerous city supplements. Each supplement outlines the local economic conditions, quality of life, present and future employment prospects, cost of living information, starting salaries and salary growth, and the growing career fields in each region or city. Our intent was to give you concrete information you can put to use now, not just another presentation of hypothetical situations.

Third, we present the business world to you through real people and real companies. In "Profiles," you will read intriguing accounts of 25 business leaders and gain insight into the thinking and actions that led to their success. Find out more about "Billionaire Boy Scout" Ross Perot. Learn about ice cream guru Ben Cohen, co-founder and CEO of Ben & Jerry's Homemade, Inc. Discover how Liz Claiborne combined creativity and good business sense into a Fortune 500 company. Learn how Fran Tarkenton has turned winning on the football field into winning at the successful Tarkenton Productivity Group. Get an inside look at Famous Amos, a successful businessman who created a world-famous cookie company. These are just a sampling of the human-interest side of business that the text presents.

In "Cases," you will gain an understanding of business through real-life corporate situations, including: "Tying Managers' Pay To Performance" (a look at high-level executive's salaries); "Permanent Replacements at Ravenswood Aluminum Corporation" (the heated confrontation between labor and management following the firm's decision to hire permanent replacements for over 1,000 employees); "100% Pure" (the ethical questions behind Beech-Nut's 100% pure apple juice claim); "Carnival Cruise Lines" (the service problems faced by this major discount cruise line); "Blockbuster Video" (an examination of the marketing strategy of one of America' newest and most successful businesses), and more.

To encourage you to form your own thoughts and opinions on business issues, we have included "Controversial Issues," "Ethical Issues," and "Critical Thinking Cases." These features invite you to think about and discuss some of the most important issues in business today, and to evaluate information, rather than accept it at face value. Employers complain that employees today are too quick to accept data, rather than make the effort to understand and interpret it. We hope to help you avoid this criticism.

A final uniqueness—and, we hope, strength—of *Business in a Changing World* is what we bring to the book as its authors. While many texts are written by professional textbook authors, this text is written by three authors and instructors who also have real-world business experience. Each of us represents expertise in one of the three major areas of business—marketing, management, and finance. We feel our backgrounds and credentials enable us to provide you with a text that is accurate and up-to-date, and reflects the current business climate.

The true measure of any text is in the students' response to it. The finest texts not only instruct and inform, but inspire, motivate, and generate enthusiasm for the material. A well-written textbook speaks to you in terms you can understand, and provides information you can use. Only then does the text rise above something you "have" to read, to something you "want" to read. We hope you will find that *Business in a Changing World* meets these criteria and, more importantly, arms you with the solid background in business you will need to enter today's changing world of business with confidence.

William H. Cunningham
Ramon J. Aldag
Stanley B. Block

ABOUT THE AUTHORS

WILLIAM H. CUNNINGHAM

Dr. William Cunningham became the 7th Chancellor of The University of Texas System in 1992. He holds the Lee Hage and Joseph D. Jamail Regents Chair in Higher Education Leadership and the James L. Bayless Chair for Free Enterprise and is a Professor of Marketing. Prior to becoming Chancellor, he served as President of The University of Texas at Austin and as Dean of its College and Graduate School of Business Administration. Dr. Cunningham is a nationally-known marketing scholar and former editor of the *Journal of Marketing*. His research interests include marketing management and research and strategic market planning. Dr. Cunningham has won seven teaching awards from The University of Texas and has written 10 books. He is a member of the Board of Directors of five major corporations. He earned his B.A., M.B.A., and Ph.D. degrees from Michigan State University.

RAMON J. ALDAG

Professor Ramon Aldag is Professor of Management and Co-Director of the Center for the Study of Organizational Performance in the Graduate School of Business at the University of Wisconsin - Madison. He has 25 years of teaching experience, and is President of the National Academy of Management, a professional organization with 9,000 members in more than 60 countries. He has published more than 50 journal articles, has coauthored five books, and is Associate Editor for the *Journal of Business Research*. Professor Aldag has served in many roles in professional organizations and as a consultant for organizations in a number of industries. He holds a B.S. degree in Mechanical Engineering, an MBA in Production Management, and a Ph.D. in Management, all from Michigan State University. He has worked as a thermal engineer on various aerospace projects. He is a Fellow of the Academy of Management and is listed in *Who's Who In America*.

STANLEY B. BLOCK

Professor Stanley Block has served on the faculty of Texas Christian University for the past 25 years, holding such positions as chairman of finance, acting dean, and Texas American Bank Distinguished Professor of Finance. He received his Bachelor's degree from The University of Texas at Austin, his MBA degree from Cornell University, and his Ph.D. from Louisiana State University. He has written 20 books and numerous articles in leading academic journals. He has served on the board of directors of the Financial Management Association and as a past president of the Southwestern Finance Association. While at Texas Christian University, he has received many honors, including the $2,500 Burlington Northern Excellence in Teaching Award. He is a Chartered Financial Analyst (CFA) and serves on a number of corporate boards. He also serves on the editorial board of the *Journal of Economics and Business*. He is listed in *Who's Who in America*.

CONTENTS IN BRIEF

PART 6

FURTHER DIMENSIONS OF AMERICAN BUSINESS   608

CONTENTS

PART 2
BUSINESS ORGANIZATION   102

PART 3
MANAGEMENT OF THE ENTERPRISE   156

7 Management of the Organization   158

8 Motivating Employees   188

9   Human Resources Management   216

10   Labor-Management Relations   245

11   Operations Management   270

12   Information Management   300

PART 4

MARKETING MANAGEMENT   336

13 Marketing: The Strategic Input   338

14   Product Management   365

15   Channels of Distribution   392

16   Pricing   421

17   Promotion   447

PART 5

ACCOUNTING AND FINANCIAL MANAGEMENT   478

18   Accounting and Financial Statements   480

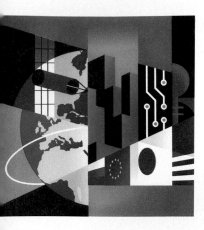

PART 6

FURTHER DIMENSIONS OF AMERICAN BUSINESS   **608**

PART 1
The American Business Environment

CHAPTER 1

Private Enterprise in America

Two decades ago, Jon M. Huntsman and his brother Blaine founded a company to manufacture plastic egg cartons. Eventually they had enough orders to open two factories. But in 1973 the oil embargo hit, and they had great difficulty in getting the chemicals necessary to manufacture the cartons. One supplier raised prices by 600 percent, and another got out of the business entirely.

The brothers were desperate. They had put up their homes and other assets as collateral to start the business. The board of directors voted 2–2 to go out of business, but Jon Huntsman gave a fiery speech. He explained that he would never be associated with a bankruptcy and that the firm would succeed no matter what happened.[1]

These were bold words. The brothers were still faced with the reality of not being able to get supplies. So what did they do? They took advantage of the chemical shortage. Overnight, the Huntsmans became chemical brokers, even though they knew little about the chemical business. When a chemical company asked for a product, the brothers would ask how to spell it and then search for it. They would find another company that had that product but needed something else. The Huntsman brothers started a whole chain of trades. In the first year, they made a $5 million profit as brokers. In the process, they were able to get the supplies they needed to manufacture their egg cartons.

Eventually the Huntsmans got out of the carton and packaging business and went into chemical manufacturing. The rest of the story is that Huntsman Chemical Company is now the largest privately owned chemical company in the U.S., with sales of more than $1.2 billion. Although Jon and Blaine Huntsman were both college graduates, they truly learned their lessons on the battlefield of business.

The point of this story is to demonstrate the benefits and dangers of a free market system, as opposed to a government-controlled economy. One has the opportunity to succeed—as well as to fail. As you read further into this chapter, you will see this point emphasized over and over again. Let's begin by examining our private enterprise economy.

Private enterprise (or **free market system**) means that business is free to organize and operate for a profit, that it is free to operate in a competitive system, and that government intervention will be limited to a regulatory role. The production of goods and services in this country—the clothes we wear, the cars we drive, the food we eat—is the responsibility of private enterprise, not the government. The economy of a private enterprise system is driven by the decisions of individuals and private organizations acting on their own behalf. Fair competition within the system is our guarantee of economic efficiency.

In the last few years, many other countries have come to recognize the virtues of the private enterprise system. The most dramatic change has occurred in the republics that once made up the Soviet Union. All of these republics have moved toward a market-driven economy and away from government allocation of resources. Grigori Yavlinsky, a Russian economist and deputy prime minister, sounded more like an American economist than a socialist when he said, "Our goal is to get ourselves out of the bottomless pit we find ourselves in. In the entire history of human existence, no one has thought of anything more efficient than the free market."[2] These words would have been considered treasonous in the Soviet Union a decade ago.

By the summer of 1991, the Soviet Communist Party had been overthrown, and a free enterprise economy was being introduced in the former Soviet Union. At the same time, Germany was in the process of reunification. The Communist policies that had prevailed in East Germany since World War II were discarded, replaced by the free market policies of West Germany.

Understanding the operations of the U.S. economy better may help you see why these great shifts are occurring around the world. We begin by defining a business.

private enterprise or free market system   a system under which business is free to organize and operate for a profit, in a competitive system with limited government intervention.

WHAT IS A BUSINESS   ❶

The barbershop downtown is a business. The steel mill, with its grimy brick walls and tall smokestacks, is a business. The electronics firms near San Jose and the computer research companies around Boston are all businesses. Along the upper Gulf Coast of Texas, the huge oil refineries that convert crude oil into chemical products are businesses. The supermarket chain is a business. So is the local dental clinic. What do all of these businesses have in common? We have seen that a business can be as small as Clyde's Barbershop or as large as the giant Exxon Corporation, but how are they all alike?

Definition of Business

We can define a **business** as an organization that combines inputs of raw materials, capital, labor, and management skills to produce useful outputs of goods and services in order to earn a profit. The key to this definition is the relationship between inputs and outputs. The transformation of inputs into outputs involves a

business   an organization that combines inputs of raw materials, capital, labor, and management skills, to produce useful outputs of goods and services, in order to earn a profit.

production process *the process by which inputs are transformed into outputs.*

production process, which can be as simple as the tools and techniques required to cut hair or as complex as the vast amount of processing equipment required to refine crude oil into unleaded gasoline. Figure 1-1 diagrams this relationship between inputs and outputs. In one form or another, all businesses manage production processes, whether those processes involve the delivery of a service or the manufacture of a product.

Economic Activity

We can deepen our understanding of the relationship between inputs and outputs by looking at the production stages involved in producing and marketing an automobile. We will keep the discussion simple by looking at four basic production stages. The first stage involves the production of sheet steel from iron ore and other raw material inputs. Sheet steel serves as the input in the second stage, in which molded auto body parts are produced. In the third stage, at the auto plant, these and other fabricated inputs are assembled into an automobile. In the fourth stage, the finished automobiles are shipped by truck to dealerships across the country, where they are sold to the public. Table 1-1 lists these production stages.

Note that the outputs of one stage serve as inputs to the next in the production chain. Note also that a different producer is involved at each stage. The output of each successive stage is more valuable than the output of the previous stage, which is to say that production adds value to inputs. Finally, the distribution of automobiles is as much a production process as the manufacture of the

FIGURE 1-1   Businesses Transform Inputs into Marketable Outputs

INPUTS

Raw Materials
Capital
Labor
Management Skills

PRODUCTION PROCESS
Technology

OUTPUTS

Goods
Services

TABLE 1-1   Stages in a Simple Production Chain

Stage	Input	Output	Producer
1	Iron Ore	Steel	Steel Mill
2	Steel	Molded Auto Body Parts	Metal Working Factories
3	Auto Body Parts	Automobiles	Auto Assembly Plant
4	Autos at Assembly Plant Lot	Autos at Retail Dealership	Automobile Dealer

cars themselves. The distribution and retail selling functions also add value to automobiles. These functions do not change the autos physically, but they do make them available to consumers at the right places and at the right time. Adding value to inputs through production or distribution is at the heart of economic activity.

Levels of Production and the Profit Motive

We are now in a position to ask: What determines a producer's level of production? That is, how much output is a firm willing and able to supply to the market? The level of production is determined by the cost of inputs (raw materials, equipment, labor, and management), the technology of the production process, and the market price of the output. This is true of both goods and services. As input costs drop, technology improves, or market prices rise, the firm will increase its level of production.

Business managers can adjust the levels of their inputs to achieve a given output level. The simplest choice might involve using more machines and fewer laborers, or fewer machines and more laborers. Efficient producers attempt to achieve the maximum dollar value of output (sales revenues) for the minimum dollar value of input (costs and expenses). The result is **profit maximization.** The choice among alternative production methods, therefore, is made on the basis of which alternatives will achieve the greatest profit. **Profit** is simply total sales revenues less all production and other costs. It is the return to the owners for undertaking the risk of operating a business.

The **profit motive**—the desire to make money—is what drives our private enterprise economy. A business, whether a small gift shop or a major international bank, cannot survive and grow unless it earns a profit. What happens when a firm cannot earn a profit? An example is the plight of the airline industry since the early 1980s. This industry was once highly regulated, but there is now direct competition between the airlines. An airline must buy the necessary aircraft and hire the personnel to fly and maintain them. At the same time, the airline must cover these high costs of operation by selling enough tickets to the traveling public. If a plane is 80 percent full at takeoff, it will probably show a profit. However, if the plane is only 60 percent occupied (and many passengers are on deep discount fares), there may not be sufficient revenue to pay for the planes, the fuel, and the personnel. Then, of course, there is no profit. If this goes on long enough, the company goes out of business. Once-great airlines such as Braniff and Pan Am suffered this fate in the late 1980s and early 1990s.

profit maximization   *the maximum dollar value of output (sales revenues) for the minimum dollar value of input (costs and expenses).*

profit   *sales revenues less all production and other costs; the return to the owners for undertaking the risk inherent in operating a business.*

profit motive   *the desire to make money.*

Role of the Entrepreneur

entrepreneur a person who starts, organizes, manages, and assumes responsibility for a business or other enterprise.

The entrepreneur has a special role in a private enterprise economy. An **entrepreneur** is a person who starts, organizes, manages, and assumes responsibility for a business or other enterprise. If the desire to earn a profit is the driving force in our economy, then the entrepreneur is the spark plug. The entrepreneur takes the lead in combining raw materials, capital, labor, and other inputs in the production of a good or service. The entrepreneur is also an innovator and a risk taker. Entrepreneurs have no guarantee that their ventures will be profitable. But in organizing a business, they risk their time, effort, and money in the hope that they will be able to earn a profit. Currently, our economy is experiencing a high level of entrepreneurial activity, in which many new businesses are being formed and many new goods and services are being introduced to the market. One such entrepreneur is Ross Perot, founder of Electronic Data Systems. This dynamic business leader is featured in the Profile section of this chapter, on page 7.

KEY ACTIVITIES OF A BUSINESS

All businesses perform eight basic activities in transforming inputs into marketable outputs. Profitable businesses perform these activities more efficiently than their competitors. Figure 1-2 lists these activities. Each is discussed briefly in the sections that follow and then in more detail in later chapters.

Develop New Ideas

Every business starts with an idea. The idea may concern an improved production technology or a new product or service to meet changing consumer needs. Ideas are a dime a dozen, but entrepreneurs turn their ideas into business ventures. At the start of this century, Henry Ford figured out a radically new way to produce automobiles efficiently. His innovation was the assembly line. Fifteen years ago, working out of a garage, Steven Jobs and Stephen Wozniak had the

FIGURE 1-2   Key Business Activities

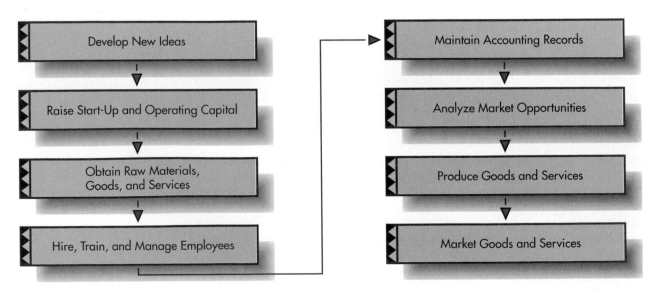

Ross Perot

Henry Ross Perot was born in 1930 in Texarkana, Texas. Perot demonstrated early the tenacity for which he is famous today, earning him the childhood nickname Henry the Hammer. After graduating from the U.S. Naval Academy, Perot spent four years in the Navy. In 1957 he joined the ranks of white-shirted computer salesmen at IBM.

The Perot visionary legend began when he failed to convince IBM that there was a huge market not just in selling people computers but in helping them figure out how to use them as well. In 1962, with $1,000 borrowed from his wife, Ross Perot founded Electronic Data Systems. Soon after EDS went public six years later, it was valued at $375 million.

During the 1970s, Perot tangled with North Vietnam on behalf of the POWs, fought the Iranian revolutionaries, and quarrelled with the Carter Administration over his lone-wolf style of high-profile private diplomacy. General Motors was the target for Perot treatment when the giant automaker bought EDS in 1984. GM chairman Roger Smith had hopes the Texas businessman could shake up the corporate hierarchy. Two years later, however, Perot publicly denounced the GM bureaucracy, saying, "I could never understand why it takes six years to build a car when it only took us four years to win World War II." The company ultimately paid him $700 million just to go away and be quiet. Perot took the money but has characteristically kept on talking.

Texas Democratic Governor Mark White recruited Perot in 1984 to head a statewide commission on educational reform. Perot responded by taking on teachers, coaches, parents, and administrators when he boldly proposed barring failing students from extracurricular activities. White, who was defeated for re-election as Texas Governor in 1986 largely due to opposition from educators, still says with admiration, "He galvanized the business leadership to get education reform done. He's a consensus player, as long as you sign up with him. He's a consensus of one."

Perot's current businesses are known collectively as the Perot Group. One of those businesses is Alliance Airport, a new, $50 million airfield northwest of Dallas. Alliance, located near 17,000 acres of Perot-owned land, embodies many criteria which make up the kind of enterprise Perot likes: It's original, it's huge, it's daring, it has a chance to be world-class. Alliance is being marketed as the world's first industrial (no passenger traffic) airport.

Another megaproject that's still in the design phase demonstrates the Perot Group's talent for coming up with unconventional solutions to everyday problems. The problem: California needs new highways but lacks the money. The Perot Group's solution: Bring in the private sector. Their idea is to build a road for $650 million, give it to the state, and then allow developers to collect tolls for 35 years. Bidders from all over the world submitted proposals. The Perots won, in large part due to their money-saving idea of building the road above an existing right of way: a creek bed. It will be an 11.2-mile-long bridge, imposing minimal environmental impact.

What makes Ross Perot so incredibly successful? By all accounts, he doesn't look the part. Perot, who loves the nickname "Billionaire Boy Scout," is a compact man with jug ears and a weather-beaten face who looks as if he might belong behind the counter in a small-town hardware store. He describes himself as the ultimate straight arrow, the billionaire who never lusted after money, a self-effacing idealist uncontaminated by personal ambition, a brilliant problem-solver who never ducked a challenge. At no time has the man had a kind word to say for management. What he admires is leadership. One of Perot's favorite maxims is from his hero Winston Churchill: "Never give in. Never give in. Never. Never. Never." Those qualities are just what provided Henry Ross Perot with the ability to shake up U.S. politics in 1992.

Source: Alan Farnham, "And Now, Here's The Man Himself," *Fortune*, June 15, 1992, pp. 68–74. Walter Shapiro, "President Perot?" *Time*, May 25, 1992, pp. 27–31.

daring idea to develop a small computer for home use. They called their business Apple Computer, Inc. In the early 1990s, annual sales at Apple exceeded $6 billion.

Successful companies begin with great ideas, but to stay in business, they must continue to develop these ideas year after year. In a market economy such as ours, firms compete with other firms that produce similar goods and services. Firms stay in business by staying ahead of the competition. All of the big three U.S. automakers—Ford Motor Co., General Motors Corp., and Chrysler Corp.—are implementing computerized and robotic assembly techniques for producing automobiles more efficiently. They also continually introduce new car models to the market in order to attract the consumer's dollar. At the heart of business growth is a spirit of competition and innovation.

Raise Start-Up and Operating Capital

It takes money to start a business and to purchase production equipment and inventory. This start-up money, called **capital,** can be obtained from a variety of sources: the owner's personal funds, other investors, and banks and other lending institutions.

capital   the money it takes to start a business and to purchase production equipment and inventory.

Ongoing businesses also need to borrow money or obtain additional funds regularly. They borrow from banks for short-term cash needs. Before the start of the Christmas selling season, for example, merchants usually take out bank loans to pay for their large Christmas merchandise inventories. They repay the loans with the profits from the Christmas sales.

When a business needs money for a longer time, such as a loan to finance an expansion program, it may borrow from a bank, issue bonds, or sell stock. It is the job of the company's finance department to find the best way to raise the needed money.

Obtain Raw Materials, Goods, and Services

Businesses obtain raw material inputs to produce their products. U.S. Steel obtains iron ore from northern Minnesota to produce steel ingots, rolled sheet steel, and other basic steel products. Wine producers in California's Napa Valley purchase grape harvests from independent growers in the area. Whirlpool Corporation buys steel, rubber and metal parts, and other materials for use as inputs to produce refrigerators. Other firms buy goods for resale to consumers. For example, Dillard's, a large department-store chain, purchases clothing, kitchenware, cosmetics, and countless other goods from thousands of domestic and foreign suppliers. Finally, firms obtain a variety of needed services, such as legal advice, long-distance telephone service, equipment repair, and advertising and graphic design services. Can you think of any other services that businesses require in order to produce their goods or services and market them to the public?

Business Career
Purchasing Agent: Buys goods and services, such as raw materials, supplies, parts, and advertising, for a business. Obtains from vendors product information, such as price, features, and delivery schedule. Evaluates product options and selects those with the best value for the firm. Maintains purchase records. *Average Salary: $25,900*

Obtaining the right goods and services at the right prices is essential for effective cost control. By keeping costs down, producers are able to keep their selling prices down. Buying the best goods and services at the lowest prices is so important that most large firms employ a staff of professionally trained purchasing agents to do this job.

Hire, Train, and Manage Employees

Many businesses employ only a few people, but others employ thousands. Every company needs a good system for finding talented people and persuading them to work for the company.

Effective training programs develop employee confidence and prepare employees for higher-paying positions. This helps keep valuable people from going to other companies.

The art of management is one of the most challenging aspects of business. Besides hiring and training new employees, managers also organize workflows, motivate employees, direct their efforts, evaluate their performance, provide leadership to the organization, and make a multitude of decisions. It can be difficult to identify future high achievers, as can be seen in the Lighter Side example on p. 10.

Successful business firms excel at management. Table 1-2 lists the most-admired large U.S. corporations. Based on a survey of executives, corporate directors, and financial analysts, the list was compiled by *Fortune* magazine, a leading business publication. All of the companies tend to be more profitable than other firms in their industries. Do you think that such companies have an easier time attracting and retaining talented employees? Why?

Maintain Accounting Records

Firms must also maintain accounting records. The most important number in these records is the one at the bottom—the "bottom-line" net profit or loss. To compute this number, the firm keeps track of the number of products sold and the amount of money spent on production, salaries, rent, insurance, interest on loans, building repairs, and other items.

Large firms produce a tremendous amount of accounting information. Managing this information and using it wisely are great challenges. All business

TABLE 1-2   The 10 Most Admired Large U.S. Corporations

Rank*	Company	Industry Group
1	Merck	Pharmaceuticals
2	Rubbermaid	Rubber and Plastic Products
3	Proctor & Gamble	Soaps, Cosmetics
4	Wal-Mart Stores	Retailing
5	PepsiCo	Beverages
6	Coca-Cola	Beverages
6	3M	Scientific and Photo Equipment
8	Johnson & Johnson	Pharmaceuticals
9	Boeing	Aerospace
10	Eli Lilly	Pharmaceuticals
10	Liz Claiborne	Apparel

* *The companies were evaluated on the basis of quality of management; quality of products or services; innovativeness; long-term investment value; financial soundness; ability to attract, develop, and keep talented people; community and environmental responsibility; and use of corporate assets.*

How to Succeed in Business the Unusual Way Warning—Please Do Not Try!

As a child, David Geffen lived in a three-room apartment in Brooklyn's Borough Park, where he slept on a couch. He got his early business training from his sweet, 4'11" mother, who ran a corset and brassiere shop. He graduated from New Utrecht High School in Brooklyn with a 66 average (65 was passing). After attending college for one year, he moved to California and eventually got a job with the William Morris talent agency. That was no small accom-plishment—at that time, the William Morris Agency hired only college graduates! Geffen simply said that he had graduated from UCLA then intercepted the letter from UCLA to his employer, steamed it open, and rewrote it to affirm his academic success.

Many people who start out with such a background end up behind bars, but not David Geffen. He is described by *Forbes* magazine as the "Richest Man in Hollywood."[3] He became an enormously successful music company exec-utive in the 1970s and 1980s, signing such pop and metal acts as Edie Brickell & the New Bohemians, Guns N' Roses, and Tesla. His stable also included performers such as Cher, Robbie Robertson, and Aerosmith. In 1990, he traded his record company to MCA for 10 million shares of MCA stock. Later that year, Matsushita Electric Industrial Co. bought out MCA for $66 per share, putting $660 mil-lion in David Geffen's pocket. Including other assets in art, real estate, and securities, his net worth is close to $1 billion.

firms—large and small alike—produce accounting information for three basic purposes: internal decision making, financial reporting to lenders and investors, and tax reporting to government.

Analyze Market Opportunities

marketing concept *the philosophy that a firm seeks to develop, produce, and market goods and services that satisfy customers.*

All businesses need to know about their markets, about changing consumer tastes and preferences, and about developments in their industries. Marketing is essen-tially a customer-oriented activity. The objective of firms is to develop, produce, and market goods and services that satisfy customer needs. This approach to business is now known as the **marketing concept.** Business managers learn more about their markets by conducting market research studies, analyzing gov-ernment data and industry reports, talking with their salespeople, and reading trade publications.

Produce Goods and Services

The real business of a business is to produce a good or service. As mentioned earlier, a business does this by manufacturing products, buying them for resale, or providing services to other firms or the public. The manufacturer has all the problems of doing business—raising money, finding good people, keeping track of sales and costs—plus the special problems involved in manufacturing a prod-uct. The reseller, such as a department store, drugstore, or appliance mart, must offer the right selection of goods at prices customers can afford. The service firm, such as an advertising agency or a neighborhood dry cleaner, must rely primarily on a reputation for high-quality work or competent service.

Market Goods and Services

Many businesses spend as much as 30 to 40 percent of their budgets on selling and marketing. Industrial firms spend most of their marketing money on first-rate salespeople. Makers of consumer goods spend heavily on advertising. In 1991,

This landscaper's business thrives because he produces a service that his customers value.

for example, Procter & Gamble, the maker of such well-known products as Tide detergent, Crest toothpaste, Ivory soap, and Sure deodorant, spent more than $1 billion on television advertising. Why? To encourage people to buy its products.

Marketing executives make decisions in four basic areas: product development and management, pricing, advertising and promotion, and distribution. Marketing is an especially dynamic part of business. In the clothing industry, fashion can change overnight. Levi Strauss & Co., the nation's largest garment maker, was nearly invincible in the sportswear industry throughout the 1970s. Levi managers focused their efforts on producing enough jeans to supply an almost limitless demand for them. In the early 1980s, sales of jeans slackened, as the market shifted to other types of apparel. In response, Levi has attempted to become more marketing-oriented by broadening its product base, increasing its advertising budget, and offering retailers volume discounts on large purchases.

OBJECTIVES OF BUSINESS

A business represents different things to different people. Each person or group associated with the business expects certain things from it. Each has certain objectives in relation to the business. The owners have their objectives; the employees have their objectives; and society has still other objectives.

A corporation is supposed to maximize its profits and its return to its owners, but other parties also have a stake in the company. To refer to them, the term **stakeholder** has evolved in the last decade. Stakeholders include employees, members of the community where the firm is located, and suppliers of the company. To operate smoothly in its environment, a business must consider the interests of all the groups affected by its business decisions.

stakeholder *any party that has an interest or stake in a company, including employees, members of the community where the firm is located, and suppliers of the company.*

Owners' Objectives

The owners of a business must make a profit on their investment; the survival of a firm depends upon its profitability. One kind of owner is someone who owns all of a business. Another is a person who simply buys stock in a business. The objectives of these two types of owners differ.

Private Owner. The basic objective of the private owner is to produce a reliable stream of cash income. The owner of a local paint supply store cannot pay the rent or buy new clothes for the family unless enough paint and painting supplies are sold. Besides the need for income, the owner of a small business has several other objectives.

Independence. Many owners of small businesses do not make as much money as they would if they worked for someone else. Being their own boss, however, is more important to them than making more money.

Family Jobs. A small business often serves as a place where the owner's children can work while growing up. The children earn extra money, and the owner has a dependable source of employees. The children may even take over the business when their parents retire.

Retirement Security. Many people sell their businesses when they are ready to retire. The cash from the sale will offer some security in their retirement years.

stockholder *owner of part of a business and its profits, through ownership of stock.*

Stockholder. A **stockholder** is someone who owns shares of stock in a business. Owning stock means owning a part of a business and its profits. It does not mean that an individual stockholder has the right to tell management how to run the company. Nor does it mean that an individual stockholder can claim ownership of any specific part of a company, such as a machine or a wall of an office building. Rather, stock ownership is the ownership of a partial interest in the company, along with many others. Stockholders are concerned with cash dividends and the value of their investments. Stocks and stockholders will be discussed further in Chapter 21.

Employees' Objectives

Sometimes, the longer people work for a company, the more their objectives tend to resemble those of the company. These objectives may be to make a profit, to produce a high-quality product that is sold at a reasonable price, to contribute to society by developing new technology, and to avoid abusing the environment. Employees also have their own personal objectives.

Income. The basic objective of most employees is to make enough money to support themselves and their families. They expect the company to provide them with employment and income. Without the steady flow of income, why work for the company?

Security. Another objective of employees is to feel secure—to believe that they will have a job in the future. They expect the company to offer this security. When a company closes down permanently, it can be a terrible shock to employees, especially to those who have worked there most of their lives.

Personal Growth. A third employee objective is personal growth. Most people want to be promoted, to take on more responsibility, and to grow in self-
esteem. Without these opportunities, many of a company's employees would
prefer to work somewhere else.

Society's Objectives

A few decades ago, society did not pay much attention to how businesses operated. Businesses were considered only sources of employment and prosperity.
They brought jobs to the community and channeled money into the local economy. This is still true, but now society expects more. Society is concerned about
how businesses operate—about whether they act fairly and responsibly.

Good Citizens. Businesses should be good citizens. They are expected to pay
their fair share of taxes and to support important local causes. Today businesses
not only contribute to charities such as the United Fund, but also collect money
for these charities from their employees who wish to donate.

McDonald's Corp. is one example of a firm that acts as a good citizen. In
several locations around the country, McDonald's has funded the development of
Ronald McDonald houses. These facilities offer inexpensive lodging for parents
whose children are being treated for cancer or other life-threatening diseases at a
nearby hospital. Nightly room rates for out-of-town guests are $10 or less.
McDonald's provides $450,000 in start-up money to build each Ronald McDonald
house and sponsors national advertising to help sustain the program. Volunteers
from the community raise the money needed to operate the houses.

Conscientious Sellers. The quality of a product should reflect the amount
spent. Not all products must be of high quality, but low-quality products should
sell for less than higher-quality products. If there are any hazards or dangers associated with the use of a product, people expect the manufacturer to inform them.
A company should stand behind its products. If a product is defective, the company should repair or replace it. If a product is thought to be unsafe, the company
should warn people, as Cadillac Seville did in 1991 with its malfunctioning steering column. In past years, Chrysler and Ford have reported similar problems to
consumers.

OUR PRIVATE ENTERPRISE ECONOMY

Business activity in the United States is organized as a private enterprise or free
market system. Private organizations own the means of production and choose
economical methods of production in order to earn a profit. Price and output
decisions are made not by government decree, but by the actions of innumerable
business firms operating under varying market conditions.

Let's begin this survey of our private enterprise economy by looking at the
basic "freedoms" of business. We will then discuss supply and demand, market
structure and competition, the role of government in our economy, and how consumers determine which goods and services are produced and sold.

Basic Freedoms

There are three basic business freedoms in this country. They are the freedom to
own property, the freedom to earn a profit, and the freedom to go out of
business.

A professional baseball club is a business, and as such it enjoys the basic freedoms of all businesses in this country—in this case, ownership of the services of the players it has under contract.

Own Property. Businesses are generally free to buy and sell land and buildings and to use their property to generate income. For instance, a real estate development firm may own an apartment building that generates income in the form of rent payments. Businesses may own the factories in which they manufacture their products. Businesses may also own other physical assets, such as office machines and delivery trucks, used in the production of goods and services. Businesses may even buy and sell the "right" to take certain actions. Examples include oil-drilling rights on a given parcel of land, motion picture rights to a best-selling novel, or the team owner's right to the services of a baseball player.

There are a great number of governmental limitations on the ownership of private commercial property. Cities often have zoning laws that prohibit some types of buildings and businesses in certain areas of town. The aim of most zoning laws is to protect residential areas. Many federal environmental laws place restrictions on the use of private property. A business may own a factory with a smokestack so long as the smokestack does not emit pollutants exceeding a level set by law.

Earn a Profit. The second basic freedom is the freedom to earn a profit. That is, businesses are free to select production methods and marketing strategies that minimize costs and maximize sales revenues. This important freedom is restricted by many rules. For example, businesses are subject to minimum wage laws. They may not cut costs by illegally dumping toxic wastes into public waterways. Nor may they distribute false information about their products to increase sales.

Government also controls profits through corporate tax laws. Usually, the more money a company makes, the more taxes it should pay. In 1991, Exxon posted before-tax profits of $15 billion. Its tax bill for that year was $6 billion.

Go Out of Business. Companies are free to go out of business. The government does not force people to stay in business if they cannot make money.

If a firm is forced into **bankruptcy,** it will sell its remaining assets (liquidate) to pay off its creditors. But what happens if, after liquidation, a business is still not able to pay all of its lenders and suppliers? Are the shareholders in the failed firm required to meet the firm's unsatisfied debts? The answer is No. The liability of the owners of a corporation is limited by law: The most shareholders can lose when a firm closes is the amount of their stock investment. The unpaid creditors in this situation remain unpaid.

Sometimes the government steps in to prevent a company from going out of business, especially when the company employs a great many people. A beneficiary of such intervention was Chrysler Corp. In 1979 it seemed clear that Chrysler would fail without massive government assistance. The U.S. Department of Transportation estimated that such a failure would cost 430,000 people their jobs—150,000 Chrysler employees, 180,000 supplier employees, and 100,000 dealer employees. The price in lost jobs was too high, so Congress guaranteed $1.5 billion in new loans to the company. Chrysler did not lose its "right" to go to bankrupt. Congress just decided it would have been against the national interest for it to do so.

By 1991, Chrysler was once again asking the government for extra protection from foreign imports, with a thinly veiled threat that failure to do so might lead to bankruptcy. This time around, the government said there would be no protection.

> **bankruptcy**   a condition in which a firm is forced out of business because it is unable to pay its debts.

Demand, Supply, and Market Price

How are the prices of goods and services determined in a free market economy? In a market free of outside controls, the market price is determined by supply and demand. In an individual business, the managers decide how much they will charge for their goods and services, but they do so in response to current market conditions.

Demand is the quantities of a good or service that consumers are willing and able to buy at various prices over a given time period. The **law of demand** says that consumers are willing to buy more of a product at a lower price than at a higher price. As the price of a good or service increases, the quantity demanded decreases. For example, if tickets to football games were $10, a fan might attend five games per season. However, if the ticket price were $30, the fan might attend only one game a season.

When the relationship between price and quantity demanded is shown on a graph, it is called a **demand curve.** Panel (*a*) of Figure 1-3 shows a demand curve. Notice that the curve is downward-sloping, because consumers demand more of the good or service at lower prices.

Supply is the quantities of output that producers are willing and able to make available to the market at various prices over a given time period. The **law of supply** says that producers are willing to produce more of a product at a higher price than at a lower price. As price rises, the quantity supplied increases. When presented on a graph, the relationship between price and quantity supplied is called a **supply curve.** Panel (*b*) of Figure 1-3 presents a supply curve that is upward-sloping, because producers will supply more output at higher prices.

> **demand**   the quantities of a good or service that consumers are willing and able to buy at various prices over a given time period.
>
> **law of demand**   an economic law stating that consumers are willing to buy more of a product at a lower price than at a higher price.
>
> **demand curve**   a graph that shows the relationship between price and quantity demanded.
>
> **supply**   quantities of output that producers are willing and able to make available to the market at various prices over a given time period.
>
> **law of supply**   an economic law stating that producers are willing to produce more of a product at a higher price than at a lower price.
>
> **supply curve**   a graph that shows the relationship between price and quantity supplied.

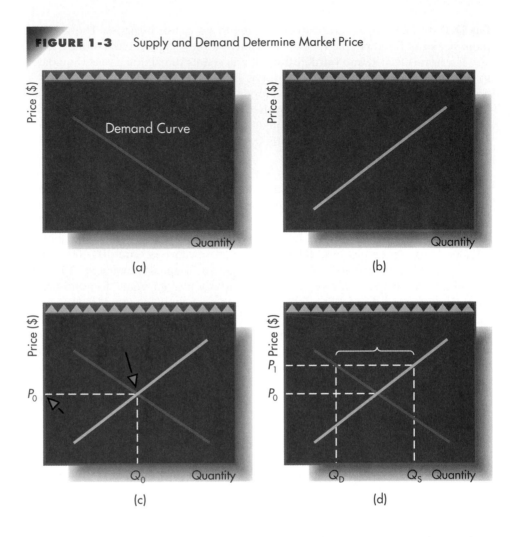

FIGURE 1-3   Supply and Demand Determine Market Price

(a)

(b)

(c)

(d)

We can combine the demand curve and supply curve on a single graph to see how supply and demand jointly determine the market price. The **market price** for a good or service is that price at which the quantity supplied to the market is equal to the quantity demanded. In panel (*c*) of Figure 1-3, P_0 is the market price.

Let's look at a real-world example of a basic commodity: petroleum. Petroleum is used to make gasoline for cars, heating oil for furnaces, and as power to generate electricity. The quantity of petroleum demanded moves in the opposite direction of price, as indicated in panel (*a*) of Figure 1-3. At high prices, the quantity demanded is lower, as people conserve their use of petroleum products. At lower prices, the quantity demanded will be greater. People will drive their cars more and turn on the furnace or air conditioner at the first sign of discomfort.

Turning to the supply side, in panel (*b*) of Figure 1-3, we can see that as the price of petroleum increases, more will be supplied to the market. Why? At higher prices, it becomes possible to drill for higher-cost petroleum. Perhaps deep wells or offshore wells can be profitably used because of the higher price that will be received for the output. Conversely, at lower prices, the quantity supplied will decrease.

Putting demand and supply together, as in panel (*c*), we see that market price, P_0, is determined by where the curves intersect. What would happen if market conditions remained the same, but the petroleum companies decided to raise the price to P_1? As seen in panel (d), at price P_1 there would be considerably more petroleum supplied than demanded. Eventually the excess supply of oil would force producers to lower the price, to get rid of their inventory. The price would return to the market level where demand and supply were once again equal. A new market price could be maintained only if the shapes or locations of the curves changed due to factors other than changes in the market price. Such things as an oil-import tax that increased the cost of producing petroleum or a recession that decreased the demand for industrial uses would cause the market price to change.

Market Structure and Competition

In our private enterprise economy, businesses operate under a variety of market or industry conditions. A **market,** in the sense considered here, is the sum total of all sales for a given kind of good among all buyers and sellers. Some industries are highly competitive; others are not so competitive. Economists identify four basic types of markets, each characterized by the degree of competition involved: perfect competition, monopolistic competition, oligopoly, and monopoly. A perfectly competitive market involves the most competition; a monopoly, the least competition. Figure 1-4 summarizes the differences among the market types.

6

market   the sum total of all sales for a given kind of good among all buyers and sellers.

Perfect Competition. In **perfect competition,** the market is made up of many small sellers and many small buyers. None of these sellers or buyers is big enough to dictate the price of the product traded in the market or the amount traded. The products of all sellers are identical, so no seller has a competitive edge in the market through product differentiation. This market type is also characterized by an absence of government regulation, freedom of movement of buyers and sellers in and out of the market, and perfect information. This last point means that all buyers and sellers share the same information about price, so that none has an advantage.

perfect competition   a market structure in which many small producers sell identical products to many small buyers, and no buyer or seller is big enough to dictate price.

Most economists say that perfect competition is an ideal rather than a reality, but a few markets in this country are close to perfect competition. For example, the markets for agricultural commodities meet some of the assumptions of perfect competition. One farmer's corn crop is essentially like any other farmer's. All farm operations are small enough that if one were to withhold its crop from the market, the market price for that commodity would not change. All farmers share the same commodity price information.

Monopolistic Competition. A second type of market structure is **monopolistic competition.** We use this name for markets in which sellers are able to achieve some product differentiation through branding, advertising, or quality improvements. Monopolistic competition is like perfect competition in that both have many sellers and buyers. Under monopolistic competition, however, firms sell similar but not identical products. This means that firms, through their marketing strategies, are able to carve out market niches for themselves with selected customer groups. For example, if a firm offers a better product than its competitors, or if it advertises to a certain group of buyers, or even if it just provides faster delivery, then it has established a niche for itself. The firm has developed a "little monopoly" position in the market.

monopolistic competition a market structure in which many sellers of similar products are able to achieve some product differentiation, enabling them to carve out market niches.

Many products today are traded in monopolistically competitive markets. At the manufacturing level, industries in which many small producers operate usu-

FIGURE 1-4   Features of Four Different Market Structures

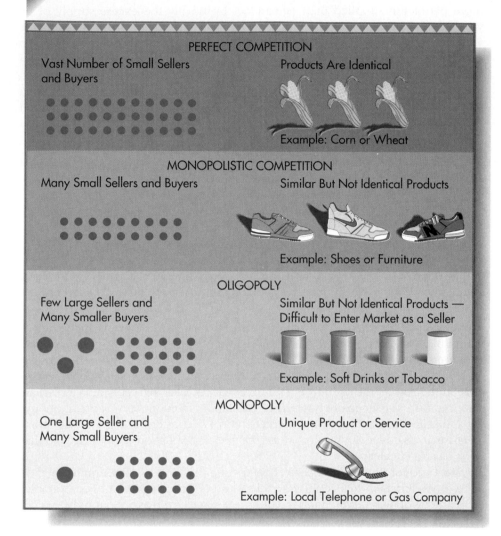

ally meet the conditions of monopolistic competition. Examples of such industries include men's and women's clothing, book publishing, shoes, and wood furniture. Most stores, especially in big cities, conduct business under conditions of monopolistic competition. Urban areas have a great number of supermarkets, convenience marts, restaurants, gift stores, barber shops, dry cleaners, and clothing stores. Although all firms of each retail type sell similar products, each retailer attempts to differentiate its product or service offering. This is done through merchandising, pricing, advertising, packaging, and product servicing decisions.

oligopoly   a market structure
in which a few large producers
sell similar but not identical
products to many small buyers.

Oligopoly. An **oligopoly** is a market made up of a few large producers selling similar but not identical products to many small buyers. Oligopolistic producers tend to follow similar pricing and product introduction strategies. For example, when one producer offers low factory-sponsored financing, other producers in the industry do the same. The federal government watches oligopolies carefully, to guard against illegal price control and to prevent any one firm from becoming too powerful.

The automobile industry is a good example of an oligopoly. The U.S. automobile market has historically been dominated by three firms—General Motors, Ford, and Chrysler. From 1950 to 1970, these firms made 95 percent of all new cars sold in the United States; General Motors alone averaged 52 percent of the new car market. The Justice Department watched GM during this period to see whether it was taking over the industry.

Today, the government is no longer so worried about the market strength of General Motors. Foreign car makers (especially Japanese and German automakers) have made strong inroads into the U.S. automobile market. Imports now account for 35 percent of the U.S. market.

Many other U.S. industries and markets are oligopolies. Examples include the steel, tobacco, soft drink, beer, household detergent, light bulb, and polyester fiber industries. When we talk about "big business," we are usually referring to the oligopolistic firms.

Monopoly. The last market model is characterized by a complete absence of competition. The market is made up of only one producer, called a **monopoly,** and many small buyers. The monopolist's product is unique, because there are no close substitutes for it in the market. In other words, the monopolist does not face any competition, with the result that consumer choice is severely restricted. Consumers either obtain the product from the monopolist or do without it. The monopolist is called a "price maker" because, by withholding the product from the market, it can control the product's price.

monopoly   a market structure characterized by a complete absence of competition: one producer and many small buyers.

It is not hard to see why monopolies have traditionally been viewed as economic and social evils. A monopolist has overwhelming market power. Operating without restraint from competitive forces, the monopolistic firm has control over supply and price. Moreover, the monopolist has no incentive to produce its output more efficiently or to innovate.

A few large firms in the United States enjoy monopolistic control in certain markets—for example, local telephone companies. Pure monopolies, however, are generally illegal in this country.

ROLE OF GOVERNMENT

We have already suggested some ways that government is involved in our private enterprise economy. In general, government has three basic economic functions. First, government provides a legal foundation and an appropriate social environment for the conduct of economic activity. For example, it defines property rights, enforces contracts and other laws, and protects the integrity of the nation's monetary system. Air and water pollution laws and product safety regulations also fall into this general category. Second, government both encourages competition in the marketplace and controls it. This is accomplished through legislation and government agency rules and regulations. Both of these general functions will be discussed at length in Chapter 3. Finally, government redistributes income from some segments of the economy to others. Government acquires revenues through **taxation**—taxes on income, property, sales, and payroll. These revenues are channeled back into the economy through spending (for example, military procurement, highway construction, and harbor dredging) and transfer payments to veterans, the aged, welfare recipients, and others in society. In short, government is a consumer of goods and services but not a producer of them.

taxation   a process by which the government acquires revenue through taxes on income, property, sales, and payrolls.

CONSUMERS RULE THE ROOST

No goods or services are produced and sold unless business managers believe that consumers are willing to buy them. Knowing what consumers want is not always an easy task. Introducing a new product to the market is a gamble in today's economy, because consumers are more value-conscious than they were a few years ago. Consumers want energy-efficient houses, better-quality food products, and longer-lasting appliances.

When we say that "consumers rule the roost," we mean that it is consumers who decide which goods and services are produced. They do this through the decisions they make in the marketplace—that is, by which goods and services they choose to buy or not to buy. Economists call this **consumer sovereignty.** Profitable businesses watch changing consumer tastes closely. Businesses that fail are those that cannot meet the challenge of the marketplace. Without the discipline imposed by a competitive market, inefficient and poorly managed firms would survive. But with this discipline, new ideas, new products, and new companies develop to meet the changing tastes of the consumer.

consumer sovereignty
the concept that consumers decide which goods and services are produced when they choose to buy or not to buy specific goods and services.

KEY TERMS

private enterprise or free market system 3

business 3

production process 4

profit maximization 5

profit 5

profit motive 5

entrepreneur 6

capital 8

marketing concept 10

stakeholder 11

stockholder 12

bankruptcy 15

demand 15

law of demand 15

demand curve 15

supply 15

law of supply 15

supply curve 15

market price 16

market 17

perfect competition

monopolistic competition 17

oligopoly 18

monopoly 19

taxation 19

consumer sovereignty 20

SUMMARY POINTS

1 A business is an organization that combines inputs of raw materials, capital, labor, and management skills in a production process, to produce useful outputs of goods and services, in order to earn a profit. A business cannot survive unless it earns a profit; it is the pursuit of profitability that makes the private enterprise system work.

2 All businesses perform eight basic activities in transforming inputs into marketable outputs. The beginning activities include developing new ideas; raising start-up and operating capital; obtaining raw materials, goods, and services; and hiring, training, and managing employees. Other activities are maintaining accounting records, analyzing market opportunities, producing goods and services, and marketing goods and services.

3 The owners' objective is to earn a profit. Employees' objectives center on income, security, and personal growth. Among society's objectives are that businesses benefit the community in which they are located and that they be conscientious sellers.

4 The three basic freedoms that are essential to our private enterprise economy are the right to own property, the right to earn a profit, and the freedom to go out of business if circumstances so dictate.

5 The law of supply says that producers are willing to produce and offer for sale more of a product at a high price than at a low price. The supply curve demonstrates this principle. The law of demand says that consumers are willing to purchase more of a product at a low price than at a high price. The demand curve demonstrates this principle. When the supply curve and the demand curve meet at a given point, the price and amount produced will be determined, because both suppliers and consumers will be satisfied.

6 The four different types of market competition are perfect competition (many small buyers and small sellers and identical products); monopolistic competition (many small buyers and sellers but differences in product); oligopoly (few large producers selling similar but not identical products); and monopoly (the complete absence of competition, with only one producer and many small buyers).

7 Government provides a legal foundation and an appropriate social environment for the conduct of economic activity. It also encourages competition in the marketplace and controls it. Finally, government distributes income from some segments of the economy to others through its powers of taxation and spending.

8 Goods and services are not produced unless business managers believe that consumers are willing to buy them. This is reflected in the marketplace by items consumers choose to buy or not to buy. Through this market discipline, new products are developed to meet the changing tastes of consumers.

REVIEW QUESTIONS

1 What is meant by the term "private enterprise"? **1**

2 What is a production process? **1**

3 What is an entrepreneur? Is the U.S. economy still benefiting from entrepreneurial activity? **1**

4 Give an example of how the desire for profit maximization dictates the choice of production alternatives. **1**

5 List the eight key activities of a business. **2**

6 What are the principal objectives of the owners of small businesses? **3**

7 Describe the three basic freedoms that businesses enjoy in our economy. **4**

8 What is the law of supply? The law of demand? Describe how supply and demand determine market price. **5**

9 What is the role of government in our private enterprise, market economy? **7**

10 Why do we say that the consumer "rules the roost"? **8**

DISCUSSION QUESTIONS

1 Explain the role of profit in our economy.

2 List some of the advantages and disadvantages of being an entrepreneur. Do you think that the risk of starting a new business is worth the effort?

3 Of the eight key activities of a business discussed in the chapter, which do you think are the most important, in your opinion? Why?

4 Can you think of some instances in which society's objectives for a business might conflict with the owners' objectives? With the employees' objectives?

5 Should the government have let Chrysler Corporation go bankrupt in 1979? Under what conditions is it appropriate for the government to step in and save a company from business failure?

6 In your opinion, does the government play too big a role in our economy? How might government involvement affect the operation of the profit motive?

EXPERIENTIAL EXERCISES

1 Review the eight key activities of a business that were discussed in this chapter. Now suppose that you are an entrepreneur who has an idea for a new product or service—for example, a home computer software program, a typing service for college students, a small retail store, or a magazine. Pick an idea and draw up a short business plan for starting your venture. In your plan, be sure to address all of the eight key activities.

2 The most common form of competition is among firms whose products are essentially similar but not identical (monopolistic competition). The firms must compete on the basis of slight product differentiation, advertising, service, pricing, location, store hours, and other factors. Pick a category of business—for example, grocery stores, restaurants, beauty or barber shops, dry cleaners, or clothing stores. Select two or three key competitors and compare them in terms of the above factors. Has any of the firms truly established a market niche for itself? Also, notice whether the firm is locally owned or is part of a national chain. Does that factor appear to make any difference?

CASES

CASE 1-1
South Texas Homebuilders

Ed Cole is the president of South Texas Homebuilders in Corpus Christi, Texas. He formed the company in 1981, during the Texas oil boom. Because Corpus Christi is a major port city for shipping oil, many people were moving to the area at the time, to take advantage of job opportunities. During his first year of operation, Ed Cole built and sold 18 homes and made a net profit of $55,000. In the second year of operation, he doubled those numbers.

By the third year, the oil boom had come to an end. Ed Cole was left with a dozen unsold houses, and he was forced to sell them at little or no profit. On two houses, Ed actually lost money—his name was on the bank loan, and he feared he might be forced into bankruptcy if he didn't take what he could get for the house and pay off the loan.

Throughout the 1980s and early 1990s, he assumed a more conservative approach and did reasonably well in his business. For the most part, he built only custom homes under a contract from the buyer. Previously, he had built "spec" (speculation) houses himself and then tried to sell them. The profit margins were smaller with custom-built homes, but Ed slept better at night.

In mid-1991, the market for housing began to improve in Corpus Christi because of more business in the port for oil shipments. Ed Cole began to wonder if his conservative policy of no longer building spec homes was causing him to lose profit opportunities. He might make $1,500–$2,000 on a custom-built home, but the profit was normally $3,000 or more on a spec house.

At the same time, Ed had some concerns. If interest rates went up substantially, he might have difficulty selling his spec houses. Federal government policy could influence interest rates in either direction. He was also concerned that state and local property taxes might go up to help fund schools. Also, he had noticed that the city building code was becoming increasingly more restrictive in specifying the type of material he could use.

As Ed Cole was attempting to make his decision, he got a call from U.S. Homes, a national homebuilding firm. U.S. Homes offered to make him the representative for the company in the Corpus Christi area. He would be in partnership with them and would follow their policies for building spec homes. At first Ed liked the idea, but he wasn't sure if that was the best route to take. He knew he had some tough decisions to make.

1. Explain the relationship between profit and risk in Ed Cole's experience. Would you say this relationship generally holds true in the private enterprise economy?
2. Although Ed was operating in a private enterprise economy, how was the government able to influence his life?
3. What might be the pros and cons of Ed going into business with U.S. Homes?

CASE 1-2
WD-40 Company

In the 1950s, a chemist at the Rocket Chemical Company discovered "Water Displacement Formula 40," a spray lubricant and water repellent. Rocket quickly realized that the lubricant was a perfect general-purpose chemical that could be used to lubricate, prevent rust, clean metal, and repel water. The company began to market the new chemical in blue and yellow cans under the name "WD-40."

Sales weren't great at first. But when the Vietnam War started, the Rocket Chemical Company (by then renamed the WD-40 Company) supplied thousands of cans of WD-40 to service personnel all over Southeast Asia. Soldiers had found that none of the lubricants offered by the Army kept their guns from rusting in the extreme heat, grime, and humidity of Vietnam. However, WD-40 worked. The Vietnam veterans continued to buy WD-40 after they returned to the United States. If it lubricated well and stopped rust in the jungle and rain forest, it had to be good. In fact, the product sold in incredible volumes.

The company dropped all its other products in order to make only WD-40. It mixes its secret formula in one large vat, packages it in drums, and then contracts with a distributor to repackage it in the familiar spray cans and market it. The company could conduct all operations itself, and even begin marketing new products, but it has chosen not to do so. The company knows the size it wants to be, and it knows the degree of complexity that best suits its operations. WD-40 makes 17¢ profit on each sales dollar after taxes and shows no sign of peaking out in its climb in sales. In 1991, annual sales exceeded $85 million.

1. Why do you think WD-40 Company chose not to expand its factory? To diversify into other products? To conduct all steps of its production (including packaging and marketing) itself?
2. What advantages that are peculiar to a private enterprise economy did WD-40 Company find for developing its product?
3. Suggest possible futures for WD-40 Company in a private enterprise economy.

OBJECTIVES

After studying this chapter, you should be able to:

1 Describe current patterns of economic change in the U.S.

2 Explain the causes and effects of inflation and deflation.

3 Discuss the effects of federal deficit spending on the economy.

4 Describe the pattern of population change in the U.S.

5 Identify key elements of social change with regard to the environment, consumerism, and other areas.

6 Discuss the increasing importance of women and minorities in the workplace.

CHAPTER 2

The Changing Business Environment

The fastest-growing group in the U.S. today is the Asian-American community. Currently, there are more than 6 million Asian-Americans in the United States, and half of all immigrants are now Asians. An Asian-American adult is twice as likely as other American adults to have a college degree. Asians are also the wealthiest U.S. demographic group, with average household incomes at least 15 percent higher than the national average.

Many businesses are now attempting to reach the Asian-American market. There are more than 200 Asian-language newspapers and magazines, and 40 radio and television stations offer Asian-language programming. Thus, entrepreneurs can choose from a great variety of media for advertising their goods and services. One carpet retailer started advertising in a Chinese-language newspaper. The number of his customers who were Asian doubled—from 15 percent to more than 30 percent. A well-known hotel and casino in Las Vegas mails out promotional literature to Chinese, Korean, and Vietnamese consumers. Businesses across the country now realize that marketing to the Asian-American community makes a lot of sense.

In this chapter, we will discuss reasons for the changing business environment and how these changes affect business.

Managers make decisions in an ever-changing environment. They are confronted daily with uncertainties and changing business conditions. Managers must choose investment programs, set prices for their products, and design advertising campaigns in spite of these uncertainties. The world of business today is a world of change.

In this chapter, we will look at change under three broad headings: economic, demographic, and social. Together, these categories define the socioeconomic context in which business people make their decisions and draw up their business plans. Individual managers have no control over the pace and direction of economic, demographic, and social change. All they can do is to adjust their business strategies intelligently in response to these changes. When reading this chapter, pay special attention to how change affects business.

ECONOMIC CHANGE

The profitability of industries and individual businesses is related to the health of our national economy. Economic change can have a powerful effect on the business outlook. Smart managers watch the economic environment continuously to spot significant changes in output, prices, interest rates, and other variables. Even the largest firms—General Motors, IBM, and Exxon—are simply too small to affect the direction of the economy, and so we say that economic change is uncontrollable. The most that managers can do is to understand how the economy affects their firm's revenues and costs and to respond accordingly. The aspects of the economy that we will study are economic growth, prices, and federal deficits and interest rates.

Economic Growth

A basic economic factor of interest to managers is economic growth. The size of the economy is measured by **gross national product (GNP)**, which is the total market value of all final goods and services produced by an economy in a given period of time. Economic growth or decline is measured by changes in GNP—positive changes for growth and negative changes for decline. Figure 2-1 shows

gross national product (GNP)   total market value of all final goods and services produced by an economy in a given period of time.

FIGURE 2-1   Gross National Product, 1960–1991

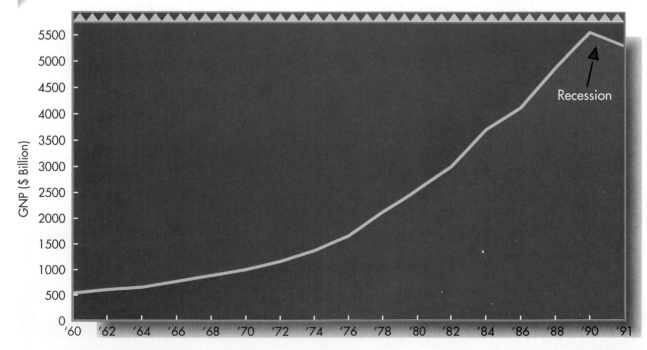

Source: U.S. Department of Commerce, Bureau of Economic Analysis.

the U.S. gross national product for the period 1960–1991. Note how dramatically the U.S. economy has grown.

This is true in spite of the fact that the U.S. economy entered a recession in late 1990. A **recession** is defined as two or more consecutive quarters of decline in gross national product (after subtracting the price increase effects of inflation). The latest recession occurred after an unprecedented eight-year period of peacetime growth. People living in the Southwest were hit particularly hard due to problems in the energy industry, and a shortage of funding for high-technology projects had severe effects in New England.

GNP Performance.   To get a clearer idea of the performance of our economy, look at the bar graph in Figure 2-2. While Figure 2-1 shows a pattern of long-term change, Figure 2-2 is a snapshot of short-term movements in the economy. The high points in the graph correspond to periods of economic expansion (new factories, higher inventories, increased employment, and rising incomes). The low points correspond to periods of economic recession (reduced capital investments, lower inventories, decreased employment, and falling incomes). In 1974, for example, GNP fell by 0.6 percent, partly in response to high energy price increases and governmental efforts to put the brakes on inflation. The economy rebounded in 1976 with a strong surge of growth, as it did again in 1983 and 1984.

Many economists believe that economic growth during the 1990s will be below historical levels. One reason is simply that the population is growing more slowly than it has in the past. Firms no longer have the easy option of increasing sales by taking advantage of overall population growth. Rather, they will have to grow by increasing their market share—that is, by taking sales away from competitors. Thus, price, product, and cost decisions will become increasingly impor-

recession   *Two or more consecutive quarters of decline in gross national product (after subtracting the price increase effects of inflation)*

FIGURE 2-2   Annual Percentage Change in Constant-Dollar GNP, 1960–1991

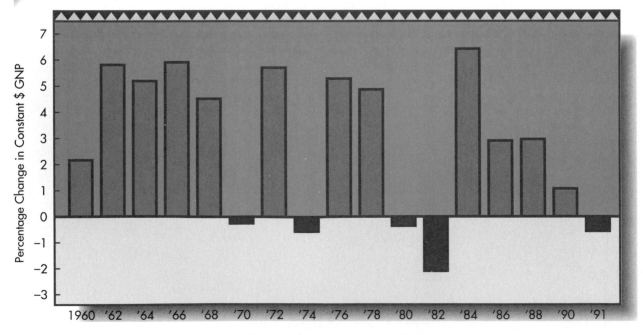

Source: U.S. Department of Commerce, Bureau of Economic Analysis.

tant. Firms must be careful to maintain acceptable profits on their products, which may mean raising prices to cover anticipated cost changes and eliminating unprofitable products from their lines.

Industrial Composition. A look at the composition of the economy by industrial sector provides insight into where the economy is growing. A **sector** is a major division of the economy. The two major sectors are goods-producing industries and service-producing industries. **Goods-producing industries** are firms that create tangible output, such as automobiles, housing, or agricultural products. **Service-producing industries** are firms that provide intangible benefits, such as financial services, medical care, travel advice, and government assistance. Table 2-1 lists the percentage of earned income accounted for by industrial sectors. The years 1965 and 1990 are shown, for purposes of comparison. Goods-producing industries accounted for 40.0 percent of the national income in 1965 but only 25.2 percent in 1990. The slack was picked up by the service sector. Earnings here increased from 59.0 percent to 74.7 percent of the national total over the same 25-year period.

Like more and more Americans, this surveyor works for a firm that provides services rather than tangible products.

sector *a major division of the economy: producers of physical goods or providers of intangible services.*

goods-producing industries *a sector of the economy that creates tangible output, such as automobiles, housing, or agricultural products.*

service-producing industries *a sector that provides intangible benefits, such as financial services, legal advice, medical care, and government assistance.*

Business Career
Travel Agent: Plans travel itineraries for customers. Talks with customers to determine desired destinations, interests, travel dates, and price range. Recommends travel packages that fit customers' interests and budget. Books accommodations, transportation, and tours. Provides information about points of interest, local customs, special events, etc. *Average Salary: $21,000.*

TABLE 2-1   Percentage of Total Earnings by Industry, 1965 and 1990

Industrial Sector	1965	1990
Goods-Producing Industries		
Agriculture, Forestry, Fisheries	3.6%	2.6%
Mining and Construction	6.4	5.5
Manufacturing	30.0	17.1
Total Goods-Producing Industries	40.0	25.2
Service-Producing Industries		
Transportation and Public Utilities	4.0	5.0
Wholesale and Retail Trade	14.9	23.3
Finance, Insurance, Real Estate	11.6	6.2
Services	11.3	24.2
Government	13.2	16.0
Total Service-Producing Industries	59.0	74.7
Other	1.0	0.1
Total	100.0%	100.0%

Source: U. S. Department of Commerce, Bureau of Economic Analysis.

One of the most remarkable economic changes over the past few decades has been the gradual transformation of the U.S. economy from a producer of goods to a producer of services. Many historians and economists believe that we now live in a "postindustrial" economy, in which the production of information and services, rather than the production of goods, is the country's chief economic activity. As Table 2-1 indicates, almost 75¢ of each dollar of national income is produced by service industries. Manufacturers now employ less than one worker in five. In 1940, agricultural workers accounted for 20 percent of total employment. Today they account for about 2 percent! Figure 2-3 projects some of the fastest-growing occupations for the year 2000. Virtually every position falls into the service sector. Note how important the medical, financial, and computer fields are expected to be in the future.

Price Changes

Price is another important economic variable that has far-reaching effects on business strategy and business decisions. Changes in the price of goods and services tell producers whether they should step up production on assembly lines or curtail it, build up warehouse inventories or draw them down, or undertake new investment projects or tighten the investment budget. Price changes also affect consumer spending and savings patterns. In this part of the chapter, we will study inflation, an index of inflation, the causes of inflation, and deflation.

FIGURE 2-3   Projected Percent Change in Employment for the Ten Fastest-Growing Occupations: 1988 to 2000

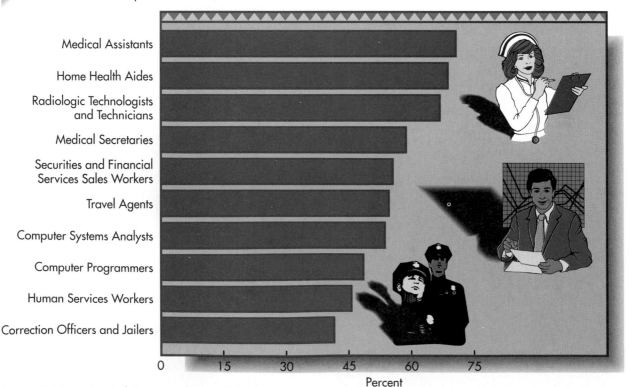

Source: U.S. Department of Commerce, Bureau of the Census.

Inflation. From the mid 1960s to 1981, the United States experienced a decade and a half of unrelieved inflation. **Inflation** is a rise in the general level of prices. Inflation itself is not new. The Romans complained bitterly about it during the reign of Diocletian. So did the Europeans in the 16th century, when gold, arriving from the New World by the shipload, sent food and other prices soaring. In this country, the greatest increase in prices since the Great Depression was experienced not during the 1970s but in 1947, when soldiers returning from World War II reentered civilian life. The demand for civilian goods and services far outstripped the ability of the economy, still gearing down from war production, to produce enough output. The result was a 14 percent rise in prices in that year.

inflation a rise in the general price of goods and services.

Historically, prices increase during times of war or periods of social upheaval and then level off during times of peace. What was new and troubling about inflation in the 1970s was its persistence.[1] According to economic theory, the cure for inflation is an increase in unemployment. During that decade, however, the U.S. experienced both high inflation and high unemployment, even as the Vietnam War wound down. The Reagan Administration, with the help of the Federal Reserve's tight credit policy and a deep recession in 1982, managed to reduce inflation, but at the expense of high unemployment, which rose above 9 percent in 1982 and 1983.

Measuring Inflation. The most commonly reported measure of inflation is the annual percentage change in the consumer price index. The **consumer price index (CPI)** tracks changes in the prices of a group of goods and services that most consumers buy. Prices are increasing when the CPI is positive and decreasing when it is negative. Figure 2-4 charts the course of inflation since World War II. Notice the stability of the CPI through the 1950s and early 1960s, except for the early Korean War years of 1950 and 1951. The index began to surge upward during the Vietnam War—a time of great military spending. It returned to its pre-1960s levels during the mid-1980s. The high values for the CPI in 1974, 1980, and 1990 coincided with dramatic increases in the price of imported oil.

consumer price index (CPI) a statistical system for measuring price changes in a group of goods and services that most consumers buy.

FIGURE 2-4   Inflation in the Postwar Period, 1945–1991

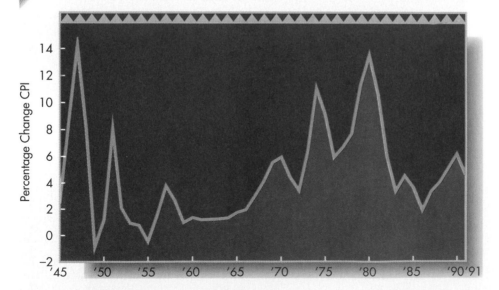

Source: U.S. Department of Labor, Bureau of Labor Statistics.

Table 2-2 shows the effects that inflation can have on the cost of items. For example, 20 years from now, with 6 percent inflation, a college textbook would cost $160.35.

Causes of Inflation.   One major cause of inflation is the relationship between wages and productivity. **Productivity** is defined as output per worker hour. When wages increase faster than productivity, the result is inflation. The amount we can consume of any product depends upon the amount we produce. When wages go up but output does not, we have more money income but not more purchasing power. This occurs because the total supply of goods available for purchase has not increased as rapidly as the amount of money in circulation. The combination of rising wages and constant or sagging output exerts an upward push on prices.[2]

Wage increases in one industry often put pressure on other industries to increase wages. When autoworkers win a 5 percent pay increase, people in other occupations are likely to demand similar pay hikes. An example of this was the professional football players' strike in 1988. The players' union argued that the salaries of football players should be more in line with NBA basketball players and major league baseball players.

Another cause of inflation is the expectation that inflation will continue in the future. Labor unions demand wage increases in anticipation of expected increases in the cost of living. Manufacturers raise the prices of their products in anticipation of future labor and raw material cost increases. Consumers borrow money to finance today's purchases in the belief that prices will be higher tomorrow. Some economists argue that inflation will subside only when people believe that it will subside.

productivity   *output per worker hour.*

TABLE 2-2   The Long-Term Effect of Inflation: Buddy Can You Spare $100 for a Meal?

Item	Price in the Early 1990s	Price 20 Years Later (Assuming 6% Inflation)
Typical Family Automobile	$11,000	$ 35,277
Mercedes	38,000	121,866
Typical 3-Bedroom House	90,000	288,630
Starting Salary (College Graduate)	23,000	73,761
Starting Salary (MBA)	35,000	112,315
College Tuition and Fees for One Year (Average Private University)	13,000	41,691
4 Years at Harvard	88,000	282,216
Typical College Textbook	50	160.35
Visit to the Doctor	25	80.18
Dinner for 2 (Reasonably Nice Restaurant)	32	102.62
Poverty Level (Family of 4)	11,800	37,843

We know that external shocks to the economy, such as the oil price increases brought about by the oil-producing cartel OPEC in the 1970s, had an effect on inflation, but how much of an effect? Between 1973 and 1981, the price of a barrel of crude petroleum increased tenfold. These huge price hikes worked their way through the economy and eventually pushed up prices of new autos, tires, plastic products, textiles, and food items. The prices of these goods increased because oil is an energy input in the production of most goods and a direct raw material input in many others. The OPEC-induced increases in the cost of energy and petroleum products may have accounted for as many as four to five percentage points in the value of the CPI for the years 1974–75 and 1979–80.

The same phenomenon occurred in August of 1990 when Iraqi troops invaded Kuwait. The threat to the disruption of world oil supplies sent the price of crude petroleum from $18 a barrel to $35 within weeks, and the CPI went up substantially in 1990. The pattern reversed itself when the war came to an end.

Deflation. A general decline in the price level is called **deflation.** Although deflation has not had a significant impact on the national economy since the Great Depression (see the box on p. 32), price declines for a particular good or service can ravage an industry and a regional economy. The collapse of oil prices in world markets in early 1986, while a windfall to most Americans, sent the domestic oil industry and the economy of Texas into a steep decline. Crude oil prices, which had been high throughout the early 1980s, dropped to a low of $10 in April 1986 (see Figure 2-5). This price decline in 1986 had a devastating effect on the Texas economy. Economists estimate that each dollar drop in the price of oil resulted in the loss of 25,000 jobs and $100 million in revenues for the state. For the first time since 1970, unemployment in Texas exceeded the national average in 1986. The slump in drilling activity spread to other industries, too. Many banks that had lent heavily to oil producers faced the danger of failure. General Motors laid off 1,700 workers at its auto assembly plant near Dallas. Nearly 1,500 businesses in Houston failed in 1985.[3] The Texas economy's return to normal after the deflationary times in the oil industry has been a slow process.

deflation *a general decline in the price level of goods and services.*

FIGURE 2-5   Crude Oil Price Per Barrel, 1972–1991.

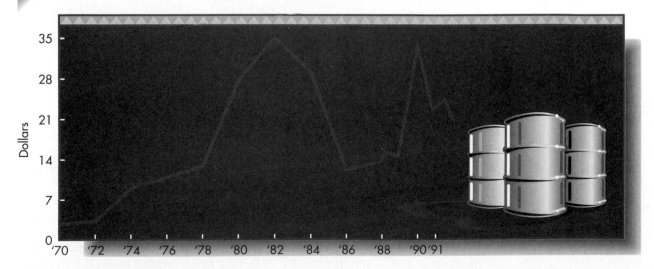

Source: U.S. Department of Energy.

The Great Depression

The U.S. economy collapsed during the Great Depression. The Depression began in 1929, and the nation did not fully recover from it until the start of World War II.

It is hard for us today to realize the magnitude of this collapse and its effect on Americans. The production of durable goods declined 80 percent from 1929 to 1933. Wholesale prices fell by one third and consumer prices by one fourth. At least one quarter of the civilization work force was out of work. Another 25 percent was working only part-time. Tables A and B show the unemployment and inflation rates for 1926 to 1940. Notice how high unemployment was in the early 1930s, the worst of the Depression years. Prices dropped by as much as 10 percent in 1932.

TABLE A
Unemployment During the Great Depression

Year	Unemployment Rate*
1926	1.8
1927	3.3
1928	4.2
1929	3.2
1930	8.7
1931	15.9
1932	23.6
1933	24.9
1934	21.7
1935	20.1
1936	16.9
1937	14.3
1938	19.0
1939	17.2
1940	14.6

* Percentage of civilian labor force unemployed, annual average.

Source: U.S. Department of Commerce, Bureau of the Census.

TABLE B
Price Changes During the Great Depression

Year	% Change in Consumer Price Index
1926	1.0
1927	-1.9
1928	-1.3
1929	0
1930	-2.5
1931	-8.8
1932	-10.3
1933	-5.1
1934	3.4
1935	2.5
1936	1.0
1937	3.6
1938	-1.9
1939	-1.4
1940	1.0

Source: U.S. Department of Labor, Bureau of Labor Statistics.

Federal Deficits and Interest Rates

Anyone who watches television or reads the daily newspaper knows about the federal budget deficit. The government collects money in the form of tax revenues and spends it on national defense, education, health, and other programs. A **budget deficit** occurs when total federal spending exceeds total tax revenues. A **budget surplus** occurs when revenues exceed spending.

Figure 2-6 shows federal tax collections, expenditures, and the resulting deficit or surplus from 1960 to 1990. The figure tells us a number of interesting things. First, the size of government, both in terms of revenues and expenditures, has grown tremendously since 1960. Federal revenues and expenditures were both about $92 billion in 1960. By 1990, they had increased to $1.05 trillion and $1.25 trillion, respectively. Second, the budget has been in surplus only one year since 1960. Third, the size of the deficit has increased dramatically. These huge

budget deficit *total federal spending exceeds total tax receipts.*

budget surplus *total tax receipts exceed total federal spending.*

What caused the Depression? Even after 50 years, it is difficult to name all the reasons. However, many economists cite two. The first reason is the stock market crash of 1929, which wiped out many investors. A speculative fever in the late 1920s sent the prices of many stocks soaring. These rapid price increases created the right conditions for a collapse of investor confidence. When investors lost confidence, they sold their stock. With just about everyone selling, the price of stocks fell dramatically.

During September and October of 1929, the average price per share of stock listed on the New York Stock Exchange dropped nearly 40 percent; by 1933, it had dropped 75 percent. This price decline nearly destroyed the capital markets; investors would not buy stock anymore. Thus, there was no money to build factories and to buy manufacturing equipment. Table C shows the stock price declines for several especially hard-hit companies.

A second major cause was bank failure. Before the Depression, bank deposits were not insured as they are today. When a bank went out of business, the bank's depositors lost all their money. The situation was so unstable that even a rumor of bank failure could *cause* a bank to fail. As a rumor of a bank failure started, panic spread, people in town rushed to the bank and demanded their money. But where was the money? It was not in the vault, of course; it was loaned out. The bank quickly ran out of cash for withdrawals, closed its doors, and declared bankruptcy. Depositors not able to withdraw their money in time were out of luck.

The failure of many banks across the country, along with the stock market crash, stopped the economy in its tracks. No one had money to invest. Factory owners had no money for plant expansion and no jobs for workers. People had no money to spend. The economy stood still.

TABLE C Prices of Selected Common Stocks, 1929 and 1933 (Dollars)

Stock	1929 Price	1933 Price
Consolidated Cigar	100	3.5
General Foods	82	20
General Motors	91	8
U.S. Steel	261	21
New York Central Railroad	256	9

Source: G. U. Axon, *The Stock Market Crash of 1929* (New York: Mason and Lipscomb, 1974), p. 93.

deficits were caused in part by the Economic Recovery Act of 1981, which scaled back income tax rates and slowed the rise in government revenues, and by the inability of government to implement deep cuts in spending. The savings and loan crisis of the late 1980s also added billions of dollars to the deficit.

In 1990, the Deficit Reduction Act was passed. Although the 1990 Act promised to bring the federal budget into balance by the mid-1990s, many remain skeptical. Why? Because of past actions. Under the 1985 Gramm-Rudman-Hollings Act, the deficit was to be reduced to zero by 1991, but it was still running at hundreds of billions of dollars in the early 1990s.

The result of these deficits—generally higher interest rates—is important. The government finances its deficits by borrowing money from the American people and from foreign investors. That is, it issues Treasury securities and sells them to investors in return for cash.

FIGURE 2-6   Federal Tax Receipts and Expenditures, 1960–1990

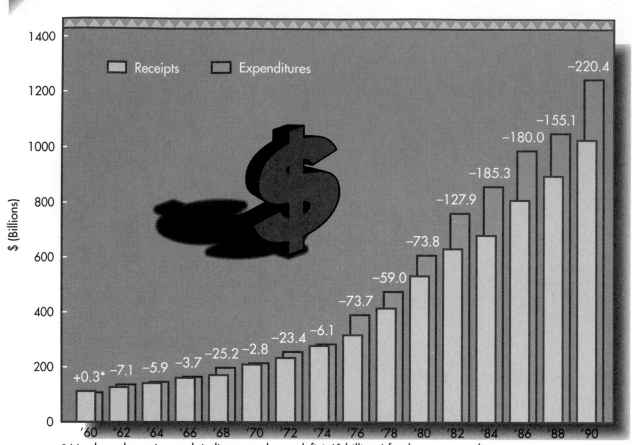

* Numbers shown in graph indicate surplus or deficit ($ billions) for the corresponding year.

Source: U.S. Department of the Treasury; Office of Management and Budget; and Department of Commerce, Bureau of Economic Analysis.

When the government borrows much money, as it has done recently, it drains the pool of funds available for investing. These funds are the amount that people are able to save from their paychecks. Obviously, this amount is limited. Borrowers in private businesses, in need of money for corporate expansion, then must compete for the remaining funds. They do this by bidding aggressively for funds, thus causing interest rates to rise. In 1983, for example, government borrowed nearly 50 percent of the available funds, with the result that interest rates climbed over the next 12 months. When interest rates are high, private business cannot obtain money to build new factories, to purchase labor-saving machinery, or to introduce new products to the market. Also hard hit is the housing industry. When home mortgage rates went above the 15 percent mark in the early 1980s, the sale of new homes slowed, and the housing industry went into a slump.

DEMOGRAPHIC CHANGE

demography *the social science that studies characteristics of human populations.*

Besides economic change, another important set of uncontrollable environmental factors is demographic change. **Demography** is a social science that studies characteristics of human populations. These characteristics include such factors as age and family structure. Managers know that demographic changes can have a dramatic effect on the markets for goods and services.

The market for new housing is especially susceptible to demographic change. It provides a good illustration of how such change can affect business strategy. For decades, the vast majority of new single-family houses constructed each year were "starter" homes—modest, inexpensive housing units for first-time buyers. By the 1990s, however, demand for new luxury homes began to increase as home-owners traded up to bigger, more expensive homes.

The reason behind this change in the housing industry is a demographic one. In the years following the end of World War II in 1945, more children were born in America than during any other time in its history. This tremendous surge in the population is called the "baby boom." The baby boomers, as they are called, began to enter the job market in the late 1960s and to buy their first homes in the early 1970s. Now, millions of baby boomers are entering their prime earning years, so they can afford bigger houses. The response of many builders around the country to this demographic change has been to switch from building starter homes to building more expensive ones.

We can now turn our attention to national and regional population growth and shifts, the changing structure of the American family, and the aging of the U.S. population. Understanding these changes can help the business person plan for the future: locate plants, market new products, and hire workers.

Population

Figure 2-7 shows the actual and projected growth of the population of the United States for the period 1940 to 2000. Our current population is roughly 250 million, up from 228 million in 1980. Demographers estimate that the U.S. population will exceed 268 million by the end of this century. However, the *rate* of population

FIGURE 2-7   Population of the United States

Source: U.S. Department of Commerce, Bureau of the Census.

growth has declined steadily since its modern peak in 1955. Currently, the population is increasing at a rate of less than 1 percent a year. Because of this slackening rate of growth, businesses must focus better on their target markets. When the population is growing rapidly, demand for new products increases constantly. There is a greater margin for error. In the new era, one company's success may come only at the expense of another company's failure.

Regional Shifts. The people of the United States are on the move, migrating from one part of the country to another in search of jobs and a better way of life. During the next five years, two out of every five American families will move to a new residence. A full 20 percent of these moves will be to a different state.

The biggest population shifts have occurred between the northern states (the Snowbelt) and the southern and western states (the Sunbelt). Each year, thousands of people leave New York, Ohio, and Illinois and move to South Carolina, Florida, and Arizona. This trend is likely to continue for years to come. Figure 2-8 shows that Alaska and the Rocky Mountain states will see the greatest rates of population increase, whereas the mideastern states will be stagnant or lose population.

Clearly, business must react to the changing shifts of the population. Hundreds of manufacturers have already relocated or opened production facilities in the Sunbelt over the past decade. Nashville, Tennessee, is quickly becoming the new Detroit. In the early 1980s, Nissan opened an $800 million assembly plant in nearby Smyrna. By the end of the decade, General Motors had built its ultramodern Saturn assembly plant in Spring Hill, just south of Nashville. The chief reasons for GM's choice of the Nashville area over many other cities were its central location, mild climate, low property taxes, and motivated, loyal work force.

FIGURE 2-8   Average Annual Growth Rate of U.S. Population by Region, 1980–2000

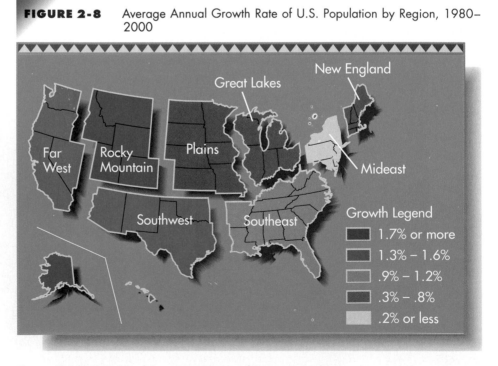

Source: U.S. Department of Commerce, Bureau of Economic Analysis.

Urban Migration Patterns. **Urban migration** refers to the movement of people to or from large cities, small cities, or rural areas, as well as shifts between the suburbs and downtown in metropolitan areas. Two distinct patterns are occurring with respect to urban migration. First, the 16 urban areas of the United States with populations of 2 million or more people are expected to grow by only .2 percent yearly during the 1990s, considerably below their 3.7 percent historical annual growth rate. Cities with populations in the 500,000 to 2,000,000 range will grow more slowly than in the past, but still more than five times faster than the larger urban areas. Nonmetropolitan areas, which actually experienced a decline in population from 1950 to 1980, along with minor metropolitan areas, will grow more than twice as fast as major urban areas.

Second, many large cities, from which the middle class fled to the suburbs during the 1970s and 1980s, are beginning to experience a rebirth of their downtown areas. Land formerly occupied by slums has become valuable because of its location. Urban property is being purchased by developers, old buildings are being razed, and high-rise office, residential, and retail complexes are being built in their place. As a result of a new spirit of government and private sector cooperation, old downtown areas are being revitalized in such cities as Baltimore, Washington, D.C., Milwaukee, St. Louis, Pittsburgh, and Detroit.

These urban migration patterns will significantly affect business decisions, too. The fact that smaller cities are growing much faster than large cities will spur retail chains to open new stores in smaller cities. The move to smaller cities necessitates a new mentality in the decision-making process. Should present employees who are used to living in large metropolitan areas be expected to shift to smaller towns? Also, what role should the corporation play in the new environment? Should the company's facility in a small town be treated as merely an extension of the overall corporate structure, or should the firm spend time and

urban migration the movement of people to or from large cities, small cities, or rural areas, as well as shifts between the suburbs and downtown in metropolitan areas.

In the past few decades, the great migration was from the large cities to the suburbs, although many people continued to work downtown, like the commuters shown above. In the future, however, it appears that more and more people will both live and work in smaller cities.

resources to become part of the community? Often a firm will ask for local property tax breaks to move into a new community. Is this an appropriate strategy from the standpoint of goodwill?

Key decisions must also be made about such factors as the adequacy of the local labor pool and the purchasing power of the people in the community. Perhaps the master of dealing with the small-town environment was the late Sam Walton, founder of the huge Wal-Mart retail chain. He is profiled on page 39.

Family Structure

Over the years, many sociologists have warned that vast social changes would bring about the extinction of the American family. This statement appeared in the *Boston Quarterly Review:* "The family in its old sense is disappearing from our land, and not only our free institutions are threatened, but the very existence of our society is endangered." It was written in 1859! Such warnings, it would seem, are not new. Although the family as an institution may not be dying off, it *is* changing.

Understanding the changing family structure is essential for business firms to target their products and services appropriately. If a company still regards dad as the breadwinner and mom as some sort of glorified domestic, the firm may soon be out of business. Let's look at some changing patterns in the family structure.

Size. The average size of the U.S. family is decreasing. It declined from 3.67 persons in 1960 to 3.15 in 1990. The average family size for whites was 3.1, for blacks 3.5, and for Hispanics 3.8. The percentage of families with 6 or more members declined from 9.8 percent in 1970 to about 2.9 percent in 1990.

Marriage. In 1990, the median age for first marriages was 24.9 for men and 22.9 for women, up from 22.5 and 20.6, respectively, in 1970. Ten percent of Americans will never marry; this percentage has doubled since 1970.

Divorce. The divorce rate in the United States nearly tripled between 1965 and 1990. In 1990, there were 3.0 million marriages and 1.3 million divorces.

POSSLQs. Three percent of the nation's households consist of unmarried "persons of the opposite sex sharing living quarters"—or POSSLQs, as they are called by the Census Bureau. The number of POSSLQs nearly quadrupled between 1970 and 1990.

Living Alone. Almost one out of every four people in the U.S. lives alone. This rate increased by more than 75 percent from 1970 to 1990. The number of people between the ages of 25 and 34 living alone quadrupled during the same period.

Single-Parent Families. The number of single-parent families has more than doubled since 1970. Five out of six one-parent families are headed by women.

Aging of the Population

The U.S. population is getting older. By this we mean that the average age of the population is increasing. The median age is currently about 33 years, up from 27.9 in 1970. In the year 2000, the median age is expected to be 36. These developments are of profound importance to the makers of consumer products and to other business planners.

Sam Walton

In this chapter, we discuss the changing business environment. No one understood the patterns of change better than Samuel Moore Walton. In 1989, he was selected by *Financial World* as the outstanding business executive of the 1980s. Before his death on April 5, 1992, he was the richest man in the U.S., with a personal and family net worth of approximately $23 billion. His career was a good lesson in how to adjust to the business environment.

Sam Walton started his business career as a trainee for J. C. Penney in the 1930s. In 1945, he opened his first retail store, a Ben Franklin franchise, in Newport, Arkansas. By 1962 he owned the largest number of Ben Franklin store franchises in the U.S., but the chain was not progressive enough to suit his desires. Walton wanted to be the most aggressive discount retailer in the country. He started over, under his own banner. With other family members, he opened the first Wal-Mart store in Rogers, Arkansas, in 1962. The strategy was to concentrate on small towns in the South and to give customers the lowest prices and the widest selection of name-brand products possible. Walton was willing to let Sears and other major retailers have the big-city market. He realized that people in small towns had different tastes from those of city people. He also realized that the migration to large cities after World War II would not continue indefinitely, and he was prepared to be a big fish in thousands of small ponds.

By the early 1990s, Sam Walton's Wal-Mart operation owned approximately 1,700 discount stores, more than 100 wholesale clubs, and other innovative retail outlets. An investor who had purchased 100 shares of Wal-Mart stock when it first became available to the public in 1970 would have holdings worth over $2 million in the spring of 1992.

Unlike many corporate executives who enjoyed great success, Walton did not live a life of luxury.

While still in his early seventies (he died at age 74), he constantly visited his stores and could often be seen driving around in his Ford pick-up truck. When new stores opened, he served as a cheerleader, exhorting the employees to give their very best.

Wal-Mart is now the largest retailer in the U.S. Over the decades, it has surpassed such household names as Sears, J. C. Penney, and K mart. Corporate sales were $43 billion in 1991, and the company's goal is to increase that figure to $125 billion by the end of the century. Wal-Mart has a long history of growing at 25 to 35 percent a year.

Even as the corporation gets larger, Sam Walton's values remain in place: patriotism and frugality. If you are going to do business with Wal-Mart, you had better put American products first. His frugality is evident in the decor of the corporate home office, which has been described as "early bus station." According to Sam Walton's philosophy, if you want to become the most successful retail operation in the country, you learn to control your costs with highly efficient management, and then you pass the benefits on to your customers. You also learn to recognize the economic patterns that exist and take full advantage of them.

Figure 2-9 shows how the age distribution of the U.S. population has changed in the last 30 years. Look at the "65 years and over" group. This group now makes up 12 percent of the population; in 1960 it accounted for 9.2 percent. Notice also how the percentage of the "under 5" population has declined and how the population percentage of 25–44-year-olds has increased. By the year 2000, people 45 and older could account for as much as 37 percent of the population!

What accounts for this gradual aging of the population? People are living longer because of improved medical care and better diet. Another reason is that fewer women are currently having children. In 1955, 118 out of every 1,000 women in the 15–44 age group had a child in that year. In recent years, fewer than 70 women out of every 1,000 gave birth to a child during the year.

What does the aging of the population mean to business? The first thing to keep in mind is the economic clout of the older age groups. Older people today have more money to spend than do younger people. Fully 77 percent of all household financial holdings—stocks, bonds, and cash savings—are in the hands of people 50 years or older. People retiring today have benefited from four decades of strong economic growth and opportunity, during which the standard of living rose more than 150 percent. To be sure, many older people live below the poverty line, but a substantial number of them enjoy high career savings, improved social security benefits, and generous private pension plans.

In response to these changes in the age distribution, we can expect to see shrinking markets for baby care products, children's toys, and record albums and much larger product and service markets for people 65 and older, particularly for women. New low-cost living accommodations that provide food service and medical care for senior citizens will be needed. Pharmaceutical firms will develop and market many new over-the-counter drugs for older people, while in-home nursing and meal services will become more popular for those people who can afford them. One manufacturer of baby foods has already begun marketing its products to senior citizens. Can you think of other product and service opportunities for this age group?

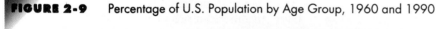

FIGURE 2-9   Percentage of U.S. Population by Age Group, 1960 and 1990

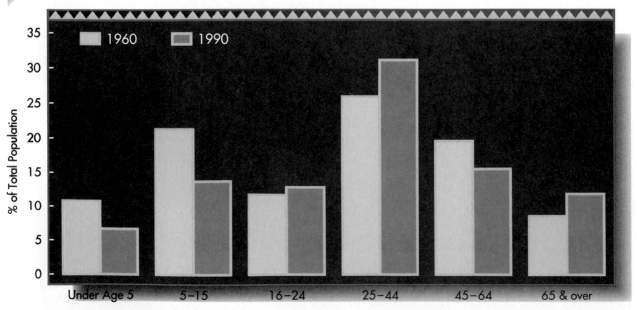

Source: U.S. Department of Commerce, Bureau of the Census.

SOCIAL CHANGE

Changes in people's attitudes can have a powerful impact on what goods and services are produced and demanded in the marketplace. In this part of the chapter, we will study how attitude changes have given rise to environmental protection, consumerism, and the changing role of women. We will also discuss some of the impacts of these changes on business.

As an example of how changing popular attitudes can influence business and markets, consider society's recent crackdown on alcohol abuse. Out of a concern for safety and health, people are drinking less or switching to less potent beers and wines. In a recent poll, 45 percent of Americans said that they now drink less than they did five years ago. Only 13 percent said that they were drinking more. Eighty-five percent of Americans support raising the legal drinking age to 21. Overall, sales in this multibillion-dollar alcohol industry have suffered from the new national temperance.

Environmental Protection

One of the characteristics of an industrial society is pollution. By the late 1960s, the immensity of this problem had become clear. Our rivers and lakes, for example, were being contaminated with hazardous wastes. People were becoming increasingly alarmed over the deterioration of the environment. In response to this growing public concern, Congress passed many environmental reforms in the

Until 1990, thousands of dolphins died each year because commercial fishermen's method of catching tuna also caught dolphins. Under pressure from environmentalists, the three major U.S. tuna companies—StarKist, Chicken of the Sea, and Bumblebee—promised not to buy or sell any tuna that was caught using the method dangerous to dolphins. In this case, what's good for the environment is also good for business.

late 1960s and early 1970s. The Environmental Protection Agency (EPA) was established to ensure that businesses would comply with the laws.

Business is obviously affected by these laws. Corporate executives must consider whether to fight the passage of a new law that might cost them millions of dollars or to go along with it. Sometimes there is little choice. In general, the effect has been to make corporations better citizens. However, business growth has been slow in the 1990s. Business leaders have argued that regulations should be kept at a low enough level that firms can afford to expand and create new jobs. Let's look at some key areas of environmental concern.

Air Quality. The amount of pollutants spewed into our air each year is staggering. According to estimates of the EPA, the volume of carbon monoxide emissions in a recent year was 69.9 million metric tons. Automobiles were responsible for most of this total. The total for sulphur oxides was 21.4 million metric tons. Electric utilities produced most of these emissions. It is hard to imagine so much material suspended in the air. Fortunately, the levels of these pollutants have dropped since the early 1970s, when the major environmental laws began to take effect.

Energy Development Trade-Offs. Supporters of energy development and supporters of environmental protection often find their goals in conflict. Should we allow oil exploration and drilling in our national parks, or should we preserve the parks for our children? Should we build dams for hydroelectric power generation on our last wild rivers, or should we leave the rivers in their natural state? Similar questions can be asked about oil shale development in the rangelands of the West, pipeline construction across the Alaskan and Canadian tundra, and the burning of "dirty" coal—which most scientists now agree is the principal cause of acid rain—by power companies.

Nearly all energy development projects involve some sort of economic problem. A major oil spill such as the one in Alaska in 1989 can leave hundreds of miles of beach spoiled for many years. An accident at a nuclear power plant, such as the one at Chernobyl in 1986, could leave a wide area contaminated for hundreds of years.

The disagreements between advocates of energy development and environmental protection groups will not go away. Any decisions in these areas involve trade-offs. For example, we can reduce air pollution from automobiles by requiring better emission-control devices. But the result is fewer miles per gallon of gasoline and, therefore, more gallons consumed. In the same way, we can become less reliant on imported oil by burning more coal. Coal is mined in the United States, and it is plentiful. The problem is that much coal has a high sulfur content, which presents a major air pollution problem.

Consumerism

Producers and consumers interact in the marketplace through the buying and selling of goods and services. Both buyers and sellers have enjoyed certain rights in this interaction. Traditionally, the seller has been allowed to introduce virtually any product to the market as long as it was not known to be hazardous. The seller has also had the freedom to design advertising strategies for its products and to price them so as to maximize profit.

Consumers have held certain rights, too. Chief among them has been the right of choice: Consumers could buy the seller's product or not. Consumers have also had the right to expect safe products and products that were essentially what the seller represented them to be. But the consumer's best protection has always been a healthy skepticism toward product claims and promises.

Buyers and sellers have always had certain rights. But could the power of the two parties ever have been considered equal? No. In response to a series of product abuses, consumerism began to gain momentum. **Consumerism** is a social movement aimed at increasing the power of consumers relative to that of sellers. Consumerism has resulted in a number of consumer protection laws. For example, automobile "lemon laws" have passed in many states. If an auto dealer fails to respond to reasonable complaints by buyers, he or she may be forced to pay them compensation and perhaps even to refund the full price they paid.

consumerism   a social movement aiming to increase the power of consumers relative to that of sellers.

Why the Consumer Movement? The consumer movement began with the great social unrest of the 1960s and 1970s. It was prompted by the sometimes irresponsible behavior of business.

Consumer dissatisfaction with defective or unsafe products, fraudulent product claims, and careless repair work contributed to the rise of consumerism and to the demand for greater business accountability. The consumer movement resulted in the establishment of the Consumer Product Safety Commission in 1972 and in the passage of a number of consumer protection laws.

Response by Business. The consumer movement is here to stay, despite a few setbacks. For example, Congress attempted repeatedly to establish a consumer protection agency in the 1970s and 1980s, without success. The lasting contribution of consumerism is greater fairness and frankness in the marketplace. But what specifically does consumerism mean for business?

Clean Up the Act. Nearly every month, another major product is recalled or a cancer-causing substance is found in food products. Every time this happens, the cry goes up for more government protection of consumers. In response to such pressure, managers have learned to look carefully at the safety of their products, the legitimacy of their advertising claims, and the sales tactics of their marketing people. Top management has no choice but to treat consumers more fairly. Without this concern, many businesses might find themselves in the position of Ford Motor Co. several years ago. It was the target of several lawsuits because the gas tank on Ford's Pinto sometimes exploded in rear-end collisions.

Take Positive Action. Rather than simply complying with the law or avoiding lawsuits, some leading companies have taken positive steps to meet the needs of consumers. Eastman Kodak Co. is an example of a company with a farsighted approach to the consumer movement. A few of its programs in that area are listed here:

- A product design philosophy that anticipates and eliminates consumer mistakes before they occur.
- A free photo advice service for consumers. This service handles more than 150,000 inquiries a year.
- Thirty-nine consumer service centers located across the country. Each center provides free advice and minor equipment repairs.
- A nonprofit publication program that distributes 100 different pamphlets and 25 books on photography.

- An assistant vice president whose primary responsibility is consumer service for all divisions.
- High standards of product quality control and an easily read and understood warranty for its products.

Other major firms, including General Electric Co., Whirlpool Corporation, and Quaker Oats Co., have set up strong consumer protection programs. As more businesses come to understand the importance of a good relationship with the consumer, we can expect an even greater degree of corporate accountability in the marketplace. Still, the battle is not over. The Ethical Issue on page 45 tells about questionable practices that are still going on in the early 1990s.

Changing Role of Women

Today, more women than ever before are choosing to work outside the home. In 1960, fewer than 22 million women in this country held jobs; by 1990, the number had risen to nearly 55 million. Figure 2-10 shows the number of women of working age who are employed. Notice that in 1960, only 37.8 percent of all women over 16 were jobholders, compared to more than 50 percent in the 1990s. The Bureau of Labor Statistics estimates that by 1995, more than 60 percent of all working-age women in the United States will be employed.

Why Women Work Outside the Home. Most women take jobs for the same reason that men do—they need the money. The increased cost of living has certainly been a reason why many women have chosen to enter the workplace. Other reasons:

- Today, more females are enrolled in college than males. In 1960, women accounted for only 36 percent of all college graduates; in each year since

FIGURE 2-10   Percentage of Women More than 16 Years of Age Employed in the U.S., 1960–1995

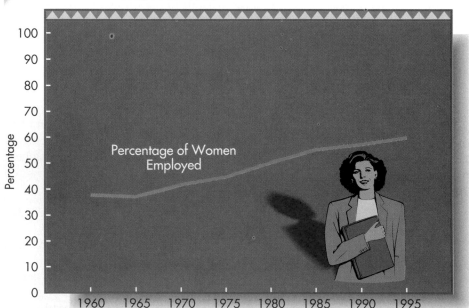

Source: U.S. Department of Labor, Bureau of Labor Statistics

When Is a Pound Really 16 Ounces?

Many ethical issues related to business are obvious. For example, if a firm cheats on its tax return or knowingly pollutes the air, its practices can easily be called into question. However, there are more subtle forms of deception and unethical behavior. Such questionable behavior may go unnoticed, so the only restraining force is the corporation's collective "conscience." Corporate executives may be leading the local United Way drive or supporting hospitals and schools, but very different activities may be going on in the background.

One area of subtle deception is the packaging and pricing of items. While the price of Charmin Squeezably Soft bathroom tissues has remained constant, the roll has been quietly reduced from 380 sheets to 300. If you like M&M candies, be prepared for a similar disappointment. While the price, appearance, and number of candies sold in small packages appears to be the same, the weight of each M&M has been reduced by 4 percent, with no notice to the consumer.[4] Was this a mere oversight by the manufacturer or an attempt to squeeze 4 percent more profit from the uninformed customer? Is this an ethical way to do business?

Another trick is to make a box appear to be full when it really is not. The candies in boxes of Andes Mint Chocolate occupy about 60 to 70 percent of their package. Yet from the outside of the see-through package, it appears as if the box is 100 percent full of chocolates.[5] Is there an ethical issue here? How would you feel if the last 100 pages of this text were blank?

Ethics thus involves other matters besides bribes to corrupt foreign governments, insider stock trading, and unsafe work environments. The way businesses treat consumers is also a question of ethics.

1980, females have accounted for more than 50 percent of all college graduates. By 1990, the figure was 54.4 percent.

- High-paying, high-status jobs are slowly opening to women.
- In addition, the number of jobs traditionally held by women has increased. The need for teachers, clerks, office-machine operators, and medical technicians is greater than ever before.
- One out of two marriages ends in divorce. This has resulted in many women entering the job market. Also, many women are choosing to remain single longer.
- More women are choosing to limit the size of their families. Births may be planned to minimize the amount of time lost from the job. Women are no longer forced to choose between family and career.
- Many women define satisfaction and self-esteem in terms of work and career advancement, just as men do.

Fair Treatment. Companies have both a moral and a legal obligation to hire and promote women. In terms of wage compensation, the principle is equal pay for equal work. That is, a female employee with the same qualifications, skills, experience, and level of performance as a male employee should be paid the same. However, women's pay still falls short of men's pay. Women's wages are currently about 68 percent of men's wages, up from 60 percent in the late 1970s. Experts predict that this figure will reach 75 percent by the year 2000. Nonetheless, top management positions are still held mostly by men. In spite of all this, there is hope for the future. Table 2-3 lists some women who have had great success in the corporate world. Note the Family Status column—over half the women in top management positions are married.

New Business Opportunities. Many households today have two wage earners. The combined earnings of the two give the household increased spending power. To illustrate, if both husband and wife worked as certified public account-

TABLE 2-3   Women in Top Management Positions

Name	Age	Company	Title	1989 Cash Compensation	Family Status
Rosetta Bailey	55	Citizens Federal Bank	Senior Vice President	$123,272	Married, Two Children
Jill Barad	39	Mattel	Division President	504,923	Married, Two Children
Ilene Beal	44	BayBanks	Executive Vice President	163,020	Single, No Children
Cathleen Black	46	Gannett	Executive Vice President	600,000	Married, One Child
Kathryn Braun	39	Western Digital	Senior Vice President	255,365	Married, One Stepchild
Jean Carrick	43	Delta Woodside Industries	Corporate Controller	76,342	Divorced, No Children
Patricia Dawley	52	Anchor Savings Bank	Executive Vice President, Secretary	139,500	Divorced, No Children
Katharine Graham	73	Washington Post	Chairman, Chief Executive Officer	739,874	Widowed, Four Children
Jane Greer	51	Delta Woodside Industries	Vice President	166,898	Divorced, No Children
Bernice Lavin	64	Alberto-Culver	Vice President, Secretary, Treasurer	513,746	Married, Three Children
Nina McLemore	45	Liz Claiborne	Senior Vice President	600,000	Married, No Children
Debbie Miede	34	Downey Savings & Loan	Senior Vice President	140,892	Married, Three Children
Maria Monet	40	Ogden	Chief Financial Officer	733,617	Married, No Children
Hazel O'Leary	53	Northern States Power	Senior Vice President	174,170	Widowed, One Child
Carole St. Mark	43	Pitney Bowes	Division President	376,946	Divorced, No Children
Mary Sammons	43	Fred Meyer	Senior Vice President	253,847	Married, One Child
Marion Sandler	59	Golden West Financial	President, Chief Executive Officer	665,357	Married, Two Children
Irene Adams Staskin	60	Kelly Services	Senior Vice President	214,500	Married, Two Children
Faye Widenmann	41	Pinnacle West Capital	Vice President, Secretary	82,889	Divorced, No Children

Source: *Fortune*, 30 July 1990, p. 46. © 1990 The Time Inc. Magazine Company. All rights reserved.

ants for an accounting firm, together they could earn more than $50,000 in their first year out of college.

Although households with two wage earners have more money to spend, the partners have less personal time. They are likely to want services and time-saving devices that make household work easier. Instead of washing clothes at home, they may send them out to the cleaners. Instead of preparing home-cooked dinners, they may buy convenience foods and pop them in the microwave oven or dine in restaurants. Working couples also have less time to shop, so many retailers have extended store hours to accommodate their schedules. Businesses take advantage of the growing number of working couples by offering products and services compatible with their lifestyles. As more women reach executive positions, businesses can target their products toward an affluent female market based on professional achievement. This might involve status symbols other than furs and jewelry, such as professional wardrobes and professional financial services for the female executive.

The Advance of Minorities

The increased prominence of minorities in the workforce is another significant development. Much of the progress of minorities is because of better education. There were 1.2 million African-American students enrolled in colleges and universities in 1990, compared to 700,000 three decades before. There were 670,000 college students of Hispanic origin, compared to a mere 230,000 in 1960. This growth took place while enrollment in colleges and universities was generally shrinking.

The Bureau of Labor Statistics projects 16.5 million blacks in the labor force in the year 2000, up by 3.2 million from 1988. Hispanic workers will number 14.3 million by the end of the century, an increase of 5.3 million from 1988. More important than the mere numbers is the advance of minorities into such formerly "all-white" domains as law, medicine, and engineering.

The advance of minorities should provide diversity, in the responses to the problems of business and society. It will certainly provide a wider range of input into the decision-making process.

SUMMARY POINTS

1 Economic change is measured through the performance of the gross national product, which represents the total market value of all final goods and services produced by the economy in a given period of time. An important consideration is which areas of the economy are producing this total output. In recent decades, the service sector has become increasingly important, while goods-producing industries have become less important.

2 Inflation is a rise in the general level of prices. It is influenced by the productivity of workers, by expectations for the future, and by external shocks such as oil shortages and wars. Deflation is a decline in the price level. It is influenced by the same factors, only in the opposite direction. Rapid rates of inflation or deflation can have a destabilizing effect on the economy.

3 Federal deficit spending means that government expenditures exceed tax revenues. The government has operated at a deficit in all but one year since 1960. High deficits generally lead to high interest rates, as the government becomes a large borrower in the financial markets to help pay its bills.

4 Another important part of the changing environment is population shifts. More people are moving into the southern and western states, where jobs are more plentiful. Also, the population is becoming older on average, and the family unit is becoming smaller.

5 Key elements of social change include an increasing concern for the environment and a movement by consumers to protect their interests in the marketplace. These factors influence the way businesses conduct their activities.

6 Women are playing a more important role in the working population. Because of the improved education of minorities, they will have a larger share of the economic pie in the future.

KEY TERMS

gross national product (GNP) 25

recession 26

sector 27

goods-producing industries 27

service-producing industries 27

inflation 29

consumer price index (CPI) 29

productivity 30

deflation 31

budget deficit 32

budget surplus 32

demography 34

urban migration 37

consumerism 43

REVIEW QUESTIONS

1 What is gross national product? What sectors of our economy are growing the fastest? The slowest? **1**

2 What is the difference between inflation and deflation? What is the consumer price index? **2**

3 Describe how wage increases that are greater than productivity increases lead to inflation. **2**

4 Why is the federal budget in deficit? How does government finance its deficits? What effect do deficits have on interest rates? **3**

5 What is demographics? Why is demographics of interest to business people? **4**

6 Where have the greatest shifts in regional population taken place recently? **4**

7 With the changing age distribution in the population, which industries (types of products) will be hurt? Which will benefit? **4**

8 Cite three examples of trade-offs between energy development and environmental protection. **5**

9 Define consumerism. What are some of the reasons for the rise of consumerism? **5**

10 How has the percentage of women attending college changed over the last three decades? **6**

DISCUSSION QUESTIONS

1 Do you think that economic growth will be as strong in the 1990s as it has been in recent decades? What effect will this have on competition between firms?

2 Discuss how the mere expectation of inflation can actually cause inflation.

3 Do you think that the migration to the Sunbelt states will slow? Are there any signs that this may already have begun to happen?

4 What are some of the economic arguments against tough environmental laws? Do you think that this country can afford the price tag for clean air and clean water?

5 Is the continued development of nuclear energy sources worth the risk? What are some of the benefits of this source of energy? What are some of the dangers?

EXPERIENTIAL EXERCISES

1 Read the daily or weekly business press (*The Wall Street Journal, Barrons, Business Week,* etc.) to track business conditions for a period of six weeks. Pay special attention to interest rates and the Dow Jones Industrial Average, a popular index for measuring stock market activity. Develop tables or graphs to keep track of any changes observed. Are any significant trends emerging? What do these trends mean for business?

2 Interview three women in business. Try to include at least one executive and one production worker. Have they observed any discrimination toward women on the job? Are women generally treated fairly? Are the pay scales for men and women in their companies comparable? Do they think that their jobs would be any easier if they were men? Write up a short report summarizing the results of your interviews.

CASES

CASE 2-1
Philip Morris

Philip Morris is one of the largest U.S. corporations. In 1990, it reported $51 billion in sales and more than $3 billion in profits. The firm employs 168,000 people. It is the biggest advertiser in the country, with twice the annual advertising budget of Pepsico, Kellogg's, Pillsbury, or Coca-Cola.

Yet, if you had been writing about Philip Morris two decades ago, you would probably have written its obituary. Its main product was cigarettes; the firm produced such brands as Marlboro, Benson and Hedges, Merit, and Virginia Slims. The Surgeon General had given repeated warnings about the dangers of cigarette smoking to a person's health. The warnings were stamped right on the pack. Furthermore, cigarette manufacturers were no longer allowed to advertise on radio and TV. The old slogan, "Call for Philip Morris," was being silenced.

But Philip Morris carefully watched demographic trends and made appropriate shifts in accordance with them. The firm reduced its dependence on the tobacco business. Philip Morris now owns the largest food-processing and food-packaging firm in the U.S., Kraft General Foods (KGF). The KGF division was formed through the multibillion dollar acquisitions of the General Foods Corporation in 1985 and the Kraft Corporation in 1988. This division of Philip Morris produces such products as Post cereals, Maxwell House coffee, Kraft cheese, Jell-O desserts, Bird's Eye frozen foods, Kool-Aid, Miracle Whip, and Oscar Mayer meats. Today, 51 percent of the corporate revenue comes from the food product division.

Philip Morris also moved into the beer business by acquiring Miller Brewing. Miller is now the second-largest brewery in the U.S., with 23 percent of the domestic beer market. Increased beer sales are projected for the future, partly because of concerns about health. People are tending to avoid hard liquor, preferring milder forms of alcohol such as wine and beer.

Philip Morris has tracked the changing demographic patterns in order to ensure its survival. Tobacco is still important to the corporation. Although it represents only 40 percent of corporate revenue, tobacco produces 72 percent of the profits. Furthermore, while U.S. consumption of cigarettes is going down, tobacco is a growth industry in the rest of the world. American cigarettes are becoming increasingly popular in Japan, Western Europe, and Russia. Philip Morris intends to take full advantage of this trend.

1. In terms of population changes, work patterns, and people's general concerns, what major strategies would you recommend for the Philip Morris food division (KGF)? What general types of products should it develop?
2. Some companies are strongly influenced by the ups and downs of the economy. Do you think Philip Morris falls into that category? Explain.
3. Once Miller Brewing was acquired by Philip Morris, it moved from fifth place to second in the brewing industry. Why do you think this took place?
4. "Institutional investors" are large investors such as mutual funds, insurance companies, and banks. Such investors are sometimes challenged about the morality of putting their funds into companies that promote smoking or other questionable activities. If you were an institutional investor, would this bother you?

CASE 2-2
Minor League Baseball Decision

In the spring of 1991, a number of investors approached Hal Dixon about the possibility of bringing a minor league baseball team to Alexandria, Louisiana. Alexandria had a rich baseball history; it had once been part of the fabled Texas League. (This was not a geographical error. There had always been non-Texan teams in the league.)

In 1958, major league baseball began to move west. The Brooklyn Dodgers moved to Los Angeles, and the New York Giants went to San Francisco. This altered not only the nature of major league baseball, but also that of the minor leagues. Cities such as Atlanta, Houston, and Kansas City went from minor-league to major-league status, and the minor leagues began to suffer. Between the late 1950s and 1991, major league baseball changed from an eastern and midwestern sport to one that involved virtually every metropolitan area in the country. For example, the state of California now has five major league teams. Every one of those California cities once sponsored a minor league team.

The number of cities with minor league baseball teams fell from 500 at its peak to slightly over 100 in 1991. Nevertheless, there is some hope for the future. After losing popularity to football through the 1960s and 1970s, baseball is enjoying a resurgence in interest at every level, from little league to the major leagues. The buying and trading of baseball cards has become an incredibly popular hobby (and investment!). Even minor league baseball got a boost from the popular movie "Bull Durham," a story about the relationship between an old pro and a young rookie.

With all of this in mind, Hal Dixon had prepared a proposal to 15 wealthy investors, calling for each to put up $20,000 (a total of $300,000) to bring minor league baseball back to Alexandria. He received the following five questions from potential investors. See how you would answer them.

1. What is the general pattern of change in the age of the population, and what effect could that have on the success of the minor league franchise?
2. Louisiana is an "oil patch" state, like Texas and Oklahoma. Since the average person spends $8 to $10 at a minor league game, is the state of the oil business an issue?
3. What effect has network television had on minor league baseball in the past? What effect is it likely to have in the future?
4. Do you think Hal Dixon should have any concern about the economic and social makeup of his group of investors?
5. The largest city in Louisiana, New Orleans, does not currently have a major league team. What influence should that have on the decision?

CHAPTER 3

Legal Aspects of Business

OBJECTIVES

After studying this chapter, you should be able to:

1 Define the three types of law—statutory law, common law, and administrative law

2 Discuss the different courts available for dispute resolution in the United States system.

3 Describe the five key elements of a contract, as well as what is meant by a breach of contract, and the Uniform Commercial Code.

4 Describe four business torts.

5 Discuss three major antitrust laws, as well as other techniques that are used by the federal government to regulate marketing activities.

6 Describe the basics of patent, copyright, and trademark law.

7 Name and explain two important collective bargaining laws.

8 Discuss federal legislation that is designed to protect the rights , health, and safety of working people.

Pennzoil and Getty Oil Company had been negotiating the sale of Getty to Pennzoil for an extended period of time. On January 5, 1984, both companies announced in The Wall Street Journal *that Pennzoil had accepted a counter-offer from Getty to purchase the company. One day later, Texaco made a higher offer to Getty, and Getty's board of directors accepted.*

What first appeared as a major Texaco victory turned out to be its worst nightmare. Pennzoil sued Texaco for interfering with the contract that had been negotiated between Pennzoil and Getty. A Texas state court jury found that the interference was intentional and in "wanton disregard" of Pennzoil's rights. The court determined that Pennzoil had suffered damages of $7.53 billion and also was entitled to $3 billion in punitive damages. Texaco appealed to the Texas Supreme Court, which found in favor of Pennzoil.

Some legal scholars felt that Texaco received bad legal advice during the time it was negotiating with Getty, while others felt the court case was poorly handled. In any case, what looked like a tremendous business opportunity for Texaco turned out to be a financial disaster of staggering proportions.

This chapter will examine the legal aspects of business. We will see that the law regulates most aspects of business, including the sale of products, the protection of ideas, and the treatment of employees.

It is possible to go through life without ever needing the services of a lawyer. But it definitely is not possible to work in business today without knowing something about the legal environment. This chapter introduces the basics of business law. A general understanding of the laws governing business can keep managers from making costly mistakes. We will begin our discussion of the legal environment of business by looking at three types of law and how they originated.

THE LAW: WHAT IT IS AND WHERE IT COMES FROM

law   *the standards of conduct established and enforced by government.*

The law of the United States can be classified in a bewildering number of ways. For the sake of simplicity, let us recognize three major types of law: statutory law, common law, and administrative law. We make this threefold division on the basis of how the law originates. We will define **law** as the standards of conduct established and enforced by government.

The United States Constitution is the supreme law in this nation. Neither the U.S. Congress nor any state legislature may pass a law that conflicts with the Constitution. The United States Supreme Court serves as the final interpreter of the Constitution. It resolves conflicts by determining whether or not the action taken by a private party, a state or local government, or the federal government is consistent with the Constitution.

Article 1, Section 8 of the Constitution gives Congress the power "to regulate commerce with foreign nations and among the several states." In an early Supreme Court case (1824), Chief Justice John Marshall wrote that commerce meant all commercial dealings within a state, as long as the activities "concerned more states than one." The Court ruled that the wheat a farmer produces to be consumed only on his farm may be regulated by the federal government, since the farmer's consumption of the product reduces the demand for wheat, which may have an impact on commerce in more than one state.

Clearly, the Supreme Court's interpretation of the constitution gives the federal government broad power to regulate business activities. However, state and local governments are also permitted to regulate private commercial activities to protect the safety and general welfare of their citizens. As a result, local and state governments regulate many commercial activities, ranging from truck safety standards to hazardous waste disposal. The Supreme Court is often asked to rule whether or not local or state government regulations place an unconstitutional burden on interstate business activities.[1]

Statutory Law

statutory law   *the legal rules and regulations enacted by legislative bodies.*

Statutory law refers to the legal rules and regulations adopted by legislative bodies, such as the Congress of the United States and the 50 state legislatures. Statutory law is also made by city governments; for example, municipal ordinances are passed by the city council in your town. Most law in this country is statutory. Individually, each law enacted by a legislative body is called a **statute.**

statute   *a law enacted by a legislative body.*

Statutory law governs a wide range of business activities including how a firm may issue stock and otherwise raise money, under what terms it may sell merchandise to the public, and how it may treat employees. Each state has laws governing the incorporation of new businesses; these are examples of statutory law.

Common Law

common law   *unwritten law or case law made by judges in reaching decisions on cases brought before their courts.*

Common law is often called "unwritten law" or "case law." Unlike statutory law, which is made by a legislative body and set forth in the text of the legislative act, common law is made by judges in reaching decisions on cases brought before them. If the appropriate legislative body has not enacted statutes in a particular area, common law governs that area.

precedents   *past court decisions used to help decide cases in the same legal area.*

In common law, past court decisions provide **precedents** for later cases in the same legal areas. That is, past decisions guide the courts in deciding similar cases in the future. Normally, these precedents are established by courts of appeal, state supreme courts, and the U.S. Supreme Court. The law relating to contracts is an example of common law. The principles of contract law evolved gradually over the years, through the case-by-case decisions issued by the courts.

Because common law is not as clearly defined as statutory law, it presents some problems for business people. It is not always clear whether a particular action could be found to be in violation of the law. Also, many courts establish and apply common law principles. Each of the 50 states has its own body of state common law. Still, the flexibility of common law does enable the courts to apply the law in ways that make sense in today's world.

Administrative Law

The third general type of law is administrative law. **Administrative law** refers to the rules and regulations issued by governmental boards, commissions, and agencies. The governmental bodies can be federal, state, or local. The National Labor Relations Board, the Securities and Exchange Commission, and the Federal Trade Commission are examples of federal agencies with rule-making powers that have the force of law. At present, there are more than 150 federal agencies with such powers. Table 3-1 lists nine of them and their primary regulatory responsibilities.

Business Career
Paralegal: Researches law sources, such as statutes, judicial decisions, and legal articles. Investigates facts to assist lawyer in preparing cases. Prepares legal documents, such as briefs, wills, and contracts. May direct law office employees. May act as a law librarian. *Average Salary: $24,900.*

administrative law   rules and regulations issued by governmental boards, commissions, and agencies.

TABLE 3-1   Important Federal Agencies with Rule-Making Powers

Federal Agency	Description
Consumer Product Safety Commission	Make safety standards for all consumer products.
Environmental Protection Agency	Develop and enforce rules that protect the nation's environment against all types of pollution.
Federal Aviation Administration	Regulate all technical aspects of civil air transportation, including establishing safety standards for airplanes, investigating airplane accidents, and operating control towers at airports.
Federal Communication Commission	Regulate the nation's airwaves(radio, television, long-distance telephone).
Federal Reserve Board	Control money supply; supply dollar bills and coins to banks; lend money to banks; help clear and collect checks; regulate federal banks.
Federal Trade Commission	Stop monopolies from forming; protect businesses and consumers from deceptive trade practices.
Internal Revenue Service	Collect federal income taxes and make administrative rules as to how taxpayers must report income and expenses.
Food and Drug Administration	Ensure that foods are safe and pure; ensure that drugs are safe and effective, cosmetics are harmless, and products are honestly and informatively labeled.
Securities and Exchange Commission	Regulate the nation's stock and bond markets to ensure that investors are not defrauded.

Although you may not have heard of administrative law before, instances of it are all around us. When your state public utility commission regulates the rates charged by the local electric company, it is making administrative law. In 1990, the Federal Aviation Administration ruled that neither passengers nor crew members could smoke on domestic commercial flights. This is another example of administrative law.

THE PROCESS OF DISPUTE RESOLUTION

② Traditionally, many disputes are resolved in the court system. As Figure 3-1 indicates, the United States court system is made up of three distinct levels: trial and special courts, appellate courts, and supreme courts. In addition, each level has both a federal and a state component. We will look briefly at each level. We will also examine several private procedures that may be used to solve disputes outside of the formal court system.

trial courts   *state or federal courts that hear civil or criminal cases involving possible violations of state or federal law.*

special courts   *state or federal courts that hear specific types of cases involving matters such as international trade, taxes, or probate problems.*

civil law   *law that defines the duties and responsibilities that exist between two or more individuals or between citizens and their governments, excluding criminal cases.*

criminal law   *law that regulates behavior against the state, as defined by local, state, and federal laws.*

Trial Courts and Special Courts

Most cases are initially heard in either **trial court** or a **special court.** Federal trial courts, or district courts as they are called, hear either civil or criminal cases that involve possible violations of federal law. **Civil law** defines the duties and responsibilities that exist between two or more individuals and between citizens and their governments, excluding criminal cases. For example, contract law is a part of civil law. **Criminal law** involves a wrong that is committed against the state. It is defined by local, state, and federal laws. The government will try to impose a penalty, involving money and/or imprisonment, on the accused party.

In a civil case, on the other hand, an individual (or possibly the government) will try to make the accused individual comply with his or her responsibilities or make restitution for the damage that was caused by the failure to comply.[2]

The state trial courts are usually called either county or district courts. They hear appeals in cases that were originally brought before a municipal justice of the peace, but most of their time is spent trying cases involving violations of state criminal law.

The special courts at both the federal and state level deal with specific types of cases, involving matters such as international trade, taxes, or probate problems. Some attorneys specialize in practice before these special courts, since they represent a narrow area of the law.

Disputes may be settled in other ways besides court proceedings. Here, Cleveland Mayor Michael White (left) confers with Jay Westbrook, president of the Cleveland City Council.

FIGURE 3-1   The United States Court System

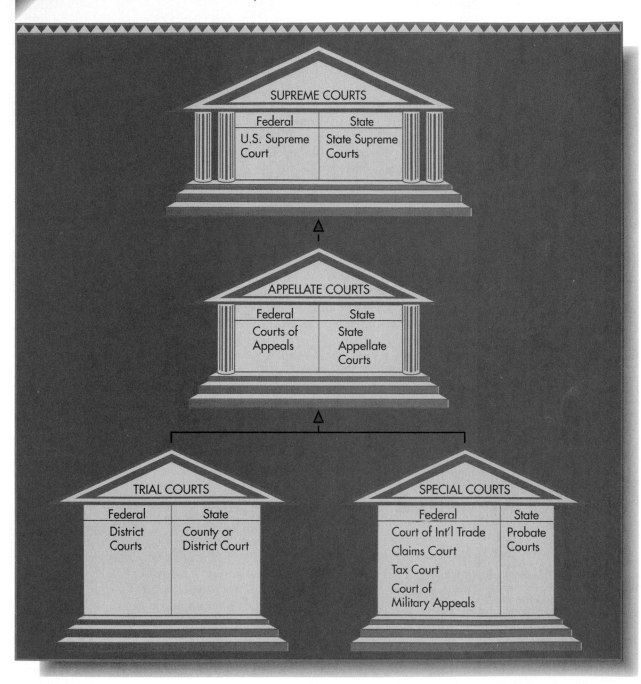

Appellate Courts

Appellate courts are federal or state courts that hear cases appealed from lower courts. The federal appellate courts are called courts of appeals.

The United States is divided into 12 judicial circuits, each with a federal court of appeals. These courts hear cases that are being appealed, either from a federal district court or a special federal court. State appellate courts hear appeals from

appellate courts *federal or state courts that hear cases from lower courts.*

lower state courts. These courts are either superior, circuit, or district state appellate courts.

Supreme Courts

supreme court *the highest court in a state or federal system; state supreme courts have final authority in all cases that have no questions involving federal law or the U.S. Constitution; the federal Supreme Court takes cases appealed from state supreme courts and handles all cases involving ambassadors to the U.S. and disputes involving states.*

A **supreme court** is the highest court in a state or federal system. The Supreme Court of the United States handles all cases that are appealed from the federal courts of appeals. In addition, it hears the few cases in which a state is one of the disputing parties, as well as all cases involving ambassadors to the U.S. The Supreme Court also hears some cases that are appealed from a state supreme court. In an average year, the U.S. Supreme Court agrees to hear less than 200 of the more than 5,000 cases that are appealed to it.

In most states, the highest court is known as the state supreme court. It has final authority in all cases that have no questions involving federal law or the U.S. Constitution. In some states, besides hearing appeals, the state supreme court also handles all matters referred directly to it by the governor of the state or by the state's legislature.

Arbitration

arbitration *a private procedure for dispute resolution, in which both parties agree to argue their case before a neutral third party and to accept this arbitrator's decision.*

The court system can be quite time-consuming and expensive. Difficult and complex trials involving one or more businesses may take several years and millions of dollars to complete. Therefore, a private procedure for resolving disputes, called **arbitration,** has developed. Both parties agree to argue their case before an arbitrator, who has no connection to the case. The disputing parties agree that the decision of the arbitrator will be final.

Arbitration is used extensively to resolve business disputes. Many contracts require both parties to employ arbitration to resolve any conflicts that may arise from the contract. An arbitrator may be a professionally trained expert in a particular field of business, such as transportation or union matters. Other arbitrators are lawyers or retired judges, whose expertise lies in ensuring that both parties to a case are given a fair and impartial hearing.[3]

CONTRACTS: MORE THAN JUST A HANDSHAKE

3

contract *a legally enforceable agreement between two or more parties that defines the responsibilities of each party in the performance of a specified action.*

Many business actions involve a contract between two or more individuals or companies. The purchase of raw materials, the sale of products, and the buying or leasing of land all usually involve a contract. A **contract** is a legal agreement between two or more parties. It defines the responsibilities of each party in the performance of a specified action. The action might be the construction of an office warehouse, or the delivery of plumbing supplies to a construction site. The agreement might be between a contractor and a group of investors, or between the contractor and a plumbing supply house.

Strictly speaking, not all agreements are contracts. Only those that a court is willing to enforce qualify as such. An enforceable contract is one that meets certain requirements, which we will examine next. Then we will discuss written contracts, breach of contract, and the Uniform Commercial Code.

Five Elements of a Contract

Figure 3-2 shows the five elements of a contract: agreement, contractual capacity, no fraud or duress, consideration, and legality. All of these elements must be present for an agreement to be a legally enforceable contract.

Agreement. The basic element of a contract is an **agreement** between two or more parties. The agreement must be reasonably clear as to what is expected of the parties to the contract. The agreement is broken down into an offer and an acceptance. An **offer** is a proposal to enter into a contractual relationship. An **acceptance** is an expression of willingness by the party receiving the offer to be legally bound by the terms of the offer. Acceptance of the offer can be signaled by signing a printed contract, by shaking hands, or by raising one's hand in agreement. The Chicago Commodity Exchange provides an example of this last type of communication: Billions of dollars of agricultural produce are bought there by people who simply raise a hand to signal their intent to buy.

agreement   the basic element of a contract; composed of an offer and an acceptance.

offer   a proposal to enter into a contractual relationship.

acceptance   an expression of willingness to be legally bound by the terms of an offer.

In 1991, Kevin Costner signed a contract with Warner Brothers. Costner's responsibilities under the contract are to develop, produce, direct, and star in motion pictures for the studio.

Contractual Capacity. Contractual capacity is the ability to enter into a legally binding contract. Not all people can enter into a contract that is legally binding. In most states, a person must be at least 18 years of age to do so. Other examples of people without contractual capacity are insane persons and persons under the influence of liquor or drugs.

contractual capacity   the ability to enter into a legally binding contract.

No Fraud or Duress. Even if a contract meets all the other requirements, it is not legally valid if there is a willful misrepresentation of fact, or if one party to the contract negotiated under duress.

FIGURE 3-2   Key Elements in a Contract

fraud *a willful misrepresentation of fact.*

A willful misrepresentation of fact is called **fraud.** For example, Sam Jones agrees to sell a building to Jane Smith. Jones tells Smith that the roof on the building is two months old, when in fact it is ten years old. Smith agrees to the sale, believing Jones's statement about the roof to be true. The fraud is the misleading information about the roof; Jones's deception renders the contract invalid.

duress *a condition in which a person is forced to enter into an agreement.*

A person who is *forced* to enter into an agreement is said to have negotiated under **duress.** Duress can be either physical or economic. An example of physical duress is a contract negotiated at gunpoint. An example of economic duress is a threat of great financial loss: "If you don't buy inventory from me, I'll make sure you lose your four top accounts." In the case of either physical or economic duress, the victim is not legally bound by the contract.

Consideration. Think about the following situation. You offer to mow your neighbor's lawn for free next week, and your neighbor accepts. Is there a contract? No. Now consider this situation: You offer to mow your neighbor's lawn for $20 next week. Agreeing to the $20 price, your neighbor accepts the offer. Is there a contract? Yes.

What is the difference between these two situations? Consideration. In the first situation, your neighbor offered nothing in return for your promise to mow the lawn. Thus, even though you offered to mow the lawn for free, you are not legally bound to do so. In the second situation, your neighbor offered something of value (it does not have to be money) in return for your promise—namely, $20. You are legally bound to mow the grass, and your neighbor is legally bound to pay you. That which each party agrees to give up—your time and effort, and your neighbor's $20—is called **consideration.** Unless each party gives up something, there is no contract.

consideration *that which each party to a contract agrees to give up.*

Legality. Finally, a contract cannot be valid if the action agreed to is illegal. Therefore, a contract calling for the commission of a crime is not enforceable. For example, a loan shark agrees to lend money to someone, at a higher interest rate than is permitted by state law. This contract would not be legal. If the person later refused to pay, the loan shark could not use the courts to collect the money.

Breach of Contract

breach of contract *the violation of one or more provisions of a contract by a party to the contract.*

When one party to a contract violates the provisions of the contract, that party has committed a **breach of contract.** The other party may ask the court to enforce the contract. For example, suppose that Sally Kendall borrows money from a savings and loan association to buy a house. The loan agreement between the two parties is a contract. The savings and loan agrees to lend Kendall the money for the house; she agrees to pay back the loan—principal plus interest—over 30 years. If Kendall stops making her monthly payments, she has committed a breach of contract, and the savings and loan can begin legal proceedings to take back the house.

Uniform Commercial Code

Uniform Commercial Code (UCC) *a comprehensive set of business laws governing commercial transactions.*

The **Uniform Commercial Code (UCC)** is a comprehensive set of business laws governing commercial transactions. It was drafted in 1952 and has now been adopted by 49 states, the District of Columbia, and the Virgin Islands. (Louisiana has adopted portions of the code.) The UCC deals with a number of business practices, including oral and written contracts and the requirements for express and implied warranties.

Oral vs. Written Contracts. There are three reasons why all contracts should be written. First, having a written contract assures that each of the five elements of a contract is present. Second, parties to a written contract know exactly what each is required to do. Third, a written contract makes it difficult for either party to deny having made the contract.

The UCC requires that all contracts for the sale of merchandise in excess of $500 be in writing. The UCC also requires written contracts in the following three areas:

- Contracts involving land
- Contracts that cannot be completed in one year
- Collateral contracts that require one party to answer for the debts or duty of another individual[4]

Contracts do not have to be written by an attorney. However, it is good business practice to have an attorney draft all important contracts, to avoid making technical mistakes. For example, Myra McDaniel is an attorney who draws on a wide variety of professional experiences when she drafts contracts for her clients. She is profiled starting on page 60.

Warranties. A **warranty** is the representation by the seller that a product has certain qualities or characteristics. The UCC defines both express and implied warranties. An **express warranty** is any "fact or promise" made by the seller to the buyer concerning a product. An example is a new car warranty requiring the manufacturer to pay for all parts and labor on repairs for the first 12,000 miles or 12 months, whichever comes first.

An **implied warranty** is the guarantee by the seller that the product sold is at least of "average quality" and is "adequately packaged and labeled." This protects the buyer in cases where the product turns out to be broken, spoiled, or otherwise unusable. When a dairy signs a contract to sell milk to a supermarket, there is an implied warranty that the milk delivered will be fresh.

warranty *the representation by the seller that a product has certain qualities or characteristics.*

express warranty *any fact or promise made by the seller to the buyer concerning a product.*

implied warranty *the guarantee by the seller that the product sold is at least of average quality and is adequately packaged and labeled.*

BUSINESS TORTS

In our free enterprise economy, businesses compete aggressively to maximize sales revenues. However, under law, businesses are not allowed to engage in certain practices intended solely to eliminate a competitor from the market. A **business tort** is any action in which the effect is to improperly interfere with the rights of another business.[5] Three business torts are examined in the sections that follow.

business tort *any action by a business in which the effect is to improperly interfere with the rights of another business.*

Wrongful Interference with Existing Contractual Relationships

The law forbids one person or business to induce another to commit a breach of contract. The burden of proof is on the plaintiff (the person or business that has allegedly been harmed). The plaintiff must show that (1) a *valid* contract existed between two parties; (2) the defendant (the person or business allegedly inducing the improper behavior) *knew* that a contract existed; and (3) the third party *intentionally* tried to induce one of the parties to break the contract.

The case between Pennzoil and Texaco cited at the beginning of this chapter, is a classic example of wrongful interference with an existing contract. The stock-

Myra McDaniel

Myra McDaniel is an excellent example of an individual who has pursued a successful career in law while devoting her life to society. As a black woman growing up in Philadelphia, Myra was exposed through her family and school to all the influences needed to make her competitive, productive, and successful. After attending the University of Pennsylvania, she worked in the Veterans Administration and the U.S. Aviation Supply Office. In these jobs, she learned how public agencies work. She also learned that good business skills are necessary in government work.

McDaniel expanded her experience with administrative jobs at Baldwin Wallace College in Ohio and at Indiana University, but she came to realize that she needed further education. After considering the alternatives, she decided to pursue a law degree. She graduated from The University of Texas at Austin School of Law in 1975.

The attorney general's office in Texas hired McDaniel, respecting her combination of experience, education, and drive. McDaniel worked her way up to chief of the taxation division in 1979. She broadened her experience further as counsel to the Railroad Commission, an extremely powerful and influential state agency in Texas.

For a brief time, McDaniel entered private practice in Midland, Texas, but her public management skills and experience made her valuable in public service. The governor of Texas offered her a position as general counsel to the governor.

In this position, McDaniel was the highest ranked black appointee in the history of Texas government. She reviewed legislation, drafted executive orders, coordinated litigation, and advised the governor on recommendations for paroles and pardons and on general legal practices. She also established procedures for the legal arm of the governor's office. A year and a half later, Ms. McDaniel returned to private practice.

The governor again called upon McDaniel in 1984, to become the first black in Texas history to serve as the state's highest-ranked appointee—Secretary of State. In that position, she administered an agency of 230 employees with a budget of $7 million a year, collecting revenues of $35 million a year.

Today, she continues her commitment to the public sector as a partner in the law firm of Bickerstaff, Heath & Smiley. Representation of public entities such as counties, cities, school districts, and water districts constitutes a significant portion of the firm's practice. The firm specializes in administrative and public law in addition to serving private businesses.

In her spare time, McDaniel and her husband host freshman athletes at the University of Texas, where she often speaks to student groups. She is active in community and legal groups and is on the Board of Trustees at St. Edward's University and the Episcopal Seminary of the Southwest. She has received numerous awards, including a tribute from the City of Austin.

Myra McDaniel is a strong believer in "putting your money where your mouth is." It is not just in her legal career that she observes the principles of social responsibility. She has made it her whole life.

holders of Texaco paid a big price for a very bad decision made by Texaco's management.

Wrongful Interference with a Business Relationship

The courts have consistently held that businesses and their owners may not interfere unreasonably with other businesses. That is, the law distinguishes between competition and predatory behavior. **Predatory behavior** exists when one firm focuses most of its attention on customers who have already shown an interest in the product or service sold by another firm. For example, a salesperson from Company A cannot follow a salesperson from Company B and call on all of Company B's customers. The courts have held that even if Company B's salesperson has not made a sale to any of the accounts, Company B has established a business relationship with them. Thus, Company A's actions are predatory. This constitutes improper interference in the affairs of another business and, therefore, is a tort.

The best defense to a charge of wrongful interference is that a firm's action merely represents acceptable competitive behavior. For example, a firm has a right to run clever, effective advertisements. If these advertisements induce a customer to move his or her business from one firm to another, this is acceptable competitive behavior.

predatory behavior the wrongful efforts of a company to focus its attention on customers who have already shown an interest in the product or service sold by another firm.

Property Disparagement

Although firms may compete in the marketplace, they may not spread false information about the products of other firms. This tort is called **trade libel.** For example, it is trade libel for one manufacturer of automobile wax to state publicly that a competitor's wax injures automobile paint if the claim is not true. To prove damages, the plaintiff must show that a third party actually refrained from doing business with the plaintiff because of the false information that was spread by the defendant.

trade libel the spreading of false information about the products of another firm.

REGULATION OF COMPETITION

We refer to our economy as a free enterprise system, but business firms are, in fact, not free to do whatever they choose. They must operate within a set of rules. Although these rules regulate and constrain business activity, their purpose is to encourage open, vigorous, and fair competition—that is, to make our economy more competitive, more efficient, and less monopolistic. A few of these rules are listed in the sections that follow.

Antitrust Law

In the years before 1890, several major corporations took unfair advantage of their economic power. These businesses (or "trusts" as they were called) operated primarily in the railroad, oil, and banking industries. In an attempt to restore competition to the marketplace, Congress passed three major laws intended to regulate trusts: the Sherman Act, the Clayton Act, and the Federal Trade Commission Act. These laws are still the cornerstone of U.S. **antitrust law.**

antitrust law laws intended to regulate businesses or trusts.

Sherman Act. The **Sherman Act** (1890) is the first and most famous of the antitrust laws. Section 1 states that "every contract, combination . . . or conspiracy, in restraint of trade or commerce among the several states, or with foreign nations, is hereby declared to be illegal." This statement means that any person

Sherman Act the first antitrust law, which declares illegal "every contract, combination . . . or conspiracy, in restraint of trade or commerce."

In this 1887 political cartoon, "The Foot of the Monopolist and the Hand of the President," antitrust action is directed at the railroads.

engaging in a monopolistic practice or conspiring to do so is guilty of a felony. The Sherman Act is enforced by the U.S. Department of Justice.

Section 2 of the Sherman Act states that a single firm may be in violation of the law if it has a monopoly position in a market. The courts have stated that a monopoly exists when one firm has a high enough percentage of the market to be able to control price and/or exclude competition. The first test always comes down to what is a market. For example, is there a single market for bleach, or are there two markets—one for liquid and one for dry bleach?

The courts have consistently held that a large market share alone is not a violation of Section 2 of the Sherman Act. If a large market share, even a monopoly, has been developed through a superior product, then the courts have been reluctant to find the firm in violation of the law.[6]

Clayton Act. The intent of the **Clayton Act,** passed in 1914, was to make the Sherman Act more effective. One provision outlaws both tying agreements and exclusive agreements. In a **tying agreement,** a seller agrees to sell a product to a buyer on the condition that the buyer also purchases other, often unwanted, merchandise from the seller. In an **exclusive agreement,** the seller, as a condition of the sale, forbids the buyer from purchasing for resale the products of competing sellers.

The Clayton Act also makes certain types of price discrimination illegal. **Price discrimination** takes place when a firm sells the same product to two or more customers at different prices. The courts have always held that price discrimination is legal if the seller can show that it costs less to sell to one customer than another and that the differences in price merely reflect the cost of doing business.

Another provision of the act prohibits companies from purchasing stock in competing companies if the effect would be to reduce competition in the mar-

Clayton Act   outlaws tying and exclusive agreements, prohibits companies from purchasing stock in competing companies if the effect would be to reduce competition, and prohibits persons from sitting on boards of directors of two or more competing companies that have sales exceeding $1 million.

tying agreement   an agreement in which a seller agrees to sell a product to a buyer on the condition that the buyer also purchases other, often unwanted, merchandise from the seller.

exclusive agreement   an agreement in which, as a condition of sale, the seller forbids the buyer from purchasing for resale the products of competing sellers.

price discrimination   the practice of selling the same product to two or more customers at different prices.

ketplace. In addition, a person may not sit on the boards of directors of two or more competing companies if the companies each have annual sales greater than $1 million.

Federal Trade Commission Act. The **Federal Trade Commission Act** of 1914 did two things. First, it established the Federal Trade Commission (FTC) to enforce the Clayton Act. Second, it gave the commission the authority to define "unfair methods of competition" and to issue cease and desist orders. A **cease and desist order** is a ruling by the FTC requiring a company to stop an unfair business practice. If the company chooses not to obey the order, the FTC can prosecute the company in federal court for violating either the Federal Trade Commission Act or the Clayton Act. Note that the FTC cannot enforce its own rulings; it must work through the courts.

Federal Trade Commission Act established the Federal Trade Commission to enforce the Clayton Act and gave the commission authority to define "unfair methods of competition" and to issue cease and desist orders.

cease and desist order a ruling by the Federal Trade Commission requiring a company to stop an unfair business practice.

Regulation of Marketing

The federal government also regulates marketing activities in the areas of pricing, personal selling, credit, credit cards, advertising, product liability, and distribution.

Pricing. **Price fixing** refers to an agreement by which two or more competing firms jointly determine the prices they will charge for their goods and services. Price fixing occurs when executives from competing firms decide in secret who should enter the lowest bid for a contract or at what level they should set their prices. Rather than letting competitive market forces determine price, they "fix" prices.

price fixing an agreement by which two or more competing firms jointly determine the prices they will charge for their goods and services.

Price fixing is an automatic or "per se" violation of the Sherman Act, and it is also a violation of the Federal Trade Commission Act. Any firm participating in a price-fixing scheme may be fined up to $1 million for each violation. Individuals involved may be fined up to $100,000 and required to spend as much as three years in prison.

Since the penalties for price fixing are so severe, why do firms still engage in price fixing? The principal reason is production overcapacity. When production capacity in an industry exceeds buyer demand, firms start slashing prices to get a higher share of the shrinking market. Lower prices usually mean lower profits for all firms in the industry. A tempting but illegal solution to this problem is for the firms to agree not to reduce their prices below a certain level. In this way, even reduced sales will generate some profits.

Personal Selling. Salespeople are often accused of using high-pressure tactics—that is, tricking people into buying products they do not want. For example, a salesperson might use one of the aggressive sales appeals shown in Table 3-2.

To protect the consumer from such tactics, the FTC adopted the **Cooling-Off Rule,** which protects the consumer from making unwise purchases at home. The rule states that anyone buying a product or service valued at $25 or more from a door-to-door salesperson has the right to cancel the purchase within 72 hours and receive a full refund. This right may be exercised merely because the purchaser has decided that he or she does not want to buy the product. There is no requirement that the product be defective, nor must the buyer show that unfair high-pressure sales tactics were used to sell the product. The seller must inform the customer of this right of cancellation.

Cooling-Off Rule a rule adopted by the Federal Trade Commission that permits anyone buying a product or service valued at $25 or more from a door-to-door salesperson to cancel the purchase within 72 hours and receive a full refund.

TABLE 3-2   High-Pressure Sales Tactics

Appeal	Statement
Timeliness	"Prices are expected to go up 5 percent next month."
	"This is the last one we have in stock. I don't know when we'll be able to get any more."
Fear	"There have been a number of burglaries in this area. You really need a burglar alarm for your home."
	"If you die tomorrow, your family could lose their home unless you buy this life insurance policy."
Flattery	"Everyone in your social position has one of these."
	"You look great in this brown suit. You are a born trendsetter."
Emotion	"If you don't buy six years of this magazine, I won't be able to go back to college."
	"Unless you give at least $60 to this cause, ten more children will die of starvation in Ethiopia."

Credit. Credit is a part of the American way of life. While some people have abused the credit system by borrowing more money than they are able to repay, others have been abused by creditors. Federal law makes it illegal to discriminate against an applicant for credit because of race, color, religion, national origin, sex, marital status, age, or because all or a portion of the applicant's income comes from a welfare program. If credit is refused, the applicant has a right to receive a written explanation.

Most states prohibit unreasonable credit collection methods. For example, many states prohibit credit collection statements that imply that a lawsuit has been initiated to collect money, if a lawsuit has not in fact been instigated. In addition, credit collectors may not use language that most people would feel was so shocking and outrageous that it exceeded reasonable bounds of decency.

Fair Credit Reporting Act gives consumers the right to be notified of credit bureau reporting activities, to have access to the information in their credit reports, and to correct misleading or false information in their credit reports.

The **Fair Credit Reporting Act** gives consumers the right to be notified of credit bureau reporting activities, to have access to the information in their credit reports, and to correct misleading or false information in their credit reports. Any negative information must have been verified within three months before it can be given to a client of the credit bureau. A bankruptcy proceeding may be reported for ten years after the bankruptcy has been finalized.[7]

Truth-in-Lending Act authorizes the Federal Reserve Board to specify how interest rates on consumer purchases are to be calculated and reported to the consumer.

Unfortunately, many consumers do not understand how interest rates are calculated. Prior to the **Truth-in-Lending Act** (1969), some financial institutions and retail stores took advantage of this fact and charged customers exorbitant interest rates. Table 3-3 illustrates how the stated interest rate can vary depending upon how the loan is repaid and how the rate is calculated. Under the Truth-in-Lending Act, the Federal Reserve Board has the power to specify how interest rates on consumer purchases are to be calculated and reported to the consumer. In this way, it is hoped, consumers will make credit decisions with a better understanding of the full cost.

Credit Cards. When credit cards were introduced, unethical banks and merchants almost instantly developed various abuses. It is now illegal to send a credit

TABLE 3-3   Differences in True Interest as a Result of Payment Schedules

	Payment at the End of One Year	Principal and Interest Paid in 12 Equal Monthly Payments
Loan	$1,000	$1,000
Interest Charges	$100	$100
Real Interest	10%	18%

Under both payment schedules, the value of the loan ($1,000) and total interest charges ($100) are the same. Under the first, however, the entire amount of the loan is borrowed for a year and repaid in one lump sum at the end of that time, but under the second, it is paid back in equal monthly installments over the year. Therefore, at the end of the sixth month, the amount of principal owed on the first is $1,000, but only about $500 on the second. As a result, the effective interest rate on the second payment schedule is higher, because the average loan balance is smaller.

card to an individual who has not applied for the card. In addition, a credit card holder cannot be held liable for more than $50 for the unauthorized use of a credit card. However, the courts have held that if a credit card holder loans his or her card to another individual, who uses it for a purpose that was not intended, the cardholder is responsible for all charges made on the card.

Advertising. The FTC protects consumers from misleading advertising. An advertisement is considered misleading if the overall impression is misleading. For example, Ocean Spray's Cranberry Juice Cocktail was advertised on national television as being good for you because it had a lot of "food energy." The FTC reasoned that many people might assume that food energy meant vitamins or proteins. In fact, food energy is nothing more than calories. Why was the ad found to be in violation of the law? Because the overall impression was misleading, even though the claim of "food energy" was literally true.

The FTC has tried to draw a line between misleading advertising and **puffery,** or innocent exaggerations used to sell a product. "We have the best used cars in town" and "No one else has better deals than we do" are examples of puffery. Most consumers probably realize that such claims are intended simply to attract their attention and not to convey meaningful information. Thus, the FTC does not view puffery as either fraudulent or misleading.

puffery   innocent exaggerations used to sell a product.

When the FTC decides that an advertisement is misleading, it usually issues a cease and desist order, which stops the firm from running the advertisement. If the ad has already misled many people, the FTC may require the firm to run corrective advertising.

The purpose of **corrective advertising** is to tell the public the truth about the product. The corrective advertisement must use the same media as the original misleading advertisement. The Ocean Spray Company, maker of Cranberry Juice Cocktail, was required to run a corrective television ad stating that food energy is just calories. The transcript of the original commercial for Cranberry Juice Cocktail and the corrective advertisement are shown in Figure 3-3.

corrective advertising serves to correct previous misleading advertising and to tell the public the truth about the product.

Product Liability. **Product liability** is an increasingly serious problem for businesses. The courts are holding them accountable to consumers for how well

product liability   accountability for a product defect, breach of product warranty, and any danger caused by the use of a product.

FIGURE 3-3 Cranberry Juice Cocktail Ads

Original Advertisement

"Cranberry Juice Cocktail is more than a new taste for breakfast. Cranberry juice is good for you. Has even more food energy than orange or tomato juice. Ocean Spray — the start of something big."

Corrective Advertisement

"If you wondered what some of our earlier advertising meant when we said Ocean Spray Cranberry Juice Cocktail has more food energy than orange juice or tomato juice, let us make it clear. We didn't mean vitamins and minerals. Food energy means calories. Furthermore, food energy is important at breakfast as many of us may not get enough calories or food energy to get off to a good start. Ocean Spray Cranberry Juice Cocktail helps because it contains more food energy than most other breakfast drinks. Ocean Spray."

and how safely their products perform. A firm may become part of a product liability lawsuit as a result of statements or actions of salespersons, print or broadcast advertisements, labeling and written instructions, and retailers' and wholesalers' actions.

Traditionally, the courts have considered two types of product liability actions: those that concern violation of a contract, such as warranty, sales claims, and advertising; and those that stem from personal injury claims. Businesses could engage in activities leading to liability claims under any of the four major theories of product liability: negligence, breach of warranty, strict liability, and misrepresentation. A brief explanation of each of these theories allows a better understanding of the responsibilities facing managers.

negligence *failure to use ordinary care in the performance of an action.*

Negligence. **Negligence** is failure to use ordinary care in the performance of an action. Businesses have an implicit duty to use reasonable care in designing and creating the product, as well as in informing consumers about any potential hazards associated with the product. Labels, salespersons' claims, and advertisements must tell consumers what they need to know about the product to avoid using it in ways that could lead to personal injury. For example, Johnson Wax sells a furniture cleaner and polisher named Complete. The spray container states, "DO NOT SPRAY OR USE ON FLOORS; IT COULD LEAVE THEM SLIPPERY." Johnson Wax recognizes its responsibility to inform customers that Complete could pose a hazard if used improperly.

Some trial lawyers have been accused of ethical violations in product liabilities cases. To earn large fees for themselves, it is said, they have exaggerated the pain and suffering that their clients experienced. These attorneys defend their actions by stating that if American businesses would simply produce better products, there would be no need for their services. The Ethical Issue (page 67) describes this problem in more detail.

Profit from Pain

Plaintiff attorneys, as they are called, represent people who are injured or killed in accidents. The cost of these cases was more than $180 billion in 1990. In addition, businesses pay more than $21 billion each year for insurance to cover losses related to product liability.

The ethical question is quite simple. Are the plaintiff attorneys taking advantage of the real pain and suffering of their clients, to line their own pockets? Plaintiff attorneys are normally paid one third of the money awarded to their clients. Most executives believe that plaintiff attorneys are nothing more than highly paid parasites. On the other hand, consumer advocates and plaintiff attorneys argue that the settlements that lawyers win for their clients would not be so high or so frequent if American companies would simply produce safer products.

A rather typical product liability case pitted Sears against Shane and Becky Sharp of Corpus Christi, Texas. The couple purchased a propane tank for their barbecue grill. Despite half a dozen warnings in the propane tank's literature to keep the tank outdoors, they left it indoors. Gas escaped from the tank and was ignited by the pilot light on their furnace. Mrs. Sharp was badly burned in the resulting explosion. The Sharps' attorney argued that the warnings in the product's literature should have been printed in larger type. Sears settled out of court for $4.8 million.

In this case, the Sharps may well have deserved everything they received from Sears. However, many people believe that Americans are spending far too much money on the legal system, and that at least some plaintiff attorneys have crossed the ethical line. Such lawyers are considered to be taking advantage of their clients' problems, or to be using various techniques to exaggerate the pain and suffering that their clients have felt.

One suggestion is to adopt the so-called English system, in which a person who brings a lawsuit and loses must pay all of the defendant's costs. Needless to say, the plaintiff attorneys oppose this suggestion. Since they have one of the most powerful and well-financed lobbying efforts in Washington, it will probably not be passed by Congress.

Source: L. Smith, "Trial Lawyers Face a New Charge," *Fortune* © 1991, The Time Inc. Magazine Co. All Rights Reserved

---

Breach of Warranty. A warranty is the representation by the seller that a product has certain qualities or characteristics. Such representation is basically a contract. Warranties are regulated by the Uniform Commercial Code and by the Magnuson-Moss Warranty Act. Advertising, product labels, salespersons' claims, and even the average quality of similar products in the market all could be viewed as warranty representations. **Breach of warranty** occurs when the seller's representation of a product's characteristics or qualities does not hold true. As an example, the container for Peters Professional Soluble Plant Food states that the product contains 20 percent nitrogen, 20 percent phosphoric acid, and 20 percent potash. The company is guaranteeing that its product contains these three key ingredients in the stated percentages. If it did not, the company could be sued for breach of warranty.

breach of warranty a violation that occurs when the seller's representation of a product's qualities or characteristics does not hold true.

Strict Liability. **Strict liability** is a relatively new theory. It claims that product liability may exist whenever the quality of the product itself is questioned. The implication of a strict liability interpretation is that people are responsible for all effects of their actions, even if the effects were unforeseen and the people exercised reasonable care. For example, a construction firm would be responsible for any personal or property injury resulting from the use of dynamite in building a road, even if the firm had used reasonable and prudent care.

strict liability a theory claiming that product liability may exist whenever the quality of the product itself is questioned.

The theory of strict liability is frequently invoked to hold manufacturers responsible for the safety of their products. If a person is injured while using a product, he or she may be able to recover damages from its manufacturer if (1) the product was defective, (2) the defect made that product unreasonably dangerous, and (3) the defect was the cause of the injury.[8]

misrepresentation *that which occurs when a consumer relies on false information from a manufacturer, seller, or their agents in making a purchase decision.*

Misrepresentation.

Misrepresentation is a theory allowing lawsuits in cases not involving negligence. Under this theory, a consumer may sue if he or she relied on false information from a manufacturer, seller, or their agents in making a purchase decision. For example, misrepresentation would occur if a used car salesperson told a customer that a particular car got 30 miles per gallon when, in fact, it got only 15. In this case, the court might determine that the misrepresentation was so important that the consumer had the right to return the car and receive a full refund.

Distribution.

Under statutory and case law, sellers have the right to choose their distributors. However, sellers may not refuse to deal with certain distributors on the basis of race, color, or creed.

Another important issue is whether or not a manufacturer has the right to restrict the sales territories of its distributors. The current opinion of the Supreme Court is that territorial restrictions are to be judged on the basis of their impact on competition. "Reasonable" restrictions—those without a negative impact on competition—are permitted. For example, Sylvania gives each of its television dealers an exclusive right to a geographic territory if the dealer agrees not to establish sales outlets outside of its territory. Sylvania's attorneys have successfully defended this territorial restriction policy before the Supreme Court, arguing that Sylvania's dealer structure is stronger because Sylvania dealers compete with other manufacturers' dealers, not among themselves.

PATENTS, COPYRIGHTS, AND TRADEMARKS

 Patents, copyrights, and trademarks are important areas of federal law for many businesses. They protect the inventions and ideas that might generate profits for the company in the future. Without this type of protection, businesses could not justify investing in scientific research or marketing techniques that might eventually pay big dividends to the owners of the business.

The pirating of intellectual property is an important problem in the U.S. It is also a very difficult and complex problem for businesses whose intellectual property is stolen by firms operating outside of this country. Unfortunately, as the International Example (page 70) points out, unless the U.S. government is willing to apply more political pressure on its trading partners than it has in the past, this problem will continue to grow. We will now examine three important areas of intellectual property law: patents, copyrights, and trademarks.

Patent Law.

The Constitution of the United States grants the federal government the power "to promote the progress of science and useful arts by securing limited times to authors and inventors concerning the exclusive right to their respective writing and discoveries." **Patent law** protects inventors by prohibiting other people from

patent law *protects inventors by prohibiting other people from making, using, or selling patented inventions for a period of 17 years.*

making, using, or selling patented inventions for a period of 17 years. The courts have held that a process, machine, manufactured article, or composition of matter may be patented. In order to be patentable, the invention must be not only new and useful, but it also must not have been obvious to a person with ordinary skills in the area of technology that is being patented.[9]

assignment *sale of a patent by its holder to another person or organization.*

Inventors obtain patents from the U.S. Patent and Trademark Office. The holder of a patent may sell it to another person or organization. This is called an **assignment.** The holder may assign patent rights for a limited period of time.

Genetically engineered forms of life may be patented, such as herbicide-resistant cotton (left) and virus-resistant potatoes (right). Even a mouse has been patented!

This is called a **license.** For example, the University of Texas at Austin developed a pulse power generator called a homopolar generator. It then licensed Parker Drilling Company to manufacture and sell that machine. The university receives a license fee each time one of the generators is sold.

license   the assigning of patent rights for a limited period of time to a particular person or organization.

Copyright Law

Copyright law protects authors, artists, photographers, designers, advertisers, and others from the unauthorized copying, duplication, or publication of their works. The Computer Software Copyright Act now gives the author of a computer code or program the same protection traditionally received by other authors.

copyright law   protects authors, artists, photographers, designers, and others from the unauthorized copying, duplication, or publication of their works.

Copyright protection is extended for a person's life plus 50 years. If the material is created by an employee of a firm and is copyrighted by the firm, the copyright is in force for 75 years from the date of publication.

It is easy to obtain copyright protection. A person need only place a copyright notice on the material. The notice is © plus the date of copyright, or the word "copyright" plus the date. Although it is normally not necessary, the person may register a copyright with the Register of Copyrights in Washington, D.C.

Trademark Law

A **trademark** is a name, term, or symbol used to identify a firm and its products. The distinctive red-and-white Coca-Cola logo is an example. The Lanham Act provides for legal protection of any distinctive name, term, or symbol registered with the federal government. According to court decisions, trademarked names that have become generic terms for products through popular usage are no longer protected by trademark law. Linoleum, aspirin, and nylon were all once trademarked products. The original producers of these products lost their trademarks when the names became generic terms.

trademark   a name, term, or symbol used to identify a firm and its products.

INTERNATIONAL EXAMPLE

The Pirating of U.S. Intellectual Property

For many years, U.S. corporations have been losing millions of dollars to international pirates. Such pirates steal computer software, formulas for new prescription and over-the-counter drugs, movies, and cassette and CD recordings. They pay absolutely no attention to U.S. and international copyright laws and patents; they make their money by stealing intellectual property.

One of Hollywood's best private investigators is Charles Morgan, whose father once played a policeman in the TV series "Dragnet." Charles Morgan, who is fluent in English, Spanish, and Portuguese, pursues pirates of movies and music on six continents. He negotiates with heads of state as well as with copycat pirates. Morgan's staff includes former police officers and government agents, who help local police in foreign countries arrest illegal operators.

Asian countries loom large in Morgan's activities. They not only have a desire to enjoy Western entertainment, but also export pirated movies, CDs, and cassettes to Africa and the Middle East. To attract public attention to the problem, Charles Morgan often uses Hollywood-style theatrics. In Japan, Morgan once stacked up 10,000 pirated cassettes and ran over them with a steamroller.

UNIONS AND COLLECTIVE BARGAINING

Until the early 1930s, both federal and state laws tended to favor management when there were labor disputes with unions. In 1932, Congress passed the Norris-LaGuardia Act, which protected peaceful labor strikes, picketing, and boycotts. In reality, this law established a national policy allowing employees to join unions and to strike. We will now briefly examine the National Labor Relations Act and the Labor–Management Relations Act.

National Labor Relations Act

National Labor Relations Act *created the National Labor Relations Board to monitor union elections and to prevent employers from engaging in unfair labor practices.*

The **National Labor Relations Act** (1935) created the National Labor Relations Board (NLRB). This board monitors union elections and prevents employers from engaging in unfair labor practices. The following practices of employers are defined as unfair and therefore illegal:

- Interference with employees' attempts to form, join, or assist labor unions.
- Interference with union elections.
- Employer domination of unions or the contribution of financial support to a union by employers.
- Discrimination in hiring or promotion of employees on the basis of their union affiliation.
- Discrimination against employees for filing charges under the National Labor Relations Act.
- Refusal to bargain in good faith with employees' representatives.

Labor–Management Relations Act

Labor–Management Relations Act *(also known as the Taft-Hartley Act) forbids unions from refusing to bargain with an employer if the NLRB has certified a specific union for a firm, from requiring an employer to pay for work not performed, and from engaging in a secondary boycott.*

The **Labor–Management Relations Act** (1947), also called the Taft-Hartley Act, was bitterly opposed by organized labor. Although it did not rescind any of the rights of labor spelled out in the National Labor Relations Act, it did forbid unions from engaging in certain activities. Three of the most important are:

- Refusing to bargain with an employer if the union has been certified for that firm by the NLRB.

Unfortunately, the pirating of intellectual property is not limited to the entertainment industry. The development of a new drug often takes more than ten years and costs more than $200 million. When a drug company applies for a U.S. patent, it must disclose its formula. This makes it easy and inexpensive for pirates to copy the drugs and sell them abroad. To complicate the problem, many developing countries do not have laws to protect drug patents. It is not uncommon for counterfeit drugs (often from Spain) to hit the street before the patented drug is available. The drug counterfeiters know that they can operate for as long as ten years before they are brought to justice. In the meantime, they have the opportunity to make many millions of dollars on the sale of illegal drugs, both in Europe and in the developing world.

U.S. corporations are facing a significant problem. Many countries simply do not believe that their people should pay for ideas that were developed in another country. Pressure from companies and trade associations seems to have some positive impact. But the problem of international piracy of intellectual property will not be solved until the U.S. government is willing to make it clear, through international police agencies and foreign trade negotiations, that its trading partners must comply with U.S. patents.

Source: F. Rice, "How Copycats Steal Billions," *Fortune* © 1991, The Time Inc. Magazine Co. All Rights Reserved

- Requiring an employer to pay for work not performed (featherbedding).
- Engaging in a **secondary boycott**—that is, a boycott of firms that do business with a firm where there is a strike.

> **secondary boycott** a boycott of a firm that does business with a firm that is being struck by a labor union.

In addition, the Labor–Management Relations Act made closed shops illegal. **Closed shops** require that a prospective employee join the union as a condition of employment. **Union shops,** on the other hand, require that the new employee join the union only after a designated period of employment. The **agency shop** is a specialized type of union shop. Employees are not required to join a union, but they must pay union dues as a condition of employment. Although union shops were not made illegal by federal law, the act did give states the authority to pass right-to-work laws that make even union shops illegal. Finally, in an **open shop,** employees are not forced to belong to a union or pay dues. However, there may be a recognized union that bargains for all employees and is permitted to bargain for a contract that binds all employees.

> **closed shops** organizations that require a prospective employee to join the union as a condition of employment, an illegal practice.

> **union shops** organizations that require new employees to join the union after a designated period of employment.

> **agency shop** a specialized type of union shop, in which employees are not required to join a union but must pay union dues as a condition of employment.

One of the most controversial parts of the Labor–Management Relations Act was the 80-day "cooling off" period. This authorizes the president of the United States to obtain a court injunction to end a strike for a period of 80 days if the strike would cause a national emergency. Various presidents have obtained injunctions to stop strikes by steelworkers, longshoremen, and coal miners.[10]

> **open shops** organizations that do not force employees to belong to a union or to pay union dues.

EMPLOYEE PROTECTION

The federal government takes an active role in protecting the health and safety of working people. Social security, unemployment benefits, and workers' compensation are all types of insurance; they are examined in Chapter 22. We begin this discussion of employee protection by examining the legislation that regulates wages and hours for a firm's employees.

The Fair Labor Standards Act

The **Fair Labor Standards Act,** which was passed in 1938, introduced both the minimum wage and the 40-hour work week. At the time of passage, the minimum wage was set at $0.40 per hour. It stood at $4.25 an hour in 1992. The law also

> **Fair Labor Standards Act** established the minimum wage, the 40-hour work week, and regulations affecting child labor.

said that workers must receive time-and-a-half pay for time spent on the job in excess of the 40-hour standard. Not all employees are covered by the Fair Labor Standards Act. People in managerial, professional, and sales positions, for example, are not protected by the act.

The Fair Labor Standards Act also regulates child labor. The minimum age for most jobs is now 16. The employment of 14- and 15-year-olds is restricted to a few types of jobs, such as filing and sales. The range of jobs for children under 14 years of age is even more restricted. They may deliver newspapers, work as actors or actresses, or hold selected farm jobs.

Occupational Safety and Health Act

The goal of the Occupational Safety and Health Act (1970) is to reduce the number of safety and health hazards in the workplace. The law established the **Occupational Safety and Health Administration (OSHA)** and gave the Secretary of Labor the authority to set health and safety standards for individual industries.

Occupational Safety and Health Administration (OSHA) *sets and enforces health and safety standards for individual industries.*

Safety Standards. The most important contribution of OSHA has been the establishment of safety standards to help prevent both job-related injuries and diseases. OSHA is permitted by law to regulate only significant risks to employees. Moreover, it must be "feasible" for employers to meet the standards.

Inspections. How does OSHA find out about safety and health hazards? One way is through unannounced inspections, which may be requested by an employee or by an employee union. Inspections may also be initiated by OSHA personnel as a part of regular inspection programs.

If the OSHA inspection turns up one or more violations, a citation is issued. The firm then has 15 days to appeal to an OSHA review board. In general, the severity of the penalty depends on the nature of the violation. Fines can be as high as $10,000 for each willful violation. An employer who totally disregards an OSHA rule may be prosecuted as a criminal and sent to jail for up to one year.

Employment Discrimination

Civil Rights Act *prohibits discrimination in hiring, training, and promotion on the basis of race, color, sex, religion, or national origin.*

Equal Employment Act *supplements the Civil Rights Act, making it illegal to discriminate in hiring, training, and promotion in local and state governments, as well as the federal government.*

Congress has passed several laws that directly address the problem of employment discrimination. Two of the most important are the Civil Rights Act (1964) and the Equal Employment Act (1972). The **Civil Rights Act** prohibits discrimination in hiring, training, and promotion on the basis of race, color, sex, religion, or national origin. The **Equal Employment Act** extends the Civil Rights Act to local and state governments, as well as the federal government.

Protected Classes. We will begin our discussion of employment discrimination by examining several classes or groups of individuals that are protected by federal legislation.

- *Race, color, or national origin.* The law clearly states that it is illegal to discriminate on the basis of race, color, or national origin. There are no exceptions.
- *Sex.* In all but a few cases, is it illegal to discriminate on the basis of sex. In such cases, it is the responsibility of the firm to prove, for example, that a person of a specific gender would not be able to perform the job in question.
- *Age.* It is illegal for a firm to refuse to hire anyone who is 40 years or older merely because of the person's age. In addition, mandatory retirement was

prohibited for most employees in 1987. The same law also required businesses to continue health care benefits to all employees, regardless of age.

- *Religion.* Federal law prohibits most types of religious discrimination. The obvious exception is that churches cannot be required to hire a minister who is of a different faith.
- *Sexual harassment.* The courts have held consistently that managers may not ask their employees for sexual favors in return for promotions or salary adjustments. In addition, employees may sue their employers for sex discrimination on the grounds that sexual harassment has created a hostile job environment. Sexual advances, repeated sexual comments, jokes, or touching may lead to a hostile job environment.

Fairness In Testing. The discrimination laws are especially important in the area of testing. The government requires fairness in any tests used for selection, transfer, promotion, or other personnel actions. When the government refers to a test, it means any method used to get information. This includes interviews and application blanks.

As the government defines it, a fair test is one that does not systematically overpredict or underpredict the performance of any subgroup of employees. For instance, if a test predicted that males would do better than females on the job when their actual performance was the same, the test would be unfair. In addition, the test must be relevant to the personnel question that is under consideration. For example, if knowing how to type has nothing to do with the job that the applicant is being considered for, then a typing test should not be administered.

Equal Pay. The Equal Pay Act (1963) requires that men and women receive equal pay for equal work. What is important is not whether the job *titles* are the same but whether the *contents* of the jobs are substantially similar. If a company pays men and women differently, it must prove that the jobs differ in terms of skill, effort, responsibility, or working conditions.

Enforcement Procedures. An individual who feels he or she has been illegally discriminated against must first file a complaint with the Equal Employment Opportunity Commission (EEOC). The EEOC will investigate the allegation and try to achieve a compromise solution that both the employee and employer can accept. If the EEOC decides in favor of the employer, or reaches another solution that the employee refuses to accept, then the employee is still free to sue the employer in federal court. However, in this case, the federal government will not intervene in the case; the employee or the employee's union must bear the expense of the lawsuit.

It is important to point out that not all forms of discrimination in the workplace are illegal. For example, it is acceptable for a firm to review a list of job prospects and hire the individual who is most qualified. In the same manner, the firm can promote or provide merit salary adjustments to its employees who work the hardest and perform the best. Finally, federal law does not protect all classes or types of people. For example, if an individual is under 40 years of age, he or she cannot claim age discrimination. Also, discrimination against homosexuals is not protected by federal law.

Affirmative Action. The federal government has encouraged and, at times, required firms to implement **affirmative action** programs to hire more minorities and/or women. These programs give special consideration in hiring and pro-

affirmative action   programs that give special consideration in hiring and promotion decisions to members of minority groups and, in some cases, women.

motion decisions to minority groups, and, in some cases, women. The intent is to overcome the effects of past job-related discrimination. The government has focused its efforts on businesses that have a history of illegally discriminating against minorities or women.

Affirmative action programs have helped provide more opportunities for minorities. For example, in 1973, AT&T settled a major lawsuit by agreeing to hire and promote more minorities. The court order expired in 1979, but AT&T has continued its commitment to affirmative action. As a result, in 1991, 21 percent of AT&T employees were minorities, and 17 percent of its managers were minorities, up from 12 percent in 1984.[11]

Affirmative action programs are often controversial. They provide preferential treatment in hiring and promotions for minorities or women for a limited period of time, to make up for past illegal discrimination. The expectation is that once women and minority groups have been given an opportunity, they will be able to compete in the marketplace. Only time will tell if affirmative action programs are able to produce the results that their proponents expect. It is clear, however, that the federal government and most major corporations are determined to do everything possible to give minorities a better opportunity to obtain the jobs that they have a legal right to.

SUMMARY POINTS

1 Laws can be classified as statutory law, common law, or administrative law. Statutory law is the set of rules and regulations created by legislative bodies. Common law is the unwritten law created by judges through their decisions in cases brought before them. Administrative law is the set of rules and regulations issued by governmental boards, commissions, and agencies.

2 In the United States, disputes can be settled within three distinct levels of both the state and federal court systems. The levels are trial and special courts, appellate courts, and supreme courts. As a faster and less expensive alternative, disputes may be settled through private procedures known as arbitration.

3 To be legally binding, a contract must have five elements: agreement, contractual capacity, absence of fraud or duress, consideration, and legality. A breach of contract occurs when one party violates the provisions of the contract. The Uniform Commercial Code regulates many business practices, including contracts and warranties.

4 In the United States, businesses are forbidden to engage in certain practices, known as torts, which are designed solely to eliminate a competitor from the market. Three types of business torts are wrongful

interference with existing contractual relationships, wrongful interference with a business relationship, and property disparagement.

5 The Sherman Act (1890), the Clayton Act (1914), and the Federal Trade Commission Act (1914) were all passed to ensure that the nation's marketplaces would not be subject to anticompetitive behavior. Specifically, contracts and combinations in restraint of trade, tying agreements, exclusive agreements, and certain types of price discrimination were all declared to be illegal. In addition, the federal government may regulate specific marketing activities, including pricing, personal selling, credit, credit cards, advertising, product liability, and distribution.

6 Patent laws prohibit people other than the inventor from making, using, or selling patented inventions for a period of 17 years. Copyright laws protect authors, artists, photographers, designers, and others from the unauthorized reproduction of their works. Trademark laws prohibit others from using a name, term, or symbol used by a firm to identify itself and its products.

7 The National Labor Relations Act established the National Labor Relations Board to monitor union elections and to

KEY TERMS

law 52

statutory law 52

statute 52

common law 52

precedents 52

administrative law 53

trial courts 53

special courts 53

civil law 53

criminal law 53

appellate courts 55

supreme court 56

arbitration 56

contract 56

agreement 57

offer 57

acceptance 57

contractual capacity 57

fraud 58

duress 58

consideration 58

breach of contract 58

Uniform Commercial Code (UCC) 58

warranty 59

express warranty 59

implied warranty 59

business tort 59

predatory behavior 61

prevent employers from engaging in unfair labor practices. The Labor–Management Relations Act defines certain practices as illegal and forbids labor unions from engaging in them.

8 The federal government has attempted to protect the rights, health, and safety of working people through several acts. The Fair Labor Standards Act provides for minimum wage and regulation of child labor. The Social Security Act provides for a minimum guaranteed income for retired or disabled persons. The Occupational Safety and Health Act is designed to reduce the number of safety and health hazards for employees. The Equal Employment Opportunity Act and the Civil Rights Act prohibit discrimination in employment on the basis of race, color, sex, religion, or national origin.

REVIEW QUESTIONS

1 What are the differences between administrative and statutory law? **1**

2 When does the Supreme Court of the United States hear a case? **2**

3 What are the five elements of a contract? Briefly explain each. **3**

4 Is an express warranty better than a implied warranty, from the consumer's perspective? **3**

5 Explain what is meant by "wrongful interference with a business relationship." How is this different from normal competition? **4**

6 What is price discrimination? How can a seller legally discriminate in the price of a product between two or more buyers? **5**

7 What rights does the Fair Credit Reporting Act give consumers? **5**

8 What constitutes a breach of warranty? **5**

9 What is the difference between a patent and a copyright? **6**

10 Explain the differences between closed shops, union shops, and open shops. **7**

11 Describe the major provisions of the Fair Labor Standards Act. **8**

12 Outline the several classes of individuals whom federal legislation protects from employment discrimination. **8**

13 What enforcement procedures are available to an individual who believes that he or she has been illegally discriminated against in the workplace? **8**

DISCUSSION QUESTIONS

1 Is a violation of a criminal law more serious than a violation of a civil law? Explain.

2 If you were involved in a dispute with your employer, would you prefer to go to an arbitrator or to court?

3 Why does the federal government try to regulate anticompetitive behavior?

4 Why is product liability a growing problem for businesses?

5 Should the government try to regulate puffery in advertisements?

6 Do you think the minimum wage should be raised or lowered? What would happen if the minimum wage requirement were repealed?

7 Do you believe that affirmative action in the workplace is in the best interest of both minority and nonminority employees?

EXPERIENTIAL EXERCISES

1 Interview an attorney who is employed by a business firm. Try to determine to whom the attorney reports and what type of issues he or she is normally involved in.

Does the attorney feel like a regular member of the firm's management team? Or does the attorney believe he or she is there only to provide specialized legal advice? Ask the attorney what legal issues businesses are are going to have to face in the next ten years.

2 Meet with the individual in your college who is responsible for ensuring that the college's personnel policies do not discriminate on the basis of race, color, religion, national origin, or sex. Ask if your college has an affirmative action plan to recruit more minorities and women as employees. Try to determine what specific steps your college has taken in such recruiting and how successful they have been. Is there anything you feel your college should do to recruit and retain more minorities and women into senior administrative and faculty positions?

CASES

CASE 3-1
Jet Manufacturing

Jet Manufacturing of Santa Barbara, California, manufactures several key components for jet engines. One valve that it makes plays an integral role in the jet engine reverser system that is used to slow down most business jets once they have touched down on the runway. If the valve failed to function properly, the plane would have a difficult time stopping. It would be even worse if a jet engine reversed itself in flight; one or both of the wings could be torn from the airplane.

More than 90 percent of the jet engines that are manufactured by General Electric, Pratt and Whitney, and Rolls Royce use the jet engine reverser valve from Jet Manufacturing. These three manufacturers together make more than 70 percent of the commercial jet engines that are used in the world.

After approximately 3,500 hours of flight, the jet engines that are used on private aircraft must be torn down and rebuilt. This work is done by specialized firms. They carefully inspect all of the engine parts and replace those that are damaged or show any signs of metal fatigue. Jet Manufacturing has traditionally ignored this market, which has been served by several specialty manufacturing companies. However, the firm's new sales manager, Linda Smith, believes that the real growth market for jet engine reverser valves is in the repair and replacement market, not in the market for new jet engines. Her current plan is to sell the firms that repair jet engines the exact same reverser valve that is sold to General Electric, Pratt and Whitney, and Rolls Royce, at a price that is 50 percent above the standard list price. She believes the repair firms will be willing to pay this premium, since they can then advertise that they use 100 percent original equipment. The price she proposes would be only 15 percent higher than that of the valves that are currently manufactured by the smaller specialty houses for the repair market.

Ms. Smith has hired two new salespeople, who will concentrate all of their time on the repair and replacement market. They will call on firms that do the repair work. They will also visit major corporations that have ten or more business jet planes, to try to convince them to specify original equipment when they contract to have their jet engines rebuilt.

1. Has Jet Manufacturing violated any of the federal antitrust laws, since it has over 90 percent of the market for jet engine reverser valves?
2. Can Jet Manufacturing be accused of illegal price discrimination if it sells to original equipment manufacturers at one price and to repair houses at a higher price?
3. Jet Manufacturing has hired two salespersons to call on jet engine repair firms that have been doing business with its competitors. Does this represent predatory behavior? Explain.

CASE 3-2
Loeb & Company, Inc. v. Schreiner

Loeb & Company, Inc. purchases raw cotton from farmers and then sells it, at a profit, to cotton mills. In April of 1973, Loeb & Company contacted Charles Schreiner, a cotton farmer, to buy 150 bales of cotton for several thousand dollars. Schreiner agreed orally; no written contract was signed. Loeb & Company did send Schreiner a written confirmation of the oral agreement, which Schreiner did not object to.

Shortly thereafter, and before the cotton was delivered and paid for, the oil crisis caused the cost of all synthetic fabrics produced from petroleum products to rise dramatically. The demand for cotton increased, since its price and availability were not dependent on the price of oil. Soon, increased demand for cotton more than doubled its market price. Schreiner decided that he could get more money for his cotton than Loeb & Company had agreed to pay. Since no written contract had been signed, he felt that no legally enforceable agreement existed. He refused to sell the 150 bales. Loeb & Company sued to enforce the sale.

A clause in Section 2 of the UCC states that if both buyer and seller are merchants, an oral agreement is legally binding as long as at least one party signs a written confirmation and the other party does not object. Loeb & Company used this argument to enforce the agreement, but Schreiner claimed that he was not a merchant. Also according to Section 2, contracts for the sale of goods valued over $500 must be in writing.

1. Did agreement exist between Loeb & Company and Schreiner to substantiate the existence of a contract? How would you attempt to show that agreement did exist?
2. Did both potential parties have contractual capacity? Why or why not?
3. Did either party have grounds for claiming fraud or duress? Why or why not?
4. What consideration was offered by Loeb & Company? What consideration was offered by Schreiner?
5. Did a legally binding contract exist? Why or why not? What would be the effect if Loeb & Company's argument (under Section 2 of the UCC) were accepted by the court? What would be the effect if Schreiner's argument were accepted? How might Schreiner support his argument?

Source: Loeb & Co. v. Schreiner, Supreme Court of Alabama, 320 So. 2d 199 (1975).

OBJECTIVES

After studying this chapter, you should be able to:

1 Discuss business ethics.

2 Suggest ways to encourage employees' ethical behavior.

3 Define social responsibility.

4 Explain the classical view of the social responsibility of business and discuss three criticisms of this view.

5 Identify groups to whom business may have social responsibilities.

6 Identify benefits and costs of socially responsible behavior.

7 Explain the social audit.

CHAPTER 4

Ethics and Social Responsibility

On November 6, 1990, unusual full-page ads appeared in The Wall Street Journal *and elsewhere. The ads took the form of a memo to "ALL INTERESTED CONSUMERS" written by Joseph L. Nicolato, President and CEO of Volvo Cars of North America. They began as follows:*

> *"LADIES AND GENTLEMEN:*
> *For nearly 35 years Volvo has earned an outstanding reputation not only for high quality products but for high quality advertising as well. Through Texas Attorney General Jim Maddox we learned that there were concerns about the validity of a recent Volvo advertisement. We have reviewed the matter in great detail and wish to share these facts with you."[1]*

The memo went on to describe Volvo ads in which "Bearfoot," a "Monster Truck," drove over a Volvo 240 station wagon and four other cars, crushing all except the Volvo. The ad failed to mention that the Volvo had a slight advantage: Its roof was reinforced with concrete and steel, and the other cars' roof-support pillars were severed or weakened. Volvo's public confession, forced by the Texas Attorney General, concluded with the promise that "corrective action" would be taken and that the incident would not be repeated. This remarkable confession is a vivid example of unethical behavior by a firm and its attempt to minimize the damage to its reputation caused by being caught.[2]

In this chapter, we will examine the closely related topics of business ethics and the social responsibility of business. First, we will discuss business ethics. We will consider the demand for ethical behavior, examine the kinds of ethical dilemmas facing business people, and highlight specific actions that firms can take to encourage their employees to behave ethically. We will then shift our focus from the behavior of employees to the social actions of the firm.

We will examine differing views on the social responsibility of business, identify parties to whom business may have responsibilities, identify costs and benefits of social actions, and discuss the social audit.

BUSINESS ETHICS

Ethics are principles of morality or rules of conduct. **Business ethics** are rules about how businesses and their employees ought to behave. Ethical behavior conforms to these rules; unethical behavior violates them.

ethics   *principles of morality or rules of conduct.*

business ethics   *rules about how businesses and their employees ought to behave.*

Demand for Ethical Behavior

Businesses, governments, and the public are all paying more attention to business ethics. The Foreign Corrupt Practices Act (FCPA) of 1977 was enacted in response to disclosures that American corporations were paying bribes to high governmental officials in foreign countries. The bribes were used in an attempt to win contracts and sell products and services. In their defense, the companies argued that firms in other countries did the same thing; the American firms had to pay bribes or risk losing sales. Congress disagreed and passed the FCPA to outlaw the practice.

Bribes and kickbacks have come under particularly close scrutiny lately. A **kickback** occurs when someone who has won a contract or made a sale through favorable treatment gives back part of the profits from the transaction to the party providing the favor. For example, a retailer hires a market researcher to find a choice location for a new store. The retailer does not know that the researcher has previously agreed to recommend the property of a real estate developer. In return, the researcher will secretly receive a percentage of the first year's rent on the property.

kickback   *a payment by someone who has won a contract or made a sale through favorable treatment to the party providing the favor.*

Could the two men be plotting something unethical? If you were the observer in the foreground, would you blow the whistle if it might cost you your job?

Ethical Dilemmas

The Wall Street Journal wanted to see how executives and the public responded to ethical dilemmas. At the request of the *Journal*, the Gallup Organization polled 1,558 adults from the general public and 396 middle-level executives of large companies. Here are four of the dilemmas they presented. How would you respond to each dilemma?

Family Versus Ethics

Jim, a 56-year-old middle manager with children in college, discovers that the owners of his company are cheating the government out of several thousand dollars a year in taxes. Jim is the only employee who would be in a position to know this. Should Jim report the owners to the IRS, at the risk of endangering his own livelihood? Or should he disregard the discovery in order to protect his family's welfare?

The Roundabout Raise

When Joe asks for a raise, his boss praises his work but says the company's rigid budget won't allow any raises for the time being. Instead, the boss suggests that the company "won't look too closely at your expense accounts for a while." Should Joe take this as an authorization to pad his expense account, reasoning that he is simply getting the money he deserves through a different route? Or should he refuse this roundabout "raise"?

Sneaking Phone Calls

Helen discovers that another employee regularly makes about $100 a month worth of personal long-distance telephone calls from an office telephone. Should Helen report the employee to the company? Or should she disregard the calls, since many people make personal calls at the office? What should Helen do if the calls totaled only $10 a month?

---

bribe *a payment made "up front" to influence a transaction.*

A **bribe** is a payment made "up front" to influence a transaction. Thus, a bribe occurs before a transaction and a kickback afterwards. Bribery is especially a problem in overseas dealings. Following a criminal investigation by the Justice Department, Lockheed Corporation pleaded guilty to charges of concealing payoffs to Japanese business and government officials. Lockheed was fined $647,000. In another instance, the Brunswick Corporation admitted to the Securities and Exchange Commission that it had paid bribes to two Latin American countries to win contracts. The Joseph Schlitz Brewing Company faced a 747-count federal indictment for giving kickbacks to beer retailers and distributors in exchange for their business. It later agreed to pay a $750,000 penalty.

More recently, General Dynamics, General Electric, and other large companies have been charged with defrauding the Pentagon. The illegal exploits of Ivan Boesky and other Wall Street traders sent shock waves through the investment community in 1987. In December 1988, the Wall Street firm of Drexel Burnham Lambert pleaded guilty to six felony counts of mail, wire, and securities fraud and agreed to pay $650 million in fines and restitution. It subsequently filed for bankruptcy. Michael Milken, head of Drexel's Beverly Hills junk bond office, agreed in 1990 to plead guilty to six felony counts and to pay $600 million in fines and restitution.[3]

Also in 1990, American Express publicly apologized for what it admitted was a "shameful" and "baseless" smear campaign against rival financier Edmund Safra. Among other things, the company had spread false rumors that Safra was connected to drug cartels. The company agreed to donate $8 million to charities selected by Safra.[4] At about the same time, the Bank of Credit and Commerce International (BCCI) scandal was exploding. Finally shut down by regulators in mid-1991, Luxembourg-based BCCI had been under suspicion since the 1970s. The collapse of BCCI, which operated in 73 countries, revealed fraud of historic proportions, involving bribery, corruption, money laundering, gun running, drug smuggling, terrorism, and more than $5 billion in lost or stolen assets.[5]

The Faked Degree

Bob has done a good job for over a year. Bob's boss learns that he got the job by claiming to have a college degree, although in reality he never graduated. Should his boss dismiss him for submitting a fraudulent resume? Or should he overlook the false claim, since Bob has otherwise proven to be conscientious and honorable, and since making an issue of the degree might ruin Bob's career?

Here's how the public and executives responded to these dilemmas. (Since some respondents were undecided, the figures don't always add up to 100 percent.)

- *Family vs. ethics.* About 49 percent of the public and 52 percent of executives thought Jim should disregard the discovery. About 34 percent of each group believed he should report the owners.
- *The roundabout raise.* About 65 percent of the public and a full 91 percent of executives rejected the roundabout raise. Only 25 percent of the public and 7 percent of executives endorsed it.

- *Sneaking phone calls.* When the employee is sneaking $100 a month worth of personal calls, 64 percent of the public and 76 percent of executives thought Helen should report it. Only 26 percent of the public and 19 percent of managers favored disregarding the calls. But when only $10 is involved, only 47 percent of the public and 48 percent of executives favored reporting the employee; 38 percent of the public and 47 percent of executives would disregard the calls.
- *The faked degree.* More executives (50 percent) recommended dismissing Bob than suggested overlooking the claim. The general public decisively (66 percent to 22 percent) favored overlooking the false claim.

In general, corporate executives seemed to apply stiffer standards in ethical dilemmas than did the general public. The public was more inclined to excuse wrongdoing if there were mitigating circumstances.

Source: Reprinted by permission of the *Wall Street Journal* © 1983 Dow Jones & Company, Inc. All Rights Reserved Worldwide.

For a survey of how executives and people in general view ethical dilemmas in business, see the Ethical Issue box on this page.

Whistleblowers

Consider now the case of an employee who learns that his or her company engages in bribery or some other illegal activity. The employee can keep quiet, report the incident to top management, or even tell the press about it. By going outside the company, the employee is "blowing the whistle." **Whistleblowers,** those who report illegal activity occurring in a firm to the press, government, or other parties outside the firm, may find their jobs and careers threatened. Several states, including New York, California, Michigan, Connecticut, and Maine, now have laws protecting whistleblowers.

whistleblower *someone who reports illegal activity in the firm to the press, government, or other parties outside the firm.*

Also, the federal False Claims Act, first signed into law by President Lincoln in 1863 and strengthened by amendments in 1986, allows whistleblowers to sue government wrongdoers in the name of the United States. This act was initiated during the Civil War to help catch contractors who were submitting fraudulent claims. For instance, they often mixed sawdust with the gunpowder provided to the armed forces. The 1986 False Claims Act bolstered whistleblowers in three important ways: It gave them more power to initiate and prosecute claims, offered them financial incentives to do so, and provided reliable protection against employer retaliation. Before it was enacted, the Department of Justice received about six whistleblower complaints a year; in 1989, well over 100 such cases were received.[6] The question of whether such protection is appropriate is examined in this chapter's Controversial Issue (see p. 82).

ENCOURAGING ETHICAL BEHAVIOR

If a firm is serious about encouraging ethical behavior, it must take concrete actions. As shown in Figure 4-1 and explained in the selections that follow, these actions can take several forms.

Should Whistleblowers Be Protected?

Yes

People who become aware of illegal or unethical practices in their firms are in a difficult position. Unless they come forward with the facts, lives may be lost, money wasted or stolen, or other injustices uncorrected. But if they blow the whistle, they could face harassment, demotion, firing, or other retribution. Either good people will get hurt for doing what they think is right, or scandalous actions will go unreported.

Consider the case of Robert Wityczak, an employee of Rockwell International. In 1985, he testified before a Senate subcommittee that his supervisors reacted angrily when he told them that he would no longer mischarge labor and other items to NASA's space shuttle project. Gradually, he was squeezed from his purchasing job at the company, stripped of his security clearance, and put to work making cotton and sweeping floors. A Vietnam veteran who had lost both legs and a hand in the war, Wityczak testified that such tasks aggravated a back problem, which forced him to take a temporary medical leave. When he returned to work, he was fired. In late 1985, Rockwell settled a wrongful discharge suit with Wityczak for an undisclosed sum.[a]

Popular movies have chillingly documented the situation of whistleblowers. "Serpico" dramatized the case of Frank Serpico, a New York City policeman who uncovered graft in the police force and took his information to the *New York Times*. "Marie" presented the story of Marie Ragghianti, the head of the Tennessee Board of Pardons and Paroles, who learned that state authorities were engaged in a conspiracy to sell early prison releases. Ragghianti took the information to the FBI. "Brubaker" was based on the story of Tom Murton, the superintendent of the Arkansas state penitentiaries. Murton discovered graft within the prison system and also found the bodies of murdered inmates buried on penitentiary grounds. Anyone who has seen these movies knows the dangers of whistleblowing: Serpico was shot, and Ragghianti and Murton were fired.

Codes of Ethics

code of ethics *a list of principles of appropriate behavior.*

More than 90 percent of U.S. companies have a written **code of ethics.** Such codes list principles of appropriate behavior. Codes of ethics generally address such topics as conflicts of interest, confidentiality of corporate information, misappropriation of corporate assets, bribes and kickbacks, and political contributions. For example, BankAmerica's "Code of Corporate Conduct" includes 77 sep-

FIGURE 4-1   Ways to Encourage Ethical Behavior

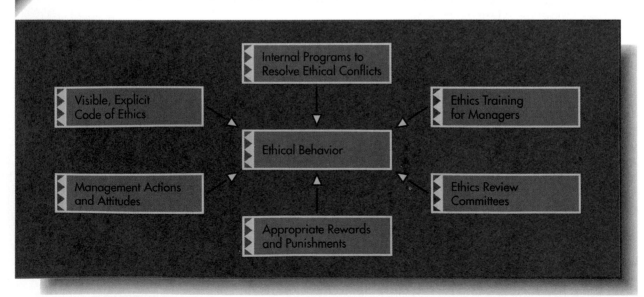

No

For several reasons, giving legal protection to whistleblowers is a serious mistake. First, many firms have internal mechanisms for reporting unethical or illegal acts. Unless internal mechanisms are used, innocent people could be hurt and unnecessary harm done to the company. Suppose an employee thinks a criminal act has occurred, when in fact it has not. If internal mechanisms are pursued, the misunderstanding might be corrected. If they are not, innocent people's names could be permanently smeared. Whistleblower protection laws discourage the use of these formal mechanisms.

Second, some people are simply malcontents who will take any opportunity to complain. Whistleblower protection laws give these people too much credibility and publicity. By encouraging them to spout their venom, whistleblower protection laws foster irresponsibility.

Third, a law of this sort can easily be abused. For instance, suppose that a marginal employee is afraid of being dismissed because of poor performance. What can he or she do? With whistleblower protection laws, the answer is obvious: Find some gossip about someone in the company, or make some up! Invoking these protective laws, the whistleblower can claim harassment when the company threatens dismissal. Furthermore, the False Claims Act provides monetary rewards for whistleblowers. This may encourage "dialing-for-dollars whistleblowers," who care more about personal gain than about justice.[b]

Finally, a fundamental premise of whistleblower protection laws is that firms are basically unethical and are trying to hide wrongdoing from the public. This is an unfair indictment of the American business system. By and large, corporate managers are hardworking and ethical.

Ethical abuses do occur in organizations, but whistleblower protection laws are not the way to correct them. There are already mechanisms to protect the public from corporate abuses and employee protection laws to prevent firms from harassing employees.

What Do You Think?

[a] "Businesses Crack Down on Workers Who Cheat to Help the Company," *Wall Street Journal*, June 1986, p. 13.
[b] "Whistleblowing While You Work," *Business and Society Review*, (Winter 1990, p. 65).

---

arate items that detail the responsibilities of the company and its employees. McGraw-Hill, Inc., has a "Code of Business Ethics," which guarantees the privacy of employee personnel and payroll records. Chevron Corp. puts out a 31-page booklet titled "Our Business Conduct: Principles and Practices." It touches on accounting and internal standards, conflicts of interest and confidential information, government relations, health and safety, antitrust concerns, multinational operations, and other matters. The section on avoiding discrimination is presented in the box on page 84. Notice how it presents the reasons underlying the policy, stresses the importance of compliance, and encourages employees to seek advice from their supervisors or others if they have questions.

If a code of ethics is to make a real difference, it must be carefully designed and implemented. Employees are more likely to accept a code if managers and others affected by it are involved in its development. For instance, Harron Communications Corporation had the company lawyers draft a code of ethics to govern many facets of employee behavior. The employees' response to the many "thou shall nots" was so negative that the code was never implemented. The company then got employees involved in developing a new code. It was worded in terms of acceptable behavior rather than forbidden actions, and response was much more favorable.[7]

Of course, employees must be aware of the code. Only about two thirds of all companies that have codes distribute them to workers. Some companies, such as Bethlehem Steel, hold annual meetings with employees to review the code of ethics and ask for clarification. When some workers asked questions about the code's moonlighting clause, Bethlehem rewrote the clause to clarify the conditions under which holding a second job would be acceptable.[8]

In addition to these steps, companies should make sure that the code specifies procedures for handling violations and that the procedures are enforced

Equal Opportunity at Chevron

Our company is subject to various federal and state laws prohibiting discrimination in employment because of age, race, color, sex, religion, national origin or handicap. Separate federal regulations require employers with contracts with the United States government to have affirmative action programs designed to provide equal opportunity for women and members of racial and ethnic minority groups, qualified handicapped persons, and Vietnam and disabled veterans. Handicapped persons must be able to perform the work without danger to themselves, fellow employees or the public. Many states have laws similar to these federal statutes and in some cases, the state laws are broader than the federal statutes.

These laws and regulations prohibit discrimination against both job applicants and employees based on any of the stated grounds (e.g., hiring, rate of pay, promotion, demotion and termination cannot be based on race, sex, age, handicap, etc.).

An essential part of our commitment to equal employment opportunity is to maintain a working environment in which the dignity of each individual is respected and in which employees may perform their job duties without physical or verbal harassment because of race, sex, color, national origin, religion, age, handicap or veteran status. It is important for all employees to know and understand that no form of harassment will be tolerated.

This company is proud of its accomplishments in assuring equal employment opportunity to all. Compliance with the equal employment opportunity laws and regulations, and company policies and instructions which implement them, is an essential part of every manager's job. Any person with a question about employment or employment discrimination should contact their supervisor or the person in their department designated to provide advice on such matters.

Source: Reprinted by permission of Chevron Corporation

fairly. Also, the code of ethics should be revised to reflect changes in the company's product line or competitive practices. Finally, the code must be internally consistent. If it contains two statements such as "Do not discriminate in hiring and promotion" and "Act affirmatively to hire and promote women and minorities," a manager's job is made more difficult.[9]

Rewards and Punishments

Research shows that how employees are rewarded or punished for ethical and unethical actions influences the likelihood of future ethical violations. In one study, 60 percent of the ethics codes of 238 companies included specific penalties for code violations. Half of the companies included termination as a potential penalty, and 30 percent included suspension. Probation, demotion, and negative comments on performance appraisals were also common penalties.[10]

Internal Programs

Besides standing behind the code of ethics and making it available and explicit, a company can encourage ethical behavior through other positive actions. IBM has had a "Speak Up!" program for more than 25 years. The program allows an employee to appeal any supervisory action and get a mailed response without having his or her name communicated to the supervisor. A meeting between the employee and management is arranged if necessary. Unfortunately, few companies currently have such internal programs for resolving ethical conflicts.

Ethics Review Committees

Other corporations have review committees made up of people specially trained to deal with ethical issues. Members of the committee come from both inside and outside the company. The committee's role is to advise the board of directors on sensitive ethical matters. Many large firms have high-level ethics committees. A few have ombudsmen, confidential hotlines for employees who are reluctant to raise ethical problems through normal channels, or formal judicial boards.[11]

Ethics Training

Ethics training is a part of some management development programs. The training usually includes discussions of real problems that the participants have faced at work. Alternative ways of dealing with the problem are explored. Probing questions are asked: "How would I feel if my family found out about my behavior? How would I feel if I saw it printed in the newspaper?"[12] In the mid-1980s, such companies as General Dynamics, McDonnell Douglas Corp., Chemical Bank, and American Can Company initiated such programs.

Top Management Actions and Attitudes

Whether employees behave ethically depends largely on the actions and attitudes of top management. For instance, if a code of ethics tells employees that bribing overseas clients is against company policy, but management looks the other way when bribes are successful in winning large contracts, the code is unlikely to be taken seriously. Also, companies must not encourage unethical behavior by setting unrealistic goals that can be met only by cutting ethical corners, and they must not condone cheating to "help" the company. In 1986, TRW Inc. dismissed or disciplined 30 employees when it was revealed that they had been overstating the time spent on military projects in order to overcharge the government.[13]

THE SOCIAL RESPONSIBILITY OF BUSINESS

On December 3, 1984, a cloud of deadly gas leaked from the Union Carbide chemical plant in Bhopal, India and covered a 25-square-mile area. By the time it cleared, 3,329 people were dead, and the lives of hundreds of thousands were

The size of bird populations is a vital indicator of the health of the environment. Leica Camera, Inc. shows social responsibility by sponsoring the annual Christmas Bird Count in conjunction with the National Audubon Society. Throughout the Americas, thousands of volunteers carefully tally each species and individual bird they see.

ruined. The company faced lawsuits totaling tens of billions of dollars, investigations into its safety procedures, and questions about how much management knew about all this. For four years, effigies of Warren Anderson, then chairman of Union Carbide, were repeatedly destroyed on Bhopal's streets. The Union Carbide plant hasn't reopened; the graffiti on the plant gate—"Carbide Kills"—is fading. In February 1989, Union Carbide reached an agreement with the Indian government to pay $470 million in compensation, to resolve all civil and criminal claims. Many called the settlement appallingly low. A company spokesperson said, "This is the end of it."[14] Unfortunately for Union Carbide, that wasn't the end. Criticism of the company continued, and in late 1991 an Indian court brought homicide charges against Warren Anderson.

Union Carbide isn't the only company to be subjected to vocal criticism in recent years. Nestle Corporation's sales of infant formula in developing countries brought charges that Nestle was contributing to malnutrition by discouraging breast feeding. Burroughs Wellcome Co., the manufacturer of the AIDS drug AZT, was stung by charges that its $198 million profit in 1988 had come at the expense of AIDS victims. Activists staged demonstrations in San Francisco, London, and New York, calling the company a corporate extortionist; "AIDS profiteer" stickers were posted on Burroughs Wellcome products.[15]

On the other hand, consider these facts. Celanese, a chemical company, gave the National Audubon Society $400,000 for research on the Atlantic puffin, the California condor, and other endangered bird species. Aetna Life and Casualty donated nearly $6 million in a single year to a bilingual community newspaper, a program of legal aid for female offenders, and a news service for Native Americans. Shell Oil contributed $2 million for testing Interferon, a drug that may be effective against cancer. Lymphomed, Inc., a drug manufacturer, announced plans to distribute, free of charge to indigent patients, a drug that can prevent a type of pneumonia that kills as many as 80 percent of all AIDS patients.[16]

Bhopal, baby formula, condors, and cancer drugs—there are many sides of the topic of social responsibility. In this portion of the chapter, we will explore viewpoints on social responsibility and identify parties whose interests must be weighed in making social decisions.

What Is Social Responsibility

social responsibility   the responsibility of businesses to pursue goals that benefit society.

Social responsibility is the responsibility of business to pursue goals that benefit society. That is, business decisions should fulfill broad social needs and expectations as well as those of the firm. Beyond these general statements, there is less agreement. Some consider the economic and social effects of business activity to be in harmony, while others see potential conflicts. Some people believe that it is socially responsible for a company to incur costs that do not relate directly to the production of goods and services. Others argue that acceptance of such costs is a violation of social responsibility. For instance, is it socially responsible to control smokestack emissions voluntarily? to build a Little League baseball diamond? We will consider opposing views on this issue next.

Views of Social Responsibility

classical view   when businesses produce goods and offer services in the most efficient way possible, they are also unintentionally promoting the social interest.

Although nearly everyone agrees that business should contribute to social well-being, there is much less agreement as to how that can best be done. In 1776, the English economist Adam Smith proposed what is now known as the **classical view** of social responsibility. Smith argued that in a private enterprise economy,

government should not set price or determine output. He believed that in pursuing their own goals, businesses would also be acting in the general interest of
society. That is, when businesses make decisions aimed at maximizing their profits, they also unintentionally promote the public or social interest. They are
guided, as if by an "invisible hand," to use society's scarce resources for the
greater good of all. According to this view, any action that is not in the best interest of the firm works against the invisible hand and reduces good to the community. In the classical view, for instance, if a firm donates funds to charity and
doesn't get a corresponding return, it cannot produce at the most efficient level,
and society suffers as a result.

Arguments in Favor of the Classical View. Proponents of the classical
view of business argue, first, that harm will result to society if a firm tries to
achieve any end except its own well-being. Classical thinkers believe that business has an implied contract with society to use resources effectively—or to use
resources to promote the business, which in turn promotes society. If a firm
begins to spend time and money directly on some social issue, such as sponsoring a community drug rehabilitation program, it will be breaking the contract to
use its resources for itself.

Second, classical thinkers believe that the voting public, not the people in
business, should set social priorities. If the public wants certain social problems
solved, then the public should work through legislative bodies to pass appropriate laws. Letting businesses set social priorities takes power away from the majority and gives it to the few.

Finally, proponents of the classical view may argue that social issues are better handled by expert social planners than by companies. Company managers
should do what they know best: running businesses. As economist Milton Fried-
man states, "The business of business is business." That is, businesses should
"stick to the knitting," not meddle in social affairs where they have little expertise.

Arguments Against the Classical View. According to its many critics, the
classical view of the role of business in society is based on narrow thinking and
outdated assumptions.[17] It assumes that individual firms have no power in the
marketplace and no control over prices. This is simply a description of perfect
competition, as discussed in Chapter 1. Perfect competition, you will remember,
is more an ideal than a reality. Critics of the classical view argue that firms must
be willing to accept responsibility in proportion to their power. Some go so far
as to argue that firms should actively divert their excess resources to social ends.
According to these critics, using company resources to protect endangered species or to further cancer research is both appropriate and necessary, even though
these activities may not lead to increased profits.

The recognition that firms have power also implies that they may abuse that
power. Many observers feel that business enterprises are largely indifferent to the
social consequences of their actions. In this view, firms tend to act irresponsibly
unless they are constrained by legal and political means. These observers call for
strict laws to govern product safety, advertising, pollution, and competitive
practices.

The classical view also assumes that businesses can stay healthy in a sick
society. But in reality, say critics, the pace of industrial activity places great stress
on the environment and on the emotional and physical health of workers. In the
long run, can a firm operate profitably if clean air and water are scarce, or if the

Investing in South Africa

U.S. firms debating whether or not to continue operating in South Africa are well aware of the complexity of social responsibility. By mid-1986, about 260 U.S. companies were doing business in South Africa, including 50 of the 100 largest industrial corporations. However, the South African government's apartheid policies and repressive acts led many of these firms to question their presence there.

Many executives see the South African issue as a no-win situation. Reasons for leaving include the deteriorating South African economy, the hostility of the black population toward the U.S. presence, opposition by many U.S. groups, and sometimes the executives' own moral stands. But things are not that simple. Many firms argue that their presence in South Africa has had a positive influence, both socially and economically, and that pulling out now would be hypocritical. Also, a pullout would abandon employees (about 50,000 of whom are black), customers, and assets. A massive pullout might even cripple the entire South African economy.

Since 1984, well over a hundred American companies—including General Electric, GTE Corp., and IBM—have sold their South African assets. It was estimated in 1990 that sanctions had cost South Africa about $40 billion over the previous five years—an amount about equal to the South African government's annual budget.

But not all firms are joining the rush. In a 1987 vote, stockholders of Johnson & Johnson defeated a proposal to stop doing business in South Africa by a resounding 12-to-1 margin. Similarly, General Dynamics refused in 1990 to stop selling aircraft to a South African distributor even after the city of Tallahassee—where it has two new plants—threatened to send the company packing because it was violating the city's anti-apartheid law.

Recent movements toward democratic change in South Africa, as well as President Bush's call for an end to sanctions, have caused some firms to rethink their positions. The South African situation shows just how complicated social decision making can be.

Sources: Based in part on C. J. LaBonte, "Should American Business Get Involved in South Africa?" *Across the Board,* July–August 1990, pp. 59–60; and A. N. Fins, "This Tallahassee Storm May Last All Summer," *Business Week,* 25 June 1990, p. 30.

work force deteriorates because of health problems? Promoting social improvement was the goal of the 51-company partnership that backed the development of the Detroit Renaissance Center. The Renaissance Center, built in a decaying section of the Detroit waterfront, has the world's largest hotel and four massive office buildings. Many critics of the classical view would see such urban renewal as a wise and forward-thinking move, regardless of whether it produced financial return for investors.

Critics also argue that the classical view does not recognize that society has certain expectations as to how businesses should act. In fact, these expectations go beyond those set down in law. Society is made up of organizations—corporations, nonprofit groups, churches—as much as it is made up of people. Just as the actions of individuals affect society, so do the actions of organizations. Therefore, if we expect socially responsible behavior from individuals, why not expect the same from organizations?

INTERESTED GROUPS

 In considering its responsibilities to society, business must weigh the interests of many groups. Some of these groups are shown in Figure 4-2 and are discussed in this section.

FIGURE 4-2   Parties to Which Business Must Be Responsible

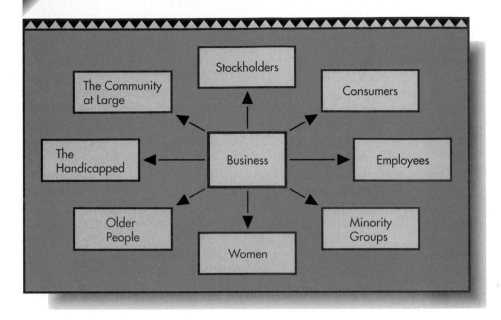

Stockholders

As explained in Chapter 1, **stockholders** (or **shareholders**) are the owners of a corporation. In light of this, we might expect that their interests always come first. In fact, the managers of corporations often take actions that are not in the best interest of stockholders. Stockholders generally have little influence over the day-to-day management of their companies. Later in this chapter, the benefits and costs of social actions to stockholders will be examined.

stockholders or *shareholders* the owners of the firm.

Consumers

Businesses must behave responsibly toward consumers. One listing of consumer rights was expressed by President Kennedy in 1962:

- The right to choose from a range of brands of products and services.
- The right to be informed of important facts about a product or service, such as quality, health hazards, and durability.
- The right to be heard by business and government, to make complaints or suggestions, and to ask questions.
- The right to be safe when using products or services.

As discussed in Chapter 2, consumerism sprang up in the 1960s to help guarantee these rights for consumers. Failing to consider consumer rights may be not only irresponsible, but also economically disastrous.

Johnson & Johnson showed its concern for consumer safety with its response to the Tylenol scares. In 1982, the company recalled all of its Extra-Strength Tylenol capsules from the market after seven poisoning deaths were caused by someone who put cyanide into the capsules. Although Johnson & Johnson was not responsible, it redesigned the Tylenol package to minimize the chances of future tampering. The total cost to the company of the recall and package redesign was $100 million. When capsules were again found to be laced with cyanide in 1986, the company decided to stop making the product in capsule form.

Source Perrier moved more slowly. In 1990, it was learned that bottles of Perrier sparkling water in North Carolina were tainted with benzene, which is known to cause cancer. At first, the company insisted that the problem was a local one, caused by cleaning fluid on bottling machinery. But then benzene was also found in Perrier water in Denmark, Japan, and elsewhere. Only then did the company admit that benzene occurred naturally in the water and that it had not been properly filtered out. Perrier then ordered a worldwide recall, at an estimated cost of $30 million. Some observers applauded the recall, but others believed Perrier's previous foot-dragging would cause lasting damage to the firm's reputation.[18]

Many other companies have conducted massive recall campaigns because of safety or quality considerations. In early 1991, the Saturn subsidiary of General Motors announced that it was recalling almost 30% of the cars it had sold, in order to fix front seats that could lurch back unexpectedly. Similarly, General Motors halted production and sales of the $64,138 Chevrolet Corvette ZR1, a car so powerful that it had been dubbed the "Corvette from Hell," when engines began to self-destruct. In other recent responses to safety concerns, Taco Bell recalled 300,000 promotional sports bottles, and Hardee's recalled 2.8 million "Ghostblaster" noisemakers, in each case because small parts could be swallowed by children.[19]

Employees

Of course, firms should protect the health and safety of their employees. Johnson & Johnson has been stepping up its efforts to become No. 1 in safety, trying to surpass Du Pont, which has long been the leader in preventing accidents and work-related illnesses. Johnson & Johnson has tough workplace safety rules, which it enforces strictly. It once spent $100 million to equip all plants and offices with sprinklers. At the company, workdays lost due to job-related illnesses and accidents have gone down more than 90% in the last decade.[20] Occidental Petroleum closed the pesticide unit of one of its chemical plants when several male workers in the unit were found to be sterile.

Worker protection has led to some controversies. For instance, in late 1988 two federal agencies—the U.S. Occupational Safety and Health Administration and the Department of Defense—launched investigations at Lockheed's Burbank, California plant. Workers there had claimed that life-threatening chemicals and materials were being used in the facility's secret projects. At least 160 workers at the Lockheed plant became ill; many of them were believed to be working on the top-secret Stealth fighter plane. About 75 workers filed a lawsuit charging that their ailments were caused by hazardous substances used in their top-secret jobs, and that Lockheed's facilities had not been adapted to the hazards. Also, many workers filed worker's compensation claims, and union officials received hundreds of grievances related to toxic substances. The workers' health problems included headaches, nausea, high blood pressure, disorientation, memory lapses, and cancer. Unfortunately, they were not allowed to discuss their work even with their doctors. They could be fired for violating laws against disclosing sensitive information. Several of the plaintiffs died.[21]

More generally, most people believe that companies have a social responsibility to offer salaries and benefits that are appropriate to the work performed as well as to the skill, knowledge, and training of the worker. Many companies also share their good fortune with their employees. When Apple Computer had an especially good quarter, it gave each of its 2,500 employees an extra week's vaca-

Business Career
Occupational Safety and Health Inspector: Government service position. Visits places of employment to detect unsafe machinery and equipment or unhealthy working conditions. Advises company managers on correcting violations to comply with government regulations. May testify in legal proceedings. *Average Salary: $37,000.*

tion. Such benefits are a great boost for employee morale. The Profile of Ben Cohen (p. 92) tells how Ben & Jerry's Homemade Inc. has recognized its responsibility to its employees and to other elements in society.

Minority Groups

As discussed in Chapter 3, certain minority groups have been treated unfairly in the past. Groups such as blacks and Hispanics have been discriminated against in hiring and promotion. Several laws now help to prevent discrimination and, in some cases, attempt to make up for past discrimination. In recent years, many discrimination lawsuits have been filed. In 1991, for instance, USX Corp. agreed to pay $41.8 million to settle a long-running case involving discrimination against about 10,000 black job applicants. The class-action suit involved violations of the Civil Rights Act. The settlement included "front pay"—that is, pay that workers would have received had they been working since the time of the discrimination.[22]

Women

Until fairly recently, most women working outside the home were employed as secretaries, nurses, teachers, receptionists, and retail sales clerks. Very few women were lawyers, doctors, or professional managers. Now, more and more women are pursuing these and other higher-paying careers. Federal law requires that businesses make a serious effort to recruit and retain female employees, as well as to treat them fairly. Otherwise, the firms risk serious legal consequences. For example, the Bechtel Corporation, a California engineering firm, settled a sex discrimination case by agreeing to pay $1.3 million in damages to former and current female employees. In another case, American Airlines agreed to rehire 300 flight attendants who had been fired because of pregnancy and to pay them a total of $2.7 million.

Another recent controversy relating to working women concerns fetal protection. In 1991, the Supreme Court ruled that employers may not bar women of childbearing age from certain jobs—such as jobs involving hazardous chemicals—because of potential risk to their fetuses. These "fetal protection" policies, affecting tens of thousands of workers, were called a form of sex bias—which is prohibited by federal civil rights law.[23] Companies are left in a difficult position, torn between worker protection and charges of discrimination.

As we will discuss in Chapter 25, companies have been taking steps to enhance career opportunities for women. Despite some successes in bringing women into management

Many firms are recruiting and promoting women and members of minority groups for important positions.

Business Career
Equal Opportunity Representative: Government service position. Evaluates and corrects unfair employment practices through consultation with employers and minority groups. Organizes federally-funded programs promoting equal opportunity. Informs minority community on civil rights laws. Encourages goodwill between employers and minority groups. *Average Salary: $37,700.*

Ben Cohen

Ben Cohen (on left in photo) is co-founder, chairman, and chief executive officer of Ben & Jerry's Homemade Inc. Before founding Ben & Jerry's with his childhood friend Jerry Greenfield, Cohen held such jobs as Pinkerton guard, pottery-wheel delivery-person, pediatric emergency-room clerk, and crafts teacher.

Ben & Jerry's began as an ice cream parlor in a renovated gas station in Burlington, Vermont, in 1978. It has grown dramatically since then, with more than 600 employees and 1990 sales of over $77 million. The company has shown a remarkable five-year annual growth rate of over 40 percent in sales and over 25 percent in earnings. Cohen sees the company as an experiment and a force for social change. The firm donates 7.5 percent of its pretax earnings to social causes. It has joined with 10 other companies in an organization called Act Now, which hopes to influence social legislation. The company's culture emphasizes fun, charity, and goodwill toward fellow workers. Cohen is personally active in social causes and has taught courses on social responsibility.

Ben & Jerry's has been noted for its social activism. For instance, it has supported committing 1 percent of the U.S. defense budget to cultural exchanges and cooperative international ventures in science, business, the arts, education, and other fields. It has also donated funds toward the preservation of Brazilian rainforests. Cohen has proposed an "Ice Cream for Peace" joint venture with Russia. American ice cream parlors would be opened in Russian cities, and any profits would finance student exchange between the two countries.

Cohen says, "I believe very strongly that business is the most powerful force in society. I see business as organized human energy and money that equal power. Add to that equation the communication resources that business has and uses and you have a superpower. So, business has a lot of potential and a lot of responsibilities." He adds, "Ben & Jerry's is incorporating that philosophy into every business decision that we make. We're looking for suppliers that share these values, such as Community Products Incorporated, which makes a product whose sales benefit rainforest and other environmental preservation efforts. Our brownies for our Chocolate Fudge Brownie are baked at the Greyston Bakery in Yonkers, N.Y. Greyston trains, employs, and counsels the homeless, the underskilled, and others in difficult situations and helps them improve the quality of their lives. These are the kinds of things business can do that are incorporated right into profitability and responsibility to the business and society." Ben & Jerry's hasn't always taken popular stands. For instance, in 1991, it made strong public statements against the Gulf war, which had strong support among the American people.

Ben & Jerry's also recognizes a responsibility to its employees. The firm even has a "Joy Committee" (renamed the "Joy Gang"), which is charged with putting more fun into the workday. The company stresses teamwork and trust and tries to put considerable power into the hands of lower management. It hires the handicapped, provides free therapy sessions to any employee who needs them, and has tables for changing babies' diapers in the men's room as well as the women's room. Cohen feels these practices and attitudes also benefit the company's bottom line. He says, "We have a saying around here at Ben & Jerry's that if it ain't fun why do it? There's no question that if you make things fun, there's a greater willingness to do things and to do them well. We really emphasize the quality of our ice cream. It takes a quality workforce to make quality ice cream."

Cohen and Greenfield have received the Corporate Giving Award from the Council of Economic Priorities for the firm's many charitable contributions. They were also named U.S. Small Business Persons of the Year in 1988 and have garnered many other honors.

roles, many people believe that a "glass ceiling" still confronts female managers; they can see the top of the organization but cannot reach it. This will be considered as the controversial issue in Chapter 9.

Older People

As seen in Chapter 2, the average age of the U.S. workforce is increasing. Among the reasons for this are longer life expectancy, the tapering off of the baby boom, the entry of increasing numbers of middle-aged women into the workforce, and the relaxation of mandatory retirement rules.

The protection of the rights of older people in the workplace is becoming more important. The Age and Discrimination Act of 1978 specifically prohibits age discrimination in hiring and promotion. But apart from legislative protection, the attitudes of employers toward older workers are important. Arbitrarily dismissing a skilled worker at age 60 or 65 hurts both the employee and the company.

Handicapped Persons

Business firms have begun to act more responsibly in hiring and promoting the handicapped. It is also the responsibility of companies to make sure that curbs, stairways, and similar obstacles do not prevent handicapped people from doing their jobs properly.

Recent legal developments have broadened the scope of the term "handicapped" to include workers with contagious diseases, including AIDS. For instance, a 1988 Justice Department ruling held that fear of contagion by itself is not a justification for federal agencies or federally assisted employers to fire or discriminate against workers infected with the AIDS virus. Such rulings, and other employees' fear of infection, will present firms with sensitive and difficult decisions in the coming years.[24]

The Community at Large

Many laws and watchdog groups now protect society from the potentially disruptive actions of businesses. One area of special concern, discussed in Chapter 2, is environmental protection. USX (formerly U.S. Steel) settled one lengthy dispute with the Environmental Protection Agency by agreeing to spend $400 million in air and water pollution cleanup at its plants in Pittsburgh. Years later, in 1991, USX faced heavy fines as the Environmental Protection Agency claimed that its plants were still releasing cancer-causing gases into the air.[25] Because of fines and negative publicity, firms must be especially careful about the effects of their actions on the environment and other aspects of community life.

A recent controversy concerning the common pencil illustrates the complexity of many social questions relating to the environment. Because of rainforest destruction, the San Francisco-based Rainforest Action Network urges a boycott of pencils made of jelutong, a wood that grows in Indonesia and Malaysia. Some U.S. pencil makers have begun using jelutong because incense cedar, which grows in California and Oregon, has risen in price. This price increase is partly due to stricter environmental rules, including protection of the spotted owl. But some pencil companies are resisting the pressure from environmentalists. Empire Berol USA is still using jelutong for 5% to 10% of the 800 million pencils it makes annually. Empire says jelutong isn't included on standard lists of rare or endangered species. It also says that the boycott may actually lead to *more* rainforest destruction—by reducing the value of jelutong below the point at which anyone would think it worth preserving.[26]

Businesses operate in a highly complex society. They affect many social and economic groups and are affected by these groups in turn. To be successful in such a setting, a company manager must have a wide range of abilities and an open mind.

BENEFITS AND COSTS OF SOCIAL ACTIONS

 Is social responsibility good for business? We'll approach this question from the perspective of the benefits and costs of socially responsible actions.

Benefits

A company may benefit directly and indirectly by taking socially responsible actions. One benefit is improved employee motivation. Workers are likely to be more satisfied on the job if they believe that their company actively contributes to community life.

Other benefits occur in the marketplace. By showing a genuine interest in social needs, a firm may become more aware of changing consumer tastes and preferences. It may spot new product opportunities, such as solar power generation or low-cost building materials for inner-city construction projects. The socially responsible company may find that its products and services are in demand simply because consumers recognize and appreciate such companies. When Toyota donated $1.3 million to a Georgetown, Kentucky community and child-care center, it devoted attractive full-page ads, such as the one shown in Figure 4-3, to publicize its actions. Presumably, the company hoped that its social responsibility would make people look more favorably on its products.

Some companies are trying to strengthen this link between marketing and social responsibility. For example, American Express Company donated $1.7 million to help restore the Statue of Liberty. It generated the gift money through a national ad campaign, by promising to donate a penny to the statue for each use of its charge card and a dollar for most of the new cards issued in the United States. During the campaign, card usage increased 28 percent over the same period the previous year.[27] Similarly, many firms are getting on the "green bandwagon," recognizing that association with environmental groups may have benefits in the marketplace. Numerous corporate offers of cash and other contributions are being made to groups such as the Sierra Club and the Natural Resources Defense Council. These groups have begun to develop guidelines regarding the sorts of gifts they will accept, and from whom.[28]

Just as consumers may favor the products of responsible firms, investors may prefer the stocks of such firms. The company with a highly visible social program may find that its stock sells at a higher market price. Several "social investing" mutual funds have emerged. These funds seek out companies with "good" social records. Three such companies are Quaker Oats Co., which makes low-sugar cereals; Dayton-Hudson Corp., which uses 5 percent of its federally taxable income for charitable purposes; and Magma Power Co., a leader in the development of geothermal energy.[29]

In the long run, socially responsible actions by business may eliminate the need for legislative controls that regulate what the company can and cannot do. Such controls often cost the firm more in lost business opportunities than the socially responsible actions would have cost.

FIGURE 4-3   Toyota Ad Stresses the Company's Social Responsibility

Courtesy of Toyota Motor Corporate Services.

Costs

Although social responsibility may be cheaper than government controls, it does have its costs. The most obvious cost is the money spent in support of social projects. A $50,000 grant to a community theater group means that $50,000 is no longer available for financing plant expansion. By diverting cash away from profitable investment opportunities, the company is not maximizing stockholder wealth. A firm's social goals are often less clearly defined than its profit goals. Therefore, it may be difficult to distinguish between good and bad management. In the long run, the market price of the stock of socially responsible companies may just as easily fall as rise.

A second cost relates to competitiveness. A company may stay on equal footing with its competitors if all of the companies support social projects. But if only one company in the market supports such projects, it may lose business if its competitors use their surplus resources to strengthen their competitive positions.

Finally, it is possible that government may step in and regulate companies' provision of social services and programs. Private companies have traditionally served society by providing goods, services, jobs, and a return on investment to stockholders. Venturing into this new area of social "product," well-intentioned companies may find that their actions bring forth more government regulation.

Comparing Benefits and Costs

Are the benefits of a proposed set of corporate social programs greater than the costs? How should a decision maker proceed? If we could clearly measure benefits and costs in terms of dollars, the answer to this question would be easy: Implement the proposed programs if total benefits exceed total costs; rethink the programs if they do not. But simple answers are not available. Many factors affect the comparison of benefits and costs. Among them are the actions of competitors, possible government controls, the amount of cash on hand, and the extent to which the social programs are in the public eye.

The USX case mentioned earlier in this chapter illustrates how difficult these decisions can be. Pollution controls at the company's mills would produce an undeniable benefit of cleaner air to people living nearby. But the costs are undeniable too. Besides the cost of installing and operating the pollution control equipment, there are the costs involved in reduced output, lost jobs, and higher steel prices. If you ran USX, what would you do? Would USX itself be better off with the pollution control equipment in place?

THE SOCIAL AUDIT

social audit *a step-by-step examination of all the activities that make up the firm's social programs.*

Our discussion so far has focused on issues of corporate responsibility and the problems of evaluating a company's social programs. One way to think constructively about these issues and problems is to conduct a social audit.

A **social audit** is a step-by-step examination of all the activities that make up a firm's social programs. The firm may evaluate its own programs in terms of goals, and it may identify new programs that it ought to pursue. Goals are then formulated for these new programs. The general aim of the social audit is to make management aware of the impact of corporate actions on society. In some countries, social audits are mandatory. In Germany, about 20 of the largest firms now publish regular social reports. In France, all firms with more than 750 employees must publish such a report, including information on 94 social indicators. Norway also requires a published social report, and many other European countries are considering such legal requirements.

Many difficult questions must be answered when conducting a social audit: What activities should be audited? How should each activity be evaluated? How should social performance be assessed? In general, these questions must answered on a case-by-case basis.

SUMMARY POINTS

1 Business ethics are principles of morality or rules of conduct about how companies and their employees ought to behave. Because of highly publicized unethical activities by businesses, the demand for ethical behavior has increased.

2 Employees' ethical behavior can be encouraged through use of written codes of ethics, rewards and punishments for ethical or unethical behavior, internal programs,

ethics review committees, ethics training, and top management's actions and attitudes.

3 Social responsibility is the responsibility of business to pursue goals that benefit society.

4 The classical view of social responsibility is that the pursuit of profits results in the greatest social welfare for all. Critics of the classical view argue that it ignores the fact that firms have substantial power, assumes that firms can remain healthy in a sick society, and ignores society's expectations about how businesses should act.

5 Ideally, businesses should be responsible to many groups: stockholders, consumers, employees, minority groups, women, older people, the handicapped, as well as the community at large.

6 Socially responsible behavior may generate both benefits and costs for a firm. Benefits may include employee satisfaction and motivation, increased demand for products and services, favorable investor re-

sponse, and reduced danger of legislative controls. Costs may include funds taken away from profit-making uses, loss of competitive position, and government regulation if the firm is thought to have overstepped its social role. The benefits and costs of a proposed social action should be carefully weighed in terms of impact on both the business and society.

7 Many companies now conduct social audits, which are step-by-step examinations of all activities, current and proposed, that make up a firm's social program. One aim of the social audit is to make management more aware of the impact of corporate actions on society.

REVIEW QUESTIONS

1 Give an example of a kickback.

2 What is a whistleblower?

3 What is a code of ethics?

4 How can firms encourage ethical behavior among their employees?

5 What does "social responsibility" mean? Give a few examples of socially responsible actions.

6 Briefly explain the classical view of social responsibility.

7 What are three criticisms of the classical view?

8 In what sense are businesses responsible to their employees? To minority groups? To women?

9 Cite three potential benefits and three potential costs of social actions.

10 What is a social audit?

DISCUSSION QUESTIONS

1 What are some of the costs to a firm if it is caught in unethical behavior?

2 Do you think it is ever justified to pay bribes and kickbacks? Why or why not?

3 In your opinion, what are the chief shortcomings of the classical view of social responsibility?

4 How are the health of society and the health of individual businesses related?

5 Do you think it is moral for extremely profitable firms not to engage in such so-

cially responsible actions as giving to charities and sponsoring community development projects? Support your view.

6 What are some of the potential benefits and costs of installing expensive pollution control equipment at production facilities? Consider both the company's and society's point of view.

7 Why should a firm undertake a social audit?

EXPERIENTIAL EXERCISES

1 Interview a corporate manager about the issue of business ethics. Be sure to include the following questions in your interview (but feel free to add others). (a) What does ethics mean to you? (b) How does your company encourage ethical behavior? (c) Please tell me about an ethical dilemma you have faced at work, and how you dealt with it.

2 Write an essay on one of the following: (a) The Michael Milken case, (b) the BCCI scandal, (c) Union Carbide and the Bhopal tragedy, (d) charges of "AIDS profiteering" by drug manufacturers, or (e) U.S. investment in South Africa.

CASES

CASE 4-1
100% Pure

There is probably no product for which quality is considered more important than baby food. Therefore, it was startling that Beech-Nut Nutrition Corporation's "100% Apple Juice" product for babies actually contained little or no apple juice. The juice, sold between 1978 and 1983, was in fact a "100% fraudulent chemical cocktail"—a cheap concoction of beet sugar, apple flavor, caramel, color and corn syrup.

The case emerged after a private investigator named Andrew Rosenzweig was hired in 1982 by a trade group. He was to investigate possible mixing of inferior ingredients in apple juices. A year later, the Food and Drug Administration received an anonymous letter from a Beech-Nut employee, signed "Johnny Appleseed," alerting it to the problem.

In fact, Beech-Nut had known since at least 1981 that the "apple concentrate" supplied by Interjuice & Universal Juice Co.—at a price 20% below the standard market rate—was bogus. Beech-Nut's director of research and development, Jerome LiCari, alerted Beech-Nut's president, Neil Hoyvald, that a "tremendous amount of circumstantial evidence" added up to a "grave case" against the supplier. He recommended terminating Beech-Nut's contract with the company. Instead, Hoyvald criticized LiCari's loyalty and judgment and threatened to fire him. In 1982, LiCari resigned.

Beech-Nut was under tremendous financial pressure, and the cheap, phony concentrate saved millions of dollars, helping to keep the company going. Beech-Nut executives apparently rationalized their behavior on two grounds, both debatable. First, they reasoned that other companies were also selling fake juice, so Beech-Nut was just remaining competitive. Second, they were apparently convinced that the fake juice was perfectly safe.

The private investigator told Beech-Nut in 1982 that he had conclusive proof that the concentrate was not apple juice. When he asked the company to join other juicemakers in a lawsuit against the supplier, Beech-Nut stalled in order to unload its $3.5 million inventory of tainted juice products. President Hoyvald ordered the inventories unloaded "fast, fast, fast," at deep discounts. Much of the product was sold in Caribbean countries.

Beech-Nut's stonewalling angered government investigators, who brought indictments against the company in 1986. In June of 1988, Beech-Nut's current president, Richard Theuer, admitted that the company had broken "a sacred trust" but assured the public that Beech-Nut baby foods were now pure. But tremendous, and perhaps irreparable, damage had been done. Two former Beech-Nut executives—Hoyvald and former vice-president for manufacturing John Lavery—were sentenced to a year and a day in prison and fined $100,000 for their roles in the scam. Federal judge Thomas Platt termed it "the largest consumer fraud case ever." Beech-Nut pleaded guilty to 215 counts of introducing adulterated food into commerce and violating the Federal Food, Drug and Cosmetic Act. The company paid a $250,000 fine to the state of New York. The Defense Logistics Agency suspended the company from all government contract work. The company also paid $7.5 million to settle a class-action suit brought by a supermarket chain, and it paid the government a $2.2 million fine. At least two civil suits are pending. The company's market share slipped from 20% to 17%, strengthening the competitive position of its rival, Gerber's. Various suppliers to the company were convicted. Perhaps worst of all, Beech-Nut's reputation, built since 1891 on purity, high quality, and natural ingredients, was forever tarnished.

1. What sorts of factors do you think might have led Beech-Nut executives to engage in these illegal and risky activities? What are your reactions to Beech-Nut's justifications for its actions?

2. In view of the widespread, blatant nature of this fraudulent activity, are you surprised that it wasn't exposed earlier? What factors may have prevented potential "Johnny Appleseeds" from blowing the whistle sooner?

3. How would you characterize Jerome LiCari's actions? Should he have acted differently, either before or after his resignation?

4. What sorts of penalties do you think are appropriate for Beech-Nut? For Neil Hoyvald?

Source: Based in part on J. Queenen, "Juice Men: Ethics and the Beech-Nut Sentences," *Barron's,* 20 June 1988, pp. 37–38; A. Hagedorn, "Two Ex-Officials of Beech-Nut Get Prison Sentences," *Wall Street Journal,* 17 June 1988, p. 39; "What Led Beech-Nut Down the Road to Disgrace," *Business Week,* 22 February 1988, pp. 124–128; and S. Kindel, "Bad Apple for Baby," *Financial World,* 27 June 1989, p. 48.

CASE 4-2
A Body to Be Kicked

A 19th-century English judge, Edward Baron Thurlow, lamented in a court decision: "Did you ever expect a corporation to have a conscience when it has no soul to be damned and no body to be kicked?" Then he whispered, "By God, it ought to have both."

A century later, assistant state's attorney general Jay Magnuson went looking for a body to kick after an elderly Polish immigrant died of cyanide poisoning in the suburban Chicago plant of Film Recovery Systems, Inc. In October 1983, after an eight-month investigation, Magnuson filed murder charges against corporate officials at Film Recovery. This might have been the first time in the United States that corporate officials had been charged with murder in a work-related death.

Film Recovery's workers used cyanide to extract silver from film scraps. Prosecutors found evidence that the workers, mostly non-English-speaking immigrants, weren't warned about the dangers of cyanide and were provided with only minimal safety equipment.

In February 1983, Stephan Golab, a 61-year-old Polish immigrant, collapsed and died near an open vat of cyanide. The Cook County medical examiner ruled that Golab died from cyanide poisoning and that his death was a homicide. The plant was closed, and federal regulators fined the company $2,425 for safety violations. A Cook County grand jury indicted five company officials for murder.

The idea of applying criminal laws to corporate executives has received worldwide attention since the mass poisoning in Bhopal, India. In the United States, the Bhopal tragedy has inspired demands for tougher laws on corporate responsibility. Under one proposed law, a company manager who knowingly concealed a dangerous product or business practice could get to up to 10 years in prison, a fine of $250,000, or both. A proponent says, "There's a growing consensus that the only way to deal with these problems is to impose very serious criminal penalties and actually put these people behind bars."

1. Is it meaningful to talk about a corporate "conscience"? Does it make sense to think of entire companies as being moral or immoral? Or is it more appropriate to say that the actions of company executives are moral or immoral?

2. Do you agree that corporate officials should be held criminally liable for the actions of their firms? Why or why not?

3. Which of the criticisms of social responsibility discussed in this chapter seems to be most clearly reflected in corporate responsibility laws? Which is least evident?

Source: Reprinted by permission of the *Wall Street Journal,* © 1985 Dow Jones & Company, Inc. All Rights Reserved Worldwide.

Intercollegiate Athletics as Big Business

Fred Willingham sat down at his large wood panel desk in his den and began writing a check for $25,000 to his alma mater. The school was one of the most prestigious private universities in the country with an endowment of almost a billion dollars. Nevertheless, the institution was concerned about funding its athletic programs and had called upon Fred and other distinguished alumni to make sizable contributions.

Before Fred actually finalized the transaction, a number of thoughts began to run through his mind. He knew college athletics was big business, and he wanted to make sure he was doing the right thing. He was somewhat concerned that his institution had gone on probation with the NCAA (National Collegiate Athletic Association) two years ago for supposedly making illegal payments to two players on the football team. The players were permanently suspended from the team. He wondered about supporting an institution that had violated the tradition of amateur athletics in the United States.

Rather than write the check immediately, he decided he would more critically analyze the situation. Was it really right to support an institution of higher education that had not followed the guidelines of the NCAA? While he was involved in the thought process over the next two weeks, he happened to read a story in a major magazine that indicated Notre Dame University would likely receive more than $38 million dollars in football television revenue plus multimillion dollar bowl contracts over the next five years.[1] Another story stated that Jim Valvano, once the head basketball coach at North Carolina State University, had made over a million dollars a year during his coaching days from his salary, speeches, and endorsements of products.[2] It was not unusual for other successful coaches to make up to half a million dollars a year.

At that point, Fred also began to wonder if it was really wrong for two college football players to accept $200 in illegal payments. The money had been given to them to fly home for Christmas vacation during their freshman year. At a time when the Rose Bowl in Pasadena, California paid participating teams five million dollars each to play on New Year's day, was it wrong for the two freshman players to accept the small payments? Afterall, college football was big business, generating hundreds of millions of dollars of revenue each year.

Fred's own son had played college football for his alma mater. His nephew had also received a football scholarship from the same institution, but wanted to transfer to another school after his sophomore year because he and the coach did not get along. The young man was told he would be allowed to transfer to another college, but would not be eligible to play for a full year. Once again Fred began to wonder who these NCAA rules were intended to protect—the players, the coaches, or the universities.

Fred was a great believer in the private enterprise system as described in Chapter 1 of this text. He thought that free competition promoted greater wealth for all and that controlled economics tended to restrict the potential for output. Even in the United States he marveled at the positive effect on services and pricing that deregulation had in such industries as air travel and banking. The strongest survived and prospered while the weakest went out of business. It was a trough system for the inefficient, but one that helped to make this country a world economic leader.

Fred also noticed that businesses in controlled industries often wanted to keep things that way. Competition and free markets were great—but that was for everybody else. They needed regulation and control to keep matters from getting chaotic and out of hand. Otherwise, the sharks would eat up the small fish. Fred wondered why the principles of open competition were not applied to intercollegiate athletics. Either they were valid or they were not. He wondered why a university that ran a multimillion dollar athletic program was different from a business that faced the same type of stiff competition. Open competition in intercollegiate athletics would mean players could be paid salaries and bonuses the same as coaches. Also, there would be no limitation on the number of scholarships a school could offer or the amount of time a team could practice. Free enterprise would be applied to an area it had not been applied to before.

As Fred was finalizing his decision about the contribution, one last thought ran through his head. He asked himself what the following eight colleges had in common: Bowdoin College, Carleton College, Haverford College, Oberlin College, Reed College, Tufts University, Wesleyan University, and Williams College. They all had freshman classes with average SAT scores of 1,250 or higher, but most of the general public had never head of them. Why? Because they did not participate in big-time college athletics at any level.

Questions

1. If you were Fred Willingham, would you make the $25,000 donation in light of the fact that the school had broken NCAA rules?
2. Who do you think the rule on losing one year's eligibility for transferring is intended to protect?
3. Given that intercollegiate athletics is big business, should there be open competition as is true of other businesses?

[1] W. Reed, "We're Notre Dame and You're Not," *Sports Illustrated* (Feb. 19, 1990), p. 56–60.
[2] Jim Valvano and Curry Kirkpatrick, *Valvano* (New York: Simon and Schuster, 1991).

PART 2
Business Organization

OBJECTIVES

After studying this chapter, you should be able to:

1 Identify the three basic forms of business ownership.

2 Discuss the features, advantages, and disadvantages of sole proprietorships.

3 Examine the features, advantages and disadvantages of partnerships.

4 Analyze the structure, advantages and disadvantages of corporations.

5 Describe six special types of corporations.

6 Describe four types of business combinations.

CHAPTER 5

Forms of Business Ownership

While Bob Greer attended Austin Community College in Austin, Texas, he worked part-time, first as a stock assistant and later as a cashier. His employer was H. E. Butt Corporation, a Texas-based grocery chain. When Bob graduated in 1988, H. E. Butt offered him a position as assistant store manager for night operations at one of its stores in Waco, Texas. Bob accepted.

One of Bob's friends at Austin Community College was Mary Gray. After Mary graduated from community college, she enrolled at Texas A&M University, where she earned a degree in landscape architecture in 1991. She learned a great deal about landscaping and the new science of xeriscape lawn maintenance and gardening. Mary wanted to start a landscape firm in Austin, specializing in xeriscape garden plants, supplies, and services. But she recognized that she knew very little about practical business affairs. In contrast, her friend Bob had studied business in community college and had also been actively involved in operating a business for three years. Mary asked Bob to join her as a partner in the new firm.

Bob had to make several important decisions. First, was he willing to think seriously about leaving a promising career with a major corporation to become a partner in a small business? If so, was there sufficient demand in Austin for low-maintenance xeriscape lawn products and services to justify this investment of his time and resources? Also, Mary Gray had been a good friend of his in college, but would she make a good business partner? Finally, if Bob and Mary decided to start a business, would they be better off creating a corporation, or would a true partnership be best for them?

This chapter will examine the advantages and disadvantages of the various forms of business ownership that are available to Bob and Mary. We will also discuss mergers and acquisitions of businesses.

T he private ownership of production is an essential characteristic of our economic system. Private business ownership generally takes one of three legal forms: sole proprietorship, partnership, or corporation. A **sole proprietorship** is a business owned by one person. A **partnership** is a business owned by two or more people. A **corporation** is a business owned by its stockholders. It is a legal entity with many of the rights, duties, and powers of a person, and it exists separately from the people who own it, manage it, and work for it. Business enterprises may be as small as a single person providing a service such as freelance writing or as huge as multinational corporation producing a product such as automobiles.

sole proprietorship   *a business owned by one person.*

partnership   *a business owned by two or more people.*

corporation   *a business owned by its stockholders; a corporation is a legal entity with many of the rights, duties, and powers of a person, but separate from the people who own and manage it.*

AN OVERVIEW OF BUSINESS OWNERSHIP

Figure 5-1 compares the three principal forms of business ownership in terms of frequency and income. Note that sole proprietorships make up 65 percent of all business concerns in the United States. But in terms of total earnings of all businesses, proprietorships are responsible for only 28 percent. Corporations, on the other hand, account for 24 percent of business enterprises but 84 percent of all earnings. Thus, sole proprietorships tend to be relatively small. In contrast, corporations, while fewer in number, can be quite large. Partnerships are less common than the other forms of ownership. Some partnerships are quite profitable, but the graph shows that partnerships as a group have not been as profitable as the other forms of ownership.

Now let's look more closely at the three basic forms of business ownership. We will present our discussion in terms of a business started by Henry Gonzalez

FIGURE 5-1   Ownership Structure of the U.S. Economy

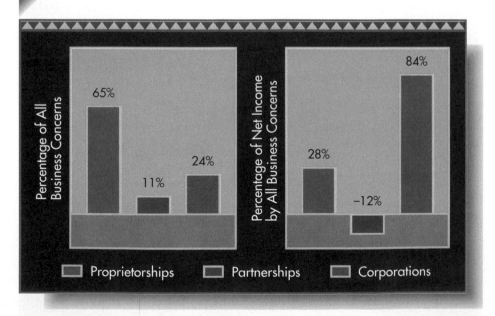

Source: U.S. Department of Commerce, Bureau of the Census, *Statistical Abstract of the United States*, 110th ed., pp. 518–545.

of Tucson, Arizona. We will watch Henry's business change from a sole proprietorship to a partnership to a corporation.

SOLE PROPRIETORSHIP

 Henry Gonzalez graduated from high school and enrolled in a community college. For the three years, he took night classes in business administration. During the day, he worked at Sears, putting on tires, replacing batteries, and doing front end alignments. Henry was working very hard, obtaining an excellent education—both from college and from Sears.

When Henry graduated, he was offered a position as assistant manager in the Sears garage, but instead he accepted a sales position in the automotive section at Montgomery Ward. Henry's dream was to own his own downtown garage. He enjoyed making decisions. Hard work never bothered him, and he wanted to keep the profits of his own ideas and work. Henry took a 10 percent cut in pay to work at Montgomery Ward, because he felt that he needed to learn more about selling.

Two years later, a small garage on the east side of Tucson went up for sale. It was not large, and it was not downtown, but it was inexpensive. Henry borrowed $10,000 from his parents, withdrew $6,000 from his savings, and received a small business development loan for $14,000 from a local bank. The term of the bank loan was five years. Henry was set: He was salesperson, purchasing agent, mechanic, and sole proprietor.

Features of Sole Proprietorships

In most sole proprietorships, the owner also acts as manager. As such, he or she makes all decisions. After all, it is the owner's money and livelihood that are at

The owner of this skateboard store in Los Angeles experiences both the advantages and the disadvantages of being a sole proprietor.

stake. In the case of Gonzalez's Garage, these decisions included ordering engine oil, filters, tune-up supplies, and miscellaneous repair parts; keeping the books current; and supervising two employees. However, some sole proprietorships are large enough that the owner can hire a professional manager to handle the day-to-day operations of the business.

Advantages of Sole Proprietorships

The sole proprietorship form of business offers many advantages. These are best understood when seen in relation to those of a partnership and a corporation, which are discussed later. Table 5-1 presents an overview of the advantages and disadvantages associated with sole proprietorships, partnerships, and corporations.

Ease of Formation.   There are no significant legal obstacles to forming a sole proprietorship. That is one reason why there are almost 19 million sole proprietorships in the United States. All Henry had to do was obtain a state sales tax number and state and federal unemployment compensation numbers. He needed to file federal social security taxes. The process was so simple that Henry started Gonzalez's Garage without even consulting a lawyer.

TABLE 5-1   Advantages and Disadvantages of Sole Proprietorships, Partnerships, and Corporations

Form of Ownership	Advantages	Disadvantages
Sole Proprietorship	Ease of Formation	Unlimited Liability
	Minimal Capital Requirements	Limited Management Talent
	Retention of All Profits	Few Opportunities for Employees
	Complete Control of the Business	Limited Credit Availability
	Tax Benefits	Instability of the Business
Partnership	Access to Capital	Unlimited Liability
	Management Talent	Personality Conflicts
	Ease of Formation	Life of the Partnership
	Tax Benefits	Adding and Removing Partners
Corporation	Limited Liability	Costs and Complexity of Incorporation
	Unlimited Life	Public Disclosure
	Transfer of Ownership	Double Taxation
	Professional Management	

Minimal Capital Requirements. One advantage of a sole proprietorship is that it requires little capital. Henry, for example, needed only $30,000 to begin operations. Although Henry was able to negotiate the $14,000 bank loan, business loans are not always easy to obtain—especially for start-ups. In Henry's case, the bank required that he present a written business plan for his proposed venture and a schedule of projected earnings for each of its first five years of operations. The bank wanted to be sure that the business could produce enough cash to repay the loan and the interest charges. In addition, Henry had to submit a statement of his personal finances and to pledge his car as security for the loan. If Henry were to go out of business, ownership of the car would transfer to the bank, which would sell it and use the proceeds to cover the unpaid loan balance.

Retention of All Profits. The sole proprietor keeps all of the profits of the business. This is a strong incentive for entrepreneurs. In contrast, the other forms of ownership require a sharing of business earnings, either with one or more partners or among corporate stockholders.

Complete Control of the Business. Another advantage is that a sole owner has complete control over the business. The owner does not have to worry about whether partners or stockholders are happy. There is no one to question such decisions as staying open until midnight or closing out a particular product. The rewards of a good decision, and the losses from a bad one, belong to the owner alone.

Tax Benefits. The sole proprietorship also offers substantial tax benefits. The owner pays taxes only on the income earned from the business. Gonzalez's Garage made $18,000 after all expenses were paid during the first year of its operation, so Henry's taxable income was $18,000. That is, the earnings of the business are the earnings of the owner. Later in this chapter, we will see that corporations pay taxes on the income they make. Then the stockholders pay taxes on the dividends they receive. Such double taxation does not apply to sole proprietorships. In addition, the owner files only one federal income tax form, since the owner and the business are one and the same.

Disadvantages of Sole Proprietorships

If sole proprietorships had no drawbacks, there would be no reason to form partnerships or corporations. But sole proprietorships do have important disadvantages. Let's take a look at them.

unlimited liability   in a sole proprietorship or a partnership, the sole proprietor or partners are liable for all obligations of the business.

Unlimited Liability. **Unlimited liability** means that the business is not separate or distinct, in any legal sense, from the person who owns it. It is the owner, not the business itself, who is legally liable in the case of accident or injury involving a customer or an employee, or any other type of liability that the business might incur. Henry Gonzalez *is* Gonzalez's Garage. The debts of the business are his debts. A customer who is injured as a result of a bad brake job can sue Henry for all of his business and personal assets. Unlimited liability is the most significant disadvantage of a sole proprietorship. It is the main reason why most entrepreneurs incorporate when their businesses get big enough.

Limited Management Talent. A second problem with sole proprietorships is that they rarely make enough money to hire competent professional managers. Therefore, they rely on the business expertise of one person only—the owner. If the sole proprietor is a thoughtful, creative, hardworking person, the firm may succeed. If not, it will probably fail, because there is little backup management support.

Also, the fact that the owner makes all the decisions can slow the growth of the business. One person can do only so much. Often, profitable opportunities cannot be pursued because the owner is already working 12 to 15 hours a day. Only about 7 percent of all sole proprietorships in the United States earn more than $100,000 annually in profits.

Few Opportunities for Employees. Sole proprietorships have a hard time attracting high-quality employees. Prospective employees often see no long-term opportunities for them in the business unless they are members of the owner's family. It is not unusual for a person to work for a sole proprietorship for several years and then to start a new sole proprietorship in the same industry.

Limited Credit Availability. Sole proprietorships face the problem of limited credit. Banks prefer to lend their money to corporations, which are usually stronger financially. This makes them better credit risks. When banks lend money to sole proprietorships, they usually charge a higher rate of interest. The extra interest compensates the bank for accepting the risk involved in such a loan. The interest rate on Henry's loan was 12 percent annually; at that time, corporations were paying only 9 to 11 percent.

Instability of the Business. Finally, sole proprietorships are unstable. If the owner becomes sick or dies, the business usually fails. Although some sole proprietorships are passed on from one generation of a family to the next, many others simply disappear when the owner is unable to continue operations.

Business Career
Credit Analyst: Analyzes credit information to determine risk involved in lending money to commercial customers. Evaluates potential borrower's financial status from financial statements, ratio analyses, and industry data. Considers such factors as income growth, credit history, liquidity, management quality, market share, and collateral. *Average Salary: $32,800.*

PARTNERSHIPS

Gonzalez's Garage was moderately successful. During the first full year of operation, Henry learned a great deal about running a business and made $18,000. He

Partners Jackie Haygood and Lou Ella Pressey run a successful shop at Florida's Palm Beach International Airport.

also realized that Gonzalez's Garage was like most small businesses—it didn't have much money and was short on talent. In order to deal with these two problems, Henry invited his friend, George Monti, to join him in a new partnership called G & M's Garage. Henry put all of his existing equipment into the partnership, while George added a much-needed cash infusion. He contributed $20,000, to be used for new electronic engine testing equipment and a modern wheel-balancing machine. They also refinanced Henry's existing bank loan in the name of G & M's Garage. The bank supported this idea, since both people were now liable for the loan. Finally, Henry and George agreed that they would both work full-time for the new enterprise.

Types of Partners

general partners partners who have responsibility for running the business and are legally liable for all of its debts.

Business partners can be either general partners or limited partners. **General partners** are responsible for running the business and are legally liable for all of its debts. All partnerships are required by law to have at least one general partner. G & M's Garage had two general partners.

limited partners partners who contribute money or capital to a partnership, play no role in its management, and are not legally responsible for the partnership's debts.

Limited partners contribute only money or capital to a partnership. Their risk in the event of loss is limited to the amount of their investment in the partnership. Limited partners share in the profits of the organization, but they do not participate in its management, nor are they legally responsible for the partnership's debts. The limitation on liability is clearly the biggest advantage of being a limited partner.

Features of Partnerships

It was not unusual that Henry and George chose to form a partnership. Many thousands of partnerships are formed each year; there are approximately 3.4 million partnerships in the United States. Still, as Figure 5-1 indicated, partnership is the least popular form of ownership.

Most partnerships share four characteristics. First, they usually have only two, three, or four members. It is difficult for a partnership to operate effectively with more than four partners, since communication among many partners becomes quite difficult and complex. In addition, there is a tendency for each partner to feel that he or she has an equal voice in making decisions that relate to the business. It is difficult to run some partnerships with two bosses, but almost impossible to operate one efficiently with five or more bosses.

The second feature is that all general partners are expected to play an active role in the management of the business. In the case of G & M's Garage, Henry took responsibility for ordering supplies, while George handled billing.

articles of partnership a legal agreement which defines the role of each partner in the operation of a business partnership and how much money each partner is expected to invest.

Third, a partnership is a legal relationship between the people involved. Therefore, it is usually a good idea for the partners to write and sign an agreement called the **articles of partnership.** This agreement defines the role of each partner in the operation of the business. The articles should always address the amount of money and time that each partner is expected to invest. Figure 5-2 shows the most common provisions of partnership agreements.

Fourth, partnerships tend to be small businesses; 75 percent have total annual sales of less than $120,000. Henry and George hired three junior mechanics to work for them during the first year of the partnership. The business plan they gave the bank called for G & M's to generate $140,000 in sales in the first year and $170,000 in the second.

FIGURE 5-2   Recommended Provisions of a Partnership Agreement

▲▼▲▼▲▼▲▼▲▼▲▼▲▼▲▼▲▼▲▼▲▼▲▼▲▼▲▼▲▼▲▼▲▼

- ▲ Date of contract and length of life of the agreement.

- ▲ Nature of business, location, and name of firm.

- ▲ Names of partners and their respective investments, and distribution of profits and losses.

- ▲ Duties of each partner and hours of personal service, and provision for salaries of partners.

- ▲ Provision for paying interest on capital and drawing account balances.

- ▲ Limitation on withdrawal of funds from the business.

- ▲ Provision for an accounting system and a fiscal year.

- ▲ Method to be followed in the case of withdrawal of a partner.

Advantages of Partnerships

Henry Gonzalez formed a partnership because he needed more money and talent than he could provide by himself. His business could not grow without it. Partnership provides a way for entrepreneurs to obtain these resources. The advantages of partnerships are listed below.

Access to Capital. Compared to a sole proprietorship, a partnership allows greater access to capital. All partners usually contribute some of their savings, and banks are more willing to extend credit. Banks prefer to lend to partnerships over sole proprietorships, because all partners are liable, individually and jointly, for the entire amount of the loan. In the case of G & M's Garage, Henry's banker was pleased to refinance Henry's loan because both Henry and George would now be responsible for repaying it. If Henry got into financial problems and could not pay his portion of the debt, George would be responsible for paying off the entire loan on G & M's Garage.

Management Talent. As the old saying goes, two heads are better than one. The best partner is one with money and good ideas or talent. Partnerships are often made up of people with complementary skills. Henry and George quickly realized that if their business was to succeed, they would have to bring in a new partner who would focus on the accounting and personnel side of the organization.

Ease of Formation. Partnerships are almost as easy to form as sole proprietorships. The most difficult task in starting a partnership is writing the partnership agreement to help avoid later misunderstandings. An experienced attorney can usually draw up a partnership agreement without much trouble.

Tax Benefits. Partners are taxed according to their percentage of ownership. For example, G & M's Garage earned $44,000 in profits during the first year of its operation. Since each partner owned half of the business, their taxable income was $22,000 each. The partnership itself does not pay taxes on its $44,000 in earned income. Also like sole proprietorships, partnerships need not file a separate federal income tax form. The partnership's profits are divided and reported on the partners' personal income tax forms. The situation is different for corporations, as we will soon see.

Disadvantages of Partnerships

Although partnerships are a good idea in some situations, they do have major disadvantages. Some of the drawbacks are the same as for sole proprietorships.

Unlimited Liability. Each general partner is legally responsible for all liabilities incurred by the partnership to the extent of that partner's personal wealth. For example, if G & M's were to go out of business, Henry would be liable for all of the partnership's debts if George could not pay his portion of the debt. Similarly, if an employee or customer were injured as the result of an error on the part of G & M's Garage, both partners would be responsible for compensating the victim.

Personality Conflicts. As long as general partners are in agreement on important issues, there is no problem. However, an argument over a major decision, such as whether another partner is needed or what piece of equipment should be purchased for the garage, could divide the partnership.[1]

Life of the Partnership. The partners *are* the partnership, so the life of the partnership is no longer than the lives of the general partners. Normally, when a general partner leaves the business, that partner's share is sold to one or more of the remaining general partners or to a new person who is acceptable to them.

Adding and Removing Partners. Investing funds in a partnership can be easy to accomplish, but withdrawing funds is sometimes not. For example, if George wanted to withdraw from G & M's Garage, and Henry was not willing to buy him out, it would be very difficult for George to get his cash investment out of the partnership. To help avoid conflicts among partners, the articles of partnership should specify procedures for adding or removing partners.

CORPORATIONS

In 1991, five local investors approached Henry and George about joining forces with them. They were forming a new corporation that would operate quick-service automobile lubrication outlets in Tucson. Three doctors and two lawyers had put together $500,000 in cash from their own savings, and they expected to borrow an additional $1 million from two local banks. The investors offered to give Henry and George each 15 percent of the business if they would agree to become president and executive vice-president, respectively, of the new company. Henry was offered a starting salary of $45,000, and George's salary would be $4,000 less.

Although G & M's Garage was doing quite well, both Henry and George quickly came to the same conclusion. They had an unusual opportunity to become involved with local investors who were willing to spend money to create a new business. Henry and George realized that if the new business became successful, they would own a significant portion of it, without having invested any

Corporations dominate the U.S. business scene.

of their own money. Within two months, G & M's Garage was sold to George's cousin, and the state of Arizona issued a charter for a new corporation called Fast-Lube. A **charter** is a legal document issued by a state creating a corporation. It contains such facts as the scope of business, the amount of money being invested, and the number of directors that the business will have.

> *charter   a certificate issued by the state, creating a corporation; contains such facts as scope of business, amount of capital, and number of directors.*

Fast-Lube, Inc. sold $500,000 worth of stock to the group of original investors and gave Henry and George their stock. A board of directors was created, consisting of the firm's five investors plus Henry, George, and a retired executive from Exxon.

Features of Corporations

The corporation is the most important form of business ownership in the United States today. Most of the products we buy are made by corporations. A few examples are Procter & Gamble (Tide detergent), General Foods (Maxwell House coffee), Kraft (cheese), Thomas J. Lipton (tea), and H. J. Heinz (ketchup). Table 5-2 ranks the 20 largest U.S. corporations by sales, lists the dollar value of their profits and assets, and shows the number of employees. Note that America's largest corporation, General Motors, lost almost $2 billion in 1991.

The first identifying feature of corporations is that they are legal entities. As Chief Justice John Marshall wrote in 1819,

> A corporation is an artificial being, invisible, intangible, and existing only in contemplation of law. Being the mere creature of law, it possesses only those properties which the charter of its creation confers upon it, either expressly or as incidental to its very existence.

As a legal entity, corporations can own assets, enter into contracts, and sue or be sued in court. **Assets** are defined as property, equipment, supplies, and other resources that are used by a firm to conduct its regular business activities. For example, *Time* magazine's assets would include its buildings, computers and other equipment, and the goodwill that it has created with its readers.

> *assets   property, equipment, supplies, and other resources used by a firm to conduct its regular business activities.*

Corporations own assets, and stockholders own the corporations, but the stockholders do not own the assets per se. Henry and George owned all of the assets of G & M's Garage. As stockholders in the new corporation, however, they

TABLE 5-2   The 20 Largest Industrial Corporations Ranked by Sales 1990

Rank	Company	Sales ($ millions)	Profits ($ millions)	Assets ($ millions)	Employees (thousands)
1	General Motors	126,017.0	(1,985.7)	180,236.0	761.4
2	Exxon	105,885.0	5,010.0	87,707.0	104.0
3	Ford	98,274.7	860.1	173,662.7	381.4
4	IBM	69,018.0	6,020.0	87,568.0	378.5
5	Mobil	58,770.0	1,929.0	41,665.0	67.6
6	General Electric	58,414.0	4,303.0	153,884.0	295.0
7	Philip Morris	44,323.0	3,540.0	46,569.0	161.6
8	Texaco	41,235.0	1,450.0	25,975.0	38.1
9	Du Pont	39,839.0	2,310.0	38,128.0	144.9
10	Chevron	39,262.0	2,157.0	35,089.0	54.5
11	Chrysler	30,868.0	68.0	46,374.0	109.9
12	Amoco	28,277.0	1,913.0	32,209.0	54.1
13	Boeing	27,595.0	1,385.0	14,591.0	161.7
14	Shell	24,423.0	1,036.0	28,496.0	NA
15	Proctor & Gamble	24,376.0	1,602.0	18,487.0	84.1
16	Occidental Petroleum	21,947.0	(1,695.0)	19,743.0	54.5
17	United Technologies	21,783.2	750.6	15,918.3	197.0
18	Dow	20,005.0	1,384.0	23,953.0	62.1
19	USX	19,462.0	818.0	17,268.0	51.5
20	Kodak	19,075.0	703.0	24,125.0	136.1

Sources: *Fortune*, 22 April 1991, p. 286, and *Forbes*, 29 April 1991, pp. 212–234.

do not own any of the assets that are used by the business. Also, corporations, like individuals, have constitutional rights: A corporation's property cannot be taken without "due process of law."

The second feature of corporations is that they often have many owners. For example, Exxon, the nation's second-largest industrial corporation, has nearly 639,000 stockholders.

Third, corporations can be classified as either closely held or publicly held. In a closely held corporation, stock is owned by only a few people. Common examples of closely held corporations are family businesses that were previously sole proprietorships or partnerships but evolved into corporations. In such situations, it is not unusual for the head of the family to own most of the stock, with the remainder divided among other members of the family. By contrast, if a corporation is publicly held, anyone can purchase its stock through a broker.

Fourth, corporations are characterized by professional management. That is, management and ownership are separate, especially in the case of large, publicly held corporations. The company's managers may own stock in the corporation, but the number of shares they own is usually small in relation to the total number issued by the company. In very small corporations, one person may own all the stock and also act as the firm's manager. But even in this case, ownership is distinct from management. In effect, the owner of the corporation hires himself or herself to manage it.

Structure of Corporations

All private corporations have the same basic structure. They are made up of stockholders, who own the company; a board of directors, which sets policy and appoints top management; and top management, which runs the company within the policies set by the board. This arrangement is pictured in Figure 5-3.

Stockholders. There are two types of stockholders: preferred stockholders and common stockholders. When a corporation goes out of business, **preferred stockholders** have the first claim on all the firm's assets once its debts have been paid. However, they have no voting right at stockholders' meetings. In contrast, **common stockholders** elect the board of directors, vote on any changes in the corporate charter, and vote on the appointment of an accountant to audit the firm's books. If the corporation ceases to operate, their claim on the corporation's assets comes last.

All corporations hold annual stockholders' meetings, but not all stockholders may live near the location of such a meeting. When stockholders cannot attend

preferred stockholders
stockholders who have first claim to the corporation's assets once its debts have been paid, but have no voting rights at stockholders' meetings.

common stockholders
stockholders who have last claim to corporate assets but have the right to elect the board of directors, vote on changes in the corporate charters, and vote on the appointment of an accountant to audit the firm's books.

FIGURE 5-3   Corporation Structure

STOCKHOLDERS
Own Company
Elect Board of Directors

BOARD OF DIRECTORS
Determines Company Policy
Appoints Top Management

MANAGEMENT
Implements Company Policies

proxy *a written statement that authorizes someone else to vote on behalf of a stockholder.*

the meeting, they vote by proxy. A **proxy** is a statement that authorizes someone else to vote on behalf of the stockholder. In most cases, proxies are requested by the management of a corporation. However, a group of stockholders who are unhappy with management's performance may attempt to solicit proxies from other stockholders in order to force a vote for a new board of directors.

At the moment, all the Fast-Lube stockholders serve on the board. However, the board would like to "go public" and sell stock to other investors if Fast-Lube is successful. These new investors would probably not sit on the board, but their financial support could be used to finance a second round of expansion of Fast-Lube outlets. At the present time, all of the stockholders hold common stock. However, if the firm does want to raise money, it will be easier to do by selling preferred stock than by selling additional shares of common stock. This is because Fast-Lube is still considered to be a rather risky investment.

board of directors *group of individuals elected by common stockholders to represent their interests, set corporate policy, and assume ultimate responsibility for management of the corporation.*

Board of Directors. The **board of directors** is elected by the common stockholders and is ultimately responsible for the management of the corporation. In the corporate structure, authority flows from the board to the firm's managers. The management powers of the board normally include the following:

1. Electing the corporation's top officers, the most important of whom is the chief executive officer (CEO).
2. Setting corporate policy in the areas of product offerings, services, prices, wages, and labor-management relations.
3. Deciding how to finance corporate expansion.
4. Deciding whether to pay a cash dividend to stockholders and, if so, how much.
5. Establishing salary levels and compensation packages for the firm's top officers.

Most boards of directors are composed of 10 to 25 people. A few are key executives from inside the organization, and several are from outside. These outside directors are usually executives from other businesses or people from the nonprofit sector (a college professor, for example). If the corporation is running smoothly, the board is usually content to monitor the progress of the company and to deal with major policy questions. However, if the firm's profits begin to fall, or if it experiences some other serious problem, the board must step in and play a more active role. Board members assume great responsibility. If they do not properly oversee the management of the firm, they can be sued by the firm's stockholders.

At the first meeting of the board of Fast-Lube, Inc., it elected Henry as president and chief executive officer (CEO). As CEO, Henry will be expected to make the day-to-day operating decisions that affect the business. The board also elected George as executive vice-president and Beth Woodson as chairman of the board. Beth will run the meetings of the board of directors. In some businesses, the chairman of the board is also the CEO.

Management. As mentioned, the officers of the corporation (top management) are appointed by the board of directors. These managers have the authority to act as agents for the firm. That is, they can sign contracts in the name of the corporation.

One particular responsibility of corporate officers is watching the marketplace. Management decides which new products to introduce, which markets to enter, or which products to stop selling. For example, General Motors was the first major corporation to market refrigerators (Frigidaire). Later, the officers of GM recommended to the board of directors that the Frigidaire business be sold. Only after the officers had researched the advantages and disadvantages of the sale was the idea presented to the board of directors for approval.

Advantages of Corporations

By now, some of the advantages of the corporate form of ownership should be apparent. Let's take a look at them.

Limited Liability. The liability of the stockholders of a corporation is limited to the amount of their stock investments. If an automobile is improperly lubricated and the engine is destroyed, the car's owner may sue Fast-Lube, Inc., but it cannot sue Henry, George, or any of the other stockholders. America West Airlines declared bankruptcy in 1991. Although its stockholders may lose the entire value of their stock, they will not have to sell their houses, cars, or other personal holdings to pay the company's billion-dollar debt. Strictly speaking, the liability of the stockholders is limited, but the liability of the corporation is not.

Unlimited Life. The corporation has a "life" of its own, continuing even after the original owners and managers are gone. Sam Barshop founded La Quinta Motor Inns in 1968. As noted in the Profile on page 118, the firm now has 211 inns and is one of the fastest-growing motel chains in the United States. If Mr. Barshop had not created a corporation to run La Quinta, it would probably be necessary to break up the company when he retires. However, because La Quinta is a corporation, it now has a life of its own that is legally separate and distinct from Mr. Barshop.

Transfer of Ownership. Transferring ownership in a corporation from one person to another can be relatively easy to accomplish. This is especially true in the case of big corporations. The New York Stock Exchange, the American Stock Exchange, various regional exchanges, and the so-called "over-the-counter" market for the stocks of smaller companies all facilitate the transfer of corporate ownership. These markets will be discussed in greater detail in Chapter 21. For now, it is important to understand that stocks can be traded almost instantaneously. The buying or selling of a stock usually requires nothing more than a call to a stockbroker.

Professional Management. The executive officers of a corporation are chosen on the basis of their managerial and decision-making skills. Fast-Lube selected Henry Gonzalez to manage the firm because he had an excellent reputation and a proven record in managing a small business. In contrast, sole proprietorships and partnerships both tend to select their management talent from the families of the founders of the business. Unfortunately, these individuals do not always have as much drive or talent as their parents. In addition, highly competent young professional managers see their way to the top blocked because of family connections, so they leave to form their own businesses or to join a corporation.

Disadvantages of Corporations

Starting a corporation is more expensive and complex than starting a sole proprietorship or a partnership. In addition, corporations must disclose a great deal of

Sam Barshop

Sam Barshop, chairman of the board, president, and chief executive officer of La Quinta Motor Inns, Inc., wears many hats. He is a financial innovator, corporate leader, municipal developer, and supporter of higher education.

La Quinta Motor Inns, with corporate offices in San Antonio, Texas, is one of the country's fastest-growing motel chains, with more than 26,000 rooms in 211 locations. Its occupancy rates consistently exceed the industry average by 10–15 percent. La Quinta uses a simple marketing concept: provide guests with quality accommodations and essential services in convenient locations at reasonable prices. It provides facilities and services that business travelers consider essential, such as 24-hour messages, same-day laundry, cable TV, and a restaurant. However, La Quinta has cut nonessentials such as banquet facilities, extensive public areas, and large meeting rooms. It is therefore able to keep prices lower than traditional convention-oriented or resort-oriented lodging establishments.

Strategically positioned between budget and luxury hotels, La Quinta concentrates on its niche and expands horizontally into new territory. Its restaurants are all run by national chains, permitting the managers of the inns to concentrate on keeping rooms clean and guests happy.

Barshop has a simple system for success: (1) Define your market and concentrate on serving it; (2) keep it simple; and (3) when you find something that works, keep doing it.

A typical La Quinta Motor Inn has about 130 rooms. The inns are usually managed by a husband-wife team who live on the premises, supported by a staff of about 15. Managers are often second-career people who treat the guests as visitors in their homes.

La Quinta pursues a strategy of building a long-term position, sometimes at the expense of short-term profits. For instance, when the southwestern United States was hit hard by declines in oil prices and devaluations of the peso in the mid-1980s, Barshop continued his policy of rapid expansion, taking advantage of reduced construction costs. This strategy and others have paid off. La Quinta's revenues rose from $179 million in 1986 to $226 million in 1990. The firm's expansion continues; plans include a total of 300 inns.

La Quinta's rapid growth requires creativity. Barshop developed an innovative financial mechanism to fuel that growth. A joint venture (or partnership) is established in which La Quinta and a co-venturer (or limited partner) share ownership of one or more motor inns. Typically, each owns a half interest. The company's partners provide equity and long-term debt or land. La Quinta operates the motor inns and receives development and management fees. The co-venturers share profits and losses and any proceeds from the motor inns at the time of sale. The system gives La Quinta tremendous leverage and reduced risk.

Sam Barshop's contributions go far beyond guiding La Quinta. He holds many directorships: Southwest Airlines Company, the San Antonio Economic Development Foundation, St. Luke's Lutheran Hospital, the National Bank of Commerce, and the Boys Club of America. He is a trustee of the Texas Research and Technology Foundation and the San Antonio World Affairs Council. He is active in the San Antonio Committee for the Arts, the Boy Scouts of America, and the local United Way campaign. He is a long-time supporter of higher education, serving currently as a member of the Board of Regents of The University of Texas System. He has funded numerous faculty endowments at The University of Texas at Austin.

information, and they are subject to double taxation of their dividends. We will now examine each of these disadvantages to forming a corporation.

Costs and Complexity of Incorporation.

State incorporation fees are not very expensive. For example, it costs a resident $400 to incorporate in Texas— $300 in filing fees and another $100 as a deposit against payment of the first year's taxes. (Out-of-state people pay $1,350.) Assets of $1,000 are required as the minimum amount of capital. Attorney's fees account for the major costs of incorporating. Each state has laws that govern the formation of corporations. A good attorney may charge $5,000 or more to form a corporation, but many people would rather hire an attorney than put up with the aggravation and time required to work through all of the state laws. To form a corporation, an application for a charter must be submitted to the appropriate state official, usually the secretary of state. The application must specify the following:

1. Name and address of the corporation.
2. Primary business objective or objectives.
3. Type of stock and number of shares to be issued.
4. Required capital of the corporation.
5. Methods for transferring shares of stock.
6. Names and addresses of the members of the board of directors.
7. Duration of the corporation.

This information would not seem difficult to collect. But in most states, the process of making the application is more complex than it should be; it is best left to an expert.

Public Disclosure.

The federal government requires that all publicly held corporations disclose a broad set of financial data to the Securities and Exchange Commission. This information is then made available to potential investors. The information concerns the company's earnings, financial condition, and product offerings, as well as the qualifications of its top managers and directors. The purpose of the disclosure is to protect investors from corporate misrepresentation of facts and conditions. From the perspective of the firm, however, disclosure can be a disadvantage if it alerts competitors to the firm's financial weaknesses or to its research and development programs.

Double Taxation.

One way that a corporation may reward its stockholders is by sending them quarterly dividends. **Dividends** are cash payments that the corporation makes to its stockholders, based on corporate earnings. Unfortunately, dividends are subject to double taxation. That is, a corporation pays dividends out of its after-tax income, and the dividends are taxed again as personal income for the stockholder.

dividends   cash payments that the corporation makes to its stockholders, based on corporate earnings.

For example, Fast-Lube earned $80,000 in profits in its second year of operation. It paid $18,500 in federal income taxes, leaving $61,500 in after-tax profit. The board felt that the firm could afford to pay $10,000 in dividends to its stockholders. Henry received a check for $1500. His personal income tax on this amount was $450. The money was taxed once as corporate income and a second time as Henry's personal income. This double taxation does not take place for sole proprietorships or partnerships.

SPECIAL TYPES OF ORGANIZATIONS

Six other forms of business ownership will also be discussed. Although important in the business world, they are not encountered as frequently as sole proprietorships, partnerships, and corporations.

Nonprofit Corporations

nonprofit corporations
organizations incorporated like for-profit corporations except that they do not exist to make a profit, they pay no dividends or income taxes, and members are protected against liability.

Many charities and other not-for-profit organizations, such as hospitals, private colleges, and religious organizations, are organized as nonprofit corporations. **Nonprofit corporations** are structured the same way as for-profit corporations, except that they do not pay income taxes or dividends. All of the nonprofit corporation's revenue in excess of the cost to raise it and administer the organization must be used to support the stated purposes of the organization. For example, in 1990 the Austin, Texas, United Way raised $5.37 million over and above its fundraising and administrative cost of $730,000. This surplus revenue was not subject to federal income tax, since the United Way is a nonprofit corporation. The United Way did not pay any dividends to its stockholders. Rather, its surplus revenue went to support a variety of charitable causes in the community. Besides not paying federal income taxes, the most significant advantage of a nonprofit corporation is that its members are protected against personal liability from the actions of the corporation.

Professional Corporations

professional corporation
an organization of professionals who incorporate to obtain liability protection.

Physicians, lawyers, accountants, and other professionals are permitted in most states to incorporate as **professional corporations** or professional associations. The professional corporation does provide liability protection for its owners. However, dividends from the corporation are subject to double taxation.[2]

Subsidiary Corporations

subsidiary corporation *a corporation in which the majority of the firm's common stock is owned by another company.*

parent company or holding company *a firm that owns a subsidiary corporation.*

When all or the majority of a firm's common stock is owned by another company, the firm is called a **subsidiary corporation.** The firm that owns the subsidiary is called a **parent company** or a **holding company.** The subsidiary corporation has its own board of directors, normally appointed by the chief executive officer of the parent company. Many subsidiary corporations are well known, such as Weight Watchers, which is owned by the H. J. Heinz Company.

S-Corporations

S-corporation *a special type of corporation that is taxed as though it were a partnership.*

An **S-corporation** (formerly called a Subchapter-S corporation) is a special type of corporation that is taxed as if it were a partnership. Forming an S-corporation is a good way for a firm to avoid the problem of double taxation of corporate dividends while retaining all the benefits of incorporation.

To qualify as an S-corporation, the business must meet all of the following tests:

1. The business cannot have more than 35 stockholders.
2. Stockholders must be private individuals who are permanent residents or citizens of the United States.
3. The business cannot own 80 percent or more of the stock of any other corporation.

4. Interest income and other income not related to the principal business of the corporation must not exceed 25 percent of its total income.

Joint Ventures

A **joint venture** is an agreement between two or more businesses for the joint production and/or sale of a product or service. The partners in a joint venture may themselves be organized as sole proprietorships, partnerships, or corporations. Each partner is expected to bring management expertise and/or money to the venture. A joint venture is taxed just like a partnership, with a proportionate share of profits or losses flowing to each partner. The International Example on page 122 involves a joint venture between American Motors' Jeep Division and the Chinese government. Although the *Detroit Free Press* once speculated that it "could turn out to be one of the shrewdest industrial strokes of the decade," it was a total failure.[3]

> **joint venture**   an agreement between two or more businesses for the joint production and/or sale of a product or service.

Cooperatives

A **cooperative,** or **co-op,** is a business that is owned by its user members. Like corporations, cooperatives are legal entities with an unlimited life, and their owners can claim the protection of limited liability. However, there are two major differences between a cooperative and a corporation. First, each member of a cooperative has one vote, regardless of the amount of stock held, while voting in a corporation is in proportion to stock ownership. Second, any profits distributed to member-owners are in proportion to their volume of business with the cooperative. In a corporation, profit distribution, like voting percentage, is in proportion to stock ownership.

> **cooperative or co-op**   a business that is owned by its user members.

The Cooperative Book Store at The University of Texas at Austin is the second-largest academic bookstore in the United States. Each student at the university is a member of the "Co-op," as it is called. At the end of each year, the Co-op pays a "dividend" to member students. Students submit receipts for their purchases during the year and receive a cash dividend, equal to 3 to 8 percent of the dollar value of their purchases.

The largest co-ops in the United States are based in agriculture. The Associated Milk Producers and California Fruit Owner's Exchange (Sunkist) are large co-ops that sell agricultural products.

MERGERS AND ACQUISITIONS

Businesses grow in one of two ways: through internal expansion or external expansion. **Internal expansion** refers to the process of growing by increasing sales and capital investment. **External expansion** takes place when a firm purchases or merges with another company. The purchase of another company is called an **acquisition.** The acquired firm may or may not retain a separate identity. Chrysler's purchase of American Motors is an example of an acquisition. Chrysler kept the Jeep line of products, but the American Motors identification as a separate company was dropped, since it was of no value to Chrysler.

Another type of external expansion is through merger. A **merger** occurs when two companies join together to form a new company. The old companies then cease to exist. For example, a playing card manufacturer could grow by merging with one of its competitors. The merged entity would then be a new

> **internal expansion**   the process of growing by increasing sales and capital investment.
>
> **external expansion**   the process of growing in which a firm purchases or merges with another company.
>
> **acquisition**   the purchase of one company by another.
>
> **merger**   the joining of two companies to form a single new company.

"The China Debacle"

One of the strangest, most highly publicized, and least successful joint ventures of all time involved American Motors' Jeep Division and the Chinese government. The opportunity seemed too good to be true. The company would build jeeps with inexpensive Chinese labor and sell them in China and the rest of the Far East.

It *was* too good to be true. In 1983, after four years of negotiations, American Motors agreed to invest $8 million in cash and $8 million in technology. China would contribute an additional $31 million in assets. Unfortunately, the contract that bound this joint venture together did not deal with many important issues:

• The contract did not specify what type of Jeeps would be built in China. American Motors wanted to produce a Chinese version of the Cherokee, but the Chinese wanted a four-door military vehicle.
• The contract did not allow American Motors to convert its profits into dollars.
• The contract did not guarantee that the joint venture would receive enough hard currency to buy parts from the U.S.
• The contract did not require the Chinese government to pay for the vehicles that they ordered.

American Motors had hoped to produce 40,000 Jeep Cherokees by 1990. Unfortunately, the plant never produced more than 3,000 Cherokees a year. On June 3, 1989, Chinese troops killed several thousand people and recaptured Tienanmen Square in Beijing. One day later, Chrysler (which had purchased American Motors) ordered all of its American employees to leave China.

China, the land of great opportunity, had once again proven too much for any one corporation to handle. The cultural and bureaucratic obstacles had destroyed the American automaker's ability to generate profits. The repressive actions of the Chinese military destroyed Chrysler's interest in trying to do so.

Source: "One Company's China Debacle" (review of J. Mann, *Beijing Jeep*), *Fortune*, © 1989, The Time Inc. Magazine Co. All Rights Reserved.

enterprise, consisting of the combined assets, workforces, earnings, and markets of the two separate companies.

We will now examine four types of business combinations, discuss some important criticisms of this approach to business expansion, and examine how a firm can avoid being taken over by another firm.

Types of Business Combinations

An acquisition can be classified as one of four types: horizontal, vertical, congeneric, or conglomerate. Each of them is discussed below.

horizontal acquisition a form of business combination in which one company buys another that is in the same industry and performs the same function.

Horizontal Acquisition. **Horizontal acquisition** is a form of business combination in which one company buys another that is in the same industry and performs the same function. Chrysler's acquisition of American Motors is an excellent example of a horizontal acquisition: Both companies sold the same products—automobiles and light-duty trucks.

vertical acquisition a business combination in which one company buys another that is in the same industry but performs a different production or distribution activity.

Vertical Acquisition. The **vertical acquisition** is a business combination in which one company buys another that is in the same industry but performs a different production or distribution activity. For example, Hart Schafner and Marx, a highly respected manufacturer of men's clothing, has purchased a number of well-established men's clothing stores. Both are in the men's clothing industry, but they perform different functions. Hart Schafner and Marx is a manufacturer, and the stores are distributors. The acquisitions provide Hart Schafner and Marx with more outlets for selling its products to the public.

Congeneric Acquisition. A **congeneric acquisition** is a business combination in which one company buys another that is in a different industry but performs a related activity. An example is the Prudential Insurance Company's acquisition of the brokerage firm Bache Group, Inc. in 1981. Both firms provided financial services, but they did not compete directly. The move allowed Prudential to broaden its range of financial services.

congeneric acquisition a business combination in which one company buys another that is in a different industry but performs a related activity.

Conglomerate Acquisition. A fourth type of business combination is the **conglomerate acquisition,** in which one company buys another that is in a different industry and performs an unrelated activity. General Electric's 1986 acquisition of Kidder, Peabody & Co., which sells stock and bonds, is an example of a conglomerate acquisition.

conglomerate acquisition a form of business combination in which one company buys another that is in a different industry and performs an unrelated activity.

Criticisms of Acquisitions

Acquisitions have been criticized by many people as a waste of scarce investment capital and management talent. Instead of devoting their attention to improving products and introducing new ones to the market, managers are forced to worry about unfriendly takeovers and possible job losses. As a result of this short-term focus on avoiding takeovers, U.S. products could become less competitive in world markets.[4]

A second criticism is that most acquisitions are accomplished through the use of borrowed money. U.S. firms currently carry a total debt of more than $1.4 trillion dollars. This "buy now, pay later" philosophy could hurt many of America's best corporations. For example, CBS spent approximately $1 billion to buy back 20 percent of its stock from stockholders. The idea was to prevent Ted Turner from acquiring the firm. CBS was forced to sell several television affiliates and its toy division to repay its debt. In an attempt to cut costs further, CBS fired 74 news division employees in a single day and offered early retirement to 2,000 other employees.[5]

Another criticism of acquisitions is that they disrupt and injure employees, families, and sometimes entire communities. T. Boone Pickens of Mesa Limited Partnership once tried to purchase Phillips Petroleum Company, which has its headquarters in Bartlesville, Oklahoma. Virtually the entire town rose up in defense of the firm. The people of Bartlesville feared that Pickens would move Phillips out of the community, or that Pickens would sell off most of the company's assets. If Pickens had taken either of those steps, many local people would have lost their jobs.

Avoiding an Unfriendly Takeover

The media often give the impression that every acquisition is an unfriendly one. The truth is that most acquisitions are friendly. That is, two corporations sit down together and decide how much one of them is willing to pay for the other. An excellent example of a friendly takeover was General Electric's purchase of RCA Corp. in 1986. After a mutual friend arranged a meeting between the chairmen of the two firms, serious negotiations began. After several weeks of negotiation, General Electric agreed to pay $66.50 per share—a total of $6.3 billion—for RCA stock. John Welch, chairman of the board of General Electric, stated, "We will have the technological capabilities, financial resources, and global scope to be able to compete successfully with anyone, anywhere, in every market we serve."

Although RCA did not object to being purchased by General Electric, many firms actively resist takeover attempts. In most cases, such resistance is based on

ESOP-LBO—Translation: Employees Left Holding the Bag

Between 1983 and 1990, 55 companies went private using LBOs, giving or selling large amounts of stock to employees. Many of these deals had three things in common: clever investment bankers, starry-eyed top executives, and poorly informed workers. All too often, the outcome was that employees lost their jobs, pensions, and health benefits, while top executives and investment bankers made substantial profits.

A typical employee-funded LBO works in the following way. Top executives terminate a company's pension plan and use the money to purchase the company's stock, thus taking the firm private. The LBO is financed by the employees' pension fund. Management then creates a new ESOP (employee stock ownership plan) pension plan and makes annual contributions to fund it.

The first fundamental flaw in the concept is that employees are gambling all of their retirement savings on the health and prosperity of the company they work for. It has been described by one expert as the "ultimate in anti-diversification." If the firm runs into financial trouble, employees may lose not only their jobs, but also their pension fund and future health insurance coverage. A second flaw in the ESOP-LBO is that the employees who become

---

what management believes is in the best interest of the stockholders. Unfortunately, however, it is sometimes based on the self-interest of managers themselves.

One way to fend off an unwanted purchaser is the **poison pill.** Target companies "swallow poison pills" by adding large amounts of new debt, which makes them less attractive to potential buyers. A second alternative is to find another buyer who is more acceptable to management. The second buyer is often referred to as a **white knight.**

poison pill *a technique for fending off an unwanted purchaser, in which the target company adds large amounts of new debt to become less attractive to the buying firm.*

white knight *a second, more acceptable buyer, which the target company locates in order to fend off an unwanted takeover.*

Alternatives to Acquisitions

A number of acquisitions take place each year, but many firms also downsize or divest themselves of major operating units. This usually occurs when a parent company needs money to pay off existing debt or to make a new acquisition. Occasionally, a firm decides that the subsidiary's business is just not consistent with the long-term strategy of the parent company. General Electric sold its small appliance division (e.g., toasters, mixers, and can openers) to Black and Decker. GE was cash-rich at the time and did not need the money. However, GE's management wanted to concentrate the firm's financial and managerial resources on other product lines that would be more profitable for the firm's stockholders. As a result, it was willing to divest itself of a well-established, profitable product line.

Most businesses are sold in the same way that other assets are sold. The purchaser uses cash generated from other businesses and borrowed funds to buy the company. This old-fashioned technique still works well in most situations, but we will examine two other forms of financing: leveraged buyouts and employee buyouts.

leveraged buyout *a purchase in which the buyer uses the assets of the firm that is being bought as security for the loan to buy the business.*

Leveraged Buy-outs. **Leveraged buyouts** (LBOs) have been used to finance the purchase of many businesses. The purchaser uses the assets of the business that is being bought as security for loans. These loans are then used to pay off the current owner of the business. If an LBO is done properly, the purchaser may not have to put any of its own money into the transaction.

Many LBOs have turned out to be a nightmare for the buyers because the businesses purchased did not generate enough cash to pay off the loans. Further-

part owners in the firm through their ESOP tend to pay too much for their stock.

Kroy, Inc., a manufacturer of lettering and label machines, went private in 1986. It created a $35.5 million ESOP to buy the firm's common stock. To complete the LBO, eight company officers and three outside investors put in $4.5 million. The ESOP put in 89 percent of the money to take the firm private, but it received only 60 percent of the shares. Management and the three investors put in 11 percent of the money and received 40 percent of the stock in the new privately held company.

Valley National Bank of Arizona, which represents the company, believes that the deal was fair, because if Kroy encounters financial trouble, the employees are not responsible for the loans. However, the U.S. Department of Labor has sued Kroy and the Valley National Bank for not giving the ESOP an adequate amount of stock in the new company.

The bottom line is very simple. Even under excellent conditions, an LBO that is financed by an ESOP is a very risky deal for the firm's employees. If the deal goes sour, the employees will bear a disproportionate amount of pain through the loss of their jobs and pensions. Unfortunately, most employees do not understand the risk that they are being asked to accept. Frequently, they are told that if they do not permit their pension funds to be used to buy the company, an unfriendly takeover will occur, and they will lose their jobs. This may occur in some cases, but in many more instances, the employees have been misled into assuming more risk than they should.

more, because LBOs tend to be quite risky, financial institutions that make the loans demand high interest rates, to compensate them for the risk they assume. The high interest rates make it more difficult for the business to make enough money to repay the creditors. All too often, LBO businesses have not had money to invest in new products and new opportunities, because all of their available financial resources have gone to pay off their loans. This makes it very difficult for them to compete in the long run.

When bonds are issued to finance an LBO, they are frequently called "junk bonds," because they are inherently riskier than other bonds issued to support an acquisition. Issuers of such bonds prefer to call them "high-yield" bonds, but all too often they become junk.

A classic example of an unsuccessful leveraged buyout was Robert Campeau's purchase of Federated Department Stores in 1988. Federated, which owned stores such as Bloomingdale's, Foley's and Filene's, could not generate enough cash to pay off Mr. Campeau's junk bonds. As a result, Federated was forced into bankruptcy. Mr. Campeau and the people who purchased his junk bonds lost a great deal of money, and one of America's greatest companies was sold off in small pieces.

Employee Buyouts. An **employee buyout** occurs when a firm's employees decide to buy their company from its stockholders or from the parent company. This technique has worked moderately well. The employees must realize from the beginning that someone still must be "boss" and make unpopular decisions, even if the person is a part owner in the firm.

One source of capital for employee buyouts has been the employees' pension funds. Unfortunately, there are major risks to the employees when these funds are used. If the firm is not successful, the employees may lose not only their jobs, but also the retirement funds they have built up over many years. The major advantage is that the new company is not saddled with an enormous amount of high-interest debt that it cannot afford to repay. Safeway, one of the nation's largest grocery chains, was bought out by its employees and is now known as Appletree.

The Ethical Issue (page 124) describes in some detail the risk associated with the use of pension funds as a source of capital in an LBO.

employee buyout *a purchase in which the employees of the firm use their own assets, frequently their pension funds, to purchase a company from its stockholders or the parent company.*

SUMMARY POINTS

1 The three basic forms of business ownership are sole proprietorships, partnerships, and corporations.

2 In a sole proprietorship, the owner acts as manager and makes all decisions. Sole proprietorships are easy to create, have minimal capital requirements, allow the owner to retain all profits, give the owner complete control of the business, and offer important tax advantages. Disadvantages of sole proprietorships include unlimited liability, limited managerial resources, few opportunities for employees, limited credit availability, and instability of the business.

3 Partnerships are businesses owned by two or more people. Partnerships offer greater access to capital, extra management talent, ease of formation, and tax benefits. However, they suffer the disadvantages of unlimited liability, potential for personality conflicts, limited life of the partnership, and difficulty in withdrawing funds.

4 A corporation is a legal entity with many of the rights, duties, and powers of a person. It is owned by its stockholders, directed by a board of directors, and separate from the people who own it and those who manage it. The chief advantages of the corporate form of ownership are limited liability for stockholders, unlimited life of the corporation, ease of ownership transfer, and professional management. Among the disadvantages are the cost and complexity of incorporation, the required disclosure of financial data, and double taxation of earnings when they are paid out as dividends.

5 Nonprofit corporations are corporations that do not exist to make a profit, such as hospitals, private colleges, and religious organizations. Professional corporations are groups of physicians, lawyers, accountants, and other professionals who are permitted to incorporate in professional associations. Subsidiary corporations are companies in which all or the majority of the firm's common stock is owned by another company. S-corporations are generally smaller corporations that are taxed as though they were partnerships. Joint ventures are agreements between two or more businesses for the joint production and sale of a product or service. Cooperatives are businesses owned by their user members.

6 A horizontal acquisition is a business combination in which one company buys another that is in the same industry and performs the same function. In a vertical acquisition, one company buys another that is in the same industry but performs a different production or distribution activity. A congeneric acquisition occurs when one company buys another that is in a different industry but performs a related activity. In a conglomerate acquisition, one company buys another that is in a different industry and performs an unrelated activity.

REVIEW QUESTIONS

1 Which form of business ownership generates the most earnings in the United States? **1**

2 What are the disadvantages of a sole proprietorship, as compared to a partnership? **2**

3 Why is unlimited liability a significant disadvantage for sole proprietorships? **2**

4 What are the important differences between general partners and limited partners? **3**

5 What points should be included in articles of partnership? **3**

6 What are the features of a corporation? **4**

7 Are corporate dividends taxed twice? Explain. **4**

8 Why would a firm be interested in becoming a partner in a joint venture? **5**

9 What is the difference between horizontal acquisitions and vertical acquisitions? **6**

10 What are two ways a corporation can fend off an unwanted takeover? **6**

11 Why have many LBOs turned out to be financial disasters? **6**

DISCUSSION QUESTIONS

1 If you were starting a new company, which form of ownership would you choose—sole proprietorship, partnership, or corporation? Why?

2 Describe the relationship that should exist between a corporation's chief executive officer and the firm's board of directors, in your opinion.

3 What are the roles of stockholders and managers in the running of a corporation?

Do their roles overlap? Is there a potential for conflict? Explain.

4 What is the most significant criticism of acquisition? Explain your choice.

5 In your opinion, what is the most effective way to stop an unwanted takeover? Explain.

EXPERIENTIAL EXERCISES

1 Interview the owner of a sole proprietorship. Ask the owner if he or she has ever considered adding a partner to the business or changing the business into a corporation. On the basis of the answers obtained, ask yourself whether the person really understands the advantages and disadvantages of a sole proprietorship.

2 Meet separately with two partners of a local business. Ask each one about the goals and objectives of the business as well as the role that each plays in it. Compare and contrast the perspectives of the two people. (Be careful—this might be very sensitive! You should not tell one partner what the other one said.)

CASES

CASE 5-1
Sam Perry's Cleaners

Sam Perry graduated from a community college in upstate New York in 1983, at the age of 20. He had worked more than 25 hours per week at a local dry cleaning plant while he was in college. Upon graduation, Sam was appointed manager of one of the dry cleaning firm's 30 retail outlets.

Sam was making $25,000 per year as a store manager, but he was restless and wanted to try something "really different." He thanked his boss, quit his job, and moved to Alaska, where he found work as an oilfield "roughneck." The working conditions were quite difficult, and his schedule was often 12 hours on and 12 hours off. But Sam saved $73,000 during his four-year stay in Alaska. Sam returned to Schenectady, New York, in 1990 and got a job selling Buicks. Although Sam did not know a great deal about cars, Buick had a good product line, and he was an outgoing, positive individual who was willing to work long hours. He quickly became one of the firm's three best salespeople. Sam's cousin Ralph Perry, who owned the dealership, was very proud of him.

A friend of Sam's, Sherry Lewis, approached him about joining her in the purchase of a small dry cleaning chain in Schenectady. Sherry had been in college with Sam. She was working as assistant manager at an interior design shop. The dry cleaning chain had one dry cleaning plant and seven retail outlets. Clothes that were brought to one of the retail outlets by 9:00 A.M. were cleaned at the plant and brought back to the retail outlet for customer pickup by 4:30 P.M. the same day. The chain was only moderately profitable, but it had a good reputation. Although Sherry's only contact with a dry cleaning establishment was dropping off her suits, she felt that if another eight to ten retail outlets were added to the chain, it could become quite profitable.

Sam and Sherry went to the Schenectady National Bank to inquire about a loan for 80 percent of the $560,000 that they would need to purchase the dry cleaning chain. The bank's vice-president was interested in helping them, but he made it clear that Sam and Sherry would have to put up a larger portion of the loan. Alternatively, they could get a third person who had well-established credit with the bank to guarantee the loan in case they could not repay it.

Ralph Perry, the Buick dealer, indicated that he would be willing to guarantee the loan, and possibly even lend them some additional money, but he wanted to own at least 10 percent of the business. Sam and Sherry were willing to have Ralph involved in the firm. But in order to reduce the personal liability associated with business, they considered hiring a lawyer to set up a corporation.

1. Should Sam, Sherry, and Ralph establish a partnership or a corporation?
2. Does the advantage of limited liability that is associated with a corporation really mean much to Sam, Sherry, and Ralph?
3. If Ralph becomes a partner in the firm, should he be made a general partner or a limited partner?
4. If Sherry and Sam create a partnership, when would the disadvantages of the partnership form become significant enough that a change to the corporation form would be desirable?

CASE 5-2
The Mississippi Band of Choctaw Indians

For generations, American Indians have been forced to live as wards of the federal government. They have been supported largely with money supplied from federal taxes. But because of cuts in government funding, many Indian reservations have begun searching for new sources of income. The Mississippi Band of Choctaw Indians, for example, decided to go into business. The Choctaws owned land that wasn't worth much, because it lacked any valuable minerals, hunting, or timber. What they did have, they realized, was their people.

The Choctaws decided to invite manufacturing companies to locate on the reservation, to provide jobs for members of the tribe. American Greetings Corp., a major greeting card manufacturer, agreed to a joint venture with the Choctaws to build a new plant. The Indians first needed money to help the firm finance a building. They didn't have money of their own to spare, and they couldn't legally issue bonds or take out large enough loans themselves. But the Choctaws persuaded a nearby township to issue bonds to finance the American Greetings plant. This reduced the card company's cost of building its new factory significantly, and the Choctaws had a factory where they could find stable employment close to home. Unemployment, which had run between 35 and 40 percent before the card factory opened, was greatly reduced.

The American Indian National Bank in Washington, D.C., is now holding seminars for more than 65 other Indian tribes, teaching them the lessons that the Choctaws learned. Tribes such as the Navajo and the Jicarilla Apaches have signed joint-venture agreements modeled after those of the Choctaws. Others, such as the Salt River Pima-Maricopa tribes, which have oil or valuable timber on their land, have been able to build their own facilities without borrowing funds. The Pima-Maricopa built a million-dollar high-security warehouse and rented it to Motorola. This rental supplies both income for the tribe as a whole and employment for many of its members. Tribal lobbyists have also pushed a bill into Congress that would make it legal for tribes to issue bonds, just as cities and counties do.

1. What are the advantages of a joint venture? Why were those advantages important to the Choctaws and to American Greetings Corp.?
2. Why did the Choctaws look for a company that wanted to build a new factory, instead of building and operating their own independent factory?
3. Describe other kinds of joint ventures that Indian tribes might attempt. Identify other American population groups that might attempt such joint ventures. Why might they succeed or fail?

CHAPTER 6

Small Business and the Franchise System

OBJECTIVES

After studying this chapter, you should be able to:

1 Describe the characteristics of a small business.

2 Explain the importance of small business to the economy.

3 Describe the sectors of the economy in which small businesses operate.

4 Evaluate whether a small business is appropriate for you.

5 Indicate the important considerations in buying a small business.

6 Explain the essential steps in actually starting a small business.

7 Describe some characteristics of a successful entrepreneur.

8 Discuss how franchising offers an opportunity for operating a small business.

Linda Rosenthal had just turned 35 when she received a $110,000 insurance check following the death of her father. She and her 10-year-old son had been living with her dad since her divorce five years before. Although she had had a number of part-time jobs in the last few years, her dad had been Linda's major source of financial support.

Linda quickly figured out that if she earned 8 percent interest on the $110,000 inheritance, that would provide only $8,800 per year. She was determined to go into business for herself. Because she had limited business experience but enough money to make a reasonably large investment, she decided to examine the possibility of buying into a well-established franchise. She read as much literature as she could find on the subject and also attended a number of trade shows featuring the products of franchisors.

After two full months of investigation, she discovered a company that seemed to be perfect for her, Nutri/System. The firm appeared to have an excellent product, and it offered extensive training to those who purchased franchises. The franchise fee for Nutri/System was based on the population of the area served. Linda lived in a community of 110,000 in Northern Florida, so her fee would be $34,000. There would also be other start-up expenses of $63,000, for a total cash investment of $97,000.

Nutri/System was founded in 1971. Its target market was the 34 million overweight people in North America. Nutri/System had 1,160 centers in the U.S. and Canada. The centers offered customers guidance in calorie-controlled, nutritionally balanced meal plans, mild exercise, and a maintenance program. The company also had a line of prepackaged, low-calorie food products.

As Linda prepared to sign the final franchise agreement, she was relieved that so much of the initial planning was being done for her by Nutri/System. On the other hand, she was apprehensive about what the future would hold. Would

Nutri/System really provide her with all the training she needed? Also, would the company give her unrealistic target levels of sales? She was paying out a lot of money on the front end. What if the cooperative spirit she sensed initially was not maintained in the long term? Whenever you go into business for yourself, as opposed to being a salaried employee for a large corporation, there are going to be greater risks and potentially greater rewards. Only time could provide the answers to many of Linda's questions. Let's take a hard look at the world of small business and the people who run it.

I n this chapter, we will first look at independently owned small businesses and eventually return to the franchise alternative as a way to owning a business.

Small businesses are normally run by entrepreneurs. As defined in Chapter 1, entrepreneurs are individuals who begin or take over businesses. They must accept the personal financial risks that go with owning businesses, but they also benefit directly from the success of their businesses. Entrepreneurs and the small businesses they own and operate are an exciting part of our economy.

Although dwarfed in size by such companies as General Electric, with 298,000 employees, or IBM, with annual profits in the billions, small businesses provide a way for people to be their own bosses. Small businesses are often very innovative companies. They can introduce new products, new management styles, and new promotional strategies.

Let's begin our discussion of small business by looking at how the government defines "small." Then we will examine just how important small businesses are in the U.S. economy.

HOW SMALL IS SMALL BUSINESS?

small business   *a business that is independently owned and operated and is not dominant in its field of operation.*

Small Business Administration (SBA)   *the principal government agency concerned with the financing, operation, and management of small businesses.*

The Small Business Act of 1953 defines a **small business** as one that "is independently owned and operated and not dominant in its field of operation." The **Small Business Administration (SBA)** is the principal government agency concerned with the financing, operation, and management of small businesses. Its many functions, including financial aid and assistance to women and minorities, are discussed in the box on page 132. The SBA uses the number of employees and sales volume as guidelines in determining whether or not a business is small. As Table 6-1 shows, this varies for different sectors of the economy.

How the SBA defines a small business is critical for firms applying for SBA loans. For our purposes, however, a small business typically has four characteristics:

TABLE 6-1   The SBA's Definition of a Small Business

Sector	Definition
Retailing and Service	Annual Sales of No More Than $2,000,000 to $7,500,000
Wholesaling	Annual Sales of No More Than $9,500,000 to $22,000,000
Manufacturing	1,500 or Fewer Employees

- The boss owns the business.
- Financing is provided by one or just a few individuals.
- Most of the people working for the business live in the same community.
- The business is small compared to the dominant firms in the industry.

HOW BIG IS SMALL BUSINESS?

What part do small businesses play in our economy? You may be surprised at just how big the world of small business is.

Small Businesses as Big Employers

Small businesses employ many people. Nearly 88 percent of all U.S. businesses employ fewer than 20 people. But in total, these small firms employ 27 percent of the U.S. workforce. Businesses with 99 or fewer employees account for 57 percent of the workforce.[1] Although big firms are also big employers, it is clear that small business, the source of nearly half the wage and salary jobs in this country, is big, too. In addition, several studies have shown that more than 65 percent of all new jobs in the United States are created by businesses with fewer than 100 employees.[2] Without small business, America would be out of work.

Sources of New Ideas

Small businesses are frequently the innovators in their industries. Big business means big bureaucracy, and big bureaucracy means that decisions are made

Small businesses are often the source of new products and services. For example, a small company can find creative ways to orchestrate meetings and events for bigger organizations, making them more rewarding for the participants. The convention center (such as The Buttes Conference Resort in Tempe, Arizona, shown above) also benefits from the innovative work of the small business that plans the events.

Small Business Administration Functions

The Small Business Administration was created by Congress in 1953 to advise and assist the millions of small businesses in the United States. Its mission "is to help people get into business and to stay in business." Let's look at the functions that the SBA performs in fulfilling its mission.

Loans

The SBA offers a variety of financial assistance programs to small business. The two most important are guaranty loans and direct loans. A guaranty loan is made by a private bank or other type of financial institution. The SBA guarantees up to 90 percent of the value of these loans. A direct loan is made directly from the SBA to a small business. Federal law prohibits the SBA from making direct loans unless private lending institutions refuse to make a loan or to take part in the guaranty loan program.

Most SBA loans are guaranty loans; the agency has relatively little money available for direct loans. The average size of an SBA guaranty loan is $115,000, and the average repayment term is eight years.

Advocacy

The SBA champions the cause of small business to the federal government. It serves as the focal point for complaints about how governmental actions might affect small business. It also regularly reports to Congress as to how existing law can be changed to help the owners of small business.

Assisting Women and Minorities

Women and minorities are eligible for all regular SBA services and for some special services as well. Starting in 1980, the SBA designated a "women's representative" in each

slowly. Also, big business is usually interested in mass production only. As a result, without the responsiveness and small production capacities of small businesses, many products would never be made—especially products with little initial demand. Remember, all successful big businesses started as small businesses.

TYPES OF SMALL BUSINESSES

 Small businesses operate in all parts of our economy. The service, retailing, and wholesaling sectors have much higher percentages of small businesses than does the production sector.

Services

service businesses
nesses that sell a service rather than a product.

Service businesses sell customers a service—advertising time on television, a few games of bowling, three hours of music—rather than a product that they can take home with them. Some examples of service businesses are advertising agencies, travel agencies, laundries, bowling alleys, amusement parks, rock bands, and motels.

One of the main features of service businesses is their small size. Only 3.7 percent of all service firms employ 50 or more people. More than 81 percent have fewer than 10 employees. This is because the success of most service-oriented businesses is based on personal contact with customers.

SBA office. Special SBA-sponsored workshops about business are held around the country to reach women. Finally, the SBA has a "mini-loan" program for women, allowing them to borrow up to an additional $20,000 easily and quickly.

The SBA has similar programs for minorities. One such program is the Capital Ownership Development Program, authorized by Congress in 1978. Its aim is to help blacks, native Americans, Hispanics, and other minority people get started in small business.

Managerial Assistance

It is no secret that most small business failures are the result of poor management. Accordingly, the SBA has an active Management Assistance Program. Through this program, SBA staff members and people from the Service Corps of Retired Executives (SCORE) and the Active Corps of Executives (ACE) provide free counseling to small business owners.

The SBA also sponsors courses, conferences, workshops, and problem clinics on a wide range of business topics. Finally, the SBA publishes a variety of booklets for small business owners. These publications are available at no charge through most SBA offices.

Procurement Assistance

The Small Business Administration tries to help all small businesses, minority and nonminority, win a fair share of government contracts. It does this in three ways. First, it employs specialists in each SBA office to show small business owners how to prepare bids for government contracts. Second, it has representatives at all major military and civilian procurement centers to refer small business owners to federal contracting officers. Finally, the SBA has a computerized listing of the names and areas of expertise of many small businesses. The computer matches the skills of these businesses with specific contract requirements.

Wholesaling

Wholesalers are firms that act as intermediaries between manufacturers and retailers or between manufacturers and industrial buyers. An intermediary serves as the go-between for other parties in a transaction. The wholesaler can alleviate problems of the other parties. For example, some manufacturers have excellent production capabilities but lack the space to store goods once they are produced. Or the manufacturer may not have the sales force necessary to promote a product to retailers. A wholesaler may be able to carry out these functions. Wholesaling is also dominated by small businesses. Figure 6-1 shows that 70 percent of all wholesalers have fewer than 10 employees. Only 4.0 percent have 50 or more.

Small wholesalers sell a variety of products, including groceries, farm produce, machinery, and industrial supplies. The small wholesaler can compete with a large wholesaler if it anticipates the needs of its customers through a hands-on approach. That means knowing the operations of retailers so well that their needs are met as soon as they arise.

wholesalers intermediaries between manufacturers and retailers or between manufacturers and industrial buyers.

Retailing

Retailers sell products to final consumers for the consumers' own use. There are a great many small businesses in retailing. Examples include drugstores, independent supermarkets, men's and women's clothing stores, bookstores, music stores, and gasoline stations. Even though large retail chains such as Dillard's and Sears dominate the larger shopping malls, nearly 35 percent of the people in retailing work for organizations with fewer than 20 employees. There is still an important

retailers firms that sell products to final consumers for the consumer's' own use.

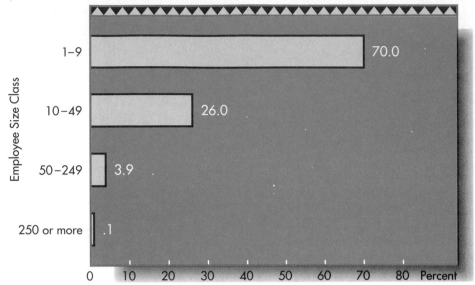

FIGURE 6-1   Sizes of Firms in Wholesaling; Percentage of Establishments by Employee Class Size, 1987.

Source: U.S. Department of Commerce, Bureau of the Census, *County Business Patterns, 1987, United States* (February 1990).

place in the U.S. economy for the one-on-one customer relationship that a small retailer can provide. How many salespeople at Sears, for example, remember your name each time you go into the store?

Production

Only 18 percent of small businesses in the United States are producers. **Producers** convert raw materials and other inputs into finished goods. This requires expensive equipment. Small manufacturers are at a great disadvantage in raising funds for the purchase of such equipment. This is because they do not have access to the public capital markets to sell stocks and bonds. As a result, it is hard for them to compete with the major manufacturers.

producers *firms that convert raw materials and other inputs into finished goods.*

IS SMALL BUSINESS FOR YOU?

 We have seen that small business offers many exciting opportunities. There is no question that small business will continue to play a vital role in our economy. But is small business right for you? To answer this question, you need to consider carefully the advantages and disadvantages of small business.

Advantages

First, you are the boss. Owning a small business is a way of life. If you enjoy taking risks and making decisions, then you would enjoy owning a small business. The small business entrepreneur has no organizational constraint and is not accountable to anyone else. Almost any decision is possible, so long as the money is there.

Second, the potential rewards are great. Few executives of large firms ever become very wealthy. Much of their companies' profits are paid to the stockholders. In contrast, the owners of small businesses help themselves to their firms' profits. A good example of this is the owner of a California Chevrolet dealership who made more money than the president of General Motors. The head of GM was responsible for a firm with 775,000 employees; the Chevrolet dealer had fewer than 400 employees.

Third, small businesses account for many of the most innovative products and services introduced to the market each year. Innovative people are sometimes happier owning their own businesses. Creative freedom is important to people like Steven Jobs and Stephen Wozniak, who founded Apple Computer before they were 30 years old. Not only did they revolutionize the computer business by introducing personal computers, but they made a great deal of money as well. In no time at all, Apple grew from a small business to a big business.

Disadvantages

Many small businesses fail each year because they are not able to pay their creditors. Business failures occur much more often when the economy is ailing. Also, new businesses are more likely to fail than older businesses. Of the businesses that fail each year, nearly 52 percent are less than five years old. In contrast, fewer than 25 percent of all business failures involve firms that have been operating for more than ten years.[3]

Small business start-up decisions are exactly like other investment decisions—the entrepreneur must examine the relationship between risk and return. The risk of business failure is great, and small business failures often result in personal bankruptcy for the owners. This is true of small businesses organized as corporations, too, because the owners are almost always required to guarantee their company's bank loans with their personal assets. On the other hand, the potential payoff—wealth, excitement, and success—is great.

Why Small Businesses Fail

Small businesses fail for many reasons. We will look at some of the more frequent problems and discuss how the small business owner can deal with them.

Economic Factors. Economic factors often lead to business failures. Most important among these factors are industry weakness, poor profitability, and poor growth prospects. Perhaps some of these items are really symptoms as well as causes.

For example, poor profitability may be a result of tough economic times, but it may also indicate a lack of planning and cost control. The small business owner is well advised to keep abreast of events taking place in the economy as well as in the firm's industry. This is particularly important in cyclical industries such as housing and construction, auto parts, and air travel.

Lack of Management Skills. As pointed out in Chapter 5, many owners of small businesses are plagued by a lack of good management talent. Most small business owners must rely on their own managerial judgment, because they cannot afford to hire management specialists. Actually, economic causes of failure may be directly linked to poor management practices. What appears to be an unfortunate economic development might have been overcome by more skillful and informed management.

A good way to overcome some management-related problems is to acquire adequate experience before jumping into a business venture. If you are going to

Operating a small business is definitely good for Densua Abayoni, owner of a successful shop in Atlanta that sells artifacts from Africa. Customers often want to know the exact origin and cultural context of merchandise in the store, and Abayoni cares enough to do the research herself.

Business Career
Restaurant Manager: Coordinates food service activities. Supervises food preparation, quality, and presentation. Plans menus. Estimates food and beverage costs and orders supplies. Manages personnel. Can specialize in such areas as catering, banquets, or coffee shop. *Average Salary: $24,000.*

open a restaurant, it is advisable to work in one for at least a couple of years. That way you can get an idea of the pitfalls and opportunities of the business. You also can assess the importance of location, the appeal of different kinds of food, the nature of traffic flow, and so on. The same principle can be applied to almost any other business.

Difficulty in Keeping Good People. Small businesses lose talent because of low salaries. In addition, many people leave small businesses because of a lack of opportunities for advancement. One reason for this lack of opportunities is that the owner's children often end up taking over the business. In such a case, about all the owner can do is to offer different kinds of challenges to valuable employees.

Aggressive Competitors. Successful businesses attract competitors. Entrepreneurs who discover previously undeveloped market opportunities may make a great deal of money at first. However, if the new market has growth potential, other businesses—large and small—will soon enter. Competition in the market becomes intense as the original entrepreneur tries to think up new product service, delivery, and promotional ideas. The small business entrepreneur must stay one step ahead of the competition to remain successful.

economies of scale   the economic principle that as more units of a product are produced, the average cost of producing each unit decreases.

Lack of Economies of Scale. As more units of a product are produced, the average cost to produce each unit decreases. This economic principle is called **economies of scale.** This means that large-scale firms produce their goods and services more cheaply than do small-scale ones. Small businesses typically produce so few units that they cannot achieve economies of scale. Larger, more efficient firms tend to drive smaller ones out of the market. The only real defense the small firm has is to produce specialized products for relatively small markets. Large firms will not be interested in the small sales potential that comes from small markets.

Excessive Government Regulation. Federal, state, and local governments require businesses to submit a vast amount of paperwork. Adequate records must be maintained about sales, expenses, salary and wage payments, disposal of waste products, safety violations, and other matters. It is expensive and difficult for small business owners to comply with these regulations. Large businesses generate enough sales revenue to hire and pay specialists whose only job is to make sure that the firm complies with government regulations. Most small businesses cannot afford to do this. Many small business owners and their families spend time at night and on weekends filling out papers to comply with government regulations.

Poor Financing. A stumbling block for most small businesses is a lack of capital and credit. It is particularly hard to obtain long-term financing. Banks rarely lend money to a small business for more than a year or two, because loans to small businesses are risky. When funds are made available, they frequently carry a high interest rate, to compensate the lender for the greater risk. It is not unusual for banks to charge small businesses 4 to 6 percent more for borrowed money than they would charge a larger customer.

One sure source of additional funds for the successful firm is profit. The Adolph Coors Co. is a classic example of a small company that grew by reinvesting its profits in the business. A second approach is to find an outside investor to buy part of the business. However, the current owner then sacrifices a certain amount of control in exchange for the needed cash.

BUYING A SMALL BUSINESS

If you want to own a small business, you should decide whether you want to buy an existing business or start a new one. This part of the chapter examines the first alternative. We begin by asking an important question.

Why Is the Owner Selling the Business?
The owner may be selling the business in order to retire. If so, the business may be healthy, and the buyer may have found a real opportunity. More typically, however, the owner has been unable to make enough money to continue. The buyer's primary concern should be to find out why the business was not a success and to determine whether the problems can be solved. Some problems cannot be corrected. For example, if a clothing store's primary appeal is to fashion-conscious, upscale shoppers, and its location is being rezoned to heavy industry, it may not be a good buy at any price.

What Does the Seller Plan to Do Next?
It is important for the person buying a small business to know what the seller is planning to do next. The customers of a small business are often more loyal to the owner than to the business. When the owner goes, all the customers might

go too. For example, if you find out that the owner of an appliance repair shop intends to open a similar store two miles away, you might be well advised to withdraw as a potential purchaser.

Establishing the Purchase Price

How much should the buyer pay for an ongoing business? How much is it really worth? Determining the value of a business can be a tricky problem. Some financial consultants spend their entire career in this area. Some basic concepts are critical for arriving at a purchase price.

assets *resources owned by a business.*

liabilities *debt and obligations owed by a business to its creditors.*

net worth *the difference between assets and liabilities.*

Assets are the resources owned by the business. For example, a business may own property, equipment, a fleet of trucks ("rolling stock"), office and store fixtures, inventory, and patents. **Liabilities** are the debts and obligations owed by the business to its creditors. Examples of liabilities are loans payable and unpaid bills. **Net worth** is defined as the difference between assets and liabilities (net worth = assets − liabilities). The assets of an ongoing business should always be greater than its liabilities, so net worth should be positive. This net worth figure becomes the basis for establishing the value, or purchase price, of a business. The buyer would expect to pay at least the difference between assets and liabilities. The fact that the business is ongoing, with trained employees and an established customer base, enhances the value of a business. Therefore, the purchase price will probably be greater than net worth.

Profit, as defined in Chapter 1, is the difference between sales revenue and expenses (profit = sales revenue − expenses). Not surprisingly, the profitability of a business is an important factor in determining its purchase price. The more profitable a business, the higher the purchase price. Suppose that the Northern Adventures Travel Co. generated $30,000 in profit, and the buyer was looking for a 15 percent return on her investment (purchase price). You can compute the purchase price as follows:

> Purchase Price = Profit/Return on Investment
> Purchase Price = $30,000/.15
> Purchase Price = $200,000

That is, at a purchase price of $200,000, the buyer could expect to see a 15 percent return on investment so long as earnings held up at $30,000 a year. If profits were $50,000, the buyer could expect to pay more for the business.

STARTING A SMALL BUSINESS

6

Starting a small business is usually much more difficult than buying one. There is simply no past history regarding the type of customer, the appeal of various products, and so on. To make this process as trouble-free as possible, the small business entrepreneur needs to follow a logical series of steps. Skipping a step can mean the difference between a successful start-up and a great deal of trouble.

business plan *a document that outlines the firm's future goals and objectives and indicates how they are to be achieved.*

Figure 6-2 shows the business start-up effort as a 12-step circular process. It is depicted as a circle because the process begins with the setting of objectives and ends with an attempt to match performance against the objectives. The 12-step process is part of the evaluation that goes into a business plan. A **business plan** is a document that outlines the firm's future goals and objectives and indicates, in detail, how they are to be achieved. Such a plan may take many months to develop. It is a powerful tool for convincing prospective investors that the

FIGURE 6-2   Twelve Steps for Starting a New Business

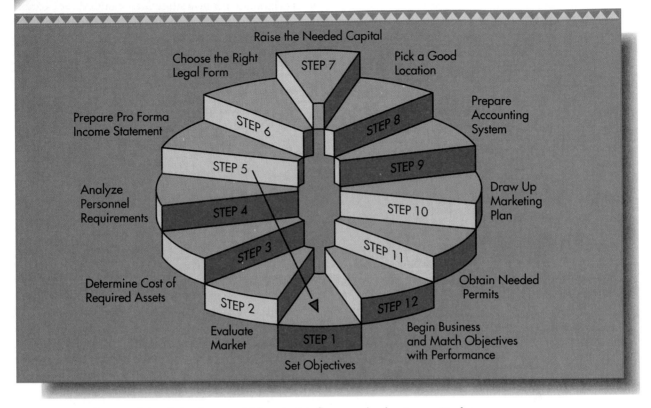

Raise the Needed Capital

Choose the Right Legal Form — STEP 7

Pick a Good Location

Prepare Pro Forma Income Statement — STEP 6

STEP 8

Prepare Accounting System

STEP 5

STEP 9

Analyze Personnel Requirements

STEP 4

STEP 10

Draw Up Marketing Plan

STEP 3

STEP 11

Determine Cost of Required Assets

STEP 2

STEP 12

Obtain Needed Permits

Evaluate Market

STEP 1

Begin Business and Match Objectives with Performance

Set Objectives

entrepreneur has evaluated the key variables that influence the business. It also helps a new business track its performance once the plan is put into action.

Step 1: Set Objectives

The first step is to establish realistic objectives for the business. The initial objective is likely to be that the business must make money. A product may be good but so expensive to produce that it is not a money maker. In a private enterprise system, a firm cannot stay in business for long without a profit. The real question is how much money the owner intends to make and over what period of time. The answers depend upon how well the entrepreneur wants to live—weekend vacations at the lake or three weeks on the Riviera—and whether the owner wants to leave a prosperous business to the children.

Step 2: Evaluate the Market

Which market needs are not currently being met? Can the entrepreneur meet these needs? What product or service of the new business is likely to be the most popular? The second step involves market research, but many small business people do not have the skills to conduct this research for themselves. Nor do they have enough money to hire a professional market researcher. Many small businesses fail because there was not a market for their new product or service.

Step 3: Determine the Cost of Required Assets

In this step, the owner must determine necessary operating assets and estimate their costs. The best procedure is to list the assets and to estimate the costs by talking with suppliers. For example, a flower shop needs display materials, a large refrigerator, delivery trucks, office furniture, and a cash register, as well as a stock of flowers. The cost of the assets depends on how they are obtained. For example, is leasing a building cheaper than buying one? The cost of assets must be accurately estimated, or else the entrepreneur may find that expenses have run out of control.

Step 4: Analyze Personnel Requirements

How many people will the firm employ? Will most of the employees be part-time college students or more permanent professional people? Once again, if personnel requirements are not accurately estimated, the entrepreneur may encounter soaring costs. As noted earlier, one of the main problems of a small business is attracting and retaining good people. The problem can be solved by formulating explicit personnel policies dealing with the training, supervision, and promotion of employees.

Step 5: Prepare a Pro Forma Income Statement

pro forma income statement   a statement estimating future sales and expenses, showing how much money the business is likely to make once it begins operations.

The entrepreneur now has enough information to prepare a pro forma income statement. A **pro forma income statement** is an estimate of future sales and expenses. It tells the entrepreneur how much money the business is likely to make, or lose, once it begins operations. In Figure 6-2, there is a line connecting Step 5 and Step 1. This means that the owner should compare the pro forma income estimates with the profit objectives (that is, compare Step 5 with Step 1). If the comparison shows that the objectives will not be met, then the owner might need to cut expenses, raise revenues, or change the profit objectives. Ultimately, the entrepreneur may have to face up to the possibility that reasonable objectives cannot be reached in the business chosen. If this is the case, the individual should look for other small business opportunities.

Many prospective business people resist drawing up pro forma income statements because the statements are nothing more than educated guesses. However, even though forecasting is not always accurate, a pro forma income statement does give a general outline of the likely profit picture.

Step 6: Choose the Right Legal Form

Should the business be organized as a sole proprietorship, a partnership, or a corporation? Most small businesses in the United States are sole proprietorships. Before an organizational form is chosen, however, the entrepreneur should carefully consider the advantages and disadvantages of each type, as discussed in Chapter 5. Talking with an accountant and a lawyer is a good idea also.

Step 7: Raise the Needed Capital

New businesses immediately face the problem of raising capital. Generally, personal resources are the largest single source of funds for purchasing or starting a business. Lenders are more generous with people buying a business than with people starting one.

Step 8: Pick a Good Location

Too many small businesses are located where the entrepreneur just happens to find an empty building. The result is often financial disaster. The right location is particularly critical for retail businesses. Retailers like to say that the three most important things in retailing are location, location, and location.

Of key importance to small retailers is the pattern of foot and auto traffic in their community. The greater the number of people who pass by a store, the greater the store's number of customers. In a shopping mall, the best location for a small retailer is next to a large store or between two large stores. Many people will pass by the small business on their way to the large one.

Step 9: Prepare the Accounting System

The small business is now getting close to the grand opening. But before that big moment, the entrepreneur should hire an accountant to set up proper bookkeeping procedures. Without an accounting system, there is no way of knowing whether the enterprise has made a profit and whether it owes any taxes.

Step 10: Draw Up the Marketing Plan

In Step 2, the entrepreneur should have evaluated the market. Now the task is to formulate a marketing strategy to reach the market. How will the new business tell the public about its product or service? Which is likely to be most effective— television, radio, or newspaper advertisements? Should the business offer price discounts? Which brands and styles of products will be most desired by consumers? What pricing strategy will work best?

Step 11: Obtain the Needed Permits

Each state, county, and city has a number of operating permits that must be obtained before a business may open its doors. For example, real estate agents and hair stylists are required to have certification from the state. In states with a sales tax, the entrepreneur will need a sales tax number. If the firm has employees, the entrepreneur must register with the state employment office and the Internal Revenue Service.

Step 12: Begin the Business and Match Objectives with Performance

The business is now ready to open its doors, and success depends largely on the flexibility of the entrepreneur. Earlier decisions may have to be changed as the business is forced to meet the test of the marketplace. It may be necessary to substitute television advertising for newspaper advertising, to employ four salespeople instead of three, or to stay open in the evenings. The assortment of products or services may need to be altered. The smart entrepreneur will adapt to changes in consumer needs and preferences. The test here is whether the business is achieving its objectives. If objectives and performance are not matched, the small business owner needs to revise some aspect of the financial, managerial, or marketing plan.

Buy a Business or Start One?

Anyone debating whether to buy or start a small business should consider five factors: profitability, risk, reputation, real property and equipment, and personnel. These factors are summarized in Table 6-2.

Clearly, buying an existing business will provide profits more quickly and with less risk. However, although starting a business has many drawbacks, that is

TABLE 6-2　Factors to Consider When Deciding to Buy or Start a Business

Factor	Buy an Existing Business	Begin Your Own Business
Profitability	Quicker Profits	Larger Profits
Risk	Less Risk	More Risk
Reputation	Established Reputation	No Reputation. Not Easy to Establish
Buildings and Equipment	Facilities and Equipment in Place	No Facilities and Equipment
Personnel	Personnel in Place	No Personnel

where the largest potential profit lies. The entrepreneur does not have to pay anyone for past contributions and gets to keep all the returns generated by his or her creativity.

THE ENTREPRENEUR AND SMALL BUSINESS

 Many psychologists and management researchers believe it requires a special type of personality to be a successful entrepreneur. If you are guessing who among your friends is a future entrepreneur, don't be too quick to pick someone with a 4.0 grade point average. An MBA from a top school is no guarantee either. These accomplishments are highly commendable, but they may simply indicate conformity to society's expectations and a willingness to carry out other's directions and assignments.

The entrepreneur is often a person of independent spirit who is always alert to opportunities. He or she normally has plenty of confidence. A classic example is H. Ross Perot, who founded Electronic Data Systems (EDS) in the 1960s. While working for IBM, Perot made his annual sales quota in the 'month of February and was told to slow down for the rest of the year. Instead, he quit and founded EDS, which he turned into a multibillion dollar company. Eventually, Perot merged the firm with General Motors. That turned out to be an unusual marriage between an entrepreneur and a bureaucratic organization—clearly a bad match. It was like placing the Green Berets under the control of the Social Security Administration. A well recognized attribute of entrepreneurs is that their creative ability works well when they are in control, but not when they are working for others.

Many of the personality characteristics of entrepreneurs may seem to be inborn, but they can be refined or complemented by educational experiences. Over 250 colleges and universities now offer courses related to small business and entrepreneurship. Clearly, it is not enough to be a risk taker. One must have the skills to accumulate financial resources, manage people, communicate ideas, and establish business plans. If you are considering becoming an entrepreneur, ask yourself how well these attributes fit you. Are you more comfortable with a guaranteed paycheck, or are you willing to take risks for a chance to accumulate great wealth? Do you prefer to be in charge, or are you more comfortable following procedures laid out by others?

Many entrepreneurs now come from the ranks of women and minorities. The number of women-owned businesses in the United States has grown as women have become more important participants in the workforce. One example is presented in the Profile on page 144. Another important development is the emergence of African-Americans, Hispanics, Asian-Americans, and other minority groups as business owners. Members of minorities have taken advantage of equal opportunity to become fully participating members of the private enterprise system.

FRANCHISING   [8]

Purchasing a franchise is another way to get into business. **Franchising** is the right to use another firm's name and products and to market them within a specified territory. Examples of successful franchises are not hard to find—just drive to the edge of almost any town and you will see fast-food restaurants, service stations, and small retail stores. Franchise outlets are also common in shopping malls.

franchising   the right to use another firm's name and products and market them within a specified territory.

Currently, there are more than 2,000 franchised systems in the United States. Banks, accounting services, dating services, skin care centers, tub and tile refinishers, funeral homes, nursing services, birdseed shops, beauty shops, child care centers, solar greenhouses, and fast-food outlets have all been franchised successfully. One franchising expert in the Department of Commerce states, "Any business that can be taught to someone is being franchised."[4]

The Parties in a Franchise Agreement

Let's examine the roles of the different participants in a franchising agreement. The **franchisor** is the business that grants the franchise license, along with exclusive territorial distribution, use of its emblem, and other benefits, such as training and marketing assistance. The **franchisee** is the person or group that buys the franchise. Most experts agree that the small business owner has a better chance of success as part of a franchise system.

franchisor   the business granting a franchise license, along with exclusive territorial distribution, use of its emblem, and other benefits.

franchisee   the person or group that buys a franchise, obtaining the right to use the franchising organization's name and trademark and paying a fee or royalty in return.

Blockbuster Video has been among the fastest-growing franchise businesses of the past decade—a hit with consumers and a moneymaker for franchisees.

Kim Gordon

She was the marketing vice president of a $2.5-billion-a-year real estate sales company in the Washington, D.C., area. Fed up with the politics and bureaucracy of corporate life, Kim T. Gordon quit the fast track two years ago and started her own business, Marketing and Communications Counsel, at her home in Silver Spring, Md.

Gordon says she used to think that corporate success would make her happy. But, she says, "I found that I was spending so much less time doing what I thought was fun, which was the *work*. I wasn't loving it anymore."

In her own business, Gordon, 35, offers clients strategic planning services in marketing and communications, and she contracts with others to implement the plans. Instead of taking a commission or a markup on the work that her subcontractors or "affiliates" do, she charges a flat fee ranging from $5,700 to $9,000 for the initial plan and then $95 an hour for her services as coordinator of the implementation. "Companies used to charge hundreds of dollars an hour for my services," she says.

Her fee structure saves her clients about 40 percent of what they would have to pay under more customary payment systems, Gordon says. In her first full year of business, she made $15,000 more in personal income than she had made as someone else's employee.

Setting up shop at home was a decision made possible by technology. With a computer and other electronic tools, Gordon says, she can do "what traditionally would have taken myself, a personal secretary, and a marketing assistant to do."

Working from home was not dictated by domestic concerns. Gordon has no children, and her husband, Stephen Mizner, media director for an advertising agency, is a gourmet cook.

She calls it "so unfair" to measure businesses primarily by the size they achieve. "We [women] don't have the same way of measuring our success," she says. For her, success means "delivering a very high-quality product to my client, feeling great about it, watching them reap the rewards of it, and also having a personal lifestyle that I enjoy. If I can do that and make money, that's what it's all about."

Gordon, whose company is a sole proprietorship, aims at growth of about 10 percent a year and expects that eventually she'll have a staff of perhaps four people. "I think this company has to grow like any other, but I never want it to be big."

Gordon is sensitive to criticism that women are creating jobs for themselves, not creating businesses. Says she: "I have created a business with a business plan, with business goals, with an ongoing marketing program, with professional signed agreements with other companies, and with ongoing contracts with clients." She expects revenues of $80,000 to $100,000 this year.

And, as her business grows, she says, she's not going to move to a location outside her home. "I'm going to buy a bigger house."

Source: Reprinted by permission, *Nation's Business,* July 1990, © 1990, U.S. Chamber of Commerce.

Franchising Is Big Business Too

Franchising is not new. The first franchise system in the United States was the Singer Sewing Machine Company. In 1898, General Motors began to market its automobiles through independent franchised dealers. By 1915, franchising had become the primary way to sell and service automobiles, as well as to distribute petroleum products. The most dramatic increases in franchising have come in the fast-food industry. McDonald's, Burger King, Kentucky Fried Chicken, and Dairy Queen are familiar elements on the American scene.

The International Franchise Association estimates that franchise retail establishments accounted for $648.9 billion in retail sales in 1991—34 percent of the retail sales in the country.[5] As indicated in Figure 6-3, the largest part of franchise retail sales (apart from the "other" category) comes from auto and truck dealers, gasoline stations and restaurants.

The International Example on page 146 deals with the international dimensions of franchising—McDonald's move into Moscow. As the formerly communist societies continue to open up to free enterprise, exciting new opportunities will arise for international franchising.

Pros and Cons of Franchising

Franchising has several distinct advantages and disadvantages. Often, what is an advantage to the franchisor is a disadvantage to the franchisee, and vice versa (see Table 6-3). Let's look at franchising first from the point of view of the franchisor and then from the point of view of the franchisee.

Franchisor's Perspective. From this point of view, the big advantage of franchising is that it allows the franchisor to expand the distribution of its product without making major capital expenditures. The franchisee is usually expected

FIGURE 6-3   *Franchise Sales in the U.S.* (Retail Sales, in Billions of Dollars)

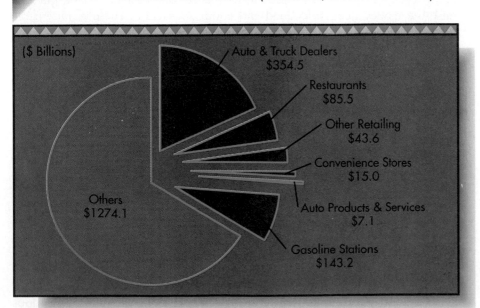

($ Billions)

Auto & Truck Dealers
$354.5

Restaurants
$85.5

Other Retailing
$43.6

Convenience Stores
$15.0

Auto Products & Services
$7.1

Others
$1274.1

Gasoline Stations
$143.2

Source: Polly Larson, "Franchising Strength Undiminished," *Franchising World* (Mar–Apr 1991), p. 6.

McDonald's in Moscow

The largest McDonald's in the world is in Moscow. Opened in January, 1990, as a joint venture between McDonald's restaurants of Canada Ltd. and the Moscow City Council, it serves about 40,000 customers per day. That translates into more than 14 million customers per year, which means a lot of Big Macs. Typically, the waiting line goes around the block several times.

McDonald's sells its hamburgers for rubles, then invests the accumulated profits in more restaurants in the former Soviet Union. This is partly because of restrictions on taking profits out of the country.

As the former Soviet Union and Eastern Europe move toward a free market, franchising may become an important factor in the development of their economies. Franchise agreements allow local business people to receive technical expertise, management training, and business skills in a relatively short period of time. Otherwise, it might take decades to move from a controlled economy to one based on individual initiative and entrepreneurship.

At the grand opening of McDonald's first outlet in Moscow, Russians were eager for a taste of the West.

Source: Reprinted with permission from *Entrepreneur Magazine*, September 1991.

not only to pay the franchisor a fee for the right to open a retail outlet, but also to raise the money needed to build and equip the facility. These requirements eliminate or greatly reduce the capital outlays required of the franchisor. In the franchisee, the franchisor also has a hardworking, highly motivated local person as its representative.

Another advantage for the franchisor is that several sources of revenue can be built into the franchise contract. These include an initial fee to obtain the franchise, a percentage of gross operating revenues, and profits from selling the necessary supplies to the franchisee. As an example, several successfully franchised hamburger restaurants charge more than $100,000 for the outlet, charge a fee of up to 5 percent of monthly sales, and supply the outlets with products ranging from hamburger meat to computer forms.

The main disadvantage to the franchisor is loss of control. If the franchisee does not keep the facility properly maintained, it reflects badly on the franchisor. La Quinta, one of the nation's fastest growing motel chains, does not franchise its properties. Why? Because top management believes that it can keep its properties cleaner and maintain them more efficiently with a system of local managers than with a system of franchisees.

The franchisor sometimes gives up potential profits by franchising. This disadvantage does not apply to every business, however, since some industrious franchisees make more money for their franchisors than the latter could make for themselves. Finally, disputes may arise between the franchisor and the franchisee

TABLE 6-3   Advantages and Disadvantages of the Franchise System

	Franchisor's Perspective	**Franchisee's Perspective**
Advantages	1. Little Capital Required	1. Initial Training by Franchisor
	2. Rapid Expansion	2. Continual Advice from Franchisor
	3. Local Orientation	3. National Marketing
	4. Highly Motivated Franchisees	4. Reputation of Franchisor
	5. Several Sources of Revenue	
Disadvantages	1. Lack of Control over Franchisee	1. Large Amount of Capital Required
	2. Must Share Profits with Franchisee	2. Too Much Money Paid to Franchisor
	3. Disputes with Franchisee	3. Franchisor May Find It Difficult to Adapt to Local Market Conditions
		4. Too Much Control by Franchisor

over such issues as buying practices, management of the outlet, and hours of operations. These disputes must be carefully resolved so as not to destroy the relationship between the two.

Franchisee's Perspective. The big advantage from this point of view is the assistance provided by the franchisor in establishing the business. Such assistance can include site-location recommendations, help in obtaining local bank financing, and instruction in the day-to-day operation of the facility.

One of the most extensive training programs for franchisees is offered by McDonald's. McDonald's requires all new operators to attend a two-week intensive course at Hamburger University in Elk Grove Village, Illinois. The program covers every aspect of how to run a McDonald's, ranging from cooking a Big Mac to proper accounting and control procedures. In addition to programs for owners of new franchises, many franchisors sponsor regularly scheduled training programs for the franchisee's staff.

The franchisee also benefits from the franchisor's national marketing efforts. This includes national advertising, market research studies, the development of new products and services, and sometimes the use of national sales offices. Finally, the franchisee benefits directly from the franchisor's reputation. For example, travelers may not know much about the Holiday Inn in Cincinnati, but they are aware of Holiday Inn's national reputation. As a result, they may be more likely to reserve a room at the Holiday Inn than at an independently operated motel.

One disadvantage is that the franchisee is normally expected to raise most of the capital required to begin operations. For example, as Table 6-4 indicates, an

TABLE 6-4   Required Investment and Number of Outlets for 12 Franchisors

Franchisor	Total Required Investment	Number of Franchised Outlets	Number of Company-Owned Outlets
H & R Block	$5,000–$8,000	4,837	3,994
Merle Norman Cosmetics	$2,000–$17,000	2,366	0
International Tours	$62,000	338	1
Burger King	$375,000	6,033	990
Baskin Robbins	$100,000–$160,000	2,987	178
Goodyear Tire Centers	$50,000–$100,000	617	919
Budget Rent-a-Car	$165,000	3,509	460
Century 21 Real Estate	$25,000–$50,000	7,052	0
Aamco Transmission	$145,000	694	0
7-Eleven Stores	$12,500 and up	3,094	6,900
McDonald's	$245,000–$290,000	11,275	3,348
Holiday Inn	Up to $5,500,000	1,398	176

Source: *Entrepreneur Magazine's Guide to Franchise and Business Opportunities, 1991 Annual Report,* Volume 5, No. 2 (Entrepreneur, Inc., Irvine, Calif., 1991).

H & R Block franchise costs $5,000–$8,000, an International Tours franchise $62,000, a Burger King $375,000, and a Holiday Inn up to $5.5 million.

Another disadvantage, particularly for successful franchisees, is that a big portion of their sales dollars is sent back to the franchisor. Also, the franchisor may not understand local business conditions. This problem is especially important if the franchisee is not allowed to make marketing strategy adjustments on its own. For example, a fast-food franchisor may require that all of its franchisees open at 7:00 A.M. to serve breakfast, regardless of whether there is a breakfast trade in a particular location.

Opportunities for Small Business Entrepreneurs

Franchising provides an opportunity for people to establish profitable businesses. But, as Table 6-4 shows, franchises are expensive. This makes it impossible for many small entrepreneurs to invest in franchises. A Chevrolet dealership (which is a small business by government standards) will cost more than $2 million. Not every small business entrepreneur can afford such a price.

Opportunities for Prospective Franchisors

So far, we have studied franchising from the perspective of the entrepreneur looking for a small business opportunity. But what about the prospective franchisors? Franchising offers a way for small businesses to grow. Most successful franchisors began with one retail outlet. Experts on franchising generally agree that there are three elements essential to success as a franchisor: sound retail concept, adequate financing, and a good relationship with franchisees.[6]

Sound Retail Concept. The retail concept must be recognizable, practical, have staying power, and be easy to replicate. McDonald's, which is one of the most successful franchise systems in the world, meets all of these criteria. The golden arches make the outlets easy to recognize. McDonald's efficient service is very much in step with our fast-paced world. The McDonald's concept has staying power, in the sense that it meets a real need in our society. An illustration of a fad-type franchise that did not have staying power was Pizza Time Theatre. This concept combined video games, singing robots, and pizza. Pizza Time's founder, Nolan Bushnell, who also started Atari, invested millions of dollars in it, but the venture collapsed. Finally, McDonald's are easy to replicate. Formulas tell franchise owners where to locate their restaurants, how to cook French fries, where to put the ice-making machine, how to hire employees, and when to clean the floors.

Adequate Financing. Most franchisors grossly underestimate the cost of building and supporting a franchise system. Even franchise fees of $50,000 or more, along with royalty income from the sales generated by franchisees, may not be enough to cover expenses. In addition, royalty income does not represent a great deal of money until there are many successful franchises. Jiffy Lube learned this lesson the hard way. The owner and his backers invested $9 million in Jiffy Lube, Inc., even though the fee for each franchise owner was only $35,000 (for each additional shop it was $25,000). To raise additional revenue, Jiffy Lube sold exclusive rights to large geographic areas for nonrefundable fees. For example, the rights to Texas were sold for $350,000.

Good Relationship with Franchisees. All too often, franchisors regard franchisees as employees, not as partners. Franchisors have legal obligations to meet. They must be willing to listen to the problems of their franchisees. Responsive franchisors will develop new procedures and products that prove useful for their franchisees.

An important question for franchisors is whether to sell franchises to absentee owners. An absentee owner purchases the franchise, recruits employees to operate it, takes the profit, but does not actively manage the franchise. The absentee owner is never available except to examine the books. Many successful franchisors will not sell franchises to absentee owners. On the other hand, the Great American Chocolate Chip Cookie Company welcomes absentee owners. Its founder believes that the franchises are easy to operate and do not require the owner to be a manager. Eighty percent of the owners of its franchises are absentee owners.

Fraudulent Practices

One of the biggest problem areas in franchising has been the purchase of worthless franchises by unsuspecting people. Many people have lost their life savings as a result of such purchases. Most of the abuses can be categorized as one or more of the following:

- Misleading information concerning profitability of the franchise.
- Refusal to show actual profit-and-loss statements for the franchise.
- Hidden charges to the franchisee.
- Improper use of celebrities' names to promote the franchise.
- Misleading promises concerning aid to the franchisee.
- Use of high-pressure sales techniques.[7]

Although several state and national laws protect the small business person from misrepresentation by fraudulent franchisors, these laws have not completely eliminated misrepresentation. The franchisee should make an effort to find out why some franchises succeed and some fail.

SUMMARY POINTS

1 A small business is one that is independently owned, has relatively few employees, and is not dominant in its field.

2 Small businesses are very important to the economy. They generate 40 percent of the gross national product. Small businesses are also responsible for much of the innovation in the U.S. economy.

3 Small businesses are most frequently found in service industries, retailing, and wholesaling. They are less important in manufacturing and production.

4 In determining whether a small business is appropriate for you, evaluate freedom of action that goes with self-employment and the opportunity to receive the benefits of your own efforts. The main disadvantage is the high risk associated with owning your own business.

5 If you are going to purchase an existing firm, you must examine the current owner's motive for selling, the current owner's future plans, and the business's potential for profitability.

6 When starting a business from scratch, the entrepreneur should follow a 12-step process. The steps include setting objectives, preparing pro forma income statements, raising money, finding a location, and preparing a marketing plan.

7 In addition to being willing to take a risk, the successful entrepreneur must have the skills to accumulate financial resources, manage people, communicate ideas, and establish business plans.

8 Franchising is a small business ownership arrangement in which the franchisor contributes management assistance, marketing expertise, and its corporate name, and the franchisee contributes capital and hard work. The big advantage to the franchisee is the expertise provided by the franchisor, but there may be high costs involved.

REVIEW QUESTIONS

1 How does the federal government define a small business?

2 Why are small businesses generally more effective than large businesses in generating new ideas?

3 Why does the production sector of the economy have relatively few small businesses?

4 Outline the advantages and disadvantages of owning your own small business.

5 What is the relationship between economic factors and poor management skills, in terms of explaining the failure of a small business?

6 What is meant by economies of scale?

7 In buying an existing business, why is it important to know what the seller is planning to do next?

8 What is a business plan? Why is it important?

9 List the 12 steps in starting a new small business.

10 What is a pro forma income statement? How can a small business person successfully use one?

11 Besides being a risk taker, what are some necessary characteristics that an entrepreneur must have?

12 What is the most important disadvantage of franchising, from the franchisor's perspective?

13 What is the biggest advantage of franchising, from the franchisee's viewpoint?

14 What are the three essential factors in the success of a franchisor? 8

DISCUSSION QUESTIONS

1 Do you believe that big business means big bureaucracy? Explain your answer.

2 Would you like to own your own small business? If so, what type of business would you like to own?

3 Is a willingness to take risks enough to become a successful entrepreneur?

4 If you were to open a small business, would you like it to be a franchise outlet? Do the advantages of franchise outweigh the disadvantages, from your point of view?

5 Does the SBA perform a valuable function for small business? Should taxpayers be forced to support the SBA?

EXPERIENTIAL EXERCISES

1 Interview the owner of a franchised fast-food outlet. Find out what services the franchisor provides the franchisee, and whether the franchisee is satisfied with those services.

2 Interview the owner of an independent small business (one that is not franchised) in the service or retail sector of the economy. Ask the owner to describe, in order of importance, the four most difficult problems that he or she faces.

CASES

CASE 6-1
Worthington's Fine Men's Wear

In late 1991, Leonard Worthington finally decided to take the plunge. He would quit his job at Nordstrom's Department Store in Seattle and begin his own business venture. Ever since graduating from the University of Tennessee in 1969, he had hoped to start his own business. He had spent ten years working for Dillard's Department Store in Little Rock, then five years with Neiman-Marcus in Dallas, and finally Nordstrom's. In each case, Leonard had started as a salesperson and progressed to the top of his group in sales volume. His specialty was in men's fashions.

Styles had changed often over the decades, but Leonard's interest never wavered from top-of-the-line, traditional apparel. This was to be the theme of his new store in Seattle. He would carry brands such as Hart, Schaffner and Marx, Hathaway, Countess Mara, Ralph Lauren, and Le Baron of California. Leonard could not hope to compete directly in price with the major department stores, but service and his own expertise would be his strong points. He would help select the proper garment to complement each customer's build, coloring, and hairstyle. He also would hire the best tailor in Seattle; nothing upset Leonard more than poorly fitted slacks or a coat that hung too short in the back.

While working at Nordstrom's, Leonard had put most of his business plan together. However, there were still many issues to consider.

1. In choosing a legal form for his business, Leonard wanted to avoid double taxation at all costs. Consult Chapter 5 and advise him how to accomplish this objective.
2. One of Leonard's financial advisers suggested that he draw up a pro forma income statement. Leonard's initial reaction was, "I haven't even opened the place. How should I know how much money I'm going to make?" What is your reaction to this?
3. Advertising is likely to play a key role in Leonard's new store. Since his funds will probably be limited at first, how would you recommend that he get the maximum impact for each dollar spent?

CASE 6-2
Gulf Bait and Tackle

Joel Loomis retired from the Navy as a full captain at age 50. He had been both a logistics officer and a flight trainer. Joel's last seven years in the Navy were spent in Europe, running one of the Navy's largest distribution centers. When Joel and his wife, Suzy, moved to Galveston, Texas, they expected to retire. Joel bought a 30-foot sailboat and started playing golf. Suzy became active in the League of Women Voters and other organizations. But Joel and Suzy soon found that they were too active to be retired, so they began to look for a business to buy.

Joel liked to fish. He had been buying all his bait and fishing tackle from Bob Witt at the Gulf Bait and Tackle store since it opened in 1980. The store was the third-largest bait and tackle store in Galveston. It had more than 2,000 square feet of sales space, plus a 300-square foot office and 1,000 square feet of inventory and general service space. Although Gulf Bait generated nearly $1 million in sales each year, it never made more than $30,000 in profit for Bob Witt.

Joel, Suzy, and Bob entered serious negotiations for the sale of Gulf Bait. In two weeks, they arrived at a mutually agreeable price of $230,000. Joel and Suzy put up $50,000 in cash from their personal assets and borrowed $100,000 from the Galveston State Bank at 12 percent per year. Bob took a five-year, interest-only note at 10 percent for $80,000. The assets of the firm were valued at $120,000 for the building and $60,000 for the inventory. The firm's only liabilities were $20,000 in unpaid bills to suppliers.

During the first six months of operations, Joel and Suzy worked almost 16 hours per day at their new store. Suzy took over the advertising and personnel functions, while Joel went to work establishing a computerized inventory control and purchase plan. The local National Cash Register (NCR) salesperson provided a great deal of advice and free consulting. Joel bought a cash register-computer terminal that gave him a daily printout on sales and an exact count of the inventory. Joel was able to cut inventory by 30 percent and to eliminate overstocked items and customer stockouts. Suzy was equally successful establishing an advertising plan and written personnel procedures.

At the end of its first year. Gulf Bait and Tackle's profits stood at $35,000. At the end of the second and third years, sales had increased 15 and 20 percent, respectively, and profits had risen 30 and 35 percent.

Joel and Suzy were then approached by Harold Kaplan, who had made a great deal of money in the oil business. He wanted to franchise Gulf Bait and Tackle all along the Gulf Coast. Harold was willing to purchase a part or all of Gulf Bait and Tackle, or to buy Gulf Bait and Tackle's first six franchise outlets.

1.   Did Joel and Suzy pay too much for Gulf Bait and Tackle when they bought it?
2.   Do you think it's possible to franchise a bait and tackle store?
3.   Should Joel and Suzy franchise their store?

The Canine Plaza

Maggie and Tex Zombrano graduated from Saddleback Community College in 1983. They concentrated their academic courses in Business Administration. Maggie enrolled at The University of Southern California and received her BBA degree in Accounting in 1986. She joined a local accounting firm of Murphy and Gonzalez. Maggie passed the California CPA examination in 1989 and began to have audit responsibility for some of Murphy and Gonzalez' smaller clients.

Tex joined Apex Insurance as an automobile and homeowner insurance salesperson. While Tex was "good on his feet" and could easily communicate with his customers, his real love was hunting and fishing. His Labrador retriever, Lex, was his constant hunting companion. Lex won several major awards for best hunting dog in Southern California. Some people felt that Lex was not only more affectionate than Tex, but also more aggressive and a harder worker.

One of Maggie's first auditing accounts was Cinci Stowell's Canine Plaza, which was located in San Diego. The Canine Plaza was opened in 1982 as an upscale "boarding house" for dogs. It had both indoor air conditioned runs and outdoor runs. Cinci hired two local dog trainers to offer obedience training as well as beginning and advanced hunting training. Cinci's operation was quite successful. She added more outdoor runs in 1988, took in cats and birds, and made $65,000 in 1991. Ten thousand dollars came from the sale of two acres of land that the Canine Plaza owned. Cinci's previous best year was 1989, in which the Plaza made $59,000.

Cinci informed Maggie when they were finalizing her 1991 income taxes that she had decided to sell the Canine Plaza. The Plaza was the fourth kennel that Cinci had worked in and the second that she had owned. Cinci told Maggie that there was a tremendous franchising opportunity for first-class, complete-service kennels. While she had decided to leave the dog training business and enter a Ph.D. program in Sociology, she felt that the next owner of the Canine Plaza could franchise her concept nationwide.

Maggie became very excited about the prospect of purchasing the Canine Plaza and about its franchising potential. Tex was not very happy selling insurance. While he was fairly good at it, he had yet to make $25,000 a year. Also, he had told Maggie on several occasions that he was either going back to school or he was going to sell new cars at his brother-in-law's Chevrolet dealership.

When Cinci found out that Maggie was interested in purchasing the kennel, she told her that she "would have to have" $433,000. Cinci knew that 100 percent bank financing would be impossible to obtain, so she indicted that she would be willing to finance $200,000 of the purchase price. Maggie and Tex had saved $50,000, so they would have to borrow only $183,000. Connie Saathoff, Vice President of the Security State Bank, indicated that she would seriously consider loaning the business $183,000 if the loan would have first call on all of the assets of the business.

Maggie did not know how much money she and Tex should expect to make on a $433,000 investment. She did know that so-called risk-free investments, such as U.S. government bonds, historically paid 6-8 percent, while riskier investments might be expected to earn their investors 15-25 percent per year. The reason the riskier investments pay more is that there is a reasonable chance the investor would lose all or a significant portion of his or her investment.

Tex and Maggie did not know which type of ownership structure would be the best for them. Tex believed that if the Plaza was structured as a corporation, their family assets would be protected in case the business was sued or they could not repay the Security State Bank or Cinci. In addition, he thought it would be easier to franchise the kennel concept if the Canine Plaza was a corporation.

Maggie also wanted to consider asking Cinci to become a limited partner in the business. Maggie and

Tex would be the general partner, and Cinci's position would be a limited partner in exchange for providing $200,000 worth of capital to the business. Maggie's main concern was that Cinci would try to interfere in the operations of the Plaza.

Questions

1. Do you believe that Maggie and Tex should purchase the Canine Plaza? How much importance do you assign to Tex's interest in dogs?

2. Can the Canine Plaza be easily franchised?

3. Does the corporate form of organization provide Tex and Maggie real protection?

4. Should Tex and Maggie seriously consider asking Cinci to join the firm as a limited partner?

5. What do you believe is a fair price for the kennel?

PART 3
Management of the Enterprise

OBJECTIVES

After studying this chapter, you should be able to:

1 Define management and describe the three levels of management.

2 Identify four criteria for assessing organizational effectiveness.

3 Discuss the principal elements of organizational design.

4 Describe organizational culture and its elements.

5 Describe the management process and identify the five functions of management.

6 Name three sets of roles that managers may assume.

7 Identify the stages of the decision-making process.

8 Cite bases of power in organizations and discuss ways that managers acquire power.

9 Describe four types of organizational changes and discuss how resistance to change can be overcome.

CHAPTER 7

Management and the Organization

Marcus Christopher had spent eight years at MarketPlace, and he had done very well. Starting as a checkout clerk, he had been given steadily more responsibility. First he had moved to the stockroom, and then he had been put in charge of merchandise in the sporting goods department. There were many things he liked about his job: the comfortable working conditions, the sense of being part of a well-run, respected organization, and the good feeling of knowing that he did his job well. Most important, Marcus loved the camaraderie with his colleagues. There were always jokes to share, helping hands when they were needed, and invitations to meet for pizza after work.

Last week Marcus had been promoted to assistant manager. He was elated at first, but now he began to worry. He would be responsible for supervising several of his former peers. He felt comfortable dealing with things, but now he would have to deal with people. Worse, these were his friends. He began to feel incompetent, and he was afraid he would soon feel lonely.

The situation Marcus Christopher faced is shared by many people in organizations. After spending years dealing with numbers or tools or products, they suddenly must deal with people. Unfortunately, they often have had no experience or formal training in managing others. Like Marcus Christopher, they often find their difficulties compounded by the fact that they must now give orders to former peers.

In this chapter, we will discuss many things that Marcus will need to know if he is to be a successful manager. For instance, we will consider the various functions required of managers and the roles they must perform. We will discuss how managers can improve the quality of their decisions. We will examine the bases of power managers can use to help ensure that their decisions are effectively carried out. We will also discuss how managers can introduce change in the organization, as well as how they can deal with resistance to such change. Before exploring these issues, we'll first define management and look at different views of organizational effectiveness.

The Great Pyramid of Cheops occupies 13 acres of desert sands in Egypt. It was built with more than 2 million stone blocks, each weighing about 5,000 pounds. Construction took 100,000 people more than 20 years. Single expeditions to find new stones and to move them back to the construction site involved as many as 8,000 people. The pyramids of Egypt are as much monuments to management as they are monuments in stone. To carry out such massive efforts, careful planning, coordination, and control were necessary. These are a few of the basic functions of management. Today, General Motors, the National Aeronautics and Space Administration, and even Fraboni's Italian Restaurant perform the same basic managerial tasks.

WHAT IS MANAGEMENT?

An early student of organizations defined **management** as "the art of getting things done through people." Managers achieve organizational goals by arranging for others to perform necessary tasks. What managers do depends on their position in the firm, the nature of the industry, and their own ingenuity. At Turner Construction Co., a nationally known construction firm, managers arrange for teams to build new office complexes and shopping centers. At Safeway Stores, Inc., store managers arrange for filling shelves with merchandise, putting out new issues of magazines each week, and adjusting the air conditioning when summer arrives.

management the art of getting things done through people.

Levels of Management

As Figure 7-1 shows, managers fall into three levels: top management, middle management, and lower management. The names of these levels suggest the main functions of the management positions in the firm's hierarchy.

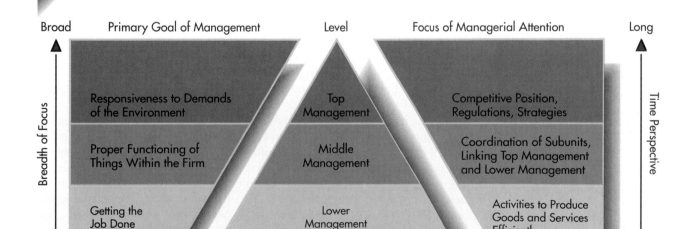

FIGURE 7-1   Levels of Management

Broad — Primary Goal of Management	Level	Focus of Managerial Attention — Long
Responsiveness to Demands of the Environment	Top Management	Competitive Position, Regulations, Strategies
Proper Functioning of Things Within the Firm	Middle Management	Coordination of Subunits, Linking Top Management and Lower Management
Getting the Job Done	Lower Management	Activities to Produce Goods and Services Efficiently

(Breadth of Focus: Broad → Narrow; Time Perspective: Long → Short)

Source: Adapted from R. A. Ullrich and G. F. Wieland, *Organization Theory and Design* (Homewood, Ill.: Richard D. Irwin, Inc., 1980).

Top Management. Top management is concerned with the overall direction of the firm. It has a broad focus, and its time perspective is long. Top management considers the "big picture" and often plans years ahead. Managers at this level watch for the kinds of developments we discussed in Chapter 2, such as changing demographics and economic trends. The job of top management is to improve the company's competitive position, to lobby government for favorable rule changes, and to develop corporate strategy. Top management must also communicate its decisions to middle management. Top management at Turner Construction keeps track of the requirements for office building construction and changes in financial markets. It also formulates plans for corporate growth and consolidation. Top management at Safeway headquarters makes such decisions as where to build new stores, which stores to close, and how much money to spend on renovations.

Middle Management. Middle management has a somewhat narrower focus than top management, and its time horizon may be months rather than years. It is concerned with the proper functioning of the organization. Middle managers coordinate the activities of the organization and act as links between top management and lower management. They are responsible for buying raw materials, selecting new employees, and planning departmental work. Middle management at Turner Construction may guide a shopping mall construction project by purchasing concrete, hiring local workers, bringing in construction engineers, and keeping track of costs. Middle managers at Safeway regional offices decide how much money to spend on advertising, how to supply regional stores with less expensive produce, and so on. Middle managers must communicate with lower managers and guide them toward accomplishment of the company's goals.

Lower Management. Lower management has a specific, narrow focus and a short time horizon. It makes sure the job gets done, and on time. Lower management works directly with the employees who provide the company's goods and services. Managers at this level make sure that machines are maintained, work is scheduled, and reports are typed. Lower management at Turner supervises employees in the day-to-day production of concrete and the delivery of construction materials to workers at the site. At Safeway stores, lower management schedules work for employees, handles cash deposits at banks, and cashes checks at the store office.

Management: An Art or a Science?

At the start of this section, we referred to management as an art. An art relies more on imagination, intuition, and practice than on an orderly system of facts and laws. In this sense, even modern management looks a lot like an art.

However, management is becoming more of a science. New management theories, refined practical guidelines, and sophisticated computer applications are all fueling this trend. For example, we will see in later chapters that managers use sophisticated computer programs to determine the best levels of inventories, to schedule work, and to help maintain product and service quality. They rely on complex robotic systems to produce a bewildering array of products flexibly and efficiently. They turn to theories drawn from psychology, sociology, anthropology, and elsewhere to motivate workers, understand consumer preferences, and make sense of financial markets.

The art of management involves difficult challenges in organizing an enormous project such as Walt Disney Company's new Disneyland in Japan.

Thus, although intuition and experience in management are still important, they must take a place beside more scientific approaches. Management is now *both* an art and a science. Successful managers must rely on their creativity, insight, and experience, but they must also work to master the increasingly complex array of tools available to them.

ORGANIZATIONAL EFFECTIVENESS

A key task of managers is to make their organizations more effective. But what is an effective organization? **Organizational effectiveness** can be defined as the degree to which the organization achieves its goals, maintains its health, secures resources needed for survival, and satisfies parties that have a stake in it. This definition suggests that effectiveness has several dimensions. On one dimension, an organization is effective if it attains its goals. The approach to defining organizational effectiveness that focuses on this dimension is called the **goal assessment** approach. It is concerned with whether the organization reaches the growth, sales, profitability, or other goals management has set for it.

    However, there are other ways to measure the effectiveness of an organization. For instance, is an organization effective if it is profitable but its workforce is unhappy? Is it effective if it has captured large markets this year but is faced with threats to its supplies of raw materials or capital? Is it effective if it boosts production capacity with new technology but in so doing upsets the local community or customers? These questions suggest three criteria, besides goal accomplishment, for measuring organizational effectiveness.

    First, **internal process assessment** focuses on organizational health. According to this approach, an unhealthy organization cannot be called effective,

organizational effectiveness   the degree to which the organization achieves its goals, maintains its health, secures resources needed for survival, and satisfies stakeholders.

goal assessment   an approach to assessing organizational effectiveness that is concerned with whether the organization reaches the growth, sales, profitability, or other goals management has set for it.

internal process assessment   an approach to assessing organizational effectiveness that focuses on organizational health.

regardless of profitability. This approach considers such measures of organizational health as employee satisfaction, levels of conflict, coordination of department activities, and production efficiency. Second, **systems resource assessment** considers whether an organization is able to acquire the resources it needs to survive and prosper. Social service agencies must acquire federal, state, or municipal funding to continue offering their services. Manufacturing firms must acquire labor and raw materials to continue operating. Biotechnology firms must have access to start-up capital and qualified scientists.

Finally, **strategic constituencies assessment** of effectiveness looks at groups inside or outside the organization that have a stake in it, such as customers, stockholders, the community, creditors, suppliers, and employees. According to this approach, an organization is effective when it has satisfied these important constituencies. The different approaches are shown in Figure 7-2. In determining whether an organization is effective, it is important to consider these various perspectives. Doing so highlights the fact that an organization, whatever its profits or losses this year or next, cannot be seen as truly effective if its workforce is dissatisfied and uncoordinated; if its sources of labor, materials, or finances are drying up; or if it is alienating important constituencies.

systems resource assessment *an approach to assessing organizational effectiveness that considers whether the organization is able to acquire the resources it needs to survive and prosper.*

strategic constituencies assessment *an approach to assessing organizational effectiveness that focuses on the extent to which important constituencies are satisfied.*

ORGANIZATIONAL DESIGN

 A fundamental task of managers is to structure the organization so that its goals are met, its employees are offered satisfying work, and other criteria of effectiveness are fulfilled. Some elements of organizational design are hierarchy of authority, division of labor, departmentalization, line and staff relationships, and span of control.

Hierarchy of Authority

hierarchy of authority *ranking of people in an organization according to their authority.*

A hierarchy is a ranking or ordering from top to bottom. A **hierarchy of authority** is a ranking of people in an organization according to their authority. A well-

FIGURE 7-2   Four Approaches for Assessing Organizational Effectiveness

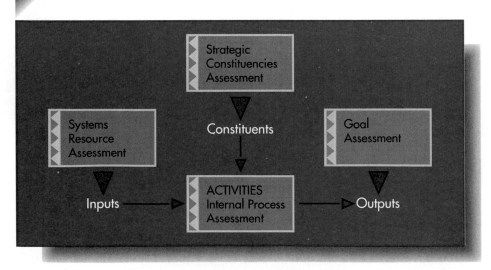

defined hierarchy is valuable because it reduces confusion about who gives orders to whom. It also defines how information flows from person to person, both upward and downward.

A firm's hierarchy is represented schematically by an **organization chart,** which maps authority relationships. The organization chart in Figure 7-3, for instance, shows that manager Grimes reports to manager Amemiya, who reports directly to the president. Managers such as Grimes, Herbert, and Ibsen, who supervise employees at the base of the organization chart, are sometimes called "supervisors." Employees W, X, Y, and Z report to Grimes. Orders, work assignments, and other information pass down along the lines. Information, ideas, and feedback flow upward along these lines as well. For example, manager Grimes gives a work assignment to employees W, X, Y, and Z. In doing the task, employee W discovers a better method. She informs manager Grimes. Grimes evaluates the method, approves it, and explains it to employees X, Y, and Z to help them to do the task better. Grimes may even tell manager Amemiya about the new method if the information might be useful to other work units in the organization.

Information can flow informally in many directions within an organization. The organization chart shows only the formal lines of communication. Efficient flow of information within the organization contributes to the organization's overall effectiveness. Information must get to the people who need it to do their jobs.

organization chart *a schematic representation of an organization's hierarchy of authority.*

FIGURE 7-3   A Simple Organization Chart

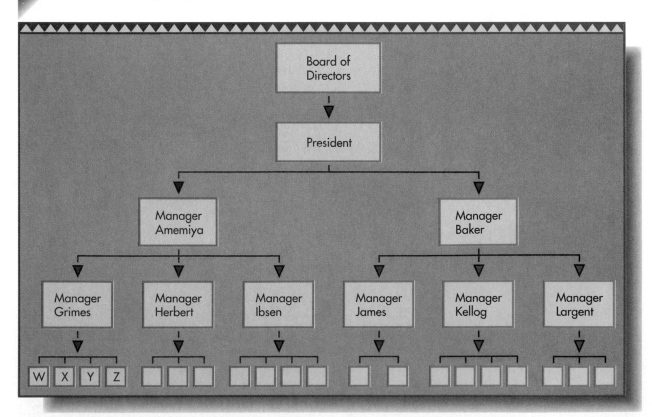

Division of Labor

The term **division of labor** refers to the way big jobs, such as assembling an automobile, are broken down into many smaller jobs, such as tightening a gasket on a radiator assembly. These smaller jobs are more easily learned and mastered.

Around the turn of the century, it was believed that jobs should be divided into very small parts, with each worker doing only a tiny piece of the overall task. This simplification of jobs was expected to increase efficiency, for several reasons. It would make it easier to learn and perform the task; it would reduce time lost moving between parts of the job; and it would be easier to replace missing workers. However, as we will see in the next chapter, many people now believe that work should be made more interesting and that employees should be given more responsibility. This is because job simplification may lead to boredom and dissatisfaction. Workers then are absent more often, quit and must be replaced sooner, and generally do work of poor quality.

Departmentalization

Any large organization must be organized into smaller units or departments. This is known as **departmentalization.** Without these smaller units, the organization would be impossible to manage. The same is often true of smaller companies. Let's take a look at three approaches to departmentalization.

Functional or Process Departmentalization. Under **functional** or **process departmentalization,** departments are organized on the basis of similar skills. One type of skill is placed in one department, another in a second, and so on. The most common form of process departmentalization is by function (see Figure 7-4). For example, a firm may have separate departments for marketing, finance, and production. The Mead Corporation features a mill products department, a packaging and distribution department, an accounting department, a sales department, and an operations and finance department. The activities of these various departments must be coordinated by top management.

This approach has economies of scale, since all employees within a function work in the same place and can share facilities. For example, a company can reduce duplication and waste by building only one production facility rather than having a separate building for each product line. If demand slows for one product line, production capacity can be used for another. Also, grouping activities in this way encourages specialization and the development of expertise. For instance, if personnel employees were spread around the organization, they would have to

FIGURE 7-4   Departmentalization by Function

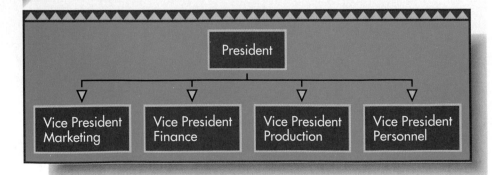

be generalists, since they would have to do all the personnel work for their respective divisions. If they are grouped together, one can focus on testing, another on training, and so on.

However, since the activities of the departments must be coordinated by top management, firms organized on this basis may be slow to react to changes in the business environment. Also, functional departmentalization may create problems of coordination across functions. Since each function is by itself, employees may identify with their functional specialties rather than with the firm as a whole. For instance, production people may feel isolated from salespeople or even hostile toward them.

Purpose Departmentalization. **Purpose departmentalization** organizes on the basis of similarity of purpose. The purpose might involve a given geographic area. For example, all manufacturing and marketing operations in Europe might be organized under a European division, as illustrated in Figure 7-5(a). The firm's line of products can also serve as the basis of departmentalization. Figure 7-5(b) shows a firm with a skateboard division, a bicycle division, and a motor-

purpose departmental-ization   *departmentalization on the basis of similarity of purpose.*

FIGURE 7-5   Departmentalization by Purpose

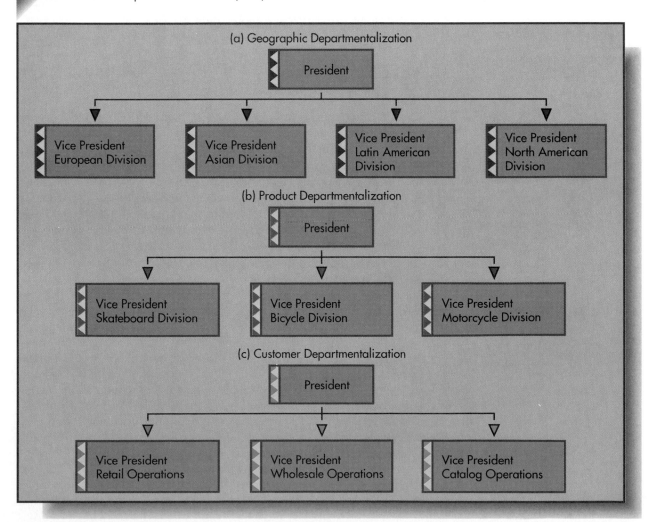

cycle division. Finally, the firm might be organized by customer orientation—retail operations might be in one department, wholesale operations in another, and catalog operations in a third. This variation is shown in Figure 7-5(c).

R. H. Macy & Co., Inc., a large retail organization, uses a geographic structure: Macy's California, Macy's Missouri-Kansas, and so on. The 3M Company has independent production and sales departments for each of its different types of products. The Ford Motor Company has separate departments for its large trucking customers, its retail passenger automobile dealers, its farm product customers, and others.

Because purpose departmentalization gathers all related activities in each department, the costs of coordinating those activities are reduced. Employees from different functions interact every day, so they can identify with the product or service. This setup also makes it easier to pay special attention to specific markets, products, or customer groups. This often makes the firm more responsive to changing needs and increases customer satisfaction. It is also easier to see where profits and losses are occurring. Thus, top management can assess the performance of each department and demand necessary changes.

matrix departmentalization *a flexible approach to departmentalization, in which the employee reports to both a functional superior and a project superior.*

Matrix Departmentalization. A more unusual approach to organizational design is **matrix departmentalization.** It is popular in rapidly changing industries such as aerospace, where organizational flexibility is needed. In essence, each employee has two bosses—one "higher up" the organizational chart in the employee's functional area, and another for the particular project being worked on.

In the matrix organization shown in Figure 7-6, employees report to supervisors in their functional areas of production, engineering, personnel, or accounting. They also report to either project manager A or project manager B, depending on whether they are working on project A or project B. When the Dutch Group of the Shell Oil Company began building offshore oil rigs in the North Sea, it had the usual finance, construction, purchasing, and accounting departments. Each oil rig also had a project manager. The project manager saw to it that the oil rig was constructed properly, at the right cost, and with the appropriate features. If the rig was not finished on time or was unsatisfactory, the project manager was held responsible. All employees were accountable both to the project manager and to their functional area managers.

The complexity of matrix organizations creates some problems. Lines of authority may be unclear, leading to conflict and confusion. The job of the project manager is especially tough. At Lockheed Corp., for instance, construction of advanced jet fighters required the interaction of physicists, aerospace engineers, financial analysts, government accountants, construction workers, and test pilots. The physicists and engineers had specialized training and wanted to operate independently of strict authority. The financial analysts knew little about aircraft design and objected to costs that the physicists thought necessary. Government accountants objected to the financial analysts' accounting procedures. Construction workers complained that the test pilots were too particular, and test pilots claimed that the aerospace engineers had not designed enough speed into the jets. Matrix project managers had to deal with all of these differences of opinion. Since the employees were also reporting to functional managers and sometimes getting conflicting orders from them, the project managers' authority was diluted.

FIGURE 7-6   A Matrix Organization Structure.

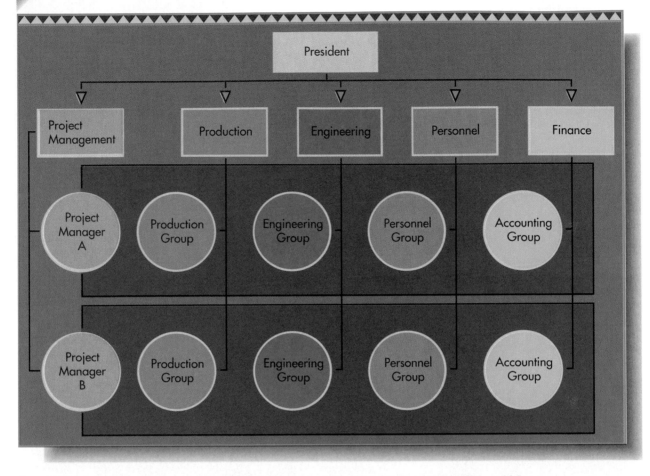

Source: D. Robey, *Designing Organizations,* 3rd ed. (Homewood, Ill.: Richard D. Irwin, Inc., 1991), p. 225.

Line and Staff Relationships

One of the fundamental concepts in management is the distinction between a line position and a staff position. A **line position** is a job in the direct chain of command that begins with the board of directors and ends with the production and sales people. Line personnel all contribute in some way directly to the company's main business. For example, assembly-line workers assemble products, a district sales manager directs the work of sales representatives who sell the products, and a lawn service employee applies fertilizer to the customers' lawns. All of these are line positions.

A **staff position,** on the other hand, is outside of the main chain of command. Staff personnel support line personnel by providing information, giving advice, or offering special services. For example, the personnel department does not contribute directly to producing or selling the company's product. Instead, this department supports the line organization by recruiting workers, handling employee benefits, and so on. Similarly, accountants occupy staff positions at many companies. They prepare financial statements, analyze cost data, and pro-

line position   a job in the direct chain of command that begins with the board of directors and ends with production and sales employees; line personnel contribute directly to the company's main business.

staff position   a position that is outside the primary chain of command; staff personnel support line personnel by providing information, giving advice, or providing specialized services.

vide information for line managers to use in planning, but they do not have direct authority over production or sales people.

Span of Control

span of control   the num-
ber of employees that a man-
ager directly supervises.

The term **span of control** refers to the number of employees that a manager directly supervises. In Figure 7-7, manager Allen has a span of control of two. Managers Benitez and Cohen have spans of control of five and four, respectively.

How big should the span of control be? Early management experts argued that a span of control of more than six or seven is too big. Coordination and monitoring of work is difficult when each manager supervises so many employees. On the other hand, when the span of control is very small, such as two or three, subordinates may feel they are being watched too closely. In fact, however, the best span of control may depend on many factors, such as the nature of employees' work and their education, training, and experience. Sears, Roebuck and Co. has utilized a span of control of 40 or more, and it has worked effectively. At BankAmerica Corp. in California, more than 600 branch managers report directly to corporate headquarters.

*classical or **mechanistic***
***organizational design**   a*
view of organizational design
characterized by heavy reli-
ance on rules and regulations,
job simplification, adherence
to the chain of command, and
the objective of efficiency.

Mechanistic and Organic Designs

Now that we've looked at the elements of organizational design, we can ask, "How should organizations be designed?" Most people in management approach this question from one of two points of view. Under the first, the **classical** or **mechanistic organizational design,** the organization is viewed as a complex,

FIGURE 7-7   Span of Control

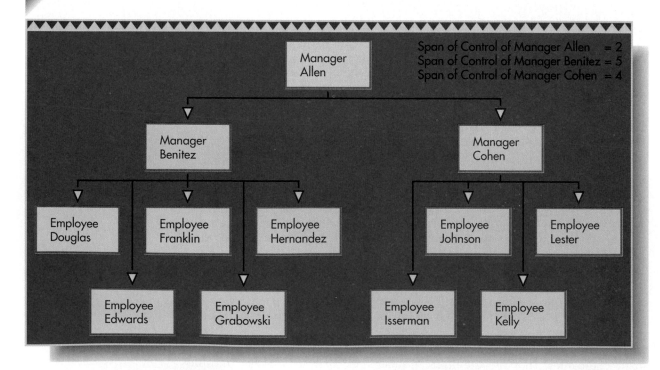

well-oiled machine. To make sure this "machine" runs efficiently, management relies heavily on rules and regulations. Employees follow the chain of command. That is, they communicate only with their direct superiors and immediate subordinates. Moreover, tasks are broken down into small parts and simplified so that employees can more easily become skilled in their jobs.

This mechanistic form was proposed long ago by Max Weber, a German sociologist.[1] Weber felt that such a form, which he called a **bureaucracy,** would have two important benefits. First, it would be efficient. Second, the rules and regulations would help ensure that everyone was treated the same, so there would be no favoritism. Despite these potential benefits, we have all heard stories of bureaucracies that were rigid and uncaring. The Lighter Side on page 170 shows how bureaucratic rules can often become ends in themselves, sometimes with unfortunate consequences. The Controversial Issue on page 172 asks whether bureaucracies have a place in modern business.

The other view, the **organic organizational design,** is that organizations must be flexible to adapt to the demands of a changing environment. One of the primary goals of management in this approach is to develop employee skills and abilities and to foster creativity as well as efficiency. Instead of behaving like a machine, the organic organization has many of the characteristics of a living organism: It senses environmental change, reacts to it, shows concern for the health of its parts, and so on.

The characteristics of each of the two approaches to organizational design are presented in Table 7-1. As a manager, which approach would you prefer? What if you were a production worker?

bureaucracy Max Weber's name for his view of an efficient, fair organization (also called the classical or mechanistic design).

organic organizational design a view of organizational design characterized by flexibility of structure, so as to ensure maximum adaptability to a changing environment and free communication among all levels of the organization.

TABLE 7-1 Characteristics of the Mechanistic and Organic Organizational Designs

Mechanistic Organization	Organic Organization
1. Jobs are broken down into small parts, and each worker does just one part of the whole job.	1. Workers are given a variety of tasks. They each do a "large" job.
2. Each worker's responsibilities are very clearly specified.	2. Responsibilities are flexible. They may change quickly as the situation demands.
3. Communications and other interactions between employees flow up and down the organizational hierarchy.	3. There are free interactions up, down, across, and throughout the organization.
4. Workers are expected to give their primary loyalty to the firms they work for.	4. Workers are primarily loyal to their professions. They tend to identify more with the profession than with the firms they work for.
5. Actions are coordinated by the organization's hierarchy.	5. Expertise, rather than formal authority, is used to coordinate.
6. There is heavy emphasis on prompt and unquestioning obedience to rules and regulations.	6. Emphasis is placed on getting the job done correctly. Rules and regulations are seen as ways to get the job done rather than as ends in themselves.

Leakers

Rules and work practices may outlive their original purposes, sometimes with bizarre consequences. For instance, when Wayne Gilbert took over as chief executive officer in Tooth & Co.'s two Sydney, Australia, breweries, he was surprised to find a "pat man" on his staff. The pat man's job was to sweep up the droppings left by cart horses—even though the breweries hadn't used horses to cart beer for more than 20 years.

A rule that only electricians could start electric motors had become so rigidly interpreted at the breweries that in some instances an electrician was required to turn on a light. "In summer, on Sundays, we had to have an electrician come in to turn on the lights so a laborer could hose down the kegs to prevent the wood from drying out and springing leaks," Mr. Gilbert recalls. But in fact, wooden kegs had been replaced by metal casks a decade earlier.

Another brewery tradition was that if a wooden keg sprang a leak, the workers were allowed to consume its contents. When metal casks were introduced the workers insisted that some kegs be designated "leakers" so they wouldn't forgo any free beer.

Source: G. Brooks, "Aussie Workplace: Theater of the Absurd." Reprinted by permission of *Wall Street Journal,* © 1987 Dow Jones & Company, Inc. All Rights Reserved Worldwide.

ORGANIZATIONAL CULTURE

organizational culture
the emotional, intangible part of the organization, consisting of the values, stories, heroes, and rituals and ceremonies that have special meaning for the people who work for a firm.

Our discussion of organizational design is concerned with the skeleton and musculature of the organization, as it were. But it reveals little about the spirit or culture of the organization. **Organizational culture** consists of the values, stories, heroes, and rituals and ceremonies that have special meaning for the people who work for a firm. Culture represents the emotional, intangible part of the organization.[2]

As an example of what we mean by organizational culture, J. C. Penney Company founder James Cash Penney laid down seven guiding principles, called "the Penney idea." The dominant values in the Penney idea are concern for the employee and customer satisfaction. Employees are encouraged to participate in decision making. Layoffs are avoided; long-term employee loyalty is valued. Usually employees are transferred rather than fired. One store manager even received a reprimand from the president of the company for making too much profit, thus being unfair to customers.

PepsiCo has had a very different culture. Its values have reflected its desire to beat Coca-Cola in the soft drink wars. Managers at PepsiCo compete fiercely to win market share and improve profits. Tiny changes in market share have made or broken careers. Employees understood the corporate culture and thrived on the tension it created. Even the company picnic featured intensely competitive team sports. However, PepsiCo management has recently become concerned about the human and organizational costs of such a culture. It is putting more effort into coaching and training of employees, career management, and feedback on performance.

We stated that culture includes values, stories, heroes, and rituals and ceremonies. Let's consider these elements in turn.

values *deep-seated, pervasive standards that influence almost every aspect of our lives: our moral judgments, responses to others, and commitments to personal and organizational goals.*

Values

Values are the things that are important to us. They are the deep-seated, pervasive standards that influence almost every aspect of our lives: our moral judgments, our responses to others, and our commitments to personal and organizational goals. Values are considered the bedrock of corporate culture. Strong

170

Corporate culture can help people feel good about working together.

organization values let employees know how they are expected to behave and which actions are considered acceptable.

Sharing of values is a key element in the development of successful organizational culture. Hewlett-Packard's sound financial condition, as well as its reputation as an excellent place to work, is often attributed to its credo, "the H-P way." The H-P way is based on a clear statement of values that all employees can understand—belief in people, freedom, respect and dignity, recognition, security, helping each other, and so forth. If values are to have a positive impact on the culture of the organization, they must become part of the daily working lives of employees. At Hewlett-Packard, units are kept small. There are no time clocks. Employees can choose which shift to work. Offices are separated by open partitions to increase accessibility and foster teamwork. In addition, Hewlett-Packard has an unwritten policy never to lay people off.[3] Thus, the company's policies and practices support its values.

Stories

Stories are another important part of organizational culture. **Stories** are narratives that are repeated among employees and are usually based on fact. Stories, or myths, help pass on a culture by acting as maps of how things are done. At 3M, for example, the eleventh commandment is "Never kill a new product idea." The importance of innovation as a 3M value is supported by a story often repeated throughout the organization. According to the story, an employee accidentally developed cellophane tape but was unable to get his superiors to accept the idea. Persistent in his belief in the new product, the employee found a way to sneak into the corporate boardroom and tape down the board members' copies of the minutes with his transparent tape. The board was impressed enough with the novelty to give it a try, and the product was incredibly successful.[4] This story not only reinforces the importance of innovation but also encourages 3M employees who believe strongly in their ideas never to take "No" as a final answer.

stories *narratives repeated among employees and usually based on fact; they help pass on a culture by acting as maps of how things are done.*

Heroes

Heroes are company role models. In their performance of deeds, embodiment of character, and support of the existing organizational culture, they highlight the

heroes *company role models whose deeds, character, and support of the existing organizational culture highlight the values a company wishes to reinforce.*

values a company wishes to reinforce. "The hero is the great motivator, the magician, the person everyone will count on when things get tough."[5] Heroes are often the main characters of the stories relayed through an organization. Thomas Watson at IBM, William Paley at CBS, and Lee Iacocca at Chrysler Corporation are all real people who have taken on heroic qualities in stories that are told in their respective companies, in some cases even after their departure.

Rituals and Ceremonies

rituals guides to behavior in daily organizational life, including evaluation and reward procedures, regular staff meetings, and farewell parties.

ceremonies similar to rituals, but more elaborate productions that occur less frequently.

Also part of an organization's culture are rituals and ceremonies, which are outward signs of what the organization values. As symbols, **rituals** guide behavior in daily organizational life. Rituals may include evaluation and reward procedures, regular staff meetings, farewell parties, parking allocations, and work-scheduling procedures.[6] **Ceremonies** are similar to rituals but are more elaborate productions that occur less frequently. Award banquets, gatherings for speeches, and presentations of promotions are ceremonies. Through rituals and ceremonies, participants can cement understandings and beliefs that are important to the organizational culture by celebrating together.[7]

For example, McDonald's holds an annual nationwide contest to select the "All-American Hamburger Maker," the best hamburger cooker in McDonald's chains across the country. The contest is widely publicized and viewed as quite important. Competition begins at the local level and progresses until the company's best cooks compete at the "All-American contest" at the national level. Cooks are judged on many details to determine whether their hamburgers are cooked quickly and to perfection. The winner gets a big trophy, a monetary award, and an "All-American" shirt patch. This elaborate ceremony communicates to all employees that McDonald's places great value on hamburger quality.[8]

Bureaucracies have had bad press, but they serve a valuable purpose. We will need them for a long time.

No

By their very nature, bureaucracies are bad for people and bad for business. They are in conflict with the needs of healthy individuals. As individuals mature, they have drives to become independent, to develop a variety of interests, and to see things in a long-term perspective. These drives are frustrated by bureaucracies, with their rules and regulations, demands for blind obedience to authority, and close supervision of workers. When workers respond to that frustration by being absent or tardy, by becoming apathetic, or by striking or filing grievances, bureaucratic firms simply tighten up on rules and regulations, demand more obedience to authority, and supervise more closely. This worsens the frustration, and the cycle continues.

Quite simply, bureaucracies don't work in the world of modern business. Research and common sense suggest that bureaucracies are suited to organizational environments that are stable, simple, and certain. By contrast, the environments facing modern business are rapidly changing. They are complex, with many elements to contend with and many interactions among those elements. They are fraught with uncertainty. Such environments require a flexible, adaptable organizational design, with opportunities for worker autonomy and participation in decision making. This hardly describes a bureaucracy!

It is faulty logic to cite examples of successful bureaucratic firms as evidence that bureaucracy works. Such firms may be successful *despite* the bureaucratic form rather than because of it. Besides, bureaucracies are often competing with other bureaucracies—a battle of the dinosaurs. In still other cases, bureaucracies have used their large size and control of markets to prevent competitive forces from working properly.

Bureaucracies are on their way out. Companies that don't recognize the inevitable will ultimately regret their shortsightedness, if they survive at all.

What Do You Think?

FUNCTIONS OF MANAGERS

It is difficult to make generalizations about managers' duties. Managers may perform many varied tasks each day, and one manager's responsibilities may be extremely different from another manager's. For instance, imagine one manager overseeing an auto assembly plant, another managing a cosmetics sales force, and a third running a local food cooperative. What do they have in common? They are all managing, so they must be doing some things in common.

To one degree or another, all managers perform the functions of planning, organizing, staffing, directing, and controlling. Together, these functions make up the **management process.** A **process** is a flow of connected activities moving toward a purpose or goal. Figure 7-8 shows how the five basic managerial functions are connected through the decisions made by managers. The aim of the management process is to put the firm in the strongest competitive or profit position possible.

management process the flow of the interconnected managerial activities of planning, organizing, staffing, directing, and controlling.

process a flow of connected activities moving toward a purpose or goal.

Planning

The term **planning** refers to determining in advance what needs to be done to achieve a particular goal. A plan includes how, when, where, and by whom a project should be done. It includes forecasting, goal setting, and selecting procedures for implementing decisions.

For instance, Trans World Airlines decided in 1991 to reduce fares for corporate travelers in an effort to pull such fliers away from its rivals. To carry out the fare reduction, TWA developed a systematic plan. It had to consider the probable demand for such fares and the potential responses of competitors. It had to determine what prices would be charged, what destinations would be covered,

planning the management function of determining in advance what needs to be done to achieve a particular goal.

FIGURE 7-8   The Management Process

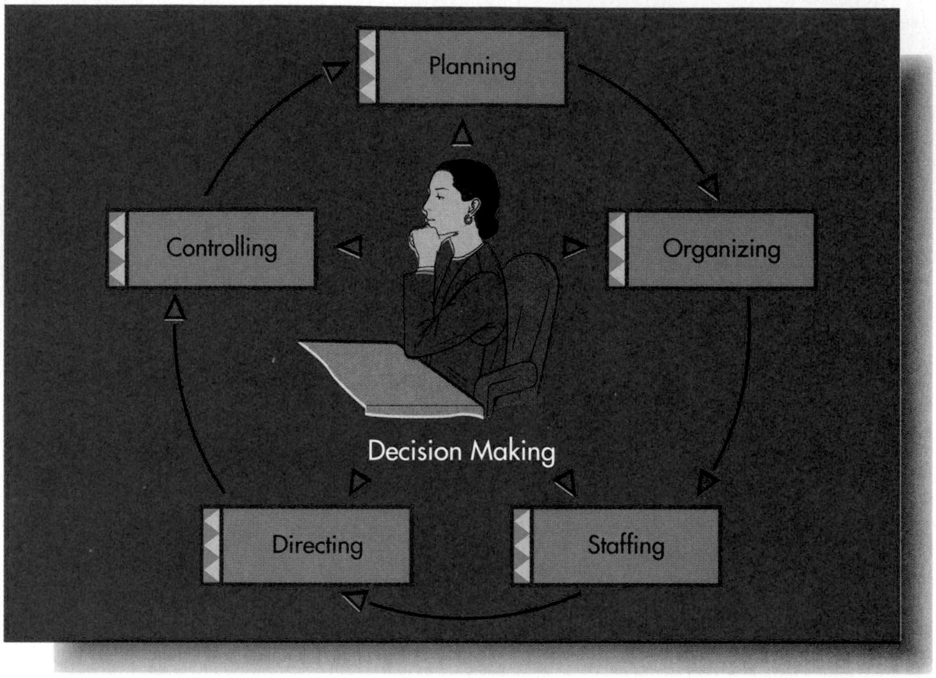

whether the tickets would be transferable and refundable, how the reduction would be publicized, and so on. TWA was experiencing severe financial problems, so it had to consider ways to reassure business travelers worried that the carrier might shut down in the middle of their trips. Achieving TWA's goal of increased corporate travel revenue called for a complex series of planning decisions.[9]

Organizing

organizing   _the manage-_
ment function of arranging and
distributing work among mem-
bers of the firm.

Organizing is the way work is arranged and distributed among members of the firm. It involves breaking down the firm into parts and then making sure that the parts mesh. As we have already discussed, departmentalization and division of labor are two important ways to "break down" the firm. At the level of the firm, work may be broken down into departments—by function, by purpose, or on some other basis. At the level of the individual employee, work may be broken down into very small parts, or each employee may be asked to complete a larger portion of the entire job. After work has been broken down, the various parts must be coordinated.

For a firm in a stable, relatively unchanging industry (such as the insurance industry), the coordination of its separate parts is not too difficult. Coordination can usually be accomplished through the formal hierarchy of authority. At the Metropolitan Life Insurance Co., decisions about whether to change life insurance premiums or to hire more insurance salespeople can be relayed up and down the organization. In rapidly changing industries, however, it is sometimes necessary to take extra steps to coordinate the decisions of each department. The Intel Corp. makes computer chips. In this dynamic industry, it is difficult to know what will happen next. Consequently, Intel employs many people to organize the company's responses to sudden technological and market changes.

Staffing

Staffing is the management function that involves the recruitment, selection, placement, training, development, and appraisal of the members of the firm. We will discuss this function in much greater detail in Chapter 9.

staffing the management function involving recruitment, selection, placement, training, development, and appraisal of members of the firm.

Directing

The term **directing** refers to those activities that guide subordinates toward the achievement of the company's goals. Some of these activities are communicating, leading, and motivating. For instance, a supervisor may communicate production goals to his or her subordinates, give the subordinates instructions about how to accomplish those goals, and provide praise and other rewards to encourage them to accomplish the goals. How well employees perform depends on how well they are led, how well they are motivated, and how well the company communicates its needs to them. We'll discuss these matters further in the next chapter.

directing the management function of guiding employee actions toward achievement of the company's goals.

Controlling

The term **controlling** refers to the set of activities that ensure that actual performance is in line with intended performance. That is, managers must make sure company goals are being met. What is it that managers control in an effort to meet goals? Managers control human resources, financial resources, inventories, and communication flows.

controlling the management function involving activities that ensure that actual performance is in line with intended performance.

To control, managers must carefully monitor developments, see whether or not they are consistent with goals, and take any necessary corrective actions. For instance, a manager might set product sales goals for a department. If it becomes clear that sales are falling short of the goal, the manager might decide to implement a new incentive program to motivate the sales force, to assign more salespeople to the product, or to revise the goals.

Sometimes, control procedures put unnecessary pressure on subordinates. The subordinates may then attempt to evade controls or, at least, develop a very narrow point of view about company goals. At Datapoint Corp., a maker of computer systems, people in the shipping department were given higher quotas each year. To meet the quotas, they often shipped goods to empty warehouses. This burdened the company with the cost of unnecessary shipping and warehouse space. Since shipping department employees were being evaluated on the basis of their quotas, they focused on shipping orders rather than on the real objective of the company—to increase sales and profits.

MANAGERIAL ROLES

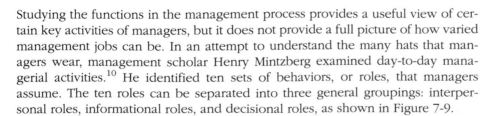

Studying the functions in the management process provides a useful view of certain key activities of managers, but it does not provide a full picture of how varied management jobs can be. In an attempt to understand the many hats that managers wear, management scholar Henry Mintzberg examined day-to-day managerial activities.[10] He identified ten sets of behaviors, or roles, that managers assume. The ten roles can be separated into three general groupings: interpersonal roles, informational roles, and decisional roles, as shown in Figure 7-9.

Interpersonal Roles

Managers perform **interpersonal roles** when they engage in interpersonal relationships. Interpersonal roles include those of figurehead, leader, and liaison. The

interpersonal roles roles managers perform when they engage in interpersonal relationships, including figurehead, leader, and liaison.

FIGURE 7-9   The Roles of Managers

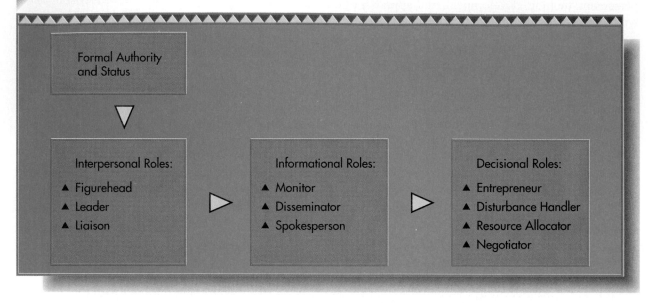

figurehead role is required for activities of a ceremonial nature. For instance, a head chef greets customers at the door, and a bank president congratulates a new group of trainees. In the leader role, the manager directs and controls subordinates' work. As liaisons, managers may contact individuals in other work groups when coordination between groups is needed. For instance, a marketing professor may meet with faculty members from other parts of a business school to coordinate efforts to incorporate more international examples into the curriculum.

Informational Roles

informational roles *managers perform when they serve as focal persons for gathering, receiving, and transmitting information that concerns members of the work unit, including monitor, disseminator, and spokesperson.*

The manager often assumes **informational roles,** becoming a focal person for gathering, receiving, and transmitting information that concerns members of the work unit. Informational roles include those of monitor, disseminator, and spokesperson. In the monitor role, the manager watches for outside information, activities, or events that present opportunities or threats to the functioning of the work unit. For instance, the manager may read in a trade journal about a new technology that would help work group efficiency.

In the disseminator role, the manager passes important information to appropriate members of the organization. For example, after reading about the new technology, the manager discusses the new equipment with the work group.

Sometimes the manager assumes a spokesperson role, representing the group to people inside or outside the organization. For instance, a lower-level manager may meet with a superior to discuss concerns voiced by his or her subordinates.

Decisional Roles

decisional roles *roles managers perform as part of the company's decision-making system, including entrepreneur, disturbance handler, resource allocator, and negotiator.*

Because managers play a major role in the company's decision-making system, they must adopt certain **decisional roles.** These roles include entrepreneur, disturbance handler, resource allocator, and negotiator.

In the entrepreneur role, managers innovate to improve their units and adapt them to the changing business environment. A manager may purchase new microcomputer software so that a department can react more quickly to market changes. In the disturbance handler role, managers respond to adversity and restore equilibrium. For example, a plant manager may have to react quickly to a cut-off of materials from a key supplier.

In the resource allocator role, managers determine the placement of resources. For instance, a manager might have to decide how much of a budget to allocate to different activities, or which employees should get new computers. Especially in times of scarcity, allocation of money, equipment, supplies, time, power, or people can be difficult. Finally, managers must sometimes adopt a negotiator role. A sales manager may have to negotiate with the personnel department to obtain employees with specialized skills, or a production manager may negotiate terms of a contract for raw materials. We will consider decision making in more detail in the next section.

Consider the profile of Rocky Aoki (page 178). Which managerial roles does Aoki seem to emphasize? Which management functions are evident in his story? On the basis of the Profile, what can we imagine about the culture at Benihana?

MANAGERIAL DECISION MAKING

Marketing, finance, accounting, management, and other areas of business all have something in common: decision making. Some decisions are obviously of great importance and involve risk. One example was RJR Nabisco's decision to stop work on its "smokeless" cigarette, Premier (discussed in Case 7-1). Another example was Drexel Burnham Lambert's decision to plead guilty to felony charges relating to insider trading and pay $650 million in fines and restitution. Other decisions, such as the size of the turkey to be given as a Christmas bonus, seem small. Together, these decisions make up the fabric of organizations. To understand what happens in organizations or to predict the behavior of employees, we must understand decision making.

Difficulties in Decision Making

Decision making is never easy, especially if the stakes are high. For one thing, we seldom have all the information we need to make a good decision. For another, we sometimes distort the information that is available. The president of Braniff Airlines did not believe the accountants who told him that he could not afford to expand Braniff's routes. He expanded anyway, and the company failed. Finally, as human beings, we have limited memory and quantitative abilities. Because of these difficulties in decision making, we sometimes put off decisions or use simple rules of thumb to make them. Often the result is a bad decision. By studying the stages in decision making, you will learn how to increase your chances of making a good decision.

Decision Stages

Successful decision makers recognize that there is more to a good decision than just choosing one option over another. They follow the five-step decision process shown in Figure 7-10.

Define the Problem.   The first step is to define the problem. This step is often skipped, because people assume that they know what the problem is. However,

Rocky Aoki

Rocky Aoki has been dubbed a "samurai restaurateur." He is the founder and chairman of the board of Benihana of Tokyo, Inc., a chain of Japanese-style steakhouses across the U.S. Aoki's recipe for success is a skillful blend of daring, vision, and sound management.

Born in 1938 in Tokyo, Rocky is a former Japanese wrestler who first saw New York on his way to the 1960 Olympics in Rome. He returned to enroll in the New York City Community College School of Hotel and Restaurant Management. In 1964, Rocky opened his first restaurant—a modest 28-seater in midtown New York—with $10,000 of his own money and a $20,000 loan.

Rocky took on the challenge of opening his own restaurant based on the age-old idea of teppanyaki (steel grill) cooking. Although worried that Americans would not accept communal dining nor a limited menu (steak, chicken, and shrimp), Rocky proceeded with his plans for having the food cooked on the hibachi table in front of his patrons.

Instructing chefs to perform with swordsman-like precision at dicing and slicing, Rocky devised a formula for creative cookery that involved both good food and theatrics. At the same time, he recognized the importance of catering to the taste buds of the American public. He set the menu and the price accordingly, to ensure that his brainchild and its novelty would not go stale.

The formula has worked. Today, Rocky and Benihana of Tokyo serve tens of thousands of customers daily in locations from New Jersey to Seattle. In 1983, Benihana of Tokyo formed Benihana National Corporation (BNC) and sold stock to the public. Rocky's other endeavors have included Big Splash seafood restaurants, wines, cooking videotapes, a line of oriental frozen foods, and several best-selling Japanese business books, to name just a few. Not all of these have been successful—for instance, the Big Splash restaurants and the oriental frozen food line have been sold—but Rocky always has new ventures planned.

Rocky is also involved in promoting cultural exchanges between Japan and the United States. These include sponsoring sporting and cultural events, becoming a backer of Broadway productions, and being a patron to young Japanese artists in the U.S. and producing films about them for release in Japan.

In 1974, Rocky's love of sports led him to the exciting and dangerous world of powerboat racing, and he became a premiere competitor on the elite circuit. After a spectacular crash under the Golden Gate bridge that nearly killed him, Rocky turned to ballooning. He was a crew member on the Double Eagle V, the first balloon to cross the Pacific Ocean. Rocky stir-fried Japanese food for the crew at 40,000 feet. However, he broke a rib when the balloon crash-landed.

Despite his flamboyant style, Rocky recognizes the importance of good management to the success of his firm. At one point, he hired a management company to run the firm's day-to-day operations while he engaged in his sporting activities. Later, he paid $3.7 million to break the long-term contract, because he felt that the company's management style clashed with his largely Oriental workforce, and he wanted to retain control over each restaurant's quality.

Rocky doesn't speak highly of the currently fashionable Japanese management style. He feels that American management is best, but that some small part of Japanese management may be helpful. Says Rocky, "American management and Japanese labor combined— that's the success of Benihana."

FIGURE 7-10   Steps in the Decision Process

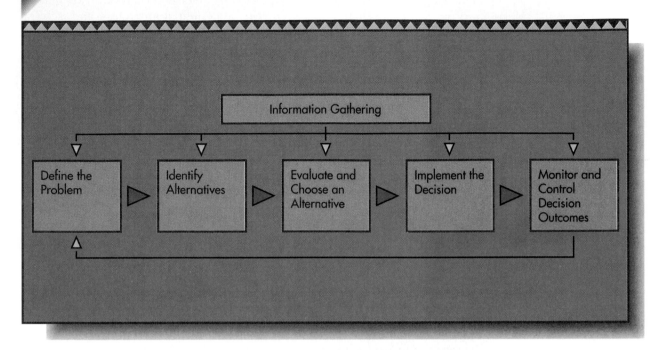

unless decision makers take proper time and care at this stage, they may solve the wrong problem. A problem occurs when there is a gap between the desired situation and the actual one. Examples are declining profits, high scrap rates, or inability to increase market share. Too often, the problem is defined in terms of its symptoms. For instance, management may define the problem as employee apathy instead of recognizing the apathy as a symptom of a deeper problem, such as an unfair reward system. Or the problem may be inappropriately defined in terms of a preferred solution. For instance, suppose sales are declining in Gloria's department. A problem statement such as "Gloria is a poor manager and should be removed" focuses on a proposed solution relating to Gloria rather than directly pinpointing the problem of declining sales. The important point here is that the problem definition should indicate what is wrong, *not* what should be done about it.

Identify Alternatives. Alternatives, or options, are the various approaches that may be taken to solving a problem. Good solutions flow from good alternatives. Unfortunately, in their rush to judgment, problem solvers often bypass the step of generating alternatives. At this stage, problem solvers should identify as many possible solutions as they can. Thus, creativity (to be discussed in detail in Chapter 24) is especially important here. The emphasis at this stage is on generating a large number of alternatives, not on evaluating them.

Caterpillar, a large manufacturer of construction equipment, started to produce farm machinery in competition with Deere & Company, a major manufacturer of farm implements. Managers at Deere were polled for ideas on how to stay ahead of Caterpillar. The managers suggested undercutting Caterpillar on price, increasing the number of models, changing model designs frequently, forcing farm machinery retailers to carry Deere equipment, and so on. Thus, top management identified several alternative courses of action.

Evaluate and Choose an Alternative. Once alternatives have been generated, they can be evaluated and the best one selected. There are two general approaches to evaluation and choice: screening approaches and scoring approaches. With a **screening approach,** each alternative is categorized as unsatisfactory or satisfactory. Unsatisfactory alternatives are screened out, leaving only those that clear all hurdles. If more than one alternative survives all the hurdles, the hurdles might be "raised" until only one alternative remains. In contrast, a **scoring approach** assigns a score to each alternative. The alternative with the best score can then be chosen.

screening approach an approach used to select from among alternatives in which each alternative is identified as either satisfactory or unsatisfactory, and unsatisfactory alternatives are eliminated.

In the case of Deere & Company, the screening approach might have eliminated some alternatives because of their cost, Caterpillar's probable responses, retailers' reactions, and other factors. The scoring approach might have evaluated each proposal in terms of expected profitability.

scoring approach an approach used to select from among alternatives in which each alternative is assigned a score, and the alternative with the best score is chosen.

Deere's actual choice was based on an alternative proposed by one of its managers. The manager suggested letting Caterpillar move into the farm equipment business. Then Deere would enter the construction equipment business and compete with Caterpillar on its own turf. Caterpillar might take this as a warning, the manager said, and get out of the farm machinery business. If not, Deere would match Caterpillar offensive move for offensive move. Since construction equipment was a more profitable business than farm implements, Deere stood to gain by the move. Caterpillar did eventually leave the farm implements business.

Implement the Decision. Some managers make the mistake of assuming that the decision process is over once they have made a choice. Unfortunately, decisions don't implement themselves; they must still be carried out. The manager must make sure that resources are available for implementation. Also, those who will be involved in implementation must understand and accept the solution. Therefore, implementers are often encouraged to participate in earlier stages of the process.

Was the decision process over when Deere decided on its competitive response? No. Much additional planning, allocation of resources, and training and motivation of employees had to be done if the plan was to work.

Monitor and Control Decision Outcomes. The final step in the decision process is monitoring decision outcomes and taking any corrective actions that are necessary. Is the decision working out as planned? Are corrective actions necessary? If the decision is not working out well, what other alternatives are available? In our example, Deere had to monitor Caterpillar's actions carefully. Deere had to be ready to respond in a variety of ways, depending on Caterpillar's actions.

Notice in Figure 7-10 that information gathering affects each stage of the decision process. Information gathering is a continuous activity; it is not done at the beginning and then forgotten. Information is needed to define the problem, identify alternatives, evaluate and choose alternatives, implement the decision, and monitor and control decision outcomes.

POWER IN ORGANIZATIONS

8

power the ability to exert force on others.

Power is the ability to exert force on others. Managers in organizations use power to accomplish their purposes. In this section, we will consider some of the ways that power is acquired.

Bases of Power

There are at least five bases of power in organizations.[11] First, **legitimate power** exists when one person believes that it is right for another to give orders or otherwise exercise authority. A worker who says, "I ought to do as my boss says," is reflecting a belief in legitimate power. Sometimes, legitimate power is culturally determined, as in a society where older people are given respect and obeyed. In other cases, it is due to acceptance of the social structure. If people accept the social structure as legitimate—whether it be the organization's hierarchy, the status ranking of a street gang, or the country's government system—they are likely to accept orders of those higher in the structure.

Reward power is based on one person's ability to administer desired outcomes to another and to remove or decrease those outcomes that are not desired. If Carlos feels that Sang controls what he wants, and that getting it depends on whether he does as Sang wants, Sang has reward power over Carlos.

Coercive power is based on a person's ability to affect the punishment that another receives. Heidi has coercive power over Brian if Brian fears a threatened punishment and if he believes that conforming to Heidi's wishes will make it less likely that he will be punished.

Referent power is derived from feelings of identity, or oneness, that one person has with another, or from the desire for that identity. If Carol says, "I want to be like my co-worker Maria, so I will behave as she does or says," this reflects Maria's referent power over Carol.

Finally, **expert power** is based on one person's perception that another has needed knowledge, skills, or perspectives in a given area. Doctors, lawyers, and computer specialists may all have expert power.

Although managers use all these bases of power, some bases are generally more effective than others. For instance, managers who rely on coercive power are likely to anger and alienate those they coerce. Such managers will encounter secret rebellion. Similarly, those who regularly "pull rank," demanding obedience simply because of their position in the hierarchy, may face resentment and begrudging acceptance.

legitimate power   *power that exists when one person believes that another has the right to give orders or otherwise exercise force.*

reward power   *power based on one person's ability to administer desired outcomes to another and to remove or decrease outcomes that are not desired.*

coercive power   *power based on one person's ability to affect the punishment that another receives.*

referent power   *power derived from one person's feelings of identity with another, or from the desire for that identity.*

expert power   *power based on one person's perception that another has needed knowledge, skills, or perspectives in a given area.*

Political Tactics to Acquire Power

Sometimes people maneuver to acquire power.[12] That is, they "play politics." One political tactic is to build coalitions with others to garner enough resources or votes to control a situation. A second tactic is to create an illusion of power. This is done by giving the impression of legitimacy, of expertise, or of the control of rewards or punishments. As long as others accept that illusion, they will behave accordingly. A third tactic is to create a sense of obligation by doing favors for others and then to ask them to "return the favor" on some important issue. Still another is co-optation, in which current or potential adversaries are somehow "brought onto the team." For instance, a critic of a company might be installed on the firm's board of directors. The hope is that the critic will then develop the perspective of the firm and treat it more kindly. Each of these political tactics may increase the manager's power base or may backfire if used carelessly. Whether or not the use of political tactics to acquire power is seen as appropriate depends largely on the culture of the organization. Whatever a company's views on these tactics, many people would argue that they are often inherently unethical and therefore not acceptable business practice.

MANAGING ORGANIZATIONAL CHANGE

Change is a fact of life for all firms. U.S. automakers face the Japanese challenge and must respond accordingly. A corner grocery store must change how it operates when a 7-Eleven opens across the street. New market opportunities cause cable TV operators to revise their business plans. In each of these instances, a change in the environment has made organizational change necessary. Bringing about change within the organization is rarely easy, and sometimes it is actively resisted by employees.

Types of Change

Let's look at four basic types of organizational change (see Figure 7-11).[13] As the figure shows, these types of change are interrelated; a change in any one will probably cause change in others. As you read, think about the difficulty of bringing about change.

purpose or task change
a form of organizational change in which the goal of the organization is changed.

Purpose or Task Change.   Under a **purpose** or **task change,** the goal of the organization is changed. At one time, the goal of the March of Dimes was to conquer polio. When an effective polio vaccine was introduced, the March of Dimes changed its organizational goal to conquering birth defects.

technological change *a form of organizational change that occurs when a new means is used to transform resources into a product or service.*

Technological Change.   A **technological change** occurs when a new method is used to transform resources into a product or service. The installation of robots on an automobile assembly line is a good example of a technological change. The use of the new technology can help the firm stay competitive.

structural change   *a form of organizational change involving alteration of the firm's formal authority structure or of job definitions.*

Structural Change.   A **structural change** involves an alteration of the firm's formal authority structure or of job definitions. Examples include a change in communication patterns, a change in the way rewards are given, a change in the

FIGURE 7-11   Types of Organizational Change

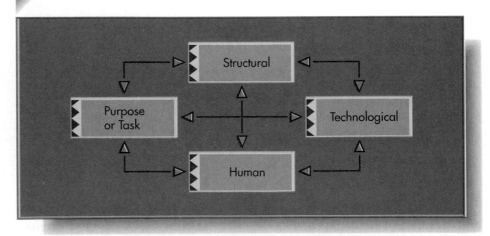

Source: Based on H. J. Leavitt, "Applied Organizational Change in Industry: Structural, Technological, and Humanistic Approaches," in J. G. March, Ed., *Handbook of Organizations* (Chicago: Rand McNally, 1965), p. 1145.

way the firm is divided into departments, and a change in the decisions that employees are allowed to make.

At the aircraft engine factories of Rolls Royce, for instance, workshop managers were not allowed to change shop assignments or to give out rewards. Therefore, workers tended to ignore the workshop managers. The factory managers, who made the decisions and gave out the rewards, spent very little time in the workshops and could not make good decisions on giving rewards. When upper management decided to let workshop managers determine shop assignments and give out rewards, productivity and quality increased dramatically.

Human Change. **Human change** involves improving employee attitudes, skills, or knowledge. Persuading employees to support the United Way, to learn how to program a computer, or to prepare for an assignment in a new department requires human change.

human change a form of organizational change that involves improving employee attitudes, skills, or knowledge.

At Hewlett-Packard, managers realized that the computer and electronics fields change so fast that everyone, from salesperson to research scientist, needs continual updating on new trends and equipment. The company started a program of seminars and lectures, designed to inform all employees within the company. Partly as a result of this forward-thinking effort, Hewlett-Packard has been one of the most profitable computer companies.

Dealing with Resistance to Change

Most attempts at change are likely to meet some resistance. Change brings about doubt. It may be seen as a threat to a worker's pay, relationships with others, authority, or skills. People may also resist change because they think it is not needed, because they think they are being manipulated, or because they do not like the person trying to introduce the change.

Managers must learn to introduce change in the least upsetting way possible. Anticipating the resistance that may occur can help managers prepare for dealing with it. Some specific approaches for dealing with resistance to change are discussed next.[14]

Education and Communication. One way to reduce resistance to change is to explain clearly the need for the change and its logic. When individuals don't understand why change is occurring, they are understandably anxious.

Participation and Involvement. When subordinates or others participate in the planning and implementation of change, they have the chance to express their own ideas and listen to the ideas of others. They gain a better picture of why some approaches to change are selected and others rejected. This reduces uncertainty and misunderstanding and increases acceptance of the change.

Facilitation and Support. It is often useful to introduce change gradually and to offer support to the people who are affected by it. Specific measures might include training programs, time off during the transition period, and emotional support when the change process is at a difficult stage.

Negotiation and Agreement. Often managers must negotiate or bargain to win acceptance or reduce resistance to change. Powerful individuals or departments in an organization may demand more resources to support the change, believing correctly or incorrectly that the change will reduce their power. Managers may want to negotiate before implementing change, in order to avoid disrupting the change process.

Manipulation. Managers may covertly steer individuals or groups away from resistance to change through selective use of information. They may also assign potential resisters to a desired position in the change process in order to ensure their cooperation. Such strategies may work, but if people recognize that they are being manipulated, future problems are likely.

Coercion. Powerful managers may simply demand that subordinates support the change or face loss of rewards and resources. Although coercion may overcome initial resistance quickly, it will probably leave people angry and may increase future resistance.

Choosing from Among the Approaches. Each of these approaches to dealing with resistance to change is widely used. Therefore, you should be aware of them. However, truly effective managers don't feel the need to resort to manipulation and coercion. These approaches are generally shortsighted and may alienate employees. Also, whatever their short-term effectiveness, manipulation and coercion may be unethical. Use of the other approaches is likely to result in a better informed, more satisfied workforce and in superior long-term performance.

KEY TERMS

management 159

organizational effectiveness 161

goal assessment 161

internal process assessment 161

systems resource assessment 162

strategic constituencies assessment 162

hierarchy of authority 162

organization chart 163

division of labor 164

departmentalization 164

functional or process departmentalization 164

purpose departmentalization 165

matrix departmentalization 166

line position 167

staff position 167

span of control 168

classical or mechanistic organizational design 168

bureaucracy 169

organic organizational design 169

organizational culture 170

values 170

SUMMARY POINTS

1 Management is the art and science of achieving organizational effectiveness by arranging for others to perform the necessary tasks. The three levels of management are top management, middle management, and lower management. Top management is concerned with overall direction of the firm, middle management with the proper functioning of the organization, and lower management with ensuring that the job gets done.

2 Organizational effectiveness is measured by looking at the degree to which the organization is achieving its goals, maintaining its internal health, assuring future supplies of needed inputs, and satisfying its various constituencies.

3 Five key elements of organizational design are hierarchy of authority, division of labor, departmentalization, line and staff relationships, and span of control. Hierarchy of authority is the ranking of people in an organization according to their degree of authority. A business firm can be departmentalized by process or function, by purpose, or through a combination of both (known as matrix departmentalization). A job in the direct chain of command from the board of directors to production and sales

people is called a line position. A job outside this primary chain is called a staff position. Span of control refers to the number of employees that a manager directly supervises.

4 Organizational culture is the emotional, intangible part of the organization. It consists of the values, stories, heroes, and rituals and ceremonies that have special meaning for the people who work in the organization.

5 The management process is the flow of connected activities performed by managers in achieving their goals. The five management functions that make up the management process are planning, organizing, staffing, directing, and controlling.

6 Three sets of managerial roles are interpersonal roles, informational roles, and decisional roles.

7 Effective decision making involves five steps: (1) defining the problem, (2) identifying decision alternatives, (3) evaluating alternatives and choosing one, (4) implementing the decision, and (5) monitoring and controlling decision outcomes.

8 Five bases of power in organizations are legitimate power, reward power, coercive power, referent power, and expert power. Managers may also acquire power by employing political tactics.

9 Four important types of organizational change are purpose or task change, technological change, structural change, and human change. Approaches to overcoming resistance to change include education and communication, participation and involvement, facilitation and support, negotiation and agreement, manipulation, and coercion.

REVIEW QUESTIONS

1 Name the three levels of management. Describe what managers do at each level.

2 What are four ways to assess organizational effectiveness?

3 Describe hierarchy of authority. Why is it necessary in most firms, especially large ones, to make authority relationships clear?

4 What is the difference between division of labor and span of control?

5 Describe the difference between a line position and a staff position.

6 What is the difference between a mechanistic approach to management and an organic approach?

7 What is organizational culture? Give three examples of elements of organizational culture.

8 List the five functions of managers.

9 What is the distinction between planning and controlling? Are staffing and directing the same thing?

10 What are three roles?

11 Identify the five stages of the decision-making process.

12 What are five bases of power in organizations?

13 Name four types of organizational change.

DISCUSSION QUESTIONS

1 Which of the approaches to assessing organizational effectiveness do you think is most appropriate? Least appropriate? Why?

2 Suppose you wanted to start your own business. Would you choose a mechanistic or an organic approach to organizing your company? Explain.

3 When you look for a job, what sort of organizational culture will you seek?

4 Of the ten managerial roles, which do you think would be most important in a computer firm? In an automobile manufacturing firm? Why?

5 Why is creativity important in decision making?

6 Why do many attempts to overcome resistance to change fail? What, in your opinion, can be done to reduce resistance to change?

EXPERIENTIAL EXERCISES

1 Interview two managers of local firms. Ask them how they spend their time on planning, organizing, staffing, directing, and controlling. Do they engage in each of the functions? Are the time distributions similar? What might account for any differences?

2 Select a firm and read magazine or book accounts about it. Based on your reading, discuss the company's culture. Try to find indications of the company's values and the extent to which they are shared. Find and discuss examples of stories, heroes, and rituals and ceremonies in the firm.

CASES

CASE 7-1
The Death of Premier

In 1989, RJR Nabisco pulled Premier, its revolutionary "smokeless" cigarette, from the shelves of stores in test markets. RJR announced that it had no immediate plans to reintroduce Premier or anything like it. Premier was dead. It was one of the biggest and most expensive new-product flops in decades.

The cigarette had taken nearly a decade to research and develop. It was designed to address many consumers' concerns about smoking. The cigarette incorporated a tobacco jacket wrapped around a flavor capsule. When "lit," a piece of carbon at the tip of the cigarette, covered with an insulating jacket, would heat, but not burn, the tobacco jacket and flavor capsule. The resulting "smoke" would be cooled by passing through two filters. This would produce much less smoke than conventional cigarettes. RJR had already spent more than $300 million on Premier and planned to spend a total of more than $1 billion on development and marketing.

In retrospect, Premier seemed doomed from the start. For one thing, RJR couldn't market Premier as a safer cigarette without undermining the industry's long-standing claim that smoking had never been proved unhealthy. Any chance that consumers might think Premier safer was doused by an intense and unexpected lobbying effort by health groups and opponents of smoking. They called the cigarette a "drug-delivery device" and urged that it be regulated by the Food and Drug Administration.

Also, researchers developing and testing the product seemed blind to some fatal flaws, such as the fact that Premier didn't taste right when lighted with a match. It didn't even taste right when lighted by most lighters. The impurities created by anything but a high-quality butane lighter settled in black specks on the cigarette's filter and on smokers' taste buds. Another problem, called the "hernia effect" by some RJR insiders, became apparent in test markets: Smokers often had to inhale furiously to get much smoke.

Even at the time of RJR's 1987 announcement of Premier—eight years after the idea of the "smokeless" cigarette was hatched—the company didn't know how to make the product in a factory. Premier required simultaneous assembly of four parts, instead of the customary two for normal cigarettes.

Although the company's board of directors was behind Premier, directors raised questions at management presentations. But the people in charge of the project never lacked for confidence or answers, according to one board member. "Management would always say, 'We can fix this; we can fix that,'" he recalled. According to another director, the project managers had insisted that they could make Premier taste however they wanted it to taste.

Wishful thinking prevailed. Everybody knew that the product had serious flaws. But many RJR managers had convinced themselves that the problems were temporary. Like decaffeinated coffee or the early diet sodas, Premier was considered a "deprivation product" that had benefits for which consumers would make big trade-offs. One tobacco employee said that she hated Premier the first time around but stuck with it until she finally began to like it. A former senior RJR scientist, who had helped mastermind Premier, added, "What happens is you get into a euphoria where you con yourself."

Source: Adapted from P. Waldman, "RJR Nabisco Abandons 'Smokeless' Cigarette, Morris and P. Waldman, "The Death of Premier." Reprinted by permission of *Wall Street Journal,* © 1989 Dow Jones & Company, Inc. All Rights Reserved Worldwide.

1. What errors or breakdowns in decision making are evident in this case?
2. What are some of the factors that led to those breakdowns?
3. What might have been done, or should be done in the future, to improve decision making at RJR Nabisco?

CASE 7-2
No Bosses

At a time when many companies in the U.S. are shrinking their hierarchies, W. L. Gore & Associates has never had much of a hierarchy to shrink. A family-held plastics company best known for the fabric, Gore-Tex, Gore represents a 33-year experiment in form-free management. Wilbert Gore was a Du Pont chemist who was frustrated because the firm wouldn't market his invention, Teflon coating for electrical wires. He left Du Pont and founded Gore with his wife, Genevieve. Vowing to avoid stifling hierarchies, he replaced the traditional chain of command with a system in which any staffer can take an idea or complaint to any other, regardless of level.

Gore's unconventional character is reflected in its remarkable variety of products, from waterproof sports wear to sutures for cardiovascular surgery, from synthetic bagpipes to fabric for space suits, from fiberoptics to filters.

Jobs are relatively fluid at Gore. For example, Ara Atkinson was a production-line worker at Gore. A co-worker noticed her knack for drawing and knew salespeople who needed artwork for presentations, but there was no artist's job Atkinson could apply for. At most companies she would have been stifled, but Gore helped her create the job of illustrating sales materials and brochures and paid for her commercial art training in night school. Her salary more than tripled.

There are no fancy titles at Gore; each of the 5,300 employees is an "associate." Robert Gore, the son of the firm's founders, accepts the title of president only for legal reasons. There are no perks such as executive parking spots or large offices. The size of plants is limited to 250 workers to encourage innovation, maintain workforce morale, and enhance customer service.

Instead of bosses, "leaders" head teams in plants or staff departments. These leaders must share the power to hire, discipline or fire associates with peer committees, personnel staffers, and "sponsors." Every employee has a sponsor, a mentor who serves as counselor and advocate. As part of the pay-setting process, groups of associates meet every six months to rank their peers in terms of contributions.

Leaders cannot give orders. Instead, they can only seek commitments from associates. For instance, when Daniel Johnson wanted to develop uses for Gore-Tex in printed-circuit boards for high-speed computers, he couldn't require anyone to work on his project. Instead, he persuaded a few associates to assist. Others then became interested and joined in, and the project team grew until it had over a dozen members. The product was scheduled to reach the market in 1991, and Johnson earned the role of leader of the electronics division.

Gore's policies and practices create some problems in dealing with the rest of the business world. For instance, one employee who needed to talk with Wall Street investment houses concerning an employee stock option plan wasn't taken seriously because he didn't have a fancy title. At Gore's suggestion, he called himself president and got the appointments he needed. Another associate's business card reads "supreme commander."

This approach has worked well for Gore. Despite recent legal challenges to some of its key patents, the company has sales of about $700 million a year, with 41 plants in six countries. It is estimated to rank in the top 5% of major companies in terms of return on assets and equity. Sales have about tripled since 1984, and are expected to top $1 billion by 1995.

Sources: Based in part on J. Weber, "No Bosses. And Even 'Leaders' Can't Give Orders," *Business Week,* 10 December 1990, pp. 196–197, and "Gore's Growth Belies Small-Company Feel," *Microwaves and RF,* July 1991, p. 134.

1. Would you describe the organizational design at W. L. Gore & Associates as mechanistic or organic? Why?
2. Which managerial roles may be especially important at Gore? Which may be relatively unimportant?
3. What bases of power are most likely to be relied on at W. L. Gore & Associates? Which might be ineffective?
4. What are some probable advantages of the management and organizational design at Gore? What are some likely disadvantages?

OBJECTIVES

After studying this chapter, you should be able to:

1 Characterize the impact of Scientific Management and the Hawthorne studies..

2 Describe how Maslow's need hierarchy, McClelland's manifest needs, learning theory, and expectancy theory relate to worker motivation.

3 Discuss categories of rewards and suggest guidelines for administering rewards.

4 Discuss job satisfaction and identify costs of employee dissatisfaction.

5 Explain the roles of leadership and identify important behaviors of leaders.

6 Identify costs and benefits of conflict in organizations and cite approaches to conflict management.

7 Explain why job redesign might be needed, and describe four approaches to job redesign.

8 Discuss how goal setting can be used to enhance worker motivation.

9 Describe ways that teams are being used in organizations.

CHAPTER 8

Motivating Employees

Katherine Swanson had been a manager long enough to have dealt with most motivational problems. She had learned to anticipate the special problems of her various subordinates, and she was generally able to get more productivity out of them than most of her peers had thought possible.

But now Katherine was frustrated. One of her subordinates, Don Aiken, had for over a decade been a self-starter, highly motivated and reliable. In the past year, however, things had changed. Don was often absent, seemed to do just enough to get by, complained about simple assignments, and generally seemed like a completely different person. Katherine had reluctantly taken him aside and leveled with him about the changes in his behavior. "You've been my best performer," she said. "I've always been able to count on you. What's wrong?"

Don glared at Katherine. "Can you blame me?" he asked. "I've worked here for almost 11 years. Eleven years of the same routine, the same deadlines, the same pressures. What do I get for it? I'm taken for granted. I'm burned out."

This chapter focuses on the roles of people within organizations. We'll begin by looking at early perspectives on motivation. Then we will discuss four views of human motivation, consider work rewards, and examine the nature and consequences of job satisfaction. We will then turn to the topics of leadership and conflict management. Finally, we will examine how job redesign and goal setting can be used to motivate employees.

There is no question that people are important to organizations. For one thing, people make the decisions; for another, they are expensive. Labor accounts for 25 percent of the cost of making an automobile and nearly 60 percent of the cost of publishing a book. Treating employees fairly, motivating them effectively, managing any conflicts, and designing jobs intelligently can lead to big gains for any firm.

EARLY PERSPECTIVES ON MOTIVATION

In this section, we will consider two early approaches to motivating employees. Scientific Management and the Hawthorne studies have had a tremendous impact on our understanding of motivation and management.

Scientific Management

Until the early 1900s, the human element was almost ignored by people writing about organizations. It was assumed that in a well-designed and well-run company, employees would act like any other pieces of machinery: They would be there when needed, and they would do as they were told. In 1911, however, Frederick Taylor introduced **Scientific Management.** The aim of Scientific Management was to find the "one best way" to perform any given task, such as the best way to make pins or the best way to shovel coal.

Scientific Management an attempt to find the "one best way" to perform a job; this approach emphasized efficiency and led to simplified jobs.

For instance, when Taylor tried to find the best way to shovel coal at Bethlehem Steel Company, he first experimented to determine the shovel load that would lead to maximum productivity without overworking the employee. He also tested shovels of various sizes and shapes to find the best tool for the job. After four months of experimentation, he concluded that a 21-pound load was optimal. Another aspect of the best way to do a job was to find the best person for the job, and Taylor stressed the importance of people in organizations. At Bethlehem Steel, the best workers were selected on the basis of their past performance and were then trained to use each of eight to ten different types of shovels for different types of coal. The cost of handling coal was cut in half, and workers' wages increased by 60 percent over what they had been earning.[1]

Taylor was talking mostly about the kinds of jobs for which strength or hand speed were important. Although he did consider the human element, nowadays Taylor's views are generally not considered very humane. Taylor emphasized worker efficiency, not satisfaction. For instance, he wrote that the kind of person who made a good pig-iron handler was "of the type of the ox." Scientific Management led to simplified jobs, with each worker going through the same few motions time after time—a boring but efficient process. The assembly line is a grim monument to Scientific Management.

The Hawthorne Studies

Despite the work of Taylor and a few early psychologists, it was not until the 1930s that the importance of the human element was really recognized. Then, in a series of studies at the Hawthorne Plant of the Western Electric Company, researchers tried to determine which level of lighting, length of workday, and length of rest periods would maximize worker productivity. What they found was surprising. As the level of light in the plant was increased, the level of production went up. But when the lights were later turned down, even to the level of moonlight, productivity kept going up!

It might be expected that productivity would increase as the lights were brightened and then decrease as the lights were lowered. What could account for the actual result? The researchers concluded that workers became more productive because they felt special. They had been singled out for the experiment and wanted to do a good job to show that they were worthy of the attention. The term **Hawthorne effect** is now used to refer to this change in behavior that results from being singled out for attention. In a more general sense, the Haw-

Hawthorne effect   a change in behavior occurring because someone is singled out for attention.

thorne studies showed that distinctly human factors may be as important as pay or working conditions in motivating employees.

THEORIES OF MOTIVATION

need   *something that people require.*

satisfaction   *the state of need fulfillment.*

motivation   *the attempt to satisfy a need.*

All people have needs. A **need** is something that people require. **Satisfaction** is the condition of need fulfillment, such as when a hungry person eats, or when a person driven by the desire for success finally achieves that goal. **Motivation** is the attempt to satisfy a need. The practice of management is largely concerned with motivating employees to work harder, more efficiently, and more intelligently. We will look at four theories of motivation and at how each relates to motivating people in the workplace. We will see that these theories have some common implications for rewarding employees.

Maslow's Need Hierarchy

Psychologist Abraham Maslow did much of the classic work on motivation theory. He believed that the key to motivating people is understanding that they are motivated by needs, which are arranged in a hierarchy of importance. This hierarchy is known as Maslow's **need hierarchy** (see Figure 8-1). Maslow theorized that people seek to satisfy needs at the lowest level of the hierarchy before trying to satisfy needs on the next higher level. What needs motivate a person depends on where that person is on the hierarchy at that time.

need hierarchy   *Maslow's view that people are motivated by needs, and that needs are arranged in a hierarchy: Needs at "lower" levels must be satisfied before needs at "higher" levels become motivating.*

Types of Needs.   Maslow believed that motivation should be examined in terms of five sets of needs.

1.   *Physiological:* the need for food, sleep, water, air, and sex.
2.   *Security:* the need for safety, family stability, and economic security.
3.   *Social or affiliation:* the need to belong, to interact with others, to have friends, and to love and be loved.
4.   *Esteem:* the need for respect and recognition from others.
5.   *Self-actualization:* the need to realize one's potential, to grow, to be creative, and to accomplish.

FIGURE 8-1   Maslow's Need Hierarchy

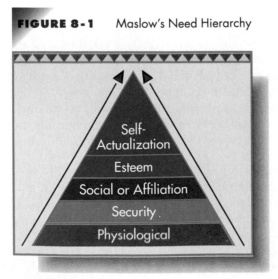

These IBM employees clearly enjoy working together. Which of Maslow's levels of needs do you think are being satisfied by their jobs?

Maslow argued that as we satisfy any of these five sets of needs, that set becomes less important to us and motivates us less. Eating, for example, satisfies the physiological need of hunger and leaves us less interested in food. In the same way, the need for affiliation and friendship is strongest for someone who feels excluded. Once this person makes friends, the need to belong becomes less important.

Climbing the Hierarchy. Maslow believed that these needs were arranged in a hierarchy from "lowest" to "highest," as shown in Figure 8-1. Maslow suggested that we "climb" the hierarchy. That is, we first satisfy our basic physiological needs. Only when we have done so are we motivated by the needs at the next higher level of the hierarchy: the need for safety and security. When this group of needs is met, we move on to the next level, and so on.

Lessons from Maslow's Hierarchy. Maslow's view of motivation shows that people have a variety of needs. People work for many reasons besides the paycheck that buys them food and shelter. They work so that they can be with others, gain respect, and realize their potential. Management must consider these needs when it designs reward systems for employees. Also, Maslow's hierarchy emphasizes that people differ in the needs that are currently most important to them. For example, a worker faced with heavy mortgage payments may focus primarily on security needs. Another, with the mortgage paid off, may now be more concerned about social needs. While the former employee might be strongly motivated by money, the latter may be more motivated by being included in a group. Finally, the hierarchy also makes clear the distinction between need importance and need satisfaction.

Maslow's need hierarchy provides useful perspectives for understanding motivation, and it has been widely accepted. However, more recent research suggests that it is not an entirely accurate portrayal of the way people's needs work.

For instance, satisfying needs at the top of the hierarchy generally does not lead to a decrease in motivation. Instead, people who are able to self-actualize become *more* motivated to take on self-actualizing activities. Also, the climb up the hierarchy is rather unpredictable; once we've satisfied needs at the lowest levels, needs at *any* of the other levels may become most important to us.

McClelland's Manifest Needs

Another way to look at motivation was offered by management theorist David McClelland. Whereas Maslow argued that people were born with a particular set of needs, which become more or less important over time depending on their satisfaction, McClelland believed that needs were acquired through the interaction of the individual with his or her environment.[3] Because these needs are not innate but rather become apparent over time, they are referred to as **manifest needs.** McClelland focused on three manifest needs: the need for achievement, the need for affiliation, and the need for power over others.

manifest needs *needs that are acquired through the interaction of the individual with his or her environment.*

need for achievement *an acquired need manifested by the desire to do well regardless of the goal pursued.*

Need for Achievement. People with a strong **need for achievement** want to do well no matter which goal they pursue. They also desire personal responsibility and want quick feedback about how well they have done at a given task. Some jobs, such as those in sales, are best for people with a strong need for achievement because of the responsibility and feedback they provide. The need for achievement, however, is not desirable in all work situations. It has been found that Nobel Prize winners, who conduct research over many years and receive very slow feedback, have only an average need for achievement.

McClelland argued that the need for achievement can be developed in people by getting them to believe that they can change and by helping them to set

For football coach John Pont, the need for achievement is the main motivator. Pont had retired from a prestigious position at a major college, but he came back to take on the challenge of motivating the players at the College of Mount St. Joseph in Cincinnati.

personal goals. This process also includes learning to "speak the language of achievement." By this we mean that people can be taught to think, talk, and act as if they were achievement oriented.

In practice, McClelland was successful in developing the need for achievement. For example, after he conducted a training session in India, the achievement activity of the trainees nearly doubled. Achievement activity meant starting a new business or sharply increasing company profits. One trainee raised enough money to put up the tallest building in Bombay—the Everest Apartments.

Need for Affiliation. The **need for affiliation** is the desire to establish and maintain friendly and warm relations with other people. It is much like Maslow's social needs. People with a strong need for affiliation welcome tasks requiring interaction with others, while those having less of this need may prefer to work alone.

> **need for affiliation**   an acquired need manifested by a desire to establish and maintain friendly and warm relations with other people.

Need for Power. The **need for power** is the desire to control other people, to influence their behavior, and to be responsible for them.[4] McClelland saw the need for achievement as most important for entrepreneurs and the need for power as most important for managers of large organizations. Those who have a strong need for power can try to dominate others for the sake of dominating, deriving satisfaction from conquering others. Or they can satisfy their need for power through means that help the organization, such as leading a group to develop and achieve goals. McClelland felt that the need for power, when exhibited in ways that help the organization, was the most important factor in managerial success. People who have a strong need for achievement might be overly concerned with personal achievement, and those with a strong need for affiliation might not take necessary actions if they could offend the group.

> **need for power**   an acquired need manifested by a desire to control other people, to influence their behavior, and to be responsible for them.

Lessons from McClelland's Perspective. McClelland's work gives us an expanded view of workers' needs. It also suggests that appropriate training might actually *develop* employees' needs in ways that might benefit both their careers and the organization. This is an important difference from Maslow's theory. Also, McClelland's perspective helps identify the characteristics of people who may be most suitable for particular kinds of jobs in organizations.

Learning Theory

A third approach to the study of motivation is called **learning theory.** The kind of learning theory used in organizations relies on the use of rewards and punishments to reinforce or change behavior.[5] This approach is based on the theory that the consequences of an act determine whether the act will be repeated. For example, if a small boy burns himself on a hot stove, he will be less likely to touch the hot stove again.

> **learning theory**   an approach to motivation, stating that the consequences of an act determine whether the act will be repeated.

Use of Rewards and Punishment. The **law of effect** states that behavior that is rewarded tends to be repeated, while behavior that is not rewarded tends not to be repeated. Thus, if managers want employees to behave in a certain way, they should reward them for acting in that way. For instance, if a company wants employees to be creative, it should be sure to reward creative behavior. If it fails to reward creativity, creative behavior is less likely to be repeated.

> **law of effect**   a learning theory law: behavior that is rewarded will be repeated, and behavior that is not rewarded will not be repeated.

Advocates of learning theory favor the use of rewards, rather than punishment, whenever possible. Unfortunately, managers sometimes find it necessary to punish behavior that must be stopped. However, although punishment may stop the undesirable behavior, it should probably be used only as a last resort. Punishment is likely to embitter employees, leaving them dissatisfied and resentful. Also, managers who frequently use punishment may find that subordinates obey their orders only when the managers are present. When they are absent, the employees may secretly rebel. Finally, since punishment only stops undesirable behavior, the task of increasing desired behavior remains.

Rewarding Poor Behavior. Unfortunately, managers often unknowingly reward poor behavior, thus causing it to be repeated. For instance, some bosses routinely "give in" to subordinates who make unwarranted demands in the hope that those demands will stop. In fact, the demands are thereby rewarded and are thus *more* likely to be repeated. As another example, a primary goal of orphanages is to place children in good homes.[6] But since the number of children in the orphanage determines the size of the budget, the size of the staff, and the director's prestige, the orphanage is actually rewarded for *not* placing children in homes. Thus, undesired behavior is rewarded, and the orphanage is less likely to try to find homes for its children. Too often, managers fail to recognize that they are "hoping for A, but rewarding B."

If, for some reason, we find that we have been rewarding poor behavior, we should stop doing so. Once that behavior is no longer rewarded, it will gradually stop occurring. The disappearance of an unrewarded behavior is called **extinction.**

extinction *the disappearance of an unrewarded behavior.*

Lessons of Learning Theory. Learning theory tells us that we should identify the behaviors that we want to see repeated or eliminated, and that we should then use rewards and punishments appropriately to reinforce or eliminate those behaviors. Learning theory also makes it clear that we are influencing behavior *anytime* we reward or punish, whether we intend to or not. For instance, suppose we reward everyone the same, rather than giving more rewards to high performers than to low performers. Since we are not rewarding higher performance, such performance is likely to decrease.

Many people see learning theory as frightening and unethical. They fear that rewards and punishments may be used to make employees blindly pursue management's goals, or to push them to exhaustion. They are also concerned that since rewards and punishments may cause employees to respond without thinking, learning theory may override free will.

Advocates of learning theory believe that managers are always manipulating behavior anyway, whether they are aware of it or not, and that the trick is to do it right. According to this view, we can reward whatever we want—quality of output, creativity, or service to society. The key is to reward desired behavior, not undesired behavior. Recent approaches to the application of learning theory in organizations rely heavily on use of social learning. **Social learning** is learning that occurs through social channels, such as conversations with the boss or with co-workers, television, memos, and so on. Thus, a parent may tell a child not to touch a hot stove rather than waiting until the child is burned; learning can occur without actual experience of the consequence. Similarly, a manager can tell his or her subordinates what sorts of behavior will be rewarded or punished. Application of social learning treats employees as intelligent individuals who are capable of adopting appropriate behaviors, once they understand which behaviors will be rewarded or punished and which will not.

social learning *learning that occurs through social channels.*

INTERNATIONAL EXAMPLE

40 Worst

In China, a land of guaranteed employment, there is plenty of recognition for a job well done. You might be named a "model worker" and awarded a television set as a special bonus. Or, like proud employees at the Xian Instruments Factory near Xian, China, you might be handed a gold plaque declaring your firm a "civilized enterprise."

But, in a country that abhors the sordid capitalist enterprise of firing, what do you do when the workers of the world won't work? The Chinese are choosing a traditional medicine: When all else fails, try humiliation.

Amid much fanfare recently, the Xian Department Store, which has about 800 employees, publicly named its "40 Worst Shop Assistants," a move meant to spur better performance from the tardy and the rude. The large retail operation in this medieval walled city even went a step further: It made the transgressor's workplace his pillory, hanging a plaque overhead, complete with picture, that proclaimed him a member of the "40 Worst."

"It's the only system we've found to pressure workers to do better," says Bai Shouzheng, the store's burly Communist Party secretary. He flashes a broad smile, showing off a solid row of silver teeth. "Those designated the 'worst' feel embarrassed," he reasons. "Otherwise, our efforts would have no effect."

Is it working? Listen to Chen Jie, a dimpled, 19-year-old salesclerk sanctioned for snapping at a customer. "I accept my punishment, since my error hurt the store's reputation," says Ms. Chen, who sells synthetic-fur coats. "Today, I view my little three-foot shop counter as a window on socialist civilization."

Consider the novel use of punishment in the International Example on this page. What behaviors is management trying to change? How might employees in the United States react to such humiliation?

Expectancy Theory

Another theory of motivation, **expectancy theory,** focuses on employees' desires and expectations. According to expectancy theory, motivating employees to perform well on the job depends on at least three things. First, the rewards given to employees should be what they want. If they don't want them, why should they try to earn them? Second, employees must be made to believe that better performance leads to rewards. If not, why do better? Third, they must believe that trying harder results in improved performance. If it doesn't, why try harder?

Clear-cut as these guides may seem, they are often forgotten. Managers sometimes assume that they know what employees want. Or they may give everyone the same rewards, no matter how well they do. Failure to reward properly can result in lack of employee motivation.

expectancy theory a theory of motivation stating that employees will be motivated to engage in an act only if they feel they can accomplish the act and that accomplishment of the act will lead to desired outcomes.

REWARDING EMPLOYEES

Our discussion of theories of motivation make it clear that different people may want different rewards, and that the way rewards are tied to behaviors is important. Let's now look at some uses of rewards, types of rewards, and guidelines for administering rewards.

Uses of Rewards

Remember that rewards may be given to reinforce any behaviors management would like to continue, including quantity or quality of performance, attendance, timeliness, creativity, and ethical behavior. For instance, Federal Express grants awards of up to $25,000 to employees who suggest useful innovations, and managers can give employees gifts and dinner parties for work beyond the call of duty. Clearly, these rewards are intended to encourage individual creativity and performance.[7] In other cases, rewards may be used to attract employees to the company and to retain them. For example, J. P. Morgan bank gives its employees free lunches. Hewlett-Packard has ten company-owned recreation areas, including mountain resorts in California and Pennsylvania, a lake resort in Scotland, a ski chalet in the German Alps, and a beach villa in Malaysia.[8] Such rewards help to make a company a good place to work.

Classes of Rewards

It is often helpful for managers to think in terms of the types of rewards they may be able to make available to their subordinates. Two useful ways to classify rewards are by source and by whether or not the reward is financial.

extrinsic rewards
rewards given to an employee by others, such as pay raises, promotions, and other symbols of recognition.

intrinsic rewards rewards related to the job itself and the pleasure and sense of accomplishment that it gives to the employee.

Theory X a theory that assumes workers are lazy and self-indulgent, require constant supervision, and work only because they get paid.

Theory Y a theory that assumes workers are responsible, like to work, and value intrinsic rewards.

financial rewards monetary rewards given to an employee, such as pay and cash bonuses.

nonfinancial rewards
rewards that do not involve money, such as praise, status, and privileges.

Extrinsic and Intrinsic Rewards. Some rewards come from the job itself; others are provided by someone else. **Extrinsic rewards** are rewards given to an employee by someone else—usually someone in management. Pay raises, promotions, and other symbols of recognition are extrinsic rewards. **Intrinsic rewards** relate to the job itself and the pleasure and sense of accomplishment that it gives the employee.

Until fairly recently, many firms and management theorists considered only extrinsic rewards—wages and salary, in particular—in the design of jobs and compensation programs. The reason may have been that employers held what is called a Theory X set of assumptions.[9] According to **Theory X,** people are lazy and self-indulgent, require constant supervision, and work only because they get paid. Employers who accept Theory X as the best explanation of employee motivation tend to watch their workers closely, treat them as inferior, and pay little attention to job satisfaction. Theory X advocates would most likely reward good performers with a pay raise or a bonus. Intrinsic rewards are of little or no concern to managers following Theory X. As an extreme example of Theory X, consider the case of the J.P. Stevens Company. At one time, this textile manufacturer actually employed company spies and watchdogs and even locked employees into their factory rooms! Fortunately, this sort of practice wouldn't be tolerated in today's business world.

The alternative to Theory X is **Theory Y,** which assumes that workers are responsible, like to work, and want intrinsic rewards. Under Theory Y, jobs are designed to be more interesting, and workers are allowed more freedom in the performance of their work. IBM is an example of Theory Y management in practice. At IBM, respect for the individual is a key corporate value, and managers are told to spend a large portion of their time on individual employees' problems. Employees who have good ideas are offered the freedom to develop them. Teams of employees are often given the authority to work by themselves on new projects. Employees respond with commitment and quality work.

Financial and Nonfinancial Rewards. Extrinsic rewards can be **financial** (those involving money) or **nonfinancial** (those not involving money). Several studies have shown that financial rewards are the key influence on choice of jobs and in requests for transfers to other jobs. There are many reasons why money is desirable. One reason is that people get pleasure out of the act of making money. Another is that a pay increase is often coupled with other desirable things, such

Rewards for achievement are not always financial. For example, this executive travels in style aboard the company jet.

as promotions or awards. A key reason, however, is that money enables people to get the other things they want. That is, money can help satisfy needs at all levels in Maslow's need hierarchy. Figure 8-2 shows how money can satisfy these needs.

To be effective, extrinsic rewards need not always involve money. Nonfinancial rewards, such as praise, status, or privileges, can be quite motivating. An example of a nonfinancial reward is a reward in the form of a status symbol. A status symbol may be a new office, a wall plaque, or travel opportunities. Granting a status reward is an inexpensive way for companies to show good employees that they are appreciated. For example, realtors often publish pictures of their most successful salespeople in the local paper. People at all levels of an organization can be motivated by status rewards, because they make them feel important to the company and in the eyes of co-workers.

Another type of nonfinancial reward is granting an employee increased input into management decisions. Many employees want to be involved in decision making. Frequently, giving employees this sense of involvement costs the firm almost nothing, makes employees feel important in the organization, and taps a source of good ideas for the company. One reason that Japanese automobile companies have been so successful is that workers are encouraged to make recommendations to management as to how cars can be produced better and more cheaply. Workers feel that they are part of the team, not just cogs in a machine. At the same time, the company benefits from the valuable ideas of its employees.

Administering Rewards

Rewards, if given properly, can improve job performance. There are at least four guidelines for administering rewards effectively. First, tie rewards directly to the

FIGURE 8-2   How Money Can Satisfy Our Needs

Time Off Work to Write a Book
(Self-Actualization Need)

Our Self Worth and Accomplishment
(Esteem Need)

Money for Social Entertainment
(Social Need)

Purchase of Insurance
(Security Need)

Buying Food
(Physiological Need)

cafeteria-style benefit plans   *benefit plans in which employees can choose from a wide range of alternative benefits, tailoring them to their particular situations.*

behavior that you want repeated. If you want high quality. If you want creativity, reward creativity. Giving people weekly or monthly paychecks rewards them only for showing up for work. Motivating the workforce may require something more. Whether the reward takes the form of a bonus, status, or public praise, it must be tied to the desired behavior to be effective. Second, let employees know what the rewards are and how they can obtain them. Third, reward desired behavior as soon as it occurs. Rewarding a person in June for a job well done in January does little to reinforce the behavior. Fourth, try to tie rewards directly to individual performance. As we'll discuss in the next chapter, there may be benefits to rewarding on the basis of such things as group performance, plant-wide productivity, or even company profits. In general, however, the more closely rewards are linked to things the individual can directly control, the more powerful the motivational effects.

In administering rewards, it is critical to keep in mind that different people desire differing rewards. One way management can learn what rewards employees want is to ask them—through surveys, for example. Then programs and rewards can perhaps be tailored to the individual or group. Another possibility is to use **cafeteria-style benefit plans.** In such plans, employees can choose from a wide range of alternative benefits. For instance, employees of differing ages or marital status may desire different benefits. One employee may choose all salary with no other benefits; another may use part of the total allowance for pension and insurance contributions. Beginning in 1992, Du Pont's 96,000 U.S. employees can choose from a menu of medical, dental, and life insurance options, as well as new offerings such as financial planning.[10]

The Lighter Side (page 199) shows how one company tried to use rewards and punishments to motivate its sales force. How do you think you would react to this "one bean motivation" if you were a high-performing sales manager? If you were not?

JOB SATISFACTION AND DISSATISFACTION

We said earlier that when people's needs are fulfilled, they are satisfied. Conversely, people are dissatisfied when they are unable to fulfill needs important to them. From the point of view of the individual, satisfaction and dissatisfaction are important. Nevertheless, some managers may say, "What I care about is my

One Bean Motivation

The sales department and special events coordinators at the La Costa Hotel and Spa Conference Center sometimes get bizarre requests. Electrolux, the national vacuum cleaner manufacturing company, has to be near the top of the list in originality for its national sales managers' meeting at the resort. At the meeting's dinner banquet, the room was divided with chicken wire, and the company's top-grossing sales managers sat separately from the others during the evening. Caterers decorated one side of the room with tables covered with white cloths, china, silver, and fresh flower centerpieces for those bringing the highest number of sales to the company.

The top sales managers dined on filet mignon, potatoes, asparagus, and chocolate mousse, while their counterparts on the opposite side of the banquet hall ate baked beans and jello, washing their meals down with a cup of hot water laced with a single coffee bean.

Source: From *The Reporter,* newsletter of the La Costa Hotel and Spa Conference Center, Carlsbad, Cal., as reported in *The New Yorker,* 2 January 1984.

employees' behavior—whether they do their jobs well, come to work (and on time), and stay with the firm. These are the things that show up on the 'bottom line,' not whether employees walk around with smiles on their faces. Why should I care about the satisfaction of my subordinates?"

One response to such a statement, of course, is that workers spend half their waking lives on the job. Management has some responsibility to ensure that the hours spent at work are tolerable. What's more, satisfaction *does* affect the bottom line. It does this directly through its impact on such work behaviors as performance, absenteeism, and turnover. It also shows up indirectly through its relationship to job stress.

Satisfaction and Work Behaviors

The evidence regarding the impact of employee satisfaction on work behaviors is clear: Dissatisfied employees are less likely to come to work, arrive on time, and stay with the firm than are satisfied employees. Also, dissatisfied workers are likely to be apathetic about their work, vent their frustration by criticizing the company or going on strike, and produce poor quality work. Further, satisfied employees are likely to go beyond the narrow requirements of the job. They might go out of their way to help co-workers with job-related problems, give extra effort to get the job done on time, and provide valuable ideas.[11] Thus, worker satisfaction influences many important work behaviors. It has been estimated that modest increases in employees' job satisfaction could result in financial benefits to the U.S. of billions of dollars.[12]

The so-called "Monday car" illustrates the costs of employee dissatisfaction. Many workers at U.S. automobile assembly plants are very unhappy with their jobs, seeing themselves as little more than machines. Consequently, many of them do not come to work on Mondays. To keep the assembly line moving, automobile manufacturers have "swing" employees, who move from job to job on the assembly line as they are needed. However, since they often cannot do the job as well as the regular employee, the quality of work suffers. As a result, a "Monday

Business Career

Employee Relations Specialist: Gathers information on workers' feelings about factors that affect morale, motivation, and efficiency. Interviews employees about attitudes toward the work environment and supervision. Discusses problems and possible solutions with management. Enrolls workers in company programs, such as pension and savings plans. Maintains medical, insurance, and other personnel records. *Average Salary: $26,400.*

Workers who are satisfied put a little something extra into their efforts. At the Quincy Market near historic Faneuil Hall in Boston, this young woman shows enthusiasm for her work. Because of her positive attitude toward the job, her employer's balloon sales are up.

car" often comes off the assembly line. These cars are referred to by their eventual owners as "lemons."

Satisfaction and Stress

stress a physiological state in which adrenaline courses into the bloodstream and then to muscles and organs, resulting in feelings of strain or pressure.

burnout a reaction to sustained stress, characterized by physical and emotional exhaustion, feelings of low personal accomplishment, and negative attitudes toward the job, others, and life in general.

Dissatisfying jobs cause stress. **Stress** is a physiological state caused by a complex set of reactions that result in the release of adrenaline into the bloodstream and then to muscles and organs. Such stress leads to a feeling of strain or pressure. People who are under stress for long periods may experience burnout. **Burnout** is a reaction to sustained stress, characterized by physical and mental exhaustion, feelings of low personal accomplishment, and negative attitudes toward the job, others, and life in general. Don Aiken, who complained at the beginning of the chapter about 11 years of routine, deadlines, and pressure, appears to be a victim of such burnout. If Don's boss, Katherine Swanson, wants to deal with his burnout, she must think about ways to make his job more satisfying.

Don's case isn't unique. Burnout and other reactions to stress are common nowadays. In fact, research suggests that job stress is linked not only to psychological problems such as depression and anxiety, but also to physical reactions such as ulcers, high blood pressure, backaches, and heart disease. The cost of stress-related disorders in this country is estimated to be $150 billion annually in health insurance and disability claims.[13]

The National Institute of Occupational Safety and Health (NIOSH) ranked 130 jobs on the basis of stress. Ten of the most stressful and ten of the least stressful jobs are shown in Table 8-1. The jobs on the "most stressful" list typically involve

TABLE 8-1   The Most and Least Stressful Jobs

Most Stressful Jobs	Least Stressful Jobs
Manual Laborer	Clothing Sewer
Secretary	Stockroom Worker
Inspector	Craftsman
Waitress/Waiter	Maid
Clinical Lab Technician	Heavy-Equipment Operator
Farm Owner	Farm Laborer
Miner	Child Care Worker
House Painter	Packer, Wrapper in Shipping
Manager, Administrator	College or University Professor
Foreman	Personnel, Labor Relations

Source: U.S. Department of Health, Education, and Welfare. National Institute for Occupational Safety and Health, *Occupational Stress* (1978).

either direct and constant supervision or a high degree of risk and responsibility. The jobs on the "least stressful" list involve freedom from direct supervision and a slower work pace.

Partly because of the impact of stress, companies are thinking more about the "wellness" of their employees. That is, they are just as concerned with keeping their employees healthy as they are with taking care of them when they are ill. The Sentry Insurance Company headquarters has a "quiet room," where employees can go to relax. The company also has an exercise room that is open to all employees. A voluntary wellness program at Johnson & Johnson, called "Live for Life," has paid off in estimated annual savings of $378 per employee by lowering absenteeism and slowing the rise in the company's health-care expenses. Employees joining the program complete a questionnaire that identifies health risks they face and suggests actions (such as exercise, dieting, or quitting smoking) to reduce them. At the company's headquarters, employees can work out in a gym, select "heart healthy" foods in the cafeteria, and check their weight in the restrooms. They are even encouraged to drop hints to fellow workers about losing weight or giving up smoking.[14]

Companies have adopted a variety of other approaches to reducing their employees' stress. In 1990, in anticipation of a 12 percent workforce reduction, Chase Manhattan Corp. initiated a program of lunchtime support groups, led by professional therapists, for employees feeling stress. At Hoffmann-LaRoche Inc., employees receive after-hours instruction in stress management techniques such as meditation and breathing exercises.[15] Ovation Marketing Inc. even provides an in-house professional masseuse to reduce employees' stress and increase their creativity.

LEADERSHIP

leadership *the use of influence to direct and coordinate the activities of a group toward goal attainment.*

Leadership is the use of influence to direct and coordinate the activities of a group toward goal attainment. Leadership plays a major role in the motivation of employees and in the direction of the firm. In this section, we will see that leaders must make many choices regarding their behaviors. Should they delegate authority to subordinates or make all decisions themselves? Should their behaviors reflect concern for employees, for productivity, or for both? Should they worry about inspiring and stimulating subordinates? These are important choices; research shows that leadership affects worker satisfaction, motivation, and performance.[16]

Autocratic and Democratic Approaches

One important dimension of leadership is the degree to which the leader involves subordinates in decision making. **Autocratic leaders** make decisions themselves, without input from their subordinates. **Democratic leaders** let subordinates participate in decision making. Autocratic and democratic leadership styles differ only in the extent to which decision-making authority is delegated to others. That is, democratic leaders are not necessarily more sensitive or caring than autocratic leaders. There are "benevolent autocrats" and uncaring democrats.

autocratic leaders *leaders who make decisions themselves, without inputs from their subordinates.*

democratic leaders *leaders who allow subordinates to participate in decision making.*

When employees participate in decision making, they tend to be more satisfied with their work and more accepting of the decisions that are made. Also, decision quality is likely to improve. More points of view usually lead to better understanding of the problems and thus better solutions. However, when a decision must be made quickly, or when employees lack information or simply do not want to participate in decision making, it may be necessary to make a decision in an autocratic way.

Consideration and Initiating Structure

In addition to delegation of decision-making authority, two other sets of behaviors are essential to effective leadership: consideration and initiating structure. The term **consideration** refers to behaviors that show the leader's friendship, trust, respect, and warmth. For instance, Carl Reinhardt, Chairman and President of Wells Fargo Bank, eliminated time cards because he felt that they insulted employees. He said, "If we don't trust them, they shouldn't be here." He encourages staff to enter his office to talk at any time, and he gives people freedom to act.

consideration *leader behaviors that show friendship, trust, respect, and warmth.*

The term **initiating structure** refers to how a leader defines and structures the way subordinates do their jobs. Giving orders, providing step-by-step directions, and carefully monitoring subordinates' performance are examples of initiating structure. Andrew Grove, President of Intel Corp., shows this orientation. Grove believes that the output of all managers can be measured, and he emphasizes results. He pays careful attention to the details of projects and regularly checks on their progress.

initiating structure *leader behaviors that define and structure the way subordinates do their jobs.*

Unlike autocratic and democratic styles, which are opposites, consideration and initiating structure are unrelated. A leader can be high in one, in both, or in neither. Leaders who exhibit high levels of consideration usually have subordinates who are satisfied. Leaders who exhibit high levels of initiating structure often have productive subordinates. Research suggests that successful leaders are concerned with both task accomplishment and the fulfillment of their subordinates' needs.

Transformational Leadership

The leader behaviors we have discussed to this point are important. However, they fail to address matters such as inspiration, vision, and stimulation, which many people consider central to successful leadership. Leaders exhibiting these qualities are called **transformational leaders.** They motivate followers to do more than they expected to do. They arouse enthusiasm, faith, loyalty, pride, and trust in themselves and their aims. They also encourage followers to transcend self-interests for the sake of the team or organization. Such leaders transform both their followers and the organizations they lead.[17]

Transformational leaders exhibit **charisma** (a Greek word meaning "divinely inspired gift"). Over 60 years ago, Max Weber wrote that charismatic leaders were perceived by subordinates to possess exceptional qualities that set them apart from ordinary people. Weber said such leaders "reveal a transcendent mission or course of action which may itself be appealing to the potential followers, but which is acted upon because the followers believe their leader is extraordinarily gifted."[18] In the business world, Lee Iacocca of Chrysler, Gordon McGovern of Campbell Soup, and Roberto Goizueta of Coca-Cola have been described as charismatic.

Transformational leadership has been shown to be associated with effectiveness of the leader's unit and subordinates' satisfaction. It seems to be especially important at times of organizational birth or rebirth.

The Profile of Fran Tarkenton (page 204) describes his leadership style as a professional football quarterback and how that style is reflected in his role as founder and head of a management consulting firm. Clearly, Tarkenton is a believer in a democratic leadership style. Most observers of his career would probably also agree that Tarkenton—and perhaps all successful quarterbacks—also displayed characteristics of transformational leadership, such as inspiring and stimulating his teammates to arouse their enthusiasm and trust.

transformational leaders leaders with behaviors and qualities that motivate followers to do more than they expected to do by inspiring enthusiasm, faith, loyalty, and pride and trust and encourage them to transcend their self-interests.

charisma from the Greek word meaning "divinely inspired gift;" charismatic leaders are seen by subordinates as being extraordinary, and they inspire subordinates to believe in a larger mission.

MANAGING CONFLICT

All organizations experience conflict from time to time. How conflict is managed determines whether it is motivating or destructive. Certainly, there are many costs of conflict. It can eat up resources, divert attention from organizational goals, and disturb necessary coordination. It can also create resentment that may lead to further conflict. On the other hand, a company without any conflict would probably be stagnant and uncreative. Conflict leads to new ideas and to change; it can be a motivating force. It may also be therapeutic, letting employees vent their frustrations. Also, conflict between groups can motivate members of each group and make the groups more cohesive. The challenge is not to eliminate conflict but to make sure that conflict is successfully managed.

Causes of Conflict

There are many potential causes of conflict. For instance, competition for scarce resources (a fixed budget or a prized promotion) can cause conflict. Conflict may also result from disagreements among employees about desirable goals or about ways to achieve goals. Communication barriers and unclear responsibilities can also produce conflict.

Fran Tarkenton

Fran Tarkenton, long known for his skill in quarterbacking NFL football teams, is now helping guide firms to greater productivity and success. With energy, openness, and personal involvement, Fran has led many successful lives.

Fran's football life put him in the public eye. A star at the University of Georgia, he led the Bulldogs to the Orange Bowl and was voted All-American. He went on to play 18 years in the National Football League as quarterback for the Minnesota Vikings and then the New York Giants. He led the Vikings to Super Bowls in 1973, 1975, and 1976 and was voted the league's most valuable player in 1975. When he retired from professional football, he had thrown more touchdown passes than any quarterback in NFL history. He has the most completions in league history; he is first in yards gained passing; and he has been elected to Football's Hall of Fame.

Fran has always understood the importance of motivation. In the huddle, he employed participatory management. For instance, he would sometimes let linemen suggest plays because they were closer to the action than the coaches on the sidelines.

Fran's activities have been varied, to say the least. He was a member of the ABC Monday Night Football broadcast team and was host to the TV shows "That's Incredible!" and "Saturday Night Live." Fran is also a successful author. His book *Playing to Win—Strategies for Business Success* was made into a movie by NFL Films. Another book, *How to Motivate People,* is a step-by-step guide to greater productivity. For a change of pace, Fran wrote a mystery novel, *Murder at the Super Bowl.*

Even during his years as a star athlete, Fran Tarkenton always considered himself to be primarily an entrepreneur. Once, while on a trip, he got the idea that airline ticket envelopes could be used for advertising. He formed a company and spent five weeks in a hotel room selling $7.5 million in advertising.

In 1970, Fran started his management consulting firm, Behavioral Systems, Inc. His college major had been business administration. Today, his firm is called the Tarkenton Productivity Group and has 50 clients. Its 63 employees include two Ph.D.s and 20 people who have master's degrees in business administration or behavioral sciences.

One subsidiary of the Tarkenton Productivity Group, called Tarkenton and Company, specializes in training and the human side of productivity. It helps companies set up worker problem-solving groups (called "quality circles") and self-managed work teams made up of workers who can hire, fire, and set work schedules. It also helps firms put together compensation programs that are linked to workers' productivity improvements.

In addition, Fran is chairman and CEO of KnowledgeWare, Inc., producers of advanced software for information systems development. He is partner and chairman of Tarkenton & Hughes advertising/marketing communications, as well as chairman and CEO of the Tarkenton Insurance Group, administrators of payroll deduction insurance plans. He has been elected to the board of directors of the Coca-Cola bottling company, Coca-Cola Enterprises, Inc., and Gen-Mar, the world's largest pleasure boat company.

Fran Tarkenton has proven that some of the same skills that led to his great success in football can play an important role in the business world. Now, instead of barking signals, he uses terms such as "human performance," "feedback," and "reinforcement," but the result is still a winning team.

Approaches to Reducing Conflict

When the level of conflict gets too high, the task of management is to reduce it. One way to do this is to emphasize larger goals on which the conflicting parties can agree. Improved communications, clarification of job responsibilities, and development of employees' negotiating skills may also help. Sometimes, third parties can serve as mediators to help manage disputes. Another option is simply to separate the conflicting parties. On the other hand, it is sometimes helpful to do just the opposite—bring the parties together so that they can get to know each other's perspective and practice cooperation. Two nonprofit groups in the Pacific Northwest used this approach to smooth the waters between environmental and timber interests, who were battling over preservation of timberland for the spotted owl. Ten men who were central to the fight, including a mill owner, a logger, a scientist, and a government official, agreed to spend three days guiding an old wooden sailboat through the San Juan Islands in Puget Sound. According to one of the organizers, "It's a cooperative effort to be on the boat, and that spills over into any kind of discussion."[19]

Approaches to Generating Productive Conflict

On the other hand, when there is not enough conflict, more can be generated in several ways. These conflict-inducing techniques are meant to overcome employee complacency, lethargy, and overconfidence. For example, sales contests create competition among marketing employees. Uncertainty can be induced by assigning new tasks, hiring new personnel, or changing the reward system. A **devil's advocate** can be given the task of finding the faults in proposed actions, so as to avoid a situation in which a group fails to evaluate its choices critically. Or individuals can act as scapegoats, coming into a situation to make unpopular but needed changes. For example, a CEO who feels that employees in one department are doing just enough to get by may assign a tough boss to the department, to "shake things up." The new boss would introduce needed changes and "take the heat" from employees they might upset. Once the changes have been implemented, the boss may be replaced.

devil's advocate an individual who is given the task of finding faults in a proposed action in order to induce necessary conflict.

JOB REDESIGN

Albert Camus wrote, "Without work, all life goes rotten. But when work is soulless, life stifles and dies." What determines whether a job is exciting and satisfying or soulless and brutalizing? Can management design jobs to be meaningful and satisfying to workers and also help the company achieve its goals?

Job redesign involves changing the scheduling or nature of employees' task-related activities in order to make them more satisfying and motivating. We will consider four contemporary approaches to job redesign: job enrichment, flextime, job sharing, and the 4/40 workweek.

job redesign changes in the nature or schedule of an employee's task-related activities.

Job Enrichment

Job enrichment is job redesign that gives employees more responsibility for the overall job. The goal of job enrichment is to make jobs more satisfying and motivating to employees. It is hoped that greater satisfaction and motivation will translate into reduced absenteeism and turnover and improved performance.

job enrichment an approach to job redesign that gives employees more responsibility for the overall job.

Job enrichment originated as a reaction to Scientific Management. Earlier, we said that Scientific Management's emphasis on the "one best way" to do a job resulted in extremely simplified work tasks. An assembly or manufacturing process was broken down into parts, and each worker was given only a small part of the overall work. The worker performed this part over and over again. Assembly-line jobs in an automobile plant are an example of such routine, simplified jobs. A worker may be responsible for tightening one bolt on each engine that passes on the conveyer belt. The idea behind such jobs is that workers have less trouble learning their jobs, do not waste time moving from one part of the job to another, and can easily be replaced if necessary.

However, such jobs lead to boredom, dissatisfaction, and other negative outcomes. This concern is reflected in a Saab advertisement from the 1970s, shown in Figure 8-3. In an enriched job, on the other hand, individual employees do a large part of the overall job rather than just a small piece of it. They are expected to make more decisions and take responsibility for doing the job well. Employees with enriched jobs have more control over their work lives and find the job more meaningful. Such employees are generally more satisfied with their work, show less absenteeism and turnover, and produce higher-quality work than those with simplified jobs.

Generally speaking, the more highly trained the workforce is, the more responsibility management can give the employees. As an example, many salespeople are simply given a list of possible customers as well as instructions about what to say during the sales call. If the sales force were well trained, however, the job of selling could be enriched by allowing salespeople to determine sales objectives and selling strategies for themselves, to decide which customers deserve extra attention, and to schedule their sales calls for the day.

Flextime

flextime *a flexible work schedule that allows employees to choose their own work hours, within specified guidelines.*

Another way jobs can be improved is through flextime. **Flextime** is a flexible work schedule that allows employees to choose their own work hours, within specified guidelines. Employees are expected to work a certain number of hours during a core work period in the middle of the day. Beyond that, they are free to decide when to come to work and when to leave, as long as they are at work for the total number of hours defined as a full day by company policy. Under flextime, one employee may decide to arrive at work at 6 A.M. and leave at 3 P.M. Another might arrive at 10 A.M. and leave at 7 P.M.

Many employees like the idea of flextime because it gives them more freedom and control over their own time. "Morning people" can choose to come in early. People can adjust their work schedules to accommodate activities outside of work. Flextime has proven particularly useful for young families. It enables working parents to get the children off to school or day care before coming to work, or to leave work early enough to attend a child's soccer game.

One company that has pioneered flextime is Control Data Corp. (CDC). CDC managers realize that their employees will work better if they can schedule work according to the availability of child care, bus or train times, and the work schedules of other family members. Flextime has solved this problem and has kept motivation and productivity consistently high.

Job Sharing

job sharing *an approach to job redesign that allows two or more people to share a single job.*

With **job sharing,** as the name suggests, two or more people share a single job. For instance, at the *St. Louis Post-Dispatch,* Margaret and William Freivogal share the job of assistant chief of the Washington bureau. Margaret works Wednesday

FIGURE 8-3   Turning Boring Work into Interesting Work

Bored people build bad cars. That's why we're doing away with the assembly line.

Working on an assembly line is monotonous. And boring. And after a while, some people begin not to care about their jobs anymore. So the quality of the product often suffers.

That's why, at Saab, we're replacing the assembly line with assembly teams. Groups of just three or four people who are responsible for a particular assembly process from start to finish.

Each team makes its own decisions about who does what and when. And each team member can even do the entire assembly singlehandedly. The result: people are more involved. They care more. So there's less absenteeism, less turnover. And we have more experienced people on the job.

We're building our new 2 liter engines this way. And the doors to our Saab 99. And we're planning to use this same system to build other parts of our car as well.

It's a slower, more costly system, but we realize that the best machines and materials in the world don't mean a thing, if the person building the car doesn't care.

Saab. It's what a car should be.

There are more than 300 Saab dealers nationwide. For the name and address of the one nearest you call 800-243-6000 toll free. In Connecticut, call 1-800-882-6500. Saab 99 L, 2-door, $3,595. 4-door, $3,695. P.O.E. Transportation, state and local taxes, optional equipment, dealer preparation charges, if any, additional.

Reprinted by permission of Saab-Scania of America, Inc.

and Thursday, William works Monday and Tuesday, and they split Friday.[20] Job sharing can be a good solution when employees can work only part-time, but the company needs someone to do the job full-time. When two people share one job, both the employees and the company get what they want.

Job sharing provides flexibility for employees and for organizations. When Motorola wanted to cut production temporarily at its 9,000-employee Phoenix plant without laying off workers, it turned to job sharing. Layoffs would have created greater hardships for many employees. They also would have meant high costs for training and recall when it was time to resume full production. By using job sharing, Motorola cut costs by $1.5 million and saved more than 1,000 jobs.

Employees can get more time with their families through job redesign approaches such as flextime, job sharing, and the 4/40 workweek.

The 4/40 Workweek

4/40 workweek *an approach to job redesign in which employees work ten hours a day for four days.*

In the United States most workers get up Monday mornings and face five days of work. However, an increasing number of American workers are working ten hours a day for four days. This is called the **4/40 workweek.** Sometimes, work schedules are staggered so that the firm can operate a full five days. Other firms stay open only four days a week, saving on overhead costs. The 4/40 workweek gives workers a three-day weekend, with the opportunity for longer vacations or even a second job. This may increase worker satisfaction and reduce absenteeism and tardiness. However, workers may be fatigued by the end of a ten-hour day, and accidents and poor performance may result. The company may also find it difficult to coordinate with firms that are working traditional, five-day schedules.

GOAL SETTING

goal setting *a motivational tool involving the selection of work-related objectives for employees.*

Goal setting involves setting work-related objectives for employees. Goals serve many purposes. They make clear to employees what they are expected to do. They motivate employees by giving them targets to strive for. They help assure that the efforts of work groups are coordinated toward achieving larger company objectives. Feedback as to whether goals are being reached allows employees to change their behavior if necessary. Employees who attain their goals feel self-confidence and pride in achievement. They are also more willing to accept future challenges. Proper goal setting can increase productivity levels and improve performance in other areas as well.

Guidelines for Setting Goals

Goal setting has been extensively studied and widely applied. Research and experience have shown that the following guidelines can help managers set goals effectively:

*   Set specific goals. Specific goals lead to higher performance than "do your best" goals. In fact, "do your best" goals have about the same effect as no goals at all.
*   Set goals that are difficult yet attainable. As long as goals are seen as achievable, more difficult goals lead to better task performance. When goals are difficult, people try harder and also attempt to find better ways to complete the task. They work both harder and smarter.
*   Be sure that employees accept the goals and are committed to their attainment. If employees are allowed to participate in the goal-setting process, they are more likely to be committed to goal attainment. Participation increases acceptance and understanding of goals.
*   Give employees feedback about how well they are doing in relation to the goals. Then they can make corrections where necessary to improve performance. If positive feedback, such as praise, is given along the way, it will serve as a reward and motivate employees to continue working toward the goal.

The power of goal setting is illustrated by an experiment in a lumber company. The company's trucks carried logs from the forest to the sawmill. Because the cut trees varied in size, the number of trees in each truckload varied from one load to the next. On average, trucks were carrying only about 60 percent of their legal net weight. Researchers, management, and the union decided that a goal of 94 percent was difficult but reachable. The drivers, who were responsible for loading the trucks, were assigned this 94 percent goal. After a month, performance increased from the initial 60 percent to about 80 percent of capacity. It later rose to 90 percent of capacity and remained at that level. Company accountants estimated that the results translated into savings to the company of $250,000 worth of new trucks alone.[21]

Management by Objectives

Management by Objectives (MBO) is a motivational technique in which the manager and employee work together to set employee goals. The employee's performance is later measured against these goals. MBO combines many of the goal-setting principles we have just described. The MBO process begins by identifying general areas of responsibility that are important to the firm. Once this has been done, the employee and manager get together and agree on specific objectives that the employee will meet during some future period of time. For example, one key responsibility area in sales management might be sales volume, and the objective might be to increase sales by 35 percent over the next six months. Once the manager and the employee have agreed on specific objectives, they develop a strategy together for meeting these objectives. The manager and the employee then meet periodically to review how the employee has done relative to the agreed-upon objectives. If there is a problem, they discuss why objectives have not been met. The final step in the MBO process is either to set new goals for the next time period or to develop new strategies to meet the previously agreed-upon goals. The entire procedure then begins anew.

Management by Objectives a motivational technique in which the manager and employee jointly set goals, against which the employee is later evaluated.

Management by Objectives may be difficult and time-consuming to implement. Sometimes the agreed-upon goals are not specific enough, resulting in employee frustration. MBO also has been faulted for encouraging people to focus only on goals that can be easily expressed in numbers (such as the number of units produced in a week or the average number of sales calls made per day), ignoring goals that are hard to measure (such as quality of products or creativity).

On the other hand, MBO does encourage planning and goal setting, and it lets employees know how they are doing on the job. Also, it allows employees to participate in setting goals, which is good for morale and motivation. It guarantees that deviations in performance from goals will be spotted before it is too late to do anything about them. In general, although MBO does not always work, successes considerably outnumber failures.[22]

USING TEAMS

Theory Z a theory developed by William Ouchi, which attempts to combine the best of Japanese and American management practices to solve human resource problems.

In his popular book, *Theory Z,* William Ouchi contrasts the typical Japanese organization with the typical American organization.[23] **Theory Z** is Ouchi's attempt to combine the best of Japanese and American management practices to solve human resource problems. According to Ouchi, a key difference between Japanese and American firms is the greater Japanese emphasis on collective decision making and collective responsibility. Teamwork, group (rather than individual) bonuses, and attention to interpersonal relationships are noticeable in the Japanese model. Ouchi suggests a hybrid organization, called a "Type Z" organization, which blends the strongest elements of the American and the Japanese forms. The Type Z organization puts a heavy emphasis on groups.

Effective management of groups is an essential part of motivation in organizations. Teamwork has become a popular management buzzword, and teams are becoming common in many organizations.[24] Problem-solving teams, such as quality circles, meet for an hour or two a week to discuss ways to improve quality, efficiency, and the work environment. Special-purpose teams introduce work reforms and new technology, meet with suppliers and customers, and link separate functions. They may collaborate with management on decisions at all levels. Self-managing work teams, a recent development, produce an entire product. Members learn all tasks and rotate from job to job. Self-managing work teams actually take over managerial duties such as work and vacation scheduling, hiring new members, and ordering materials.

A General Electric Company plant in Salisbury, North Carolina produces many different models of lighting panelboards each day. Using a team system, along with "flexible automation" and other computerized systems, the plant can switch back and forth between models throughout the day. Productivity at the plant rose 250 percent over GE plants that made the same products four years earlier. After A. O. Smith Corp. reorganized its production workers into work teams that essentially manage themselves, the company's productivity growth rate doubled, and defects plummeted by 85 percent.

Teamwork offers potential benefits to both management and workers. For management, work teams provide flexibility and, often, productivity improvements. Robert Erskine, manager of production services at GE, says, "When you combine automation with new systems and work teams, you get a 40 to 50 percent improvement in productivity." Also, the spirit of cooperation fostered by teamwork may serve to reduce labor strife. Workers are given more say in decision making, and they have more enriched jobs. They exercise greater autonomy on the job and can use more of their valued skills. Because of such benefits, as well as demonstrated results, many U.S. companies have adopted the team idea, including Procter & Gamble, General Motors, Ford, LTV Steel, General Foods, Boeing, and Champion International.

SUMMARY POINTS

1 The aim of Scientific Management, an early approach to job motivation, was to find the "one best way" to perform any given task. The lesson of the Hawthorne studies was that distinctly human factors may be as important in motivating employees as are pay and working conditions.

2 Maslow identified five sets of needs as a basis for human motivation: physiological, security, social or affiliation, esteem, and self-actualization. McClelland looked at motivation in terms of the need for achievement, the need for affiliation, and the need for power. According to learning theory, the consequences of an act determine whether or not the act will be repeated. Unrewarded behavior eventually stops occurring. This is a process known as extinction. Under expectancy theory, rewards should be consistent with employee desires and should be tied to desired behaviors. Together, these theories provide a set of useful guidelines for motivating employees.

3 Rewards may be categorized as extrinsic or intrinsic and as financial or nonfinancial. Extrinsic rewards include pay raises, promotions, and other symbols of recognition. Intrinsic rewards flow from the job itself and the pleasure and sense of accomplishment that it gives the employee. Financial rewards are monetary; nonfinancial rewards are nonmonetary, including status, praise, and the opportunity to participate in making decisions. When administering rewards, it is important that rewards be tied to desired behaviors, that employees know what the rewards are and what behaviors are rewarded, that rewards be given as soon as the behavior occurs, and that rewards be tied directly to individual performance.

4 Job satisfaction is important for many reasons. Employees spend much of their lives at work, so management has some responsibility to make their jobs satisfying. Also, dissatisfaction may result in worker stress, absenteeism, turnover, apathy, negativism, and poor-quality products and service. Dissatisfied workers are less likely to benefit the firm by behavior such as helping co-workers, giving extra effort, and providing valuable ideas.

5 Autocratic leaders make decisions themselves; democratic leaders let subordinates participate in decision making. Consideration includes leader behaviors that show friendship, trust, respect, and warmth. Initiating structure includes leader behaviors which define and structure the way subordinates do their jobs. Transformational leaders motivate followers by arousing enthusiasm, faith, loyalty, pride, and trust in themselves and their aims. They also encourage followers to transcend self-interests for the sake of the team or organization.

6 There are many costs of conflict. Conflict may consume organizational resources, divert attention from organizational goals, disrupt coordination, and lead to lingering resentment. However, a company without conflict would be stagnant and uncreative. Conflict may be reduced by stressing larger goals, improving communication, mediating, separating conflicting parties, or getting conflicting parties together to work things out. It may be increased by staging contests, introducing change, and employing devil's advocates. The way conflict is managed determines whether it is motivating or destructive.

7 Job redesign involves changing the scheduling or nature of employees' task-related activities in order to make them more satisfying and motivating. Four approaches are job enrichment, flextime, job sharing, and the 4/40 workweek. Job enrichment involves giving employees a greater degree of authority and more responsibility in deciding how particular tasks should be done. Under flextime, employees are free to decide when to come to work and when to leave for home, within stated guidelines.

KEY TERMS

Scientific Management 189
Hawthorne effect 189
need 190
satisfaction 190
motivation 190
need hierarchy 190
manifest needs 192
need for achievement 192
need for affiliation 193
need for power 193
learning theory 193
law of effect 193
extinction 194
social learning 194
expectancy theory 195
extrinsic rewards 196
intrinsic rewards 196
Theory X 196
Theory Y 196
financial rewards 196
nonfinancial rewards 196
cafeteria-style benefit plans 198
stress 200
burnout 200
leadership 202
autocratic leaders 202
democratic leaders 202
consideration 202
initiating structure 202
transformational leaders 203
charisma 203
devil's advocate 205
job redesign 205
job enrichment 205
flextime 206
job sharing 206
4/40 workweek 208
goal setting 208
Management by Objectives 209
Theory Z 210

They still work a full day but are allowed to vary starting and quitting times. With job sharing, two or more people share a single job. With the 4/40 workweek, employees work ten hours a day for four days.

8 Goal setting involves setting work-related objectives for employees. Used properly, it increases employees' motivation and performance. Goals should be specific and difficult, yet attainable. Feedback should be provided about goal accomplishment. Employee acceptance of goals is critical. Management by Objectives is the process of employees and management jointly setting work objectives and reviewing performance against those objectives.

9 Teams are increasingly being used in organizations. Quality circles are teams that meet to discuss ways to improve quality, efficiency, and the work environment. Special-purpose teams introduce work reforms and new technology, meet with suppliers and customers, and link separate functions. Self-managing work teams actually take over many managerial duties. A team approach can enrich employee jobs and improve productivity for the company.

REVIEW QUESTIONS

1 Describe Scientific Management. **1**

2 What did the Hawthorne studies show? **1**

3 Into which of Maslow's need categories does hunger fall? Friendship? Self-worth? **2**

4 What is learning theory? **2**

5 What is the difference between intrinsic and extrinsic rewards? Give two examples of each type of reward. **3**

6 What are some guidelines for giving out rewards? **3**

7 Identify some of the costs of worker dissatisfaction. **4**

8 What is consideration? How does it differ from initiating structure? What is transformational leadership? **5**

9 What are three costs of conflict? Three benefits? **6**

10 Cite some advantages of enriched jobs; of flextime; of the 4/40 workweek. **7**

11 Give four guidelines for goal setting. How is Management by Objectives related to goal setting? **8**

12 What are some ways that groups are used in organizations? What are some benefits of teamwork? **9**

DISCUSSION QUESTIONS

1 Discuss how satisfaction relates to motivation.

2 What are some characteristics of people with strong needs for achievement? In view of those characteristics, can you think of a job which would *not* be suitable for a person with strong need for achievement?

3 Of the theories of motivation presented in this chapter, which do you think offers the best explanation of human behavior in organizations? Why?

4 If you ran a company, would you try to be a Theory X manager or a Theory Y manager? Explain.

5 Of the leadership approaches discussed in this chapter, which do you think you would try to adopt as a leader? Why?

6 Do you agree that it is sometimes desirable to increase conflict in organizations? Why or why not?

EXPERIENTIAL EXERCISES

1 Interview a local businessperson. Structure your interview in such a way that you can ask questions concerning each of the needs identified by Maslow and McClelland. For each need, attempt to determine (1) the extent to which the need is important to the businessperson and (2) the extent to which the job provides opportunities to satisfy the need. Also, ask questions concerning (1) the factors that led the businessperson to choose his or her current job and (2) the sorts of things he or she would change about the current job. Analyze the answers to these last two questions in light of the responses concerning needs.

2 Here are five characteristics of enriched jobs:

- *Skill variety:* the degree to which the job provides the opportunity to use a variety of valued skills and abilities.
- *Autonomy:* the extent to which employees have a major say in scheduling their work, selecting the equipment they will use, and deciding on procedures to be followed.

- *Task identity:* the extent to which employees do a whole task and can clearly identify the result of their efforts.
- *Task significance:* the extent to which the job has a substantial impact on the lives and work of other people.
- *Feedback:* the degree to which employees receive information as they are working that reveals how well they are performing on the job.

Think about one of your current or past jobs. Use the following scale to rate it on each of the above dimensions:

1	2	3	4	5
Completely lacking		Present to a moderate degree		Present to a very high degree

—Skill variety   —Task significance
—Autonomy   —Feedback
—Task identity

Based on your responses, would you say your job was enriched? Did you find the job to be satisfying? Would you have liked to change any of the above dimensions? How?

CASES

CASE 8-1
Riding the Product Through the South Bronx

Robert Felts was a veteran line operator at Bethlehem Steel Corp's Sparrows Point, Maryland, plant. When his supervisor asked him to visit a customer, Felts jumped at the chance. But there was one problem: The client was in eastern Texas, and Felts had to fly for the first time in his life. "I didn't like that. And they put me on four planes to get me there," he recalled with a shudder.

Felts' adjustment is only a small part of a general upheaval in traditional management–labor roles in the country's basic industries. Increasingly, management is turning to hourly workers for help with problems formerly handled only by field engineers and select executives. Employees like Felts are calling on customers and sometimes even visiting foreign competitors to determine firsthand how their own products stack up.

Whether the concept is called "employee involvement" or "worker education," the goals are the same: to improve quality, increase competitiveness, and open up a new channel for client relations. Says a senior executive at Aluminum Co. of America, "It's useless to ask employees to do a better job if they aren't empowered to take steps toward that goal."

Jobs are becoming so specialized that decisions about products often have to be made closer to the workbench. Thus, more companies are ensuring that hourly employees understand how their products or services are viewed by customers or compare with those of competitors.

Workers are sometimes sent as far afield as Japan. A trip by Clay Adams, a machine operator at a Westinghouse Electric Corp. turbine plant, left him with the impression that "the Japanese aren't going to slack up."

Westinghouse sent 30 hourly workers who produce subway generating equipment to New York to appraise the performance of their products on the city's transit system. The trip underscored the importance of reliability. "There's a difference between putting wires into a black box and riding the product through the South Bronx," contends Jack Geikler, general manager of Westinghouse's transportation business unit near Pittsburgh.

The changes are difficult for both management and labor. Management delayed bringing wage earners into the bigger picture, and workers and their unions were hesitant to drop the adversarial role. A mill supervisor at Bethlehem Steel explains that many workers who agreed to visit customers were hounded during their shifts by co-workers who claimed they were "turncoats."

At Bethlehem Steel's facility at Sparrows Point, general manager John G. Roberts is largely credited with starting the employee visitation program. "Management still has to make the tough economic decisions. But they are easier to make when employees understand the issue and also trust management," he says.

1. How is worker motivation likely to be altered by "employee involvement" of the kinds discussed in this case?
2. What rewards do employees receive from the kinds of changes identified in this case?
3. In addition to motivation, what are other probable positive consequences of such employee involvement? Possible negative consequences?
4. What sorts of conflict have these changes introduced? How might the conflict be dealt with?

Source: Adapted and abridged from T. Roth, "Employee Involvement Gains Support." Reprinted by permission of *Wall Street Journal* © 1984 Dow Jones & Company, Inc. All Rights Reserved Worldwide.

CASE 8-2
The Death of the Assembly Line?

By most measures, Volvo was a notable success. Its sales totaled $16.1 billion in 1988, a 50% increase since 1983, and operating profits totaled $1.2 billion. Volvo had no net debt and had a healthy return on equity of over 15 percent. But the company knew that it must streamline and internationalize to meet continuing challenges. Also, it had a problem that haunted all Swedish manufacturers: The country's highly educated, well-trained labor force doesn't like to work in factories.

Volvo's Swedish plants suffered absenteeism of 20 percent, and almost one-third of its workers quit yearly. More pay does not motivate Swedes; taxes take up to 70 percent of any overtime pay. With unemployment at 1.6 percent, there was no lack of jobs. The problem of Swedish firms was to keep a workforce.

Volvo's new, worker-designed assembly plant in Uddevalla, Sweden, is a response to this problem. At full capacity, it can produce 80,000 of the company's top-end 700 Series cars a year. If Uddevalla seems quiet for an auto plant, it is because there are almost no machines. The plant looks like the service area of a huge car dealership.

In full production since early 1989, the plant employs teams of seven to ten hourly workers. Each team works in one area and assembles a complete car in about two hours. Team members are trained to handle all assembly jobs and work an average of three hours before repeating the same task. This avoids the short work cycles of only one or two minutes on conventional assembly lines and the resulting boredom, inattention, poor quality, and high absenteeism.

Uddevalla is divided into six assembly plants, each of which has eight teams. The teams largely manage themselves, handling scheduling, quality control, hiring, and other duties normally performed by supervisors. Indeed, there are no first-line foremen and only two tiers of managers. Each team has a spokesperson/ombudsman, who reports to one of six plant managers, who in turn report to Leif Karlberg, president of the entire complex.

Morale seems high at Uddevalla. Absenteeism is only 8 percent. Workers have a spectacular view of a fjord. The plant is well lighted, and noise is subdued. Volvo gives its workers 16 weeks of training before they are allowed near a car, and on-the-job orientation lasts 16 months more.

The volume at Uddevalla is relatively small compared with that of most auto plants. Other Volvo plants produce all of the model 740's components and perform the major operations of stamping, welding, and painting car bodies that are shipped to Uddevalla.

After entering the plant, the car bodies glide noiselessly on magnetic tracks to the assembly points, where Volvo-designed machines lift and tilt the body to any angle. More than 80 percent of the assembly can be done from a comfortable working position, with no bending or stretching. Tools have been redesigned with narrower grips and more internal torque and power, to accommodate the 40 percent of the workforce that is female. Teams determine how long they'll work on a car and take responsibility for fixing defects. Volvo's Karlberg says, "This isn't just new production technology. It is the death of the assembly line. We've brought back craftsmanship to automaking."

But skeptics question whether Volvo's approach will spread. Uddevalla can achieve a high level of quality, they say, but it cannot match efficient mass-production systems, Japanese or American. Indeed, Volvo could have achieved at least 15 percent to 20 percent lower costs with a traditional plant design.

Source: Based on S. Kindel, "Check Your Brakes," *Financial World,* 31 October 1989, pp. 32–34; and J. Kapstein, "Volvo's Radical New Plant: 'The Death of the Assembly Line'? *Business Week,* 28 August 1989, pp. 92–93.

1. What are some benefits of the job design at Uddevalla?
2. What are some likely costs or difficulties associated with Uddevalla's design?
3. Do you think this approach would be successful in U.S. auto plants? In your answer, be sure to consider relevant similarities and differences between the situation in the U.S. and Sweden.
4. Is Uddevalla likely to herald "the death of the assembly line"? Justify your position.

OBJECTIVES

After studying this chapter, you should be able to:

1 Explain the steps in human resource planning.

2 Describe the three basic stages of staffing.

3 Discuss the trade-off between recruiting, selection, and placement on the onehand, and training and development on the other.

4 Identify six sources of job applicants and describe the realistic job preview.

5 Identify approaches to selection and hiring and explain their relative benefits and problems.

6 Describe elements of placement.

7 Explain why job training and development are needed and identify training and development methods.

8 Discuss why performance appraisal is important to the firm and how employee performance can be measured.

9 Describe how job worth, employee performance, labor market conditions, and pay systems determine levels of employee compensation.

CHAPTER 9

Human Resources Management

Over the years, recruiting, hiring, and promotion policies had evolved naturally at Allied Biological Sciences. Current employees recommended friends and family members for entry-level positions, and these individuals were given preference in hiring. Employees all began at the bottom of the organization and worked their way slowly but steadily to the top. Gary Wasilewski, Allied's current Chief Executive Officer, was especially proud that he and the two previous CEOs were "home grown". They had started out by "getting their hands dirty" in entry-level jobs, had worked hard to rise in the company, and had never worked anywhere but Allied.

In the past five years, Allied had been expanding rapidly, but its traditional sources of workers were drying up. Also, increased foreign competition, tighter government controls, and the sheer size of the company were placing new demands on management. The policy of promoting from within was no longer viable. New perspectives and skills were needed, and they were not available within the firm. Gary Wasilewski realized that Allied had to pay much more attention to human resources.

In this chapter, we will look at human resource planning, staffing, and training and developing employees. We will close by discussing approaches to appraising employee performance and to compensating employees.

From the local delicatessen to the largest international bank, business firms are made up of people. It is critical to get good people into the right jobs and then develop them properly. Recognizing this, companies have developed some novel staffing methods. For instance, it is said that retailer J. C. Penney invited candidates to breakfast and served them eggs. If a candidate salted or peppered the eggs before tasting them, Penney concluded that he or she was inclined to make decisions without enough information and was not suitable for the company.[1] As we will see, such salt-and-pepper approaches to human resources management are no longer viewed as acceptable or successful.

Some decisions concerning human resources—such as the choice of a chief executive—may be more important than others. Some—such as the selection of players in the pro football draft—may receive more attention than others. Together, the human resource decisions made by a firm, whether involving chief executives or entry-level employees, play an important role in the firm's success.

HUMAN RESOURCE PLANNING

It would be unthinkable for a company not to plan for its future needs for materials, plant capacity, or financing. Similarly, firms must plan for their human resource needs. **Human resource planning** is the process of analyzing an organization's human resource needs and developing a program to satisfy them. Human resource planning begins by analyzing where the firm is in terms of staffing and where it wants to be. Then strategies can be developed to move toward the desired situation.

human resource planning
the process of analyzing an organization's human resource needs and developing a program to satisfy them.

The need for human resource planning is evident in the chapter-opening example. Allied recognizes that external forces are placing new demands on management, which will translate into human resource needs. It also knows that hiring from its traditional sources and promoting from within will not meet its future needs. Thus, it must develop a plan to acquire and develop human resources.

The first step in human resource planning is to list human resource objectives. The objectives specify the goals and directions for human resource management decisions and activities. Next, planners do an inventory of the firm's current personnel and estimate the supplies of labor available outside the firm. Then planners consider the firm's strategic growth plan and the mix of employee skills it will require. They then estimate demand for labor—the number of people required and the skills needed—as well as when these needs must be met. Finally, human resource plans are developed. In the plans, estimates of future labor supply are coordinated with future labor demand. This may involve changes in the rates and policies of hiring, promotion and transfer, and termination. The steps in human resource planning are shown in Figure 9-1.

As a simple example, let's take a computer software firm, Softhouse. The firm has marketed very simple computer programs that help the users manage their personal finances. Now the company has decided to expand its offerings, to include more sophisticated computer programs for corporate financial planning. Softhouse thus needs to focus its human resource efforts on upgrading programming skills. Next, Softhouse would survey the skills of its current programmers and estimate the external supply of programmers with various skills. Then the firm would make specific projections of the numbers of programmers needed with specific skills, as well as the timing of those needs. Finally, Softhouse would consider various changes in human resource policies to mesh the employees' skills with the new skill needs. This might involve training of current programmers, hiring of new programmers with required skills, and other steps.

STAFFING THE FIRM

Staffing is a vital part of human resource management. It involves bringing new people into the organization and then moving them through, and perhaps out of, the firm. Staffing consists of three stages: recruiting, selection and hiring, and

staffing   the management function dealing with the recruitment, selection, and placement of the members of the firm.

FIGURE 9-1   Human Resource Planning Steps

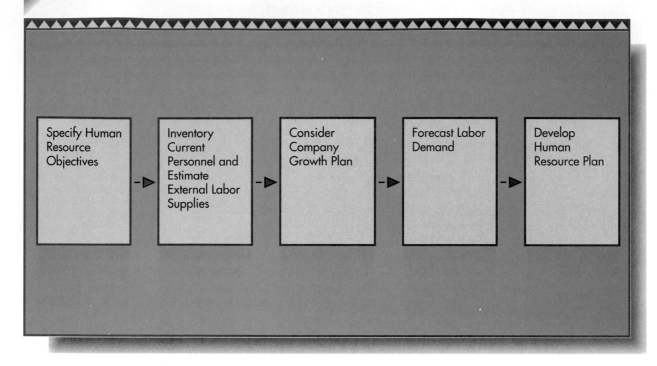

placement. These staffing activities are coupled with the training and development function to match the abilities of the job candidate with the needs of the firm. This matching process is most clearly seen when the new employee enters the firm or when the requirements of the job change.

Staffing or Training?

 Figure 9-2 illustrates the balancing act necessary between the staffing activities of recruiting, selection, and placement on the one hand and training and development on the other. In its personnel practices, should a firm tip the balance to one side or the other? More specifically, should a firm hire people who are ready to step into their jobs, or should it "groom" them through training programs?

Careful selection and placement certainly have their advantages. The new employees can begin work immediately, showing results right away rather than in six months, after a training program. For example, offshore drilling companies such as SEDCO like to hire undersea welders who are already competent and can do their jobs safely. Acquiring these skills takes years of experience. Individuals are hired because they already have proven skills; the firm does not have to gamble that they will learn them properly. Brokerage companies such as Prudential-Bache Securities offer big bonuses to brokers who come from other companies.[2] These brokers already have the needed skills and have proven their ability.

Training and development also have advantages. For one thing, people can be hired at lower rates of pay if they come to the firm untrained. Also, training and development can be tailored exactly to the company's needs. For example, Westinghouse hires students with degrees in advertising and then retrains them completely. Ford, Bell Telephone, and McDonald's have similar training programs for employees who need special skills that cannot be obtained elsewhere. In

FIGURE 9-2 Balancing the Staffing Mix

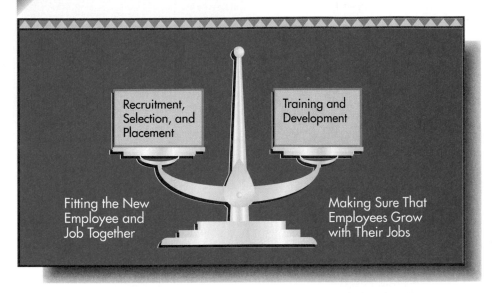

addition, people trained by a firm often feel loyal to it. Sales and service personnel trained by IBM feel strong loyalty to their company; they ar renowned for their dedication to IBM's interests. Bankers Trust New York Corp. placed ads in magazines for chess and bridge enthusiasts, in order to recruit trainees for bond trading positions. The company reasoned that bond traders, like bridge and chess players, make moves as part of a calculated game plan. One of the ads is shown in Figure 9-3. Bankers Trust believes that it can teach individuals with these skills the specifics of bond trading.

In the remainder of this section, we will consider the three staffing functions of recruiting, selection, and placement. In the next section, we will examine training and development.

Recruiting

The first of staffing's three stages is recruiting. The term **recruiting** refers to all activities involved in finding interested and qualified applicants for a job opening. No matter how employees are later selected, trained, and motivated, it is important to start out with a good group of job applicants. The greater the number of applicants and the better their qualifications, the more likely it is that the firm will build a solid personnel base. As indicated in the International Example on page 221, recruiting has increasingly become a global activity.

recruiting all activities involved in finding interested and qualified applicants for a job opening.

Sources of Applicants. Job applicants can be found in many ways. We'll look at six sources of applicants, which differ in ease of use, cost, and the quality of applicants obtained.

Newspaper Advertisements. One simple way to publicize a job opening is through newspaper and magazine advertisements. For instance, when McDonald's planned in 1990 to open a restaurant in Shenzhen, China, it placed two newspaper ads displaying McDonald's striped shirts with matching caps. The ads read, "More than 200 youths in Shenzhen are going to put on this uniform,

FIGURE 9-3   Bankers Trust Ad in Chess Magazines Seeking Currency and Bond Traders

HERE'S A MOVE THAT COULD CHANGE YOUR LIFE.

Chess at its top level requires certain finely-honed skills.

The ability to predict an opponent's future moves.

Courage to take short-term risks for long-term gains.

Patience to assess every option available and strike accordingly.

Interestingly enough, these are the exact skills necessary to succeed as a trader in the global currency and securities markets.

Allow us to introduce ourselves.

We're Bankers Trust and this is basically a fancy 'Help Wanted' ad.

Bankers Trust is one of the most successful traders of foreign exchange and debt securities in the world.

Every day we trade over $35 billion in volume and we've made money doing this every year for the past twenty years.

Most of our competitors just hire MBAs right out of school but we're predicting that "a few good chess players" have what it takes to win in our highly competitive world.

The idea came to us from several of our best traders who are themselves, games players, one of our most successful in particular being an international master.

He is still moving pieces to form a calculated game plan, but now it is Yen and Deutchmarks as well as Rooks and Knights.

If you are interested in this quite unique job opportunity, send your resumé and/or a letter about yourself to Allen R. Beyer, Bankers Trust New York Corporation, 31st floor, One Bankers Trust Plaza, New York, New York, 10006. It doesn't really matter what your background is and it could be the best move you'll ever make.

Source: *Chess Life*, August 1990, Vol. 45, No. 8, p. 5.

the symbol of a prosperous future. As an aggressive person, what are you waiting for?" The ads drew more than 6,000 applicants for 240 part-time jobs.[3]

Although advertisements often bring in many applicants, they do not function as a screening device. **Screening** is the identification of obviously unqualified applicants before gathering additional selection information on those applicants. Newspaper ads may attract many job seekers, but only a few of them may be qualified for the position advertised. The others must be screened somehow.

screening *the identification of obviously unqualified applicants for a position before gathering additional selection information on those applicants.*

Referrals. Current and past employees sometimes refer their friends and relatives to the firm. Because these employees usually understand the firm's personnel needs, referrals can be a very good source of job applicants. When companies in the computer industry need new executives, they routinely ask current employees for referrals. The assumption is that the employees will know the best people in the industry.

Private Employment Agencies. Private employment agencies are in the business of matching job seekers with suitable jobs. They charge a fee for their services—sometimes to the job seeker and sometimes to the hiring firm. In effect, when a company contracts with an employment agency, it is turning over the task of recruiting and screening applicants to someone else. Many private employment agencies specialize in finding people to fill top management positions.

INTERNATIONAL EXAMPLE

The Global Talent Search

International staffing has become increasingly common as companies become more global in their operations and strategic thinking. Firms once looked only as far as their national borders to find qualified managerial talent, but they now look beyond.

For instance, Gillette's International Graduate Trainee Program has helped groom local talent in the countries where the company has business operations. Training includes an 18-month term at the company's Boston headquarters, followed by an entry-level management position at the division in the home country. While at the headquarters, the trainee focuses on two major disciplines, such as marketing, finance, or manufacturing. An executive mentor is responsible for overseeing his or her training and education in Gillette's operations. About half of the trainees have moved into executive positions, and many have returned to the U.S. or moved to other countries to pursue international careers.

As another example, in 1990 Coca-Cola Company transferred more than 300 members of its professional and managerial staff from one country to another under its leadership development program. The company now has operations in 160 countries and employs nearly 400,000 people. It seeks to develop people who have the experience, skills, and values to help the company achieve its objectives. The company prefers job applicants who are fluent in more than one language, since such people can adapt more easily to another country. Of the directors of the company's 21 divisions, only four are American.

Public Employment Agencies. In most cities, there is an office of the state employment agency. Its role is to find jobs for unemployed people and to keep track of people receiving unemployment compensation. Some of these agencies also offer training programs.

Educational Institutions. Universities, colleges, community colleges, junior colleges, vocational schools, and high schools may all be good sources of job applicants. If there are many jobs available, companies may send recruiters to campuses for the purpose of finding and interviewing job applicants.

Labor Unions. For blue-collar and some professional jobs, labor unions are often a good source of applicants. Some unions have hiring halls, where employers and job seekers are brought together. Builders and contractors sometimes hire trade construction workers in this way. Union halls function as centralized labor exchanges, where employers and job seekers jointly determine the allocation of people to specific job slots.

Realistic Job Preview. Most companies present a rosy picture of themselves and their job openings in order to attract job applicants. Partly as a result, many new employees are dissatisfied when they learn the "truth" about the company. Some may even quit after a short time. To avoid this, some companies now use realistic job previews. The aim of the **realistic job preview (RJP)** is to give the recruit an accurate picture of what the company and the job are like. For example, films of people on the job and uncensored comments of current employees may be used to acquaint new employees with the day-to-day reality of the job. Exxon prints brochures describing the kinds of jobs available for people with varying educational backgrounds, the promotion and salary opportunities of the jobs, and where in the world an individual might work. Because of its highly developed preview, Exxon has one of the lowest employee turnover rates in the petroleum industry.

Business Career

Personnel Recruiter: Seeks Recruits, screens, and interviews job applicants to fill company openings. Contacts colleges to arrange on-campus interviews. Provides information on company job opportunities to applicants. Checks references. Recommends applicants for follow-up interviews. *Average Salary: $26,400.*

realistic job preview *information given to the recruit, describing what the company and the job are actually like, rather than presenting an overly rosy picture.*

Selection

Consider the case of Korbel Champagne Cellars. Since consumption of champagne is often associated with romantic situations, Korbel has a Romance, Weddings, and Entertainment Department, presided over by a Director of Romance. When the Director of Romance resigned, the company was faced with the task of selecting a successor. The ideal candidate, according to a company spokesperson, should "personify romance in some highly visible or glamorous way."[4] How might you go about selecting such a person?

selection the process of evaluating each candidate's qualifications and hiring the one whose skills and interests best match the job requirements.

The role of recruiting is to locate job candidates; the role of **selection** is to evaluate each candidate's qualifications and pick the one whose skills and interests best match the job requirements. Some firms use informal selection procedures, such as reviewing application blanks and resumes. Others ask their job candidates to take personality and ability tests. Still others have assessment centers, where procedures for selecting and hiring new employees are very systematic.

Careful selection procedures can be time-consuming and costly. However, they are probably worthwhile if the costs of a wrong decision are high, if there are many applicants and few openings, and if selection tools are accurate. Some companies now use expensive selection procedures even for positions that would traditionally have been filled without much screening. For instance, when Toyota Motor Corp. wanted to fill positions at its new auto assembly plant in Kentucky, it received 90,000 applications from 120 countries for its 2,700 production jobs, and thousands more for the 300 office jobs. The company wanted to select workers who would conform to its emphasis on teamwork, loyalty, and versatility. Toyota required applicants to spend as much as 25 hours completing written tests, workplace simulations, and interviews, in addition to undergoing a physical examination and a drug test. The tests examined not only literacy and technical knowledge, but also interpersonal skills and attitudes toward work. At each stage of the selection process, more applicants were screened out. Only 1 in 20 made it to the interview.[5] Let's look at some of the ways in which firms determine whether the qualifications of a job candidate are in line with the requirements of the job.

Application Blanks. The first source of information about a potential employee is the **application blank.** It provides the hiring firm with information about educational background, work experience, and outside interests. Much of this information is especially useful for screening purposes. For example, an applicant for a position as a computer analyst should have had courses in data processing. The application blank would tell the employer right away whether the applicant had the needed training.

application blank a selection tool in which a form is completed by job applicants to provide the hiring firm with information about educational background, work experience, and outside interests.

However, there are at least three problems with application blanks as sources of information about potential employees. First, the information provided by the applicant may not be relevant to performance on the job. Second, job applicants may give incorrect or misleading information on their application blanks or in resumes. The National Credit Verification Service has found that about one-third of the job applicants whose credentials it has investigated somehow misrepresented their educational backgrounds. Sometimes these misrepresentations are discovered many years later, when employees are considered for promotion. Third, the law places many restrictions on what can and cannot be asked on a job application. Figure 9-4 lists questions considered to be unfair by the Washington State Human Rights Commission. Clearly, firms must be careful to avoid questions on application blanks that violate state or federal law.

FIGURE 9-4   Some Unfair Preemployment Inquiries

- Any inquiry that implies a preference for persons under 40 years of age.

- Whether applicant is a citizen. Any inquiry into citizenship which would tend to divulge applicant's lineage, ancestry, national origin, descent, or birthplace.

- All inquiries relating to arrests.

- Inquiries which would divulge convictions which do not reasonably relate to fitness to perform the particular job or which relate to convictions for which the date of conviction or prison release was more than seven years before the date of application.

- Specific inquiries concerning spouse, spouse's employment or salary, children, child care arrangements, or dependents.

- Any inquiries concerning handicaps, height, or weight which do not relate to job requirements.

- Whether the applicant is married, single, divorced, engaged, widowed, etc.

- Type or condition of military discharge.

- Request that applicant submit a photograph.

- Sex.

- Any inquiry concerning race or color of skin, hair, eyes, etc.

- All questions as to pregnancy, and medical history concerning pregnancy and related matters.

- Any inquiry concerning religious denomination, affiliations, holidays observed, etc.

- Requirement that applicant list all organizations, clubs, societies, and lodges to which applicant belongs.

- Inquiry into original name where it has been changed by court order or marriage.

References. References are another popular selection tool. **References** are information provided by previous employers, co-workers, teachers, or acquaintances concerning an applicant's credentials, past performance, and qualifications for the current position. The reference givers may be contacted in person, by phone, or by mail. The evidence suggests that references are generally of little value in the employee selection process. The people asked to provide references sometimes do not really know much about the person requesting the reference. Sometimes they are not frank because they do not want to say anything uncomplimentary about a person, especially in writing. As a result, references are generally biased in the applicant's favor.

references a selection tool in which information is provided by people who have had previous experience with a job applicant, such as former employers, co-workers, teachers, or acquaintances, concerning the applicant's credentials, past performance, and qualifications for the current position.

Interviews. The hiring firm generally asks candidates that pass the initial screening process to participate in an interview. In an **interview,** a representative of the hiring firm asks the candidate a series of questions. The goal of the interview is to determine how well the candidate's skills and interests match the job

interviews a selection tool in which a representative of the hiring firm asks a job candidate a series of questions to determine how well the candidate's skills and interests match the job requirements.

requirements. The interviewer may be a member of the firm's Human Resources Department or the supervisor who has an open position.

Interviews can be conducted in many ways. Two types often used are structured interviews and unstructured interviews. In a structured interview, all candidates are asked the same list of questions in the same order. A structured interview helps ensure that all questions are related exclusively to job duties and requirements critical to job performance. By sticking to the questions in the structured interview, the interviewer gives each applicant the same chance as every other and makes it easier to compare candidates. The fact that all applicants are treated the same also makes it less likely that the company will be sued for discrimination in hiring. An unstructured interview, on the other hand, is a looser exchange between the interviewer and the job candidate. The interviewer often asks questions that are not on the planned list, to follow up on the candidate's comments. This sometimes results in a more complete picture than would otherwise be possible.

Advantages of Interviews. Interviews are widely used. More than 90 percent of all people hired for industrial positions are interviewed at least once. There are many reasons for the popularity of interviews. For one, it is easier to ask someone a series of questions than to develop a test. For another, interviewing makes the selection process more personal and gives the interviewer an overall idea as to whether the applicant is right for the job. Also, companies may use interviews to give the applicant information about the duties of the position to be filled and about the organization in general. Interviews may be used to "sell" the company to the applicant. They may also be used to complete the information about job candidates. Finally, good candidates might be unwilling to consider a job seriously unless they had the chance to ask questions and gather information.

Problems with Interviews. Despite the popularity of interviews, a successful interview does not always mean that the recruit will perform well on the job. Interviewers sometimes show many biases, disagree with one another over which recruits are likely to do best, and ignore much of the information available. The success of an interview in identifying the best candidate for the job depends on the skill and good judgment of the individual interviewer.

Improving Interviews. Steps can be taken to increase the likelihood of a successful interview. Interviewers should always prepare for an interview by making a list of specific topics to be covered and/or specific questions to be asked. Interviewers should be trained in preparing questions that relate to the job requirements, probing for details, listening carefully, and avoiding discriminatory questions. Written records of the interview should be kept. Whenever possible, multiple interviewers should be used, so that the selection will depend on the judgment of more than one person. Interviews should never be the sole basis for selection of a candidate. They should be used along with other selection devices to provide additional information on candidates' strengths and weaknesses.[6]

test *a systematic and standardized procedure for obtaining information from individuals.*

Testing. A **test** is a systematic and standardized procedure for obtaining information from individuals. Testing is a relatively objective way to determine how well a person may do on the job. Many human resources experts and personnel managers believe that testing is the single best selection tool. Tests yield more information about a person than does a completed application blank, and they are less biased than interviews.

Types of Tests.   Human resources managers use many types of tests today. Let's examine four types: ability tests, personality tests, interest tests, and work sample tests.

• **Ability tests** measure whether the applicant has certain skills required to perform the job tasks. Mental ability tests assess memory, problem-solving speed, verbal comprehension, ability to deal with numbers, and so on. Here are some typical mental ability test items:

1.   What number is missing in this series?

> 4-7-11-16-22-?

2.   Using the letters in the word "Connecticut," write as many four-letter words as you can in the next two minutes.

_____   _____   _____   _____

_____   _____   _____   _____

_____   _____   _____   _____

3.   Carry out the following calculations:

| 234 | 9843 | 528×24 = _____ |
| +768 | −1256 | 1460/5 = _____ |

Mechanical ability tests measure spatial relations—the ability to see how parts fit together into a whole. Such spatial relations skills might be useful, for instance, in putting a carburetor back together, or for drafting or interpreting blueprints. Psychomotor ability tests assess reaction time and dexterity. They might assess speed of limb movement, coordination, and finger dexterity. Psychomotor ability tests are given to people applying for jobs involving mostly physical tasks. Professional football teams use them to assess athletes.

• **Personality tests** measure the strength or weakness of personality characteristics that are considered important for good performance on the job. Job applicants are asked to describe themselves in terms of traits or behavior. The Ghiselli Self Description Inventory, for example, lists 64 pairs of adjectives. Applicants are asked to pick the trait in each pair that best or least describes themselves.:

_____ capable   _____ defensive   _____ weak
_____ discreet   _____ touchy   _____ selfish

On the basis of responses to such pairs, scores are given on personality dimensions such as initiative, decisiveness, and self-assurance.

Personality tests have been used for managerial jobs for a long time. They are now becoming more popular when hiring people for entry-level jobs, such as customer sales representatives and sales clerks, and for blue-collar positions. This is especially true at companies that practice participatory management, where workers are given responsibility in running operations. Also, many financial service and insurance firms, trying to improve service in the face of competition, are looking harder for workers with "people" skills such as empathy, the ability to communicate, and motivation to please others.

ability tests   *tests measuring whether the applicant has certain skills required to perform the job tasks.*

personality tests   *tests measuring the strengths or weaknesses of personality characteristics that are considered important for good performance of the job.*

interest tests *tests measuring a person's likes and dislikes for various activities.*

• **Interest tests** measure a person's likes and dislikes for various activities. A person whose interests don't fit well with the characteristics of a particular job would probably find the job boring and unsatisfying. One popular interest test is the Kuder Vocational Preference Record, in which the person is given sets of three activities and told to pick his or her favorite. A typical set is:

_____ play baseball
_____ work a puzzle
_____ watch a movie

The responses result in scores on ten interest categories, such as literary, outdoor, and mechanical.

work sample tests *tests measuring how well applicants perform selected job tasks.*

• **Work sample tests** measure how well applicants perform selected job tasks. An applicant for a job that requires typing skills is usually given a typing test; a police officer candidate might be given judgment tasks involving realistic job situations. Work sample tests generally predict subsequent job performance quite well.

Test Validity. Although testing works well, it is not without problems. First, the value of a test is based on its validity. **Validity** is the degree to which predictions from selection information are supported by evidence. Thus, a test that accurately predicts employee performance is valid, while one that does not is invalid. Valid tests are expensive to develop. Also, some jobs, such as those of top management, are hard to describe, and the abilities and interests required may be all but impossible to predict on the basis of test results.

validity *the degree to which predictions from selection information are supported by evidence.*

As a result of concerns about validity and invasion of privacy, a 1988 federal law outlawed most private uses of pre-employment polygraph (or "lie detector") tests aimed at assessing employee honesty. However, written "honesty" or "integrity" tests are now often given instead. Many of them may be even less valid than the polygraph tests they replace.[7] Many firms, including Abbott Laboratories, J. C. Penney, and Nordstrom Inc., are also trying to judge the integrity of applicants by performing credit checks. Critics question the validity of credit checks and charge that firms may use them to obtain personal information they aren't supposed to consider, such as age or marital status.[8]

Faking Tests. There is also the danger that tests can be faked. William H. Whyte wrote about "How to Cheat on Personality Tests" in his classic 1957 book, *The Organization Man*.[9] He suggested that companies want conservative people who are neither very "soft" nor very dominant. Accordingly, test takers were advised in his book to check these kinds of responses:

• I like things pretty much the way they are.
• I never worry much about anything.
• I loved my father and my mother, but my father a little bit more.
• I love my spouse and children, but I don't let them get in the way of company work.

Test Fairness. Some tests may be unfair to certain groups, such as women or blacks. Everyone agrees that tests should be fair, but few agree on a definition of fairness. To some, a test is unfair if it includes questions about things that might be unfamiliar to some people because of their race or ethnic origin. To others, a test is unfair if it measures things that aren't needed on the job but that serve to block some people from being hired.

In the eyes of the law, a fair test is one that does not underpredict or over-predict performance of one group of employees relative to another. For instance, if a test predicts that white males will do better than black males on the job, when in fact both groups do equally well, the test is unfair.

As indicated in this chapter's ethical issue (page 228), critics of a new form of testing—genetic testing—argue that it may introduce a new kind of unfairness to the workplace: exclusion of employees with certain genetic characteristics.[10]

Assessment Centers. Instead of just using an interview or a test, about 2,000 large companies approach the employee selection process more systematically. They use various procedures, combined in the form of an **assessment center.** Assessment centers are part of the firm; they are a collection of systematic procedures rather than a physical place. The centers employ psychologists and other experts on human behavior as well as providing tests, interviews, group discussions, and other approaches for evaluating job candidates. Often, managers from within the firm serve as assessors.

assessment center *a center employing human resources experts and a variety of selection procedures to systematically evaluate the qualifications of job candidates.*

One approach used in assessment centers is **role playing,** where job recruits pretend to be actual employees in a real decision situation. Another approach to discovering how recruits hold up under fire is the **in-basket.** The recruit is given a basket piled high with memos, phone messages, letters, and other matters requiring attention. Each person's performance is evaluated in terms of how the tasks are sequenced, how promptly they are completed, whether the most important ones in the pile are finished, and how good the proposed solutions are.

role playing *an approach to employee selection in which job recruits pretend to be actual employees in job situations.*

in-basket *an assessment approach in which the job recruit's performance is evaluated in terms of how well and how quickly the recruit organizes a series of tasks and makes decisions concerning them.*

Assessment centers have many uses besides selection. They may help to spot management potential early. They may pinpoint areas of weakness where employees should improve to enhance their career prospects. When the assessors are managers within the firm, the training they receive on how to run assessment centers is also valuable in helping them understand the firm, observe and rate behavior, and make judgments.

Assessment centers, on the average, cost over $100,000 to maintain each year. But they may be worth the cost to the large firms that use them, such as AT&T, IBM, and General Electric, which can spread the costs over many employees. AT&T alone runs more than 40,000 people through its center each year. Studies of assessment centers show them to make better predictions of employee performance than other approaches to selection. Also, employees usually report that assessment centers have given them a fair chance to show their abilities.

Placement

6

Placement means fitting people and jobs together after the people have become employees of the firm. It includes everything from helping new employees feel at home in the firm to promoting them to positions of greater pay and responsibility or demoting them to less demanding positions when necessary.

placement *the process of fitting people and jobs together after the people have become employees of the firm.*

Orientation. Orientation involves introducing new employees to their jobs and to the company. It is their first "inside" look at the company, and it can make an important impression. The job orientation reduces uncertainties, makes company policies and expectations clear, and provides a good idea of what the firm, plant, and co-workers are like. Often, both the personnel department and the new employee's supervisor are involved in the orientation efforts. Orientation may include such elements as an explanation of job procedures and responsibilities, criteria for performance appraisal, organization and work unit rules, safety

orientation *the process whereby new employees are introduced to their jobs and to the company.*

Genetic Testing

A new form of testing has been introduced into the workplace. Full of promise and peril, it applies the expanding science of genetics to the testing of workers for chromosomal damage or susceptibility to disease.

Genetic testing of workers comes in two varieties: monitoring and screening. They differ in their purposes and in the way they have been received.

Genetic monitoring involves periodically testing groups of employees to see whether they are showing any alarming chromosomal abnormalities that might have been caused by their environment. Monitoring has the approval of most observers, including labor leaders. It provides an early warning of danger from the work environment and indicates when workplaces need cleaning up.

Genetic screening is the one-time analysis of DNA taken from blood or other body fluids. It is aimed at finding genetic "markers" that indicate that a person may be especially susceptible to harm from a particular substance. Advocates of genetic screening say that screening could identify those with a special susceptibility to a disease and steer them away from work with dust or fumes that might trigger it. But screening worries many critics. They argue that if employers know that certain workers are susceptible to a disease caused by workplace hazards, they will simply get rid of those workers rather than clean up the workplace. Critics also warn that such screening could be used to screen out employees who are likely to develop debilitating or fatal genetic diseases such as Huntington's chorea or Alzheimer's. Susceptible workers may find their privacy violated, their careers ruined, and their health insurance terminated.

regulations, the chain of command for reporting purposes, where to turn with problems or questions, and so on. Often, the new employee is given an orientation packet containing organization charts, maps of the facility, the company policy handbook, copies of performance appraisal forms, lists of holidays and employee benefits, phone numbers of key personnel, and copies of insurance plans.

Lateral Move. Firms sometimes move employees laterally—that is, neither up nor down in the organizational hierarchy, but sideways. One type of lateral move, systematic job rotation, may build worker skills. At Union Carbide, three executive vice presidents traded jobs to get a better feel for the total organization and to prepare for the presidency. Such lateral moves can provide valuable learning experiences, building a more solid base for later promotions. W. R. Grace & Company, a chemical and consumer products company, has been moving managers laterally, some to special projects for the company's future, others to fill slots at locations far from their current posts, and others to newly created jobs in other countries. According to Paul Zeller, the firm's vice president for corporate administration, "They get new challenges, and we get broadened managers—something a global, decentralized company must have."[11] Sometimes lateral moves are dictated by organizational changes. For instance, when IBM reorganized its staff to reduce costs, its plan required several thousand people to change jobs, often from staff positions to the sales force.

promotion *a move up in the organizational hierarchy, generally to a new title, more responsibility, and greater financial rewards.*

Promotion. The most pleasant job move is the promotion. A **promotion** is a move up, generally to a new title, more responsibility, and greater financial rewards. Most employees would like more status, challenge, and pay, so promotions are attractive to them. But good promotion decisions also benefit the firm. An individual who has demonstrated competence and loyalty to the firm and shows promise for further accomplishment is moved to a position with greater impact on the firm's success. Promotions also demonstrate to other employees that good performance and potential are rewarded, thus serving as a motivating device.

Promotions must be handled carefully. For one thing, the fact that the promoted individual did well at the old job is no guarantee that he or she will do well at the higher-level job. Jobs at different levels may require vastly different skills and interests. All too often, a good salesperson or engineer becomes a poor manager. This tendency is called the Peter Principle. The **Peter Principle** asserts that good workers are repeatedly promoted to positions of greater authority. Eventually, they reach their "level of incompetence" and will not be promoted again. Most managers can point to examples of the Peter Principle in their firms. Good promotion decisions prevent capable salespersons or engineers from becoming poor managers.

Peter Principle   a principle stating that there is a tendency for good workers to be promoted to positions of greater authority until they eventually reach a "level of incompetence" and will not be promoted again.

Promotions can also cause problems for the people promoted. Some employees may be happier in their current jobs than they would be in positions requiring greater responsibility, new skills, and geographic moves. Such changes can cause stress. To make the move a bit less scary, some firms have instituted fallback positions. Employees accepting promotions are guaranteed that if they are unhappy, they can "fall back" to their old positions or positions of equal stature.

However, most people certainly welcome promotions. Some employees may even experience an "inverse Peter Principle," performing better as they take on increased responsibility and challenge.

An important controversy regarding promotions focuses on the very small number of women in top management positions in the U.S. The Controversial Issue on page 230 asks whether there is a "glass ceiling" that prevents women and minorities from moving into executive positions. Similar arguments have been presented with regard to minorities.

Demotion. A move down in the organizational hierarchy to a lower title, less responsibility, and lower salary is called a **demotion.** Demotions are stressful for employees, of course, and they are likely to be resisted by unions. Still, demotions are often necessary. For example, companies may demote individuals who are performing poorly, rather than fire them. Also, especially during recessions, employees may prefer demotion to unemployment. Some companies have experimented with demoting employees temporarily so that they can relate better to their subordinates. Also some employees ask for their old jobs back if they are unhappy with their promotions.

demotion   a move down in the organizational hierarchy, to a lower title, less responsibility, and lower salary.

Termination. Another painful reality in business is the need to fire employees. Sometimes firings are necessary because employees have continued to perform poorly, or because they have been unmotivated or uncooperative. Firings are traumatic for the terminated individual and costly for the firm. For instance, the firm will have to bear the costs of recruiting and training a replacement. Therefore, employees who are performing below standards should be counseled and given written performance goals and plans for meeting them. They should have a probationary period and should receive regular feedback over that period. Firing should be used only if such corrective efforts fail, as a last resort.

In recent years, many employees have been fired as a result of factors having little to do with their motivation or performance. Due to technological changes, mergers, changes in strategy, foreign competition, or other factors, firms may have to cut costs by reducing the size of their workforce. This is called "downsizing." Sometimes downsizing has serious consequences, even at the executive

Is There a Glass Ceiling?

Yes

There is certainly a glass ceiling—an invisible barrier of attitudes, prejudices, and "old boy networks" blocking women who seek important corporate positions. It's not surprising that this glass ceiling exists. There are many stereotypes about women that don't fit the image of a successful chief executive officer. For instance, women are often seen as emotionally unstable, passive, and lacking in confidence and "toughness." These false stereotypes, together with behaviors that reinforce male advantage—such as informal mentoring systems that favor males and company-paid memberships in all-male clubs—make up a recipe for discrimination.

The numbers make this very clear. A *Fortune* magazine listing of directors and top executives at 799 major corporations included 3,993 men—and 19 women! In a recent survey, 79 percent of CEOs acknowledged that women face barriers in advancing to top management, and 91 percent said that their companies should change their cultures to meet women's career needs. Even when women do make it to the level of vice president, Chamber of Commerce figures show that they earn 42 percent less than their male peers.

The effects of the glass ceiling are so obvious that in 1990 U.S. Labor Secretary Elizabeth Dole launched a "glass ceiling initiative" to investigate the reward systems, training and development programs, and job-assignment procedures of major corporations. The investigation has been continued by her successor, Lynn Martin. Companies found to have a glass ceiling may lose their government contracts. If companies are unwilling or unable to shatter the glass ceiling, the government may do it for them.

Companies had better stop denying that the glass ceiling exists and move to do something about it. They should focus on systematic programs to train and promote qualified females, provision of child care facilities and flexible work schedules (since women often have heavy family responsibilities), and a complete reexamination of the corporate culture. There will be a glass ceiling as long as that

level. For example, N. V. Philips, a major Dutch electronics firm, announced in late 1990 that it would eliminate 35,000 to 45,000 jobs, or about 16 percent of its workforce, in a worldwide "efficiency drive." The cuts were made in response to a 1990 loss of over $1 billion. In the face of huge losses, Ford, General Motors, and Chrysler each announced plans in 1991 to make major workforce reductions. In early 1992, GM made the somber announcement that it would eliminate 71,000 jobs and close 21 plants.

It was probably inevitable that companies would come up with some innovative jargon to avoid using terms such as "firing" and "layoff." Employees who are terminated are now likely to hear that their firms are engaging in a "skill mix readjustment," "rightsizing," or "workforce imbalance correction." Other workers may find that they have been subjected to "indefinite idling," "outplacing," "dehiring," "degrowing," "decruiting," or a "career-change opportunity."[12]

Whatever they are called, firings are extremely stressful to individuals and firms. In some cases, the firm hires outplacement companies to assist people who are affected. These firms help the employer with the dismissal—offering advice and sometimes getting involved in the termination interview—and then counsel the individual on how to carry out a job search and cope with the period of transition between jobs. They may also actually help the individual find a job.

Due to recent changes in the law and its interpretation by the courts, companies can no longer fire employees anytime they want. Although courts generally recognize management's right to terminate employees who are incompetent, lazy, or uncooperative, they are increasingly attacking firings for certain other reasons. For instance, courts have challenged firings for reasons of convenience, to make the employee a scapegoat, or to avoid pension costs. Nevertheless, critics argue that workers in the United States are still much more likely to be fired

culture reflects and reinforces traditional male values, attitudes, and practices.

No

There is no argument about the numbers. There *are* relatively few women at the top of firms in the U.S. The argument is about whether this is because of invisible barriers or other, more legitimate reasons.

In fact, what looks like glass is just a reflection of the fact that it takes time to move to the top in corporate America. Chief executive officers of firms have often had decades of managerial experience. For whatever reason, relatively few women have entered the ranks of managers until recent years. There simply hasn't been enough time for those women to reach the corporate pinnacle.

The question is, how could women possibly be fully represented at the top levels of organizations when few have had the time to acquire the skills and experience to succeed there? There seem to be at least two solutions. One would be to promote women very rapidly, giving them preference over equally qualified men. There are at least two problems with this answer. First, such preferential treatment will create charges of favoritism and a backlash of resentment among men. Second, to move women too quickly to these positions would be to set them up for failure. From the point of view of women in organizations, this would be disastrous. Such failures would simply fuel arguments that women aren't ready for top positions. The other approach to getting women into top positions, despite their disadvantage in time of service, is to place them in special, accelerated programs. Such programs may seem condescending, but they work. However, they don't work overnight, and they don't work miracles.

It is understandable that women are anxious to move up rapidly in their firms. When people enter a new situation and see how well others are doing there, they naturally want the same for themselves. Unfortunately, such desires are often unrealistic, at least in the short run. There is every indication that the numbers of women at the top will change for the better. The percentage of women in managerial positions is growing rapidly, and these women are on the move. However, the drive to the top must be guided by realistic expectations and patience.

What Do You Think?

unjustly than workers in other democratic, industrialized nations. They call for national laws providing general protection against such treatment.

TRAINING AND DEVELOPMENT

The training of employees and the development of their skills and careers have many advantages for the firm. First of all, they help the firm meet its immediate human resource needs. Over the long run, training and development ensure that the firm's employees are ready to meet future challenges. A wide range of approaches to training and development have been devised; some have had considerable success.

Determining Training and Development Needs

Training and development needs may arise for many reasons. In general, training and development should follow a systematic needs assessment. The needs assessment should consider three sets of factors:

1. *The organization.* What is the environment for training in terms of the organization's goals, resources, and climate for training?
2. *The task.* What is the work to be performed and the conditions under which it will be performed?
3. *The person.* What personal capabilities are needed to do the job, and what are the people like who will do the job?

The needs assessment may indicate a requirement for specific skills that are not readily available, such as computer programming, accounting, and mechanical

As part of their training, some companies now send employees to programs that don't relate directly to the job. However, the teamwork these employees are learning through mountain climbing can translate into better cooperation at work.

skills. Or it may suggest needs for future career development among employees. Also, firms often set up special training programs for women, minorities, and the handicapped, in order to correct imbalances in management positions and meet affirmative action goals.[13]

Sometimes training takes the form of counseling employees on how to handle stress, overcome dependence on alcohol or other drugs, or manage their time. More than half of the Fortune 500 companies have such employee assistance programs. Illinois Bell Telephone Co., Navistar, and Control Data Corp. have reported favorable results from such programs, including fewer cases of illness disability, reduced grievances and disciplinary actions, and improved performance. Control Data estimates that its program saves the company $3.5 million annually.[14] In the face of the AIDS epidemic, firms such as Wells Fargo and IBM have initiated policies and programs to educate employees about AIDS, suggest how they can offer support, and even help them deal with death and the grieving process.[15]

On-the-Job Training

on-the-job training *training conducted while an employee performs job-related tasks.*

As the name says, **on-the-job training** is conducted while employees perform job-related tasks. They are not taken out of the workplace or put in a classroom. Employees learn the job by doing it, with coaching and feedback from a supervisor or more experienced employees. On-the-job training is the most direct approach to training and development. It offers both employer and employee the quickest return in terms of improved performance. Such training is also conducted in anticipation of future job requirements. For example, many large companies rotate their employees through a variety of positions to broaden their knowledge of the company so that they will be equipped to handle jobs in other areas. Other on-the-job training for employees includes regular coaching by a superior, committee assignments to involve individuals in decision-making activities, and staff meetings to broaden employee understanding of company activities outside their immediate areas.

Off-the-Job Training

It is often necessary to train employees away from the workplace. Such off-the-job training may take place elsewhere within the firm or outside the company. Role playing and in-baskets, which we discussed in conjunction with assessment centers, are often used for training purposes. Let's consider five other popular off-the-job training techniques.

Classroom Training. Classroom training is a popular off-the-job training technique. Many trainees can be handled by a relatively small number of instructors. Some large organizations have sophisticated classrooms for training purposes; films, videotapes, and other audiovisual media are used. Classroom training might also include case studies. Case studies start by presenting information about a business problem, such as how to finance the expansion of a new plant. Trainees are then asked to analyze the material and present recommendations. This may enhance their knowledge about specific issues and improve their decision-making skills.

Programmed Instruction. With **programmed instruction,** subject matter is broken down into organized, logical sequences. The trainee is presented with a segment of the information and responds by writing an answer or by pushing a button on a machine. When a correct response is given, the trainee is presented with the next segment of material. An incorrect response is met with an explanation and the suggestion to "try again." Computer-assisted instruction (CAI) is a more sophisticated version of programmed instruction, in which the memory and computational ability of computers permit more complex topics to be taught.

programmed instruction an off-the-job training technique in which subject matter is broken down into organized, logical sequences; when the trainee gives a correct response, he or she is presented with the next segment of material.

Management Games. **Management games** present trainees with a simulated business situation. Trainees make a series of decisions, such as how much of a product to manufacture and what price to charge. Generally, trainees are members of teams competing with other teams. The performance of each team is evaluated, and trainees get feedback, often from a computer. The games give a feeling of "real" decision making and generate considerable enthusiasm.

management games an off-the-job training technique in which trainees are presented with a simulated business situation requiring some type of decision to be made.

Sensitivity Training. **Sensitivity training** is used with small groups, called "T" (training) groups. In extended sessions, group members share their feelings and learn to be open to the views of others. Sensitivity training is designed to develop participants' sensitivity, self-insight, and awareness of group processes. Sensitivity training is controversial. For one thing, it has not been conclusively proved that sensitivity training leads to improvements in performance on the job. Also, some people feel stressed when asked to "open up" to others. Sensitivity training is still a part of many training programs, but its popularity has faded since the 1970s. The Profile of Erroll B. Davis, Jr. on page 234 discusses how sensitivity training is used at WPL Holdings.

sensitivity training an off-the-job training technique designed to develop participants' sensitivity, self-insight, and awareness of group processes.

Behavior Modeling. **Behavior modeling** gives supervisory trainees an opportunity to deal with the sorts of employee problems they may face on the job. They are given immediate feedback on their performance. With behavior modeling, trainees view videotapes in which a model supervisor is shown attempting to improve or maintain an employee's performance. The model shows specifically how to deal with the situation. Trainees then take the role of the supervisor and practice, in front of the trainer and other group members, the behaviors demonstrated by the models. As the trainee's behavior comes closer to

behavior modeling an off-the-job training approach in which supervisory trainees deal with actual employee problems and are given immediate feedback on their performance; trainees observe the behavior of a model supervisor and then imitate that behavior.

Erroll B. Davis, Jr.

Erroll Davis is the president and CEO of WPL Holdings. With over $600 million in annual operating revenues, WPL is the holding company of Wisconsin Power & Light Co. (WP&L) and of Heartland Development Corp., a real estate investment and development concern that provides low-cost affordable housing for Wisconsin communities. WPL also has an environmental consulting business, with offices across the country, which advises companies on how to comply with environmental regulations.

Trained in electrical engineering at Carnegie-Mellon University, Davis later received an MBA in Finance from The University of Chicago. He served on the corporate finance staffs at Ford Motor Company and Xerox Corp. before joining the utility in 1978 as vice president of finance.

Davis took over the reigns of WPL in 1990. He assumed leadership at a time of tremendous change and challenge in the utilities industry. Utility firms were previously regional monopolies and could focus primarily on reliability of service. Now they face deregulation, competition, environmental concerns, and the need to find innovative ways to meet future energy demands. Davis recognized that it was necessary to transform the culture of the company to make it more market-driven and more oriented toward quality and customer service. He had to do this while sharply cutting costs.

An avid tennis player, Davis carries his competitive spirit into his leadership role. He is taking aggressive steps to improve cost efficiency and enhance quality and has rallied his top management team to assist in that effort. Davis regularly meets with his 12 top executives to reemphasize company goals, give status reports, and develop long-range business plans. Most decisions are made by consensus. Davis has also reduced the number of employees handling some jobs, resulting in company-wide staffing reductions. Under his leadership, the company has also implemented new billing and customer information systems. Some managers worry that quality increases will be costly. But Davis says that quality doesn't cost; it saves.

Davis practices an open, friendly leadership style. He often walks the hallways at headquarters, calling many of his employees by name and discussing their work, families, and questions.

As the only African-American chief executive of a major public utility company, Davis is committed to strengthening the company's affirmative action policies and to helping it retain more blacks. WPL is struggling with diversity like every other company, but Davis says, "I confront this issue head-on. I set a tone that intolerance of difference will not be accepted within this company." Toward this end, the company instituted mandatory sensitivity training for all first-level managers and has made plans to incorporate diversity seminars into management training programs.

Davis has a special interest in education. He is a member of the University of Wisconsin System Board of Regents and the Carnegie Mellon University Board of Trustees. He regularly addresses groups of disadvantaged teens. Davis also serves on several other boards, including those of Amoco Corp., Sentry Insurance Company, and the American Gas Association. He has received many honors, including the 1988 "Black Engineer of the Year Award" from *U.S. Black Engineer* magazine.

Davis feels that understanding people is as important as understanding the dynamics of his industry. He combines an arsenal of competitive skills with a people-oriented management style, to transform WLP into an aggressive and successful 21st-century utility.

Source: Based in part on M. S. Scott, "Erroll Davis Has the Juice," *Black Enterprise,* June 1991, pp. 304–308.

that of the model, the trainer and other trainees provide praise, approval, encouragement, and attention. The behavior is videotaped to add feedback and reinforcement.

High-Tech Training

Sophisticated new tools are being used in training. For instance, simulation in training once meant using expensive replicas of job situations. Now, 300 law enforcement agencies across the country use complex computer-based simulations. On a ten-foot video screen, patrol officers watch criminals "respond" to their actions. If officers use their laser guns to shoot a criminal, the attacker can die on the screen. If not, the suspect might escape or even shoot back, "killing" the officer. After the simulation is completed, the computer rates the officer on the accuracy of any shooting and the wisdom of the decision. Other computerized simulations are used as part of the training of airline pilots and operators of nuclear power plants. The newest simulations employ "artificial reality." In one version, trainees wear fiber-optic helmets. They see 3-D images through the lenses of the helmet and hear stereophonic sound. As the trainee's head moves, the computer senses it and adjusts the image accordingly. Although such techniques are expensive, they typically cost only about 10 percent as much as training on real equipment.[16] We will discuss other computer applications to training in Chapter 12, Information Management.

APPRAISING PERFORMANCE

Performance appraisal is the process of measuring employee performance against established goals and expectations. Before we look at techniques for performance appraisal, let's consider why performance should be appraised in the first place.

performance appraisal
the process of measuring employee performance against established goals and expectations.

Why Appraise Performance?

There are many reasons to measure how well employees are performing. First, many administrative decisions, such as those dealing with promotions, salary increases, and layoffs, depend on performance appraisals. Second, if employees are to do their jobs better in the future, they need to know how well they have done them in the past. Then they can make adjustments in their work patterns as necessary. Third, appraisal can have powerful motivating effects. When employees know that their performance will be evaluated, they try harder to meet performance goals. Finally, performance appraisal is necessary as a check on new policies and programs. For example, if a new pay system has been put into effect, it is useful to see whether it has had a positive effect on employee motivation.

Types of Performance Measures

Performance may be appraised in at least three major ways. Appraisal can focus on employee traits, behavior, or accomplishments.

Trait Approaches. Under these approaches, a manager or performance appraiser rates an employee on such traits as friendliness, efficiency, and punctuality. The assumption is that these traits are related to performance. One such approach asks the appraiser to check the word or phrase (such as "outstanding," "average," or "poor") that best describes how an employee rates on each trait.

Trait approaches are very widely used in business, but they suffer from a number of problems. For instance, words such as "superior" and "average" may mean different things to different people. Also, the people appraising performance are sometimes biased in their ratings. They may also feel uncomfortable giving a coworker a low score on efficiency, decisiveness, or supervisory ability, especially if the ratings will be shown to the person being rated. As these problems suggest, trait approaches should never be used alone, if at all.

Behavioral Approaches. These approaches involve the rating or recording of specific employee actions. In the critical incidents method, for example, the performance appraiser keeps a list of all the employee's actions that were especially good or bad. A newer approach, the behaviorally anchored rating scale, presents a list of possible employee actions, rated on a scale ranging from very desirable to very undesirable. The rater checks the action on the scale in which the employee would be most likely to engage. By focusing on specific actions, this approach improves on the earlier trait approaches. However, behavioral approaches sometimes give employees the feeling that the rater is always looking over their shoulders.

Outcome Approaches. Rather than considering traits or actions, some appraisal techniques rate what the employee is supposed to accomplish on the job. One of these approaches, Management by Objectives, was discussed in Chapter 8. As noted there, this approach is time-consuming and may cause people to focus only on objectives that can be easily expressed in numbers. However, it does get directly at the things that the company cares most about.

COMPENSATING EMPLOYEES

The wages paid to employees, as well as other job benefits, depend in part on how well those employees perform on the job. Other factors influencing employee compensation are the relative worth of each job within the firm, labor market conditions and prevailing wage rates, and the type of pay system used. Let's take a closer look at these determinants of employee compensation.

Job Analysis

job analysis the systematic study of a job to determine its characteristics.

The systematic study of a job to determine its characteristics is called **job analysis.** One common method of gathering information about a job is to observe workers on the job, noting which tasks they perform, the order in which the tasks are done, and the time it takes to perform each one. Another method is to interview employees about the nature of their work. Sometimes employees are asked to supply the needed information by filling out written questionnaires. The value of this information is that it allows a job specification and job description to be written. A **job specification** is a summary of the qualifications needed in a worker for a specific job. It is especially useful in recruiting job applicants and making hiring decisions.

job specification a summary of the qualifications needed in a worker for a specific job.

Job Description

job description a short summary of the basic tasks making up a job.

A **job description** is a short summary of the basic tasks making up a job. A job description usually includes the title of the job, the supervisor to whom the employee reports, all major categories of work activities involved in the job, and working conditions. An example of a job description is shown in Figure 9-5.

FIGURE 9-5   Example of a Job Description

Job Identification

JOB TITLE: Employment Assistant

Division: Southern Area
Department: Human Resources Management
Job Analyst: Virginia Sasaki
Date Analyzed: 12/3/90
Wage Category: Exempt
Report to: HR Manager
Job Code: 11-17
Date Verified: 12/17/90

Brief Listing of Major Job Duties

JOB STATEMENT

Performs professional human resources work in the areas of employee *recruitment* and *selection, testing, orientation, transfers,* and maintenance of employee human resources files. May handle special assignments and projects in *EEO/Affirmative Action, employee grievances, training,* or *classification and compensation.* Works under general supervision. Incumbent exercises initiative and independent judgment in the performance of assigned tasks.

Job Duties and Responsibilities

JOB DUTIES

1. Prepares recruitment literature and job advertisements for applicant placement.
2. Schedules and conducts personal interviews to determine applicant suitability for employment. Includes reviewing mailed applications and résumés for qualified personnel.
3. Supervises administration of testing program. Responsible for developing or improving testing instruments and procedures.
4. Presents orientation program to all new employees. Reviews and develops all materials and procedures for orientation program.
5. Coordinates division job posting and transfer program. Establishes job posting procedures. Responsible for reviewing transfer applications, arranging transfer interviews, and determining effective transfer dates.
6. Maintains a daily working relationship with division managers on human resource matters, including recruitment concerns, retention or release of probationary employees, and discipline or discharge of permanent employees.
7. Distributes new or revised human resources policies and procedures to all employees and managers through bulletins, meetings, memorandums, and/or personal contact.
8. Performs related duties as assigned by the human resources manager.

Source: A. W. Sherman, Jr., and G. W. Bohlander, *Managing Human Resources,* 9th ed. (Cincinnati, Ohio: South-Western Publishing Company, 1992), p. 121.

Job descriptions serve a number of important functions. First, they clarify organizational structure by specifying who is to perform each task. They also minimize job overlap (in which two people are assigned the same task). Second, job descriptions can be used to introduce new employees to their jobs. In this way, they are given a good idea of what to expect on the job before they actually start work.

Job descriptions are also important in developing performance standards and criteria for job evaluations. **Performance standards** define the goals to be achieved by a worker over a specified period of time. The purpose of a **job evaluation** is to determine the relative worth of a job in the firm. The more important the job, the higher the level of pay. The result of the job evaluation process is a rank ordering or rating of job importance, which is useful in setting wage and salary scales.

performance standards *standards used to define the goals to be achieved by a worker over a specified period.*

job evaluation *an evaluation performed to determine the relative worth of a job in the firm.*

Labor Market Conditions

Supply and demand cause the wages for some jobs to be higher than the wages for others, even though the jobs may be of similar difficulty, responsibility, and so on. For example, in an area where many teachers but few nurses are looking for work, employers may have to pay more to hire a nurse than a teacher, even if the jobs are considered equally responsible. The level of wages is also influenced by what other local firms pay. For example, machine shops in the same town will tend to pay the same wage, especially if a union contract is in effect. Because of this tendency, some companies conduct surveys of local wage rates to make sure that their own are in line.

As Table 9-1 shows, there is considerable variability in average hourly wage rates for the same job in different parts of the country. On average, for example, the hourly wage rate for truck drivers is $3.96 more in Providence, Rhode Island, than in Raleigh-Durham, North Carolina. For secretaries, the wage differential between Oxnard-Ventura, California, and Providence, Rhode Island, is $3.23. Notice that although workers in most categories in Table 9-1 are paid more in Oxnard-Ventura, California, than in Madison, Wisconsin, forklift operators and guards are paid less. Geographic differences in factors such as cost of living and labor supply and demand play important roles in determining wages.

Pay Systems

Even after the value of a job is determined and the local and regional wage differences are taken into consideration, one person may be paid more for the same

TABLE 9-1   Average Hourly Wage Rates for Selected Jobs, by City

Job	Providence, R.I.	Stockton, Calif.	Raleigh-Durham, N.C.	Madison, Wis.	Oxnard-Ventura, Calif.	Savannah, Ga.
Secretary	9.88	10.52	10.53	10.71	13.11	10.36
Truck Driver	13.79	11.16	9.83	11.64	12.31	10.34
Forklift Operator	9.56	11.61	8.78	9.91	9.10	9.25
Drafter	12.78	10.38	12.72	11.43	12.07	11.52
Accounting Clerk	8.34	9.06	9.04	8.48	10.53	8.63
Key Entry Operator	7.53	7.04	7.70	7.29	8.44	8.25
Computer Operator	10.29	9.96	10.23	10.11	11.27	10.02
Guard	5.78	5.27	5.20	6.71	6.01	4.91
Computer Programmer	14.51	14.09	16.73	13.98	14.44	14.04

Wage quotations for Savannah are for March 1990; for Providence, April 1990; for Raleigh-Durham, May 1990; for Stockton and Oxnard-Ventura, August 1990; and for Madison, September 1990.

Source: U.S. Department of Labor, Bureau of Labor Statistics, *Area Wage Surveys* (1990).

job than another person. We can identify at least five other factors that account for wage differentials.

Individual Performance. How much individual employees are paid is often based largely on how well they do on the job. Under a **piece-rate system** of compensation, total wages paid are tied directly to output. For example, a worker in a toy factory may get one dollar for every puppet produced. Piece-rate systems are often justified because they motivate employees. As we discussed in Chapter 8, rewards that are directly based on desired outcomes have the strongest motivating effects. About half of the firms in a 1991 survey had performance-based pay plans.[17]

piece-rate system   a compensation plan in which total wages are tied directly to output.

Performance may be defined in various ways in compensation plans. For instance, at firms such as GTE and Sony, customer service representatives are rewarded on the basis of the speed and courtesy with which they respond to phone calls from customers.[18] Also, employees may be rewarded with things other than cash. Some firms give high performers vacation time or gifts such as VCRs and bicycles.[19] Some employees are rewarded with stock options—the right to purchase stock at some specified price, typically well below the market price. Stock options were once reserved for executives at the top of the corporate ladder, but they are increasingly being made available to middle and lower-level managers, and even to employees who are not managers.

Seniority. The term **seniority** refers to the number of years spent with the company. Generally, the more years of service, the greater the level of pay. The idea is that seniority reflects loyalty to the company as well as valuable experience.

seniority   the number of years spent with the company.

Group Performance. Workers performing similar or related tasks are sometimes organized into work groups. In such situations, pay scales are often tied to group performance. How much each person takes home is based on how well the group as a whole does. Such group performance systems encourage cooperation. Also, because wages for one worker are determined by the efforts of others, group members have an incentive to push slow workers to do better. Again, we see that compensation systems and motivation are related.

Plant-Wide or Company-Wide Productivity. Employee pay rates can be based in part on the productivity of the entire plant or organization. For instance, at Borden in 1990, 28,000 workers at 180 plants had the opportunity to win bonuses ranging from $250 to $800 each, depending on how their individual plants performed in relation to measures of attendance, safety, quality, production, and financial goals.[20] At Monsanto's chemical plant in Luling, Louisiana, workers earned bonuses of $760 each in 1990 when the plant met goals for reducing injuries and preventing pollutants from escaping into the outside air.[21] One form of productivity plan is the Scanlon Plan, under which groups of employees suggest to management how productivity might be improved. Then, at regular intervals, the productivity of the organization is evaluated. If productivity is up, each worker is rewarded with a bonus. Some Japanese companies have adopted an interesting variation of this plan. They have annual picnics at which new ideas, inventions, and improvements devised by the employees are exhibited and demonstrated by the company president.

FIGURE 9-6   The Wage Determination Process

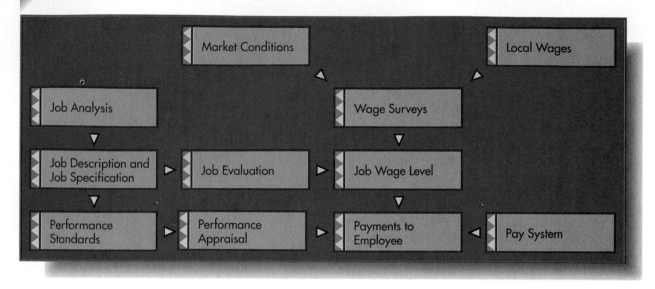

profit-sharing plans
bonus plans that tie employees' bonuses to levels of, or increases in, company profits.

Company Profit. Many companies today feature **profit-sharing plans.** Under such plans, employees are given a bonus, in the form of either a cash payment or company stock, if company profits are high. For instance, in 1988 General Motors paid out a total of $90 million in bonuses to 450,000 blue-collar and salaried workers, based on a profit-sharing formula. A nice feature of profit-sharing plans is that firms make payments only when they can afford them.

One problem with profit-sharing plans, as well as with tying bonuses to plant productivity, is that employees are not rewarded on the basis of individual performance. Research clearly shows that the more closely rewards are tied to individual performance, the more strongly the employee will be motivated. Also, employees do not like to be penalized for things outside their control, such as low company productivity or profit. For instance, Du Pont introduced an ambitious "achievement sharing" plan in 1988, involving nearly 20,000 employees in its fiber plants. However, poor performance of Du Pont's fiber business, primarily due to a weak economy, caused employees to face pay losses, and the plan was ended in late 1990.[22] In general, plant-wide productivity plans and profit-sharing plans may result in more positive employee attitudes toward the company, but they may not have much impact on individual performance.

Figure 9-6 shows where each of the factors we have discussed fits into the process of setting employee wage and salary rates.

SUMMARY POINTS

1 There are several steps in human resource planning. They include listing human resource objectives; making an inventory of the firm's current personnel and estimating outside labor supplies; considering the firm's strategic growth plan and the mix of employee skills it will require; estimating demand for labor in terms of the number of people required and the skills needed, as well as when these needs must be met; and developing human resource plans to match estimates of future labor supply with future labor demand.

2 The aim of the staffing process is to match the abilities and interests of the job candidate or employee with the changing needs of the firm. The three stages of the staffing process are recruiting, which refers to all activities involved in finding applicants for a job opening; selection, which involves evaluating candidates and picking one; and placement, which means fitting people and jobs together.

3 Careful recruiting, selection, and placement have advantages: New employees can begin work immediately, with no time needed to develop skills, and they can be hired with proven skills, reducing the risk that they may not learn properly. Training and development also have advantages: People can be hired at lower rates of pay if they come to the firm untrained; training and development can be tailored exactly to the company's needs; and people trained by a firm often feel loyal to it.

4 Six sources of job applicants are (1) newspaper advertisements, which draw many applicants but do not serve as a screening device; (2) referrals, which are useful because current and past employees usually understand the firm's human resource needs; (3) private employment agencies, which charge fees for their services and take over some recruiting tasks from the hiring firm; (4) public employment agencies, which find jobs for unemployed persons and keep track of them; (5) educational institutions, such as colleges and high schools, which may invite recruiters to campus; and (6) labor unions, which have hiring halls and may be good sources for blue-collar and some professional jobs. The realistic job preview tries to give recruits an accurate picture of the company and job, rather than an unrealistically rosy view.

5 There are several approaches to selection and hiring. Application blanks provide a variety of information, which is often useful for screening purposes, but some of it may not be relevant to performance on the job or may be incorrect. Also, some information cannot be legally collected by application blanks. References are popular, but the people providing the information may not be frank or may know little about the

applicant. Interviews are easy to use, and they personalize the selection process, but they are subject to many biases and errors. Tests are relatively objective and provide considerable information, but it may be hard to develop fair and valid tests, and some tests can be faked. Assessment centers use a variety of procedures and make better predictions of employee performance than other approaches to selection, but they can be expensive.

6 Placement involves fitting people and jobs together once the people are employees of the firm. This may involve moving employees laterally, promoting them to positions of more responsibility, or demoting them to positions of less responsibility. In some cases, termination may be necessary.

7 The two basic goals of training and development are to help the firm meet its immediate human resource needs and to prepare employees for future job challenges. Approaches to training and development include on-the-job training, classroom training, programmed instruction, management games, sensitivity training, and behavior modeling.

8 Performance appraisal is needed as an input to administrative decisions, to help employees improve their performance in the future, and to check on whether new policies and programs are working. Performance can be measured by the trait, behavioral, or outcome approaches.

9 The wages paid to employees depend on their performance on the job, the relative worth of jobs, labor market conditions, and the type of pay system used. Job analysis is the study of the essential characteristics of a job; job description is the systematic listing of the tasks making up a job. Five pay system factors that account for wage differentials are individual performance, seniority, group performance, plant-wide or company-wide productivity, and company profitability.

REVIEW QUESTIONS

1 Define human resource planning.

2 What is the basic goal of staffing?

3 How do recruiting and placement differ from training and development?

4 What is the aim of the realistic job preview?

5 Name six sources of job applicants.

6 In the selection and hiring process, how does a personality test differ from an interest test?

7 What is a fair test?

8 Explain how the Peter Principle works. Give an example.

9 What are five types of off-the-job training?

10 What are some reasons why it is necessary to appraise employee performance?

11 Describe some problems with trait approaches to performance appraisal.

12 What is a job description? What is it used for?

DISCUSSION QUESTIONS

1 In what ways are human resources like other resources of the firm? In what ways are they different?

2 Discuss factors that would influence the relative desirability of recruiting, selection and placement, on the one hand, and training and development, on the other, for effective human resource management.

3 Under what conditions might letters of reference be useful in the selection and hiring process?

4 What role should personality testing play in the selection and hiring process? Is there a danger with these tests? If so, in what ways could they be misused?

5 Cite some situations in which demotion would be preferable to firing an employee.

6 How important should seniority be in determining the wage paid to an employee? Does tying pay to years of service punish some workers unfairly?

EXPERIENTIAL EXERCISES

1 Read the classified advertisements for positions available in a recent copy of *The Wall Street Journal*. For three of the positions, list the qualifications specified in the advertisement (for example, "extensive accounting and auditing knowledge," "self-directed and independent," "experience with sales of all types of medical equipment"). Then discuss how the firm that placed the advertisement could best measure how well the applicants meet each of those qualifications.

2 Select four different sorts of jobs (such as night watchperson, professional basketball player, secretary, and lawyer). Then list the factors that you feel are considered in determining the wages for each of those jobs. To what extent are the lists similar or dissimilar?

CASES

CASE 9-1
Tying Managers' Pay to Performance

Time Warner CEO Steven J. Ross had a very good year in 1990. The merger of Time, Inc. with Warner Communications led to a $74.9 million bonus for Ross, bringing his total compensation for the year to $78,176,000. This was an extreme case, but executive bonuses are becoming larger and more common. Very often they exceed base salaries. Supporters of such bonuses say that since the bonuses are tied to some aspect of company performance, they are appropriate rewards for a job well done. Karyl Lynn, personnel director at Colt Industries, says of generous bonuses at her firm, "We have no shame or trepidation about the fact that our people are highly paid. They've earned it."

A similar attitude can be found in increasing numbers of boardrooms across the country. After years of regularly receiving hefty increases in salary and bonus—regardless of their companies' success or failure—more top executives are now finding their compensation linked directly to corporate performance. The trend is even extending to division managers. "There's been so much scrutiny that boards have been taking a closer look" at compensation, says Pete Smith, national director of Wyatt Co.'s compensation consulting business. Companies are now relying less on salary and more on bonuses and other performance-linked compensation to reward executives. They are also tightening the criteria for earning those rewards.

Bonuses and other long-term compensation are becoming more important. In 1975, salary made up 60 percent of the pay of a chief executive officer of a company with $1 billion to $2 billion in sales. By 1985, the proportion had fallen to 50 percent.

Also, during economic downturns and times of low profits, a bonus plan offers a way to trim compensation costs quickly. "Salaries are a fixed cost; bonuses are a variable cost," says Charles Peck, a compensation specialist. Some executives have found their compensation sharply cut by hard times. For instance, Barry Sullivan, chairman of First Chicago Corp., did without a cash bonus for 1990. This cut his cash compensation by 50 percent, to $735,632 (although he also received 65,000 stock options, as well as 25,000 restricted shares valued at $662,500).

Traditionally, executive bonuses were supposed to be tied to growth in earnings per share or similar measures, but many executives have come to look on the bonuses simply as additional salary. "The past standards were so loose that bonus plans were designed to pay off no matter what," says a corporate compensation manager. Such plans also gave executives an incentive to maximize short-term profits at the expense of long-term corporate goals. Now, however, more compensation is linked to three-year or five-year gains in such performance measures as return on equity, return on assets, and earnings per share.

1. What impact do you think the changes noted in this case will have on executive motivation?
2. Do you see any potential dangers with this approach to rewarding executives?
3. In view of the potential benefits of performance-based bonuses, why do you think they are not universally applied?

Source: Based on A. Bennett, "More Managers Find Salary, Bonus Are Tied Directly to Performance," *Wall Street Journal,* 28 February 1986, p. 23; A. Bennett, "Hard Times Trim CEO Pay Raises," *Wall Street Journal,* 17 April 1991; and J. A. Byrne, "The Flap Over Executive Pay," *Business Week,* 6 May 1991, pp. 90–96.

CASE 9-2
How Does Disney Do It?

Walt Disney Company has been tremendously successful, with 1991 revenues of $6.2 billion and sharply rising returns to stockholders. Central to that success are the "cast members" in its theme parks, which contribute over half of Disney's revenue. These members are primarily high school and college students, and they must be trained and motivated to perform repetitive, sometimes routine work at low pay while conveying the Disney fantasy and creating happiness. This is even more challenging because Disney is heavily unionized; Disneyland alone has 24 unions. Disney has made a concerted effort to develop a sense of community and shared values. It does this largely through selection, training, and socialization, and it has developed Disney University to help in the process.

Disney's philosophy is a comprehensive approach to employee relations. It is reinforced with activities, management style and language. For example, employees are called "cast members," and they don't work at a job, they're cast in a role. Cast members work either onstage or backstage, and they wear costumes, not uniforms.

Because of the company's clean-cut image and conservative reputation, it usually attracts the type of applicants it wants. To narrow the field even more and make sure that everyone knows what's expected before the interviews proceed, would-be employees may be shown a film that details the discipline, grooming, and dress code. People know in advance that they must conform if they want a role in the show.

Virtually all of the 39,000 cast members begin their Disney career with an orientation. Rather than a single program, this orientation is an ongoing process that continually reinforces the company's values, philosophies, and guest service standards.

Orientation is the core of the company's training. It is designed to be sensitive to new cast members. Teachers at Disney University reflect the group they're instructing. Outstanding cast members, dressed in full costume, lead a group of new college-age employees through the park.

When orientation is completed, cast members begin a series of learning experiences on-site and classes at the university. In the next step—paired training—exceptional cast members act as role models. The benefits are twofold: The new cast member rehearses with a respected member of the troupe, and the veteran gets recognition from management, as well as his or her peers.

To encourage enthusiasm and commitment, Disney offers service recognition awards, peer recognition programs, attendance awards, and milestones banquets for 10, 15 and 20 years of service. In addition, informal recognition parties, during which root beer floats are served in employee cafeterias, help boost morale. During the Christmas holiday, the parks reopen one night just for cast members and their families. Management says "happy holidays" by dressing in costume and operating the parks. All events are designed to build a sense of camaraderie and identification with the organization.

1.   What factors make human resource management especially difficult at Disney? What factors might facilitate it?
2.   To what degree does Disney rely on recruitment, selection, and placement on the one hand rather than training and development on the other?
3.   How do you think human resource practices at Disney are likely to influence employee satisfaction and motivation, loyalty to the firm, and performance?

Source: "How Does Disney Do It?" by C. M. Solomon, © Dec. 1989. Reprinted with the permission of PERSONNEL JOURNAL, Costa Mesa, California; all rights reserved.

CHAPTER 10

Labor-Management Relations

OBJECTIVES

After studying this chapter, you should be able to:

1 Describe the role of labor unions in today's economy.

2 Explain how labor unions are structured.

3 Describe the process by which unions are organized.

4 Identify the key issues in collective bargaining and discuss the collective bargaining process.

5 Discuss the use of mediation and arbitration for settling labor–management disputes.

6 Explain how contract administration takes place.

7 Identify the sources of negotiating strength for labor and for management.

8 Discuss new approaches to labor–management cooperation.

On March 19, 1990, a settlement was reached between major league baseball players and the owners of the teams. The baseball season could finally get underway, although opening day was delayed by a week. After a final marathon meeting, representatives of players and owners signed a collective bargaining agreement to end a 32-day lockout by the owners. In the new agreement, a player's minimum salary would be $100,000—up from $68,000 under the old contract. The players also gained bigger owner contributions to the players' pension plan and some strengthening of players' ability to negotiate individual salaries. In each case, the terms represented a compromise between the initial positions of management and labor. The delay caused by the dispute crushed the hopes of young players still in the minor leagues, who had hoped to prove their talent during spring training. The delay also forced the cancellation of some of ESPN's coverage of spring training and regular-season games, hurt local economies (since most exhibition games were canceled), and raised the ire of countless fans. Still, things could have been worse.[1]

This chapter examines how labor and management deal with each other in order to achieve their individual and joint goals. We'll begin by examining the nature and role of labor unions in today's economy. We will then consider how workers organize into unions, and we will discuss the collective bargaining process. Next, we'll examine how disputes are settled and discuss the sources of negotiating strength of labor and management. We will close with a look at new approaches to labor–management cooperation.

In the opening years of the 1990s, labor–management relations were in flux. The power of unions continued its long decline, but unions tried innovative initiatives. A new nursing union, the United Nurses of America, was formed. Some union contracts led to very favorable outcomes for employees. For instance, agreements between the United Auto Workers union (UAW) and General Motors resulted in substantial improvements in workers' job security, pension benefits, a reduction of the minimum retirement age to 50, and many other gains. In return, GM was given more flexibility in assigning work, eliminating expensive work rules, and reducing the workforce through attrition.[2]

In other cases, employees were less happy. Continental Air Lines pilots actually filed suit against their union, claiming that its settlement with the company to resolve a lengthy strike and lawsuit had left the pilots worse off than if they had simply offered to return to work.[3] Bitter labor disputes took place at Eastern Airlines, Greyhound, and the Pittston Coal Co. This was in stark contrast to the cooperative negotiations in the auto industry, which some hailed as "the dawn of more mature and cooperative labor–management relationships in the industry."[4]

The ways in which labor and management settle their differences—and recognize their common interests—largely determine whether their relationship is productive or ends in hostility, strikes, or employee firings and plant closings.

LABOR UNIONS

labor union   an organization made up of workers who have united to achieve their job-related goals.

A union is a collection of people or organizations joined together for a common purpose. A **labor union** is an organization made up of workers who have united to achieve their job-related goals. Labor unions work to ensure that their members get a fair "price" for their services, safe working conditions, more interesting work, and job security. By forming unions, workers can bargain more effectively than if each worker dealt with management separately.

Role in Today's Economy

The labor union plays an important role in our economy. Most of this country's basic industries (steel, automobiles, rubber, glass, machinery, mining) are heavily unionized. Earlier in the century, union membership in the United States rose

Many manufacturing industries are union strongholds, such as carpet fiber manufacturing.

dramatically, from under 4 million in 1930 to more than 14 million in 1950. Membership peaked at 23.7 million in 1975 and then slid to about 17 million in 1990. About 40 percent of those members were government employees. Union membership as a percentage of the labor force peaked in 1953 and then declined; it is currently about 16 percent. Next we'll examine labor unions from the perspective of their impact on workers and on management.

Impact on Workers. Labor unions affect workers in many ways. Successful bargaining results in economic security and fair treatment for union members. Unions give workers a sense of belonging and a feeling of having some control over their work lives. They also provide a formal channel through which workers' grievances can be aired. But not all employees want to be in a union. For one thing, unions charge membership dues to cover their expenses. Some employees do not believe that the benefits of membership are worth those dues. Many employees also believe that their companies are already doing the best they can for workers and that a union would only tie the hands of management. The employees of Lincoln Electric System have agreed for years that they do not need a union. They earn more money under the firm's profit-sharing plan than they would if they were unionized. Moreover, the company provides a good measure of job security. It has not laid off an employee since 1951.

Impact on Management. It is safe to say that managers of most companies in the United States would prefer that their companies not be unionized. The presence of a unionized workforce generally weakens management's control over how work is staffed and organized, how performance is appraised, and how wages are set. For example, some municipal bus drivers' unions are very strong. These unions can dictate route schedules, numbers of buses per route, and hours of operation. They also set the standards by which management evaluates drivers and establishes wage rates and seniority systems.

The presence of a labor union can often create a power struggle between labor and management. Such a struggle has the potential to harm the company economically, through strikes and other means. If workers vote to join a union, this may be perceived by management as a "slap in the face."

Union contracts also limit management's ability to cut costs during slack periods. For instance, although General Motors lost $1.4 billion in the fourth quarter of 1990, union contracts required the company to continue providing laid-off workers with nearly full pay and benefits.

Still, the picture is not one-sided. In the long run, a union, by helping to meet employee needs, may lead to a stronger, more satisfied, more highly skilled workforce. A union can also serve as a communication channel, providing a way for management to learn of employee concerns. Moreover, some unions may take over responsibility for disciplining employees, one of the more unpleasant functions of management.

Labor Union Structure

There are three main levels of labor organizations. They are national unions, local unions, and union federations.

National Unions. Most U.S. unions are organized on a national basis. The biggest national union is the National Education Association, with 2 million members, followed by the Teamsters, Chauffeurs, Warehousemen and Helpers of America (commonly referred to as the Teamsters), with 1.6 million members. The ten largest U.S. labor unions are listed in Table 10-1.

TABLE 10-1   10 Largest U.S. Labor Unions in Terms of Total Membership

Union	Members (Thousands)
National Education Association	2,000
Teamsters, Chauffeurs, Warehousemen and Helpers of America	1,600
Food and Commercial Workers	1,300
State, County, and Municipal Employees	1,200
Automobile, Aerospace & Agricultural Workers of America	1,000
Electrical Workers	1,000
Service Employees	850
Steelworkers of America	750
American Federation of Teachers	750
Communications Workers of America	700

Source: Bureau of Labor Statistics, 1991.

By law, the leaders of national unions must be elected at least every five years. These elections are usually held during national labor conventions.

The structure of a national union can be as complex as the structure of a corporation. For instance, the United Steelworkers of America (USW) has units to handle membership records, pensions, dues, investments, and negotiations. In addition, departments and committees deal with such matters as civil rights, education, organizing, contract research, and safety and health.

What does a national union do for its members? Consider the United Mine Workers (UMW). To help local UMW affiliates, UMW representatives periodically visit small independent mines to encourage miners to sign up with the union, and they monitor large mining operations to be sure that the union holds its strength there. To help individual members, the UMW maintains a pension fund for mine workers, as well as health programs, special disability programs, and extensive welfare programs for the families of miners killed at work. The national union spends millions of dollars each year researching black lung disease and other occupational hazards of mining. When a mine disaster occurs, or when economic conditions shut down a mine, the UMW comes into town and provides emergency loans, unemployment compensation, special counseling, and other help for miners and their families. Meanwhile, the union conducts economic research to improve its bargaining position in Congress and with mining companies. There are at least six functions that national unions perform for their members and local affiliates.

- Assist with organizing campaigns.
- Manage pension funds and other benefit programs for members.
- Conduct economic and social research to use in collective bargaining.
- Give financial aid and emergency assistance to member locals.
- Lobby legislatures for labor's point of view and economic interests.
- Negotiate contracts with management that serve as a model for other unions.

This chapter's profile of Vicki Saporta of the International Brotherhood of Teamsters (page 250) provides further insights into the roles of national unions.

Local Unions. Local unions are usually affiliated with a national labor organization. Local unions represent workers in a particular geographic area. They may be organized by craft (such as plumbers or electricians), according to the particular industry (such as steelworkers), or both. Locals may represent a single plant, all plants in a geographic area, or several smaller companies in an area. Most workers have direct contact with their local, rather than with the national organization.

The members of a local are represented in a plant by **union stewards,** whom they usually elect. The responsibilities of stewards include interpreting the contracts between labor and management for members of the local, acting as spokespersons for employees in disputes with management, and working out acceptable solutions to these disputes. Union stewards at the Ford Motor Co. are assigned to each assembly line or manufacturing department. They monitor safety standards, report contract violations or complaints both to Ford and to their unions, and act as mediators between Ford managers and union representatives.

union stewards individuals who represent members of a local union in a plant.

Union Federations. Most national unions in the United States have joined federations. The largest of these, the American Federation of Labor–Congress of Industrial Organizations (AFL–CIO), has about 14 million members in more than 80 member unions. AFL–CIO member unions include the Federation of State, County, and Municipal Employees, the United Mineworkers, the American Federation of Teachers, the United Steelworkers of America, and the Ladies' Garment Workers. Labor federations provide such services for member unions as research, education, lobbying, and public relations.

THE ORGANIZING PROCESS

Workers organize into unions in two basic ways. Dissatisfied workers may decide on their own to join a union, or professional union organizers may come into a plant to convince workers that a union would advance their interests. In either situation, the following steps usually take place.

Organizing Campaign

At the start of the organizing process, some workers will favor the idea of joining a union. These workers try to persuade others to sign authorization cards. An **authorization card** designates the union as the worker's bargaining agent. The organizing campaign continues until the majority of employees have signed up. When the union believes that it has a majority, it may ask the employer for official recognition. If the employer refuses, the union can then petition the National Labor Relations Board (NLRB) for an election.

authorization card a card signed by a worker, which designates the union as the worker's bargaining agent.

This organizing process is often the most difficult part of introducing a union. There were two stumbling blocks to unionizing the textile firm of J. P. Stevens & Co. The first was persuading a majority of employees to sign up; the second was getting the company to recognize the union. Similarly, banks still fight vigorously against any attempts to enroll their employees in unions; fewer than 1 percent are organized.

Vicki Saporta

When Vicki Saporta was appointed Director of Organizing for the International Brotherhood of Teamsters in 1983, it was quite a change for the male-dominated union. The Teamsters broke with tradition by appointing the first female organizing director of a major union.

Saporta is a graduate of the School of Industrial and Labor Relations at Cornell University, where she was on the women's basketball and sailing teams. She also received training at the London School of Economics.

After joining the Teamsters in 1974, she spent nine years on the road, traveling over 200 days per year organizing new members. She has organized in virtually every part of the country and in most sectors of the economy, including airlines, public service, health care, trucking, and manufacturing.

Achieving unusual success early in her career, she won ten straight victories for union representation in ten months in the anti-union state of North Carolina. Getting employees involved was instrumental to her campaigns. She led rallies, parades, and meetings and dressed her supporters in bright yellow "Go Teamsters" T-shirts. You could find your way to any plant Saporta was organizing by the trail of phosphorescent Teamster stickers.

Teamster locals have traditionally been given the responsibility for organizing in their communities. Saporta structured the Organizing Department to give the union's 650 locals needed assistance. The help took the form of training programs; advice in formulating, and assistance in implementing, organizing corporate campaign strategies before, during, and after elections; development of surveys and polls; information regarding organizing issues, company profiles, and management consultants; assistance with cases before the National Labor Relations Board; materials, including videotapes, leaflets, and organizing items; experienced organizers; evaluation of grant requests; assistance with affiliations; decertification election assistance; and coordination of industry-wide and company-wide campaigns. Such assistance from the international union has enabled the Teamsters to organize both small and large units.

In 1991, Saporta made another breakthrough. She was placed on a slate of candidates for the executive board of the Teamsters. Though 30 percent of Teamster members are female, no woman had held a position on the board in the history of the union. Saporta's slate did not win the election, but the changing nature of the Teamsters was reflected by the fact that the winning slate did include one woman.

Saporta is a committed and vocal advocate for labor. She freely criticizes management when she feels that it is ignoring workers' needs. She hopes some day to organize hundreds of thousands of workers a year. In these times of declining union membership, this is clearly an ambitious goal. It will require energy and the ability to delegate authority and to motivate subordinates. Given Vicki Saporta's abilities and track record, nobody is betting against her. She is helping shape a new image for the Teamsters, and she is changing many people's stereotypes of unions.

Determining the Bargaining Unit

After the NLRB receives a petition, it conducts a hearing to determine the appropriate bargaining unit. The **bargaining unit** is the group of employees whom the union will represent if it receives a majority of votes. For instance, the bargaining unit could be defined as all employees in technician job categories in a particular plant, or it could be all nonmanagerial employees in several locations. Since some employees are likely to want the union more than others, how the bargaining unit is defined—that is, who is included in the unit—often affects the outcome of the election. Therefore, both union and management argue for units that improve their chances of winning the election. To determine the most appropriate bargaining unit, the NLRB considers worker demands, the geographical distribution of workers, the similarity of interests among workers, and how other bargaining units are defined in the industry.

bargaining unit   the group of employees whom the union represents if it receives the majority of votes.

Representation Election Campaign

Both labor and management work hard to win employees over to their sides. Union people argue that workers will be treated more fairly under a union and that they will have better benefits and more power. Management argues that workers can do just as well without a union and that union dues will cost more than the union will return in benefits.

If the union wins the election, it becomes the exclusive representative of all employees in the bargaining unit, including those who do not belong to the union. If it loses, it can try for recognition again in a year. Both the frequency of elections and union success in the elections that are held have been declining. For instance, blue-collar unions won 40 percent of 1,066 organizing votes in 1990, as against 54 percent of 4,361 elections in 1970.[5]

Decertification Election

Winning a representation election doesn't necessarily guarantee that the union will remain in place. If employees have second thoughts about the desirability of keeping the union's services, they can—after a period of one year—petition the NLRB for a decertification election. A majority vote in the decertification election ousts the union.

In a well-publicized 1991 case, employees in Seattle-area stores of Nordstrom Inc., a major retailer, voted by more than a two-to-one margin to decertify United Food and Commercial Workers Local 1001, the union that had represented them for six decades. The fight was begun by Nordstrom, which demanded in contract talks two years earlier that union membership be made optional. The union attracted national attention by disclosing that Nordstrom doesn't fully compensate salespeople for providing some of the extra service on which the company has built its reputation. During the decertification campaign, the company ran a 24-hour telephone hotline and produced anti-union videos.[6]

Unions are losing an increasing number of decertification elections. By 1989, over 700 such elections were being held annually, and unions were losing about three out of four.

COLLECTIVE BARGAINING

Collective bargaining is the process by which representatives of labor and management negotiate an agreement governing pay scales and terms of work. The negotiations leading to a labor contract are often time-consuming, difficult, and

collective bargaining   the process by which representatives of labor and management negotiate an agreement covering pay scales and terms of work.

Vacation time is among the fringe benefits unions can achieve through collective bargaining.

heated. A contract between a large union and an industry such as automobiles or steel is of considerable economic consequence, involving thousands of workers and billions of dollars in wages.

Key Issues

Collective bargaining focuses on issues that are important to management and to workers. Let's look at several of the key issues.

Union Security and Management Rights. The union and management are each concerned with preserving and strengthening their relative positions. The union generally wants some form of security. **Union security clauses,** now appearing in about 83 percent of contracts, specify whether union membership is required for all employees in the bargaining unit. From the point of view of the union, the most advantageous of these clauses is called the closed shop. As discussed in Chapter 3, employees must join the union as a condition of employment in a closed shop. Closed shops are unusual nowadays; they are generally prohibited by law for firms engaging in interstate commerce. With a union shop, the employer may hire anyone, whether or not they are members of the union. However, new employees must then join the union in order to stay employed. This is now by far the most common form, appearing in 72 percent of contracts. In a maintenance-of-membership shop, the worker is free to elect whether or not to join the union. However, a worker who does join the union must maintain membership in the union for the duration of the contract period or forfeit the job. During an "escape period," the employee may drop the membership before it becomes effective. Once quite common, the maintenance-of-membership shop is now rare. Two other uncommon forms are the agency shop and the preferen-

union security clauses
clauses in labor contracts that specify whether union membership is required of all employees in the bargaining unit.

tial shop. With the agency shop, employees are not required to join the union but must pay a fee to the union to help support it. The preferential shop gives union members preference in hiring but allows the employment of nonunionists.

The union may also demand a checkoff. With a **checkoff,** the worker's union dues are deducted directly from the paycheck. A **management-rights clause** lists the areas of operation in which management may take actions without having to obtain permission from the union.

Compensation. Wages are almost always a major concern in collective bargaining. Wage rates, determination of pay grades, incentive systems, and pay for particular jobs are all vital matters. Generally, a union tries to get the same pay for its members as other workers receive in similar jobs.

Some recent contracts have provided unprecedented unemployment benefits for laid-off workers. For instance, a contract signed in 1990 by GM and the United Auto Workers provides laid-off workers with 85 percent of regular take-home pay for up to three years. More than 100,000 autoworkers who are laid off either temporarily or indefinitely will receive these benefits.

Because of the impact of inflation on real purchasing power, many unions have pushed for **cost-of-living adjustments (COLAs).** Under a COLA, wages are adjusted during the life of the contract in accordance with changes in the consumer price index (CPI). For example, if the CPI went up by 5 percent, wages would automatically increase by the same percentage. COLA clauses were contained in the contracts of 39 percent of workers under 1990 settlements.[7] This was down from a peak of 61 percent in 1977. During 1990, about 1.4 million workers received average wage increases of 2.7 percent because of COLAs. Almost all COLAs are in private industry.

Fringe Benefits. This is another important issue to both labor and management. **Fringe benefits** are any benefits received by employees in addition to their regular pay. They include paid vacation, sick leave, welfare programs, and health and life insurance. The cost of fringe benefits is increasing much more rapidly than wages. One fringe benefit that unions have been stressing recently is the pension. Pension funds are certainly not small: The pension fund of the United Mine Workers is currently valued at over $4 billion.

Job Security. Beginning in the early 1980s, there was a sharp increase in the number of agreements calling for employee givebacks. **Givebacks** are reductions in wages and benefits or delays in receiving increases that were negotiated previously. Because of hard economic times, employees are willing to make such sacrifices in return for more job security. In recent years, an unprecedented number of contracts have contained job security clauses.[8] National Steel Corp. promised the United Steelworkers that it would not lay anybody off during the life of its new contract, barring an economic "disaster." A Pacific Telesis Group unit made a similar guarantee to the Communication Workers of America, with a promise to provide training for workers moving to new positions if necessary. Typically, the price of such security clauses has been pay cuts or other financial sacrifices.

Hours of Work. Important issues to be negotiated are the length of the workday, the length of the workweek, and the nature of work shifts. For instance, in a 1991 agreement with General Motors, the United Auto Workers union agreed to let GM operate an Ohio car plant with three assembly crews on an expanded

---

checkoff an automatic deduction of union dues from a worker's paycheck.

management-rights clause a clause in a labor contract that lists the areas of operation in which management may take actions without having to obtain permission from the union.

cost-of-living adjustment (COLA) the adjustment of wages during the life of the labor contract in relation to changes in the consumer price index.

fringe benefits any benefits received by employees in addition to regular pay.

givebacks in labor-management bargaining, a reduction in wages and benefits, or a delay in receiving increases previously negotiated; typically accepted by the union in exchange for greater job security.

work schedule. In return for this flexibility, GM agreed to hire all additional work-ers from an adjacent assembly plant the company planned to close later in the year.[9] How employees are compensated for extra work (for example, time and a half for overtime) is also an important negotiating issue. Some unions are press-ing now to strip management of the right to make workers accept overtime assignments even when they do not want them.

Safety and Health.   Private industry workers sustained 6.5 million injuries and illnesses on the job in 1989. The 60 million workdays lost to injuries and illnesses cost billions of dollars in lost wages and production slowdowns and billions more in medical and administrative expenses.[10] Company payments for employees' medical costs are often tremendous. For instance, General Motors spent $2.9 bil-lion in medical costs in 1989.

With rising health care costs and growing concern about environmental dan-gers, unions have begun to place greater emphasis on contract provisions dealing with employee health and safety. A major oil workers' strike occurred because employers refused to cover the full cost of medical insurance. In other industries, special contract provisions cover safety equipment, health safeguards, and train-ing programs on health and safety. The UAW and General Motors formed a joint committee to study health care issues and to experiment with various health care approaches.

Quality of Work Life.   Until fairly recently, unions pushed for "hard" gains, such as wage increases. Job enrichment and democracy in the workplace were thought to have little meaning for the average worker. Today, as discussed in the Controversial Issue on page 256, quality of work life (QWL) clearly has a major impact on employee health, satisfaction, and behavior, so some unions are paying closer attention to it. Major QWL programs at General Motors and elsewhere have had promising results.

Prenegotiation

Unions and management engage in months of preparation before bargaining begins. The union gathers information about other contract settlements, inflation rates, and worker demands. Management tries to anticipate what the union will ask for. It also assesses its own needs, how much it can afford to give up, how various settlements would affect its competitive situation, and so on. If a contract is currently in effect, union and management may use it as a starting point. Each then tries to improve its position and to clarify areas of confusion or controversy.

Negotiation

Negotiations usually begin with a presentation by the union of a list of demands. For bargaining purposes, management may also write up a list of its own. Through the process of bargaining, the sides come closer and closer together. Various demands of each side are dropped, revised, or traded off. The negotiation of a labor contract is a give-and-take process. Both parties get something and give up something in return. At some point in the process, the union may call for a strike vote as a show of member support.

The negotiating atmosphere may range from genuine cooperation to outright hostility. Each side attempts to win the "game." Some examples of negotiating behaviors are presented in Figure 10-1.

FIGURE 10-1   Negotiating Behaviors

DE-EMPHASIZING DIFFERENCES

"Who won?" was the question as the two parties proceeded to the next room for the formal announcement and picture taking (after the completion of the 1955 Ford Motor-UAW negotiations). "We both won," Reuther (union leader) replied. "We are extremely happy to announce that we have arrived at an agreement...Both the Company and the Union have worked very hard and very sincerely at the bargaining table."

Source: B. M. Selekman, S. K. Selekman, and S. H. Fuller, *Problems in Labor Relations*, 2nd ed. (New York: McGraw-Hill Book Co., 1958), pp. 428-429.

PUNISHING OPPONENT'S BEHAVIOR

A union delegate to management: "We have been very reasonable this year; if the company does not take advantage of it, *things will be different.* It appears to me that the company is not sincere; General Motors has settled, John Deere has settled, and yet the company has done nothing."

Source: R. E. Walton and R. B. McKersie, *A Behavioral Theory of Labor Negotiations* (New York: McGraw-Hill Book Co., 1965), p. 254.

COMPLIMENTING OPPONENT'S BEHAVIOR

Management negotiator during bargaining: "I might inquire as to the job-evaluation committee. I want to say that you people have gone along in pretty fine style there. It is new to you and the reason you are doing well is because you have an open mind."

Source: A. Douglas, *Industrial Peacemaking* (New York: Columbia University Press, 1962), p. 331.

SEPARATING NEGOTIATORS FROM THEIR BEHAVIORS

Management negotiator during bargaining: "I have found that your union representatives, even when they were angry and sore and mean—and they get that way just the way we get that way, because we are all human—even in their worst moments, they were all men whose word could be trusted."

Source: Selekman, Selekman, and Fuller, p. 550.

Source: R. E. Walton and R. B. McKersie, *A Behavioral Theory of Labor Negotiations*, 2nd ed. (New York: ILR Press, 1991). Reproduced with permission.

Typically, bargaining continues until the last minute, just before the existing contract expires. Both sides want to show their supporters that they have done everything possible to have their demands met. Once a tentative agreement is reached, it must generally be agreed to by union members and by a management body, such as a board of directors.

Mediation and Arbitration

Attempts by the union and management to work out an agreement may reach a dead end, either before or after the start of a strike. Then mediation or arbitration may be necessary.

Mediation. In **mediation,** an experienced and knowledgeable neutral person, the mediator, helps the union and management reach an agreement. State agencies or the Federal Mediation and Conciliation Service provide the mediator if requested. The mediator clarifies each side's position, suggests possible compromises, and tries to bring the sides together. However, mediators make recommendations only; neither management nor labor has to accept the recommendations.

Arbitration. Some disputes between labor and management cannot be resolved through mediation. In such cases, arbitration may be necessary. As discussed in Chapter 3, **arbitration** is the process in which an arbitrator (again, an

mediation   *a process in which an experienced and knowledgeable neutral person helps the union and management reach an agreement.*

arbitration   *a process in which an arbitrator listens to the arguments of labor and management, weighs the merits of each argument, and then makes a binding judgment.*

Are Unions Dying?

Yes

Statistics and simple observation clearly show that unions are dying. The percentage of the U.S. workforce in labor unions is sharply declining. Unions are winning fewer representation elections than in the past and losing more decertification elections. In 1990, union membership dropped to 17.0 million, almost a 30 percent decline from the peak of 23.7 million in 1975. This left unions with only 16 percent of nonfarm employment—down from 33 percent at its peak in 1953. For some unions, the decline has been even more dramatic. Membership in the United Steelworkers plummeted by almost 50 percent between 1980 and 1990. Interestingly, the decline of unions is virtually a worldwide phenomenon.

One survey showed that 44 percent of Californians believe that unions do more harm than good, up from 28 percent 15 years ago. Nearly three out of four Californians feel that unions are mainly responsible for the inability of U.S. firms to compete internationally. Surveys also show that most managers in the U.S. feel that union strength is declining.

These numbers shouldn't be a surprise. The workforce is changing. Unions have had their greatest success in organizing blue-collar workers, but white-collar workers now account for two-thirds of the workforce. Unions have traditionally focused their demands on wages and working conditions. But the workforce is now better educated than in the past and is increasingly concerned with responsibility, challenge, and other noneconomic issues.

Also, nonunion wages are usually lower than union wages, and thus more competitive in the world market. The public recognizes that union wage demands have been a major cause of inflation and related problems.

Finally, companies have become more enlightened and are acting to make unions unnecessary. They are paying attention to issues that unions have long ignored, such as the quality of work life.

Business Career

Arbitrator: Mediates disputes between labor and management to bind both to terms of a labor contract. Evaluates contentions of both parties, using knowledge of facts involved and industry practices. Renders binding decision to settle dispute. *Average Salary: $29,000.* **6**

contract administration *interpreting and following the union contract on a daily basis.*

grievance procedure *a set of steps contained in the labor contract, specifying what must be done when disputes over contract provisions arise.*

experienced neutral person) listens to the arguments of labor and management, weighs the merits of each argument, and then makes a judgment. This judgment is binding; that is, both sides must accept it. Since most managers and labor leaders do not want to risk a third party's judgment on crucial contract issues, arbitration is not commonly used to resolve collective bargaining stalemates.

CONTRACT ADMINISTRATION

After a contract has been signed by labor and management, the process of **contract administration** begins. The contract has to be interpreted and followed on a daily basis. Contracts usually list a set of steps to be followed when disputes over contract provisions arise. These steps make up the **grievance procedure.**

For example, an employee disagrees with a supervisor over the interpretation of the contract as to which duties the employee is to perform. If the employee and the supervisor cannot work out a solution themselves, the disagreement becomes a formal grievance, and the employee contacts the union steward. The

No

It is true that union membership is down, but the decline reflects many factors that are largely outside the control of unions. For example, traditional union strongholds such as the "smokestack" industries are in decline. Employment in the largely nonunion southern states is increasing, and the less organized service sector is growing rapidly.

If unions are to prosper, they must follow these occupational trends. In fact, an increasing number of professionals and other white-collar workers—including teachers, nurses, and government employees—are joining unions to fight inflation and to gain greater control over their work lives. For instance, the number of unionized government employees has risen almost 700 percent since the mid-1950s. The American Federation of Teachers, the American Federation of State, County and Municipal Employees, and many other unions representing professional and civil service employees have shown dramatic growth.

Union leaders are not blind to reality. They recognize that issues such as autonomy, job challenge, and participation are important to current and prospective members, and they are beginning to take appropriate action. For example, unions at organizations as diverse as Boeing, Ford Motor Co., the U.S. Postal Service, the Philadelphia Zoo, and the New York Sanitation Department are working with management to improve the quality of work life.

This doesn't mean that economic issues should be or will be ignored. Recent cases have shown that companies will cut back on economic benefits when given a chance. For instance, hundreds of companies, including Northwest Airlines, Safeway Stores, and Dow Chemical Co., have implemented two-tier contracts, in which current workers retain their present wages, but new workers receive much lower pay.

Surveys show that union members themselves overwhelmingly support unions, as does a substantial percentage of the general public. The same studies that show the public blaming unions for driving up prices also show that the public recognizes that unions have been primarily responsible for getting improved wages and benefits for workers.

This is a time of tremendous opportunity for unions. If they assess their strengths and weaknesses and adopt flexible recruitment and bargaining strategies, they may ultimately grow stronger than ever before.

What Do You Think?

---

steward tries to work things out with the supervisor. If that fails, the steward can put the grievance in writing and submit it to management.

Then representatives of the union's grievance committee and management's grievance committee meet to settle the matter. If the results of this meeting are unsatisfactory, a grievance committee made up of union and management representatives discusses the issue. The last step, if all others fail, is that the grievance goes to arbitration and is settled by an independent third party.

SOURCES OF NEGOTIATING STRENGTH

Labor and management both approach the negotiating table with certain weapons, or sources of strength, at their disposal. These sources give each side leverage during the negotiating process.

Labor

Labor can use its financial and political power to help achieve its goals. Strikes, picketing, boycotts, and corporate campaigns are sources of labor's financial strength. In addition, labor's sheer numbers provide political clout.

Strike. The ultimate source of labor's strength is the strike. A **strike** is a temporary work stoppage by employees. By refusing to work, employees hope to pressure management to agree to their demands. Each day that workers are off the job, the firm loses money. At some point, the cost of meeting worker demands becomes less than the cost of letting the strike go on.

Most strikes end with an agreement between labor and management. In recent years, more than 80 percent of all strikes have ended either with all issues resolved or with a procedure set up to handle any remaining differences. It is rare

strike a temporary work stoppage by employees, aimed at pressuring management to agree to their demands.

Striking workers picket the Boeing plant at Everett, Washington.

that strikes end with the employer going out of business. It is also unusual that a strike is "broken"—that is, the workers go back to work without their demands being met.

Of course, a problem with striking is that strikers pay a price, too—mostly in terms of lost wages. Also, some firms see strikes as an opportunity to bring in replacements and permanently lay off workers. Since it is still legal for firms to hire permanent replacements for striking workers (as discussed in Case 10-2), the firm's incentive to yield to union demands is reduced. The president of the North Carolina AFL-CIO went so far as to claim that "Strikes are now a weapon of management. In a lot of cases, management wants you to go on strike so they can bust the strike and bust the union."[11] The International Example on page 261 illustrates the difficulties that Soviet workers have encountered in their attempts to use strikes to further their interests.

As shown in Figure 10-2, the number of work stoppages has dropped dramatically in recent years. The percentage of time lost to stoppages has shown similar declines.

picketing *a union tactic in which workers march back and forth in front of the entrances to the workplace, carrying signs listing their grievances and demands.*

Picketing. Union members often picket when striking. **Picketing** means that workers march back and forth in front of the entrances to the workplace, carrying signs listing their grievances and demands. The idea is to make the views of the union known, to generate sympathy for the strike, and to persuade nonstrikers not to work. Many nonstriking union members show their support for the union by refusing to cross the picket line into the workplace. As a result, a small striking union may get enough support to cause major problems for a company or an industry.

Britain's economy has suffered for years from the strong support that small independent unions can stir up among the British people. Striking British transport workers are often joined by workers from other transportation firms. Consequently, nearly all passenger and commercial transportation across England comes to a stop.

FIGURE 10-2   Major Work Stoppages

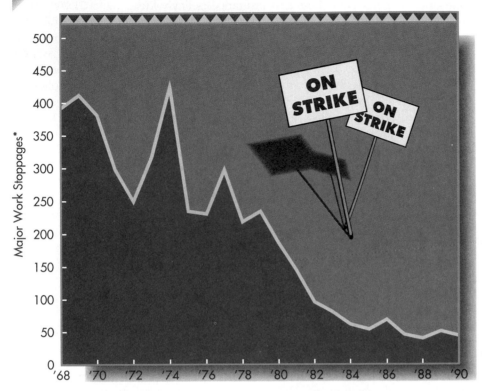

* Work stoppages include all known strikes or lockouts involving 1,000 or more workers and
lasting a full shift or longer.

Source: U. S. Department of Labor, Bureau of Labor Statistics, *Current Wage Developments* (April
1991), p. 30.

Boycott. In a **boycott,** union members and other people who agree with the
union's goals refuse to purchase or handle the company's goods or services. This
can result in tremendous financial pressures on a company. The AFL-CIO called
off a decade-long boycott against Coors Brewing Company only after Coors
agreed to permit a union election. A **primary boycott** occurs when a union tells
its members not to patronize a business involved in a dispute with labor. When
the union goes even further and persuades other parties, such as suppliers and
customers, to stop dealing with the company, it is called a **secondary boycott.**
Secondary boycotts are generally prohibited by law. This does not apply to the
United Farm Workers, however. That union has used secondary boycotts to
restrict the sale of grapes, lettuce, and wine of growers from whom the union was
trying to gain recognition.[12]

Corporate Campaign. An aggressive new labor weapon is called the corporate campaign. In a **corporate campaign,** the union attacks the company by
pressuring people or organizations important to that company—such as institutional stockholders or creditors. The corporate campaign was first used against
J. P. Stevens & Co. The Amalgamated Clothing & Textile Workers Union (ACTWU)
had been able to organize only 10 percent of the workers at Stevens using traditional tactics. The ACTWU put pressure on Stevens' major creditor, on outside

boycott a tactic by which
union members and other people who agree with the union's
goals refuse to purchase or
handle a company's goods or
services.

primary boycott a type of
boycott in which union members refuse to patronize a business involved in a dispute with
labor.

secondary boycott a type
of boycott in which nonunion
members, such as suppliers
and customers, support the
union by refusing to deal with
a business involved in a labor
dispute.

corporate campaign a
tactic in which a union attacks
a company by pressuring people or organizations important
to that company.

directors of the firm, on a firm that managed $1 billion of Stevens' pension funds, and on other parties linked to Stevens. For instance, by mobilizing the support of thousands of bank depositors and insurance policyholders, the ACTWU forced two insurance companies to drop Stevens' chairman from their boards of directors and forced outside directors to resign from Stevens' board. In addition, to pressure Metropolitan Life Insurance Co., Stevens' major creditor, the ACTWU employed a little-used New York law. By proposing candidates for Metropolitan's board, the union threatened to make it conduct a vote of its 23 million policyholders that would have cost $9 million. Metropolitan Life's chairman then communicated his hope to Stevens that an accord would be reached with the ACTWU. In 1980, the ACTWU signed its first contract with Stevens.

In a more recent example, Beverly Enterprises, the nation's largest nursing home chain, had regularly challenged union organizing victories in court and taken a hard line in bargaining. Unions finally won concessions after they published studies criticizing the quality of Beverly's patient care and questioning its levels of administrative costs. The corporate campaign is becoming more common, and it has gained the support of the powerful AFL-CIO. Unions are writing letters directly to the stockholders of corporations with which they are dealing or to the depositors of target banks. They are even testifying against the firms in government hearings.

Corporate campaigns are often used during the organizing process. They may also be employed instead of strikes or to reinforce strikes. Thus far, it appears that corporate campaigns have been considerably more effective as part of organizing drives than as either complements or substitutes for strikes.[13]

Political Influence. Many unions can use the size of their memberships as a potent political weapon. For instance, they can endorse and provide financial support to "pro-labor" candidates for political office. Even though all unions may not support the same candidates, union members form an important voting bloc. Interestingly, former President Ronald Reagan was the first union member to be elected president of the United States. He is a former president of the Screen Actors Guild.

Management

Management also has a variety of resources that it can draw upon to protect its interests. Let's look at those that are most commonly used.

lockout a management tactic in which the company prevents union members from working, often by shutting down its operations.

Lockout. A **lockout** occurs when a company prevents union members from working, often by shutting down its operations. Sometimes, when a union strikes against one employer, other firms lock out their employees to show solidarity and to weaken the union's position. The premise is that "A strike against one is a strike against all." In other cases, a company may lock out its workers before they strike, thus controlling the timing of the work stoppage. For instance, Roundy's Inc., a food wholesaler, locked out its employees after its contract with the Teamsters union local expired in 1991. Roundy's said the lockout was a way to prepare for the possibility that the union might strike, endangering perishable food in the warehouse. Also, as noted at the beginning of this chapter, baseball owners locked out the players during the 1990 major league baseball contract dispute. This was largely to force serious negotiation immediately, thus preempting a strike by players that might come right at the beginning of the season and severely damage team revenues.

Strikes Fail to Unite Soviet Labor Unions

In January of 1991, the heat failed at the Lublino steel factory in the Soviet Union. About 1,000 employees, a quarter of the workforce, decided they'd had enough and walked off the job.

Emotions were running high, and the list of complaints was long. More than 100 workers in the past ten years had contracted job-related illnesses. The factory wasn't supplying enough shoes for those working on the oily factory floor, and each worker was allotted only two uniforms a year. More immediately, the government was going to raise food prices in April and had frozen salaries.

Railway Ministry officials, fearful that a prolonged strike at the country's only producer of spare railway parts would throw the nation into chaos, offered concessions: a 50 percent pay increase and a further 40 percent in a few months, subsidized lunches and three additional vacation days.

In six days, the strike was over. By the following week, even the strike committee had disbanded. The short-lived strike is typical of the Soviet labor movement today. For the first time in the history of the communist state, thousands of workers are now taking to the picket lines—and then abandoning longer-range demands in exchange for economic concessions doled out by the government.

If ever there was a time to organize a labor movement in the Soviet Union, this is it. Coal miners showed the power of a strike with their two-month walkout in the spring of 1991. Glasnost has permitted a certain freedom of expression. Democratic politicians, such as Russian President Boris Yeltsin, have advocated workers' rights. Some intellectuals are trying to organize a Polish Solidarity-type movement that could spur democratic reform. The American AFL-CIO has recently stepped up its aid, offering trips to Washington for labor leaders, providing computer links and promising to expose any harassment from the KGB as human rights violations.

But a Soviet version of Solidarity seems a remote possibility. Polish workers saw a clear enemy in the Communist Party, but many Soviet workers still depend on the party to look after their welfare. Despite glasnost, there is an air of political uncertainty that scares many workers. Mikhail Gorbachev (then President of the Soviet Union) banned strikes and decreed that strike leaders would be subject to criminal prosecution.

Source: Excerpted from L. Hays, "Strikes Fail to Unite Soviet Labor Unions," *Wall Street Journal*, 24 July 1991, p. A9.

Lockouts may also be used to prevent employees from continuing actions that are harmful to the company, such as slowdowns, damage to property, or violence. For instance, grain companies in British Columbia imposed lockouts after some employees had deliberately worked slowly in support of contract demands.[14]

A landmark 1986 National Labor Relations Board ruling greatly increased the value of the lockout as a management tactic. The ruling stated that an employer can hire temporary replacements during a lawful lockout as long as it continues to bargain in good faith. Thus, the employer can continue operations while pressuring the union to give in to its demands.[15] Although this ruling makes lockouts a more potent management tool, they are still rarely used, largely because of the "bad press" they may receive.

Injunction. An **injunction** is a court order requiring someone to do or stop doing something. Injunctions can be used to make striking employees return to work or face a penalty. At one time, injunctions were frequently issued to stop any strike that might interfere with business. Recently, court injunctions have been used by local governments to stop illegal strikes by public employees. The president can issue an injunction to halt strikes if the strikes are believed to be harmful to the public interest. For example, in 1981 President Reagan invoked a no-strike law (applicable to federal employees) to order the 15,000 members of the Professional Air Traffic Controllers Association (PATCO) to go back to work.

injunction a court order requiring someone to do or stop doing something; management can use an injunction to make striking employees return to work or face a penalty.

261

PATCO argued that the government's contract offer did not include a big enough pay increase. Moreover, PATCO said, the contract did not provide for early retirement and a shorter workweek—both critical issues in an industry characterized by tremendous job stress. The union went out on strike anyway, disobeying the president's order. His response was to fire all striking workers.

"Business As Usual."

strikebreakers workers hired by the company to replace workers on strike.

"Business As Usual." Firms can sometimes carry on "business as usual" during a strike. One way is by having managers take over strikers' duties. Another is by hiring **strikebreakers,** workers who are willing to cross the picket line and replace striking workers. This can cause considerable bitterness. Strikebreakers are referred to as "scabs" by striking employees and their sympathizers. On the other hand, keeping a plant in operation by whatever means does minimize loss of revenue. Management may even gain a better understanding of workers' jobs. Contract terms after a strike are generally more favorable to management when operations continue than when the union is able to force a plant shutdown.

When the New York *Daily News* faced the possibility of a strike by its union, executives of the parent Tribune Co. spent more than a year and $24 million preparing for the showdown. They set up a mock newsroom to practice publishing under strike conditions. They also trained nonunion drivers to deliver the paper and hired security guards to protect them. The company continued to operate during a four-month strike, but it still suffered huge losses. When mediation subsequently failed, the Tribune agreed to sell the *Daily News* to British media baron Robert Maxwell.[16]

Agreements and Organizations. Just as some unions have banded together for their mutual benefit, some companies have formed associations to help one another in the event of a strike. For instance, if one company is struck, others may provide financial and other support to help it hold on against the union. The National Association of Manufacturers is one national organization that helps companies in their mutual struggle against unions.

To illustrate, many newspapers share printing facilities, computer equipment, and even delivery trucks when one newspaper is crippled by a strike. Newspaper management places a high priority on continuing operation, and only rarely will it stop publication. Similarly, the Shipowners' Mutual Strike Insurance Association helps shipping companies continue operation during strikes.

Employee Relations Programs. One way companies try to avoid problems with unions is by making unions unnecessary. That is, the firm tries to keep its employees so satisfied that they see no need to join a union. One company that has been successful with this approach is Du Pont. By stressing employee well-being and keeping wages competitive, Du Pont has successfully held off more than 17 years of attempts by the steelworkers union to win a company-wide election.

ombudsman an individual employed by a company to check out and resolve employee complaints.

Some companies attempt to forestall unionization of their workforce, or at least to keep the workforce satisfied, by employing an **ombudsman,** whose job is to check out and resolve employee complaints. Ombudsmen are now found in corporations and in governmental and educational organizations. General Electric Co. and Xerox Corp. have both used them successfully. When employees have complaints, they go to the ombudsman, who maintains confidentiality, so that employee identity is protected. The ombudsman then presents the complaint to management. Ombudsmen help ensure that employees are treated fairly. They also give management another way to diagnose problems in the workforce.

APPROACHES TO LABOR-MANAGEMENT COOPERATION

As this chapter has suggested, relations between unions and management in the U.S. have traditionally been primarily adversarial. This is unlike the situation in Japan, for instance. Haruki Shimizu, the head of Nissan Motor Co.'s union, has said that labor peace "has been a driving force of Japanese economic development and social progress. Union members want to protect their jobs and preserve their livelihoods. The best way to do that is to cooperate with the company."[17] Mr. Shimizu notes with pride that his union hasn't struck since 1953. When Japan's economy faced a slowdown in the mid-1980s, the government wanted to push companies to boost wages to stimulate the economy. Management resisted, and the labor unions supported management.

In fact, instances of labor–management cooperation are becoming more common in the United States. This may be due in part to a recognition that unions and management must work together if they are to meet foreign challenges successfully. Also, both labor and management recognize that cooperation rather than conflict may help them find "win-win" solutions, enlarging the pie rather than just dividing it. Unions, facing difficult times, recognize that they may have to embrace new strategies. Firms may also gain from such cooperation. A recent study looked at 56 unionized manufacturers that either ousted unions or developed cooperative relations with them in 1974 and 1975. The researchers found that, after adjusting for changing market conditions and other factors, employers that had tried teamwork—about half of the sample—reported a 19 percent increase over the decade in value added per employee. The combative employers reported a 15 percent decline.[18]

In this section, we will examine approaches to labor-management cooperation. We will first discuss some recent examples of cooperative efforts. We will then consider two developments that are transforming the face of labor–management relations: codetermination and employee purchase of companies.

Cooperative Efforts

Let's look at just a few recent examples of labor-management cooperation:

In 1990, Chrysler closed an 84-year-old factory, and many workers were unemployed. In the year following the plant closing, 51 employees died, a toll that officials of the plant's employee-assistance department attributed in part to the stress of being out of work. As the death toll mounted, the union sponsored a "Health Day," during which laid-off workers got free blood pressure and cholesterol examinations and were urged to seek professional help for their adjustment problems. The company and union are trying to reduce the pressures by encouraging workers to keep busy. For laid-off workers, Chrysler pays for courses ranging from computer programming to truck driving.[19]

In its effort to redefine and revitalize the North American automobile industry, General Motors' new Saturn division is stressing consensus-building and teamwork. A unique power-sharing agreement between GM and the UAW describes the union as a "full partner" in the operation of the plant and says that all decisions must be made by consensus. UAW members helped to choose Saturn's suppliers, dealers, and advertising agency. Union members are also responsible for interviewing and hiring all new employees, who are selected from 135 other GM plants throughout the United States.[20]

At General Motors' new Saturn plant in Tennessee, labor and management work together to improve the car and the way it is made.

In addition, many other leading firms—including AT&T, Philip Morris, Xerox, and Johnson & Johnson—have taken important steps toward creating more participative workplaces. Workers are involved in making major decisions regarding work rules and job design, or share in profits, or have important job security agreements.[21]

Codetermination

codetermination *formal worker participation on the governing bodies of companies.*

Codetermination is formal worker participation on the governing bodies of companies. As part of a 1980 wage-concession package, then United Auto Workers president Douglas A. Fraser was given a seat on the board of directors of Chrysler Corp. Western Airlines, Pan American World Airways, and Hyatt Clark are among the firms that have subsequently elected union-proposed directors. Other examples of codetermination are found in the steel, trucking, and food industries.

Although codetermination gives labor a voice in the management of the company, some unions oppose it. They fear that workers may begin to identify with management and see unions as unnecessary. Similarly, they are concerned that union members who sit on the board of directors may begin to sympathize with management, taking their point of view rather than that of the workers. Many managers and directors of large corporations also oppose codetermination. They are uncomfortable with the idea of sharing decision-making responsibilities with workers.

Employee Purchase of Companies

One way for workers to understand the concerns and views of management is to become owners of the firm. Since 1970, hundreds of thousands of employees in the United States have acquired stock in their companies, either through purchase or in exchange for concessions on pay and benefits. **Employee stock owner-ship plans (ESOPs)** make company stock available to workers as part of the menu of benefits. More than a quarter of the Fortune 500 companies have at least 4 percent of their shares in workers' hands. Hundreds of U.S. corporations are at least 51 percent owned by employees. Such buyouts have also taken place in other countries, including Canada, the United Kingdom, and France. In 1990, the AFL-CIO created a union-backed fund to help finance employee buyouts of companies. Of course, these plans have risks to employees who participate in them. Their financial welfare is closely tied to the company's fortunes, and workers at firms declaring bankruptcy have seen the value of their shares plummet.

employee stock owner-ship plans (ESOPs) plans in which workers receive company stock as part of the menu of benefits.

Sometimes these employee stock purchase programs can rescue a troubled company—but not always. In July 1980, for example, members of a Waterloo, Iowa meatpackers' union agreed to buy a majority ownership share in Rath Packing Company. The union members did this by putting part of their wages into company stock. The company was temporarily saved from bankruptcy. If Rath had closed, 2,200 jobs would have been lost. Productivity increased at the plant, and the company showed its first profit in six years. But market conditions continued to worsen, and Rath began to sustain mounting losses. By 1983, the company was forced to declare bankruptcy.

However, employee purchase of the ailing Weirton Steel Corporation, of Weirton, West Virginia, saved the company. It is cited as a notable success story in a troubled industry. Similarly, workers purchased The Okonite Company, a wire and cable manufacturer in Ramsey, New Jersey, through contributions to an employee stock ownership plan. The 1,600 workers put in no money up front, took no pay cuts, and kept their regular pension plan. Employees now have an average of $22,000 in their stock accounts. Interestingly, employee ownership has not eliminated labor strife at Okonite. Employees have gone on strike (essentially against themselves) four times since the stock plan was put into effect.[22]

Ironically, firms sometimes use ESOPs to place more of their stock in friendly hands, to help prevent hostile takeovers. They may also get substantial tax breaks in the process. Thus, to safeguard the firm from raiders and to secure tax benefits, management is transferring ownership to workers. As one observer noted, "Ah, capitalism."[23]

SUMMARY POINTS

1 A labor union is an organization of workers who have united to achieve their job-related common goals. By so doing, they hope to increase their bargaining power with management. Successful bargaining by unions results in economic security and fair treatment for their members and gives the members a sense of belonging and control. Unions generally weaken management's control over procedures and limit management's flexibility. They may also create a power struggle with management. However, unions may also assist management by helping provide a more highly skilled workforce, serving as a communication channel, and taking over some disciplinary responsibilities.

2 The three main levels of labor organization are national unions, local unions, and union federations. Most union power rests at the national level. Local unions represent workers in a particular geographical area and are usually affiliated with a national union. In turn, most national unions in the United States have joined federations, which provide research, education, lobbying, and public relations services.

KEY TERMS

labor union 246

union stewards 249

authorization card 249

bargaining unit 251

collective bargaining 251

union security clauses 252

checkoff 253

management-rights clause 253

cost-of-living adjustment (COLA) 253

fringe benefits 253

givebacks 253

mediation 251

3 Union organizing involves several steps: the signing of authorization cards by workers, petitioning the National Labor Relations Board for an election, determining the bargaining unit, and holding a representation election. Employees may also vote to decertify a union.

4 Collective bargaining is the name for the negotiations leading to a work contract between labor and management. Some important collective bargaining issues are union security and management rights, compensation, fringe benefits, job security, hours of work, safety and health, and the quality of work life. The collective bargaining process may include prenegotiation, negotiations, and sometimes mediation or arbitration.

5 When negotiations between labor and management reach a stalemate, the parties involved often turn to mediation or arbitration to find the solution. A mediator serves as a facilitator. An arbitrator may actually make a final, binding decision regarding the dispute.

6 Contract administration is the day-by-day process of interpreting and following a work contract after it has been signed by labor and management. When disagreements arise in the interpretation, labor and management follow a prescribed grievance procedure for settling the disputes.

7 The sources of negotiating strength for labor are strikes, picketing, boycotts, corporate campaigns, and political influence. The sources of negotiating strength for management include lockouts, court injunctions, strikebreakers, trade associations, and employee relations programs.

8 There have been many recent examples of a spirit of labor–management cooperation. These include more cooperative contract negotiations, joint union–management programs, and power-sharing agreements. In addition, new developments such as codetermination and employee purchase of companies are transforming the nature of labor–management relations.

REVIEW QUESTIONS

1 What are the goals of labor unions with respect to their members? **1**

2 What does the national union organization do for its members? **2**

3 What is a union steward? What does this person do? **2**

4 Explain why the definition of the bargaining unit is important to both labor and management. **3**

5 How does a cost-of-living adjustment in a labor contract work? **4**

6 Why are unions sometimes willing to sign labor contracts calling for employee givebacks? **4**

7 What are some reasons for organized labor's recent decline in membership? **4**

8 How does mediation differ from arbitration? **5**

9 Describe the steps in the grievance procedure. **6**

10 Explain the difference between a strike and a boycott. **7**

11 Describe the major sources of management's strength in contract negotiation. **7**

12 What is codetermination? Why do some unions oppose it? **8**

DISCUSSION QUESTIONS

1 Management generally resists unionization of its facilities. How might the presence of a union actually benefit the firm?

2 In your opinion, has organized labor become too strong? Have its wage demands in the auto industry become excessive? If so, what can management do about it?

3 Both labor and management come to the negotiating table with certain advantages, or sources of strength. Which party, in your opinion, is usually in a better position?

4 What are some of the probable consequences of codetermination in the United States? Do you see any benefits of codetermination for management?

5 Do you think that organized labor will become a more or less important force in our society in the years ahead? Why?

6 What are some possible dangers to unions of cooperating with management?

EXPERIENTIAL EXERCISES

1 Select a particular union and gather information concerning its history and current status. Write an essay on the topic. In the essay, identify the factors that influenced development of the union, as well as the factors that are shaping its current actions and probable future directions.

2 Using the *Business Periodical Index* or some other source, find information about a recently negotiated labor contract. Analyze the contract in terms of the collective bargaining issues discussed in this chapter.

CASES

CASE 10-1
Flexible Work Rules

American industry is saddled—some say crippled—with a large number of work rules. Work rules are regulations that govern the workplace and specify precisely what each employee is allowed and not allowed to do. Over the years, work rules have become increasingly restrictive, handcuffing management and making jobs limiting and often boring.

At General Motors, for instance, an electrician could rewire an electric socket but could not take the screw out of the cover plate—a millwright was needed to do that! When both welding and milling were required on an engine block, both a union welder and a union millwright were involved. Each did part of the job while the other waited. GM management argued that the jobs should be combined, because the welder and millwright share each other's skills. Some experts claim that the specialization of tasks reflected in such work rules is more in step with the early 20th century, when the principles of Scientific Management were in vogue, than with the realities of today. They claim that these work rules result in billions of dollars in excess labor costs. Rapidly changing technologies and market conditions have rendered many of these principles obsolete.

Work rules can cover virtually all aspects of work, including job assignments, wages, hours of work, and other areas. Because of increased foreign competition and other pressures, many firms and unions are taking a hard look at these rules. Unions in various industries are granting work rule changes. In industries such as steel, railroads, and airlines, unions have permitted jobs to be enlarged by adding duties, thus cutting the size of crews. In the trucking, textile, meatpacking, and rubber industries, unions have allowed changes in hours of work, such as giving up relief and wash-up periods and giving management more flexibility in scheduling daily and weekly hours. In the meatpacking, auto, and steel industries, unions have agreed to work rule changes that restrict use of seniority in filling job vacancies and picking shifts. In the rubber and steel industries, unions have granted changes that reduce incentive pay to reflect changing job conditions. In the auto supply and several other industries, unions have given management more flexibility regarding how work teams are formed, paid, and changed over time.

These changes have paid off. For instance, oil refiners claim that easing of work rules has increased their output per worker by 10 to 15 percent. At Jones & Laughlin Steel Corp., the number of person-hours needed to make a ton of steel has been cut from six to three and a half as a result of work rule changes.

Some unions have fought hard against relaxation of work rules. They wonder whether the benefits of eased work rules will be passed on to employees. But in recent hard economic times, companies have issued an ultimatum: Either make these concessions or the plant will close.

1.   What, if anything, do the revisions in work rules suggest about the changing roles of labor unions? How do you think unions should respond to requests for work rule changes?
2.   Which of the changes described in the case do you think unions would oppose most strongly? To which of the changes might they be most sympathetic?
3.   Which of these changes, if any, do you think will benefit workers in the long run? In the short run? Why?

CASE 10-2
Permanent Replacements at Ravenswood Aluminum Corp

Federal law decrees you can't fire a striking worker—but it doesn't stop you from hiring a permanent replacement. Though that subtle legalism has governed the nation's labor relations for half a century, the nuance is lost on Dan Stidham.

"What's the difference?" demands Mr. Stidham, the local United Steelworkers union president in Ravenswood, West Virginia, who with 1,700 others has been permanently replaced in a dispute between the union and Ravenswood Aluminum Corp. "It's the same as if they came out and fired us—either way we don't have a job."

At first glance, this eight-month-old labor dispute is much like any other in a small, one-factory town, with cousins and neighbors squabbling and local businesses struggling. But this hamlet of 4,000 on the Ohio River is also a symbol of an emerging national debate over the hiring of permanent replacements for strikers.

Companies insist that they must sometimes offer permanent-replacement status to keep their businesses going. But labor groups, pointing to long strikes at Greyhound Lines, Eastern Airlines, and International Paper Co., say that management increasingly uses permanent replacements to break unions and to prevent collective bargaining. They argue that there is little incentive for management to bargain in good faith if it can hire permanent replacements for strikers.

Monsignor Sylvester Staud of Ravenswood's St. Matthew's Church preaches in Sunday sermons to both management and labor: "The position taken by management to hire permanent replacement workers is nothing short of immoral."

Ravenswood's top executive says the union left him no choice. "I get upset when I'm called a union buster or when this is called premeditated," says Chairman R. Emmett Boyle. He says he warned the union that "our responsibility to bankers and customers will drive us to run the facility in a strike." After failing to win enough recruits by offering temporary status, the "only way I could do it was with permanent-replacement workers."

It all began in mid-1990, months before the labor contract expired, when Ravenswood began installing new security cameras and clearing brush from the hillside bordering the plant, to remove sniper cover. The company told its unionized security guards that they must become salaried employees or be transferred to production jobs. It installed steel plates to protect the plant's electrical equipment from bullets and hauled in truckloads of food and supplies so that managers could live inside the plant. Before negotiations began, Ravenswood advertised in Ohio for replacement workers, boarded up its front-office windows and encircled the plant in barbed-wire fence.

Negotiations got under way on September 25. The company declared an impasse on Oct. 31. The union says that the company acted even though the union had narrowed the cost gap between the two sides by 80 percent. As soon as the contract expired on November 1, the temporary replacements stepped in. Ravenswood met again with the union but declared another impasse on November 29 and soon after gave permanent status to its temporary replacements—who now number 1,030—without first notifying union workers.

The union says that the company made the replacements permanent even though the steelworkers withdrew more than 20 demands. The union also charges that Ravenswood refused to bargain on certain safety issues, although five workers had been killed in the 18 months since current management bought the plant from Maxxam Inc.'s Kaiser Aluminum & Chemical unit. (Ravenswood claims that the deaths weren't because of management's negligence.)

"This company has used permanent replacements in an effort to rid itself of the union," asserts Carl B. Frankel, associate general counsel for the steelworkers. Not so, counters Ravenswood's Mr. Boyle, who led a buyout of the plant in 1988 with two partners. He concedes that the company's position didn't budge much during negotiations, but he says Ravenswood can't afford the rich labor contracts of its larger rivals.

Boyle also maintains there remains an $80 million difference between the two sides' proposals over the life of the proposed three-year contract. "I think that's an impasse," he says. Further, he argues, "the history of the union indicated there was the strong possibility of a strike," given wildcat strikes in the past and the plant's 69 percent vote against ratification of the last contract with Kaiser in 1988.

Since the strike began, local businesses say sales have dropped by one third, and clergy report shouting matches at services. At weekly picnics for union faithful, many in attendance wear "Scab Hunter" T-shirts featuring the barrel of a gun. In front of the union hall, replacement workers hang in effigy.

There has also been violence. The company won an injunction limiting the number of picketers, claiming some 2,000 acts of union violence, including bombings and barn burnings. A security guard lost an eye when a sniper's bullet pierced his windshield, although the union denies responsibility for this.

1. How would you characterize the prenegotiation stage of collective bargaining in this case? The negotiation stage?
2. Do you think the hiring of permanent replacements by Ravenswood Aluminum Corp. was an acceptable practice? Why or why not?
3. What did management gain by carrying on "business as usual" in this case? What did it lose?
4. Who are the apparent "winners" in this case? Who are the apparent "losers"?

Source: Abridged and adapted from D. Milbank, "Row Escalates Over Striker Replacements," *Wall Street Journal,* 3 July 1991, p. 9.

CHAPTER 11

Operations Management

Hewlett-Packard executive George Henry got a startling bit of advice on a 1982 trip to Japan. "You Americans are so good at agriculture," said a Japanese business executive. "Why don't you go back to agriculture and leave manufacturing to us?"[1] Events of recent years suggest that American firms have in fact been leaving manufacturing more and more to foreign competitors, however reluctantly. For the last two decades, the "Made in America" label has been vanishing as overseas manufacturers dominate entire industries. In 1969, U.S. manufacturers produced 82 percent of the nation's television sets, 88 percent of its cars, and 90 percent of its machine tools. Today, they produce almost no TVs; half of the domestic machine-tool market and almost 30 percent of the auto market belong to foreign firms. Even in the new area of semiconductors, the U.S. world share has plunged from 85 percent in 1980 to about 15 percent at present.[2]

Maintaining satisfactory productivity and quality are among the most pressing challenges facing American business today. As we saw in Chapter 2, productivity is defined as the amount of output per worker hour. An individual worker is more productive if he or she can produce 100 units of output in a 40-hour workweek than if only 90 units are produced. The absolute level of productivity in the United States is still quite high relative to other nations. But in recent decades, the rate of growth in productivity has not compared so favorably. Output per worker grew at a rate of more than 2 percent per year in the 1960s, but the annual growth rate since 1973 has averaged less than 1 percent. Over that period, productivity growth rates in countries such as West Germany, Japan, France, and the United Kingdom were considerably higher.[3] A "productivity paradox" exists. American manufacturers have been putting almost $20 billion a year into automation, and there are productivity czars, committees, and campaigns across the country. But the results have been relatively skimpy. Although there has been an upturn in productivity since 1982, it has been less impressive

*than other postwar upturns, and many doubt that it will be sustained.[4] Also, as
will be discussed later in the chapter, American business must respond to perceptions that the quality of some products and services is unacceptably low, at least
in relation to that of foreign competitors. (Such perceptions have plagued the U.S.
auto industry, for instance.) Our ability to meet these challenges in productivity
and quality will depend largely on operations management.*

I n this chapter, we will explore the nature of operations and operations management. We will examine capacity planning, facility location, and facility
design and layout. We will discuss materials purchasing, inventory control,
and the production planning process. Then we will consider quality control and
maintenance policies. Finally, we will take a look at the factory of the future.

OPERATIONS AND OPERATIONS MANAGEMENT

Before we begin examining specific issues in operations management, an overview may be useful. Let's consider the nature of operations and operations management and the tasks of the operations manager.

Operations

The term **operations** refers to any process that accepts inputs and uses resources
to change those inputs in useful ways. A basic operations process is shown in
Figure 11-1. Inputs to the process include labor, capital, and materials. The transformation process alters the inputs in some useful way. The outputs are goods or
services. By evaluating the resulting outputs, management gains feedback about
how well the process is working. If necessary, management can adjust the inputs
or the transformation process to improve the outputs.

Inputs may be transformed in a variety of ways. An assembly line, in which
automobiles, radios, or other products move from one workstation to the next, is
an example of a process involving a form transformation. Whenever materials are
processed and converted into finished products, a **form transformation** occurs.

operations *any process
that accepts inputs and uses resources to change those inputs
in useful ways.*

form transformation *the
processing or conversion of
materials into finished
products.*

FIGURE 11-1   The Transformation Process

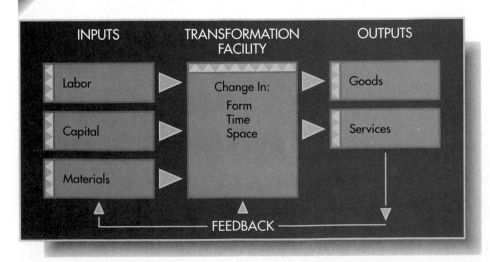

synthetic transformation
a production process in which basic parts, components, or chemicals are combined to form a finished product.

analytic transformation
a production process in which a basic material is broken down into one or more final products.

temporal transformation
the process whereby inputs are transformed in time, such as the storage of goods.

spatial transformation
the process whereby inputs are transformed spatially, such as in the movement of goods from one place to another.

Two types of form transformation are synthetic transformation and analytic transformation. In a **synthetic transformation** process, basic parts, components, or chemicals are combined to form a finished product. The production of appliances from steel, plastic, and other inputs is an example of a synthetic transformation. In an **analytic transformation** process, a basic material is broken down into one or more final products. Examples include the refining of iron ore or crude oil and the milling of logs into lumber, plywood, composite board, and other building materials.

Inputs can also be transformed in time or space—**temporal transformation** and **spatial transformation,** respectively. Storage is an example of a temporal transformation. Rental warehouse space is the output, and it is purchased for a period of time. A transportation service, such as a commercial airline or a package delivery service, is an example of a spatial transformation. Here, the transformation process involves the movement of people or packages from one place to another.

As these examples show, operations may include both production operations and service operations. The goal of production operations is to produce goods. Goods producers include such organizations as computer manufacturers, building contractors, and coal mines. The goal of service operations, such as hospitals, universities, or banks, is to provide personal services. Examples of production and service operations are shown in Figure 11-2.

operations management
the systematic direction of the processes that transform inputs into finished goods and services.

Operations Management

Operations management is the systematic direction and control of the processes that transform inputs into finished goods and services.[6] As we will see, operations management includes such activities as purchasing, inventory control,

FIGURE 11-2 Examples of Operations

Type of Operation					
Production			Service		
Manufacturing	Converting	Repairing	Protection	Logistics	Well-Being
Paper Mill	Electrical Power Plant	Water Treatment Plant	Prison	Gas Pipeline	Hospital Intensive Care Ward
Automobile Assembly Plant	Open-Pit Coal Mine	Large Auto Paint Shop	U.S. Secret Service	Airline	Public School
Winery	Scrap-Metal Reduction Plant	Road-Repair Contractor	Traffic Court	Grain Elevator	Military Basic Training Camp
Furniture Maker	Custom Slaughterhouse	Auto Body Shop	Fire Department	Trucking Firm	Travel Tour Guide
Office-Building Construction Firm	Ship Salvage Company	Major Ship Repair Yard	Lloyds of London (Insurance)	House Mover	Management Consulting Firm

Source: Stephen E. Barndt/Davis W. Carvey, *Essentials of Operations Management,* © 1982, p. 9. Reprinted by permission of Prentice Hall, Inc., Englewood Cliffs, New Jersey.

quality control, and maintenance. **Production management** is the process of managing all aspects of the production operation. Although operations management is often associated with production operations (partly because people treat the term "production management" as synonymous with "operations management"), it also applies to service operations. Figure 11-3 presents typical problems of operations management in service organizations.

production management
the process of handling and managing all aspects of the production operation.

Tasks of the Operations Manager

Economists make a basic distinction between the short run and the long run. In the short run, the basic plant and equipment cannot be changed in size or design. In the long run, they can. That is to say, production capacity is fixed in the short run but variable in the long run.

The operations manager's task in the short run is to use existing facilities efficiently through proper maintenance, inventory control, and production scheduling. In particular, the operations manager can:

1. Vary the amount or type of inputs, such as by purchasing more raw materials.
2. Use the facility more effectively through multiple shifts, overtime, or improved work methods.
3. Temporarily add capacity by hiring another company to do part of the work ("subcontracting").

Over the long run, the operations manager's job is to improve existing facilities and to modify or expand them as needed. This important function, capacity planning, is discussed later in the chapter.

FIGURE 11-3   Service Operations Management Problems

Organization	Typical Problem Areas	
	Before Operation	During Operation
Outpatient Clinic	Design facility and staffing plan	Schedule patients and employees
Hospital	Design facility and staffing plan	Schedule operating room; schedule elective patients; staff emergency room; schedule employees; maintain quality audit; maintain inventories of blood and supplies
School Board	Design or modify facilities and geographic coverage	Design bus routes; schedule classes; operate lunch programs
Retail Store	Design facilities and product-line strategy	Maintain inventories; schedule employees
Mail-Order House	Design distribution system (capacity and location of warehouses and transportation links); design order-entry system	Maintain inventories; expedite late orders; develop transportation plans
Bank	Design information-flow system; locate and design branch banks	Maintain and audit quality of information; plan employee schedules

Source: John O. McClain/L. Joseph Thomas, *Operations Management: Production of Goods and Services*, 2nd ed., © 1985, p. 7. Reprinted by permission of Prentice Hall, Inc., Englewood Cliffs, New Jersey.

Mathematical Models

Because operations management is complex, sophisticated mathematical models have been developed. Several of these models are discussed later in the chapter. **Management science,** or **operations research** as it is also called, is concerned with the development and application of these models to business problems.

management science or operations research *the development and application of mathematical models to business problems.*

Manufacturing Focus

Operations management techniques are widely applied to both production operations and service operations, as we will show throughout the chapter. However, large manufacturing complexes are a key focus of operations management. There are at least two reasons for this. First, the quantitative tools of operations management are easy to apply to manufacturing. Second, large manufacturing complexes play an important role in our economy. Consider the fact that the 50 largest U.S. manufacturers together account for about 24 percent of the total value added by manufacturing. The 200 largest companies account for 44 percent. **Value added** is the sales dollar value of the finished product minus the cost of all the raw materials and semifinished inputs bought from other manufacturers. The resulting figure is the value added to the product by the production process. Some value is added to a product at each stage of production.

value added *sales value added to the product by the production process, computed as the sales dollar value of output minus the cost of raw materials and semifinished inputs brought from other manufacturers.*

Since the Industrial Revolution of the 18th and 19th centuries, machine operations have increasingly replaced handwork in the production of goods. That is, we have mechanized. Mechanization is probably most characteristic of **continuous manufacturing** processes, which produce a flow of goods at a predetermined rate. Such processes are used in chemical plants and large food-processing facilities, for example.

continuous manufacturing *a mechanized manufacturing process that produces a flow of goods at a predetermined rate.*

Another type of mechanized manufacturing process is **intermittent manufacturing,** in which a product is processed in lots rather than in a continuous flow. The most common form is the **job shop,** in which products are manufactured or assembled to a customer's purchase order or specification. Custom-built cars and custom-designed jewelry are examples. Intermittent manufacturing does not permit the high level of mechanization found in continuous processes.

intermittent manufacturing *a type of mechanized manufacturing process in which a product is processed in lots rather than in a continuous flow.*

job shop *a type of intermittent manufacturing in which products are manufactured or assembled to a customer's purchase order or specification.*

At the end of this chapter, we will see how modern manufacturing facilities have evolved into technological marvels, integrated by computers and populated by robots, in order to meet competitive demands.

Strategic Role

Many people view operations management as a dull subject, something to do with keeping the boilers running. However, as we will see throughout the chapter, operations management decisions are among the most important ones facing American business. Capacity planning decisions, inventory policies, procedures to enhance quality, and technological changes all have a strong impact on the survival and success of a firm. They influence not only its productivity, but also its innovativeness, responsiveness to customers' needs, and adaptability to demands of the environment. Also, they affect the satisfaction, motivation, performance, and job security of individual workers.

It would be wrong to suggest that operations management bears the blame for inferior quality and disappointing rates of productivity growth, or that it alone can improve them. Nevertheless, many of the conspicuous differences between American firms and their Japanese counterparts are to be found in the area of operations management.

響き合い　心と力で　目標達成！
RESPOND QUICKLY WITH ALL OUR HEART AND STRENGTH TO ACHIEVE OUR TARGET.

Operations management plays an especially important strategic role for firms that face international competition. Shown above is Panasonic's assembly line for television sets in Japan.

In fact, operations management is increasingly viewed as an important weapon in a firm's strategic arsenal. Throughout the chapter, we will see examples of how U.S. firms are using operations management to respond to foreign threats and opportunities. This is especially evident in the case of manufacturing firms. The term **world-class manufacturing** describes a set of processes designed to achieve a sustained global competitive advantage through the continuous improvement of manufacturing capability. In particular, world-class manufacturing combines many of the practices we will consider in this chapter—including heavy reliance on robotics and innovative approaches to the control of inventories and quality—with human resource management practices (such as group reward systems) and organization characteristics (such as decentralized decision making). World-class manufacturing employs "high-tech—high-touch." That is, it combines sophisticated technologies with concern for individuals and teams. World-class manufacturing rejects the traditional view that plants should focus on a single goal, such as low cost or high quality. Instead, it seeks continuous improvement of manufacturing capabilities, to develop product lines that are innovative, flexible, high-quality, low-cost, and delivered on time. World-class manufacturing is discussed in Case 11-1, pages 297 and 298 "Meeting Foreign Challenges with Operations Management."

world-class manufacturing   *a set of manufacturing processes designed to achieve a sustained global advantage through the continuous improvement of manufacturing capability.*

CAPACITY PLANNING

Capacity is simply the maximum possible output of a firm. Capacity planning reflects a firm's long-range operations strategy. In capacity planning, the firm must consider many issues, such as market size and trends, probable technological changes, the possible addition of new products or services, the likelihood that new production methods will be developed, and the choice between a single facility and several facilities.

The process of capacity planning involves several steps. First, future demand must be predicted. Then the physical capacity needed to meet future demand is determined. Next, alternative capacity plans are generated. Possible alternatives to meet increasing demand might be to add capacity, use overtime or multiple shifts, employ outside sources, or not add capacity and absorb lost sales. If demand were expected to decrease, the capacity alternatives might include closing plants, consolidating some operations, or retooling assembly lines to handle more profitable company products. The economic effects, risks, and strategic effects of these alternative plans are then analyzed. Plans may have an impact on economies of scale, competition, flexibility of operations, market location, labor policies, market share, and so on. Finally, a plan for implementation is formulated.

Capacity planning involves the operations manager in decisions that have strategic implications. These decisions require coordination with such areas as marketing, finance, and engineering.

FACILITY LOCATION

For most companies, the decision of where to locate (or relocate) a facility is critical. How close a manufacturing facility is located to raw materials, a skilled labor force, or markets can mean the difference between success or failure. Firms compete with one another by keeping transportation, labor, and distribution costs low. A bioengineering firm without a nearby supply of college graduates or a sod farm located far from its customers would be at a severe competitive disadvantage.

Table 11-1 suggests some important factors in decisions about facility location. As the figure shows, the decisions involve both cost and noncost factors. When General Motors was deciding on the location of its new Saturn plant, it used computers to weigh the many relevant variables. States competed aggressively for the facility.

In times of economic slump, states and localities work hard to attract desirable industries because of the jobs they will create in the community. Many states now grant tax breaks to attract firms. In addition, Ireland, Puerto Rico, and Canada are actively vying for new facilities. Federal minimum wage laws and other nationwide standards may make facility location outside the United States more attractive in years to come.

FACILITY DESIGN AND LAYOUT

Business Career
Facilities Planner: Plans use of space in a business facility for efficient operation. Draws design layout, showing location of furniture, equipment, doorways, electrical outlets, etc. Plans space for each staff member. *Average Salary:* $26,400

process layout *a facility layout that groups work of a similar function in a single department or work center.*

The goal of facility design and layout is to develop a plan for a businesslike environment that promotes efficiency. Specifically, facility design and layout efforts try to reduce idle time for machines and employees. Idle time can result from unnecessary movement, bottlenecks, and uneven utilization. Good design and layout also minimizes in-process inventories, materials-handling costs, and facilities operation and maintenance costs. Of course, they help provide a safe and pleasant place to work.[7]

Depending on the function of the facility, facility layouts may be classified as process, product, group-technology, or fixed-position layouts. A **process layout** groups work of a similar function in a single department or work center. In a clinic, for instance, radiology may be in one location, occupational therapy in another, and internal medicine in yet another.

TABLE 11-1 Factors in Deciding Facility Location

Factor	Industry in Which This Might Be Especially Important	Recent Developments
Cost Factors		
Labor Costs	Apparel	Because of rising labor costs, firms are making greater use of part-time employees and two-tier contracts. Minimum wage laws tend to even out costs across the country. Labor costs tend to be higher in unionized areas.
Transportation Costs	Cement	These have gone up very rapidly in the last two decades, making location near resources and markets more important.
Construction Costs	Warehousing	These have risen sharply since 1975. They tend to be lower in areas where unions are less dominant, such as the South and West.
Utility Costs	Steel	Energy sources are quickly being used up. Costs are skyrocketing. The Clean Air Act of 1990 will increase the cost of electric power in some areas, especially the Midwest.
Taxes	Oil	Many states and territories (particularly Puerto Rico) are now trying to attract industries with substantial tax breaks.
Noncost Factors		
Environmental Conditions	Paper	New laws and social pressure have had great impact on many companies. Industry has spent tremendous amounts on air pollution and waste disposal equipment.
Living Conditions	High Technology	Many employees are no longer willing just to go where the company tells them. Quality of life in the community is becoming more important.
Availability of Resources	Canning	Industrial use of water will increase substantially by the year 2000. Supplies are low in Chicago, Denver, Las Vegas, and Los Angeles. The Gulf Coast from Texas to Alabama suffers from a shortage of groundwater.
Availability of Skilled Labor	Genetic Engineering	Some argue that the shortage of qualified labor will be the primary location-related challenge of the 1990s. The Northeast is the tightest labor market, followed by the West Coast. The South Central region and the Midwest are in the best shape.

In a **product layout,** the location of workstations follows the sequence of steps needed to produce the end product. Parts proceed from one operation to the next with a minimum of movement. Product layouts are usually set up to produce only one kind of product at a time. The auto assembly line is an example.

product layout *a facility layout in which the location of workstations follows the sequence of steps needed to produce the end product.*

group-technology layout
a facility design that gathers dissimilar machines into work centers (or cells) to work on products having similar shapes and processing requirements.

A **group-technology layout** groups dissimilar machines into work centers (or cells) to work on products having similar shapes and processing requirements. A group technology layout is similar to a process layout, in that cells are designed to perform a specific set of processes. It is similar to a product layout, in that the cells are dedicated to a limited range of products. This layout permits companies that produce a variety of parts in small batches to achieve some of the economies of the product layout without product standardization. Although group technology was applied extensively in the Soviet Union and Western Europe since the 1950s, its use in the United States is quite recent.

fixed-position layout *a facility design in which the workers, rather than the material or parts, move from one work center or machine to another.*

Finally, in a **fixed-position layout,** the workers, rather than the material or parts, move from one work center or machine to another. Such a layout is used when the product is very large, such as an aircraft carrier, or could be damaged by movement. The fixed-position layout is costly, since tools and skills are duplicated across projects. Therefore, it is generally used only when there is no good alternative.

MATERIALS PURCHASING AND INVENTORY CONTROL

Purchasing is the link between the firm and its suppliers. It involves decisions about which supplies to buy, when, from whom, and for how much. Inventories act as a cushion between the firm and its environment. The challenge of inventory control is to balance the various costs involved to achieve the lowest total cost. Let's examine materials purchasing first, and then we'll take a close look at inventory control.

Materials Purchasing

Most people in operations management would agree that purchasing and materials handling have a big impact on company profits. For instance, it has been estimated that moving materials from one place to another (say, from a pipe company to a plumbing supply house) accounts for 20 to 50 percent of all production costs. The total amount of money spent on supplies and raw materials in any given year exceeds the gross national product, and 50 percent of the sales dollar of most big firms is spent on purchasing. Clearly, even a small savings in the purchasing budget can be very important.

Understanding the purchasing cycle is the key to understanding materials purchasing. The purchasing cycle begins with a decision to buy materials for production and ends when the materials are accepted by the department requesting the order. There are six steps in the cycle:

1. *Requisitions.* Personnel from the various production units turn in purchase requisitions to the purchasing agent or buyer. The requisitions indicate the type and number of items needed.
2. *Value analysis.* The purchasing agent conducts a systematic appraisal of each purchase requisition. The idea is to find the least-cost way to satisfy the request. Management asks several types of questions at this stage. Do the requested items include too many unnecessary features? Can packaging or shipping requirements be reduced? How available are these items in the forms needed?
3. *Supplier selection.* A list of approved suppliers is developed. The list rates suppliers on the basis of price, quality, reliability, and services. The purchasing agent then obtains quotes on prices and delivery times.

4. *Order placement.* A formal purchase order is completed. The purchase order describes the goods requested, unit prices, quantities desired, shipping instructions, and so on. The purchasing agent can often obtain quantity discounts by ordering large amounts of requested materials at one time. Buying more than is needed right away is called **forward buying.**

5. *Order monitoring.* The purchasing agent regularly checks important orders to make sure they are on schedule. Communicating with the supplier is crucial at this stage.

6. *Order delivery.* A receiving clerk checks the delivered goods against a copy of the purchase order. If the shipment is correct, the purchase is recorded and payment is made.

forward buying   in materials purchasing, the buying of more of a good than is immediately needed for production.

Inventory Control

Most firms keep plenty of inventory on hand. In this way, they are protected from threats to their supply lines, such as a strike by the employees of a supplier. Also, if a firm has an ample inventory of finished goods, it can meet a sudden surge of demand. So we say that inventories cushion against both supply-side and demand-side shocks. Holding inventories is expensive, however. The operations manager must weigh the benefits of large inventories against the costs. This trade-off is pictured in Figure 11-4, along with other typical operations management trade-offs.

Inventory Costs. Three types of costs must be considered for proper inventory control: holding costs, ordering costs, and stockout costs. The term **holding costs** refers to the expense of storing, or holding, the inventory in the firm's warehouse or on its stock shelves. Examples of such costs are warehouse rental and utility bills on the storage facility. **Ordering costs** are the expenses involved in placing an order—mostly paperwork and management time. **Stockout costs** result when the firm runs out of inventory. The dollar value of lost production time or the value of a lost sale and the possible decline in customer goodwill are examples of stockout costs.

holding costs   the expense of storing, or holding, the inventory in the firm's warehouse or on its stock shelves.

ordering costs   the expenses involved in placing an order.

stockout costs   the expenses incurred when a firm runs out of inventory.

As an example, holding costs for a Toyota retail dealership include the interest on loans required to purchase an order of cars from the factory, the cost of showroom space, and the cost of accessories (such as radios and tape decks) that are mounted in the cars and cannot be sold separately. Ordering costs include the cost of paperwork, customs fees, arranging shipping to the dealer's lot, taxes and title fees, and so on. If the dealership runs out of a certain model, stockout costs include the profits lost when customers give up on a Toyota and buy a Honda instead. It is a long-term cost of stockout that those customers do not return to the Toyota dealer when they buy another car. Also, repeated reports of stockouts may spread to other potential customers.

Reorder Point and Reorder Quantity. The total of the three inventory costs depends on the size of inventories at the **reorder point** (when an order is placed) and the **reorder quantity** (size of the order). Figure 11-5 shows variation in inventory level over time, the reorder point, and the reorder quantity. If demand is known and steady from one day to the next, the reorder point is chosen so that new supplies are delivered just as the last product moves off the shelf. In the figure, average daily demand is ten units, and the time from order placement to delivery (called **lead time**) is three days. The firm reorders when the level of inventory drops to $10 \times 3 = 30$ units. The reorder quantity is 80 units. It

reorder point   the point in the inventory order cycle at which an order is placed.

reorder quantity   the size of the inventory order.

lead time   the time from order placement to delivery.

FIGURE 11-4   Production Management Trade-offs

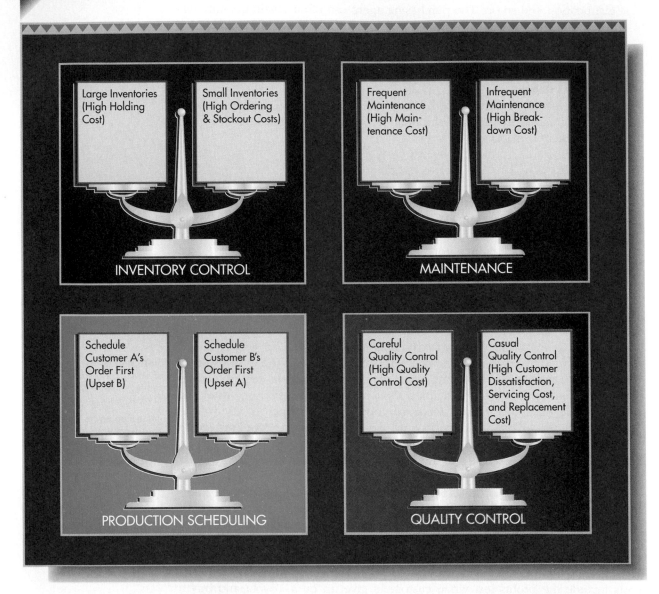

is usually best to build some slack into an inventory control system. For example, it might be safer to reorder when the inventory level drops to 40 units rather than 30.

Economic Order Quantity. The choice of the best reorder quantity requires a balancing of the various inventory costs. If the reorder quantity is large, average inventories will be high, so holding costs will be high. If the reorder quantity is small, the number of separate orders will be high, so total ordering costs will also be high. If demand is not known with certainty (which is almost always the case), small inventories may result in disappointed customers. Thus, a small reorder quantity may lead to high stockout costs. Holding costs on the one hand versus ordering and stockout costs on the other determine the least-cost reorder quantity, or the **Economic Order Quantity (EOQ).**

Economic Order Quantity
(EOQ) the least-cost reorder
quantity.

FIGURE 11-5   Inventory Levels

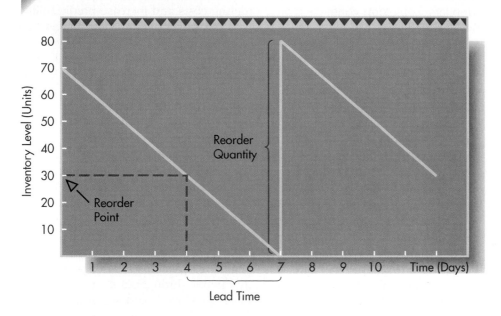

A Safeway store, which holds inventories of perishable goods, must determine an accurate EOQ for each of its products. Accuracy is especially important because profit margins are extremely small in the grocery trade. Profits are quickly eaten up if inventories are too large, so that the products spoil, or if inventories are too small, so that customers are lost to other stores. The EOQ for fresh lettuce will be different from that for canned soups or dried beans.

Keeping Track of Inventories. Many companies keep a running count of their inventory levels. This is called a **perpetual inventory.** Under such an inventory system, the firm knows exactly how much inventory it has at any moment. Both additions to inventory and drawdowns are immediately noted on the inventory records. This continuous method of accounting for inventory is maintained on a transaction-by-transaction basis. Computers are often used for this.

perpetual inventory an inventory system that keeps a running count of inventory levels.

Under a **periodic inventory** system, the firm does not keep a continuous count of inventory. Rather, at the end of each accounting period (six months or a year), the firm takes a physical count of the inventory. Some firms use periodic counts as a check on the accuracy of a perpetual inventory system.

periodic inventory an inventory system in which a physical count of inventory is done at the end of each accounting period.

New Developments in Inventory Control. Two recent developments are changing the nature of inventory control. They are just-in-time and material requirements planning.

Just-in-time (JIT), or **kanban** (a Japanese term for the control cards used in the process), is a method of inventory control in which the firm maintains very small inventories.[8] When an order is received for a finished product, a kanban (card) is issued, instructing workers to produce the item. The finishing department chooses components and assembles the product. The kanban is then passed back to predecessor workstations to replenish the components. This process continues all the way back to the material suppliers. At each stage, parts and other materials are delivered "just in time" for use.

just-in-time (JIT) a method of inventory control in which the firm maintains very small inventories and obtains materials for production just in time for use.

kanban another term for just-in-time inventory control, named for the Japanese word for the control cards used in JIT.

JIT keeps inventory levels extremely low, thereby reducing holding costs. It also fosters a stable, mutually supportive relationship between the producer and suppliers. Long-term contracts reduce ordering costs and increase predictability. Because deliveries are much more frequent, some suppliers devote themselves exclusively to one purchaser and move nearby. Using JIT principles, Huffy Corp., a bicycle maker, was able to cut its inventories almost in half, from $69 million to $36 million. Ford and Chrysler have saved hundreds of millions of dollars by applying JIT techniques. Analysts believe that General Motors could cut its annual costs for maintaining inventories from $3 billion to about $1 billion.

Just-in-time management was credited with softening the economic downturn that began in the mid-1980s. Many manufacturers kept inventories so lean by use of JIT that they could track swings in demand and avoid getting stuck with large stockpiles. Thus, it wasn't necessary to lay off workers while inventories were gradually reduced. Firms such as Corning Inc., General Electric Co., Motorola Inc., Rubbermaid Inc., and various automakers used inventory control procedures so effectively that inventories have never been lower since such records were first kept.[9] This permits firms to control the rhythm of production and reduces the dangers of a deep recession.

JIT doesn't work everywhere. It is difficult to implement when a product line is very diverse and when demand is highly variable throughout the year. Also, JIT may limit flexibility in the range of products produced, and suppliers must be willing to locate nearby. Suppliers are very vulnerable to manufacturers' demands and, perhaps, whims.[10]

materials requirement planning (MRP) an inventory control technique that uses a computer to coordinate information about orders for the finished product, the amount of various materials on hand, and the production sequence, to make sure that the right materials are available at the right time in the production cycle.

Materials requirement planning (MRP) is another new inventory control technique. When component parts are assembled into products, such as automobiles, they are not used independently of one another. Instead, they are needed at exact times in the production cycle. They have to be ordered to fit into that cycle. In MRP, a computer coordinates information about orders for the finished product, the amount of various materials on hand, and the production sequence. It then formulates a master schedule that makes the right materials available at the right time in the production cycle. MRP practitioners report substantial reductions in inventory levels, total labor costs, and overtime costs. On-time deliveries have increased sharply.[11]

PRODUCTION PLANNING AND CONTROL

6 Production planning and control is concerned with the ordering and monitoring of work in process. It includes control of the flow of materials, people, and machines. The aim is to use these resources in the most efficient way possible.

The Planning and Control Process

Effective planning and control involves seven basic steps or actions, as shown in Figure 11-6. Let's take a close look at each of them.

routing the process of determining workflows in production.

Routing. The movement of a mechanical part or other piece of work from one operation to the next traces out a route. **Routing** is the process of determining these workflows. In the case of an assembly line, the routing of work is built into the design of the plant itself. Volvo, for example, is famous for the efficiency of its automobile assembly lines. Even the Japanese automakers have inspected Volvo plants closely before building their own factories.

FIGURE 11-6   Steps in the Planning and Control Process

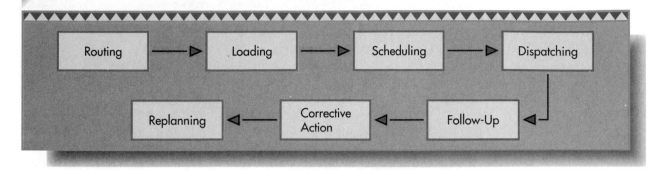

Loading. The term **loading** refers to the process of determining the amount of time each machine or workstation will operate. The planner first determines how long a particular operation takes at a machine or workstation and then adds that amount of time to the time for work already scheduled there. The result is a "load chart" that shows how much each machine or workstation will be used. Because of setup time, maintenance, and other factors, most machine tools cannot be used for more than seven hours of an eight-hour shift.

General Electric faces heavy production schedules for its Hotpoint air-conditioner assembly plants just before the summer starts. The company prefers to schedule its maintenance around this busy period so that it can load its plant as fully as possible. When the assembly line has to be set up for a new product, maintenance work is often done at night so that it won't interfere with normal shift operations.

Scheduling. The planning and controlling function of **scheduling** is the process of determining *when* an operation is to be performed at a machine or workstation. At McLouth Steel, foundries sometimes have to be booked weeks or months in advance for an operation that may take only a few hours. If the facilities are not available on time, an expensive batch of iron can be lost.

Dispatching. After the routing, loading, and scheduling functions are performed, the start of each operation on the shop floor is authorized through **dispatching**—the preparing and issuing of work orders. For example, if four machine operations are required, work orders for each operation are prepared and issued at this point.

Follow-up. Another function in production planning and control is keeping track of work completed and any time lags or delays that may have occurred. This is called **follow-up.** Some jobs will run behind schedule, and others will always run ahead. With effective follow-up procedures, the time savings from jobs running ahead of schedule can subsequently be used to bring lagging jobs back on schedule.

Corrective Action. We might think that a well-managed plant would have everything running on schedule. Actually, a plant that does not encounter production delays is probably not being used efficiently. Because delays have to be

loading *the process of determining how many hours each machine or workstation will operate.*

scheduling *the process of determining when an operation is to be performed at a machine or workstation.*

dispatching *the preparing and issuing of work orders.*

follow-up *the process of keeping track of work completed and any delays that may have occurred.*

Planning and control includes the scheduling function, which is critical in the printing industry. Expensive printing equipment must be used with great efficiency, so print runs are booked months in advance.

corrective action *action taken by management to get lagging production jobs back on schedule.*

expected, management should be ready to deal with them. It may take such **corrective action** as scheduling overtime or shifting work to other machines to get lagging jobs back on schedule.

The United States Postal Service, for example, usually operates at maximum capacity. When delays are encountered, post office managers schedule overtime or send part of their volume to post offices with additional automation, where sorting and delivery can be completed more efficiently.

Replanning. New plans may sometimes be needed in response to changing market conditions, manufacturing methods, or labor force availability. The development of new routing, loading, and scheduling is called **replanning.** In the semiconductor industry, operations managers have to develop new production schedules for new products weekly or monthly.

replanning *the development of new routing, loading, or scheduling plans in response to changing conditions.*

Analytical Tools for Planning and Control
Operations managers have several analytical tools available to help them with production planning and control. We'll examine two such tools.

Schedule Charts. One simple way to keep track of work in process is with a schedule chart. The **schedule chart** shows when each job order is to be performed at each machine, workstation, or department. One such schedule chart, a **Gantt chart,** helps managers monitor the flow of work and the status of work in process. Figure 11-7 is an example of a Gantt chart. According to this figure, the operations manager has scheduled several job orders on each of three lathes over a six-week period. Notice that lathe #1 is frequently idle and that the operations manager has anticipated maintenance time and delays on lathes #2 and #3. Also, job order #16 is ahead of schedule. With scheduling charts such as a Gantt chart,

schedule chart *a planning and control diagram that shows when each job order is to be performed at each machine, department, or workstation.*

Gantt chart *a schedule chart for monitoring flow of work and schedule status of work in process.*

FIGURE 11-7   A Gantt Chart

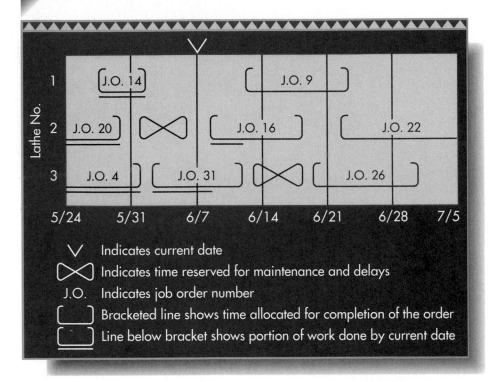

operations managers are able to monitor the flow of materials through a production process or the flow of work through a job shop. The manager then always knows the status of work performed in relation to the work schedule.

PERT and the Critical Path.   Many times, an operations manager has a major project to finish by a contract deadline. The project is made up of many separate activities or steps, each of which requires a certain amount of time for completion. Usually, one activity cannot be started until another is completed. This activity, in turn, is followed by still others. The problem is to coordinate all activities. Most projects, from the company picnic to the construction of an offshore oil drilling platform, fit this description. Some projects involve thousands of separate activities.

The operations manager who is faced with such a project often develops a **Project Evaluation and Review Technique (PERT) chart.** It depicts each activity required to complete a project, the sequence of the activities, and the time allotted for each. Figure 11-8 is an example of a PERT chart.

Whenever possible, it is desirable to carry out several activities at the same time ("in parallel") rather than one after another ("in series"). In Figure 11-8, activities B and C can be performed at the same time, because the start of one does not depend on the completion of the other. However, activity A must be completed before B and C can begin. Thus, activity A and activities B and C must be performed "in series." In a marketing research project, for example, the choice of research goals must precede the writing of the survey questionnaire and the selection of data analysis methods.

The aim of a PERT network is to minimize project delays through effective scheduling of project activities. Such scheduling depends on the identification of

Project Evaluation and Review Technique (PERT) chart *a planning and control diagram that depicts each activity required to complete a project, the sequence of the activities, and the time allotted for each activity.*

FIGURE 11-8   A PERT Chart

The diagram shows nodes Start, 1, 2, 3, 4, 5, Finish connected by activities:
- A (time 1) from Start to 1
- B (time 4) from 1 to 2
- C (time 3) from 1 to 4
- D (time 2) from 2 to 3
- E (time 1) from 4 to 5
- F (time 1) from 3 to 5
- G (time 2) from 5 to Finish

Legend:
- ─────▷ Activity
- ● Completion of Activity
- 1 Activity Time Shown below Activity
- ⇒ Critical Path

critical path — *the sequence of in-series activities requiring the longest time for completion.*

the **critical path.** This is the sequence of in-series activities requiring the longest time for completion. In Figure 11-8, the sequence of activities along the critical path is such that the project cannot be completed in fewer than ten weeks. Activities B and C are "in parallel," but activity B is along the critical path because that path (ABDFG) takes the most time to complete. Activity C is on a path (ACEG) that takes only seven weeks to complete. So activity C could be delayed as much as three weeks (10−7) without slowing project completion. Because activity C can be delayed somewhat without slowing down the project, it is not on the critical path.

The completion of a project on time depends on the careful management and control of activities along the critical path. Delay in any activity along the critical path will delay the project. When necessary, the operations manager can divert resources from noncritical activities to critical activities to complete them more quickly. Also, the operations manager can look for other opportunities to schedule activities in parallel which are now in series.

QUALITY CONTROL

At one time, the term "Made in Japan" was synonymous with cheap products and inferior construction. It was usually written on the bottom of products found in discount bins. Now, however, consumers speak with pride about their Japanese autos, cameras, televisions, stereo systems, watches, and porcelain dinnerware. More often than not, it is U.S. products that are thought to be of inferior quality. For instance, one researcher visited every Japanese manufacturer of room air conditioners and all but one American manufacturer. He found tremendous variations in failure rates among the companies—sometimes by a factor of 500 or 1,000. The average Japanese plant had an assembly-line defect rate 70 times lower than that of the average American plant. First-year service call rates were almost 17 times better for the Japanese plants. The poorest Japanese company had a failure rate less than half that of the best American manufacturer.[12]

Many companies in this country have responded to the problem of declining product quality by setting up quality improvement programs for employees. Such programs often use a combination of posters, slogans, pep talks, and praise to encourage employees to work more carefully. Companies have also increased emphasis on **quality control,** the process of setting standards and measuring the quality of products and services against these standards.

quality control *the process of setting standards and measuring the quality of products and services against these standards.*

Total Quality Control

Many companies are adopting quality as a primary goal and guiding philosophy. This concept, called **total quality control** (in Japan, "companywide quality control") is based on the premise that everyone at every level of the company is responsible for quality—not just quality control departments and formal control systems. Also, instead of settling for an "acceptable" level of quality, where some defects are expected, the target is zero defects. This approach encourages efforts toward continuous improvement rather than just being "good enough." This constant improvement, called **kaizen** in Japan, is a key element of the Japanese success story.[13] Nearly half of the large U.S. companies in one survey reported that they had created executive-level quality posts since 1988.[14]

total quality control *a concept based on the premise that everyone from the top to the bottom of the organization is responsible for the quality of goods and services.*

kaizen *the Japanese term for constant improvement of products and processes.*

Quality Circles

Quality circles (QCs) are a popular approach to quality control and improvement. QCs are committees of workers who analyze and solve problems relating to quality. Typically, the committee consists of 6 to 12 volunteers from the same work area. Committee members receive training in problem solving, statistical quality control, and group processes. A specially trained manager instructs members and sees to it that the committee runs smoothly. The circles typically meet for about four hours a month on company time. QC objectives include quality improvement, productivity enhancement, and employee involvement.

quality circles (QCs) *committees of workers who analyze and solve problems relating to quality.*

Widely adopted in Japan since the 1950s, quality circles first appeared in the United States at Lockheed Missile and Space Company in 1974. Lockheed estimates that QCs may have saved the company $3 million. Experts estimate that there are now more than 3,000 quality circles in U.S. companies, that over 200,000 U.S. employees have participated in quality circles, and that more than 90 percent of the Fortune 500 companies now have QC programs.[15]

Many successes of quality circles have been reported, and workers who are involved in them often have positive work attitudes.[16] Nevertheless, many people question whether the culture of the United States is right for QCs. American management and workers differ in many ways from those in Japan, and a transplant may not take. Also, there is evidence that many initially successful QC programs were no longer in operation within a few years.[17]

The bottom line seems to be that quality circles often work and they often fail. Managers who consider using QCs must have realistic expectations and must consider their costs—often $20,000 or more for a modest effort—as well as their potential benefits. To be successful, quality circles need the support of top management, and they can't be forced onto organizations. Last but not least, quality circles will not remedy problems caused by poor management planning or an inappropriate product mix.

Inspection

We defined quality control as the process of setting standards and measuring the quality of products and services against these standards. The term **inspection** refers to the second part of this definition: It involves comparing products against the standards, approving those that meet them, and rejecting those that do not. Inspection serves as a check on the quality of incoming material and finished goods.

Many advanced techniques, including ultrasonic and magnetic tests, X rays, computerized scanners, and television cameras, are used for inspection. But some judgments, such as whether a wine tastes "bad" or a flaw is "serious enough" to cause rejection, cannot be made so objectively.

Statistical Quality Control

Statistical quality control was first applied in the Bell Telephone Laboratories in the early 1920s. W. Edwards Deming, whose accomplishments are discussed in this chapter's International Example (see page 290), introduced statistical quality control concepts to Japan in 1950. He is widely credited with the stunning improvement of Japanese product quality in just a few years. The assumption behind **statistical quality control** is that most quality problems (perhaps as many as 85 percent) are the result of flaws in manufacturing systems, not of errors by production workers.

Random Variation or Out of Control. The goal of statistical quality control is to determine whether something has gone wrong with the manufacturing system. It relies on the laws of probability to do this. By checking a sample of the output of a process and applying the right statistics, a manager can tell whether the system is "out of control."

To illustrate, suppose that our plant produces a machine part for oil well pumps. The part is designed to be 6" in diameter, but we know from experience that it is sometimes slightly more than or less than 6" for individual parts. Now suppose we pull one of the finished parts off the assembly line and find its diameter to be 6.01". Is this deviation of .01" simply a random, unimportant variation? Or is the deviation a sign that the production process is out of control, therefore requiring adjustment?

The Control Chart. To answer this question, we need to look at the past outputs of our production process and determine their average characteristics (such as the average diameter of 6") and the typical variation around these averages. We also need to know the probability that various deviations may have occurred by chance alone.

For example, we might know that a part with a 6.01" diameter occurs ten times in a hundred by chance alone. Thus, our sampled part with the 6.01" diameter does not concern us very much, because the deviation is very likely due to chance. But suppose the diameter of the sampled part were 6.03", and we know that the probability of this occurring by chance is only one in 10,000. What then? In this case, we can be fairly sure that the production process is out of control and that more defective parts will be produced.

A control chart is usually used in conjunction with statistical control. A **control chart** shows the average and the upper and lower control limits of critical production parameters. A control chart for our example is shown in Figure 11-9. The chart shows the average diameter of the part as well as the upper and lower control limits for the diameter. If a part has a diameter greater than the upper

FIGURE 11-9   A Control Chart

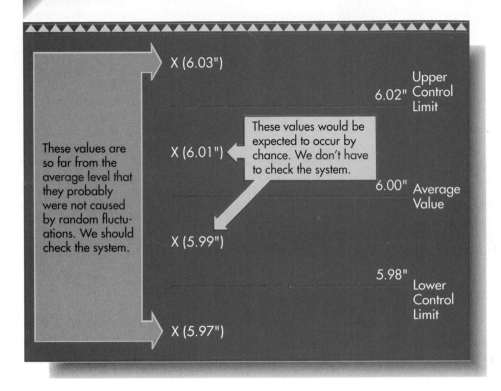

control limit of 6.02″ or smaller than the lower control limit of 5.98″, the production system is somehow flawed. If the diameter is within that range, then the system is operating satisfactorily. These control limits might be measurements (such as the diameter in our example), frequencies (such as the number of bad light bulbs in a sample), or number of defects per unit (such as the number of flaws on a piece of glass).

Monitoring the Quality of Supplies

Quality control problems in production are often the result of poor quality inputs. Some companies have strong programs for ensuring the quality of incoming production materials and supplies. Xerox has a four-point program to assist suppliers. From the beginning of its new product development process, Xerox involves its suppliers in writing specifications for production materials and components. Xerox makes sure that its suppliers understand these specifications before supply orders are placed. It also operates a hotline for suppliers who have any last-minute questions. Finally, Xerox uses statistical quality control on its suppliers' manufacturing systems, and it uses a team approach for a check on the packing and handling of materials. Significant quality improvements have been attributed to Xerox's program.

MAINTENANCE POLICIES

Breakdowns of production machinery can be expensive in terms of lost production time and repair costs. Keeping production equipment in good repair is a big job. More than $14 billion a year is spent on maintenance by companies in the United States. Maintenance can take one of three forms.

Deming and the Japanese Experience

W. Edwards Deming is a man with a mission. This 90-year-old statistician from Sioux City, Iowa wants American industry to adopt the statistical quality control techniques that he so successfully introduced to Japan more than 40 years ago.

During World War II, Deming developed his ideas while teaching ways to improve the quality of production through statistical control. When the war ended, the concern in the United States was with meeting pent-up demand, not with quality. But Japan was more receptive. The postwar economy was shattered, and product quality was very low. In July 1950, Deming conducted the first of a series of meetings with leading Japanese industrialists.

He argued that improved quality was within their reach: "Don't just make it and try to sell it. But redesign it and then bring the process under control . . . with an ever increasing quality." He told the industrialists that with application of statistical quality control techniques, Japan would capture many world markets within five years.

According to Deming, they beat that prediction. By 1951, in fact, the London Express ran a banner headline stating, "And Now Come Japanese Nylons: And They Are of Good Quality." In recognition of Deming's contributions to Japanese industrial growth, Japanese companies now present an annual Deming award to one of their industries that has achieved the most significant quality improvements.

Despite these developments, Deming's work drew little interest outside Japan. Then, in June 1980, an NBC-TV documentary titlled "If Japan Can . . . Why Can't We?" was aired in the United States. The program compared Japanese and American quality and highlighted Deming's role in the Japanese turnaround. Since then, many U.S. firms—including Ford Motor Company and General Motors' Pontiac Division—have turned to Deming for guidance in quality control.

1. Corrective maintenance—fixing a machine that is not working properly.
2. Preventive maintenance—designing, inspecting, and servicing machinery so that breakdowns are less likely.
3. Predictive maintenance—using monitoring instruments to estimate when machine failures are likely.

Preventive maintenance is usually less costly than corrective maintenance, so it is preferred by most operations managers. Predictive maintenance is especially appropriate for complex, highly automated production processes.

Management should answer several questions concerning maintenance. How much maintenance is needed? Can computers and statistical methods be of help? Should an in-house maintenance staff be used, or should outside people be brought in? Would preventive or predictive maintenance be less expensive?

Most maintenance policies are just good common sense. For instance, it is usually best to try to schedule maintenance for periods when things are slow. If much maintenance is needed during peak periods, perhaps some work should be contracted out. Also, there is usually a "best" time to service equipment. If it is done too soon, money is wasted; if done too late, repair may be costly or impossible.

THE FACTORY OF THE FUTURE

factory of the future the computer-based integration of design, process, and control functions in the manufacturing environment.

Because of the increasing competition in world markets, American producers are keenly aware of the need to become more efficient and effective. To do so, some U.S. firms are making major technological investments in what has been called the factory of the future. The **factory of the future** is a term referring to the computer-based integration of design, process, and control functions in the manufacturing environment. It uses robots and other modern technologies and practices to achieve high-quality, low-cost, flexible manufacturing. Thus, the factory of the future is intimately linked to world-class manufacturing. As indicated in the Ethical Issue (page 292), modern manufacturing technologies can reduce pollution and waste at the same time that they improve production.

Historically, manufacturing has been based on economies of scale. Large numbers of identical products were manufactured on automated equipment in order to achieve low unit production costs. In contrast, the factory of the future tries to capture **economies of scope**—those that occur when the same raw materials and production facilities are used to produce a variety of products.[18] In the factory of the future, computerized controls result in economies of scope by allowing the same automated machinery to produce a variety of goods cheaply. As a fanciful example, if three specialized machines designed to produce unicycles, rollerblades, and skateboards could be replaced with one computer-controlled machine able to switch almost immediately from one product to another, the savings could be considerable. Thus, the cost of the machinery could be spread over many products. The advantages would be short lead times, product variability, and reasonable costs.

economies of scope an objective of the factory of the future; computerized control allows automated machinery to produce a variety of goods cheaply.

Robotics

One of the authors attended a week-long conference on new developments in operations management. Of the many topics covered, perhaps the most thought-provoking was a simple photograph. It was solid black, with only a pinpoint of light in the lower right-hand corner. The photograph showed the third shift at a Japanese auto plant. No lights were needed by the robots that ran the plant. The pinpoint of light was from the flashlight of the lone guard.

Robots play a key role in the factory of the future. The term "robot" comes from a Czech word meaning drudgery, servitude, or forced labor. Czech playright Karl Capek introduced the term about 70 years ago. His satirical play "R.U.R." raised questions about the dehumanizing impact technological progress could have on humankind. Today, a **robot** is defined as a machine that can be programmed to do a variety of tasks automatically.

robot a machine that can be programmed to do a variety of tasks automatically.

The variety of robots on the job is remarkable. There is now a bureaucratic robot that stamps signatures on letters, a nurse robot to assist the handicapped in wheelchairs, and a talking robot to advertise products. Some industrial robots are mobile and have many arms, but most are nothing more than a mechanical arm attached to a stationary base. A programmable computing device controls the operations of the arm. Robots in U.S. factories are now performing such manufacturing tasks as spray painting, arc welding, die casting, assembling, and materials handling. In 1990, the robot population of the U.S. was estimated at between 75,000 and 150,000 units.[19]

The science fiction aspects of robots have captured the public's imagination. Robots can be used for dangerous or unpleasant jobs, such as cleanup of nuclear power plants, excavation of hazardous-materials sites, bomb detection and disposal, space exploration, and military reconnaissance.[20] They can handle heavy loads, work odd hours, and provide flexibility. However, the great growth in the number of robots on the job is largely the result of simple economics. About 25 years ago, an assembly-line robot cost $4.20 an hour to operate, or slightly more than the hourly pay of an average factory worker. By 1988, auto manufacturers were able to operate robots for $5 to $6 per hour (including maintenance and depreciation), as compared to $23 to $24 for skilled labor. Moreover, each robot may do the work of as many as five or six humans, and robots have down time of only 5 percent, versus 25 percent of the average blue-collar worker.[21] Roger

Clean Manufacturing

According to conventional wisdom, clean-air laws willl burden U.S. industry with billions of dollars in pollution-control costs and raise prices for many commodities and finished goods. However, many firms are actually reducing some costs as they install new pollution-cutting technologies. These benefits come primarily from new manufacturing techniques rather than waste and emission treatment processes.

American companies produce five times as much waste per dollar of goods sold as Japanese companies and more than twice what German firms do. Clearly, waste reduction can have a major impact on profits and competitiveness. The congressional Office of Technology Assessment estimates that U.S. manufacturing wastes can be cut in half using existing technologies. Another 25 percent could be reduced with research and development.

For instance, Carrier Corp. decided in 1987 to adopt "clean" technologies. In manufacturing air conditioners, the biggest source of hazardous wastes is the "degreasing" line. There, copper and aluminum parts pass through tanks of solvents to be cleaned of oils and debris accumulated during cutting and soldering. The company first developed a nontoxic lubricant that evaporated. Next, it fine-tuned its cutting presses to cut metal coils more precisely, with less friction and less waste. The company also designed air conditioners with fewer parts, reducing the need to cut and rejoin metal. Thus, Carrier eliminated the "degreasing" line, increased automation, reduced scrap, eliminated down time, and increased product quality. The $500,000 costs incurred in 1988 for these changes resullted in annual production cost savings of $1.2 million.

American Telephone & Telegraph Co. had traditionally cleaned soldering debris and rosins from circuit boards with chlorofluorocarbons (CFCs), which are believed to deplete the earth's protective ozone layer. AT&T has been installing new cleaning lines that use solutions similar to household detergents. The new solutions are less expensive than CFCs, resulting in a $3 million annual saving, but still require treatment before disposal. Now, by switching to a rosin that is completely harmless and evaporates, AT&T expects to eliminate the cost of cleaning entirely.

Another notable success is Whyco Chromium Co. The Company developed a new alloy to eliminate harmful byproducts from its process for coating nuts and screws, trimming the cost by 25 percent. Also, 3M Corp. estimates that manufacturing changes to control pollution have saved it $41 million in the past three years. As these examples demonstrate, firms that address environmental challenges intelligently may clean up both their profits and the air we breathe.

Smith, former chairman of the board of General Motors, stated, "Every time the cost of labor goes up $1 per hour, 1,000 more robots become economical."[22]

GM's Lordstown, Ohio, plant features advanced Unimate robots that apply 450 welds to every car that comes off the assembly line. The Unimates have "super seniority"—they stay in the plant during layoffs and shutdowns and are back at work as soon as they are needed. A Unimate costs $45,000 and pays for itself in less than ten months by replacing two $28,000-a-year welders.[23]

Since robots replace human labor, many workers see them as a threat. In the past, some people were at least comforted by the belief that someone would have to build the robots. Now, there are instances of reproductive robotics, in which robots build themselves. Unemployment is a possibility that can't be ignored. One study concluded that the current generation of robots has the technical capability to perform nearly 7 million existing factory jobs—one third of all manufacturing employment. How much unemployment will ultimately result from automation is hotly debated. Some analysts argue that automation will steadily eliminate manufacturing jobs in the U.S. Others counter that the negative effects of automation are overstated and will be short-term anyway. According to this view, automation will result in higher productivity and, with it, new jobs.[24] Many people agree with the view that long-term effects may well be beneficial. But someone has accurately pointed out that in the long run, we're all dead. There will almost certainly be major short-term displacement of workers as a result of automation. Companies, unions, and government will have to seek creative ways to deal with it.[25] The profile of Deborah Coleman on page 294 discusses how Apple Computer used advanced automation, along with modern techniques of inventory control and quality control, to cut production costs.

Design for Manufacturability

One of the most exciting developments in modern factories is design for manufacturability.[26] **Design for manufacturability (DFM)** is based on the philosophy that the best-engineered part is no part at all. For instance, although screws and bolts cost only pennies apiece, the associated costs, such as the time needed to align components while screws are inserted and tightened, may drive the price of these parts to 75 percent of total assembly costs. Therefore, NCR Corp. used DFM to design its new electronic cash register. The register uses no screws or bolts and has 85 percent fewer parts, from 65 percent fewer suppliers, than the company's previous low-end model, and it takes only 25 percent of the previous assembly time. DFM makes good use of computer models. Such models can fashion three-dimensional parts on the computer screen, analyze the overall product and its elements for performance and durability, and assemble simulated components on the screen to make sure they fit properly. NCR used DFM programs to get its simplified terminal to market in record time. The product remained a computer model until all members of the development team were satisfied.

Ford, General Motors, Whirlpool, and Motorola are also among the firms that are enthusiastic about DFM. Since 1981, General Electric Co. has used DFM in more than 100 development programs, from major appliances to gearboxes for jet engines. It estimates that benefits from use of the concept have totaled $200 million. Several years ago, IBM used DFM computer programs to analyze printers it was buying from Japan. IBM decided that it could do far better. Its Proprinter has 65 percent fewer parts, and assembly takes a remarkable 90 percent less time.

design for manufacturability (DFM) a design concept that uses computer programs to simplify product design and minimize the number of component parts in the product.

Status of the Factory of the Future

Although the factory of the future has great promise, some firms are rejecting this approach. They prefer to go "back to the basics," focusing more on employee motivation and on teaching workers quality-control techniques.[27] Many companies have spent millions of dollars on expensive technology, with disappointing results. To a large extent, this is the result of overly optimistic estimates of the impact of robotics and other technology. Also, firms have often tried to install new technology on top of the same old structure—paving an old road instead of building a better road from scratch.

Now firms are recognizing that if the factory of the future is to realize its potential, reorganization must take place from the ground up. The goal is to work smarter rather than faster. To accomplish this, new computer approaches and programs are being used.

Using these approaches, many U.S. firms are recording remarkable successes. At the General Dynamics Corp. plant in Forth Worth, Texas, the expertise of a master machinist has been installed in a system that oversees a cluster of machine tools and robots. The operation has never scored less than 100 percent quality. At Digital Equipment Corporation, savings from new technology are $135 million annually—on an investment of $30 million annually. These savings are the result of reduced inventories, higher productivity, and faster cycle times for billing and

Deborah A. Coleman

Deborah Coleman is a champion of American manufacturing and a remarkable Silicon Valley success story. At Apple Computer, Inc., she has held the titles of controller of the Macintosh special task force; controller of the Macintosh division; group controller of the Apple 32 product group; director of operations, Macintosh division; director of worldwide operations; vice president for operations; vice president for finance and chief financial officer; and vice president of information systems and technology. In the process, she has helped to make Apple a model of what American manufacturing can be.

Apple Computer does business in more than 80 countries. Apple had net sales in 1990 of $5.58 billion, net income of $475 million, and 14,500 employees. Its stated goal is to provide easy and affordable access to information and computing power for everyone.

Debi Coleman can speak comfortably with engineers and technicians, but her academic training was in other areas, including an undergraduate education in English at Brown University and an MBA at Stanford. She worked at General Electric after graduating from Brown and at Hewlett-Packard after Stanford, in each case in the area of finance. Her knowledge of manufacturing was gained by observation and reading. Such "stretching" is common at Apple, where many employees work in areas outside the strict definition of their fields.

Debi Coleman joined Apple Computer in 1981 as a member of the special Macintosh task force. As controller of the new Macintosh division, she helped then-chairman Steve Jobs select the first two managers for the Macintosh factory. When neither of those managers worked out, Ms. Coleman mentioned to Jobs that she wanted to run the factory. He laughed at first, but then they made a deal. If Coleman built the best finance organization and management information system in the industry, Jobs would hand her the Macintosh factory. A year later, she had the position. When Debi Coleman took over, the plant was falling far short of its goals, and she took firm action. She eliminated computer-driven equipment that wasn't "people friendly," reduced inventories, and called everyone in the plant together to set monthly goals and "foster a shared vision."

A year after taking over the plant, Debi Coleman was named director of worldwide manufacturing. Ms. Coleman's challenge was to salvage the manufacturing organization. She soon closed one plant and sold another, advanced automation, implemented just-in-time techniques, improved quality control, and strengthened relationships with vendors. Production costs were cut 25 percent.

In 1987 Debi Coleman—then 34 years old—was offered the title of vice president for finance and chief financial officer. She accepted the challenge and became responsible for Apple's planning, internal financial controls, management information systems group, and treasury functions. Some people might view her dual careers in manufacturing and finance as an odd combination, but Ms. Coleman saw no conflict. By rotating between functional areas, she was able to get a broader view of the company.

Debi Coleman currently serves as Apple's vice president of information systems and technology and directs the company's internal information systems. Her mission is to make Apple's information system—using Apple's technology—the most advanced and effective of any company in the Fortune 100.

Debi Coleman has been described by John Sculley (Apple's chairman, president, and CEO) as "a national treasure," and she has made no secret of the fact that her dreams extend beyond Apple. Her long-term goal is to run General Electric Corporation, which she describes as "the most vertically integrated and multiproduct range of manufacturing there is." The personalized plates on her Toyota van make that goal clear: GECEO2B.

distributing products. The B-2 Stealth bomber is one of the most complex products ever made. Using a computer model, Northrup Corp. was able to build the bomber without a mock-up. Ninety-seven percent of the B-2's parts fit perfectly the first time. The best Northrup had ever done previously was 50 percent.[28] These and other successes show the potential of the factory of the future. Nevertheless, new technology carries high start-up costs and risks, and changes in technology may require corresponding changes in structure and management practices.

SUMMARY POINTS

1 The term "operations" refers to any process that accepts inputs and uses resources to change those inputs in form, time, or space. Operations management is the systematic direction and control of the processes that transform inputs into finished goods and services. Operations managers must be concerned with both the short-term and long-term effectiveness of their production or service facilities. Many operations management decisions, such as those relating to capacity planning, inventory policies, and procedures to improve quality, are important for the survival and success of the firm and the satisfaction, performance, and job security of its members.

2 The capacity planning process involves several steps, including prediction of future demand, translation into capacity requirements, generation of alternative capacity plans, consideration of costs and benefits of the alternative plans, and development of steps for implementing the selected plan.

3 Both cost and noncost factors are considered in deciding facility location. Cost factors include labor, transportation, construction, and utility costs, as well as taxes. Noncost factors include environmental and living conditions and availability of resources and skilled labor. Firms compete by keeping transportation, labor, and distribution costs low, so facility location is critical.

4 The goal of facility design and layout is to plan a businesslike environment that will promote efficiency. It tries to minimize idle time, in-process inventories, materials-handling costs, and facilities operation and maintenance costs, and to provide a safe and pleasant workplace. Four basic types are process, product, group-technology, and fixed-position layouts.

5 The steps in the materials purchasing cycle include requisition, value analysis, supplier selection, order placement, order monitoring, and order delivery. Inventory control involves balancing the costs of maintaining inventories, placing orders, and losing sales because of stockouts. Total costs are minimized by choosing an optimal reorder point and reorder quantity. Inventory levels may be monitored continuously or periodically. Two new developments in inventory control are just-in-time (JIT), in which parts and materials are delivered just in time for use, and material requirements planning (MRP), in which a computer coordinates information about orders for the finished product, the amount of various materials on hand, and the production sequence. It then formulates a master schedule that makes the right materials available at the right time in the production cycle.

6 Production planning and control coordinates work in process so that materials, people, and machines are used efficiently. This requires determining routes for parts, loading and scheduling of operations on machines, and subsequent control. Schedule charts and project planning methods help with production planning and control. A Gantt chart is a type of schedule chart used for monitoring the flow of work and the status of work in process. A PERT chart is a diagram of the activities required to complete a project, the sequence of the activities, and the time needed to complete each one. The critical path of the PERT chart is the path of in-series activities requiring the longest time for completion. A delay in any activity on the critical path will delay the completion of the entire project.

7 Quality control is the process of setting standards and measuring the quality of products and services against those standards. Many companies are adopting the total quality control philosophy, based on the premise that everyone at every level of the company is responsible for quality. Quality circles, inspection, and statistical quality control are useful in maintaining quality. Quality circles (QCs) are committees of workers who analyze and solve problems relating to quality. Inspection involves the comparison of products aainst standards, approving those that meet them and rejecting those that do not. Statistical quality control is a method of monitoring production quality. It assumes that flaws in manufacturing systems, not errors by production workers, are the primary cause of quality problems. Since quality control problems are often the result of poor inputs, some companies have strong pro-

grams for ensuring the quality of incoming materials and supplies.

8 Maintenance may be corrective, preventive, or predictive. Corrective maintenance involves fixing machines that are not working properly. Preventive maintenance uses design, inspection, and service of machinery to minimize breakdowns. With predictive maintenance, monitoring instruments are used to anticipate failures.

9 The term factory of the future refers to the computer-based integration of design, process, and control functions in the manufacturing environment. The factory of the future seeks to attain economies of scope. It relies heavily on computerization, including robotics.

REVIEW QUESTIONS

1 What is operations management? What is the operations manager's task in the short run? In the long run? **1**

2 Describe three ways that operations transform inputs into outputs. **1**

3 What is world-class manufacturing? **1**

4 Describe the steps in the capacity planning process. **2**

5 Explain three cost factors and three noncost factors that should be considered in deciding facility location. **3**

6 Identify four types of facility layouts and indicate when each might be used. **4**

7 List and describe the steps in the purchasing cycle. **5**

8 Describe four key trade-offs in operations management. **5**

9 Discuss the three costs associated with inventory control. **5**

10 List and explain the seven steps in the production planning and control process. **6**

11 Discuss two sets of analytical tools for production planning and control. **6**

12 Explain how a control chart is used. **7**

13 Describe three forms of maintenance. **8**

14 What is the factory of the future? How do economies of scope differ from economies of scale? **9**

DISCUSSION QUESTIONS

1 Give two example of goods or services resulting from (a) synthetic transformation processes, (b) analytic transformation processes, (c) temporal transformation processes, and (d) spatial transformation processes.

2 Which three tools or approaches discussed in this chapter do you consider most important for service sector organizations? Least important? Why?

3 Which of the facility layouts discussed in the chapter would seem to be most appropriate for continuous manufacturing processes? For intermittent manufacturing? Why?

4 Consider the characteristics of the modern manufacturing facility. How do you think those characteristics affect efficiency? Worker satisfaction? Flexibility?

5 Describe a product for which stockout costs might be especially important. Describe one for which stockout costs might be unimportant.

6 Do you think the quality of products made in the U.S. is higher or lower than that of products made in Japan? In South America? In Germany? Do you think the differences in quality have more to do with statis-tical quality control, worker motivation, or other factors?

7 The chapter notes that some firms are rejecting the factory of the future to go "back to basics." Do you think robots and other complex technologies will be used more or less in the future? What are some factors that might influence the desirability of such technologies?

EXPERIENTIAL EXERCISES

1 Visit a local manufacturing firm. Guided by the material discussed in this chapter, interview the operations manager concerning the firm's (a) inventory control procedures, (b) quality control techniques, (c) production planning and control procedures, and (d) maintenance policies. Write a summary of your findings. What works particularly well for this company? What did the manager identify as problems for the company?

2 Select some project that you will have to complete in the future (such as planning a party, choosing a job, or organizing a baseball team). Develop a PERT chart for that project.

CASES

CASE 11-1
Meeting Foreign Challenges with Operations Management

Stiffer competition from foreign firms forced General Electric Co. to restructure the company's circuit breaker business from top to bottom. Moving quickly, they decided to consolidate the circuit breaker's unit at one automated assembly plant in Salisbury, N.C., shutting five others. They also simplified the design of the breaker box, reducing its total parts from some 28,000 to 1,275. Furthermore, they installed a computerized system: With each order, the machines were automatically programmed to make the boxes. In addition, GE eliminated all line supervisors and quality inspectors and gave those middle-management responsibilities to production workers. These changes in people and process have sparked impressive results. Productivity jumped 20 percent, and manufacturing costs declined 30 percent in a year. Best of all, it now takes just three days—rather than three weeks—to fill an order, and the plant's backlog has dropped from three weeks to two days.

Corning Glass Works undertook a similar approach with two new factories that manufacture pollution-control devices. The Corning, N.Y., company examined each of the 235 manufacturing steps involved. It eliminated 115 unnecessary operations to cut production time from four weeks to three days. At the same time, Corning insisted on just two job classifications at the plant: operations associate and maintenance engineer. Plants now have just a single layer between workers and plant managers. The plants are unionized, but all workers receive bonuses for achieving goals.

Some manufacturers are edging toward so-called small-batch manufacturing, using advanced computer technology to make a broader variety of products more quickly. Surprisingly, one is a casket manufacturer: Hillenbrand, based in Batesville, Ind. has used automated equipment to slash the time in which it can turn out a casket model from an array of designs. On a larger scale, a plant in Charlottesville, Va., operated jointly by General Electric and Japan's Fanuc Ltd., has automated the production of sophisticated programmable logic controllers used in factory automation equipment. The plant is capable of custom-making each individual controller—at a competitive price—to fit customers' needs.

Source: Adapted by permission of *The Wall Street Journal,* © Dow Jones & Company, Inc. (May 2, 1989). All Rights Reserved Worldwide.

1   Which elements of the factory of the future can be seen in the examples discussed in this case? What other new developments in operations management are suggested?

2   The chapter noted that world-class manufacturing seeks to achieve many goals simultaneously. It tries to develop product lines that are innovative, flexible, high-quality, low-cost, and delivered on time. Which of these goals are reflected in this case?

3   Considering the successes discussed in the examples in this case, why do you think more firms haven't adopted such procedures?

CASE 11-2
Project Saturn

General Motors decided on "Project Saturn" as the name for its $3.5 billion attempt to build a competitive small car. The company borrowed the name from the U.S. effort to be the first nation to put a man on the moon. If Saturn fails, GM is likely to give up U.S. small car production and sharply increase its purchases of small cars from affiliates in Japan, South Korea, and elsewhere.

As initially proposed in 1983, GM's Saturn effort was extremely ambitious. The company wasn't just talking about *building* a new car; it wanted to design a new way to *produce* cars. The company hoped to abandon the assembly line that has been standard in the industry since the days of the first Henry Ford, to decrease dramatically the number of parts and the amount of labor needed to build cars, and to leapfrog competitors in the use of highly sophisticated robots. If GM succeeds in this effort, it could establish itself as one of the world's lowest-cost auto producers and force its U.S. competitors to revamp their operations, at huge cost.

The overriding idea was to compensate for the Japanese advantage in labor costs ($8 to $10 an hour) by cutting drastically the number of person-hours needed to build a car. GM's goal was to slash the number of person-hours per car to 30, compared to its current 175 and about 100 for Japanese automakers.

The biggest single change slated for Saturn is so-called modular construction. With modular construction, the parts are first subassembled into a few fairly large components called "modules." The final assembly isn't done on an assembly line at all. Instead, workers or teams of workers posted at stationary workstations put the modules together. Instead of having one or only a few tasks to do, they perform a whole cluster of tasks, such as building an entire fender or front end. Trolleys carry the partly completed cars from station to station.

In building the subassemblies, GM initially planned to rely heavily on so-called intelligent robots. Currently, robots are used only in the final assembly process for spot welding and materials handling, or for such relatively simple tasks as attaching a tire to a wheel. That is because current robots have sharply limited abilities. In contrast, intelligent robots would be able to "see" that a part is out of position, calculate how far out of position it is, and adjust its own operations on the part accordingly. Thus, such robots could perform complex assembly steps such as installing interior trim. As robots get even more intelligent, they could do quick quality control checks on the dimensions and tolerances of parts as well.

To make Project Saturn work, GM knew it needed cooperation from the United Auto Workers. A contract agreed upon in 1985 gave GM needed flexibility. It sharply reduced the number of job classifications, allowing a single worker to do various assembly, inspection, and equipment-maintenance tasks required under modular construction. In return, workers were given greater job security, annual salaries, and benefits.

Another hurdle for GM was to persuade its thousands of suppliers to make the necessary sacrifices. To cut inventory costs and improve quality, suppliers would have to invest in new equipment and to locate plants close to GM's Saturn facilities. But many were wary. They feared they would be stuck with big losses if Project Saturn failed.

GM board chairman Roger Smith's pledge to drive a Saturn car off the assembly line before his retirement in August 1990 was realized. But much had changed. GM's market share had tumbled from 44 percent to 37 percent, and its profits had been badly squeezed. So Saturn's budget was cut, and the emphasis changed from exploring leading-edge technology to building a high-volume car that would capture lost customers. Instead of costing $6,000 as originally planned, the lowest-priced Saturn had a base price of $7,995. Despite Smith's wishes, there are no workerless "lights out" factories, nor any 50-mile-per-gallon engines.

Nevertheless, freed of the encumbrances of the GM bureaucracy, workers and management already appear to have taken giant steps toward defining a new way of building and marketing cars. Japan wrote the book on high quality, low cost, and relentless productivity gains in auto manufacturing, but Saturn is busily developing its own translation. The offices in the Detroit suburb of Troy have open cubicles, and executives eat off paper plates in a spartan cafeteria. Consensus and teamwork are the management bywords. Policy is set by an 11-man Saturn Action Council that includes a United Auto Workers union representative.

The most dramatic evidence of Saturn's Japan-like approach can be seen at the factory complex in Spring Hill, Tennessee. The largest single construction project in GM history, the mile-long installation combines all the essential operations on one site, much as the Japanese have done. In addition to the usual sheet-metal stamping and body assembly, Spring Hill includes a foundry for casting engine blocks, a power-train assembly line, a plastics-molding unit, and an interior trim shop. Surrounding each operation are dozens of loading docks, so that materials and parts can be delivered close to the assembly lines, kanban-style.

Spring Hill represents a big change from recent GM efforts to boost factory productivity and quality. There are fewer robots and automatic car-carrying vehicles than in GM's other new plants. Instead, Saturn is pouring its money into people management. It plans to hire exceptionally motivated workers, put them through intensive training, give them more and more say in how their jobs get done, and pay them a salary plus a performance bonus—just like Saturn executives.

Relations with Saturn suppliers are, in the Japanese style, a partnership. Saturn has fewer primary suppliers and buys fewer parts from other GM operations. Its suppliers have to work in lockstep with the plant. Some figure out what to ship by reading production schedules for the coming week. A single miscue could foul the assembly process. "This assumes everybody is going to do jobs right the first time," says Joseph A. Chrzanowski, a Saturn finance manager. "If there is a problem, we inflict pain on the source until it gets fixed."

By mid-1991, the early verdict on Saturn was mixed. Production was far below first-year goals; there were many production glitches; and losses were substantial. One company executive quipped that GM would be losing less money if instead of developing Saturn it had given every Saturn buyer a free Chevrolet. However, customers were pleased with their purchases, production levels were increasing, and various cost-cutting efforts were underway. Some observers said it would be five years before conclusions could really be reached about Saturn's success.

1. What are some of the factors that might work for or against success of Project Saturn?
2. Which operations costs (associated with inventories, quality, and maintenance) do you think will be lower in the Saturn facilities than in traditional assembly plants? Which might be higher?
3. Do you think that ventures such as Project Saturn will someday make the assembly line obsolete? Why or why not?

Source: Adapted from *The Wall Street Journal,* 14 May 1984, pp. 1, 41; A. Taylor III, "Back to the Future at Saturn," *Fortune,* 1 August 1988, pp. 63–64, 68, 72; and J. B. White, "GM Struggles to Get Saturn Car on Track After Rough Launch," *The Wall Street Journal,* 24 May 1991, pp. A1, A5.

OBJECTIVES

After studying this chapter, you should be able to:

1 Define information, discuss the field of information management, and describe a management information system and how it can be designed.

2 Explain what a computer is and why it is used.

3 Describe the major pieces of computer hardware.

4 Describe the main types of computer software.

5 Explain personal computers, including their applications and how they can communicate with one another.

6 Discuss computer applications to manufacturing, management, marketing, accounting and finance, and other aspects of business.

7 Explain how computers can be used to improve decision making.

8 Discuss some of the potential problems associated with the use of computers.

CHAPTER 12

Information Management

- *Frito-Lay was concerned that its centralized decision-making structure was damaging its ability to track sales and respond promptly to competitive pressures. In 1989, it introduced a new system . More than 10,000 route salespeople equipped with hand-held calculators now feed detailed sales and inventory information to 200 managers. When Frito-Lay launched its new "Light" line of snack foods in 1990, the system permitted it to track sales and make "mid-course" corrections as needed. When sales lagged in one region, the system quickly pinpointed the problem to one store, determined that the culprit was a generic store-branded competitive product, and developed a successful counter-strategy. The system has saved millions of dollars. Also, because it gives middle managers more information quickly, most decisions formerly reserved for top management can now be made at lower levels.[1]*

- *Staring across the table at an intimate cafe, Humphrey Bogart lifts his glass and utters that line: "Here's looking at you, kid." Marilyn Monroe raises her glass and smiles seductively. But what is Marilyn Monroe doing in "Casablanca?" Actually, this is a scene from "Rendez-vous à Montréal." Bogart and Monroe are computer-generated likenesses. Computers are now capable of such sophisticated graphics that director George Lucas predicts that such technology may soon replace human actors with "fresher faces." Businesses are now using computer-animated humans in a variety of applications. For instance, Deere & Co. is using them to "test-drive" tractors, permitting designers to visualize what the operator would see and what controls could be reached on a tractor that has not yet been built.[2]*

- *Xerox Corp. is reaping the rewards of faster information—savings of almost 20 percent of the manufacturing costs in its copier division. It now exchanges quality-control information with its suppliers via computer terminals, to eliminate the expensive inspection of incoming parts. In turn, the copier maker gives suppliers its master manufacturing schedule so that they can ship parts at precisely the time Xerox needs them in its production line, thus keeping inventories thin.*[3]

These examples suggest just a few of the revolutionary applications of computers in business, but they provide some glimpses of the power of new information technologies. In this chapter, we'll examine information management and the role of the computer in business. First, we will consider the nature of information and information resource management. Then we will discuss computers—including uses, types, and hardware and software—and we'll examine the growing role of microcomputers. Next, we will consider business applications of computers and take a look at computer-assisted decision making. We will close with a discussion of problems with computers.

Time magazine's "Man of the Year" for 1982 was not a man, woman, or child. The contributions of any individual, *Time* concluded, were small in comparison to the contributions of the computer—*Time's* choice for 1982's "greatest influence for good or evil." Events of the subsequent decade have confirmed the wisdom of the choice.

In 1890, 46 percent of the population of the United States was involved in agriculture and 4 percent in information services. By 1979, the percentages had reversed, with 4 percent of the population in agriculture and 46 percent in the information business.[4] It is estimated that 67 percent of the workforce will be engaged in information work by 1995.[5] This is the age of information. It is an age made possible, in part, by the computer.

INFORMATION AND MANAGEMENT

Over a billion pages of computer printout. Hundreds of millions of photocopies, letters, and faxes. These are the *daily* output of U.S. offices. But these figures don't even include managers' phone calls, meetings, or day-to-day observations. Information is the lifeblood of organizations. Flows of information allow organizations to function, coordinate their parts, and respond to new challenges. Clearly, managing information is an important and difficult task.

Information Defined

The dictionary defines **information as** "knowledge communicated or received concerning a particular fact or circumstance." Thus, information is not just facts and figures and charts and maps. Rather, it is *knowledge* that is passed along in order to enlighten or inform. Many, if not most, of the figures, calls, and data that managers receive are not really information. Rather than informing, they overwhelm. Still, the problem is not just one of cutting down on paperwork, phone calls, and the like. Much of the information managers need simply does not reach them, or else it comes too early or too late.

information   knowledge communicated or received concerning a particular fact or circumstance.

How Managers Get Information

Henry Mintzberg, a noted researcher in the field of business management, studied managers as they went about their day-to-day work. What he saw was surprising. Rather than finding long-range planners who blocked out days to analyze important issues, he found managers performing a wide variety of brief, often unrelated tasks. Instead of getting all information from a single all-knowing computer ter-

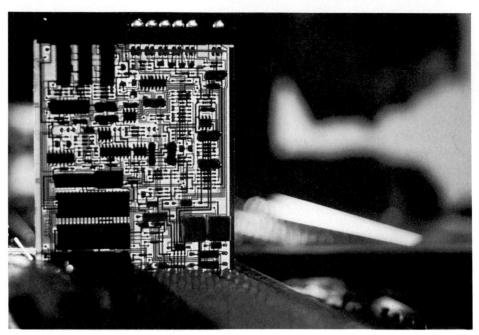

The information that keeps organizations functioning comes from many sources and is transmitted in many ways.

minal, managers used five different media: documents, telephone calls, scheduled meetings, unscheduled meetings, and observational tours. Of these, managers strongly favored telephone calls and meetings. The manager's job emerged as hectic, overloaded, and fragmented. What's more, Mintzberg concluded, things will only get worse.[6]

Information as a Resource

information managers
managers responsible for designing and controlling the systems that gather, process, and distribute information.

Information management is the name given to a field that has developed in recognition of the fact that information is a valuable resource in need of systematic management. **Information managers** design and control the systems that gather, process, and distribute information. Information has all the characteristics of a resource. It is clearly a valuable asset to the firm. It costs money to collect, store, transmit, and display information. Like other resources, information has qualities—it may vary in timeliness, accuracy, and form. Also, the amount of these qualities can be altered. Information handling systems can be designed to deliver information sooner or later, of higher or lower quality, in the form of text, numbers, or images.

Several factors determine the value of information to a decision maker:

- *Accuracy*. Information should be free from error and bias. This may require multiple, independent checks on accuracy.
- *Timeliness*. Information should be available when needed, not a day or a month later. Tardy information can cause costly errors or delays.
- *Relevance*. Information should help answer the specific questions the decision maker is addressing. Information may be accurate and timely yet fail the test of relevancy.
- *Form*. Information should match the form required by the decision maker. Information that uses an unfamiliar format or jargon will often be ignored.
- *Accessibility*. Information should be easily accessible to the decision maker.

Management Information Systems

To organize and exploit information more effectively, many firms are developing management information systems (MIS). As Figure 12-1 shows, a **management information system** is a system for gathering information, transforming it into forms needed for decision making, and distributing it to those who need it. As indicated above, good management information is accurate, timely, relevant, in appropriate form, and easily accessible.

Many firms are now harnessing the power of information management. For instance, at Xerox Corp., corporate leaders use their information systems to send and receive electronic mail, review reports, check financial statements, study customer and market information, and keep up with world news.[7] Information technology also plays a key role in the efforts by Minnesota Mining & Manufacturing Co. (3M) to encourage and capitalize on innovation while cutting costs. With more than 60 different business units, 3M has developed information technology emphasizing decentralization and flexibility. Although most of the business units' key applications programs are developed locally rather than centrally, 3M boasts several companywide information systems that tie critical aspects of the firm together. Financial, human resource management, engineering project management, and other data can be swapped between units located anywhere in the world and then consolidated at headquarters. Such worldwide integration of decentralized efforts results in substantial savings in time and cost.[8]

Design of the MIS. To design an MIS, it is necessary to set objectives, identify constraints, determine information needs and sources, and put the system together. Systems designers should interact with users throughout the design process. The purpose of an MIS is to help managers be more effective decision makers by making sure that:

- They get early warning signals of trouble ahead.
- They get information to assist in decision making.

Management information system (MIS)   a system for gathering information, transforming it into useful forms, and distributing it to decision makers.

FIGURE 12-1   A Management Information System

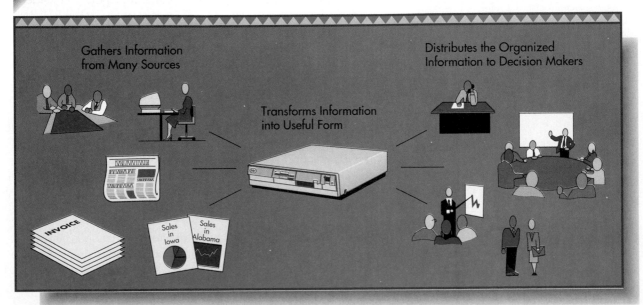

TABLE 12-1 Examples of MIS Objectives

Purpose of an MIS	Typical MIS Objective	Related Company Objective
1. Early Warning Signals	Prevent surprises due to technological breakthroughs affecting the firm's products	Avoid crash development programs or loss of market share
2. Decision-Assisting Information	Supply financial trends and ratios to management	Make good cash and capital investment decisions
3. Programmed Decision Making	Allocate advertising expenditures among selected magazines	Provide economic and broad support for sales force
4. Automation of Routine Clerical Operations	Automate payroll computations	Timely and accurate pay of employees at minimum cost

Source: R. G. Murdick and J. E. Ross, *Introduction to Management Information Systems* (Englewood Cliffs, N.J.: Prentice Hall, 1977), p.147.

- The system automatically makes certain decisions that do not require managerial input.
- Routine clerical operations are automated.

Specific objectives should be set to help accomplish these purposes. Table 12-1 shows how these purposes tie in with MIS objectives and related company objectives.

Constraints on MIS design may be externally or internally imposed. External constraints may include government regulations, customer demands, or supplier needs. Cost, computer capacity, availability of personnel, and policy considerations are four possible internal constraints.

Once MIS goals and constraints have been identified, the next step is to write a clear statement of information needs. These needs depend on the manager. Some managers want a sophisticated, computerized system; others want to "keep things simple." Some say, "Get me all the facts"; others say, "Get me only what I need to know." After needs are determined, the sources of the desired information can be found.

Then the system must be put together. This involves charting the necessary flows of information, such as marketing and sales information and reports, and determining how the information is to be stored, how inputs to the MIS (such as personnel information) will be coded, and which type of equipment (such as computers and terminals) will be needed. Since different systems may be proposed, their relative technical feasibilities, acceptability to the end user, and costs must be considered.

Once the system is in place, everyone who is affected by it should be trained and educated concerning their individual system responsibilities and what the system provides them. Periodic evaluations and reviews of the MIS are important in order to maintain and improve the system.[9]

COMPUTERS IN BUSINESS   **2**

In 1952, a new device called the electronic computer predicted that Dwight Eisenhower would win the presidential election by a landslide. Viewing the prediction with disbelief, the programmers changed the results. But the computer was right—Eisenhower was a landslide winner. The public was awed. Here was a machine that was smarter than humans. The computer had captured the people's imagination. Society and business would never be the same.

Computers are now used in virtually every area of business. Business and government spend an estimated $75 billion a year for computer equipment, materials, and staff. In the future, an inability to deal effectively with computers may be seen as a sort of illiteracy.

What is a Computer?

A **computer** is a machine that can carry out complex and repetitious operations at very high speeds. It receives data and instructions, processes the data into desired information, and provides results in a form that can be read by a person or another machine.

computer *a machine that carries out complex and repetitious operations at very high speeds.*

Why Use Computers?

Computers have at least five advantages over the human decision maker. First, computers are fast: The speed of some modern computers is measured in nanoseconds (billionths of a second)! The fastest computer currently clocks 8.6 gigaflops (billion operations a second), and a 128-gigaflop computer is in the works.[10] Second, they can perform operations that are far too complex for human minds. Travel into space would probably have been impossible without them. Third, computers have a vast memory capacity. Even the computers now being bought for home use are able to store many millions of pieces of information. Fourth, computers are unemotional when performing mathematical calculations or analyzing decision alternatives. Computers will not put off making a decision and will not distort facts to build a case. Finally, computers do not get bored. They find the same challenge in adding two numbers as in guiding an exotic robot.

These strengths of computers suggest the kinds of tasks for which they are most useful: tasks demanding fast completion; very complex jobs, with many tricky computations; repetitive, boring tasks. However, as we'll see, a computer is really a very fast, efficient simpleton. It can only follow orders given in the simplest possible language. However, with the advent of artificial intelligence (discussed later in the chapter), this is changing. Computers are even starting to have some creative capabilities.

A Short History of Computers

Computers as we know them may be fairly recent developments, but they do have an interesting family tree. The earliest "computer" was a counting device called the abacus. The abacus was developed as early as 1000 B.C. by the Greeks and Chinese and is still used by Chinese merchants. It is made up of a series of beads strung in a frame on parallel vertical bars.

A variety of devices developed over the past 350 years provided the groundwork for the modern computer. For instance, around 1641, Blaise Pascal, a young French scientist and philosopher, developed a simple adding machine to help carry out computations for his father's tax office. The machine had a series of wheels, each with teeth representing the digits 0 through 9. When a wheel rotated past 9, the next wheel automatically rotated. When it in turn reached 9, the next rotated, and so on. This simple "tens carrying" feature made the machine very popular.

Fifty years later, Gottfried Leibnitz, a German mathematician and philosopher, improved on Pascal's adder. The Leibnitz calculating machine could perform multiplication and division as well as addition.

Joseph-Marie Jacquard, a French inventor, developed the Jacquard loom in 1801. The Jacquard loom used punched cards to control the patterns that were woven into cloth. Instructions for a particular pattern could be stored on a set of punched cards, saving weeks of set-up time. If a hole appeared on the card inserted in the loom, the loom was instructed to lift a thread. If there was no hole, the thread would be depressed. This one-zero or yes-no system is the basis for the modern computer.

Charles Babbage, a 19-century English mathematics professor, is sometimes called the father of early computers. He developed two devices that provided many of the ideas for modern computers. The first, the difference machine, was designed around 1822 to produce mathematical tables that previously had taken expert mathematicians years to compute. Although it could serve only this single purpose, Babbage saw the possibility of a general-purpose calculating machine. That machine, the analytical engine, was developed in the 1880s and was like modern computers in many ways. It had a memory, an arithmetic device, punched card input, automatic printing of results, and a programmed set of instructions.

Herman Hollerith, a statistician at the U.S. Census Bureau, invented the first practical punched card tabulating machine for the taking of the 1890 U.S. census. Data were stored on cards by punching holes in them. Because of the tabulating machine, the 1890 census took only two and one-half years, less than a third of the time previously needed. The tabulating machine company that Hollerith founded in 1886 later merged with others to become what is now the International Business Machines Corporation (IBM).

The Mark I computer, completed at Harvard University in 1944, was remarkably similar to Babbage's analytical engine. It could perform a lengthy series of arithmetic and logical operations without any human intervention after start-up. However, since many of its parts were mechanical, it was not nearly as fast as was desired.

Modern Computers

Modern computers are electronic. That is, they rely entirely on electronic pulses to function. Early electronic computers used vacuum tubes. Because the tubes were bulky and generated quite a bit of heat, the computers were often huge and had to be kept in air-conditioned rooms.

The first big electronic computer, ENIAC (Electronic Numerical Integrator and Calculator) was built in 1946. It took up 1,500 square feet of floor space, weighed 30 tons, contained 18,000 vacuum tubes, ate 140,000 watts of electricity, and cost a fortune. It was quickly made obsolete by the development of the transistor. Transistors allowed computers to be smaller, more reliable, and easier to maintain and repair. Computers also became faster, had greater memory capacity, and could use a variety of languages.

microprocessors tiny wafer-shaped chips that can hold millions of pieces of information.

Most computers now use integrated circuits, called microprocessors, instead of transistors. **Microprocessors** are tiny wafer-shaped chips that can hold tremendous amounts of information. A single chip of this type is more powerful than its ancestor, ENIAC. Unimaginable a few decades ago, these chips are now a part of our lives; such everyday products as digital watches, pocket calculators, and video games could not have been built without them. These products are not only getting more sophisticated, they're getting cheaper too. Pocket calculators that sold for $400 in 1970 now retail (in fancier versions) for about $10. It has been estimated that if automobile technology had improved as fast as computer technology, a Rolls-Royce today would cost less than $5, and it would travel several thousand miles on a gallon of gas.

Computers come in various sizes and capabilities, including very powerful and expensive mainframes and supercomputers. However, microprocessors have made it possible to develop the intermediate-sized, less expensive, yet powerful **minicomputers** and even the typewriter-sized microcomputers that are finding extensive use in businesses and homes. **Microcomputers,** often called **personal computers** or PCs, are the smallest, slowest, and least expensive computers on the market today. Complete microcomputer systems capable of performing statistical analyses, text editing, and many other business-related chores are now available for under $1,500. Computers are getting even smaller; "Laptop" and even "notepad" computers are now available.

minicomputer an intermediate-sized computer whose speed, capacity, and cost fall between those of the mainframe and the microcomputer.

microcomputer the smallest, slowest, and least expensive computer; often called a personal computer.

personal computers (PCs) microcomputers.

COMPUTER HARDWARE

The computer and its support equipment are called **hardware.** This is the collection of metal, plastic, nuts, and bolts that we see when we look at a computer. As shown in Figure 12-2, the hardware includes input units, a central processing unit, and output units. As a group, input and output units are referred to as **peripheral equipment.**

hardware the computer and its support equipment.

peripheral equipment the input and output units of a computer.

FIGURE 12-2   Typical Computer Hadware Components

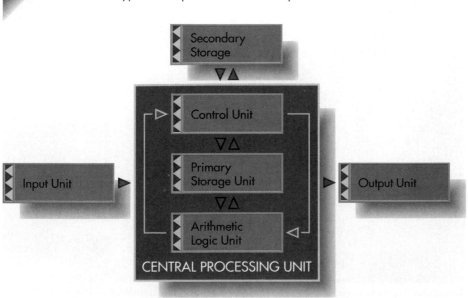

Secondary Storage

Control Unit

Primary Storage Unit

Arithmetic Logic Unit

CENTRAL PROCESSING UNIT

Input Unit

Output Unit

Input Units

input unit *the means through which data and programs enter a computer system.*

storage media *the "machine readable" form on which data and programs are stored for computer processing at a later time.*

batch processing *a type of data processing in which data are collected for some period of time and then processed all at the same time.*

visual display terminal *computer hardware that includes a keyboard to input data and instructions and a television-like screen for displaying output.*

on-line processing *instant input and output processing as a result of a direct hook-up of all input and output units to the main computer.*

time-sharing *in data processing, the hook-up of many different terminals to the same main computer.*

Data and programs are entered into a computer system through **input units.** Before this happens, however, the data and programs are put in "machine-readable" form on magnetic tape, diskettes, cassettes, cartridges, digital audio tape, or other **storage media.** Disk drives, magnetic tape drives, and keyboards are examples of input units. Other input devices are graphic tablets, consisting of a pad and a special pen for producing illustrations, and voice activators, which enable computers to understand spoken words. Generally, data are collected for some period of time, such as an hour or a day, and then processed all at the same time. This is called **batch processing.**

Nearly everyone has seen **visual display terminals (VDTs)** in offices, airports, or banks. A VDT includes a keyboard for inputting data and instructions and a television-like screen for displaying output. Two common types of screens are the cathode ray tube (CRT) and the liquid crystal display (LCD). As data and instructions are entered on the typewriter-like keyboard, they appear on the screen. After the computer processes the data, the resulting output appears on the screen.

Visual display terminals allow for **on-line processing**—all input and output units are hooked directly to the processing unit for instant input and output. Such terminals also permit **time-sharing,** in which many different terminals are hooked to the same main computer, so that many people can use the computer at the same time. Because the main computer processes data so quickly, each user gets very rapid response.

HAL, the computer in "2001: A Space Odyssey" and "2010: Odyssey Two," communicated with two humans by speaking and listening. Some computers now have this voice input capability. One computer has been developed that can even tell the difference between a Texas drawl and an English accent. United Parcel Service has a sorting computer that interprets spoken destination codes

Computer hardware and software have revolutionized the handling of information in the business world.

and then directs a mechanical arm to move packages accordingly. In an IBM advertisement, a computer is able to do a correct translation of the spoken sentence, "Write a letter right now to Mrs. Wright."

Processing Unit

The **central processing unit (CPU)** is the "brain" of the computer. It does the "thinking" and "memorizing"—that is, the CPU processes and stores information. The CPU has three main parts: the arithmetic/logic unit, the control unit, and the primary storage unit. The **arithmetic/logic unit** performs the mathematical operations (such as adding and subtracting) and logical operations (such as comparison) on the data. The **control unit** directs what happens within the computer. For instance, it indicates where data should be stored. The **primary storage unit** is the computer's main information storage area, or **memory.** It stores data and program instructions.

central processing unit (CPU)   the part of the computer that processes and stores information.

arithmetic/logic unit   the part of the CPU that performs the mathematical and logical operations on the data.

control unit   the part of the CPU that directs the internal operations of the computer.

primary storage unit   the computer's main memory, where data and program instructions are stored.

Output Units

Output units present the results of computer operations to the user. Sometimes, results are presented in a form that can be read by the user, such as on a computer printout. In addition, plotters may create drawings, diagrams, or graphs, or audio devices may produce spoken words through a telephone or loudspeaker. In other cases, results are put in a form that is easy to store or to use for further operations.

memory   the part of the computer that stores all information.

output units   units that present the results of computer operations to the user.

Secondary Storage

Secondary storage is extra memory outside the primary storage unit of the central processing unit. Magnetic tapes and disks are examples of secondary storage devices.

A relatively new storage device is the CD-ROM (for compact disk, read-only memory), which is read by a laser beam. A single CD-ROM has the capacity to store an entire set of encyclopedias or 500 typical books. Data requiring 4,222 yards of shelf space in print requires only 1.3 yards in the CD-ROM format. The entire 18,000-page Boeing 757 parts catalog is now on a single CD-ROM. Once it is on a CD-ROM, information can be quickly searched and cross-referenced.[11]

secondary storage   extra memory outside the primary storage unit of the central processing unit.

COMPUTER SOFTWARE

Computer **software,** or **programs,** are step-by-step instructions that tell the computer what to do. Software must be prepared before the computer is used. Without it, hardware is useless.

There are two general types of software: system software and application software.[12] **System software** is a set of programs that manages the resources of the computer, such as processing time and storage space, so that they are used efficiently. This set of programs provides routine services, such as copying data from one file to another, and helps with the development of application programs. The computer's operating system, which controls the execution of programs and provides services such as data management, scheduling, and input/output control, is a form of system software. DOS, for *D*isk *O*perating *S*ystem, is the operating system used by IBM computers and IBM clones.

Application software performs specific tasks for the computer user. There are many types. For instance, word processing software, such as XYWRITE III

software or programs   step-by-step instructions that tell the computer what to do.

system software   set of programs that manages the resources of the computer, such as processing time and storage space, so that they are used efficiently.

application software   programs that perform specific tasks for the computer user, such as balancing a budget or computing statistics.

PLUS, which was used in writing this book, permits the user to enter, edit, and print text material. Spreadsheet software, such as LOTUS 1-2-3, lets the user manipulate columns of figures to prepare budgets, tax analyses, and sales and profit projections and to deal with other financial problems. File management software, such as PFS:File, replaces the file drawer. Users can construct forms on the screen similar to the paper forms they had been filing, enter data on the screen version, and then store it on a device such as a diskette. They can also search and sort data and prepare reports. Statistical software, such as SPSS-PC, permits various statistical analyses of data and often displays the results in graphic form, such as pie, bar, or line charts. Application software is also available for project management, desktop publishing, preparing reports drawn from data in multiple files, and many other purposes.[13]

Flowcharts

program flowchart a diagram showing the sequence of operations to be performed by the computer.

Software development often begins with flowcharting. A **program flowchart** is a diagram showing the sequence of operations to be performed by the computer. Suppose we would like to write a program instructing the computer to figure a weekly paycheck. We might first draw a flowchart such as the one shown in Figure 12-3. Then we would use the flowchart as the basis for writing a computer program.

Computer Languages

Computer programs are written or "coded" in a language that the computer can understand. Computers can read any of several languages. Some can even understand English. Below are some common computer languages used in programming.

binary system a system that is composed of two digits, 0 and 1; machine language is based on this system.

bits the two digits that compose the binary system.

bytes strings of eight bits, which are used to represent characters on the computer keyboard.

procedure-oriented language a language in which the programmer gives instructions to the computer that are in turn translated into machine language by a compiler.

compiler a component inside the computer that translates symbolic language into machine language.

BASIC a computer language that is easy to learn; used frequently by small computers.

COBOL a computer language that processes data in a language something like English.

Machine Language. Machine language, popular among programmers in the early days of computers and still used by some, is based on the **binary system**—that is, on only two digits, 0 and 1. These digits (called **bits** from *bi*nary dig*its*) are combined into strings (called **bytes**). Bytes, in turn, are used to represent characters on the keyboard. Computers operate by turning on and off many electrical circuits. The digit 1 tells the computer to switch a circuit on. The digit 0 tells the computer to switch a circuit off. A different combination of 1's and 0's represents each character on the keyboard.

Since machine language is hard to learn and use, other "higher level" languages have been developed. A **procedure-oriented language** is a language in which the programmer gives instructions to the computer. Inside the computer, a language translator, called a **compiler,** translates procedure-oriented language into machine language so that it can be understood by the computer. Let's take a look at some of the more popular procedural languages.

BASIC. As its name suggests, the **BASIC** language (short for *B*eginners *A*ll-purpose *S*ymbolic *I*nstruction *C*ode) is easy to learn. BASIC is the language most often used by small computers. Figure 12-4 shows what BASIC looks like. It is based on the flowchart shown in Figure 12-3.

COBOL. **COBOL** (*C*ommon *B*usiness-*O*riented *L*anguage) was developed so that data could be processed in a language something like English. Despite being rather difficult to learn, COBOL is widely used in business. This chapter's profile of Grace Murray Hopper (p. 314) describes her leading role in developing the COBOL language.

FIGURE 12-3   A Flowchart for Computing Weekly Pay

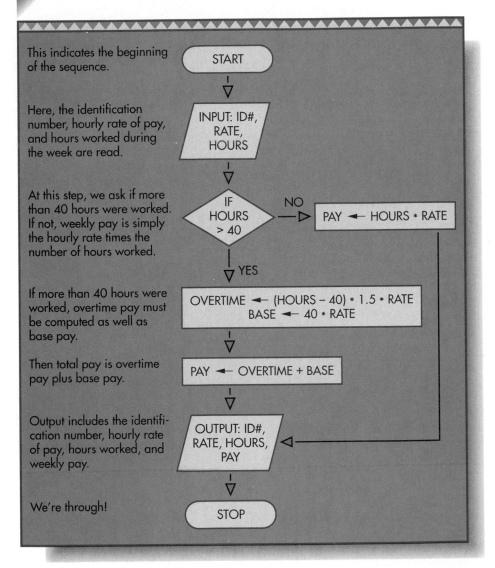

This indicates the beginning of the sequence.

Here, the identification number, hourly rate of pay, and hours worked during the week are read.

At this step, we ask if more than 40 hours were worked. If not, weekly pay is simply the hourly rate times the number of hours worked.

If more than 40 hours were worked, overtime pay must be computed as well as base pay.

Then total pay is overtime pay plus base pay.

Output includes the identification number, hourly rate of pay, hours worked, and weekly pay.

We're through!

START

INPUT: ID#, RATE, HOURS

IF HOURS > 40 — NO → PAY ← HOURS * RATE

YES

OVERTIME ← (HOURS – 40) * 1.5 * RATE
BASE ← 40 * RATE

PAY ← OVERTIME + BASE

OUTPUT: ID#, RATE, HOURS, PAY

STOP

FORTRAN. **FORTRAN** (*FOR*mula *TRAN*slator) was developed by IBM in the 1950s and is still widely used for mathematical and statistical applications. Although similar to BASIC, and somewhat more flexible, it is harder to use.

C. C, a new challenger to COBOL and FORTRAN, is often called a "programmer's language." One reason for C's growing popularity is its portability. That is, software developers using C can write programs to run on one computer and then adapt them for other types of computers with relative ease.[14]

Canned Programs. Fortunately, using a computer hardly ever means starting from scratch and writing a program in BASIC, COBOL, FORTRAN, or C. Many **canned** (or **packaged**) **programs** are available. These programs may perform statistical analyses, find optimal solutions to a problem, provide a convenient

FORTRAN *a computer language used for mathematical and statistical applications.*

C *a popular computer language, noted for its portability between different computer systems.*

canned (packaged) programs *computer programs that are already written and available for purchase.*

FIGURE 12-4 A Basic BASIC Program to Compute Weekly Pay

These statement numbers tell the computer the order in which the statements are to be executed.

This statement serves as a reminder of the purpose of the program.	10 REM PROGRAM TO COMPUTE WEEKLY PAY
Identification number, hourly rate of pay, and hours worked are read.	20 READ ID, R, H
This IF-THEN statement allows branching. If hours worked are greater than 40, it branches to statement 60. If not, it moves on to the next statement.	30 IF H > 40.0 THEN 60
If no more than 40 hours were worked, this statement computes pay.	40 P = H * R
This statement tells the program to go to statement 90. (Otherwise, pay would be computed again).	50 GO TO 90
Here, overtime pay is computed. (Notice that we get here only if more than 40 hours were worked).	60 OV = (H − 40) * 1.5 * R
Base pay for 40 hours is figured here.	70 B = 40 * R
Total pay is overtime pay plus base pay.	80 P = OV + B
This statement prints out the identification number, hourly rate of pay, hours worked, and pay.	90 PRINT ID, R, H, P
The end. That wasn't too bad, was it?	100 END

form for keeping track of records, or help perform any of hundreds of other tasks. The various application software packages noted above are examples. Often, canned programs are reasonably priced and have been thoroughly "debugged" to make sure they contain no errors.

Documentation

The term **documentation** refers to the process of providing a permanent record of a computer program. Generally, documentation indicates why the program was written and includes the program flowchart, the program, sample input and output, and comments. Good documentation makes it easier to find flaws in programs. It also helps new users understand the program.

documentation   *the process of providing a permanent record of a computer program.*

MICROCOMPUTERS

Microcomputers, or personal computers or PCs, are usually typewriter-sized computers. They have made remarkably fast inroads into the business world. Like larger computers, a PC contains an operating system that controls or defines the computer's basic operations and functions. Often, a hand-held pointing device called a mouse is used to move a cursor around the computer's screen and select different functions from a menu. In 1990, 23.3 million personal computers were sold worldwide. It is estimated that PCs will become a $50 billion market in the U.S. by 1995, with a continued growth rate of 8 to 12 percent.[15]

The most common business applications of personal computers are for accounting, financial analysis, and word processing. How much PCs are used, and how they are used, varies by level in the organization. Executives use them mainly for accessing electronic mail and other information. At other levels, PCs are used more for planning and analysis and for writing.

Microcomputer Communications

Although microcomputers are marvels of technology, their applications and potential are even greater when they are linked with other computers in an information network.

Modems. A **modem** (short for *mo*dulator-*dem*odulator) is a device for connecting microcomputers via telephone lines. Using a modem, a microcomputer user in one city can transmit letters, financial data, or other information to a user in another city. The microcomputer user can also "call" a mainframe computer, carry out computations on the mainframe, and display the output on the microcomputer screen.

modem   *a device for connecting microcomputers via telephone lines.*

The powerful combination of a microcomputer and a modem also allows access to electronic bulletin boards. **Electronic bulletin boards** are message and information services that provide microcomputer users with a wide array of information.[16] Electronic bulletin boards display financial information, job opportunities, newspapers and magazines and encyclopedias, airline schedules and prices, status of pending legislation, weather data, and almost anything else imaginable, for about 2 million users each day in the United States. The most popular on-line information service, Prodigy, permits its members (more than a million of them) to select from a screen with a lengthy list of topics, much like a newspaper. The screen changes at least once a day. Some services also provide bulletin boards devoted to member messages about the latest software, programs they have written, and so on. Users can read messages from the board or add messages to it. Some also offer "chat" sessions, like telephone conference calls, where members type in their conversations.[17] They may allow users to book airline reservations and purchase stocks, bonds, and mutual funds.

electronic bulletin boards   *message and information services that microcomputer users can access through a modem.*

Grace Murray Hopper

Born in 1906, Grace Murray Hopper continued to enrich the field of computer science until her death in 1992.

Hopper graduated from Vassar College and then received M.A. and Ph.D. degrees from Yale. After teaching at Vassar and at Barnard College, she enlisted in the United States Naval Reserve in 1943. Her husband was killed in the war. By then, Hopper was heavily involved with computers and committed to the Navy, and she charged ahead with her remarkable career. She was commissioned a lieutenant and assigned to the Bureau of Ordnance Computation Project at Harvard University. There, she helped tame the Mark I computer, learning to program the unwieldy device dubbed "the monster," as well as its successors. Hopper subsequently worked on the UNIVAC I, the first large-scale commercial electronic computer.

Early in her career, Hopper contributed to the terminology of computing. When a computer failed one day in 1945, Hopper found the cause: a dead moth in one of the computer's parts, which she removed with tweezers. After that, when Hopper was asked if she was accomplishing anything, she said that she was "debugging" the computer. Now, the term "bug" refers to a computer problem, and "debugging" means getting rid of that problem.

Hopper firmly believed that programming languages should be more like everyday language, so that many people could use computers. To help achieve that goal, she published the first paper on compilers, in 1952. She went on to publish more than 50 articles on computer software and languages. Hopper also led the team that developed the first completed compiler. Called the A-0, it was developed for use on the early UNIVAC computers. Subsequently, Hopper directed the work that eventually led to the COBOL language. She remained a prime mover in the refinement of COBOL throughout her life.

Hopper received many awards and honorary degrees. For instance, in 1969, the Data Processing Management Association selected her as as its first Computer Sciences Man of the Year. In 1971, in recognition of her contributions, the Grace Murray Hopper award for young computer professionals was initiated.

In addition to her many technical and managerial contributions, Hopper was a strong and convincing voice for progress in computing. She played a major role in presenting the case for compilers and English-like languages and was an advocate of standardization of computer languages. A popular speaker, she was active on the lecture circuit and was once featured on the television program "60 Minutes."

Hopper retired from the Navy in 1986 with the rank of Rear Admiral but continued to look toward the future of computer science. She argued that computers have only begun to realize their potential for such uses as predicting weather patterns, managing energy resources, and increasing agricultural output. Hopper always encouraged the involvement of young people in computing; she said that her greatest contribution was all the youth she had trained. In her final years, she also actively encouraged the increased involvement of women in new computer technologies such as artificial intelligence.

314

Networking. New developments in technology are now linking computers to large-scale computational and information-sharing networks. **Networking** ties computers together and enables them to communicate with each other, share resources, and access tremendous amounts of information. Local area networks (LANs) allow users who are near each other (in the same room or building) to share expensive resources such as data storage, computing power, and printers. Wide area networks (WANs) connect LANs to distant offices or other locations. As an example of networking, The Travelers Corp., a large insurance company, spent $10 million to lay 2 million feet of cable in its Manhattan headquarters building in order to link computers for 8,000 employees. A senior vice president at Travelers predicts that some day 400,000 machines, including 30,000 home computers, will be linked to 60 data and claims centers and 300 field offices, allowing one-stop shopping at the computer screen for auto, health, and life insurance.[18]

networking the linking to-gether of computers to enable users to communicate with each other, share resources, and access tremendous amounts of information.

BUSINESS APPLICATIONS OF THE COMPUTER

Computers are being used today in virtually every area of business. Here, we'll survey some notable examples in manufacturing, management, marketing, accounting and finance, banking and credit, word processing, and data processing.

Manufacturing

Computers now design products, run production lines, check product quality, control machine loads, and automatically guide machines. As discussed in Chapter 11, computers are essential to material requirements planning and to the factory of the future. Here, we will consider computer-aided design and computer-aided manufacturing.

Computer-Aided Design. To produce many of the special effects in the movie "The Abyss," the dimensions of real objects were fed into a computer. The computer then displayed on a screen an image of each object from any distance and from any perspective. These processes are what computer-aided design is all about. **Computer-aided design (CAD)** is the use of computer graphics programs to design new products or processes. CAD is a popular tool with automakers and architectural firms. It speeds up design projects by reducing drafting time. CAD has also been used in the fast-paced sportswear industry, where product lines may change as often as five times a year.[19]

computer-aided design (CAD) the use of computer graphics programs to design new products or processes.

Computer-Aided Manufacturing. **Computer-aided manufacturing (CAM)** is the use of computer programs to control production machinery. Many businesses use computers to run manufacturing processes. Lathes, looms, and riveting machines are often run by computers. Computers have been used extensively in chemical production, oil refining, and other industries that involve large-volume processing. Computers also apply a layer of dye only a few 10,000ths of an inch thick on Polaroid film.

computer-aided manufacturing (CAM) the use of computer programs to control production machinery.

Coupled with computer-aided design, CAM enables engineers to design mechanical parts rapidly, analyze them to close tolerance, and generate machining instructions directly. This avoids time-consuming and expensive manual work on the shop floor. Therefore, companies can markedly reduce the cost and time of developing new products.

To enter "virtual reality," this man has put on a special pair of goggles that allow him to interact with a computer-generated environment as if he were actually part of it. Today, virtual reality is commonly regarded as an expensive toy. In the future, however, it may be used for such business purposes as teleconferencing, improved computer-aided design, training simulations (as discussed in Chapter 9), and product testing.

Computer-aided manufacturing is revolutionizing the textile industry. Robots lift and unpack cotton bales. Computers direct the tugs and conveyor belts feeding mill assembly lines. Electronic eyes spot and cut out defects in weaving yarn. Such innovations allow the industry to compete with imports. They also free employees from the more boring, repetitive jobs to do more creative tasks.

Management

Computers are being used in a wide variety of ways in management. Some applications reduce costs and increase efficiency; others are more novel. Here are some examples.

Training. As discussed in Chapter 9, computers can help train employees more rapidly, economically, and enjoyably than other job training approaches. Computers train mechanics at Ford dealerships, teach inventory control techniques at J.C. Penney, and train IBM repair people.[20] Chase Manhattan Bank NA used computer-based training (CBT) to train 500 data center managers at 60 locations worldwide. The entire course, titled "The 39 Elements of Data Center Management," fit on one disk and was shipped to Chase Manhattan data centers around the world.[21]

Directing. When Victor Sloan, president of Victor Aviation Services, needed advice on how to motivate an employee, he asked his personal computer. He thought the employee was shy and needed encouragement, but the program said otherwise. "It told me to let him work alone. So I did, and his performance went up 30 percent," says Sloan.[22] Computer programs now advise managers on interpersonal relations, conflict management, leadership, group processes, and personality assessment.

Communications. Computers and other information technologies have revolutionized organizational communications. For instance, **electronic mail**—software that enables users to send and receive written messages through their computers—is a fast, inexpensive, and efficient means of communication. An electronic mail system at the Metropolitan Life Insurance Co. streamlined message and reporting capabilities and saved the company more than $100,000 annually.[23]

electronic mail   software that enables users to send and receive written messages through their computers.

As another example, **teleconferencing**—two-way audio and video communication among distant locations—offers tremendous savings in time, energy, and money. Many firms conduct sales meetings, editorial conferences, and job interviews via teleconference. ARCO developed a $20 million teleconferencing network that links eight regional centers by satellite. A manager in the New York teleconferencing room can walk down the hall to meet with a life-sized image of a colleague sitting in an identical room 3,000 miles away. ARCO has cut travel costs by 20 percent with the new technology—an annual savings of $10 million.[24]

teleconferencing   two-way audio and video communications among distant locations.

Career Planning. As we will see in later chapters, many firms are now actively managing their employees' careers. Computers can play a big role in this process. Personnel specialists use computers to plan successions, to regulate affirmative action programs, and to track junior managers on their way up. Personnel experts claim that computers increase objectivity, allow a larger number of candidates to be considered for positions, and reduce the need for hiring people from outside the firm. For instance, Southland Corp., owner of the 7-Eleven convenience store chain, has computerized its search for "fast-trackers." Twice a year, Southland managers file reports on the promotability of their subordinates. The computer consolidates the reports and evaluates whether enough bright young people are coming up through the ranks. Another program produces career-development plans for employees, notes career weaknesses, and, when applicable, suggests such solutions as university courses, in-house training, and special assignments.[25]

Job Design. Computers have brought about fundamental changes in the design of jobs and organizations. For instance, supervisors once walked around the plant and checked on employees' performance, but they can now stay in one place and perform the same task over a computer screen. With the arrival of modems and microcomputers, the electronic cottage has become a reality. By **electronic cottage** we mean the home linked via telecommunications and computer technologies to large centralized databases and production centers. With the home turned into an electronic cottage, a person can perform tasks on a computer at home instead of traveling to the office to perform the same work on a computer there. The work is transmitted via phone line to the office, where it may be evaluated and integrated with other work. Workers in these situations are typically paid at a piece rate (that is, according to how much they produce). Stay-at-home computer work provides opportunities for those who are unable or unwilling to work away from home.

electronic cottage   a home that is linked via telecommunications and computer technologies to large centralized databases and production centers.

Marketing

Computers have been applied to many routine marketing activities, such as processing customer orders and compiling and reporting sales data. Recently, some more refined applications have been developed.

bar coding *patterns of bars and spaces printed on products or other materials to represent information; the bars and spaces are read by computers equipped with special scanning devices.*

Bar Coding. With **bar coding,** patterns of wide and narrow bars and spaces are printed on products. These patterns represent information, such as product identification and price, which can be read by computers equipped with special scanning devices. Scanning bar codes instead of manually keying in the information speeds checkouts and reduces human error. Bar codes also permit automatic tracking of what was sold, when and where, and perhaps to whom. First used in the late 1960s, bar coding is now employed in thousands of stores. The National Grocers Association estimates that chains using the systems have had as much as 50 percent increases in operating profits. In view of such figures, it isn't surprising that bar coding is finding other uses. It is being used to track inventory on an aircraft carrier and blood in blood banks, monitor the flow of products during manufacturing, sort airline baggage, and identify people in cafeterias, libraries, and even marathons.[26] Bar codes will be discussed further in Chapter 14.

Sales Analysis. With a computer, sales data can be readily analyzed in terms of product line, territory, customer, and salesperson. Salespeople for Hoffmann-La Roche, Inc., a pharmaceutical firm, take terminals with them on sales calls, to help answer doctors' questions.

Sales Forecasting. Because computers are able to process data quickly and to detect and analyze relationships among variables, they are well-suited to sales forecasting. Past relationships among variables can first be evaluated and then extended into the future. Detailed, individualized forecasts, often for many products and different sales regions, can be generated instantly.

Point-Of-Sale Advertising. Computers are being used to revolutionize the shopping experience. For instance, the Videocart is a normal shopping cart with a small computer screen mounted to the front rail. Activated by infrared "triggers" placed around the store, the Videocart screen flashes ads as the customer approaches certain products. The Videocarts also give shoppers access to information, using a simple keyboard, relating to recipes and nutritional information as well as a detailed index of the store. When the cart reaches the checkout line, local news and weather reports are automatically triggered. Plans are in the works to provide "electronic coupons" and automatic check-cashing devices as part of the Videocart. In one supermarket chain, sales of Videocart-promoted items were 5 percent to 60 percent above normal levels. Procter & Gamble, Pepsi, Nabisco, and other firms are placing the computerized ads.[27]

Accounting and Finance

In most companies, the accounting department was the first one to adopt computer technology. Accountants found the computer ideal for storing and processing the vast amounts of data for which they were responsible. Payroll preparation, accounts payable processing, and customer billing are examples. Three other applications relate to financial simulation, securities trading, and financial planning.

Financial Simulation. It is often helpful to determine what a company's financial situation would be like if certain events were to occur—for example, a jump in sales or an increase in the price of raw materials. In a financial simulation, a mathematical model of the firm's financial flows is developed. The model typically includes such factors as costs, revenues, income, and cash flows. Once the model is completed, the numerical values of any of these factors can be changed to see their impact on the values of the other factors. For instance, the impact of a 2 percent sales increase on profits could be assessed.

Securities Trading. Another financial application is in the area of securities trading. Stock price quotations, news items, and data on mergers are all transmitted by computerized equipment. Computerized trading systems are already having a far-reaching impact on securities markets. Launched in 1984, the International Futures Exchange, or Intex, is a Bermuda-based computerized market that lets participants enter orders from their homes or offices anywhere in the world. A dealer enters an order into a trading terminal. The order is received in Bermuda, and the dealer receives an acknowledgment. Execution of the order occurs when the computer system matches buy and sell orders at the same price. The entire trading sequence takes $3\frac{1}{2}$ seconds![28]

Financial Planning. Financial planning software is now available to balance checkbooks, draft budgets, track investments, and otherwise assist with personal finances. Some of these programs have features that link PCs via modems to electronic checking services. These services automatically transfer bill-payment information to the Federal Reserve System's automated clearinghouse, an electronic service linked to all U.S. consumer banks. No stamps or envelopes are needed.[29]

Banking and Credit

Banks were among the first businesses to reap the benefits of computers. Many banks computerized their accounting and bookkeeping operations in the early 1960s. Once that was done, many other applications became possible.

On-Site Computers. A wide range of bank processes have been computerized. The processing of checks and handling of time deposits, installment loans, and real estate loans are all examples. Also, many banks make their computers available to small businesses.

Electronic Funds Transfer. Various computer applications are changing the way people conduct financial transactions. Grouped under the name "electronic funds transfer," these applications are detailed in Chapter 19. They include the automated teller machines that give out cash, take deposits, and report account balances for bank depositors and the point-of-sale terminals used in retail stores to verify checks. In addition, dozens of automated clearinghouses around the country handle such large-volume transactions as payrolls, transferring funds without the use of checks.

Word Processing

Microcomputers are rapidly replacing typewriters in businesses for preparing written documents. With word processing software, a person can input, output, and store written information in one easy operation. Corrections can be made easily and words or sections inserted, deleted, or shifted around. Word processing programs are often complemented by grammar checkers and spelling checkers. These programs analyze written material and provide specific suggestions for improvement. As an example of how such programs can be especially valuable to companies, consider a program called Corporate Voice. Some companies have established writing styles for their documentation. Once existing documents used by the company are read by Corporate Voice, it analyzes sentence structure and builds a style model from the samples. Later, any text can be compared with this model, and changes required to tailor the text to the model are suggested.[30]

Data Processing

data processing *manipulating data into some usable form.*

Another important application of computers is data processing. **Data processing** is manipulating information into some usable form. The information could be of many types: names of customers, prices of products, economic indicators, or units in inventory. Let's consider some of the operations that may be performed on data.

Computation. The term "computation" refers to the adding, subtracting, multiplying, or dividing of numbers. For instance, to calculate gross profit for each of a company's 200 products, the computer subtracts selling costs for each product from its total sales revenue. This type of repetitious task can be done efficiently and accurately by a computer.

Classifying. Many times, it is useful to classify ideas, objects, or people into groups. For example, we might want to group employees by their job classifications, such as sales clerk, district manager, or personnel manager. This process, called classifying, is an ideal application for computers.

Sorting. Sometimes, sales orders, inventory items, or the like may need to be put in a sequence. Sorting is arranging a list into a desired order. For instance, we might want to sort the numbers 3, 8, 6, 2, 1 into the ascending order 1, 2, 3, 6, 8, or we might want a customer list arranged alphabetically. Arranging invoices according to their due dates is another task for which computers are ideal.

Merging. Merging, or collating, refers to the combining of two or more sorted files into a single file in the same sequence. Table 12-2 shows two sorted files and the file into which they were merged.

TABLE 12-2   Merging of Files

Territory A Customer Numbers	Territory B Customer Numbers	Merged Customer Numbers
116	86	86
188	112	112
245	181	116
312	356	181
		188
		245
		312
		356

Moving and Editing. The modifying of data into a more useful form is called moving and editing. For instance, data may be moved from disk storage to an output device, or the figure 001765 in storage may be edited to $17.65 when it is displayed.

COMPUTER ASSISTED DECISION MAKING   ◆7

Computers can improve decision making in many ways. Various applications of computers to specific types of decisions have already been discussed. Here, we will consider two important, innovative, and more general applications of computers for decision making: decision support systems and expert systems.

Decision Support Systems

The term **decision support system (DSS)** refers to a class of systems that help managers make decisions. A type of MIS application, decision support systems allow managers to ask a series of "what if" questions about business problems. With a decision support system, a manager and computer essentially engage in a dialogue. The manager asks the computer a series of questions, to which the computer responds. The computer does not make a decision, but it provides information about different situations and alternative courses of action, which the manager can use for decision making. Thus, decision support systems support, rather than replace, the manager as a decision maker.

decision support system (DSS) a class of systems that help managers consider alternatives in making decisions.

There have been many impressive examples of savings and other benefits derived from decision support systems. For instance, the Delco Electronics Division of General Motors has plants in Wisconsin and Mexico. The plants ship finished goods such as radios and speakers to an Indiana facility. There, they are consolidated and shipped to 30 GM assembly plants across the country. Delco could ship directly from the Delco plants to the GM assembly facilities, saving some inventory costs. But this would increase shipping costs, since loads would be less than full and schedules would be irregular. Delco developed a decision support system called TRANSPART to examine the trade-off between its inventory costs and shipping costs. Shipment sizes, shipment frequencies, shipping routes, and other variables were included in the model. TRANSPART was used to examine the total costs of various shipping strategies, resulting in annual savings of $2.9 million. It has now been applied at more than 40 GM facilities, with documented savings of $35,000 to $500,000 per year for each application.[31]

The ability of decision support systems to help decision makers cope with complex tasks is illustrated by the International Example, "Decision Support for the 1992 Barcelona Olympics" on p. 322.

Expert Systems

At the National Aeronautics and Space Administration (NASA), turnover in top and middle-level managers, engineers, and scientists threatened to cripple operations within five years. NASA turned to intelligent computers to replace its skilled humans.[32] An **expert system** is a computer program that helps solve problems by applying decision rules and information provided by an expert in the field. Using an expert system, a non-expert can achieve performance comparable to that of an expert in a particular area of work. Expert systems are a sort of decision support system. Their distinguishing characteristic is the **knowledge base,** the data and decision rules that represent the expertise. These expert sys-

expert system a computer program that helps solve problems by applying decision rules and information provided by an expert in the field.

knowledge base data and decision rules contained in expert systems representing the needed expertise.

Decision Support for the 1992 Barcelona Olympics

To prepare for the 1992 Olympic Games, the city of Barcelona had to prepare a schedule of the games. This was not a trivial task. At the outset, a huge number of schedules were possible, as more than 2,000 events had to be scheduled in a 15-day period. Several well-defined constraints helped to bring that number down. Some were obvious: Semifinals had to be held before the finals, and two events could not be scheduled at the same time and place. Some were less obvious. For example, it is a tradition that the marathon is run on the last day of the games, and that swimming and track and field don't go on at the same time. However, the problem was still very large.

In such an environment, selecting the best possible schedule was not a well-defined problem at all, mainly because it was not clear what was meant by "best" in this context. The problem was one of multiple criteria. One criterion would be that the schedule should ensure the maximum audience for each Olympic event. Another might be to avoid inconveniences for the athletes (which could conflict with the first criterion). The overall rhythm of the games—including the pacing of the sequence of finals in various events—would be another criterion. At the same time, constraints on available equipment and personnel had to be considered. Also, traffic jams could be caused by two or more events scheduled near each other at approximately the same time. In addition, TV would be broadcasting live. The time in Barcelona is equivalent to different times in different countries, where interest in particular sports could vary widely.

To help prepare the schedule, a DSS was built. It allowed the schedulers to develop alternative schedules and to evaluate them in terms of various criteria. The DSS, now called SUCCCES92, was very complex internally, containing information about the nature and duration of events, facilities and equipment, traffic flows, TV and live audience characteristics, effectiveness criteria, and many other variables. Despite its internal complexity, SUCCCES92 was easy to use. It was interactive and contained graphical aids to help compare certain characteristics of a given schedule with ideals established at the outset. The result was a well-planned 1992 Olympics.

Source: Adapted from R. Andreu and A. Corominas, "SUCCCES92: A DSS for Scheduling the Olympic Games," *Interfaces*, (September-October 1989), pp. 1-12.

---

artificial intelligence (AI)
computer programs that simulate human reasoning.

tems rely on **artificial intelligence (AI).** With artificial intelligence, a computer can simulate human reasoning, as well as learn from experience and communicate in human language. Complete artificial intelligence has not been achieved, but developments are promising. Researchers have developed programs to play backgammon, make generalizations, draw inferences and make analogies, and mimic the human brain in other ways. The difficulty of developing artificial intelligence is suggested by the Lighter Side, "Time Flies" on p. 323.

There are now many business applications of expert systems.[33] For instance, an expert system at Hewlett-Packard advises how to manufacture integrated circuits, and at Digital Equipment Corp., an expert system manages scheduling on the shop floor.

American Telephone & Telegraph Co.'s expert system, called ACE, quickly locates faults in telephone cables. In an hour, it does a job that previously took a team of technicians a week to accomplish. Digital Equipment spent two years building an expert system that its salespeople use to configure computer systems for their customers. The system has cut error rates from 25 percent to 5 percent, for an estimated annual savings of more than $10 million. Expert systems are also ideally suited to a variety of insurance underwriting and banking tasks, to medical diagnosis, and to almost any other area in which decision rules can be developed to simulate human expertise.

THE LIGHTER SIDE

Time Flies

The controversy over whether computers are really capable of artificial intelligence highlights the tremendous complex-ity of the mind and of learning. For example, could a computer understand the line from Shakespeare's play, Othello, when Othello, preparing to extinguish the bedroom candle and to kill his wife, says, "Put out the light, and then, put out the light"? This would require programming to give an understanding of figures of speech as well as jealousy, love, and madness.

Or imagine preparing a computer to deal with these sentences: "Time flies like an arrow. Fruit flies like an apricot."

Source: Abridged and adapted from Susan Chace, "Mind Machines: Scientists Are Laboring at Making Computers Think in Artificial Intelligence Research," Reprinted by permission of *The Wall Street Journal*, © 1983 Dow Jones & Company, Inc. All Rights Reserved Worldwide.

Expert systems may one day be more common than people on the factory floor. They will be the brains that make robots intelligent and flexible. They will assist engineers and managers in such diverse tasks as designing products, supervising orders and inventories, and coordinating production. Expert systems are difficult to develop, and they take considerable time and effort. Also, experts are sometimes reluctant to share their valuable knowledge.[34] Despite these problems, expert systems are a promising and exciting new development.

PROBLEMS WITH COMPUTERS

Inevitably, any new development with great potential for good also has great potential for harm. This is certainly the case with computers. Let's take a look at six problems commonly associated with computers.

Malfunctions

All of us have heard about computer malfunctions. A computer error caused false alarms on the Air Force's NORAD missile detection system, moving the nation to the brink of war. On a smaller scale, computer malfunctions can be devastating for businesses. The heavy reliance of firms on computers creates dependence. For instance, business organizations were surveyed to find out how long they could operate without the information-processing capabilities of computers. Many firms reported that they would quickly be immobilized by a major computer failure. After five and a half days without a computer, only 28 percent of business activities could continue; after ten and a half days, only 9 percent. We have developed a machine that is so efficient that we are almost helpless without it.

Because of the dangers of malfunctions, some firms are spending millions of dollars to develop backup operations, work out contingency plans, and otherwise prepare for electronic disasters. Nevertheless, specialists say that most firms are ill prepared to cope with failures of their computer facilities.

Often, of course, computers are blamed for human mistakes. By simply saying, "We had computer problems," it is easy to shift responsibility to a computer. Such a statement is typically greeted with a resigned nod and the unspoken understanding that "these machines aren't as smart as they think they are."

Are Computers a Threat to Personal Privacy?

Yes

The amount of personal information that is kept on computers has reached threatening proportions. Records on personal health, finances, traffic violations, and travels abroad are available from government computers. Businesses may also have sensitive information on past arrest records, military discharge status, and medical records. Together, this and other computerized information could prove extremely damaging to many individuals if revealed. Some medical information, for instance, may give clues about sexual preferences, and information concerning arrest records, personal loans, and military discharge status could be misused.

Moreover, the computerized information may simply be wrong. An error by a programmer or a computer glitch could destroy a person's credit rating, alter a medical status report, or create an incorrect arrest record. There is little if anything that most people can do to check on the accuracy of such information. They generally aren't even aware that it exists!

It is also hard to accept assurances that the information will be kept strictly confidential when we know that businesses' computer files are often subject to the prying of hackers and the manipulations of computer criminals. Who knows how many people are secretly accessing these personal files, or what they do with the information? Some firms, such as Cummins Engine Company, have recognized the magnitude of this problem and have refused to computerize their personnel records.

In the last few years alone, threats to personal privacy have become depressingly clear. Federal prosecutors in Kentucky, after selling used computers to a local dealer, learned that the computers still contained sensitive information about potential witnesses, confidential information, and continuing legal cases. Employees using electronic mail systems often think their messages are private; in fact, many others—including management—often routinely monitor such messages. The million subscribers to the Prodigy information network who use electronic bulletin boards have their messages screened. Also, computers radiate electromagnetic waves that can be intercepted and reproduced up to a mile away. One guidebook for hackers outlines some of the benefits of this snooping, including obtaining client lists, access codes, passwords, and personal information. Amazingly, such computer tapping apparently violates no federal law. A new product from Lotus Development Corp. provides a variety of information on 80 million U.S. households. The product, called Lotus Marketplace, packs data on palm-sized compact disks. This is a big step toward complete loss of control over personal information.

A massive network called FEDNET was proposed to tie together all government computers, but it was scrapped because of fears that it could be misused. Nevertheless,

Invasion of Privacy

Many people are concerned that the vast amount of personal information stored on computers makes invasion of privacy possible. The seriousness of this threat is examined in this chapter's Controversial Issue, "Are Computers a Threat to Personal Privacy?" (above).

Hackers

hackers   computer buffs who illegally gain access to, and sometimes tamper with, computer files.

Hackers are computer buffs who illegally gain access to, and sometimes tamper with, computer files. Hackers are a growing threat to business. Some people see hackers as fun-loving pranksters. Others see them as angry rebels, and still others as wanton criminals. Some hackers' actions, such as interrupting another computer user's work and flashing "Gimme Cookie!" on the screen, may seem harmless, but others are very costly to organizations. Over half of the readers of one computer magazine who responded to a survey said their companies had suffered losses of critical data, costing an average of $14,000 per occurrence.[35]

The potential danger of hackers was vividly illustrated by a series of incidents in November, 1988. Between 9 and 10 P.M. on a Wednesday evening, computers

such networks are developing almost on their own, without plan.

At the very least, we need stronger laws governing computerization of personal information, greater publicity about the nature of the information that is now maintained on such files, and easier access to our own files to correct errors. Perhaps we should even think seriously about simply banning such computerization of files.

No

Those who claim that computers pose threats to personal privacy are confusing the writing with the blackboard. It may well be that storing some types of information is inappropriate, but it is just as inappropriate to store it in a file drawer as on a computer chip.

In fact, computers may help guarantee the accuracy and relevance of personal information. When information is stored in a computer, it can easily be accessed to check its accuracy, whereas files kept manually may never be available for careful scrutiny. If for some reason it is concluded that certain information should not be stored, it can be quickly and totally erased from a computer file, unlike manual records.

Also, hackers and computer criminals have been widely publicized, but people have been stealing confidential information from file cabinets for a long time. If anything, storage on computers makes stealing information more difficult. Stealing passwords and tapping into databases requires more expertise than opening a file drawer.

Let's not forget all the benefits of computerization of personal information. Firms can quickly determine who is best qualified for jobs. They can track the career progress of minorities. They can see that retirees get their pension checks on time. Marketers can better match products and services to customers' needs and wants. All of this can be done at a remarkably low cost.

Finally, let's remember that a tremendous amount of the information that firms have on their computers is there precisely because the government insists on it. Firms must show, for instance, that they are dealing fairly with women and minorities, so they must keep supporting records. It would be ironic if the government stepped in and took action against firms because they are keeping the very information it demands.

This is the computer age. The issue is not whether information should be computerized, but how it can be done right. Most firms are doing all they can to ensure the accuracy of their records. For instance, General Electric, Eastman Kodak, and Caterpillar Tractor give employees access to their files.

To some extent at least, the reaction to computerization is an irrational response. Some primitive people resisted having their photos taken, fearing that their souls would be captured. Modern society apparently has the fear that personal information is our essence and that we thus are threatened when it is "taken" from us.

In sum, there is no reason to believe that computers pose any real threat to personal privacy. Quite the opposite!

What do you think?

in Berkeley, California and Cambridge, Massachusetts slowed to a crawl, the victims of a surprise attack. Shortly thereafter, Princeton University was struck. Before midnight, the National Aeronautics and Space Administration Ames Research Center, in California's Silicon Valley, and the Los Alamos National Laboratory in New Mexico were targeted. Then John Hopkins University in Baltimore and the University of Michigan in Ann Arbor were hit. In each case, computers mysteriously slowed and ran strange programs. At 2:28 A.M., a Berkeley scientist sent a bulletin around the nation: "We are currently under attack." A "worm," a self-contained program that entered computers via a communications network, had been developed by a Cornell University hacker. The worm was a form of **computer virus,** which is a program that automatically copies itself, "infects" other programs, and then plays some trick or otherwise disrupts computer functioning. When the worm entered a computer, it used information in the computer to establish links with other computers in the network, and it spread rapidly. Fortunately, this virus was relatively benign; it merely used empty storage space. However, it could have just as easily wiped out files, or it could have been programmed to wreak havoc on systems days or months later. Ultimately, a "vaccine" was developed to counter the attack, but not before computer operations had

computer virus *a program that automatically copies itself, "infects" other programs, and then plays a trick or otherwise disrupts computer functioning.*

been widely disrupted and hundreds of person-years of work had gone into purging the virus.[36]

Hackers are now using computers to steal company passwords and tap into computer switchboards, permitting them to make phone calls at the companies' expense. The total cost to companies of these calls is estimated to be $500 million annually.[37]

To fight hackers, firms are using security software, which restricts access to files and disk drives and provides audit trails. The audit trails keep track of who uses computers, as well as of invalid log-in attempts. Firms are also using anti-virus programs, which detect, identify, and purge computer viruses.[38] Such programs gained popularity in early 1992 to counter the "Michelangelo virus," which would attack a computer when its internal clock registered March 6—Michelangelo's birthday. There have been some well-publicized crackdowns on hackers, but criminal convictions are very rare.[39]

Errors in Using Computers

Unfortunately, many people operate computers without proper training. Also, managers who routinely check their own computations and information may fail to do so when using a computer. One California executive used a personal computer to project sales for one of his company's new products. According to the projection, the product would generate $55 million in sales in its first two years on the market. Based on that figure, other managers began making aggressive plans to add staff and inventory. Unfortunately, the executive had failed to include in the program a price discount planned for one key component. This oversight inflated the sales estimate by $8 million. If the executive's mistake had not been caught, it would have cost the company profits and investor confidence.[40]

In another case, a corporate chief executive hit the wrong key while on a public electronic-mail network and misaddressed a note intended for the firm's head of product development. As a result, he sent a total stranger the company's product plans for the next year and a half.[41]

Computer Crime

A 25-year-old computer terminal operator used computer trickery to receive pension checks under 30 different names. An accountant working for a fruit wholesaler used a computer to inflate prices on invoices and to send the extra money to dummy vendors. He amassed $1 million over six years. In the infamous Equity Funding fraud, computers were used to build a confusing pyramid of fake assets. By the time the fraud was uncovered, $185 million in fake assets had been created.

Computers have spawned a whole new class of criminals. Often computer experts, these criminals take advantage of flaws in systems or of access to files to steal an estimated $300 million a year. The FBI figures that the average armed bank robbery nets about $10,000, but computer crimes often bring in more than $1 million.

Many companies do not report computer crimes to the authorities, out of embarrassment at being a victim. A security consultant says, "The bigger the theft, the greater the embarrassment to the company," and the lower the likelihood of prosecution. One of his clients, an insurance company, lost $38.1 million to a crooked senior officer and never reported the crime to police.[44]

Terminal Tedium

Some people regard computers as the new assembly lines. People who once interacted with one another and carried out at least some physical activities now may sit and stare at video displays for eight or more hours a day. There is concern that such "terminal tedium" may be stressful, and even that there may be health hazards associated with constant exposure to the display. Although most claims of health hazards are just speculation at this point, fears about the consequences of stress and social isolation are harder to dismiss.

Negative Reactions to Computers

People's reactions to computers run to extremes. Some view them as all-knowing. They treat anything coming out of a computer as "truth," beyond challenge. In fact, of course, what the computer produces is no better than what is put into it and how it is instructed to process it. This "garbage in-garbage out" principle is too often forgotten.

Other people fear the computer, believing it will threaten their jobs, either by replacing them or by requiring skills they don't have. Others are concerned that they will become too dependent on computers. For still others, the computer represents change and the unknown. Each of these sources of fear may lead to resistance.

To some extent, computers are becoming more "user friendly." In his science-fantasy story, "I Sing the Body Electric," Ray Bradbury wrote of an "electric grandmother," a computerized robot designed to look, talk, and act like a warm, supportive grandmother. Computers are rapidly becoming more "grandmotherly."

Still interested in computers after hearing about these problems? If so, take a look at Figure 12-5, which lists some important factors to consider when buying a computer.

FIGURE 12-5   Selecting a Computer

There is more to choosing a computer system than just picking the one that is biggest, fastest, or most expensive. Instead, it is important to carefully assess your needs first and to then set up selection criteria. These might include:

▲ *Service level* — the ability of the system to work quickly and reliably.
▲ *Flexibility* — whether the system can be used for a variety of applications.
▲ *System support* — the quality of maintenance and emergency service.
▲ *Ease of use* of hardware and software.
▲ *Cost* of installation and operation.
▲ *Quality of supplier management.*
▲ *Delivery time, space requirements, and compatibility* with equipment now in use.

SUMMARY POINTS

1 Information is knowledge communicated in order to inform. Information management is a field that has developed in recognition of the fact that information is a valuable resource in need of systematic management. A management information system is a system for gathering information, transforming it in ways needed for decision making, and distributing it to those who need it. To design an MIS, it is necessary to set objectives, identify constraints, determine information needs, and put the system together.

2 A computer is a machine that can carry out complex and repetitious operations on data at very high speeds. Computers are often used because of their advantages over individuals: They are fast, can perform complex operations, have tremendous memory capacity, can make unemotional decisions, and don't get bored.

3 Computer hardware, the "nuts and bolts" of the computer, includes input units, output units, and a central processing unit. The input unit is the means through which data and programs enter into a computer system. Output units present the results of computer operations to the user in some form. The central processing unit is the "brain" of the computer.

4 Computer software, or programs, are step-by-step instructions that tell the computer what to do. System software is a set of programs that manages the resources of the computer so that they are used in the best possible way. Application software performs specific tasks for the computer user, such as computing budgets or calculating statistics. Software preparation involves flowcharting, programming in a computer language, and documenting.

5 Personal computers, or microcomputers, are usually typewriter-sized computers. They can be used for a wide array of applications. A modem is a device to permit microcomputers to communicate with other microcomputers, mainframes, or electronic bulletin boards via telephone lines. Networking ties together computers, either locally or at distant locations, to allow them to communicate with each other, share re-

sources, and access vast amounts of information.

6 Computers have numerous applications in business. Some manufacturing applications include computer-aided design and computer-aided manufacturing. Managers are using computers for training, directing, communicating, career planning, and job design. Some marketing applications include bar coding, sales analysis, sales forecasting, and point-of-sale advertising. Financial simulation, securities trading, and financial planning are among the accounting and finance applications. Banks use computers both on-site and for electronic funds transfer. Computers are also widely used for word processing and data processing.

7 Decision support systems and expert systems are two ways computers are used to assist decision making. Decision support systems are interactive MIS applications that help managers consider alternatives in making decisions. Managers can ask the computer a series of "what if" questions about business problems, in order to explore the probable impacts of alternative choices. Expert systems are computer applications that guide nonexperts in tasks requiring expertise. These systems apply decision rules and information (provided by an expert in the field) to the problem situation. Expert systems rely on artificial intelligence, in which computer programs simulate human reasoning.

8 Some of the problems associated with computers are malfunctions, invasion of privacy, hackers, errors in use, computer crime, terminal tedium, and negative reactions. Our society is becoming computer-dependent. Computer malfunctions can paralyze a business, and errors in computer use can lead to costly mistakes. Personal information, which is often stored on computers, has the potential to be misused. Hackers and other computer criminals can disrupt computer functioning and even steal from businesses. Individual users risk health problems from staring at a computer screen constantly. Also, people's reactions to computers can range from treating them as "all knowing" to viewing them as a threat.

REVIEW QUESTIONS

1 What is information? Why is it important? **1**

2 What do information managers do? In what ways is information a resource? **1**

3 What is a management information system? Why is it important? **1**

4 List four purposes of a management information system. **1**

5 What is a microprocessor? Why is it important? **2**

6 List three types of computer input units and three types of output units. Then list the three main parts of the central processing unit. **3**

7 What is the difference between hardware and software? **3** **4**

8 Name four computer languages. **4**

9 What is a modem? An electronic bulletin board? **5**

10 Give applications of computers in manufacturing, management, marketing, accounting and finance, banking and credit, word processing, and data processing. **6**

11 Explain two ways that computers can be used to improve decision making. **7**

12 List seven problems that may occur with the use of a computer. **8**

DISCUSSION QUESTIONS

1 In what ways is information management similar to the management of other resources? In what ways is it different?

2 What are some potential problems with the electronic cottage?

3 Can you think of business decisions for which computers would not be helpful? What might be the characteristics of such decisions?

4 Do you think computers can ever really have artificial intelligence? Why or why not?

5 Which of the problems associated with use of computers do you think is currently most important? Which do you think will be most important in the year 2010?

6 Do you think computers are a threat to business? To society? Why or why not?

EXPERIENTIAL EXERCISES

1 Go to your school's microcomputer lab, to a local computer store, or wherever a microcomputer and application software are available for your use. Choose any piece of application software other than a word processing program, such as a spreadsheet, file management program, or statistical program. Apply the software to a problem or application with which you are familiar or to a hypothetical program or application. Submit the printed output, along with a description of the problem or application and a discussion of your reactions to the software. In the discussion, indicate whether or not you thought the software was interesting, helpful, and easy to use.

2 Go to the library of your school and find the most recent edition of the *Business Periodicals Index*. Look under the following headings for recent information about computers and information systems: computers, data processing, information storage and retrieval systems, information systems, personal computers, microcomputers, and supercomputers. Then read at least two of the articles and write a one-page summary of each.

CASES

CASE 12-1
Productivity Spies

Vaughn Foster had U.S. 85 all to himself as he swung his truck onto the highway for his last trip of the day. To his right, the sun was disappearing behind the Rockies; ahead, the empty road stretched straight for miles. With one eye on the speedometer, he eased into the right lane and started creeping ahead at 50 miles an hour.

"I've been out all week," he said. "My wife's home, my kids are home, and I'd just as soon be there with them. There's no doubt about it: If it weren't for that computer, I'd be running 60 easy."

Vaughn Foster is talking about a black box the size of a dictionary that sits in a compartment above his right front tire. At the end of his trip, his boss at Leprino Foods Co. in Denver will pull a cartridge out of the box and pop it into a personal computer. In seconds the computer will print out a report showing all the times Foster exceeded the speed limit. "It's like a watchdog," Foster grumbles. "You just can't get as far away from that supervisor as you used to."

Computers are transforming thousands of jobs at companies like Leprino in a significant new way: They are watching employees and monitoring their productivity. The Office of Technology Assessment estimates that in 1988, more than 10 million workers were subjected to concealed observation.

Typists in word processing pools generate reports that show how many pages they produce in a day and how many keystrokes they make in a minute. Telephone operator supervisors scan summaries of how many calls each operator answers and how long each call takes. In production plants making everything from spark plugs to Tupperware, supervisors glance at terminals and see instantly which machine operators are ahead of schedule and which are behind. Many companies use software that keeps tab on how many keystrokes VDT workers make in a day and how long they keep their hands on the keyboard.

To many managers, computer monitoring has brought wondrous results. They say it motivates employees to meet company standards and makes them more productive. Some managers also find that computer monitoring leads to more objective performance evaluations. At least one employer has used monitoring technology to investigate an episode of apparent office sabotage and to build a case against the suspect.

But as electronic watchdogs move into the workplace, they are stirring up concern among a growing number of unions, government officials, and labor experts, who worry that the practice breeds stress and dehumanizes employees. For instance, there is evidence that video display terminal workers who labor under the constant scrutiny of secret monitoring devices suffer boredom and heightened levels of stress-related medical problems such as ulcers, heart disease, fatigue, and depression. A union, the Communications Workers of America, contends that, "In essence, concealed surveillance combines the worst features of 19th century factory labor relations with 20th century technology, creating an electronic sweatshop." Many other unions have adopted positions against monitoring, and many states are considering restrictive legislation.

1. Do you agree that computer monitoring motivates employees to meet company standards and makes them more productive? Do you agree that computer monitoring breeds stress and dehumanizes employees?
2. For what sorts of jobs do you think computer monitoring is most appropriate? Least appropriate?
3. Do you think it is right for states to consider legislation to restrict computer monitoring? Why or why not?

Source: Abridged and adapted from M. W. Miller, "Productivity Spies: Computers Keep an Eye on Workers and See If They Perform Well," *The Wall Street Journal,* 3 June 1985, pp. 1, 15; and J. A. Lopez, "When 'Big Brother' Watches, Workers Face Health Risks," *The Wall Street Journal,* 5 October 1990, p. B2. Dow Jones & Co., Inc. All Rights Reserved Worldwide.

CASE 12-2
Computers Cut Through the Service Maze

Service with a smile just isn't good enough anymore. Instead, service with a computer is becoming the norm. Recent improvements in computer technology can provide speedy response to telephone inquiries and provide customers with answers at any hour of the day or night. Developments in expert software and image processing shorten the game of telephone tag and cut the number of times customer calls get shunted from person to person. Improvements in laptop computers are sending more companies' representatives into the field to speed the handling of insurance claims, mortgage applications, elevator repairs, and even cocktail orders.

Among the biggest breakthroughs to improving customer service have been systems that let telephone switches and standard computers speak the same language. That means for example, that someone calling with a question on a credit-card bill can punch in an account number while on hold. The telephone switch would relay the number to the computer, which would fetch the caller's records. The records would be relayed back through the phone switch and would appear on the customer-service person's computer screen as soon as he or she answered the call.

Such systems can be especially important for callers when they get passed from one person to another. The records simply become part of the call. When the call is transferred, the files appear on the computer terminal of the service representative who grabs it, so the information doesn't have to be taken down all over again.

These systems also make it easier to reroute phone calls. In one firm, callers after business hours on the East Coast used to get a recorded message, but now they're shifted to the West Coast and answered in person by someone there. Moreover, the computers automatically track all sorts of indicators—how long the caller was on hold, how many times he or she was transferred, etc.—so that problem areas can be spotted quickly. Using such systems, callers can get information on accounts at any time, without waiting for an operator. One software firm recently unveiled a system that lets golfers reserve tee times by dialing a computer and following the voice prompts.

Image processing—in which documents are scanned by a computer and stored electronically—is also becoming widely used to cut the time a customer spends on the phone with a company. One study found that with image processing, companies can more than halve the time it takes to respond to an inquiry, because pulling files together electronically is so much faster than fetching them from drawers. According to the study, a big insurance company cut the time it took to resolve complex claims from more than six months to ten days. A manufacturing company cut the parts-ordering process from an average of 20 minutes to three. One new system has cut the time it takes a hospital to find a patient's chart from half an hour to less than a minute.

Some companies are also beginning to use expert systems, which collect knowledge, to help answer customers' questions, especially on technical matters. Turnover in customer-service operations can be high, and it can take a long time to bring a new person up to speed, so companies use the software systems to store answers as people uncover them and build a base of expertise that won't walk out the door when an employee does.

Otis Elevator Co., a subsidiary of United Technologies Corp., is using an expert system with laptop computers to speed up repairs. Otis has devices that work like airplane flight recorders, collecting information on the behavior of many of its elevators. When an elevator isn't working, an expert system provides a list of possible problems, which the repairperson can call up on a personal computer.

As laptops have shrunk, systems such as NCR Corp.'s "palmtop" order-entry systems have become available. The computer lets a waiter take an order at a table and immediately send it over a radio frequency to the bar or kitchen, trimming the time people have to spend waiting for their orders.

The march of technology isn't always seen as progress, of course. Customers frequently complain about reaching a computer when they're trying to call a company. Customers may get a sales pitch when they call for service, since consolidated data on the customer can alert the company to what products a caller might possibly be interested in.

Also, people who appreciate being able to call late at night to get a tee time wouldn't necessarily like having to walk through the same series of voice prompts in the middle of the afternoon.

In many instances, however, these technologies really will save customers a minute here, an hour there.

1. What do you think firms gain by use of this information technology? What do they lose?
2. The chapter discusses five factors that determine the value of information to the decision maker. Discuss how the systems in this case might influence these factors.
3. Which types of customers do you think would respond most favorably to such systems? Least favorably?

Source: Abridged and adapted from P. B. Carroll, "Computers Cut Through the Service Maze," *The Wall Street Journal,* 1 May 1990, p. B1. Dow Jones & Co., Inc. All Rights Reserved Worldwide.

Sniffing Out the Bottom Line

As founder and President of Dynachow, a small but rapidly growing pet food producer, Elizabeth Robertson was anxious to find ways to improve company profitability. With a bachelor's degree in business and over ten years of related work experience, Robertson felt she was well qualified to lead the company through the future challenges of a dog-eat-dog industry. She felt, though, that she was missing something. She had read texts on business and management. They seemed to provide good information, but they were filled with qualifiers—do X only if Y; consider A, B, and C before doing D. She had also followed various practitioner's journals. They helped her make better sense of topical issues and kept her informed of important trends, but they were somehow not authoritative and convincing. Still, though, her basic question—how to improve company profitability—wasn't directly and unambiguously answered. What, she asked, are some concrete steps to the bottom line?

Robertson decided to carefully look into the issue of company profitability, and she seemed to have quickly struck paydirt. She found a book on the bestseller list titled *Everything I Needed to Know About Profitability and Didn't Learn in Business School: The Five Rule Manager*. It claimed to identify five ironclad rules for company profitability. According to the authors, who based their recommendations on many years of consulting experience, these rules would work for any company in any industry. The rules were:

Rule 1. Motivate your employees with challenge and interesting work rather than with money.

Rule 2. Let employees participate in important decisions.

Rule 3. Respect your employees and customers.

Rule 4. Treat all employees the same.

Rule 5. Constantly improve product quality.

Robertson was pleased to read these guidelines. They seemed reasonable and they were consistent with her own values and beliefs. They also seemed to apply in general, rather than just in a few settings. Still, Robertson wasn't going to be satisfied with the recommendations of a single book, however popular. Instead, she did three things.

First, she read *Fortune*, *Business Week*, *Forbes*, and other business magazines to find discussions about profitable firms. She found articles about three very successful and profitable companies and tried to discern whether of not they followed the five rules for profitability. The evidence seemed clear to Robertson. She found no discussion in any of the articles of policies or practices contrary to the rules. Respect, involvement, participation, and quality were often mentioned as characterizing the firms.

Second, Robertson decided to get her employees' opinions. She asked ten of her employees:

1. What is more important to you, money or challenge and interesting work?

2. Do you like to be involved in important decisions?

3. Does it really matter to you if you are respected? Do you think respect for customers is important?

4. Do you think it is ever appropriate to treat one employee better than another?

5. Is improving product quality really important?

Her employees' responses seemed to confirm the guidelines. Virtually all the employees said they were more concerned with job interest and challenge than with money. They also said that involvement, respect, and equitable treatment were important to them, and they believed that pursuit of quality was critical.

Third, Robertson asked an assistant to find research studies which related the rules to company profitability. The assistant found two surveys which seemed relevant. One found that job challenge and employee involvement were each significantly statistically related to firm profitability. The other found statistically significant relationships between profitability and concern for quality. While Robertson was certain there was much more research on this subject, she felt that she had dug far enough. She had three solid pieces of evidence in support of the five rules:

1. Three highly publicized and profitable firms appeared to use practices and policies consistent with the rules.

2. Employees of Dynachow agreed with the rules.

3. Two scientific surveys showed some of the rules to be statistically related to company profitability.

Based on all this, Robertson began to consider how she could change policies and practices to implement the rules. First, she decided that money which might have been used for raises would instead be used to implement a job enrichment program. Second, supervisors would be sent to training programs designed to encourage them to treat subordinates with more respect. Third, employees would be routinely involved in all important decisions. Fourth, any policies and practices resulting in differential treatment of employees would be absolutely forbidden. Finally, immediate steps would be taken to increase product quality, regardless of short-term costs.

Questions

1. Does the evidence regarding the three profitable organizations provide compelling evidence in support of the rules?
2. Should the employees' responses to Robertson's questions enhance confidence in validity of the rules?
3. Do the survey results provide conclusive evidence that following the rules will lead to higher profitability.?
4. Given all the evidence, should Robertson go ahead with her planned changes?
5. What dangers associated with lack of critical thinking can be seen in this case?

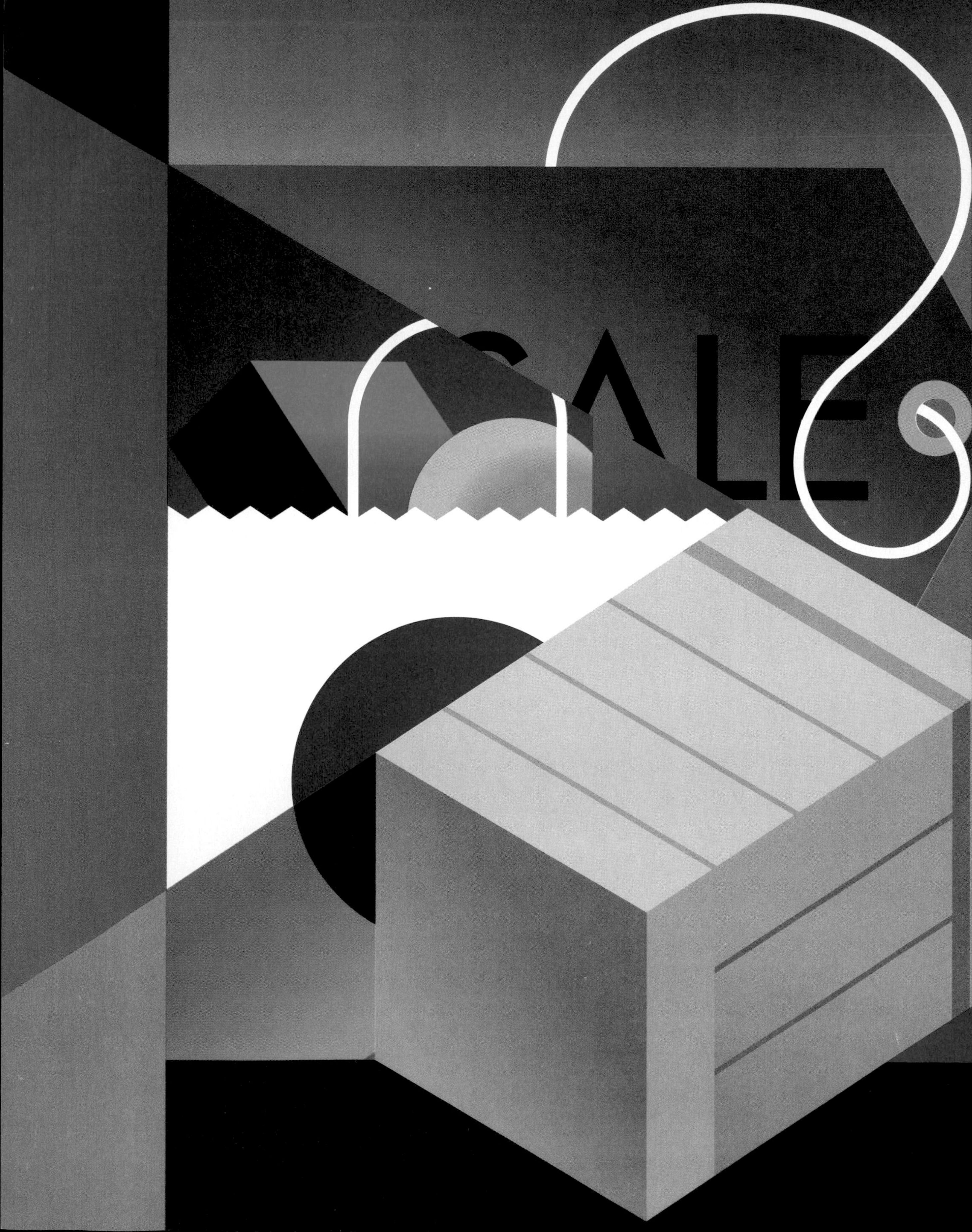
SALE

PART 4
Marketing Management

27100 0601

OBJECTIVES

After studying this chapter, you should be able to:

1 Define marketing.

2 Discuss the four functions of macro-marketing.

3 Explain the marketing concept.

4 Describe the three steps in strategic market planning and discuss market segmentation and uncontrollable environmental factors.

5 Define the four key elements in the marketing mix.

6 Identify the five stages of the purchase decision process and describe the differences between final consumers and organizational buyers.

7 Explain the uses and limitations of marketing research.

8 Discuss the role of the marketing concept in nonprofit organizations.

CHAPTER 13

Marketing: The Strategic Input

IBM had successfully dominated the computer/data processing industry for almost 30 years. The company's formula for success was amazingly simple; it was based on three principles. First, its computers were sold exclusively by a highly trained sales force that was supported by an excellent technical staff. Second, IBM regularly introduced new lines of larger, faster mainframe computers that made its previous models obsolete. Third, its software was state of the art. If a firm wanted to have the very best computer capability, it probably would be built around an IBM mainframe.

Then IBM's whole world changed with the introduction of personal computers by firms such as Apple. It became painfully obvious to IBM that if it was not willing to make radical changes in its marketing strategy, it would be reduced to a bit player in the computer market. The company was successful in revamping its marketing strategy. Today, IBM personal computers are sold in IBM-owned stores as well as a wide variety of retail outlets that sell personal computers. This chapter will focus on marketing as a key element in business strategy.

The old saying, "Nothing happens until a sale is made," contains more than just a grain of truth. A business can make the right decisions about investment, production, and management, but if it does not have the right product available for the market at the right time and place, then all of its other efforts have been wasted. Even though marketing may not be any more important than the other business functions, the success of the enterprise is determined in the marketplace. We will begin by defining marketing.

MARKETING DEFINED

Most people define marketing as either advertising or selling. Although these are important components of marketing, they represent only a limited view of marketing and its relative importance to most organizations.

The American Marketing Association defines **marketing** as "the process of planning and executing the conception, pricing, promotion, and distribution of ideas, goods, and services to create exchanges that satisfy individual and organizational objectives." According to the definition, marketing managers not only make advertising and selling decisions, but also decide which products are brought to the marketplace. In addition, marketing managers are active in the distribution of goods and services *and* of ideas, information, and recommended practices. For example, the American Cancer Society has a sophisticated marketing program to encourage individuals to stop smoking. It consists in part of technical literature given to physicians, advertisements placed on television and in magazines, and campaigns for smoke-free days.

marketing   *the process of planning and executing the conception, pricing, promotion, and distribution of ideas, goods, and services, to create exchanges that satisfy individual and organizational objectives.*

MACROMARKETING

The purpose of marketing is to create time and place utility for the buyer. What do we mean by "time and place utility"? **Utility** is a general measure of the extent to which a product or service satisfies consumers' needs. It is created when the characteristics of a product match the needs of the buyer. **Time utility,** therefore, is a measure of the degree to which a product is available *when* buyers want it. **Place utility** is a measure of the degree to which a product is available *where* buyers want it. All purchases are attempts by buyers to maximize time and place utility.

Time and place utility are created by marketing. For example, think of fresh bread at the bakery. The product itself creates utility—bread is nutritious, it tastes and smells good, and purchasing it is easier than baking it yourself. But what if you could buy bread only on Mondays at a bakery located 30 miles from your house? Now imagine that the same bakery sold its bread through several nearby supermarkets, and they were open seven days a week. Doesn't the second situation, in which the product is more actively marketed, bring an added convenience to the buyer? This added benefit or convenience is time and place utility.

The creation of time and place utility is responsible for about one half of the cost of consumer products. If a product costs $1.00, then raw materials, labor, and overhead account for approximately $.55, and moving the product from the factory to retail shelves accounts for $.45. This is not to say that marketing simply inflates the price of products. Marketing adds value to products in the form of time and place utility. The extra $.45 in our example is a measure of that added value.

The cost of marketing products and services can be reduced through gains in efficiency. There are four major ways that marketing makes the sale of goods and services more efficient. They are the functions of information, inventory, exchange, and the routine transaction. Together, these four functions make up **macromarketing**, the study of how goods and services are distributed from buyers to sellers. Macromarketing concerns the economy as a whole. Let's take a closer look at the four functions of macromarketing.

utility   *general measure of the extent to which a product or service satisfies customers' needs.*

time utility   *a measure of the degree to which a product is available when buyers want it.*

place utility   *a measure of the degree to which a product is available where buyers want it.*

macromarketing   *the study of how goods and services are distributed from buyers to sellers.*

Information Function

An effective marketing system acts as an information network linking together producers and consumers. Information flows between producers and consumers in a continuous, back-and-forth pattern. This information is important if producers are to meet the changing needs of consumers in a cost-efficient manner, and if consumers are to maximize the utility of their purchases.

The automobile industry is an example of how this information function works. Automobile manufacturers look to the market to see which features and options people want in a new car. Manufacturers analyze the safety and mileage standards required by the government. They also check with their suppliers to find the lowest-cost combination of glass, steel, rubber, and other production inputs. To get the best buy, the public examines model prices, dealer information, and studies of product quality and reliability in magazines such as *Consumer Reports* and *Road and Track.* The more timely and accurate the information flowing through the network, the more efficient the market. Figure 13-1 illustrates the information flows in the automobile market.

Inventory Function

Merchandise does not move in an even stream from producers to consumers. Both supply and demand change over time, sometimes surging ahead and at other times dropping off. The ups and downs of the production cycle are not always matched with the ups and downs of the consumption cycle. The task of equating supply and demand falls on the marketing system—specifically, on the inventory function.

Inventories are built up when production is strong and demand is slack. Inventories are drawn down when production is weak and demand is brisk. If the entire United States wheat crop were put on the market immediately after the autumn harvest, the price of wheat would fall so low that most farmers would be

FIGURE 13-1   The Automobile Information Network

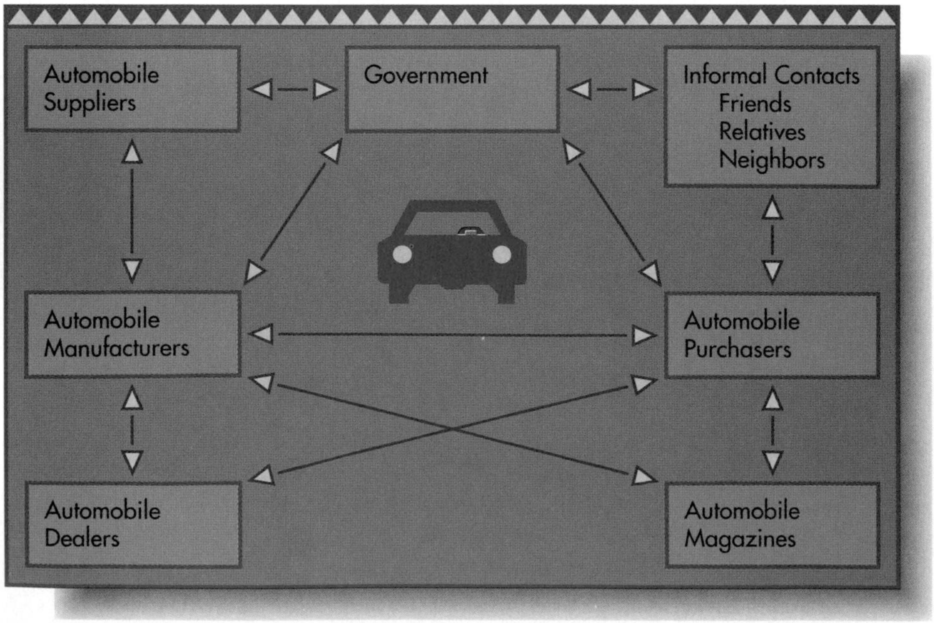

wiped out. The problem for the wheat farmer is that demand is fairly constant over the year, but production peaks in certain months. As a result, much of the wheat crop is stored for several months and only gradually released to the market. This keeps supply and demand in line and makes the price of wheat fairly stable. The trade-off for the farmer is between the increase in price that results from temporarily withholding wheat from the market and the added cost involved in warehousing it. In this example, these storage costs are more than offset by the higher market price.

Exchange Function

The marketing system also centralizes the exchange of goods and services. This increases distribution efficiency for society and creates time and place utility for individual buyers. Consider an economy consisting of five businesses. Each business produces an extra amount of a product and trades that surplus for some of the products made by the other businesses. Figure 13-2(a) shows that ten separate exchanges are required if our miniature economy has no central market. Figure 13-2(b) shows that only five exchanges are needed when centralized exchange is introduced.

For many years, the market was a physical location where buyers and sellers came together to exchange money for produce or products. This was particularly true when our economy was largely dependent on agricultural goods. Today, this centralized physical market still exists in facilities such as the Dallas World Trade Center. There, buyers and sellers of many different types of products, ranging from clothing to furniture, come together several times per year. However, the

FIGURE 13-2   Exchanges in Decentralized and Centralized Markets

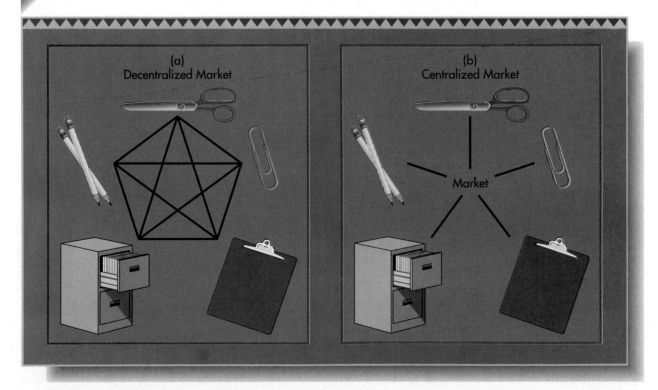

concept of a market has now been expanded to include wire transfers of instructions and money from people all over the world to a central location. A classic example would be the New York Stock Exchange, which frequently trades more than 200 million shares of stock in a single day, quickly and efficiently, for people located all over the world.

Routine Transaction Function

The marketing system not only centralizes the buying and selling of goods and services but also provides routine or standardized mechanisms for exchange. Without routine buying practices, buyers and sellers would have to develop a new set of exchange procedures each time they did business. This would be expensive, time-consuming, and inefficient. Instead, standardized procedures make it easy to buy and sell goods and services. For example, imagine the confusion and delays that would exist if the New York Stock Exchange did not have routinized stock trading procedures and exchange mechanisms. It would take buyers and sellers days rather than seconds to complete a transaction, and the costs would be much higher than they are today.

THE MARKETING CONCEPT

marketing concept   *a philosophy that marketing is a customer-oriented activity and that the overall objective of a firm is to develop products and services that satisfy customer needs.*

The **marketing concept** is a contemporary philosophy of business. It says that marketing is a customer-oriented activity. The objective of the firm (and of its marketing department) is to develop products and services that satisfy customer needs, not just to produce high-quality goods and services.

British Airways and the Marketing Concept

In the early 1980s, British Airways was considered by many frequent flyers to be among the world's worst airlines. According to John Bray, an airline consultant, the attitude among most British Airways employees was, "This would be a great place to work if it wasn't for those bloody customers."

A dramatic shift took place in the mid-1980s, when the firm adopted the marketing concept. A marketing research study indicated that a friendly, supportive airline crew was twice as important to most customers as operational factors such as food service and speed of check-in. The problem was how to communicate to all British Airways employees that travelers must be treated as individuals rather than commodities to be shuttled around. The firm adopted mandatory training programs, led by the president of British Airways, focusing on this need to treat the customer as king. The program took a great deal of effort and time, but it did succeed. A recent poll of frequent travelers ranked British Airways among the finest airlines in the world. In addition, profits and sales have increased dramatically.[1]

Satisfaction, Substitutes, and Profits

The marketing concept is based on three important principles. Understanding them can save a firm from the kind of problem that British Airways encountered.

Customer Satisfaction.   At the very heart of the marketing concept is the notion of customer satisfaction. If the firm is dedicated to maximizing profit at the expense of satisfying customer needs, it will not prosper in the long run. The key ingredient in satisfying customers is listening to what they have to say. The Four

Seasons Hotel is a textbook example. The firm requires that each of its regional vice presidents serve as a general manager of one hotel, so that he or she will stay close to the customer. In addition, the hotel is now installing a computerized database that will keep track of information about each customer. The data will include preference for smoking or nonsmoking room, the need for a nonallergenic pillow, and what type of tea the customer wants at night. One Four Seasons Hotel manager said, "We've got to mother you [the customer] to death."[2]

According to the marketing concept, customer satisfaction is the key to enduring success.

Belief in Competitive Substitutes.

A firm that practices the marketing concept realizes that even its most profitable product will someday be obsolete. It monitors the changing needs of its customers. Such a firm will be the one to bring out the new product that replaces the original. Success, however, makes many firms complacent, and they stay with the same old products year after year. They may be surprised when their products are no longer wanted by the buying public.

Federal Express faces a critical test. The firm that founded overnight delivery is being challenged by the proliferation of independently owned fax machines. Businesses that once used Federal Express for time-sensitive documents can now fax them. Often, the price is lower and delivery is completed not by ten o'clock the next morning but within minutes. It is unclear how Federal Express will adjust. But it is evident that a new competitive substitute, the fax machine, will have a tremendous impact on the future of the company.

Concern with Profit, Not Sales.

Businesses must make a profit if they are to continue serving the needs of the market. A firm must make enough money to pay all of its expenses and to provide income for its investors. According to the marketing concept, the task of marketing is to increase profits, not simply to increase sales. British Airways found that there was a direct relationship between customer satisfaction and profits.

STRATEGIC MARKET PLANNING

If an organization is to be successful, it must have a strategic plan to guide its overall marketing efforts. As the introduction to this chapter pointed out, IBM was forced to develop a whole new marketing strategy to market personal computers.

If it had not been flexible and willing to adjust to changes in the market as a result of new products (personal computers) and new competition (Apple), it would not be a major player in a large segment of the computer market today. The first step in the development of a strategic market plan is to define the market segment that the company is trying to reach. Then the firm must determine what factors beyond its control will affect its ability to market products or services. The final step is to blend the four primary variables in the marketing mix (discussed in the next section of this chapter) into a strategy that will permit the firm to meet its marketing objectives.

Market Segmentation

market segmentation
the process of identifying groups of customers with similar characteristics and modifying the product or selling strategies to match the characteristics of each group.

market segment   *a limited group of customers whose wants and needs most closely match the product's characteristics.*

Most firms realize that they cannot sell their products to all of their potential customers. To narrow the focus, they go through a process called **market segmentation,** in which they identify groups of customers with similar characteristics and needs. They then modify the product or selling strategies to match the characteristics and needs of each group. Firms thus focus their efforts on **a market segment**—a limited group of customers whose wants and needs most closely match the product's characteristics. For example, the Waterman Pen Company sells expensive pens that have been "painstakingly tooled and balanced to absolute precision." The firm's advertisements state, "Pens write. A Waterman pen expresses." Clearly, Waterman has selected a relatively small, high-income market segment for its products.

In contrast, Ford's Mercury division introduced the Tracer, which is "the new small sedan from Mercury." The firm's advertisements are directed at a large consumer market that wants a small, efficient, comfortable, affordable automobile. The Tracer's advertisements state that although the car's price starts as low as $8,969, it has "more room inside than Civic, Corolla, or Sentra." Mercury advertises Tracer with a different theme and in different magazines than its Lincoln Town Car, a very expensive automobile that appeals to a relatively small target market. The key point is that in both cases, the Waterman Pen and the Mercury Tracer, the marketing strategists have aimed the product at selected market segments. One segment is just larger than the other.

Segmentation is the key element of marketing strategy for many companies. Segmentation is demand-oriented, because it involves modifying business strategies to fit the needs of individual market segments rather than those of the entire market. We will now look at why firms segment markets.

Rationale for Segmentation.   Firms adopt market segmentation strategies for three reasons: (1) their markets are diverse, (2) consumers respond differently to different promotional appeals, and (3) market segmentation is consistent with the marketing concept.

Diverse Markets.   In theory, a market can be divided into as many segments as there are people in the market. This extreme form of segmentation is practiced in custom job shops that make products to the exact specifications of buyers, but it is not applicable for goods produced in large quantities. At the other extreme, a firm can provide a single product to one undifferentiated set of buyers. Most marketing managers realize that different customer groups have different needs and wants. The marketer's goal is to identify and develop those segments of the market that are large enough to be served profitably.

The Coca-Cola Company is an example of a firm that switched from selling one product to an entire market to selling several products to distinct market segments. Until 1960, the Coca-Cola Company produced only one soft drink. Today, Coca-Cola practices market segmentation. As Table 13-1 indicates, the company produces a variety of products that are distinguished by three features: flavor, number of calories, and caffeine content.

Varied Marketing Appeals.   A strategy of market segmentation does not necessarily mean that the firm must produce different products for each market segment. Instead, the firm may decide to build flexibility into its promotional strategy rather than expanding its product line.

For example, many political candidates sell themselves to the electorate by emphasizing one message to labor, another to business, and a third to farmers. In the same manner, New York plays often charge one price for a Saturday afternoon performance and a much higher price for the Saturday night performance. The market is segmented based on price.

Consistency with the Marketing Concept.   Market segmentation is consistent with the marketing concept. Market segmentation recognizes the existence of distinct market groups, each with a specific set of needs. Through segmentation, the firm directs its product and its promotional efforts at those markets that appear most promising. This is the heart of the marketing concept.

Four Approaches to Market Segmentation.   The R. J. Reynolds Tobacco Company tried to aim a new cigarette directly at black consumers. As the Ethical Issue (p. 348) shows, the company found out that using ethnicity to segment markets can be very controversial. Four traditional and less controversial methods

TABLE 13-1   Coca-Cola Company Products

Taste: Calories:	Cola		Non cola
	With Caffeine	**Without Caffeine**	
Diet	Diet Coke Diet Cherry Coke Tab	Caffeine-Free Diet Coke Caffeine-Free Tab	Diet Sprite Diet Minute Maid Orange Soda
Non diet	Coca-Cola Coca-Cola Classic Cherry Coke Mr. Pibb	Caffeine-Free Coke	Sprite Mello Yellow Fanta Hi-C Fresca Minute Maid Orange Soda

Source: Coca-Cola Company Annual Report, 1990, pp.4–5.

Training Wheels.

Sammy Markowitz isn't a champion. Yet. But now that he's training with a Team Hall chair, better watch the sports pages.

Bob Hall, who creates chairs for world champions, packs the same performance into his kid-sized racers.

For starters, the chair's custom-built for your child. So it soars to the finish line safely.

Its aircraft-certified tubing is tough on the track, but not on your child — chairs average just 10 pounds.

The three-position seatback helps it keep pace with a growing youngster. And easy-off wheels make it a snap to stash in your car.

You can even pick the chair's colors. From super subtle shades to screaming neons.

Get your kid rolling. Phone 617/628-7955. Or write P.O. Box 784, Cambridge, MA 02238.

Kid-sized? Yes.

Kid's stuff? No way.

Sammy Markowitz, six years old, 35 pounds, just possibly, aspiring racer.

Hall's Wheels
Get your rear in gear

Electric Chair.

Nothing juices up your performance like a Team Hall chair.

Just ask Craig Blanchette. His chair powered him to four world records in a single year.

You'll feel electricity instantly, as Bob Hall's racing geometry zaps you off the starting line.

Sleek aerodynamics help keep your speed sizzling.

And the spring-loaded steering with fine-tune directional trimmer keeps you from short circuiting.

Naturally, every Team Hall chair is built to your precise body measurements.

So you get a perfect fit. Without throwing one.

Charged up?

Call Bob Hall at 617/628-7955 to find out what's current. Or write P.O. Box 784, Cambridge, MA 02238.

Or talk to red hot Craig Blanchette. If you can catch him.

Craig Blanchette, world champion racer and rapid racer racer, Olympic bronze medalist.

Hall's Wheels
Get your rear in gear

■ In an extreme example of market segmentation, Hall's Wheels of Cambridge, Massachusetts will make a racing wheelchair tailored exactly to the body measurements of each customer.

of segmenting markets are by demographics, geographay, user rate, and benefits that people receive from the product.

Demographic Segmentation.

The most widely used segmentation variables are demographic, such as income, age, and sex. Family income is often very useful in segmenting markets. The German statistician Ernst Engel first noticed that as family income increases, the percentage spent on clothing and transportation increases, the percentage spent on food decreases, and the percentage spent on housing remains constant. The producers of expensive cars, homes, and vacations therefore aim their marketing campaigns at high-income families.

High-income families are easy to identify. Research has shown that high-income families, when compared with the population as a whole, have a head of the family between 45 and 64 years of age who went to college, works as a professional or manager, and lives in the suburbs.[3]

Many marketing managers find that segmenting markets by age works well for their products. Families with infants are the primary market for baby foods. People over 65 years of age are the principal users of medical services and prescription drugs. Other aspects of age are not quite so obvious. For example, the average teenager spends more than $2,300 per year. This amounts to approximately $55 billion nationwide. In addition, teenagers influence the purchase of another $183 billion in goods and services annually, ranging from breakfast cereals to stereos and automobiles. Polaroid's Cool Cam is designed for the 9- to 14-year-old market ("tweens"), while Delta Airlines' Fantastic Flyers program is aimed at the 2- to 12-year-old market segment.[4]

It is also important for the marketing manager to define both the percentage and the geographic distribution of the age group of interest. In other words, how big is the target age group and where do its members live? The percentage of the United States population under the age of 5 increased until 1990 but is projected to decrease through the year 2000. Such a population change will have a major impact on manufacturers of baby food, diapers, toys, and children's breakfast cereals.

It is also important for the marketing executive to remember that age is not always a good predictor of the timing of life's events. We all know some 70-year-old people who are very active. They play tennis, jog, and work ten hours a day. In contrast, some 70-year-old individuals have been retired for five or more years and participate in little or no physical exercise. Likewise, some 35-year-old parents have a child in college, while other 35-year-olds are preparing for the birth of their first child.[5]

Gender has been an excellent segmentation variable for many products, such as clothing, cosmetics, and magazines. In recent years cigarette manufacturers have begun to segment some of their markets by gender. Although both men and women smoke most cigarette brands, feminine brands such as Capri, Eve, and Virginia Slims have been successfully introduced. The marketing campaigns included appropriate packaging, flavor, and advertising cues to reinforce the appeal to women. In the same manner, cigarettes such as Marlboros are aimed at macho males.[6]

Geographic Segmentation.

Another relatively easy way to segment markets is geographically. The demand for many products varies from one section of the country to another, because of historical and cultural distinctions. For example, consumption of Mexican food is highest in southern California, Arizona, New

R. J. Reynolds Tobacco Company

R. J. Reynolds dropped plans in January, 1990, to test-market a new cigarette named Uptown. The cigarette, which was packaged in slick black and gold packaging, was aimed directly at the African-American market. Dr. Louis Sullivan, the Secretary of the U.S. Department of Health and Human Services, stated, "Uptown's message is more disease, more suffering, and more death for a group already bearing more than its share of smoking-related illness and mortality."

Market segmentation has become more and more important in the tobacco industry as the percentage of Americans who smoke keeps declining. This is a particularly acute problem for R. J. Reynolds, because its two leading brands, Winston and Camel, have not been targeted at one particular market segment.

The company's marketing executives debated how subtle they should be in their marketing approach. They decided that they would be accused of being underhanded and devious if they did not explicitly state that Uptown was aimed directly at blacks. Marketing specialists seem to agree that Reynolds made a mistake in its blatant attempt to segment the cigarette market by race. The company probably would have run into a similar firestorm of criticism if it had targeted other groups such as women, Hispanics, or young people.

Mexico, and Texas, because of the large Hispanic populations in those areas. Hallmark sells a great many engagement cards in the Northeast, where engagement parties are traditional. Birthday cards saying "Daddy" sell best in the South, where many adults tend to call their fathers "Daddy."[7]

Changes in climate may also account for variations in demand. Residents of Michigan, Wisconsin, and Minnesota will not purchase the same winter clothing as people in Florida and Georgia. A national retailer such as Sears must take these demand differences into consideration, so as to match its merchandise to the needs and preferences of its customers.

User Rate Segmentation. This type of segmentation sorts customers into heavy and light users of the product. The firm then focuses its advertising and personal selling efforts on the customers who account for most of its sales. Many salespersons for industrial products concentrate most of their efforts on one or two large accounts. In these situations, the salesperson almost becomes an external consultant to the buyer.

One major problem with this approach is that light users may be ignored. Although this strategy might be wise in the short run, the seller could lose market opportunities. For example, light users might develop new applications for the product.

Benefit Segmentation. Practitioners of benefit segmentation look to the attributes, or "benefits," that people seek in a product. For example, a product may have two benefits: style and low cost. Consumers favoring style as the primary benefit make up one segment; consumers favoring low cost make up the other. Although people would like to get as many benefits as possible from a product, certain benefits are usually given much greater weight in purchase decisions.

Once these key product benefits have been identified, the next step is to compare each benefit segment with the rest of the market. Do the segments have unique demographic or locational characteristics, consumption patterns, or media habits? Answers to such questions provide many clues about how to reach each segment and about which advertising appeals might prove most effective.

The market for toothpaste provides a good illustration of how benefit segmentation works. This market can be segmented in terms of four product benefits: flavor and product appearance, brightness of teeth, decay prevention, and price. (See Table 13-2.) Four variables describe each segment. People concerned with the brightness of their teeth tend to be young, usually in their teens. Many people in this segment are also smokers, worried about cigarette stains. Generally more "sociable" than people in other segments, they often buy such products as Gleem or Ultra Brite. If we were to introduce a new product to the "brightness" market, our advertising should stress the "social success" that users of our brand can expect. The media selected should be appropriate for teens and young people.

Market segmentation is an example of the marketing concept in action. It recognizes the existence of market groups that have different sets of product or service needs. Firms use segmentation strategy to aim their marketing programs at those groups that will benefit most from product or service offerings.

Uncontrollable Environmental Factors

Uncontrollable environmental factors are circumstances outside the firm's control that influence the way the firm markets its products. They are uncontrollable because no one firm can have a significant impact on them. The marketing executive must carefully identify the uncontrollable environmental factors that affect the firm's business, analyze them, and adjust the firm's marketing strategy accordingly. A classic example would be demographic changes, which are discussed in some detail in Chapter 2. Other uncontrollable environmental factors examined in this chapter that impact on marketing decisions include competition, economics, social trends, and technology.

uncontrollable environmental factors circumstances beyond the firm's control that affect the way it markets its products, including demographic changes, competition, economics, social trends, and technological changes.

TABLE 13-2   Benefit Segmentation for Toothpaste

Principal Benefit Sought	Demographic Strengths	Special Behavioral Characteristics	Personality Characteristics	Brands Disproportionately Favored
Flavor, Product Appearance	Children	Users of Spearmint-Flavored Toothpaste	High Self-Involvement	Colgate, Stripe
Brightness of Teeth	Teens, Young People	Smokers	High Sociability	Gleem, Ultra Brite
Decay Prevention	Large Families	Heavy Users	High Hypochondriasis	Crest
Price	Men	Heavy Users	High Autonomy	Brands on Sale

Competition.   The competitive environment for most products changes very quickly. U.S. automakers once had 97 percent of the domestic market. Now they have less than 65 percent and are fighting for their very survival in the most competitive automobile market in the world. Strategic market planners must constantly examine the market to identify their present and future competitors and determine their strengths and weaknesses. Some analysts tend to underestimate the strengths of the competition. In reality, they do their company a great disservice if they fail to look objectively at what the competitors can be expected to accomplish in the future. Shelby Carter, who is profiled on page 351, has been a senior executive at several companies and has always made sure to position his company appropriately with respect to the competition. For example, he helped Xerox refocus on high-quality products, which enabled the company to compete successfully with challengers from Japan.

Economics.   There are many stories that make fun of the inexact science of economics. The truth is that economics is much more of an art than a science. Marketing executives understand that the health of the economy has a great deal to do with the profitability of most businesses. Since the economy is so large, no single firm can have a direct effect on its health. What marketing managers can do is, first, to understand how the uncontrollable ups and downs of the short-term business cycle affect their firm's sales and, second, to evaluate how long-term economic growth can be expected to affect sales.

Many economists forecast that economic growth in the United States will be below historical levels during the 1990s. One reason is that the rate of U.S. population growth has declined. In addition, the new focus on protecting and cleaning up the environment will require a major redirection of capital resources away from the development of new products and the creation of new technology. Finally, our domestic businesses will have to cooperate with the newly united Europe as well as with Japan.

If the above scenario concerning the United States economy is correct, how should U.S. firms adjust their business and marketing plans? Clearly, no one answer will apply to all businesses. However, it does seem apparent that foreign markets represent real opportunities for American corporations. Businesses producing goods and services that are in demand in world markets, if they are willing to invest time in learning to compete in Europe, Japan, and less-developed nations, may find the next 20 years to be the most profitable period in their history.

Social Trends.   Social trends have a major impact on which products and services will be in demand, who buys them, and which promotional campaigns will be the most effective. For example, a major social trend has been the increased concern about protecting the environment from hazardous chemicals and other products. The data is very clear and quite disturbing. Survey after survey indicates that the American public is very concerned about the environment. However, when consumers are asked to pay more for products that do not damage the environment, only a very small fraction of them are willing to do so. It seems quite apparent that there is a market for environmentally sensitive products (such as household cleaners). However, they will not sell unless they are priced competitively with traditional products. Successful marketing executives will identify social trends and adjust their products and services to fit these changes in society.

Shelby H. Carter., Jr.

Shelby H. Carter, Jr., is an influential figure in American and international business. During his diverse career, he has distinguished himself as a senior corporate executive, a recognized educator, and a successful founder and developer of promising companies.

Today, Carter divides his time between teaching and his business interests, including his responsibilities as Chairman of the Board and Director of SynOptics Communications, Inc., a successful, publicly traded, high-technology company that he co-founded in 1985.

Carter's teaching responsibilities are centered at The University of Texas at Austin, where he is Adjunct Professor in the Graduate School of Business and the College of Business Administration. He has received numerous awards for outstanding teaching from academic groups, marketing organizations, student groups, and magazines.

Before assuming his current responsibilities, Shelby Carter rose through the management ranks of Xerox Corporation, from which he retired in 1985. His career included numerous professional honors, such as being named one of "The Ten Greatest Salespersons" in the book of the same name by Robert Shook. With Xerox, Carter rose to the position of Corporate Vice President and General Sales Manager of its worldwide operations. He also served as a member of the Corporate Operating Committee.

Carter has been involved for more than three decades with dynamic marketing companies. Before joining Xerox, he had spent 14 years in marketing and line management positions with IBM. Throughout his career, Carter has constantly held fast to certain fundamentals of strategic marketing. (1) *Customers* are the key asset to any business. (2) Marketing is a qualitative act, not a quantitative science. (3) Strategic marketing must focus on *creation* of markets and opportunities, not on dividing and sharing existing markets.

Shelby Carter views marketing as the "mother science," a dynamic force based on capitalism, which is by nature a form of constant change and can never be stationary. In 1991, in response to the dynamic developments in Mexico, Carter created Futura Enterprises, Inc., an infrastructure development and marketing company that will respond to the new commercial opportunities between the United States and Mexico.

Carter graduated from The University of Texas at Austin with a Bachelor of Business Administration and attended law school at The University of Texas at Austin and the University of Maryland. He served as an officer in the United States Marine Corps from 1953 to 1956, with his last two years as aide-de-camp to the Commanding General of the Second Marine Division.

This distinguished citizen has served on the boards of numerous corporations and community organizations. Carter contributes to his community and to his university by teaching in the business school and giving of his time in generous amounts to many student activities and counseling. He is a longtime supporter of higher education and has funded several endowments at The University of Texas at Austin.

Says Carter, "A completely happy man's best investment is the time he spends with his family. My family has been, and is, my first priority, my greatest joy, and my most-fun 'management' challenge." Shelby Carter carefully balances his immensely busy schedule in order to spend maximum time with his wife, Patricia, and his six children and eight grandchildren.

Technology.   High-technology businesses are at the cutting edge of our economy. Research and development efforts in these firms are uncontrollable in the sense that no one knows whether such efforts will result in useful products. What is clear is that the United States is operating in a new, restructured economy. Smokestack industries such as steelmaking, which helped create much of the nation's wealth, no longer offer a competitive advantage in the international marketplace. In contrast, the United States is unmatched in high-technology research. The ultimate test will be this nation's ability to translate output from these research laboratories into products that are in demand throughout the world.[8]

THE MARKETING MIX

The third step in developing a strategic market plan involves decisions in four key areas: product (which products to make available to the marketplace), distribution (where to sell them), price (how much to charge for them), and promotion (what to tell the public about them). These four key elements—product, distribution, price, and promotion—make up the **marketing mix.** The firm cannot make marketing mix decisions until it decides at which market segment to aim its product and what impact the uncontrollable environmental factors will have on the sale of the product.

marketing mix   *the four key elements in marketing decisions: product, distribution, price, and promotion.*

The marketing mix for each product is different. Table 13-3 shows the decisions about product, distribution, price, and promotion for automobile batteries and for men's shaving cream. Let's take a closer look at the elements of the marketing mix.

Product

Decisions in the product area involve developing a product that people are willing to buy. The product must satisfy a customer need; otherwise, people won't want it. Specific product decisions concern size, color, brand name, packaging,

TABLE 13-3   The Marketing Mix for Automobile Batteries and Men's Shaving Cream

	Automobile Batteries	Men's Shaving Cream
Product	Short-, Medium-, and Long-Lived Batteries	Regular, Mentholated, etc. Shaving Cream
Distribution	New Car Manufacturers; Replacement Battery Market— Gasoline Stations, Sears, Montgomery Ward	Drug Stores, Supermarkets, Discount Stores
Price	$20.00–$120.00	$0.59–$1.85
Promotion	Direct Sales to Automobile Manufacturers; Primarily Newspapers for Replacement Market	Primarily Television and Magazines; Store Displays

and product options. But the marketing manager is concerned about more than just physical features. A product is made up of all the factors a customer considers in making a purchase. For example, how is the product to be serviced? What about installation? Should the product carry a warranty? If so, what kind of warranty? What kind of reputation will the product have? Chapter 14 focuses on product management.

Distribution

The distribution element of the marketing mix involves decisions about where the product is sold, how it is delivered, and by whom. Distribution decisions involve manufacturers, such as Procter and Gamble; retailers, such as Kroger; and a variety of wholesalers. An excellent example of a wholesaler would be a local Budweiser distributorship, which buys beer from Budweiser and sells it to retailers such as Appletree and 7-Eleven stores. The wholesalers and retailers that link the manufacturer and the consumer make up the **channel of distribution.**

channel of distribution
the wholesalers and retailers that link the manufacturer with the consumer.

The right distribution decisions create time and place utility for the buyer, which means more profit for the seller. Marketing managers need to answer many questions when constructing a channel of distribution. Who should sell the product? Should the manufacturer own the distribution network? Should an independent wholesaler be used? How much inventory should be kept at the retail level and at the wholesale level? What types of stores should sell the product?

The difference between success and failure for a new or an existing product frequently comes down to the distribution system. The International Example (page 354) describes a joint venture between Nestle and Coke to sell canned coffee in South Korea. This product has an excellent chance of success, largely because Coke's powerful distribution system will ensure that most convenience stores in South Korea will carry the product. Chapter 15 will examine important questions relating to channels of distribution.

Price

How much to charge for a product is one of the most important decisions facing managers. Pricing decisions involve more than the number on the price tag. They also have to do with discounts, markups, and delivery terms. We will look at these factors in Chapter 16.

The pricing decision can be simple if the product is similar to others on the market. Then the firm sets the selling price near the prices of competing products. However, if the product has features that make it different from competing products, or if it is an entirely new product, the decision is much more difficult. Should the product be priced to earn immediate profits or long-term profits? Should price be based on demand or on cost factors? Would a higher price or a lower one earn greater total profits? Do buyers believe that price is a direct indication of product quality? How should one model of the product be priced in relation to a slightly different model?

Promotion

Even a great product cannot sell itself. People must be told about the product before they can buy it. **Promotion** includes all techniques that are available to the firm to communicate to its potential customers about its products or services.

promotion   all techniques available to the firm to communicate to its potential customers about its products or services.

Nestle, Coke, and South Korea

Nestle S.A. of Switzerland and Coca-Cola have created a new joint venture to market canned liquid coffee in South Korea. The product carries the name Nescafe, can be served either hot or cold, and comes in "rich" and "regular" flavors. It will be promoted as an alternative to carbonated soft drinks, and the Coca-Cola brand name is not featured on the product.

Nestle and Coca-Cola will be very tough competitors in South Korea. Nestle is a well-known firm, thanks to its heavy promotion of its traditional Nescafe coffee. Coke has a strong distribution system that will get the new product into every convenience store in the country. "Oh sure, we will carry Nescafe," says 7-Eleven manager So-Chung Sub. "We will have to because we have Coke; the Coke salesman will make sure of that." In addition, the joint venture has installed 2,700 vending machines that will serve both hot and cold Nescafe.

The advertising campaign for Nescafe canned liquid coffee was created by a well-known U.S advertising firm, McCann-Erickson. The advertisements feature traditional Korean music and a man and a woman who are rushing down a rain-swept street. They notice a Nestle coffee-warming device in a store at the exact same moment. Their eyes meet and they flirt for just a second and the advertisement states, "It's a coffee moment."

If the product is successful in South Korea, the new joint venture may introduce it in the United States. The product, which tastes like a coffee milkshake, may well appeal to many people in America.

Some businesses promote their products through personal selling—that is, through direct face-to-face interaction between a salesperson and the customer. Avon sells its cosmetic products this way. However, most makers of consumer products rely on advertising to reach their markets. In addition, they may supplement their advertising with point-of-purchase displays, free samples, and coupons.

Whatever the methods used, the firm must communicate with the public. Otherwise, its products will grow old on the shelf. This is just as true for service organizations as for product manufacturers. Airlines tell the public about new routes, changing ticket prices, and the comfort of their flights. Even the United Way advertises to convey its service messages to the public. Businesses and nonprofit organizations ask themselves many questions. Should we advertise directly to the final consumer, or should we direct advertisements at wholesalers? How much should we spend on advertising? Should we give away free samples? How should we pay salespeople? How should we select new salespeople? What about plant tours and other publicity devices? Chapter 17 examines the major variables that make up the product's promotion strategy.

Marketing Mix Interaction

Just as managers must work together as a team if the firm is to operate efficiently, so must the elements of the marketing mix work together. A decision with respect to one element has an impact on decisions about the others.

Many products fail in the marketplace because the firm does not coordinate its marketing mix decisions. Toyota introduced the Lexus in the fall of 1989. The advertising was well-timed to notify potential customers about Toyota's exciting new luxury car. In contrast, Nissan's new luxury automobile, the Infiniti, was introduced ten weeks after the Lexus, but the advertising for Infiniti was running full-speed months before the new brand was ready for sale. The lack of coordination between the Infiniti's promotional campaign and the availability of the product hurt the sales of the new car significantly.[9]

This type of mistake could have been avoided if the manufacturer had considered the interactions among the marketing mix elements. The firm should have considered some combination of higher price and less promotion in order to control demand until its distribution system was improved.

BUYER BEHAVIOR

Some social critics suggest that corporations have hidden powers of persuasion. The impression given suggests marketing technicians in the employ of corporate giants conducting research on buyer behavior with the cool precision of scientists studying the behavior of laboratory mice. These critics believe that big corporations are able to manipulate the market behavior of people in any way they choose.

It is true that firms do study human behavior, to find out what consumers want and to find better ways to tell buyers about the merits of their products. Keep in mind, however, that people are unpredictable, as suggested by a study done at Purdue University. Researchers asked 264 subjects to rank soft drinks, from their most favorite to their least favorite. A few days later, the same subjects were given a free soft drink sample. They were then asked to come up with a new list of their favorite soft drinks. Surprisingly, more than half of the subjects changed the order of their preferences and put a different soft drink at the top of the list.

Considering the unpredictability of people, it is difficult to argue that marketing managers understand human nature well enough to manipulate the market. On the contrary, the study of buyer behavior is still an inexact science. At its base is the purchase decision process.

Purchase Decision Process

The act of buying is a significant part of everyone's life. It is such a routine activity that we rarely consider in detail the mental process involved in product purchases. Just what are the steps in the purchase decision process? As Figure 13-3 illustrates, buyers usually pass through a five-stage process when they buy a good or service.

- *Stage 1: Problem recognition.* The buyer recognizes a need, desire, or problem. The marketer tries to determine which needs, desires, or problems stimulate the buyer to begin the purchase process.
- *Stage 2: Information search.* The buyer collects information about purchase alternatives. The successful marketer knows the sources of buyer information and their relative importance to the buyer.
- *Stage 3: Alternative evaluation.* The buyer evaluates purchase alternatives in light of various criteria. Since these criteria may differ in each purchase decision, the marketer determines which criteria are appropriate to that decision.
- *Stage 4: Purchase decision.* The buyer selects a product from among the purchase alternatives. Up to this point, the marketer has done as much as possible to influence the buyer to buy his or her product.

FIGURE 13-3   The Purchase Decision Process

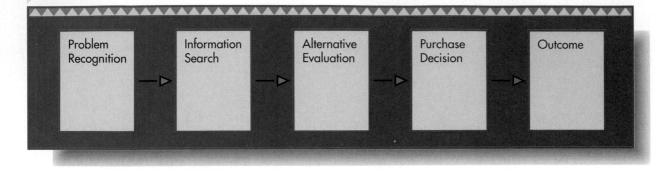

- *Stage 5: Outcome.* The buyer experiences some degree of satisfaction or dissatisfaction with the purchase decision. Knowledge of this satisfaction or dissatisfaction is crucial to the marketer.

Only when this decision process is understood can an effective marketing program be developed. This analysis of the decision process in five distinct stages draws attention to the fact that the buying process begins before the purchase decision is made and continues for a period of time thereafter. Figure 13-4 illustrates the purchase decision process for a new car purchase.

Final Consumer vs. Organizational Buyers

This portion of the chapter has focused on buyer behavior. It is important to understand that there are two types of buyers—final consumers and organizational buyers. **Final consumers** are individuals who purchase products for their own use or for the use of a family member or friend. When you purchase a tomato in the supermarket to eat at home, you are acting as a final consumer. In contrast, an **organizational buyer** purchases products or services that are used to produce other products that are sold or rented to other individuals. The Campbell's Soup production facility in Paris, Texas purchases as much as 70,000 pounds of carrots per day. The purchasing agent for Campbell's is acting as an organizational buyer.

Both final consumers and organizational buyers go through the same mental purchase decision process illustrated in Figure 13-4, but final consumers are more likely to be affected by psychological, social, cultural, and family influences than are professional buyers. For example, a woman purchases an Anne Klein II outfit. Promotional material describes as follows: "A billowy blouse, wide leg pants, and cropped jacket all come together for a casual look of incredible style." The woman who buys it is not just interested in functional clothing. Rather, the style, which is described in more detail by Klein as "sheer brilliance," is important to the final consumer, and the acceptance of such a product is influenced by the consumer's family and friends.

Other differences between consumers and organizational buyers are as follows:

- Organizational buyers purchase more products than consumers.
- Organizational buyers are more technically qualified than consumers.

final consumers   individuals who purchase products, usually in small amounts, for their own use or for the use of a family member or friend.

organizational buyer   an individual who purchases products in large quantities, to be used in the production of other products.

FIGURE 13-4 Automobile Purchase Decision Process

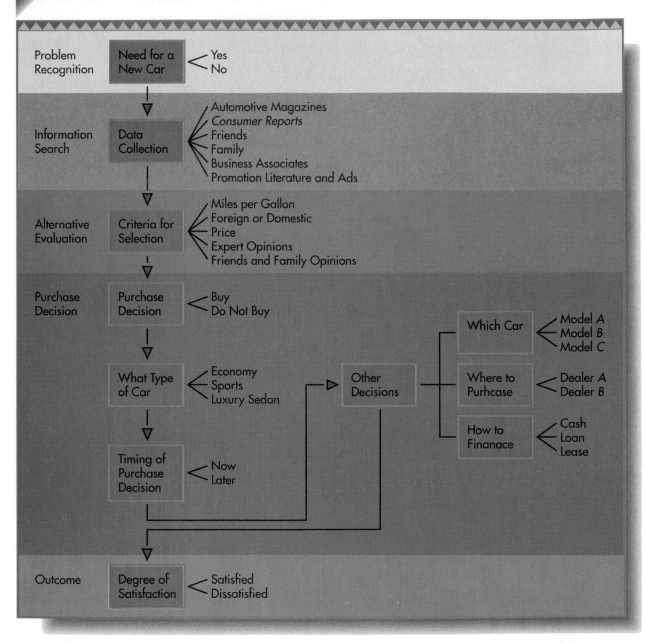

- Organizational buyers work with committees in making purchase decisions for large firms, whereas the consumer often acts alone.
- Organizational buyers follow purchasing policies and requirements that are not used by consumers.
- Organizational buyers tend to be more rational than consumers, since they try to buy products and services that will help their firms make a profit.

Organizational buyers frequently develop personal relationships with their suppliers. However, these relationships flourish only if the supplier is able to provide the buyer with high-quality products, delivered on time and at a competitive price. Organizational buyers realize that the success or failure of their businesses often rests with their skill in purchasing products.

MARKETING RESEARCH

7

marketing research the systematic gathering, recording, and analyzing of data about problems relating to the marketing of goods and services.

Business Career
Market-Research Analyst: Researches market conditions in local, regional, or national area to determine potential sales of product or service. Designs format for data gathering, such as surveys, opinion polls, or questionnaires. Collects data on consumer preferences and buying habits. Analyzes data to forecast marketing trends. *Average Salary: $35,000.*

The American Marketing Association defines **marketing research** as "the systematic gathering, recording, and analyzing of data about problems relating to the marketing of goods and services."[11] Marketing research acts as an intelligence unit for the firm, identifying and solving market-related problems, spotting new product opportunities, tracking the changing composition of the market, and monitoring the legal, social, and economic environment. The right marketing mix decisions depend on accurate research.

This portion of the chapter discusses the uses and limitations of marketing research, as well as one type of information gathering—focus groups.

What Marketing Research Tells the Firm

Business firms conduct marketing research when they have a question that is too important to be answered by guessing alone. Often they conduct research to determine how satisfied their customers are with their products, to estimate future sales, and to study alternative promotional strategies. Although these activities are closely related to each other, it is best to look at them separately.

Examines Customer Satisfaction.   The marketing concept is based on the philosophy that the customer is king. Thus, the firm's marketing executives need to know if the king is happy. Ford Motor Company surveys 2.5 million customers per year to determine their satisfaction with their Ford products. In addition, the company regularly invites owners to meet with engineers and dealers to discuss quality problems.[12]

Evaluates Sales Potential.   As discussed in Chapter 1, a market can be defined as the total number of units of a product sold in a given period of time, such as one year. How big is the market for a particular product? How fast is the market growing? A market can range in size from the highly competitive multibillion-dollar market for personal computers in the United States to the relatively small market for advanced physics textbooks.

Information on the size and growth rate of a market is essential in making the decision to develop a new product. Firms like to enter fast-growing markets. A business also needs to know how many units of its product it can expect to sell. Forecasts based on research of company sales, especially short-range forecasts, tell the firm how much raw material it should order and how many units it should produce. A firm's sales forecast is usually made on the basis of a marketing plan. The greater the level of marketing effort involved in the plan, the higher the expected sales level.

Evaluates Promotional Strategies.   Marketing research can be very effective in determining which advertising messages are most effective. An advertiser may test the effectiveness of different messages by showing a group of people five trial television commercials for its product. The advertiser will pick the best commercial based on the response of the sample group.

Focus Groups

There are several highly structured ways to collect marketing research data. Most of us have responded to mail questionnaires or telephone interviews asking whether we used a product, how satisfied we were with it, how we learned about it, who purchased it, where it was purchased, and the demographic characteristics of the head of the household in which the product was used.

Another type of marketing research tool that works very well is **focus groups.** A small group of people, usually 10 to 20, are asked to participate in an open-ended discussion of a particular subject. The subject might be why they shop at particular stores, what process the family goes through when it buys a new car, or what types of advertisments are the most effective for a bank to use.

The moderator's role is to stimulate discussion, take notes, and try to draw conclusions at the end of the session. The moderator must be very careful not to lead the participants to any specific conclusions.

Focus groups are inexpensive and easy to do. In addition, they tend to produce responses concerning specific problems or marketing opportunities that might not have emerged from more structured marketing research questionnaires. Therefore, focus groups are frequently used to help define a problem that will eventually be investigated by a mail questionnaire or a telephone interview. The biggest problem with focus groups is correctly interpreting the information that has been obtained. The more experienced the moderator is at running focus groups, the easier it is to draw meaningful conclusions from the research.

focus groups   *a method of marketing research in which a small group of people, led by a moderator, are asked to participate in an open-ended discussion of a particular subject regarding buyer behavior.*

Limitations of Marketing Research

Marketing research is concerned with tomorrow. Research findings serve as inputs to business decisions that will change the future course of the firm. Some business executives do not believe in the value of marketing research because the predictions are occasionally wrong. We can think of at least two reasons why such skepticism is not justified.

First, marketing research is concerned with the behavior of people in the market. It aims to forecast future behavior based on current behavior. But even the most powerful marketing research tools allow us to understand only a small part of human behavior, since people are very complex and often change their minds.

Second, the uncontrollable factors that affect business change all the time. A prediction based on one set of assumptions about the future may turn out to be wrong if any single assumption is incorrect. Imagine a five-year forecast of the number of new housing starts in the United States, based on a 9 percent mortgage interest rate. Now, let's assume that the government, in an attempt to slow inflation, adopts a tight credit policy. As a result, the mortgage rate climbs to 13 percent, and fewer families can buy houses. Thus, a forecast based on the 9 percent interest rate would overstate the actual number of housing starts at the 13 percent rate.

We must remember that the purpose of marketing research is to reduce the risk of making a bad decision. It is not possible to eliminate this risk completely. But the more timely, accurate, and relevant the information provided by the marketing research staff, the better the resulting business decisions will be.

THE MARKETING CONCEPT AND NONPROFIT ORGANIZATIONS

This chapter has examined a broad set of marketing issues: the marketing concept, market segmentation, uncontrollable environmental variables, the marketing mix, buyer behavior, and marketing research. Many people assume that these concepts are applicable only to the selling of products and services on a for-profit basis. But they can also help managers of nonprofit organizations market their services to the public.

Nonprofit institutions, such as hospitals, colleges and universities, and charities, all face marketing problems. Consider the college that you attend. First, it must address basic issues of market segmentation. Is it a four-year or a two-year college? If it is a two-year college, is it trying to attract students who want to complete a two-year basic education and then transfer to a four-year college or university? Or do its students want a two-year vocational program that will allow them to enter the job market with an associate's degree?

The second marketing factor that must be examined is the uncontrollable environmental factors that affect the college. The school must examine the demographics of the market that it serves. Is the number of students increasing or decreasing? What is the average age of the potential student body, and is it likely to change in the near future? Is the state, and/or the community, providing adequate financial support?

Third, your college faces four basic questions about the marketing mix. Price: How high should tuition be? Promotion: How should the college tell the public about its curriculum? Distribution: Where should it teach courses? Product: What courses should it teach?

Fourth, the college must also understand the purchase decision process. Problem recognition: How do students recognize the need to enroll in college? Information search: Where do students get their information about various colleges? Alternative evaluation: How do they compare colleges? Once the prospective college student selects an institution of higher education (purchase decision), how does the college or university measure whether or not the student has had a successful academic experience (outcome)?

Finally, a college needs to do marketing research. It should examine student records to determine where its students live, their age distribution, and their ethnic background. It may also survey the community to find out what courses should be taught and whether they should be taught during the day or in the evening.

Both for-profit and nonprofit organizations need to understand the importance of marketing. If they do not take marketing seriously, they may not accomplish their mission.

KEY TERMS

marketing 339
utility 339
time utility 339
place utility 339
macromarketing 339
marketing concept 342
market segmentation 344
market segment 344

SUMMARY POINTS

1 Marketing is "the process of planning and executing the conception, pricing, promotion, and distribution of ideas, goods, and services to create exchanges that satisfy individual and organizational objectives." Marketing executives are also actively involved in deciding which products are brought to the marketplace.

2 Macromarketing is the study of how goods and services are distributed from buyers to sellers. The information function links buyers and sellers together in a continuous back-and-forth pattern. The inventory function helps equate supply and demand. The exchange function stimulates efficiencies in distribution by bringing buyers and sellers together at one place. The routine transaction function creates standardized techniques that permit products to be sold in an efficient manner.

3 The marketing concept is a contemporary philosophy that marketing is a customer-oriented activity based on three principles: customer satisfaction, belief in competitive substitutes, and concern with profit rather than sales.

4 Successful marketing includes a strategic plan that identifies the market segment at which the firm is aiming its product or service, examines environmental factors beyond the control of the organization that will affect on the sale of the product or service, and blends the four primary marketing mix variables into a strategy that will permit the firm to meet its objectives. Market segments are the limited group of consumers that the firm is trying to reach with its product. The strategic market plan must include how the firm will deal with uncontrollable factors, including competition, demographic changes, the state of the economy, social trends, and technological changes.

5 Every marketing strategy is made up of four marketing mix decision areas: product, distribution, price, and promotion. Product decisions involve developing products that consumers are willing to purchase. Distribution decisions focus on where the product is sold, how it is delivered, and by whom. The pricing questions relate to how much to charge for the product, and the promotion area includes all techniques that

are available to the firm to communicate to its customers about its products.

6 The purchase decision process is composed of five stages: problem recognition, information search, alternative evaluation, purchase decision, and outcome. Final consumers purchase products for themselves or their families, whereas organizational buyers purchase products that are used to produce other items. Organizational buyers are more rational, more technically qualified, work more with buying committees, and are more likely to follow specific purchasing procedures than are final consumers.

7 Marketing research acts as an intelligence unit for the firm, identifying and solving market-related problems, spotting new product opportunities, tracking the changing composition of the market, and monitoring the legal, social, and economic environment. This research faces certain limitations, including the unpredictability of human behavior and the changes that inevitably take place in the uncontrollable environmental factors.

8 Marketing is as valuable a tool for nonprofit organizations as it is for profit-making institutions. It helps the nonprofit group focus on specific market segments, identify uncontrollable environmental factors that will affect the organization, and make marketing mix decisions. Marketing can also help nonprofit organizations understand the decision-making process that potential users of their services will go through.

REVIEW QUESTIONS

1 Is marketing limited to advertising and selling? **1**

2 How does marketing create time and place utility? **2**

3 What is meant by macromarketing, and what are its four key functions? **2**

4 What is the marketing concept? **3**

5 What is the rationale for market segmentation? **4**

6 Differentiate between demographic segmentation and benefit segmentation. **4**

7 How do uncontrollable environmental factors affect a firm's ability to market its products? **4**

8 What are the four elements of the marketing mix, and what does each contribute to the marketing decision? **5**

9 What are the five steps in the purchase decision process? **6**

10 Do final consumers and organizational buyers go through the same mental process when purchasing products? Explain. **6**

11 What does marketing research tell the firm or organization? **7**

12 What are the major limitations to marketing research? **7**

13 What role does marketing play for nonprofit organizations? **8**

DISCUSSION QUESTIONS

1 Should a firm be more concerned with profits or with sales? Explain.

2 What is the value of coordinating the firm's marketing mix? Give an example of how you would coordinate the marketing mix for inexpensive cordless telephones.

3 Are firms able to manipulate the buying behavior of their customers? Why or why not?

4 Why do some firms decide not to do any formal marketing research?

5 How can marketing be applied to nonprofit organizations?

EXPERIENTIAL EXERCISES

1 Interview the manager of your college bookstore. Does the manager embrace the marketing concept? What market segments is the bookstore trying to serve? Has the bookstore done any formal market research to understand the needs of its customers? What are the uncontrollable environmental factors that affect the store's business?

2 Ask ten to twenty of your classmates to meet outside of class to participate in a focus group session. The focus group should examine the quality and number of services that your college is providing to its students. When you are finished, ask to meet with the Dean of Students to discuss the results of your research.

CASES

Case 13-1
Blockbuster Video

Blockbuster Video created its industry in the same way that McDonald's created the fast-food industry. Prior to Blockbuster, most video stores were small, seedy, rental shops. In contrast, Blockbuster stores are like supermarkets. They are well-lit, attractive, and conveniently located. Their selection of tapes ranges from classic Groucho Marx to CPR techniques to current hit movies. Blockbuster stores have approximately 8,000 titles, all easily accessible, even to the first-time Blockbuster customer. Blockbuster introduced rapid computerized check-out, and its friendly staff are always knowledgable about current and classic movies. The stores do not have a porno section, because it would not be consistent with the family orientation that Blockbuster strives for.

Blockbuster's growth has been nothing short of spectacular. The company opened its first store in 1985, and five years later it was operating 1,582 retail outlets, of which 787 were owned by Blockbuster and 795 were franchised. Blockbuster opens a new store every 17 hours.

Blockbuster's management feels that the company will continue to grow rapidly, increasing its 11 percent share of the video market by opening 400 stores a year for the foreseeable future. Independent market analysts are not so sure. They say that Blockbuster's growth has largely paralleled the spread of the VCR. More than 65 million VCRs were sold between 1984 and 1990, and approximately 70 percent of the households in the United States now have at least one VCR. It is unreasonable to believe that the sale of VCRs will continue at such a rapid pace. In addition, new technology, including 150-channel fiber-optic cable systems, may be a reality in a few years. Such systems will need to show a great many movies if they are to fill up the channels. This could affect Blockbuster's business.

Blockbuster, like McDonald's, now has a number of major competitors. Retail stores such as Turtle's, Movietime, Tower Video, and Video Factory offer a large number of videotapes in attractive, convenient locations. The United States has more than 28,000 video stores and the biggest markets are saturated. Although Blockbuster introduced the three-night, three-dollar rental price, which has been very popular with customers who are late returning their videos, the firm has not had to face a major price war. Unfortunately for Blockbuster, as the number of competitors has increased, there has been a natural tendency to drop the price of rental videos. Supermarkets have led this change with $1.50 videos and even 99-cent one-night specials.

Blockbuster is looking for new products and new services that will help it sustain the growth that it experienced during the second half of the 1980s and into the 1990s. It is test-marketing film processing in some stores and the sale of compact disks and audio tapes in others. However, it is quite clear that the firm feels that its future is tied to the videotape.

1. What are the uncontrollable environmental factors that may make it difficult for Blockbuster to sustain its past level of growth?
2. Does Blockbuster believe in the marketing concept?
3. What market segment does Blockbuster focus most of its attention on?
4. What are the future growth markets for Blockbuster?

Reprinted by permission of *The Wall Street Journal* © 1991 Dow Jones & Company, Inc. All Rights Reserved Worldwide.

Case 13-2
Frito-Lay

The potato chip market is booming in the United States. The average American eats over six pounds of potato chips a year. More than $4 billion was spent on potato chips in 1991. George Rosenbaum, a marketing consultant from Chicago, said, "Young people are learning to graze on potato chips, the way cows eat grass."

Frito-Lay, which is a division of PepsiCo, has over 35 percent of the market for potato chips, up from approximately 25 percent in 1981. The firm has 10,000 salespeople, each of whom sells the firm's 85 varieties of potato chips and monitors the market. If a competitor such as Borden introduces a new flavor, or if there is a shortage of Frito-Lay potato chips, the home office will know about it in a matter of hours, if not minutes.

Frito-Lay is obsessed with product and market research. The firm spends between $20 and $30 million on research each year, even though the firm's advertising budget is decreasing as a percentage of sales. It has a $40,000 aluminum simulated mouth, which measures the jaw pressure that it takes to crunch a potato chip. Quality-control engineers constantly measure the thickness of chips, to 36 thousands of an inch. Other engineers test the 50 chemical compounds that are found in every potato chip. Frito-Lay develops 24 new flavors of potato chips each year. They are tested by more than 6,000 consumers; on the average, only six of them will reach the market.

Frito-Lay has segmented the market for its potato chips. Consumer research shows that Lay's Potato Chips consumers are seen as "affectionate, irresistible, casual, and a fun member of the family." Advertisements for Lay's Potato Chips show puppies, flowers, streams, and a couple exchanging wedding vows. In contrast, Ruffles Potato Chips buyers were found to be "expressive, aware, confident enough to make a personal statement." Their advertisements illustrate a man and his new BMW, wind-surfers, and a woman exercising in a fashionable outfit.

Frito-Lay is very concerned about the health movement. One ounce of potato chips has 150 calories and 10 grams of fat (or 14 percent of the recommended daily allowance). Michael Jacobson, who is with the Center for Science in the Public Interest, says, "As a vegetable, the best thing you can say about the potato chip is it's better than ketchup."

Frito-Lay has reduced the amount of salt in its products significantly. The company is heavily promoting its new Lite Ruffles chips. This new product uses one third less vegetable oil than regular Ruffles. The firm has found that if it reduces the oil any further, the chips taste lousy. Research has shown that consumers will not trade taste for health in snack foods.

Frito-Lay portrays its products as just a little naughty. In 1966, a line was introduced on Frito-Lay potato chip packages and can still be found there today: "Betcha Can't Eat Just One." Frito-Lay spends a great deal of money on developing just the right packages for its products. It used focus groups to test 1,000 shades of blue to find the right bold, cheerful color for its Ruffles packages.

Potato chips were first made for Cornelius Vanderbilt, the railroad magnate, in 1853—as a joke. Vanderbilt might have done better investing his money in potato chips than railroads.

1.   Has Frito-Lay adopted the marketing concept?
2.   Do you believe that the firm's segmentation strategy is appropriate for the market?
3.   How important is the healthy food movement to Frito-Lay?
4.   Do you approve of the line on the package for Frito-Lay potato chips that says, "Betcha Can't Eat Just One"?

CHAPTER 14

Product Management

OBJECTIVES

After studying this chapter, you should be able to:

1 Discuss the classification of consumer products.

2 Explain the differences between the five types of industrial products.

3 Examine the special characteristics of services.

4 Explain the product mix.

5 Discuss the stages of the product life cycle and how this concept benefits marketing managers.

6 Analyze what is new about a new product and why firms develop new products.

7 Explain the process of developing new products and what makes a new product successful.

8 Discuss the importance of branding and the features of a good brand name.

9 Describe the functions of packaging.

In 1984, Mobil Oil's Hefty trash bags had a hefty 23 percent of the market for plastic waste bags, second only to Glad. However, the firm came under tremendous pressure and criticism that year from environmentalists and supermarket operators. The complaint was that Hefty bags were damaging the environment because plastics are not degradable.

The results of Mobil consumer research were very clear. Consumers wanted degradable trash bags that did not cost any more than traditional bags. Mobil modified its bags in 1989 with an ingredient that would make them 25 to 40 percent more degradable when exposed to the sun. The new Hefty packages told consumers that Hefty bags were now "degradable" if they were exposed "to elements like sun, wind, and rain."

Everything looked great for Mobil until the Environmental Defense Fund called for a boycott of many degradable products, including the Hefty trash bag. They stated that since most trash bags end up being buried in landfills, the elements don't reach them, so degradation is limited. Even though Mobil quickly abandoned its claims of degradability, the company was sued by several state attorneys general for consumer fraud and false advertising. The Minnesota Attorney General said, "Unfortunately, Mobil's advertising claims break down faster than their garbage bags."

Mobil has refused to settle the cases. It feels that it acted in good faith. The firm does admit that "environmental issues are extremely sensitive" and that "today's answer may not be tomorrow's answer."[1]

Product management is one of the most exciting and fast-moving areas in business. Firms that do not focus attention on how existing products are managed, as well as on the development of new products, may well find that they are no longer competitors in the marketplace.

A few years ago, marketing people had relatively little to do with product development. Engineers designed products; marketers sold them. For firms that have adopted the marketing concept, this has changed. Now marketers work together with designers to develop products that are closely matched to the needs of the market. The new goal is to make products that meet customers' needs and are easy to sell. We'll begin our discussion of product management by looking at how marketers classify their products.

PRODUCT CLASSIFICATION

 Different kinds of products are marketed in different ways. How products are classified tells us a lot about how they can be marketed. Product classification recognizes that people buy a product for various reasons. This is why it is said that a product is more than the sum of its physical attributes. A product classification also involves consideration of servicing, warranties, and delivery terms, as well as the important image attributes of prestige, reputation, and perceived quality. In a product classification, buyer perceptions are just as important as the manufacturer's specifications.

The most basic distinction is between consumer products and industrial products, because they are marketed in different ways. Since we are more familiar with consumer products, we will begin our discussion with them.

Consumer Products

consumer products
goods produced for sale to individuals and families for personal consumption.

Consumer products are goods produced for sale to individuals and families for personal consumption. Consumer products are further classified as convenience goods, shopping goods, or specialty goods. Table 14-1 lists the differences among them in terms of replacement rate, shopping time, profitability, distribution, and sales techniques.

convenience goods *consumer goods that are purchased frequently, immediately, and with little shopping effort.*

Convenience Goods.   **Convenience goods** are purchased frequently, immediately, and with little shopping effort. The cost for the consumer of making price and quality comparisons is much greater than the benefits that would result from

TABLE 14-1   Characteristics of Convenience, Shopping, and Specialty Goods

Characteristics	Convenience Goods	Shopping Goods	Specialty Goods
Example	Milk, Candy Bars	Refrigerators, Vacuum Cleaners	Expensive China and Jewelry
Replacement Rate	Frequently Purchased	Occasionally Purchased	Seldom Purchased
Searching Time	Low; First Available Product Is Purchased	Significant; Customer Analyzes Characteristics of Several Brands	Customer Looks for a Particular Brand
Per-Unit Profit	Low	Moderate	High
Distribution	Many Retailers	Several Retailers	Few Retailers
Sales Techniques	Mass Advertising	Mass Advertising and Personal Selling	Highly Trained Sales Force

such comparisons. Some examples of convenience goods are milk, magazines, soap, and cigarettes.

The key to marketing convenience goods successfully is availability. Most people buy convenience goods at the nearest store. This is why Southland Corporation has more than 7,000 7-Eleven stores. Southland's strategy is to make it as convenient as possible for people to shop at one of their outlets.

Convenience goods are sold primarily by mass advertising, not by personal attention or sales technique. When people buy milk or cigarettes, they don't ask the clerk which brand is best. They realize that the sales clerk's job is to take their money, not to give them advice on such products.

Convenience retailers must keep in mind that other nearby stores sell the same products. Pricing is about the only way for such

Before gasoline can be sold as a consumer product, crude oil (an industrial product) must be refined.

retailers to differentiate their merchandise from that of the competition across the street or down the block. People tend to be price conscious when they shop for convenience goods. If the price of aspirin, potato chips, or masking tape is too high, the store may lose business to a nearby competitor. Accordingly, the profit margin on convenience goods is quite small. **Profit margin** is the difference between a product's cost and its selling price.

Shopping Goods.   In the case of **shopping goods,** the buyer actively considers price, quality, style, and value before making a purchase decision. The buyer believes that the benefits of an intelligent purchase decision are worth the extra shopping effort. Examples of shopping goods are refrigerators, microwave ovens, vacuum cleaners, and stereo equipment.

Selling shopping goods successfully depends on retail advertising and personal selling. The retailer must tell the public which brands it carries. Salespeople should be able to explain the advantages and disadvantages of the various brands. Since customers rely on this information, it is essential for the retailer of shopping goods to have a good sales staff.

Shopping goods are usually marketed through a combination of the manufacturer's advertising and the salesperson's efforts. A manufacturer runs expensive national advertising campaigns on television or in magazines to tell people why they should purchase its products. Ford's advertisements for its Thunderbird SC focus on the following product features: "one of the most powerful production engines," five-speed overdrive transmission, ride control system, and four-wheel anti-lock disc brakes, as well as sleek exterior and bucket seats. The advertisements' theme is, "Parking is such sweet sorrow."

profit margin   the difference between a product's cost and its selling price.

shopping goods   consumer goods for which the buyer actively considers price, quality, style, and value before making a purchase decision.

As a percentage of selling price, the profit on shopping goods is usually much higher than it is on convenience goods. The retailer needs a higher profit margin in order to cover the costs of more expensive sales staffs, store fixtures, and advertising budgets required to sell shopping goods.

Specialty Goods.

specialty goods *consumer goods for which shoppers are willing to make a special shopping effort; these goods generally command brand loyalty.*

Specialty goods are products for which shoppers are willing to make a "special" shopping effort. Whether a product is a specialty good or not depends on whether shoppers know which brand they would buy before actually feeling the need to purchase the product. If the next watch you intend to buy is a Rolex—even though you have no intention of buying a watch now—then a Rolex watch is a specialty good for you. Specialty goods command brand loyalty. It is important for manufacturers of specialty goods to select retailers that will present their products properly. Specialty goods are promoted on the basis of product quality, reliability, and image. Thus, the image of the retailer should be consistent with the image of the product.

Profit margins are quite high for specialty goods, because competition among retailers tends to be limited. Relatively few stores in a given community sell the same specialty goods. In addition, people who can afford expensive specialty goods are usually more concerned about buying the "right" product than about price.

Industrial Products

2

industrial products
goods and services sold to private businesses or public agencies, to be used in turn to produce other goods and services.

Industrial products are goods and services sold to private businesses or public agencies; these organizations then use them to produce their goods and services. The buyers of these goods are not final consumers, but professional purchasing agents. The market for industrial goods includes utility companies, manufacturing firms, contractors, mining firms, wholesalers, and retailers, as well as local, state, and federal governments. Examples of industrial goods are iron ore, petrochemical products, cleaning fluids, machine tools, and computers for office use.

What makes the selling of industrial goods unique? First, most industrial goods are sold by salespeople who call on buyers in their places of business. Second, mass advertising is generally limited to trade journals such as *Hardware Age* or *Milling Record,* which are read by people in specific industries. Third, the markets for industrial goods are more concentrated than the markets for consumer goods. There are about 250 million people and 93 million households in the United States, but only 18 million businesses.[2] Organizations within an industry tend to cluster in certain parts of the country. The automobile industry is centered in Detroit; the apparel industry, in New York City and South Carolina. Finally, purchase decisions are often made by teams or committees, not by individuals. There are five major types of industrial products: installations, accessories, raw materials, components, and supplies.

Installations.

installations *industrial products that are major capital items, such as buildings and expensive pieces of equipment.*

Major capital items such as buildings and expensive pieces of equipment are called **installations.** The buyer can expect to earn a profit on an installation if it is operated in a cost-efficient manner. For example, IBM dramatically expanded its Austin, Texas manufacturing facility so that it could efficiently produce the new RISC System/6000 line of computer workstations.

Accessories.

accessories *industrial products, including tools or equipment, that have a fairly short life and are used in the production of a firm's products or in its offices.*

Tools or equipment that have a fairly short life and are used in the production of a firm's products or in its offices are called **accessories.** For example, IBM computers that are used to control production systems and design new products are accessories. Other examples include Xerox copying machines, Hewlett-Packard calculators, and General Electric diamond-cutting tools. The final purchase decision concerning an installation is usually made by the firm's senior management, but accessories are routinely purchased by purchasing agents or other mid-level managers.

Raw Materials.   **Raw materials** are inexpensive, unprocessed items, such as wheat, sugar cane, coal, and iron ore, that become a physical part of the product that the firm is producing. Producers of well-known high-quality products must have access to high-quality raw materials if they are to produce the products that their customers expect. For example, Smucker's could not produce excellent jams without using use high-quality berries. Therefore, buyers of raw materials often sign long-term contracts with suppliers to ensure that they will have access to the supplier's output.

> ***raw materials***   *industrial products that are inexpensive, unprocessed items that become a physical part of the product the firm is producing.*

Components.   Expensive processed items that become part of the finished product are called **components.** Disk drives for computers and electric motors for refrigerators are examples of components. The market for components is frequently highly competitive and the profit margins low.

> ***components***   *industrial products that are expensive, processed items that become a physical part of the product the firm is producing.*

Supplies.   **Supplies** are items that are used in the production of a product but do not become part of the product. Maintenance supplies include items such as light bulbs and paint. Repair supplies consist of items such as filters, bearings, and gears for the production equipment. Operating supplies include lubricating oils, typing paper, paper clips, and electricity. Supplies are important to the success of the firm, but they are usually not vital to its immediate continued operations. Therefore, when the firm is trying to cut costs, orders for supplies are frequently the first to be cut back.[3]

> ***supplies***   *industrial products that are used in the production of a product but do not become part of the product, such as maintenance supplies.*

WHAT ABOUT SERVICES?

A product can be characterized as a tangible object or device, whereas a **service** is an intangible deed or performance. The purchase of a refrigerator is the acquisition of a product, but the purchase of a maintenance agreement secures a service to make sure that the refrigerator works properly. There are many examples of services in the public and private sectors. Henry Cisneros, who is profiled on page 371, has been successful because he understands the importance of providing consistently high-quality services to his clients. Cisneros first demonstrated this as mayor of San Antonio and then translated his drive for excellence into a highly successful privately owned company that provides asset management, communications, and insurance services.

> ***service***   *intangible deed or performance.*

In addition to intangibility, services have three other characteristics that differentiate them from products. These characteristics are examined in the next three subsections.

Services Cannot Be Inventoried

Products are manufactured, inventoried, and then sold; businesses keep products in inventory to meet future demand. In contrast, services are produced and then consumed immediately. The electric company provides electricity when it is used. Since a service cannot be inventoried, sellers of services must be concerned with

Freeze-Dried Pets

Andrew Dachisen is touting the virtues of a bull terrier poised motionless atop a workbench. The terrier is just about as undemanding as a pet can be. "You don't have to feed him, you don't have to worry about him going on the rug, and you don't have to worry about him barking at the neighbors," Dachisen says.

But you do have to dust him occasionally with a hair dryer. He is all dog, but he is also dead—and freeze-dried.

The terrier, a specimen owned by the American Kennel Club, is a fine example of state-of-the-art taxidermy, and Dachisen is a taxidermist. A bear rug at the foot of his $25,000 freeze-dryer lends a homey touch to Mr. Dachisen's workshop, where he is currently freeze-drying a German shepherd, as well as a deer, a red fox, a gray fox, a wood duck, a mink, a squirrel, and some fish.

Used during World War II to preserve plasma, freeze-drying is giving a boost to the profession of taxidermy. The taxidermists aren't freeze-drying only game and other wild animals, but also departed household pets for their bereaved owners. Taxidermist Nick Coppola says that with freeze-drying, "you don't have to worry what happened to Spot. Spot is right there on the pillow."

Coppola's most exotic job was to have been the freeze-drying of a sacred mongoose kept by an Indian resident of New York. But the customer decided that the process "would freeze the spirit out." Coppola advertises his service as "eternalizing" pets and other animals—or parts of them. He was recently given a heap of deer feet to be eternalized as coat hooks.

peak loads and excess capacity, because fluctuations in demand cannot be met by adjusting inventory.

Buyers Are Dependent on Sellers

When a seller transfers title to a product, the buyer has control over it. In contrast, the purchase of a service does not involve transfer of ownership. Consumption of the service is not possible without the participation of the seller, whether the

The services of this tour guide enhance his clients' enjoyment of the Greek Theater at Taormina, Italy.

Henry G. Cisneros

Ask residents of San Antonio, Texas, to cite examples of outstanding public service, and their response is likely to include "Henry." Henry G. Cisneros served as mayor of San Antonio from 1981 to 1989. During his tenure, the dynamic Cisneros promoted his city to leaders on the national and international stage. He has always seemed equally comfortable conversing with heads of state, presidents of major corporations, or employees at the local cafe. Cisneros is fondly known by his many admirers as simply "Henry."

Cisneros is a product of San Antonio's predominately Hispanic west side. He was the first of five children born to George Cisneros, an Air Force reserve officer, and Elvira Cisneros. Mrs. Cisneros gave her children an appreciation of their hometown by attending cultural and educational events. She planned daily creative ventures to ensure that the youngsters gained an understanding of San Antonio's arts and cultural opportunities. Young Henry and his siblings developed a deep affection for the San Antonio community and its heritage.

During his terms of office, Cisneros showed a keen desire to give something back to his hometown. He worked tirelessly to bring the 300-year-old city of San Antonio to the cutting edge among 20th-century communities. His first act as mayor was to seek ways in which city government could encourage the formation of a network of daycare providers. The issue spoke directly to the quality of life of San Antonio's citizenry, like many issues adopted by Mayor Cisneros: tax-exempt bonds for affordable housing; a municipal "Environmental Court" to tackle such problems as weedy lots, junk vehicles, run-down structures, and noise violations; and expansion and improvements of the city's police and fire departments.

As he worked to improve daily living in San Antonio, the mayor also directed the city's economic development toward biotechnology, high technology, finance, and tourism. The city attracted such firms as Advanced Micro Devices, the VTI-VLSI computer chip manufacturing plant, Nippon Colin Electronics, Signtech Corporation, and the Catalogue Communications Center of Sears Roebuck.

To promote tourism, Mayor Cisneros worked to renovate the city's historic central shopping district, expand the convention center, to build a domed multipurpose facility, and to get Sea World of Texas to locate in San Antonio.

Cisneros left municipal government in 1989. Since then, his public service has broadened and diversified. He has emerged as a leader of the nation's growing Hispanic population, which the 1990 census estimated to total about 22.4 million. The former San Antonio mayor heads the National Hispanic Leadership Agenda, an organization that aims to assemble a platform for future presidential elections.

Cisneros's career interests also focus on service. He now oversees the Cisneros Group, which has three components: Cisneros Communications, Cisneros Benefit Group (an independent insurance agency), and Cisneros Asset Management Company. Although his company demands a great deal of his time, Cisneros remains committed to his civic agenda. He is Chairman of the National Civic League and serves on the board of the Enterprise Foundation, an organization that provides housing and services to low-income families. He also volunteers time to many other worthy organizations.

Asked if he would run again for public office, Cisneros responded, "Yes, but only if I can make a difference." A city report summarizes Cisneros's contribution to San Antonio: "He has raised our aspirations—and it is for this that he will be best remembered."

Sources: S. Harrigan, "Cisneros at Forty," *Texas Monthly,* September 1987, pp. 87–91, 134–142; *The Cisneros Years,* City of San Antonio Report, April 1989.

seller is a public utility, a lawyer, or a football team. CBS paid $1 billion to the National Football League for the right to broadcast games from 1990 to 1993. CBS does everything in its power to produce a high-quality show and to make the experience as entertaining as possible. There are special pregame, postgame, and halftime segments, staffed by articulate announcers and former football players and coaches. CBS realizes that if it is going to make a profit on its $1 billion investment, it must provide a total entertainment package for the consumer.

Performance Standards Are Difficult to Maintain

Finally, except for a few machine-intensive service industries such as automated telephone systems, it is very difficult to maintain uniform performance standards for services. The quality of service varies not only among firms in the same industry, but also from one transaction of a firm to the next. The basic reason for such variation in quality is that service industries are people-intensive. Sam Barshop, Chairman of La Quinta Motor Inns, stated, "The reason we invest so much time and money on our live-in, on-site management team is that these individuals are responsible for ensuring that our rooms are always immaculate and our customers are treated in a warm and friendly manner. The bottom line is that in our business there is no substitute for a hard-working local management team that is dedicated to meeting our quality-control standards."

PRODUCT MIX

product item   an individual product (either a good or a service).

product line   a group of related products.

product mix   all the product lines that a firm sells.

A **product item** is an individual product, which can be a good or a service. Gillette produces a single-edge razor, a double-edge razor, a twin-blade razor, and an adjustable twin-blade razor. Each of these is a separate product item. A **product line** is a group of related product items. All of Gillette's razor products together represent one product line. The *depth* of a product line refers to the number of items making up a line.

The **product mix** consists of all the product lines that a firm sells. Gillette's product mix includes shavers, replacement blades, shaving creams, deodorants, lighters, hair and skin care products, writing instruments, correction fluid, travel clocks, and oral care products. Normally, a firm will try to maintain a certain consistency among the products in its mix, so that customers will associate new items with the firm's reputation in that area. In the case of Gillette, many of its product lines involve personal-care products.

The firm must continually analyze its product mix, product lines, and product items. Most executives realize that consumers' attitudes and perceived needs change rapidly. If they do not carefully monitor their markets to create new products, or modify existing products to meet changing needs, both sales and profits will soon fall dramatically. Even though Gillette already dominated the non-electric, refillable razor market, it introduced a new product to that market—the Sensor razor. Gillette hoped that the Sensor would help maintain or expand the firm's market share well into the 1990s.

product life cycle   a marketing concept that the life of any product passes through the stages of introduction, growth, maturity, and decline before disappearing from the market.

PRODUCT LIFE CYCLE

The **product life cycle** is another important concept in marketing. The basic idea is that products pass through several stages from the time they are introduced to the market to the time they disappear. We will analyze a four-stage model of the product life cycle. Then we will look at what the model has to say about how products should be marketed.

Stages in the Product Life Cycle

Research has shown that most products move through four separate stages, as shown in Figure 14-1. First, the product is introduced into the market, and sales increase slowly. Sales begin to pick up during the second stage, as more people discover the product. In the third stage, sales rise and fall with the health of the economy. The fourth stage arrives when people begin to switch to new products. Eventually, the product is no longer profitable and is taken off the market. Figure 14-2 shows the current stage of the life cycle for several types of products.

Introduction.   In the **introduction stage,** a product is truly new, and a market usually does not yet exist for it. During this time, there is little or no direct competition. Therefore, the firm's primary objective during the introduction stage of the product life cycle is to develop a market for the product—that is, to attract a sufficient number of customers to make product introduction and development feasible. Without this, it is difficult to justify spending money for further product research and development and for the creation of a long-term distribution structure. However, most products, even successful ones, lose money at first, because of high production and marketing costs.

introduction stage   the first stage in the product life cycle, when a product is truly new, a market usually does not as yet exist, and competition is scarce.

In the early 1990s, flushable cat litter was in the introduction stage. Catsanova advertised its Scoop Away brand extensively, in an attempt to develop a market for the product

FIGURE 14-1   The Product Life Cycle

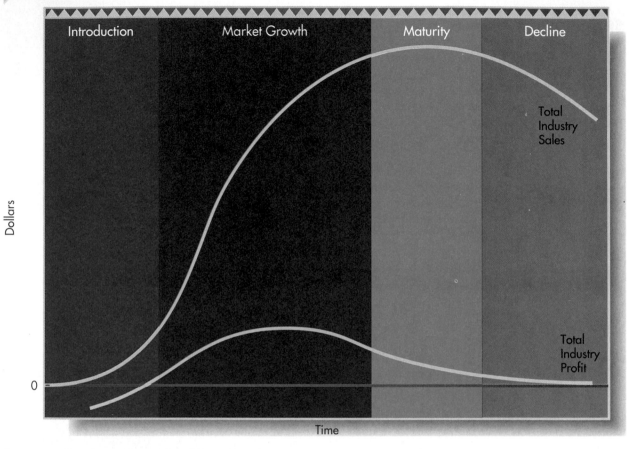

market growth stage
the second stage in the product life cycle, which is characterized by rapid sales increase, supply that falls short of demand, and eventually intense competition.

Market Growth.   Product sales increase rapidly at the beginning of the **market growth stage,** as the product catches on in the market. Other firms introduce competing products, but industry supply still falls short of demand. This helps keep the price of the product high during early market growth. If costs are kept under control, profits can rise rapidly. Smart firms establish strong distribution networks during this stage.

Competition begins to stiffen late in the market growth stage. Firms slash prices, offer more product options, cut delivery time, and redesign packaging—all in an attempt to increase their share of the profit pie. Although sales increase throughout the market growth stage, intense competition pushes down profits for the product, as shown in Figure 14-1.

maturity stage   *the third stage in the product life cycle, which is characterized by peaking sales, declining profits, and few entries into the market.*

market share   *the percentage of total industry sales controlled by a firm.*

Maturity.   The **maturity stage** may last a long time. Industry sales hit their highest level during this stage, although profits begin to decline. Weaker firms have left the market. Very few firms enter the market at this point, because a large amount of capital is required and because other firms have a head start.

The basic goal of the firm during the maturity stage is to hold on to **market share**—that is, to maintain its current percentage of industry sales of the product.

FIGURE 14-2   Life Cycles of Various Products

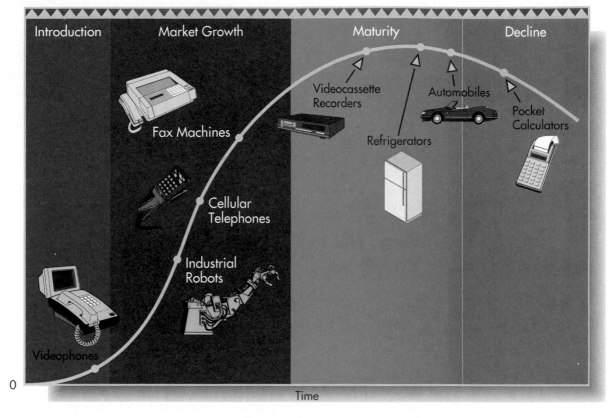

A great year for a "mature" product is a gain of 1 or 2 percent in market share. Profits can still be made during this stage if the economy is strong and the product is selling well. A sales slump, whether induced by a recession or a change in consumer tastes, can wipe out profits entirely.

The automobile is clearly in the maturity stage of its life cycle. Throughout the 1970s, Ford was one of the most profitable companies in the nation. Yet the auto giant lost $1 billion in 1981, when Ford sales dropped 12.1 percent below the 1979 level. In 1988, as a result of economic growth and consumer optimism, Ford once again experienced record sales and profits of $4.7 billion. In 1991, however, the firm lost almost $2 billion as the nation's economy remained in a recession. Sales and profits for firms whose products are in the maturity stage often fluctuate with the general health of the economy.

Decline.   By the time a product enters the **decline stage,** its glamor days are over. Demand for the product has lessened, so there are only enough sales to keep a few firms in the market.

A firm with a product in the decline stage should invest only enough money to keep the production lines running. It does not make sense to buy new high-speed production equipment for a product that may soon disappear from the market. The firm should also try to make as much cash as possible on the product, by keeping it on the market as long as enough demand exists to provide some profit. The goal here is to maximize short-run profits.

decline stage   *the fourth and final period in the product life cycle, which is characterized by lessening demand for the product and few firms in the market.*

Product Life Cycle—a Powerful Tool

The concept of product life cycle can be a useful tool for managers in making marketing decisions. Let's look at three ways in which managers use the life cycle idea.

Forecasting Sales.   One area in which the product life cycle is applied is product sales forecasting. When dot matrix printers were first introduced in the early 1970s, sales skyrocketed. An inexperienced forecaster might have assumed that this high rate of sales growth would continue indefinitely. However, company planners knew that competition from unannounced, undeveloped, or even unimagined new products would reduce the demand for dot matrix printers sooner or later and send them into the maturity stage of the product life cycle. The product that eventually did push the dot matrix printer into the maturity stage was the relatively inexpensive laser printer, introduced in the late 1980s by Hewlett-Packard.

Introducing New Products.   The level of profit for a product depends on how long it has been on the market. As Figure 14-1 indicates, profits are highest in the market growth stage, when the firm and the industry face relatively little competition. Profits they decline in the maturity and decline stages. Therefore, when a product enters the maturity stage, the firm should have another new product ready for the market. The older, more mature product then keeps the firm in business as the new product moves into the profitable stages of its life cycle.

Motorola was one of the first businesses to mass-market cellular telephones in the United States. The firm kept improving its car phone throughout the 1980s with innovations such as programmed dialing, call waiting, and speakerphone options. Each of these product improvements helped keep Motorola among the leading manufacturers of cellular phones. In 1991, Motorola introduced its Cellular One phone, which is no larger than a person's hand, weighs 7.7 ounces, and has a totally self-contained, rechargeable energy system. The user is no longer tied to an automobile or to a cumbersome battery pack.

Extending the Product Life Cycle.   The concept of the product life cycle tells us that a sequence of actions is required to maintain a product's sales and profits. The goal of planning is to stretch out the life of the product, thus keeping it profitable longer.

Figure 14-3 shows an extended life cycle for a product. Notice that at point A, when original uses for the product leveled off, the firm took action to push product sales upward. The firm repeated its product-extension tactics at points B, C, and D, thereby maintaining sales and profits. In effect, the firm pushed the product life cycle curve to the right. The following techniques are often effective in extending a product's life cycle:

1. *New or extended uses.* The sales of rugged four-wheel drive sport-utility vehicles, ranging from relatively inexpensive Jeeps to $40,000 Range Rovers, increased dramatically once they became accepted as family automobiles.[4]
2. *Reduce price and build volume.* Tylenol became a much more successful product after Johnson & Johnson reduced its price.
3. *Increase frequency of use.* Trade associations that are connected to the poultry and fish industries have been successful in informing the public that their

FIGURE 14-3   Extensions of a Product Life Cycle

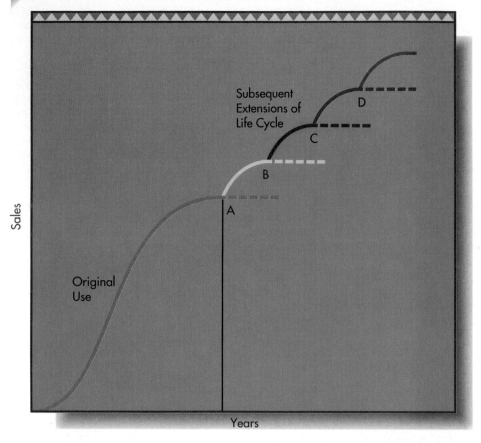

Source: Reprinted by permission of the *Harvard Business Review*. An exhibit from "Exploit the Product Life Cycle" by Theodore Levitt (November/December 1965). Copyright © 1965 by the President and Fellows of Harvard College; all rights reserved.

products are low in cholestrol and should be eaten frequently as part of a healthy diet.

4. *Broaden the target market.* As the Ethical Issue (page 378) indicates, American tobacco firms have successfully enlarged the market for American cigarettes by focusing on Japan. They have also been very successful in expanding the market for tobacco products in Europe and South America.

NEW PRODUCT DEVELOPMENT

The introduction of new products to the market is essential for the survival and financial success of most businesses. Today's profits come from products currently on the market; tomorrow's profits come from products currently on the drawing boards.

When firms run into financial problems, they sometimes reduce the number of people working on new product ideas. In 1992, the American automakers laid off many of their engineers. This move may have been necessary because of their financial crisis, but it will make it harder for them to develop new cars for the future.

The Japanese Market for American Tobacco Products

American tobacco manufacturers have had to deal with a federal government that has placed more and more restrictions on the marketing of tobacco products. The result has been a slow but steady reduction in the amount of tobacco products consumed in the United States. Most of the tobacco firms have responded by diversifying into other consumer products. For example, Phillip Morris, which sells Marlboro, Benson & Hedges, and Virginia Slims, also sells coffee (Maxwell House), Post Cereals, packaged foods (Jell-O, Kraft), and beer (Miller Lite and Lowenbrau).

On the other hand, sales of American-made cigarettes are skyrocketing in Japan. In 1987, U.S.-made cigarettes accounted for less than 3.5 percent of the Japanese market. In 1991, their sales exceeded 15 percent of the market.

Advertisements for American cigarettes in Japan are very professionally done. They normally feature a couple engaged in some type of fun activity, such as riding a motorcycle or singing a song. In contrast, a typical Japanese advertisement shows a man smoking a cigarette by himself.

Partly because of the American-style advertisements, the smoking population in Japan grew by almost 900,000 people in 1990 alone, with women accounting for most of the increase. It does not seem likely that the Japanese government will take any strong steps to reduce the consumption of tobacco. One Japanese health official stated, "In the U.S. and European countries, smokers are a minority. But in our country, smokers are still the majority, so it is difficult to take a compulsory step across the board."

The ethical question is obvious. American tobacco firms are exporting products that most medical experts believe cause cancer, heart disease, and emphysema. No responsible public official has seriously suggested an outright ban on the sale of tobacco products in the U.S. or abroad. But in many people's eyes, it seems unethical to use slick professional advertisements to increase smoking in foreign countries when similar types of advertisements are prohibited in the U.S.

What's "New" About a New Product?

new product *a product that performs a new function for the buyer or represents a significant improvement over existing products.*

A **new product** is one that performs a new function for the buyer. Since relatively few new products are able to do this, we extend the definition to include products that represent a significant improvement over existing products. When Hewlett-Packard introduced the laser printer, the product did not perform a new function. Line printers and dot matrix printers had been displaying computer output for many years. Yet the laser printer was "new," because it represented a significant improvement over existing technologies and products. The information was displayed more quickly and legibly, and the printer was much quieter to operate than the products it replaced.

New products that are priced lower than those already on the market and perceived to be more dependable and more convenient to use are relatively easy to sell. In contrast, complex products, featuring what the public perceives to be unimportant benefits, are harder to sell.

Hewlett-Packard recognized the importance of price, product improvements, and dependability when it introduced its HP DeskJet PLUS printer. The advertisements that appeared in *The Wall Street Journal* stated, "Step up in print quality at a dot matrix price." It went on to say, "No dots. No ragged curves. Just sharp, smooth, laser quality text and graphics" and to proclaim the "first three-year warranty as your assurance of reliability."[5]

Why Introduce New Products?

Businesses introduce new products primarily to earn profits year after year. But there's more to the strategy of new product introduction. We'll now look at three more reasons why there are so many new products on the market.

Achieve Sales Growth Objectives.   Businesses like to see their sales grow at a rate of 10 to 20 percent annually. Sometimes it is easier to meet such ambitious growth objectives by introducing new products than by selling more of the firm's old products. For example, approximately 32 percent of 3M's sales come from products that have been introduced during the past five years.[6]

Match the Competition. When a firm introduces a new product into the market, its competitors are often forced to introduce versions of their own. Companies that are late getting into a market realize that they made a mistake by not seeing the potential of the new product sooner. In much the same way, a firm may choose to enter a market to prevent a competitor from exploiting the market first. In this case, it is the threat of a competitive action that inspires the firm to act.

The chapter-opening vignette describes a situation faced by Mobil Oil. Mobil realized that the market was demanding modification of its Hefty trash bags so that they would be biodegradable. Mobil's competitors were facing

Ethicon, Inc., of Blue Ash, Ohio, has helped pioneer the development of new products for endoscopic surgery. Instead of opening up a large incision in the patient to expose the affected area, the surgeon makes small punctures, through which tiny instruments can be inserted to perform the surgery. Patients feel less pain, recover faster, and have lower rates of infection. In a few short years, a billion-dollar market for endoscopic surgery surgery products has developed, and Ethicon is investing heavily to maintain its share of this new product market.

the same pressure. The first firm to introduce a biodegradable plastic trash bag would not only help solve a major environmental problem but would also have a significant marketing advantage over the competition.

Complete a Product Line.   The third reason for introducing new products is to complete a product line. As the International Example (page 380) illustrates, Ford Motor Company and its old rival, Nissan of Japan, formed a partnership to assemble front-wheel-drive minivans in Ohio. Ford had a successful rear-wheel-drive minivan, but no front-wheel-drive minivan. The partnership gave Ford access to Nissan's successful front-wheel-drive minivan technology at a lower price than if it had been forced to develop the new minivan on its own.

Developing New Products

Firms that introduce successful new products usually aren't just lucky; they have a system. Any system for developing new products should have three features. First, it should encourage as many new product ideas as possible. Second, it should allow company analysts to screen new product ideas quickly and inex-

New Alliances with Foreign Competitors

American companies are forming alliances with foreign competitors to obtain new technology, new products, and access to new markets. Ford Motor Company has formal ties with its old enemies, Nissan of Japan and Volkswagen of Germany. According to Philip E. Benton, Jr., president of Ford's automotive group, these new relationships come about because of an "insatiable consumer appetite for more variety than any one company can handle."

In late 1991, Ford and Nissan began producing a new front-wheel-drive minivan in Ohio, using Nissan's technology. Both firms sell the minivan through their own dealer networks. The new front-wheel-drive vehicle complements Ford's rear-wheel-drive minivan.

Ford merged its operations in Brazil and Argentina with Volkswagen's and created a new company called Autolatina. The firm is designing a new common engine for their cars, and the Ford plant in Argentina is assembling both Ford and Volkswagen products.

International arrangements sometimes have strange beginnings. Texas Instruments successfully sued Japan's Hitachi for selling memory chips in the United States at a lower price than in Japan. During negotiations, both Hitachi and Texas Instruments learned a great deal about each other, and a certain level of mutual respect was established. It resulted in a cooperative arrangement between the two firms to develop a 16-megabit dynamic RAM chip. Each firm felt that it needed a partner, to minimize risks. The relationship with Hitachi has changed the corporate culture at Texas Instruments. Now, rather than trying to invent all of its new products, the firm has arrangements with other companies, from small U.S. firms to innovative Taiwanese businesses. Pat Weber, president of Texas Instruments' semiconductor group, said, "We've become more realistic about what it takes to be successful in the complexities of global markets."

pensively. Third, it should be rigorous, so that only the best ideas are brought to market.

Figure 14-4 depicts a six-stage model of the new-product development process. Each stage will be discussed briefly.

Stage 1: Idea Generation.

idea generation the first stage in the development of new products, in which new product ideas from all sources are collected.

New product ideas from all sources are collected in the **idea generation** stage. Management should encourage as many new product ideas as possible. Some businesses, such as Du Pont, Westinghouse, AT&T, General Electric, and IBM, have large, well-funded basic research departments. Although such departments have been responsible for such revolutionary new products as nylon and computer chips, most new product ideas come from customers, salespeople, and competitors.

IBM has an Installed User Program Department, which coordinates the acquisition of user-developed software. This department takes referrals from salespeople and forwards them to the appropriate product divisions.

Stage 2: Product Evaluation.

product evaluation the second stage in the development of new products, in which new product ideas that are not feasible or not consistent with the firm's objectives are eliminated.

The development of new products is a very expensive process. The firm must not permit itself to spend precious resources on products that have little or no chance of being successful. The purpose of the **product evaluation** stage is to eliminate new product ideas that are not feasible or not consistent with the firm's long-term objectives. Factors usually considered when a firm evaluates a new product idea are potential sales volume, impact of existing and future competition, expense and availability of raw materials, and the compatibility of the new idea with the firm's current marketing and production procedures. Most new product ideas do not make it past the product evaluation stage.

To illustrate, a large manufacturer of industrial cleaning compounds developed a new product for cleaning bathrooms. Top management saw that the prod-

FIGURE 14-4   New-Product Development Process

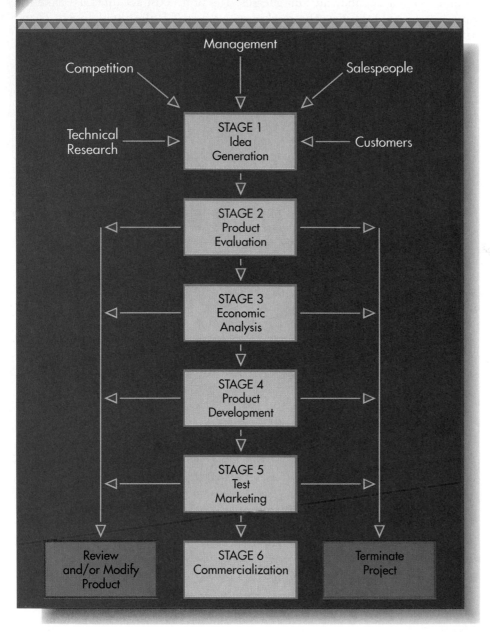

uct could be highly profitable in the consumer market. However, the firm decided to sell the formula to a consumer products firm. There was no question that the new product had a strong sales potential and that the firm could easily produce it. What was at issue was the ability of the firm, which was primarily a maker of industrial products, to market the new product successfully at the consumer level. The firm simply had no experience in or structure for serving the consumer market. It avoided a potentially disastrous mistake by considering this and other criteria.

Stage 3: Economic Analysis.   The likely profitability of the product is estimated during the **economic analysis** stage. To do so, it is necessary to make

economic analysis   *the third stage in the development of new products, in which the likely profitability of the product is estimated.*

guesses about production costs and sales revenue. These guesses are based on careful analysis, but they are still guesses. The firm's cost accountants make the production cost estimates. The market research staff is the usual source of the sales estimates.

product development
the fourth stage in the development of new products, in which a prototype of the product is developed.

prototype *a physical model or a custom-made first version of a new product.*

Stage 4: Product Development.   At the **product development** stage, the product becomes more than just an idea. The firm's production design engineers develop a prototype of it. A **prototype** is a physical model or a first, custom-made version of the product. It enables the firm to see what the product will look like and whether it can be produced at an acceptable cost. It also gives the marketing research people something to show prospective customers.

test marketing *the fifth stage in the development of new products, in which there is limited introduction of a new product to a few selected geographic markets, for a short time, under controlled conditions.*

Stage 5: Test Marketing.   Next, the marketing research staff evaluates the product by test marketing. In **test marketing,** the firm introduces the new product to a few selected geographic markets, for a short time, under controlled conditions. The marketing research team hopes the test market will provide answers to several question. How many consumers or businesses are likely to buy the product? How much will they pay for it? What product features do they like best? What forms of promotion will be most effective? How many units of the product can be sold in the first year?

Some firms bypass the test market stage of the process because competitors may learn about the product from the test market and introduce similar products of their own. This is particularly a problem for trendy products, such as bike shorts, air-pump athletic shoes, splatter-paint pants, and home video games. Also, test marketing is expensive. A large-scale test can easily cost more than $300,000, or as much as $3 million. Many firms simply do not have the financial resources to perform tests on this scale.

commercialization *the sixth and final stage in the development of new products, in which the product is made available to the market.*

Stage 6: Commercialization.   The last step in the new-product development process is **commercialization,** in which the product is made available to the market. The firm begins this stage by designing its promotional strategy in light of what was learned during the test-marketing stage.

It also is necessary to decide how to distribute the product. Many firms have the ability to distribute a product nationwide but prefer to "roll" the product out to the market. This means that the product is first sold in one part of the country only. As the firm learns more about the product and which selling strategies work best, it introduces it to other parts of the country until, eventually, it is sold from coast to coast.

What Makes A New Product Successful?

The failure rate of new products in the United States is astonishing. Up to 30 percent of new industrial products are unsuccessful, and the figure for consumer products is close to 50 percent. These percentages are particularly surprising because only 1 to 3 percent of the new product ideas that are introduced in the idea generation stage are ever marketed commercially. Also, a failure is defined as a product that is pulled off the market. Many other products are left on the market even though they do not earn much money for the company.

Why do so many new products fail? Let's look at four important reasons why some products succeed and others do not.[7]

Timely Introduction.   Businesses that are successful with new products make every effort to bring their new products to the marketplace as quickly as possible and at the appropriate time. McKinsey & Co., an internationally known management consulting firm, found that new high-tech products that come to market six months late earn 33 percent less profits over five years than do products that arrive on schedule. Recognizing the need for speed, AT&T cut the development time for new telephones by 50 percent.

There are also certain times of the year when specific types of new products should be introduced to the market. For example, the best month to bring a new college textbook to the market is October. Most new textbook adoption decisions are made in March or April. If the new textbook comes out in October, it will carry the next year's copyright date, and the company's salespeople will have five to six months to try to convince faculty members to adopt the book for the following year. Other examples of timely introductions include new cars in the fall and new movies in December and June. The fall introduction schedule for automobiles seems to be a matter of tradition. The December and June release dates for movies coincide with holidays and vacations, when people are more likely to have time for movies.

Significant Price or Performance Advantage.   The McKinsey report also found that 74 percent of all successful new consumer products offer the public better performance than competing products.[8] It is interesting to note that price was not a critical factor when the product was perceived to be superior. It seems that people are willing to pay higher prices for better products.

Significant Differences from Other Products.   New products that are different from existing ones have a greater chance of success than those that are mirror images. However, we can qualify this statement in two ways. First, product distinctions or improvements must be readily visible to the buyer. Highly technical differences, understood only by experts, may not contribute to success at all. Second, the differences must not be so great that buyers feel uncomfortable purchasing the product. For example, what if you invented a new typewriter with an entirely different keyboard arrangement? Instead of the letters "q," "a," and "z" being at the left of each row of keys, they would be someplace else. Would people feel comfortable with this machine? Would they be willing to learn the new keyboard arrangement? Do the benefits of the changes justify this effort? Would customers buy the typewriter? Many new products have failed because management neglected to answer such questions.

Special Attention for New Products.   Successful firms give their new products extra attention. When Toyota introduced its new line of luxury automobiles, the Lexus ES 250 and LS 400, the firm held intensive seminars for its sales and service people. The emphasis was on personal attitudes, not product attributes. After 2.7 million test miles, Toyota was convinced that its cars would work. But the company was not sure that they would sell in the highly competitive luxury car market unless dealer representatives embraced the Lexus "vision" for the future. The participants were told that they must have the same high level of product knowledge as BMW dealers, respect their customers the way Mercedes representatives did, and avoid the backslapping used by Cadillac salesmen. Toyota was willing to invest in expensive marketing training programs. It realized that its $3 billion investment could easily be stalled by ill-mannered, unprofessional sales and service personnel.[9]

BRANDING

brand *any name, symbol, or design that identifies a firm and its products.*

A **brand** is any name, symbol, or design which identifies a firm and its products. Chevrolet, Adidas, the Izod alligator, and the Purina checkerboard are all brand names, symbols, or designs. A brand/symbol that has been granted legal protection, so that it cannot be used by anyone else, is a trademark (discussed in Chapter 6). In this section, we'll consider the objectives of branding and the characteristics of a good brand name.

Why Branding?

A brand name identifies the seller and establishes a limited form of control over the buyer. The term "control" means that the buyer learns to associate a particular brand name with a need or a class of products. Consider the case of photocopiers. When most people think of photocopiers, they think of Xerox: "Would you xerox this for me, please?" In the same way, Coke is synonymous for some people with soft drinks, and Kleenex is synonymous with tissues. Consumers will pay more for the product if they are familiar with the brand name, and they will tend to select it with little or no comparative shopping. Specifically, branding has two main objectives: repeat sales and new product sales.

Repeat Sales. If you liked your last pair of Reebok tennis shoes, you are more likely to purchase another pair of the same brand. Branding fosters repeat sales; satisfied customers seek the company's products for future purchases. Branding is also important in word-of-mouth communications. Satisfied customers are a seller's best friends. They tell other people about the product and their positive experiences with it. Word-of-mouth promotion works best for shopping and specialty goods such as televisions, refrigerators, and automobiles.

Branding can help the company sell an image rather than a mere product. Who doesn't associate excitement with the name "Corvette"?

New Product Sales.   A firm with a well-established brand name often has an easier time introducing new products. Consumers and industrial buyers believe that a firm with a reputation for quality products will continue to offer such products in the future. For example, when Reebok introduced its Energy Return System (ERS) tennis shoes, many consumers who had had a good experience with Reebok products in the past assumed that Reebok's new ERS shoes would be good for them. Reebok's reputation for quality helped the new ERS shoes become a successful new product.

It is important to point out that even a strong brand name will not always help a new product. Levi Strauss introduced a line of slacks and blazers under the name Daniel Hunter. They were promoted as "classically tailored clothes from Levi's." The line was a total failure, partially because consumers did not see a logical connection between classically tailored clothes and Levi Strauss.[10]

Family Brands vs. Individual Brands   When most or all of a firm's products bear the same brand name, they are said to be sold under a **family brand.** An example is the Heinz 57 Variety brand name, which is carried on many Heinz products. We just saw that a brand name makes new product introduction easier. It may also stimulate the sales of other products in the firm's line. Then why do some firms sell each of their products under a different, **individual brand** name? We can cite two reasons: to protect existing products and to stimulate internal competition.

family brand   the same brand name used for most or all the firm's products.

individual brand   a different brand name used for each of a firm's products.

Protect Existing Products.   Shoppers sometimes regard two or more of a firm's products as almost the same, even though they have different technical characteristics and vary considerably in price and quality. In such situations, the firm usually tries to differentiate its products from one another—especially when introducing a new, inexpensive product to the market. The concern is to prevent the new product from jeopardizing the sales of an older, more expensive product.

Stimulate Internal Competition.   A second reason why a firm might adopt an individual branding strategy is to stimulate competition within the organization. In the highly competitive laundry soap business, successful manufacturers offer a variety of products to the market. Each product stands alone in the market and competes against the products of other firms as well as against the other detergents produced by the same company and sold under different names. Procter & Gamble produces such well-known laundry soaps as Tide, Cheer, and Bold.

What Makes a Brand Name Good?

Choosing the right brand name involves a combination of creativity, market research, and good luck. However, four rules of thumb can be helpful.

1. The name should be short, easy to spell, and easy to understand. Examples: Ziploc, Jell-O, Wisk, Raid, Glad.
2. The name should be appropriate for the product and emphasize its major attributes. Examples: Easy-Off, Kitty Litter, Right Guard.
3. The name should be distinctive. Examples: Exxon, Zest, Calgon, Spaghettios.
4. The name should be easy to remember. Examples: Odor Eaters, Betty Crocker, Uncle Ben's, Log Cabin.

Two problems commonly occur when selecting a brand name. First, the name chosen may have already been used by another company. When Budweiser introduced Natural Light beer, the Miller Brewing Company sued Budweiser, saying that Miller had trademarked the term "lite." The courts ruled that Miller did not have exclusive rights to the word "lite," but only to "Miller Lite."

A second problem is top management indecision. Many years ago, Ford was attempting to name a new car. The company wanted a name that fit the car's image and "personality." Not wanting to pick the wrong name, Ford tested 2,000 different names for the car on people in New York, Chicago, and Ann Arbor. The people were asked to state what the sample names brought to mind. One of the names, "Edsel" (the name of Henry Ford II's father), was associated with "pretzel," "diesel," and "hard sell." Despite these negative associations, the company named its new car Edsel.[11] The rest is history: The car was a fiasco, and the name Edsel is now synonymous with business failure.

Generic Products

Generic products are unbranded, plainly packaged products. These products are often lower in quality than branded products, and they often sell for 10 to 30 percent less. Staple items such as paper towels, canned peas, and dog food are frequently available in generic versions in supermarkets. The manufacturer or processor of generics saves money by using lower-quality ingredients and by not advertising its products.

Most manufacturers of branded items have targeted customers who want quality and consistency in their purchases and are willing to pay for it. Other options are to reduce the price of the branded item to compete with generic products or to introduce a new line of low-cost branded items. Procter and Gamble uses the Banner brand to sell paper products that are somewhat lower in quality than its nationally advertised brands, Charmin and White Cloud, but are priced to compete with generic brands.

The success of generic products varies according to the income level of the people who shop at particular stores. Supermarkets in high-income communities do not sell as many generics as do stores in middle- and lower-income communities. Nationally, the sales of generic products represent about 5 percent of their respective markets.

PACKAGING

Packaging is more important today than it was 30 years ago. The main reason for the "packaging revolution" has been the spread of self-service retailing. In a self-service world, packaging describes and sells the product—functions that were once handled by salespeople. Next, we will look at the functions of packaging and the distributor's perspective on packaging.

Functions of Packaging

Protection of the product is still the most important function of packaging. In recent years, great strides have been made in developing materials that provide added protection at reduced cost. Today, packaging also performs three marketing functions: product differentiation, product information, and symbolic image.

Product Differentiation.   Producers often use packaging to differentiate their products from those of competitors. When a consumer walks through a supermarket stocked with several thousand items, the package must catch the eye, hold the attention, and stimulate interaction between the consumer and the product. Consider the phenomenal success of L'eggs hosiery and the role packaging has played in it—truly an example of product differentiation through packaging.

Product Information.   The label on the package frequently provides a great deal of information to the shopper. The label may list detailed instructions on how to use the product, or it may give information about contents, value, and price. Del Monte, for example, led the way in providing nutrition-related information on its canned food products. The information on the label may also warn about potential hazards associated with use of the product.

Symbolic Image.   Packaging may also help give a product an image. Elizabeth Taylor's Passion, an expensive perfume, is packaged in a beautiful purple bottle. This is not because such a container will protect the perfume better than plain glass, but rather so that the package can relay the message that this product is of high quality. In the same manner, a fine liqueur requires a bottle that is considerably different from the one used for a container of cheap jug wine. The image conveyed by the package must be consistent with the image of the product.

Universal Product Code (UPC)

Government and industry representatives worked together to create the **universal product code** (UPC), so that products (especially convenience goods) could be identified or "read" by electronic scanners. A small bar code is printed on each package, identifying the product and its price. At the checkout station, the cashier runs the code across the scanner instead of keying in the information. A computer matches each code to the product and its price. The seller does not have to place a price sticker on each item. Checking out is fast and virtually error-free, since cashiers do not key in information. In addition, it is very easy to monitor inventory levels, since the computer keeps track of each item that is sold.

The major advantage of the UPC for the consumer is that it helps keep the retailer's costs down, which keeps the prices of products lower. Also, it reduces the amount of time that the customer must wait in line to check out of the store.

Blockbuster Video assigns a UPC to each customer and to each videotape. The sales clerk uses a laser instrument to read first the customer's identification card and then the UPC on the videotape that the customer wants to rent. Checkout is quick, and the store has a low-cost, highly accurate system for monitoring which videotapes are in high demand.

Business Career
Package Designer: Designs containers for products, considering factors such as ease in handling and storing, distinctiveness for customer identification, and simplicity to minimize production costs. Confers with engineering, marketing, and other departments to determine packaging requirements and the product's market. Sketches design and then creates a model in paper, wood, glass, plastic, or metal. *Average Salary: $27,000.*

universal product code
    a system developed by government and industry representatives, in which products can be identified or "read" by electronic scanners from a bar code printed on the product's packaging

SUMMARY POINTS

1   Consumer products are produced for sale to individuals or families. They are classified as either convenience goods, shopping goods, or specialty goods. Convenience goods are purchased frequently and with little shopping effort (e.g., milk or cigarettes). Buyers actively consider price, quality, style, and value when purchasing shopping goods (e.g., refrigerators or stereo equipment). Specialty goods are items that consumers are willing to make a "special" shopping effort to find, since they know which name brand they want to purchase before they have the need to purchase the product (e.g., expensive watches).

2   Industrial products are used to produce other goods and services. Installations are major capital items (e.g., buildings and expensive pieces of equipment). Accessories are tools or equipment that have a short life (e.g., copying machines or cutting

KEY TERMS

consumer products 366
convenience goods 366
profit margin 367
shopping goods 367
specialty goods 368
industrial products 368
installations 368
accessories 368
raw materials 369
components 369

tools). Raw materials are inexpensive, unprocessed items (e.g., wheat or iron ore). Expensive, processed items that are part of the finished product are called components (e.g., disk drives or small motors). Supplies are used in the production process, but they do not become part of the finished product (e.g., light bulbs or filters).

3 A service is an intangible deed or a performance. Characteristics of services are that they cannot be inventoried, that buyers are dependent on sellers, and that performance standards are difficult to maintain.

4 The product mix consists of all the product lines that a firm sells, including individual products (product items) and groups of related products (product lines).

5 Most products move through four stages in their life cycle. During the introduction stage, the product is truly new, and there is little, if any, direct competition. Product sales increase rapidly during the market growth stage. Other firms enter the market during this stage, but prices remain high, and if costs are carefully controlled, the product is very profitable. In the maturity stage, industry-wide sales are higher than in any other stage, and profits are declining. Very few firms will enter the market. During the decline stage, the demand for the product falls to the point where only a few firms can continue to produce it. The concept of the product life cycle helps marketing managers to forecast sales, understand the profitability of products at different stages in their life cycles, and know how to extend the life cycle of products.

6 A new product is one that performs a new function for the buyer or represents a significant improvement over existing products. Businesses introduce new products so that they can earn long-term profits, achieve sales growth objectives, match existing and future products from competitors, and complete a product line.

7 There are six stages in the new-product development process. New product ideas are collected from all sources during the idea generation stage (1). The objective of the product evaluation stage (2) is to eliminate any new product ideas that are not feasible or consistent with the firm's objectives. The likely profitability of the product is estimated during the economic analysis stage (3). A prototype model of the product is made in the product development stage (4), and the market research staff evaluates the product during the test marketing stage (5). The last step is commercialization (6), in which the product is made available to the market. A product is more likely to be successful if it is brought to the market quickly and at an appropriate time and if it has significant performance advantages over its competitors. The product's chances of success are also better if its new features are easily seen by the buyers and if its differences from existing products are not so radical as to make buyers uncomfortable.

8 Brand names identify the seller, foster repeat sales, and facilitate new product introduction. A firm's product line may be sold under one family brand name or be branded individually. A good brand name should be short, easy to spell, appropriate for the product, distinctive, and easy to remember. Generic products are unbranded, plainly packaged, and generally of lower quality than branded products.

9 The main function of packaging is to protect the product. However, packaging also serves to differentiate products, provide product information, and project an image. Bar codes are printed on the packages of many products so that a scanner can identify the product and its price at the checkout station.

REVIEW QUESTIONS

1 What are the major considerations in marketing convenience goods?

2 Why is advertising important in the sale of shopping goods?

3 What makes the selling of industrial products unique?

4 What characteristics differentiate services from products?

5 Differentiate between a product item, a product line, and a product mix. 4

6 What are the stages of the product life cycle, and what is the firm's primary objective during each stage? 5

7 What are three ways that the concept of the product life cycle is useful to management? 5

8 Why are there so many new products on the market? 6

9 What are the six stages in the new-product development process? 7

10 What makes a new product successful? 7

11 Why do companies use branding on their products? 8

12 What makes a brand name good? 8

13 What are the functions of packaging? 9

14 How has the universal product code (UPC) helped sales? 9

DISCUSSION QUESTIONS

1 What is meant by the statement, "A product is more than just the sum of its physical attributes"?

2 What was the last specialty good you purchased? Was brand loyalty important to you in the purchase decision? Why?

3 How would you develop a marketing plan for a service?

4 Why is careful monitoring of the product life cycle vital to the success or failure of a business?

5 What was "new" about the last new product you purchased?

6 What are some of the potential new products that you can foresee being introduced in the next year? Do they complete a product line, or are they the beginning of a completely new product line? What features might make them successful?

EXPERIENTIAL EXERCISES

1 Visit a store that sells shopping goods. Ask the manager what role local and national advertising play in the success of the store. Try to determine whether the store manager believes that customers want low prices or that value is more important in the purchase of shopping goods. Ask the store manager to describe the training programs that are made available to the store's sales-people. Find out whether they are sponsored by the store or by manufacturers.

2 Select three products in your home. Examine their packages carefully. What functions does each package perform? Look carefully at the products' brand names. Which products seem to have particularly appropriate brand names? Explain your answer.

CASES

Case 14-1
McDonald's

McDonald's created the fast-food industry in 1954. Today, more than $66 billion worth of fast foods are sold in the U.S. every year, and McDonald's share of that exceeds $7.5 billion. Much of the firm's growth in recent years has come from company-owned restaurants overseas. There are now almost 3,000 McDonald's outlets in 51 foreign countries. They represent approximately 26 percent of the firm's outlets, but they account for 34 percent of its sales and 30 percent of its profits. Moscow's Bolshoi Mac seats 900 customers.

McDonald's is facing several major problems. It has new competition from supermarkets, convenience stores, and Mom-and-Pop delicatessens, which sell prepackaged foods that can be quickly reheated in microwave ovens. Second, American consumers are becoming much more health-conscious. Not only does a greasy hamburger fail to provide much in the way of vitamins and minerals, but it may actually be bad for us because of its high fat content. For example, a Big Mac has 560 calories, 32.4 grams of fat, and 950 milligrams of sodium. A Filet-O-Fish sandwich is not much better. McDonald's is sensitive to this problem; it now cooks all of its fried food in vegetable oil, with the exception of french fries. A third problem is that the 1991–1992 recession reduced consumers' appetites for fast foods. McDonald's had always stayed away from price discounts and price promotions. However, as a result of the slowdown in the economy, McDonald's implemented a "value menu" that offered low prices on certain items, to try to stimulate sales. Finally, the cost of opening and operating a McDonald's outlet has increased dramatically in the last few years. The new restaurants are more comfortable and have larger tabletops, movable chairs, and less of a prefab look and feel. As a result, the cost of opening a new McDonald's increased from $983,000 in 1986 to more than $1.4 million in 1991.

McDonald's is trying to adjust to the environment of the 1990s by introducing new products. McDonald's salads, which are prepackaged in plastic containers, now account for 7 to 9 percent of the chain's sales. The new McLean Burger has fewer calories and significantly less fat than a Big Mac. McDonald's is also considering the pizza market, which it first tested in 1984 with a McPizza. It was a dough envelope stuffed with tomatoes, cheese, and sausage; the product failed in its test market. A second, oval-shaped McPizza, designed for one person, was introduced in 1986. It also failed. McDonald's third attempt at the pizza market is a 14-inch pie made from frozen dough and fresh toppings. It may not be a gourmet pizza, but it is competitively priced ($5.84 for plain cheese to $9.49 for the deluxe). Also, it takes only 5½ minutes to bake (compared to the usual 10 to 20 minutes), thanks to a new oven created by McDonald's engineers. The initial test market results indicate that the McPizza is quite good. One customer stated, "It's faster here, and on our schedule that is important."

McDonald's has been attracted to selling pizzas for obvious reasons. It is a $21 billion market, and it represents the fastest-growing segment of the fast-food industry. It is also a whole new market for McDonald's. When the firm introduces a new hamburger, the result is all too often that it merely "cannibalizes" one of the firm's existing products. That is, customers switch from one of McDonald's existing hamburgers to the new product. Although they may be more satisfied customers, they have not created any new revenue for McDonald's. In contrast, pizza gives the chain a chance to attract new customers who have been spending their fast-food dollars in other restaurants.

McDonald's has several big advantages over most fast-food firms. It has more outlets, located in attractive locations, run by experienced managers and owners, than any other fast-food company. In addition, the firm spends almost $1 billion per year promoting the McDonald's brand name. As a result, the American public is well aware of McDonald's. However, even with these advantags, McDonald's may find that selling pizzas at a profit is not as easy as may seem. National chains such as Pizza Hut realize that they must respond in an aggressive manner to the threat from McDonald's. Pizza Hut has aired commercials in McDonald's test cities, poking fun at "McFrozen" pies. Other national chains will surely respond with similar advertising themes and more aggressive advertising strategies and budgets.

1. Is McDonald's being too cautious in introducing its new McPizza?
2. Will the McDonald's brand name and reputation help or hurt the sales of McPizza? Explain.
3. What is the firm's biggest asset in the sale of McPizza?
4. Should McDonald's discount the price of McPizza?
5. Do you feel that McDonald's should enter the pizza market? What other opportunities do you think McDonald's should pursue?

Source: R. Henkoft, "Big Mac Attacks with Pizza," Fortune, 26 February, 1990, pp. 87–90. ©1991, The Time Inc. Magazine Co. All Rights Reserved.

Case 14-2
Carnival Cruise Lines

"Cruises are for the very rich and for the almost dead." This is a myth that has been destroyed by Carnival Cruise Lines. The company, which was founded by Ted Arison, an Israeli-born billionaire, sails the Caribbean, the South Pacific, the Mediterranean, and the Alaskan coast. Each of its ships carries approximately 1,500 passengers and weighs 48,000 tons.

Arison realized that he could not compete with the most expensive premium cruise lines, so he targeted consumers with an average household income of $25,000 to $50,000. Many of his clients are blue-collar entrepreneurs such as owners of auto supply shops and dry cleaning establishments. Most people pay a package fare of $1,200 for a Caribbean cruise, which includes airfare from their home cities to Miami. Unlike most other cruise lines, Carnival rarely discounts the price of its cruise packages.

Carnival Cruise ships are called "fun ships" by many of the firm's clients. Rather than focusing on where the ship goes, the firm emphasizes having a good time while on board. Each cruise ship has a disco, a casino, a movie theater, several nightclubs, eight or more bars, wading and swimming pools, and 24-hour room service. Three meals are served each day, plus a midnight buffet. The ships are luxuriously furnished throughout.

The passengers are overwhelmed with service. There is one crew member for every two guests. Room stewards serve breakfast in bed and lay out women's negligees in the shape of a female body. On deck, waiters quickly learn passengers' names and drink preferences. Hundreds of activities are available. Passengers can play bingo or shuffleboard, shoot skeet, gamble, participate in organized pie-eating events or pillow fights, or help select the woman with the shapeliest legs or the man with the hairiest chest.

Carnival uses very aggressive marketing techniques to sell its services. Carnival spends $15 million per year on television advertising, which is more than all of the other cruise lines combined. The theme is always the same: A fabulous vacation at sea is within the reach of almost everyone. Carnival also depends heavily on travel agents to promote and sell its service. The firm sends out its own employees to pose as customers. If the travel agent recommends a cruise first, the "client" gives the agent $10. However, if the travel agent recommends Carnival cruises, he or she is given $1,000. Carnival has awarded more than $500,000 to travel agents since it began this promotional package.

Carnival has been very successful. It has identified a new market segment that other cruise lines had ignored. The company is now the largest cruise line in the industry, and its profits have been growing steadily every year. The firm introduced a new superliner in 1991, called the *Fantasy,* which holds over 2,000 passengers and should help the firm's profits continue to grow.

1. Can the concept of the product life cycle be used to help explain Carnival's success?
2. Should Carnival be more aggressive in discounting the price of its cruise packages when a particular cruise is not sold out?
3. How can Carnival expand its revenue base in the future?
4. The chapter states that buyers of services are dependent on the seller. Is this true in the case of Carnival cruises? Explain.

CHAPTER 15

Channels of Distribution

Phar-Mor is the nation's newest, fastest-growing deep discount retail chain. Its name is a play on words for the store where customers get "far more." Phar-Mor began operations in the early 1980s. By 1991, the chain had 250 stores, located in 27 states, and sales in excess of $3 billion.

Phar-Mor focuses its attention on keeping the price of its products as low as possible. It buys only in large quantities and only when it can get a special discount. As a result, one day a Phar-Mor store will have boxes of Crest toothpaste, and the next day the Crest display may be replaced by 100-pound sacks of dog food.

The firm has developed a reputation not only for hard-nosed negotiating with suppliers, but also for very aggressive marketing techniques. Phar-Mor blitzes consumers with television, radio, and full-page newspaper advertisements, driving home only one message: low prices. The stores resemble brightly lit warehouses. In-store promotional videos, along with banners hanging from the ceiling, reinforce the message that Phar-Mor's prices are low. Each Phar-Mor store provides prominent displays of well-known products to illustrate Phar-Mor prices. For example, Coke machines sell canned soft drinks for 35 cents, and videotapes cost only 99 cents for two nights' rental.

It is too early to predict how successful Phar-Mor will be, but it is apparent that the store has discovered a market that was not being adequately served.[1] This chapter will examine, among other things, how retailers find a niche in the market, enabling them to be successful.

A channel of distribution is like a river. Each begins at a source—for a channel of distribution, the manufacturer. Each flows along until it reaches its destination—the sea or the industrial and consumer markets. Each encounters obstacles along the way and attempts to overcome them in the most efficient manner possible. Water flows around granite bedrock and cuts its way through softer sedimentary stone. Goods and services, ideally, flow around warehousing bottlenecks and follow a course involving the lowest transportation costs and the greatest delivery efficiency.

This chapter examines channels of distribution—what they are, what they do, and how they do it. We will look at the role of wholesalers and retailers in the channel. We will then explore topics relating to shopping centers, transportation, and inventory management.

TYPES OF CHANNELS AND THEIR FUNCTIONS

The image of a channel of distribution as a river may seem a bit contrived, but it does emphasize the idea of a *flow* of goods and services. Not surprisingly, marketing channels are also frequently referred to as "conduits" and "pipelines." Let's now look at a more exact definition of a channel of distribution.

Distribution Channel Defined

A **distribution channel** is an organized network of people and businesses, through which goods and services flow from producers to end users. These channel members, called **intermediaries** or middlemen, can be wholesalers, retailers, or other intermediaries. It is through distribution that goods and services are made available to buyers at the right place and at the right time.

distribution channel an organized network of people and businesses through which goods and services flow from producers to end users.

intermediaries members of the distribution channel between the manufacturer and the consumer.

Channel distribution management is dynamic. Consumer tastes and preferences change rapidly, and new selling and transportation opportunities present themselves almost daily. Prescription drugs were once sold almost exclusively in neighborhood drugstores. Today they are available in many supermarkets and large chain pharmacies such as Eckerd, Ace, and Walgreen, as well as in local family-owned drugstores.

What Kinds of Channels Are There?

Figure 15-1(a) shows channels of distribution for consumer and industrial products. The distribution channels for consumer products usually feature both a wholesaler and a retailer. That is, the manufacturer sells its products to a wholesaler (sometimes through an agent), and the wholesaler then sells the products to retailers. However, some manufacturers of consumer products, however, sell directly to retailers, and a few even sell directly to final consumers. IBM owns many of its retail establishments. Avon and Fuller Brush have well-established sales forces that call on customers in their homes.

Channels of distribution for industrial goods often have only one intermediary between the manufacturer and the user. Figure 15-1(b) shows industrial wholesalers and agents providing the only links between a manufacturer of industrial goods and its buyers.

Figure 15-2 shows the channel of distribution for Champion Spark Plugs. To succeed in the marketplace, Champion supplies spark plugs to large and small retailers, engine makers, and automotive repair shops. These customers buy in different quantities and require different services from Champion. For example, Champion's own sales force calls on some very large retail accounts such as Sears, as well as engine manufacturers such as General Motors. There are relatively few large retail accounts and engine manufacturers that buy large quantities of spark plugs. Champion can give them a great deal of technical advice and service—as well as low prices, since they purchase large quantities of plugs.

FIGURE 15-1   Channels of Distribution for (a) Consumer and (b) Industrial Goods

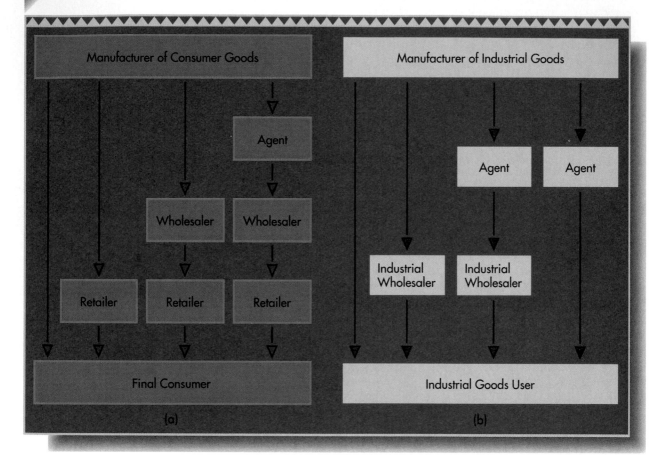

In addition, Champion uses regional and local wholesalers to reach some large retailers (those that are not serviced directly by the company's own representatives) as well as small retail stores and automotive repair stores. These wholesalers carry a broad line of products to meet their customers' needs. Highly technical advice on spark plugs or a very low per-unit price are not as important to the wholesaler's customers as quick delivery of a broad range of products. The use of multiple channels reflects Champion's desire to reach many market segments.

Functions of the Channel

Are intermediaries really needed in the channel of distribution? Would products be cheaper if there were no wholesalers? Do channel members make money for themselves at the expense of an unwary public? Before answering these questions, let's look at what intermediaries actually do in the channel.

Contact Potential Customers.   The most important function of a channel of distribution is to link producers and consumers. To understand the importance of this function, look at Figure 15-3. The top of the figure shows a distribution channel made up of three manufacturers and three retailers. The bottom portion

FIGURE 15-2   Channel of Distribution for Champion Spark Plugs

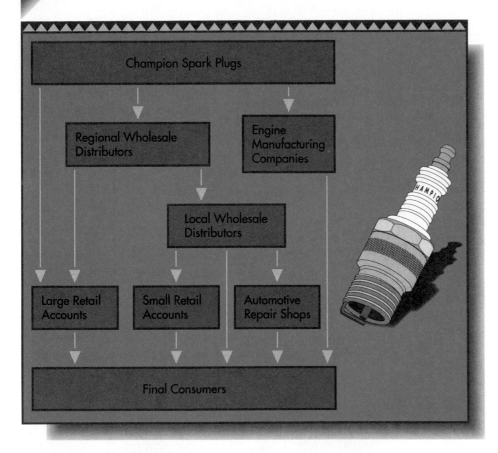

shows the same channel with a wholesaler added. In the channel without the wholesaler, a total of nine contacts or exchanges are needed for each manufacturer to link up with each retailer. In the channel with the wholesaler, the number of contacts needed drops to six. Distribution costs decrease as the number of contacts required decreases. The Gillette Company distributes its products through 3,000 wholesalers and more than 500,000 retailers. The costs of contacting and supplying all of these retailers would be astronomical if Gillette did not rely on wholesalers.

Cut Transportation Costs.   Transportation costs are a major portion of total marketing costs. Using intermediaries in the channel of distribution allows transportation costs to be reduced significantly. Retailers and wholesalers minimize overall transportation costs by buying goods in large quantities and breaking these bulk purchases down into smaller amounts for resale.

Suppose there is an electrical supply wholesaler in Albuquerque, New Mexico. The wholesaler buys a truckload of 45,000 light bulbs from a General Electric plant in Louisville, Kentucky. The bulbs are shipped directly to the wholesaler's warehouse in Albuquerque. From there, they are distributed to retailers, who sell them to people around the Southwest. Now imagine this alternative: Every time people in the Southwest need light bulbs, they phone the GE plant and order a half dozen. GE then mails each order to the customer.

FIGURE 15-3   Number of Contacts in a Distribution System

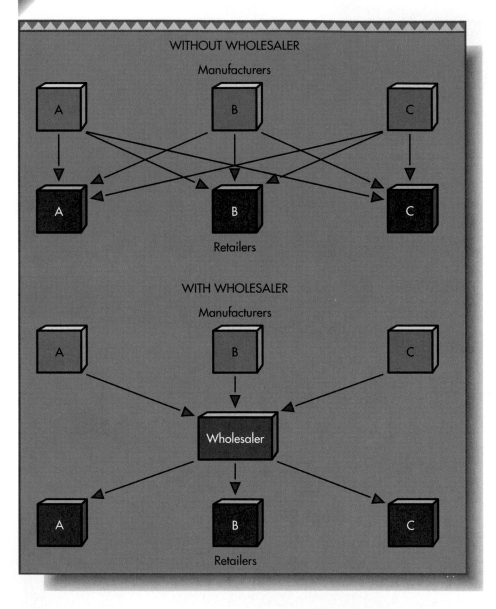

Which of these two alternatives involves lower transportation costs? Obviously, the first one. Shipping the bulbs in one large truckload, warehousing the shipment in Albuquerque, and then selling the bulbs in smaller quantities to retailers makes much more sense economically. The transportation cost savings and greater convenience benefit consumers.

Stimulate Demand.   Wholesalers and retailers help encourage people to buy the manufacturer's products. They do this because their success depends on the success of the products they carry. Gillette's wholesalers employ more than 22,000 salespeople to call on retailers. These salespeople promote Gillette products, along with the other products the wholesalers carry.

Wholesalers also run product advertisements in magazines directed at retailers. The purpose is to convince retailers to stock the advertised product. Similarly, retailers spend a great deal of money advertising locally. All of these promotional efforts, whether launched by the manufacturer, wholesaler, or retailer, serve to stimulate demand for the manufacturer's products.

Maintain Inventory.   The success of a manufacturer depends largely on its ability to deliver products rapidly to consumers. Manufacturers like to see their products inventoried close to the consumer—that is, at wholesalers' warehouses around the country and in retail stores. In this way, the product is available where and when the consumer wants it.

Relay Market Information.   Wholesalers and retailers also relay market information to and from the manufacturer. Product information—such as advertisements, sales promotions, and product demonstrations—flows down the distribution channel, from manufacturers to wholesalers to retailers to consumers. Information about changing consumer tastes and preferences moves up the channel, from consumers and retailers to wholesalers to manufacturers. These information flows are shown in Figure 15-4.

Channel Intermediaries: Who Needs Them?

Who needs intermediaries? Both consumers and manufacturers do. We consumers need intermediaries if we want the right products available at the right placeand at the right time. Manufacturers need intermediaries for at least two reasons. First, most businesses cannot afford to own the entire channel of distribution. General Motors, for example, has more than 15,000 independent dealers in the United States. The average dealership is worth about $3.5 million, so GM would have to pay nearly $43 billion to buy all its dealers. Even the world's largest car maker does not have that much cash. Second, some manufacturers know a great deal about production but very little about wholesaling and retailing. Therefore, most manufacturers let intermediaries—who have wholesaling and retailing expertise—distribute their products for them.

Even if a manufacturer elected to "eliminate the middleman and pass the savings on to you," someone would still have to perform the intermediary's functions. That someone

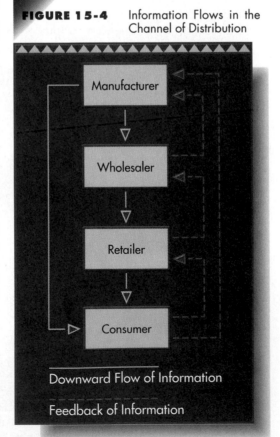

FIGURE 15-4   Information Flows in the Channel of Distribution

Manufacturer

Wholesaler

Retailer

Consumer

Downward Flow of Information

Feedback of Information

would be the manufacturer. It is only reasonable that the manufacturer would then charge its customers for performing at least some of these functions.

Selecting a Channel of Distribution

2 In selecting a channel of distribution, the most important considerations are market needs. If consumers demand that a particular product be easily available to them, the channel must have conveniently located stores to meet their needs. In contrast, if an industrial purchaser wants to discuss directly with the manufacturer the technical features of a product, then the channel may have to go directly from the manufacturer to the industrial user.

Product features also play an important role in determining the channel of distribution. Large, expensive, complex products are often sold directly by the producer to the end user. In such cases, selecting the correct product, installing it, and servicing it require a great deal of technical expertise, which can best be provided by the manufacturer. In contrast, less complex products can be sold and serviced by an intermediary rather than a manufacturer. To illustrate, Cray sells its supercomputers, which cost as much as $25 million each and do more than 4 billion calculations per second, directly to corporations and university research laboratories. Apple, on the other hand, sells most of its personal computers through retail stores.

The financial and managerial strength of the manufacturer may also affect how its products can be sold most efficiently. A firm that has limited marketing resources can expand its marketing capabilities by using intermediaries to sell its products. For example, most foreign manufacturers of tool and dye equipment use agents to sell their products in the American marketplace. These firms might prefer to call on their American customers themselves, but they realize that they

The channel of distribution must make goods available in the right place at the right time. The customer expects bread that is fresh, and effective distribution provides it.

do not have enough salespeople. Also, the sales potential in the American market may not be great enough to justify hiring more salespeople or spending the money necessary to service the market directly. In contrast, an agent can represent several noncompeting firms and thereby spread its cost over a number of products.

Vertical Marketing Systems

Traditionally, in most channels of distribution, manufacturers, wholesalers, and retailers are totally independent from one another. When they cooperate, they do so because it is in the best interests of all of them. Unfortunately, cooperation is often lacking, and a great deal of duplication and inefficiency may exist within the channel. This leads to higher prices for the consumer and fewer sales for the members of the channel of distribution.

A **vertical marketing system** establishes a mechanism that will permit the channel members to cooperate on a long-term basis. Each member realizes that its success is interrelated with the success of the other channel members. The assumption is that an integrated vertical marketing system will permit the members to provide better service at lower prices. This will permit the members of the channel to be more competitive and to make larger profits. We will now examine three types of vertical marketing systems.

vertical marketing system a mechanism that permits members of a distribution channel to cooperate on a long-term basis.

Corporate Vertical Marketing Systems.
For some time, large corporations have been attempting to gain control of their distribution systems. One way to control the system is to own it. A **corporate vertical marketing system** is a distribution channel in which most or all of the members are owned by one firm. The owner can be a manufacturer, wholesaler, or retailer. The Sherwin-Williams Co., a paint manufacturer, operates more than 2,000 retail paint stores. Hart Schaffner & Marx, a well-established manufacturer of men's clothing, has purchased more than 100 clothing outlets. Sears Roebuck, a retail chain, partially owns various production facilities that supply 30 percent of its merchandise. These corporate vertical marketing systems often completely displace independent intermediaries, thereby allowing the firm to dictate a product's marketing strategy.[2]

corporate vertical marketing system a marketing system in which all or most links in the system (manufacturer, wholesaler, retailers) are owned by one firm.

Administered Vertical Marketing Systems.
Under an **administered vertical marketing system,** channel coordination is achieved through the leadership of a member firm, not through ownership of the entire channel. The makers of popular consumer brands, for example, usually experience little difficulty in obtaining strong support for their marketing programs from both wholesalers and retailers. Thus, they tend to assume leadership roles in their distribution systems. In addition, many small manufacturers have been able to gain the cooperation of wholesalers and retailers by using liberal distribution policies, including price discounts, financial assistance, and large advertising allowances. These policies encourage resellers to accept the manufacturer's marketing programs and thus reduce channel conflict.[3] For example, a small producer of high-quality industrial paints in Houston administers its channel by permitting wholesalers to pay up to 90 days after delivery and providing technical help to the wholesaler's salespeople when they call on industrial buyers.

administered vertical marketing system a marketing system in which channel coordination is achieved through the leadership of a member firm, not through ownership of the entire channel.

Contractual Vertical Marketing Systems.
The fastest-growing type of vertical marketing system is the contractual system. Under a **contractual vertical marketing system,** independent organizations enter into a formal contract to

contractual vertical marketing system a marketing system in which independent organizations within the channel enter into a formal contract to coordinate their marketing efforts.

coordinate their marketing efforts. It differs from an administered system, in which leadership serves as the primary source of power. In a contractual system, legal contracts provide the power to make each member live up to its responsibilities. The nationwide network of McDonald's restaurants is an example of a franchise organization that uses a contractual vertical marketing system.

WHOLESALING

wholesaler *a firm that helps a manufacturer sell its products to other businesses for eventual resale to final consumers.*

For some people, buying at wholesale simply means paying significantly less than the list price for a product. But this use of the term "wholesale" doesn't shed much light on the role of wholesalers in a distribution channel or wholesalers' contributions to economic efficiency. We define a **wholesaler** as any firm that helps a manufacturer sell its products to other businesses, usually retailers, for eventual resale to final consumers. Wholesalers are intermediaries in the channel of distribution. They do not deal with final consumers.

How Big Is the Wholesaling Industry?

Wholesalers are certainly an important part of our economy. In 1990, wholesale sales amounted to more than $2.5 trillion, while retail sales barely exceeded $1.4 trillion. The reason for this difference is that products are often sold by wholesalers several times en route from manufacturers to retailers and final consumers. There are about 466,000 wholesale firms, employing nearly 5 million people, in the United States. The total inventory of wholesale firms is valued at more than $165 billion.[4]

Are All Wholesalers the Same?

Wholesalers are successful only if they are able to serve the needs of their customers. Since customer needs differ, wholesalers differ in the type and scale of their operations.

Most wholesalers have always offered product delivery services for their customers. Today, many of them also perform some or all of the channel functions discussed earlier—contacting, transportation cost savings, demand stimulation, inventory maintenance, and market information. Let's look at four major kinds of wholesalers and the services they offer.

full-service merchant wholesalers *wholesalers who take title to and possession of the products they sell and who perform the functions of contacting and transporting, providing market information to their suppliers, and offering credit and managerial services to their customers.*

Full-Service Merchant Wholesaler.

offer a broad range of services to their customers and suppliers. These wholesalers take title to and possession of the products they sell. A full-service merchant wholesaler also makes contact with potential buyers of the product, achieves transportation efficiencies through volume purchasing, and stimulates demand for the manufacturer's products. More than 80 percent of U.S. wholesalers are full-service merchant wholesalers.

In addition, full-service merchant wholesalers provide market information to their suppliers about what types of products final consumers are buying and how these products can best be advertised and sold. They also relay information back to manufacturers about how consumers like the products. This information helps manufacturers modify their products so that more people will want to buy them. Finally, these wholesalers often finance their customers' purchases and provide them with general managerial advice.

In the meat industry, stockyards serve a wholesale function. These sheep are brought to market in Indonesia, but the meat may well be sold in Europe or North America.

Rack jobbers are examples of full-service merchant wholesalers. They specialize in fast-moving nonfood merchandise sold in supermarkets, such as toys, health and beauty aids, and books and magazines. They provide the racks or point-of-purchase displays. In addition, they stock and restock the merchandise, price the product, and generally maintain the space.

Limited-Service Merchant Wholesaler.   **Limited-service merchant wholesalers** also take title to the merchandise, but they do not perform all of the functions that a full-service merchant wholesaler provides. For example, although they do perform the function of contacting, they rarely provide market information to their suppliers or credit and managerial services to their customers.

limited-service merchant wholesalers wholesalers who take title to the products they sell but do not perform all the functions of a full-service merchant wholesaler.

An example of a limited-service merchant wholesaler is a drop shipper. A drop shipper takes legal title to merchandise, but never takes physical possession of it. Rather, merchandise is ordered by the customer through the drop shipper. The drop shipper transmits the order to the producer, who then ships the order to the customer. The drop shipper is responsible to the buyer for any delays in delivery and to the producer for collecting payment from the buyer. The products sold by drop shippers are large, bulky items, such as building materials, which would be too expensive to transport to the wholesaler before their delivery to the consumer.

Manufacturer-Owned Wholesaler.   A **manufacturer-owned wholesaler** is a wholesale business owned and operated by the product manufacturer. We have already talked about why many manufacturers prefer to let other people handle the wholesaling function for them. So why do some manufacturers choose to act as their own wholesalers? First, it may be less expensive than using an

manufacturer-owned wholesaler a wholesale enterprise owned and operated by the product manufacturer.

independent wholesaler. Second, it may be hard to find a reliable, efficient wholesaler to sell the manufacturer's products. Third, the manufacturer may want to retain full control over the selling of its products.

Agent.   Unlike full-service and limited-service merchant wholesalers, **agents,** or brokers as they are sometimes called, do not buy merchandise. That is, they do not take title to the product and hold it for resale. Instead, they are paid a fee for bringing buyer and seller together. In addition, an agent often plays an important role in facilitating the actual transaction. For example, a real estate agent not only brings the buyer and seller together but also may help the buyer obtain a mortgage. Normally, the seller pays the real estate agent a commission, between 3 and 6 percent of the sales price.

Agents normally have a great deal of knowledge about the marketplace. They share this information with both the buyer and the seller. Agents are common in a variety of industries, including textiles, industrial machinery, chemicals, and canned foods. They are sometimes referred to as manufacturer's agents.

RETAILING

Retailers are businesses that sell products to the final consumer. Retailers vary in size, style, and character. Some are small mom-and-pop outlets that sell convenience goods. Some are one-of-a-kind boutiques that market expensive specialty goods. Others are multibillion-dollar corporations that sell a wide variety of consumer goods nationwide.

Retailers such as Sears, J.C. Penney, Wal-Mart, and Neiman Marcus are sophisticated, professionally managed firms. They use the most modern business techniques to generate profits for their stockholders. The managers of these firms devote a great deal of time and money to analyzing their markets, studying social and cultural trends, and designing advertising and promotion strategies.

One of the most exciting things about retailing is the many career opportunities it provides. Perhaps you would like to work for yourself. If so, take note of the fact that 85 percent of all retail stores in the United States are individually owned. Or you may want to work for a very large business. If so, look at Table 15-1, which shows that the 20 largest U.S. retailers sell more than $308 billion in goods annually and employ over 3 million people.

What Kinds of Retail Stores Are There?

Think of the different retail stores found in your hometown or in a nearby shopping mall. Although they sell many goods, the stores themselves can be classified into six major categories: supermarkets, superstores, convenience stores, specialty stores, department stores, and discount stores.

Supermarket.   **Supermarkets** are the primary sellers of food and other regularly purchased household products in the United States. Each supermarket is large—normally over 25,000 square feet—and sells more than $1.5 million of merchandise each year. Supermarkets usually carry over 8,000 brands of convenience goods. They provide free parking and are open long hours, sometimes even 24 hours per day, for the convenience of the shoppers.

Modern supermarkets are highly efficient businesses. Their executives manage their inventory closely. They must keep down their investments in inventory yet still stock the products that consumers demand. Supermarket executives also

TABLE 15-1   The 20 Largest Retailing Companies, Ranked by Sales, 1990

Rank	Company	Sales ($mil)	Net Income ($mil)	Net Income as Percentage of Sales	Number of Employees
1	Sears Roebuck	55,971.7	902.2	1.6	460,000
2	Wal-Mart Stores	32,601.6	1,291.0	4.0	328,000
3	K Mart	32,080.0	756.0	2.4	370,000
4	American Stores	22,155.5	182.4	0.8	163,900
5	Kroger	20,261.0	82.4	0.4	170,000
6	J.C. Penney	17,410.0	577.0	3.3	196,000
7	Safeway Stores	14,873.6	87.1	0.6	114,514
8	Dayton Hudson	14,739.0	412.0	2.8	161,000
9	Great Atlantic & Pacific Tea	11,164.2	146.7	1.3	91,000
10	May Department Stores	11,027.0	500.0	4.5	116,000
11	F.W. Woolworth	9,789.0	317.0	3.2	142,000
12	Winn-Dixie Stores	9,744.5	152.5	1.6	101,000
13	Melville	8,686.8	385.3	4.4	119,590
14	Albertson's	8,218.6	233.8	2.8	58,000
15	Southland	8,037.1	(276.6)	(3.4)	45,665
16	R.H. Macy	7,266.8	(215.3)	(3.0)	76,000
17	McDonald's	6,639.6	802.3	12.1	177,000
18	Supermarkets General Holdings	6,126.0	(41.5)	(0.7)	46,000
19	Walgreen	6,063.0	174.6	2.9	48,500
20	Publix Super Markets	5,820.7	149.0	2.6	66,000

Source: Reprinted by permission of *Fortune*, © 1991 The Time Inc. Magazine Company. All Rights Reserved.

realize the importance of location. Most people will not drive past one supermarket just to go to another.

One factor that differentiates supermarkets is the quality of their meats and produce. Items such as Campbell's canned soup or Kleenex paper napkins do not vary from one supermarket to the next, but well-displayed fresh produce and attractive, high-quality meat do separate supermarkets in the minds of many consumers.

Superstore. **Superstores,** or **hypermarkets** as they are sometimes called, are very large supermarkets that carry a full line of food products, as well as numerous other items that are often purchased by consumers. When the buyer in the family makes a trip to the superstore, he or she can purchase food items as

superstores or hypermarkets   *very large supermarkets that carry a full line of food products, as well as numerous other items often purchased by consumers.*

well as many other products that have traditionally been purchased at clothing, hardware, drug, and liquor stores.

Superstores are a logical extension of a concept called "scrambled merchandising," which began in supermarkets almost 20 years ago. It is the practice of selling unrelated products in one store. The reason supermarkets began selling diapers, motor oil, and cosmetics was very simple. The per unit profit on these items was often twice as much as on food and food-related items. The profit situation has not changed today. Superstores are able to attract customers regularly to purchase food products in their stores. Once they are inside the store, they are more likely to purchase unrelated products such as sweaters, prescription drugs, or power sanders.

Superstores make every effort to keep costs down so that their prices are very competitive with discount stores. It is too early to tell how successful superstores will be, but it does appear that the combination of convenience and low prices will make superstores very competitive in the 1990s.

convenience stores *small supermarkets that offer a limited selection in terms of brands and package sizes.*

Convenience Store.

Convenience stores are actually minisupermarkets. They carry many of the same food and nonfood items that are sold in supermarkets, but they offer a limited selection of brands. The products are normally packaged in small sizes, to allow shelf space for other items. Convenience stores, such as 7-Eleven or Stop-N-Go, do not have meat or fresh produce departments. One of the most significant changes in convenience stores has been the addition of gasoline. Many such stores now offer not only the convenience of easy shopping but also the opportunity to get gasoline at a competitive price.

Since convenience store prices on nongasoline items are typically higher than supermarket prices, we should ask why people shop at them. You can probably answer this from your own experience. Many shoppers tolerate the higher prices because the total of their convenience store purchases is quite small (averaging less than $4). They are willing to pay a little extra for the convenience of being able to make purchases quickly and easily—no lines at checkout counters, no parking problems. In addition, while purchasing gasoline, it is easy to pick up a gallon of milk, a six-pack of Coke, or even a can of shaving cream. Consumers recognize that they are paying a little more for these products than they would at a supermarket. But most people are not willing to invest the extra time and effort to go to the supermarket to save a few cents on one or two items. In effect, the convenience store retailer charges the consumer a premium for this time savings.

specialty stores *retail stores that meet the needs of a particular market segment, usually selling only one type of product.*

Specialty Store.

Specialty stores meet the needs of a particular market segment. They usually sell only one type of product, such as clothing, jewelry, or furniture. Although many smaller specialty stores are owned and managed by one person, most of the larger ones are members of a chain. A chain is a group of stores owned by one individual or firm. Four examples of successful chains of specialty stores are The Limited, Banana Republic, Waldenbooks, and Computerland.

The successful specialty store is able to compete against larger stores by spotting new trends in the marketplace and making the right inventory adjustments quickly. Large department stores, which have much more money available for buying merchandise, are sometimes slow to react to market changes because of inflexible bureaucratic procedures.

department stores *large retail stores, divided into a number of specialty units or departments that sell a wide variety of mostly nonfood merchandise.*

Department Store.

Department stores sell a wide assortment of mostly nonfood merchandise, ranging from women's dresses to kitchen appliances. They are divided into free-standing units, or departments; such stores often appear to be a collection of individual specialty shops. The appeal of a department store is that the consumer can go to one large store and purchase a wide variety of items, using one credit system. In addition, many department stores have developed excellent reputations in their communities. They are known as highly reputable stores that always back up the products they sell.

Before World War II, traditional downtown department stores such as Foley's in Houston, Dayton's in Minneapolis, and Macy's in New York dominated the retail markets. But these stores lost their markets as people moved to the suburbs. Sears was among the first department stores to build in the suburbs. The older, more established downtown stores eventually realized the impact of this population move and established branch stores in fast-growing suburban areas. Today, more than 85 percent of most department stores' sales are from suburban branch stores.

A significant problem in our society is that large, efficient retailers no longer serve many poor neighborhoods. Thus, our most economically disadvantaged citizens have relatively few places to shop. The Ethical Issue (page 407) describes this problem in more detail.

Discount Stores.   During the last 30 years, the term **discount store** has meant several things. When discount stores first appeared on the retail scene in the early 1950s, they sold primarily name-brand products at low prices. Popular items included jewelry, luggage, and electrical appliances. One reason they could afford to feature such low prices was that they did not offer buyers delivery or credit services. This cuts costs.

> **discount store**   a retail store that offers popular items at low prices by keeping operating costs down.

In the early 1960s, a dramatic change occurred in the discount world: Kresge's, K Mart, Jupiter, Korvette, Shopper's Fair, Gibson's, and other such stores began to sell little-known brands at low prices. Today, discount stores focus a great deal of attention on keeping their costs as low as possible so that they can sell both name brands and little-known brands at low prices. The merchandise lines of discount stores are limited to the most popular items and colors, so that they do not have to stock slow-moving items. Other characteristics include self-service, long operating hours, Sunday business hours, inexpensive interiors, and ample parking. We will look briefly at four types of discount stores.

Gray market stores purchase products at a deep discount from other retail outlets that need to sell their merchandise, either because they purchased too many items or because they must liquidate their inventory to meet a cash problem. Most manufacturers disapprove of gray market outlets, since they tend to undermine the firm's dealer structure. For example, gray market stores do not provide warranty service, cooperate in advertising programs, or participate in special seminars designed to train salespeople. These factors, along with the low price that they pay for their products, permit them to sell merchandise at relatively low prices. Electronics products tend to end up in gray market stores more than most other products.

> **gray market stores**   retail stores that buy products from other retailers that purchased too much merchandise or must raise cash quickly; the stores then sell the products at a considerable discount.

Warehouse stores represent the newest concept in discount retailing. Merchandise on store shelves is often stacked to the ceiling. Although the stores are clean and well-lighted, they present a very spartan look. The main characteristic of warehouse stores is that they offer products purchased in large quantities, such as cases of Diet Coke or 100-pound sacks of Purina dog food, at significant discounts.

> **warehouse stores**   discount stores that stack large quantities of merchandise on the shelves and have an interior resembling a warehouse more than a retail outlet.

The Phar-Mor chain, discussed at the beginning of this chapter, is the fastest-growing warehouse store in the United States. The firm focuses its attention on

The Blue Light Special

"Attention, K Mart shoppers, the blue light is rolling. . . . Get six-packs of 16-ounce Coke. Not $3.19! Not $2.89! Not even our own sale price of $1.99. But $1.39!" The Thursday night shoppers stop and crane their necks at the familiar call. They spot the moving blue light and close in with eager determination. But several savvy regulars have already reached the island of six-packs in the store aisle. Their shopping carts are piled with Coke, and they await the little blue tags that transform their six-packs into the consumer's equivalent of a big-game trophy.

It has been more than 20 years since a K Mart assistant manager put a police light on a pipe and initiated one of the most peculiar rites in American retailing. Now, when the blue light starts to flash, mothers sometimes abandon babies. Shoppers have pushed clerks up onto counter tops and ripped merchandise to shreds. The prices are low at blue-light specials, but that is just part of their appeal. The sales are highly dramatic: They are never officially announced in advance, and they normally last from 15 to a mere 5 minutes. Stocks are limited.

Ernest Reed, the manager of a Southfield, Michigan, K Mart, recalls the time toys were mistakenly marked down 90 percent instead of 10 percent. The blue light started to flash, and hysteria swept the customers and the workforce alike. "Girls wanted to shut their cash registers down to get their toys," Reed says. "Luckily, the store wasn't too busy, but they still sold a lot of bicycles that day."

The Reverend Thomas A. Barbret of the Lutheran Church of the Master, adjacent to K Mart headquarters in Troy, Michigan, borrowed a blue light for his church's fund-raising campaign several years ago. "We rolled the blue light right down the aisle," he says, to a litany familiar to many of his parishioners: "K Mart shoppers, we call your attention to the pulpit." "Reaction was very positive," says Mr. Barbret. "That particular year the giving went up about 32 percent."

selling products at the lowest possible price. Many of the store's customers have only one complaint: The prices are so low that it is difficult not to purchase items that they really don't need.

Factory outlet discount stores are owned by manufacturers. They are used to sell merchandise that has been discontinued, did not pass inspection, or is last year's model that simply did not sell. The store may mark down the merchandise as much as 60 to 80 percent in an effort to sell it as quickly as possible. Factory outlet discount stores do not usually allow the consumer to return merchandise once it has been purchased.

Catalog showrooms are large retail stores that feature a wide assortment of sample merchandise on display but make their sales from stock kept in a warehouse. Catalog showrooms offer reduced prices because of economies of scale. Relatively little merchandise is stolen, since most items are kept in the warehouse. In addition, catalog stores do not offer free delivery or similar customer services. Selling and display expenses are considerably below those of traditional department stores. Best Products is an example of a catalog showroom store. One of the newest showroom stores on the retail scene is IKEA, a home furnishing chain featuring contemporary European design and low prices.

Nonstore Retailing

We often think of retailing and stores practically as synonymous. Actually, Americans regularly purchase a wide variety of merchandise through **nonstore retailing**—selling in ways other than through stores. We will briefly examine selling by mail, vending machines, door-to-door selling, and cable television and computer services selling.

factory outlet   a discount store owned by a manufacturer and used to sell merchandise that has been discontinued, did not pass inspection, or is last year's model.

catalog showrooms   large retail stores that feature a wide assortment of sample merchandise on display but make sales from stock stored in a central warehouse.

nonstore retailing   methods of selling merchandise to final consumers other than through retail stores.

Distribution in the Ghetto

During the last 30 years, large, efficient private retailers have fled ghetto communities such as Harlem, Watts, and Chicago's South Side. The companies believed that there was more money to be made in the suburbs and that their investments and employees were in danger if they stayed in the ghetto. The unfortunate result is that the nation's poorest population segment is being served by inefficient, expensive small retail outlets. It is not unusual for many people living in the poor sections of our cities to travel several miles on public transportation to buy groceries.

It is important for our nation's best and most efficient retailers to understand three key points. First, although a community such as East Harlem has a median household income of only $14,500, which is approximately half the national median, the total neighborhood income still exceeds $1 billion per year. Second, the suburbs are virtually saturated with new stores. Growth in retail business will have to come from nontraditional areas such as poor urban communities. Third, experiments in modern inner-city retailing, such as the Concourse Plaza Shopping Center in the Bronx, appear to be quite successful.

Major retailers have a responsibility to their stockholders to generate a profit. But they also have a responsibility to the community to provide adequate shopping facilities for all of our nation's citizens. If they are unwilling to accept this dual responsibility, they will fail to take advantage of a significant profit opportunity for their stockholders.

Source: M. Alpert, "The Ghetto's Hidden Wealth," *Fortune*, 29 July 1991, pp. 167–174.

Selling by Mail. **Mail-order houses** are retailers that reach customers primarily through the mail. They present their products to customers in attractive catalogs and fill orders by mailing products directly to customers. Some mail-order firms specialize in a narrow range of products. For example, REI's products all relate to outdoor recreational activities. Other mail-order houses, such as Spiegel's, are mass merchandisers.

__mail-order houses__   retail businesses that display their merchandise in catalogs and fill orders through the mail.

Some mail-order houses, such as L. L. Bean and Eddie Bauer, also do some store selling. On the other hand, some retailers whose main business is through stores also have a mail-order business. Sears has the largest mail-order business in the United States. It distributes more than 60 million of its catalogs every year and has catalog sales of more than $4 billion.

Vending Machines. Vending machines play an important role in the sale of certain types of convenience goods, for which easy access is most important to the consumer. For example, cigarettes, soft drinks, coffee, and candy are routinely sold in this manner. Vending machines are open 24 hours a day and can be found in many convenient locations.

Products sold in vending machines are usually more expensive than the same items bought in a store. Vending machines are quite expensive to maintain, and they are often vandalized. The prices of their products have to be high to cover these costs and to provide a profit to the owner of the machines.

Vending machines are much more sophisticated than they were a few years ago. They can be designed to handle both hot and cold foods, as well as make change for paper currency or take credit cards. Although sales from vending machines have grown consistently during the last decade, their relative market share has remained at approximately 1.5 percent of the nation's retail sales.

Door-to-door Selling. In **door-to-door selling,** salespeople call on prospective customers in their homes. This technique has been very successful for many firms, such as Avon, Mary Kay Cosmetics, and Tupperware. A big advan-

__door-to-door selling__   retail efforts in which sales are made by visiting prospective customers in their homes.

tage of door-to-door selling is that there is a personal touch to the selling process. Salespeople talk to customers face-to-face. Often the salesperson is a neighbor, further adding to the personal nature of the transaction.

Although door-to-door selling is still common, it has been partially replaced by salesperson-sponsored "parties." At Tupperware parties, for example, a host or hostess supplies refreshments in return for a gift from the sponsoring company. The value of the gift depends on the amount of the company's products sold at the party.

Although many different products are sold door-to-door, successful ones have the following four characteristics:

1. Dependable quality
2. Unconditional guarantee
3. Product demonstration
4. Potential for repeat sale

The first two characteristics reassure the customer as to the quality, dependability, and reliability of the product. Such reassurance is essential because most people tend to be skeptical (perhaps justifiably so) about the quality of merchandise sold door-to-door. The third characteristic is important, because one of the advantages of door-to-door selling is that the salesperson is there to show precisely how the product can be used. This is why Avon and Mary Kay Cosmetics train their salespeople to be fashion consultants, not just order takers. In general, if the sales of a product are not enhanced by a demonstration, it should not be sold door-to-door. Finally, in order to take advantage of the personal contact established between the customer and the salesperson, the product should be the kind of product that people buy repeatedly. Fuller Brush has been successful at developing repeat sales by encouraging its representatives to call regularly on their customers.

Cable Television and Computer Service Selling.   Cable television and computer service selling are emerging technologies. QUC, Shopping Network, and Home Shopping Network are national cable television stations that sell merchandise. They all began with relatively inexpensive gift items such as gold chains and earrings. Consumers view the items on television and call a toll-free 800 number to purchase the products, using a credit card. If the consumer is not satisfied with the purchase, he or she may return it for a full refund.

There are several computer shopping services that consumers can use. The consumer must have a personal computer and a modem to connect it via telephone lines to a host computer. Prodigy, which is a joint venture between IBM and Sears, and Genie, which is owned by General Electric, are two of the best-known systems.

These computer services offer home shoppers a wide variety of merchandise including garden supplies, airline tickets, photographic equipment, flowers, and men's and women's apparel. In some cases, a color image of the product or service appears on the screen. Otherwise, the consumer must rely on a brief written description of the item. The consumer pays for the product through a credit card.

wheel of retailing a theory that most new types of retailers begin as low-cost, low-price operations and evolve to higher-cost, higher-service, more expensive operations.

Wheel of Retailing

The **wheel of retailing** is a theory that most new types of retailers begin as low-cost, low-price operations and then evolve into higher-cost, higher-service, more expensive operations. Here is how the evolution works. When existing retail stores mostly fill the high-price, high-service niche, there is an opportunity for new retail stores to enter the market to serve the low-price customers. These new retailers can offer lower prices than the established stores by providing fewer services, selling lesser-known brands, accepting a smaller profit margin to gain market share, and holding down the cost of facilities.

As these new retailers become successful, they begin to add more services, handle more popular brands, and upgrade their facilities to gain broader appeal. To cover the costs of these improvements, the firms then raise prices. Since they are now established, they can also sell at a higher profit margin, again resulting in higher prices. Now these retailers are no longer discount stores, as they were originally. Opportunity again exists for new market entrants who offer low prices, and the cycle begins again.

For example, Holiday Inn began as a motel chain priced to attract traveling families on a modest budget. The rooms were clean but not elegant, and there was little else beyond the room to attract customers. Gradually, Holiday Inn evolved to appeal to the business traveler and convention business. The rooms became more elegant. The company added meeting rooms, cocktail lounges, and services such as shoe shining and room service. To cover these added costs, prices increased, so Holiday Inn now attracts the traveler who is less price-conscious. Other motels, such as Motel 6 and Budgetel, have replaced Holiday Inn as the place for families with limited means.

Market Coverage

The term **market coverage** refers to how readily available a product is to consumers—that is, whether the product is sold through most retail outlets or through only a few. The issue is how far consumers can be expected to travel to buy the product. Let's look at three levels of market coverage: intensive, exclusive, and selective.

market coverage   *the extent to which a product is readily available to consumers.*

Intensive.   When a product is made available through as many stores as possible, **intensive distribution** is being used. This approach to retailing is based on the idea that sales of a product are greatest when it is sold nearly everywhere. Intensive distribution usually means that the manufacturer or wholesaler of the product must have a large sales force, to stay in touch with each retail store. Examples of products sold intensively are candy, milk, and cigarettes. These are primarily convenience goods.

intensive distribution   *a retailing approach whereby a product is made available through as many stores as possible.*

Exclusive.   If a product is made available through one or only a few stores in a geographic market, **exclusive distribution** is being used. Exclusive distribution is the opposite of intensive distribution. Exclusive distribution involves lower costs, because the manufacturer needs only a few salespeople to service the smaller number of stores carrying the product. Two products often sold by exclusive distribution are expensive watches and fine china. These are specialty goods.

exclusive distribution   *a retailing approach whereby a product is made available through only a few stores in a geographic market.*

Selective.   Selective distribution falls between intensive and exclusive distribution. **Selective distribution** involves selling products through several—but certainly not all—retailers in a market. Shopping goods, such as television sets, refrigerators, and furniture, are examples of such products.

selective distribution   *a retailing approach whereby a product is made available through several, but not all, retailers in a market.*

The Level of Market Coverage.   The answer to the question of which distribution strategy is right for a product depends on where shoppers expect to find the product. If consumers expect to see it at nearby stores, then it should be sold intensively. We know, for example, that consumers expect to be able to buy milk at convenient, nearby locations. Most people will not drive great distances for a particular brand of homogenized milk. Likewise, consumers will not go very far out of their way to purchase even a really good chocolate chip cookie. Famous Amos, who is described in this chapter's Profile (page 411), distributes his cookies through his own specialty stores and also through convenience stores, department stores, and supermarkets around the country. In contrast, people expect expensive watches to be sold in fine jewelry stores by experienced salespeople. So manufacturers do not display their watches next to the soft-drink cooler at the local convenience store.

SHOPPING CENTERS

 Today's shopping centers are designed to generate pedestrian traffic. Most large centers have two or more "anchor" stores, such as Sears, Bloomingdale's, or a large local department store. These stores are placed so that shoppers must pass many small stores in order to get from one anchor store to another. The smaller stores, perhaps without much drawing power of their own, benefit from the increased foot traffic.

Locating together in well-planned shopping centers benefits all of the stores in several ways. So much merchandise is on display that more people are attracted to the center than would be to any individual store. The stores within a planned center participate in cooperative programs designed to attract people to the center. These activities include sales, special promotions, and mall events.

However, shopping center retail space is expensive. To receive all the benefits of a well-planned shopping center, the store owner may have to pay more than $50 per leased square foot annually—up to 40 percent more than in comparable free-standing stores. Many retailers also believe that stores located in a mall lose some of their identity, especially if the center requires all stores to adhere to rigid design criteria.

There are three basic types of shopping centers: neighborhood, community, and regional.

Neighborhood Shopping Centers

neighborhood shopping center *the smallest type of shopping center, consisting of a strip of stores along a main roadway, with the major tenant being a supermarket or drugstore.*

The **neighborhood shopping center** is the smallest of the three types. The major tenant is usually a supermarket or a large drugstore. The center consists of a strip of stores along a major roadway. Most neighborhood centers do not sponsor regular shopping center events; they rely on the convenience of the center to compete against the larger malls.

Community Shopping Centers

community shopping center *a shopping center that is likely to feature a drugstore or supermarket, that a medium-sized department store, and several specialty stores.*

A **community shopping center** is designed to serve about five times the number of people that a neighborhood center serves. In addition to a supermarket or drugstore, the community center is likely to feature a medium-sized department store and five to fifteen smaller specialty stores. The attraction of the community center is its diversity of merchandise and convenient location. The center may have several major center events each year to generate publicity and attract customers.

Wally (Famous) Amos

Wally Amos, who is known either as Wally or as Famous Amos, exemplifies how an individual can have a satisfying and enjoyable career with hard work, "smarts," and the willingness to pursue innovative marketing strategies.

Amos is the founder of the Famous Amos Chocolate Chip Cookie Corporation. He first tasted chocolate chip cookies when he moved to New York City, at age 12. Deciding that he wanted to be a cook, Amos attended Food Trades Vocational High School, but he later lost interest in cooking. He joined the Air Force for four years and then worked at Saks Fifth Avenue. After four years he left Saks, where he had risen to manager of the supply department. Amos then entered the training program, as a mailroom clerk, at the William Morris Agency, a theatrical talent agency. Amos took the initiative to reorganize the mailroom and was soon appointed secretary to a company vice president.

When the agency set up a rock-and-roll department, Amos joined that department, displaying an unerring sense for talent. He invited his boss to a local club to audition two young singers he had heard—Paul Simon and Art Garfunkel. He also worked with such artists as Dionne Warwick, the Beach Boys, and the Temptations. Finally, he moved to California and started his own personal management company. Although he acquired an impressive list of clients, Amos really didn't like the Hollywood crowd and the problems of being a personal manager.

Amos had become well known for bringing little bags of chocolate chip cookies as calling cards when he visited producers and executives in Hollywood. A friend suggested that he open a store selling chocolate chip cookies. Amos liked the idea and wrote up his financial plan. The Small Business Administration and banks turned down his loan request, but Amos knew singer Helen Reddy and her husband, Jeff Wald. Wald and Reddy, along with singer Marvin Gaye and the president of United Artists Records, decided to invest in his business. On March 10, 1975, Amos opened his first store.

Wally Amos was a natural at promoting his cookie. He dropped the tailored banker's suits and started wearing Indian gauze shirts, loose-fitting pants, and a panama straw hat. Cookie samples were given to passersby in Beverly Hills and Hollywood, and orders were taken for more, which Amos delivered personally. Soon he opened more stores. He now has stores throughout the U.S. (including Hawaii) and in Japan, Malaysia, and Singapore. He has wholesale baking operations in California and sells cookies to specialty, convenience, and department stores and supermarkets throughout the country. Amos plans his marketing strategies around the exclusive reputation his product enjoys.

Amos is proud of what he has accomplished: "I feel good about my achievements. I think it shows that success is possible, regardless of your color. Success is directly related to a positive mental attitude. I truly believe that."

In a nonstop promotional campaign, Wally Amos makes public appearances not only for cookies but also for the adult reading program of Literacy Volunteers of America, his favorite charity. The Famous Amos Chocolate Chip Cookie is head-and-shoulders above any other cookie in the market. In leading stores, Famous Amos cookies can be found alongside Godiva Chocolates and Bill Blass Truffles. Wally Amos has made a place for himself in the world—a place built on savvy, energy, and marketing.

Regional Shopping Centers

regional shopping center
the largest type of shopping
center, featuring three to five
anchor stores and more than
100 specialty stores; the center
frequently sponsors events to
attract the public.

A **regional shopping center** is designed to attract large numbers of people from the surrounding area. These centers often feature three to five anchor stores and more than 100 specialty stores. They sponsor events almost every week to attract the shopping public. Because of their size and the automobile traffic they generate, it is important that regional shopping centers have access to major cross-community streets, if not expressways. For many communities, regional centers have almost become new central business districts.

PHYSICAL DISTRIBUTION

physical distribution   the
movement of products from the
manufacturer to the final buyer.

Now let's examine how products are actually moved from the manufacturer to the final buyer. This activity is called **physical distribution.** How should products be transported to the buyer? Which transportation mode—truck, rail, airline—is the least costly? What about the trade-off between delivery speed and cost? Should the firm own or rent its warehouses? These are just a few of the challenging questions that physical distribution managers must attempt to answer.

We begin our discussion of physical distribution by examining its relationship to marketing. We then look at the total-cost approach to distribution decisions, alternative transportation carriers, and inventory management.

A prime example of a regional shopping center is the West Edmonton Mall in Alberta, Canada. At the time of its completion, it was the world's largest shopping center. With 800 stores and parking for 20,000 vehicles, the mall is a major tourist attraction.

Physical Distribution and Marketing

An efficient physical distribution system makes it easier for the firm to sell its products. How? By reducing product delivery time and making the order cycle more consistent. We will examine each of these very important concepts in the next two subsections.

Reducing Product Delivery Time.   Most people want to buy high-quality products at fair prices. The same is true of businesses, whether they buy coal for the production of power or televisions for resale to the consumer. Equally important, firms like to have their purchases delivered quickly.

To see the importance of physical distribution, picture yourself as the purchasing agent for the Amerex Climate Control Company. Your job is to choose a supplier of galvanized metal sheeting that your company will use to make heating and cooling ventilation ducts—one of your top-selling products. You've narrowed your choices to two suppliers. One of them promises three-day delivery on all shipments. The other can offer no better than two-week delivery. All else being equal, which supplier would you pick? Obviously, the one offering faster delivery.

It is not difficult to see that in a competitive marketplace, the supplier with an efficient physical distribution system wins more new customers and sells more of its products.

Improving Order Cycle Consistency.   The **order cycle** is the length of time between the placing of a purchase order and the delivery of the merchandise to the buyer. The phrase "order cycle consistency" refers to whether ordered products are regularly delivered on schedule. A supplier's promise of three-day delivery means three-day delivery, not ten-day delivery or even five-day delivery.

order cycle   *the length of time between the placing of a purchase order and the delivery of the merchandise to the buyer.*

Returning to the Amerex example, let's assume that your fabrication plant has limited room for storing sheet metal. You have enough warehouse space for only three days' worth of production. To keep the production line running, you need to receive a new shipment of metal sheeting at least every three days. If the shipment is even a day late, you have to shut down the production line and send the workforce home at full pay until the sheeting arrives. In this instance, consistent three-day delivery means the difference between operating the plant and closing it down temporarily. If the supplier cannot promise consistent delivery, Amerex should buy from another supplier who can.

So what is the precise connection between physical distribution and marketing? The connection is quick delivery and order cycle consistency. These are two of a supplying firm's most effective sales tools. Especially when competing products are essentially alike, the supplier with the best distribution system usually has the greatest sales and (more important) the greatest profits.

How Are Products Transported?

The five major modes of transporting merchandise and materials are airlines, trucks, railroads, pipelines, and waterways. Railroads still handle a greater percentage of intercity freight in the United States than any other type of carrier. However, as Figure 15-5 shows, their share of the freight market has declined steadily since 1960, whereas the shares of airlines, pipelines, and trucks have all increased. The percentage of the market for inland waterways has remained surprisingly stable. Let's take a brief look at each type of carrier.

FIGURE 15-5   Trends in Transport Mode Usage as a Percentage of the Total Intercity Ton-Miles Hauled

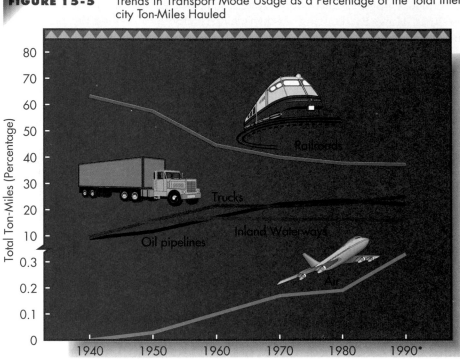

Source: U.S. Bureau of the Census Statistical Abstract, 1971 and 1990.

Airfreight.   Air transport specializes in the movement of high-value, lightweight, perishable products, such as flowers and medicines. As Table 15-2 indicates, airfreight is much more expensive than any other way of transporting merchandise.

With the development of the jumbo jet, airlines have begun to haul bulk cargo. United Airlines has its "Soft-Touch" container service. The container is a sealed box holding up to 10,000 pounds in 457 cubic feet. Soft Touch is now used by computer companies as an alternative to truck transportation.

TABLE 15-2   Freight Transportation Costs

Mode	Price (Cents/Ton-Mile)
Air	92.4
Truck	33.9
Rail	2.9
Pipe	1.3
Water	2.1

Source: *National Transportation Strategic Planning Study* (Washington, D.C.: U.S. Department of Transportation, March 1990), pp. 5-26.

Truck.   After airfreight, truck shipment is the most expensive form of transportation. Trucks tend to compete more directly with railroads than with airlines. The major advantages of truck transportation are door-to-door service, frequency, convenience, and flexibility of service.

The major disadvantage of highway shipment is cost—33.9 cents per ton-mile, as compared to 2.9 cents per ton-mile for rail shipment. Also, some products are too large to be sent by truck. The nation's trucking industry is pushing hard for new federal legislation that will permit triple-trailer trucks to operate on the nation's expressway system. These train-like trucks would be 99 feet long and would be much more efficient than today's 48-foot trailer trucks. However, they are actively opposed by the American Automobile Association, which claims that they are unsafe.[5]

Railroad.   Railroads are used primarily for shipping products over very long distances, especially products that do not need to arrive quickly at their destinations. Forty years ago, trains carried a wide variety of products, but today they haul mostly heavy manufactured goods and raw materials.

Recently, railroads have tried to regain lost markets by developing special cars for hauling complete truck trailers ("piggy back"), as well as automobile-carrying freight cars ("stack-back" and "vert-a-pac"). The railroads have also developed special rapid "run-through" freight trains, which reduce product delivery time significantly. If railroads are able to repair their rail beds and upgrade their equipment, they should continue to be competitive in the long-haul shipment business.

Pipeline.   Pipelines are used for moving products such as crude oil and natural gas. Although the product moves slowly—3 to 4 miles per hour—it moves all the time, and the result is inexpensive transport. Transportation via pipelines is also

Railroads are still the number one means of physical distribution of goods between U.S. cities.

very dependable. They are almost completely automated and are therefore unaffected by labor problems or the weather.

Inland Waterway.

Shipment on inland waterways is one of the oldest ways of moving freight. Although inexpensive, shipment by water has two disadvantages. First, inland waterways are affected by the weather. The Great Lakes are shut down for up to four months each year because of ice. Similarly, floods render navigation impossible on some rivers in the spring. Second, water transportation is very slow. Barge traffic moves at 6 to 9 miles per hour.

Inventory Management

inventory management
the process of balancing holding costs and stockout costs.

One of the most important functions performed by physical distribution people is **inventory management.** Holding too much inventory can cost a firm a great deal of money. Keeping too little inventory also costs the firm, in terms of lost sales.

Inventory managers balance holding costs and stockout costs. Holding costs are the costs involved in maintaining and warehousing inventory. Holding costs may account for as much as 30 to 40 percent of the value of the firm's inventory. Stockout costs are the costs that result when sales are lost because of inadequate inventories. If a firm has a unique product with little competition, stockout costs are typically low, because buyers cannot get the product elsewhere. In contrast, if the product has much competition, disappointed shoppers will buy the product from someone else. If their disappointment is great enough, they will not return to that store.

A firm could minimize inventory holding costs by reducing inventory levels drastically, but this would cause lost sales and high stockout costs. Likewise, a firm can minimize stockout costs by stockpiling inventory. But holding costs would then rise. Inventory managers attempt to balance these two cost concerns by minimizing the sum of holding and stockout costs.

KEY TERMS

SUMMARY POINTS

1 A channel of distribution is an organized network of individuals and businesses through which goods and services flow from manufacturers to consumers. Key functions of the channel are to contact potential customers, cut transportation costs, stimulate demand, maintain inventory, and relay market information. The distribution channel for consumer goods usually has both a wholesaler and retailers, although some manufacturers of consumer goods sell directly to retailers, and a few sell directly to final consumers. Industrial goods often have only one wholesaler and are more likely to be sold directly to the final user than are consumer goods.

2 The most important factor in selecting a channel of distribution is the needs of the user of the product. In addition, product features (e.g., complexity and technical service requirements) and the financial and managerial strengths of the manufacturer are important factors. Vertical marketing systems establish a way for channel members to cooperate over the long term.

3 There are four types of wholesalers. Full-service merchant wholesalers offer a broad range of services to their customers. A limited-services wholesaler takes title to the merchandise but may not take possession of it and may not provide credit or market information to customers. A manufacturer-owned wholesaler is owned and operated by the manufacturer. Agents do not take title to the products they sell.

4 Retail stores sell products to the final consumer. Supermarkets are the primary sellers of food products, while convenience stores offer a limited selection of products found in supermarkets. Superstores are very large stores that carry a full line of food products, as well as many other products frequently purchased by consumers. Specialty stores usually sell one type of product to a particular market segment, and department stores consist of a number of specialty units that together offer a wide selection of goods. Discount stores focus on keeping the prices of their products as low as possible. Mail-order houses present their products to the customer through attractive catalogs. Vending machines are useful for selling some products for which easy access is the most important marketing variable. Door-to-door selling is particularly useful for products that can be demonstrated in the home. Cable television and computer service selling use new and emerging technologies to sell relatively inexpensive gift items.

5 The wheel of retailing theory states that most new retailers begin as low-cost, low-price operations and evolve to higher-cost, higher-service, more expensive operations. In intensive distribution, a product is sold through as many stores as possible; in exclusive distribution, a product is made available through one or only a few stores. Selective distribution involves selling products through several retailers in a market.

6 A neighborhood shopping center usually has a supermarket and several specialty stores. It relies on the location and convenience of the center to compete. A community shopping center may have both a supermarket or drugstore and a medium-sized department store and five to fifteen specialty shops. A regional shopping center has three to five major anchor stores and more than 100 specialty stores.

7 An efficient physical distribution system makes it easier for a firm to sell its products by reducing product delivery time and improving order cycle consistency.

8 The five major modes of transportation are airfreight, truck, railroad, pipeline, and inland waterway. Inventory management is important because holding too much inventory is expensive for the firm, and keeping too little inventory results in lost sales.

KEY TERMS (cont.)

superstores or hypermarkets 403
convenience stores 404
specialty stores 404
department stores 404
discount store 405
gray market stores 405
warehouse stores 405
factory outlet 406
catalog showrooms 406
nonstore retailing 406
mail-order houses 407
door-to-door selling 407
wheel of retailing 408
market coverage 409
intensive distribution 409
exclusive distribution 409
selective distribution 409
neighborhood shopping
   center 410
community shopping center 410
regional shopping center 412
physical distribution 412
order cycle 413
inventory management 416

REVIEW QUESTIONS

1 What is a channel of distribution? **1**

2 Describe the functions of a channel of distribution. **1**

3 Identify the objective of a vertical marketing system. What are the types of vertical marketing systems? **2**

4 What is the role of the wholesaler in the distribution channel? **3**

5 Describe the different types of retail stores. **4**

6 Cite some examples of nonstore retailing. **4**

7 What are the differences between the three levels of market coverage? **5**

8 Why would a retail business want to locate in a neighborhood shopping center, a community shopping center, or a regional shopping center, respectively? **6**

9 How does an efficient physical distribution system make it easier for a firm to sell its products? **7**

10 What are the major modes of transporting merchandise and materials? **8**

DISCUSSION QUESTIONS

1 Would the absence of wholesalers and retailers reduce price? Explain.

2 What criteria should be considered when a manufacturer selects members of the channel of distribution?

3 What is the future of convenience stores in the next century? Will their sales increase or decrease? Why?

4 What are the advantages and disadvantages of having products distributed through nonstore retailing? What products are best suited to this type of distribution?

5 What factors should be considered when a firm is attempting to manage its inventory costs?

EXPERIENTIAL EXERCISES

1 Visit a real estate agent. Try to determine what services the agent provides the buyer and the seller. How does the agent try to differentiate himself or herself from other real estate agents? What factors tend to make one agent successful and another a failure at selling real estate?

2 Visit the manager of a regional shopping center. What are the biggest problems the

manager faces? Has the manager been able to keep the right mix of stores in the center? Do the stores cooperate with shopping center promotional programs? Do the store owners or managers see themselves as part of a community, or as just a group of independent retailers?

CASES

CASE 15-1
Dell Computer

Mail-order computer sales is the fastest growing segment of the personal computer market, and the Dell Computer Corporation is the most successful mail-order computer company in the United States. Michael Dell started the company when he was a freshman at The University of Texas. His strategy was simple: Sell IBM-compatible personal computers to consumers who did not want to pay retail computer store prices. Dell's sales went from zero to over $400 million in just seven years.

Consumers phone in their orders to salespeople in Austin, Texas. The salespeople, or account representatives as they are called at Dell, must complete an intensive four-week training program before starting work. They are tested on technical questions relating to Dell products, as well as on the firm's marketing strategy. Each telephone order is customized to include the exact options the customer specifies. Dell then ships the completed personal computer in five days or less. Michael Dell calls this "direct relationship marketing." He feels that Dell's sales costs are less than his traditional competitors', and his firm also has the advantage of having direct contact with each customer.

Although Dell began by focusing all of its attention on individuals who wanted to purchase one computer, the firm now generates 40 percent of its total sales from major corporate, government, and educational customers. These accounts are assigned a salesperson who calls on them in their place of business. The salesperson can get help from highly trained, specialized technical staff to design a package of computers that will solve the customer's needs.

Dell offers over-the-phone service to its customers. The firm solves 90 percent of customer problems in this manner. Dell also offers next-day on-location service through a service unit of Xerox Corporation. Michael Dell believes that the company's personal interaction with its customers helps build a unique database of information concerning the needs of the market and ways in which products can be improved.

Michael Dell does not want his firm to be thought of as just a mail-order distributor. Dell's research staff, which has already applied for 15 patents, has helped the firm earn a reputation for developing high-quality, reliable products. For example, Dell's new 386SX system, which was developed internally, provides access to a 32-bit software and can process information as much as 33 percent faster than comparably priced machines. Dell's battery-powered laptop computer (316LT) was one of the first systems based on the 386SX chip. It provides full desktop capabilities and features a continuous power battery system, which permits the user to replace a battery pack that is running low with a fully charged battery.

A key element of Dell's strategy has always been customer satisfaction. In 1990, the firm was ranked first in customer satisfaction in three polls taken by *PC Week* magazine. Also in 1990, the Dell System 325 was voted Computer of the Year by PC journals from around the world. Michael Dell believes one major reason for the firm's success is that it listens to its customers. Direct relationship marketing helps Dell accomplish this. Michael Dell also encourages customers to write to him directly if they are having any problem with their machine or if they have an idea for a Dell computer product innovation.

1. Is price the most important factor in the purchase of a computer for most of Dell's customers?
2. Why has direct marketing worked well for Dell when it has failed for so many other firms?
3. Will Dell's direct sales force be successful in marketing Dell's computers to large corporations? Are there some retail stores that should carry Dell's products?

Sources: S. A. Forest, "PC Slump? What PC Slump?" *Business Week,* 1 July 1991, pp. 66-67; and personal conversation between Michael Dell and William H. Cunningham.

CASE 15-2
Adolph Coors Co.

Adolph Coors Co. believes that it should produce and market only the highest-quality beer. To accomplish this objective, Coors uses ingredients grown on Coors-supervised farms. No artificial ingredients are used in the brewing of its beers. In addition, Coors has the longest and most expensive brewing cycle in the industry.

The Coors philosophy has made the firm successful. During the 1960s and 1970s, the firm was among the most profitable brewers in the United States. Through the mid-1970s, Coors dominated the beer market in the Rocky Mountain and West Coast states. However, competitors added new brewing capacity and began to move into the company's traditional markets.

In response to these challenges from other brewers, Coors decided to sell its products nationally. By 1987, Coors beer was sold in 47 states. According to Peter Coors, the company made this move to take advantage of the economies of scale associated with a national marketing effort. In the brewing industry, beer is sent from the brewery to local distributors. These distributors then sell the beer to both retail accounts and subwholesalers, who also sell to retail accounts. Normally, subwholesalers sell to those accounts that the distributor considers too small to be worth its own attentions. Coors uses the same channel of distribution as all other beer distributors, but it expects a great deal more from its distributors than does any other major brewer.

As part of the Coors quality control program, the company ships all its beer in refrigerated railroad cars or trucks to its distributors. When the beer arrives, it must be stored in a refrigerated warehouse at no more than 40°F. The Coors distributor delivers the beer to its retail accounts in refrigerated trucks. The distributor must convince the retail account that Coors beer will last longer and taste better if it is kept refrigerated. The distributor must then visit all of its retail accounts regularly to rotate the beer. The beer that was delivered first to the retail account is moved to the front of the retailer's display case, and any newly delivered beer is placed at the back of the case. Finally, all Coors beer is dated so that the local distributor knows when it was brewed. If any beer older than 60 days is discovered at the retail level, it is bought back by the Coors distributor and destroyed. This requirement ensures that all Coors beer in stores is fresh.

No other brewery requires that its wholesalers spend as much time and money as Coors to maintain the product once it arrives at the local level. For example, Anheuser-Busch is the only other national brewer that requires its product to be refrigerated when it arrives at the wholesale level. But Budweiser is not refrigerated when it is shipped to the wholesaler, and the wholesaler is not required to deliver Budweiser to its retail accounts in refrigerated trucks.

Until 1976, Coors sold only one beer. In that year, it introduced Coors Light. In 1991, Coors Light was the nation's third best-selling beer. The firm's new, popularly priced products, Keystone and Keystone Light, introduced in 1989, have done extremely well.

Coors executives are very pleased with the company's position. The firm's sales growth rate in 1990 was 9 percent, which was more than three times the industry's growth. Coors demands a great deal from itself and its distributors, but it does seem to be paying off for the company.

1.   Is Coors market-oriented?
2.   Has Coors adopted the best plan for distributing its beer?
3.   What conflict does Coors face in its channel of distribution?

Sources: S. Hume, "Coors Pores Over Plans to Expand," *Advertising Age,* 15 April 1985, pp. 4, 58; F. Paul, *Beverage World,* November 1983, pp. 148–149; B. Lowry, "Coors Plans Ad Series," *Advertising Age,* 19 August 1985, p. 6; *Wall Street Journal,* 19 February 1985, p. 41; and B. A. Collins, *Value Line Investment Survey,* 22 February 1991, p. 1539.

CHAPTER 16

Pricing

OBJECTIVES

After studying this chapter, you should be able to:

1 Discuss fixed and negotiated prices and the role of price in our economy.

2 Explain three common pricing objectives.

3 Examine how price is set under perfect competition..

4 Identify the five factors that are important in setting prices, and explain how cost and demand information is used to establish prices.

5 Explain three pricing policies.

The invasion of Kuwait by the Iraqi army in 1990 had major geopolitical consequences for the entire world. One of the nonmilitary impacts of the invasion was a dramatic rise in the price of jet fuel. Although there was never any real danger of a worldwide shortage of jet fuel, psychological pressure on the market was so great that the price skyrocketed from 60 cents per gallon in August to $1.30 per gallon in October. To put this number in perspective, each increase of one cent in the price of jet fuel costs the airline industry approximately $150 million each year.

American Airlines, which is one of the best-run U.S. corporations, responded to the increase in the price of jet fuel by increasing the price of its tickets. Unfortunately, the economy was just then sliding into a recession, which reduced the amount of domestic business travel. In addition, international travel dropped dramatically because people feared terrorist attacks on U.S. airlines. These two factors forced the company to offer various special discount fares to attract customers. Because of the price increases in jet fuel and the price discounts in tickets, American Airlines, which had earned $454 million in 1989, lost $39 million in 1990.

Pricing decisions are among the most difficult for business managers. The selling price of a product influences the public's image of the product, who buys it and how often, and how much profit the firm earns on the product. We'll begin this chapter by examining the meaning of price in our economy.

MEANING OF PRICE

Price is what the buyer pays for a product or service. Most prices are fixed by the seller, but for some products, the price is negotiated between the buyer and

price   *what the buyer pays for a product or service.*

the seller. This section of the chapter looks at fixed and negotiated prices and at the role of price in our economic system.

Fixed vs. Negotiated Price

fixed price   *a price that is not negotiable between the buyer and seller.*

Most consumer products are sold at a **fixed price**—namely, the figure on the price tag. The price of the good may be reduced during a sale. Nonetheless, the designated price is the price the buyer pays. There is no bargaining between buyer and seller. When buying a gallon of milk, for example, you don't approach the supermarket manager to try to negotiate a better price. If the price is too high, you don't buy milk there.

negotiated price   *a price that can be negotiated between the buyer and the seller.*

In contrast, there are a number of products for which buyer and seller bargain with each other until they agree on a price. This is called the **negotiated price**. When you buy a new car, you are very likely to negotiate with the seller. Depending on the make of the car, the time of the year, and competition in the market, you may be able to buy the car for considerably less than the price shown on the sticker. The more you know about the product, the better your negotiating position will be. In the case of an automobile, for example, you may find it helpful to know how much the dealer paid for it. You can obtain this information by looking in *Edmund's New Car Price Buying Guide.*

Role of Price in Our Economy

The price mechanism serves many important functions in a free economy. It enables consumers to compare value, stimulates production and demand, and allocates scarce goods and resources among competing buyers. As the International Example (page 423) points out, there are major distortions in the market-

The Waldorf Astoria Hotel in New York City sets its prices high. Its customers are willing to pay a premium for elegance and prestige.

The Ruble and the Dollar

No area of the world changed faster or more dramatically than did the Russian Republic in 1991. To illustrate this point, in August of 1991, the official exchange rate of the ruble (Russian currency) was $1.70 for one ruble, but the unofficial, or black market, rate was 3 cents for one ruble.

The distortion in the marketplace caused by such a wide difference between official and unofficial rates was staggering. For example, a Sony Video 8 video camera sold for approximately 40,000 rubles in Moscow in August 1991. If the purchaser bought rubles with dollars on the black market, the video camera would cost $1,200 (40,000 × $.03). However, if the rubles were purchased from the government at the official prices, the video camera would cost $68,000 (40,000 × $1.70).*

In 1991, if you had dollars, and were not caught exchanging them on the black market, you could live quite comfortably. To illustrate, the video camera that sold for $1,200 in Moscow at the black market rate sold for approximately the same amount in the United States in August 1991. Unfortunately, most Russian citizens did not have any dollars, and if they were caught exchanging what few dollars they had on the black market, they might be sent to jail. Of course, most Russian citizens could not even dream of purchasing a video camera.

The difference in the exchange rates was due to several factors, including the confidence the Russian people had in their economy. Until the Russian economy is able to generate enough real wealth by selling high-quality, competitively priced products in the world marketplace, Russian citizens will continue to prefer dollars to rubles, which will drive the price of dollars up and the price of rubles down.

*P. Galuszka and P. Kranz, "Welcome to the Moscow Shopping Mall," *Business Week,* 19 August 1991, p. 44.

---

place when price is not permitted to reflect the real value of products and services. We will now take a closer look at the three key functions of price.

Comparison. The price of a product allows the buyer to estimate its value, or worth, relative to other products. A pineapple may be worth two oranges, three guavas, and one and a half papayas, but it is more convenient to express value in terms of dollars and cents. That way, all goods have a common measure of value. A higher price is generally thought to mean greater product quality. Which camera is of higher quality? Probably the more expensive one.

Stimulation. Price also performs a stimulation function. It acts as a signal, telling producers whether they should produce more goods and consumers whether they should buy more of them. All else being equal, a price increase, by increasing sales revenue and profits, stimulates production. A price decrease, by extending the consumer's purchasing power, encourages more spending on goods and services. That is, it stimulates demand.

Rationing. Finally, the pricing mechanism is said to "ration" scarce goods and resources. Imagine a society in which there is no scarcity. All goods are infinitely abundant and therefore free. Since all goods are freely available, they have no particular value, and people take as much as they want.

Now imagine a society in which all goods are scarce to one degree or another. Each good has value and therefore has a price. The buyer who wants a good must purchase it. Buyers with limited amounts of money compete for scarce goods. This is what we mean by rationing. Who purchases each particular good is determined by the price of the good, the income of the buyer, and the expected utility of the purchase to the individual buyer.

PRICING OBJECTIVES

According to theory, businesses in an economy such as ours select a price for each good so as to maximize profits from the sale of that good. We say that the rational business person is a profit maximizer. In reality, however, businesses have other pricing objectives besides maximizing profits. It may be that they lack the information needed to make profit-maximizing decisions. Or perhaps their goal in making pricing decisions is somewhat less ambitious—satisfactory profits rather than maximum profits. Some of the more common pricing objectives are pricing to achieve a specified return on investment (ROI), pricing to obtain a target market share, and pricing to meet or match the competition.

Achieving a Target Return on Investment

target-return-on-investment pricing *the practice of setting price to achieve a specified yield on an investment.*

Target-return-on-investment pricing is the practice of setting price to achieve a specified yield on an investment. For example, if a company has a $20,000 investment in productive assets and wants a 25 percent before-tax return, the product should be priced to earn expected profits of $5,000 ($20,000 × .25).

Achieving Target Market Share

target-market-share pricing *the practice of setting price to obtain a specified share of the market.*

Many firms use **target-market-share pricing**, in which they price their products with the goal of achieving a certain share of the overall market. Such a goal might be 15 percent of all transistor sales in the United States in the upcoming business year. In general, a price reduction leads to an increase in market share, and a price hike leads to a decrease in market share.

A second quantity objective would be to maximize sales of a product. If this is the objective, the product price would be set as low as possible while still making a profit. For example, it is clear that a low price alone will not place a book on the *New York Times* best sellers list, but a relatively low price certainly helps improve the sales of a book that is good to begin with.

Meeting or Matching the Competition

Some firms do not have a specific pricing policy of their own. They let other firms make their pricing decisions for them. The firm raises or lowers its prices in response to the actions of its competitors. Du Pont, for example, has a policy of adopting the market price on products for which it is not the industry leader.

SETTING PRICE—PERFECT COMPETITION

As you learned in Chapter 1, perfect competition is a theoretical model of the economy in which prices are established by the marketplace, not by the action of any one buyer or seller. Three conditions must exist for a market to be perfectly competitive. First, there must be many producers selling products that are exactly alike to many buyers. Second, there must be no government intervention in the marketplace. Third, each buyer and seller must have perfect information. That is, they must always be aware of all of the activities of the other buyers and sellers.

In the world of perfect competition, supply and demand work together to set product price. To illustrate, as demand for a product increases, the price of the product increases, and more firms enter the market to take advantage of the high profit potential associated with the product's price. As product supply increases,

Competition has a strong effect on pricing. This family could buy the same products in many other places, so the grocery store must be careful not to overprice.

the price stabilizes and may even decline. As the price goes down, more people demand the product and fewer firms supply it, because it is no longer as profitable as when the price was higher.

In the real world, no markets meet all the criteria for perfect competition. However, some are competitive enough that the basic forces of supply and demand have a significant impact on prices. For example, the demand for oil-field drill pipe increased significantly in 1990; as a result, its price increased dramatically. Then the price of drill pipe stabilized, as marginal steel producers began to produce more of it to take advantage of the high prices.

SETTING PRICE—THE REAL WORLD

Now that we have examined how prices are set in a perfectly competitive economy, we can examine five factors that are important in setting prices in the real world. We will then look at how firms set prices using cost and demand information.

Choosing a Price

What factors do sellers consider in making pricing decisions? As shown in Figure 16–1, the cost of the product, the objectives of the company or store, competition, customer needs and characteristics, and economic conditions all affect pricing decisions.

Product Cost. The manufacturing or purchase cost of a product is the basic factor in establishing its selling price. Goods and services are generally sold above cost, unless the seller is attempting to close out a line or the merchandise has been damaged in some way. Another exception is the loss leader—a product

FIGURE 16-1   Factors in Setting Price

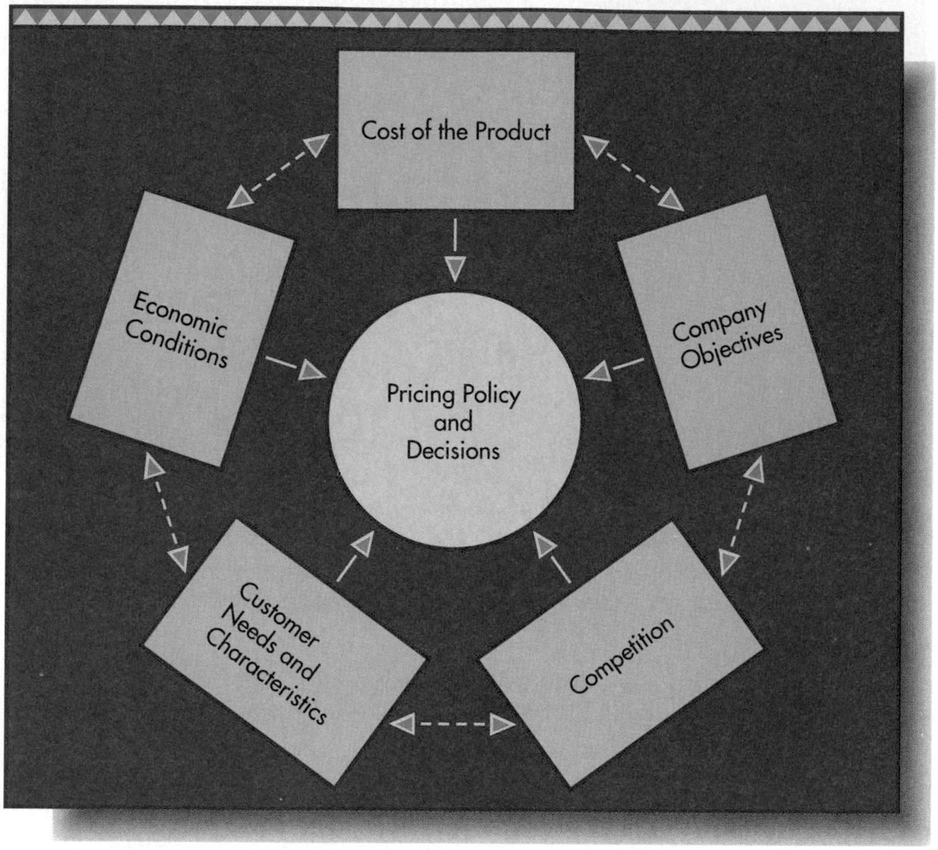

sold at or below cost so as to promote the sale of other products. Loss leaders are discussed later in this chapter.

Company Objectives. Company objectives also play an important role in pricing decisions. One of the objectives General Motors had for the Saturn was to capture a large share of the price-conscious market for automobiles. Accordingly, GM priced the car as low as possible. The redesigned 1992 Buick Roadmaster, on the other hand, is designed to appeal to a much smaller, less price-conscious segment of the market for new cars. The typical Roadmaster buyer is more concerned about quality, elegance, comfort, performance, and prestige than about price. Thus, the Roadmaster could be priced further above cost than the Saturn.

Competition. The greater the competition in the marketplace, the more care a firm should take in making pricing decisions. In addition, the greater the similarity between a firm's products and those of its competitors, the more it must depend on price to sell its products. One reason the Mercedes-Benz has been so expensive is that other companies have only recently introduced cars designed to compete with it. For years, Mercedes-Benz stood alone in its product class. Therefore, it was able to command a high price in the market. Competition from new high-priced, high-quality Japanese automobiles such as the Lexus will make it harder for Mercedes-Benz to raise the price of its products.

Customer Needs and Characteristics. Consumer tastes and preferences, shopping habits, income levels, and other demographic characteristics all have an impact on pricing decisions. Affluent shoppers are not particularly price conscious. Indeed, they may seek out products with high price tags. Young people have different need for products and services than do elderly people.

Economic Conditions. For many goods and services, sales volume depends on the health of the economy. In a vigorous and expanding economy, income levels are high, and both consumers and businesses buy more goods and services. They can also afford to pay higher prices for them. In a recession, income is down, and profitable investment opportunities are few. Sellers may reduce prices in an attempt to get people to buy. For example, as the economy began to slip into a recession in late 1990, retailers put on unusually large pre-Christmas sales in hopes of stimulating demand.

We will now examine how cost and demand factors are used to establish prices.

Cost Pricing

It stands to reason that firms consider product-related costs in making their pricing decisions. The selling price must be greater than the cost of production if the firm hopes to make a profit. Under the **cost pricing** approach, production or purchase cost is the starting point in making pricing decisions.

cost pricing a philosophy of pricing in which production or purchase cost is the starting point in making pricing decisions.

Markup Pricing. **Markup pricing**, or **cost-plus pricing**, is the practice of establishing price by adding a predetermined percentage to the cost of manufacturing or purchasing the product. The **markup** is the amount added to production or purchase cost. The cost plus the markup equals the selling price. The box on page 428, "Setting Prices According to the Markup Method," illustrates how the markup method is used to set the final selling price of a product.

markup pricing or *cost-plus pricing* the practice of establishing price by adding a predetermined percentage to the cost of manufacturing or purchasing the product.

Because it makes sense and is easy to understand, markup pricing is used by many retail firms, especially those that sell a variety of products. The markup percentage varies from one product type to another. In a grocery store, the markup on canned food might be 15 percent; on meat, 25 percent; and on frozen foods, 30 percent. Three things determine the markup percentage: the level of competition, the level of risk associated with selling the products, and the amount of overhead expenses that the seller needs to cover.

markup the amount added to production or purchase cost to arrive at the selling price.

Markup is normally stated as a percentage of selling price, but it can also be stated as a percentage of cost. Suppose that a furniture store paid $300 for a chair and added a $100 markup to that purchase cost. The chair would sell for $400. As Table 16–1 indicates, the markup is 25 percent if stated in terms of selling price but 33.33 percent if stated in terms of purchase cost. Ideally, the markup percentage, however defined, should reflect both the demand for the product and the cost of stocking and maintaining it.

Business Career

Cost Clerk: Calculates cost of labor, material, time, and overhead, and the relationship of revenues to costs. Gathers data for calculations from time and production sheets, payrolls, and schedules. Prepares reports showing total costs, selling prices, and profits. *Average Salary: $16,000.*

The mechanical application of markup pricing involves two important problems. First, markup pricing does not consider demand for the individual product. If a firm applies the same markup to all its products, it may underprice some and overprice others. As an example, the manager of a women's junior clothing store knows that there is strong demand for the current styles of designer jeans. These products can be marked up more than dressier slacks. A store that applied a single markup to all women's slacks would miss the opportunity to make additional profits from the high-demand item. Also, it could lose sales of the dressier slacks, which might benefit from a lower markup.

Setting Prices According to the Markup Method

Markups are typically stated in terms of selling price. The accompanying illustration shows how a markup chain is calculated. Notice how the product, a table lamp, moves down a distribution system from the manufacturer to a wholesaler and then to the retailer. The markup chain follows the same path. At each stage in the chain, the selling price of the lamp increases as markups are added to the purchase cost.

Direct and Indirect Cost

The cost figure used in marking up a product—that is, in setting its selling price—is the direct cost of producing or acquiring it. In the case of our markup chain, this is the $40 production cost for the manufacturer, the $60 purchase cost for the wholesaler, and the $80 purchase cost for the retailer. We know that this cost plus the dollar markup equals selling price. The markup in dollars at each stage must be big enough to cover all the indirect costs associated with the production, acquisition, and sale of the lamp. Indirect costs include rent on buildings, insurance and utility costs, telephone bills, and salaries. Also, the dollar markup must allow for a profit on each unit sold. For example, the retailer buys the lamp from the wholesaler for $80. The retailer's accountant has estimated per-unit indirect cost at $60. The retailer selects a selling price of $160, marking up the product $80. This leaves a per-unit profit of $80 − $60 = $20. Remember: Profit per unit equals selling price minus the sum of indirect cost and direct cost. $160 − ($60 + $80) = $20.

Calculating the Markup Percentage

To calculate the markup percentage, we need to know the direct cost of the product and the selling price. For the lamp manufacturer, the production cost is $40 and its selling price is $60. The dollar markup is $60 − $40 = $20. When expressed as a percentage of selling price, the markup percentage equals the dollar markup divided by the selling price. The markup percentage for the manufacturer is $20 ÷ $60 = 33.33 percent.

Setting Price with the Markup Percentage

Now we're ready to use a markup percentage to set selling price. Assuming a customary practice in the wholesaling industry of marking up products 25 percent, we can easily

A second problem is that overhead may vary substantially from one product to another. Men's suits usually command a higher markup than men's dress shirts, since it takes more of the salesperson's time to sell a suit than a shirt. In addition, once the suit is sold, the store may have to pay for the cost of alterations, which it would not have to do with a shirt. Allocation of overhead is always a difficult task.

TABLE 16-1 Markup Calculation

	Percentage of Selling Price	Percentage of Cost
Retailer's Cost	$300.00	$300.00
Markup	100.00	100.00
Price	400.00	400.00
Percent Markup =	$\dfrac{\text{Dollar Markup}}{\text{Selling Price}}$	$\dfrac{\text{Dollar Markup}}{\text{Cost}}$
	$\dfrac{100}{400} = 25\%$	$\dfrac{100}{300} = 33.33\%$

calculate the selling price. The wholesaler buys the product for $60. If the markup percentage is to be 25 percent, then the direct cost to the wholesaler must equal 75 percent of its selling price. This is because cost plus markup equals selling price. Therefore, the wholesale price of the lamp is set using the following formula:

$$.75x = \$60$$
$$x = \$60 \div .75$$
$$x = \$80 = \text{Selling Price}$$

The wholesaler buys the lamp for $60 and, knowing that the appropriate markup percentage is 25 percent, computes the selling price of $80. The retailer would follow the same steps in setting the retail selling price.

Markup Chain for a Table Lamp

	$	%
Manufacturer		
Cost	40	67
Markup	20	33
Selling Price	60	100
Wholesaler		
Cost	60	75
Markup	20	25
Selling Price	80	100
Retailer		
Cost	80	50
Markup	80	50
Selling Price	160	100

Break-Even Analysis. A second approach to cost pricing, **break-even analysis**, shows how alternative prices affect the firm's profit on a product. Before we see how break-even analysis works, two terms need to be defined: variable costs and fixed costs.

Variable costs, as the name indicates, vary with the level of production or sales of the product. Increases in production or sales make total variable costs go up. An example of a variable cost is the cost of the cotton-polyester material used in the manufacture of sport shirts. As more shirts are produced, the total cost of the fabric increases. If production is stopped completely, variable costs will drop to zero.

Fixed costs are costs that do not vary with the level of production or sales. If our shirt manufacturer stops making shirts, it will still have to pay its fire insurance premiums and the salaries of its executives. These are fixed costs. Table 16–2 lists other examples of costs that are usually classified as variable and fixed.

Break-even analysis determines a product's **break-even point**, which is the volume of sales at which total revenue exactly equals total cost, both variable and fixed. When sales of any product are greater than the break-even point, the product earns a profit. When sales are less than the break-even point, the product loses money. The break-even point is calculated using this formula:

break-even analysis an approach to cost pricing that shows how alternative prices affect the firm's profit on a product.

variable costs costs that vary with the level of production or sales of the product.

fixed costs costs that do not vary with the level of production or sales.

break-even point the volume of sales at which total revenue exactly equals total cost.

$$\text{Break-Even Point in Units} = \frac{\text{Total Fixed Costs}}{\text{Unit Selling Price} - \text{Unit Variable Cost}}$$

TABLE 16-2   Examples of Fixed and Variable Costs

Fixed Costs	Variable Costs
Management's Salaries	Heating Expenses
Trade Association Dues	Labor Costs
Building Security	Raw Materials
Depreciation on Plant and Equipment	Shipping Expenses
Property Taxes	Electricity to Run Machines

Consider the case of a product with an $80 selling price, variable costs of $30 per unit, and fixed costs of $10,000. The break-even point for this product is 200 units, calculated as follows:

$$\frac{\$10,000}{\$80 - \$30} = \frac{\$10,000}{\$50} = 200 \text{ Units}$$

margin   *the unit selling price minus the variable costs per unit.*

Let's state this relationship another way. The **margin** is the unit selling price minus the variable costs per unit—in the above example, $80 − $30 = $50. If the firm sold 200 units at a margin of $50 per unit, it would generate $10,000 in revenues. This is just enough to cover the product's fixed costs. The break-even point can be calculated for any price level by substituting that price (say, $75 or $90) into the formula.

The break-even relationships are shown in Figure 16–2(a). The fixed-cost curve is horizontal, indicating that fixed costs do not change with the level of production. Variable costs are added to the fixed costs and increase as the level of production increases. The total-cost curve is the sum of variable costs and fixed costs. Finally, the total-revenue curve is the price per unit multiplied by the number of units sold. The higher the price, the steeper the angle of the revenue curve. The total-revenue curve intersects the total-cost line at the break-even point—in this case, at 200 units and at total revenue of $16,000, which is simply the price of the product ($80) times the number of units that it takes to break even (200 units).

Notice what happens in Figure 16–2(b) when the price of the product is raised to $130. The fixed costs and the variable costs are the same as in part (a). All that has changed is the price of the product. The total revenue line does increase at a faster or steeper rate than it did when the price was only $80, and it intersects the total cost curve at 100 units. The break-even point in dollars is $13,000, which is the new higher price ($130) times the number of units that it takes to break even (100).

Break-even analysis is a good tool for examining the relationship between costs and revenue. Note, however, that break-even analysis does not determine a product's price. Rather, it enables management to determine the effect of a price change on the number of units the firm must sell in order to break even. The higher the price, the lower the break-even point will be; the lower the price, the higher the break-even point. It is also useful for evaluating the impact of a change in fixed or variable costs.

FIGURE 16-2(a) and (b)   Break-Even Analysis

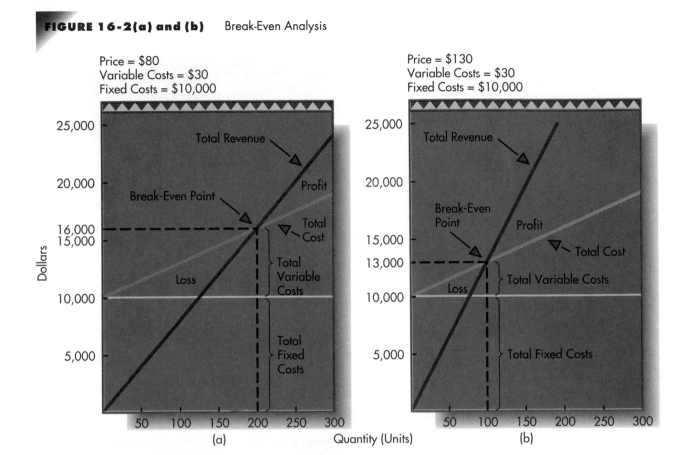

Price = $80
Variable Costs = $30
Fixed Costs = $10,000

Price = $130
Variable Costs = $30
Fixed Costs = $10,000

The biggest problem with break-even analysis is that it is based strictly on costs. That is, after conducting a break-even analysis, we know how many units must be sold to break even, but we do not know whether consumers will buy the product at the price used to calculate the break-even point. This can be determined only after studying the market for the product or service.

Target-Return-on-Investment Pricing   Earlier in this chapter, achieving a target return on investment was described as an important pricing objective for many businesses. With a target-return-on-investment pricing policy, the manager tries to set a price for a product that will achieve a specific target return. This technique is often used when a business is introducing a new product to the market. The manager wants to know if enough of the product can be sold at the price necessary to achieve the target return. If the market will not accept a price high enough to meet the target return, management may decide not to introduce the product.

Target-return-on-investment pricing can be implemented with break-even analysis. The first step is to estimate the amount of money needed to introduce the product and then specify a required rate of return. The dollar return figure is calculated and then added to the fixed-cost figure in the numerator of the break-even formula. To illustrate, again suppose that selling price is $80, unit variable costs are $30, and fixed costs are $10,000. Suppose further that the required investment is $20,000 and that the firm desires a 25 percent return on investment—that is, a $5,000 return ($20,000 × .25) before taxes. The target-return-on-investment break-even point is calculated as follows:

$$\text{Target-Return-on-Investment Break-Even Point} = \frac{\text{Fixed Costs} + \text{Required Return}}{\text{Price} - \text{Variable Costs per Unit}}$$
$$= \frac{\$10,000 + \$5,000}{\$80 - \$30}$$
$$= \frac{\$15,000}{\$50}$$
$$= 300 \text{ Units}$$

Note that 300 units is not the break-even point. Rather, it is the number of units that the firm must sell at the $80 price to achieve a 25 percent return on investment. Sales greater than 300 units would contribute more to profits than the 25 percent return on investment. If total sales were less than 300 units, the firm would be falling short of its target-return-on-investment objective. Figure 16–3 diagrams target-return-on-investment break-even analysis. It is important to note that the required return of $5,000 is added to the fixed cost of $10,000. The rest of the break-even analysis is graphed in the same manner as Figure 16–2(a).

The next step in the analysis is to decide whether the target figure of 300 units is reasonable, given a selling price of $80 and current demand conditions. It may be necessary for the firm to lower the selling price, thereby increasing the

FIGURE 16-3   Target-Return-on-Investment Break-Even Analysis

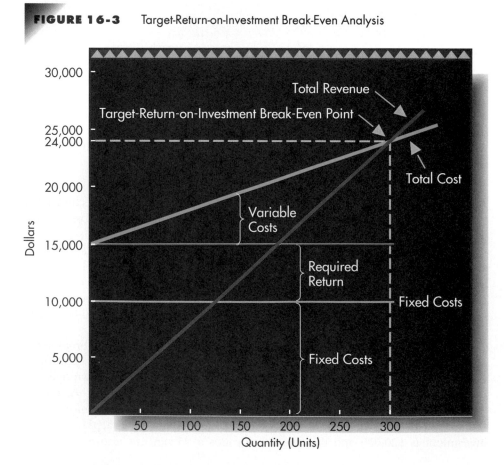

number of units that must be sold before the firm reaches its return objective of $5,000.

Demand Pricing

The second basic approach to making price decisions is **demand pricing**. Under this approach, managers set the price of a product to reflect the level of demand for it. Products in great demand tend to be more expensive; products for which demand is weak tend to be less expensive. We'll look at the demand curve as an introduction to demand pricing. Then we'll turn to two demand-pricing techniques: psychological pricing and differential pricing.

demand pricing   a method of pricing in which price is determined by the level of demand for the product.

The Demand Curve.   As discussed in Chapter 1, the demand curve is the fundamental tool of economic analysis. It shows the relationship between the price of a product and the amount of the product sold. The demand curve slopes downward—that is, as the price of a product decreases, more of the product is demanded and sold. Figure 16–4 shows a typical demand curve. In this example, the firm can sell 50 units of the product at a price of $10. At a price of $5, the firm can sell 175 units. As you can see, the firm can sell more when it lowers the price and less when it raises the price.

Psychological Pricing.   Many marketing executives believe that psychological or non-economic factors play an important role in how much people will pay for a particular product. When executives consider psychological factors in setting prices, they are using **psychological pricing**. For example, many people associate quality with price. Therefore, if they are looking for high quality, or want to impress someone with their good taste, they are more likely to purchase a product if it has a higher price. This emphasis on prestige can be illustrated with wine. Since most of us are not wine experts, if we want to take a high-quality wine to our boss's home for dinner, we will want and expect to pay more per bottle than if we were using it to cook with at home. Thus, winemakers must not charge too low a price for their better wines, since many people associate budget price with poor quality and will not buy the wine at all.

psychological pricing   a method of pricing in which psychological or non-economic factors are considered in determining price.

FIGURE 16-4   The Demand Curve

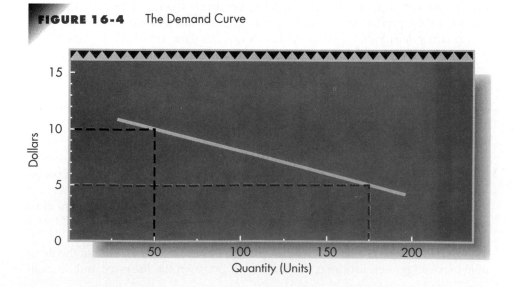

odd/even pricing *giving a product an odd price, rather than an even amount, so as to attract potential buyers.*

A second psychological consideration is **odd/even pricing**. Are shoppers more likely to buy a product at an odd price, such as $1.95, than at an even price, such as $2? Whether or not it is actually true, retailers certainly believe so and price their products accordingly. In a study of 1,865 supermarkets in 70 cities, 64 percent of the prices investigated ended in a 9 and 19 percent ended in a 5. Only 1 percent of the supermarket prices ended in a 0.[1] Most practitioners of odd/even pricing do so in the belief that consumers perceive $1.95 as a much lower price than $2. In any case, odd/even pricing has become standard practice in most retail stores.

differential pricing *the practice of pricing products differently to match varying levels of demand in different market segments.*

Differential Pricing. The other major demand-pricing technique is **differential pricing**. It is used when the market for a product is made up of several distinct segments. (Market segmentation was discussed in Chapter 13.) The product is sold at a higher price to people who are willing to pay more for it. That's one segment. The same product is sold at a lower price to people who value it less. That's another segment. The important point is that the difference in price does not result from any difference in cost. It reflects only a difference in demand.

Differential pricing is normally based on time or location. The demand for a product often varies with the season of the year or the time of day. For example, resort hotels in Florida charge higher rates in the winter, when demand is greatest, than in the summer, when demand falls off. Location-based differential pricing is also common. Theater tickets are an example. A seat close to the stage is more expensive than one in the back. The difference in ticket price is again a function of demand, not of cost. The more heavily demanded tickets are more expensive. The cost of installing and maintaining the seats is the same regardless of their location.

As we have seen, a firm can use either a cost or a demand approach for setting price. We will now look at the pricing policies that guide managers in making pricing decisions.

PRICING POLICIES

Pricing policies provide the framework for making consistent, realistic pricing decisions. Although policies are hard to develop, a firm that has a good set of pricing policies will make better pricing decisions than a firm that does not. Unfortunately, there is no perfect set of pricing policies that works all of the time. The policies must be tailored to the needs of each firm. Let's look at three of the most important aspects of pricing policy: price discounts, new product pricing, and geographic pricing.

Price Discounts

list price *the publicly stated price for which a firm or store expects to sell a product.*

Most products have a list price. A **list price** is the publicly stated price for which a firm or store expects to sell a product. It is called a list price because many manufacturers publish a list of prices for their products in a book or folder, which is given to their customers. As discussed in the Ethical Issue (page 435), it may be legal for a manufacturer to try to control the reseller's price for its products, but this practice presents significant ethical questions. For one thing, consumers must spend more for the manufacturer's products than if the goods were sold at a discount.

When a reseller, whether a wholesaler or a retailer, charges less than the manufacturer's suggested list price, the difference between the list price and the sell-

Anti-Discount Policies

Many manufacturers try to control the prices of their products at the retail level. For example, Prince Manufacturing, maker of Prince tennis racquets, provides its dealers with "suggested ranges" for six of its lines of racquets. In a July 30, 1990, pricing directive, Prince stated:

> Prince will not supply these racquets to accounts which we believe will sell them at a price below the suggested range of retail pricing listed above. In the event Prince becomes aware of a dealer pricing a racquet below these guidelines, it will, following receipt of verification acceptable to Prince, suspend shipment to that account of that racquet and in its sole discretion, any or all other racquets on this pricing policy.*

Manufacturers defend this type of policy by stating that if they do not control the retail price of their products, stores will discount them to obtain quick sales in the short-run. Manufacturers consider this to be a short-sighted strategy that will result in retailers not making enough money to continue to be able to sell their products.

It is clearly legal for a manufacturer to try to control the final price of its products, as long as it does not conspire with one or more of its retailers to set prices. However, the situation does present several ethical problems.

Such a pricing policy assumes that manufacturers know more about establishing retail prices than retailers do. This canot be substantiated by any research. Also, it smacks of a "big brother" approach to business. The reason our market system works well is that it is able to adjust quickly and efficiently to market conditions. For example, if there is not sufficient demand for Prince racquets in a certain community, the market dictates that their price would fall to the point at which the retailer could sell them. If Prince's pricing policies keep racquet prices from being discounted, the market will not function efficiently. Highly efficient, low-cost discount stores will not be able to pass their savings on to the consumer. This means that consumers will inevitably pay more for Prince racquets than they would have if the product were available in discount stores. When price competition is taken out of the retail environment, the consumer will inevitably pay more for a product.

*P. M. Barrett, "Anti-Discount Policies of Manufacturers Are Penalizing Certain Cut-Price Stores," *Wall Street Journal*, 27 February 1991, p. B1.

---

ing price is referred to as the **discount**. Discounts are usually based on the quantity purchased, the season of the year, the firm's sales objectives, or the terms of payment.

discount the difference between the list price and the selling price.

Quantity Discounts. Most firms offer discounts on large orders. **Quantity discounts** encourage customers to purchase a larger order than they otherwise might. Quantity discounts not only help sell more products but also reduce the cost of making a sale. One large order of 100 units requires much less paperwork than 10 orders of 10 units each. Also, a large order does not take much more of a salesperson's time than a small order.

quantity discounts discounts offered to encourage large orders.

Quantity discounts can be either cumulative or noncumulative. Buyers qualify for **cumulative discounts** when their total purchases over a period of time reach a certain amount—say, $5,000. Usually, the greater the total amount purchased, the greater the cumulative discount will be. Cumulative discounts encourage customer loyalty and repeat purchasing. Some hardware stores, for example, offer a 10 percent discount off the list price on a gallon of paint when customers buy more than six gallons of paint during any three-month period.

cumulative discounts discounts offered when total purchases over a period of time reach a certain amount.

Buyers qualify for **noncumulative discounts** when an individual purchase exceeds a specified amount, not when total purchases over a period of time exceed a certain level. For example, a home improvement contractor might receive a 20 percent discount for buying 15 five-gallon buckets of drywall compound in a single purchase. The discount would not be offered if each bucket were purchased one at a time. Noncumulative discounts reduce sellers' paper-

noncumulative discounts discounts offered when an individual purchase is larger than a specified amount.

work, but they do not foster customer loyalty in the same way that cumulative discounts do.

Seasonal Discounts.

seasonal discount *a discount based on the time of year.*

A price reduction is called a **seasonal discount** when it is based on the time of year. The sales of many firms vary dramatically in different seasons. A retailer of swimsuits may sell 80 percent of its suits in May and June. Beginning in late June, the retailer offers shoppers a seasonal discount in order to sell off the remaining suits in stock. Alternatively, the retailer could hold the line on price, sell a few swimsuits, and keep the rest in inventory until the following May. The problem with this approach is that the retailer must pay inventory costs on the leftover stock. Moreover, styles may change, and customers may not want last year's fashions.

Promotional Discounts.

promotional discounts *discounts offered to encourage customers to buy particular products.*

markdown *a discount designed to encourage customers to buy a product that they otherwise would not purchase at that time.*

loss leader *a product that is sold at or below cost in order to stimulate the sales of other products.*

Promotional discounts are offered to encourage sales of particular products. There are two types of promotional discounts: markdowns and loss leaders. A **markdown** is a discount designed to encourage customers to buy a product that they would not otherwise purchase at that time. At the beginning of this chapter, it was pointed out that American Airlines was forced to discount, or mark down, its tickets to encourage people to fly in 1990. Unfortunately for the airline industry, the market remained slow in 1991. During that year, more than 90 percent of all airline tickets were sold at a discount.

A **loss leader** is a product that is sold at or below cost in order to stimulate the sales of other products. Grocery stores regularly advertise loss leader items, such as a package of hotdog buns for 15 cents or a gallon of milk for $1.60. Store managers know that they would be in big trouble if shoppers purchased only the hotdog buns and the milk. However, managers hope that the low prices on these goods will bring in people who will then buy a week's worth of groceries. It is on these additional purchases that the store will make its profits.

Cash Discounts.

cash discount *a discount offered when the buyer pays for the product within a certain period of time.*

It is a common practice in many industries for the seller to offer a discount when the buyer pays for the product within a certain period of time. This is called a **cash discount**. For example, some invoices read "2/10, net 30." This means that payment is due in 30 days but that a discount of 2 percent on the amount due can be taken if the entire bill is paid within ten days. An invoice that reads "net 30 days" means that payment for a purchase is due in full within 30 days, with no discount offered.

Firms offer cash discounts to encourage prompt payment of bills and rapid turnover of accounts payable into cash. These discounts also give the firm a competitive edge if few of its competitors also offer them. Smart buyers take cash discounts whenever they can. Although a 2 percent discount, as in "2/10, net 30," may not seem like much at first glance, it amounts to a 36.5 percent return if expressed on an annual basis! To see how this works, suppose the buyer takes the discount on the tenth day rather than paying the full invoiced amount on the thirtieth day. This 2 percent discount can be viewed as a 2 percent return for a 20-day period. Since there are 18.25 20-day periods in a year, this amounts to a 36.5 percent annual return (.02 × 18.25). Where else can you earn this much at no risk?

New Product Pricing

There are two common strategies that firms use when pricing new products: price skimming and penetration pricing. We examine these two strategies in the subsections that follow.

Price Skimming. The term **price skimming** refers to the policy of giving a new product an artificially high price. An "artificially" high price is one that the firm will not be able to hold as other sellers move into the market with products of their own.

Figure 16–5 shows how price skimming works. Suppose that the market price for Avalon Electronics' new household video projection system is expected to stabilize at $300 a unit. Avalon introduces its system at $600; during the first year, it sells 1,000 units at this price. Then competitors begin to introduce models of their own. Now Avalon starts cutting price, and eventually the long-run price of $300 is reached. Thereafter, Avalon sells 6,500 units annually. Price skimming, in effect, enables Avalon to segment its market according to how much consumers are willing and able to pay for its video projection system. Avalon initially sells its system to that segment of the market that is willing to pay a little extra to own the product when it first comes out. Then, as competitive pressures develop and producers saturate the market with their offerings, Avalon successively cuts price to appeal to a broader market.

As we suggested, the successful price skimmer can expect competitors to introduce similar products. The Reynolds Pen Company is a classic example of a firm that used price skimming successfully. Reynolds introduced the ballpoint pen in 1945, with an initial investment of only $26,000. The pen cost 50 cents to produce but was originally priced at $12.50. In less than a year, new competitors had driven the market price for ballpoint pens to under $1.00, but not before Reynolds claimed total after-tax profits of more than $1.5 million. More recently, home computers and cellular telephones have been introduced with a price-skimming strategy.

Penetration Pricing. **Penetration pricing**, the opposite of skimming, is the practice of introducing a product to the market at a relatively low price. In most

price skimming   *the policy of pricing a new product artificially high, to earn extra profits before competition drives the price down.*

penetration pricing   *the practice of introducing a product at a relatively low price, to sell a large quantity to a price-sensitive market.*

FIGURE 16-5   Price Skimming

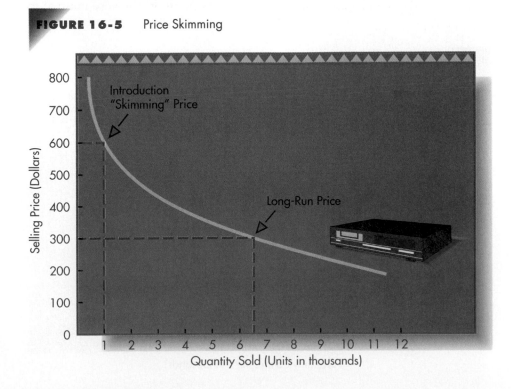

cases, the penetration price is set at the level the firm considers to be the long-run price of the product. In some cases, a firm using very aggressive penetration pricing may even sell its new product at slightly below the expected long-run market price.

Figure 16–6 shows how penetration pricing works for the Snowdrift Company, which is introducing a new laundry detergent with a water-softening additive. The long-run price of the product is expected to be $4. Snowdrift could adopt a penetration pricing strategy and introduce its new laundry detergent at this price. However, the company could be even more aggressive, charging only $3.50 for the product. By adopting an aggressive penetration strategy, Snowdrift discourages other firms from entering the market segment for detergents with water-softening additives. Instead of selling 30,000 units at $4 the first year, Snowdrift sells 60,000 units at $3. Snowdrift may eventually raise its price to $4 and sell 30,000 annually. However, if the detergent has features that encourage brand loyalty, many of the original buyers may continue to purchase it at the higher long-run price.

Evaluation of New Product Pricing. It is impossible to say which strategy is the best. In fact, some multiproduct firms use both strategies. The best approach depends on the situation.

Price skimming works best when there are many buyers willing to pay a high price—a "premium"—to be among the first owners of the product. This occurs only when there is something unique or exotic about the product. For example, when Callaway introduced the Big Bertha driver in 1991, many golfers felt that they just had to have one. They hoped and sometimes prayed that Big Bertha would enable them to hit a golf ball straighter and farther than they could with a conventional driver. Whether or not this was true was unimportant. During the first year that Big Bertha was sold, it carried a premium price above what normal cost and market conditions would dictate. What's more, it was very unusual to

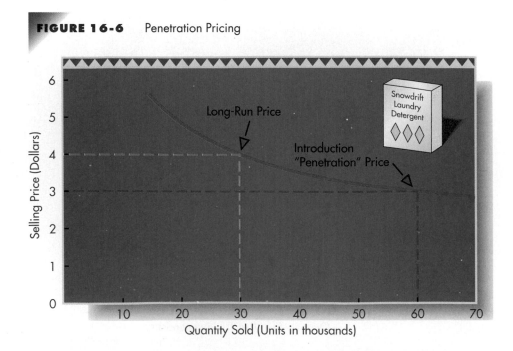

FIGURE 16-6   Penetration Pricing

find Big Bertha sold at even a small discount, whereas most clubs are regularly sold at a discount.

Price skimming minimizes the risk involved in new product introduction. Most firms cannot pump money into a new product indefinitely, and a skimming strategy enables them to recover their initial product investment quickly, thereby freeing funds for investment in other projects. The shorter the payback period for a new product, the less risk is involved. This quick payback feature is especially important to a small company without much cash. The major problem with price skimming is that the initial high price tends to attract potential competitors, who want the early profits for themselves.

The penetration pricer expects to sell a large number of units to a price-sensitive market. Everyday staple goods are normally introduced using penetration pricing. For instance, very few people are willing to pay a premium to be the first buyers of a new brand of household starch. Realizing this, a starch manufacturer must introduce its new product at or below what the market will be able to sustain in the long run.

Penetration pricing has two major advantages. First, profits are small in the beginning because of the low price. Small profits are not desirable in and of themselves, but they do tend to discourage competitors from entering the market, and that is desirable. As we said before, large profits attract competitors. Small profits do not.

The second advantage relates to the first. Penetration pricing often results in greatly increased sales, because the low price attracts many buyers. Heavy sales mean large production runs. At some point, the firm begins to benefit from economies of scale; that is, as the volume of production increases, the per-unit cost of production goes down. Thus, at a constant selling price, unit profit increases as unit product cost decreases.

Herb Kelleher, the founder and chairman of Southwest Airlines, adopted a low-price strategy in the airline business. As indicated in the Profile on page 440, Kelleher felt that there was a large market for inexpensive, efficient airline transportation. His objective was to attract the budget-minded business traveler as well as people who normally traveled between cities by automobile. His formula of keeping his cost as low as possible and attracting a large segment of the market as a result of low fares has made Southwest Airlines one of the most successful airlines in the United States.

Geographic Pricing

One more pricing policy issue to consider is delivery cost. After a sale has been made, who pays the cost of shipping the product to the buyer? Does the buyer or the seller pay? It all depends on the geographic pricing policy of the selling firm. The policy is called "geographic" because the buyers are assumed to be located at some distance from the seller's place of business. Also, the products are assumed to be too big for buyers to carry home in their pockets, so the product is shipped by a suitable carrier. We'll look at four approaches for allocating transportation costs: FOB-factory, FOB-destination, uniform-delivered, and zone-delivered pricing.

FOB-Factory Pricing. "FOB" is a common term in transportation. It means "free on board." Usually, the price is stated as "FOB factory." Under an **FOB-factory pricing** policy, the seller is responsible for loading the product aboard a carrier, but the buyer is responsible for paying all transportation charges after the

FOB-factory pricing *a pricing policy in which the buyer pays all costs of shipping the merchandise once it leaves the seller's place of business.*

Herb Kelleher

Herb Kelleher thinks people should be able to travel quickly and efficiently from one city to another without having to pay a king's ransom. In fact, he has built a billion-dollar corporation based on low-cost travel. Kelleher is known throughout the travel industry as the co-founder, president, chief executive officer, and chairman of Southwest Airlines, the country's most successful low-cost airline. Southwest was the first airline to abandon in-flight meals and offer a bag of peanuts instead.

In the late 1960s, Kelleher was a senior member of a law firm in San Antonio, Texas. When a friend suggested that they start an airline, he eagerly agreed. The two mapped out an initial plan to serve Dallas, Houston, and San Antonio. Air travel between these cities was already available through well-established carriers, but it was expensive. Normally, flying was only for business travelers and those who could afford luxury. The idea behind the new airline was to offer no-frills air transportation at a price much lower than the competition's. It was designed to attract the budget-minded business traveler, as well as individuals who traditionally drove rather than flew between cities.

Southwest Airlines was born in 1971, with three aircraft and $148 in the bank. Twenty years later, it is the country's seventh largest airline in terms of passengers carried. It now flies east as far as Cleveland, west to San Francisco. In between, it serves an additional 30 cities across 14 states. Southwest has identified its niche and is a master at its task. It is the nation's most successful high-frequency, short-distance, low-fare airline.

The key to the company's success is low overhead, low prices, and simplicity. The company's frugality is symbolized by the bag of peanuts. There are no seat assignments. Passengers find their own seats on a first-come, first-served basis. All of the company's planes are Boeing 737s. Using only one type of aircraft, the company saves money by reducing training and maintenance costs. Flight attendants and even pilots pick up trash between flights. The company enjoys the best on-time performance, the best baggage-handling record, and the fewest customer complaints among airline carriers.

A primary factor in keeping costs down is the high level of productivity among Southwest's personnel. The all-union staff maintains a family-like relationship with management. Officers of the company spend one day each quarter working as baggage handlers, ticket agents, and flight attendants, so they knew what it is like on the front lines. Kelleher himself often drops by to chat with employees about the operation. Executives and employees receive the same percentage raises in salary. Employees also have special incentive to give extra, since they own 12 percent of Southwest.

The effort has paid off. Southwest has a dedicated, highly efficient workforce that is willing to make sacrifices. This company spirit is attributed in part to Kelleher's management style, which includes valuing each employee equally and making the entire operation fun both for employees and customers.

Immediately after it was organized, the young company advertised itself as: "The Airline That Love Built." Its commercials featured flight attendants in hot pants lavishing attention on customers. The hot pants of the '70s have since given way to shorts and sneakers for the '90s, but the fun continues. Kelleher himself has been known to show up in bunny costume on Easter Sunday flights.

Herb Kelleher's concept of a low-cost, no-frills airline has yielded rewards for everyone. Corporate leaders enjoy continued profits; employees are happy in their work; customers travel affordably and arrive at their destinations on time; and everyone enjoys the peanuts.

Sources: "Herb Kelleher: The Zany Captain of Southest Airlines," *Best of Business Quarterly*, Vol. 12, No. 3, Fall 1990; "Southwest Airlines: A Model of Superb Management," *Forbes*, 16 September 1991; "A Busy Boss Can Never Fly Solo," *Business Month*, August 1990.

Christmas-tree farming is a large-scale industry in the Pacific Northwest. Customers there pay less for their trees than customers in the East, because of lower delivery costs.

merchandise leaves the seller's place of business. In short, "FOB factory" means that the buyer pays shipping costs.

There is one big problem with FOB-factory pricing. The farther the buyer is from the seller's place of business, the more the buyer pays for the product. The buyer's total cost equals selling price plus transportation costs. Therefore, a seller may have a hard time marketing its products to customers located closer to another supplier of those products.

FOB-Destination Pricing. Under **FOB-destination pricing**, the seller pays all transportation costs. This type of geographic pricing policy is appropriate for products with relatively low transportation costs. A wholesaler of expensive diamonds probably would not bill its retail buyers for shipping costs. It seems unlikely that a firm selling a product worth more than $10,000 would worry about a $30 transportation fee.

Uniform-Delivered Pricing. Under **uniform-delivered pricing**, the seller charges its customers the same delivered price, regardless of where the customers are located or how much it costs to ship the merchandise. Every buyer pays the same price for the product. In setting its price, the seller figures in an amount equal to the average shipping cost.

Uniform-delivered pricing is used most often when transportation costs are small in relation to selling price. In addition, some businesses, such as furniture stores, assume that "free" delivery improves their competitive position.

Zone-Delivered Pricing. **Zone-delivered pricing** is a modification of uniform-delivered pricing. The seller assigns each customer to a geographic zone and charges the customers within each zone the same delivered price for the

FOB-destination pricing *a pricing policy in which the seller pays all costs of transporting the goods to the buyer.*

uniform-delivered pricing *a pricing policy in which the seller charges its customers the same delivered price, regardless of where the customers are located or how much it costs to ship the merchandise.*

zone-delivered pricing *a pricing policy in which the seller assigns each customer to a geographic zone and, within each zone, charges the same delivered price for the goods.*

product. Each customer within the zone pays a price that includes the average cost of shipping the product to buyers in that zone.

Let's assume the following system for a department store in Cincinnati, Ohio. All people living within 20 miles of downtown Cincinnati would belong to the primary market, which is called Zone 1. People living outside a 20-mile radius would be assigned to other zones. The store delivers merchandise free to all its Zone 1 customers but charges a transportation fee equal to 2 percent of the product's selling price for people living in Zone 2, 4 percent for people living in Zone 3, and 6 percent for those living in Zone 4. Thus, customers living outside the seller's primary trading area pay the cost of having their purchases delivered.

SUMMARY POINTS

1 ...st consumer products are sold at a nonnegotiable, fixed price. The consumer either pays the stated price or doesn't buy the product. However, the price of some products can be negotiated between buyer and seller. Price serves three important functions. It allows consumers to compare value between products, stimulates production and demand, and allocates scarce goods and resources among competing buyers.

2 In theory, firms set prices so as to maximize profits on the sale of their products. In reality, however, firms often pursue other goals in their pricing. Some firms set prices so as to achieve a specific return on the firm's investment. A second goal would be to achieve a target market share; prices are then set accordingly. A third goal would be simply to meet or match the competition. A firm pursuing this goal lets other businesses set prices; it merely copies the other firms' prices.

3 Perfect competition is a theoretical model of the economy in which prices are established by the marketplace, not by the action of any one buyer or seller. For perfect competition to exist, there must be many producers selling products that are exactly alike, there must be no government intervention, and each buyer and seller must have perfect information. Under perfect competition, supply and demand work together to set price.

4 The five factors that affect pricing include the cost of the product, the objectives of the company or store, competition, cus-tomer needs and characteristics, and economic conditions. Three cost-oriented pricing techniques are commonly used: markup pricing, break-even analysis, and target-return-on-investment pricing. Markup pricing (or cost-plus pricing) is based on adding a predetermined percentage to the cost of manufacturing or purchasing the product. Break-even analysis examines different pricing alternatives to show how they would affect the firm's break-even point. Target-return-on-investment pricing is similar to break-even analysis, except that the firm adds a predetermined profit to the fixed cost to calculate a target-return-on-investment break-even point. Two demand-oriented pricing techniques are psychological pricing and differential pricing. In the first, non-economic factors play a major role in setting price. In the second, the firm can sell the product at different prices to different market segments.

5 Important aspects of pricing policy include price discounts, new product pricing, and geographic pricing. Quantity discounts are given for large orders; seasonal discounts are based on the time of year. Promotional discounts are designed to stimulate the sales of a product, and cash discounts encourage buyers to pay for products in a specified period of time. Price skimming is a pricing policy for a new product, in which the price is set artificially high. With penetration pricing, on the other hand, a new product is introduced to the market at a relatively low price. "FOB factory" is a geographic pricing term meaning that the buyer must pay the cost of transportation. In contrast, "FOB destination" means that the seller pays all of the transportation cost. Under uniform-delivered pricing, the seller charges all of its customers the same price regardless of their geographic area. Zone-delivered pricing means that all the customers in each specific geographic zone or area pay the same transportation cost.

REVIEW QUESTIONS

1 What is the role of price in our economy?

2 How does the price mechanism ration scarce goods and resources?

3 Explain the differences between target-return-on-investment pricing and target-market-share pricing.

4 Explain what is meant by perfect competition.

5 How do company objectives affect pricing considerations?

6 Identify two important problems associated with the mechanical application of markup pricing.

7 Why is break-even analysis a good tool for examining the relationship between costs and revenue?

8 What is the rationale behind differential pricing?

9 Differentiate between cumulative and noncumulative discounts.

10 What is the difference between a markdown and a loss leader?

11 Define what is meant by "2/10, net 30."

12 Why would a firm use a price-skimming strategy in introducing a product?

13 What is meant by FOB-factory pricing? What is the major problem with this pricing technique?

DISCUSSION QUESTIONS

1 Why are fixed prices most common in our economy?

2 Discuss the most critical considerations in setting the price for a new piece of electronic technology such as the compact disk player.

3 What is the major problem in using break-even analysis to set the price of a product?

4 Why does psychological pricing work for some products and not for others? Name

a product that lends itself to this pricing technique. Explain your answer.

5 In introducing a new line of health food snacks to the market, what would be the best strategy for pricing—price skimming or penetration pricing? Why?

6 In the case of office supplies and office furniture, which geographic pricing strategy would you apply—uniform-delivered pricing or zone-delivered pricing? Why?

EXPERIENTIAL EXERCISES

1 Telephone four airlines and ask about round-trip coach fare between New York and San Francisco, with one stopover for one day in a city of your choice. Now ask the airline representative about discount fares. Is there a discount for purchasing the

ticket 30 days before departure? Is there a discount depending on which day of the week you travel? Is there a student or military discount? Does first class have its own set of discounts? Are some discount tickets sold on a nonrefundable basis? After you have completed your research, what recommendations do you have for the airline industry in terms of its pricing structure?

2 Visit the managers of three local automobile dealership. Ask them to identify

their pricing objectives. Are they profit maximizers? Do they seek a target return on investment? Do they want a certain market share, or do they merely meet or match competitors' prices?

CASES

CASE 16-1
Specialty Products

Harold Simpkins and his brother Edward own and operate Specialty Products, a Denver manufacturing firm specializing in high-quality metal outdoor furniture. The firm's line includes round and rectangular tables, chairs to go with them, and several styles of poolside lounge chairs. The products are always tastefully finished. Over 90 percent of the firm's sales are in Colorado, Idaho, New Mexico, and Texas. Specialty Products has a small sales force that sells directly to its retail customers.

For some time, Harold has felt the need to generate additional revenue. The firm is considering expanding the distribution of its current line of products into California and/or adding one or more new products. Edward feels that the firm should exploit its knowledge of how to use steel and aluminum to manufacture furniture.

Edward has done some tentative market analysis. He believes that there is a good market for metal bunk beds for children's rooms. The beds would be made out of steel tubing, which could be painted in a variety of eye-catching colors.

As the accompanying table indicates, the total fixed cost for the project is $180,000. The firm would have to spend $50,000 on new manufacturing equipment and $15,000 to hire a consultant to design the bunk beds. The administrative cost of $20,000 represents a portion of the executives' time that would be reallocated to the bunk bed project. The marketing fixed costs are additional marketing expenditures required to market the bunk beds.

Fixed Cost Analysis

Product Fixed Cost		$ 50,000
Design Cost		15,000
Administrative Cost		20,000
Marketing Costs		
Salaries	$60,000	
Advertising	20,000	
Sales Promotion	15,000	
Total Marketing		95,000
Total Fixed Cost		$180,000

The variable production cost of the bunk beds is $150 per unit. The firm will also have to spend $75 for two mattresses and pay 10 percent sales commission (based on the sales price) for each unit that the sales force sells. Although Edward does not know how much to charge for the beds, he is aware that similar products sell for $400 to $600 at the retail level.

1. How many units of the bunk beds would the firm have to sell to break even if the price to the retailer were $400?
2. How does the sale of the bunk beds affect the break-even point of Specialty Products' other items?
3. If the Simpkin brothers' goal was to make at least $100,000 profit on the sale of the bunk beds, how many units would they have to sell?
4. If the average retailer had a markup of 40 percent, what would be the price to the final consumer, assuming that Specialty Products sold the bunk beds for $400?
5. Should Specialty Products introduce its bunk beds to the market?

CASE 16-2
General Motors

The pricing of new automobiles has always been complex, from the perspectives of both the retailer and the final consumer. Federal law requires that every new automobile carry a sticker (or list) price, attached to the window. However, very few models are consistently sold at sticker prices. Consumers who would never think about bargaining with a retailer about the price of other products expect to negotiate with the dealer for a discount from the list price of a car.

Invoice prices, which are the prices dealers pay for the cars, are sometimes used in dealers' advertisements. The theme is usually that for a limited period of time, a specific model will be sold for only $100 or $200 above invoice. The consumer who reads the advertisement carefully usually finds that "dealer incentives," or holdbacks, ranging from $250 to $1,500 per car, will be retained by the dealer. Simply put, this means that the dealer will get an incentive from the manufacturer for every car that has been sold, which reduces the actual cost to the dealer to a level below the price stated on the invoice. This, of course, permits the dealer to sell a car below invoice or "dealer cost" and still make a profit.

To complicate the matter further, most dealers sell the previous year's model, as well as the new model, from August through December of every year. Since there may not be much of a change in the new model, many consumers do not understand why the new model costs 3 to 6 percent more than the previous year's. Dealers also sell "demonstrators," which are used by their salespeople as personal cars as well as for test drives, and "factory cars," which have a varied background. Such cars are usually sold at a significant discount, yet they retain their new-car factory warranty. Finally, optional equipment can be purchased as a package or on an item-by-item basis. If the package from the manufacturer contains options that the consumer wants, he or she can save a significant amount of money by purchasing the package rather than each of the items individually.

General Motors and the rest of the American automobile industry had a very difficult time in 1991. GM had a record loss of almost $6 billion, and the prospects for the world's largest automobile company are not very encouraging through the mid-1990s. The chairman of GM, Robert Stempel, announced in December of 1991 that 20 plants would be closed permanently by 1995, reducing the company's workforce by 150,000 people in an attempt to reduce costs and restore the firm to a profitable position. Clearly, some of the factors contributing to this situation were beyond GM's control, such as the recession of 1991 and the war in Iraq. However, Stempel pointed out that GM is the world's high-cost producer of automobiles, taking as much as 40 percent more time than its competitors to produce a car. In addition, many consumers believe that although the quality of American cars has improved significantly, foreign cars are still more trouble-free and easier to maintain.

In an effort to sell its automobiles, GM began offering a wide variety of pricing options to its customers. Some models carry low-interest (2.9 percent), 48-month loans, and others have a factory discount or factory rebate, as well as a discount from the dealer. A factory discount is applied directly to the purchase price of the car, whereas a factory rebate is sent to the car buyer after the car is purchased. However, most dealers will permit the consumer to assign the rebate to the dealer, thereby reducing the price of the car at the time it is sold.

Factory-sponsored leases are another pricing option that is now available to consumers. The lease may be for up to 60 months. At the end of that time, the customer may purchase the car or return it to the dealer. Most leases contain a penalty for driving the car more than a specified number of miles. The cost of the lease varies with interest rates and market demand for certain models. A model that is not selling well may be leased at a lower rate than a comparable car that has met General Motors' sales expectations.

General Motors announced price increases on its 1992 automobiles in August of 1991. Cost was the reason given for some of the price increases. For example, the Chevrolet Cavalier's sticker price increased by $904, or 11.3 percent. The company stated that this price increase would allow GM's "low cost" anti-lock braking system to be offered on new Cavaliers.[2] Other cost increases were rationalized on the basis of overall inflation or costs associated with new government regulations.

1.   How do you think the public reacted to General Motors' price increases for the 1992 model cars?
2.   Does General Motors have a well-coordinated pricing strategy?
3.   Should GM continue to offer rebates, discounts, and low-interest loans on its automobiles?
4.   Why is the lease option of interest to a large number of customers?
5.   What will General Motors have to do next to stimulate the sales of its automobiles?

CHAPTER 17

Promotion

OBJECTIVES

After studying this chapter, you should be able to:

1 Identify the elements in the promotion mix.

2 Discuss advertising objectives and five types of advertising.

3 Evaluate the use of alternative types of advertising media and explain the relationship between the product life cycle and the stages of an advertising campaign.

4 Discuss how advertisements are evaluated and describe the role of advertising agencies.

5 Discuss career opportunities in selling.

6 Describe the roles and responsibilities of salespeople, as well as the stages in the sales process.

7 Explain how sales promotions contribute to the firm's marketing strategy and discuss sales promotion techniques.

8 Discuss the role of publicity in the promotion mix.

The Gillette Company's Sensor shaving system was one of the most visible product launches of 1990. Over the previous ten years, Gillette had spent more than $200 million developing the product. Sensor was advertised during the Super Bowl telecast with "teaser" ads. The advertisements called the product revolutionary because of its system of two blades, individually mounted on springs that enable them to move independently. Sensor's advertising campaign was planned as a $25 million media blitz, but consumer response was so great that Gillette pulled some of its ads, since it could not fill demand for the product.

Nine months later, Sensor had captured an 8.8 percent dollar share of the wet-shave market. This was a remarkable feat in such a competitive segment. The advertising campaign for Sensor was one of the most successful introductions of a new product ever.

In developing a promotional strategy for its new product, Gillette faced the same questions that all firms face. What are the advantages of its product or service? (A close, comfortable shave.) To whom should the communication be directed? (Men who are willing to pay extra for a close, comfortable shave.) What are its major competitors? (Other, less expensive Gillette razors and Schick and Bic products.) How should it reach its potential customers? (TV and print advertisements and point-of-purchase displays.) This chapter will focus on how firms effectively advertise and sell their products.

THE PROMOTION MIX

A company must communicate with its markets. How else are people to know about its products, services, and way of doing business? Between a firm and its markets flows a continuous stream of communication. The old saying goes,

"Build a better mousetrap and the world will beat a path to your door." In truth, the saying should read, "Build a better mousetrap, communicate it properly, and the world *might* beat a path to your door."

There are four major tools that any firm can use to communicate with its market:

1. *Advertising:* any paid nonpersonal presentation of product information to the market.
2. *Personal selling:* oral presentation to a prospective customer or customers, either in person or by phone, for the purpose of selling a product.
3. *Sales promotion:* short-term incentives designed to encourage prospective customers to purchase a product or service.
4. *Publicity:* nonpersonal communication that is not paid for by the sponsor and is designed to stimulate the demand for a product or service or to enhance the general reputation of a firm.[1]

promotion mix *the combination of advertising, personal selling, sales promotion, and publicity used by a firm to communicate product or company information to the market.*

The **promotion mix** is the combination of these tools that a firm chooses to use to communicate product or company information to the market. This chapter will examine each of these four critical elements in the promotion mix.

ADVERTISING

advertising *any paid, nonpersonal presentation of ideas, goods, or services to the market.*

Advertising is any paid, nonpersonal presentation of ideas, goods, or services to the market. The purpose of advertising is to tell the public about the firm and its products and to persuade potential buyers that the firm's products are better than those of its competitors. Stated another way, the purpose of advertising is to stimulate demand. It does this by showing how the product meets a consumer need or by describing product attributes.

Who Advertises?

Most business people believe that good advertising increases both sales and profits. Table 17–1 shows the amount of money spent on advertising in 1990 by ten of the largest U.S. advertisers. In addition to commercial firms, many nonprofit organizations use advertising. The Sierra Club promotes conservation practices. The American Cancer Society discourages smoking. The United Way encourages donations for charitable purposes. Advertising is also used to promote political candidates. A few years ago, only people running for national office regularly bought television and radio time. Today, it is common for a candidate for city council in a large city to spend more than $100,000 on political advertising in a single campaign. A candidate for governor can spend more than $7 million on political advertising in one race.

Advertising Objectives

The ultimate objective of most business advertising is to sell products. This may be approached in different ways. For example, some advertisements encourage people to use the advertised product more often. Greater frequency of use naturally implies greater frequency of purchase. One marketing executive for a popular brand of toothpaste said, "If we could just get people to brush three times a day, our sales would increase almost 33 percent and the American public would be much better off." Another common advertising objective is to introduce a new product to a product line. Marketing managers know that if their firm has a good

TABLE 17-1   The Leading National Advertisers

Rank	Company	Advertising Expenditures
1	Proctor & Gamble Co.	1,224,263,600
2	Philip Morris Companies Inc.	1,199,733,400
3	General Motors Corp.	1,100,929,200
4	Sears Roebuck & Co.	590,765,500
5	PepsiCo, Inc.	546,964,400
6	American Telephone & Telegraph Co.	505,433,300
7	Ford Motor Co.	471,335,200
8	McDonald's Corp.	426,044,400
9	Chrysler Corp.	412,717,300
10	Toyota Motor Corp.	406,538,300

Source: *Ad $ Summary*, published by Leading National Advertisers Inc., January–December 1990 issue.

reputation for a particular type of product, it will be easier for them to add a new product to their line. In such cases, marketing managers hope that the firm's reputation for quality will carry over to the new product.

Types of Advertising

Not all advertising is the same. It can aim to sell a specific product or a category of products. It can be directed at a member of the channel of distribution or at the general public. We will look at five types of advertisements, differing significantly in their objectives and their formats.

Brand Advertisements. **Brand advertisements,** also known as **product advertisements**, are aimed directly at final consumers. These advertisements promote specific brands of products. They create awareness of new products and services, reinforce or establish brand loyalty for a particular product or service, and inform consumers about product changes or new uses for old products or services. Brand advertising is especially important in markets where many products are offered to the public. Brand advertising aimed at consumers can be seen on television at any time of day or night.

brand advertisements or product advertisements advertising that promotes specific products to final consumers.

Nearly all prime-time television commercials focus on the merits of a particular product or service. Such advertising tries to stimulate **selective demand,** which is desire for a particular product or service. In contrast, the California Avocado Growers have engaged in a nationwide advertising campaign to popularize avocados. The purpose of this campaign is not to sell a specific producer's brand of avocado, but rather to sell more avocados from all producers. These advertisements aim to stimulate **primary demand**—the desire for a general product category.

selective demand   desire for a particular product or service.

primary demand   desire for a general product category.

institutional advertising *advertising designed to build a positive image for a company.*

Institutional Advertising. The objective of **institutional advertising** is to build a positive image for a company rather than to communicate the merits of a particular product. Freeport McMoRan, an international oil, gas, and mining company, ran a series of television and print advertisements designed to demonstrate to the public that the company is a good corporate citizen. The advertisements focused on what Freeport McMoRan has done to reclaim the land that it has mined, its efforts to rebuild and equip a park for children in New Orleans, and the economic impact of a new sulphur mine that it recently opened in the Gulf of Mexico. The Profile on page 456 describes the energetic and charismatic chairman of Freeport McMoRan, Jim Bob Moffett, and Case 17–1 presents the dilemma that Freeport McMoRan faced as it created its institutional advertisements.

advocacy advertising *institutional advertising designed to present a firm's position on a public issue, to influence public opinion or educate the public.*

Institutional advertising that is designed to present the firm's position on a public issue is called **advocacy advertising.** The goal is to influence public opinion or educate the public in a way that will benefit the company. Continental Insurance ran a series of advertisements that focused on car theft. The goal was to reduce car theft claims by educating the public about how to minimize the risk of car theft. Several of Unocal's institutional advertisements examined the air pollution problem in southern California. The ads told the public how Unocal was trying to reduce pollution by producing cleaner fuels and by purchasing and then scrapping 7,000 pre-1971 automobiles. Figure 17–1 shows an institutional advertisement for Freeport-McMoRan.

trade advertising *advertising designed to influence members of the channel of distribution to carry the firm's products.*

Trade Advertising. The purpose of **trade advertising** is to communicate with members of the channel of distribution, including wholesalers and retailers. Manufacturers run advertisements in trade papers and magazines in order to persuade wholesalers and retailers to carry their products. Examples of such publications include *Hardware Retailer*, *Supermarket News*, and *Advertising Age*. Figure 17–2 shows a typical trade advertisement.

Trade advertising is much more informative and detailed than the advertising consumers encounter in popular magazines and newspapers. Trade advertisements describe the product offered, make suggestions as to how it can be properly displayed, and point out reasons why the wholesaler or retailer should carry the product. Trade advertising often mentions sales contests and sales training courses.

industrial advertising *advertising designed to tell industrial customers how they can use the advertised product to make their businesses more profitable.*

Industrial Advertising. As mentioned in Chapter 14, many firms sell industrial goods—machinery, tools, parts, and fabrication equipment—to other firms, which then use these goods in manufacturing their products. The makers of industrial goods also advertise to reach their markets. This type of advertising, known as **industrial advertising,** tells customers how they can use the advertised product to make their businesses more profitable.

It is the job of industrial buyers to understand the technical characteristics of the products they buy. Therefore, an effective industrial advertisement must be informative above all else. It acts as a "stand-in" for a sales representative, answering the kinds of technical questions that an industrial buyer would ask if a sales representative were present. Emotional appeals, often used in consumer advertising, are generally not used in industrial ads. Figure 17–3, page 452, presents an industrial advertisement.

retail advertising *store advertising designed to encourage people to buy consumer products at the sponsor's retail outlets.*

Retail Advertising. **Retail advertising** is sponsored by retail stores. The aim of retail advertising is to encourage people to buy consumer products at the sponsor's retail outlets.

FIGURE 17-2   Trade Advertisement

FIGURE 17-1   Institutional Advertisement

FIGURE 17-3 Industrial Advertisement

Some retailers advertise both locally and nationally. J.C. Penney and Sears advertise products through national television and magazines as well as through local newspapers. The idea behind national retail advertising is to tell the public that the national retailer is a good company with which to do business. Its aim is to make shoppers, wherever they live, more loyal to the retailer and its products. In contrast, local retail advertising is directed at shoppers in a particular retail market. Its aim is to increase sales at a specific store. Thus, local advertising stresses the styles, prices, and types of products carried at that store, along with the image that the store would like to convey to the public. Figure 17–4 shows a local retail advertisement.

FIGURE 17-4   Retail Advertisement

Many manufacturers and retailers engage in **cooperative advertising** programs, in which advertising costs are shared by the retailer and the manufacturer. A 50–50 arrangement is common. Cooperative advertising is widely practiced in the United States and offers many benefits for manufacturers. Specifically, it motivates retailers to promote the manufacturer's products. It also gives manufacturers a local tie-in and reduces their advertising costs. Cooperative advertising benefits retailers by lowering their advertising costs and by providing them with professional-quality advertisements. It also gives retailers a tie-in with a national campaign, which may enhance their image and prestige.

cooperative advertising
advertising promotions in which costs are shared by the retailer and the manufacturer.

Advertising Media

A critical decision that all advertisers must make is what media to use to communicate their message. The media that are normally available include newspapers, television, radio, magazines, direct mail, and outdoor advertising. Table 17–2 presents the advantages and disadvantages of each of the major media.

TABLE 17-2   Advantages and Disadvantages of Major Advertising Media

Media	Advantages	Disadvantages
Newspapers	Timely	Short Life
	Local Market	Limited Color Opportunities
	Excellent Positioning	Limited Careful Review
	Wide Readership	
Magazines	Highly Segmented	Expensive
	Excellent Color Opportunities	Long Lead Time
	Long Life	
Television	Wide Reach	Expensive
	Sight and Sound	Long Lead Time
	Vast Creative Opportunities	Consumers Tune Out
		Short Exposure
		"Clutter"
Radio	Wide Reach	Only Sound
	Highly Segmented	Short Exposure
	Inexpensive	
	Quick Response Time	
Direct Mail	Highly Segmented	Expensive
		Maintaining Quality Lists
		Junk Mail
Outdoor	Highly Visible	Limited Use with Complex Messages
	Repeat Exposure	

Newspapers. As Table 17–3 shows, 24.3 percent of yearly advertising expenditures go to newspapers, which makes them second only to network television in attracting advertising dollars. Newspaper advertisements are timely and can be directed at the needs of a local market. Most newspapers will run advertisements within two to three days of their placement. In addition, it is possible to position the advertisement in a particular section or even a specific page of the newspaper. The most widely read portion of most daily newspapers is the sports section, so an advertiser may be willing to pay a premium to place its advertisement on the second page of that section. Finally, newspapers tend to have a wide readership. Most people do not read the daily paper from cover to cover, but a large number of people in the community at least scan the paper each day.

TABLE 17-3   Advertising Expenditures (in Percent, 1991)

Network Television	25.4%
Spot Television	23.5%
Newspapers	24.3%*
Magazines	16.5%
Syndicated Television	3.9%
Cable Television	2.8%
Network Radio	2.0%
Outdoor	1.7%

* *Includes Sunday magazine.*

Reprinted with permission from the Feb. 11, 1991 Issue
of Advertising Age. © Crain Communications, Inc. 1991

The biggest disadvantage of daily newspapers is that they are "history" after one day. Advertisements that are not seen during the day they appear will not be seen at all. Also, most newspapers still find it difficult and expensive to utilize color to improve the appeal of advertisements. Finally, although readership is high for newspapers, most people do not invest the time to review the entire contents of the paper carefully. Thus, a poorly placed advertisement may not be seen by very many people.

Magazines. A great advantage of magazines is that they appeal to highly segmented markets. Canadair advertises its executive jet, the Challenger, in magazines such as *Fortune*, rather than in *Outdoor Life*, since a larger percentage of *Fortune*'s readers may be in a position to influence the decision to buy a private jet. Magazines that are published on high-quality paper are excellent vehicles for the use of color to produce attractive, eye-catching advertisements. In addition, many magazines remain in circulation for several months or even years. Possibly the best illustration of this is *National Geographic*, which seems to remain in many homes and offices indefinitely.

Unfortunately, magazines are often too expensive for small businesses. Although magazines such as *Time* and *Newsweek* are able to produce regional editions, they are still far too expensive for a local dry cleaning store to use to promote its services. Also, newspaper advertisements can be run a few days after the order is placed, but magazines normally have a much longer lead time from placement until the advertisement runs.

Television. Television is an intimate part of most families' lifestyle and thus serves as an important vehicle for advertising. A big advantage of television is that it provides an opportunity to communicate with a large audience. An advertisement that appears in prime time will reach a very large audience. For example,

Jim Bob Moffett

James Robert Moffett knows all about taking risks. He's been challenging the odds and reaching for his dreams since he was a boy. Jim Bob, as he is known to his friends and business associates alike, is the son of an itinerant oil-field worker and a clerk at Montgomery Ward department store. At public school, he was a good student and an avid athlete. The poor boy earned an athletic scholarship at The University of Texas. It seemed the answer to his future.

However, Darrell Royal, the Longhorn football coach, wasn't sure that Moffett could make the team. Moffett set out again to challenge the odds. He had no choice; he needed the financial support of the football scholarship to remain in school. Even with that assistance, he had to carry more than the regular load of classes in order to complete his education as quickly as possible. Majoring in geology, Moffett learned to juggle football practice with 21 hours of classes and three science labs. He also found time to play baseball and to join Army ROTC and a fraternity. Putting in long hours of hard work, he proved the coach wrong and became a strong member of the Longhorn football team. He also graduated with special honors. Moffett now says that the experience was instrumental in teaching him principles of patience and perseverance. In 1963, he received a Master of Science degree in geology from Tulane University.

After graduation, Moffett married his high school sweetheart and settled in New Orleans, working in the oil exploration business. Life was better than he had dreamed, but soon the desire for a challenge overtook him, and he decided to start a new company. He went into partnership with Ken McWilliams to form an oil exploration firm, McMoCo. With the addition of a third partner, B. M. Rankin, the company's name was changed to McMoRan Exploration. Business boomed, thanks to some major oil finds near Corpus Christi, Texas.

By 1980, Moffett had become the firm's chairman and chief executive officer. He engineered one of the largest mergers in corporate history, between his McMoRan Oil & Gas Co. and Freeport Minerals. Freeport was a New York-based company more than twice the size of McMoRan, with operations in Louisiana, Florida, Nevada, Indonesia, and Australia. Under Moffett's leadership, the new corporation flourished. In 1990, it was ranked by *Fortune* as the 251st largest industrial firm in the nation. Since Moffet

has been in charge, its assets have almost tripled, to $4 billion. Today the company has 6,000 employees in the United States and overseas. In 1991, Freeport-McMoRan revenues reached $1.5 billion.

New Orleans has prospered from the economic boost brought to the local economy by the corporation. Moffett's fellow citizens in New Orleans soon learned that he is an untiring crusader for community needs and a staunch believer in philanthropy. He organized and chaired the New Orleans Business Council, and has served as head of the Chamber of Commerce and the Metropolitan Arts Fund, to which his company pledged $5 million. Moffett has been particularly noted for his personal philanthropy and company charitable activities in Louisiana and Austin.

Moffett's principal causes involve helping young people. This is probably because he looks back on his own youth, when he worked hard to earn his spurs but also received a friendly hand from time to time. Moffett's philanthropic efforts include every area of the nonprofit sector, from the arts to public television to human service organizations to education to a multitude of civic endeavors.

In honor of his rise from modest circumstances to the chief of a worldwide Fortune 300 company, Jim Bob Moffett was given the Horatio Alger Award in 1990. In appreciation of this very great honor, Moffett is devoting his time to helping the Alger Association raise funds to continue giving scholarships to students throughout the 50 states. Moffett is chairing the annual fundraising dinner in 1992.

Once again, life is sweet for Jim Bob Moffett, but a new challenge undoubtedly waits just around the corner. Without fail, Jim Bob Moffett will meet it with gusto.

there were 92.1 million TV homes in the U.S. during the week of April 1–7, 1991. Of these homes, 20 million were tuned in to the number-one show, NBC's "Cheers." Even the lowest-ranked show for that week, "Against the Law" (Fox), drew 2.8 million homes. Likewise, a television spot on a local news or entertainment show has the potential to be seen by a significant percentage of the local audience. Other advantages of television are that it permits both sight and sound to be used and that it provides creative opportunities to communicate with potential consumers of a product or service.

The most significant disadvantage of television is its high cost. For example, 30 seconds of air time for a commercial on national prime-time televison may cost as much as $130,000. The Super Bowl, which is normally the most-watched television program of the year, charged $850,000 in 1992 to run a 30-second television advertisement.

Another problem with television is that television advertisements may take as much as six months to create and produce. If a firm is trying to make quick changes in how a product is perceived, the time it takes to produce a television advertisement is a significant drawback.

Consumers have learned to tune out commercials, either by leaving the room when they are played or by using their remote control devices to "zap" to another program. Research indicates that the average household with a remote control zaps once every three minutes and 26 seconds.[2] Obviously, many consumers are not sitting in front of the televison watching everything that is presented to them.

A related problem is that exposure time is quite limited. If the viewer misses a 30-second commercial, the firm's time and effort have been wasted with respect to that individual. Finally, there are a great many television commercials on the air every day. This clutter, as it is called in the industry, makes it difficult for consumers to perceive one particular firm's advertisements. To overcome this problem, advertisers try to present interesting, at times humorous, advertisements. The firm must also be prepared to run the advertisement more than once if it is to be seen by many people.

Television has been attacked by social critics for many years. The usual theme is that America's youth are being corrupted by spending as much as five hours a day watching worthless, tasteless television shows. Critics of television may be overly harsh, but the networks must address an important ethical question. Should they accept advertisements from condom manufacturers? As the Ethical Issue (page 458) points out, AIDS is a national crisis, and it may be time for TV networks to modify their advertising policies.

Radio. There are at least 500 million radios in the United States. Some people listen to the radio only in their cars, while others listen to the radio as background music or entertainment all day. Radio has the advantage of reaching a wide audience. A radio station in New York City has the potential to communicate with as many as 15 million people.

Most radio stations focus on a particular format, such as country and western music, popular music, talk radio, or news and sports. Since particular stations attract listeners of different ages and ethnic and socioeconomic backgrounds, an advertiser can focus its advertising efforts on the station that best reaches a particular market segment. Radio is also relatively inexpensive, and it takes a short period of time to create and produce a new radio commercial.

Condom Advertising

The three largest television networks, NBC, CBS, and ABC, have historically refused to accept paid advertising from condom manufacturers. They have believed that condom advertisements would offend large segments of their viewing populations, so it was not in their best interest to run the advertisements.

Fox Broadcasting announced in November 1991 that it would run condom advertisements, as long as they focused on the prevention of sexually transmitted diseases.

The first commercials were for Ramses condoms from Schmidt Laboratories. The ads were controversial because they were used to introduce a new condom, called Ramses Safe Play, which was aimed directly at the teen and college student markets. The condom box featured day-glo lettering and contained a free condom-holder key chain. The package indicated that the product is "for young lovers."*

The network executives realize that AIDS is a terrible disease that may eventually kill millions of people. They also understand that sexually active young people represent the segment of society that is most at-risk for AIDs and other sexually transmitted diseases. Also, times have changed, and their own networks run love scenes that would have been banned from movie theaters a few years ago, not to mention televison sets. The major networks must face the ethical question of whether or not to run condom advertisements. If they decide to do so, what advertising themes should they permit?

*Reprinted by permission of the *Wall Street Journal* © 1991 Dow Jones & Company, Inc. All rights reserved worldwide.

The main disadvantage of radio is that only sound can be utilized. Although some radio commercials are very creative and fun, the advertiser faces limitations because a visual presentation cannot be incorporated. Radio commercials, like television commercials, also have a limited life. A listener who misses a particular ad may never be exposed to it again.

direct mail *advertisements sent through the mail.*

Direct Mail. Advertisements that are sent through the mail are called **direct mail.** They range from postcards or leaflets, addressed "Occupant," to elaborate catalogs or sales letters addressed to a specific individual in the family. The biggest advantage of direct mail is that the advertiser can segment its market in a way that is not possible in any other medium. For example, a local dry cleaner can send an inexpensive flyer directly to consumers who live in a specific area of town. On a national scale, J. P. Morgan uses sophisticated, expensive market research techniques to identify wealthy individuals who could benefit from its private banking program. A national motel chain uses an American Express mailing list to reach people who stay in hotels or motels more than 20 nights per year but have not stayed in one of the chain's properties during the past year. This type of segmentation is just not possible with any other advertising medium.

There are three major problems associated with direct mail. First, it tends to be relatively expensive. The cost of mailing and the cost of producing the message and segmenting the consumer base can make it the most expensive form of advertising per prospective customer reached. Of course, this may not be a problem if the firm is able to reach its target market. Second, it is difficult and expensive to maintain high-quality mailing lists. For example, The University of Texas at Austin makes more than 166,000 changes of address on its alumni mailing list every year. Finally, most Americans are tired of receiving "junk mail." If a direct mail piece is to be effective, it must somehow differentiate itself from the other direct mail that consumers receive each day.

Outdoor. Billboards, signs, and posters are examples of **outdoor advertising.** Most businesses that sell products or services to final consumers have at least a sign above the door. The sign may present the name of the business in small letters, or it may thrust a huge, elaborate design 60 feet above the highway. The main advantage of outdoor advertising is that it is highly visible to the public. It gives the advertiser an opportunity to get repeat exposure for its advertising themes. American Airlines has used billboards and signs located in airports, emphasizing the number of flights the company has each day to Europe from New York. The theme is very simple: American flies to European airports at times that are convenient to passengers.

The biggest problem with outdoor advertising is that it cannot communicate a long or even modestly complex message. American, Europe, and convenience is just about all American Airlines could hope to communicate in a billboard advertisement.

outdoor advertising billboards, signs, and posters used to convey advertising messages.

Other Media. Other advertising media include the yellow pages and **specialty advertising,** which appears on products such as calendars, T-shirts, coffee mugs, and ballpoint pens. Local shopping centers often produce some form of shopper's guide that includes information and discount coupons to attract consumers. These are frequently delivered to households by a private delivery service.

specialty advertising advertising messages that appear on products such as calendars, T-shirts, coffee mugs, caps, and ballpoint pens.

Advertising and the Product Life Cycle

In Chapter 14, the product life cycle was discussed. We identified four stages in the life of a product—introduction, market growth, maturity, and decline—and mentioned that advertising changes over the life of a product. Now we are ready to discuss the relationship between the product life cycle and advertising messages and objectives.

Figure 17–5 shows the product life cycle curve and the three stages in the life of an advertising campaign. Notice the correlation between the four stages of the product life cycle and the three advertising stages. As a product moves through its life cycle, it requires three distinct stages of advertising. These stages differ in their messages and in their objectives. The stages make up what we shall call the **advertising spiral.**[3]

advertising spiral the three stages of the advertising campaign that are used as the product moves through the product life cycle; the pioneering, competitive, and retentive stages.

Pioneering Stage. The **pioneering stage** in the advertising spiral corresponds to the introduction stage of the product life cycle. Here, the advertiser introduces the product to the public. Generating interest in a product—or causing people to recognize a need for it—is called primary demand stimulation.

A classic example of primary demand stimulation was RCA's campaign introducing color television to the American public in the 1950s. RCA's pioneer advertising stated:

pioneering stage the first stage in the advertising spiral, when the product is introduced to the public.

See the World Series Baseball in Living Color. . . . Rarely in the lifetime can you share a thrill like this. . . . You can see baseball's greatest spectacle come alive in your own home in color. . . . You'll sense a new on-the-spot realism in every picture of the crowd, the players, the action. . . . Made by RCA—the most trusted name in electronics.

FIGURE 17-5   Advertising and the Product Life Cycle

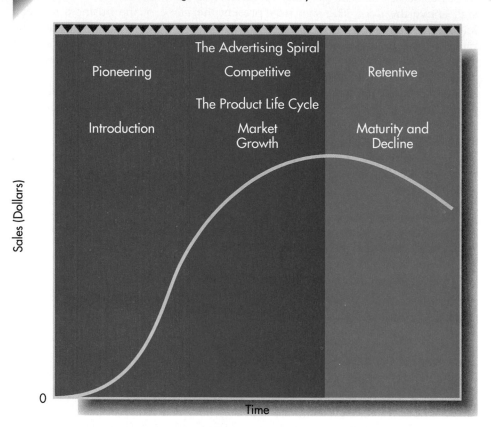

Source: Thomas Russell/Glenn Verrill, OTTO KLEPPNER'S ADVERTISING PROCEDURE, 11/e, © 1990, pp. 54–58. Adapted by permission of Prentice Hall, Inc., Englewood Cliffs, New Jersey.

Note how this ad emphasized the benefits of color television in general, with only minor mention of the RCA name. The purpose of the ads was to sell people on the "idea" of color television. The problem of selling the RCA brand name was left for later advertisements.

competitive stage the second stage in the advertising spiral, which stresses the unique features of a product, especially the features most desired by buyers.

Competitive Stage. The **competitive stage** corresponds to the market growth stage of the product life cycle. By this time, the need for the product is well established in the minds of buyers. People no longer ask, "Should I buy the product?" Instead they ask, "Which brand should I buy?"

Many of the products we buy are in the competitive stage of the advertising spiral. Competitive advertising stresses the unique features of the product, especially the features most desired by buyers and supposedly missing in competing products. Here are the competitive advertising themes for several products:

- Engineered like no other car in the world. (Mercedes-Benz)
- Making it all make sense. (Microsoft)
- The Smart Window TV. (Magnavox)
- You deserve national attention. (National Car Rental)

The idea behind each of these slogans is that the advertised brand is better than other brands. Figure 17–6 shows another example of a competitive advertisement.

Retentive Stage.

The **retentive stage** of the advertising spiral corresponds to the maturity and decline stages of the product life cycle. By now the product is used by many people, so the aim of advertising in this stage is to foster brand loyalty. That is, the firm, through its advertising, attempts to hold on to as many current customers as possible.

Typically, the firm relies on name advertising during the retentive stage of the advertising spiral. The goal of **name advertising** is to put the name of the product (or the company's trademark) in front of as many people as possible. Think of the familiar red-and-white signs that encourage you to drink a Coke. Why does Coca-Cola advertise? It can't be to increase brand awareness, because everyone has already heard of Coke. Coca-Cola advertises in order to keep the name of the product in front of you. This makes you just a little more likely to reach for a Coke the next time you're thirsty. The makers of Pepsi-Cola, Dr. Pepper, 7-Up, and Royal Crown Cola also advertise their products heavily, for the same reason. All of these companies are fighting for market share in the intensely competitive soft-drink industry. Thus, another objective of name advertising is to take market share away from competitors. Figure 17–7 shows a good example of name advertising.

retentive stage   the final stage of the advertising spiral, when the ads aim to foster brand loyalty.

name advertising   advertising designed to put the name of the product or the company's trademark in front of as many people as possible.

Measuring Advertising Effectiveness

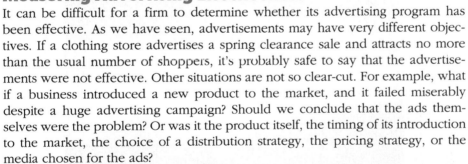

It can be difficult for a firm to determine whether its advertising program has been effective. As we have seen, advertisements may have very different objectives. If a clothing store advertises a spring clearance sale and attracts no more than the usual number of shoppers, it's probably safe to say that the advertisements were not effective. Other situations are not so clear-cut. For example, what if a business introduced a new product to the market, and it failed miserably despite a huge advertising campaign? Should we conclude that the ads themselves were the problem? Or was it the product itself, the timing of its introduction to the market, the choice of a distribution strategy, the pricing strategy, or the media chosen for the ads?

Although the measurement of advertising effectiveness can become quite complex, there are at least two ways to approach it: reach and frequency. **Reach** is a measure of how many people actually saw or heard the advertisement in a given medium. However, reach in itself may not mean much. What if very few of the people who see the ad are interested or qualified buyers? A few years ago, The University of Texas advertised a new type of program leading to a Masters degree in Business Administration. The program, designed for business executives, was advertised in local newspapers and in the southwest edition of *The Wall Street Journal*. Of the 475 applicants to the program, more than 300 read about it in local papers. Only 75 read about it in the *Journal*. The other 100 heard about the program from other sources. However, of the 300 who read the local newspaper, only 10 were qualified applicants, whereas 62 of the 75 who read *The Wall Street Journal* were qualified. The *Journal* was the more effective medium in this case, even though the local paper's advertisements had greater reach.

reach   a measure of how many people actually saw or heard an advertisement in a given medium.

FIGURE 17-6   Competitive Advertisement

CHEVY EQUIPS MORE 1992 MODELS WITH STANDARD ANTI-LOCK BRAKES THAN ANYONE.

Anti-lock brakes (ABS) may be one of the most important safety features to come along in a decade. That's because ABS helps you to maintain steering control of your car even while braking on slippery roads. Whenever your wheels begin to lose traction during braking, the ABS computer "pumps" your brakes on and off up to 15 times a second. That's faster than even the most experienced driver could pump them. And the result is both better control for you and shorter stopping distances. ◆ But anti-lock brakes are only one part of a total safety system developed for your Chevrolet. We have more M.D.s and Ph.D.s at GM involved in automotive safety than any other car company in the world. At Chevrolet, we give you even more than you would expect to protect you from the unexpected. ◆ No wonder Chevrolets are the cars more people depend on.

THE 1992 CHEVROLET CAVALIER RS

FIGURE 17-7   Name Advertising

frequency   *the number of times a person is exposed to an advertisement.*

Frequency is the number of times a person is exposed to an advertisement. Advertisers know that the more often people see or hear an advertisement, the more likely they are to remember it. Therefore, an ad with greater frequency has a better chance to achieve its objective.

Advertising Agencies

advertising agencies
companies that develop advertising strategies and campaigns for other companies.

Advertising agencies are companies that develop advertising strategies and campaigns for other companies. Advertisers choose agencies they think can create advertisements that will tell their story in an effective manner. Agencies range in size from local specialty houses servicing a few small clients to giant multinational organizations such as Ted Bates Worldwide, which places more than $2.5 billion in advertising for thousands of clients each year.

The process begins with a series of meetings between the client and representatives from the agency. The agency must have a clear understanding of what its client hopes to accomplish with the advertisement. Therefore, the advertising agency's personnel must be thoroughly informed about what makes the product unique and how it compares with its competition. Once this process is completed, the agency's creative people can begin to form the basic concept of the advertisement, write the words or copy, and design the layout for a print ad or the sequence of filming for a TV commercial.

The advertising agency does not actually produce the advertisement. Rather, it contracts with specialized organizations to make the recording or films or prepare the final print advertisement. However, agency personnel monitor the entire process until an advertisement that is acceptable to the client is finished.

Business Career
Advertising Copywriter:
Writes advertising copy for use in publication or broadcast media to promote sales of goods and services. May work freelance or for an agency. Consults with client to obtain product information and discuss style and length of ad. Reviews advertising trends, consumer surveys, and other data regarding marketing of related goods to formulate presentation approach. *Average Salary: $26,600.*

Another important function of the agency is to place the advertisement with the media. This service includes examination of available media schedules, purchase of time or space, and actual placement of the advertisement. Most advertising agencies also provide their clients with a variety of market research services. These include studies that range in scope from measuring the success of competing products to determining what type of advertisements are likely to be most effective in reaching particular market segments.[4]

Advertising agencies normally create the advertisement and oversee its production at no cost to the client. The agency can afford to price its service in this manner because it is able to purchase television or radio time, or print coverage, at a substantial discount. The agency then sells the client the air or print advertisements at "book" price and thereby covers its costs and makes a profit. Marketing research studies are normally paid for separately by the client, as is the cost of actually producing the advertisment.

A number of major advertising blunders could have been avoided if international businesses had used advertising agencies in the country where the ads would run, to review their appropriateness for the foreign culture and their proper translation. The International Example on page 465 describes this problem in some detail.

PERSONAL SELLING

 As we stated at the start of Chapter 13, "Nothing happens until a sale is made." At least that's what many salespeople tell their friends in production and accounting. What they are saying is that making a sale is the most important thing a business does. Without a sale, what good were the long hours spent by the firm's

Translations in an International Marketplace

International firms that sell consumer products in several countries can get into trouble by trying to translate an advertisement that works in one culture and language into another. For example, in Great Britain, Electrolux advertises its vaccum cleaners very successfully using the theme, "Nothing Sucks Like an Electrolux." If this ad were run in the United States, it might easily qualify as the advertising blunder of the year. Another example was General Motors' theme, "Body by Fisher," which translated into a Flemish advertisement as "Corpse by Fisher." A third example was Braniff's Spanish advertisement that invited the international airline's Spanish customers to try its leather seats. Unfortunately, what was supposed to be translated as "to be seated in leather" came out "to be seated naked."

The best way to avoid translation mistakes is for the international firm to use a good local advertising agency in the target country to review the advertisement and its translation to make sure that it is appropriate for the country. A useful technique is called back-translation. A second linguist translates the translation back into the original language, to determine whether it really says what the original language said. The point is that translation mistakes can be avoided only if the international firm is willing to make an effort.

Sources: M. R. Czinkoto and I. A. Ronkainen, *International Marketing*, 2nd ed. (Chicago: Dryden Press, 1990), pp. 136–137; and "Braniff Inc.'s Spanish Ad Bears Cause for Laughter," *Wall Street Journal*, 9 February 1987, p. B5.

production engineers to design an efficient manufacturing process? Or the efforts of the finance people to raise money for a plant expansion? Or the work of the advertising staff to develop an ad campaign for the firm's products?

Let's begin our discussion of personal selling by examining opportunities in selling. We will then look at attributes of successful salespeople, sources of new salespeople, what salespeople do, and how the sales process works.

Opportunities in Selling

Personal selling involves promoting products through oral presentation to prospective customers, either in person or by phone. Many men and women in business work as salespeople. They sell everything from office supplies to satellite dish antennas. Their goal is to make money for themselves and their companies by enabling their customers to get what they need at a price they can afford. There are many career opportunities, as well as career rewards, in selling.

personal selling promoting products through oral presentation to prospective customers, either in person or by phone.

Career Opportunities. In many firms, the people working in the marketing department began their careers with the sales force. This is not so much an accident as it is a matter of policy. Why do firms want their marketing staffs to have sales experience? The answer is simple: Sales experience gives them an understanding of the problems faced by salespeople. The people who design the marketing strategy must understand exactly how the products are sold. It does not make much sense for managers in the marketing department never to have seen a customer. In the same way, it is absolutely necessary for anyone seeking a position as a sales manager to have had sales experience.

In personal selling, ego drive is important to the salesperson—especially in the case of high-priced products such as automobiles.

Financial Rewards. Many salespeople earn a good living. Often, they are paid on a **commission** basis. That is, their pay is in proportion to the amount they sell. It is not unusual for salespeople on commission to make more money than their sales managers. Such people may turn down jobs in marketing or sales management because they can't afford the cut in pay.

commission compensation in proportion to the amount of sales generated.

Freedom from Direct Control. Selling provides an excellent opportunity for people who do not like close supervision but who still want the security of working for an organization. Many salespeople operate virtually as independent business people. They plan their own schedules, develop their own sales strategies, and often go several weeks without face-to-face contact with their supervisors. Sales reps often work in whatever way they choose. For example, they may decide to work 13 hours on Thursday and take Friday off. For people who want to be their own bosses, selling positions can come close to providing them with the independence they seek.

Qualities of Successful Salespeople

empathy the ability to understand someone else's problems.

Successful salespeople have two basic qualities—empathy and ego drive. **Empathy** is the ability to understand someone else's problems. In the case of a salesperson, this means seeing problems as the customer sees them. Empathy enables the salesperson to anticipate the customer's reaction to a sales presentation and to adjust the presentation accordingly.

Ego drive is a special kind of motivation. Ego-driven people feel a personal stake in completing each task successfully. Ego-driven salespeople see the potential in each sales prospect to fulfill their desire for recognition, success, and personal achievement. In effect, each sale becomes a conquest. The self-image of a salesperson improves dramatically when a sale is made and diminishes when a sale is lost. Salespeople must have strong egos, because even the most successful salespeople fail on many sales attempts.

ego drive   a special kind of motivation, in which people feel a personal stake in completing each task successfully.

Salespeople: Roles and Responsibilities

The most important function of the salesperson, of course, is to sell the firm's products. We'll look more closely at this particular function when we get to the end of this section. Right now we'll examine four other roles of the salesperson.

Credit Reviewer. Most products sold to businesses are sold on credit. Regardless of how soon payments are to be made, it is the salesperson's job to determine whether the buyer can afford to make the purchase and pay the bill. In the case of a small company, the salesperson may have to look at the company's financial statements and obtain a letter of recommendation from the company's bank. This process is referred to as "qualifying" the prospect.

Team Manager. Often, products are sold not by one person but by a team of people in the company. For example, IBM divides its mid-range business computer sales geographically, but the firm also has both technical and industry specialists available to help the salesperson complete the sale. However, the local IBM salesperson is the team manager. He or she is given the clear responsibility of determining if either technical or industry help is needed, and at what point in the sales process the IBM consultants should call on the customers.

External Consultant. The salesperson also acts as an adviser, or external consultant. Customers rely on the advice of a salesperson as to which products are best for them. In short, the buyer has a problem—which product to buy—and the salesperson has a solution. National Chemsearch, for instance, sells high-quality cleaning supplies to other businesses. The salesperson for National Chemsearch calls on the purchasing agent at the buying firm and on the person who actually uses the cleaning materials. National Chemsearch believes that it is important for its salespeople to explain to the user how its products can best be utilized.

Glad-Hander. This role involves listening to the customer's problems, some of which are personal and some business-oriented. A salesperson also takes customers out to lunch. Why? To talk business and to build and maintain a good personal relationship.

Order Processer. The final role involves physically processing the order. Once the salesperson and the customer have agreed on what is to be purchased, the salesperson must complete the required paperwork. In cases where there is a great deal of money involved and where purchases are made infrequently, such as the purchase of a coal-fired power plant by a city, lawyers and financial advisors play a major role in completing all of the paperwork. In contrast, when an order is a routine transaction, neither the buyer nor the seller can afford to spend much time processing the order.

Selling the Firm's Products

The sales process is pictured as a circle in Figure 17–8. The circular nature of the sales process means that the last stage leads back to the first. Let's take a look at the six stages of the sales process.

Stage 1: Finding New Customers. The salesperson begins the sales process by locating new customers—that is, by **prospecting.** Sometimes new customers are found by making **cold calls.** The salesperson walks into a company and tries to sell the product without having called on anyone there before and without knowing much about the business. Cold calls are not usually very successful. At other times, current customers recommend new customers. The salesperson then follows up on the recommendations.

Stage 2: Approaching Customers. During the second stage, the salesperson decides how best to approach the prospective customer. The salesperson will need to find out what kind of products the customer needs and determine who makes the purchase decision. If the salesperson has a good personal relationship with someone inside the buying firm, this information is not hard to obtain.

Stage 3: Presenting the Product Line. At this stage, the salesperson presents the firm's product to the customer. The presentation may include charts, graphs, or even slides. If possible, it is a good idea to demonstrate the product too. If a picture is worth a thousand words, a well-planned demonstration is worth even more.

Stage 4: Answering Questions. Very few sales are made without the customer asking questions or raising objections. These are usually nothing more than an attempt to learn more about the product. The salesperson who has a good

prospecting *locating new customers.*

cold call *a visit by a salesperson to a prospective customer with whom he or she has not previously done business.*

FIGURE 17-8   The Sales Process

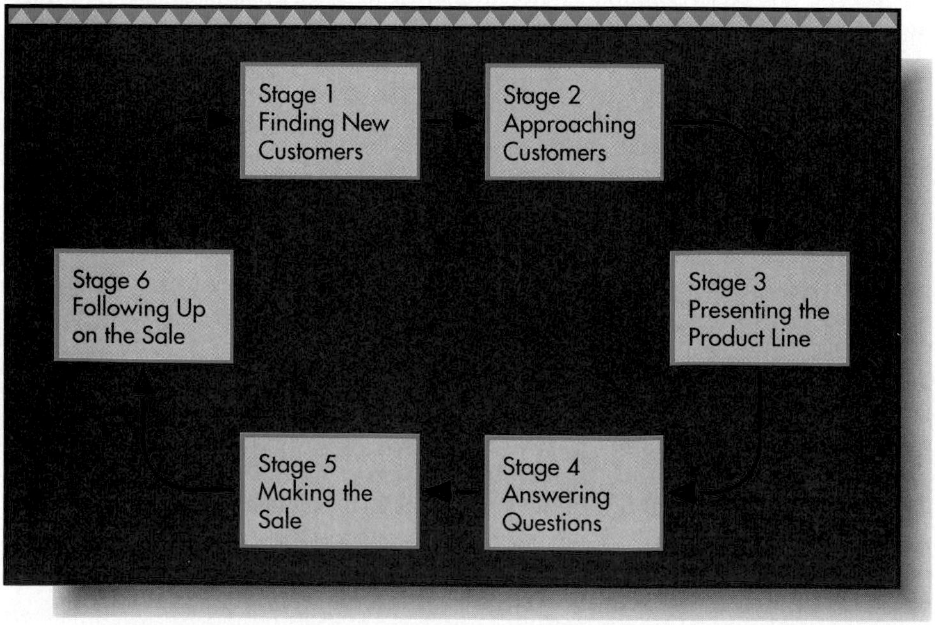

- Stage 1 Finding New Customers
- Stage 2 Approaching Customers
- Stage 3 Presenting the Product Line
- Stage 4 Answering Questions
- Stage 5 Making the Sale
- Stage 6 Following Up on the Sale

product and a good understanding of it has no reason to fear such questions and objections. However, a good salesperson will anticipate customer objections and come to the presentation prepared with information to overcome them.

Stage 5: Making the Sale. If the salesperson answers the customer's questions well, the customer may buy the product. Unfortunately, some customers have a difficult time making decisions. Therefore, the salesperson may need to end the presentation by asking for the order. This is called **closing the sale.** The salesperson attempts to make it as easy as possible for the customer to say yes. The salesperson does this by asking such questions as: "Whom should I see about filling out the order?" "Do you want to purchase one or two months' supply?" "Would you like to pay for the product in 30 days or 45 days?"

closing the sale   the sales technique of concluding the presentation by asking the customer to purchase the product or service.

Stage 6: Following Up on the Sale. The last stage is follow-up. At this stage, the salesperson pays a return visit to the customer after the sale has been made. The idea is to see whether the buyer is happy with the product. If there are any problems with the product, the salesperson can help solve them.

Notice the dotted line in Figure 17–8 between the follow-up stage and the prospecting stage. This line closes the circle and means that if the salesperson takes good care of the customer after the sale, it will be much easier to do business with the customer in the future. This is why the sales process is pictured as a circle.

SALES PROMOTION

Sales promotion is any direct inducement to purchase a product. These inducements may be free samples, coupons, gifts, sweepstakes, etc. Sales promotion is essential for most businesses. It is impossible to know exactly how much money is spent each year on sales promotion, but there were as many as 130 billion coupons in circulation in the United States in 1991—and coupons are only one sales promotion tool. In general, sales promotions have four objectives: (1) to get people to buy a product that they have not bought before, (2) to encourage people who already purchase a product to buy it more often, (3) to suggest new uses for a product, and (4) to give a product a good image. In the subsections that follow, we will discuss some common types of sales promotions: point-of-purchase displays, free samples, coupons, gifts, product demonstrations, sweepstakes, and trade shows.

sales promotions   direct inducements to purchase a product, such as free samples, coupons, gifts, and sweepstakes.

Point-Of-Purchase Displays

Point-of-purchase displays are product advertisements or displays placed near the product on the store shelf or in another high-traffic area in the store. By placing displays in retail stores, advertisers can get their message to consumers right where the buying decision is made. Almost any product can benefit from such a display. However, they are vital for products sold in supermarkets, where customers are expected to find products for themselves.

point-of-purchase displays   product advertisements or displays placed in retail stores where the buying decision is made.

An excellent example of a point-of-purchase display was provided by Budweiser during the 1991 NCAA basketball tournament. Budweiser worked with supermarkets to create a 15-foot hallway made out of 12-packs of Budweiser beer, with a basketball goal at the top. This point-of-purchase display was timely, and it was seen by most people who entered the supermarkets.

Samples

samples *small portions of a product, given away to encourage potential customers to try the product.*

Manufacturers and retailers sometimes give away small portions of the product, called **samples**, to encourage people to try it. Sampling may be used to rekindle interest in an old product, but it is most often used to introduce a new one. For samples to be an effective promotional device, they must be given to as many people as possible. Therefore, sampling is a very expensive way to promote a product. Sampling is most effective if the product sampled is obviously superior to competing products. Food and household products have been sampled successfully by many firms.

Coupons

coupon *a piece of paper entitling its holder to a discount on a particular product.*

A **coupon** is a piece of paper entitling its holder to a discount on a particular product. Most coupons are printed in local newspapers. They may also be sent directly to people's homes.

Coupons are a good way to get people to switch from one brand to another. Many people do not feel much loyalty to any particular brand of a product, especially if it is a convenience item. If they have a chance to buy a laundry soap at 35 to 75 cents off, many of them will do so.

Gifts

Businesses often use gifts to attract new customers or to hold on to existing customers. Car dealers may present a small gift to people who come in for a test drive, or a printing company may give each of its important customers a gold-plated pen-and-pencil set for Christmas. An interesting gift idea was Coca-Cola's MagiCan, which was introduced in 1990. Randomly distributed with regular Coca-Cola Classic cans were identical cans that contained money rather than a soft drink. Unfortunately, the new cans had to be withdrawn in only a few weeks because a series of problems developed. For one thing, most consumers just did not understand the advertisements that stressed that there really was money in some of the Coca-Cola cans. The concept of giving cash away in a can of Coca-cola was just too complex for most consumers. As a result, the cash gift program had to be suspended.[5]

Product Demonstrations

product demonstration *a sales promotion in which a salesperson actually shows the customer how the product works.*

A **product demonstration** is a sales promotion in which a salesperson actually shows the customer how the product works. Demonstrations are most often conducted at a point-of-purchase retail outlet, but they may also take place in the customer's home or office. Many of us have been called on in our homes by vacuum cleaner salespeople, who offer not only to vacuum all the floors but also to shampoo the living room rug and to bathe the dog—all with the same machine. Sewing machines, microwave ovens, dishwashers, and new types of food products are frequently demonstrated in stores. The key to a successful demonstration is getting the customer involved with the product. This is why automobile salespeople want you to test drive their cars.

Sweepstakes

sweepstakes *a contest in which prizes are awarded on the basis of chance.*

A **sweepstakes** is a contest in which prizes are awarded on the basis of chance. Businesses spent nearly $250 million on nationally advertised sweepstakes in 1991. The primary objective of sweepstakes is to build interest in a product or service that is being sold. Some of the biggest users of sweepstakes are magazine distributors. It seems as if every home in America receives a package of material featuring Ed McMahon once or twice a year from American Family Publishers. McMahon makes it very clear that you do not have to buy a magazine subscription to enter the sweepstakes, but you are certainly given an opportunity to do so.

In the 1960s, an investigation by the Federal Trade Commission uncovered widespread abuses by sweepstakes promoters. Since then, promoters have been required by law to disclose the odds of winning the sweepstakes, to show that winners are picked fairly, and to make sure that winners are located and prizes delivered. The success of a sweepstakes depends on the quantity and value of the prizes awarded, as well as the amount of advertising supporting it. Consumers play sweepstakes for the same reasons that people buy lottery tickets. They hope to "hit it big" without having to work hard. Therefore, a successful sweepstakes must give away exciting prizes, such as a dream home or $10 million, and it must be heavily promoted. Without a great deal of advertising, people will lose interest in the game. This is why Ed McMahon appears so frequently on television prior to the mailing from American Family Publishers, hyping the prizes and the contest.

Trade Shows

A **trade show** is a gathering of many producers in the same industry, to display their products to customers. This sales promotion tool is normally used to communicate with firms who purchase a product with the explicit objective of using it in their own production process or reselling it to another organization or a final consumer. For example, book illustrators, typesetters, and printers might exhibit in a large pavilion, to demonstrate their services to publishers. Customers have an opportunity to come to one location and view the products of many different sellers. Sellers use videotape as well as live demonstrations of their products. Trade shows are critically important to many industries, including electronics, boating, fashion, furniture, and textbooks.

trade show *a gathering of many producers in the same industry, to display their products to customers.*

PUBLICITY

Publicity is unpaid media coverage about the firm or its products. Since the firm does not pay for publicity, it is outside the firm's control. Therefore, publicity can be bad as well as good. Most large firms have publicity or public relations (P.R.) departments. The objective of the publicity department is to promote positive media coverage for the firm, so as to enhance its image with customers, suppliers, employees, stockholders, governmental entities, and the general public.

During the 1991 mideast war, the Patriot missile was widely publicized for destroying incoming SCUD missiles from Iraq. It was the first real test of an anti-missile system, and it appeared to work. Raytheon, the manufacturer of the Patriot, did an excellent P.R. job when President Bush visited the plant and met publicly with the firm's management and its employees. Everything was properly orchestrated to communicate to the public what a great job Raytheon was doing, to demonstrate to the federal government that it had made a wise decision by investing in the Patriot defense system, to make the firm's employees feel that they were making a major contribution to the nation's defense, and to show the stockholders what an excellent job management was doing.

Businesses seek publicity that reflects positively on their products, their contributions to society, or their management team. In the case of the Patriot missile,

publicity *unpaid media coverage about the firm or its products.*

Business Career
Public-Relations Representative: Plans and directs communication of information designed to inform the public of employer's programs, accomplishments, or point of view. Prepares and distributes fact sheets, news releases, scripts, recordings, etc. to the media and other interested parties. Promotes goodwill through speeches and exhibits. Represents employer at public gatherings. Purchases ad space and time. Consults on production of TV and radio ads. *Average Salary: $26,100.*

Raytheon's public relations department wrote short articles that served as ideas or even stories for newspapers. The P.R. department arranged for the firm's management to be interviewed on national television. It also arranged for thorough TV and print coverage of President Bush's visit, resulting in major news stories on national television and in daily newspapers. Good publicity is particularly effective because the public is more likely to believe a news story than a paid advertisement that communicates the same message. In this case, cheaper is definitely better.

SUMMARY POINTS

1 The promotion mix consists of the four major tools that a firm uses to communicate with its markets: advertising, personal selling, sales promotion, and publicity.

2 Advertising is designed to increase sales or profits by showing how a product can satisfy a consumer need or by providing information about the product. There are five types of advertisements. Brand advertisements promote a specific product, whereas institutional advertising is designed to build a positive image of the company. Trade advertising is used to communicate with members of the channel of distribution, and industrial advertising is aimed at the purchasers of industrial products. Retail advertising encourages people to buy consumer products.

3 There are seven types of advertising media. (1) Newspapers are timely and can be directed at local markets. (2) Magazines can be used to target specific markets, and (3) television is very useful for reaching a large audience. (4) Radio reaches a wide market, although many people listen to it only in their cars. (5) Direct mail targets prospects through the mail, and (6) outdoor advertising consists of signs, billboards, and posters that are highly visible to the public. (7) Other media include such specialty advertisements as the yellow pages, T-shirts, coffee mugs, and ballpoint pens.

As a product moves through its life cycle, it requires three distinct stages of advertising. The pioneering stage of the advertising spiral corresponds to the introduction stage of the product life cycle. During the competitive stage, the advertising stresses the unique features of the product. The retentive stage corresponds to the maturity and decline stage of the product life cycle. The objective of ads in this stage is to keep the name of the product in front of the consumer.

4 Reach and frequency are the two measures that are most widely used to evaluate advertising. Reach is the measure of how many people see an ad, and frequency is the number of times a person is exposed to it. Advertising agencies develop advertising strategies and campaigns for their clients and purchase advertising space for them.

5 Many marketing people begin their careers in business as salespeople, because marketing executives need to understand the problems that salespeople face. Other salespeople stay in selling because they can make a great deal of money in commissions. Another advantage of a career in selling is that salespeople often operate independently of supervision.

6 The salesperson is responsible for reviewing the credit of the prospective customer, acting as a team captain coordinating the work of support personnel who help in the sale, advising the customer as to which products are best for him or her, building a personal relationship with the customer, and processing the customer's order. There are six stages in the sales process: (1) finding new customers, or prospecting, (2) approaching the customers, (3) presenting the product line to the customers, (4) answering any questions or objections from the customers, (5) making or closing the sale, and (6) following up on the sale to make sure the customer is happy.

7 Sales promotions contribute to a firm's marketing strategy by providing direct inducements to purchase a product. There are seven common sales promotion techniques. (1) Point-of-purchase displays communicate directly with customers in the store. (2)

Samples are small portions of the product given away to potential customers. (3) A coupon permits its holder to receive a price discount on the purchase of the product. (4) Gifts are given to the customer when the product is purchased. (5) A product demonstration lets the salesperson actually show the customer how the product works. (6) A sweepstakes is a contest in which prizes are awarded. (7) Trade shows are gatherings of producers in the same industry to show their products to customers.

8 Publicity is unpaid media coverage about the firm or its products. Positive publicity helps the firm to enhance its image with customers, suppliers, employees, stockholders, governmental entities, and the general public.

REVIEW QUESTIONS

1 What are the elements in the promotion mix and what role does each one play? **1**

2 What is the difference between selective demand and primary demand? **2**

3 What is cooperative advertising? **2**

4 What are the main advantages and disadvantages of direct mail advertising? **3**

5 How would advertising for a product differ in the pioneering stage and in the retentive stage? **3**

6 What is the difference between reach and frequency in measuring advertising effectiveness? **4**

7 What are the roles of advertising agencies in marketing products or services? Describe the functions they serve for the client. **4**

8 Why do many people in marketing have sales backgrounds? **5**

9 What are the primary incentives for individuals to seek careers in sales? **5**

10 What are the stages of the sales process? **6**

11 Why do companies engage in sales promotions? **7**

12 What is the role of an effective public relations department? **8**

DISCUSSION QUESTIONS

1 Describe differences in promotion strategy for heavy-duty copiers for industrial use and for personal copiers for home use. What types of advertising techniques and media outlets would you use for each?

2 What are the characteristics of a good salesperson? Would you make a good salesperson?

3 What would be the most effective promotion for a new soft drink? Why?

4 Are there times when the public relations department can handle a situation or issue better than the marketing department? Describe one.

EXPERIENTIAL EXERCISES

1 Visit a retail store. Meet with the manager of the store or, if the store is large enough, its advertising manager. Find out what advertising media the store uses to communicate its message and how it measures the effectiveness of its ads. Ask the store executive whether or not the store is able to take advantage of cooperative advertising. Ask about the store's use of point-of-purchase displays and coupons. Finally, try to determine whether or not the store has a well-developed plan to communicate with its existing and potential customers.

2 Spend a day with a salesperson. Determine how much time the salesperson spends preparing for the day's sales calls. Does the salesperson make many cold calls,

or are most of the calls follow-ups to previous contacts? How much authority does the
salesperson have to make pricing and delivery commitments? Does the salesperson appear to be primarily motivated by a commission? What suggestions would you make
to the salesperson to improve his or her
effectiveness?

CASES

CASE 17-1
Freeport-McMoRan Incorporated

Freeport-McMoRan is one of the most successful American companies that extract natural
resources. The company began as a sulfur producer and has expanded into oil and gas,
gold, copper, and agricultural minerals. The firm's Agrico division is now the nation's second largest producer of agricultural fertilizers. In Indonesia, Freeport-McMoRan owns one
of the world's largest and richest open-pit copper mines. The mine also contains more gold
than any other in the world. Off the coast of Louisiana, Freeport-McMoRan has discovered
the largest sulfur reserve in the United States, and also one of the largest oil and gas discoveries in the Gulf of Mexico.

Freeport-McMoRan does not produce any consumer products. However, the company
recognized that it did have a need to communicate with the public—a problem that could
most easily be solved by advertising. Vice President for Communications Garland Robinette
said, "We don't feel like we have been communicating very well in the past, and we intend
to improve that in the future." Specifically, Robinette felt that a high-quality institutional
advertising program could be successfully aimed at the general public, the legislature, and
the media. Robinette's corporate communication philosophy is that if people do not know
what Freeport-McMoRan is or what it stands for, they are likely to believe the first piece of
negative publicity that they hear about the company. However, if Freeport-McMoRan is
able to communicate a positive image that is "entirely truthful and dependable," then people are much more likely to give Freeport-McMoRan a fair hearing if a problem should
develop. Freeport-McMoRan's public image is also important because it must often obtain
permits from regulatory agencies, which are sometimes more influenced by public opinion
than by scientific evidence.

In 1991, Freeport-McMoRan created three commercials that focused on the firm's philanthropic efforts, its environmental program, and the economic importance of its new offshore sulfur mine. The philanthropic advertisement described the company's efforts to
help rebuild a playground in New Orleans. The firm donated $1 million to the New Orleans
Recreational Department to rebuild and maintain the playground. Chairman and Chief
Executive Officer Jim Bob Moffett believed that if the city's children have attractive playgrounds, they are much more likely to avoid criminal behavior. Moffett hoped that publicity
about McMoRan's efforts would stimulate other businesses to support the city's
playgrounds.

The second commercial showed how the company transformed vast open-pit phos-
phate mines in Florida into valuable wetlands, where migratory birds spend the winter and
other birds, alligators, and deer live all year. Although the law now requires Freeport-
McMoRan to reclaim its open-pit mines, the company was already doing so, and its activities still go far beyond what the law requires. The main theme of the second commercial
was that big business and the environment can coexist. The commercial showed how
indigenous animals live in the newly created wetlands, which was named Morrow Swamp.

The third commercial depicted how important the new sulfur discovery in the Gulf of
Mexico is to the Louisiana economy. It did this by creating a mythical town called Promise,
Louisiana. The town has 21,000 new jobs, and the people of Promise pay millions of dollars
in state and local taxes. The total economic benefit of the sulfur project will eventually be
$31 billion for the state of Louisiana. The commercial showed that the people of Promise
have a good life with a high standard of living as a result of the discovery and operation of
the sulfur mine.

In addition to the three commercials, Freeport-McMoRan made a series of short videotapes for public schools on how oil, gas, and sulfur are commercially developed. Freeport-

McMoRan also created a 15-minute tape describing its efforts to help rebuild public parks in New Orleans. The tape was given to the local television stations the day a park was reopened for the public. The television stations were given permission to use any portion of the videotape on their evening news broadcasts, and each of them did so.

Freeport-McMoRan's efforts seemed to pay off. In late 1991, the firm's polls indicated that more than 50 percent of the people of Louisiana believed Freeport-McMoRan to be "responsible," "environmentally minded," and "committed to Louisiana's future." These results were particularly impressive because Freeport-McMoRan's approval ratings rose dramatically at the same time as other natural resource companies' reputations were falling.

1. Do you believe that Freeport-McMoRan should invest in television commercials that are aimed at the general public?
2. Why is it in Freeport-McMoRan's best interest to make tapes on the discovery and production of oil, gas, and sulfur for the public schools?
3. Was Freeport-McMoRan trying to manipulate the press when it gave television stations the tape showing the renovation of the park in New Orleans?
4. Do you feel that the corporate communication strategy that Freeport-McMoRan has developed will work in the long run? If so, can it be used successfully by other companies?

CASE 17-2
Coca-Cola Classic Comes Back

In May 1985, Coca-Cola chairman Robert Goizueta announced one of the boldest gambles in marketing history: Coca-Cola would make a significant flavor change in Coke, the world's best-selling soft drink. Coke's 99-year-old formula would be modified to make it slightly sweeter and less filling. The idea, according to one of Coke's leading strategists, "was to take all the positive qualities associated with the current product, its heritage and so on, and transfer that to an improved tasting product."

Coca-Cola introduced "New Coke" to the market in an attempt to win back market share from Pepsi. Supermarket sales of Coke had slipped behind Pepsi by almost two percentage points, and Pepsi was consistently winning blind taste tests. The advertising campaign for New Coke emphasized improved flavor.

Coca-Cola spent nearly $4 million to taste-test its new product on 200,000 consumers. Some of the taste tests were blind, and others had brand names associated with them. When the brands were not identified, the taste tests of 40,000 people done in 30 communities showed that 55 percent chose the new Coke over the old, and 52 percent chose it over Pepsi. Subjects were not told during any of the tests that the product being tested would take the place of the traditional Coke.

During the first month of New Coke's introduction, shipments to Coke bottlers set a record, and more people tried the new product than had ever sampled any new product. However, the entire picture changed suddenly. Consumers began to demand the old Coke. Sales were dropping rapidly. There was even talk of a class-action suit by a Seattle-based organization, Old Coke Drinkers of America. Coca-Cola headquarters received thousands of protest letters such as, "Dear Chief Dodo: What ignoramus decided to change the formula of Coke?" Coca-Cola bottlers meeting in Dallas signed a petition demanding that the company restore the traditional formula.

On July 5, Coca-Cola announced that it would bring back the old formula. The firm's marketing research department quickly tested several alternative names: Original Coke, Coke 100, Coke 1886, Old Coke, and Coke 1. On July 10, Coca-Cola announced that it would reintroduce the original formula under the name Coca-Cola Classic. Within hours of the announcement, a national phone survey indicated that 68 percent of the people were aware of that move and 66 percent approved of it. The Coca-Cola Classic package was designed only two days before the announcement.

The media had given a lot of coverage to what had been labeled the "new Coke failure." ABC News covered the story on its "World News Tonight" report, again on "Nightline," and on "20/20." ABC-TV also interrupted its "General Hospital" soap opera to tell the public that the old Coke was coming back.

PepsiCo, bottlers of Pepsi-Cola, couldn't resist the temptation to poke fun at Coca-Cola's misfortune in its advertising. Pepsi's first advertising campaign in response to its competitor's move stated that Pepsi's own better taste had forced Coca-Cola's move. The second campaign talked about the confusion of Coke products, emphasizing the split between new Coke and old Coke. The confusion and controversy between the two cola-market leaders grew. By September, Coca-Cola decided to change its approach once more by bringing back the kind of traditional soft-drink advertising that it had been trying hard to get away from. The new ads did not address the differences between the new Coke and Coca-Cola Classic but rather, focused on a return to traditional values.

The ads showed consumers drinking both the new Coke and Coca-Cola Classic in the same scene, to tie the two brands closely together. In 1986, according to some sources, Coca-Cola Classic was outselling the new Coke by a four-to-one margin. Three of the new spots were vignettes showing people enjoying Coke as a refreshment during the course of everyday activities. The fourth spot was the type of emotional spot more common among soft drink advertisements. The new theme line was "We've got a taste for you."

1.   What mistakes, if any, did Coca-Cola make in the introduction of New Coke?
2.   Should Coca-Cola have reintroduced the old Coke flavor drink?
3.   Was the increase in consumer awareness of Coca-Cola products good or bad overall for the Coca-Cola Company? What type of overall long-term effect would it have on the Coca-Cola Company's marketing program?
4.   Do you approve of company's changes to its ad campaign in September 1985? Discuss your opinion in detail, and indicate whether such changes would affect overall sales of Coca-Cola products. If so, how?
5.   Did Pepsi make a mistake by making fun of the problems that Coca-Cola was having?

Sources: Material for the case was drawn from S. Scredon, "Brian Dyson Takes the New Coke Challenge," *Business Week*, 26 May 1986, p. 81; J. Kotel and S. Kilman, "How Coke's Decision to Offer 2 Colas Undid 4½ Years of Planning," *Wall Street Journal*, 15 July 1985, pp. 1, 8; A. B. Fisher, "Coke's Brand-Loyalty Lesson," *Fortune*, 5 August 1985, pp. 44–46; J. Fierman, "How Coke Decided a New Taste Was It," *Fortune*, 27 May 1985, p. 80; N. Gigs, "Coke Back to 'Traditional' Ads," *Advertising Age*, 16 September 1985, p. 1.

A&H Manufacturing Marketing Management

A&H Manufacturing is headquartered in Phoenix, Arizona. The firm is a major producer of private label cleaning and detergent products. A&H's best selling product is a low cost laundry detergent that is sold in several of the large regional supermarket chains in the Southwest. The company also sells private label liquid hand soap, window cleaning products, and tub and tile cleaner.

The laundry detergent market has changed radically during the last twenty years. At one time, national firms such as Procter & Gamble heavily advertised products such as Tide and Cheer in an attempt to differentiate their products from other laundry detergents. While some detergents are still advertised on television and in newspapers and magazines, more and more household detergent manufacturers are turning to price discounts and coupons to increase the market share for their products. As a result, the market has become very price competitive. This has led to lower per-unit profit margins and lower overall profits for most detergent manufacturers.

A&H has never promoted its products directly to final consumers. The firm has sponsored several cooperative advertising programs where it has agreed to pay 30 percent of the cost of advertising any of its products. The program has been very simple to understand and approximately 35 percent of the supermarkets that sell its products have participated in the program.

A&H's senior marketing executive, Joyce Moos, feels that A&H should consider bringing out its own line of consumer detergents and household cleaning products. She believes that A&H's salespeople could sell its private label products to supermarkets as well as its own line of products. Joyce believes that by having two separate and distinct lines to sell, A&H's salesperson's time would be spent more efficiently since they would be selling two lines of products instead of one. In addition, if A&H could develop in consumers' minds that its new products have some important distinguishing features, then they could be sold at a higher price and potentially a higher per-unit profit margin.

The new line of products, which has tentatively been called Wonder products, would be only slight modifications from existing products. The ingredients would be somewhat more expensive and since initially A&H would not sell very many units of its new products, it would not achieve any significant economies of scale. This means that the products will be more expensive per unit to produce.

Joyce is working with two advertising agencies to design local television advertisements to sell A&H's new line of Wonder products. While the advertisements will stress the line's expensive ingredients that will clean better than traditional household cleaners while not injuring the environment, they will focus most of their attention on the new Wonder Detergent. The advertising agency executives are confident that they will be able to create an advertising theme that will add some excitement and "punch" to the new products.

Joyce's boss, Harold Shapiro, is concerned that supermarkets may not be very interested in carrying the new Wonder line of products. He realizes that shelf space is the most important commodity that any supermarket has and they are very reluctant to "spend" it on new unproven products. Joyce believes that the combination of a cleaver advertising campaign that will focus on high quality environmentally sensitive products will attract customers to the Wonder products, plus a higher profit margin for the supermarket, will encourage retailers to carry the Wonder line of products.

Questions

1. Why did the national household detergent manufacturers begin using coupons to sell their products?
2. How successful has A&H's cooperative advertising been?
3. Should A&H introduce its own line of household detergents? What problems must it address to do so?

PART 5

*Accounting and
Financial Management*

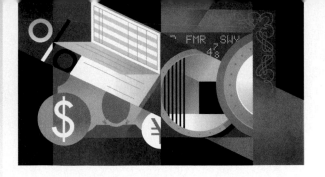

OBJECTIVES

After studying this chapter, you should be able to:

1 Discuss the role of the accountant, both public and private, as well as the importance of accounting information.

2 Explain how management uses accounting data for decision-making purposes and how computers are used in this process.

3 Describe two accounting concepts—the accounting equation and double-entry book-keeping—and the relationship between them.

4 Discuss each major item on a balance sheet.

5 Describe how expenses are subtracted from revenues on the income statement to yield "bottom-line" net income after taxes.

6 Explain the various methods of valuing inventory and their impact on the financial statements of a firm.

7 Interpret financial statements through comparative analysis and ratio analysis.

8 Explain how the statement of cash flows enables a firm to tell whether it has adequate resources to meet its obligations.

9 Describe the impact of aggressive (rather than conservative) accounting in reporting the operations of a firm.

CHAPTER 18

Accounting and Financial Statements

Harold Bridges spend his first two years of college at St. Petersburg Community College in Florida, where he worked part-time for a local CPA firm. He received a BBA in accounting from the University of Alabama in 1983. Bridges took particular pride in the fact that he financed 80 percent of the costs of his schooling through his own work efforts. He passed the various parts of the CPA exam in 1984.

Following graduation, Bridges worked for five years at a major accounting firm. During the early part of his employment, he worked mainly in auditing the books of the clients of his firm. As time passed, he became more involved in tax and financial planning.

In 1988, Bridges and two other young accountants formed their own CPA firm in Birmingham, Alabama. By 1992, they had hired five other full-time accountants and three part-time employees. The practice had grown rapidly because Bridges and his partners were able to service the needs of small clients so well. They were particularly adept at dealing with retail firms. Recently, the firm landed the account of a major manufacturing company whose shares are traded on the over-the-counter market. Bridges knew that to hold on to the account in the highly competitive world of accounting, he and his partners would need to expand their skills. They now would have to compete with Arthur Anderson, Price Waterhouse, and other major firms in providing a wide range of services.

This chapter will show you the type of data that Harold Bridges deals with and its importance to the business firm.

Accounting is one of the most important activities of a firm, and it is also one of the fastest-growing career fields today. Why are accountants in such demand? Because without good financial records, a business would not know how much income tax it owes the government, how much money it can safely borrow, whether it has invested its money wisely, or even whether it has made a profit. In this chapter, we'll look at the accounting process and at how financial statements are interpreted. Let's begin by examining the role of the accountant.

ROLE OF THE ACCOUNTANT

Many people confuse bookkeeping and accounting, or they think that accounting is nothing more than glorified bookkeeping. The two are related, but they are not the same thing. The bookkeeper is responsible for keeping a company's financial records. Much of a bookkeeper's work is clerical.

The job of the accountant is to design a system for keeping financial records, to prepare financial statements, and to interpret these statements. An accountant's first job frequently involves some bookkeeping, because it is important for accountants to understand exactly what bookkeepers do. Bookkeepers are usually supervised by accountants.

There are two main areas of accounting. **Managerial accounting** is concerned with providing management with the financial information needed to operate the firm. For example, General Motors' management may need to know how many Buick Park Avenues it sold with leather interiors in a period of three months and exactly how much the leather interior added to the production cost of each car. **Financial accounting** is concerned with providing financial information to people outside the firm. Examples of such information are financial statements (income statements, balance sheets, and statements of cash flow, discussed in this chapter) and tax statements prepared for local, state, and federal governments.

managerial accounting a type of accounting that is concerned with providing management with the financial information necessary to operate the firm.

financial accounting a type of accounting that is concerned with providing financial information to people outside the firm.

Public accountant Judy Chiao Smith of San Rafael, California often advises small companies on which form of business organization is best for them from the standpoint of taxation.

Public vs. Private Accounting

There are also two types of accountants: public and private. Although their roles in a business differ, they often work closely together.

Public Accounting. The public accountant, rather than working for a single employer, makes his or her services available to the public. Each state has laws that govern the licensing of **certified public accountants (CPAs).** The requirements for becoming a CPA vary in different states. In general, the CPA applicant must be a U.S. citizen, 21 years of age or older, of good moral character, and a college graduate with a major or concentration in accounting. The applicant must pass a 2½-day examination prepared by the American Institute of Certified Public Accountants. The examination covers accounting theory, accounting practice, auditing, and business law.

> **certified public accountants (CPAs)** licensed accountants who make their services available to the public.

There are approximately 400,000 CPAs in the United States, and the number grows by about 35,000 every year. Actually, there are 1.3 million people providing accounting functions of one form or another. (Not all accountants are certified as CPAs.) There are two accountants for every lawyer in this country. For a Profile of Charles Solomon, a successful CPA, see page 483.

Public accountants provide a variety of financial services to their clients, including helping prepare income tax returns and analyzing the merits of a property purchase or other asset acquisition. The public accountant's role as external auditor is probably the most important. An **auditor** verifies the records and transactions of a firm.

> **auditor** an accountant who verifies the records and transactions of the firm.

Many public accountants are self-employed or are members of locally owned accounting firms. A large number of public accountants work for one of the "Big Six" accounting firms shown in Table 18-1. The Big Six firms audit the nation's largest corporations and also provide audit services for many small- and medium-sized businesses.

Private Accounting. Other accountants work for only one firm. They supervise bookkeepers, prepare financial statements, and advise top management as to the financial position of the firm. Many private accountants take an examination prepared by the National Association of Accountants. Those who pass the exam are awarded a Certificate in Management Accounting (CMA). The exam tests the person's knowledge of managerial accounting.

Some private accountants also work as internal auditors. In this capacity, they make sure that the firm's accounting procedures are being followed properly. Internal auditors often serve as the eyes and ears of top management. The Insti-

Table 18-1   The Big Six Accounting Firms

The Big Six Accounting Firms
Arthur Andersen & Co.
Coopers & Lybrand
Deloitte & Touche
Ernst & Young
KMPG Peat Marwick
Price Waterhouse

Charles M. Solomon

Charles M. Solomon is a certified public accountant (CPA) practicing in Baltimore, Maryland. Solomon operates his own small public accounting firm in downtown Baltimore. The goal of Solomon's team of six accountants and support staff of four is "to provide quality accounting services to clients in a timely, efficient manner at an equitable cost."

Solomon attended the Wharton School of the University of Pennsylvania and graduated in 1958 with a degree in economics. He became a certified public accountant a year later and earned a law degree in 1965. While attending law school at night, Solomon worked for the Internal Revenue Service (IRS) during the day. His four years as an IRS agent taught him much about tax law. As Solomon points out, however, there have been a least 20 major changes in federal tax law since 1954, and these changes are occurring faster and faster.

Public accounting firms such as Solomon's audit or produce financial statements for their business clients in one of three ways. In a certified audit, the accountant examines the financial records of a business to determine the accuracy of its financial statements. An audit is concerned with the discovery of material misrepresentations of fact. Accountants also review financial statements. In a review, the accountant performs similar but less complete tests to determine whether the statements conform to generally accepted accounting principles. In a compilation, the accountant produces financial statements using information provided by the managers of the business, but he or she does not express any opinion about the quality or accuracy of the information provided. Although hired by the client, the public accountant always acts independently when conducting an audit, a review, or a compilation.

Solomon's company occupies a special market niche in relation to the much larger "Big Six" firms. In effect, Solomon operates as his clients' part-time financial controller. Most of his clients are small companies, so Solomon's job may be to advise them about insurance coverage, tax planning, cash flow management, bank borrowing strategies, computerization, personnel recruiting, or other matters. Solomon views his job as one of helping his clients achieve their business or financial goals.

Because of the recent downturn in the national economy, CPAs have opportunities to work with bankruptcies and complicated cases of debt restructuring. Another niche that looks challenging to Solomon is providing support to lawyers who need financial information to litigate cases.

According to Solomon, success as an accountant requires self-discipline, a logical mind, and the ability to concentrate for long periods of time. Interestingly, accounting is now considered to be the most stressful professional occupation in America. This stress stems, in part, from the repeated changes in tax law and the resulting need to keep current with new accounting standards and theory. Accountants work under strict deadlines, and this causes stress, too, as does the recent increase in the number of malpractice suits filed against accountants.

Nonetheless, public accounting remains one of the most satisfying career choices for students today. Says Solomon, "The potential in accounting is unlimited for people who work hard and who are willing to accept responsibility. The accountant meets interesting people and deals with new challenges every day. No two businesses are alike, each of our clients is a fascinating case history."

tute of Internal Auditors administers an examination similar to the CPA exam. The accountant who passes the exam is designated as a Certified Internal Auditor, or CIA.

Who Uses Accounting Information?

A complex society such as ours can function efficiently only if reliable financial information is available to the people and organizations that need it. All users of accounting information are interested in "bottom-line" profit or loss, but many people need more detailed information. Bankers and other creditors, for instance, want to know about a firm's financial status before making a loan. Therefore, they need information about the firm's assets and long-term and short-term debts.

People in the securities industry, such as stockbrokers, need information to help them determine the appropriate price for a firm's common stock. Government agencies need financial information to regulate the firm's business activities. The government is primarily concerned with the firm's tax obligations and the protection of its employees. Labor unions use financial information in negotiations with management for wage increases.

Who else uses accounting information? The owners and stockholders of a business use it to find out whether the business has invested its money wisely and whether it is in a position to raise more capital. Management is concerned with the firm's ability to meet immediate cash needs. Does the business have enough money to pay off its creditors and to purchase needed assets?

The accounting information that is provided to all of these parties is based on **generally accepted accounting principles (GAAP).** This term refers to broad rules adopted by the accounting profession for measuring and reporting the financial activities of a firm.

generally accepted accounting principles (GAAP) *broad rules adopted by the accounting profession for measuring and reporting the financial activities of a firm.*

Accounting and the Management Function

2

Throughout the chapter, we will explain many of the financial statements that the accountant prepares. Though many students using this text may not actually become accountants, you are almost certain to use this type of data as future managers. Managers who cannot read and understand financial statements are at a severe disadvantage when carrying out their functions. If your boss lays a balance sheet or income statement on your desk, you will be expected to interpret and respond to the data that is in front of you. You may also be expected to do comparative analysis, in which you relate the results of a firm for this year to those for last year and to those of other firms in the industry.

These expectations will apply whether you are in finance, marketing, management, production, or any other area of business. For example, a marketing manager may have very creative ideas but fail in his or her task because of an inability to translate the ideas into clearly developed projections of profitability.

A basic understanding of accounting is also important to completing coursework in a business school curriculum. Accounting is normally a prerequisite for taking courses in finance, and it is also essential for courses in other areas. A potentially outstanding student may get B's and C's in business courses because of a weakness in accounting.

Computers and Accounting

One of the areas most affected by the development of computers is accounting. Because of the repetitive nature of recording accounting information and the need for instant access to data, the industry has become more and more dependent on the computer. It is now possible to have a computer continuously audit, testing the reliability and accuracy of financial statements. Major accounting firms are actually linking their computers to those of clients, to share data instantaneously. For the smaller accounting firm, the computer is also important as an aid in decision making and tax preparation.

TWO ACCOUNTING CONCEPTS

To understand how modern accounting works, we must understand the accounting equation and how transactions are recorded in a double-entry bookkeeping system. A discussion of both follows.

The Accounting Equation

As you learned in Chapter 5, assets are all the properties owned by a firm. The rights or claims against the firm are called **equity.** Any property that the firm owns must have a corresponding claim; assets do not suddenly appear without another party being responsible for financing them. If a firm has $100,000 worth of assets, then it must have $100,000 worth of equity. Hence,

equity   rights or claims against the assets of the firm; indicates how the assets have been financed.

> Assets = Equity
> $100,000 = $100,000

The equity side of the equation is divided into the rights of owners and the rights of creditors. Since the rights of creditors are debts for the firm, we call them liabilities. **Liabilities** are legal obligations to pay in the future. The value of the owners' investment in the company is called **owners' equity.** The **accounting equation,** then, is:

liabilities   legal obligations to pay in the future.

owner's equity   the value of the owners' investment in the firm.

accounting equation   Assets = Liabilities + Owners' Equity.

> Assets = Liabilities + Owners' Equity

If our firm owed $25,000 to a bank, we would write the accounting equation as follows:

> Assets = Liabilities + Owners' Equity
> $100,000 = $25,000 + $75,000

We normally place liabilities before owners' equity in the accounting equation. We do this to show that creditors have first rights to assets. That is, if a company were forced out of business, its creditors would be repaid before the owners were given back their investments. It is sometimes useful in this regard to move liabilities to the other side of the accounting equation.

> Assets − Liabilities = Owners' Equity
> $100,000 − $25,000 = $75,000

This shows that owners' equity is a residual amount—in other words, what is left over, in the event of liquidation, for distribution among the owners after all debts have been repaid.

Double-Entry Bookkeeping

Double-entry bookkeeping is a record-keeping method based on the accounting equation. Each transaction requires two entries in the books. These entries
show the effect of the transaction on the assets side and the equity side of the
accounting equation. This keeps the equation balanced at all times. That is, assets
always equal liabilities plus owners' equity. Suppose a business borrows $5,000
from the bank to buy a car. The firm's assets increase by $5,000, because it now
owns a car valued at $5,000. Its liabilities also increase by $5,000, because it owes
the bank $5,000 for the car. To illustrate, we'll continue with the example pre-
sented in the last section. Before purchase of the car:

$$Assets = Liabilities + Owners' Equity$$
$$\$100,000 = \$25,000 + \$75,000$$

After purchase of the car:

$$Assets = Liabilities + Owners' Equity$$
$$\$105,000 = \$30,000 + \$75,000$$

Note that the accounting equation is still in balance. Both sides of the equation
were equally affected by the transaction, because both increased by $5,000. Let's
now look at how a series of five transactions were recorded by Joel Snyder when
he established Snyder's Pizza House and Dance Hall. These five transactions are
shown in the box below.

Transaction (A): Establish the Business. To start his business, Joel used
$20,000 of his own money to open a bank account in the name of Snyder's Pizza
House and Dance Hall. This created $20,000 worth of assets for the firm and, at
the same time, $20,000 worth of owners' equity.

Snyder's Pizza House and Dance Hall

Transaction (A)

$$Assets = Equity$$
$$Cash = Owners' Equity$$
$$\$20,000 = \$20,000$$

Transaction (B)

Assets	=	Equity	
Cash + Building	=	Liability +	Owners' Equity
$20,000			$20,000
$20,000 + $60,000	=	$60,000 +	$20,000

Total left-hand side $80,000 = $80,000   Total right-hand side

Transaction (C)

Assets		=	Equity	
Cash + Building	+ Supplies	=	Liabilities +	Owners' Equity
$20,000 $60,000			$60,000	$20,000
−$ 2,000	+ $2,000			
$18,000 + $60,000	+ $2,000	=	$60,000 +	$20,000

Total left-hand side $80,000 = $80,000   Total right-hand
                                             side

Transaction (B): Buy a Building. Joel's next step was to buy a building. The best building available cost $60,000. Fortunately for Joel, the bank was willing to lend him the entire amount. Note that although assets went up by $60,000, liabilities, which represent the debt to the bank, also went up by $60,000.

Transaction (C): Buy Supplies. Joel then bought pizza dough and tomato paste. He spent $2,000 cash on these supplies. All changes occurred on the asset side of the equation. Simply stated, $2,000 cash was converted to $2,000 worth of supplies, leaving equity unaffected. Note also that the equation is still in balance.

Transaction (D): Record Sales Revenue. After one week, Snyder's Pizza House and Dance Hall was a hit, selling a total of $3,000 worth of pizzas. This revenue is treated as an increase in cash and an increase in owners' equity. Again, we see that the equation remains in balance.

Transaction (E): Record Expenses. Joel incurred four expenses while selling his pizzas: He paid $1,200 in wages to servers and to members of the band, $150 in utilities (electricity and water), and $100 in other bills. In addition, he used $750 worth of supplies. These expenses reduced Joel's cash, supplies, and owners' equity accounts. Total assets still equal total equity: The expenses reduced the assets and equity sides of the equation equally.

In summary, Joel's business began with assets and equity both equal to $20,000. It ended up with assets and equity equal to $80,800. It is important to restate two things. First, each transaction required two entries. That is why the accounting system is called double-entry bookkeeping. Second, if assets do not equal equity, then an error has been made in recording a transaction.

Transaction (D)

	Assets			=	Equity	
	Cash +	Building +	Supplies	= Liabilities +	Owners' Equity	
	$18,000	$60,000	$2,000	= $60,000	$20,000	
	+$ 3,000				$ 3,000	
	$21,000 +	$60,000 +	$2,000	= $60,000 +	$23,000	
	Total left-hand side		$83,000 =	$83,000	Total right-hand side	

Transaction (E)

	Assets			=	Equity	
	Cash +	Building +	Supplies	= Liabilities +	Owners' Equity	
	$21,000	$60,000	$2,000	$60,000	$23,000	
(Wages)	−$1,200				−$1,200	
(Util.)	−$150				−$ 150	
(Misc.)	−$100				−$ 100	
(Supp.)			−$750		−$ 750	
	$19,550 +	$60,000 +	$1,250	= $60,000 +	$20,800	
	Total left-hand side		$80,800 =	$80,800	Total right-hand side	

BALANCE SHEET

balance sheet a financial "snapshot" of the business showing the balance of the firm's assets, liabilities, and owners' equity at one moment in time.

There are three major financial statements prepared by the accountant: the balance sheet, the income statement, and the statement of cash flows. The **balance sheet** presents a financial "snapshot" of the business at a particular moment in time. It, too, is based on the accounting equation: Assets = Liabilities + Owners' Equity. The balance sheet shows the value of a firm's assets as well as the value of its liabilities and owners' equity. The balance sheet is in balance only when assets equal liabilities plus owners' equity.

The balance sheet is used by a firm's creditors in deciding whether to lend more money to the firm. Most firms prepare a balance sheet at the end of each calendar year. This gives the firm and its creditors a picture of its financial position at the same time each year.

Some business firms use a fiscal year instead. Under this approach, the annual accounting period may begin on any day of the year rather than on the first day of January. For example a fiscal year might begin on July 1 and run through June 30 of the next year. Figure 18-1 presents a calendar year balance sheet for Nevada Cement, Inc., dated December 31, 1992. Nevada Cement's balance sheet is in balance because its $2,513,000 in assets equals its $2,513,000 in liabilities and owners' equity. Let's look at the sections of the balance sheet individually.

Assets

current assets cash and other liquid assets that the firm expects to use, sell, or turn into cash within one year.

cash the most liquid of all business assets; includes checking account balances as well as currency and coin.

marketable securities company holdings in stocks, bonds, money market accounts, and other securities readily convertible to cash.

accounts receivable the amount owed to the firm as a result of credit sales.

allowance for bad debt a special account set up to reflect the amount of accounts receivable that may not be collectible in the future.

note receivable a signed note in which one party promises to pay another a certain amount of money over a designated period of time.

merchandise inventory a balance sheet current asset category that includes finished goods, work in process, and raw materials.

finished goods products that are ready for shipment or sale to a buyer.

There are two basic types of assets: current assets and fixed assets. We can also distinguish between tangible and intangible assets. It is important for a firm's accountants to classify its assets correctly.

Current Assets. **Current assets** are cash and other "liquid" assets that the firm expects to use, sell, or turn into cash within one year. **Cash** is the most liquid of all business assets. It includes money held as currency or coins in a safe or strong box as well as checking account balances. Cash would not include money deposited in a two-year time deposit, because the firm does not have access to it quickly. The term **marketable securities** refers to company holdings in stocks, bonds, money market accounts, and other securities readily convertible to cash.

Firms often sell their products on credit. The amount owed to the firm at any moment in time as a result of these credit sales is listed under the entry called **accounts receivable.** Accountants treat accounts receivable much as they do cash: Both are current assets. As Figure 18-1 shows, Nevada Cement has $223,000 in receivables. It also has $28,000 listed as **allowance for bad debt.** This indicates that Nevada Cement does not believe that it will be able to collect all of its receivables. In effect, Nevada Cement is telling the reader of its balance sheet that its accounts receivable are really worth only $195,000.

A **note receivable,** on the other hand, is a signed note in which one person or company promises to pay another person or company a certain amount of money over a designated period of time. Nevada Cement has a note receivable of $25,000. The company sold one of its railroad cars to another company, which promised in writing to pay $25,000 for the car within six months.

Three types of **merchandise inventory** are also listed on the balance sheet as current assets: finished goods, work in process, and raw materials. As discussed in Chapter 11, **finished goods** are products that are ready for shipment

FIGURE 18-1   Nevada Cement Balance Sheet

NEVADA CEMENT, INC.

Balance Sheet

December 31, 1992

CURRENT ASSETS
Cash		$ 80,000	
Marketable Securities		25,000	
Accounts Receivable	$223,000		
Less Allowance for Bad Debt	28,000	195,000	
Notes Receivable		25,000	
Merchandise Inventory			
Finished Goods	450,000		
Work-in-Process	330,000		
Raw Materials	280,000	1,060,000	
Prepaid Expenses		18,500	
TOTAL CURRENT ASSETS			$1,403,500

FIXED ASSETS
Land		400,000	
Building	550,000		
Less Accumulated Depreciation	135,000	415,000	
Equipment	360,000		
Less Accumulated Depreciation	125,500	234,500	
TOTAL FIXED ASSETS			1,049,500

INTANGIBLE ASSETS
Goodwill		40,000	
Patents		20,000	
TOTAL INTANGIBLE ASSETS			60,000
TOTAL ASSETS			$2,513,000

LIABILITIES AND OWNERS' EQUITY
Current Liabilities
Accounts Payable		$ 320,500	
Notes Payable		65,000	
Accrued Expenses		92,000	
Income Tax Payable		160,000	
TOTAL CURRENT LIABILITIES			$ 637,500

Long-Term Liabilities
Long-Term Notes Payable		340,000	
Bonds Payable		475,000	
TOTAL LONG-TERM LIABILITIES			815,000
TOTAL LIABILITIES			1,452,500

Owners' Equity
Common Stock (17,600 shares at $25)		440,000	
Retained Earnings		620,500	
TOTAL OWNERS' EQUITY			1,060,500
TOTAL LIABILITIES AND OWNERS' EQUITY			$2,513,000

work in process *unfinished products that still need to move through one or more stages in the manufacturing process.*

raw materials *inputs from which the firm makes its products.*

prepaid expenses *a balance sheet current asset category consisting of expenses paid in advance.*

fixed assets *nonliquid assets that the firm expects to hold for the long term or permanently.*

or sale to a buyer. **Work in process** refers to unfinished products. These products still need to move through one or more stages in the manufacturing process. **Raw materials** are the inputs from which the firm makes its products. Sand is a finished good for a sand company, but it would be a raw material for Nevada Cement. The value of each component of Nevada Cement's merchandise inventory is listed in its balance sheet.

Expenses paid in advance, another current asset, are called **prepaid expenses.** An example of a prepaid expense is automobile insurance and building insurance. Insurance companies require businesses to buy their insurance in advance—normally, six months or one year. Because the firm pays in advance of the period of coverage, this expense is recorded on the balance sheet as a current asset.

The prepaid expense account is confusing to many students, because it is an "expense" that is called an asset. The reason that it is an asset is that it is already paid for before it is used. Although the firm cannot sell a prepaid expense as it can many other current assets, such as marketable securities or inventory, it does have the benefit of having taken care of an obligation before it is actually due.

This makes it an asset to the firm. Of course, as the prepaid expense is used (during the period of the insurance coverage for example), the asset will be reduced and converted into an expense for the period. By the end of the period of insurance coverage, there will not longer be a prepaid expense on the books.

Fixed Assets. **Fixed assets** are "long lived" or permanent assets. They are not sold during the ordinary course of operations. Fixed assets include land, buildings and machinery, and equipment. There is no standard for how long an asset must be used in order for it to be called "fixed." Fixed assets, however, must be capable of repeated use, and they are normally expected to last several years.

Note on Nevada Cement's balance sheet that its building is listed at $550,000 minus accumulated depreciation of $135,000. Fixed assets get used up or become obsolete over

Which of these items shown above are current assets and which are fixed assets?

time. To reflect this fact on their financial statements, firms deduct portions of the asset's original cost each year of its useful life instead of deducting the entire expense at the time of purchase. This gradual write-off of fixed assets is called **depreciation.** On the balance sheet, **accumulated depreciation** is the sum of all depreciation expense to date. When accumulated depreciation is subtracted from the original value of the building, the balance sheet shows a "net" value of $415,000. The same procedure was also used for equipment. Federal tax law regulates the rate at which fixed assets may be depreciated.

Intangible Assets. Patents, licenses, trademarks, and goodwill are all examples of **intangible assets.** All these assets have a common trait—intangibility. That is, none of them is really a physical object.

Goodwill can be a reputation for producing high-quality products. Such a reputation is certainly worth something. Nevada Cement enjoys goodwill because its reputation for quality encourages people to buy its products. How can you tell whether a firm has goodwill? The real test is whether the firm earns a return on its assets greater than those of other firms in the industry. Goodwill may be added to a firm's balance sheet only when ownership changes hands.[1] Nevada Cement was sold to its current owners in 1991. At that time, the new owners paid $40,000 more for the business than its net assets (assets minus liabilities) were worth. Accordingly, $40,000 was assigned as goodwill on Nevada Cement's balance sheet.

Liabilities and Owners' Equity

This part of the balance sheet shows the amount of money a firm owes its creditors, as well as the value of the owners's investments in the business. We'll begin this discussion by looking at current liabilities.

Current Liabilities. As explained earlier in this chapter, a liability is a legal obligation requiring payment in the future. **Current liabilities** must be paid within one year. Normally, current liabilities are paid out of current assets. The most common types of current liabilities are accounts payable and notes payable.

Accounts payable represent purchases for which the firm has not yet paid. Suppose a firm buys computer paper on credit in April and pays for it in May. At the time of the purchase in April, the cost of the paper is entered as an account payable. In May, the account payable is removed from the books, and the payment is deducted from the cash account. Nevada Cement has a total of $320,500 in accounts payable as of December 31, 1992.

Notes payable are like accounts payable except that the firm signs a legal document stating exactly when the amount due is to be paid. Nevada Cement has $65,000 in notes payable for a cement truck it recently purchased.

Some services are paid for only after they are performed. The amounts owed for such services are listed on the balance sheet as **accrued expenses.** A good example of an accrued expense is the labor provided by employees. You think of employees as earning a small part of their salaries each minute or hour they work. But employees are paid on a weekly or monthly basis. The amount of money that a firm owes its employees for work already performed is listed as an accrued expense on the balance sheet.

The final category of current liabilities listed on Nevada Cement's balance sheet is income tax payable. This could be classified as a type of accrued

depreciation   the gradual write-off of the value of a fixed asset over its useful life, rather than writing off the entire cost at time of purchase.

accumulated depreciation   the sum of all depreciation to date.

intangible assets   assets that are not physical objects, including patents, licenses, and goodwill.

current liabilities   liabilities that must be paid within one year.

accounts payable   purchases for which the firm has not yet paid.

notes payable   purchases for which the firm has signed a legal document stating when payment is due.

accrued expenses   money owed for services, to be paid after their performance.

income tax payable *the estimated amount of money owed to the government on income already earned.*

expense. **Income tax payable** is to the estimated amount of money owed to the government on income already earned. Nevada Cement's accountants estimate that the firm owes $160,000 in federal income taxes.

Long-Term Liabilities. Debts that do not have to repaid for at least 12 months are called **long-term liabilities.** Typically, they represent borrowings from a bank, insurance company, or other financial institutions. Nevada Cement owes $340,000 in long-term notes payable. This represents money the firm borrowed from a Nevada bank to pay for three new railroad cars. **Bonds payable** are an obligation to repay long-term bonds. The bonds payable were issued to purchase land three years ago.

long-term liabilities *debts that do not have to be paid for at least 12 months.*

bonds payable *an obligation on the books of the issuing firm to repay long-term bonds.*

Owners' Equity. As discussed earlier, the term "owners' equity" refers to the value of the owners' investment in the company. Owners' equity is usually broken into three subaccounts on the balance sheet: common stock, preferred stock, and retained earnings. As we will see in Chapter 20, common stock and preferred stock represent the amount of money invested in the company by its owners; retained earnings is the cumulative amount of earnings, after payment of dividends, that has been left in the business. Nevada Cement has no preferred stock.

It is important to notice once again that the balance sheet for Nevada Cement is in balance: Assets equal liabilities plus owners' equity.

INCOME STATEMENT

income statement *a financial statement that shows all the firm's revenues and expenses over an interval and the resulting profit or loss for that period.*

The balance sheet was described as a snapshot of a firm's assets, liabilities, and owners' equity at one moment in time. The **income statement,** on the other hand, records all of a firm's revenues and expenses that have occurred over an interval of time. It shows how much money was made or lost during, say, the last 12 months.

Income statements are drawn up each year—at the same time the firm draws up its balance sheet. Additionally, many firms provide quarterly and monthly income statements. Nevada Cement's annual income statement is shown in Figure 18-2. Note that it contains several types of income and expenses. The "bottom line" of the income statement shows the firm's profit or loss for the year. The income statement arrives at the profit or loss by starting with revenues and systematically subtracting all expenses.

Gross Sales

gross sales *revenue received from selling the firm's products or services, including cash sales and sales charged or made on account.*

Gross sales represent revenue received from selling the firm's products or services, including cash sales and sales made on account or charged. To arrive at net sales, all returns and allowances are subtracted from gross sales. **Returns** are products that customers return to the firm, for which they receive a full refund. **Allowances** are partial refunds—for example, giving a customer a 20 percent refund because the product purchased was slightly damaged. **Net sales,** therefore, are gross sales minus returns and allowances. Net sales for Nevada Cement during 1992 were $2,495,700.

returns *products that customers return to the firm, for which they receive a full refund.*

allowances *partial refunds to customers for products that they return to the firm.*

net sales *gross sales minus returns and allowances.*

Cost of Goods Sold

cost of goods sold *the amount of money spent by the seller to produce or buy the merchandise sold.*

The amount of money spent by the seller to produce or buy the merchandise is known as **cost of goods sold**. Retailers and wholesalers use one procedure for calculating cost of goods sold; manufacturers use another.

FIGURE 18-2   Nevada Cement Income Statement

NEVADA CEMENT, INC.

Income Statement

for the Year Ended December 31, 1992

Sales			
Gross Sales	$2,570,700		
Less Returns and Allowances	75,000		
Net Sales		$2,495,700	
Less Cost of Goods Sold		950,000	
GROSS PROFIT			$1,545,700
Operating Expenses			
Selling Expenses			
Sales Salaries	$230,000		
Advertising	20,000		
Sales Insurance	2,200		
Depreciation—Sales Equipment	45,000		
Miscellaneous	2,900		
Total Sales Expenses		$300,100	
Administrative Expenses			
Salaries	380,400		
Taxes	21,000		
Depreciation—Office Building and Equipment	345,000		
Insurance	20,200		
Miscellaneous	3,000		
Total Administrative Expenses		769,600	
TOTAL OPERATING EXPENSES			1,069,700
INCOME FROM OPERATIONS			476,000
Other Income			
Dividends	3,000		
Interest	1,800	4,800	
Other Expenses			
Loss from Land Sale		(12,000)	
NET INCOME BEFORE TAXES			468,800
Federal Income Taxes			147,642
NET INCOME AFTER TAXES			$321,158

The procedure used by retailers and wholesalers is illustrated in the left side of Figure 18-3. The accountant begins by determining how much inventory the firm had at the beginning of the period—in this case, $150,000 as of January 1, 1992. The dollar value of the inventory purchased during the year ($319,000) is then added to this figure. The sum $469,000 is the value of the inventory available for sale during the year; it is called "goods available for sale." The accountant then subtracts the year-end inventory ($125,500) from the goods available for sale to obtain the cost of goods sold during the year ($343,500).

In contrast to a retailer or wholesaler, both of which buy products for resale, a manufacturer makes the products it sells. How does this affect the computation of cost of goods sold for a manufacturer such as Nevada Cement? First, the accountant determines the value of finished goods inventory at the beginning of the year. The next step is to add the costs of labor, raw materials, and overhead to determine the cost of goods manufactured.

The calculation of the cost of goods sold for Nevada Cement, a manufacturer, is shown in the right side of Figure 18-3. Note that Nevada Cement's accountant added finished goods inventory at the beginning of the year ($185,000) to the cost of goods manufactured ($1,215,000). This gives the dollar value of manufactured goods available for sale during the year ($1,400,000). The accountant then subtracted finished goods inventory left at the end of the year ($450,000) to obtain the cost of goods sold ($950,000).

Gross Profit

gross profit the difference between net sales and cost of goods sold.

Gross profit is the difference between net sales and cost of goods sold. It is called gross profit because operating expenses still have not been considered. As shown in the income statement in Figure 18-2, the gross profit of Nevada Cement is $1,545,700.

Operating Expenses

operating expenses selling and administrative expenses.

The operating expenses of a business can be classified in a number of ways. Nevada Cement and most other companies classify **operating expenses** under the two general headings of selling expenses and administrative expenses.

FIGURE 18-3   Calculation of Cost of Goods Sold for Retailers, Wholesalers, and Manufacturers

Retailers and Wholesalers		
Beginning Inventory (January 1, 1992)		$150,000
Inventory Purchased	$345,600	
Less Purchase Discounts	(26,600)	319,000
Goods Available for Sale		$469,000
Less Ending Inventory (December 31, 1992)		125,500
COST OF GOODS SOLD		$343,500

Nevada Cement, Manufacturer		
Beginning Finished Goods (January 1, 1992)		$185,000
Cost of Goods Manufactured		1,215,000
Goods Available for Sale		$1,400,000
Less Ending Finished Goods Inventory (December 31, 1992)		450,000
COST OF GOODS SOLD		$950,000

Selling Expenses. As the name implies, **selling expenses** result directly from the firm's sales efforts. They include advertising expenses, insurance on sales force automobiles and office buildings, and salaries of salespeople. Some selling expenses represent the cost of depreciating any physical assets used by sales-people in selling the firm's products. Nevada Cement incurred $300,100 in sales expenses in 1992.

selling expenses expenses that result directly from the firm's sales efforts.

Administrative Expenses. Administrative expenses are expenses incurred in the administration of general operation of the business, such as administrative salaries, federal income taxes, insurance, and depreciation. Administrative expenses are also called "general overhead" by some accountants. In the case of Nevada Cement, they include the salaries of the company president, the president's staff, and the accounting and personnel departments. These are all included under the salaries entry of administrative expenses. The taxes entry brings together all taxes paid by the firm except for federal income tax. For many firms, local property taxes are the most important item under this category. The depreciation entry is used to record the yearly write-off of the cost of the physical assets, such as office building and equipment. The insurance entry includes all the insurance the firm must carry to protect its assets. Total administrative expenses for Nevada Cement are $769,600.

administrative expenses overhead expenses incurred in the administration or general operations of the business.

Income from Operations

The accountant next calculates **income from operations** by subtracting total operating expenses from gross profit. When gross profit is greater than operating expenses, the firm has made a profit on its operations. If gross profit is less than operating expenses, then the firm has lost money from operations.

income from operations gross profit minus total operating expenses.

Income from operations is a very important line on the income statement, because it tells us whether the firm is making money from its principal business. Nevada Cement is making $476,000 from the manufacture and sale of cement. We obtained this figure by subtracting total operating expenses of $1,069,700 from the gross profit of $1,545,700.

Other Income

Revenue from sources other than the primary activity of the firm is called **other income**. Examples include interest income, dividends received, or gains from the sale of physical assets. Nevada Cement made $3,000 from dividends and $1,800 in interest income in 1992.

other income revenue from sources other than the primary activity of the firm.

Other Expenses

All expenses that cannot be directly associated with the operations of the firm are called **other expenses**. Nevada Cement sold some land it had purchased two years earlier. Nevada paid $130,000 for the land and sold it for $118,000—a $12,000 loss. Because Nevada Cement's primary activity is not the buying and selling of land, the loss from the sale is recorded as other expense.

other expenses all expenses that cannot be directly associated with the operations of the firm.

Net Income Before Taxes

Net income before taxes is determined by subtracting other expenses from other income and adding the result to income from operations. When other expenses are subtracted from other income, if the result is positive, income from operations is increased by this amount to arrive at net income before taxes. If the

net income before taxes income from operations plus other income minus other expenses.

result is negative, income from operations is reduced by this amount to arrive at net income before taxes. Since other expenses were greater than other income by $7,200, Nevada Cement's net income of $468,800 before taxes is less than its income from operations of $476,000.

Federal Income Taxes

After considering all the firm's expenses and revenues, the accountant estimates the amount owed in federal income taxes. Table 18-2 shows that the more money a business makes, the more taxes it pays. A business making $50,000 a year pays 15 percent of this amount to the government. A firm making $10 million a year pays 34 percent of its profits to the government as income tax.

Net Income After Taxes

net income after taxes
the amount of money the firm made during the period; net income before taxes minus federal income taxes.

The real bottom line on the income statement is **net income after taxes.** It is the amount of money the firm made or lost during the year. It is calculated by subtracting federal income taxes from net income before taxes. The term "net income after taxes" is generally shortened to simply "net income." Net income for Nevada Cement in 1992 was $321,158.

Footnotes

The financial statements also include a set of footnotes. The footnotes indicate which accounting methods the firm uses for items such as inventory valuation and depreciation, and they give additional information that the financial statement user may find helpful, such as the market values of some of the company's assets.

INVENTORY VALUATION

As we saw from our discussion of the income statement, the accountant cannot calculate net income without first calculating the cost of goods sold. To calculate this figure, the accountant must determine the value of the firm's ending inventory. Two commonly used methods for valuing inventory are FIFO and LIFO.

Table 18-2   Income and Income Taxes

Yearly Income	Federal Income Taxes	Federal Income Taxes as Percentage of Income
$ 25,000	$ 3,750	15.0%
50,000	7,500	15.0
75,000	13,750	18.3
100,000	22,550	22.6
500,000	163,250	32.6
1,000,000	332,250	33.2
20,000,000	6,792,250	34.0

Inventory valuation must be done before a firm can determine its cost of goods sold.

Before discussing them, let's first take a closer look at the inventory valuation problem.

The Valuation Problem

Additions to inventory and the selling off or using up of inventory occur continually throughout the year. Your local supermarket sells many tubes of toothpaste every day. At regular intervals, a clerk restocks the toothpaste display. Thus, inventory supplies are continuously being both drawn down and replenished.

The problem is one of determining the value of the toothpaste inventory on the day for which the supermarket draws up its balance sheet. Which tubes of toothpaste are left on the shelf: the ones the supermarket purchased last week for $1.20 a tube, or those it bought three weeks ago for $0.95? This problem is not as trivial as it may seem. Large cost changes from one inventory purchase time to another can have a dramatic effect on total inventory valuation. LIFO and FIFO deal with this problem. Obviously, if per-unit inventory purchase cost does not vary over the year, then there is no valuation problem. Total value of inventory in this case is the number of units left on the shelf at year-end multiplied by the purchase cost per unit.

FIFO

The **first-in, first-out (FIFO)** method is based on the idea that the first items put into inventory are the first ones taken off the shelf and sold. As a result, inventory on the shelf at the end of the year is assumed to be made up of the most recently purchased items. Ending inventory is therefore valued at the cost of the most recent additions to inventory.

Figure 18-4 shows how FIFO works during a period of rising prices. The firm in this example, as a January 1, had 200 units of inventory on hand. It purchased

first-in, first-out (FIFO) *a method that values inventory based on the premise that the first items put into inventory are the first ones sold.*

FIGURE 18-4   Inventory Valuation

Available Inventory

January 1	Inventory	200 units at $8.00	$1,600
March 1	Purchase	500 units at $9.00	4,500
May 17	Purchase	450 units at $10.00	4,500
September 19	Purchase	500 units at $11.00	5,500
December 15	Purchase	100 units at $11.50	1,150
Available for Sale		1,750 units	$17,250

FIFO Inventory Valuation

Most recent costs, December 15	100 units at $11.50	$1,150
Next most recent costs, September 19	200 units at $11.00	2,200
TOTAL ENDING INVENTORY	300 units	$3,350

LIFO Inventory Valuation

Earliest costs, January 1	200 units at $8.00	$1,600
Next earliest costs, March 1	100 units at $9.00	900
TOTAL ENDING INVENTORY	300 units	$2,500

additional units of inventory on four occasions during the year. On the last day of December, 364 days later, the firm counts 300 units left in inventory. These 300 units, under the FIFO method, would be valued at $3,350. Figure 18-4 shows that the first 100 units of ending inventory are valued at the December 15 unit purchase cost of $11.50. Since only 100 units were purchased then, the other 200 units of ending inventory are valued at the September 19 cost of $11.00, at which time 500 units were purchased. Total inventory value, then, is the sum of $1,150 and $2,200, or $3,350.

LIFO

last-in, first-out (LIFO) a method that values inventory based on the premise that the last items put into inventory are the first ones sold.

The other valuation method is **last-in first-out** (LIFO). The LIFO approach assumes that the last items put into inventory are the first ones sold. Ending inventory is assumed to consist of items purchased first. Thus, the earliest inventory purchase costs determine the value of ending inventory. This is the opposite of FIFO.

The bottom of Figure 18-4 shows the LIFO calculation of ending inventory value for the same inventory purchase history. Of the 300 units of ending inventory, the first 200 are valued at the January 1 unit cost of $8.00. Two hundred units were purchased at that time for $1,600. The other 100 units are valued at the next earliest unit purchase cost of $9.00. The total LIFO valuation is the sum of $1,600 and $900, or $2,500. Note that LIFO will produce a smaller ending inventory value than FIFO during a period of rising prices.

INTERPRETING FINANCIAL STATEMENTS   **7**

You should now understand the difference between a balance sheet and an income statement. The next question is how to interpret these statements to gain greater insight into a firm's financial performance. Has a firm improved its financial position? Is it strong relative to its competition? The answers are in the income statement and balance sheet. The task is to pull them out. There are two basic ways to do this: comparative analysis and ratio analysis.

Comparative Analysis

One way to evaluate financial statements is to compare, for example, one year's balance sheet with the balance sheet of the previous year. The goal is to interpret changes that have occurred between the two years. These changes indicate whether the company is getting stronger or weaker. The annual reports of many companies show balance sheets and income statements for the current year and for nine preceding years. The reader of these comparative financial statements is thus able to spot performance trends.

Figure 18-5 shows two years of balance sheet data for the Snap-on Tools Corporation. Note that current assets increased from $504,980,000 in 1988 to $564,623,000 in 1989. What caused this sizable increase? The biggest jump was in accounts receivable, from $336,588,000 in 1988 to $403,926,000 in 1989. It appears that the firm had to extend more credit to customers to expand sales. At the same time, the firm was able to reduce the amount tied up in inventory by over $2,000,000. Perhaps Snap-on Tools is managing its inventory flow more efficiently. There was also a sizable jump in plant and equipment, from $146,371,000 in 1988 to $195,020,000 in 1989. This was part of Snap-on Tools' long-term commitment to modernizing its facilities.

In terms of liabilities, the largest increase was in notes payable. In 1988, there was no such debt, but $37,000,000 was borrowed in 1989. The large increase in retained earnings, from $464,394,000 in 1988 to $526,449,000 in 1989, indicates that the company was quite profitable during the year.

To summarize the data, the large increase in accounts receivable is a matter of some concern. However, the fact that the firm had a substantial increase in profitability (as reflected in the retained earnings account) makes future problems seem less likely. Snap-on Tools appears to be enjoying healthy growth.

The data for Snap-on Tools Corporation came from its annual report. To get a better understanding of annual reports, read the box entitled "How to Read an Annual Report" on page 502.

Ratio Analysis

A great deal can also be learned about a firm's financial performance by looking at certain financial ratios. These ratios are developed from balance sheet and income statement data. The advantage of ratio analysis is that it allows us to assess the performance of one firm against that of others in the same industry. Comparative analysis, on the other hand, typically involves an evaluation of year-by-year performance for a single firm. The usual procedure for ratio analysis is to look at a firm's financial ratios in relation to industry averages.[2] Let's look at several of these financial ratios, using the information in Nevada Cement's balance sheet and income statement (Figures 18-1 and 18-2).

FIGURE 18-5   Comparative Balance Sheets for Snap-on Tools Corporation

SNAP-ON TOOLS CORPORATION

Comparative Balance Sheets
(in thousands)

	Dec. 31, 1989	Dec. 31, 1988
ASSETS		
Current Assets		
Cash	$5,078	$16,895
Accounts Receivable	403,926	336,588
Inventories	137,106	139,460
Prepaid Expenses	18,513	12,037
Total Current Assets	$564,623	$504,980
Plant and Equipment	195,020	146,371
Goodwill	17,960	16,187
TOTAL ASSETS	$777,603	$667,538
LIABILITIES AND OWNERS' EQUITY		
Current Liabilities		
Accounts Payable	$40,259	$30,962
Notes Payable	37,000	0
Accrued Expenses	58,895	67,311
Other Current Liabilities	43,322	44,064
Total Current Liabilities	$179,476	$142,337
Long-term Debt	7,700	8,125
Other Long-term Liabilities	17,770	11,874
TOTAL LIABILITIES	$204,946	$162,336
Owners' Equity		
Common Stock	$41,117	$40,911
Other Equity	5,091	(103)
Retained Earnings	526,449	464,394
TOTAL OWNERS' EQUITY	572,657	505,202
TOTAL LIABILITIES AND OWNERS' EQUITY	$777,603	$667,538

current ratio *a measure of whether a firm can pay its short-term debts, calculated as current assets divided by current liabilities.*

Current Position. Current position analysis tells us whether the firm is able to meet its short-term debt obligations. An important ratio here is the **current ratio,** which is calculated by dividing the firm's total current assets by its total current liabilities. Nevada Cement's current ratio is:

$$\text{Current Ratio} = \frac{\text{Current Assets}}{\text{Current Liabilities}}$$

$$= \frac{\$1,403,500}{\$\ 637,500}$$

$$= 2.20$$

This means that Nevada Cement has $2.20 in current assets for every dollar of current liabilities.

Is Nevada Cement's current ratio of 2.20 acceptable? Would a smart banker make Nevada Cement a short-term loan? Unfortunately, there is no simple answer to this question. Of course, 2.20 is better than 1.85, but it is also not as good as 3.15. Many accountants believe that a company with a current ratio of 2.00 or higher is a good risk for a short-term lender.

A second ratio for assessing a firm's current position is the **acid-test** or **quick ratio.** Whereas the current ratio includes all current assets and all current liabilities, the acid-test ratio includes only those current assets that can be quickly converted to cash. The numerator of the acid-test radio includes cash, marketable securities, and accounts receivable, but not notes receivable, merchandise inventory, or prepaid expenses. The acid-test ratio is always smaller than the current ratio. Nevada Cement's acid-test ratio is shown here:

acid-test or quick ratio measure of whether a firm can pay its short-term debts from liquid assets, calculated as cash plus marketable securities plus accounts receivable divided by current liabilities.

$$\text{Acid-Test Ratio} = \frac{\text{Cash} + \text{Marketable Securities} + \text{Accounts Receivable}}{\text{Current Liabilities}}$$

$$= \frac{\$80,000 + \$25,000 + \$195,000}{\$637,500}$$

$$= \frac{\$300,000}{\$637,500}$$

$$= .47$$

Although several ratios are important in assessing a firm's current position, an acid-test ratio of 1.0 or greater is considered quite good. It means that the firm is "liquid" in that it is able to raise cash quickly to pay its current liabilities. Nevada Cement's acid-test ratio of .47 might make some conservative bankers nervous.

Inventory Turnover. A firm should have enough inventory to meet the needs of its customers. However, too much inventory ties up money that could be used more productively in other ways. The **inventory turnover ratio** measures how many times a year the firm sells off, or "turns over," its inventory. It is computed by dividing cost of goods sold by average inventory. Because monthly inventory data is usually not available for analysts outside the firm, it may be necessary to use the average of the inventory at the beginning of the year and at the end of the year. The inventory turnover ratio for Nevada Cement is based on data from Figures 18-2 and 18-3.

inventory turnover ratio a measure of how many times a year the firm sells its inventory, calculated as cost of goods sold divided by average inventory.

$$\text{Average Inventory} = \frac{\text{Beginning Inventory} + \text{Ending Inventory}}{2}$$

$$= \frac{\$185,000 + \$450,000}{2}$$

$$= \$317,500$$

$$\text{Inventory Turnover} = \frac{\text{Cost of Goods Sold}}{\text{Average Inventory}}$$

$$= \frac{\$950,000}{\$317,500}$$

$$= 2.99$$

How to Read an Annual Report

If profitable stock investments are your objective, take time to read the annual reports of the firms in which you are interested before you invest your money. Here's how to go about obtaining and reading annual reports so that you know how to recognize a good investment prospect.

Locating Annual Reports

If your school library does not have the report you want on hand, the library may subscribe to an annual report microfiche service. Also, most libraries and local stockbrokers have the names and addresses of the officers of large corporations. Write to the treasurer of the company in which you are considering a stock purchase and request a copy of the firm's annual report.

Beginning Your Analysis of the Company

Turn to the back page of the report. Examine the statement of the certified public accountant. If the firm's financial statements are believed to reflect its true financial position, the accountant will say that the financial statements presented in the report conform to generally accepted accounting principals.

Look carefully for the words "subject to." They mean that the statements are accurate only if you are willing to accept certain management assumptions. Since the term "subject to" does not often find its way into the final report issued to stockholders, you should be very suspicious if you see these words in the report.

Also, you should examine the footnotes to the financial statements. The real story behind a firm's financial strength or weakness often is told in the footnotes. For example, the reason profits are down may be a change from LIFO to FIFO. If so, the firm may not have much of a problem. On the other hand, profits may be up simply because the firm has sold off some of its assets. The footnotes will supply this information.

Reading the Chairperson's Comments

Turning to the front of the report, you should find the letter from the chairperson of the board. The letter is as much a reflection of the chairperson's personality as it is a statement of the financial well-being of the firm. It usually includes an appraisal of the firm's profitability as well as an explanation of why it made or lost money. If the letter is full of sentences that begin, "Except for . . ." and "Despite the . . .," beware!

On the positive side, the letter may also discuss new opportunities and how they affect the firm's various business ventures. Ask yourself whether management really understands the challenges ahead.

Working Through the Financial Statements

In the financial statements, you can see for yourself how the company performed. Make a comparative analysis of the balance sheet. Is working capital (current assets less current liabilities) growing or shrinking? If it falls too low, the firm may not be able to pay dividends. How about long-term debt? A growing company may need to take on more debt. A firm without growth prospects, however, could choke on the interest charges of additional debt.

Nevada Cement turns over its merchandise inventory approximately three times a year.

Once again, it is hard to define a good inventory turnover ratio. But we do know that the higher the inventory turnover ratio, the less inventory the firm usually has on hand. Although this may indicate efficiency, a high turnover ratio may also mean that the firm is not always able to meet the product needs of its cus-

Also look at the income statement. Most people care only about net earnings per share. But this figure may fool you. You need to know where the profits came from so that you can tell whether they will keep coming in the future. Is net income from operations up or down? If the firm is able to maintain profits only from unusual activities that are not related to its principal operations, it may face big problems in the future. Have sales increased from year to year? Are sales increasing faster than inflation? If not, sales are declining in real dollars.

Now you need to conduct a ratio analysis. Calculate the current ratio, acid-test ratio, inventory turnover ratio, debt to net worth ratio, return on sales, and return on equity. If possible, compare these ratios with those of other leading companies in the industry.

Deciding Whether to Buy the Stock

At this point, you are ready to decide whether or not you should buy the company's stock. What is the stock's current selling price? Is the price in line with your analysis of the company? For example, if the price is down and your analysis indicated that the company's prospects are favorable, then the stock may be a good buy. On the other hand, if the price is high and your analysis uncovered some financial weaknesses, then there is a good chance that the price will fall soon.

Stock prices are very much influenced by what the "market" thinks will happen. Of course, you cannot know the future by reading a firm's annual report. Since the report focuses on past years' activities, you will have to watch the firm's industry to determine its growth prospects and to read the *The Wall Street Journal, Forbes, Business Week, Fortune,* and other business publications.

Source: Adapted from J. B. Quinn, "How To Read an Annual Report," International Paper Company.

tomers because of out-of-stock situations. Nevada Cement's inventory-turnover ratio should be compared to the same ratio for other firms in the cement industry to see if it is in line.

Debt to Net Worth. This ratio is calculated by dividing total liabilities by net worth. **Net worth,** or owners' equity, is simply total assets minus total liabilities.

net worth *owners' equity calculated as total assets minus total liabilities.*

The **debt to net worth ratio** measures the amount of money owed to creditors relative to the equity value of the company. A high debt to net worth ratio indicates that the company has a substantial amount of debt, which means that its interest payments will be large.

The debt to net worth ratio for Nevada Cement is calculated in the following manner:

$$\text{Debt to Net Worth} = \frac{\text{Total Liabilities}}{\text{Owners' Equity}}$$

$$= \frac{\$1,452,500}{\$1,060,500}$$

$$= 1.37$$

Nevada Cement has borrowed a lot of money, but total debt is still only slightly more than owner's equity. That is, the company has $1.37 in debt for every dollar of owners' equity. Thus, it is probably still a good credit risk.

Profitability Analysis. A profitability measure frequently used by investment analysts is **earnings per share** of common stock. In general, the more money a firm makes per share of common stock, the more money people will pay for each share of stock. Earnings per share is calculated by dividing net income by the number of shares of common stock outstanding. For Nevada Cement, it is calculated in this way:

$$\text{Earnings Per Share} = \frac{\text{Net Income}}{\text{Shares of Common Stock Outstanding}}$$

$$= \frac{\$321,158}{17,600}$$

$$= \$18.25$$

Another measure of profitability is **return on sales**—that is, the amount of profit generated by each dollar of sales. It is calculated by dividing net income by net sales. From Nevada Cement's income statement, the ratio would be as follows:

$$\text{Return on Sales} = \frac{\text{Net Income}}{\text{Net Sales}}$$

$$= \frac{\$\ 321,158}{\$2,495,700}$$

$$= .129 \text{ (or } 12.9\%)$$

Return on sales tends to vary by industry. For example, a jewelry store sells relatively few items, so its return on sales needs to be high. A supermarket sells many products in a highly competitive market. Its return on sales is low—often less than 5 percent.

A third measure of profitability is rate of **return on owners' equity.** This ratio tells how effective the firm has been in earning money on the invested capital of owners. It is calculated by dividing net income by total owners' equity.

return on owners' equity
a measure of profitability that tells how effective the firm has been in earning money on owners' invested capital, calculated as net income divided by owners' equity.

$$\text{Return on Owners' Equity} = \frac{\text{Net Income}}{\text{Owners' Equity}}$$

$$= \frac{\$\ \ 321,158}{\$1,060,500}$$

$$= .303 \text{ (or 30.3\%)}$$

In other words, Nevada Cement earned about 30 cents on each dollar of owners' equity.

The rate of return on owners' equity is evaluated in relation to comparable investments. For example, assume that money market funds are paying 5 to 6 percent, and high-quality corporate bonds are paying 10 to 12 percent. Before investing in Nevada Cement, you would ask yourself how favorably its return compares to these other investment choices, assuming equal risk all around. It appears from this analysis that Nevada Cement may be a good investment.

The statement of cash flows lists all movements of resources in and out of the firm. For example, AT & T's statement of cash flows would reflect the resources the company gained when it acquired NCR Corp. Above: officials of the two companies shake hands on the deal.

STATEMENT OF CASH FLOWS

statement of cash flows
a financial statement that reflects the movement of cash resources in and out of the firm.

accrual method of accounting   *the method normally used for financial statements, in which revenues and expenses are recognized when they occur rather than when cash changes hands.*

The analysis of financial statements so far has focused on the balance sheet and income statement, but there is a third important financial statement that we now consider. This is the **statement of cash flows,** which reflects the movement of cash resources in and out of the firm. The financial statements previously presented normally use the **accrual method of accounting,** in which revenues and expenses are recognized as they occur rather than when cash changes hands. For example, a $50,000 credit sale made in December 1991 may be shown as revenue for that year, in spite of the fact that the cash payment will not be received until April of 1992. When payment is received under accrual accounting, no revenue is recognized, because it has already been accounted for. The primary advantage of accrual accounting is that it allows the firm to report revenues in the same period as it reports the expenses incurred in earning those revenues. The result is a fairly accurate picture of profit. A disadvantage is that it does not allow the firm to know its actual cash position—that is, the amount of cash it actually has on hand.

The statement of cash flows concentrates specifically on the cash position of the firm. Unlike the income statement (which concentrates on profit) and the balance sheet (which emphasizes the amount of assets owned and how they are financed), the statement of cash flows indicates the ability of the firm to pay its bills from cash resources.

To understand the workings of the statement of cash flows, examine Figure 18-6 for Johnson and Johnson, the medical supply firm. The firm recorded $1,082 million in earnings in 1989. However, it spent $750 million on plant, property,

Annual reports can advertise a company's image, as in this photo of a mother and child with Johnson and Johnson products.

FIGURE 18-6   Johnson & Johnson Statement of Cash Flows

JOHNSON & JOHNSON AND SUBSIDIARIES

Consolidated Statement of Cash Flows
(Dollars in Millions)

	1989	1988	1987
CASH FLOWS FROM OPERATING ACTIVITIES			
Net earnings	($1,082)	974	833
Adjustments to reconcile net earnings to cash flows from operating activities:			
Depreciation and amortization of property and intangibles	414	391	356
Tax deferrals	(8)	(6)	(58)
Changes in assets and liabilities, net of effects from acquisition of businesses:			
Increase in accounts receivable, trade, less allowances	(179)	(214)	(5)
Increase in inventories	(82)	(149)	(76)
(Decrease) increase in accounts payable and accrued liabilities	(42)	47	(39)
(Increase) decrease in other current and non-current assets	(103)	(110)	10
Increase (decrease) in other current and non-current liabilities	168	(45)	73
NET CASH FLOWS FROM OPERATING ACTIVITIES	1,250	888	1,094
CASH FLOWS FROM INVESTING ACTIVITIES			
Additions to property, plant and equipment	(750)	(664)	(515)
Proceeds from the disposal of assets	71	95	137
Acquisition of businesses, net of cash acquired	(131)	(39)	(286)
Other, principally marketable securities	(87)	(89)	130
NET CASH USED BY INVESTING ACTIVITIES	897	(697)	(534)
CASH FLOWS FROM FINANCING ACTIVITIES			
Dividends to stockholders	(373)	(327)	(278)
Repurchase of common stock	(153)	(611)	(225)
Increase (decrease) in short-term debt, net	52	195	(698)
Proceeds from long-term debt	451	540	523
Retirement of long-term debt	(453)	(114)	(45)
Proceeds from the exercise of stock options	47	55	51
NET CASH USED BY FINANCING ACTIVITIES	(429)	(262)	(672)
Effect of exchange rate changes on cash and cash equivalents	(1)	(22)	54
Decrease in cash and cash equivalents	(77)	(93)	(58)
Cash and cash equivalents, beginning of year	529	622	680
CASH AND CASH EQUIVALENTS, END OF YEAR	$ 452	529	622

Source: Reprinted with permission of Johnson & Johnson.

and equipment; paid $373 million in dividends to stockholders; and retired $453 million of long-term debt. Together with other positive and negative factors, this caused a decrease of $77 million in Johnson and Johnson's cash position.

Johnson & Johnson is a strong company and could handle the decrease in cash balances, but this is not always the case. A classic example of the importance of cash flow analysis was the bankruptcy of W. T. Grant in the mid-1970s. The

Should Accounting Data Be Reported on the Basis of Current Value Rather Than Historical Cost?

Yes

Currently, most financial statements are calculated on the basis of historical cost. This means that an asset is carried on the books of the firm at the value at which it was purchased, less depreciation, rather than at its current market value. This is amazing to people who are looking at financial statements for the first time. It means that what you see on the company's books may have little to do with what an asset is worth.

Suppose a firm constructed a new plant five years ago for $20 million. Over the five-year period, $5 million in depreciation may have been written off, so now the plant is carried on the books at $15 million. Let's further assume that oil has been discovered on property near the plant. Perhaps the firm has received two offers of $100 million for the site in anticipation of the discovery of oil on the property. The firm probably would laugh at an offer of $50 or $75 million, but this very same piece of property will continue to be carried on the books for $15 million.

Of course, it could go the opposite way. Perhaps a nuclear waste dump is constructed nearby, in spite of protests by the firm. Now the plant is virtually worthless. What will be the recorded value on the company's books? You guessed it: $15 million.

These are pretty dramatic examples, but lesser events can also have an impact. Perhaps a new highway is constructed. Or the town in which the plant is located experiences an economic upsurge due to a new government contract for a nearby aerospace firm. Conversely, the town may face an economic downturn because of the closing of a military base.

Even more routinely, inflation is likely to have an impact. With 5 percent annual inflation, the plant that was built five years ago for $20 million would now cost $25.5 million to replace.

firm showed a profit every year between 1970 and 1973, but shortly thereafter had to take bankruptcy and liquidate its assets. Several years of heavy investments in inventory and other assets had used up all the firm's cash.

Now that you have read and learned about the three major financial statements, you may wish to read the Controversial Issue on this page. It deals with the critical valuation problems that accountants face. The message is that you can never rely on a number just because it is published.

AGGRESSIVE VS. CONSERVATIVE REPORTING

No discussion of accounting would be complete without pointing out the dangers of blindly accepting the numbers in a firm's financial statements. Although accountants are guided by generally accepted accounting principles, as pronounced by the American Institute of Certified Public Accountants, Financial Accounting Standards Board, and rulings of the Securities and Exchange Commission, there is still flexibility in financial reporting. Aggressive accountants attempt to put the financial statements of the company in the best possible light by claiming every revenue item possible and deferring the recognition of expenses whenever possible. Conservative accounting takes just the opposite approach. Although the use of aggressive reporting is limited to some extent by regulatory

In order to reflect these and other changes that can take place, representation of value on financial statements should be based on current worth, not historical costs.

No

Arguments for current-cost accounting make great sense from a theoretical viewpoint, but they simply would not work in reality. Who is going to determine the current value of the property? The firm, its accountants, or perhaps professional appraisers. Everyone knows, that there are high appraisers and low appraisers, so you merely turn to the yellow pages and pick the one that suits your mood. The courts are full of lawsuits over this, related to estate settlements or divorces. One party brings in an expert to claim that a piece of property is worth a certain amount, and the other side brings in an equally qualified expert, who reaches and entirely different conclusion.

With current-value accounting, you would never know who to believe. In reading Exxon's annual report, for example, you would see the supposed "current value" of its assets and then be left to wonder how honest the firm, its accountants, or appraisers were in sharing data with you.

If the firm were about to sell new stock, it would undoubtedly want to show a high value. On the other hand, if the property values given were used to assess property taxes, low values would be more likely to appear.

Although historical-cost reporting does have drawbacks, at least it is objective. There is a piece of paper on file to indicate the price at which the initial transaction took place. Nobody is in a position to manipulate the values. In this day and age, when accountants are already under criticism for using too much flexibility in reporting results, why open up an area of great potential controversy?

Perhaps the proof is in the pudding. In October of 1979, the Financial Accounting Standards Board (the rule-making body in accounting) issued a ruling that required 1,300 large companies to disclose inflation-adjusted accounting data in their annual reports. The information was supplemental to the historical-cost data that are normally presented. There was so little interest in the inflation-adjusted data that its inclusion was later made optional by the Financial Accounting Standards Board. Would you have wanted to see the data?

What do you think?

bodies, readers of financial statements must be sensitive to the methods employed.

As an example, accountants may be slow to deduct valueless inventory from profits. An even more aggressive practice is to claim sales before they are absolutely certain. The point is that a million dollars worth of earnings may not have the same meaning for two companies if one has an aggressive accounting firm doing its books and the other has a more conservative one. It's like getting a B from the toughest professor at your college; it may actually be worth more than an A in a snap course.

Accounting firms generally recognize their responsibility to provide accurate numbers, but sometimes they fall short of the mark. (Consider the Ethical Issue on page 510, "The Accountant's Dilemma.") For example, during the mid-1980s, Arthur Andersen & Co., a highly prestigious accounting firm, was required to pay $67 million in damages to the creditors of Drysdale Securities Corporation for failing to uncover the firm's problems, which eventually led to bankruptcy.

One of the most publicized cases of overly aggressive reporting in the last decade involved Blockbuster Entertainment Corporation, the popular distributor of videocassettes. Lee Seidler, a respected analyst for Bear Sterns and Company (a stock brokerage house), demonstrated that Blockbuster's reported earnings per share of $.57 in the banner year of 1988 would have been only $.07 if appropriate accounting practices had been used. That's like being told that your A+ is only worth a C− on a tougher grading scale.

The Accountant's Dilemma

How ethical are accountants? There is an old story about two job applicants who interviewed with the president of a company for the position of chief accountant. The first candidate appeared eminently qualified. She held an MBA from a top Ivy League school, had passed all four parts of the CPA exam in one sitting, had worked five years for Price Waterhouse, and had installed comprehensive management information systems for large Fortune 500 companies.

The second candidate was considerably less qualified. He had taken a bookkeeping course (for non credit) and had worked the night shift for a defense contractor. There, only about 25 percent of his work had to do with accounting. The company president conducting the interviews became so unhappy with the second candidate that he said to him, "You are so unqualified that I bet you don't even know what two plus two equals." The candidate quickly smiled and said, "anything you want it to." Guess who got the job?

Accountants are in the unusual position of reporting on and measuring the performance of the people who pay their fee. For large public accounting firms, the situation is even more complicated. Firms that the accountants are auditing also represent large sources of revenue for their consulting and tax services. If they are too rigid in insisting that the firm follow a tough accounting rule in reporting earnings, they may lose a very lucrative account.

Although the accounting profession has generally been allowed to oversee its own actions, some members of Congress have clamored for tighter government regulation. That would be ironic, for no one engages in more questionable accounting practices than the U.S. government itself. In order to cover up the ever-growing federal deficit, the government uses every controversial practice known to the accounting profession. For example, quasi-government agencies are used to hide expenditures, and Congress borrows from the Social Security Trust fund to cover shortages in revenue.

KEY TERMS

managerial accounting 481

financial accounting 481

certified public accountants (CPAs) 482

auditor 482

generally accepted accounting principles (GAAP) 484

equity 485

liabilities 485

owners' equity 485

accounting equation 485

double-entry bookkeeping 486

balance sheet 487

current assets 488

cash 488

marketable securities 488

accounts receivable 488

allowance for bad debt 488

note receivable 488

merchandise inventory 488

finished goods 488

work in process 489

raw materials 489

prepaid expenses 489

SUMMARY POINTS

1 The public accountant, rather than working for a single employer, makes his or her services available to the public. Most public accountants are self-employed or are members of locally owned or "Big Six" accounting firms. The private accountant, on the other hand, actually works for a specific company and helps prepare its accounting data. Whether prepared by a public or a private accountant, accounting information is used by bankers, investors, government regulators, labor unions, and others to judge the profitability of a firm.

2 Understanding accounting concepts is important not only to accountants, but also to the managers of a firm. Accounting data may be used to determine whether or not a new project is undertaken. People who cannot read and interpret financial statements may be at a severe disadvantage when competing with those who can. Providers and users of accounting data should also understand and appreciate the use of the computer in the process. Computers can handle many of the repetitive tasks in accounting, provide instant access to data, audit data for accuracy, and make it possible for accounting firms to share data with clients through linking.

3 The accounting equation is Assets = Liabilities + Owners' Equity. It may also be written as Assets − Liabilities = Owners' Equity. Double-entry bookkeeping is based on the accounting equation. Each transaction requires two entries to keep the accounting equation in balance.

4 A balance sheet shows the firms assets, liabilities, and owners' equity at one point in time. On a balance sheet, assets may be classified as current, fixed, or intangible. Current assets are expected to be sold or used within one year. Fixed assets, such as plant and equipment, are not normally sold during the ordinary operations of a business. Intangible assets are assets that are not physical objects, such as licenses, trademarks, and goodwill. On the other half of the balance sheet are liabilities and owners' equity. Liabilities represent short-term and long-term debt obligations of the firm, whereas owners' equity is the value of the owners' investment in the company.

5 The first item on the income statement is revenue (gross sales). After deducting returns and allowances, net sales are determined. From this value, the accountant subtracts cost of goods sold to arrive at gross profit. The next step is to deduct selling and administrative expenses to determine income from operations. Then other income is added and other expenses subtracted to arrive at income before taxes. When taxes are subtracted, income after taxes is determined.

6 The two main methods of valuing inventory are FIFO (first-in, first-out) and LIFO (last-in, first out). If prices are rising, FIFO requires that lower-cost items be written off first, which results in a higher value for ending inventory. With LIFO, higher-cost items would be written off first, which means a lower value for ending inventory.

7 Comparative analysis allows you to compare a company's performance over time. The goal is to uncover performance trends by analyzing changes that have occurred from year to year, as shown in the statements. A great deal can also be learned about a company by computing financial ratios from balance sheet and income statement data. These ratios can be compared to those of other firms in the company's industry to see how well the firm is performing.

8 The statement of cash flows concentrates on the cash position of the firm. Unlike the income statement (which concentrates on profit) and the balance sheet (which emphasizes the amount of assets owned and how they are financed), the statement of cash flows indicates the ability of the firm to pay its bills from cash resources.

9 Aggressive accountants attempt to put the financial statements of the company in the best possible light by claiming every conceivable revenue item and deferring the recognition of expenses whenever possible. Conservative accounting takes just the opposite approach. The use of aggressive reporting is limited to some extent by regulatory agencies, but readers of financial statements must be sensitive to the methods employed.

REVIEW QUESTIONS

1 Compare and contrast the duties of the bookkeeper with those of the accountant.

2 How does an external auditor differ from an internal auditor?

3 Who are the primary users of accounting information?

4 Assume that a business has $70,000 worth of assets and $20,000 worth of liabilities and that it buys a new microcomputer for $10,000 cash. Show what happens to the accounting equation as a result of the purchase.

5 Explain why an understanding of accounting may be important to a marketing manager.

6 When do assets not equal owners' equity in the accounting equation?

7 Describe the different types of current assets.

8 How does the accountant calculate gross profit?

9 A retailer has beginning inventory of $90,000, purchases $185,000 worth of merchandise during the year, and ends up with $105,000 in inventory. What was its cost of goods sold?

10 Define the current ratio and the acid-test ratio. Which is the best ratio for evaluating a firm's financial position?

11 What is the main emphasis of the statement of cash flows?

12 What is the difference between aggressive accounting and conservative accounting?

DISCUSSION QUESTIONS

1 Describe how the accounting equation works.

2 How is the balance sheet used by a firm and its creditors?

3 Why do some firms list prepaid expenses on their balance sheets as current assets?

4 Explain the differences between LIFO and FIFO. Which method of evaluating inventory do you feel most businesses should use?

5 Why is the statement of cash flows important? In your answer, consider the fact that many firms use the accrual method of accounting.

EXPERIENTIAL EXERCISES

1 Go to the library and ask to see *Standard and Poor's Corporate Reports* for New York Stock Exchange firms. Turn to the information sheet for IBM. Using the financial information presented on the back of the first sheet for the firm, comment on the pattern of IBM's performance, based on the following ratios. Use the last five years of data. Has the firm been generally improving or not?

a. % net income of revenue (which is the same as return on sales)
b. Current ratio

c. Return on assets (net income divided by total assets)
d. Return on owners' equity

2 Meet with a certified public accountant. What types of services does his or her firm provide for its clients? Specifically, how much of the firm's time is spent doing bookkeeping, tax preparation, auditing, financial consulting, etc.? Also inquire about the job opportunities in accounting and the skills necessary to be a successful accountant.

CASES

CASE 18-1
Apple Computer, Inc.

Apple Computer's financial information for 1988 and 1989 is shown in the accompanying financial statements. Also included below is comparative industry information for 1989.

1. Compute the current ratio, the quick ratio, and the ratios for debt to net worth, return on sales, and return on owners' equity for 1989 and 1988. Total liabilities are $1,258,153 (thousands) in 1989 and $1,078,661 (thousands) in 1988. Total liabilities represent the sum of current liabilities and deferred income taxes (taxes owed but not yet paid). The firm has no long-term liabilities.
2. Comment on the pattern of change in the ratios for the two years. Disregard the comparative industry data for now.
3. Compare the 1989 ratios for Apple to the 1989 industry data. What important observations can you make?

Comparative Computer Industry Data

Current Ratio	2.25
Quick Ratio	1.34
Debt to Net Worth	.802
Return on Sales	8.61
Return on Owners' Equity	18.23%

APPLE COMPUTER

Consolidated Balance Sheets
(Dollars in thousands)
September 29, 1989, and September 30, 1988

	1989	1988
ASSETS		
Current assets:		
Cash and cash equivalents	$ 438,300	$ 372,360
Short-term investments (marketable securities)	370,650	173,357
Accounts receivable, net of allowance for		
doubtful accounts of $35,512 ($24,149 in 1988)	792,824	638,816
Inventories	475,377	461,470
Prepaid income taxes	117,179	88,711
Other current assets	100,098	48,280
Total current assets	2,294,428	1,782,994
Property, plant, and equipment:		
Land and buildings	88,897	62,104
Machinery and equipment	303,658	186,238
Office furniture and equipment	111,950	76,693
Leasehold improvements	138,868	95,307
	643,373	420,342
Accumulated depreciation and amortization	(309,146)	(212,985)
Net property, plant, and equipment	334,227	207,357
Other assets	115,244	91,735
	$2,743,899	$2,082,086
LIABILITIES AND SHAREHOLDERS' EQUITY		
Current liabilities:		
Notes payable	$ 56,751	$ 127,871
Accounts payable	334,157	314,668
Accrued compensation and employee benefits	106,666	82,632
Income taxes payable	85,790	62,465
Accrued marketing and distribution	167,022	113,175
Other current liabilities	144,857	126,282
Total current liabilities	895,243	827,093
Deferred income taxes	362,910	251,568
Shareholders' equity (same as owners' equity)		
Common stock, no par value; 320,000,000 shares authorized;		
126,270,216 shares issued and outstanding		
in 1989 (122,768,343 shares in 1988)	315,279	226,239
Retained earnings	1,175,899	776,453
Accumulated translation adjustment	(1,868)	4,266
	1,489,310	1,006,958
Notes receivable from shareholders	(3,564)	(3,533)
Total shareholders' equity	1,485,746	1,003,425
	$2,743,899	$2,082,086

Source: Courtesy of Apple Computer, Inc. Annual Report, pp. 24, 25.

APPLE COMPUTER			
Consolidated Statements of Income (In thousands, except per share amounts) Three fiscal years ended September 29, 1989			
	1989	1988	1987
Net sales	$5,284,013	$4,071,373	$2,661,068
Costs and expenses:			
Cost of sales	2,694,823	1,990,879	1,296,220
Research and development	420,083	272,512	191,554
Marketing and distribution	1,207,464	952,577	655,219
General and administrative	327,330	235,067	146,637
	4,649,700	3,451,035	2,289,630
Operating income	634,313	620,338	371,438
Interest and other income, net	110,009	35,823	38,930
Income before income taxes	744,322	656,161	410,368
Provision for income taxes	290,289	255,903	192,872
Net income	$ 454,033	$ 400,258	$ 217,496
Earnings per common and common equivalent share	$ 3.53	$ 3.08	$ 1.65
Common and common equivalent shares used in the calculations of earnings per share	128,669	129,900	131,615

Source: Courtesy of Apple Computer, Inc. Annual Report, pp. 24, 25.

CASE 18-2
Texaco

On January 1, 1979, Texaco Oil Company shifted its accounting system to LIFO. Its financial reports for 1979 were the first to show the effects of the change. Texaco, like most large oil companies, was reporting incredibly high profits and naturally did not want to pay hundreds of millions of dollars in taxes to the government if these dollars could be saved. In its financial report for 1979, Texaco cited a net income of $1,759,069,000. Had Texaco not switched to LIFO, its income would have been $732,200,000 higher. LIFO saved Texaco almost $300 million in 1979—over a dollar of taxes per share of common stock.

One problem with LIFO is that it works well only in an inflationary and growing economy. LIFO produces a "cushion" of long-standing inventory that remains on the books at a very old and very low price. Unless the company has to sell off its inventory, that cushion stays in place forever. However, if a company has to lower its inventory, it will have to sell part of this cushion and report its cost of goods sold at a very old and low value. This drives taxable income up dramatically.

In 1980, Texaco was hurting from a glut of oil inventories in the United State. It had to lower its inventories, producing an increase in taxable income of $98,900,000. This increase in income was *not* due to increased sales but only to the failure of LIFO to cope with recessionary conditions. Thus, in 1980, Texaco had to pay almost $46 million extra in taxes because it had chosen to value its inventory by LIFO. In 1981, Texaco again had to cut its inventories—this time by 16 percent. Although the increased income reported meant that Texaco showed a profit for 1981, the company actually lost money in 1981 (if one ignored the effect of LIFO). In fact, Texaco lost very badly, since it had to pay a huge tax penalty for its use of LIFO.

The federal government doesn't allow companies to switch back and forth between LIFO and FIFO as conditions change. Texaco has stayed with LIFO accounting throughout the 1980s and into the 1990s. During this period, it has both helped and hurt the firm at different times.

1. Is LIFO a better valuation method than FIFO in the oil business?
2. Describe the impact of LIFO accounting on ending inventory when prices are rising rapidly. Would the value of ending inventory tend to be higher or lower than under FIFO accounting?
3. Given your answer to Question 2, indicate which of the following ratios would look better, worse, or unchanged under LIFO as compared to FIFO.

   a. Current ratio
   b. Quick ratio
   c. Inventory turnover ratio

CHAPTER 19

Money and Banking

Ken Herrick was very proud to become president of a medium-size Kansas City bank in the fall of 1992. His career had come a long way since he graduated with a degree in finance from the University of Missouri in 1974. After spending his first year in the training program for credit analysts, he became a junior loan officer at a Kansas City bank in December of 1975. For the next 17 years, Ken progressed up the ladder, becoming senior vice president and the bank's most experienced lending officer. He was particularly adept at working with businesses that had $10 to $25 million in sales. Having lived in Missouri all his life, he was familiar with the factors that influenced the local economy. He had also strengthened his skills by attending the post graduate summer banking program at Rutgers University and proudly displayed his certificate in his office.

When Robert Harrison stepped down as the bank's CEO in the fall of 1992, Ken hoped he would be picked to fill that position, and he was. Robert had served ably as chief officer of the bank for more than two decades. Though the world of banking had changed rapidly over that time, Robert had remained a traditionalist. He maintained that the primary purpose of the bank was to pay a reasonable return on deposits and to make solid loans that would help the community.

As Ken took the presidency, he knew that changes would have to be made rapidly. The bank had fallen behind the times. Other banks were providing more services, including trust management, cash management, bank-sponsored credit cards, and insurance. Ken called his management team together. Most of the officers agreed with his proposed changes, but others suggested that he remember what happened to the savings and loan industry when S&Ls became too aggressive, trying to generate big numbers quickly. Ken, however, decided that the bank must move forward in modernizing its activities. Many topics relating to the decisions that Ken must make will be discussed in this chapter.

AN OVERVIEW OF BANKING

After 10,000 commercial banks failed during the Great Depression of the 1930s, the industry became highly regulated. In the simple world of those times, 3–6–3 was the formula. Bankers paid 3 percent interest on deposits, which they could then lend out at 6 percent and be on the golf course by 3 o'clock. How times have changed! Now banking is one of the most competitive industries in the world. The hometown bank has to compete not only with other local banks, but with large regional and New York City banks as well. What's more, 27 percent of commercial loans in the United States are made by foreign bankers. There is a Japanese banking presence in virtually every major metropolitan area. Furthermore, banks no longer merely compete with other banks. Their competition now includes savings and loans, credit unions, stock brokerage houses, insurance companies, credit card issuers, and other organizations.

The primary function of today's banker is still to take deposits from one group at a relatively low rate and convert them into loans to a second group at a relatively high rate, in order to make a profit. However, the banker no longer makes a 3 o'clock tee-off time. The staid, conservative banker in his mid-sixties, wearing a three-piece suit and carrying a pocket watch, is just a memory. Today's banker is young, well educated, highly compensated, and above all competitive.

We will begin our discussion of the banking system by examining how money is supplied to the system. We will then discuss the vast array of services that bankers offer. The deregulation of the banking industry since 1980 will also be considered. Because the U.S. financial system extends far beyond commercial

Local banks must now compete with large banks from across the nation and around the world.

banks, we will also look at other financial institutions, such as savings and loans and credit unions. Finally, we will examine how the Federal Reserve System attempts to maintain a healthy economy.

The Banking System of Today

More than 14,000 commercial banks are in operation today. Approximately two thirds are granted charters to operate at the state level and one third at the national level. Though national banks are fewer in number, they dominate the banking scene. The 25 largest banks in the U.S. are all national banks.

The banking system controls more than $3 trillion in assets. One reason depositors are willing to leave funds with banks is because they are insured through the **Federal Deposit Insurance Corporation (FDIC).** The FDIC was established in 1934 to protect depositors from bank failures; generally, it has served its purpose. Deposits in state banks as well as in national banks can be covered for up to $100,000 by the FDIC. In practice, the FDIC has not stopped at the $100,000 limit but has covered all deposits regardless of size. Whether this generous "over coverage" policy will continue in the future remains to be seen.

Before we go much further into a discussion of banking, you should have an understanding of the raw product with which the banker works: money.

Federal Deposit Insurance Corporation (FDIC)   Federal agency that protects depositors against losses up to $100,000 in federally insured accounts at financial institutions.

Money

We are accustomed to using money every day, but what does it really represent? **Money** is anything generally accepted as payment for goods and services. Money is the lifeblood of an economy. Even a basic understanding of money will take us a long way toward comprehending how our financial system works. Most of us spend a good deal of our lives chasing after money. We talk about it nearly every day, and we work hard for it. But have you ever considered what actually makes money valuable? Let's explore this question by considering the functions of money.

money   anything that is generally accepted as payment for goods and services.

Functions of Money. Money's primary function is to serve as a **medium of exchange,** which makes exchanging goods and services easier by eliminating the need for a barter system. Rather than trading goods directly for other goods, goods and services can be exchanged for money and the money exchanged for other goods.

medium of exchange   a function of money; makes exchanging goods and services easier by eliminating the need for a barter system.

Money also serves as a **standard of value,** in that it provides a means of comparing the values of different things. We routinely compare the value of objects by how much each is worth in dollars: A $10,000 car is more valuable than a $5,000 motorcycle. Money also acts as a **store of wealth.** After goods or services are exchanged for money, the value represented by the money can be saved for any length of time before it is exchanged for other goods or services. Money is thus a measure of savings. Through investment, this accumulated wealth can be stored in the form of land, steel ingots, gold bullion, famous works of art, or corporate stocks and bonds. When kept as cash, wealth is said to be "liquid," because it can readily be used in exchange for needed goods and services.

standard of value   a function of money; a standard by which the values of objects can be compared.

store of wealth   a function of money; a way of saving purchasing power until it is needed to buy something.

What gives money its magic is that it is generally accepted throughout the economy as a medium of exchange, a standard of value, and a store of wealth. The paper on which a dollar bill is printed is not worth much more than a few square inches of newsprint. A dollar is valuable because it is believed to be valuable. If people lost confidence in our currency, it would no longer perform its three functions and would become worthless.

The Money Supply. In the United States, money consists of the amount of currency in circulation (paper money and coins) and checking account balances at commercial banks and other financial institutions. Only about 26 percent of the nation's money supply is in the form of circulating currency. The rest is in the form of checking account balances. Growth in the money supply for the period from 1979 through 1990 is shown in Figure 19.1. The amount of money now in circulation is about $800 billion.

How Banks Create Money. One of the most interesting things about commercial banks is that they "create" money. How do they do this? To answer this question, we must first explain demand deposits. A **demand deposit** is a checking account at a commercial bank or other financial institution. Demand deposits are part of the money supply because they can be withdrawn "on demand" and converted immediately into currency at the option of the holder of the account. As we can see from Figure 19-1, demand deposit balances are the leading component of the nation's money supply. A **check** is a piece of paper legally authorizing the bank to withdraw the specified amount of money from the account and to pay it to the person or organization to whom the check is written.

Banks create money when they make loans. In making a loan, a bank does not take cash out of its vault and hand it over to the borrower. Rather, it credits the borrower's checking account for the amount of the loan. The borrower, then,

demand deposit a checking account at a commercial bank or other financial institution.

check written authorization for the bank to withdraw the specified amount of money from the account and give it to the person or company to whom the check is written.

FIGURE 19-1   Money Supply Movements (Seasonally Adjusted, Monthly), 1979–1990

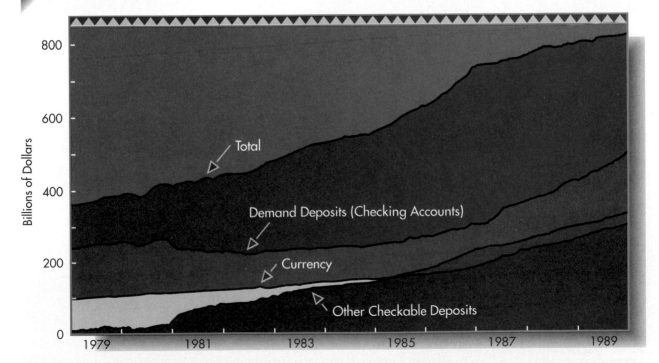

Source: *Federal Reserve Bulletin*, June 1990, p. A13.

may write checks on the account. Figure 19-2 illustrates this process of money creation.

In Step 1, Ms. Appel deposits $1,000 in the First State Bank, joining thousands of others in her city who hold checking and savings accounts there. The Federal Reserve, which regulates the banking system, requires that 12 percent of deposits in banks be kept on deposit.[1] Thus, when the First State Bank receives Ms. Appel's $1,000 in deposit, $880 can be lent out again. It can now lend $880 to Mr. Ramirez for a home repair loan. These funds are deposited in Mr. Ramirez's account at the Second State Bank. That bank may lend 88 percent of its newly received funds, or $774.40. As can be seen in Figure 19-2, this process can be carried out many times; the initial $1,000 deposit creates money far in excess of the original amount. The figure carries the process through only five steps, but it can be repeated until the amount under "Money to Lend" reaches zero.

THE SERVICES THAT BANKS OFFER

 The basic functions of a bank are accepting deposits and lending money. We shall now examine these in greater detail and then discuss the many other services that banks perform. Many of these services are performed by other financial institutions as well.

FIGURE 19-2   How Banks Create Money

		Deposit	Money Held in Reserve by Bank (12%)	Money to Lend	Total Money Supply
Step 1	Initial Deposit by Ms. Appel	$1,000.00	$120.00	$880.00	$1,880.00
Step 2	Loan and Deposit by Mr. Ramirez	$880.00	$105.60	$774.40	$2,654.40
Step 3	Loan and Deposit by Next Borrower	$774.40	$92.93	$681.47	$3,335.87
Step 4	Loan and Deposit by Next Borrower	$681.47	$81.78	$599.69	$3,935.56
Step 5	Loan and Deposit by Next Borrower	$599.69	$71.96	$527.73	$4,463.29

Types of Deposit Accounts

Checking Accounts. The basic, no-frills checking account is losing its popularity. A traditional checking account allowed you to write some number of checks per month for a small service fee. If an excessive number of checks were written, the fee increased. This setup was a great source of cheap funds for a bank, and it was mandated by law. Banks were not allowed to pay interest on checking accounts. You might get a free toaster or a couple of tickets to the ballgame, but no actual interest was paid on your checking account.

The consumer movement in the late 1970s and early 1980s forced changes in the nature of checking accounts. This trend was intensified by the Reagan administration's emphasis on deregulation. In 1980, legislation was passed allowing interest to be paid on checking accounts for the first time. Many new types of accounts flooded the marketplace.

NOW Accounts. The first product to be offered after the passage of the legislation was the **NOW account.** "NOW" stands for "negotiable order of withdrawal." A NOW account allows unlimited check writing privileges and pays interest but requires the account holder to maintain a minimum balance of a few hundred dollars. NOW accounts are still popular today. Banks compete fiercely for these funds, but they are not nearly as profitable for the banks as the old non-interest-paying checking accounts.

NOW account   a bank account that allows unlimited checkwriting and pays interest but requires a minimum balance of a few hundred dollars.

Super-NOW Accounts. Quickly following the NOW account was the **Super-NOW account,** which has two added features. Higher interest rates are paid, but a higher minimum balance is also required. Whereas a NOW account might pay 4½ to 5 percent interest, a Super-NOW account might pay 6 percent, but the required balance in the Super-NOW account might be $1,000 higher. These numbers are merely illustrative; they change, sometimes daily. They also vary at different financial institutions, so the potential depositor should check around carefully.

Super-NOW account   a bank account similar to a NOW account, but paying higher interest and requiring a higher minimum balance.

Money Market Accounts. Although the NOW and Super-NOW accounts were popular at the time they came into existence and are still widely used, they are no longer competitive with other financial products for depositors who have larger amounts ($5,000 and over). In 1982, the Depository Institutions Act enabled banks to offer **money market accounts.** As checking accounts, these are limited (three checks per month), but they have the advantage of paying fully competitive interest rates. They came

Banks make loans to consumers for special purposes, such as to pay for college.

money market accounts   limited checking accounts (three checks per month) that carry interest rates competitive with those offered by brokerage houses for their money market funds.

into existence to compete directly with money market funds offered by brokerage houses such as Merrill Lynch. A money market fund is a form of a limited checking account offered by a nonbanking institution. (Money market funds will be discussed in more detail in Chapter 21.) During normal times, money market accounts and money market funds might pay 7 percent interest. Of course, all rates move up or down in accordance with the going interest rate in the economy. One advantage that the bank-offered money market account has over a money market fund is that the funds are insured by the FDIC.

certificates of deposit (CDs) *interest-bearing certificates, offered by financial institutions, that have a fixed maturity date and a penalty for early withdrawal.*

Certificate of Deposit.   Banks and other financial institutions also offer **certificates of deposit (CDs).** The depositor provides the funds to the financial institution and receives an interest-bearing certificate in return. Unlike the accounts described previously, CDs have a fixed maturity date—six months, a year, five years, and so on. Although CDs pay rates of interest that are competitive with money market accounts and money market funds, they have one feature that makes them less desirable. There is a penalty for withdrawing the funds before the maturity date. For example, if you buy a one-year CD and decide that you need your funds after ten or eleven months, you may lose up to three months of interest. With a money market account or a money market fund, you would merely use one of your checks to withdraw the funds, without a penalty. An advantage of a CD is that the required minimum is smaller than on a money market account or a money market fund. Sometimes CDs pay higher rates, but not always. Generally, longer-term CDs pay higher rates of interest than short-term CDs.

savings account *a low-paying bank account that does not allow checkwriting.*

Savings Accounts.   The oldest interest-earning product, the **savings account,** is still in existence, but it is not generally competitive. It pays low rates of interest on savings and does not allow checkwriting privileges.

Types of Loans

Once banks take in a deposit, the majority of the funds are loaned out to bank customers. Banks make short-term loans, from 90 days to a year, to help finance the temporary needs of an individual or a firm. For the most part, banks are not in the business of providing permanent financing for a firm. The owners generally contribute the initial funding to get a business started; they look to the bank to cover seasonal and growth needs. For larger, more prosperous businesses, banks are willing to make loans for longer periods. These are called **term loans**—usually extended for one to seven years. Banks also make specialized loans directly related to consumer purchases: auto loans or home mortgage loans, home improvement loans, educational loans, and even loans for vacations.

term loans *longer bank loans, normally for one to seven years.*

Rates on loans may be fixed or variable. On **fixed-rate loans,** the interest rate is specified at the outset and never changes over the life of the loan. On a **variable-rate loan,** the interest rate changes according to market conditions over the life of the loan. Types of bank loans are discussed more fully in Chapter 20, Financial Management.

fixed-rate loans *loans on which the interest rate is specified at the outset and never changes.*

variable-rate loan *a loan in which the interest rate changes with market conditions.*

Other Banking Activities

The only banks that restrict themselves to taking deposits and making loans are found in isolated communities of 25,000 or less. A modern financial institution is likely to be involved in five or six additional activities, depending on its size. These are discussed in the subsections that follow and are shown graphically in Figure 19-3.

Trust Management. In **trust management,** a department of the bank manages money for pension funds, university endowments, and wealthy individuals. The bank trust department receives a fee of ¼ to 1 percent of the funds in a trust account. The trust department normally invests the funds in stocks, bonds, real estate, and other assets and makes regular disbursements to the trust account customer.

trust management a bank program that manages investments for pension funds, university endowments, and wealthy individuals.

Cash Management. Banks often advise firms on the management of their cash balances. In a **cash management program,** the bank establishes a system for tracking cash flow. If a firm has multiple bank accounts, excess balances from one account are shifted to cover deficits in another.

cash management program bank program for advising firms on managing their cash balances by establishing a system for tracking cash flow.

FIGURE 19-3   Some of the Services a Bank Might Provide

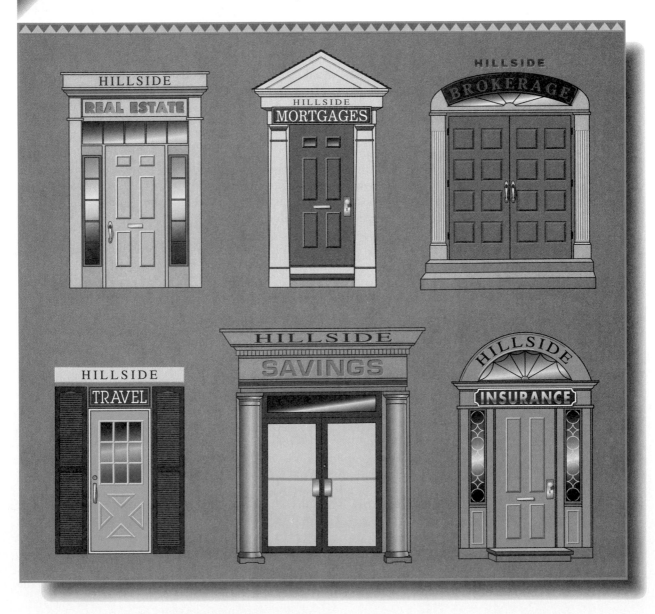

Discount Brokerage. Many banks have a discount brokerage subsidiary that can help customers buy and sell stocks at a discount of 30 to 50 percent from what a full service broker (such as Merrill Lynch or Dean Witter) would charge. The intent is to encourage the customer to use the bank for a complete range of financial services.

Insurance. Many banks also have subsidiaries that can underwrite insurance. Some loan arrangements require insurance to be carried on property that serves as collateral for a loan. In the past, banks always looked to outside insurers to provide this coverage, but many banks now do so themselves.

Credit Cards. The early issuers of credit cards were companies such as American Express, Diners Club, Mobil, Sears, and J. C. Penney. Now, however, banks are in the credit card business in a big way, issuing cards through MasterCard and Visa. For example, Citicorp, the largest U.S. banking institution, has 27 million MasterCard and Visa accounts, representing over $20 billion in annual business. Once you begin earning a steady income, a banking institution will very likely be willing to grant you a credit card. Why not? Businesses pay a processing fee of 1 to 5 percent on credit card sales. Credit card users pay anywhere from 14 to 20 percent interest on their unpaid balances and may also pay a membership fee of $25 to $75 annually. This "plastic money" may be expensive, but over 70 percent of the households with incomes of $15,000 to $25,000 use MasterCard or Visa. For higher-income consumers, the rate is higher.

Traveler's Cheques. Banks also have products for the use of travelers. Rather than carrying cash, the traveler can get guaranteed checks, accepted anywhere in the world. Banks' **traveler's cheques** may be offered through MasterCard, Visa, or American Express. If the cheques are lost or stolen, the issuing company will reimburse the customer the full value.

traveler's cheques a guaranteed check accepted anywhere in the world and, if lost or stolen, reimbursed at full value by the issuing company.

Electronic Funds Transfer. Another form of service to bank customers is **electronic funds transfer (EFT),** in which funds are moved instantaneously between accounts by electronic means. The computerized system works in many ways. One is **point of sale terminals.** A retailer puts your electronic card in a slot in the cash register, and a signal is sent to the bank, immediately transferring funds from you account to the store's account. There is no need for you to write a check. EFT can also be used by an employer to process the payroll, by instantaneously transferring funds from the firm's bank account to those of the employees.

electronic funds transfer (EFT) the movement of funds instantaneously between accounts by electronic means.

point-of-sale terminals computer terminals at retail stores, which immediately transfer funds from customers' bank accounts to the store's to pay for purchases.

Many firms have jumped at the opportunity of electronic funds transfer. General Electric now makes 50 percent of its payments through EFT. Of course, the banks also like EFT. The banking system is now called upon to process 50 billion checks annually, and EFT offers hope for a reduced burden. Later in this chapter, you will see how complicated it is for the Federal Reserve System to clear handwritten checks. Furthermore, the cost of moving funds through EFT is $.10 per transaction, versus $.79 for a check.

Nevertheless, there is still some resistance to EFT. First, many bank customers are hesitant to allow electronic impulses to move funds in and out of their accounts. There is also a potential loss of privacy, since outside sources have access to a person's account information. Furthermore, when you pay your bills, there is not the paper evidence that a check provides. Finally, with EFT a bank customer loses the advantage of **float.** Float represents the use of funds from the

float the use of funds from the time you write a check to the time it clears your account.

time you write a check to the time the bank records it as removed from your account. Almost everyone has written a check and put it in the mail knowing full well that the account will not be debited for a couple of days. With EFT, the movement of funds is instantaneous.

A related item is the **automated teller machine (ATM),** which allows customers to make cash withdrawals, deposits, and transfers between accounts at any time by using an access card. ATMs can be found in bank lobbies, outside bank buildings, in shopping malls, in airport terminals, and in many other places. Over 100,000 ATMs currently exist. However, some customers prefer the smiling face of a live teller.

automatic teller machine (ATM) *a machine that allows customers to make cash withdrawals, deposits, and transfers between accounts anytime by using an access card.*

BANKING AND DEREGULATION

Before the Depression, banks were free to engage in virtually any activity they desired. They were heavily involved in trading stocks and selling and underwriting new stocks and bonds. They also made highly risky loans. With the stock market crash of 1929 and the Depression of the 1930s, thousands of banks failed. President Franklin Roosevelt and the Congress addressed the banking issue with the **Glass-Steagall Act of 1933.** The act limited the rights of banks to engage in investment activity, and this law and subsequent legislation created highly specialized institutions. The legislation defined the business that banks and savings and loans were to engage in and granted them exclusive rights to conduct their business. Essentially, banks and savings and loans were treated as "protected species." Banks provided checking accounts and made personal and business loans. Savings and loans accepted savings deposits and lent out the funds for home mortgages. No financial institution was allowed to cross a state line. Furthermore, the government established the maximum amount of interest that could be paid on a savings account in a bank or savings and loan. S&Ls were allowed to pay slightly more, to compensate for the stricter limits on their activities.

Glass-Steagall Act of 1933 *a law that limited the rights of banks to engage in investment activities.*

Everything was controlled. To get government permission to open a new bank or savings and loan, the founder had to prove that the new institution would not cause harmful effects to existing institutions. In the highly regulated environment that prevailed through the 1970s, only the most foolish of bankers could fail.

Changing Economic Forces

All of this began to unravel in the late 1970s. Tight government regulation could not protect the banks and savings and loans from new economic forces. It all began with the double-digit inflation of the late 1970s. With inflation at 10 to 12 percent, depositors became very disgruntled with the 4½ percent interest they were receiving in savings accounts at banks or the 5 percent at savings and loans. If you receive 5 percent interest on $100 in savings, you will have $105 in your account at the end of the year, but with 10 percent inflation, it will buy only about 95 percents as much as it did at the beginning of the year. Because interest rates on savings accounts were mandated by the government, they could not be raised to satisfy depositors. Also, because bankers were used to having ready access to low-cost deposits, they were not clamoring to have the government raise the rates. Bankers hoped that inflation and consumers' desire to be compensated for inflation would soon go away. This was not to be.

Merrill Lynch, the huge brokerage house, decided to fill the gap between what consumers were demanding and what financial institutions were paying.

Since Merrill Lynch was not a bank or a savings and loan, it was unrestricted as to what interest rates it could pay. It introduced the money market fund, which allowed investors to deposit funds and receive whatever interest rate Merrill Lynch chose to pay. Merrill Lynch began offering investors double-digit interest. The firm also provided a thinly disguised form of a checking account and even offered credit cards. Brokerage houses such as E. F. Hutton and Bache soon followed suit, and mutual funds also began offering similar high-yielding arrangements.

As the bankers watched their customers march out the door with a substantial part of their savings, they finally began to demand that the government deregulate the banking industry so that they could pay competitive interest rates.

New Legislation in the 1980s

Depository Institutions Deregulation and Monetary Control Act of 1980 a law that deregulated the banking industry by phasing out interest rate ceilings and allowing interest to be paid on checking accounts.

The first piece of legislation to deregulate the banking industry was the **Depository Institutions Deregulation and Monetary Control Act of 1980**. Commonly referred to as the Banking Act of 1980, this law phased out interest rate ceilings at financial institutions by 1986 and also allowed interest to be paid on checking accounts at these institutions. A series of legislative and judicial actions followed. The effect was to break down the barriers to competition in the financial services industry.

The impact of this legislation has been enormous. First, banks and savings and loans have had to become much more competitive. This has not been easy. As the government removed the ceiling on interest rates paid by banks and savings and loans, the rates went up rapidly. Although the financial institutions were better able to hold onto old deposits and attract new ones, higher interest rates put pressure on their profitability. They would have to invest funds more aggressively to achieve higher returns. All of these factors forced the financial institutions to take greater risks. For the commercial banks, it meant going beyond normal personal and business loans, into loans to the oil and real estate industries, and also extending credit to unstable foreign countries. Savings and loans went a step further. Not only did they make increasingly risky loans to try to generate high returns, but they actually began investing directly in real estate on their own. All of these actions led to thousands of failures in the banking and savings and loan industry (to be addressed in the next section). Deregulation had led to a tremendous shakedown in the industry. The weaker institutions have failed, and the stronger, competitive institutions have grown and prospered. Banks such as Citicorp, Chase Manhattan, and BankAmerica can compete with any business in the world.

Superregional Banking

superregional bank a bank holding company which crosses state lines in a specific region of the country to gain increased power.

As barriers to interstate banking came down in 1985, the **superregional bank** emerged—a bank holding company that crosses state lines in a specific region of the country in order to gain increased power. This is accomplished by increasing the number of banks affiliated with the firm. Although superregional banks are not as large as the East and West coast money center banks (such as Citicorp and BankAmerica), they are often more profitable because of their dominance in a region. This dominance allows them to offer banking services over a wide geographical area, leading to lower costs for advertising, data processing, and loan servicing. The superregional bank seems to be the trend of the future, with the development of NCNB Corp. of Charlotte, North Carolina (Southeast and Southwest), PNC Financial Corp. of Pittsburgh (Northeast), and Banc One Corp. of Columbus, Ohio (Midwest and Southwest).

THE CRISIS IN THE SAVINGS AND LOAN INDUSTRY

Savings and loans were originally set up to encourage thrift and to provide funding for the housing industry. A similar type of institution, the mutual savings bank, was established for the same purpose. **Mutual savings banks** differ from S&Ls in that they are member-owned. Deposits in mutual savings banks are actually stock purchases in the banks. There are approximately 2,500 savings and loans throughout the country, but there are only 600 mutual savings banks, mostly in the northeast. Both types of institutions have suffered from the competitive pressures described in the previous section.

During the period after World War II, savings and loans provided approximately 70 percent of the home financing in the United States. Since the success of an S&L depended largely on local goodwill, S&Ls tended to be exemplary citizens. Savings and loans contributed to local charities, and their officers were often active in the Chamber of Commerce, local government, and other community organizations. If you were to go through the files of your hometown newspaper or read *Time* or *Newsweek* from the 1970s, you would have to read for a long time to find even one negative story associated with savings and loans.

If your research concentrated on the late 1980s and early 1990s, quite the opposite would be true. The challenge would be to find a positive news story about S&Ls. No industry was hit harder than the S&Ls by the economic conditions and the deregulation described in the preceding section. S&Ls had committed themselves to 20- and 30-year home mortgage loans at 6 and 7 percent interest. Then the cost to fund those home loans—that is, the interest rates they had to pay depositors to compete for their money—suddenly went up to twice and three times that amount. It was an impossible situation.

The eventual solution was worse than the problem. Under deregulation, savings and loans began offering higher and higher interest rates to depositors. In order to cover their costs, they moved out of low-risk home mortgage lending to high-risk commercial lending on shopping centers, condominiums, raw land, and so on.[2] They took part of their funds and made direct investments in real estate. Thus, savings and loans became involved in designing and building new real estate developments, some of which were only slightly less risky than a high-stakes midnight poker game.

The land or property swap also became popular. Savings and loan A would buy a piece of property for $100,000 and sell it to savings and loan B for $120,000. This appeared to be a successful investment that produced a $20,000 profit. Shortly thereafter, savings and loan B would sell the property back to savings and loan A for $150,000. Now savings and loan B had brilliantly made a gain of $30,000, which it could proudly report to stockholders and government regulators. This process might be repeated four or five more times until the property was bid up to $500,000. Enormous paper profits were being made on a piece of property that had no more real value than when it was bought for $100,000. (For more about questionable industry practices, read the Ethical issues on page 528.)

It was the federal government's job to monitor the industry, because S&L deposits were insured by the government for up to $100,000 through the Federal Savings and Loan Insurance Corporation (FSLIC). It was the worst regulatory mis-

mutual savings banks *financial institutions similar to S&Ls except that they are member-owned.*

Business Career
Real Estate Agent: Rents, buys, and sells property for clients on commission basis. Stays informed on housing market in the community. Solicits new listings. Accompanies prospective buyers to property sites, quotes price, and describes features. Facilitates price negotiations between buyer and seller. Draws up real estate contracts. Assists buyer in obtaining financing. *Average Salary: $18,000.*

S&Ls: Is This an Industry Without Ethics?

The justice department estimates that fraud may have taken place in as many as 30 percent of the failed savings and loans. In no other industry has unethical behavior been exposed to this extent. Besides such well-known S&L executives as Charles H. Keating, Jr. of Lincoln Savings and Loan and Thomas Spriegel of the Columbia Savings and Loan Association, government probes have implicated Neil Bush, the son of President Bush. The younger Bush served on the board of a Denver S&L that made highly questionable loans to "special friends" of the financial institution.

Some industry practices appear even more outrageous because the funds were acquired through the use of federally insured deposits. Indirectly, the government was bankrolling S&L purchases of yachts, airplanes, and prostitutes to enable the industry to entertain its clients and peddle its influence. In the case of Sunrise Savings and Loan, funds that were suppose to be used for a construction loan instead financed the purchase of a $1.3 million diamond ring for a client.

There is an old saying, "You can't legislate morality." In the savings and loan industry, the government didn't even try. During the heyday of the high rollers, almost nobody was refused permission to run a savings and loan. It didn't matter if they had engaged in unethical activities in other phases of their business life.

match of the century. Wheeler-dealer S&L operators with 20 years of real estate experience, with high-priced lawyers to back them up, were going against S&L regulators who were fresh out of college, making $18,000 a year and still completing their on-the-job training.

By the mid- to late 1980s, the savings and loan industry fell apart. Over 500 of the 3,000 savings and loans failed. (Another 1,000 may eventually fail.) Because the federal government insured the deposits of these institutions, it had to take them over when they failed, pay off the depositors, and sell off the assets. As an alternative, the government might find a stronger institution to take over the failed institution but would have to compensate the stronger institution for its efforts. With so many S&Ls going under at the same time, much of their property was dumped on the market. This meant that property values for *all* real estate declined, because of the excess supply. Eventually, even well-managed S&Ls were caught up in the process. Perhaps they had made a legitimate $80,000 loan on a $100,000 piece of property. Because of the overall dumping on the market, the property was now worth only $60,000. If the property was sold, the borrower could not pay off the loan, and the "good" savings and loan was now in trouble too.

This process, repeated over and over again, has cost the government billions of dollars annually for the past few years. However, you should not feel sorry for the government, but rather for yourself. The eventual cost to bail out the savings and loan industry is estimated to be between $300 billion and $500 billion over the next 40 years. That translates to about $2,000 per taxpayer or $8,000 per family of four. One person who attempted to correct his process was Ed Gray, who is profiled on page 530.

Current Regulation and Reform

The industry losses in the 1980s broke the federal insurance fund that was set up to cover the losses. The Federal Savings and Loan Insurance Corporation (FSLIC) was as insolvent as the savings and loans it was organized to insure. A slow panic settled over the economy as depositors became concerned about the safety of their accounts, which were insured for up to $100,000 by the FSLIC. The president and Congress had to move in to ease the fear. The government proclaimed that

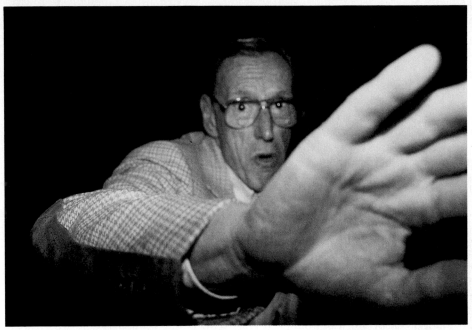

Lincoln Savings and Loan was among the biggest of the S & Ls that failed in the late 1980s. Owner Charles Keating is shown during his 1991 trial in Los Angeles.

the "full faith and credit" of the federal government would be used to cover deposits in the savings and loan industry. If the FSLIC could not cover its obligations, the U.S. Treasury itself would raise the funds to cover the deposits. The same commitment was made to the banking industry, where depositor funds are insured by the FDIC.

The most important piece of actual legislation passed to help solve the problems of the savings and loan industry is officially known as the **Financial Institutions Reform, Recovery and Enforcement Act of 1989 (FIRREA).** It is more simply referred to as the Financial Institutions Reform Act.

The most important provisions of the Act were that it:

- Provided funding to close failed S&Ls and pay off depositors.
- Established the **Resolution Trust Corporation (RTC)** to handle the closing of failed institutions and to dispose of their assets.
- Eliminated the Federal Savings and Loan Insurance Corporation (FSLIC) and replaced it with the Savings Association Insurance Fund.
- Placed the Savings Association Insurance Fund under the supervision of the FDIC. Banking regulators would now be responsible for overseeing the activities of the savings and loan insurance fund.
- Strengthened regulators' enforcement powers.
- Raised the capital requirements (the amount of ownership funds that savings and loans must have) to levels similar to those applied to banks.

The basic intention of the law was to raise enough money to close down or reorganize failed savings and loans and to pay off depositors where necessary.

One of the important implications of the Act was to strengthen the role of the FDIC. As shown in Figure 19-4, the FDIC now monitors the activities of the entire banking and savings and loan industries. That includes overseeing their insurance funds, supervising their operations, and providing accounting and legal services to both industries.

Financial Institutions Reform, Recovery and Enforcement Act of 1989 (FIRREA)   the most important legislation passed to help solve the problems of the savings and loan industry.

Resolution Trust Corporation (RTC)   a government organization established to handle the closing of insolvent savings and loans and to dispose of their assets.

Edwin G. Gray

Ed Gray was the chairman of the Federal Home Loan Bank Board (FHLBB) from 1983 to 1987. Until 1989, the FHLBB supervised the activities of the Federal Home Loan Bank system, which supported federally chartered savings and loans across the country. Gray had the unenviable task of presiding over the industry at the height of the S&L crisis.

Ed Gray was born in Modesto, California and graduated from California State University at Fresno in 1957. For the next ten years, he held various positions in journalism and public relations. In 1967, Gray became a staffer for California Governor Ronald Reagan. He left the governor's staff in 1973, spent the next seven years as a senior vice president of San Diego Federal Savings and Loan Association, and then joined the Reagan presidential campaign in 1980. After Reagan became president, Gray was appointed to a White House post. He left the administration in 1982 to become first vice president of Great American Federal Savings Bank in San Diego but returned a year later when he was appointed to head the FHLBB.

It wasn't long before Gray became convinced that the deregulation of savings and loans had backfired. The S&L industry's original problem was that the institutions could not make money on low-interest mortgage loans and could not obtain enough funds through deposits because inflation had driven interest rates up higher than the S&Ls were allowed to pay. By 1984, however, the situation was different: Deregulation legislation had allowed the S&Ls to engage in high-risk commercial loans and direct investments in real estate and junk bonds, and many of these investments were going bad.

Gray started saying publicly that the S&Ls weren't growing out of their problems. He warned that the increasing number of S&L failures could bankrupt the FSLIC and jeopardize the entire industry. Gray's comments did not make him popular with the S&L industry.

Gray's FHLBB published a new regulation in early 1985, limiting direct investments by S&Ls to 10 percent of assets. This angered S&L executives, particularly Charles Keating of Arizona's Lincoln Savings and Loan. Keating pulled strings, trying to get Gray to exempt Lincoln Savings & Loan from the regulation. Gray refused. Keating twice visited Treasury Undersecretary George Gould, trying to get Gray fired. Gould refused to comply. Next, Keating tried to hire Gray for $300,000 a year. Again, Gray refused. Keating hired several top law firms to leak reports about Gray's acceptance of travel and entertainment expenses from the U.S. League of Savings Institutions. Gray's reputation suffered. As early as 1984, Gray had pleaded for more examiners and regulators to deal with the S&L industry's growing problems, but his pleas fell on deaf ears. White House chief of staff Donald Regan disagreed publicly with Gray, saying that appointing more regulators would be equivalent to re-regulating the S&L industry. Many members of Congress were also hostile. One Congressional aide threatened that Gray would not be able to get a job after his bank board term ended if he didn't stop talking about the industry's problems.

It is not hard to see why Gray faced so much resistance. Closing down all the S&Ls that were insolvent would cost the FSLIC billions more than it had in its insurance fund. This would drive the fund into bankruptcy, raising questions about the competence of regulators, Congress, and everyone connected with the industry.

In July 1987, Gray's term as chairman of the FHLBB ended, and he left to become chairman of Chase Federal Bank in Miami, Florida. In 1989, Congress finally came to grips with the issues Gray had raised years before. The FHLBB was stripped of its powers. The bankrupt FSLIC was also abolished and its functions replaced by the Savings and Loan Insurance Fund, managed by the FDIC. The damage was already done, however, and nobody was thanking Ed Gray for trying to prevent it.

Sources: Marquis *Who's Who in America,* Volume 1, ©1990–1991; "The Man Who Tried to Buy Washington," *U.S. News & World Report,* 27 November 1989, p. 18: "When Hell Sleazes Over," *New Republic,* 26 March 1989, p. 26.

FIGURE 19-4   The Regulatory Chart Under the Financial Institutions Reform Act of 1989

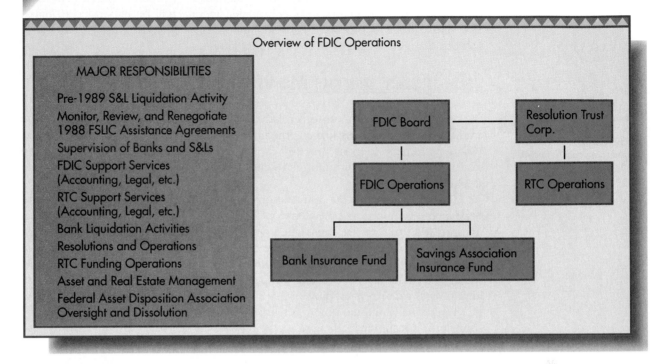

Source: *ABA Banking Journal*, October 1989, p. 79.

The Resolution Trust Corporation, created by the Act, has responsibility for taking over failed savings and loans and selling off their assets. By mid-1990, the RTC held 35,908 pieces of property for future sale. Although the property was valued at $14.92 billion at the time of the seizure, the true market value was though to be 30 to 40 percent lower. This property included homes, shopping centers, condominiums, and office buildings, as well as such unique assets as a pool hall in Houston and two uranium mines. Anyone can bid for property held by the RTC, and a lot of investors have attempted to do some bargain-basement shopping.

Only time will tell if the Financial Institutions Reform Act of 1989 has cured the problems of the savings and loan industry or whether we will need to pass other legislation in the future.

Similar Problems in Banking

In the early 1990s, banks have unfortunately developed a number of the same ills as their cousins in the savings and loan industry. During the recession, a number of banks failed as their energy and real estate loans went sour. Also, the industry's insurance fund, the FDIC, fell short of cash.

Banks have not failed at the same rate as S&Ls or been accused of the many improper activities that went on in that industry. However, bankers are likely to face some tough times in the future. They have responded by being ultra-conservative in making loans during the early 1990s. Some have named this as the cause of the "credit crunch," which made it difficult for customers to borrow funds under reasonable terms.

Legislation to correct problems in the banking industry is almost sure to come. Banks will be required to have more capital to protect against risky loan losses. Also, the framework in which banks operate will be expanded to make U.S. banks more competitive in world markets. The FDIC, with its expanded powers, also has an increasing need for funding.

THE CREDIT UNION MOVEMENT

6

credit union *a member-owned, nonprofit financial institution.*

We now turn our attention to a relatively new kind of financial institution, the credit union. A **credit union** is a member-owned, nonprofit financial institution. When customers "deposit" money in a credit union, they are actually buying stock in it. Since a credit union is owned by its depositors, there are no outside stockholders.

There are over 14,000 credit unions in the United States, with a total membership of 60 million people. One out of every three adults belongs to a credit union. Credit unions are most often sponsored by a company, labor union, or religious or professional group. They are also popular with military and state employees. Who may join a credit union is usually defined by where people work. For example, the University Federal Credit Union in Austin is exclusively for University of Texas employees.

Traditionally, credit unions engaged in limited activities, such as making short-term consumer loans and accepting savings deposits. However, they also participated in the deregulation movement of the 1980s. Now they offer interest-bearing checking accounts, termed **share-draft accounts,** which compete directly with NOW accounts at banks and savings and loans. Some credit unions also offer mortgage loans, life insurance, credit cards, financial counseling, and many other services.

share-draft accounts *interest-bearing checking accounts offered by credit unions.*

One of the reasons for the growing popularity of credit unions is that their loan rates to members are often slightly lower than banks or savings and loans, and interest paid on deposits is slightly higher. How can they accomplish this?

⬤ver the past decade, credit unions have become competitive with banks.

First, they are nonprofit in nature. They may also enjoy low rent and overhead through the sponsoring institution.

In spite of the growth of the movement, credit unions have considerably fewer assets than banks or savings and loans. In 1990, credit unions controlled $200 billion in assets, while savings and loans had over $1 trillion and banks over $3 trillion. Although 70 percent of American credit unions have assets of $5 million or less, there are exceptions. For example, the U.S. Navy Credit Union manages more than $3.5 billion in assets, has 1 million members, and employs 2,200 people.

Credit unions are regulated by the National Credit Union Administration (NCUA), and deposits are normally insured by the National Credit Union Insurance Fund. As with banks and savings and loans, deposits are insured up to $100,000.

PRODUCTS OFFERED BY FINANCIAL INSTITUTIONS

Table 19-1 presents an overview of the features and services offered by financial institutions. Many of these institutions have already been discussed, and others will be covered later in the text. Notice that the first four categories (banks, savings and loans, savings banks, and credit unions) offer virtually every product

How safe is your money? Are the funds in your financial insitution federally insured?

TABLE 19-1 Competitive Products offered by Financial Institutions

	Checking Accounts	Savings Accounts	Loans	Insurance	Credit Cards	Brokerage Services
Commercial Banks	Regular Checking Plus NOW Accounts and Super-NOW Accounts	Certificates of Deposit, Money Market Accounts, Passbook Savings. Funds Are Federally Insured up to $100,000	Personal, Commercial, Auto, Home Improvement, Mortgage	Credit Life and Credit Disability, Accidental Life and Health	Normally MasterCard and Visa	Discount Brokerage Affiliate
Savings and Loans	NOW and Super-NOW Accounts	Certificates of Deposit, Money Market Accounts, Passbook Savings. Funds Are Federally Insured up to $100,000	Personal, Auto, Home Improvement, Mortgage	Credit Life and Credit Disability, Property and Casualty	Normally MasterCard and Visa	Discount Brokerage Affiliate
Savings Banks	NOW and Super-NOW Accounts	Certificates of Deposit, Money Market Accounts, Passbook Savings. Funds Are Federally Insured up to $100,000	Personal, Auto, Home Improvement, Mortgage	Credit Life and Credit Disability, Property and Casualty	Normally MasterCard and Visa	Discount Brokerage Affiliate
Credit Unions	Share-Draft Accounts, Similar to NOW and Super-NOW Accounts	Certificates of Deposit, Money Market Accounts, Passbook Savings. Funds Are Federally Insured up to $100,000	Personal, Auto, Home Improvement, Mortgage	Credit Life and Credit Disability, Group Life Insurance	Only Offered in Larger Credit Unions	Discount Brokerage Affiliate—But Only in Larger Credit Unions
Stockbrokers	Checking as Part of Money Market Fund	Certificates of Deposit, Money Market Funds. Funds Are Not Federally Insured.	Margin Loan on Stock and Bond Purchases	Fixed and Variable Annuities	May Offer MasterCard or Visa as Part of a Cash Management Account	All Brokerage Services Provided
Consumer Finance Companies	Not Directly Offered	Not Directly Offered	Small Personal Loans, Generally at High Interest Rates. Also, Auto and Home Improvement Loans. Qualification for Credit Is not Hard.	Credit Life and Credit Disability	Not Provided	Not Provided

and service covered in the table. Also, the deposits for each of these four are federally insured up to $100,000. So why even look elsewhere? For one thing, stockbrokers may offer higher rates because of a wider variety of product offerings (discussed more fully in Chapter 21). Also, consumer finance companies are willing to make loans that more traditional financial institutions turn down. If three banks turn you down for a loan, you may be willing to pay the high rate that a consumer finance company charges because it is your only available source of financing.

Having examined some of the financial institutions in the U.S. economy, we shift our attention to the federal government's role in controlling the banking system in particular and the economy in general, through the Federal Reserve System.

FEDERAL RESERVE SYSTEM

The **Federal Reserve System** (**the Fed**) operates as the central bank of the United States. The Fed was established in 1913 to provide a source of short-term funds to banks and to add stability to the nation's banking system. In effect, the Fed operates as a bank for bankers. Although each regional Federal Reserve bank is owned by its member banks, of which there are now more than 5,500, the Federal Reserve is a government agency, operated in accordance with the public interest. Let's examine the structure of the Fed and some of its important functions.

Federal Reserve System (the Fed) a government agency that acts as the central bank for the U.S. and controls the money supply through reserve requirements, open market operations, and discount rates.

Structure of the Fed

The activities of the Federal Reserve System are coordinated and directed by a seven-member Board of Governors, who are appointed by the president and confirmed by the Senate. Each member of the board serves a 14-year term. Because of the long, guaranteed period of service, political pressure on the policy decisions of the board members is minimized.

Geographically, the Federal Reserve System is made up of 12 districts, each with is own Federal Reserve District Bank. The 12 districts and the locations of the Fed's branch banks are shown in Figure 19-5. The Board of Governors of the Federal Reserve is located in Washington, D.C.

Controlling the Money Supply

The primary activity of the Federal Reserve System is controlling the rate of growth of the nation's money supply. The goal of the Fed's monetary policy is to promote economic growth while holding down inflation.

The rate of growth in the supply of money has a direct effect on credit availability and interest rates. The more money flowing through the economy, the lower the rate of interest on borrowed funds will be, and the greater the rate of economic expansion. Unfortunately, when the economy grows too fast, prices start going up too. Table 19-2 lists the Fed's three major policy tools and how each affects the money supply, interest rates, and economic growth.

Reserve Requirements. Commercial banks create money when they make loans. The Federal Reserve, through its reserve requirements, controls the rate at which a bank can create money. **Reserve requirements** are the percentage of total deposits that a bank must hold as cash in its vault or as deposits in the regional Federal Reserve bank. That is, a bank cannot lend all of its depositors'

reserve requirements the percentage of total deposits that a bank must hold as cash in its vault or as deposits in the regional Federal Reserve bank.

FIGURE 19-5   The Federal Reserve System: Boundaries of Federal Reserve Districts and their Branch Territories

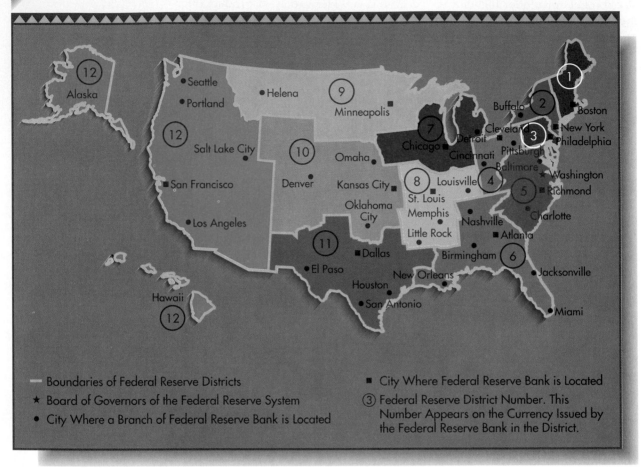

Source: *Federal Reserve Bulletin*, January 1983, p. A88.

money. Reserve requirements change periodically, in response to the health of the economy and the goals of the Fed's monetary policy. In the early 1990s, banks were required to maintain reserves equal to 3 percent of their first $40 million in deposits and 12 percent of their deposits above that amount. In this way, the bank has cash on hand to meet withdrawals.

To see the impact of the reserve requirement on the money supply, look at Figure 19-2 again. When Ms. Appel deposited her $1,000 in First State Bank, the bank was required to keep $120 (12 percent) in reserve, so it could lend out only $880.

Now suppose the Board of Governors of the Federal Reserve decided that the economy was growing too fast, with an unwanted rise in prices. To slow the rate of inflation, the Fed might raise the reserve requirement to 14 percent. Ms. Appel's bank could now lend only $860. This slows the rate of money creation, making credit less available. Interest rates begin to rise as borrowers compete for loanable funds. The result is that investment in new factories, housing projects, and office buildings begins to decline, thereby slowing the rate of economic expansion and the general rise in prices.

TABLE 19-2   How the Federal Reserve Controls the Economy

Federal Reserve Action	Impact on Money Supply	Impact on Interest Rates	Impact on the Economy
Reserve Requirements			
Lower Reserve Requirements	Increase Money Supply	Reduce Interest Rates	Foster Economic Growth
Raise Reserve Requirements	Decrease Money Supply	Increase Interest Rates	Discourage Inflation
Open Market Operations			
Buy Securities from the Public	Increase Money Supply	Reduce Interest Rates	Foster Economic Growth
Sell Securities to the Banks	Decrease Money Supply	Increase Interest Rates	Discourage Inflation
Discount Rate			
Lower the Discount Rate	Increase Money Supply	Reduce Interest Rates	Foster Economic Growth
Increase the Discount Rate	Decrease Money Supply	Increase Interest Rates	Discourage Inflation

In the example, the $20 difference in the amount of money created when the reserve requirement was raised to 14 percent may not seem like much. However, when all deposits in all banks across the country are considered, the impact can be substantial. For this reason, the reserve requirement is the Fed's most powerful weapon for controlling the money supply. Because the reserve requirement has such an impact, the Fed does not often change it.

Open Market Operations. A second and more common way of controlling the money supply is through **open market operations**—that is, through the buying and selling of U.S. government securities on the open market. This trading is done through specialized dealers in New York.

Figure 19-6 shows how open market operations work. Suppose the Fed wanted to inject more money into the economy. The Federal Reserve Bank of New York, under the direction of the Federal Open Market Committee,[3] might purchase $100 million in short-term Treasury notes from a dealer in these securities. The bank writes a cashier's check for the amount, and the dealer hands over the securities and deposits the check in a commercial bank. This exchange of money for government securities adds more money to the economy, because the Fed itself created $100 million and because the dealer's bank now has $100 million (minus the reserve requirement) more in loanable funds on deposit. Figure 19-6 also shows how the Fed reduces the money supply by selling off government securities from its holdings of such securities.

Discount Rate. From time to time, commercial banks borrow short-term money from their regional Federal Reserve bank to meet the reserve requirement or to cover other cash obligations. The **discount rate** is the name for the interest rate charged on these loans. Only member banks may borrow from the Federal Reserve at the discount rate.

A lowering of the discount rate raises the rate of money creation and economic expansion. Funds borrowed from the Fed and on deposit in the commercial bank's account with the regional Federal Reserve bank act just as the bank's other deposits do—they increase the amount of money available for lending. A

open market operations the buying and selling of U.S. government securities by the Fed to influence the money supply.

discount rate the interest rate charged when commercial banks borrow short-term money from their regional Federal Reserve Bank.

FIGURE 19-6   How Open Market Transactions Affect the Economy

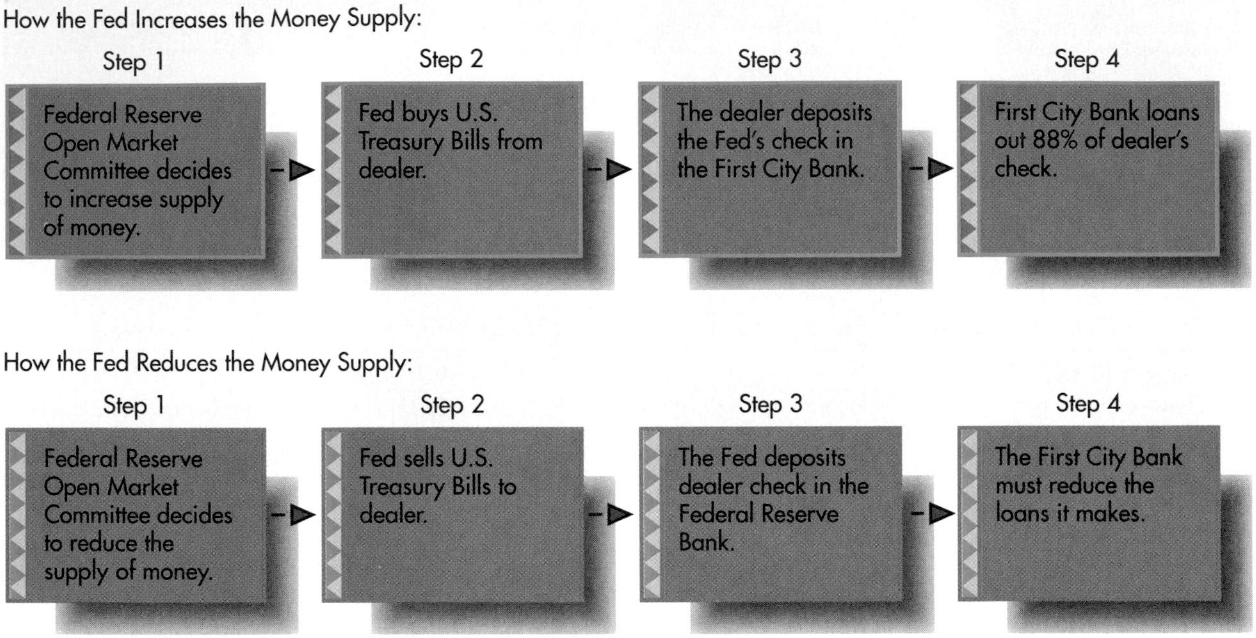

How the Fed Increases the Money Supply:

Step 1	Step 2	Step 3	Step 4
Federal Reserve Open Market Committee decides to increase supply of money.	Fed buys U.S. Treasury Bills from dealer.	The dealer deposits the Fed's check in the First City Bank.	First City Bank loans out 88% of dealer's check.

How the Fed Reduces the Money Supply:

Step 1	Step 2	Step 3	Step 4
Federal Reserve Open Market Committee decides to reduce the supply of money.	Fed sells U.S. Treasury Bills to dealer.	The Fed deposits dealer check in the Federal Reserve Bank.	The First City Bank must reduce the loans it makes.

reduction in the discount rate, therefore, encourages bank lending. The subsequent decline in interest rates throughout the financial sector promotes economic growth. By similar reasoning, raising the discount rate discourages inflation. The discount rate was as high as 13 percent in 1980. By the early 1990s, it had fallen to 3½ percent, as the Fed tried to stimulate the economy by lowering interest rates.

Check Clearing

Have you ever wondered what happens to a check after it is deposited in a bank? Since a fully implemented EFT system is still decades away, this remains an important issue. Suppose that Nick and his sister Annie have checking accounts at the same bank in Baltimore. Nick writes a check to Annie for $60. In this situation, the processing of the check is simple. The bank subtracts $60 from the balance in Nick's account and adds $60 to Annie's account.

The processing of a check becomes much more complicated when the bank on which the check is drawn and the bank at which it is deposited are in different cities. The Fed plays a major role in clearing intercity checks to ensure that the nation's banking system works efficiently. Each year, it processes billions of checks.

Figure 19-7 details the path of a check drawn on an account in a Chicago bank and written to a merchant in San Francisco. Two Federal Reserve banks, as well as two commercial banks, are involved in the transaction. The Fed is normally able to process a check such as this in just a few working days—quite an accomplishment when you realize how many checks it processes each day.

FIGURE 19-7   How a Check Travels Through the Federal Reserve System for Inter-city Collection

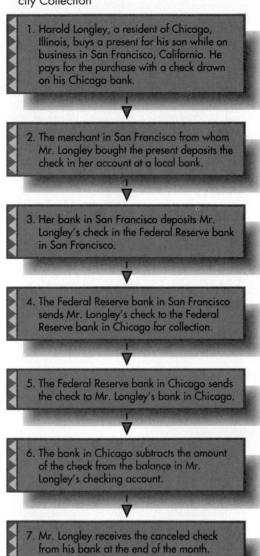

1. Harold Longley, a resident of Chicago, Illinois, buys a present for his son while on business in San Francisco, California. He pays for the purchase with a check drawn on his Chicago bank.

2. The merchant in San Francisco from whom Mr. Longley bought the present deposits the check in her account at a local bank.

3. Her bank in San Francisco deposits Mr. Longley's check in the Federal Reserve bank in San Francisco.

4. The Federal Reserve bank in San Francisco sends Mr. Longley's check to the Federal Reserve bank in Chicago for collection.

5. The Federal Reserve bank in Chicago sends the check to Mr. Longley's bank in Chicago.

6. The bank in Chicago subtracts the amount of the check from the balance in Mr. Longley's checking account.

7. Mr. Longley receives the canceled check from his bank at the end of the month.

SUMMARY POINTS

1 Banking is one of the most competitive industries in the world. A bank competes not only with other local banks, but also with banks from all over the country and the world. There is competition from savings and loans, credit unions, stock brokerage houses, insurance companies, credit card issuers, and other institutions.

2 Money can be defined as anything that is generally accepted as payment for goods and services. Money serves as a medium of exchange, a standard of value, and a means of storing wealth. Banks play an important role in the creation of money, as shown in Figure 19-2.

KEY TERMS

Federal Deposit Insurance Corporation (FDIC) 518

money 518

medium of exchange 518

standard of value 518

store of wealth 518

demand deposit 519

3 Besides accepting deposits and making loans, banks also provide services such as trust management, cash management, discount brokerage, insurance, credit cards, traveler's cheques, and electronic funds transfer.

4 The stock market crash of 1929 and the Depression of the 1930s caused thousands of banks to fail. Strict regulation was put in place to protect against such events happening again. However, with the hyperinflation of the late 1970s, the industry was deregulated, in hopes of improving the banks' profitability.

5 Deregulation in the 1980s also extended to the savings and loan industry. The increased power that savings and loans were given to expand their activities was not well used. They made high-risk loans, and some engaged in shady practices such as property swapping. These practices, coupled with falling property values, caused hundreds of savings and loans to fail in the 1980s. In order to deal with these problems, Congress passed the Financial Institutions Reform Act in 1989. This Act established the Resolution Trust Corporation to handle the closing of failed institutions and shifted the industry's insurance fund to the supervision of the FDIC. The cost to bail out the industry is likely to reach hundreds of billions of dollars.

6 Credit unions are member-owned nonprofit financial institutions. They are growing rapidly because they provide many services. Also, they generally make loans to their members at slightly lower rates than banks and S&Ls and pay slightly higher interest on deposits. These attractive features are possible because credit unions are nonprofit.

7 Banks, savings and loans, savings banks, and credit unions offer a wide range of similar financial products. Stockbrokers sometimes offer higher rates of return. Consumer finance companies specialize in making loans that other institutions would turn down.

8 The Federal Reserve System is responsible for controlling the money supply and thereby the national economy. Measures used to control the money supply include changing reserve requirements, buying and selling securities in the open market, and changing the discount rate.

REVIEW QUESTIONS

1 What are some of the nonbanking institutions with which banks compete? **1**

2 What are three main functions of money? **2**

3 Assume that a depositor places $4,200 in the Bank of New Orleans. If the reserve requirement is 12 percent, (a) how large a dollar loan can the bank make? (b) If the proceeds from the loan are then placed in the Bank of Baton Rouge, how large a loan can this second bank make? **2**

4 What are the differences between a NOW account and a Super-NOW account? **3**

5 What is the disadvantage of a certificate of deposit? **3**

6 If interest rates are expected to go down, would you prefer a fixed-rate loan or a variable-rate loan? Why? **3**

7 Is there a profit motive for banks offering credit cards, or is it a mere service activity? **3**

8 How did Merrill Lynch's aggressive policy of paying high rates for deposits indirectly affect the regulation of the banking industry? **4**

9 What is a superregional bank? How does it compare with a money center bank in terms of profitability? **4**

10 What government act created the Resolution Trust Corporation? What purpose does the RTC serve? **5**

11 Why are credit unions sometimes referred to as "financial institutions with a heart"? Why have they grown so rapidly? **6**

12 Suppose the Federal Reserve makes a large purchase of government securities on the open market. Does this add or subtract from the money supply? **8**

DISCUSSION QUESTIONS

1 Discuss how commercial banks create money.

2 What is float? Will it become more common or less common as electronic funds transfer becomes more prevalent?

3 Explain how Merrill Lynch helped to change the nature of the banking industry.

4 Has deregulation been a positive factor in the savings and loan industry?

5 How might the Board of Governors of the Federal Reserve System move the economy out of a recession? Present your answer in terms of all three of the Fed's monetary policy tools.

EXPERIENTIAL EXERCISES

1 Assume that you have $1,000 that you wish to deposit. Call three different financial institutions to find out what their terms are. The institutions may include banks, savings and loans, and credit unions. Inquire about the rates they pay, checkwriting privileges, minimum deposit requirements, penalties for early withdrawal, and so on. Ask about NOW accounts, Super-NOW accounts, money market accounts, savings accounts, and certificates of deposit. (These accounts may be called by slightly different names at some financial institutions.)

2 At a local bank or savings and loan, check the rates for fixed-rate mortgages and variable-rate mortgages. How far apart are the rates? If you were purchasing a house, given your expectations about future earning power and all you can learn about probable interest rates in the future, which sort of mortgage would you choose? Why?

CASES

CASE 19-1
Citicorp

Citicorp is the largest bank holding company in the United States. In 1990, the New York bank had more than $230 billion in assets and $150 billion in loans. It is also a major money center bank, which means that it collects deposits and makes loans throughout the country and even the world. When John Reed, a 1960s graduate of the MIT Sloan School of Management, became president of Citicorp in 1984, he said, "This job is like getting to paint the Sistine Chapel."*

With the deregulation of the banking and financial services industry, Reed saw numerous exciting opportunities for the bank. Citicorp had a long-standing commitment to increase earnings per share by 15 percent per year, and Reed envisioned new ways of accomplishing this task. The bank already had major commitments of loans to companies in less-developed countries throughout the world. Now it was determined to expand its real estate lending and its participation in leveraged buyouts.

By the early 1990s, almost all of these activities had gone sour. In 1990, the firm's earnings per share had dropped to $.57, from a peak of $4.87 in 1988. Furthermore, during 1990 the annual dividend was decreased to $1.00 from its prior level of $1.78, and 8,000 employees were laid off. Citicorp's stock price dropped from a high of $35 per share in

Source: C.J. Loomis, *Fortune* © 1991 The Time Inc. Magazine Company. All Rights Reserved.

1988 to a low of $10.75 in 1990. That represented a total loss to investors of almost $1 billion. During this same period, Citicorp was further embarrassed by having $275 million in loans outstanding to Donald Trump. 1990 was the year that Trump's successful real estate empire came to an end.

Stronger banks in New York City, such as J. P. Morgan, indirectly encouraged customers to switch their business away from Citicorp through ads stressing "the importance of the security of the customers' deposits." Though no one really thought Citicorp was in any danger of failing, such scare tactics can be effective. Citicorp lost some of its business and had to pay more in interest for the business it kept.

If Citicorp were to get into serious trouble, it might be able to rely on "the too big to fail" doctrine. The federal government has a history of not letting major banks go under, because of the shock-wave effect such bankruptcies would have on the financial system. Thus, Continental Illinois of Chicago was bailed out by the government a decade ago, and the pattern has been repeated several times since then.

In looking to the future, Citicorp knew that it would have to sell more stock to raise needed capital. It would also need to reduce losses on bad loans it had made in the past and more carefully pinpoint areas of future activity. The bank needed to determine how far it could afford to stray from the traditionally profitable consumer banking functions that it had engaged in for decades.

1. Would further deregulation of the financial services industry be likely to solve Citicorp's problems?
2. What are the advantages and disadvantages of having a commitment to a high rate of growth for the future, as Citicorp did with its 15 percent growth rate in the 1980s?
3. What drawback can you see to Citicorp's selling a large amount of new stock in the situation discussed in the case?
4. Do you think the "too big to fail" doctrine is good?

CASE 19-2
AT&T, "The Credit Card Company"

Although there are already 260 million credit cards in circulation in the United States, there is still tremendous opportunity for card issuers. Originally, owning a credit card was a prestigious thing. Having a Diners Club or American Express Card to flash around at a restaurant was the equivalent of belonging to a top country club. Of course, all that has changed. Most American families have credit cards—usually two or three. The credit card business has traditionally been very profitable to the issuer. People are sometimes shocked to find out that major banks make up to 50 percent of their total profits from their credit card business.

AT&T has now entered the business. The long-distance phone company decided to get a piece of the lucrative credit card business in 1990. Ma Bell, as AT&T is sometimes called, had a head start because it had access to the credit histories of 70 million long-distance callers. That was a great target list for potential customers; AT&T could get a credit card customer at an average promotional cost of $6 to $10 instead of the industry standard of $25 to $80. Also, AT&T was not hung up on the high profit margins that the banks and American Express were enjoying. Ma Bell decided not to charge a membership fee, as many other card issuers do. Also, a 10 percent discount would be allowed on long-distance calls utilizing the new credit card. Of course, the card is meant for much more than long-distance calling; it covers every type of credit purchase that other cards do.

Other participants in the credit card industry were not happy to have AT&T join them. Banks filed petitions with the Federal Reserve Board and Federal Communications Commission, arguing that a telephone company should not be allowed to enter the consumer credit business. However, the company was allowed to continue issuing credit cards, and it has forged ahead aggressively.

With or without AT&T, the credit card business continues to look for new ways to grow. Be prepared for credit cards at fast-food restaurants, toll booths, and movies. Perhaps in your lifetime, cash will be something you see only in museums.

1.   What particular advantages does AT&T have over existing credit card companies?
2.   Do you think that credit cards are generally beneficial to the buying public?
3.   Since AT&T is not a financial institution, do you think it should be barred from the credit card industry?
4.   Some credit card companies are starting to promote their cards to college students. Do you think this policy is advisable?

OBJECTIVES

After studying this chapter, you should be able to:

1 Explain the generally accepted goal of financial management.

2 Describe the functions of the financial manager.

3 Define budgets and discuss the importance of budgets and controls to a firm.

4 Explain why firms need sources of funds beyond their own profits.

5 Describe the techniques and considerations that are used in managing the assets of a firm.

6 Describe the sources of short-term financing that are available to a company.

7 Describe the sources of long-term financing available to a company.

8 Discuss the advantages and disadvantages of the main sources of financing that are available to a firm.

CHAPTER 20

Financial Management

Pam Estes resigned after 10 years as vice president of operations at Sun Nurseries. At the time, the plant and garden chain was generating sales of $100 million a year and profits of $4 million. Pam had an MBA from a leading educational institution in the southwest and felt confident in her ability to start her own business. She was simply tired of working in a large bureaucracy and reporting to others.

Two other associates also left Sun Nurseries at the same time as Pam. The three pooled their funds to start a chain of stores called Hillcrest Nurseries.

After a couple of years of getting established, the company became highly profitable in the third year. In the fourth year, Hillcrest sold shares of its stock to the public to raise additional capital. Pam was thrilled with all the growth and progress the company had made but she sometimes got tired of hearing her investment banker talk about the responsibilities she had to the stockholders, even though she was aware that this outside funding was essential to keep the business growing. She also knew that the company needed continued bank financing to carry the large inventory that is essential to the nursery business.

Pam and the two other founders decided that the time was right to hire a full-time chief financial officer. In time, they would also need a treasurer, a controller, and many other financial people. If they were to meet their long-term goals, they had to develop a full-scale financial organization. Just how financial management helps in running a firm like Hillcrest Nurseries will be carefully examined in this chapter.

n this chapter, we first look at the goal(s) of financial management and the functions of the financial manager. We then consider how the firm manages its assets and attracts the capital to keep functioning. A particularly important distinction is made between short-term and long-term financing.

THE GOAL OF FINANCIAL MANAGEMENT

Financial management involves the acquisition of funds for the firm and the management of those funds. The generally accepted goal of financial management is **stockholder wealth maximization.** This means that the overriding purpose in managing the financial affairs of a firm is to maximize the value of the firm for the owners—the stockholders. The importance of meeting this goal has been highlighted in recent years by many unfriendly takeovers of companies by investors who thought the company was failing to meet the goal of achieving maximum value in the marketplace. So-called corporate raiders such as T. Boone Pickens (profiled on page 546) have repeatedly challenged management to put stockholders' interests first.

In a classic example involving this goal, American Express once made an offer to acquire McGraw-Hill Publishing Company. At that time, McGraw-Hill common stock was selling at $26 per share. American Express made an offer worth $34 per share, and many investors viewed this as a marriage made in heaven. Not only would McGraw-Hill be joining forces with the largest credit card company in the world, but each McGraw-Hill stockholder would enjoy an immediate increase of more than 30 percent in the value of his or her holdings. Such a gain might normally take three or four years.

The investor was dismayed to learn, later that same day, that the board of directors of McGraw-Hill was turning down the offer that contained the $8 per share immediate gain. The McGraw family felt that it would be inappropriate for a "prestigious publishing company" to join forces with an aggressive finance company such as American Express. The integrity of the press might be sacrificed. This was not a very convincing argument to the individual stockholder, who wanted to see the value of his or her shares go up dramatically.

American Express increased the offer to $40 a share—a potential gain of $14 per share. Once again, the McGraw-Hill board of directors refused. Was McGraw-Hill following the first commandment of finance—maximize the wealth of stockholders? The answer is probably no.[1]

It might be suggested that managers do not always try to maximize stockholders' wealth because it might end their own positions of power. If a merger took place, the stockholders would gain, but managers might lose their jobs. Under most circumstances, managers do attempt to accommodate the wishes of stockholders. In many corporations, executives have options to buy stock and also participate in profit-sharing programs. Only when their own jobs are threatened are they likely to depart from the concept of stockholder wealth maximization.

financial management the acquisition and management of funds for a firm.

stockholder wealth maximization maximizing the firm's value for stockholders, which is the overriding goal in managing the firm's financial affairs.

FUNCTIONS OF FINANCIAL MANAGEMENT

Financial managers are responsible for acquiring a firm's funds and managing those funds. In some respects, financial management picks up where accounting leaves off. Accounting is responsible for providing the data that are used to make financial decisions. The accountant is like a skilled technician who takes a patient's blood sample and runs other tests to measure results. The financial manager is like the doctor who then acts on that information. If the tests indicate a healthy patient, the status quo is maintained. If there are imbalances and malfunctioning parts, the financial manager must prescribe corrective action.

T. Boone Pickens, Jr.

T. Boone Pickens, Jr. is one of the most controversial people in business. Some fear him as a "corporate raider." To others he is a stockholder advocate and corporate activist. Everyone agrees that he has had a tremendous impact on the oil industry and on American business in general.

Born in 1928 in Holdenville, Oklahoma, T. Boone Pickens, Jr. is a 1951 graduate of Oklahoma State University. In 1954, he left the security of a major oil company to strike out on his own as an independent geologist. He formed his first company with only $2,500 in equity capital. In 1964, he founded Mesa Petroleum, now America's largest independent oil and gas producer. A $10,000 investment in Mesa in 1964 would be valued at more than $300,000 today.

Mesa has explored for oil and gas in the United States, Canada, Australia, and the North Sea; acquired three other independents; formed two pioneering royalty trusts, and earned more than $500 million in profits for Mesa stockholders from investments in other companies. In 1985, Pickens received stockholder approval to transform Mesa into Mesa Limited Partnership.

Over the years, Pickens has led several huge takeover attempts against major corporations, including Gulf, Phillips, and Unocal. In each of these cases, he made sizable profits for Mesa and for the stockholders of the target firms.

In August 1986, Pickens founded the United Shareholders Association. The Washington-based organization champions the rights of America's 50 million stockholders. Although more people own stock in American corporations than ever before, they have very little power. Corporate managers, fearful of being ousted in hostile takeovers, have installed a variety of "shark repellents" that have weakened stockholders' rights. Such measures, according to Pickens, handcuff potential acquirers and shield poor management from the corrective powers of the market.

In the late 1980s, Pickens turned his interest to Japan. He purchased a 26.4 percent stake in Koito Manufacturing, a car-parts associate of Toyota. Pickens quickly found that Japanese firms were even less sensitive to stockholder needs and desires than U.S. companies. He has been denied a seat on the Koito board, and access to company books and corporate documents has been refused. No doubt this advocate for stockholder rights will continue to draw attention to the closed system for outside stockholders in Japanese companies. The Ministry of International Trade and Industry (MITI) in Japan is watching him closely.

At Parker Hanafin Corp. Michael J. Hiemstra is Chief Financial Officer and Vice President for Finance and Administration.

To maximize stockholder wealth, the financial manager must constantly assess the trade-off between risk and return in the organization. **Risk** is the uncertainty about future outcomes and the potential for future losses. The prudent financial manager must consider not only how much he or she could make from an investment, but also the chances for loss and how large that loss could be. A project that promotes a potential 20 percent return, but with only a 50 percent chance of success, may be less desirable than a project with a virtually guaranteed return of 12 percent.

risk   the uncertainty about future outcomes and the potential for future losses.

Figure 20-1 shows the breakdown of jobs in the finance area and how they fit into a corporate structure. The Chief financial officer (CFO) usually has the title of vice president of finance and has operating responsibility similar to that of the vice president of marketing and the vice president of management. Normally, the finance function is further broken down into those activities conducted by the corporate treasurer and by the corporate controller. The treasurer's staff carries out the activities involved in the management of corporate funds, and the controller's staff handles tax- and accounting-related tasks.

The organization chart in Figure 20-1 applies to a medium-size or large organization. In a smaller organization, the 12 finance-related positions shown in the chart might be compressed into one or two positions, and these finance persons must carry out all the activities on their own. Nevertheless, the finance function is just as important in a small organization as in a multimillion dollar company.

Figure 20-2 is a flowchart showing the progression of financial activities toward the overall goal of maximizing stockholder wealth. In reading from left to right, the first step toward achieving this goal is to acquire accounting data. This information is then used to establish budgets that enable management to measure its performance in meeting corporate objectives. The three boxes running from the bottom to the top of the chart involve operational activities that ensure that budgets and goals will be carried out. That is, management must acquire the necessary financial resources for the firm and put them in place. The next step on

FIGURE 20-1   Organization Chart Highlighting the Finance Function

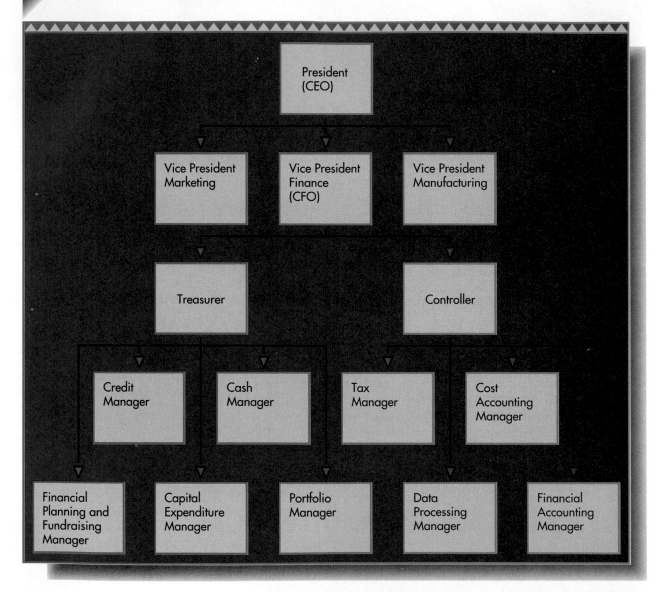

the right goes beyond the normal operating activities of the firm to consider periodic decisions: whether to pay cash dividends, acquire other companies, or the like. In carrying out the steps shown in Figure 20-2, management must determine the appropriate trade-off between risk and return in order to achieve stockholder wealth maximization. The remainder of this chapter will examine these financial activities more closely.

ESTABLISHING BUDGETS AND FINANCIAL CONTROLS

 If there is one skill that is essential to the financial manager, it is the ability to plan ahead and make necessary adjustments rather than simply reacting to events after

FIGURE 20-2   Financial Activities Toward Maximizing Stockholder Wealth

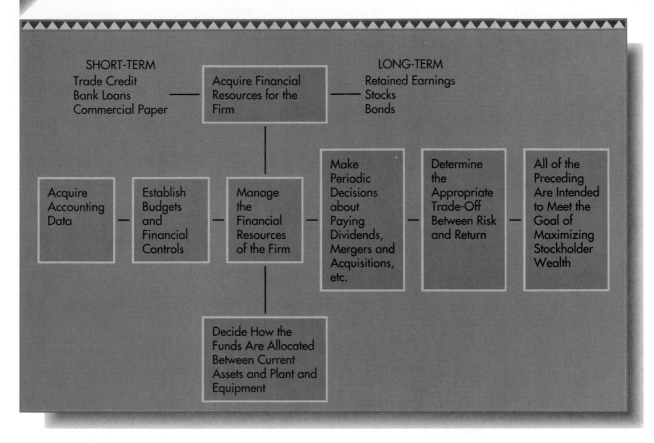

they occur. If we imagine two firms faced with the same set of external events (recession, inflation, strong new competition, and so on), it is very possible that one would survive while the other would not. The outcome might be a function not only of their tendencies to take risks but also of their ability to hedge against risks by careful planning.

The need for such planning is particularly important in a seasonal business. For example, a swimwear company does most of its selling and generation of cash flow in the summer months, but it must spend large amounts on design and production in the late winter and early spring. A similar cash flow dilemma might exist for a Christmas card manufacturer, as depicted in Figure 20-3. During the first two or three months of the year, the company's artists design the Christmas cards that will appear in stores that December. In March, the company starts producing cards and inventorying them in its stockroom. Retailers begin placing their orders in June, but the cards are not shipped until September.

Not until November and December does the company see any cash for its production run of that year. Yet the company incurred production, inventory, insurance, and other costs throughout the year, which had to be paid long before the selling season. To meet these obligations, the Christmas card manufacturer takes out short-term loans from a local bank. The cash received from retailers at the end of the year is then used to pay back the loan. These activities call for very careful financial planning.

FIGURE 20-3   Business Activities and Short-Term Money Needs for a Christmas Card Manufacturer

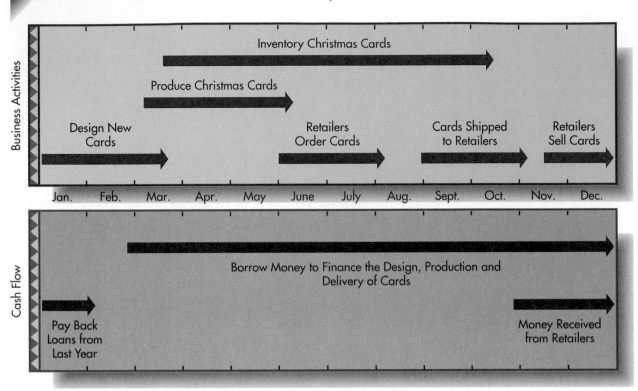

Budgets

budget *a detailed financial plan showing estimated revenues and expenses for a specified future period, usually one year.*

operating budget *a budget that allocates dollar amounts to costs and expenses needed to run the business.*

capital budget *a budget that estimates expenditures related to long-term asset acquisitions, such as machinery and equipment.*

cash budget *a budget used to forecast cash balances at the end of each month and for the entire year.*

master budget *a budget that ties together the operating budget, the capital budget, and the cash budget, ensuring that there is consistency in their projections and outlook.*

A **budget** is a detailed financial plan showing estimated revenues and expenses for a specified future period, usually one year. Five budgets are essential to the financial manager. The **operating budget** allocates dollar amounts to the various costs and expenses needed to run the business. It lists expected outlays for such items as salaries, rent, and supplies. It usually has a one-year time horizon but is broken down by month. An abbreviated operating budget for the Christmas card manufacturer is shown in Table 20-1.

A **capital budget** estimates expenditures related to long-term asset acquisitions, such as machinery, equipment, or the site for a new plant. Although the budget is only for one year, its implications may stretch well into the future.

The **cash budget** forecasts cash balances at the end of each month and for the entire year. Through this budget, the peaks and valleys of financial need can be determined. The firm can then determine how much money must be borrowed at any point in time and how and when it will be paid back. For a firm that has tight financial needs, the cash budget is the most critical of all—the one the banker will ask to see first.

A **master budget** simply ties the other budgets together. It ensures that there is internal consistency in their projections and outlook. For example, the master budget makes sure that estimated expenditures in the capital budget for machinery and equipment are also properly reflected in each of the other budgets. To the extent that supplies, rental space, or employees will be required to operate the new equipment, the master budget builds these assumptions into the other budgets.

TABLE 20-1   Operating Budget for a Christmas Card Manufacturer

	March	April	May
Purchase of Card Stock	$290,000	$220,000	$185,000
Salaries	260,000	280,000	350,000
Rental Expense	50,000	50,000	50,000
Supplies	15,000	13,000	16,000
Quarterly Tax Payment	150,000	0	0
Total Monthly Expense	$765,000	$563,000	$601,000

The five-year financial plan goes well beyond the annual budgetary process. Whereas banks and short-term lenders are interested in the annual budgets, stockholders and bondholders care more about longer-term prospects. The accuracy of five-year plans is necessarily limited, because they forecast so far into the future, but they are absolutely essential for attracting long-term funding to a firm. Stockholders, security analysts, and investment bankers demand to see anticipated earnings per share several years ahead, and bondholders want to see how well interest and other fixed obligations will be covered. The difficulties of doing long-term forecasting are exemplified in the box on page 552, "Financial Planning in Search of Excellence (or Disaster)."

five-year financial plan
a plan that lays out a five-year forecast of the firm's earnings and expenses.

The capital budget covers expenditures for long-term assets, such as these production robots.

Financial Planning in Search of Excellence (or Disaster)

In 1982, Thomas J. Peters and Robert H. Wasserman wrote the runaway bestseller *In Search of Excellence: Lessons from America's Best-Run Corporations* (published by Harper & Row). The authors identified what seemed to be the best American corporations. Among the 29 firms honored were IBM, Texas Instruments, Procter and Gamble, Merck, and Eastman Kodak. Not only did the firms have excellent records of asset growth, equity growth, return on equity, and a number of other quantitative factors, but they also were known as companies that were innovative, had a bias toward action, were customer driven, employed lean staffs, and practiced hands-on management. The companies were chosen for their superior performance for the five-year period from 1976 through 1980.

What happened after these firms were singled out for praise by Peters and Wasserman? From 1981 to 1985, 86 percent of them experienced declines in the rate of asset growth, 93 percent had a decline in the rate of equity growth, and 79 percent saw a similar reduction in return on equity. Only 17 of the 29 publicly traded companies did as well as the popular stock market averages.

What was going on here? Stock market researcher Michelle Clayman decided to find out. She went down the same path as Peters and Wasserman had followed, except that Clayman decided to conduct a search for disaster. She identified the worst companies that

Financial Controls

Without some type of monitoring process, merely establishing budgets would be a useless process. Progress in meeting the budget must be continually monitored so that deviations from plan can be identified and corrective action taken. However, as pointed out in Chapter 7, goals should not be followed so rigidly that employees pursue targets that are no longer valid. The microcomputer, with its flexible spreadsheet programs, is extremely useful in the ever-changing environment of budgeting and control. What was valid in January may have little meaning in September if a new competitor has moved into the market or a recession has hit the economy.

MANAGING THE FINANCIAL RESOURCES OF THE FIRM

 As Figure 20-2 showed, once budgets and financial controls have been established, the next step is to manage the firm's financial resources. The management of these resources is critical to the success of the firm. In most new businesses, buildings and equipment are acquired, then inventory is purchased or manufactured, and finally sales must be generated to provide profits. Since not all sales are cash, accounts receivable are also built up.

At the time these assets are acquired, funds must be obtained to pay for them. Who is to put up the funds for the building? How is the inventory to be financed? Even if the business is successful, these issues will continue to be important. A growing business always needs financing to support its activities.

The need for new funds may be greater at some times of the year than others. You will recall our earlier discussion of the Christmas card manufacturer who spent the first three quarters of the year designing, producing, and shipping Christmas cards but did not receive payment until November and December. Financial managers must manage the firm's finances so that the right amount of money is available at the time it is needed.

she could possibly find, using Peters and Wasserman's criteria, and selected 39 companies for the period from 1976 to 1980. The "unexcellent companies" included such firms as Bethlehem Steel, B.F. Goodrich, J.P. Stevens & Co., and F.W. Woolworth. The firms in the disaster group generally had terrible performances during the period in which Peters and Wasserman were "in search of excellence." Knowing how poorly the firms chosen by Peters and Wasserman had performed in the five-year period after they were picked, Clayman examined how her "disaster" firms had done over the same five-year period after being singled out for their incompetence (according to the Peters and Wasserman criteria). Most showed improved asset and equity growth. More significantly, 25 out of 39 outperformed the popular stock market averages. Actually, the entire disaster group had an average annual market return of 12 percent a year above the Standard and Poor's Stock 500 stock index—a remarkable performance.

What is the lesson? When you are doing financial budgeting and forecasting, be very cautious about automatically carrying the past into the future. Good companies sometimes become complacent, and poorly performing companies are forced to improve or lose their independent existence.

Source: M. Clayman, "In Search of Excellence: The Investor's Viewpoint," *Financial Analysts Journal*, May–June 1987, pp. 54–63.

A common misconception is that profits alone are sufficient to provide the necessary financing for a firm. Even companies with high profits must constantly look to their bankers, trade creditors, or elsewhere to fill the financing gap. Of course, the problem is even more acute for firms that do not make good profits. The issue is not normally whether a firm is planning to use outside financing, but how it is going to do it most efficiently. What is the firm willing to pay? Is it going

Financial resources must be managed in such a way that the firm has enough goods available for sale when the best selling season begins. For example, the Nursery Annevore in Namur, Belgium has plenty of flowers in stock for the spring because it has managed its finances well during the months when sales are slower.

to acquire short- or long-term financing? Is it going to use a combination of debt and equity (stockholder funds)?

The management of the firm's financial resources can be better understood by examining the abbreviated balance sheet for the Fletcher Corporation in Figure 20-4. Many of the items in Figure 20-4 were introduced in Chapter 18. In the following sections, we will discuss the management of the assets on the left-hand side of the balance sheet and then shift our attention to the means of financing on the right-hand side.

MANAGING OF ASSETS

 As explained in Chapter 18, cash includes checking account balances as well as currency and is the most liquid of all assets. However, it is also the lowest-yielding asset a firm can have. Therefore, the cash balance should be kept at an absolute minimum. In managing cash balances, financial managers first determine the minimum amount of cash necessary to support short-term needs. Then, when the cash balance rises above this minimum, managers transfer some cash into higher-yielding investments. Many firms now have desktop computers linked to banks so that they can immediately determine their cash balances anywhere in the country or the world. They can also instantaneously transfer funds from accounts that have excess cash to other, more profitable investments. For firms that are involved in international operations, cash management is critical. The firm must try to keep excess balances in strong currencies rather than weak ones. For example, if the Japanese yen is going up in value relative to the dollar, while the British pound is going down, funds should be immediately shifted to Tokyo from London.

FIGURE 20-4   Fletcher Corporation: Abbreviated Balance Sheet

FLETCHER CORPORATION

Balance Sheet

December 31, 1992

ASSETS	LIABILITIES AND STOCKHOLDERS' EQUITY
Current Assets:	Current Liabilities:
Cash	Trade Credit (Accounts Payable)
Marketable Securities	Notes Payable (Unsecured)
Accounts Receivable	Secured Debt
Inventory	
Total Current Assets	Long-Term Liabilities
	Bonds Payable
Fixed (Long-Term) Assets	Total Liabilities
Plant and Equipment	
Less: Accumulated Depreciation	Retained Earnings
Net Plant and Equipment	Stock
Total Assets	Total Liabilities and Stockholders' Equity

Sophisticated cash management also calls for collecting cash amounts due at the earliest point in time and paying at the latest acceptable time. A corporation may have collection centers across the country, which immediately process a check when it comes in, but the same firm may have only one payment center. Often, the payment center may be instructed that if an invoice says payment is due in 60 days, then it is to be paid as close as possible to day 60. Obviously, this principle should not be carried too far. Alienating a key supplier just to hold on to the cash for one more day is hardly good business.

Marketable Securities

As explained in Chapter 18, marketable securities are stocks, bonds, money market accounts, or any other securities that can be easily sold when cash is needed. Any excess cash should be immediately invested in marketable securities so that it will earn interest while remaining quickly accessible to the firm. The financial manager has a virtual supermarket of securities from which to choose. Among the factors influencing the choice are yield, maturity, minimum amount required, safety, and marketability. Under normal conditions, the longer the maturity of the security, the higher the yield. Also, securities rated lower in terms of safety tend to pay higher returns. However, companies generally use marketable securities to "park" excess funds only temporarily. Those funds will later be needed for deployment elsewhere, so risk-taking is not acceptable.

Managing Accounts Receivable

As explained in Chapter 18, accounts receivable represent credit that a firm has extended to customers. It indicates the extent to which the firm is waiting to convert credit sales to cash. Because the firm may have to go to the bank (or another

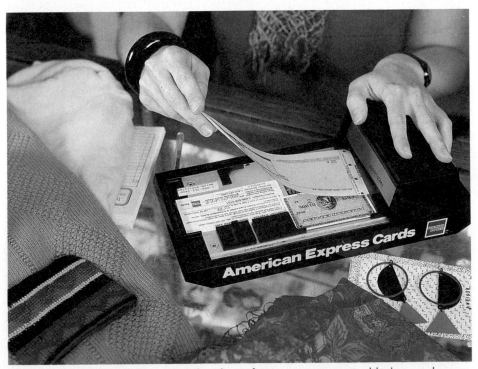

Credit card sales are among a merchandising firm's accounts receivable that can be converted to cash.

source) to borrow funds until the receivables are converted into actual dollars, most firms try to keep accounts receivable under close control. This can be accomplished through the credit terms that are offered (such as 30 days or 60 days to pay), the credit standards that are applied, and the collection policy.

Credit Standards. Most suppliers of credit use guidelines or rules to decide who receives credit. Criteria include the ratio of income to debt payments and the trend in income over the last few years. The customer's prior record of payment is also likely to be examined. Because large firms often have accounts that are dispersed throughout the country or the world, an extensive network of credit information has been developed. The most widely accepted source is Dun & Bradstreet, which publishes *The Dun & Bradstreet Reference Book of American Business,* listing millions of business establishments. The book presents information on the firm's line of business by Standard Industrial Classification code. The Dun & Bradstreet (D&B) rating is also presented when available. An illustration of the rating system used by Dun & Bradstreet is shown in Table 20-2. A rating of 3A3 would mean an estimated financial strength between $1,000,000 and $9,999,999 and a composite credit appraisal of "fair." Besides *The Dun & Bradstreet Reference Book of American Business,* D&B can also provide more extensive individualized credit reports on specific customers.

Collection Policy. After credit is approved, the payment patterns of customers must be closely monitored. The firm's collection policy will determine what steps must be followed if the customer falls behind in his or her payments. Note that no matter how conscientious a firm is in collecting its accounts, a rapidly growing

An important facet of the management of assets is managing inventory so that the firm has enough goods on hand to satisfy demand, but not so many that the firm incurs excessive inventory costs. (See "Managing Inventory" on page 557.)

TABLE 20-2   Dun & Bradstreet's Rating System for Credit

D&B Ratings and Symbols

D&B Rating System
The D&B Rating System is a widely used tool that uses a two-part code to represent a firm's estimated financial strength and composite credit appraisal. A Rating may be based on a book financial statement or on an estimated financial statement submitted by the company.

	Estimated Financial Strength				Composite Credit Appraisal			
					High	Good	Fair	Limited
Estimated financial strength, based on an actual book financial statement.	$50,000,000	and over		5A	1	2	3	4
	$10,000,000	to	$49,999,999	4A	1	2	3	4
For example, if a company has a Rating of "3A3," this means its financial strength is between $1,000,000 and $9,999,999 and its composite credit appraisal is "fair."	$1,000,000	to	$9,999,999	3A	1	2	③	4
	$750,000	to	$999,999	2A	1	2	3	4
	$500,000	to	$749,999	1A	1	2	3	4
	$300,000	to	$499,999	BA	1	2	3	4
	$200,000	to	$299,999	BB	1	2	3	4
	$125,000	to	$199,999	CB	1	2	3	4
	$75,000	to	$124,999	CC	1	2	3	4
	$50,000	to	$74,999	DC	1	2	3	4
Estimated financial strength, based on either an actual book financial statement or an estimated financial statement.	$35,000	to	$49,999	DD	1	2	3	4
	$20,000	to	$34,999	EE	1	2	3	4
	$10,000	to	$19,999	FF	1	2	3	4
	$5,000	to	$9,999	GG	1	2	3	4
		up to	$4,999	HH	1	2	3	4
Estimated financial strength, based on an estimated financial statement (when an actual book financial statement is not available to us).	$125,000	and over		1R		2	3	4
	$50,000	to	$124,999	2R		2	3	4

Symbols in the Rating column — what do they mean?

-- (Absence of a Rating)
A Business Information Report is available on this business, and other information products may be available as well. However, a D&B Rating has not been assigned. A "--" symbol should not be interpreted as indicating that credit should be denied. It simply means that the information available to Dun & Bradstreet does not permit us to classify the company within our Rating key and that further inquiry should be made before reaching a credit decision.

In many cases, a "--" symbol is used because a current financial statement on the business is not available to us. Some other reasons for using a "--" symbol include:
☐ Unavailability of the source and amount of starting capital — in the case of a new business
☐ A deficit net worth ☐ Bankruptcy proceedings ☐ A critical financial condition

firm is almost certain to show an increase in accounts receivable. The question then becomes, is the growth pattern reasonable? That is, is the growth in the firm's receivables caused by increased sales or by its customers' deteriorating ability to pay? In the first case, it is normally justified to extend additional credit; in the latter case, it is not.

Managing Inventory

Besides providing credit to attract customers, a firm must maintain adequate inventory as well. The investment in inventory may necessitate bank financing or other forms of credit. A build-up in assets on the left-hand side of the balance sheet almost always creates a need for additional financing on the right-hand side.

Capital Budgeting

Capital budgeting is the process of managing the long-term asset decisions of the firm. The time horizon is normally at least one year, but many assets have an anticipated life that is considerably longer. A chemical or steel company may purchase equipment with a life of 10 to 15 years, and a public utility may design a new plant with a 30-year life. Because large dollar amounts are often involved in the purchase of such fixed assets, particular care must be taken to ensure that the appropriate decision is made. When a firm such as Disney makes foreign investments, as described in the International Example on page 559, careful analysis becomes even more important.

A capital budgeting decision normally involves comparing an immediate cash outlay with benefits that the firm hopes to receive over time. Two aspects of this situation require particular attention. One is the fact that inflows received in the future will come in dollars that are worth less than the dollars expended today. Certainly, you would not agree to pay $1,000 that you have in your bank account today for the right to receive the same $1,000 ten years from now. If invested instead at 10 percent compound interest, your original $1,000 would be worth $2,594 after 10 years. Financial managers must keep this in mind and discount the value of future inflows, so as to put them on the same scale as current dollars.

A second factor in a capital budgeting decision is that it involves much more uncertainty than a shorter-term decision, such as the purchase of inventory in anticipation of next month's sales. When General Motors built its Saturn plant in Tennessee, analysts had to guess at the key factors that would influence auto sales for decades in the future. By the time the cost of the plant is fully recaptured, a vastly different type of vehicle may have made all current automobiles totally obsolete.

Financing the Assets of the Corporation

A firm must invest in the various assets just discussed: marketable securities, accounts receivable, inventory, and plant and equipment. Now it is time to examine the sources of financing for these assets. Look back at Table 20-2. The sources of financing are on the right-hand side of this abbreviated balance sheet. Generally, the firm may acquire funds on a short-term or a long-term basis. In an ideal world, short-term assets would be financed on a short-term basis and long-term assets on a long-term basis. However, many smaller firms have difficulty in attracting long-term capital. Let's look at the various sources of funding that are available. First we will examine short-term financing.

SOURCES OF SHORT-TERM FUNDS

 Short-term financing is normally for one year or less. A major part of the financial manager's time is spent in meeting the short-term financing needs of the firm. As seasonal inventory requirements increase or bills come in, various sources of short-term funds must be examined: trade credit, unsecured bank loans, commercial paper, and secured (collaterized) borrowing related to accounts receivable and inventory.

Trade Credit

When one company buys a product or service from another, it pays for the purchase either with cash at the time of delivery or with credit. Most suppliers offer

Disney Goes Worldwide

Financial management in the international arena carries all the problems and risk of domestic activities and then some. Nevertheless, firms such as Dow Chemical, Exxon, Gillette, IBM, and Mobil receive over 50 percent of their revenue from foreign sales.

When Walt Disney Company established theme parks in Japan and other countries, the chief financial officer of the firm had to consider such complications as exchange rates, debt flows, and potential political problems.

Exchange-Rate Exposure

Sales and profits made in foreign currency have to be translated back to U.S. dollars. If the yen is declining in value relative to the dollar, profits initially recorded in yen will be worth fewer dollars.

Capital Flows

Disney and other multinational companies must also decide where they are going to get their funds for foreign investments. They can borrow Japanese yen or German marks locally, or they can transfer dollars to foreign banks and convert them into foreign currency. Some countries restrict the flow of foreign currency in and out of their territory, which can cause added problems. Perhaps an initial investment is allowed, but five years later, the foreign government announces that all outflows will be restricted.

Political Problems

In extreme cases, foreign regimes take over corporate property without compensation. The political environment of the country considered for investment must be carefully assessed, along with the potential for returns. Oil companies and other natural resource firms have learned this lesson only too well.

It will require a lot more than great entertainment for Disney to be successful in its international operations over the next decade.

trade credit to their business customers. **Trade credit** means that the supplier finances the purchase by giving the buyer 30 days or more to pay. In effect, the buyer obtains financing from the supplier rather than from a bank.

Even a small manufacturer of housewares, such as coffee mugs and kitchen aprons, would have several sources of trade credit. The production of kitchen aprons, for example, involves the purchase of raw materials and services from fabric brokers, contract sewing companies, and offset and silkscreen printers. Each of these suppliers is a potential source of credit for the housewares manufacturer.

trade credit financing of a purchase by the supplier, who gives the buyer 30 days or more to pay.

This company has an open account with its supplier. These newly arrived goods can be stocked and sold immediately, but they don't have to be paid for until 30 days from now.

Types of Trade Credit.

open account   an informal credit arrangement by which a buyer makes purchases and pays for them later.

There are three basic types of trade credit. Most merchandise purchases are made on **open account**. Under this informal credit arrangement, a buyer makes purchases and pays for them later. An invoice usually accompanies the shipment of goods to the buyer. The invoice specifies which products were purchased, how many, at what price, and when the buyer is expected to pay the seller. This type of credit purchase is "open" in the sense that the buyer is not required to sign a written repayment agreement for each purchase. Open-account buying contributes to the smooth flow of business transactions in our economy.

promissory note   a form of trade credit in which the buyer draws up a note promising to pay a specified amount by a specified date.

The **promissory note** is another form of trade credit. A promissory note is a signed "promise to pay." The note indicates in writing the amount of money owed by the buyer and the repayment date. It is drawn up by the buyer in advance of the purchase. Promissory notes are a common way of obtaining credit in the fur and jewelry businesses.

trade acceptance   a form of trade credit in which the seller draws up a note, which the buyer signs.

A third type of trade credit is the **trade acceptance**. This credit instrument is similar to a promissory note except that it is the seller rather than the buyer who draws up a trade acceptance. The customer indicates acceptance of the credit agreement by signing it. Trade acceptances are often used by manufacturers when shipping merchandise to customers with doubtful or unknown credit standings.

Terms of Trade.

terms of trade   the conditions the seller gives the buyer when offering short-term credit.

net period   the length of time for which the seller extends credit to the buyer.

The conditions the seller gives the buyer when offering short-term credit are called **terms of trade**. The **net period** is the length of time for which the seller has extended credit. The Hi-Tone Paint Company sells its heat-resistant latex paint to retail customers for $6 a gallon. The terms of trade may be net 30 days, 2/10, n/30, or 3/20, n/60. Do you remember how to compute pay-ments with such terms? If not, review Chapter 16.

From the customer's perspective, it makes sense to take a discount and pay a bill early. Also, by paying the bill on the last day of the discount period rather than on the first or the second, the buyer obtains as much cost-free credit as possible without losing the benefit of the cash discount. If unable to take the discount, the buyer should wait until the end of the net period to pay the bill—for example, on the 30th day rather than earlier when the terms of trade are "2/10, net 30." Why? In order to use interest-free credit for as long as possible. This practice is referred to as stretching accounts payable.

Trade credit is an important source of short-term funds for most firms. It is "free" in that the firm is not required to pay a finance charge. The danger of trade credit is that the firm may overextend itself by taking too much.

Unsecured Bank Loans

Commercial banks are the second most important source of short-term business funds. The real business of most banks is lending money to commercial borrow-ers, such as retail stores, manufacturers, service companies, and construction firms.

Types of Bank Lending. The three forms of bank loans that we will examine are lines of credit, revolving credit, and transaction loans. A **line of credit** is an agreement between a bank and a borrower, specifying how much the bank is willing to lend the borrower over a certain period of time. For example, a bank might establish a $500,000 line of credit over a 12-month period for one of its customers. The quoted interest rate might be 9 percent. At any time during the year, the customer can automatically obtain funds from the bank, so long as the total amount borrowed does not exceed $500,000.

line of credit *an agreement between a bank and a bor-rower specifying how much the bank is willing to lend the bor-rower over a certain period of time, although the bank can lower the amount if conditions warrant.*

The advantage of a line of credit for the borrower is the ease of obtaining funds. However, the bank is under no obligation to lend up to the maximum amount. If the borrower's credit rating deteriorates, the bank may refuse a request for another loan. It may also reduce the customer's line of credit.

A **revolving credit agreement** is similar to a bank line of credit. Again, a credit limit is specified. However, under a revolving credit agreement, the bank is obligated to extend funds up to the credit limit. Revolving credit agreements are usually negotiated for periods of twelve months to three years. Some banks charge a fee for a revolving line of credit, normally ½ to 1 percent of the value of the credit agreement.

revolving credit agreement *an agreement similar to a line of credit ex-cept that the bank is obligated to extend funds up to the credit limit.*

When a borrower needs money for a specific purpose, such as to finance a seasonal variation in inventory, a capital equipment purchase, or a construction project, it may approach the bank for a **transaction loan**. To illustrate, a builder may need to borrow $100,000 for the construction of a house. When the house is sold, the loan is repaid. The bank considers each loan request from the builder on a case-by-case basis. A transaction loan is called a note payable on the bor-rower's books.

transaction loan *credit ex-tended by the bank for a spe-cific purpose.*

Interest Rates. Banks make money by charging interest on their loans. The **interest rate** is the price paid for the use of money over a stated period of time. Assuming an annual interest rate of 10 percent, the total cost of borrowing $200,000 for a year would be $20,000. From the perspective of a firm in need of

interest rate *the price paid for the use of money over a stated period of time.*

short-term funds, the big difference between a bank loan and trade credit is that the firm pays interest on the bank loan but not on trade credit.

prime rate *the interest rate that a bank charges its best customers.*

The interest rate that a bank charges its best customers is called the **prime rate**. The prime rate is usually set by one or more of the nation's largest banks. This rate goes up or down as the cost of money to the bank itself goes up or down.

Commercial Paper

commercial paper *unsecured short-term promissory notes issued by large corporations.*

The term **commercial paper** refers to unsecured short-term promissory notes issued by large corporations (usually industrial firms, bank holding companies, or public utilities). In recent years, state and municipal governments have also begun to issue commercial paper. Only the largest and most creditworthy firms— such as Allied-Signal Inc. with $45 million of commercial paper outstanding at year-end 1990—are able to sell commercial paper. The number of issuers is currently about 1,200.

Commercial paper is purchased by money market funds, life insurance companies, pension funds, bank trust departments, and other large investors. Most paper matures in 30 to 90 days, with a maximum maturity of 270 days. It is usually sold in blocks of $25,000.

Discount on Commercial Paper. Strictly speaking, commercial paper is non-interest-bearing. That is to say, it is sold at a discount below par and matures at par. Suppose that Mobil Oil issues $10 million in commercial paper. Through a commercial-paper dealer, such as Merrill Lynch Money Markets, Inc., several investors purchase the paper for $9.8 million. This is the amount that Mobil receives. In 60 days, when the paper matures, Mobil buys it back at par for $10 million. Thus, Mobil has the use of $9.8 million for 60 days at a total cost of $200,000. This $200,000 is the discount. Figure 20-5 shows the interest rate on commercial paper for the period from 1979 to 1991. Note that the commercial paper rate is always lower than the prime rate.

Uses of Commercial Paper. An issue of commercial paper is a substitute for a bank loan. The purpose of commercial paper is to cover immediate cash needs. Many firms use commercial paper to finance inventory buildup for seasonal sales. Others "roll over" commercial paper to obtain a continual source of funds. That is, when one issue of paper is about to mature, the firm sells another to pay for the maturing issue.

Secured Borrowing

Trade credit, bank lines of credit, revolving credit agreements, and commercial paper are all examples of unsecured loans. That is, the firm borrows money on the basis of its earnings potential and credit history; it does not put up property or other valuable assets as collateral. Transaction loans from commercial banks, on the other hand, can be either secured or unsecured, depending on the credit standing of the borrower, the amount of money advanced, and the purpose of the loan. A **secured loan** requires that the borrower pledge some form of asset as payment for the loan in case the borrower cannot repay the loan. Let's look at some of the assets that are frequently pledged as security for short-term loans.

secured loan *a loan that requires the borrower to pledge some form of asset as payment for the loan in case the borrower cannot repay it.*

Accounts Receivable. Borrowing against accounts receivable is a common practice for firms in need of short-term funding. In this instance, the loan is tied

FIGURE 20-5   Short-Term Interest Rates, 1979–1991

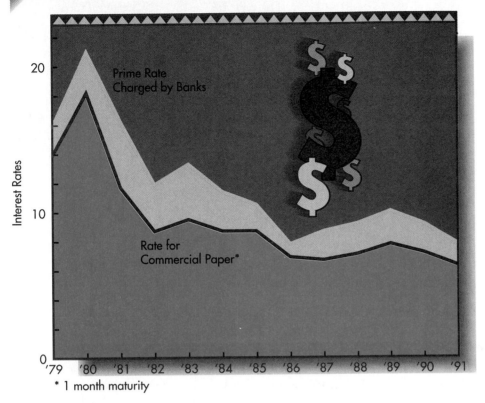

* 1 month maturity

Source: Federal Reserve *Bulletin*.

directly to the asset that the loan is financing. Once again, the right-hand side of the balance sheet is tied to the left-hand side.

Actually using accounts receivable as security, or collateral, for short-term loans is called **pledging accounts receivable**. Here's how pledging works: The borrowing firm gives the lender a list of its current receivables. The lender then decides which of them it will accept as collateral. As these receivables come due, the cash received as payment is forwarded to the lender until the loan (plus interest) is repaid. The firm is liable for the entire value of the loan, even if one or more of its customers should default on its debt.

Commercial banks regularly make accounts-receivable loans. Other financial institutions, such as General Motors Acceptance Corporation, General Electric Credit Corporation, and Transamerica Financial Corporation, are also involved in this type of lending.

Some firms take accounts-receivable financing a step further and factor their accounts receivable. **Factoring accounts receivable** means selling them to a financial institution, called a "factor." Business firms factor their accounts receivable to obtain cash immediately; financial institutions buy them in order to make money. Factors are usually paid a fee of 3 to 10 percent for their services. A retail department store selling $10,000 in receivables would net $9,500 if the factor fee were 5 percent. It is also common for factors to charge interest on the funds advanced. Therefore, factoring receivables is an expensive way for a firm to obtain short-term funds.

pledging accounts receivable   *using accounts receivable as security, or collateral, for a short-term loan.*

factoring accounts receivable   *selling accounts receivable to a financial institution.*

Factoring accounts receivable is a form of secured borrowing that is common in the sporting goods industry.

Here's how factoring works: A firm makes a credit sale (net 30 days) to a customer. It then sells the receivable to the factor for an amount less than the face value of the receivable—say, for 5 percent less. The customer is directed to pay its bill directly to the factor. The value of factoring to the firm is that it obtains its money from credit sales immediately. Factoring was once used only by firms with major cash problems. Today, however, many firms in industries such as sporting goods, automotive accessories, plastics, building materials, and communications equipment regularly factor their receivables.

Some larger firms sell their accounts receivable in a somewhat different fashion. They package a large volume of accounts receivable together and sell them to the public in the form of a security. The first such **asset-backed security offering** of accounts receivable was made by General Motors Acceptance Corporation in 1985, for $500 million. The receivables are sold at a discount from actual value, so when payments by customers take place, the investor receives a return on investment, normally 10 to 12 percent.

The sophisticated market for asset-backed security offerings now includes firms such as Mack Trucks (truck loan receivables) and Unisys (computer receivables). BankAmerica actually packaged together 836,659 "Classic Visa" credit card balances, containing over $655 million in receivables, and sold them to the public.

Inventory Financing. Inventories are second in importance to accounts receivable as collateral for short-term loans. We should first identify three different types of inventory:

- **Raw materials inventory**—basic inputs a manufacturer uses to produce other goods. For example: sheet steel for the production of Chevrolet auto bodies.
- **Goods-in-process inventory**—products or inputs that have already undergone some stages in a manufacturing process. For example: sheet steel shaped into fenders, hoods, and other Chevrolet body parts.

asset-backed security offering *a large volume of accounts receivable sold as a package to the public in the form of a security.*

Chrysler Chairman Lee Iacocca has helped the company find long-term funds for modernization.

- **Finished goods inventory**—products that have undergone all stages in a manufacturing process. For example: new Chevrolets waiting in a GM lot for shipment to dealers.

These distinctions are important. The lender needs to know the nature of the inventory involved before deciding whether to accept it as collateral. Most lenders will lend against raw materials and finished goods inventories only. In assigning a dollar value to collateralized inventory, most banks first determine the original cost of the inventory and then lend up to 65 to 75 percent of that amount.

When the DeLorean Motor Car Company went bankrupt in 1982, a market still existed for the completed DMC cars. Some of the raw materials, such as stainless steel and special plastics, also had resale value. But the half-finished De-Loreans had little value as collateral.

SOURCES OF LONG-TERM FUNDS

For a firm's needs for financing related to long-term assets, such as plant and equipment or new product development, long-term financing is required. The primary sources of long-term financing are retained earnings, bonds, common stock, and preferred stock.

Retained Earnings

The first source of long-term financing for a corporation is the surplus of revenues over costs after all expenses have been paid. As we saw in Chapter 1, this excess amount is called profit. Successful firms can use their accumulated profits to fund long-term expansion programs. An operating surplus also makes it easier for a firm to raise money in the capital markets—that is, to sell stocks and bonds. This is because investors perceive profitable firms as being good investments.

Retained earnings are the amount of money left at year-end after all expenses, interest payments, taxes, and dividends have been paid. It represents

retained earnings *the amount of funds left at year-end after all expenses, interest payments, taxes, and dividends have been paid.*

the accumulation of past and present profits that may be plowed back into the business. How important are retained earnings as a source of capital? In 1991, total after-tax profits of all U.S. corporations were about $165 billion. Of this total, nearly $92 billion was paid out to stockholders as cash dividends. The remainder, about $73 billion, was available for new investments by the corporations. For many smaller companies, retained earnings are just about the only source of long-term capital.

Perspective of the Firm. Should a successful firm retain its earnings or pay them out to shareholders? In theory, a firm should pay cash dividends only when it cannot find a better use for the money. According to this rule, the firm examines investment opportunities at the end of the fiscal year. If it finds a productive use for its surplus, such as a new assembly plant in a fast-growing part of the country, it retains the surplus, plowing it into the proposed investment. Otherwise, it distributes the surplus as dividends.

For many years, Lotus, the software development firm, has had a policy of investing all of its operating profit. From 1983 to 1991, the company did not pay out a single penny in dividends. During this time, its annual profits increased from $15 million to $68 million, and the price of its stock jumped from $2 to $30.

Perspective of the Investor. In practice, dividend policies are affected as much by stockholder expectations as they are by investment prospects. If the main concern of investors is increase in the stock price, not cash dividends, then investors neither expect nor want dividends. Lotus stockholders, for example, are clearly more interested in the value of their stock than in yearly dividend income, or they wouldn't buy Lotus stock. Not all investors and not all companies are the same, however. Maytag stockholders look for dividend income. Maytag has paid out an average of 60 to 70 percent of its after-tax profits as dividends since the mid-1970s. Many Maytag stockholders are older people who rely on cash dividends as a source of income. If the company failed to pay such dividends, it might weaken investor confidence.

Bonds

bond *a contract between the issuer and the buyer. The purchase price represents a loan to the issuing firm for which the firm pays the buyer interest.*

The second source of long-term financing is bonds. A **bond** is a contract between the issuer and the buyers. The purchase price of the bond represents a loan to the issuing firm. In return for this loan, the issuer promises to make regular interest payments to the buyers of the bond—individuals, pension funds, or other corporate investors—in specified amounts. The issuer also promises to repay the principal at a stated maturity date. The terms of the lending agreement are specified in the **bond indenture**. A bondholder is a creditor rather than an owner of the issuing firm. In short, a bond indicates a debt. Bonds are usually sold in units of $1,000, $5,000, $10,000, or $100,000.

bond indenture *the terms of the lending agreement associated with a bond.*

Secured vs. Unsecured Bonds. **Secured bonds** are backed by the pledge of a specific asset in case the issuer fails to pay. The security may be real estate or a specific claim to other assets. Unsecured bonds are termed **debentures;** they are not backed by specific collateral but rather by the overall strength of the corporation. Only corporations with relatively strong reputations are able to issue unsecured bonds.

secured bonds *bonds that are backed by the pledge of a specific asset in case the issuer fails to pay.*

debentures *bonds not backed by specific collateral, but rather by the overall strength of the corporation.*

If a firm is eventually liquidated because of failure to make payment on its bonds, the secured bondholders stand first in line to receive payment from the sale of the pledged assets. If funds are available from the sale of other assets, the unsecured bondholders will also receive some payment. In a typical liquidation, secured creditors might receive 60 to 70 cents on the dollar, while unsecured creditors get 20 to 30 cents.

Bond Interest Rates. To calculate the interest paid on a bond, multiply the principal or face amount of the bond by the bond interest rate. For example, on a $1,000 corporate bond, a 10 percent interest rate would indicate that $100 a year in interest would be paid. Since the interest payments are normally distributed semiannually, the two $50 payments would be made during the year.

The interest rate that is paid on a bond is based on the risk associated with the issue. Highly regarded companies pay the lowest rates. If a firm is poorly regarded in the marketplace, the interest rate demanded by bond investors is much higher. There are a number of private agencies that rate bonds based on their quality. The two most important agencies are Standard and Poor's and Moody's. Their rating standards are presented in Table 20-3.

In mid-1991, AAA corporate bonds provided investors with an average yield of 9.15 percent, and AAs were paying 9.26 percent. What about lower-rated issues? A BBB bond paid 10.70 percent, and a CCC bond yielded 15.5 percent.

Business Career

Securities Clerk: Compiles and maintains records of firm's securities transactions. Verifies accuracy of transaction statements for purchases and sales of securities and enters details in journals. Computes cash balances, dividends, gains and losses, and other investment data to verify records. Distributes investment income to various accounts, according to budgeted percentages. Prepares vouchers to transfer funds as needed to make payments. *Average Salary: $16,000.*

TABLE 20-3   Standard and Poor's and Moody's Bond Ratings

Standard and Poor's	Moody's	Description
AAA	Aaa	Highest rating; capacity to pay interest and repay principal is very secure.
AA	Aa	High quanity; differ from highest rated bonds only to a small degree.
A	A	Upper medium grade; interest and principal payments may be in jeopardy when a long, deep economic recession occurs.
BBB	Baa	Medium grade; adequate capacity to pay interest and principal in normal economic periods.
BB	Ba	Quite risky; modest capacity for interest and principal payments.
B	B	Poor investment, highly speculative; assurance of interest and principal payments over a long period are quite small.
CCC	Caa	Poor standing, may be in default; purchased for speculative purposes only.
CC	Ca	Highly speculative, often in default.
C	C	Very poor prospects for ever being a good investment.
D	—	Default; relatively little chance of ever being paid.

Source: *Standard and Poor's Register* (New York: Standard and Poor's Corporation, 1986); *Moody's Handbook* (New York: Moody's Investors Services, Inc., Winter 1985-1986).

Nowhere in the world of investments is the trade-off between risk and return more evident than in the bond market.

Low-rated, high-yield bonds became popularly known as **junk bonds** in the last decade. Although they provide exceptionally high quoted yields, the high return will never materialize if the firm fails to meet its interest obligations and goes into bankruptcy.

junk bonds   low-rated, high-yielding bonds.

Common Stock

common stock   stock whose owners have last claim to corporate assets but have voting rights.

As explained in Chapter 5 holders of **common stock** are the primary owners of the corporation. By purchasing a share of stock, an investor is buying a "share" of the ownership pie. Thus, common stock is an equity security. The total number of shares held by all investors represents the total ownership of the corporation. At the time of purchase of a stock, the investor receives a **stock certificate,** which signifies ownership of a share of the company.

stock certificate   a document signifying ownership of shares in the company.

Firms sell common stock for the same reason they issue bonds: to finance long-term expansion projects. Stocks differ from bonds in several important respects. Let's look at common stock in terms of liability, maturity, and the voting and income rights of stockholders.

Limited Liability.   One of the most important characteristics of common stock is that it carries limited liability. **Limited liability** means that the stockholders cannot be sued by the corporation's creditors for payment of the creditors' claims. If the corporation declares bankruptcy, the loss to stockholders is limited to the value of their shares. Individually or jointly, they are not liable for the corporation's debts.

limited liability   stockholders' exemption from being sued by the corporation's creditors for payment of claims.

Maturity.   Another characteristic of common stocks is that they never mature. Stocks are held forever unless the investor can find another buyer. This feature

The New York Stock Exchange is a prime source of long-term funding for many major U.S. corporations.

makes the secondary market especially important to stockholders, as discussed in the next chapter.

Voting Rights. The common stockholders of a corporation elect the board of directors, who in turn choose the firm's chief executive officer. Even though stockholders are the owners of the corporation, they in no way act as its managers. Stockholders have only indirect control, through their choice of the corporation's board of directors.

Holders of common stock are sometimes asked to approve certain actions proposed by the board. They may be asked to vote on the board's choice of a certified public accountant (CPA) to audit the firm's financial records, or to approve the acquisition of another company through an exchange of stock.

In each of these instances, the stockholder may cast one vote for each share of stock held. A stockholder with 5,000 shares has 5,000 votes. Stockholders who cannot vote in person at a corporate meeting of stockholders are given a chance to vote by proxy. When stockholders sign proxy statements, they give the managers of the corporation the right to vote their shares for them. If stockholders are pleased with the way the company is performing, they willingly give management their voting rights.

Income Rights. As the owners of the company, common stockholders are entitled to receive a share of its after-tax earnings. When distributed to stockholders, these earnings are called dividends. There is no legal requirement that a corporation pay dividends. The decision to do so is made by its board of directors. As explained in the preceding section, whether dividends are paid depends on the earnings record of the firm, its need for capital, and the expectations of stockholders.

Stock Dividends and Stock Splits. In the case of a **stock dividend**, the investor receives additional shares of stock rather than cash. A 10 percent stock dividend involves the distribution of one additional share for every ten shares held. An investor with a hundred shares would receive ten more shares.

stock dividend dividend paid in additional shares of stock rather than cash.

Under a **stock split,** one or more new shares are distributed to stockholders for every share held. A "two-for-one" split is the most common. Here, the investor with 500 shares receives an additional 500 shares. Put another way, 500 old shares have become 1,000 new shares—hence, a two-for-one split. By splitting its shares in this way, the issuing corporation doubles the total number of its shares outstanding.

stock split distribution of one or more new shares to stockholders for every share they already hold.

Figure 20-6 shows how a two-for-one split works. Each investor owns the same percentage of the company after the split as before. Note also that the market price of the stock has been cut in half.

The Reason for Stock Splits. Stocks are most actively bought and sold when their prices fall within a certain range—typically $30 to $90 a share. When the price is too high, many investors buy fewer shares. The Indivisible Diamond Company might split its stock two-for-one when the price reaches $100 a share, bringing it down to a more attractive $50 a share.

Preferred Stock

As explained in Chapter 5, owners of **preferred stock** have first claim to corporate assets once debts have been paid, but they have no voting rights. Preferred stock represents a cross between the other two types of long-term financing we

preferred stock stock whose owners have first claim to corporate assets once debts have been paid but who have no voting rights.

FIGURE 20-6 A Two-for-One Stock Split

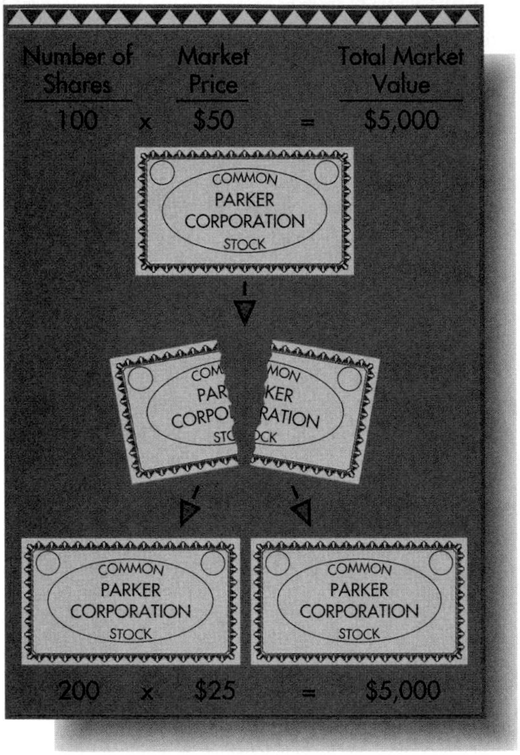

have discussed—corporate bonds and common stock. Like a bond, preferred stock carries a fixed income payment or dividend. But the dividend represents a distribution of corporate profits, not payment of interest on a debt. Consequently, failure of the firm to pay this dividend does not mean default, just as nonpayment of common stock dividends does not mean default. If dividends are not paid to preferred stockholders in a given year, they cannot be paid to common stockholders either. Compared to retained earnings, bonds, and common stock, preferred stock accounts for a small percentage of new corporate financing. In 1990, $7 billion of new preferred stock was sold in the United States, compared to $210 billion in bonds and $36 billion in common stock.

cumulative preferred
preferred stock that carries forward to the next year any dividends not paid in the previous year.

As mentioned, a corporation is not required to pay a preferred stock dividend in any particular year. However, if the stock issue is **cumulative preferred**, dividends not paid in one year are carried forward to the next year. The corporation cannot pay a dividend to its common stockholders until it pays all past and current dividends due to its preferred stockholders. Suppose the Eleusis Pharmaceuticals Company has an issue of cumulative preferred stock paying $2.50 annually as its fixed dividend. Three years pass before the company can afford to pay a dividend. In the fourth year, it must pay $10 per share of preferred stock (4 years × $2.50 a share) before it can pay *any* dividends on common stock.

WHICH SOURCE OF FINANCING IS BEST?

8 We have just looked at four sources of long-term funding for a business: retained earnings, bonds, common stock, and preferred stock. Which source is best? What are the pros and cons of each? Is there a single best mix of long-term funding sources? There are no easy answers to these questions, but let's look at some of the main issues involved. These points are summarized in Table 20-4 from the viewpoint of a corporate treasurer.

Sources of Funds: Pros and Cons

For many smaller businesses, the option of issuing bonds, common stock, or preferred stock is not feasible. They cannot offer the investor a proven record of stability, because they are too small. Such companies rely on retained earnings, personal funds, or family borrowing to fund growth. Moreover, sole proprietorships and partnerships are prohibited by law from issuing common or preferred stock. Only corporations may do so.

Retained Earnings. The big advantage of retained earnings as a way to fund growth is that they are safe. If sales and profits decline, the firm does not need to worry about interest or debt repayment, as it would with bonds. Reinvesting retained earnings is also much less costly than raising money in the stock market.

As a source of funds, however, retained earnings are not without problems. First, they may not be sufficient for the firm to take advantage of all good investment opportunities. Second, a policy of relying on retained earnings may conflict with the dividend expectations of investors. A dollar retained and reinvested is one less dollar paid out in dividends. To the extent that investors expect hefty

TABLE 20-4   Pros and Cons of Sources of Long-Term Financing from the Issuing Corporation's Viewpoint

	Retained Earnings	Bonds	Common Stock	Preferred Stock
Pros	No Repayment Obligation	Interest Is Tax Deductible	No Financial Risk — Dividend Payments Are Not Legally Required	No Financial Risk — Dividend Payments Are Not Legally Required
	Less Costly Than Selling Stock	No Ownership Interest Is Sold		
		Potentially Improves Return On Stockholders' Equity		
Cons	Limited to Past and Current Profits	Bond Interest Payments Are Legally Required	Dividend Payments Are Not Tax Deductible	Dividend Payments Are Not Tax Deductible
	Accumulation of Retained Earnings Means That Dividends Are Not Being Paid		Sale of Additional Shares Dilutes the Ownership of Current Stockholders	

quarterly dividends, the firm may have to look to the capital markets for long-term money.

Bonds. Bonds have at least three advantages as a source of funds. First, they are less expensive than equity securities. Bond interest payments are treated as a business expense and are therefore tax deductible. Also, issuing bonds does not involve a possible loss of control through a takeover, as does the selling of common stock. The firm borrows money rather than trading ownership for money. Finally, issuing bonds allows the firm to increase its rate of return on equity. As discussed earlier, this is known as leverage.

Bonds are not perfect, however. The main problem with them is the risk from the firm's point of view. If the firm cannot make the interest payments on the bonds, it can be taken over by its creditors.

Common Stock. The advantage of issuing common stock is that it does not add to financial risk. Payment of dividends is voluntary, whereas payment of interest charges on bonds is mandatory. At least in this respect, common stock has one big advantage over bonds. However, common stock can be expensive to the firm. One reason is that dividends are paid out of profits, and profits are calculated after payment of income taxes. Unlike bond interest payments, which are tax deductible, dividend payments are not. Also, depending on conditions in the stock market and the confidence of investors, the firm may have to sell many shares of stock to raise the amount of money needed. The more shares issued, the more the price of the stock falls, and the more control is sacrificed by the original stockholders.

Preferred Stock. Our last source of long-term money is preferred stock. Like the buyers of bonds, preferred stockholders do not share in the control of the business; the holders of preferred shares cannot vote on major issues unless the firm is in real trouble financially. This leaves more control in the hands of the common stockholders. Like issuing common stock, issuing preferred stock does not add more risk to the firm. However, preferred stock can be expensive, because dividends are paid with after-tax dollars.

Capital Structure

capital structure   a firm's long-term financing mix, showing the breakdown between debt and equity financing.

Most large companies do not rely on one source of long-term financing but rather on a mix of all four. **Capital structure** is the term used to describe a company's long-term financing mix. Most commonly, it describes the amount of debt capital (bonds) in relation to total equity capital (retained earnings, common stock, and preferred stock).

The right capital structure for a firm depends on many factors. Among them are the type of industry in which the firm operates, the nature of the assets purchased, the prevailing interest rate on debt, and the firm's earnings record.

SUMMARY POINTS

1   The goal of financial management is to maximize the wealth of the stockholders of the firm. Although managers generally follow this goal, they may take a different position when their jobs are threatened because of a possible merger.

2   A financial manager is responsible for acquiring funds and managing them. He or she must also evaluate the trade-off between risk and return in the financial decisions of the firm.

3 Budgets are detailed financial plans showing forecasted revenues and expenses over a specified period. Budgets and control are important because financial managers must plan for events before they occur and then determine if goals have been met. Key budgets include the operating budget, the capital budget, the cash budget, the master budget, and the five-year financial plan.

4 Firms need funds to purchase assets such as equipment and inventory to conduct day-to-day business and support growth. Also, the need for funds may be greater at some times of the year than others. Profits alone are generally not sufficient to support a firm's growth or seasonal need for funds. Financial managers must constantly consider sources of outside financing, so that the right amount of money will be available to the firm at the time it is needed.

5 The financial manager must oversee the management of the firm's cash balances, marketable securities, accounts receivable, inventory, and fixed assets. Prudent cash management involves holding a minimum cash balance to support the firm's short-term needs and transferring additional funds into higher-yielding investments, which are termed marketable securities. To manage accounts receivable, the firm must establish credit standards and monitor customer performance against those standards. Investments in inventory and fixed assets involve tying up funds for a longer time and must be carefully evaluated.

6 Sources of short-term financing include trade credit, unsecured bank loans, commercial paper, and borrowing against receivables and inventory. Trade credit is generally the least expensive and the easiest to acquire, but other sources are also necessary to meet the needs of the firm. Unsecured bank loans can be obtained for up to a specified limit or for a specific purpose. The largest, most creditworthy corporations can cover immediate cash needs by selling commercial paper. Firms can also obtain short-term funds by pledging assets as collateral for secured loans.

7 Long-term financing is important to take care of the permanent financing needs of the firm. Smaller firms may be highly dependent on retained earnings (earnings not paid out as dividends), whereas larger firms also have the option of selling bonds, common stock, or preferred stock. Bonds represent a contractual obligation by the corporation to pay interest to bondholders on a regular basis. Common stockholders represent the primary ownership interest in the firm, and preferred stockholders have a legal position between those of the bondholders and common stockholders.

8 In deciding which sources of financing are best, the financial manager must consider such factors as costs, tax advantages, legal liabilities, and restrictions on the corporation. Retained earnings are safe and less costly than other options, but they may not be sufficient to meet all needs, especially if dividends must be paid. Bonds are a less expensive form of financing than stocks, involve less loss of control, and increase the firm's leverage, but they are risky. Common stock and preferred stock are both expensive but not risky.

REVIEW QUESTIONS

1 What is the generally accepted goal of financial management? What might happen to companies whose financial managers do not follow this goal? **1**

2 What does the term "risk" mean within the context of financial management? Should a firm always invest in the project that promises the highest return? **2**

3 For a firm in a tight financial position, which of the budgets is most important?

4 Are profits alone normally sufficient to provide the necessary financing for a firm?

5 Use Table 20-3 to describe what a DD3

rating by Dun & Bradstreet would tell about a company.

6 What are the three types of trade credit?

7 What is the difference between a line of credit and a revolving credit agreement?

8 What is the difference between pledging accounts receivable and factoring accounts receivable?

9 What are the four major sources of long-term funds?

10 Define retained earnings.

11 What is meant by limited liability as it pertains to common stock?

12 What is meant by cumulative preferred stock?

13 Suggest an advantage and disadvantage for a corporation in issuing bonds.

DISCUSSION QUESTIONS

1 Why do sophisticated financial managers often try to keep their cash balances at a minimum? How can this be accomplished through computers and the banking system?

2 In doing capital budgeting analysis, explain why funds received in the future are worth less than funds held today.

3 How do investors' desires for return affect the dividend policy of a firm?

4 Explain the importance of an investor's owning secured debt as opposed to unsecured debt in the event a company is forced into liquidation.

5 What are three advantages for a corporation in issuing bonds as a source of long-term financing? What is one disadvantage?

EXPERIENTIAL EXERCISES

1 Select three large companies in different industries. Then go to the latest edition of *Moody's Industrial Manual* and look them up. For each company, list the amounts of long-term debt, common stock, preferred stock, and retained earnings shown on the balance sheet. To what factors do you attribute the different capital structures of the three companies?

2 Go to the "Dividend News" section of *The Wall Street Journal,* which normally has one or two short stories daily about companies changing their dividend policy. The stories might refer to changing the amount of the dividend or declaring a stock split or stock dividend. Then look up the company in *Value Line* or *Standard and Poor's Stock Reports.* Does the change in policy reported in the *Journal* appear to be reasonable, based on the information you looked up?

CASES

CASE 20-1
Union Carbide

In November of 1986, Union Carbide Corp. announced a series of moves to reduce interest expenses and restore flexibility in selling assets and entering other businesses. It said it planned to buy back as much as $2.53 billion of its debt and to issue about 65 million shares of common stock.

Earlier in the year, Carbide had taken steps to prevent a takeover by GAF Corp. It had issued a huge amount of debt, bought back 56 percent of its common stock shares, and deliberately made itself less attractive by selling valuable assets.

The debt Carbide now intended to repurchase consisted of high-risk, high-yield "junk bonds" paying an average interest rate of 14.2 percent. To make the purchases, Carbide would borrow money at interest rates of 10 percent to 11.5 percent. The company planned to buy back the securities at premiums of 15 percent to 33 percent above face value. Carbide said it planned to finance about $2 billion of the planned buyback through a bank credit agreement. The borrowings would be repaid with proceeds from the planned sale of less important divisions and the sale of common shares. The borrowings could include restrictions on Carbide's ability to pay future dividends, but these borrowings were not expected to interfere with the company's current dividend.

Because Carbide would be buying back the securities at a higher price than it carried them on the books, the plan would result in an after-tax charge of as much as $401 million. But analysts were generally pleased with the plan. They said the step would give Carbide the flexibility to make major moves into new businesses. The plan could slice $100 million from annual interest payments.

1. Why was Carbide willing to accept an after-tax charge of over $400 million in order to make these changes?
2. What would be the benefits to Carbide of replacing junk bonds with new debt? The drawbacks?
3. What would be the benefits to Carbide of issuing more common shares? The drawbacks?
4. If you were a current holder of Carbide common stock, how would you feel about Carbide's moves? Why?

Source: B. Meier, "Carbide Plans Debt Buyback of $2.53 Billion," *Wall Street Journal,* 5 November 1986, p. 3.

CASE 20-2
Houston Drilling Company

Houston Drilling Company builds offshore fixed platforms and marine pipelines for the oil and gas industry. The company works primarily in the Mideast, Mexico, and Alaska.

The company has had a long-standing policy of paying a cash dividend. Because earnings did not improve from 1987 to 1990, the dividend remained constant at $.80 per share. For the preceding decade, the annual dividend payment had grown by approximately 10 percent per year.

With 16,540,000 shares outstanding, the $.80 dividend was costing the firm $13,232,000 per year. Earnings for 1991 were projected to be $28,500,000, so dividend payments would represent 46.4 percent of earnings. The remaining $15,268,000 in retained earnings was to be set aside for investments in new equipment.

The only problem was that the $15,268,000 to be set aside for investments fell far short of the amount needed for potentially profitable projects. New investments costing $24 million, all with return potential of over 20 percent, could be undertaken in 1991. Al Delgado, the chief financial officer, thought about cutting back dividend payments so that the extra funds could be redeployed in the firm. On the other hand, he was concerned about how current stockholders would react to a reduction in dividend payments. Another alternative was to keep the dividends at their current level but borrow additional funds. Texas Commerce Bank in Houston was willing to engage in a revolving credit agreement, in which up to $10 million could be borrowed at 10.25 percent interest.

Since the firm had never issued preferred stock before, this was also considered as an alternative. The firm's investment banker, A. G. Edwards and Sons, figured that $10 million in cumulative preferred stock could be issued at $100 per share, with a dividend requirement of $9 per share. Under this arrangement, there would be 100,000 shares of preferred stock outstanding.

Because Houston Drilling Company had received unsolicited buyout offers from both Dresser Industries and Halliburton in the last twelve months, it was very concerned about how its dividend/investment policy would affect the value of its shares. The management of Houston Drilling Company was afraid that if the firm's stock price declined from its current trading range of $25 to $30, the takeover offers (which were in the range of $35 to $40 per share) would appear too attractive to turn down.

1. In your opinion, what factors might determine whether cutting the cash dividend would have a negative effect on the stock price?

2. If the firm decides to continue paying its current dividend but borrows funds to carry out all its desired investments for this year, how much must be borrowed? What will the interest expense be for the year?

3. What is the tax advantage of issuing debt instead of preferred stock?

4. If $10 million of cumulative preferred stock is issued, and the firm fails to make dividend payments for four years, how much will Houston Drilling Company be behind in its dividend payment obligation? Can it continue to pay dividends to common stockholders while it is behind on dividend payments to preferred stockholders?

5. Does the management of Houston Drilling seem to be concerned about stockholder wealth maximization?

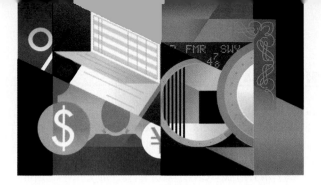

CHAPTER 21

The Securities Markets

OBJECTIVES

After studying this chapter, you should be able to:

1 Explain how the securities markets allow a firm to raise capital.

2 Describe the seven objectives of a personal investment program.

3 Describe the major U.S. security exchanges.

4 Explain the process through which stocks are bought and sold.

5 Describe speculative trading tactics by which the investor tries to make money on rapid movements in the market.

6 Discuss how stocks are valued in the marketplace.

7 Describe other investments besides stocks, such as bonds, options, and financial futures.

8 Explain the characteristics of different types of mutual funds.

9 Describe the role of stock market indicators in assessing how well an investor is doing compared to the market.

Rita Jensen was a junior at Texas Christian University (TCU), majoring in finance. Two weeks before the end of spring term, Rita was excited to hear that she had been accepted into the student-managed Educational Investment Fund. This meant that she would get six hours of academic credit in her senior year for helping to manage $1.2 million dollars of the university's endowment fund. Although this represented only a small percentage of the university's total funds, it seemed like all the money in the world to the 16 students who were selected to participate in the program.

Part of Rita's responsibility would be to analyze six stocks or bonds. She would write a report on each firm and actually make a buy or sell recommendation. She was aware that each recommendation would involve $30,000 to $40,000 of the university's money. This represented a lot of responsibility and pressure for Rita, whose prior job experience was as a bookstore employee making $4 an hour. She had already taken a number of finance courses, and now she planned to spend the summer before her senior year reading everything she could find about what was going on in the stock market. Rita kept asking herself, "What do I really need to know?"

In this chapter, we will look at what Rita will need to know about the securities markets. We will examine the stock exchanges, discuss how stocks are bought and sold, and consider some speculative trading tactics. Then we will discuss mutual funds and close by presenting some stock market indicators. We will look at the securities markets from the perspectives of both the firm and the investor.

PERSPECTIVE OF THE FIRM

securities *stocks and bonds, issued by corporations and government bodies, that can be bought and sold in securities markets.*

securities markets *a central place where organizations can sell stocks and bonds to raise money for expansion and where investors can buy and sell stocks.*

primary market *the use of securities markets by firms to sell new issues of stocks or bonds to investors.*

investment bankers *companies that help firms raise needed capital in the securities markets by underwriting the sale of new stock or bond issues.*

underwriting *the agreement by investment bankers to buy new issues of stocks or bonds from the issuing corporation and resell them to the public.*

Securities are stocks and bonds, issued by corporations and government bodies, that can be bought and sold in securities markets. **Securities markets** perform two essential functions for a business. First, they provide a ready way for the firm to raise money for industrial expansion. Second, they provide a central place where the firm's stocks and bonds can be traded.

New Issues

As stated in Chapter 20, businesses raise long-term money through retaining earnings, selling common or preferred stock, or issuing bonds. When a firm sells a new issue of stocks or bonds in the securities markets to raise capital, it is said to be using the **primary market**.

Investment Bankers as Underwriters. **Investment bankers** help firms raise needed capital in the securities markets by underwriting the sale of new stock or bond issues. **Underwriting** means that the investment banker agrees to buy stocks or bonds from the issuing corporation and resell them to the public. If the price of the security falls during the distribution process, or part of the issue remains unsold, then the investment banker bears the loss. The investment banking firm is essentially the risk taker during the distribution of securities.

Since a stock offering may be for hundreds of millions of dollars, investment bankers often form partnerships when underwriting issues. In this way they reduce their loss if the security does not sell for as much as expected.

Other Investment Banking Services. Investment banks perform other services, too. They help the issuing firm register the stock or bond sale with the Securities and Exchange commission. They also market some of the shares to large investors, such as pension funds and insurance companies, as well as to smaller investors through their brokerage offices around the country. The fee charged by investment banks is usually about 1 to 3 percent of the total value of the security issue.

Outstanding Issues

outstanding issues *securities already sold by the issuing firm, which can now be bought and sold by investors.*

secondary market *the use of securities markets by investors for buying and selling securities with each other.*

The main reason why people are willing to buy *new* securities is that the securities can eventually be resold to other investors. **Outstanding issues** are securities already sold by the issuing firm, which can now be bought and sold among investors. All trading that takes **place** between investors is referred to as the **secondary market.** Secondary trading is not a source of new capital for a firm. It involves transactions between investors, not between an issuing firm and an investor. If you bought 100 shares of Westinghouse stock through your broker, you would probably be buying stock that someone else previously owned. Accordingly, your payment would indirectly go to the previous owner, not to the company that issued the stock. Active trading in the outstanding shares of a firm's stock makes it easier for the firm to issue new shares in the future, because it indicates interest in the firm's stock.

Secondary trading in the securities markets is also important to the firm because its new stock and bond offerings are priced in relation to its currently traded securities. Investment bankers generally advise that new stock offerings be priced at least 5 percent below their current market price and new bond offers 3 percent below their current price.

PERSPECTIVE OF THE INVESTOR

Most of the 50 million people who own shares in U.S. corporations are not looking to make a "killing" in the market. Rather, their aim is to make a reasonable return on their investments. This is as true of stock investors as it is of bond investors. Other buyers of securities try to maximize short-term gain. These people, called **speculators,** are willing to accept greater risk if it means a potentially greater profit.

speculators *those who are willing to accept greater risk in the securities market if it means a potentially greater profit.*

Ultimately, most investors tend to allocate their investments based on their situation in life. After you have read this chapter, refer to the box on page 582, the Investor Profile, to see where you or your family fits in terms of investor characteristics and types of investments. Some students choose to send a copy of the material to their main financial supporter (mom or dad), then compute their score and follow this up with a suggestion for the most appropriate type of investments.

Let's look at the seven objectives of a personal investment program. Although their order of importance depends on the particular investor, the first is of great importance to all investors.

By choosing investments carefully, a person can achieve the combination of safety, liquidity, stability, inflation protection, tax advantages, appreciation, and ease of management that is right for him or her. Which of the investments pictured above is riskiest? Which is most liquid? Which might offer the greatest tax advantages?

Safety of Principal

All investors are concerned about the safety of their investments. The price of a stock or bond sometimes falls below the amount paid for it, but there is always the hope that the price will bounce back.

There are two basic ways to safeguard investment principal: careful analysis and diversification. Most smart investors examine various financial, managerial, and marketing characteristics of each company in which they are considering buying stock. They want to know how strong a company is and what its prospects are. They look at the general health of the industry in which the firm operates. In this way, they avoid investing in risky companies or in industries without much growth potential.

Smart investors also use **diversification** to protect their investments—that is, they don't buy too much of any one stock or bond. Instead, they buy a variety of stocks and bonds in many different companies, representing many different industries. Thus, if the price of one stock falls, the investor has not lost all of his or her money.

diversification buying a variety of stocks or bonds in many different companies in different industries, to reduce risk.

Liquidity

Most investors like to have some assets that they can quickly turn into cash—cash that might be used for a family emergency or to take advantage of an unusual investment opportunity. One of the big advantages of stocks and bonds as an investment is that they are liquid. That is, they can be converted to cash quickly, especially if they are regularly traded in one of the big securities markets. Normally, it takes only about five business days for the seller to receive the money from the sale of a security.

Stability of Income

Some investors buy stocks and bonds because they pay high dividends. Many retired people, for example, supplement their social security and retirement incomes with dividend income. If dividends are a large part of the investor's income, stability of dividend payment over time can be an important investment objective. This type of investor looks to such companies as IBM, Wisconsin Electric, and General Electric. These companies have long histories of paying dividends regularly. Figure 21-1 shows the dividend payments of IBM for 1970 to 1990.

Protection Against Inflation

Investors are concerned about inflation. If you are going to tie up money for a period of time in an investment, you want to make sure that when you withdraw the funds, you will have increased purchasing power. This consideration is particularly important to people who are on fixed incomes or are approaching retirement age. However, inflation is also an important consideration to a student completing college. Do you realize with 6 percent inflation over the next 40 years, the cost of a meal at a nice restaurant would go from $25 to $257? That means a dinner for four would cost $1,028 (before the tip). Also, a $55 textbook would be marked up to $563.75. Furthermore, the average price of a house in the U.S. would increase from $90,000 to $925,740. Investments must be able to keep up with inflation over both the short term and the long term.

FIGURE 21-1   Dividends per Share of IBM Stock, 1970–1990.

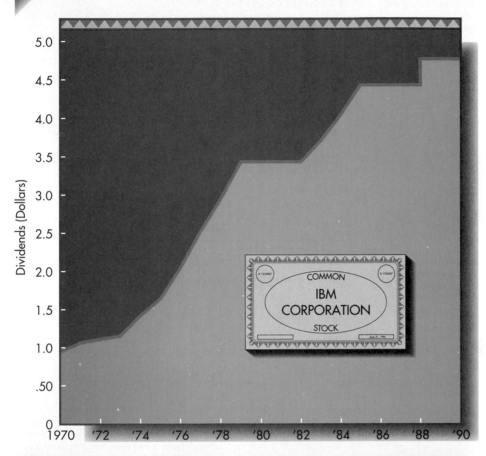

In times of rapidly rising prices, tangible investments such as fine art are especially attractive, since their value is not eroded by inflation.

Investor Profile

Profile Analysis: What Should You Invest in Now?

Directions: Circle the answer that most nearly applies to you or your family. Write the number in the space at right. Then add up the numbers and divide by 9 to get a median score.

AGE—My age is closest to:

(9) 30	(7) 40	(5) 50	(3) 60	(1) 70	_____

INCOME—My present annual income from all sources is nearest to (in thousands):

(2) 10	(4) 20	(5) 30	(6) 40	(8) 50	_____

ANNUAL EXPENSES—In relation to income, my annual expenses approximate:

(1) 100%	(3) 90%	(5) 80%	(7) 70%	(9) 50%	_____

NUMBER OF DEPENDENTS—I presently have these dependents:

(9) 0	(8) 1	(6) 2–3	(4) 4–5	(1) 6 or more	_____

ESTIMATED VALUE OF ASSETS—My house, insurance, savings, and investments total (in thousands):

(1) 50	(3) 100	(5) 250	(7) 350	(9) 500 or more	_____

LIABILITIES—My bills, mortgages, installment payments, and debts in relation to assets approximate (in thousands):

(9) 30%	(7) 50%	(5) 75%	(3) 90%	(1) 100%	_____

SAVINGS—I have cash on hand in savings or other liquid assets to equal this amount of expenses:

(1) 1 month	(3) 2 months	(5) 3 months	(7) 4 months	(9) 6 months or more	_____

LIFE INSURANCE—My life insurance coverage equals (in thousands):

(9) 250	(7) 150	(5) 100	(3) 50	(1) 25 or less	_____

HEALTH INSURANCE—My health insurance coverage includes:

(9) Basic, major medical, catastrophic	(5) Major medical plus basic	(1) Basic	_____

Add up your scores and divide by 9 to get the average. Then consider the investment strategies that follow.

The investment strategy rating numbers below correlate with the average score you got from the profile analysis. The investment strategy ratings indicate investment categories ranging from (1) ultraconservative to (9) highly speculative. By matching the profile score with the nearest investment strategy numbers, you get some feel for investments that may be appropriate for you. You would probably choose from two or three categories.

1. Insured savings accounts.
2. High-grade government securities.
3. High-quality corporate and municipal bonds, preferred stocks, investment trusts, and annuity income.
4. Lower-rated corporate and municipal bonds, preferred stocks, investment trusts, convertible bonds and preferred stocks, and variable insurance.
5. Higher-rated common stocks and investment trusts and investment annuities.
6. Lower-rated common stocks and investment trusts.
7. Speculative bonds, stocks, and investment trusts.
8. Gold and silver-related investments and foreign investment trusts.
9. Rare and exotic investments: stamps, rare coins, art, antiques, gems and jewelry, rare books, autographs, prints, and lithographs.

Source: Excerpts from HOW TO MAKE MONEY DURING INFLATION RECESSION by the Editors of Consumer Guide with Peter A. Dickenson. © 1980 by Publications International Ltd. Reprinted by permission of Harper Collins Publishers.

Tax Considerations

You cannot always predict whether your investment will go up or down, but you can generally determine the tax consequences. If you are in a relatively high tax bracket (such as 31 percent), you will want investments that have tax advantages. An example might be a **municipal bond** issued by a city or state, because the interest is exempted from federal taxation (and in many cases state taxation as

municipal bond a bond issued by a city or state on which the interest is exempted from federal taxation.

well). Also, for the young investor, an **individual retirement account (IRA)** might be desirable. Why? Because the contributions that go into the IRA are tax deductible, and the taxes on all future returns on the funds in the IRA are not due until retirement.

individual retirement account (IRA)   a savings plan in which all contributions are tax deductible and all future returns on the funds are not taxed until retirement.

Appreciation in Value

People buy stocks and bonds not only for safety of principal, but also because they hope the price of the security will rise. The stock and bond markets are highly irregular. The price of the average security fluctuates by as much as 20 percent a year. By purchasing the right stock at the right time and by selling it at the right time, the investor can make a very good return indeed.

Ease of Management

Speculators spend a great deal of time watching their investments. They read *The Wall Street Journal* every morning and visit their stockbroker several times a week. However, many investors buy stocks or bonds and hold them for a long time. The last thing they want is constant worry over whether they should sell their shares and buy something else.

The less hassle an investor is willing to tolerate, the better the grade of stock or bond that should be purchased. Even with high-grade ("blue-chip") stocks, however, it is sometimes necessary to sell the stock and buy something else. For many years, the automobile companies were a growth business—the stock of Ford, General Motors, and Chrysler all performed very well. In recent years, the U.S. auto industry has taken a beating as more and more consumers have chosen imported cars. This was particularly evident in 1991, when the Big Three automakers had their largest operating losses in history, and their stocks declined accordingly. Many investors switched to other industries that involved less stress in the management of their portfolios.

THE STOCK EXCHANGES

Ownership shares in corporations are bought and sold through stock exchanges. The New York Stock Exchange and the American Stock Exchange are the two national exchanges. Several regional exchanges and the over-the-counter market also play a vital role in the buying and selling of securities.

New York Stock Exchange

The New York Stock Exchange (NYSE), founded in 1792 only a few blocks from its current location on Wall Street, is an association of 1,469 members, 1,366 of whom own "seats" on the exchange. A seat on the New York Stock Exchange sells for as much as $500,000. The other 103 members pay an annual fee to have access to the trading floor. The purpose of the New York Stock Exchange is to help its members buy and sell stock for their customers. To accomplish this, the exchange provides a building for conducting stock transactions, modern communications equipment for reporting those transactions, and a set of regulations governing all transactions.

In the frenetic activity of the New York Stock Exchange, the financial health of many major corporations is assessed, and the value of many people's investments changes accordingly.

Only stocks listed on the exchange can be traded there. Today, more than 1,500 companies are listed on the New York Stock Exchange. They are generally the older, bigger companies. To be considered for listing on the "Big Board," as it is called, a company must have at least 1.1 million shares of common stock outstanding and $2.5 million in pretax income for the preceding year. Although the New York Stock Exchange traded the stocks of less than one quarter of 1 percent of the nation's corporations in 1990, the value of stock traded on the exchange during that year was more than $2 trillion.

American Stock Exchange

The American Stock Exchange (AMEX) is like the New York Stock Exchange, except that the companies listed there are not nearly as large or as powerful as those listed on the NYSE. They are generally small to medium-size businesses with potential for growth. Each of the 780 companies listed on the AMEX has at least 500,000 shares of stock outstanding. Also, to be considered for listing, a company must show a pretax income of $750,000 or more for the preceding year.

Many companies try to move from the AMEX to the NYSE in the belief that the Big Board attracts more attention. However, many large companies are listed on the AMEX, including Imperial Oil Limited, Wickes Companies, The New York Times Company, and Wang Laboratories. In 1990, the volume of trading in common stock was over $50 billion.

Regional Exchanges

regional exchanges *stock exchanges located outside of New York City.*

There are several **regional exchanges** in the United States, located in Chicago, Boston, Cincinnati, Philadelphia, and San Francisco. Early in their existence, the regional exchanges traded securities of local firms only. As the firms grew, they

TABLE 21-1   *Breakdown of Trading Between the New York Stock Exchange and Other Markets*

By Market	Thur	Wed	Week Ago
New York	155,140,000	172,330,000	164,770,00
Midwest	9,979,800	9,711,600	9,213,500
Pacific	6,236,700	6,694,200	6,613,100
NASD	11,107,770	8,766,710	14,111,080
Phila	3,226,400	3,339,700	2,864,500
Boston	3,337,600	3,340,800	2,874,400
Cincinnati	1,176,200	1,077,900	1,077,700
Instinet	118,800	317,100	227,100
Composite	190,323,270	205,578,010	201,751,380

Source: *Wall Street Journal,* 25 May 1990, p. C2.

would be listed on the national exchanges but also continued to trade on the regional exchange. A classic example is Sears, which started in Chicago.

Most of the trading volume on the regional exchanges today involves securities that are also listed on the New York Stock Exchange. This is referred to as **dual trading**. Table 21-1 shows the number of shares of firms listed on the New York Stock Exchange that were traded there and elsewhere. (The American Stock Exchange does not allow dual trading with stocks on the New York Stock Exchange, so it is not shown in the table.) The figures represent total shares traded. Typical daily volume is 150 to 200 million shares, so these were normal days in terms of market activity.

dual trading   *trading in the same security on the New York Stock Exchange and on regional exchanges.*

Why would some stocks trade on two or more exchanges? Perhaps a better price can be found at one exchange or the other at different times of the day. Another reason is that some markets are in different time zones. Because the Pacific Exchange in San Francisco is three hours behind New York, investors can still trade on the Pacific Exchange well after the New York Stock Exchange has closed at 4 P.M. Eastern Standard Time.

Over-the-Counter Market

The term **over-the-counter (OTC) market** is misleading: There is no counter and there is no market in the sense of one place where traders come together to buy and sell stock. It is a way of trading stocks rather than a central place for trading them.

over-the-counter (OTC) market   *trading stocks through a computerized service that transmits information from various locations instead of through a central marketplace.*

The over-the-counter market was originally a complex network of brokers who communicated with one another by telephone. Today, the OTC market has an automated computer service called NASDAQ (the National Association of Securities Dealers Automated Quotations). This service collects, stores, and displays on computer terminals in brokers' offices the prices of about 5,000 of the most actively traded OTC stocks. All other OTC stocks are still sold the old way.

Approximately 30,000 stocks are periodically traded on the over-the-counter market. This compares to approximately 1,500 companies listed on the New York Stock Exchange and fewer than 800 on the American Stock Exchange. Although many firms whose stocks are traded over the counter are small, there are many exceptions, including Apple Computer, Coors Brewing, Intel, MCI Communications, Liz Claiborne, and Mack Trucks. Actually, 700 of the 30,000 over-the-counter firms could meet the rigorous listing requirements of the New York Stock Exchange if they so chose, but they prefer the NASDAQ system, in which there is open competition for trades.

HOW STOCKS ARE BOUGHT AND SOLD

 The way in which stocks and bonds are sold is fascinating. Just as with any other good or service, there must be a buyer, a seller, and an agreed-upon selling price. The buying and selling of stocks and bonds is different from the buying and selling of consumer goods in that securities' prices are not set by the seller alone.

Post Trading and Price Setting

post trading *a system of stock trading in which each stock traded is assigned to a specific "post" or trading area.*

Most stock exchanges use a **post trading** system; that is, each stock traded on the exchange is assigned to a "post," or trading area. Any broker with an order to buy or sell walks over to that area and attempts to make a trade for the stock.

Prices in the secondary market are determined in an auction. Buyers and sellers converge at the trading area and bid on a particular stock. For example, at 2:30 on Wednesday afternoon, suppose five traders want to buy Delta Air Lines stock and ten want to sell it. Unless at least one buyer and one seller agree upon a price, there won't be a sale. It is important to remember that a stock exchange does not buy and sell stock itself, nor does it even set the price of stocks. It is

Commission brokers are the ones who actually carry out customers' stock transactions on the floor of the exchange.

FIGURE 21-2   Reading a Stock Quotation Reported in *Wall Street Journal*,
31 May 1990.

52 Weeks		Stock	Div.	Yd. %	P-E Ratio	Sales 100s	High	Low	Close	Net Chg.
High	Low									
$75\frac{3}{4}$	$54\frac{1}{2}$	Pfizer	$2.40	3.8	15	4861	$62\frac{3}{4}$	$62\frac{7}{8}$	$63\frac{5}{8}$	$+\frac{1}{2}$
(1)	(2)	(3)	(4)	(5)	(6)	(7)	(8)	(9)	(10)	(11)

(1) The highest price paid for Pfizer common stock in the past year.
(2) The lowest price paid for Pfizer common stock in the past year.
(3) The name of the company, or an abbreviation.
(4) The annual dividend per share.
(5) The current annual yield, computed by dividing the dividend by the closing price.
(6) The price-earnings ratio, computed by dividing the current price of a share by annual earnings per share.
(7) The number of shares sold for the day reported, expressed in lots of 100.
(8) The highest selling price for the day.
(9) The lowest selling price for the day.
(10) The price per share when the exchange closed that day.
(11) The change from the closing price of the previous day.

merely a place for traders to come together to buy and sell. What determines the selling price of a stock is the strength of demand for it in relation to the extent of supply. In other words, selling price depends on how much buyers are willing to pay and how much sellers are willing to accept. Figure 21-2 explains how to read stock price quotations in the *Wall Street Journal*.

Role of the Stockbroker

As Figure 21-3 shows, the process of buying or selling a stock begins with a call to a **stockbroker**. The stockbroker wires the investor's buy or sell instructions to a commission broker on the floor of an exchange. The **commission broker** is the one who walks over to the trading area and buys or sells the stock for the stockbroker's customer. The commission broker often works for the same company as the stockbroker.

Besides relaying messages to commission brokers, many stockbrokers perform other services for their customers. They make available expensive financial periodicals and reporting services, such as *Value Line Investment Survey*. Some brokerage firms have research departments that study the stock market and selected companies, sharing the results with the brokers' customers. Some firms have a trading room where traders can watch reports from the stock market.

Type of Order

We mentioned earlier that the stockbroker wires the investor's instructions to a commission broker who works on the floor of the exchange. These instructions specify the name of the stock to be traded, the number of shares to be traded, and type of order—that is, how the stock is to be traded. The three different types of stock orders are market order, limit order, and stop order.

stockbroker   the person who initiates the buying or selling of a stock by wiring the instructions to a commission broker on the floor of an exchange.

commission broker   the person on the floor of the exchange who walks over to the trading areas and fulfills the instructions of a stockbroker's customer.

FIGURE 21-3   How Stocks Are Bought and Sold

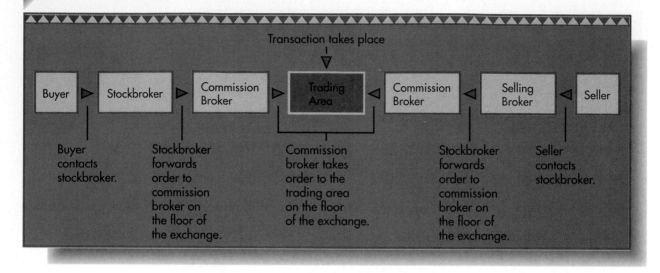

market order *an investor's instruction that authorizes the commission broker to buy or sell a stock at the best possible price.*

Market Order. Under a **market order,** the most common type of stock order, the commission broker has the authority to buy or sell the stock at the best possible price. If the stock involved is traded actively, the investor knows that the selling or purchase price of the stock will be roughly the same as it was when the stock was last traded. Market orders can usually be carried out in fewer than five minutes.

limit order *an investor's instruction that requires the commission broker to purchase the stock only at a certain price, or lower, or sell it at a certain price, or higher.*

Limit Order. A **limit order** "limits" the action that the commission broker can take. Specifically, the customer, working through a stockbroker, instructs the commission broker that the stock in question is to be purchased at a certain price, or lower, or sold at a certain price, or higher. For example, an investor, believing that Circuit City is a good buy at $35, issues a limit order to purchase 200 shares of Circuit City at $35 or below. This type of order prohibits the broker from paying more than $35 for the stock.

stop order *an investor's instruction that requires the commission broker to buy or sell stock when the price reaches a specified figure, to protect a gain or minimize a loss.*

Stop Order. A **stop order** is an instruction to protect a stock price gain or to minimize a price loss. For example, suppose that six weeks ago, you purchased stock in Union Carbide at $23 a share. The price of the stock is now $27 a share. Believing the stock will go even higher, you decide to hold on to it for a while, but you're also concerned about a possible price decline. Since you want to make at least some profit on your stock purchase, you place a stop order at $25. That is, you tell your stockbroker to issue a sell order to the commission broker if the price falls to $25. You're protected against a severe price decline, because the commission broker automatically sells the stock when it hits $25. The problem with a stop order is that the stock price might slide to $25 once during the day and bounce back to $29 by the close of the afternoon trading. In that case, you would have been ahead $4 a share if you hadn't given the stop order.

Round Lots and Odd Lots

round lots *stock traded in lots of 100.*

Stock trading is usually conducted in **round lots** of 100: 100 shares, 200 shares, 300 shares, and so on. These round-lot transactions are handled by commission brokers. Round-lot purchases are often too expensive for the individual investor. On July 16, 1990, it would have cost over $60,000 to buy a round lot of 100 shares of Capital Cities/ABC Inc. Not many small investors could afford that much and still make an attempt to diversify their holdings.

Odd lots, on the other hand, refer to transactions involving fewer than 100 shares. The problem with odd-lot transactions, such as nine shares of Motorola stock, is that it is not always possible to find someone who wants to buy or sell exactly nine shares.

odd lots   stock transactions involving fewer than 100 shares.

To trade odd lots effectively, stock exchanges employ the services of odd-lot brokers. These brokers combine several odd lots to make a round lot, which can then be sold all at once. Most stockbrokers charge an extra fee for handling odd-lot transactions.

Trading Specialists

Another important person in the making of a market for securities is the specialist. The job of the specialist is to stay at one trading area and watch all trading in a particular stock. Specialists perform two vital functions. First, they assist commission brokers trying to buy or sell a large number of stocks. As part of the process, they keep a "book" on all existing orders. When a commission broker for a buyer or seller approaches them, they are able to match the order in most cases. Generally, commission brokers and specialists work for different firms, each emphasizing its own particular function.

Second, specialists help to stabilize the price for their particular stock by buying and selling it on a regular basis. If a commission broker wants to buy a stock at $41 but sellers won't take anything less than $42, the specialist will offer to buy or sell stock at a price between $41 and $42. Although specialists cannot prevent all short-term fluctuations in stock prices, they do minimize such fluctuations.

The profile in this chapter describes the career of Ralph Wright, a successful specialist on the New York Stock Exchange.

Transaction Costs

Securities transactions are not without cost to investors. Until the mid-1970s, there was little mystery as to the cost of buying or selling securities. A well-publicized fee schedule prevailed throughout the brokerage industry. That changed in 1975, when the Securities and Exchange Commission (SEC) ruled that investors had the right to negotiate transactions costs with their stockbrokers. The Securities and Exchange Commission is a powerful federal agency that regulates the sale of securities in the United States.

Many informed people in the industry thought that this ruling would bring down the established brokerage houses and encourage cutthroat price competition. However, it is now clear that the SEC's pricing decision did not cause panic in the stock market or destroy any of the big brokerage houses. They adjusted to the new market rules.

Full-Service Brokers.   Earlier in this chapter, we pointed out that stockbrokers not only buy and sell stocks but also provide research and other services to their customers. This type of stockbroker is referred to as a **full-service broker**. Merrill Lynch, Pierce, Fenner & Smith is the largest full-service firm in the brokerage industry.

full-service brokers   stockbrokers who buy and sell stocks and also provide research and other services to their customers.

Ralph Wright

Ralph Wright is the son of a Newark, New Jersey, automobile assembly plant worker. When he graduated from high school, Ralph needed a job. On the recommendation of his future brother-in-law, he went to the New York Stock Exchange to look for a position.

When most people think about the Stock Exchange, they see only the brokers rushing about the floor of the Exchange. They fail to realize that hundreds of people back up the trading on the floor. Wright knows these people, because he has moved up to the specialist position from the very bottom of the ladder. He started as a carrier, then became a page, a tube clerk, and finally an Exchange reporter. The first three positions all involved moving documents on the floor of the exchange. As a reporter, he accompanied a specialist at his post, recording the specialist's purchases and sales.

Specialists employed by Carl H. Pforzheimer & Co., one of the oldest firms trading on the floor, recognized Wright's skills and asked him to join their company. He started as a clerk again and after three years had worked his way to senior clerk. In 1981, when he was a clerk for a specialist who had been trading in Standard Oil (Indiana) stock, Wright's diligence in fulfilling his duties during the dramatic rise in Standard Oil's stock brought him to the attention of the managing partners of the firm. As a result, Wright became the first black specialist on the floor of the New York Stock Exchange, at the age of 30.

As a specialist, Wright was responsible for overseeing all transactions relating to several major stocks listed on the Exchange and allocated to Pforzheimer. Specialist firms, like Pforzheimer, authorize their traders to buy and sell stock of their client companies (such as Standard Oil) regularly, using Pforzheimer's capital, in order to stabilize the stock price and minimize price fluctuations. When brokers give limit orders, the specialist makes commissions on these purchases or sales. Wright recorded orders in a book he kept for each stock. His records had to be in meticulous order and perfectly accurate at every moment.

A specialist firm hopes to make a profit on its own ownership positions, which—in the case of the several companies mentioned above—were managed by Wright. When he wasn't committed to buying stock for limit orders, he could make purchases for his company with credit extended by his firm. Often he would buy and then resell the stock on the same day, or even within the same hour, if prices changed dramatically. He might also buy stock at times just to give liquidity to the market while also fulfilling his specialist function.

Specialists are not chosen right out of business schools. They spend years in lower positions, learning the ropes of trading on the floor and contributing to their firm's success. The main factor that gets a clerk promoted to specialist is the ability to make money. Ralph Wright has demonstrated that ability.

When you make money, you are in demand. This is true of Ralph Wright, who parlayed his prior work experience into an even better position with the J.J.C. Inc. specialist division of Quick and Reilly, a New York Stock Exchange firm.

Discount Brokers. One outcome of the 1975 SEC ruling on commissions was the development of the so-called discount brokerage houses. The fees that **discount brokers** charge their customers are 30 to 70 percent lower than the fees that the full-service brokers charge. Not surprisingly, therefore, discount stockbrokers do not usually offer research services to their customers. Most of them also do not maintain local offices. Buy and sell orders are executed over the telephone via a toll free long-distance number, and the stock is distributed through the mail.

discount brokers stockbrokers who offer only a few services to customers but charge considerably lower fees for handling stock transactions than full-service brokers.

SPECULATIVE TRADING TACTICS

Most investors buy securities and hold them for a reasonably long time. Others are interested in turning a profit within a few months, weeks, or even hours. Speculative trading, as it is called, is quite risky. One speculator who got carried away in his questionable trading activity was Michael Milken, as indicated in the Ethical Issue on page 594. Normally speculators stand to make a great deal of money very quickly or lose a great deal of money just as quickly—all honestly. Speculators use different trading tactics depending on whether they believe stock prices are heading up or down. Two of the most popular trading tactics are selling short and buying on margin.

Selling Short

We usually cannot sell something until we have first bought it. In a short sale, however, the investor first sells the stock and then buys it! **Selling short** is an ingenious tactic, because it gives the investor a chance to make money when stock prices are falling. Investors normally make money when their stocks increase in value.

selling short a speculative technique that involves selling stock before purchasing it, to try to make money when stock prices are falling.

To sell short, the investor borrows the stock from the brokers and then sells it. The proceeds from the sale are held by the broker as collateral on the borrowed stock. On instruction from the investor, the broker later buys the stock back. The broker keeps the stock, and the investor keeps the difference between the high selling price and the low purchase price.

Investors sell short when they think that the price of a particular stock will fall. Suppose Polaroid is currently selling at $50 a share. Investor Dan Daring believes that the price will soon slide to $40. Dan borrows 100 shares from a broker and sells them at the current price of $50 in the hope of buying the shares back in a few weeks for only $40. The difference between the selling price, $50 a share, and the purchase price, $40, is Dan's profit.

But suppose that Dan Daring is wrong, and the price of Polaroid goes up instead of down. What happens then? Dan loses money.

Buying on Margin

When **buying on margin,** the investor finances part of a stock purchase with borrowed money. Currently, investors may borrow up to 50 percent of the purchase price. Margin requirements are set by the Board of Governors of the Federal Reserve.

buying on margin a speculative practice in which an investor finances part of a stock purchase with borrowed money.

Table 21-2 shows how margin trading works. The investor in the figure, Francine Fearless, wants to buy 100 shares of AT&T stock at $50 a share. She can either put up the $5,000 herself ($50 × 100 shares) or borrow up to $2,500 from her stockbroker. Suppose that AT&T goes to $60 in a year. If Francine

TABLE 21-2   Impact of Buying Stock on Margin in Good Times and Bad Times

	Initial Cash Purchase	Initial Margin Purchase	Cash Purchase One Year Later		Margin Purchase One Year Later	
			Good Times	Bad Times	Good Times	Bad Times
Selling Price	$ 50	$ 50	$ 60	$ 40	$ 60	$ 40
Number of Shares	100	100	100	100	100	100
Total Value of Investment	$5,000	$5,000	$6,000	$4,000	$6,000	$4,000
Investor's Cash	$5,000	$2,500	$5,000	$5,000	$2,500	$2,500
Borrowed Cash	None	$2,500	None	None	$2,500	$2,500
Interest Charges			None	None	$ 250*	$ 250*
Net Profit (Loss)			$1,000	($1,000)	$ 750	$1,250
% Return on Investment			$\frac{1,000}{5,000}$ =20%	$\frac{(1,000)}{5,000}$ =(20%)	$\frac{750}{2,500}$ =30%	$\frac{1,250}{2,500}$ =(50%)

* *Interest charge in the example is 10% of $2,500, or $250.*

had put up all the money herself, she would have made a return of $1,000 ($6,000 − $5,000), or 20 percent ($\frac{\$6,000 - \$5,000}{\$5,000}$). But if she had invested $2,500 of her own money and borrowed the other $2,500 from her broker, paying a total of $250 in interest charges on this borrowed money, the return on her investment of $2,500 would have been $750 ($1,000 − $250), or 30 percent ($\frac{\$1,000 - \$250}{\$2,500}$). Conversely, as Table 21-2 shows, if the price of the stock had fallen to $40, Francine's loss would have been 20 percent on the full cash transaction and 50 percent on the margin transaction. It's not hard to see why margin trading is both exciting and risky.

VALUATION OF SECURITIES

 Investors are always trying to decide whether a stock is a good buy or not. This is particularly true if the stock is purchased on margin, as described in the last section.

What determines value? For most companies it's their ability to produce earnings and cash flow. A firm's earnings capabilities are regularly evaluated in the marketplace through a statistic called the **price/earnings ratio**. This is the current market price per share of stock divided by earnings per share. Using this ratio, the value of a stock can be calculated by the following formula:

price/earnings ratio *the premium investors are willing to pay for a firm's earning potential.*

Market Value of Common Stock = Earnings Per Share × Price/Earnings Ratio

Valuation of securities often involves statistics, but it is more of an art than a science. For example, in mid-1990, the price/earnings ratio of Wal-Mart stock was 32, while that of American Airlines was only 11. Was Wal-Mart stock really worth so much more?

Earnings per share are directly determined from the company's financial statements, but the price/earnings ratio is the result of the collective wisdom of the investors in the marketplace. It represents the premium investors are willing to pay for the firm's earning potential. It's actually an easy concept to understand. As an example, suppose you were considering purchasing a clothing store in your college town. There are two choices. One is located on a highly visible street corner with a great traffic flow. It has the best clothes in town and has been a successful business for 30 years. You might be willing to pay 20 times last year's earnings per share to acquire this business. (Thus, the price/earnings ratio is 20.) The second store you are examining is on the outskirts of town and has out-of-date clothing. Furthermore, the store has an unattractive exterior. Even though you think you could improve the second store with the passage of time, for now you might not be willing to pay more than five times last year's earnings per share to acquire it (a price/earnings ratio of 5).

Basically, the same process takes place on a larger scale when investors evaluate stocks in the marketplace. They are willing to bid the price up and pay a high price/earnings ratio if the company has a strong record of growth, is in a good industry, has able management, knows how to market its product, and so on. The opposite is true for companies with poorer prospects.

In mid 1990, the average company on the New York Stock Exchange had a price/earnings ratio of 15. That means that a firm that had $2 in earnings per share would be valued at $30, and one with $3 of earnings would be valued at $45.

Market Value of Common Stock = Earnings per Share × Price/Earnings Ratio
$30 = $2   × 15
$45 = $3   × 15

Of course, 15 was merely the average price/earning ratio on the New York Stock Exchange. Wal-Mart, a firm highly favored by investors, was selling at 32 times earnings at one time, whereas AMR (American Airlines) was selling at only 11 times earnings. The first time you call a stockbroker, the topic of price/earnings ratio and valuation is likely to come up, so now is the time to become familiar with the concept. Also be aware that just because a stock has a high price/earnings ratio now does not mean that it will continue to be high indefinitely.

Business Career
Investment Analyst: Analyzes financial information to forecast business, industry, and economic conditions for use in making investment decisions. Reviews financial publications and company financial statements. Interprets data concerning price, yield, stability, and future trends of investments. Recommends investment timing and buy-and-sell orders for company. *Average Salary: $30,000.*

A Verdict on Greed

Was Michael Milken's sentence too harsh? Milken was the founder of Drexel Burnham Lambert's famous high-yield junk bond department. He had helped thousands of small companies raise vast amounts of capital to finance their growth. Without Milken, they would probably have had to go without adequate funds to create new products and jobs. A graduate of the Wharton School of Business, Milken had special skills for putting together deals that were beyond the imagination of others. In court proceedings, he was described as a devoted husband, father, and friend. He had given millions of dollars to charity.

Yet Milken received the harshest sentence ever given out to a stock market participant by Judge Kimba M.

Wood. Wood had graduated from Harvard Law School and had been a prominent corporate attorney before moving to the bench, so she was well qualified to assess the penalty.

Milken had been found guilty of manipulating stock prices, bribing investment fund managers, illegally trading on insider information (information that was not known by the public) and destroying key documents. His sentence was 10 years in jail and $600 million in fines. His most famous partner in crime, Ivan Boesky, another widely publicized Wall Street white-collar criminal, had received only a three-year jail sentence for crimes that seemed more serious.

Milken's verdict came some years after Boesky's. It could be argued that Milken was not only being punished for his criminal acts but was also serving as a symbol for society's "verdict on greed for the 1980s." In part, a new morality has arrived on Wall Street in the 1990s, and Milken's sentencing on November 21, 1990 was a signal that accumulation of wealth was not sufficient justification for circumventing legal and ethical codes of conduct.

Price/earnings ratios change over time as earnings and stock prices change. Some people question whether stocks are ever correctly valued, as discussed in the Controversial Issue on page 596.

OTHER TYPES OF INVESTMENTS

 The informed investor may wish to consider other types of investments besides stocks. Here we will examine bonds and stock options.

Investing in Bonds

The characteristics of bonds were discussed in Chapter 20. How do bonds stack up as an investment outlet? If you want a steady stream of income for a long period of time, bonds may be the answer. However, as implied in Chapter 20, there is always a danger of default in payment. This can normally be avoided by purchasing higher-rated bonds, but they carry lower interest payments.

Many investors do not understand that the price of bonds can change, just like the price of stocks. Let's examine why this is the case. Suppose you buy a $1,000 bond that pays 10 percent annual interest over the next 20 years. That would represent $100 in yearly interest payments, plus the return of your $1,000 investment after 20 years. Now assume that because of changing economic conditions, new $1,000 bonds are paying 12 percent (or $120 per bond). You tell your broker that because of unexpected needs, you want to sell your bond now for the best price you can get. Will the broker be able to sell it for the original $1,000 you paid? The answer is No! Since economic conditions caused subsequent bond issues to go up to 12 percent, your 10 percent bond will sell for only $850. While the actual calculation is beyond the scope of this book, the general principle is that a bond's value depends on bond interest rates in the market at that time, not on the face value. After you bought your bond, if interest rates on new bond issues *fell* to 8 percent, your bond would be worth more at that time than the $1,000 you paid for it.

Another factor to consider in buying bonds is whether the interest payments are taxable or not. On municipal bonds (those issued by state and local governments), there is no federal tax obligation (and in many cases, no state taxation either). For an investor in a 31 percent tax bracket, a 7.5 percent municipal bond is the equivalent of a 10.87 percent taxable investment. Some people complain that municipal bonds represent "welfare payments" to the rich.

Trading on the Options Market

An **option** gives its holder the right to buy or sell a specified stock at a given market price for a certain period of time. Speculators trade options in much the same way as they trade stocks. A **call** is an option to buy, say, Chevron at $70 a share anytime within the next nine months. Using the same example, a **put** is an option to sell Chevron at $70 anytime in the next nine months. The option itself may cost only a few dollars, so don't confuse the purchase of an option with the purchase of a stock. The Chicago Board Options Exchange is the only exchange now trading exclusively in stock options, although the American, Philadelphia, and Pacific stock exchanges also handle them.

How can a speculator make money playing the options market? To answer this question, let's return to our Chevron example. Suppose Chevron is currently selling for $70 a share. Our speculator in this case, Ingrid Intrepid, buys 100 options at $2.35 an option. That is, she acquires the right to buy 100 shares of Chevron at $70 until the options expire. If the price of Chevron stock climbs to $85 within the option period, she has made a profit. By exercising her options, she can buy stock for $70 that is currently selling for $85. Her profit is $100(\$85 - \$70) - 100(\$2.35) = \$1265$.

Also, the options themselves have value. The value is the difference between the 100 shares at $70 and the 100 shares at $85, or $1500. Instead of exercising the options, she could sell them to another speculator. But if the price of Chevron, rather than climbing, were to sink to $55, her $235 in options ($2.35 × 100 options) would be worthless.

MUTUAL FUNDS   **8**

To evaluate all the investments that are available to investors, you should also consider the mutual fund. A **mutual fund** is an association of many small investors, who pool their funds and buy securities. Here's how a mutual fund works. Suppose you have 19 good friends, each of whom, plus yourself, has $1,000 to invest. You could pool your money and buy $20,000 worth of stock in a variety of companies. Many small investors thus have become one bigger investor. If the value of your stock purchases climbed to $25,000, each person's share of the "fund" would be $25,000 ÷ 20, or $1,250. That means a gain of $1,250 − $1,000, or $250 for each investor.

Now suppose that you and your 19 friends decide to restrict membership in the fund to yourselves. In so doing, you are creating what is called a **closed-end fund.** If you decide to admit new investors into the investment pool at its current per share value, you are creating an **open-end fund.** If each new investor then pays $1,250 to join the fund, the value of a share will not be diluted, and there will be more money available to invest. Open-end funds are more prevalent than closed-end funds.

option   the right to buy or sell a stock at a given market price for a certain period of time.

call   an option to buy shares of stock at some specified price during a certain period of time.

put   an option to sell shares of stock at some specified price during a certain period of time.

mutual fund   an association of many small investors, who pool their funds and buy securities.

closed-end fund   a type of mutual fund in which the membership (as represented by number of total shares) is restricted.

open-end fund   a type of mutual fund in which the membership (as represented by number of total shares) is unrestricted.

Do Stock Prices Move in a Random Fashion?

Yes

Some stock market analysts and academicians who do research in finance believe that stock prices change without rhyme or reason. It's like spinning a top on the middle of a slick surface. Where will it end up? Who knows? Likewise, just because a stock moves up or down for a few days does not necessarily predict its pattern for the future.

This theory is sometimes carried a step further by comparing the performance of professional money managers to results that could be achieved by throwing darts at a listing of stocks from the *Wall Street Journal*. In many cases, the results are remarkably similar.

Why do many professional money managers have difficulty beating the market on a regular basis? It may not be because they are bad at managing money, but rather because they are so good. If you have 10,000 professional analysts following the market every minute of the day, it's hard for anyone to get a true advantage. Most of the analysts have MBAs and six-figure salaries and are prepared to react immediately to any new information.

Furthermore, because of the modern electronic transfer of information, there is very little opportunity for one investor to have substantially more information than another, as was the case a decade or two ago. Through Reuters News Service or the Dow Jones News Retrieval System, an investor in McAllen, Texas or Monroe, Louisiana can be informed of an event or transaction almost as quickly as someone on Wall Street. Also, program trading, which utilizes computerized trigger points to initiate large-scale buying and selling activity, further increases the ability of the market to react quickly to new events.

The first mutual funds were formed in the mid-1920s, but they did not become popular until the late 1970s. Figure 21-4 shows the growth in the total value of all assets held by mutual funds from 1950 to 1990. It is truly impressive.

Reasons for Popularity of Mutual Funds

Many people do not invest in the stock market because, by themselves, they cannot diversify their stock holding sufficiently. A few thousand dollars is not enough money to achieve a reasonable degree of diversification. Moreover, they may want more professional advice than they can get from a stockbroker. When the small investor is looking for diversification and professional advice, a mutual fund is generally the answer.

load fund *a mutual fund that charges a commission.*

no-load fund *a mutual fund that does not charge a commission.*

A **load fund** is one that charges a commission, whereas a **no-load fund** does not. Generally speaking, the investor should always look for a no-load fund in preference to a load fund when there is a choice. The load or commission may run as high as 8½ percent on a load fund. This means that on a $1,000 investment, $85 will go toward commissions and only $915 toward the purchase of the mutual fund shares. Even if your mutual fund goes up by $50 or $60 dollars after you purchase the shares, you will still be behind. With a no-load fund, your full $1,000 goes toward the purchase of mutual fund shares and is all working for you. If the fund goes up by $50 or $60, it is all profit.

low-load fund *a mutual fund that charges a commission lower than that of a load fund.*

In recent years, some funds have taken an in-between position by offering **low-load funds**. Here the commission is normally 2 to 3 percent. If the fund has a truly unusual investment strategy, it may be worth it to pay the small commission. As a general rule, however, always look for no-loads first, then low-loads, and last full-load funds.

Types of Mutual Funds

Not all mutual funds have the same purpose. Let's look at a number of different classifications.

No

Stock prices do not move in a random fashion. The truly wise investor can win the most chips. It's hard to believe that stocks can be correctly priced at any point in time when the Dow Jones Industrial Average, an important measure of market movement, can go down 509 points in one day, as it did on October 19, 1987. The drop represented a 22 percent decline in value. It's pretty difficult to accept that stocks were correctly priced on the day before the decline.

Furthermore, all this talk about sophisticated professional market participants competing with each other is subject to challenge. Instead of being the cutthroat profit maximizers described above, they are really a bunch of lemmings that follow each other over a cliff. Many investment advisors are afraid of being out of step with the majority, so they merely mimic the actions of others, confident that they will have plenty of company in the event they guess wrong.

Also, all the up-to-date information in the electronic age tends to spew in many directions at any one time. Just because you see something coming over the newswire does not necessarily mean it's true. There are false reports about presidential assassinations, spectacular new product discoveries, and so on. The few really smart investors and analysts can determine the truth, while the masses are in a state of confusion. They may make enormous profits from undervalued stocks. To suggest that all analysts are equal (and therefore that all markets are random in nature) is like suggesting that a famous attorney has no better than a 50-50 chance of beating an untried lawyer fresh out of law school.

Another reason why stock price movements are not random is that in spite of all the government regulation, there is still a lot of insider trading going on. It's not just the Boeskys and Milkens who take advantage of inside information to make large profits; it's also third cousins to corporate presidents and even people who set the printing presses for news releases.

What Do You Think?

Bond and Stock Funds. Remember that a mutual fund is a diversified portfolio of investment securities. These securities can be either stocks or bonds. Bond funds are characterized by conservative investment policies and a fairly stable rate of return. Even with a bond fund, however, a profitable investment is not guaranteed.

FIGURE 21-4   Growth in Mutual Fund Assets (in billions of dollars)

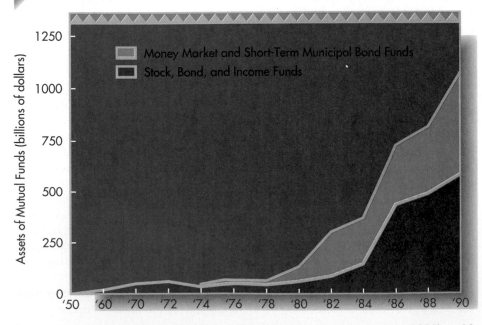

Source: *Mutual Fund Fact Book* (Washington, D.C.: Investment Company Institute, 1991), p. 19.

In contrast to a bond fund, the aim of which is to generate a steady interest stream, a stock fund can have any of several objectives. For example, some stock funds attempt to outperform the market as a whole. They are made up of a variety of high-quality stocks that are expected to do well. Others are composed of stock from small companies with strong growth potential. These are called **growth funds.** Of course, some funds consist of both stocks and bonds. Smart investors always consider their investment objectives carefully before selecting a fund.

growth funds *mutual funds that specialize in small companies with strong growth potential.*

Foreign Funds. Investors seeking participation in foreign investments confront a number of obstacles, but the rewards can be outstanding. The International Example on page 602 illustrates this point. The mutual fund industry has made overseas investing convenient by establishing **foreign funds** that invest worldwide or in special regions of the world. Examples include the Fidelity Magellan Fund (worldwide), Kemper International Fund (worldwide), and G. T. Pacific Fund (Japan and Hong Kong). Foreign mutual funds have consistently outperformed U.S. funds in the past decade.

foreign funds *mutual funds that specialize in worldwide investments.*

Specialty Funds. Some funds have unique approaches that do not fall into any of the preceding categories. They are referred to as **specialty funds.** Specialty funds may invest in special causes or a given industry. Examples include the Calvert Social Investment Fund and the Medical Technology Fund. There is even a mutual fund that does nothing but invest in other mutual funds (Fund Trust).

specialty funds *mutual funds that have a unique approach to investments, such as investing in a special cause or a given industry.*

Money Market Funds. **Money market funds** have been one of the brightest new stars in the financial heavens. They are made up of short-term, high-yield government notes ("T-bills"), commercial paper, and negotiable certificates of deposit. Because of their investment policies, money market funds are just about risk free, offering their investors a return only a few percentage points below the prime rate. (The prime rate is the rate of interest that the leading banks in the country charge their biggest, most reliable corporate borrowers.)

money market funds *funds that invest in short-term, high-yield investments.*

It is not an exaggeration to say that money market funds revolutionized the way small investors save their hard-earned dollars. The total amount invested in these funds went from practically zero in 1975 to more than $350 billion in 1990.

Mutual Fund Performance

As an example of mutual funds and their performance, examine Table 21-3. This is an excerpt from the annual *Forbes* magazine mutual fund survey that comes out in early September. In the first two columns after the fund name, you can see the fund's performance over the last 10 years as well as over the last 12 months. For example, the Neuberger & Berman Manhattan Fund was up 15.7 percent over the last 10 years and 20.3 percent in the last 12 months.

In the far left-hand column, you can observe how *Forbes* magazine grades the various funds in up and down markets. The grading scale is from A+ to F. The Neuberger Berman Manhattan Fund gets an A rating in up markets, but only a C in down markets. This would indicate that it has an aggressive investing attitude that is great in advancing markets but sometimes leaves the investor overexposed to risk in down markets.

Lastly, note the second column from the right, which shows the maximum sales charge or commission. Can you identify some of the no-load funds?

TABLE 21-3   Forbes Annual Fund Survey

| Performance | | | Total Return | | | Assets | | | |
In Up Mkts	In Down Mkts	Fund/Distributor	Annual Average '80 to '89	Last 12 Months	Yield	6/30/89 (millions)	% Change '89 vs '88	Maximum Sales Charge	Annual Expenses per $100
		Standard & Poor's 500 Stock Average	14.8%	20.4%	3.2%				
		FORBES Stock Fund Composite	12.1%	15.0%	2.3%				$1.58
D	•D	Nautilus Fund/Eaton Vance	—*	–3.4%	none	$ 13	–16%	4.75%	$1.87p
B	C	Neuberger & Berman Guardian[1]/Neuberger	14.6%	17.0	2.6%	556	4	none	0.84
Ⓐ	Ⓒ	Neuberger & Berman Manhattan[2]/ Neuberger	⟨15.7⟩	⟨20.3⟩	1.5	382	–8	none	1.20
D	A	Neuberger & Berman Partners[3]/Neuberger	15.9	17.5	3.4	743	3	none	0.97
D	C	Neuberger & Berman Select Energy[4]/ Neuberger	8.5	19.8	2.6	412	6	none	1.01
A	D	Neuwirth Fund/National Finl	9.9	16.9	0.1	29	8	none	1.92
•D	•C	New Alternatives Fund/Accrued Eq	—*	21.7	1.6	9	63	5.66	1.24
		New Economy Fund/American Funds	—*	23.4	2.0	805	8	5.75	0.81
D	A	New England Equity Income/New England	13.4	10.5	3.2	58	12	6.50	1.52
A	B	New England Growth Fund/New England	18.0	7.2	2.9	505	4	6.50	1.26
C	A	New England Retirement Equity/New England	14.7	9.0	3.7	139	–3	6.50	1.29
A	C	New York Venture Fund/Venture	16.6	24.6	2.4	299	80	4.75	1.01

• Fund rated for two periods only; maximum allowable grade A. * Fund not in operation for full period. *Expense ratio is in italics if the fund has a shareholder-paid 12b-1 plan exceeding 0.1% (hidden load) pending or in force.* p: Net of partial absorption of expenses by fund sponsor. [1]Formerly Guardian Mutual Fund. [2]Formerly Manhattan Fund. [3]Formerly Partners Fund. [4]Formerly Select Fund.

Source: *Forbes*, 4 September 1989, p. 224.

Money market funds became extremely popular with small investors during the 1980s.

STOCK MARKET INDICATORS

Most investors follow the fortunes not only of selected stocks of interest but also of the stock market as a whole. They do this so that they can judge the perfor-mance of a particular stock against the performance of the market. Indexes show-ing stock market performance are called **stock market indicators.** Let's look at four of the top stock market indicators.

Dow Jones Industrial Average

The Dow Jones Industrial Average is the most widely quoted stock indicator. One feature of evening network newscasts is the quotation of the closing value of the Dow Jones Industrials for the day's trading. The Dow Jones Industrial Average is made up of a cross section of 30 well-established companies traded on the New York Stock Exchange. Each company is considered to be an industry leader.

Figure 21-5 shows how the Dow Jones is displayed in the *Wall Street Journal*. The Dow Jones Industrial Average moved up and down by almost 350 points for the six-month period. Note the listing of the companies that make up the average inside the box of the figure.

The investor can readily measure the performance of his or her individual stocks against the Dow Jones. For example, the average dropped significantly in the months of January and April. Did the individual investor's stocks drop as much or less than the market did? Did the performance of investor's stocks then match the market's upturn in March and May?

FIGURE 21-5 The Dow Jones Industrial Average, December 1989–May 1990.

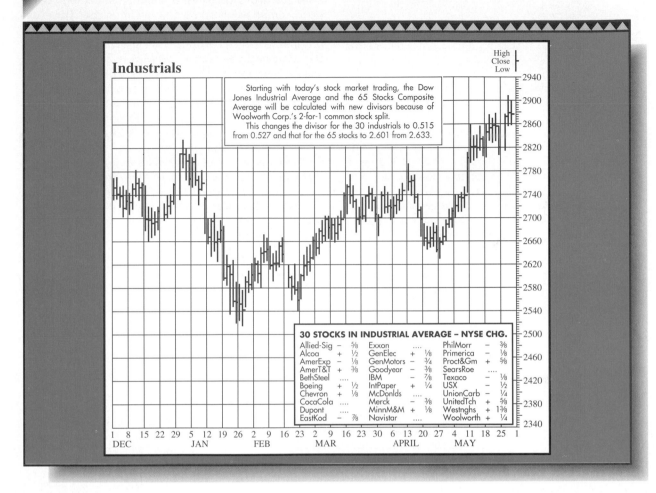

Source: *Wall Street Journal*, 1 June 1990, p. C3.

Standard & Poor's 500 Index

Another stock market indicator is Standard & Poor's 500 Index. The S&P Index, covering 500 NYSE companies in 88 industries, is much more broadly based than the Dow Jones. It is made up of 400 industrial companies, 40 public utilities, 20 transportation companies, and 40 financial institutions. Therefore, many people believe that Standard & Poor's Index provides a more representative measure of market activity.

NYSE Composite Index

The NYSE Composite Index includes all common stocks listed on the New York Stock Exchange. It was developed in 1966, partly because investors did not believe that the Dow Jones reflected market activity. The base value for this index was set at 50, which approximated the average NYSE stock price for 1966. In June 1990, the index stood at 198. In other words, the average stock on the New York Stock Exchange has risen 148 points, or 296 percent, since the index was first reported.

Table A compares the performance of nine different world stock markets between 1969 and mid-1990. Each started out with a base value of 100. Stocks on the Hong Kong exchange increased by 2,261.7 percent, from the base value of 100 up to 2361.7. Japanese firms enjoyed a growth of 1,269.2 percent, up to 1369.2. U.S. firms did not do nearly so well, as indicated in the first line of the table.

The wise money manager should consider the entire world as part of the market basket of investments to choose from. There are great opportunities for return and also excellent opportunities for diversification. By spreading funds over many countries, a recession in one part of the world can be balanced by a boom in another. For example, if world oil prices drop dramatically, oil-producing countries will suffer, but oil-consuming countries will benefit. The losers might be firms in the Middle East and Mexico, and the winners would be in Japan and Europe. The opposite is true for oil price increases, as happened in 1990.

All this sounds inviting, but there are potential problems. For example, investments on foreign exchanges are normally made in foreign currency. A 20 percent gain on the Tokyo Stock Exchange might be partially wiped out if the Japanese yen goes down relative to the U.S. dollar. There are also special political risks involved in investing in less stable countries. Finally, there can be tax problems and information difficulties. (Can you read an annual report in French?)

TABLE A *Index of Values for Stock Markets Throughout the World—Increase in Value from 1969 to Mid-1990 (100 = Beginning Value for Each Country in 1969)*

United States	334.9
Britain	704.6
Canada	395.6
Japan	1369.2
France	584.9
Germany	296.8
Hong Kong	2361.7
Switzerland	226.8
Australia	307.6
World Index	528.0

The good news is that many of these problems can be reduced or eliminated by investing in internationally oriented mutual funds.

ASE Market Value Index

The ASE Market Value Index is made up of the stocks listed on the American Stock Exchange. Its base value was originally 100. In 1983, the index was adjusted to half its previous level, changing the base to 50. Since the index was first reported in 1973, it has fallen to a low of 29 (using a base of 50) and risen to a high of 365. The volatility of this index in comparison to the NYSE Composite Index reflects the dramatic stock price changes that occur on the American Stock Exchange.

Other Indexes

Other indexes include the NASDAQ Composite Index, which tracks the performance of major over-the-counter stocks; the Wilshire Index, which covers virtually all U.S. stocks; and the Nikkei Index, which measures the performance of stocks on the Tokyo Stock Exchange.

SUMMARY POINTS

1 Securities are stocks and bonds that can be bought and sold in securities markets. Firms sell securities to raise capital for expansion. Firms issue new securities in the securities markets with the help of investment bankers. After the securities are issued, they are traded between investors in the secondary market.

2 The seven objectives of a personal investment program are as follows. *Safety of principal* means maintaining the initial value of the investment through careful analysis and diversification. *Liquidity* is the ability to turn an investment into cash quickly for emergency purposes or to take advantage of a new investment opportunity. *Stability of income* involves establishing a steady stream of cash receipts for the investor. *Protection against inflation* means shielding the investor against a loss in purchasing power due to inflation over the life of the investment. *Tax considerations* involve minimizing the tax obligation associated with an investment. *Appreciation in value* requires purchasing a stock or bond at the right time so that it will gain in value. *Ease of management* means tailoring the investment portfolio to the amount of time that the investor wishes to spend monitoring performance; some investments are easier to track than others.

3 The major stock exchanges in the U.S. are the New York Stock Exchange, the American Stock Exchange, the regional exchanges, and the over-the-counter market. The stock of larger firms is normally traded on the New York Stock Exchange, while that of smaller firms is traded in the other markets. However, there are exceptions. Some firms prefer the over-the-counter market, where there is more competition between brokers in the trading of the securities.

4 Stocks are bought and sold through customers contacting stockbrokers, who then place orders through commission brokers on the floor of the exchange. Customers can use market orders, limit orders, and stop orders, all of which may be placed through full-service brokers or discount brokers.

5 Investors may use speculative trading tactics to try to make money on anticipated short-term movements in the market. One example is the use of a short sale, in which the investor borrows stock from a broker and sells it. On instruction from the investor, the broker later buys the stock back. If the stock has gone down in value, the investor has made a profit. Another speculative trading tactic is to buy stock on margin, which means that the investor finances part of the purchase with borrowed funds. This allows the investor to buy more shares and magnifies the potential for gains and losses.

6 Stocks are valued in the marketplace by multiplying earnings per share times the price/earnings ratio. The price/earnings ratio is based on the collective wisdom of investors in the marketplace. It reflects the premium investors are willing to pay for the overall quality of a firm and its future outlook.

7 Although stocks are often thought of as the most important investment for individuals, the well-informed investor should also consider other securities such as bonds and put and call options. These investments may have different degrees of risk than stocks and offer special tax advantages.

8 Mutual funds combine the money of many small investors under professional financial management. They can be closed-end (restricted) or open-end (unrestricted). Some funds charge a commission (load), while others do not. Different funds invest in different financial instruments, depending on their purpose. Some funds may emphasize stocks or bonds, while others specialize in foreign investment or in specific industries.

9 Stock market indicators allow the investor to measure overall changes in the market and to compare the performance of individual investments against market changes. Key stock market indicators include the Dow Jones Industrial Average, the Standard & Poor's 500 Index, the NYSE Composite Index, the ASE Market Value Index, and other indexes that measure stock performance both in the U.S. and abroad.

REVIEW QUESTIONS

1 What is the difference between the primary market and the secondary market?

2 What is the role of investment bankers in the sale of common stock?

3 Give two examples of tax-advantaged investments.

4 What is the over-the-counter market?

5 Explain the difference between a limit order and a stop order.

6 How do investors make money by selling short? Is selling short very risky? Why or why not?

7 Why is buying on margin so risky?

8 Would a company with a favorable outlook for the future tend to have a high price-earnings ratio or a low one?

9 Would you buy a call or a put option if you thought a stock was about to go up in value?

10 What is the difference between a closed-end fund and an open-end fund?

11 Name two characteristics of stocks that are part of the Dow Jones Industrial Average.

DISCUSSION QUESTIONS

1 What are the seven objectives of a personal investment program? Which would be the most important to you?

2 What is the main reason why many investors diversify their holdings? If you had a million dollars and wanted to invest it, would you diversify or not?

3 How important are trading specialists in the buying and selling of stocks? What risks do they take?

4 Would you rather do business with a regular stockbroker or with a discount stockbroker? Explain.

5 Explain why the price of bonds goes up and down in the market.

6 How do speculators make money by trading in the options market?

EXPERIENTIAL EXERCISES

1 Turn to the section of the *Wall Street Journal* or some other periodical that gives daily price quotations for securities on the New York Stock Exchange. Select three stocks that you think will do better than average over the next month. Plot the prices of those stocks on a sheet of graph paper. Also plot the current Dow Jones Industrial Average (adjust the level so that it fits on your scale). Over the next month, plot the prices of each of your selected stocks and the Dow Jones. At the end of the month, calculate which of your stocks did better than the Dow Jones and which did worse.

Then try to determine the factors that contributed to the performances of each of your stocks. Also, did the values of your stocks seem to fluctuate more or less, on a percentage basis, than the Dow Jones?

2 Watch your daily newspaper for a company that has been involved in some major event. Check the price of its common stock on the day prior to the event, the day of the event, and each of the few days following the event. Did the price changes seem to be linked to the event?

CASES

CASE 21-1
Hewlett-Packard Company

There couldn't be a better address for a high-tech company than Palo Alto, California. That city is the home of Stanford University and its renowned School of Engineering, and countless successful firms are located nearby. Just a stone's throw from Hewlett-Packard are such firms as Apple Computer and Sun Microsystems.

Hewlett-Packard (HP) was founded in 1939 by Bill Hewlett and David Packard. It has continued to grow rapidly over five decades. For example, from 1980 to 1990, sales increased from $3.1 billion to $13.2 billion and net profit from $269 million to $739 million. The firm specializes in precision electronic equipment and computers; it is a world leader in both categories.

In 1990, the investment community was somewhat surprised when David Packard, who still owns one-sixth of the company's stock and is 78 years old, announced that he was coming out of semiretirement to take control of the firm once again. What motivated him to take such action? First, HP stock had fallen by half in value. Its price/earnings ratio had declined to a mere 12 from its lofty levels of over 30 in the 1970s and a steady 18 to 25 in the 1980s. Although the firm was not losing money, its earnings per share of $3.06 in 1990 were projected to grow only to $3.10 in 1991. This would not qualify HP as a growth company, a term reserved for firms that are growing at 10 to 15 percent per year or higher.

David Packard was very determined to get the firm back on track. HP had 92,000 employees, and the word was that Packard intended to lay off a few thousand of them to help boost earnings in the future. Packard also observed that HP had become too bureaucratic; in the fast-moving world of electronics and computers, slow decision making is costly. Recently, HP had purchased Apollo Computer, a move that temporarily gave HP market share leadership in the market for computer workstations, but the firm had since fallen behind Sun Microsystems. Packard intended to correct these and other problems.

The company was certainly not in a desperate position. HP still had $951 million in cash and only $235 million in debt. The only question was whether this once-glorious company would become a dinosaur or recapture its past glory.

Assume you are considering HP as a potential investment.

1. Should you be concerned by the firm's low price/earnings ratio?
2. Assume you are convinced the company can turn the situation around, so you buy 100 shares of Hewlett-Packard stock at $36 per share. If the stock price goes to $50, what will be the percentage of return on your investment?
3. Suppose when you call your stockbroker, he suggests that you buy the stock on margin. His suggestion is that you put up half the purchase price in cash and borrow the balance. The broker anticipates that the interest cost on the borrowed funds will be $200 over the time you hold the stock. If the stock price goes to $50, what will be the percentage return on the cash that you put into the investment?

    To answer the question, fill in the blanks below:

1.	Value of investment	100 shares × $36 =	$3,600
2.	Investor's cash (50 percent of investment)		
3.	Proceeds from sale	100 shares × $50	$5,000
4.	Value of investment (same as line 1)		− 3,600
5.	Profit before paying interest		
6.	Interest		− 200
7.	Profit after paying interest		
8.	Return on cash investment (divide the answer to line 7 by the answer to line 2)		

4. Right before you make the decision to buy the stock, you receive a call from another stockbroker. She says that one of HP's key suppliers, Motorola, will not be able to deliver its newest microprocessor, which is used in HP workstations. Although you do

not necessarily understand all the technical jargon, you know that this is bad news for HP. You feel that the stock price will definitely go down. Even though you do not currently own the stock, you wish to take advantage of this predicted decline. How might you be able to accomplish this?

CASE 21-2
GTE Corporation

In late 1986, the board of directors of GTE Corporation, a large telecommunications company, wondered how it should deal with a threatened takeover of the company. Although the board did not know exactly who was attempting the takeover, it did know that an investor had been accumulating large numbers of the company's shares. Analysts were saying that, at about $62 a share, GTE's stock was undervalued and should be selling above $70 a share. Since GTE's total market value was more than $13 billion, a takeover could result in huge profits for anyone attempting it.

In view of the highly regulated nature of GTE's principal business—local telephone service—it would have been difficult for someone to take over the company and dismember it, selling off its assets and reaping a big gain. Nevertheless, GTE's board of directors believed that some preventive action was necessary. Faced with just such a situation, many other firms agree to pay "greenmail"—that is, to buy back stock from the takeover artist at a higher-than-market price. In this case, it was not clear who the suitor was, or if others would follow.

In November 1986, GTE's board announced its decision: It would take a series of steps to raise the price of its stock shares and to make a takeover more difficult and less attractive. It increased its quarterly dividend to 91.5 cents a share from 81 cents. It also authorized a buyback of as many as 10 million of its outstanding shares, announced plans for a 3-for-2 stock split, and called for a special meeting to vote on anti-takeover changes in its corporate charter. The company would buy back the 10 million shares in the secondary market, but it would not buy back any particular investor's shares. It would then resell 5 million shares to employees through GTE's various employee stock ownership, savings, and dividend reinvestment plans.

GTE stockholders voted in December 1986 to approve the proposed 3-for-2 stock split, which would raise the number of shares outstanding to 330 million from 220 million, as well as requirements that elections of directors would be staggered and that a takeover would require an 80 percent vote. These changes would make any planned takeover much more difficult and expensive.

1. Which of the proposed changes do you think would increase the price of GTE's shares? Which, if any, do you think might depress share price?
2. If you were a GTE shareholder, would you have voted for the proposed changes? Why or why not?
3. Do you think these proposed changes would make GTE stock more or less attractive to mutual funds? Why?
4. An analyst reviewing the GTE moves said, "This is probably one of the most beneficial ways to pay greenmail I have ever seen." Evaluate this statement.

Sources: J. Guyon, "GTE Corp. Acts to Boost Share Value, Thwart Suitors," *Wall Street Journal,* 7 November 1986, p. 2; J. R. Norman, "Can GTE Keep Foiling the Raiders?" *Business Week,* 6 April 1987, p. 100.

Coleman Diversified Industries (CDI)

In January, 1993, Coleman Diversified Industries (CDI), a firm with holdings in the entertainment, aerospace, and housing industries, was considering making a major acquisition of a company involved in magazine and general publishing. CDI had recent sales of $5 billion a year and was located in Nashville, Tennessee. The primary target was the Rollins Company, which was founded in 1954 and had total corporate sales of $2.5 billion in 1992. Its home office was in Pleasantville, New York. Approximately 30 percent of the firm's sales were accounted for by the *Intellectual Conservative Digest,* with the balance coming from books, newspapers, and cable TV revenue.

Al Corwin, the vice president of finance at CDI, was particularly excited about the potential merger because he thought it would go a long way toward achieving financial management's goal of maximizing corporate sales. Although CDI had looked at a number of other acquisition candidates in the publishing industry, no other firm could get CDI up to $7.5 billion in sales as quickly as the Rollins Company.

As an experienced financial manager, Al Corwin knew that not only past sales and profits were important, but future projections as well. Although employees of the Rollins Company were hesitant to share future projections with him, he was able to obtain information from two other firms in the magazine/publishing industry. These were Galaxy Enterprises (which publishes a magazine targeted for the independent working woman and owns a pay TV service) and Mega-Pub (which publishes a popular news magazine and owns extensive cable TV systems). Over the next 5 years Galaxy's sales were projected to grow by a total of 38 percent and its earnings by a whopping 300 percent. For Mega-Pub, the total sales increase over the five years was projected to be 28 percent and the earnings increase 35 percent. These numbers led Al Corwin to be particularly optimistic about the prospects for the Rollins Company.

The Rollins Company currently had 1992 earnings of $241 million on its sales of $2.5 billion. It was the intention of top management to move the operations of the Rollins Company to Nashville in order to eliminate overlapping functions with CDI, and Al Corwin thought this action alone would increase the current earnings of the Rollins Company by $20 million.

CDI was proud of its own current return on stockholders' equity of 20 percent.

$$\frac{\text{Net income}}{\text{Owner's Equity}} = \frac{\$400,000,000}{\$2,000,000,000} = 20\%$$

Al Corwin anticipated that the purchase price for the Rollins Company of around $4 billion dollars could be all paid for out of newly borrowed funds. CDI currently had $2,500,000,000 on its books in debt. The average debt to owner's equity ratio for diversified companies similar to CDI was 1.10 as reported by leading financial data publications such as *Standard and Poor's Industry Survey.*

Preliminary estimates were that 1993 earnings per share would increase by 15–20 percent for CDI as a result of the merger. It was thought that the stock price would go up by a like amount.

If this merger went well, Al Corwin thought the next major step might be to acquire Galaxy Enterprises. He was impressed with managerial talents of Gloria Holmes, who is a leader in the national women's rights movement and owns 71 percent of the stock. She started the company 10 years ago.

QUESTIONS

1. Do you think the fact that the acquisition of the Rollins Company could bring total corporate sales up to $7.5 billion is particularly significant?
2. Discuss all fallacious assumptions that Mr. Corwin may be making.
3. What do you think of his other future plans for acquisitions?
4. What additional information about the Rollins Company would you like to have besides that presented in the case?

PART 6

Further Dimensions of American Business

CHAPTER 22

Risk Management and Insurance

Gentex is a small biotechnology and genetics research firm in Los Angeles. The business was started by three scientists: George Johnson, Sam Winters, and Harriet Arnold. Each of the founding partners has a Ph.D. and an M.D. degree. Before forming Gentex, they worked as research scientists at a research and teaching hospital.

Gentex performs basic research on viruses, such as AIDS. The federal government currently provides more than 80 percent of its funding. The remaining revenues come from a number of small contracts with pharmaceutical companies.

After Gentex had been in operation for two years, the three founding partners hired Terrence Ford to run the company. Ford had earned a B.A. degree in business from the University of Wisconsin. The first task that he addressed was the establishment of an efficient and accurate accounting system. Next, he made several key staffing decisions and designed an employee compensation plan. Then he turned to the issue of insurance. Almost immediately, Ford could see that the founders had taken no actions to protect themselves from the risks associated with operating their business. The company had no product liability insurance to protect itself in the event that one of its products injured someone. Nor had the founders purchased directors and officers insurance or life insurance on themselves. Moreover, the company's fire insurance protection was inadequate, and several employees in positions of trust were not bonded. This chapter will examine many important issues dealing with risk management and insurance.

The need for people to protect their homes against loss became painfully evident in 1666. In that year, a fire in London destroyed 14,000 buildings and left more than 200,000 people homeless. The first fire insurance company was formed the next year. In the United States, Benjamin Franklin started the first successful fire insurance company in 1752. The company is still in existence. Today, we can buy insurance to protect ourselves against many such calamities.

RISK MANAGEMENT

Risk is defined as the uncertainty of loss. Risk is the possibility that events will not turn out as we want. We face risk every day. When Oscar tries to register for a college course, he faces risk: The course might be full, so he cannot take it. When Alicia drives to work or school, she faces the risk that another driver will run into her.

> **risk**   the uncertainty of loss.

Anticipated risk is not a problem. For example, to cover the cost of spoilage, supermarkets charge a little extra for their vegetables. This replaces operating risk by building in some additional profit margin. Unanticipated risk, however, exposes an individual or a company to sudden and unexpected loss.

As a prelude to our discussion of risk management and insurance, let's identify two basic forms of risk: pure risk and speculative risk.[1] Understanding the difference between the two is important, because insurance companies protect against only one of them.

Pure Risk

Pure risk exists in situations in which the only possible outcomes are loss or no loss. There is no possibility of gain. When a person buys a house, there is a chance that the house will be destroyed by fire, that a burglar will break in and steal the furniture, or that a windstorm will blow out all the windows. All of these possibilities are examples of pure risk. There is no way that the homeowner can reasonably gain from any of these misfortunes. Insurance companies are prepared to protect people against this sort of risk.

> **pure risk**   situations in which the only possible outcomes are loss or no loss; there is no possibility of gain.

In the industrial setting, the risk of accidents can be reduced by enforcing appropriate safety measures. For example, special garments protect this sandblaster from certain kinds of injury.

Speculative Risk

Speculative risk involves the possibility both of loss and of gain. It is the risk of either making money or losing it. Gambling is the classic example of speculative risk. Mike bets his friend Sally that the Washington Redskins will beat the Dallas Cowboys in a football game. The bet is $10, and the odds are even. Mike is risking a loss of $10 in the hope of winning $10.

The introduction of a new product also involves a great deal of speculative risk. The product could be either very popular or a total market failure. The entrepreneur accepts the risk because of the possibility of earning a profit.

Insurance companies will not protect people or businesses against speculative risk. General Motors' Buick Division introduced an expensive two-seater sports car, the Reatta, in 1989. Buick executives believed that there was a small but profitable market for a luxury sports car that was significantly less expensive than the Mercedes SL line. Unfortunately, the Reatta did not appeal to many buyers, and Buick lost money on the project. Production of the car ceased in 1991. Insurance companies do not insure against this type of loss. Too many things can go wrong for an insurance company to accept the speculative risk involved with new product introduction.

Managing Pure Risk

The rest of this chapter is concerned exclusively with pure risk—that is, risks that are insurable. There are five ways a person or firm can manage, or protect against, pure risk.

Risk Avoidance. Risk can be avoided completely. An individual can avoid drowning by not getting near water, avoid a divorce by not getting married, or avoid being mugged in Detroit by not going to Detroit. In the same manner, an insurance company can avoid the risk associated with selling automobile insurance by not selling automobile insurance. Although risk avoidance does work, it obviously reduces the alternatives that are available to an individual and the profit options that are available to businesses.

Risk Reduction. One way to manage pure risk is to reduce it. A family concerned about the risk of burglary can take several steps to reduce risk before leaving on a trip. The family can stop delivery of newspapers and mail, lock the house securely, ask neighbors to watch the house, and plug several lights into timers so that they come on in the evening and give the house a lived-in look.

A business can reduce its risk by training its employees and establishing high standards of quality for production. For example, Campbell's Soup Co. spends millions of dollars each year monitoring its kitchens to ensure that its products not only taste good but also are free from impurities that could harm consumers.

Self-Insurance. Another way to manage pure risk is to put money aside each month to cover unexpected losses. Instead of buying fire insurance, a business could deposit money into a savings account. This would establish a fund to pay for losses in the event of a fire. Self-insurance may be appropriate for a large business that faces a similar type of risk in many different locations. For example, a company that has production plants all over the world might decide to self-insure against the risk of damage caused by fire. It is highly unlikely that a company would experience major fire losses in several of its plants during the same year. Although some firms do benefit from self-insurance, it does not provide adequate protection in most cases.

Current Income. Some people and business organizations pay for losses out of current income rather than out of a special account or fund. For example, most states do not insure their government office buildings against fire or wind damage. If fire destroys a state building, the state legislature simply appropriates money to construct a new one. A private firm could replace a truck destroyed in an accident with a new one. This is probably the least satisfactory way to manage pure risk, especially when the loss is potentially great.

Insurance. Most people and organizations choose insurance as the way to protect themselves against pure risk. Even with insurance, however, there is still the risk that the insured house will be destroyed by fire or that the firm's delivery truck will slide into a ditch. What the insurance company does (within the limits of the policy issued) is to reimburse the owners for all or part of their losses.

PRINCIPLES OF INSURANCE—THE COMPANY'S PERSPECTIVE ②

The insurance business is based on a set of seven principles. Insurance companies have learned that if they follow these principles, they can both pay damage claims on insured losses and earn money for stockholders. Let's look at each of these principles.

Because of the principle of catastrophic hazard, an insurance company does not want to issue too many policies in the same geographic area. This 1991 fire destroyed several adjacent buildings in Los Angeles, and an insurance company would have suffered a severe loss if it had insured all of them.

Insurable Interest

insurable interest *a principle of insurance: the only accidents that are insurable are those that would cause the policyholder a real financial loss.*

The first principle of insurance is that buyers of insurance policies must show that they would suffer financial loss from an accident of the type covered by the policy. This is called an **insurable interest**. Let's say that Mr. Jones wants to insure Ms. Smith's house against fire, naming himself as the beneficiary of the policy. Mr. Jones would not suffer a loss if Ms. Smith's house burned down. In fact, he would profit from the insurance policy. He might even be tempted to set Ms. Smith's house on fire to obtain the insurance money. An insurance company would not issue such a policy. The only accidents that are insurable are those that would cause the policyholder a real financial loss.[2]

The Principle of Indemnity

principle of indemnity *a principle of insurance: the insured person or firm cannot collect more in damage claims than the dollar loss sustained.*

The aim of insurance is to protect the insured against loss. As we have said, insurance is not speculation or gambling. The **principle of indemnity** says that the insured person or firm cannot collect more in damage claims than the dollar loss sustained. For example, suppose a house is insured for $80,000, but its true replacement cost is $60,000. What happens if the house is totally destroyed by a tornado? The insured may collect only $60,000, because this represents the real dollar loss caused by the tornado.

Law of Large Numbers

law of large numbers *a principle of insurance: the probability of an event occurring in the future can be predicted from the past rate of occurrence.*

The third principle of insurance is the **law of large numbers.** This principle holds that the probability that a particular loss-causing event will occur can be predicted from the past rate of its occurrence. The event could be a flood, a hurricane, or death. From statistical or actuarial tables summarizing past occurrences, insurance companies know roughly how many houses will burn down this year in the United States and how many automobile accidents will occur in a particular city.

actuaries *people employed by insurance companies to develop statistics from historical data and predict future losses based on those statistics.*

Table 22-1 illustrates the law of large numbers. Insurance companies employ people called **actuaries** to develop statistics from historical data and predict future losses based on those statistics. Actuaries do not know how long each of us will live, but they do know approximately how many deaths will occur per 1,000 people in a given year. They also know the life expectancy of people in different age brackets. As the table shows, only 1.12 out of 1,000 people who are 19 years old are expected to die this year. In addition, the average 19-year-old will live 56.40 more years. This type of information allows insurance companies to set rates for life insurance policies in such a way that they can pay off a reasonable number of claims each year and still earn a profit.

Definite and Measurable Risk

Insurance companies protect against measurable losses that result directly from a specific event that occurs at a definite time, such as a collision between two cars or the theft of a car from a firm's fleet. Insurance protection does not apply to losses that occur gradually over time, such as the gradual loss in value resulting from the daily operation of a company car.

Insurance companies also need to know when the loss occurred and the extent of loss involved. In the case of an automobile accident, the company must know the time of the accident and the estimated cost of repairing or replacing the damaged vehicle.

TABLE 22-1   Mortality Table

Age	Deaths Per 1,000	Expectation of Life (Years)	Age	Deaths Per 1,000	Expectation of Life (Years)
0	12.60	73.88	51	6.42	27.10
1	.93	73.82	52	6.99	26.28
2	.65	72.89	53	7.61	25.46
3	.50	71.93	54	8.30	24.65
4	.40	70.97	55	9.02	23.85
5	.37	70.00	56	9.78	23.06
6	.33	69.02	57	10.59	22.29
7	.30	68.05	58	11.51	21.52
8	.27	67.07	59	12.54	20.76
9	.23	66.08	60	13.68	20.02
10	.20	65.10	61	14.93	19.29
11	.19	64.11	62	16.28	18.58
12	.25	63.12	63	17.67	17.88
13	.37	62.14	64	19.11	17.19
14	.53	61.16	65	20.59	16.51
15	.69	60.19	66	22.16	15.85
16	.83	59.24	67	23.89	15.20
17	.95	58.28	68	25.85	14.56
18	1.05	57.34	69	28.06	13.93
19	1.12	56.40	70	30.52	13.32
20	1.20	55.46	71	33.15	12.72
21	1.27	54.53	72	35.93	12.14
22	1.32	53.60	73	38.82	11.58

Source: *Life Insurance Fact Book* (Washington, D.C.: American Council of Life Insurance, 1990), pp. 122–123.

Law of Adverse Selection

Insurance companies would like to believe that there is an equal proportion of good risks and bad risks in any group of people or organizations that they insure. Unfortunately, this is not the case. People or organizations that are more likely to need insurance are also more likely to want insurance. For example, people who are unhealthy or who work in hazardous occupations are more likely to want health insurance than are other people. This tendency is called the **law of adverse selection.**

law of adverse selection
a principle of insurance: people or organizations that are more likely to need insurance are also more likely to want insurance.

Adverse selection may prevent an insurance company from offering insurance. For example, Jefferson-Pilot Life Insurance Company requires that all applicants for life insurance submit to a urine test to screen out HIV-positive individuals. If Jefferson-Pilot did not follow this practice, the law of adverse selection would predict that they would insure a disproportionate number of HIV-positive individuals. This would lead to large claims losses that the company might not be able to sustain.

Accidental Loss

accidental loss *a principle of insurance: only losses that may or may not happen—that are accidental—are insurable.*

According to the principle of **accidental loss,** only a loss that may or may not happen is insurable. That is, it must be accidental. If an insurance company knew that an arsonist was planning to burn down a building, it would not insure that building against fire loss.

Likewise, life insurance policies prohibit payment if the insured person commits suicide within the first year or two of coverage. Insurance companies insure only against losses that occur by chance, not those that are planned by the insured.

Catastrophic Hazard

catastrophic hazard *a principle of insurance: insurance companies must spread their risk so that no single disaster forces them to pay all their clients at once.*

Insurance companies expect losses to occur, and they expect to pay damage claims to some of the people they insure. However, they do not expect to pay everyone at once. The principle of **catastrophic hazard** dictates that insurance companies must spread their risk so that no single disaster forces them to pay all their clients at the same time. Many insurance companies have violated this principle and have paid dearly for doing so. For example, a tornado may destroy all the houses in a five-block area, or a hurricane may wipe out an entire city. If one company insured all the houses in the affected area, it would suffer an extremely large loss.

PRINCIPLES OF INSURANCE—THE INSURED'S PERSPECTIVE

3 The seven principles that have just been examined deal with insurance from the perspective of the insurance firm. Two principles of insurance from the perspective of the insured must also be followed.

Large Loss Principle

People and businesses should insure potentially serious losses before they insure minor losses. Otherwise, the person or business will spend more money on insurance than is prudent. In general, if an individual can pay for a loss from current income, it probably does not make sense to purchase insurance as a method of handling the risk. A classic example is that many people insure an old car for $1,000 but do not purchase life insurance. Unfortunately, if they were to die, their families could lose hundreds of thousands of dollars in income that would have been earned by the individuals during their lives.

Insuring Highly Probable Losses

A second principle is not to insure against highly probable losses. The more likely a loss is to occur, the more expensive the insurance premium will be to manage the risk. For example, individuals over 80 years of age find that life insurance is very expensive. Insurance companies' actuaries know that the average 80-year-old male will live only 5.4 more years.[3] Therefore, the full cost of the insurance coverage, plus administrative cost and profit for the company, must be charged to the insured during only 5.4 years. Clearly, life insurance should be purchased when an individual is relatively young.

SOURCES OF INSURANCE

The two basic sources of insurance are government agencies and private insurance companies. We'll begin our discussion by looking at federal and state governments, which are the largest source of insurance in the United States.

Federal and State Government Agencies

The federal government provides two basic types of insurance. First, it offers voluntary insurance programs to U.S. citizens. These programs provide protection against such disasters as floods, nuclear accidents, and damage to farm crops from drought or hail. Table 22-2 lists several types of voluntary insurance programs offered by the government.

TABLE 22-2   Selected Voluntary Federal Insurance Programs

Program	Protection
Federal Crop Insurance Corporation	Protects farmers' incomes by reducing losses from natural disasters. Insures 23 commodities including drought, flood, hail, insects, frost, and disease.
Federal Deposit Insurance Company (FDIC) and Savings Association Insurance Fund	Provides insurance protection for deposits up to $100,000 in banks, savings and loan associations, and credit unions.
Federal Flood Insurance	Protects homes and small businesses against floods. Protection limited to $35,000 for a single-family home and $10,000 for a business.
Federal Home Mortgage Loan Insurance	Protects private savings and loans and banks from loss resulting from default on the part of the borrower. The program promotes home ownership by encouraging loans.
Federal Crime Insurance	Protects businesses and homes against burglary, robbery, and theft (other than auto). Available only in states where there is a shortage of crime insurance at affordable rates.
Nuclear Energy Liability Insurance	Provides liability coverage to power companies for nuclear accidents. Maximum coverage is $560 million, with a $140 million deductible.
Post Office	Provides protection against the loss of mail. The post office sells loss insurance on registered mail, parcel post, and express mail.

The federal government also provides insurance that many people are required to purchase. The most important example of required insurance is social security, which will be discussed later in this chapter. Another example is federal pension insurance, which is issued by the Pension Benefit Guarantee Corporation. Each employer is required to pay a premium for each employee who is a part of an employer-sponsored pension plan.

State governments also provide several types of insurance. The most important are worker's compensation and unemployment insurance, both of which also are examined in the next section of this chapter.

Private Insurance Companies

Private insurance companies can be either stock companies or mutual companies. Both types offer a variety of insurance. Insurance agents sell insurance for both stock and mutual companies. Some agents are independent business people and sell insurance for several companies, while others work for only one company. Bonny Pearson, who is profiled in this chapter, is one of Jefferson-Pilot Life Insurance Company's most successful agents.

stock insurance companies private insurance companies organized to provide insurance for policyholders and profits for stockholders.

Stock Insurance Companies. **Stock insurance companies** are organized to provide insurance for policyholders and profit for stockholders. Stock companies operate very much as other private companies do. If profitable, they pay a dividend to their stockholders; if unprofitable, their stockholders may see the price of their stock drop.

Stock insurance companies are highly regulated by state insurance laws and agencies. Each state decides how much money insurance companies operating within its jurisdiction must have available to pay losses. Some states permit stock companies to sell all types of insurance except life and health insurance.

mutual insurance companies nonprofit insurance companies owned by the insurance policyholders.

Mutual Insurance Companies. **Mutual insurance companies** are nonprofit corporations owned by the insurance policyholders. There are no stockholders. The policyholders elect a board of directors, which oversees the operation of the company.

When a mutual company has revenue in excess of its costs, it pays a dividend to its policyholders, reduces the costs of insurance premiums, or keeps the money for company expansion. When a mutual company does not have enough money to meet its expenses or to pay losses, the law allows the company to collect an assessment from policyholders to offset company losses.

TYPES OF INSURANCE

Insurance can be classified in many ways. We have divided insurance into seven categories: property, homeowners', liability, loss-of-earning-power, employee, directors and officers, and life. Table 22-3 describes the protection provided by each type of insurance.

Property Insurance

property insurance insurance that protects against damage to real estate and other property.

Property insurance covers damage to real estate and other property. Most individuals and businesses need property insurance. In fact, many businesses simply could not operate without it. Five types of property insurance are discussed below.

TABLE 22-3   Types of Insurance

Policy	Protects Against
Property	
Fire	Losses to building and contents from fire and subsequent smoke and water damage.
Extended Coverage	Losses to building and contents from nine major risks, including windstorm, hail, civil commotion, explosion, and damage from aircraft, automobiles, and trucks.
Marine	Losses to ships and property being moved from one place to another.
Automobile	Injuries to people and damages to property from automobile accidents.
Burglary, Robbery, and Theft	Losses from crimes involving either employees or nonemployees.
Homeowners'	
Dwelling	Losses to private residence from fire, smoke, lightning, wind, hail, explosion, civil strife, vandalism, and accidents involving automobiles, trucks, or airplanes.
Other Structures	Losses to buildings separated from the dwelling.
Unscheduled Personal Property	Losses to the insured's personal property anywhere in the world from perils listed in the dwelling section of policy.
Additional Living Expenses	Cost of living expenses if dwelling is damaged to the point of being uninhabitable.
Personal Liability	Claims resulting from injuries to nonfamily members while on the insured's premises.
Renter's	Losses to personal property within rented dwelling where the insured lives.
Liability	
Public Liability	Losses relating to the ownership and maintenance of property and the acts of a company's employees.
Product or Service Liability	Damage from products or services purchased by consumers.
Loss-of-Earning-Power	
Business-Income	Losses from not being able to sell a product or service because of some extraordinary event.
Extra-Expense	The high cost of keeping a business operating after a major accident has occurred.
Rain	Losses resulting from rain.
Employee	
Social Security	Hardship in old age (by providing retirement benefits) and losses resulting from disability; Medicare pays most medical bills for people over 65, and Medicaid provides health care insurance for low-income people.
Fidelity Bond	Losses resulting from dishonest employees.
Worker's Compensation	Accidents to employees or work-related diseases.
Unemployment	Losses resulting from involuntary unemployment.
Health	Expenses related to the loss of health.
Disability Income	Loss of income resulting from illness, disease, or injury.
Directors and Officers	Losses to company directors and officers from stockholders' suits.
Life	
Term Life	Losses from premature death.
Whole Life	Losses from premature death (also creates a cash value for the insured).
Universal Life	Losses from premature death (also creates a variable-rate cash value for the insured).
Variable Life	Losses from premature death (also creates a cash value that fluctuates with the value of the securities purchased).

Bonny Pearson

Bonny Pearson's life is the stuff of which Hollywood movies are made. Born in Clayton, New Mexico, in December 1937, she was raised in a three-room sandstone house. To reach the house, people had to travel a narrow dirt road and ford a rather formidable creek. Her family worked the hostile land to grow its own food. Bonny wore dresses her mother had fashioned from flour sacks, as did the other young girls in her community. Survival in this beautiful but rugged land depended on personal determination, long hours, and neighbor helping neighbor. Along the way, Bonny developed a strong work ethic, a love of independence, and the attitude that people can accomplish anything they desire.

After high school, Bonny married and moved with her new husband to Pueblo, Colorado, where they both enrolled in junior college and began their quest for a better life. Bonny's formal education was delayed when she gave birth to the couple's first child one year later.

Over the next few years, many things changed in Bonny's life. She welcomed a second child, moved with her family to Texas, and began working at the candy counter in a variety store to help keep the family afloat. Throughout it all, however, she maintained her faith that anything can happen if a person is willing to work hard enough for it.

Bonny returned to night school. She took an entry-level position with a company specializing in insuring crops against hail. With the strong work ethic of her youth to guide her, Bonny set out to prove that she could master the daily operations of the company. Over the next few years, she accomplished this, gained experience, and expanded her knowledge of insurance when the company merged with another.

By 1969, Bonny was a single parent. She made what turned out to be the move of her lifetime, accepting a position as a "girl Friday" in the south Texas office of the Pilot Life Insurance Company. Later, she wrote, "There were two salespeople in the office. There was something about these two young men—something special—and I wanted to be a part of it." She proceeded to learn all she could about the life insurance business.

Within a year after Bonny took the job, the company moved into a larger office and doubled its sales force. She assumed a leadership position and became office manager. By 1973, the south Texas office had prospered to such an extent that Bonny could no longer handle the mounting workload alone, so additional staff members were hired for her to supervise.

In 1979 the agency was incorporated. Bonny married one of the men who had been a part of the original sales force. In early 1985, she assumed the title of general agent and began managing her own successful agency. In 1987, Jefferson Standard Life Insurance Company and Pilot Life Insurance Company merged to form Jefferson-Pilot Life Insurance Company. Bonny found herself once again in the position of needing to prove her leadership abilities. She succeeded in winning the trust of the new management. Today, Jefferson-Pilot Life Insurance Company is recognized as one of the best-managed insurance companies in the United States.

Life along the Texas-Mexico border, where Bonny Pearson's agency is located, has much more in common with her roots in New Mexico than with the world of Jefferson-Pilot's corporate offices on the East Coast. Bonny is now seeing the payoff for her hard work and her faith in her own abilities. Under her leadership as general manager, her south Texas offices have led the corporation nationwide in productivity for six of the past seven years, and the success shows no sign of diminishing.

The lessons of her childhood have produced big dividends for Bonny. She has traded flour-sack dresses for designer fashions. Bonny Pearson has met the challenge, and she is enjoying the rewards.

Fire. **Fire insurance** protects the insured building and its contents against financial loss caused by fire or subsequent smoke and water damage. The more risk underwritten by the fire insurance company, the more expensive the policy. A wooden building without a sprinkler system costs more to insure than a brick building that has a sprinkler system.

The New York Standard Fire Policy of 1943 is now used in nearly all states. It has been widely adopted because it is so easily understood. Before the adoption of this standard, fire insurance policies were written specially for each client. As a result, policies were very complex and could often be understood only by legal experts.

Most fire insurance policies for commercial buildings carry a **coinsurance clause**. This clause requires the policyholder to purchase sufficient insurance to cover a specified percentage of the property value to obtain full reimbursement for loss in the event of a fire. The percentage required is usually 80 percent. To illustrate, suppose a commercial building is valued at $1 million and sustains $400,000 in fire damage. The insurance company would be required to pay the insured the full $400,000 if the building were insured for at least $800,000 (or 80 percent of its value). On the other hand, if the building were insured for only $600,000, the insurance company would pay only $300,000 of the loss, and the insured would pay the remaining $100,000 to repair the building. The calculations are done as follows:

- The coinsurance clause requires that the building be insured for $800,000 (80 percent requirement × $1,000,000 value of the building).
- The insured purchased only 75 percent of the required insurance coverage ($600,000 insurance divided by the $800,000 requirement).
- To compute its obligation, the insurance firm multiplies the 75 percent by the amount of the loss (75 percent × $400,000 = $300,000).

The standard fire policy has four exclusions. Fire insurance does not:

1. Cover losses resulting from fire intentionally started by the owner of the building.
2. Cover new, potentially risky plant additions if the insurance company has not been previously informed of them.
3. Protect against losses to a building left vacant for 60 days or more.
4. Protect against a fire caused by explosion, riot, invasion, rebellion, civil war, or an order by a civil authority.

If a loss does occur, the insured must give notice to the insurance company as soon as possible. In addition, the insured must complete a claim form for the insurance company within 60 days of the loss. This form will ask detailed questions concerning when the loss occurred, why it occurred, the cash value of the property that was destroyed, and the amount of the loss being claimed. Finally, the insured is required to protect the property from further loss. For example, if a commercial building is damaged by fire, the owner must protect it by boarding it up or securing it somehow. The purpose of this requirement is to minimize further damage to the property.

The insurance company has the option of paying the claim in cash or repairing the structure. This option protects the company from claims for inflated amounts.

Finally, most fire insurance policies contain a **subrogation provision** that gives the company the right to recover damages from the party who caused the loss. For example, if faulty wiring causes a building to burn down, the insurance

fire insurance insurance that protects the insured building and its contents against financial loss caused by fire or subsequent smoke and water damage.

coinsurance clause a clause in most fire insurance policies that requires the policyholder to purchase enough insurance to cover a specified percentage of the value of the property in order to obtain full reimbursement for loss in the event of a fire.

Business Career
Claim Adjuster: Investigates damage or loss claims involving insurance company clients. Examines claim form and other records to verify that loss is covered by the policy. Inspects property damage, interviews witnesses, and consults police and hospital records to determine extent of liability. Negotiates settlement or recommends legal proceedings to settle claim. *Average Salary: $22,300.*

subrogation provision a clause in most fire insurance policies that gives the company the right to recover damages from the party who caused a loss.

company may sue the electrician who installed the wiring to recover the funds paid to the building owner.[4]

Extended Coverage. Fire insurance is the basic business property insurance policy, but it is also possible to "extend" a fire insurance policy to protect against other risks. **Extended coverage** protects a building and its contents against windstorm, hail, explosion, smoke, civil strife, riot resulting from a strike, and damage from aircraft, automobiles, and trucks. For example, extended coverage made it possible for some businesses to rebuild after the Los Angeles riots in May, 1992 (discussed in the box on p. 623). The firm's cost of protecting itself against these risks with an extended policy is much less than if a policy for each were purchased separately.

extended coverage insurance that protects a building and its contents against windstorm, hail, explosion, smoke, civil strife, riot resulting from a strike, and damage from aircraft, automobiles, and trucks.

Marine. **Marine insurance** protects ship owners against damage to the ship and/or its cargo. The two types of marine insurance are ocean marine and inland marine. Ocean marine, the oldest form of insurance, protects shipowners against damage to vessels and property being transported by ships at sea. Most movable property can be protected by inland marine insurance, which covers losses on property being transported from the ports as opposed to on the ocean. It may include coverage for transportation by rail, truck, and inland waterway.

marine insurance insurance that protects ship owners against damage to the ship and/or its cargo; can also be extended to cover property being transported by truck and train.

Automobile. **Automobile insurance** protects against injuries to people and damage to property from automobile accidents. There are nearly 30 million automobile accidents each year in the United States. These accidents result in 50,000 deaths, 5 million injuries, and $60 billion in losses. Deaths related to automobile accidents account for almost half of all accidental deaths in the United States.

Young drivers are involved in a disproportionate number of automobile accidents. For example, drivers under age 25 made up 18.6 percent of all drivers in 1990, yet they were involved in 32.1 percent of all traffic accidents.[5] This is why automobile insurance for young people is quite expensive.

Personal Automobile Policy, or PAP, is the most common type of automobile insurance. Although PAPs differ slightly from company to company and state to state, the basic PAP coverage has four components.

automobile insurance insurance that protects against injuries to people and damage to property from automobile accidents.

1. *Liability:* The insurance company agrees to provide money to protect the policyholder against claims for injuries to pedestrians, passengers, or people in other cars. The protection applies to the owner of the car that was involved in the accident or to anyone else driving the car with the owner's permission. In addition, the insurance company will pay the cost of damage to other people's property resulting from an auto accident. This coverage applies not only to cars but also to property, such as lamp posts, telephone poles, and buildings.

2. *Medical:* This portion of the PAP covers medical expenses resulting from an automobile accident injury. This insurance protects the policyholder, family members living at home, and any guest riding in the car. If you are driving an automobile that you do not own, your PAP medical coverage will protect you, but not anyone else who is riding in the car. In this situation, passengers must rely on their own medical coverage or on the vehicle owner's medical coverage.

3. *Uninsured motorist:* The insurance company agrees to pay the owner of the car or any occupant of the car medical expenses resulting from an automobile accident that was caused by an uninsured motorist or hit-and-run driver.

Loss from Civil Strife: Rodney King and the Los Angeles Riots

On May 1, 1992, a verdict of not guilty from a jury of ten whites, one Hispanic, and one Asian-American shook South Cenral Los Angeles and the rest of the nation. Rodney King had led the Los Angeles Police Department on a 115 mile-per-hour chase. When he was apprehended by more than 20 Los Angeles police officers, he refused to cooperate. Mr. King was shot twice with taser darts, which produce 50,000 volts of electricity. In addition, he was beaten unmercifully by several Los Angeles police officers. The event was video-taped for the entire world to watch over and over again. To most Americans, it was a classic case of police violence.

The results of the verdict were quick, deadly, expensive, and disastrous for South Cen-tral Los Angeles. Rioters immediately took to the streets. The police were ill-prepared and ill-equipped to deal with the problem. Much of the initial violence was directed at Korean-American-owned businesses in the South Central community. However, it quickly spread to virtually all neighborhood grocery stores, gasoline stations, liquor stores, and household appliance outlets. Signs that read "Black owned—do not burn" had virtually no impact. The bottom line was hundreds of millions of dollars in damage, thousands of jobs lost, the economic infrastructure of a community destroyed, and more than 50 people dead.

A few of the South-Central merchants carried extended coverage for fire insurance. These policies protect policy holders against risks associated with civil strife. As a result, these retailers did recover most of their immediate losses from their insruance companies. However, very few of these policies contained any loss-of-earning power insurance. As a result, the merchants were not able to recover any lost revenue or profits from their busi-nesses that were destroyed. All of the policies did carry a subrogation provision. Unfortu-nately, the police were not able to identify very many people who actually destroyed a specific piece of property and who also had enough money to repay the insurance com-pany for the damages that it incurred. As a result, the insurance companies had to bear the expense.

Some merchants elected to practice risk reduction by protecting their businesses with shotguns and barricades made up of any material that was available, ranging from shop-ping carts to automobiles. While this type of protection worked in some cases, it was very dangerous for the store owners, and if they were unfortunate enough to injure an innocent party, it would be much more expensive than extended coverage fire insurance.

This is important coverage because, regardless of state laws, many people drive automobiles with no liability insurance coverage.

4. *Physical damage:* Physical damage to an automobile is divided into two types of coverage—collision and loss other than collision. Collision pays for dam-age to the policyholder's car in the event of an accident. Such damage may result from colliding with another car or with a building, or from rolling the car over. Collision insurance is normally sold with a deductible of $100 to $500. A **deductible** is a specified amount that the policyholder must pay toward a loss before the insurance company pays anything. In this example, the policyholder pays the first $100 to $500 in damages, and the insurance company pays the rest. If the other driver is at fault, his or her company pays for any damages suffered. In this case, the driver not at fault is totally reim-bursed for the cost of repairing the car.

Policies that cover loss other than collision include losses resulting from the theft of an automobile. They also pay for damages resulting from fire, glass breakage, falling objects, explosion, earthquake, windstorm, flood, and vandalism. This type of automobile insurance usually has a deductible in the range of $100 to $250.

deductible *a specified amount that the policyholder must pay toward a loss before the insurance company pays anything.*

no-fault insurance *automobile insurance under which parties to an accident recover medical and hospital expenses and any losses in income from their own insurance companies, regardless of who was at fault.*

In addition to the standard PAP automobile insurance coverage, **no-fault insurance** was introduced in the early 1970s. Today approximately half of the 50 states permit no-fault insurance to be sold. Under no-fault insurance, the parties to an accident recover their medical and hospital expenses and any losses in income (resulting from the accident) from their own insurance companies. Medical and related expenses are paid to each person by his or her insurance company, regardless of who was at fault. Expensive litigation is thereby avoided.

Burglary, Robbery, and Theft. Crime is a major problem in the United States. It is also a very expensive problem. As Table 22-4 shows, crime has increased since the early 1970s. **Burglary,** defined as forced entry, increased by approximately 5 percent, and **robbery,** defined as the taking of property by force, by almost 30 percent. Automobile theft was up 37 percent.

burglary *forced entry.*

robbery *taking property by force.*

Homeowners' Insurance

One of the most important and most often purchased types of insurance is **homeowners' insurance.** It permits the homeowner to purchase, in one policy, a broad range of coverage for a relatively low price. In addition to insuring the home, this coverage protects against many perils that could cost a great deal of money.[6] This section will review the five basic coverages included with homeowners' insurance. Like other types of insurance, homeowners' policies differ depending on the state and the company that is issuing the policy.

homeowners' insurance *an insurance policy that provides a broad range of coverage to protect the policyholder's home, other structures, personal property, etc., at a relatively low price.*

Dwelling. A dwelling is defined as a structure on the property that is used primarily as a private residence. It also includes structures that are attached to the dwelling, such as a patio roof, a carport, or a greenhouse. This coverage provides protection against such perils as fire, smoke, lightning, wind, hail, explosion, civil strife, vandalism, and accidents that involve automobiles, trucks, or airplanes.

Other Structures. Buildings that are separated from the dwelling are also protected. It is usually to the insured's advantage if a separated building is defined as an "other structure" if both buildings are damaged, since the total coverage is usually 110 percent of the dwelling coverage. The "other structure" coverage is designed to protect personal property, so structures that are used for business purposes or to provide rental income are not protected.

unscheduled personal property insurance *a portion of a homeowners' insurance policy that protects property owned or used by the policyholder anywhere in the world against theft, damage resulting from fire, vandalism, or other perils.*

Unscheduled Personal Property. **Unscheduled personal property insurance** is the most complex portion of any standard homeowner policy. It

TABLE 22-4   The Grim Statistics of Crime (rates per 100,000 inhabitants)

	1971	1985	1990	Percentage Increase
Burglary	1,175	1,280	1,236	5.2
Robbery	198	202	257	29.8
Motor Vehicle Theft	480	495	658	37.0

Source: U.S. Department of Justice, *Crime in the United States* (Washington, D.C.: U.S. Government Printing Office, 1990), pp.18, 27, 38.

The largest single asset of most American homeowners is their house. It makes sense to protect it by getting homeowners' insurance. When Hurricane Hugo pushed a tree onto this North Carolina house, the damage was covered by a homeowners' policy.

covers personal property owned or used by the insured anywhere in the world. This means that personal property is protected against theft or damage resulting from fire, vandalism, or the other perils that are listed in the dwelling portion of the policy, while the insured is away.

The amount of unscheduled personal property coverage is normally 50 percent of the dwelling's insurance coverage. Therefore, if a home is insured for $100,000, the total unscheduled personal property insurance would be $50,000.

There are a number of exceptions, as well as limitations, to this form of insurance. For example, there is a $200 limit on money and a $1,000 limit on both trailers and silverware. In addition, animals, motor vehicles, and the property of boarders are specifically excluded. Under most homeowners' policies, it is possible to increase the dollar amount of unscheduled personal property insurance, as well as to obtain insurance to cover specific property such as a valuable coin collection.

Additional Living Expenses. This portion of the policy covers the cost of living if a dwelling is damaged to the point that it is uninhabitable. The objective of this insurance policy is to permit the policyholder's family to maintain its normal standard of living while the damaged dwelling is repaired or replaced. Most policies permit the insured to select one of two options: receiving additional living expenses or the fair rental value of the home. With the first option, the insured is given enough money each month to pay the additional expenses required to maintain the family's normal standard of living. However, the insured may elect to take the fair rental income option and live with family or friends and keep the living allowance provided by the company.

Personal Liability. The basic homeowners' policy provides $100,000 worth of comprehensive personal liability coverage and $1,000 worth of medical insurance. This protects the insured and his or her family against claims from other individuals while they are on the insured's premises. In addition, most medical coverage provides protection for the insured if he or she injures someone at another location. For example, if you injure a friend playing racquetball, your homeowners' medical insurance should help defray your friend's medical expenses. Individuals who want additional personal liability protection may increase their coverage by paying increased premiums or by purchasing an umbrella liability policy.

Personal umbrella policies are designed to protect well-to-do people against catastrophic lawsuits. Most firms will write personal umbrella insurance coverage ranging from $1 million to $10 million. The coverage takes over from standard homeowners' policies for liability associated with accidents related to dwellings, boats, automobiles, and recreational vehicles. The coverage is normally inexpensive, since it is drawn upon only after the limits on the homeowners' policy have been reached.

Renters' Insurance. The standard homeowners' policy is designed to provide a broad spectrum of insurance for an individual who owns his or her home. Most states also permit insurance companies to sell a homeowners'-type policy to people who are living in a rented dwelling. The policy is similar to the standard homeowners' policy except that it does not protect the dwelling or any other structures. The rest of the coverage, including the contents of the dwelling and other structures, is very similar to the standard homeowners' policy.

Liability Insurance

liability insurance insurance that protects against losses resulting from harm caused to people or their property.

An important risk for all businesses is financial loss resulting from harm caused to people or their property. **Liability insurance** protects against losses resulting from such harm. Employees of a business are protected through worker's compensation, which will be discussed later in the chapter. However, a firm also needs to protect itself against damage claims filed by the public due to failures of the products or services that it provides.

Liability insurance has become even more important because the courts have accepted the concept of strict liability. This means that individuals or businesses are responsible for the consequences of their actions, regardless of their motives or their use of reasonable care. A purchaser of a product will usually prevail in court against a manufacturer of a defective product, and even against the retailer who sold the product, if it can be shown that (1) the product was defective, (2) the defect made the product unreasonably dangerous, and (3) the defect was the cause of the injury.[7]

We will examine two forms of liability: public liability and product or service liability. Both can be covered by a comprehensive, general liability insurance policy.

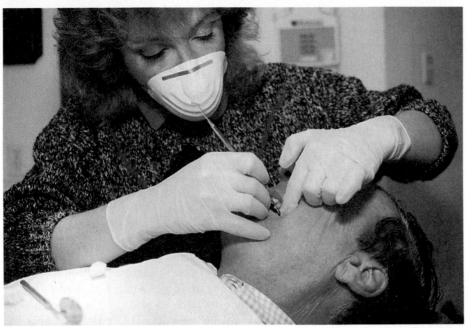

Dentists nowadays exercise special care to avoid transmitting infectious diseases such as AIDS. Even so, they need liability insurance, because they can be held responsible for millions of dollars in damages, no matter how careful they have been.

Public Liability. **Public liability insurance** protects against business risk associated with the ownership and maintenance of property and the actions of a firm's employees. If a customer in a retail store stumbles on torn carpeting and breaks a leg, the retailer is usually held responsible for the injury. The retailer, or the retailer's insurance company, must pay all medical expenses and possibly monetary damages as well—to compensate for the "pain and suffering" experienced by the injured person as a result of the fall. Public liability also relates to the conduct of a firm's employees. That is, the firm is responsible for any harm caused to the public by one of its employees.

public liability insurance insurance that protects against business risk associated with the ownership and maintenance of property and the actions of a firm's employees.

Product or Service Liability. **Product liability insurance** covers losses resulting from product defect, breach of product warranty, and any danger caused by use of a product. Until a few years ago, manufacturers were held responsible only for product defects and breaches of warranty. Today, courts hold manufacturers liable for product safety even when the victim contributes to the injury.[8] For example, not long ago a manufacturer was successfully sued for $111,000 when one of its products caught on fire. The trouble started when a person using roofing primer heated it over a fire. This "thinning" procedure was not recommended by the manufacturer. The court ruled that the manufacturer was liable for damages suffered by the user, because it did not print a warning that the roof primer would release explosive gases when heated.[9]

product liability insurance insurance that covers losses resulting from product defect, breach of product warranty, and any danger caused by use of a product.

An individual offering a service is responsible for correctly administering that service. **Service liability insurance** covers losses resulting from a service that was improperly provided. A doctor cannot provide medical services without liability protection. A misdiagnosis could cost hundreds of thousands of dollars in damages. Doctors are not alone in this regard. Other professionals, such as law-

service liability insurance insurance that protects against losses resulting from a service that was improperly provided.

yers, accountants, insurance agents, and even hairstylists, must also carry liability insurance. One beauty salon had to pay $15,000 because of damage to a customer's hair when a cold wave was applied incorrectly.[10]

Loss-of-Earning-Power Insurance

loss-of-earning-power insurance *insurance that protects businesses against lost income caused by some unusual event.*

Many businesses buy **loss-of-earning-power insurance** to protect themselves against lost income because of some unusual event. An accident may not only destroy the property of a business but also make it impossible for the business to meet its regular expenses. The most common form of loss-of-earning-power insurance is business-income insurance. Let's take a closer look at this type of insurance, as well as extra-expense insurance and rain insurance.

Business-Income Insurance. Businesses face many types of risk. One type of risk, as mentioned above, is that uncontrollable events will temporarily disrupt regular operations of a business. **Business-income insurance** protects a business from losses when some unusual event prevents the business from selling its product. For example, imagine a major strike at Worthington Industries, a major producer of steel for the automobile industry. The strike could quickly cause a division of Ford Motor Company to stop the production of cars—no steel, no cars. In this situation, business-income insurance pays all of Ford's continuing expenses even though operations have halted. These expenses might include the cost of fire insurance, plant security, and layoffs. In addition, business-income insurance would pay Ford for the loss of normal profits. These are the profits that Ford would have made if there had not been a steel strike.

business-income insurance *insurance that protects a business from losses incurred from not being able to sell a product because of some extraordinary event.*

Extra-Expense Insurance. Certain businesses cannot afford to shut down when their facilities are destroyed or heavily damaged. Banks, newspapers, public utilities, oil dealers, and dairies must somehow continue to make their services available. Even a short-term shutdown of any one of these businesses would injure the public.

extra-expense insurance *insurance that protects against the high cost of keeping a business operating after a major accident has occurred.*

   Extra-expense insurance allows a business to meet the needs of the public, even after its property has been severely damaged. It pays such expenses as rent on temporary office space and office machines. It also pays overtime allowances for employees working long hours to keep the business operating.

rain insurance *insurance that protects against losses resulting from rain.*

Rain Insurance. April showers bring May flowers, but they can also drown a firm's profits, no matter in which month the showers occur. For example, outdoor concerts depend on good weather for their success. **Rain insurance** protects the entrepreneur for a short period of time against financial losses resulting from sudden rainstorms. When rain results in the cancellation of an event, the insurance company does not pay the policyholder unless the U.S. Weather Bureau verifies that at least one tenth of an inch of rain fell during the time the insurance was in effect.

Employee Insurance

Most business executives believe in the importance of high-quality insurance for their employees and their families. Besides protecting the health and safety of employees, such insurance can also protect the firm from employee dishonesty. The most important and widely held employee insurance is the federally mandated and operated social security system.

Social Security. **Social security** is required insurance, through which the federal government provides benefits to the elderly and the disabled. When social security began, its primary aim was to provide income to retired workers. The amount of money each person received was based on the worker's previous average monthly earnings. Now, to protect the elderly from inflation, the government increases the size of benefits if annual inflation exceeds a certain percentage. In 1990, the average monthly benefit for a single retired worker was $1,023; for a family, $1,390.

Social security retirement payments are thought of as insurance by most people. In reality, however, they are retirement benefits paid by the government from funds contributed by currently employed individuals.

The social security program does provide insurance to workers between the ages of 50 and 64 who become disabled. In case of death, retirement benefits transfer to the surviving spouse. The most significant change in social security was Medicare insurance. This mandatory federal health insurance pays most medical bills for people 65 years of age or older. It costs the employer and the employee 1.45 percent of the employee's wages up to $125,000. Medicaid provides health care coverage to low-income people. (See page 630 for a discussion of the Controversial Issue, "Should Health Insurance Be Nationalized?")

Social security is a very expensive program. Both the employer and the employee pay 7.65 percent of the employee's first $53,400 of income. This means that a total of $3,060 is contributed annually for each employee who makes $20,000. Self-employed individuals must contribute 15.3 percent of their income up to a maximum income of $53,400. Most experts believe that social security will become even more expensive in the future. The number of retired people will increase, and the number of employed people who pay the cost of the social security program will remain relatively stable.

Fidelity Bonds. **Fidelity bonds** protect an employer from losses resulting from employee dishonesty. They are particularly important for businesses handling significant amounts of cash, such as banks. However, even convenience stores, such as 7-Eleven or Stop-N-Go, purchase fidelity bonds, since most of their transactions involve cash.

There are two types of fidelity bonds: individual and blanket. An **individual fidelity bond** protects a business against losses from dishonesty by one or more specified employees. A **blanket bond** protects the business against losses caused by dishonesty of any of its employees. With blanket bonds, the employee responsible for the theft need not be identified by name. The business will be able to collect on its policy if it can show that the loss resulted from employee theft.

Worker's Compensation. **Worker's compensation insurance** pays benefits to employees who suffer job-related accidents or disease. It is based on the premise of liability without fault. That is, employers are held liable for any accident or disease that is related to their employees' jobs, regardless of who is at fault. The law provides for quick payment to injured employees according to a schedule of benefits that is established by law.[11]

Today, all 50 states have worker's compensation laws. Roughly nine out of ten employed people in the United States are covered by some form of worker's compensation insurance. Although the specific benefits vary from state to state, the following forms of protection are usually provided:

- *Medical*—payment for hospital, doctor, and other medical expenses.
- *Disability*—payments of lost income to an injured employee unable to work.

social security *required insurance, through which the federal government provides benefits to the elderly and the disabled.*

fidelity bonds *insurance that protects an employer from losses due to employee dishonesty.*

individual fidelity bond *insurance that protects a business against losses from dishonesty by one or more specified employees.*

blanket bond *insurance that protects the business against losses caused by dishonesty of any of its employees.*

worker's compensation insurance *government insurance that pays benefits to employees who suffer job-related accidents or disease.*

Should Health Insurance Be Nationalized?

Legislators have suggested that the federal government create a national health insurance program, funded from taxes and taxpayer contributions, to ensure that everyone is guaranteed protection from extensive medical bills. Is such a system of national health insurance the best choice?

Yes

Health insurance should be nationalized. A major risk problem Americans face today is how to cover the costs of medical treatment for injury or disease. Medical costs have reached unreasonable levels, and medical insurance premiums have risen to cover those costs. Many people spend more on health insurance than they save for retirement!

We must either lower medical costs themselves or lower the costs of insuring for them. To lower medical costs,

the only effective approach would be to nationalize (or socialize) medical care. People disagree as to how efficient this remedy has been in countries where it has been tried. Also, there would be serious constitutional questions about the legality of socialized medicine. So we are left with reducing the cost of insuring for medical costs.

Health insurance could be handled very efficiently and quite economically by the federal government. Premiums could be withheld from paychecks along with social security taxes and income taxes. Consistent premiums could be charged across the country. Older people would not be charged more for insurance than they can afford, and poor-risk individuals would not have to forego health insurance. National health insurance could also be a powerful tool of social policy. It could be used, for example, to penalize cigarette smoking. It could be used to provide part of the aid required in natural disasters, and it could include special insurance clauses for drug or alcohol rehabilitation. The poor and unemployed could be covered by national health insurance, with the government picking up some or all of the costs.

Health insurance taxes would be collected to pay for current expenses, unlike social security taxes, which must be collected to pay for expenses the government incurs after many years. In an era of erratic economic changes, a national health insurance program would never face the

---

- *Rehabilitation*—payment of the cost of therapy designed to return the injured worker to the job.
- *Survivor benefits*—payment to surviving family members in the case of death resulting from a work-related accident or disease.

unemployment insurance
government insurance that provides cash benefits to involuntarily unemployed individuals and helps unemployed people find jobs.

Unemployment Insurance. Unemployment insurance programs are operated jointly by federal and state governments. Each state's program varies slightly, but they all have two common objectives: provide cash benefits to involuntarily unemployed individuals and help unemployed people find jobs. To be eligible for unemployment benefits, the individual must have been continually employed during the base period. This is normally one year before the unemployed person lost his or her job. In addition, the individual must be capable of working, must register for work at a public employment office, and must be actively seeking employment. Unemployment insurance benefits are not available to an individual who quits his or her job or who was terminated for good cause.

Unemployed workers usually receive benefits for up to 26 weeks at approximately 50 percent of their wages when they became unemployed. In addition, each state has a minimum and maximum amount of coverage, with an average benefits package of approximately $200 per week. The federal government has created an extended benefits program that permits an individual who has not found a job to receive benefits for an additional 13 weeks.[13]

health insurance *insurance that covers medical costs resulting from injury or disease.*

Health Insurance. Health insurance covers medical costs resulting from injury or disease. Many businesses offer employees and their families free health insurance, or at least an opportunity to buy health insurance at reduced rates.

prospects of deficits that the social security system now faces. Yes, national health insurance is a good idea.

No

The United States has the best system of health care in the world. It is true that our system is expensive and that doctors frequently make well over $100,000 per year—but they do spend as much as ten years studying medicine before they can earn a living. One of the objectives of any national health care system would be to reduce the cost of health care. This is a noble objective, but if the earning potential of our doctors is significantly reduced, the nation will not be able to attract as many of our best and brightest citizens into the medical profession.

A second problem with cost containment is that everyone is for it until it involves a friend or a family member. Then most of us want to do everything humanly possible to solve the immediate medical problem. Cost is usually not much of a concern. Therefore, the real question is whether you want private doctors making key medical decisions that affect your friends and family members, or whether you want even the best-intentioned government bureaucrat making them. The bureaucrats may be able to reduce the cost of medical care by denying some forms of treatment because they are too expensive, too experimental, or offered in too many hospitals. Unfortunately, this type of cold, hard logic will seem cruel when someone who is important to you is being denied needed medical care.

An additional issue involves future cost containment. National health care will be subject to the same damage from inflation that our social security program has experienced. From 1980 through 1989, the maximum amount that both employees and employers put into social security insurance more than doubled. Also, consider the scandals surrounding Medicare, or even the government-supervised savings and loan industry. Who is to guarantee that a national health insurance program won't be corrupted like these and other governmental welfare and social care systems have been? Mismanagement or fraudulent use of funds would require additional tax support of the health insurance program, and then everyone would have to pay more.

Let's keep government out of the health insurance business. Our current program is not broken, so let's not try to fix it. Health insurance is too important to have it botched the way social security has been. In the end, national health insurance will cost more money and might cost us some of our valuable freedoms. Let's keep things the way they are.

What Do You Think?

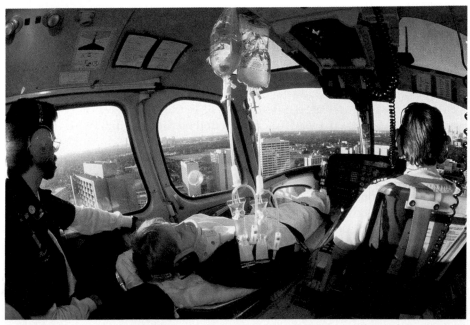

Good health insurance coverage is important to every worker, even those who may never need a dramatic helicopter transport to the hospital.

Health Maintenance Organizations

health maintenance organization (HMO) private group of physicians that provides members with medical and hospital care for a fixed, prepaid fee.

A **health maintenance organization (HMO)** is a private group of medical doctors that provides its members with medical and hospital care for a fixed, prepaid fee. The HMO is a type of health insurance that competes directly with traditional health insurance companies. Many HMOs are sponsored by private insurance companies. For example, Prucare is sponsored by the Prudential Life Insurance Company.

The major differences between HMOs and other types of group health insurance plans are listed below.

1. The regular monthly payments that HMOs receive are not directly tied to how many people use the HMO's services. That is, with the exception of a nominal fee such as $2 per visit, HMOs are not paid for on a fee-for-service basis. Instead, a fee is set for member employees of a company in a contract that may run for several years.
2. HMOs stress regular health care, early diagnosis, and disease prevention. Traditional group insurance plans pay for losses only when a sickness or accident occurs.
3. HMOs control costs by providing incentives for doctors to be good managers. Since the HMO regularly receives a specified amount of money, it benefits directly by holding down costs. In contrast, traditional insurance companies cannot really control costs, which are determined by doctors and hospitals.
4. HMOs offer a variety of medical services under one roof. Under most regular health insurance plans, the patient must seek different types of medical care from different sources. That is, no single health care provider is responsible for the total health of the patient.

Many people refused to enroll in HMOs when they were first established. The concern was that patients could not choose their own doctors and that they would receive "assembly line" medical care. However, many HMOs provide excellent medical care at a cost that is lower than traditional group insurance plans. It is likely that HMOs will continue to increase their share of the health insurance market.

This second option is becoming increasingly common, because health insurance is so expensive that many businesses simply cannot afford to pay the entire cost of their employees' insurance coverage.

More than 80 percent of the U.S. population is covered by some form of health insurance. Being covered by a health insurance policy is very important, because if a family is not well insured, a major illness can wipe out a lifetime of savings. Total health expenditures in the United States amount to approximately 12 percent of GNP, up from 4.4 percent in 1950. (See the boxes on health maintenance organizations (page 632) and preferred provider organizations (page 633) for two alternative approaches to health insurance.)

Five types of health insurance benefits may be offered as separate or combined contracts.

Hospitalization. A hospitalization contract protects the insured against the major costs of a hospital stay, including room and board, laboratory fees, use of the operating room, and medicines and supplies. Many insurance contracts establish upper limits for each area of the coverage. For example, a hospitalization contract might allow payment for a semiprivate room, but not to exceed $150 per day for 120 days. Likewise, most hospital plans limit miscellaneous fees, such as laboratory charges, X rays, and the cost of drugs, to a multiple of the room rate (e.g., 10 times the day rate) or a maximum per-day charge (e.g., $2,000 per day).

Surgical. A surgical contract sets allowances for different surgical procedures. For example, the contract may state that an appendectomy will be covered for up to $1,000 and a tonsillectomy for $1,500.

Preferred Provider Organizations

A **preferred provider organization (PPO)** is a network of health care providers who have agreed to provide medical care to specific groups of people at a reduced cost. The PPO is an alternative to the HMO. Its objective is to hold down medical costs while guaranteeing patients high-quality medical care. A business may establish a PPO network by contracting with area physicians, hospitals, and other providers of health care to care for its employees at a reduced fee. In return for the discount, the business agrees to encourage its employees to use the PPO system and to ensure that payments are made promptly to the health care providers.

There are two major differences between PPOs and HMOs.

1. Medical care is not provided on a prepaid basis. HMOs are paid whether people use their services or not, whereas PPOs receive payment only when medical care is provided.
2. If an employee has selected an HMO, he or she must use it exclusively during the period of the contract. In contrast, employees who are in a PPO system may decide on a case-by-case basis whether or not to use the PPO system. Although there is a clear economic incentive to use the PPO system, there is no obligation on the part of the employee to do so.

The most important difficulty with PPO systems is in getting doctors and other health care organizations to join the system. Health care providers are concerned that once discounts begin with a certain group of patients, they will spread to other patients. However, firms that have a large number of employees in any one community have been quite successful in establishing PPO networks.

Regular Medical. This coverage pays for physician services other than surgical procedures. It usually allows for physician visits in the hospital, at home, or in the doctor's office. Normally, regular medical insurance is written as a part of other types of insurance, not as a separate contract.

Major Medical. This type of coverage protects the insured against very large medical bills. A major medical policy might establish a maximum payment of $200,000 for any one illness or accident. It might also feature a small deductible, such as $300, and stipulate that the insurance company will pay 90 percent of all medical costs above the deductible. Major medical will cover a wide variety of expenses, including hospital room and board, nursing care, miscellaneous hospital services, physician expenses, prescription drugs, and wheelchairs.

Dental. Dental insurance covers oral examinations, X rays, cleaning, fillings, bridgework, root canal therapy, and orthodontics. Dental coverage is usually part of a group insurance plan. Traditionally, such insurance has a set of maximum allowances limiting the coverage for particular dental services.

Disability-Income Insurance. Another form of insurance is **disability-income insurance,** under which the issuing company pays all or part of a person's salary when he or she is unable to work due to illness, disease, or injury. These policies offer a great deal of protection to the disabled worker's family. Most disability-income plans pay the insured person for a specified number of years only, although lifetime protection can also can be obtained.

Disability-income insurance is quite inexpensive and may be the most important type of insurance coverage an individual can obtain. It will protect the insured's family against loss of income. Without this protection, a family may face the double catastrophe of having to take care of a disabled person without the income that person has traditionally generated.

Directors and Officers Insurance

Directors and officers (D&O) insurance is purchased to protect the directors and officers of a corporation from damages associated with being personally sued by stockholders who feel that the firm has been mismanaged. D&O insurance is very expensive and is difficult to obtain for most small firms. In addition, the insurance is normally written with a substantial deductible and costs much more today than it did a few years ago. D&O insurance does not protect the directors and officers of a firm from lawsuits if they engage in illegal actions or conspire to do so.

Prospective directors who are not officers and employees of a corporation often refuse to join its board of directors if they are not provided with adequate D&O insurance. "Going naked," or serving as a director without adequate D&O coverage, can be a very expensive proposition if directors are sued successfully.

Life Insurance

Life insurance pays a cash benefit to a designated person, called a **beneficiary,** when the insured person dies. The purpose of life insurance is to partially offset the income lost when a wage earner dies. As Figure 22-1 shows, the value of the average family's life insurance is almost three times as great as its annual disposable income. Thus, if the primary wage earner in the family were to die, the family could live for approximately three years on the insurance money.

Some of the largest companies in the United States sell life insurance. The 15 largest life insurance companies have more than $4 trillion of life insurance in force. These 15 companies employ approximately 309,000 people.[14]

Most families cannot afford to buy enough life insurance to protect themselves completely against the loss of income resulting from the death of the primary wage earner. To help provide adequate coverage, many firms offer their employees the opportunity to purchase some form of life insurance through group plans. In families where both spouses have good-paying jobs and substantial assets, complete protection is less important.

Life insurance comes in various forms. Let's look at them and at some of the questions that need to be asked before buying life insurance.

Term Life Insurance. **Term life insurance** pays a death benefit if the insured person dies within the specified period when the policy is in force. The death benefit is the amount of money paid to the beneficiary of the policy. Typically, a family purchases term life insurance to protect itself against the premature death of the breadwinner. A term life insurance policy has no savings element in it. It is worth nothing if it expires before the death of the insured person.

Term insurance generally provides more insurance per dollar of premium paid than any other type of life insurance. For a person 25 years old, a $120 annual premium will buy approximately $100,000 in term life insurance for one year. In contrast, it would cost approximately $670 per year for the rest of the insured's life to purchase $100,000 worth of whole-life insurance.

FIGURE 22-1   Value of Life Insurance and Annual Disposable Income

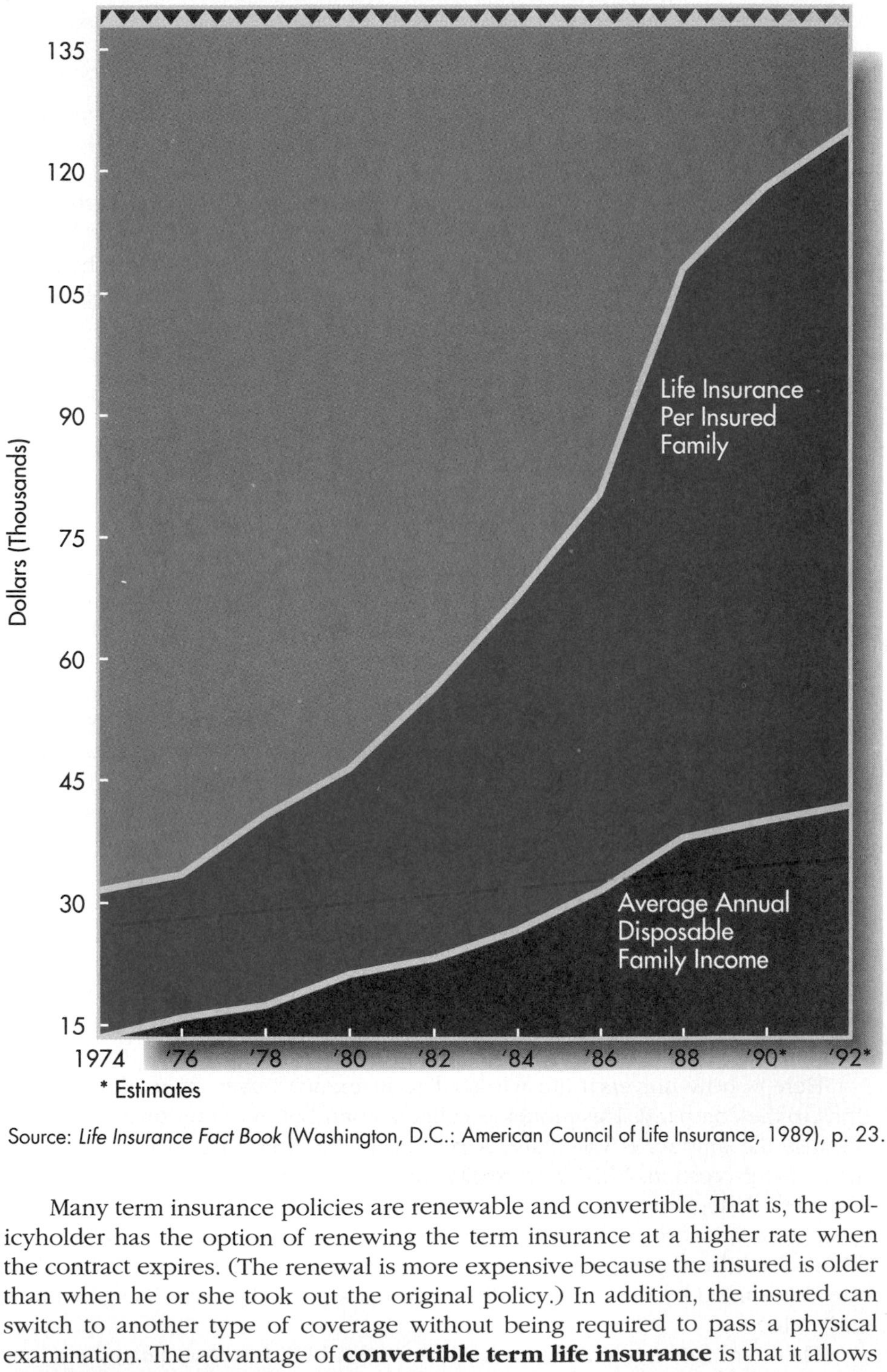

Source: *Life Insurance Fact Book* (Washington, D.C.: American Council of Life Insurance, 1989), p. 23.

Many term insurance policies are renewable and convertible. That is, the policyholder has the option of renewing the term insurance at a higher rate when the contract expires. (The renewal is more expensive because the insured is older than when he or she took out the original policy.) In addition, the insured can switch to another type of coverage without being required to pass a physical examination. The advantage of **convertible term life insurance** is that it allows the holder to buy the most protection when the need is greatest and then convert to a more permanent type of life insurance later.

Level term life insurance provides the same amount of protection during each year of the term contract. **Decreasing term life insurance** provides

convertible term life insurance   *term life insurance that may be changed to a permanent type of life insurance.*

level term life insurance   *term life insurance in which the amount of protection is the same during each year of the term contract.*

decreasing term life insurance   *term life insurance in which the amount of protection decreases during the term of the contract.*

decreasing protection over the life of the policy. It is written to cover specific obligations such as mortgage payments. For example, as the mortgage decreases with each mortgage payment, the face value of the insurance also decreases. When the decreasing term is associated with a credit obligation, it is also called credit life insurance.

whole life insurance *life insurance that gives lifetime protection to the insured person.*

ordinary or straight life insurance *whole life insurance in which the policyholder pays premiums for life.*

limited life insurance *whole life insurance in which the policyholder pays higher premiums, but only until the policy is paid up.*

single-premium life insurance *whole life insurance in which the insured makes one payment and the insurance is fully paid.*

cash value *the savings portion of a life insurance policy.*

Whole Life Insurance.
Whole life insurance protects the insured person for his or her lifetime. Unlike term insurance, a whole life policy does not automatically expire after a certain number of years.

Whole life insurance comes in three forms. Under **ordinary (or straight) life insurance,** the policyholder pays premiums for life. In contrast, with **limited life insurance,** the policyholder pays higher premiums, but only until the policy is paid up. Most limited life policies are fully paid in 20 to 30 years. The insured makes one payment with **single-premium life insurance,** and the insurance is fully paid. To illustrate, one insurance company would provide a 25-year-old male the following three options in purchasing $100,000 worth of whole life insurance.

1. Ordinary life: $650/year for the rest of his life.
2. Limited life: $950/year for the next 20 years.
3. Single-premium life: $12,500 one-time payment.

One advantage of whole life insurance is that it generates a cash value for the insured. A **cash value** is the savings portion of a life insurance policy. Figure 22-2 shows the cash value of a $100,000 ordinary life policy, a $100,000 limited life policy, and a $100,000 single-premium life policy. The single-premium life policy generates cash value most quickly, since the premium paid is greatest.

The holder of a whole life insurance policy can benefit in one of two ways. The insured's family can collect in the event of the policyholder's death, or the policyholder can cash in the policy. In addition, the insured person may borrow against the cash value of the insurance policy. The cost for such borrowing is stated in the policy; it is usually quite low.

universal life insurance *term life insurance with a savings component.*

Universal Life Insurance.
Universal life insurance is term life insurance with a savings component. It was first introduced in the United States in 1979. Today, more than 20 percent of the life insurance sold each year is universal life. It is designed to give the buyer the protection of term insurance and, at the same time, the opportunity to earn a high yield on funds invested with the insurance company.

Here is how universal life works. The insurance buyer makes a "contribution" to the company. This money is called a contribution rather than a premium because the amount is voluntary. A portion of the contribution is a charge for insurance protection. This is, in reality, the term insurance premium. Next, the company deducts an amount for expenses and profits. The expenses cover the agent's commission and the cost of establishing and maintaining the policy. After all fees have been paid, the insurance company invests the remaining funds at a rate determined by the company. This money is the policy's savings portion or cash value.

There are four major advantages of universal life insurance. First, the contribution is variable. If the policyholder does not want to invest enough money to generate cash value, there is no requirement to do so. In addition, both the timing and the amount of the yearly premium can be adjusted to fit the insured's financial situation. Second, the insurance company lists all of the fees, so that the pol-

FIGURE 22-2   Types of Whole Life Insurance

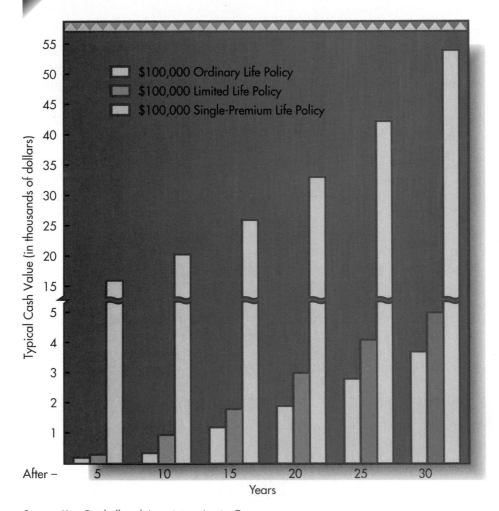

Source: Ken Gutshall and Associates, Austin, Texas.

icyholder knows exactly how much is going for insurance, expenses, and the build-up of cash value. Third, the cash value part of the policy is invested at a rate that has been averaging almost twice as much as the rate for whole life policies. (However, when interest rates go down, the rate paid on the cash value of the policy also goes down. This does not happen with whole life policies.) Finally, in most policies, the insured may adjust the size of the death benefit if he or she is still in good health.

Variable Life Insurance. **Variable life insurance** is a form of whole life insurance. It provides a death benefit and cash value that fluctuate with the value of the securities purchased with the premiums. If the securities increase in value, the benefits will rise. If the securities decline in value, the benefits will fall. Policyholders are given a substantial amount of flexibility as to how their premiums are invested.

 Variable life insurance was designed to help protect the consumer against inflation. People who are concerned about inflation should also consider pur-

variable life insurance a whole life policy in which the death benefit and cash value fluctuate with the value of the securities purchased with the premiums.

chasing a cost-of-living option or rider, which is available on most traditional forms of life insurance.

Evaluation of Life Insurance

Which type of life insurance is best for you? The answer depends on your income and your needs. If your income is limited but your insurance needs are large, you should consider term insurance. A term policy offers a great deal of insurance at relatively low cost. Whole life policies provide a significant amount of protection while creating cash value for the insured. If you have the interest and the skills to manage your own investments wisely, variable life insurance policies are an option that you should consider.

Finally, universal life insurance is similar to whole life except that there is more flexibility in the payments. In addition, most universal life insurance policies pay a higher return on the money invested with the insurance company than do similar whole life policies. Table 22-5 compares the alternative life insurance programs.

Business Application of Life Insurance

The death of an important person in an organization may make it difficult for the organization to survive. Therefore, many small and some large companies purchase life insurance on senior executives as well as chief scientists and engineers.

TABLE 22-5   Comparisons of Alternative Life Insurance Programs

| | Term | Whole Life | | | |
	Insurance	Ordinary Life	Limited Life	Variable Life	Universal Life
Premium	Lowest available	Higher than term insurance	Higher than ordinary life	Comparable to limited life	Higher than term; may vary from one payment period to another
Premium Payment Period	Specified number of years—normally 5, 10, or 15	Life of the insured	Specified number of payments—normally 20 to 30 years	Specified number of payments—normally 20 to 30 years	Specified period
Cash Value	None	Some cash value	More cash value than ordinary life	Cash value depends on the value of the securities purchased	Varies with amount invested by the insured
Collection Time	Upon the death of the insured	Upon the death of the insured	Upon the death of the insured	Upon the death of the insured	Upon the death of the insured
Objectives	Protection for a specified period of time; to cover specific and temporary risks	Protection for life, some cash value for insured	Protection for life; some cash value for insured	Protection for life; some cash value; protection against inflation	Life insurance plus high rate of return on savings component

639

If the insured person dies prematurely, the firm receives a cash death benefit, which helps it cope with any financial problems that may arise as a result of the loss of the person.

In the same manner, partnerships often purchase life insurance on each of the partners. Typically, the surviving partners are named as beneficiaries. The aim of such policies is to provide the surviving partners with enough money to buy out the deceased partner's share of the business from his or her estate.

SUMMARY POINTS

1 Risk is the uncertainty of loss. Pure risk exists in situations in which the only possible outcomes are loss or no loss with no possibility of gain. Speculative risk involves the possibility both of loss and of gain. Firms and individuals can manage pure risk by simply avoiding it or by taking steps to reduce it. Other options are setting money aside to cover unexpected losses or planning to pay for losses out of current income. Most firms and individuals choose insurance to protect against pure risk.

2 From the insurance company's perspective, the insurance business is based on seven principles. According to the principle of insurable interest, only accidents that would cause real financial loss to the policyholder should be insured. By the principle of indemnity, the insured individual may not claim more in damages than the dollar loss sustained. The law of large numbers permits companies to predict the probability that a particular loss-causing event will occur, based on the past rate of its occurrence. The principle of definite and measurable risk means that the company protects against measurable losses that result directly from a specific event that occurred at a definite time. By the law of adverse selection, those most likely to need insurance are also the ones most likely to purchase it. According to the principle of accidental loss, a loss must be accidental, not previously planned. The principle of catastrophic hazard means that the company must spread its risk so that no single disaster forces it to pay all its clients at once.

3 From the perspective of the insured, the decision to buy insurance should be based on two key principles. The large loss principle is that potentially serious losses should be insured against before minor losses. The second principle is that highly probable losses are expensive to insure against and should not be covered.

4 The two main sources of insurance are government agencies, which offer both voluntary and required programs, and private insurance companies, which include both stock and mutual companies.

5 Seven basic categories of insurance are property, homeowners', liability, loss-of-earning-power, employee, directors and officers, and life insurance. Property insurance protects against damage to real estate and other property. It includes fire, extended coverage, marine, automobile, and burglary, robbery, and theft. Homeowners' insurance protects against risks involved in owning a home. It covers dwellings, other structures, unscheduled personal property, additional living expenses, and personal liability. Property in a rented dwelling may be covered by renter's insurance. Liability insurance protects against losses for harm caused to people or their property. It includes public and product or service liability. Loss-of-earning-power insurance protects against lost income due to some unusual event. It includes business-income, extra-expense, and rain insurance. Employee insurance, such as social security, fidelity bonds, worker's compensation, unemployment, and health insurance, protects the health and safety of workers and protects the firm from employee dishonesty. Directors and officers insurance protects executives and directors from stockholder suits. Life insurance pays a cash benefit to a beneficiary when the insured dies. Term life insurance pays a death benefit when the insurance is in force. Whole life insurance protects the insured person during his or her lifetime. Universal is a form of term insurance with a savings component. Variable life is a whole life policy in which the death benefits and cash value fluctuate in accordance with the value of the securities purchased.

KEY TERMS

risk 611
pure risk 611
speculative risk 612
insurable interest 614
principle of indemnity 614
law of large numbers 614
actuaries 614
law of adverse selection 615
accidental loss 616
castastrophic hazard 616
stock insurance companies 618
mutual insurance companies 618
property insurance 618
fire insurance 621
coinsurance clause 621
subrogation provision 621
extended coverage 622
marine insurance 622
automobile insurance 622
deductible 623
no-fault insurance 624
burglary 624
robbery 624
homeowners' insurance 624
unscheduled personal property insurance 624
liability insurance 626
public liability insurance 627
product liability insurance 627
service liability insurance 627
loss-of-earning-power insurance 628
business-income insurance 628
extra-expense insurance 628
rain insurance 628
social security 629
fidelity bonds 629
individual fidelity bond 629
blanket bond 629
worker's compensation insurance 629
unemployment insurance 630

REVIEW QUESTIONS

1 How can people or businesses protect themselves against pure risk?

2 What is the principle of indemnity?

3 Explain the law of adverse selection.

4 Analyze the large loss principle.

5 Explain what types of insurance are provided by federal and state government agencies.

6 Describe extended coverage insurance policies.

7 What is the difference between automobile liability insurance coverage and automobile physical damage insurance coverage?

8 What is unscheduled personal property?

9 Briefly describe the three types of loss-of-earning-power insurance.

10 How do fidelity bonds protect a business?

11 Describe the main differences between whole life insurance and term life insurance.

12 What are two applications of life insurance for business organizations?

DISCUSSION QUESTIONS

1 Why do insurance companies insist on the principle of insurable interest?

2 What is a coinsurance clause in a fire insurance policy? Why do most fire insurance policies carry this clause?

3 Discuss the development of no-fault insurance. What are the benefits of this type of coverage to the insurance company? To the policyholder?

4 Would you advise someone who is renting an apartment to purchase renter's insurance?

5 What is social security insurance? Who pays for it, and who benefits from it? What do you see as the future of this form of insurance?

EXPERIENTIAL EXERCISES

1 Meet with a life insurance agent. (Make sure that the agent knows you are working on a class project and are not interested in purchasing insurance.) Ask the agent what factors should be considered when determining how much life insurance an individual should own. Does the agent sell term life, whole life, universal life, and variable life? Which types of life insurance does the agent recommend for most of his or her clients? What kinds of changes does the agent see occurring in the insurance industry in the next ten years? Ask the insurance agent what he or she considers the most important factors in determining whether an individual will be successful in selling insurance. Write a report on your findings.

2 Arrange a meeting with an individual who handles a business's insurance program. Find out what types of group insurance the firm offers its employees. Does the firm pay the total cost of employees' insurance, or do the employees pay a portion of it? Does the firm believe that its employees are adequately insured? Explain. If the firm is a corporation, does it carry directors and officers insurance, and are the firm's directors and officers adequately protected from stockholder suits? Write a report on your findings.

CASES

CASE 22-1
Interminco

Several companies have been formed to search for oil on the continental shelf of the United States. Other firms, such as Sedco, finance and manage the actual construction of huge offshore oil rigs—floating platforms that are towed to a drilling site, moored, and then serve as the base of operations for large drilling operations. These platforms are highly sophisticated and very expensive. The most expensive rigs cost about $250 million to build and more than $1 million a week to rent.

Many companies rent rigs rather than build them. One company that rents oil rigs is International Mining Company, or Interminco. Its traditional line of business was nickel mining, but the company decided to go into offshore oil drilling when the price of nickel fell. To do so, it chose to rent six offshore drilling rigs.

Interminco contacted insurance companies to see about adequate insurance coverage for the rigs. Interminco executives remembered that an offshore drilling platform rented to the Mexican government by Sedco had broken down in the Gulf of Mexico, spilling millions of gallons of crude oil into the ocean and polluting over 1,000 miles of beach. Legal claims resulting from that pollution were immense. Another rig off Newfoundland, Canada, sank in a storm. More than 100 workers were drowned, and the rig was lost. Lawsuits against the renting company are still in progress, but the families of the dead workers expect to receive over $1 billion before all the suits are settled. Interminco was concerned that its workers be well insured and that the company be adequately insured against claims if another rig should fail.

Interminco would also like insurance against fire, arson, terrorism, delays due to bad weather or mechanical breakdowns, and the possibility that no oil will be discovered. Interminco must have special marine insurance to cover the towing of the rig out to its drilling site, as well as insurance against worker injury.

1. What kinds of risk does Interminco face?
2. In what ways could Interminco reduce the risk it faces?
3. Before issuing a policy what constraints will any insurance company put on Interminco and the property it wants to insure?
4. What kinds of insurance should Interminco consider purchasing?

CASE 22-2
Cindy Carr and Associates

Cindy Carr graduated from Arizona State University in 1983. She immediately went to work as an insurance salesperson for Allstate Insurance Company. After four years with Allstate, she joined an independent insurance agency, Dave Dillow and Associates, in Phoenix. Dave's firm represented three life insurance companies, as well as two firms that sold automobile and business insurance. Dave's philosophy had always been to represent his clients' interests first. He did this by trying to find the most cost-effective insurance options for his clients, based on their unique needs.

In 1991, Dave announced that he was going to retire in September, 1992. Cindy and Dave worked out an arrangement for Cindy to buy Dave Dillow and Associates for $350,000. Dave agreed to let Cindy pay $25,000 down, with the rest to be paid from profits she expected to earn from future commissions. The day she took over the business, Cindy changed the name of the agency to Cindy Carr and Associates.

Three clients are typical of many of the people Cindy serves. Mike Millsap has been married for less than a year and has no children. Mike is 26 years old and works for Arizona State University as an accountant. He just passed the CPA examination. Mike's wife Susan is 27 years old and works as Assistant Vice President for Valley National Bank. The Millsaps hope to have their first child within the next two years. They both have term life insurance, provided by their employers, equivalent to twice their current annual income.

Cindy's second client, Martha Mantovani, is a single woman with two children aged 14 and 17. Martha was divorced from her husband of 13 years. She is a secretary for an office contractor and builder. She also works part-time on Saturdays as a cashier at a local carwash.

The third client is Jack Walters. Jack is 52, and his wife Sarah is 49. The Walters have two grown children. Jack is the senior partner of Walters and Smith, a successful Phoenix law firm, and Sarah writes novels under an assumed name. The Walters make over $650,000 per year. They own a 1,000-acre ranch outside of Phoenix, which the family enjoys a great deal. The ranch is said to be worth almost $2 million.

Cindy wants to continue providing the same type of insurance service that made Dave Dillow and Associates one of Phoenix's most successful insurance agencies.

1. Should Cindy continue to operate her firm as an independent agency, or would she be better off to try to associate with one major national firm?
2. Should Cindy have changed the name of the insurance company?
3. What type of life insurance coverage or coverages would you suggest for Cindy's three clients?

CHAPTER 23

International Business: A Growing Sector

OBJECTIVES

After studying this chapter, you should be able to:

1 Explain why it is important to study international business.

2 Explain the principles of absolute and comparative advantage in the production of goods.

3 Discuss the concept of balance of trade.

4 Discuss some barriers associated with international trade.

5 Describe five different ways of selling products in foreign markets.

6 Discuss the advantages and disadvantages of developing a standardized international marketing strategy.

7 Discuss the role of multinational corporations in the world economy.

8 Discuss the role of international institutions and economic communities.

Overseas markets have become the new growth opportunities for U.S. brewers.[1] The growth of the domestic market for beer has been slow, but the growth rates have exceeded 15 percent per year in some Asian markets, making them very attractive. However, to be successful, U.S. brewers will have to deal with tough local competition and sometimes hostile environments.

Coors announced in 1991 that it will build a $200 million brewery in South Korea in a joint venture with Jinro, a Korean distiller. For the agreement to go into effect, the joint venture must obtain a license from the Korean government to produce and sell beer. The company believes that the joint venture will be successful. Coors will not have to ship its beer great distances to reach the Korean market, yet Coors will be heavily involved in the brewing, marketing, and distribution of the beer.

Coors has been selling beer in Japan for some time. It licenses the production, distribution, and marketing of its product to Asahi, a Japanese firm. It is very difficult to gain access to the distribution system to sell beer in Japan, so building a new brewery is not a realistic option. There is simply too much risk that new beer will never reach the market in sufficient quantity to justify the investment in capital that would be required.

In this chapter we will discuss international business—an exciting development in the world economy.

Three decades ago, most business textbooks did not even mention international business. Not many U.S. corporations had large investments in foreign countries. Few U.S. citizens had been overseas, and even fewer had worked in foreign countries. Today this has all changed. U.S. citizens and corporations now play a major role in many businesses in foreign countries. In addition, foreign-owned businesses such as Toyota and Nissan are not only selling their products in the United States but also operating major production facilities here.

WHY STUDY INTERNATIONAL BUSINESS?

 Studying international business is more important now than ever. The U.S. and world economies are becoming increasingly interdependent. Over the last decade and a half, the U.S. has purchased more products from the rest of the world than other nations have from the U.S. Also, total U.S. corporate investment overseas has increased dramatically during this period. As Table 23-1 indicates, these investments appear to be paying off, since some of the largest and best-known U.S. companies now earn a significant portion of their revenue in foreign countries. International trade now plays a major role in the U.S. economy. We will begin this chapter by examining the principles of absolute and comparative advantage.

ABSOLUTE AND COMPARATIVE ADVANTAGE

 Natural and economic resources are distributed unevenly around the globe. Some nations have an oversupply of one resource but barely enough of another to take care of their populations. An **absolute advantage** exists when one country can clearly produce a product more cheaply than another country can. For example, the cost of producing a barrel of oil in Saudi Arabia is less than $4 per barrel. In contrast, it costs approximately $10 to produce a barrel of oil in the most efficient U.S. fields. Adam Smith stated in 1776 in his classic text, *The Wealth of Nations*, that countries should specialize in the production of products in which they had an absolute advantage. They could then trade with nations producing other products, to maximize the total wealth of all countries. This concept is called the principle of absolute advantage.

This principle breaks down in the real world. For one thing, some nations have virtually no absolute advantages with respect to important products. However, every country can produce some products more cheaply than it can produce other products. A country is said to have a **comparative advantage** in the products it produces cheaply compared to other products. In 1817, David Ricardo for-

absolute advantage *a country's ability to produce a product more cheaply than another country can.*

comparative advantage *a country's ability to produce some products more cheaply than other products.*

TABLE 23-1   Percentage of Sales Revenues Earned From Exports (1991)

Company	Exports as % of Sales
Boeing	58.3
Eli Lilly	40.0
General Motors	16.0
General Electric	35.0
IBM	52.0

Source: *Value Line Investment Survey*, 1992.

mulated the principle of comparative advantage. According to this principle, countries should produce those products that they can produce most efficiently (cheaply), even if they do not have an absolute advantage in them. They can trade those products in the world market to generate buying power for other products that they cannot produce efficiently. Ricardo demonstrated that even a relatively poor nation will benefit from free trade if it specializes in the products that it can produce most efficiently.

Toys "R" Us Vice Chairman Robert Nakasone has masterminded the company's successful expansion into such countries as Japan, the United Kingdom, Singapore, and France.

The trade relationship between the United States and Brazil illustrates the principle of comparative advantage. Both nations can produce sugar and jet planes. Although the United States has an absolute advantage in producing both products, Brazil is relatively more efficient in producing sugar than jets. Therefore, it should focus its efforts on sugar and leave jet plane production to the U.S. The result of our simple two-product, two-country economic model is that Brazil's standard of living will not be as high as that of the United States, but it will be better off if it specializes in the production of sugar and uses its profits from sugar to purchase jet planes.

Both absolute and comparative advantages change over time. At the end of World War II, Japan quickly developed an absolute advantage relative to the United States in the production of a wide variety of inexpensive electronic devices. This advantage existed primarily because of Japan's low-cost labor. As the Japanese economy matured and wages increased radically, Japan lost its advantage with respect to low-cost items. The country's leaders were wise enough to encourage investments in education, engineering, and research, and today Japan is a leader in the production of many high-tech, state-of-the-art electronic devices.

INTERNATIONAL TRADE

Any product made in one country and sold in another is both an export and an import. The product is an **export** from the point of view of the country making and selling it and an **import** from the point of view of the country buying it. Wheat grown in Kansas and sold in London is an export for the United States and an import for England.

Each year, all the nations of the world add up their exports and their imports to determine their trade balances. The **balance of trade** measures the dollar volume of exports relative to the dollar volume of imports over a defined period.

export *a domestically produced good or service that is sold in another country.*

import *a foreign-made good or service that is purchased domestically.*

balance of trade *a measure of the dollar volume of exports relative to the dollar volume of imports over a defined period.*

trade surplus *a situation in which total exports exceed total imports.*

trade deficit *a situation in which total imports exceed total exports.*

In recent years, the United States has almost always imported more than it has exported, resulting in a trade deficit that makes people worry about the health of the American economy.

When total exports are greater than total imports, the difference is called a **trade surplus**. When imports are greater than exports, it is called a **trade deficit**. Nations prefer a trade surplus to a trade deficit, because a deficit represents a drain on its currency and income. During the last 20 years, Japan has been the world's leading export nation and has experienced the largest trade surplus.

Before 1970, the United States consistently showed an end-of-the-year trade surplus. That is, each year it exported more than it imported. Figure 23-1 shows the difference between total exports and total imports for the period from 1970 to 1990. As long as exports exceeded imports (the way we would like things to be), the curve was above the zero line. When exports were fewer than imports, the curve fell below the line, indicating that the U.S. had a trade deficit. This relationship between exports and imports indicates how well U.S. products compete in world markets. In only 3 out of the 20 years shown in Figure 23-1 did the U.S. economy show a trade surplus. In all other years, U.S. imports exceeded exports. Also note how the trade deficits increased steadily until 1988.

Figure 23-2, page 648, illustrates that the U.S. had a trade surplus in 1989 in agricultural products, crude materials, and chemicals. It had significant trade deficits in such categories as mineral fuels and lubricants (primarily crude oil), manufactured goods, motor vehicles, and machinery (the largest single category of imports and exports).

The common perception is that Japan has a substantial trade advantage with the United States. For once it seems that our perception is actually supported by the data. Of the 15 countries or areas of the world examined in Figure 23-3, page 649, Japan has by far the largest trade surplus with the United States. Only Britain, France, Spain, and Australia have a trade deficit with the United States.

Ambassador Robert Strauss, who is profiled on page 650, has worked tirelessly to reduce the U.S. trade deficit. As President Carter's trade ambassador, he was able to get the Japanese to open more of their markets to U.S.-manufactured products. As the first United States ambassador to the new Russian Republic, he has invested a great deal of time trying to open the Russian market to American products.

BARRIERS TO INTERNATIONAL TRADE

Many businesses are reluctant to enter foreign markets. Sometimes this is due to a lack of knowledge about these markets, but in other cases it is because of real

FIGURE 23-1   U.S. Merchandise Trade Balance, 1970—1990

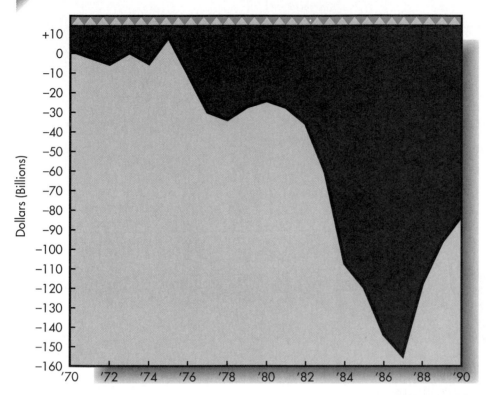

Source: U.S. Department of Commerce, Bureau of Economic Analysis, *Survey of Current Business* (1991).

problems that businesses face abroad. Table 23-2, page 649, lists some of these problems. Let's look at them.

Planning Problems

A good business plan relies on accurate market information. What kind of people are likely to purchase a new product? How much will they pay for it? How big is the market? Is style important, and what characteristics do consumers want in the product? Such questions are hard to answer even in the United States, where a great deal of up-to-date information exists about business conditions. In many less-developed foreign countries, it is almost impossible to answer even basic marketing questions. For example, Saudi Arabia says that its population is approximately 10 million. In reality, the country's population is probably somewhere between 5 and 10 million. More accurate information is needed to estimate the size of the market for particular products.

Inadequate marketing data makes planning difficult, but political instability can make it impossible. A sudden change in the political leadership of a foreign country can send the value of the local currency plummeting. Many U.S. companies have concluded that they just do not understand the market or political structures that exist in foreign countries, so they limit themselves to domestic operations.

Government Regulations

Foreign government regulators are often accused of being overly bureaucratic, to the point that it is difficult for a firm to do business in a foreign country. In addi-

FIGURE 23-2   U.S. Exports and Imports (1989) (in Billions of Dollars)

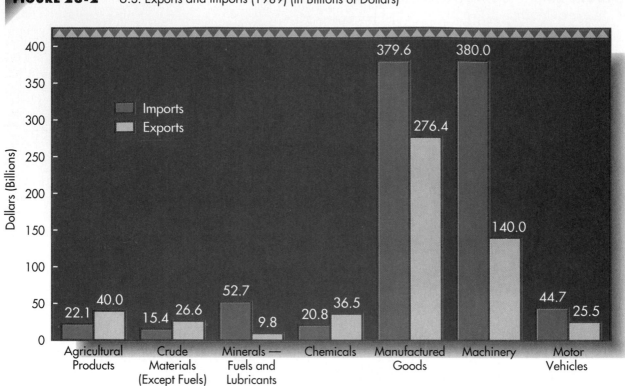

Source: U.S. Bureau of the Census, *Statistical Abstract, 1991*, p. 805.

tion to being inefficient, foreign governments often introduce trade and monetary restrictions that make it very expensive for foreign firms to operate profitably. Many governments try to protect their domestic businesses from foreign competition.

Tax Controls. Many countries try to limit the amount of goods they import by imposing a tax, which is called a **tariff**, on imported products. These countries assume that economic growth and employment depend on their ability to protect their home industries from foreign competition. Argentina places a tariff of more than 200 percent on many imported products. The effect of such a tariff is to make imported goods more expensive, which discourages people from buying them.

The Ethical Issue on page 651 examines dumping, which is the practice of selling products at artificially low prices in foreign markets. When this occurs in the U.S., an import tax may be imposed to ensure that the imported product is sold at a fair market price.

Another type of tax that creates problems for firms doing business abroad is a tax on profits. Many countries encourage U.S. private investment but attempt to limit the flow of earned income back to the United States. Sending profits back home is known as **repatriation**.

Many people believe that such profits should stay in the country where they were earned. Some countries either forbid repatriation of profits or tax them heavily. In Sweden, for example, foreign companies must pay an additional 5 percent in taxes in order to take profits out of the country. To soften the impact of such actions, many countries offer special loans, tax breaks, and other benefits

tariff *a tax on imported products.*

repatriation *sending profits from an international company back to the country of origin rather than leaving them in the country in which they were earned.*

FIGURE 23-3   Balance of Trade With Selected Nations and Areas of the World (in Millions of U.S. Dollars)

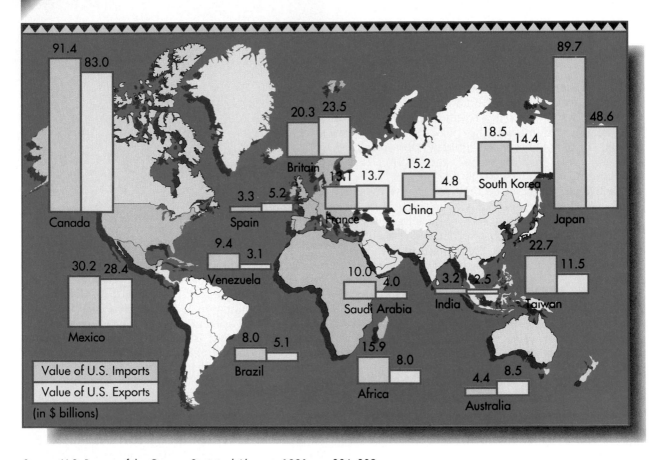

Source: U.S. Bureau of the Census, *Statistical Abstract, 1991*, pp. 806–809.

TABLE 23-2   Barriers to International Trade

Barriers	Specific Problems
Planning Problems	• Inadequate Market Information • Unstable Governments
Government Regulations	• Tax Controls • Quotas and Embargoes • Offset Agreements • Export Subsidies • Standards on Imported Products
Cultural Factors	• Negotiating Practices • Language Differences • Distribution Practices • Worker Loyalty
Political Instability	• Coup d' Etat • Expropriation Without Reimbursement
Economic Conditions	• Infrastructure • Rate of Inflation

Robert S. Strauss

In the roaring twenties, life wasn't so roaring in tiny Stamford, Texas. Young Robert Strauss spent his days as many boys do—playing marbles, climbing trees, and hanging around with his pals. Headline news events, bright lights, and golden opportunities seemed far removed from the West Texas community.

Bob's parents expected their son to give his best at school. However, they taught him that life's real lessons come from doing and from being involved, not always from getting the top marks in the classroom. Young Strauss took their philosophy to heart and became involved in everything around him. As a result, he was voted "best liked" by his high school classmates before leaving Stamford in 1935 to attend The University of Texas at Austin.

At the university, Bob continued to embrace his parents' words of wisdom. He was a doer. Along the way, he formed ties with some fellow students, which would prove all-important to his career.

Shortly after graduation from The University of Texas Law School, he and former classmate Richard Gump opened a law practice in Dallas. Their first case involved a $150 lawsuit over a wagonload of onions. Today the firm of Aikin, Gump, Strauss, Hauer & Feld employs more than 400 attorneys in offices in Washington, D.C., four Texas cities, and Brussels, Belgium. The client list includes a page and a half of Fortune 500 companies. By being involved, Strauss not only fine-tuned his law skills but also learned well the principles of big business. Bob Strauss is well-versed in the art of the deal. For example, he was able to help secure the purchase of MCA by Matsushita Electrical Industrial Company over Thanksgiving dinner in a New York restaurant.

Strauss is quick to point to his parents' philosophy of involvement when discussing the secret of his success. Many of his present business associates and clients were originally friends and acquaintances in law school and in his subsequent interests, including government.

In the 1950s, Strauss experienced his first taste of politics when he agreed to help raise funds for the campaign of his former college classmate, John Connally. Strauss's talents came to the attention of the Democratic National Committee. In 1970, he was hired to oversee the party's financial affairs. After two years as treasurer, he served an additional four years as party chairman.

In 1977, President Jimmy Carter made Strauss his special trade representative. In that cabinet-level job, he was responsible for negotiating the Tokyo Round of tariff reductions. In 1978, he got a taste of shuttle diplomacy as special envoy to the peace talks between Egypt and Israel. In 1980, Strauss chaired the Carter-Mondale reelection committee. In this role, Strauss demonstrated his finesse in making a deal. Representatives from both political parties were amazed when Strauss and Ronald Reagan's campaign manager, Jim Baker, emerged from a 15-minute session with an agreement for a presidential debate. Other representatives of the two campaigns had negotiated for hours without being able to break the deadlock.

Robert Strauss's most recent government appointment, and perhaps his biggest challenge in the worlds of politics and business, came in 1991, when he was named ambassador to the Soviet Union by another old colleague, President George Bush. One Washington observer said it was the point "where American capitalism meets Soviet Communism." Shortly after President Bush announced the Strauss appointment, the Soviet government began to crumble, and Strauss was named the first U.S. ambassador to the new state of Russia. Strauss has his work cut out for him as he sets out to help the former Soviets with their economic woes.

In Washington circles today, this West Texas native is a leading expert in the art of the deal in politics and in business. He can most often be found on the telephone talking with government leaders, politicians, and campaigners around the globe. His parents' advice has proven a successful lifelong philosophy for Robert Strauss.

Dumping

The practice known as "dumping" is blamed for many U.S. economic problems. What is dumping? How does it hurt the U.S. economy? Should it be stopped? Is it unethical?

Dumping is the export and sale of goods to other countries at prices below manufacturing cost, or at least far below market prices. When a foreign company sells its products at an artificially low price in the United States, it hurts domestic companies that must try to compete with the dumped products. If the practice is permitted to continue very long, U.S. companies will be forced out of business,

leaving only the foreign producers. The end result will be a loss of U.S. jobs and domination of the market by a foreign producer, which can raise the price of the product at will, since the U.S. producers have been eliminated.

In the United States, if an American manufacturer believes that competing products are being dumped, it can ask the U.S. Department of Commerce to investigate. If dumping is found to have occurred, the International Trade Commission (which is a U.S. government agency) will be asked to determine if the import in question has hurt U.S. manufacturers. The commission has the power to apply special taxes or duties that will raise the price of the dumped products.

The United States is not the only country that worries about dumping. The European Community imposed dumping duties, ranging from 23 to 43 percent, on Japanese computer printers that were being sold for 20 percent less in the European Community than in Japan.*

Dumping is not fair and must not be permitted. Not only is it unethical; it also strikes at the heart of free trade.

*D. A. Ball and W. H. McCullock, Jr., *International Business*, 4th ed. (Homewood, Ill.: BPI Irwin, 1990), p. 81.

---

to foreign corporations so that they will continue to invest there. Denmark has a special banking agency that lends money at low interest rates to foreign companies building factories there. Similarly, Ireland places a hefty tax on repatriated profits but gives big tax breaks and loan assistance to companies planning to invest in Ireland.

Quotas and Embargoes. An **import quota** is a specific limit placed on the number of units of a product that may be imported into a country. Many developing nations impose import quotas on various products to protect local businesses.

An **embargo** is a complete prohibition on the importation of a product. Embargoes are often imposed to protect a nation from health hazards. For example, certain types of animals may not be imported into the United States because they may carry diseases. Embargoes are also used for political reasons. For example, Saudi Arabia has boycotted Ford Motor Company because Ford does business with Israel.

Offset Agreements. Host governments sometimes force foreign suppliers to agree to reciprocal trade arrangements with their customers. These arrangements are called **offset agreements**. For example, Colombia may require a Spanish firm to buy its coffee, or else it will not buy buses from the Spanish firm. Offset agreements are little more than outright protectionism—one country trying to protect its domestic businesses from foreign competition. When a seller is forced to purchase a product in return for a sale, competition is not free. The U.S. Department of Commerce estimates that 20 to 30 percent of worldwide trade involves some type of offset agreement.[2]

Export Subsidies. Some governments provide direct cash incentives to local businesses if they export their products. This is clearly unfair, because it enables

> **import quota** a specific limit placed on the number of units of a product that may be imported into a country.

> **embargo** a complete prohibition on the importation of a product.

> **offset agreement** a policy in which host governments force foreign suppliers to agree to reciprocal trade arrangements with their customers.

the exporting company to sell its products at a lower price in foreign markets than it does in its domestic market and still make a profit. The European Community provides an export subsidy of $196 per metric ton of chicken broilers. Importing countries often impose tariffs to offset the advantage that the subsidy provides. Other less obvious export incentives include low-interest loans to the exporter's customers, reduced income taxes on profit generated from exports, and subsidized freight charges on government-owned ships and airplanes.[3]

Standards on Imported Products. For many years, government agencies have established standards on imported products, designed to protect the health and safety of their nation's citizens. Unfortunately, standards can also be used unfairly, to exclude foreign products. For example, Australia requires imported livestock to be quarantined, yet it has no quarantine facilities. Denmark requires that all beverages be sold in returnable bottles, which protects its soft-drink industry from foreign competition.

Economic Impact. The government restrictions and subsidies discussed above do little more than distort the world economy and increase prices of products. Americans want to believe that only other countries participate in such practices, but the truth is that our country also subsidizes a number of special interest groups and the products they produce. One recent study found that Americans pay more than $100 million annually to protect 31 groups of products, ranging from automobiles to textiles. The study also found that it is very expensive to use government restrictions on imported products to protect domestic jobs. For example, it cost $220,000 per year to protect one U.S. job in the dairy industry.[4] Unfortunately, research done on other nations' economies tends to substantiate this information.

Cultural Factors

culture   a set of values, ideas, and attitudes that shape human behavior.

Culture is a set of values, ideas, and attitudes that shape human behavior. Cultural attitudes vary dramatically among countries. Many business executives choose not to sell their products in foreign countries because they do not understand the cultures of those countries. Without cultural understanding, they are likely to make a series of costly mistakes.

There is no question that culture affects business decisions. For example, in the Mideast, even a simple agreement may take several days to negotiate, because Arabs often engage in lengthy discussions of unrelated issues. The abrasive style of Russian negotiators and their tendency to try to change a deal at the last moment is difficult for Americans to understand.[5]

Cultural differences are reinforced by language differences, and many business blunders abroad have their roots in inaccurate translation. For example, in a new car promotion, Chrysler-France translated the phrase "the original" that had been used in England to "the example" for its advertising campaign in Germany. The literal translation of "the original" into German, "die original," was not appropriate, because the phrase in German connotes "strangeness" or "oddness"—surely not what the automaker was trying to communicate to the German car buyer.

Culture also affects how a product is distributed. In the United States, Avon and Tupperware use homemakers as an in-home sales force. This approach would not work in Europe, because most people there perceive door-to-door sales and gimmicks such as "Tupperware parties" as violations of privacy.

I'll Drink to That

Coca-Cola has changed the name of its soft drink in China after discovering that the word means, in Chinese, "Bite the wax tadpole." The new name translates to "May the mouth rejoice."

Finally, culture has an influence on how a product is made. Many automobile workers in the United States are more loyal to their union, the United Auto Workers, than to their companies. In Japan, auto workers feel a personal bond to their employers.

Political Instability

We take for granted the stability of our political system, as do the people of Canada and most of the Western world. Unfortunately, such stability tends to be the exception rather than the rule. One need only remember August 18, 1991, when Soviet leader Mikhail Gorbachev was arrested in an unsuccessful coup attempt. The Dow Jones industrial average dropped 100 points, world leaders met, and talk of nuclear civil war could be heard on every evening newscast. Fortunately for the former Soviet Union and the world, the coup ended almost as fast as it began. If it had not, all of the political reforms that had taken place in that region and the movement toward a free economy would have been lost.

In times of political unrest, the host country's government sometimes takes over the assets of a foreign firm without offering compensation. Such **expropriation without reimbursement** does not occur very often, however, because it discourages other companies from investing in that country. Still, the dangers of political instability are real. They are difficult to measure, even for highly trained

expropriation without reimbursement a takeover of the assets of a foreign firm by the host country's government without offering compensation.

Despite the unstable transition from the Soviet Union to the sovereign Russian Republic, Pizza Hut has managed to run a successful operation in Moscow.

political scientists. The factors that must be considered include inflation, balance of payments, real growth rates of the gross national product, characteristics of population groups, the quality of life of the nation's citizens, and the tendency for orderly transitions of power from one government to the next.[6] In retrospect, it is not hard to understand that the former Soviet Union was ripe for a coup attempt in 1991, and it will remain so until it is able to solve its fundamental economic problems.

Most businesses that operate in politically risky environments have learned that their chances of surviving are enhanced dramatically if they give local citizens and their governments reasons for wanting the companies to continue operations. The easiest ways to do this include training and promoting local citizens, paying taxes, permitting local citizens to invest in the company, supporting local charities, protecting the environment, and remaining neutral in national and local elections. These practices, which add up to nothing more than being a good corporate citizen, help most companies get along well with their host governments.

Economic Conditions

Economic conditions vary greatly among countries and place certain limits on business activities. The most fundamental of these conditions is the country's state of economic development. In the United States, we are favored with good highways, railroads, and air transport systems. We have a telephone system that works. The benefits of such systems for conducting business are almost immeasurable. Not all countries are so fortunate. When a country lacks basic communication and transportation facilities, known as **infrastructure**, the options available for developing markets are severely limited.

infrastructure basic communication and transportation facilities.

Another economic condition is inflation, which was discussed in Chapter 2. It has been a terrible problem for many countries. For example, the former Soviet Union, Brazil, and Yugoslavia all experienced rates of inflation in excess of 200 percent in 1991. Multinational firms can deal with inflation by investing in material, equipment, and buildings that are expected to increase in value. In addition, they should hold relatively little cash, because it loses value quickly.

ENTERING FOREIGN MARKETS

5 Many firms earn large profits without ever operating abroad. However, more and more U.S. firms now recognize just how profitable foreign markets can be. Figure 23-4 shows six ways of selling products in foreign markets. Each way involves a different degree of investment in the foreign country. Generally, the level of profit from these markets depends upon the level of investment. The greater the investment, the greater the potential profit can be. Of course, it also is true that the greater the investment, the greater the risk. If the overseas operation falls apart, the firm suffers a big loss. The firm also is more vulnerable to such political actions as expropriation. Let's look at each of the six ways of entering foreign markets.

Exporting

The simplest way to enter foreign markets is to export products. A Chicago-based machine tool company might manufacture its products in this country and ship them to Canada, Mexico, Taiwan, and other foreign countries.

FIGURE 23-4   Alternative Ways to Sell Products in Foreign Countries

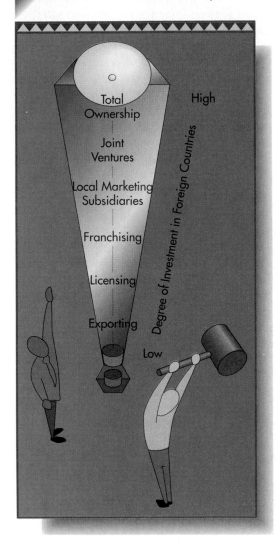

Exporting is an attractive strategy, because it involves very little risk. The manufacturer has no money invested in plant and facilities abroad. In addition, exports are good for the exporting country because they are a source of foreign exchange. Vigorous export activities also mean jobs for local workers. These are three reasons why our government wants United States-based firms to market products abroad. To encourage exports, the federal government provides information about foreign markets. State Department personnel also help exporters find overseas distributors for their products.

However, business managers frequently encounter two barriers to export activities. First, production and export costs may be too high. Exports compete with products that are made in the country of interest. Local firms may be able to produce and sell more cheaply than the exporter. The exporter also incurs transportation costs in moving the product to the foreign market. Second, as mentioned earlier, the foreign country may place a very high tax on imported prod-

Business Career

Foreign Clerk: Calculates duties or tariffs to be paid on merchandise. Converts foreign currency figures into U.S. monetary equivalents, or domestic currency into foreign equivalents. Examines documents, such as invoices, bills of lading, and shipping statements, to verify conversion of merchandise weights or volumes into system used by other country. May correspond with foreign companies. *Average Salary: $16,300.*

ucts. This makes imported products very expensive in relation to products manufactured locally.

Some domestic firms use export management companies (EMCs) to sell their products abroad. Some EMCs take title to the product in question; others act as sales agents. In the second capacity, they assist the domestic firm in developing its foreign sales strategy, contact potential buyers, and try to complete the sale, but they do not take title to the merchandise. EMCs have the distinct advantage of quickly providing the domestic firm with international expertise. Unfortunately, since EMCs that act as sales agents are paid only when they make a sale, they tend to take on too many clients and thereby dilute the amount of attention that they can give any one exporter.[7]

Licensing

licensing an approach to selling products in foreign countries in which a firm in one country agrees to allow a firm from another country to use its intellectual property for a fee.

Licensing is another way to sell products in foreign countries. Under this approach, a firm in one country (the licensor) agrees to allow a firm from another country (the licensee) to use its intellectual property for a fee. The property could include patents, trademarks, copyrights, technology, marketing skills, or manufacturing processes. For example, a French licensee of a new industrial cleaning solution could build a manufacturing plant using the processes developed by the licensor. It could then distribute the product under the trademark of the licensor, using the licensor's marketing strategy, all for a fee paid to the licensor.

Licensing has several advantages. The licensor is able to earn additional revenue with little extra cost and virtually no risk, since the licensee provides the investment capital. The licensee can take advantage of earlier research developed for a different market. Licensing also sidesteps many tariff laws, since the product is made in the host country. Finally, licensing can be used to test the viability of a foreign market without the cost associated with a major market test. If the product is successful, the licensor may decide to enter the market once the license agreement has expired.[8]

Licensing does involve two problems. First, the licensor is paid out of the profits made by the licensee on the product. Since many licensees lose money, they pay nothing to the licensor. The licensor might have been able to show a profit had it marketed the product itself. Second, the licensee receives the benefit of much production and marketing advice from the licensor. Eventually, licensees can become so skilled in their markets that they can break away and compete directly with the licensor. It is very hard to draw up a contract that will prevent this from happening.

Franchising

Franchising is a type of licensing in which the franchisor grants the franchisee the right to do business in a certain manner. As was discussed in Chapter 6, franchising has been very popular in the United States. For example, most major fast-food outlets are franchises. In the international sector, the use of franchises is growing. Researchers are finding new ways to use the franchise management system to merchandise products or services abroad.

The biggest advantage of franchise contracts is that they permit the franchisor to make sure that the product is manufactured and/or sold in a manner consistent with the franchisor's quality standards. In this sense, franchising is more of a commitment on the part of the franchisor than the typical licensing arrangement. The franchisor expects to provide advice, counsel, and supervision to the franchisee, to help ensure the success of the franchise. The franchisor must make larger investments in capital and personnel than would be required in the typical licensing agreement, since the franchisor must supervise the franchisee's quality control systems and standards.

Local Marketing Subsidiaries

A fourth way to market products abroad is to establish a **local marketing subsidiary**. That is, the firm rents office space in the foreign country, hires and trains a local staff, and sends a few of its executives to manage the facility. It then ships its products to the foreign country, where the staff of the marketing subsidiary directs the selling effort. This approach is more expensive than exporting, licensing, or franchising.

Very few firms choose to set up local marketing offices or subsidiaries. The major reason is not the cost involved, which can sometimes be high, but rather the lack of information about local market conditions. Rather than hire a local distributor, the firm acts as its own marketer under this approach. This means that the firm must learn about its new markets quickly if it is to have any chance of earning a profit.

Not all firms are against setting up local marketing subsidiaries. High-technology firms are especially concerned about having qualified people sell and service their products. For example, IBM's mainframe computer division operates in many foreign markets through a network of local subsidiaries. These subsidiaries sell and service nothing but IBM computers. The employees of these subsidiaries, most of whom are nationals of the host country, receive special IBM training. In this way, the company is able to stand behind its mainframe computers that are sold abroad. Computers are sophisticated products—they can't be exported as if they were textile products or wheat. Nor does it make much sense to license someone to manufacture them abroad because of the technology and investment involved. Thus, whatever marketing information IBM loses by not hiring a local distributor is more than balanced by greater management control and improved service.

local marketing subsidiary a means of market products abroad in which an office is established in the host country, staffed by local residents but managed by executives from the parent company.

Joint Ventures

A joint venture is yet another way to enter foreign markets. As mentioned in Chapter 5, a joint venture is a partnership between two or more businesses. Most international joint ventures begin when one company, wishing to expand its markets, buys a percentage of a local company operating in the foreign country of interest.

Joint ventures offer several advantages for the company looking at foreign markets. The local partner provides the foreign company with information about products, promotion, and pricing in the market. Sometimes the local partner also has physical facilities, access to a distribution system, a pool of trained labor, and valuable contacts with local officials and businesses. In return, the foreign company offers managerial, technical, and financial assistance to the local partner. Finally, in some developing countries, the government requires that local investors be given a chance to participate in the business. In this case, if the foreign firm wants to own a portion of the business, it may have no choice but to agree to the creation of a joint venture.

Unfortunately, there are some problems with joint ventures. As in any partnership, there is always the possibility that the partners will disagree on important issues. This is even more likely to happen with an international joint venture, because the people involved are often from very different cultures. For example,

To enter the Japanese telecommunications market, IBM chose to form a joint venture with Nippon Telephone & Telegraph Company.

marketing research is seldom used in developing countries. This is partly because market data are hard to collect and partly because many foreign business people have not seen how marketing research can be of use. The U.S. partner in a joint venture might insist on marketing research, and the local partner might insist just as strongly that such research is a waste of time. Other potential sources of disagreement might be dividend policy, new products, and the financial contribution of each partner to the joint venture.

Total Ownership

Total ownership involves the greatest commitment to a foreign market. One example would be a manufacturing plant in the U.S., owned and operated by a Swiss corporation. Another example would be a factory in Argentina owned by a U.S. corporation. In short, the multinational firm owns all of the business located in the foreign country. It does not just ship the products to the country and sell them through a subsidiary; it manufactures them there as well.

Some advantages of total ownership are clear. Compared with a joint venture, total ownership means that neither profits nor decision-making authority need to be shared with a foreign partner. Compared with licensing or franchising, the company has more managerial control and a greater probability of making a profit.

The advantages of total ownership in comparison to simple exporting are not quite so apparent but are important nonetheless. As mentioned before, many countries discourage imports. Rather than having foreign companies manufacture products elsewhere and then market them to their people, these countries prefer that the companies build factories within their borders and make the products there. This creates jobs for the national workforce. To encourage such investment, these countries often offer tax incentives, low-interest loans, labor guarantees, and special export arrangements.

There are several disadvantages to total ownership. The most significant is that the firm loses the knowledge of local market conditions that a good local partner can provide. This can be partially overcome by hiring local managers to run the company. Another disadvantage is that total ownership involves a great deal of risk. If the product fails in the foreign market, or if the host government becomes anti-business, the firm could lose its entire investment. Under total ownership, all the profits belong to the firm—but so do all the risks.

INTERNATIONAL MARKETING STRATEGY

When a firm decides to sell its products abroad, it must also decide whether to fashion an international marketing strategy. The first step is to determine just how big foreign sales are expected to be. If the idea is to sell surplus products abroad on a one-shot basis, it makes little sense to develop an entirely new marketing strategy for the product. But if the idea is to open up new, permanent markets abroad, then the firm should develop an international strategy.

This decision is made more difficult when the firm wants to open up markets in several countries. Should it come up with a separate strategy for each country, or should it use the same strategy in all countries? Since most large firms look to several overseas markets at the same time, we'll confine our attention to this situation.

Advantages of Standardization

There are two advantages to using the same marketing strategy (that is, a **standardization strategy**) in all markets. They are production cost efficiency and advertising consistency.

> **standardization strategy**
> the practice of using the same marketing strategy for all of a firm's foreign markets.

Production Cost Efficiency. Usually, the more of a product a firm manufactures, the lower will be the unit cost of manufacturing it. As discussed in an earlier chapter, this is brought about by economies of scale. Modern capital-intensive production plants are designed to operate most efficiently at high levels of production. Thus, if the firm can sell basically the same product in each country, it may be able to produce all of its output at one location. The firm sells the same product everywhere, manufactures it cost-efficiently, and relies on the same general marketing strategy from one country to the next. Individually tailored marketing strategies might increase total sales, but the great advantage of a single standardized strategy is that it reduces costs.

Advertising Consistency. When the firm uses the same advertisements in all of its markets—the same, that is, except for language differences—it creates a consistent image for its product. This is important in Europe because many Europeans travel regularly from one country to another. By seeing the same advertisement as they travel, they are more likely to believe that the firm's product claims are genuine. This can lead to higher product sales.

Marketing ideas that work in one country may work in others. Certain advertising themes that were developed in the United States seem to have a universal appeal. Advertisements for Levi's jeans have a casual flavor wherever Levi's are sold. In the same way, the Marlboro man rides out of the West to sell Marlboro cigarettes in Tokyo, Toledo, Tours, and virtually every city in the world. Likewise, Coca-Cola ads stress the freshness and sparkle of youth in all its markets. Good advertising ideas are relatively scarce. If an idea works in one market, why not try it in another?

Disadvantages of Standardization

Standardizing the marketing strategy for a product does pose some problems. The greatest problem is that cultural and social differences among nations may make it impossible to rely on a single strategy. Many business managers do not realize how significant, and sometimes how subtle, the effects of culture can be. Disaster may result from using a single strategy when a better choice would be to use a different strategy for each national market.

When to Standardize

When should a firm standardize its marketing strategy? What factors should it consider in making this decision? Ideally, it should consider the type of product involved, the similarity of people and cultures across national markets, the availability of marketing services in each target market, and government restrictions.

Type of Product. Generally, it is easier to standardize marketing strategies for industrial goods than for consumer goods. Also, it is easier to standardize strategies for consumer goods with a truly universal or an obviously simple function. Razor blades, electric irons, automobile tires, and ballpoint pens are sold mostly on the basis of feature or function. Such products are readily marketed with a standardized strategy. In contrast, some consumer products, such as perfume and deodorant, are sold on the basis of image or emotional appeal. These products usually require customized marketing strategies for each country.

Similarity of People and Cultures. The more alike people are across national markets, the more likely they are to buy the same products for the same reasons. For example, the income, education, and even the cultural characteristics of people show certain resemblances in Western European countries. Therefore, it is sometimes appropriate to use a single strategy for selling products there. However, it may not be appropriate to take a strategy developed for Europe and apply it without modification to China or Peru.

Availability of Marketing Services. Not all countries can provide the same level of marketing services and marketing data. A marketing strategy developed in the United States may be based on good market research data and on television and radio commercials for advertising. However, in some countries the government owns the broadcast stations and does not allow commercial advertising. In others—for example, Burundi, Suriname, Syria, and Mauritania—it is nearly impossible to conduct market research studies. The greater the differences among nations in terms of the availability of marketing services, the more advisable a separate marketing strategy is for each nation.

Government Restrictions. All nations have laws that regulate the market. These laws determine how products are priced, promoted, and distributed. The greater the differences in these laws among nations, the more advisable are separate marketing strategies.

MULTINATIONAL CORPORATIONS

A **multinational corporation (MNC)** sells its products anywhere in the world where there is a market for them. A multinational corporation may be headquartered in Houston with an English president; manufacture products in Africa and Japan; sell them in Europe, South America, and the United States; and have its stock traded in Hong Kong, London, and New York. Many businesses that we think of as U.S. corporations are really multinational corporations. Table 23-3 lists the world's 15 largest industrial corporations, as well their home country, sales, and number of employees. It is interesting to note that four of the five largest companies are U.S.-based.

multinational corporation
a corporation that sells its products anywhere in the world where there is a market for them.

Benefits of MNCs
The well-known economist John Kenneth Galbraith, a frequent critic of business, has said that MNCs have been both economically and socially beneficial.[9] The International Example on p. 662 discusses the purchase of the Seattle Mariners by a group led by Japanese MNC Nintendo. While foreign ownership in baseball is distasteful to many Americans, Nintendo did bail out a financially troubled business.

TABLE 23-3   World's 15 Largest Industrial Corporations (1990)

	Company	Home Country	Sales (Millions of Dollars)	Employees
1.	General Motors	U.S.	$125,126.0	761,400
2.	Royal Dutch/ Shell Group	Britain/ Netherlands	107,203.5	137,400
3.	Exxon	U.S.	105,885.0	104,800
4.	Ford	U.S.	98,274.7	370,400
5.	IBM	U.S.	69,018.0	373,816
6.	Toyota	Japan	64,516.1	96,849
7.	IRI	Italy	61,433.0	419,500
8.	British Petroleum	Britain	59,540.5	116,750
9.	Mobil	U.S.	58,770.0	67,300
10.	General Electric	U.S.	58,414.0	298,000
11.	Daimler-Benz	Germany	54,259.2	376,785
12.	Hitachi	Japan	50,685.8	290,811
13.	Fiat	Italy	47,751.6	303,238
14.	Samsung	South Korea	45,042.0	NA
15.	Philip Moris	U.S.	44,323.0	168,000

Source: "The World's Biggest Industrial Corporations," *Fortune*, 29 July 1991, p. 245.

Nintendo Hits Home Run

Only a month after baseball adopted a policy that banned foreign ownership of any team, Major League Baseball owners approved the sale of the Seattle Mariners to a group whose majority investor is a Japanese company. The investor group, called the Baseball Club of Seattle, is led by Hiroshi Yamauchi. Yamauchi is president of Nintendo, the world's biggest video-game company, which has its headquarters in Redmond, Wash.

What prompted this dramatic policy reversal? First, baseball backed away from its long-time reluctance to allow foreign interests when it became obvious that local ownership was the prime consideration. Second, the group, which also includes several Northwest business leaders, agreed to decrease its effective interests to less than 50 percent. And finally, the Seattle group agreed to put control of the club in the hands of John Ellis, North-American born and a Seattle resident.

Baseball commissioner, Fay Vincent, termed the $125 million transaction, "a triumph for baseball." Few of the owners expressed similar enthusiasm. Most merely accepted the situation as the best possible, maybe the only, solution to baseball's economic reality. The ten other major league teams for sale are attracting little notice. Awareness is increasing that the league may be forced to welcome foreign interests to bail out small-market teams. Only time will tell what long-term effect foreign interests will have on America's favorite pastime . . . maybe the concession stands will sell sushi alongside the hot dogs.

Source: Claire Smith, "Baseball Will Allow Sale of Seattle Team," *The New York Times* (June 10, 1992).

We will begin our examination of MNCs by examining the contributions they have made to the world economy.

Lessening of Tariffs. MNCs have worked hard for tariff reduction and for the elimination of other trade barriers. High tariffs (import taxes) inhibit the movement of goods and services across borders. High tariffs also lead to higher prices in the country imposing the tariffs. Thus, a lessening of tariffs is generally considered to be a good thing.

Peaceful Influence. During the last century, steel, coal, and shipbuilding industries had a strong interest in creating international tension. The more hostility between countries, the greater the demand for armaments and other war material. Today the opposite is true. MNCs operate in many countries, and a war—or even the threat of war—could cost them a great deal of money in terms of lost trade. Many MNCS, therefore, work to reduce international tensions.

Capital Transfer. Many developing countries do not have access to the financial resources needed to develop their countries. MNCs have access to the world capital markets. For example, Freeport MacMoRan borrowed more than $500 million from Japanese banks to build a copper and gold mine in Indonesia. Without Freeport's participation in the project, the Japanese banks would probably not have provided Indonesia with the capital to build the mine.

Local Managerial Development. MNCs are not run by their owners or stockholders, but by professional managers. Often, decision-making authority is delegated to local managers who know and understand local conditions. Employing local people not only makes the business more effective but also looks good in the eyes of the host country government officials. In many developing nations, such hiring practices have created a new class of professional managers. For example, in Brazil, General Electric has 10,000 full-time employees, fewer than 20 of whom are U.S. citizens. These employees contribute to their company as well as to the economic growth of their country.

MNCs are clearly not perfect organizations. They are imperfect organizations in an imperfect world. Some are better than others; some make more money than others; but all of them, in one form or another, contribute to world economic efficiency.

Criticisms of MNCs

We have looked at some of the most important benefits of MNCs; now let's look at the other side of the coin. They have been accused of exploiting the poor in developing nations, exporting jobs and capital from the U.S., and contributing to U.S. trade balance problems. Their critics also claim that they are not loyal to any government and will do anything to make a buck. Let's take a closer look at a few of these allegations.

Morality and Political Influence. In a well-known case, the Lockheed Corporation admitted to spending more than $12 million to influence military purchasing policy in Japan. This action may not have been bribery in the strictest sense, but it was clearly an attempt to affect government policy. What standard of behavior can we reasonably expect from MNCs? Did Lockheed act unethically? The answer to this question may vary from nation to nation. Regardless, the stockholders of the firm, as well as the local government officials, have a right to expect that the MNC will act in a manner that is consistent with the laws and ethical standards of the host country. Anything less will result in a perception that the firm is a poor corporate citizen that is not welcome in the country.

The Management of Technology. Most multinational firms concentrate their basic research efforts in one country, and frequently one city. AT&T's world-famous Bell Labs has located much of its research efforts in Murray Hill, New Jersey, for more than 50 years. Most businesses realize that their basic research units are more productive when a significant number of scientists and research engineers are able to interact easily every day.

The problem with this centralized approach to research and development is that the host country may conclude that its long-term development is being retarded because few, if any, of its citizens are participating in developing state-of-the-art technology. Many countries are now demanding that multinational firms create research laboratories in their countries. Western Europe is taking a somewhat different approach. Western European countries have decided to pool much of their basic research and development efforts for both private industry and government agencies. This pan-European research project, Eureka, has the potential to do world-class research.[10]

Impact on Balance of Payments. Many people believe that multinational corporations are responsible for the U.S. balance of payments problem. The charge is that U.S.-based multinationals are taking money out of the U.S. and buying businesses in foreign countries. However, the facts do not really support this claim. Since 1955, U.S. MNCs have generated more than $3 billion in inflows per year, with only a $2 billion average annual outflow. In addition, the value of U.S. corporate assets in foreign countries has more than doubled during the past ten years, which increases the national wealth of this country. The causes of recent U.S. balance of payments problems are too complex to be explained simply as a matter of MNC-induced cash inflows and outflows.

Exploitation of Cheap Labor. MNCs have been accused of locating operations in developing countries to take advantage of cheap labor. Wages paid in these countries are lower than U.S. wages, but MNCs are typically among the highest-paying firms in foreign countries. They frequently offer fringe benefits that are not provided by most local employers. In addition, one of the key reasons that MNCs are willing to invest substantial amounts of money in developing countries is that the cost of labor is lower than it is in the U.S. or Europe. If the labor cost differential did not exist, MNCs would not be willing to accept the additional risk involved in investing in a developing nation.

Maquiladora plants, which are located in Mexico along the California, Arizona, and Texas borders, have been accused of being sweatshops that exploit local labor. Electrical subsystems for many automobiles are manufactured in the U.S. and then shipped to Mexico for final assembly in maquiladora plants, after which they are sent to U.S. automobile factories to be installed in new cars. It is true that these plants, which are owned by firms such as General Electric, Westinghouse, Ford, and General Motors, do pay lower wages than would be paid in the U.S. However, the employees are doing largely unskilled labor, and they receive a competitive wage, as well as a benefits package that frequently includes paid vacations, free transportation back and forth to work, medical insurance for themselves and their families, and free English lessons. Most of these benefits are unheard of for unskilled labor in Mexico.

Now let's see how various nations have joined together to promote greater economic cooperation.

INTERNATIONAL INSTITUTIONS AND ECONOMIC COMMUNITIES

 After World War II, several groups of nations decided to create international organizations and economic alliances to stimulate trade. They believed that economic cooperation would lead to economic prosperity for their citizens. We will examine several of the international institutions that were created, and we'll look briefly at the most important economic and political alliance—the European Community (EC).

International Institutions

General Agreement on Tariffs and Trade (GATT)
a 1947 international accord that established rules for settling trade disputes and aimed to stimulate international trade by developing nations.

The **General Agreement on Tariffs and Trade (GATT)** is a 1947 international trade accord that has now been signed by 96 nations. Its objective was to establish a set of rules to settle international trade disputes and to stimulate the participation of developing nations in international trade. The organization established by GATT is headquartered in Geneva, Switzerland, and it is supported by contributions from the member nations.

GATT was initially very successful in reducing tariffs on more than 50,000 products. The eighth round of GATT negotiations began in 1986 and is scheduled to conclude in the mid-1990s. The negotiations are focused on trade in services, further reductions of traditional trade barriers, and the protection of copyrights and patents.

The **International Monetary Fund (IMF)** is an international bank created at the end of World War II. The primary objective of the IMF has been to help stabilize the international monetary system. It has done this by monitoring exchange rates between IMF members and by making short-term loans to help ease balance-of-payments problems of member countries.

The **World Bank**, officially named the International Bank for Reconstruction and Development, was also created at the end of World War II. The World Bank lends funds to developing nations for long-term projects to stimulate economic development. It borrows these funds from international capital markets or wealthy member countries. Some of the loans must be paid off in 15 to 25 years, at current interest rates. Others are financed over 50 years, with the first 10 years free of both interest and principal payments. The World Bank has operated profitably since 1947. Although the World Bank has never had a country fail to repay its loans, it has on several occasions been forced to reduce the interest rates of a loan and extend the repayment period.

International Monetary Fund (IMF)   an international bank that helps stabilize the international monetary system by monitoring exchange rates and making short-term loans to members with balance-of-payments problems.

World Bank   an international bank that makes long-term loans to developing countries to stimulate economic development.

Economic Communities

Economic communities are groups of nations that form alliances to reap economic benefits from mutual cooperation. The primary advantage of economic communities to businesses is that they open up large markets—markets without tariffs and other trade restrictions. The member nations benefit because the economic community stimulates trade, economic development, and productive jobs that will improve the quality of life of the citizens. Table 23-4 lists five major economic communities.

economic communities groups of nations that form alliances to reap economic benefits from mutual cooperation.

The European Community (EC), also known as the Common Market, was established on January 1, 1958, and today consists of 12 countries: Belgium, Denmark, France, Germany, Greece, Ireland, Italy, Luxembourg, the Netherlands, Portugal, Spain, and the United Kingdom. The goal of the EC is to promote European growth and stability by establishing common economic policies among member nations.

The EC's first step was to reduce tariffs on industrial goods and to place a common external tariff on all industrial products imported into EC countries. Today, the EC has reduced or eliminated virtually all tariffs among its members on industrial and agricultural products. In addition, it has established common transportation, monetary, and antitrust policies.

The EC is hard at work pursuing a program called Europe 92. The objective of this program is to eliminate all barriers between the 12 member nations, so that merchandise, people, and capital can move freely among them. The potential of Europe 92 is very exciting for European companies, as well as for American firms that have businesses operating inside the EC. The EC's population exceeds that of the U.S. by almost 80 million people, and its GNP is approximately 85 percent of that of the U.S.

It is too early to know whether Europe 92 will succeed. Each of the 12 nations has its own culture, history, language, tax system, and currency. There will probably not be a true United States of Europe in 1992, but great progress will have been made toward the economic and political unification of Europe. This will help stimulate economic development in Europe and improve the standard of living of its citizens.

TABLE 23-4   Economic Communities

Name and Starting Date	Countries	Level of Integration
European Community (EC), 1958	Belgium Denmark France Germany Greece Ireland Italy Luxembourg Netherlands Portugal Spain United Kingdom	The nations are highly integrated, both economically and politically
European Free Trade Association (EFTA), 1960	Austria Finland Iceland Norway Sweden Switzerland	Free trade area; few political ties among members
Latin American Integration Association (LAIA), formerly Latin American Free Trade Area (LAFTA), 1960	Argentina Bolivia Brazil Chile Colombia Ecuador Mexico Paraguay Peru Uruguay Venezuela	Some economic integration
Central American Common Market (CACM), 1961	El Salvador Nicaragua Guatemala Costa Rica	Some economic integration
Caribbean Free Trade Association (CARIFTA), 1968	Jamaica Trinidad Tobago Montserrat	Some economic integration

KEY TERMS

absolute advantage 644

comparative advantage 644

export 645

import 645

balance of trade 645

trade surplus 646

trade deficit 646

tariff 648

repatriation 648

SUMMARY POINTS

1 It is important for Americans to understand international business, because international trade plays a major role in the U.S. economy. We have purchased more products from the rest of the world during the last 15 years than other nations have bought from us. U.S. corporate investment overseas has increased dramatically during the same period. The U.S. and world economies are becoming increasingly interdependent.

2 A country has an absolute advantage in a product that it can produce more cheaply than another country can. According to the principle of absolute advantage, a country should specialize in the products in which it has an absolute advantage and trade with other countries for other products. A country has a comparative advantage in the products it can produce more cheaply than it can other products. By the principle of comparative advantage, a country should produce the products that it can produce most efficiently, even if it does not have an absolute advantage over other countries.

3 Balance of trade measures a country's dollar volume of exports compared to its dollar volume of imports over a period of time. The United States has been running a trade deficit most of the time since the mid-1970s.

4 Businesses wanting to enter foreign markets face many trade barriers. Some involve lack of knowledge about the foreign country's political and market structures and culture. Others involve government roadblocks, such as tariffs, taxes on repatriated profits, quotas, embargoes, offset agreements, export subsidies, and unfair standards on imported products. Foreign countries may be politically unstable. Changes of government in some countries can lead to expropriation of the investing firm's assets without reimbursement. Lack of systems of good communication and transportation and inflationary conditions in foreign countries can also limit business activities.

5 Products can be sold in foreign markets through exporting, licensing, franchising, local marketing subsidiaries, joint ventures, or total ownership. Each method entails a different degree of investment in the foreign country. The greater the investment, the greater the risk and the greater the potential profit.

6 A standardized international marketing strategy enables a company to produce products efficiently and to employ consistent advertising. However, it may also present problems because of the type of product, cultural and social differences, unavailability of marketing services, and foreign government regulations.

7 Multinational corporations help the world economy by working to eliminate tariffs and other trade barriers, lessening the tensions between countries, making financial resources from developed societies available to developing countries, and encouraging development of a new class of professional managers in developing countries. On the other hand, MNCs have been accused of exploiting inexpensive foreign labor, exporting jobs and capital from the U.S., and contributing to the U.S. trade balance problem. They have also been criticized for not being loyal to any single government and being willing to do anything to make a profit for their stockholders.

8 International institutions and economic communities stimulate trade between countries by developing rules to settle international trade disputes, opening up large markets free of tariffs and other trade restrictions, and stimulating participation of developing nations in international trade. The International Monetary Fund and World Bank lend funds to member nations. The most well-developed economic community, the European Community (EC), is an alliance of 12 European nations. The EC is working toward further economic and political unification of Europe.

REVIEW QUESTIONS

1 Why is it becoming increasingly important for Americans to understand the international business world?

2 If a country has no absolute advantages in trade, how can an understanding of comparative advantage help the country develop its international market strategy?

3 How does a country determine its trade balance?

4 What are some of the government regulations that work to restrict trade? Why would a country impose such restrictions?

5 What are the advantages and disadvantages of licensing and of franchising goods in foreign markets? Which method gives the parent company the greater level of control?

6 What factors should be considered in deciding whether to standardize a marketing strategy across several foreign markets? Are there factors that make a standardized international marketing strategy less desirable? If so, what are these factors? **6**

7 What are some criticisms of multinational corporations? **7**

8 What is an economic community? What are the benefits that would draw a country into an economic community? **8**

DISCUSSION QUESTIONS

1 In your opinion, what has been the overall effect on the U.S. economy of increased international dealings by American corporations?

2 What are some ways that the United States could go about increasing its export levels?

3 How could cultural and social differences among nations affect the marketing of big-screen televisions?

4 What is the relationship between risk and potential profit for the six ways of entering foreign markets?

5 Do you see multinational corporations as a positive or negative force in the international economy? Why?

6 Assuming that Europe 92 succeeds, what will be the effect on U.S. efforts to market goods within the 12 member nations? Will the overall outcome be positive or negative to American interests within the countries? To American firms that have no business operations inside the countries?

EXPERIENTIAL EXERCISES

1 Arrange to meet with an executive of a manufacturing firm that exports at least some of its products to other countries. Ask the executive what percentage of its products the firm exports, why there is a market for its products in other countries, and how the firm exports its products. Also ask whether the decline of the dollar, relative to other world currencies, has made it easier for the firm to export its products. Finally, ask the executive if the firm has standardized its marketing strategy. Has Europe 92 made any differences in the firm's strategy with respect to export sales to Europe?

2 Meet with the manager of a wholesaler or retailer that regularly imports products to the U.S. Does the firm deal with other U.S. wholesalers, or does it import its products directly from foreign manufacturers? What problems has the firm encountered in importing products? Has the firm ever been accused of selling products that were being dumped in the U.S.? Why does the executive believe that his or her imported products are able to compete successfully against U.S.-made products?

CASES

CASE 23-1
Japan Inc.

The nation of Japan has been called "Japan Inc." by both its detractors and its admirers for many years. Japan is the model of a well-run country (if not a company) with a clear mission and established goals.

After World War II, Japan, with help from the United States, began rebuilding its economy. Much of what Japan has accomplished has been the result of a workaholic attitude on the part of its citizens, a willingness to sacrifice and save for the next generation, and a desire to dominate certain world markets. Japan's leaders have also recognized the importance of protecting Japan's traditions and domestic markets from foreign invasion.

In January 1992, President Bush led a delegation to Japan. It consisted of the usual foreign policy advisors from the State Department plus several executives from the automobile industry and other corporate officials. The trip was highly controversial from the beginning. It was perceived by the press and the public as primarily a P.R. venture. Unfortunately, the president became ill, the executives were seen as overpaid whiners, and nothing very substantive was accomplished.

Why did the president visit Japan? The answer is simple. The trade deficit between Japan and the U.S. had grown steadily for several years and reached $38.5 billion in 1991. It is clear to almost everyone that the United States buys too many consumer electronic goods, cars, and machine tools from Japan. If something is not done to reduce U.S. imports from Japan or increase U.S. exports there, the United States runs a real risk of becoming a commercial outpost for Japan.

Japan has been accused by its detractors of having predatory ambitions. They believe that Japan is not interested in mere competition; rather, its goal is to conquer markets. The Japanese government's economic policies are designed to stimulate the economy and make Japan a dominant player in certain world markets. In addition, Japan's antitrust laws are weak. In contrast to the U.S., Japan's central government tries to bring businesses together to help them compete against foreign-owned businesses.

Government and industry planners have targeted specific industries that Japan wants to dominate. Two examples are consumer electronics and automobiles. There are indications that Japan is now targeting the computer industry. The Japanese government also protects new and established domestic industries from competition. A classic example is the country's rice growers. Rice can be grown efficiently and inexpensively in the United States and shipped to Japan. However, the Japanese government will not permit any significant amount of rice to be imported. The rice market is simply off-limits.

Very few U.S. corporations have been successful against Japan Inc. once their industry has been targeted. One company that has competed effectively against Japan's best-known firms is Motorola. Motorola has outdone Japan Inc. at its own game. It has actively pursued market share, dramatically increased the quality of its products, and reduced its manufacturing costs. In addition, Motorola has invested billions of dollars in research and development, training, and capital improvements. Motorola has also been a strong supporter of industry-wide research and development consortiums, such as Sematech. Sematech is a partnership of thirteen of America's leading semiconductor manufacturers. Sematech's goal is to develop the best computer chip manufacturing technology in the world.[11] Only U.S.-owned firms may belong to Sematech.

It is popular now among politicians to criticize Japan. The theme is that Japan has taken advantage of the U.S. for too long. We gave the Japanese our technology and advice, restructured their political system, and paid virtually all of their defense costs. The United States opened up its domestic markets to Japan. Now, when the U.S. needs help, what we hear from the prime minister of Japan is that America's workers are lazy, illiterate, and do not care about quality. These comments seem to indicate a level of contempt for America that is quite shocking.

1. Should there be any changes in America's foreign trade policy with respect to Japan?
2. Can America's automobile industry compete with Japanese automakers?
3. How should small and medium-sized American businesses try to compete with the Japanese?

CASE 23-2
TechCo

Cellular telephones have become one of the hottest-selling electronic products in the United States. Cellular phones, which are not much bigger than a human hand, sold for $3,000 to $4,000 apiece in 1989. In 1992, they sold for $300 to $400. In addition, the cost of operating such a phone has declined from over $1 per minute to less than 25¢ per minute in many markets.

TechCo was founded in 1983 in Los Angeles by Doug Smith. It manufactures private-label consumer electronic products, such as pagers and cellular telephones. TechCo cellular telephones are sold in the United States by discount stores, department stores, and specialty electronics stores under private label brand names. The company's phones are priced the same or lower than competitors' products. TechCo does not try to compete with the latest cellular phones produced by firms such as Motorola. TechCo's business philosophy is based on value: It tries to produce a good product at a low price. TechCo customers are willing to sacrifice the most modern product features in return for a relatively low price.

This strategy worked well until 1991. Then, as the U.S. market for cellular phones began to mature, the prices of cellular phones dropped dramatically. TechCo found itself competing directly with the industry giants such as Motorola. Unfortunately for TechCo, when consumers were given the choice of purchasing a private-label phone or a Motorola cellular phone at the same price, they purchased the Motorola phone almost every time.

One way for TechCo to escape the profit squeeze that was occurring in the domestic market was to sell its products in South America, specifically Brazil and Argentina. These two countries were selected because they were setting up cellular phone systems in their largest cities, and they did not have a U.S. or Japanese firm producing cellular phones in their countries.

TechCo met with an electronics wholesale firm in Brazil. It said that if it could purchase TechCo cellular phones for under $700, it would be able to sell as many as 500,000 phones over three years. However, it costs $250 to produce the hand-held TechCo phone, and the import tax on the phones would be almost $300 each. After transportation costs and overhead, that would not leave much room for profit.

TechCo also talked with a firm in Argentina that would like to license TechCo's technology. TechCo would provide the Argentine firm with its cellular phone technology at no cost. TechCo would receive 10 percent of the price that each phone is sold for. The American firm would also pass on new cellular phone technology at no cost as it develops. Negotiations for this deal are still continuing.

1. Will TechCo be able to escape its profit squeeze by selling cellular phones in South America?
2. What are the major barriers to the introduction of TechCo cellular phones in Brazil?
3. Should TechCo export or license its cellular phones in South America?
4. Would a joint venture be a viable way to introduce TechCo phones to South America?
5. Will TechCo be able to standardize its marketing strategy?

CHAPTER 24

The Future of American Business

OBJECTIVES

After studying this chapter, you should be able to:

1 Discuss the importance for business of forecasting and planning.

2 Describe long-term trends in population and income for this country and for the world and discuss the implications of these trends.

3 Identify trends that are shaping the industrial composition of the American economy and discuss the decline of basic industries.

4 Explain the role of technology in economic growth and speculate about the future of four high-technology industries.

5 Discuss how firms will achieve the creativity and flexibility they need to respond to future challenges.

American firms are facing a world that was unimaginable even a decade ago. Consider the following developments:

- *Tobacco plants are being used as living chemical factories. They are producing, among other things, an AIDS drug, a human blood protein, and an enzyme used in the food industry.[1]*
- *Wind farms, long a common sight in California, are sprouting up in the midwest. Wind power costs have dropped by a factor of ten since the early 1980s. New developments put the cost of wind power at five cents a kilowatt hour—on a par with the cheapest traditional alternative, coal power, and less expensive than coal when environmental costs are taken into account.[2]*
- *The collapse of Communism in Eastern Europe and the Soviet Union is presenting tempting but uncertain opportunities for American businesses. This collapse was so complete that several small securities markets—prime symbols of capitalism—opened in the Soviet Union in 1991. The failed 1991 Soviet coup saw a temporary krakh, or crash, of all three stocks listed on the Moscow Central Stock Exchange.[3]*
- *Researchers are reporting incredible breakthroughs in miniaturization. At IBM they have demonstrated a tiny switch that depends on the motion of a single atom, making it the smallest electronic device in existence.[4] At Hitachi's Central Research Laboratory (HCRL) they have shown that they can write atomic-sized words, moving atoms around to spell "PEACE '91 HCRL." The procedure may become the basis of next century's computer memories.[5] Gears on motors developed at the University of Wisconsin are a few dozen microns (millionths of a meter) in diameter. Such motors may be used in tiny robots with a bewildering array of potential applications.[6]*

> • *Demographic changes are dramatically reshaping American workplaces and markets. For example, it is predicted that white males will constitute only 15 percent of net additions to the workforce in the year 2000, down sharply from 45 percent in 1985.[7]*

This is just a sampling of the remarkable opportunities and challenges facing business today. As we will see in this chapter, many changes are taking place in the environment of business. If firms are to succeed—indeed, to survive—in this startling new world, they must recognize and respond to these developments. In this chapter, we will discuss the future of American business.

Human beings are fascinated with the future. They think about it. They dream about it. They worry about it. They even plan for it. What will the weather be like tomorrow? Where will I be living in five years? What can we do today to make the world a better place tomorrow? Indeed, a French philosopher once remarked that what distinguishes human beings from other animals is our love of wine with dinner and our fascination with the future.

This is an exciting time for American business. Our society may be on the brink of an economic and technological revolution as far-reaching in its impact on human life as was the industrial revolution of 200 years ago. Some experts foresee an era of great prosperity ahead: a doubling of our standard of living, the elimination of poverty and industrial pollution, the creation of a new economic dynamism through the emergence of high-technology industries, an overall increase in worker productivity, and a halt to inflation. Others are less optimistic about our ability to solve economic and social problems. Today, more than ever before, a concern with the future is essential because of the rapid pace of change and because of our power to influence the direction of change for better or for worse.

Let's begin our study of the future of American business by looking at how business managers make educated guesses about the future. Then we will gaze into the crystal ball to see what the future might have in store for us. We'll make a few educated guesses of our own about population trends, economic developments, and new technological industries.

FORECASTING AND PLANNING

forecasting *predicting the future using analytic techniques.*

forecast *a prediction of future values of a variable based on known or past values of the variable or of other related variables.*

All thinking about the future is to some degree guesswork, because no one knows today what will happen tomorrow. However, in an attempt to understand the direction and magnitude of change, we can think about the future analytically. **Forecasting** is predicting the future using analytic techniques. A **forecast** is a prediction of future values of a variable based on known or past values of the variable or other related variables. Forecasts may be based on historical data, expert opinion, or experience; they may involve the use of sophisticated mathematical techniques.

Let's see how forecasting works. Population is a variable. A prediction that the population of the United States will reach 268 million in the year 2000 is a forecast. This prediction was made by examining known rates of population growth over the past few years and projecting those rates into the future.

Housing starts is another variable. By studying economic and population data, we could define a relationship between the number of new houses built (one variable) and population growth (a related variable). At its simplest, this

The age mix of the population will be changing as we enter the new century. Senior citizens, like these participants in the National Senior Olympics in St. Louis, will make up an ever larger and more important market for products and services.

relationship would tell us that as population increases, the number of new houses built increases. If our understanding of the relationship were good enough, we would be able to predict the number of new housing starts for every increase of 1,000 people in the population. With a forecast of population, therefore, we could produce a forecast of new housing starts. The forecast could be for a period of one year, five years, ten years, and so on. We could perform this analysis for the entire country or for a regional economy—say, that of Atlanta, Georgia. Builders in Atlanta would want to know how predicted population changes in their area are likely to affect the construction industry there. Such information would help them develop budgets for obtaining building supplies and for hiring new workers.

Going Out on a Limb

Of course, not all predictions about the future are right. In 1902, one popular magazine stated confidently: "The actual building of roads devoted to motor cars is not for the near future, in spite of the many rumors to that effect." Today, if all the paved roads in this country were joined end to end, they would reach to the moon and back many, many times. Predictions about society and the way we live have also been off the mark. What ever happened to an autogyro in every garage, boxing robots as a popular form of entertainment, 250-story skyscrapers, mid-ocean cities served by dirigibles and hydroplanes, and inexpensive atomic energy? Consider the following examples of notoriously faulty predictions:[8]

> "Well-informed people know it is impossible to transmit the voice over wires and that were it possible to do so, the thing would be of no practical value." Editorial in the *Boston Post,* commenting on the arrest for fraud of Joshua Coppersmith (who had been attempting to raise funds for work on a telephone), 1865.

"When the Paris exhibition closes electric light will close with it and no more will be heard of it." Erasmus Wilson (professor at Oxford University), 1878.

"Everything that can be invented has been invented." Charles H. Duell (Commissioner of U.S. Patents), urging President William McKinley to abolish his office, 1899.

"If we are to begin to try and understand life as it will be in 1960, we must begin by realizing that food, clothing and shelter will cost as little as air." John Langdon-Davies (British journalist and Fellow of the Royal Anthropological Institute), 1936.

"This is the biggest fool thing we have ever done. . . . The bomb will never go off, and I speak as an expert in explosives." Admiral William Daniel Leahy, advising President Harry S. Truman on the impracticality of the U.S. atomic bomb project, 1945.

"Video won't be able to hold onto any market it captures after the first six months. People will soon get tired of staring at a plywood box every night." Darryl F. Zanuck (head of 20th Century-Fox Studios), circa 1946.

"With over 50 foreign cars already on sale here, the Japanese auto industry isn't likely to carve out a big slice of the U.S. market for itself." *Business Week*, January 17, 1958.

"There is no reason for any individual to have a computer in their home." Ken Olson (President of Digital Equipment Corporation), Convention of the World Future Society in Boston, 1977.

Business managers face a very difficult forecasting task. They must make decisions today based on certain assumptions or expectations about the future. A strategic planner for a retail firm could decide to open new stores in 12 downtown markets this year, but if consumer demand for the firm's goods does not materialize, then the decision will be a costly one. Consumer demand for goods and services is a function of income levels, the rate of inflation, and interest rates. If a prediction about any of these variables is wrong, then any prediction about consumer demand and the resulting sales revenues could be wrong, too.

Forecasting these fairly simple relationships is hard enough, but when planners try to predict technological breakthroughs or turning points in economic trends or political events, forecasting becomes even riskier. Who would have predicted the developments noted at the beginning of the chapter? A good forecast involves just the right combination of observation, analysis, instinct, and luck! Faith Popcorn, profiled on page 678, has made a career of this difficult task.

Reducing Uncertainty

Despite our mistakes in reading the future, forecasting and planning are essential activities of all firms. Profitable firms are better forecasters and planners than unprofitable ones. Our forecasts become more accurate as our understanding of economics, markets, and business conditions increases and as our forecasting techniques improve. The aim of all forecasts is to reduce decision uncertainty by telling us something about the future. Thus, forecasts serve as guides to decision making. Organizations establish goals and objectives; attempt to predict economic, social, or technological change; and then select actions that they hope will result in achievement of the goals and objectives. With an accurate interest rate forecast, indicating a drop in mortgage rates and an end to a housing slump, a wood products company could gear up production capacity in anticipation of future demand.

INTO THE NEXT CENTURY

In the year 2050, the United States will be a very different place than it is today. Chapter 2 examined the changing socioeconomic environment of business. Let's take a second look at the most important population and income trends, both national and global, and at where these trends are taking us.

U.S. Population Size

The population of the United States is still growing. Our current population is about 250 million, up from 205 million in 1970. According to census experts, the population will climb to 268 million in the year 2000 and will continue to increase until about 2040, at which time it will peak and then begin a decline. These population projections are shown in Figure 24-1. However, as Figure 24-2 shows, the rate of population growth is already declining and has been since the 1950s. Whereas the population grew by 10.6 percent during the 1970s and 10.2 percent in the 1980s, it may actually decline by 0.7 percent between 2040 and 2050. Could this slowdown in population growth eventually mean an end to unemployment? As the size of the labor pool shrinks, will there be fewer people competing for available jobs? The slowdown in population growth also suggests that, since markets will not be growing rapidly, competition for customers may increase. Growth-oriented firms may have to enter new markets aggressively to meet their goals.

FIGURE 24-1   U.S. Population Growth, 1950—2050

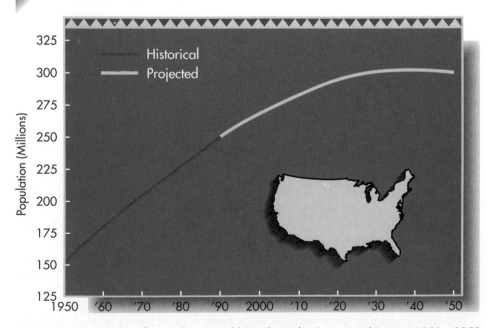

Source: U.S. Department of Agriculture, *World Population by Country and Region, 1950 – 2050* (Washington, D.C., 1990).

FIGURE 24-2   Rate of Growth of U.S. Population, 1950—2050

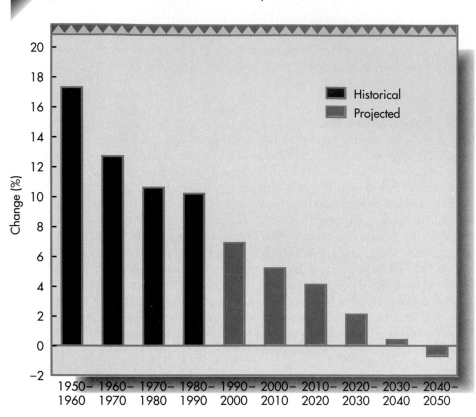

Source: U.S. Department of Agriculture, *World Population by Country and Region, 1950 – 2050* (Washington, D.C., 1990).

Age Mix

The median age of Americans at the turn of the century was only 23 years. It had grown to 30 years in 1980 and 33 in 1990. By the end of this century, the median age is projected to be 36, increasing to 42 in the year 2050. The proportion of the population 34 years of age or younger will decline to 45 percent by the year 2010, down from 58 percent in 1980. Census experts say that proportion could drop to 42 percent by 2050. Moreover, it is now estimated that older Americans will live longer than ever. The typical 65-year-old man can currently expect to live to 80, and the typical 65-year-old woman to 83.[9]

What does the aging of the population mean for the makers of youth-oriented products? It means that the markets for their products will tighten in years to come. At the same time, the markets for products aimed at middle-aged and elderly people will expand. We can expect to see more demand for home-improvement products, pharmaceutical products, hospital and medical services, financial services, travel services, and fitness services. Services now play a big part in our economy, and they are likely to play an even bigger part in years to come. Perhaps as much as 80 percent of all employment will be in services by the year 2000.

This aging trend also suggests that firms will incur increasing costs for employer-sponsored pension plans and retiree health benefits, as well as for social security and Medicare. Of course, firms will also be benefiting from a relatively stable and experienced workforce.

Family Size and Family Income

As our population grows bigger, average family size will get smaller. In 1980, 16.6 percent of all U.S. families consisted of five or more people. By 1995, however, such large families will account for only 9.4 percent of the total. The average family size fell from 3.67 in 1960 to about 3.15 in 1990, and the downward trend is expected to continue through the year 2000.

Barring a worldwide recession or other economic disaster, families of all sizes should have higher incomes in real terms through the 1990s. The percentage of all families earning $50,000 or more should rise to 24 percent by 1995, up from 10 percent in 1980. Demographers expect this increase to be greatest for four-person families. The main reason for these higher incomes is that the output of our economy will continue to grow. Technological innovation will be the driving force behind the increase in national wealth. Also, dual-career families will be more common. In Chapter 2, we observed this trend, and it should continue. Finally, the baby boom generation—the subject of Case 24-2—will have grown up, formed families, and entered the years of greatest productivity and earnings.

Smaller families coupled with higher incomes should result in more discretionary income and fewer responsibilities. Therefore, there may be more flexibility to pursue interests such as travel and hobbies. The shrinking size of families may also influence such things as the sizes of cars, homes, and even of "family size" packages. Also, dual-career families will have less time for housework, so premium-priced convenience products are likely to continue to gain market share.

Household Composition

The traditional two-parent, multichild household is becoming less common. In 1970, over 85 percent of children under the age of 19 were living with both parents, but that figure had dropped to 70 percent in 1990. The fastest-growing household type is people living with nonrelatives, which rose 46 percent during the 1980s. While some of these are unmarried couples, others are nonromantic partners, such as friends sharing apartments.[10] The number of people living alone—now about 25 percent of households—will continue to rise as more people are widowed, divorced, or simply opt not to get married. These single-person households have increased in number by almost 5 million since 1980. Increasingly, too, there are fewer children living at home. Historically, the number of families with children living at home outnumbered those without children at home, but that changed around 1985, and the trend is continuing. Interestingly, though, the number of older children living at home is increasing.

Firms will have to rethink the nature and marketing of their offerings in view of these changes. Although traditional families will still dominate, other forms will create opportunities. For instance, the Hyatt hotel chain sees the growing number of singles as a prime target. The chain figures that singles have traditionally gotten a bad deal when traveling, and it is considering a program of special prices for them.

Ethnic Mix

The coming decades will present firms with the tasks of managing diversity in the workforce and responding to diversity in markets. For example, from 1981 to 1991, while the total U.S. population grew by slightly more than 10 percent, the number of Hispanics increased four times as fast. It is estimated that 40 percent of U.S. population growth in the 1990s will be accounted for by persons of His-

Faith Popcorn

Faith Popcorn, the founder and CEO of BrainReserve, Inc., is a futurist. She helps firms such as Campbell's Soup, Pillsbury, and Eastman Kodak spot changing values, needs, lifestyles, and other trends that might influence consumer preferences and company practices. Based on that information, she helps firms formulate marketing plans, develop new products, and reposition old ones. Because of her predictions, *Newsweek* has called Popcorn "one of the most interviewed women on the planet." Her insights are not inexpensive: The price tag for her speeches is up to $20,000, and corporate projects may cost $1 million.

Popcorn says that it is important for firms to distinguish between fads and trends. Fads, she says, appeal to a limited audience, come and go quickly, and often run counter to other happenings. Trends, on the other hand, affect a wider audience, last long, and are consistent with other social and economic indicators. To forecast trends, Popcorn and her colleagues at BrainReserve interview more than 2,000 consumers a year, keep abreast of movies and TV shows, read nearly 300 trade and consumer publications, and keep an eye on powerful trendsetters. The firm once even signed on a psychic.

Popcorn has identified many trends relating to fitness, downsizing, return to tradition, and "grazing"—doing everything, including eating, in short takes. She is perhaps best known for identifying a trend she calls "cocooning." According to Popcorn, rapid change and a variety of threats have caused consumers to "run home and pull the covers over their heads," the way caterpillars wrap themselves in cocoons. Popcorn sees cocooning as a way to protect oneself from a harsh, unpredictable world. Because of this intense focus on home life, she says, Americans are reading more, having babies, spending more time with their children, and engaging in other household activities. Although people want security, they seek out fantasies and adventures that can be experienced either in the home or in a safe environment. The popularity of pick-up trucks, ethnic foods, and adventure movies reflects this desire for safe adventure.

Popcorn predicts that consumers of the future will go beyond cocooning: They will be "burrowing," leaving their homes as little as possible. Thus, companies will be able to sell subscriptions for basic products such as soap, with a new bar arriving each month along with the magazines and bills.

panic origin.[11] Hispanics will account for 10.5 percent of the U.S. population by the year 2000. This remarkable growth is due to a constant stream of immigrants and to the relatively high birth rate among Hispanics. The Asian population grew by 65 percent between 1980 and 1990. It is predicted that the Asian population will attract increasing attention from marketers, since it will continue to grow in numbers and affluence. Overall, minority-group members will make up 30 percent of the U.S. population in the year 2010, up from 20 percent at the beginning of the 1980s.[12]

The growth of the ethnic population will create opportunities to market products and services that are preferred by particular ethnic groups. In addition, advertising will have to take cultural differences into consideration. For example, Hispanics place heavy emphasis on the family. Thus, Ford Motor Company stresses the family rather than singles in its ads aimed at Hispanics.

Workforce Composition

As noted at the beginning of this chapter, it is predicted that white males will constitute only 15 percent of net additions to the workforce by the year 2000, down from 45 percent in 1985. Labor-force participation rates have increased for all women under age 65, but especially for women in their 30s and 40s. The rate for women aged 35 to 44 is now 78 percent, up from 65 percent in 1980. Furthermore, over 50 percent of women who have had a child in the preceding year are now in the workforce—up from 31 percent in 1976.

These and other trends in workforce composition, as well as related social changes, will have important implications for the hiring, training, management, and compensation of employees. For instance, 42 percent of companies report engaging in minority recruiting, though just 12 percent currently train minorities for supervisory positions. Also, firms are rethinking their policies on such issues as leaves and insurance plans. For example, many firms now give paternity leave to new fathers. In another development reflecting changing attitudes, Lotus Development Corp. attracted attention when it decided in 1991 to extend health insurance to partners of gay and lesbian employees.[13]

The growing ethnic population noted above will also create challenges in the workplace, as cultures with different attitudes toward time, relationships, life, and work interact. For instance, Asians and Hispanics typically show greater deference to authority than do white North Americans. Hispanic cultures generally regard music, family members, and food as welcome additions to the workplace. Also, tones of voice, facial expressions, physical distance maintained between people, and types of interaction with the opposite sex have very different meanings in different cultures.

Global Population and Income Trends

The population and income outlook is much more favorable nationally than worldwide. Most demographers now have little hope that world population growth will be brought under control in the foreseeable future. Between 1990 and the year 2000, world population will increase from 5.3 billion to 6.3 billion, an average increase of about 100 million people a year. By 2020, it is estimated to rise to 8.1 billion—more than triple the 1950 level. Of this growth, 90 percent will occur in the developing countries. **Developing countries** are countries where per capita income and standard of living are far below those of other countries. Because these countries are so poor, they are least able to provide for such a large population growth. By 2025, over 84 percent of the world's population

developing countries
those countries, predominantly in Asia, Africa, and Latin America, whose per capita incomes and standards of living are far below those of other countries, but whose population growth rates are among the highest in the world.

will live in these nations, compared to 77 percent in 1990. Food production in the developing countries is not expected to keep pace with population growth there.

If current population growth were to continue indefinitely, the world's pop-ulation would approach 30 billion by the end of the next century. However, many factors influencing birth and death rates may alter these trends. For instance, some nations, such as China, have already made significant strides in slowing the rate of population growth. In other countries, however, the birth rate is still very high. In nations such as Mali and Uganda, only about 5 percent of married women of reproductive age use contraceptives.

Another big uncertainty in the population equation is the threat of Acquired Immune Deficiency Syndrome (AIDS). Although the growth rate in new AIDS cases in the U.S. and Europe is expected to taper off around 1995, it will continue to rise in Africa and Asia beyond the year 2000. The World Health Organization estimates that 5 to 6 million Africans carry the AIDS virus, out of an estimated total of 8 to 10 million infected people worldwide.[14]

Figure 24-3 shows the distribution of world population by region in 1990 and 2025. Compare population growth in the industrialized West with that of the developing countries of Latin America, Africa, and Asia and Oceania. Given these high rates of growth, what are the chances that such developing countries will be able to lift themselves out of poverty?

FIGURE 24-3   Distribution of the World's Population, 1990 and 2025

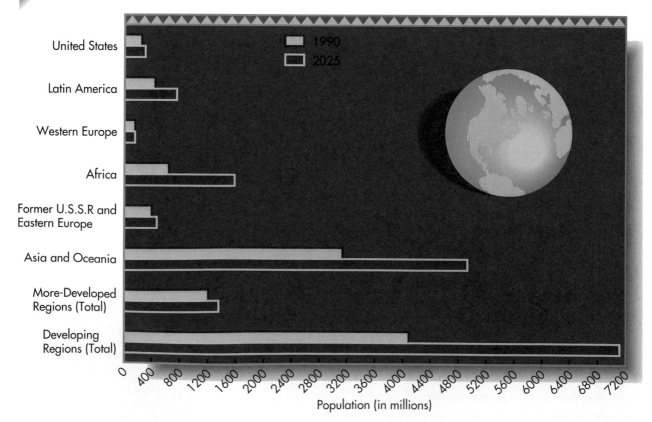

Source: United Nations Population Fund (UNFPA), *The State of World Population 1990* (New York, 1990).

The economies of the developing countries, especially in Latin America, are expected to grow faster than those of the wealthier Western nations. One reason is that they are just beginning to undertake widespread industrialization. The early stages of industrialization tend to produce higher rates of national economic growth than the mature stages. The United States and the Western European nations are examples of nations in the mature stage of industrialization. The nations of Africa and Asia, despite their efforts at industrialization and economic growth, will experience only modest gains in per capita wealth. In Africa, for example, per capita GNP will scarcely rise above the equivalent of $600.

This continuing income gap between the rich and the poor nations will place pressure on the world community for a more equitable division of wealth. It will also present opportunities for American business expansion as U.S. firms help developing countries industrialize and supply them with food and other critical resources. However, the instability of the developing countries adds risk. American businesses may be taken over without warning by the host country's government, or political changes may cause anti-American hostility and even violence. American firms can reduce such risks by making a positive impact on the local economy—providing jobs for locals, buying local raw materials, and supporting local charities. This combination of opportunity and danger is also faced by American firms hoping to help the former U.S.S.R. become capitalistic, as discussed in the International Example on page 682. Increasingly, the global trend is one of economic interdependence, and the world is the marketplace.

INDUSTRIAL OUTLOOK   3

Two trends that are reshaping the industrial composition of our economy are the decline of basic industries—the so-called smokestack industries—and the rise of high-technology industries. **Basic industries** are heavy manufacturing industries such as steel, automobiles, airplanes, chemicals, machinery, rubber, and glass. They employ about one third of the U.S. labor force. The rapid expansion of these industries produced the great economic boom that followed World War II. Now that these industries are in decline, however, we must look toward the new high-technology industries if the United States—and, indeed, all of the industrialized West—is to enter another long period of economic growth.

basic industries *heavy manufacturing industries, such as steel, automobile, airplane, chemical, machinery, rubber, and glass.*

Decline of Basic Industries

The plight of basic industry in this country is best exemplified by the steel industry. In the early 1980s, American steel mills were operating at only 30 percent of capacity. That is, for every 100 tons of steel that the mills were equipped to produce, they were producing only 30 tons because of slack demand. Unemployment in the industry was running at an astronomical 60 percent. By 1990, steel producers had cut capacity by 27 percent and slashed their workforces by more than half. Because of these cuts in capacity, mills were able to operate at 78 percent of capacity in 1991. However, most analysts believe that even with aggressive cost cutting and new production technologies, there is not much chance that U.S. steelmakers will ever dominate world markets again.

Labor Costs and Cheaper Imports.   Two reasons for the steel industry's troubles are high labor costs and increased competition from foreign steel producers. Labor costs—which make up more than a third of total steel costs—are

A New Revolution

It had the appearance of a new revolution. The former Soviet Union was disintegrating. U.S. President George Bush and Russian President Boris Yeltsin formally declared an end to the Cold War. Russia, Ukraine, and other republics in the newly formed Commonwealth of Independent States that succeeded the Soviet Union, led by Yeltsin's bold steps in 1992 to revive Russia's economy, moved toward a market-based system. For the first time since the early 1920s, price controls were eliminated in Russia on all but the most basic commodities, and Yeltsin announced that he would cut off state subsidies to unprofitable enterprises. All this represented both promise and peril for American business.

Many American firms moved quickly to take advantage of the tremendous opportunities created by these changes. Joint ventures were announced or discussed in telecommunications, energy, and food. Even the hallowed grounds of the Kremlin were opened for the first time to permit Scottie McBean Inc., a gourmet-coffee dealer from Columbus, Ohio, to open cafes inside the medieval Russian citadel.

At the same time, the changes bred tremendous uncertainties. Just six weeks after the announcement of the economic liberalization plan, prices had increased 350 percent, many store shelves were bare, and the black market was thriving. There was no comprehensive economic plan, no taxation system to bring the government revenue, and no monetary policy to control the budget deficit and halt the unbridled printing of money. There was no real privatization of industry; the economy was still run by great state monopolies. In addition, Russian managers had never studied pricing theory, cost containment, marketing, or labor relations.

U.S. Secretary of State James Baker declared that we might be seeing "the economy collapse with no bottom in sight." Pravda saw impending "total pauperization of the people and final collapse of the monetary system." The situation created unrest, as well as the possibility of massive strikes or even a coup. Yeltsin urged patience and promised major corrections. He put his chief critic in charge of reorganizing Russia's troubled agriculture, in order "to occupy his time to the limit." The world watched and waited, checkbooks in hand, anxiously gauging the shifting balance of risk and return.

usually much cheaper abroad, so steel producers in Japan, South Korea, Spain, and other countries are able to undercut the prices of U.S. producers.

Politically, the issue is quota agreements with foreign countries. A quota sets an upper limit on the amount of steel that foreign producers may ship to this country. Quotas in effect in 1991 permitted imports to capture no more than 20.1 percent of the U.S. market (in fact, they made up 17 percent), but President Bush vowed to remove import protection by 1992.[15]

Two Views on Industrial Investment. In the long run, the problem with many basic industries is the aging of their capital equipment. Two views prevail as to what sort of investment policies should be undertaken. According to one view, insufficient investment is the cause of the decline of basic industries. Proponents of this view favor a "reindustrialization" of traditional industries through a combination of tax incentives, import quotas, government-directed investment strategies, and other measures. Indeed, some U.S. companies are actively experimenting with new technologies. For instance, Nucor Corp. has developed a new technology to produce steel slabs, cutting energy costs by 20 percent to 40 percent and reducing work hours per ton by half.

The other view holds that such policies are badly misguided. Rather than pouring our resources into these "sunset" industries, which are fading as a result of economic forces, we should be investing in "sunrise" industries—namely, high-technology industries.

This second view is supported by the **long wave theory** of economic growth and decline. The theory holds that economic growth follows a pattern of

long wave theory *a theory of economic growth: that 50-year "waves" alternate between economic prosperity and decline; economic growth is theorized to be technologically driven.*

682

"waves" that alternate between global prosperity and economic decline. Each wave, lasting 50 years or so, is driven by a new cluster of technological innovation. These 50-year cycles have been noted in various biblical accounts and several past civilizations, including those of the Mayans, Aztecs, Romans, and Babylonians.[16] One wave reached its peak around 1920, when the railroads and other early industries produced a period of widespread economic prosperity. The economies of the world went into decline thereafter. Another wave peaked around 1970, and was driven by innovation in such basic industries as steel, chemicals, and transportation.[17]

Figure 24-4 illustrates the long wave theory. Interestingly, according to this view, we have barely begun the next wave. Most of the benefits of computers and related technologies are still ahead of us. If this wave pattern of growth and decline operates as almost an unchanging law of history and economics, as proponents of the theory believe, then government attempts to prop up basic industries only postpone the arrival of the next wave.

Emerging High-Technology Industries

The 1980s were a time of great activity with respect to scientific discovery, applied research, and high-tech business start-ups. It was a decade of innovation and entrepreneurship. The opening years of the 1990s have been at least as exciting. Keeping current with technological change and adjusting business strategy accordingly is one of management's most essential tasks. No one expects technological change to slow down in the years ahead, so this task will become even more important in business planning.

Role of Technology. Technological innovation is the engine of economic growth. Technology drives our economy by enabling us to produce more output from limited resource inputs. The results may include more and better goods and services, more efficient capital equipment, a higher standard of living, and greater opportunities to realize human potential.

FIGURE 24-4   Long Waves of Economic Growth and Decline

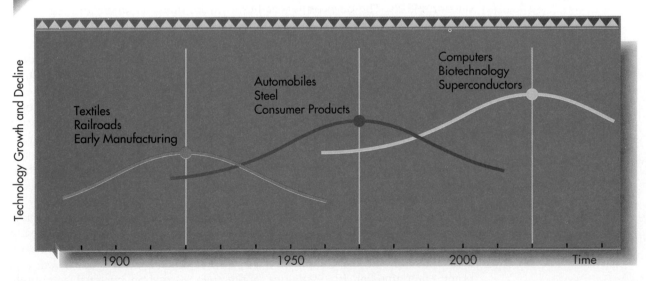

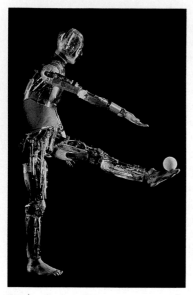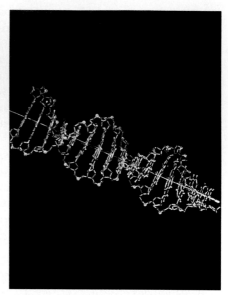

Technology will continue to transform the economy and our lives in the years ahead. Shown above: the robotic mannequin "Manny," used in research and development of improved robots for industrial use; a superconductor, which promises great efficiencies in production; and a magnified section of a strand of DNA, the genetic material that serves as the basis for the burgeoning field of biotechnology.

production possibilities curve   *a graphic display of the various combinations of goods that can be produced in an economy with the available resources and technology.*

In all economies, technology is applied to the fixed supply of natural resources to produce goods and services. Economists use a **production possibilities curve** to depict the various combinations of goods that can be produced in an economy with the available resources and technology. For that economy to produce more output, some change must occur that makes it possible to use the available resources more efficiently. Such changes are often technological advances. For example, imagine an economy with a fixed supply of natural resources from which it produces its output of goods and services. To keep the discussion simple, let's say that the economy produces only two goods: hammers and loaves of bread. The economy can produce varying quantities of these two goods, depending upon how it decides to allocate its natural resources and production efforts. The decision is whether to make more hammers and less bread or to make fewer hammers and more bread. The maximum output of the total of hammers and bread depends on the state of technology at the time. Figure 24-5(a) shows a production possibilities curve for hammers and bread. The curve represents various output combinations of the two goods. Two possible output combinations are shown as points on the curve.

What effect does technological innovation have on maximum possible output? It pushes the curve to the right, as shown in Figure 24-5(b). The outward movement of the curve indicates that the economy, using the new technology, is able to produce more output with the same amount of natural resources. Specifically, it can produce more hammers *and* more bread. More efficient production technologies result in less waste and more total output. The result is greater economic wealth and a higher standard of living.

The high-technology sector of our economy makes headlines every day. Think about the vitality of the electronics industry, as indicated by the steady stream of innovations pouring out of its research labs and assembly plants each year. Think about how computers have revolutionized business, education, and home entertainment. In 1990 alone, more than 23 million personal computers

FIGURE 24-5   Production Possibilities Curve

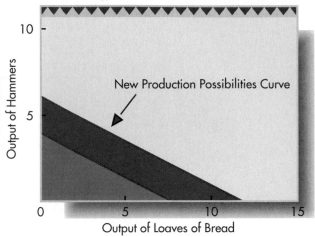

(a) Total output of hammers and bread with a given technology.

(b) Advancing technology pushes the curve to the right; society produces more total output of hammers and bread with its higher level of technology.

were sold worldwide. Not only were laptop computers being seen everywhere, but sophisticated new palmtop computers weighing as little as 8 ounces were becoming popular.[18] There is even a computer that lets users write directly on the screen with special pens. These "pen computers" promise to improve the productivity of executives, field workers, and others who don't want to hassle with a keyboard to enter data.[19] Think about how the linking of telecommunications and computer systems could change the way we live and work. Consider the possibilities of research and production in space, the subject of this chapter's Controversial Issue (see page 688). Four new industries on the frontier of technological innovation are biotechnology, robotics and factory automation, materials science, and superconductors.

Biotechnology.   A new and exciting industry is **biotechnology,** in which new products are developed through recombinant genetics, or gene splicing. Only a dream 20 years ago, biotechnology involves moving genes from one organism to another. Genes are located in the cells of all living organisms and are responsible for determining and transmitting inherited characteristics. By manipulating genes, geneticists can create new bacteria, yeasts, and plants that may benefit humanity. The names of some of the biotechnology firms—Genentech, Biogen, and Chiron—may sound as if they belong in a science fiction novel, but recombinant genetics is one of the brightest spots in our business future. Case 24-1 illustrates the potential of "Pharming."

biotechnology   a field in which new products are developed through recombinant genetics, or gene splicing.

Table 24-1 shows a sampling of products developed through biotechnology that are now on the market in the United States. Already in production is a bacterially produced human insulin (a drug used in treating diabetes). Other promising commercial products include human growth hormones, antibodies for fighting viral infections, and aspartame (a sugar substitute). In the long run, recombinant genetics is expected to have a revolutionary impact on the pharmaceutical, medical, agricultural, food processing, chemical, and petrochemical

TABLE 24-1   Some Products Developed Through Biotechnology That Are on the Market in the United States.

	Product	Treatment or Use (Year First Approved)
Human Health Care	Alpha interferon	Hairy cell leukemia (1986); Kaposi's sarcoma (1988); non-A non-B hepatitis (1990)
	Erythropoietin	Anemia associated with kidney disease (1989)
	Human growth hormone	Dwarfism (1986)
	Insulin	Diabetes (1982)
	Tissue plasminogen activator	Dissolve blood clots (1987)
	Vaccines	Hepatitis-B (1986)
	Monoclonal antibodies (MAbs)	Treat kidney transplant rejection (1986); purify blood clotting agents (1987)
	Diagnostic tests (MAbs and DNA probes)	Diagnose pregnancy and fertility; bacterial and viral infections; cancer; genetic diseases; DNA fingerprinting; forensic and paternity testing; etc.
Agriculture	Animals:	
	Vaccines	Colibacillosis or scours (1984); pseudorabies (1987)
	Diagnostic tests	Bacterial and viral infections, pregnancy, presence of antibiotic residues
	Plants:	
	Diagnostic tests	Diagnose plant diseases (e.g.,turfgrass fungi)
Food Processing	Diagnostic tests	Diagnose food and feed contaminants
	Chymosin or rennin	Enzyme used in cheesemaking (1990)
Other	Transgenic mice	Cancer research
	Luciferase TM	Detection agent used in food and medical diagnostic tests

Source: U.S. Dept. of Commerce, International Trade Administration, *U.S. Industrial Outlook 1991—Advanced Materials* (Washington, D.C.: U.S. Government Printing Office, 1991), p. 18-3.

industries. Eventually, the market will see a wealth of new industrial products that make waste treatment, oil refining, chemical synthesis, and food production more efficient and less costly.

Biotechnology's remarkable breakthroughs pose many challenging ethical questions. Some people argue that it is immoral to manipulate life and to patent new life forms. Others fear that genetically engineered plants or animals may somehow run amok and endanger the environment. Biotechnology and other scientific developments pose ethical challenges, even as they present new possibilities and dangers. Increasingly, these involve difficult tradeoffs, as discussed in the Ethical Issue on page 690.

Robotics and Factory Automation. The industrial robots of today bear little resemblance to the mechanical wonders of 1950s outer space movies or the computerized image of Max Headroom in 1980s TV commercials. As discussed in Chapter 11, a robot is a machine that can be programmed to do a variety of tasks automatically. Some industrial robots are mobile and have many arms, but most are simply a mechanical arm attached to a stationary base. A programmable computing device controls the operation of the arm. Robots in U.S. factories are already performing such manufacturing tasks as spray painting, arc welding, die casting, assembling, and materials handling. An industrial robot costs an average of $115,000.

Robotics is the field of study concerned with the construction, maintenance, and application of automatically controlled mechanisms in production processes. Two of the most important benefits of robotics and automation technology are greater productivity and improved cost control, both of which can make U.S. producers more competitive in world markets. Other benefits include more consistent product quality, around-the-clock output, improved inventory control, and more efficient use of capital equipment. Also, robots are able to toil where humans dare not tread—cleaning up waste in nuclear power plants and hazardous materials sites, detecting bombs, conducting underwater maintenance of offshore oil rigs, and carrying out dangerous missions in space.[20]

robotics   *a field of study concerned with the construction, maintenance, and application of automatically controlled mechanisms in production processes.*

The resurgence of American industry will depend on the widespread adoption of robotics and computer-automation technologies. Unfortunately, American industry is lagging behind some foreign competitors in adopting robots. It was estimated that there were between 175,000 and 275,000 robots operating in Japan in 1990, but only 37,000 in American factories.[21]

Although American firms are far behind the Japanese in their use of robots, American robot orders have continued to increase, to over $514 million in 1990. However, American business has decided to drop out of robotics manufacturing, at least for now. There were once more than 60 American makers of robots, including Cincinnati Milicron, Westinghouse, and General Electric, but now only a few small American firms remain in the field.

Materials Science. Imagine ceramic knives that stay sharp for years and never rust or corrode. Imagine friction-free truck engines that get 100 miles to the gallon. Imagine road bridges made of plastic. Imagine cements so strong and pliable that they can actually be formed into flexible springs. Imagine plastic composite materials both lighter and stronger than steel. These are just a few of the wonders coming from a branch of technology research called **materials science,** which develops super-materials. The 19th century was the era of iron and wood. The 20th century, through the post-World War II period, was the era of steel and plastics. The decades ahead may be the era of composite materials.

materials science   *a branch of technology that deals with the development of super-materials.*

Business Career
Materials Engineer: Determines which metals, plastics, ceramics, and other materials work best for product applications. Considers factors such as strength, weight, and cost. Tests materials and develops new materials to meet design objectives. *Average Salary: $29,200.*

Scientists are now learning how to engineer desirable traits into materials by manipulating substances at the molecular level. Such traits may be lightness, strength, flexibility, hardness, or heat resistance. An example of the latter would be ceramic engine parts that withstand the high heat generated by an internal combustion engine without needing to be cooled by a circulating water system.

As is the case with many new discoveries, the path to commercial introduction of these new super-materials may be harder than the course of research in the laboratory. For example, there are many obstacles to the introduction of these new materials in automobile assembly processes, including the cost of rebuilding assembly lines and potential liability problems. However, you may already be using products made with super-materials and not know it. Do you play tennis?

Should American Business Invest in Space?

Part of the intention behind the massive federal support of NASA's space program during the 1960s and 1970s was to increase the feasibility of starting industrial research and production facilities in space. Now that space technology is coming of age, should businesses start investing in such programs?

Yes

The early success of the space shuttle program demonstrated that all the tools are available to establish industrial programs of research and production in space. NASA has demonstrated the capability to build permanent space stations, and a major space station program is now in progress. The space stations could house factories for work that is expensive, hazardous, or inefficient on earth. For example, plants and molds, when suspended in a weightless environment, produce great quantities of many kinds of drugs, so space is the perfect environment for new drug factories. Many electronic techniques involving new semiconductor systems require assembly in a vacuum and a far cleaner dust-free environment than earth's atmosphere can offer; again, space is perfect. A single shuttle flight can deliver enough supplies to construct literally hundreds of millions of dollars worth of products for a shuttle return trip. The prospects are staggering.

Also consider that a factory in space can obtain almost limitless supplies of energy from the sun. Reduced expenditures for power may make further economic efficiencies possible.

Remember that the American government is still subsidizing much of the cost of space development. Companies that hop on the bandwagon now can get carried into space for very little. The government is even assuming the incredible risks, so firms don't have to worry about getting Prudential to insure a space factory. (Can you imagine what the premiums would be like?)

There is no indication that NASA is running out of exciting ideas for space development. Along with the space station, NASA has launched interplanetary probes and earth-orbiting astronomical laboratories, and others are nearing completion. Plans for lunar bases and human travel to Mars are in the works.

Do you use a graphite tennis racket? If you do, then welcome to the world of super-materials!

superconductor a special material that conducts electricity without resistance.

Superconductors. Scientists have known about superconductors for a long time, but not until 1987 did these exciting new substances begin to receive a lot of public attention. A **superconductor** is a special material that conducts electricity without resistance. Normally, when an electric current flows through a copper wire, it encounters resistance and releases energy as heat. With superconductors, no energy is released. The catch is that these materials act as superconductors only at extremely low temperatures—near absolute zero, minus 460 degrees Fahrenheit! Because of the great expense involved in cooling materials to that temperature, there once seemed to be little hope that superconductors could be used in commercial applications.

Recently, however, research scientists have succeeded in producing ceramic materials that superconduct at much higher temperatures—minus 320 degrees and up. This is still very cold, of course, but it is much less expensive to cool materials to this temperature range than to absolute zero. The pace of research in this area is frenzied, as scientists work to produce materials that superconduct at much warmer temperatures, some even at room temperature.

Low-cost, room-temperature superconductors could revolutionize world industry in as far-reaching a way as computers revolutionized information processing. Power lines made of superconducting wire could lower electric bills greatly, because the superconductors would minimize the amount of energy lost in distributing electric current through power grids. Another intriguing prospect

Most of all, America has the technological capacity and the freedom to begin space industry. With the adoption of the National Space Policy and Commercial Initiatives in 1988, the commercial space industry was left free to exploit the heavens with little or no government intervention. Already, American firms have been privately launching payloads into space, especially communications satellites. American companies have been falling behind Japan and other industrialized powers, but the advantages gained from space ventures can propel us back into the lead.

No

No, space industrialization is not feasible. There are some industrial procedures that are better performed in space, but these methods change from month to month as technology advances. Long before space can be developed commercially, scientists will have figured how to improve these techniques for operation on earth.

There will also be economic and political problems. The government almost scrapped NASA before the space shuttle revived interest in space development. What will happen to the space budget during the next economic downturn? It will be cut. For instance, faced with projections that NASA's proposed space station could have a final price tag of more than $100 billion, Congress threat-ened to cut out funds for that project in 1991. No company, no matter how large, can afford to go it alone. Also, the explosion of the Challenger demonstrated just how dangerous space flight is.

Then there's the problem of space politics. For example, to whom will taxes be paid? Will taxes be higher on space-produced products because they have been produced with tax subsidies? In a war, will space stations be protected? International law and political agreements will have to be completely rethought and rewritten. Meanwhile, producing goods in space will be very risky.

What about the cost of space life to employees? When the Soviets sent astronauts aloft for many months, they returned home so weak they couldn't even lift a paper cup of orange juice. They had to learn how to walk again, and they were ill and disoriented for months. If employees are to endure these problems, they will expect extra compensation. There's no efficiency in that! If firms try to automate procedures entirely, to avoid having employees in space, there will still be horribly expensive breakdowns, and a repair crew will have to be sent out to fix them.

No, space travel is a tool for the government and for scientific research. Private investment in space just isn't worth it.

What Do You Think?

---

is a highly efficient battery that produces energy indefinitely. Some researchers even talk about trains that zoom along at 300 miles per hour on a cushion of air.

One of the most exciting new scientific developments is the buckyball. Buckyballs are molecules resembling soccer balls, made of pure carbon, which were first identified in 1985. The molecules' formal name—buckminsterfullerene—honors Buckminster Fuller, the inventor of the geodesic dome, which the buckyball resembles. The buckyballs are only the third pure form of carbon ever found—the others are diamond and graphite. In 1990, scientists discovered a way to make buckyballs easily. This sparked what some observers called a "feeding frenzy" among researchers, who were excited about their potential to make new lubricants, batteries, and high-strength polymers, among other things. With the discovery in 1991 that buckyballs could be made into superconductors when mixed with potassium, the race to capture the promise of the buckyball took on new energy.[22]

ORGANIZATIONAL CHANGES TO MEET FUTURE CHALLENGES

We have discussed how forces for change have led to the decline of some industries and the rise of others. Existing firms may have to change their structures and practices to compete effectively in the modern setting. Forces for change may call for many specific changes in the design of firms as well as in their marketing, financial management, and other policies. In general, however, two things are quite clear: Firms will have to be creative, and they will have to be flexible.

Tree Of Life

Once worshiped as a tree of death by the Greeks, and clipped for funeral wreaths by the English, the yew has now become a tree of life. One ironic result is that Bristol-Myers Squibb Co. finds itself at the center of a major controversy.

The controversy illustrates the painfully difficult trade-offs that will face American business in the future as it tries to balance the interests of many constituencies. Bristol-Myers has been named by the National Cancer Institute to develop taxol, an experimental drug. Taxol has shown dramatic success in the treatment of advanced ovarian cancer, which kills 12,000 women each year, and may be effective against other malignancies that affect hundreds of thousands of patients. Some call taxol the most promising new chemotherapy in a decade.

Unfortunately, taxol is derived from the rare Pacific yew tree, and the drug is scarce. Because of restricted supplies, 50 of 65 proposed studies of its effects on humans have been put on hold. Federal scientists need ten times their current supply for so-called compassionate-use treat-ment of the dying and to complete research necessary for approval of broader use of the drug. Medical researchers say that the only way to produce quickly all the taxol needed for treatment and testing would be to chop down tens of thousands of yews. Bristol-Myers set a goal of about 760,000 pounds of Pacific yew bark for 1991, requiring that 38,000 trees be cut. If taxol is approved as a practical treatment for cancer, demand—and the number of trees needed—will increase dramatically.

However, conservationists are successfully opposing any large-scale harvesting of the tree, which grows in the ancient forests that are the habitat of the endangered Northern spotted owl and other wildlife.

Bruce Chabner of the National Cancer Institute, sponsor of the studies, says "This is the ultimate confrontation between medicine and the environment. It's the spotted owl vs. people. I love the spotted owl, but I love people more." Conservationists reply that it's not that simple. They are concerned about saving the spotted owl and the yew trees as part of their overall goal of preserving the diversity and integrity of threatened forests. Destruction of the Pacific yew is, in their eyes, like killing the goose that lays the golden egg. Once the yew is gone, so is the source of taxol. What's more, says Wendell Wood of the Oregon Natural Resources Council, "Ancient forests that gave us the yew may give us answers to medical problems we haven't thought to ask."

Source: Based on M. Chase, "Cancer Drug May Save Many Human Lives—At Cost of Rare Trees." *Wall Street Journal,* 4 April 1991, pp. A1, A6.

Encouraging Creativity

Creativity is important in any business, but it is critical in rapidly changing or competitive industries. This is because firms in such industries must make decisions quickly, often, and with important consequences. To increase creativity, firms are making structural changes, employing creativity enhancement techniques, and instituting company programs.

Structural Changes. Some firms are setting up relatively independent units to enhance creativity. The idea is that this will free them from all the rules, hierarchy, and other bureaucratic entanglements of the parent firm. For instance, Convergent Technologies, a Silicon Valley computer maker, decided to build a new personal computer.[23] It named employee Matt Sanders as the leader of a "strike force" to develop the computer and then kicked him out of his office. His boss said, "If you get in trouble, call me, and if you get good news, call me too. But I ain't calling you." Sanders was being cut loose from day-to-day routines to form his own "company within a company." On a larger scale, when General Motors launched its Saturn project, the first new nameplate in the GM line since 1918, it wanted a clean-slate approach, not old ways of designing, engineering, manufacturing, or selling the product. Therefore, it set up a new organization to free Saturn from the inefficiencies and overstaffing of the current GM bureaucracy.

Creativity Enhancement Techniques. In addition to such structural changes, firms are recognizing that creativity can be improved if employees are encouraged to think in new and less constraining ways. They are using various techniques to do this.

For instance, **brainstorming** is a technique used to come up with as many original ideas as possible. The key to brainstorming is to set up the right atmosphere for relaxed, creative thinking. A small group of employees is brought together in a room, presented with the problem, and asked to propose as many free-wheeling solutions as possible. Participants are instructed that they should not criticize or evaluate others' ideas. Further, they are encouraged to improve upon and combine other participants' ideas. Brainstorming is an especially good way to develop new product ideas and creative advertising strategies.

brainstorming   a creativity enhancement technique in which individuals are encouraged to generate many free-wheeling ideas, building on the ideas of others and avoiding evaluation.

Another creativity enhancement technique, called **retroduction,** involves asking the question, "What if?" For example, "What if our firm were to diversify its line of products? How would that affect sales of our leading product?" Or "What if we could acquire the ailing steel producer in Ohio? How would that lower the production and distribution costs for our other plants?" Or "What if our employees could design their own jobs?" Retroduction helps free people from mental ruts.

retroduction   a creativity enhancement technique that uses "What If?" questions to help free people from mental ruts.

Finally, **listing** involves asking a series of questions about how we might use something that we already have. For example, "Can we put our nickel-plated gizmo to other uses?" "What would happen if we made it larger?" "Smaller?" "Would zinc-plating improve durability?" Listing techniques have been used to invent fiberglass, freeze-dried foods, tapered roller bearings, and many other products.

listing   a creativity enhancement technique that involves asking a series of questions about a currently available alternative.

Company Programs. Firms are using special programs to foster their employees' creativity.[24] Many send their employees on retreats and outings to jolt them out of routine ways of thinking. Quaker Oats Co. executives go horseback riding when they need fresh approaches to budget and marketing problems. American Greeting Co.'s licensing unit, Those Characters From Cleveland, which created Strawberry Shortcake and the Care Bears, has a half dozen weekend retreats in the woods each year, where its creative personnel brainstorm, play games, sketch, and generally try to come up with creative ideas.

Fostering Flexibility

Many firms have become so large and rule-bound that they cannot respond to changes in the environment. Organizations in the future will require flexibility. To be flexible, they will have to scan the environment. They will need open flows of communication. They will have to be leaner and more streamlined, with fewer levels of management. During the 1980s, U.S. businesses slashed more than 1 million management jobs, a practice that is expected to accelerate. By some estimates, by the year 2010, the typical large business may have half as many management levels as today, and only one third as many managerial positions. With fewer levels, decision making will be pushed down to lower levels of the firm. The firm will change from a pyramid to a pancake.[25]

YOU AND THE FUTURE

In this chapter, we have discussed some of the trends currently shaping our world. One key ingredient, however, has been left out of our discussion of the future: you. In our forecasts, we have focused on the next ten years, somewhat beyond the year 2000. This is the same period of time in which you will be beginning your career and growing into your most productive years. You will be assuming the lead in building this imagined future.

How you will affect the future is largely determined by your choice of a career. The ideas and skills that you learn today, as well as the career decisions that you have already made or will be making shortly, will determine your role in tomorrow's world. In the next chapter, we will examine some of the issues involved in career choice and various career options in business.

SUMMARY POINTS

1 An essential activity of any business is to forecast or predict the future. The aim of business forecasting is to reduce uncertainty in the decision environment by telling the business manager something about the future.

2 The population of the United States is growing, but the rate of population growth is slowing. The population of the United States is gradually getting older. The median age could increase from 30 in 1980 to 42 in the year 2050. In the years ahead, average family size in this country will decrease, while average family income will increase. The traditional two-parent, multichild household will become less common. Minority-group members will make up a growing proportion of the population. More women and minorities will enter the workforce. The population of the world's developing countries will grow at a faster rate than the population of the industrialized Western countries. These developments will create challenges and opportunities in the marketplace and the workplace.

3 The two primary trends reshaping the industrial composition of the U.S. economy are the aging of basic industries and the emergence and growth of high-technology industries. Basic industries are declining, due in part to increased labor costs and foreign competition. According to one view of industrial investment, such investment should be directed toward basic industries to revitalize them. Another view, the long wave theory, suggests that basic industries should be allowed to continue their natural decline, and investment should be directed

toward emerging industries, such as high technology.

4 Technological discovery and innovation is the engine of economic growth. New technologies enable us to produce more output from limited resource inputs. Four important high technology industries are biotechnology, robotics, materials science, and superconductors. Biotechnology is based on recombinant genetics and gene splicing. Future applications of bioengineering will be in the areas of cancer treatment, oil refining, chemical synthesis, food production, and waste treatment. An industrial robot is a computer-guided machine that is capable of performing a variety of manufacturing tasks automatically. Industrial robotics and automation technologies offer the benefits of greater productivity and improved cost control in America's factories. Materials science research is enabling scientists to engineer desirable traits into manufacturing materials by manipulating them at the molecular level. Such research will result in lighter, stronger, harder, and more durable manufacturing materials. A superconductor is a special material that conducts electricity without resistance and without losing energy as heat. Commercial applications of superconductors could revolutionize the power industry as well as transportation and biomedicine.

5 Firms will need creativity and flexibility to respond to future challenges. To be creative, they may make structural changes, use creativity-enhancing techniques such as brainstorming and retroduction, or use approaches such as retreats and outings. To be flexible, they will have to scan the environment, have open channels of communication, and be lean and streamlined.

REVIEW QUESTIONS

1 How is forecasting useful to a business?

2 What is the relationship between forecasting, objectives, and uncertainty?

3 Summarize the major population and income trends in the United States.

4 Which areas of the world are likely to experience the slowest growth in per capita income in the years ahead?

5 What is a basic industry? Give some examples of basic industries.

6 What are some of the reasons for the current problems of our basic industries? How has competition from abroad contributed to these problems?

7 Name four fast-growing high-technology industries.

8 Discuss three ways that firms can become more creative.

DISCUSSION QUESTIONS

1 Some futurists foresee a world in which nearly all of us will work at home. What problems do you see in such a development? What opportunities?

2 The decline of basic industries has left millions of people out of work. Many of them may never get their old jobs back. What can be done to move these workers into the fast-growing "sunrise" industries?

3 What, in your opinion, is the most likely outcome of the race between population growth and food production? Will we be able to grow enough food to feed everyone? Will we be able to slow the rate of population growth?

4 What potential social and ethical questions does recombinant genetics raise? More specifically, do you think that private companies should be able to patent new life forms, just as they are able to patent other inventions?

5 What is the role of private business in building a better tomorrow? Do you think that we will still have private businesses in the 21st century, or will all our production facilities be owned and operated by the government?

EXPERIENTIAL EXERCISES

1 Produce a forecast of your own about consumer lifestyles in the year 2010. What types of products will people buy? Where will they shop? How will they pay for their purchases? What types of recreational activities will people seek? How much of their budgets will they spend on these recreational activities? What new electronic devices will people have in their homes? How might computers, telecommunications, and other technologies affect the average household? Write up your predictions as a short report, as if you were a special staff assistant in the planning department of a large consumer products company and your boss was drawing up a long-range strategic plan for the company. Be *creative* in your predictions.

2 What does the future hold for America and for the world? Will we and our children live in a better world or a worse one? Take a piece of looseleaf paper and divide it down the middle with a line. Label the top of the left side of the page "optimistic future" and the top of the right side "pessimistic future." Now develop two possible scenarios for economic and social change over the next 25 years. Present your optimistic scenario on the left side and your pessimistic scenario on the right. Be sure to consider population trends, income trends, economic and social change, and technological advances. In your opinion, which scenario is the most likely to occur?

CASES

CASE 24-1
Pharming

Forget the goose that laid the golden eggs—researchers have genetically engineered animals to produce drugs in their milk worth tens of thousands of dollars a day. Scientists say that the development proves the commercial feasibility of "pharming"—using herds of animals as living pharmaceutical factories. Pharming may give the biotechnology industry a cheaper, better way to make genetically engineered drugs.

Reports by U.S. and British teams said that they have developed genetically altered goats and sheep, respectively, that secrete sizable amounts of useful drugs in their milk. In a third report, scientists in the Netherlands said that they had developed the first practical technique to put foreign genes in cattle, which eventually could lead to an even more productive source of drugs in milk.

Researchers had previously inserted foreign genes in mice and some other animals, to cause them to produce in their milk tiny amounts of proteins that are potentially useful as medicines. It remained to be seen whether the technique would work in farm animals, to make possible large-scale production of therapeutic proteins. Besides making genetically engineered drugs cheaper (they cost $1,000 or more a gram), pharming may lead to better variants of existing drugs.

Scientists made the "transgenic" animals—those that carry a foreign gene—involved in the studies by injecting genes for human proteins into their early-stage embryos along with genetic switches that turn on the genes only in mammary glands. The switches prevent the human genes from being activated in blood cells or other tissues, which could harm the animals. The method also makes it easier to retrieve drug molecules, because they are excreted in milk and don't have to be extracted from tissues.

Pharming promises to make available certain proteins that are potentially valuable as medicines but that currently can't be made cheaply enough for widespread use. An example is human serum albumin, a blood protein used by patients with liver damage.

The U.S. team has developed transgenic goats that produce 2 to 3 grams of the drug TPA per liter of milk. TPA, or tissue plasminogen activator, dissolves blood clots and is used to clear blocked arteries in heart-attack patients. The safety and effectiveness of the goat-produced TPA hasn't been established in humans. The U.K. team reported that it had developed transgenic sheep whose milk contains alpha-1-antitrypsin, an enzyme used to prevent mucus from building up in the lungs of people with emphysema. The Netherlands group reported that it had developed a technique to insert foreign genes in cattle and had created the first transgenic calf. The animal, a bull, carries a gene for human lactoferrin, an antibacterial substance that could be useful in medicines for patients with weakened immune systems—including those with acquired immune deficiency syndrome (AIDS).

Source: Abridged and adapted from D. Stipp, "Animals Altered to Make Drugs in Their Milk," *Wall Street Journal,* 27 August 1991, pp. B1, B8.

1. What are some ways that such "pharming" might influence American business in the future?
2. What sources of resistance do you see to such genetic engineering?
3. Do you feel that there are ethical issues associated with such genetic engineering?

CASE 24-2
Baby Boomers

They will be rich and poor. They will embrace family values, and they will not. They will get religion, and they won't. They will have homes with Jacuzzis—or maybe not. Only one thing is sure: Robots will cook their dinner.

They are the baby boom, the largest generation in American history, and this is their life. Born between the end of World War II and 1964, the baby boom's 76 million members have wreaked havoc with American culture, confounding demographers with their size, affluence, education, politics, and feminism.

So naturally, predictions about what they will do in middle age are as common as thinning hair. Boomers will demand gourmet ice, ancient cubes chipped from Alaskan ice floes, one forecaster predicts. Boomers won't want waiters to recite the specials; they will want to hear "about omega-3 fatty acids," another says. Velcro fasteners will replace zippers on boomers' clothes to baby their gnarling fingers, says a third.

Even in the simplest times, predicting the behavior of an entire generation is an act of courage. This is doubly true for the baby boom, whose immense size makes the task and the stakes even larger. If forecasters are right about what the boomers are going to buy—as The Gap, MTV, Toys "R" Us and BMW were—fortunes will be made. If they aren't, fortunes will also be made. "It's foolhardy to make predictions about the baby boom, but that's where the big bucks are," says Paul Light, associate dean of the Hubert Humphrey Institute at the University of Minnesota.

Forecasters of the baby boom—including marketers, advertisers and consultants of all kinds—use a combination of statistics, interviews, history and gut instinct. Generalizations that involve simple aspects of aging—they will have more health problems; their children will leave home—are almost certainly true. However, when it comes to more specific predictions—they will play croquet and live in boardinghouses—only time will tell.

Source: Abridged from Cynthia Crossen, "I Want Stocks, Sister; Golf Clubs, Brother; and Hair, Hair, Hair," *Wall Street Journal,* 16 September 1991, pp. A1, A11.

1. What are some of the factors that make predictions about the baby boomers so difficult?
2. Can you think of any businesses that are *not* influenced by forecasts about a major population group such as the baby boomers?
3. The case suggests that forecasters may do well whether or not their forecasts are correct. Do you agree? If so, how is this possible?

OBJECTIVES

After studying this chapter, you should be able to:

1 Explain what a career is and why it is important, and describe the process of self-analysis that one must go through in making a career choice.

2 Identify what employment information you need and where to go to get it.

3 Describe the steps in a job search campaign.

4 List the five career stages that most people go through.

5 Discuss the "rules" of success chess—that is, what you need to do to get ahead.

6 Explain what some companies do to help their employees achieve their career objectives.

CHAPTER 25

You and Your Career

Janice Rubin had returned to college after 15 years. She felt proficient at managing a household and raising two children, but was she really prepared to take useful notes and pass difficult exams? About 70 percent of the students in her class were full-time students straight out of high school. Her first thought was that she was going up against experienced pros. However, Janice did an excellent job, making the dean's list in every term.

As graduation approached, Janice began her job search. The career counseling and placement office at her college suggested that the first step was to do a careful self-analysis. She took a series of tests relating to intelligence, personality, and motivation; they indicated that she had a strong aptitude for sales and marketing. She then began preparing a resume, writing letters of application, obtaining recommendations, and lining up interviews.

Janice was somewhat disappointed when she had not received a job offer after her first six interviews. Finally, an offer from Southern Monthly *magazine came along. Janice was offered a position calling on mid-size corporate accounts to sell advertising space. She would have a salary at the start, but her success would ultimately depend on bringing in new accounts, for which she would receive commissions. This might seem pretty risky, but Janice had already taken on longer odds when she decided to return to school.*

After two months on the job, it was clear that the organizational skills Janice had developed in managing a family were paying off in the workplace. She knew what it meant to accept responsibility and to live with an occasional crisis. Janice Rubin turned out to be the star performer of the sales staff. She was proud that both her years as a homemaker and her time at college had been well spent.

ach year, more than a third of a million business graduates enter the job market. Fortunately, business is one field that offers both a rich diversity of interesting job opportunities and a favorable job market. Business graduates will take jobs as sales representatives, personnel assistants, research analysts, accountants, purchasing agents, and loan officers. They will earn an average of $23,000 with a bachelor's degree and $34,000 with an MBA degree.

WHAT IS A CAREER?

Certainly, a career has something to do with getting jobs, and perhaps with moving between jobs, places, and levels of responsibility and challenge. However, a career means more than that. It also involves a person's self-fulfillment and personal growth.

Why Are Careers So Important?

Most people would agree that careers are important. Unfortunately, many business students leave college without knowing much about how to manage their own careers. We can think of at least two reasons why people should be concerned about their careers:

- The career represents a person's entire life in the work setting, and work is a key factor in influencing the quality of a person's life. Work has the potential to satisfy almost all human needs, directly or indirectly.
- Work is a way to get social equality and social freedom. For example, the fact that more women are entering the workforce has changed the way society views women, how much power they have, and the rhythm of family life. Similarly, as more blacks and members of other minority groups obtain high-prestige jobs, their roles in society will change too. It is already happening. Nothing speaks louder than success. A successful career brings recognition, respect, and freedom from economic want.

It's best to start planning for your career even before you graduate.

Managers should understand the career interests of their subordinates. Doing so gives them a better grasp of what motivates people and enables them to manage more effectively.

Quest for the Ideal Job

It would be nice to find a job that's perfect in all ways, but this hope is not very realistic. Instead, we generally have to make trade-offs. We may have to take lower pay to get a more "meaningful" job. Or we may have to put up with poor working conditions if we want higher pay.

So you must ask yourself, "What do I really want from a job?" Figure 25-1 presents a list of job characteristics that many people seek. Which one is most important to you? Least important? Do the things you want have anything in common? Would you give up the less important things to get those you have rated as most important?

FIGURE 25-1   What Do You Want From a Job?

A variety of job characteristics are listed below. Rate how important you feel each characteristic is to you by using the following scale:

1	2	3	4	5
Not Important	Slightly Important	Somewhat Important	Quite Important	Crucial

Job Characteristic	Importance Rating
Salary	_____
Challenge and Responsibility	_____
Type of Work	_____
Friendly Co-Workers	_____
Opportunity for Promotion	_____
Job Difficulty	_____
Geographical Location	_____
Job Security	_____
Training	_____
Opportunity for Personal Growth	_____
Clear Job Responsibilities	_____
Opportunity to Travel on the Job	_____
Opportunity to Help Others	_____
Work Hours	_____
Opportunity to Participate in Decision Making	_____
Fair Treatment by Employer	_____
Fringe Benefits	_____
Company Reputation	_____
Freedom to Work on Your Own	_____
Job Title	_____

Stages of Job Choice

People's career choices develop over a long period of time, often progressing through three stages.[1] The fantasy stage generally occurs between the ages of 6 and 11 and is seldom realistic. It is the stage at which a child wants to be an Indian chief or a firefighter. The tentative stage usually occurs between the ages of 11 and 16. This is the stage when people first realize that they must make important decisions about their future. They start to consider how various professions might fit their abilities, interests, and values. Finally, in the realistic stage, people seriously explore occupational options; firm up their preferences, and choose an occupation. In this stage, people recognize that they must make compromises between what they want and what is available. This realistic stage often lasts for years—even for a decade or more.

Self-Analysis: Be Honest

Don't panic if you are still exploring career options, but do start to think about a realistic job choice. To do this, honest self-analysis is crucial.

Ideally, you will choose a career that offers a good fit to your abilities, values, and interests. A job that is really not "right" for you may seem attractive in the short run but will almost certainly lead to problems. Try to step back from yourself, take an objective look, and assess your abilities, values, and interests.

Your Abilities. It is important to recognize both what you can do well and what you can't do well. Figure 25-2 may help you assess your strengths and weaknesses.

Your Values. What is really important to you in life? Answers might include family, security, status, popularity, love, freedom, power, leisure, wealth, glamour, affection, social welfare, and achievement. What do you really want? What things repel you? Jobs will differ in the extent to which they are consistent with your values.

Your Interests. Interests are the things that you like or dislike. Interests often develop from more general values. Some interests are shown in Figure 25-3. Think hard about your interests and how various jobs might fulfill them.

EMPLOYMENT OPPORTUNITIES

To make an intelligent career choice, you need information about opportunities for various jobs, about industries, and perhaps about clusters of related jobs. The Careers Appendix gives detailed information about current and future job opportunities. Throughout the 1990s, professions expected to be in high demand include accountants, actuaries, health services administrators, marketing researchers, securities sales workers, human resources managers, travel agents, receptionists, wholesale and retail sales workers, hotel managers, lawyers, computer operators and programmers, and systems analysts. People who will find their skills in less demand include bank tellers, wholesale and retail buyers, typists and data entry keyers, and blue collar supervisors.

Figure 25-4, page 701, shows projected employment growth by industry. Services, retail trade, and finance, insurance, and real estate are expected to show the greatest percentage of growth, while employment in manufacturing and mining is projected to fall.

FIGURE 25-2   Ability Profile

	Far Below Average	Below Average	Average	Above Average	Outstanding
Intelligence					
Leadership					
Motivation					
Direction					
Self-Confidence					
Energy Level					
Self-Knowledge					
Competitiveness					
Creativity					
Perseverance					
Initiative					
Goal Achievement					
Willingness to Accept Responsibility					
Interpersonal Skills					
Ability to Handle Conflict					
Sensitivity					
Ability to Communicate					
Flexibility					
Writing Skills					
Organizational Ability					
Public Speaking Skills					
Persuasiveness					

Use this checklist to get a better picture of your strengths and weaknesses. It may help you find a job for which you are suited as well as prepare you for job interviews. Also, make a list of your abilities that may be important in particular jobs. Such abilities might include knowledge of electronics, real estate, payroll procedures, or foreign languages.

FIGURE 25-3   What Are Your Interests?

Traveling	Helping Others
Working with People	Being Outdoors
Competing	Relaxing
Acting	Using Skills
Speaking	Thinking
Being Alone	Supervising
Working with Data	Solving Puzzles
Writing	Moving
Learning	Organizing

FIGURE 25-4   Projected Employment Growth by Industry, 1988–2000

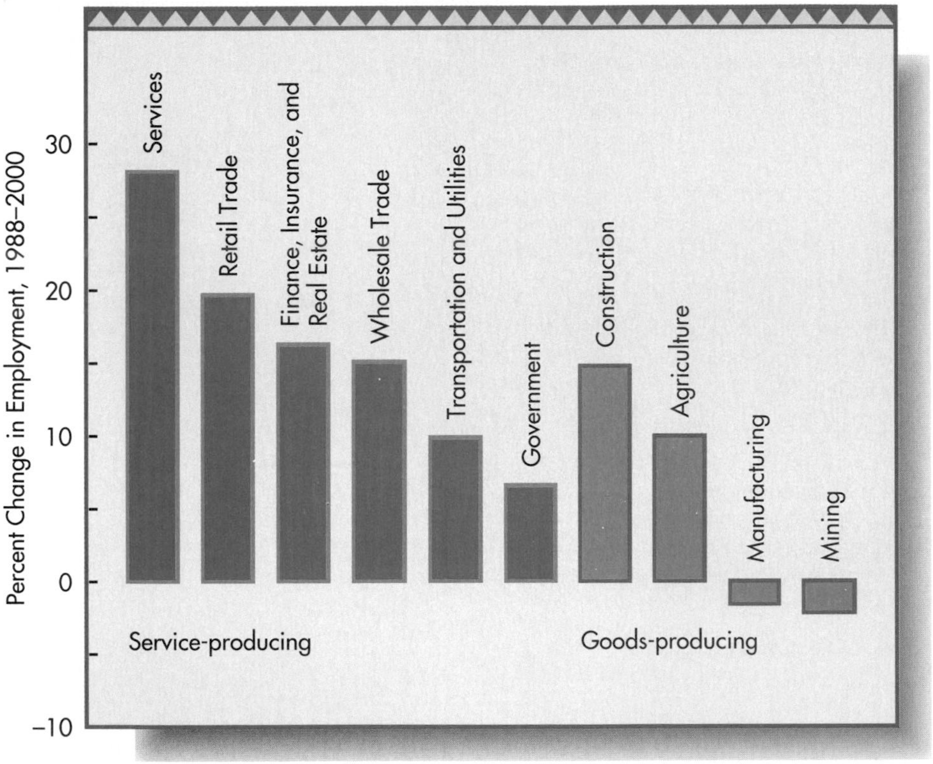

Source: U.S. Bureau of Labor Statistics.

Career Clusters

Your skills and knowledge would probably be useful in any of several jobs. So if opportunities for a particular job dry up, you may be able to find another kind of job elsewhere. The U.S. Office of Education has identified 15 "career clusters." Each **career cluster** is a group of related jobs. Sample clusters are presented in Figure 25-5. When preparing for a career, it may help to think in terms of career clusters as well as in terms of specific jobs.

career cluster   *a group of related jobs in which a person's skills and knowledge would probably be useful.*

Employment Information Sources

There are many sources of information about employment opportunities. Here are some to keep in mind:

- *College placement services.* Most colleges and universities have placement services. Check yours out. Ask what services it provides, when you should register your credentials, what percentage of past graduates were placed through the service, and so on.
- *Ads.* Read the help-wanted ads in newspapers or trade journals. The Sunday edition often has many pages of these ads. Check ads in papers of cities where you might want to work. The *New York Times* and *Wall Street Journal* list many ads for business positions.

FIGURE 25-5   Sample Career Clusters

Marketing and Distribution:
Marketing management, marketing research and analysis; purchasing; selling; physical distribution; related business services.

Business and Office: Accounting; computer; secretarial science; management; personnel; finance; insurance; real estate; office (clerical).

Environment: Pollution prevention and control; disease prevention; environmental planning; resources control.

Hospitality and Recreation: Commercial and noncommercial travel bureaus; travel agencies; transportation; public, private, and industrial recreation; recreation concerned with natural resources.

Source: U.S. Office of Education, 1988.

Business Career
Employment Counselor: Helps clients make wise career decisions. Helps them evaluate their education, training, work history, interests, skills, and personal traits. May arrange for aptitude and achievement tests. Helps clients with job-seeking skills, such as resume writing and interviewing. Assists in locating and applying for jobs. *Average Salary: $34,000.*

- *The United States Employment Service (USES).* This service has about 2,400 offices throughout the country. You can ask the office in any city or state about opportunities in other locations.
- *Private employment agencies.* There are about 8,000 private employment agencies in the United States. Some of them specialize in certain types of clients (such as executives) or in particular fields (such as data processing). These agencies charge a fee that is payable when and if the job seeker is hired.
- *Local organizations.* Many cities have business directories that provide basic information about firms (products, services, number of employees, key executives, etc.) and about the community in general. You can write to the local chamber of commerce for employment information in that area.
- *Personal contacts.* Ask friends and relatives about job opportunities. College professors may also have useful suggestions.

Information from the College Placement Council

No student should approach the job market without becoming familiar with material produced by the College Placement Council (CPC). Virtually every placement office in the country has this highly informative material. If you need to write away for it, the address is College Placement Council, Inc., 62 Highland Avenue, Bethlehem, PA 18017.

The CPC publishes four booklets of 100 pages annually. The first booklet covers virtually every facet of the job search. It discusses not only careers in business but also such topics as jobs in government, international careers, and the graduate school option. The other three booklets list job openings and positions

Interest in a certain area could lead a person to pursue various career opportunities. The woman above loves science and teaches it to fifth graders. The man expresses his scientific interest by working in a laboratory.

at over 1,000 companies. An example for Alcoa Corporation is presented in Figure 25-6. The CPC booklets allow you to find openings by the field of your choice and by the location you desire. Summer job possibilities are also indicated. The CPC is a potential source for international positions, as described in the "International Example" on page 706. Furthermore, the CPU publishes salary data four times a year. The January 1992 salary data for business majors is shown in Table 25-1. The information is gathered from 428 placement offices throughout the country.

HOW TO OBTAIN A POSITION IN BUSINESS

The job search is a challenging, important, and time-consuming process. If done right, it may start you on a rewarding career. Be willing to take the time, effort, and expense to do it right.

Planning the Job Search

A job search should be thought of as a campaign. You are looking for the job that best fits your needs and qualifications. You should plan your job search strategies and then actively carry them out. A key step in any job search is to identify potential sources of employment. The information already given in the section on Employment Information Sources can get you started. Then it is up to you to put your data together in a way that reflects your abilities, interests and strengths.

Preparing a Resume

The **resume** is a written presentation telling the prospective employer who you are, what you know, what you have done, what you can do, and what kind of job you would like. It should provide a complete picture in a compact, convincing way. To write an effective resume:

* Be concise. Keep the resume to one or two pages, if possible. Avoid narrative format.

resume *a written presentation telling the prospective employer who you are, what you know, what you have done, what you can do, and what kind of job you would like.*

FIGURE 25-6   Sample Company Data Sheet from the College Placement Council

ALUMINUM COMPANY OF AMERICA

Alcoa Building
Pittsburgh, PA 15219
Contact: Manager, Professional Employment

Date established: 1888; number of employees: 62,000.

Sales Offices

Los Angeles, Calif.; New Canaan, Conn.; Washington, D.C.; Atlanta, Ga.; Chicago, Ill.; Detroit, Mich.; Minneapolis, Minn.; St. Louis, Mo.; Charlotte, N.C.; Cincinnati and Cleveland, Ohio; Philadelphia and Pittsburgh, Pa.; Nashville, Tenn.; Dallas and Houston, Tex.; and Seattle, Wash.

R&D Headquarters

Alcoa Technical Center, Alcoa Center, Pennsylvania.

ABOUT ALCOA FOR THE NONTECHNICAL PERSON

Alcoa didn't invent aluminum. It had been around for a long time as a precious metal. But Charles Martin Hall (the first Alcoan) invented a successful process for producing aluminum in commercial quantities. That was over one hundred years ago.

Today, Alcoa continues to be the world's leading producer of aluminum products. Operations—in addition to mining, refining, smelting, fabrication, and recycling—include shipping, producing alumina chemicals, licensing technology, and selling engineering services. Alcoa has more than 100 operating locations and sales offices worldwide.

Primary markets are in packaging and containers, transportation, aerospace, electrical, construction, consumer durables, and machinery and equipment.

Specific opportunities include:

Financial/Management Information Systems

Qualifications: BA, MA, or MS accounting, business administration, finance, mathematics, computer science. **Preferred:** Broad academic background, range of interests, capacity for early responsibility, strong analytical and communication skills. **First assignment:** In accounting, probably at a plant, monitoring and reporting production/financial performances. In information systems, software analyst or systems developer. **Career paths:** Product Accounting Supervisor, Corporate Cost Accountant, Plant Controller, Senior Analyst, Project Analyst Manager.

Procurement

Qualifications: BA engineering, BA or MA business administration, or other technical/mathematical disciplines. **Preferred:** Tact, integrity, capacity for detail, ability to integrate technical and commercial aspects of complex operations. **First assignment:** Industrial Buyer, probably at a plant, finding best sources that meet specific cost/quality requirements. **Career paths:** Materials management, inventory control, purchasing research, information systems—leading to top procurement management.

Human Resources/Industrial Relations

Qualifications: BA or MA personnel/labor relations, psychology, organizational behavior. **Preferred:** Tact, communications skills, ability to balance Alcoa's needs with those of individual employees. **First assignment:** Probably at a plant, recruiting and selection, benefits administration, training and development, and industrial relations. **Career paths:** Advancement in human resources or industrial relations.

Sales/Industrial Marketing

Qualifications: BA or BS, MA or MS liberal arts, business administration, or technical discipline. Ideal: technical BS and marketing MBA. **Preferred:** Good listener, responsive to people's needs. Disciplined self-starter, able to explain customer's changing needs to engineers and production people. **First assignment:** After training (both in Pittsburgh and the field), posting to a Business Unit as a Sales Representative or Marketing Assistant. **Career paths:** Alcoa promotes from within; prospects excellent for advancement to sales management, marketing management, or other areas, such as personnel, public affairs, procurement, finance.

SALARY AND BENEFITS

Alcoa offers one of the best benefits programs in American industry. It includes hospital, vision, and dental coverage; short- and long-term disability income; excellent vacation and retirement plans; participatory savings, company matched savings and stock ownership programs; company-paid and contributory life, accident, and travel insurance. Alcoa offers a competitive salary structure plus profit sharing.

EDUCATIONAL OPPORTUNITIES

Alcoa's Tuition Aid Program covers the cost of study at accredited colleges and universities.

Source: *CPC 35th Annual; Volume 2: A Guide to Employment Opportunities for College Graduates* (Bethlehem, Pa.: College Placement Council, 1991/92), p. 117.

TABLE 25-1   College Placement Council Data on Salary Offers to College Graduates in Business for 1991

By Curriculum, for All Types of Employers	Number of Offers January 1992	Average $ Offer	
		January 1992	September 1991
BUSINESS			
Accounting	795	$27,493	$26,642
Business Administration (including Management Science)	147	23,433	24,019
Distribution Management	2	26,500	27,081
Economics & Finance (including Banking)	161	24,827	25,819
Hotel/Restaurant Management	14	19,395	21,220
Human Resources (including Labor Relations)	9	21,364	23,812
Management Information Systems	61	28,166	28,237
Marketing/Marketing Management (including Research)	176	23,897	23,713
Real Estate	1	26,000	21,693

Source: Excerpted from the January 1992 *Salary Survey*, with the permission of the College Placement Council, Inc. copyright holder

- Include a brief career objective. The **career objective** may indicate your area of interest (such as finance or sales), the sort of organization you would like to work for (such as banking or manufacturing), and the level of the position you want. If you have not made up your mind about your career objectives, a more general statement of objectives may be best. Figure 25-7 presents two sample career objectives.

  career objective a statement describing your area of interest, the type of organization for which you would like to work, and the level of position you want.

- Include educational experience and work experience, starting in each case with the most recent. When describing your experience, use action verbs, such as:

accomplished	achieved	budgeted
classified	controlled	counseled
designed	evaluated	increased
managed	operated	proposed
researched	sold	trained

- List relevant personal data. These can include extracurricular activities in which you are involved. Be selective: Omit items that could be misinterpreted, are unnecessary, or do not strengthen your case.
- Point out those skills that are relevant to the position you are seeking.
- Indicate that references are available upon request, or (especially if they are very good) list them. References from people who know your abilities as an employee or student have more impact than references from friends.
- Make sure the resume looks good. Work on the layout. Proofread the resume, have a friend proofread it, and then proofread it again! Have the resume duplicated on high-quality bond paper in white or a subdued color.

Looking Abroad for a Job

For those who wish to work in a foreign country, knowledge of job markets is even more critical than in this country. The College Placement Council (CPC) identifies companies that hire U.S. citizens under the title of "Foreign Employment Offered to U.S. Citizens." Some of the major employers listed are Schlumberger, Goodyear Tire & Rubber Company, and National Semiconductor. Financial institutions such as Citibank, BankAmerica, and Manufacturers Hanover are also included.

There are positions in the not-for-profit sector as well, including the Peace Corps, American Field Service, and the Care and IVS volunteer programs. For those who go on to graduate degrees, there is the possibility of positions in the foreign service, the U.S. Agency for International Development, or the International Trade Commission. One highly regarded graduate program training students for international careers is the American Graduate School of International Management (known as "Thunderbird") in Glendale, Arizona.

Anyone seeking a job overseas should be prepared to master one or more foreign languages. (Japanese might be the best choice for the future.) An ability to adjust to different cultural norms, eating habits, and methods of doing business is critical.

* Generally, do *not* state salary requirements, give reasons for leaving past employers, or indicate your race, religion, or political affiliation. A sample resume is presented in Figure 25-8.

Writing the Application Letter

letter of application *a letter accompanying a resume that states the position for which you are applying and your most significant qualifications, with the goal of obtaining an interview.*

Always include a letter of application when you mail a resume. The purpose of a **letter of application** is to state the job you are applying for and to persuade the employer to grant you an interview. To do this, the letter should begin by getting the employer's attention, follow with a brief summary of your most significant qualifications, and end with a request for an interview. The letter must be brief—certainly less than a page—and carefully constructed. It should be typed on the same type of paper as your resume. It should be addressed to a specific person. Keep a copy of the letter for your files. Figure 25-9 shows the components of an application letter.

Obtaining Letters of Recommendation

Letters of recommendation are an important part of the job application process. Your letters of recommendation should be favorable, of course, and should be

FIGURE 25-7   Two Sample Career Objectives

Human Resources—To begin my career in human resources as an assistant with exposure to recruiting, training and development, benefit administration, and compensation administration. Eventually wish to become a human resources manager.

Brand Assistant—Seeking position with responsibility for coordinating and advertising, pricing, packaging, and distribution channels of a consumer goods product line. Eventual goal is to become a product manager.

FIGURE 25-8   A Sample Resume

PERCIVAL R. MESSMER

1130 Odana Road
Madison, WI 53711
(608) 281-0527

JOB OBJECTIVE
Wish to join the audit staff of a public accounting firm with the eventual
goal of becoming a partner.

EDUCATION
University of Wisconsin-Madison
Earned the Bachelor of Business Administration degree in May 1992.
Majored in Accounting and Finance.   3.1 GPA

WORK EXPERIENCE
Jerred & O'Day, CPAs, Madison, Wisconsin
Accounting Clerk (20 hours/week)   June 1991 – Present
Maintain accounts payable and accounts receivable. Supervise payroll
and payroll tax reporting functions. Assist staff accountants with client
work when time permits.

Leonies' Restaurant, Madison, Wisconsin
Part-time Bartender (25 hours/week)   September 1989 – May 1991

Baraboo Inn, Baraboo, Wisconsin
Desk Clerk   Summers 1987, 1988, 1989

ACTIVITIES
Active member of Beta Alpha Psi, Delta Sigma Pi, and the Hoofer Ski &
Sailing Club.

SKILLS AND INTERESTS
Have well-developed writing and public speaking skills. Speak German and
French fluently. Enjoy traveling, reading, and sailing.

REFERENCES
Professor Jon Smart, Accounting Department, University of Wisconsin-Madison,
1155 Observatory Drive, Madison, WI 53706   (608) 252-1111

Professor Helen Smith, Mathematics Department, University of Wisconsin-Madison,
1155 Observatory Drive, Madison, WI 53706   (608) 252-1234

Mr. James Jones, Manager, Jerred & O'Day, CPAs, 202 West Washington Avenue,
Madison, WI 53702   (608) 255-9988

Source: School of Business, University of Wisconsin-Madison, *Placement Manual.* Used with permission.

FIGURE 25-9   A Sample Letter of Application
Placement Manual. Used with permission.

Opening paragraph:
Attract attention—state the position you are applying for and mention how you learned about it. Make the employer want to read on!

Second paragraph:
Indicate when and from where you will be graduating. State why you are interested in working for the company (avoid excessive flattery) and specify your reasons for desiring this type of work.

Third paragraph:
Refer the reader to your personal resume. Point out college or work experiences that might be of particular interest to the company. Do not repeat what is on the resume!

Closing paragraph:
Show appreciation and ask for action, i.e., request an interview and state when you would be available. Mention if you are going to be in the area at a particular time. Remember to include your telephone number. Try to portray a tone of modest confidence without being overbearing.

> 1320 Odana Road
> Madison, WI 53711
> January 17, 1992
>
> Mr. Thomas Williams
> Human Resources Director
> Zimmer, Thomas and Zimmer, CPAs
> 1424 Commerce Street
> Milwaukee, Wisconsin 53715
>
> Dear Mr. Williams:
>
> I recently read an exciting article about Zimmer, Thomas and Zimmer in a local business magazine. The article characterized your company as innovative, market-driven, and successful. I would like to apply for a position on your auditing staff. I believe my skills and interests would fit well in your progressive organization.
>
> I will graduate from the University of Wisconsin at Madison in May 1992. I have chosen auditing and public accounting as my career because I enjoy working with numbers. The article indicated that your firm uses personal computers extensively. My computer skills are strong, and I am very interested in using them in my work.
>
> As you will see from the enclosed resume, I have accumulated substantial work experience while in college. My current job is in accounting, and I believe I have gained a broad knowledge of accounting and the business world that will enable me to adjust quickly to a new work environment.
>
> I will be in Milwaukee during the first week in February and would welcome an opportunity to demonstrate how my skills fit your company's needs. My phone number is (608) 281-0527. I look forward to hearing from you.
>
> Sincerely,
>
> *Percival R. Messmer*
>
> Percival R. Messmer

Source: School of Business, University of Wisconsin-Madison, *Placement Manual.* Used with permission.

written by people who are in respected positions and who know you reasonably well. College professors and past employers are natural choices. Make sure that they have copies of your resume and of any other materials that will help them write better informed and more complete letters. Send these letters of recommendation to the prospective employer along with your resume and letter of application.

Preparing for the Job Interview

The initial interview may be held on your college campus or in the company's offices. If it goes well, you may be offered a visit to the prospective employer, or even a job. If it goes badly, your chances of getting the job are poor.

FIGURE 25-10   Some Typical Interview Questions

- ▲ What are your strengths? Your weaknesses?
- ▲ Tell me about yourself.
- ▲ Why should we hire you?
- ▲ What are your hobbies and interests?
- ▲ Why do you want to work for our company?
- ▲ Are you willing to travel or relocate?
- ▲ What do you want to be doing in two years? Five? Twenty?
- ▲ How will you choose among the various job offers you receive?
- ▲ Why did you choose your major? Do you wish you had chosen differently? Which courses did you like? Dislike? Why?
- ▲ What kinds of extracurricular activities have you participated in? Which did you enjoy the most?
- ▲ What percentage of your college expenses did you earn?
- ▲ Do you plan to further your education? Why or why not?
- ▲ Does your grade point average reflect your intelligence? Your potential? Your motivation? Why or why not?
- ▲ What questions do you have about our company?

Make sure that you prepare carefully for the interview. Read everything you can find that might be useful. Research the industry and the company thoroughly. Check company annual reports and look in the *Business Periodical Index.* Also, anticipate questions that you may be asked, such as those in Figure 25-10. Work out answers and practice them. Finally, put together an "interview folder" to take to your interviews. Include extra copies of your resume, questions you have about the company and position, any information you've gathered on the company, a copy of your transcript, and a pen and paper. A few interviewing tips are listed in Figure 25-11.

Visiting Your Prospective Employer

If an employer offers you a visit to the company, you know that you have been evaluated favorably. Such visits are typically for one day. Expect to meet some people in management positions.

During the visit, try to act natural and relaxed. Dress well. Ask questions you have prepared in advance. Keep track of the names of the people you meet. Near the end of the visit, ask what you should do next and what actions the employer will take next. When you get home, write thank-you letters to the employer and others you met during the visit.

Analyzing Job Offers

If you are lucky, you may get a number of job offers. If so, you have a tough decision. Don't look just at starting salary. Job security, potential for growth and challenge, the sorts of people you would be working with, and many other factors should also be considered. Look back at the job characteristics listed in Figure 25-1 and the importance you attached to each. Then ask yourself how much

FIGURE 25-11   Interviewing Tips

▲▲▲▲▲▲▲▲▲▲▲▲▲▲▲▲▲▲▲▲▲▲▲▲▲▲▲▲▲▲▲▲▲▲▲▲▲▲▲

- ▲ Be on time for the interview.
- ▲ Be positive. Show interest and enthusiasm.
- ▲ Speak clearly and maintain good eye contact.
- ▲ Listen to what is being said and follow the interviewer's lead.
- ▲ Think before speaking.
- ▲ Be well groomed.
- ▲ Show a knowledge of the company. Ask questions that couldn't have been answered by reading the recruiting literature. Ask about such things as training programs, opportunities for advancement, structure of the organization, and fringe benefits. Don't make it seem that you're concerned only with money.
- ▲ Don't act evasive if asked about unfavorable parts of your record.
- ▲ Don't act conceited, overbearing, or overly aggressive.

of each of these factors you are likely to get from each prospective job, using the following scale:

1	2	3	4	5
None	Very Little	Some	A Moderate Amount	Very Much

Now multiply the importance rating you gave each job factor by the amount of that factor you are likely to get from the job. Add these up across all the job factors. The job prospect with the highest total is probably your best bet.

CAREER STAGES

All careers may be different, but they do have a few things in common. A person's career development typically occurs in distinct stages. Let's look at these stages now.[2]

1. *Preparatory period.* In the preparatory stage, an individual's early experiences and adjustments in school, at home, and in the community help develop mental and physical maturity. For instance, hearing one of your parents talk about a day at work over the dinner table may give you an idea of what to expect when you get a job.
2. *Initial work period.* The initial work period is characterized by part-time and occasional jobs. It usually begins when an individual seeks a first job while still in school. In this stage, the job is seen as temporary.
3. *Trial work period.* During the trial work period, people usually in their 20s and early 30s, take a regular full-time job and begin to settle into a stable field of work. This stage sees people moving between jobs and finding out what they like. Sometimes employees are faced with unexpectedly tough decisions, as described in the Ethical Issue on page 712.
4. *Stable work period.* Employees who have become settled in their jobs have entered the stable work period. In this period, people believe that they have found the jobs they will stick with for the rest of their careers.

At every career stage, cooperation and attention to detail are important.

5. *Retirement*. Retirement is seen as a blessing by some people and as a curse by others. Those happiest in retirement are the people who have prepared for it over a period of time and made plans for the retirement years.

   Some people go through all these stages. Others may skip stages or may never get beyond the trial work period. It is important to understand that when you start your career, you probably won't enter the stable work period right away. A lot of job searching—and soul searching—will probably take place first.

SUCCESS CHESS

Managing a career is like playing a complex, high-stakes game of chess, probably against some very tough opponents. One career expert set down nine rules, designed to help people win that game. His rules of **success chess** are summarized as follows:[3]

success chess rules suggested for managing your career successfully.

- *Rule No. 1.* Maintain the widest possible set of options. Don't get stereotyped. Don't stay in technical work too long. It may be necessary to get staff experience, but a good line reputation is also necessary.
- *Rule No. 2.* Don't get trapped in a "dead-end" position. Try not to work under a superior who hasn't moved in more than three years. Check to see that there are job routes open upward. If there are not, try to get out of the situation.
- *Rule No. 3.* Become a crucial subordinate to a mobile superior. A crucial subordinate is one that the boss needs as much as that person needs the boss. A crucial subordinate will move when the boss moves.
- *Rule No. 4.* Always try for increased exposure. "Exposure" means how often you are seen by those above you in the organization. Decades ago, people were told that the best way to get to the top was to have a desk near the

Should You Ask the Tough Question?

Tony had just completed his third year of employment at Union Chemical Company. He got an unusually positive job evaluation from his immediate superior, as well as a whopping 12 percent salary increase. That's why he was particularly upset when he read a story in a business journal about a division of the firm manufacturing deadly nerve gas. Tony had heard talk about ethical issues in his dormitory while he was in college, but he had never become personally involved. Now he wondered if he should ask his supervisors whether the story in the journal was true. Would such an inquiry bring his loyalty to the firm into question, in the eyes of his superiors? What would you do?

boss's door. This advice—that you don't get promoted if you aren't noticed—is still valid.

- *Rule No. 5.* Be willing to practice self-nomination. That is, let people in power know when you want a job. Generally, at least two moves in a career are due to self-nomination. Don't just wait for your boss or someone else to determine your options.
- *Rule No. 6.* If you decide to leave a company, do it at your convenience. Leave on the best of terms. Don't wait for the situation to get really bad or for a nasty confrontation to occur. Quit while you're ahead.
- *Rule No. 7.* Rehearse before quitting a job. Don't leave in a state of high emotion. Write out your resignation and wait a week. Think the decision through. Tell your family, take a week-long vacation, and bring your biographical data sheet up to date. After a week, decide whether or not to quit. However, don't just keep on rehearsing; one way or the other, make up your mind.
- *Rule No. 8.* Think of the corporation as a marketplace for skills. Learn which skills are in demand in a particular company or industry. Read business periodicals, such as the *Wall Street Journal* or *Business Week,* to find out which companies need your skills.
- *Rule No. 9.* Don't let success cut off your options. Successful people in one area often can be successful in other areas. Consider new careers. Don't spend your life in a rut.

As an example of a person who has achieved a high degree of success in her career, see the profile of Liz Claiborne on page 713.

CAREER MANAGEMENT BY FIRMS

Some companies are taking steps to ensure that their employees' careers are not left to chance. At Fairfield Control Systems Company, each of ten experienced managers is assigned as a mentor to one high-potential protege. The mentor and protege meet monthly. They put together a two-year development plan focusing on ways to enhance the protege's education, exposure, responsibility, and skills training. The mentor develops goals for the protege, which are reviewed every two years, and the mentor monitors goal completion.[4]

Another company, Syntex, operates assessment centers (discussed in Chapter 9) that provide management candidates with information about their abilities and about opportunities for career planning. Syntex has also developed a career-plan-

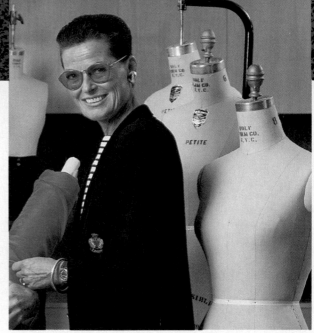

Liz Claiborne

Until her retirement in 1989, Elizabeth Claiborne Ortenberg was president, chief executive officer, and chairperson of Liz Claiborne, Inc., the second-largest clothing firm in the United States. Renowned manager Harold Geneen of ITT once said "decide what it is you want to do, and then start doing it." The career of Liz Claiborne is a perfect illustration of this advice.

Born in Brussels, Belgium, in 1929, Liz gained an appreciation of art, drawing, and painting from her father, Omer Villère, a banker for Morgan Guaranty Trust Company. She learned to sew from her mother, Louise Carol (Fenner) Claiborne. Her father sent her to study fine arts in Brussels and Nice, France, in 1947 and 1948, expecting that she would become a painter. Liz had other ideas. Because she liked to draw and sew, she had decided to become a clothing designer. In 1950, she took a job in New York City's garment district. She spent the next 25 years designing clothes for various firms. While working in Milwaukee, Liz met design executive Arthur Ortenberg, whom she married in 1957.

From 1961 to 1976 Liz was the chief designer for the junior dress division of the Jonathan Logan Company. There, she developed the idea of starting her own firm. The trouble with the women's clothing market, Liz thought, was that little was available for women who were too old for teenwear and too young for the standard navy business suits. Up-and-coming women in fields and places where suits weren't necessary, such as teachers, doctors, and women in Southern California or Florida, had little to choose from, and what was available was outrageously expensive. So, Liz thought, a woman ought to be able to buy something in between. "I'm a great believer in fit, in comfort, in color," Liz said. "I was working myself, I wanted to look good, and I didn't think you should have to spend a fortune to do it."

In 1976, she started Liz Claiborne, Inc. Liz was the head designer and president, her husband Arthur was the secretary and treasurer, and Leonard Boxer was in charge of production. Right away, the company was a success. The firm was in the black within nine months and achieved sales of $2.6 million in its first year of operation. In 1986, they reached $1.2 billion, which qualified Liz Claiborne, Inc. as one of the Fortune 500 (the first one started by a woman).

Liz credits her firm's success to the fact that she *listened* to her customers. She would work on the floor as a saleswoman, go into the fitting room, and hear what the customers liked and didn't like. She used a computerized system to get weekly reports on which styles, colors, and sizes were sold. Liz's creative ability and her husband's managerial talent made a winning combination. Their firm's average annual return on equity from 1979 to 1988 was 40.3 percent, better than any other Fortune 500 firm.

In 1989, Liz and Arthur retired from active management to devote themselves to personal pursuits. Today they run the $10 million Liz Claiborne Foundation, which supports environmental causes, including the Wilderness Society, the Greater Yellowstone Coalition, and the "Nature" series on PBS. In retirement, as in her career, Liz Claiborne knows what she wants to do, and she does it.

Sources: *Current Biography Yearbook* (1989), p. 110; *Fortune,* 24 April 1989, p. 50; *Fortune,* 12 March 1990, p. 118; H. Geneen and A. Moscow, *Managing* (New York: Doubleday, 1984), p. 7; and *Sales and Marketing Management.* March 1991, p. 48.

Special Problems for Women in Business

The number of women in business is growing dramatically. As we pointed out in Chapter 2, such increases result in part from changing cultural norms. It was once believed that "a woman's place is in the home," but people now recognize that women have an important and legitimate role in the workplace. Also, federal policies and regulations prohibit sex discrimination in organizations.

Current Status of Women in Business

To date, the results of these changing norms and regulations have been mixed. Women with business degrees, such as the MBA, are earning higher starting salaries than men with comparable degrees, but their later salary increases do not keep up with those of men. Women are increasingly moving into management positions, but mostly in the entry-level and some middle-level ranks. It is still unusual to find women in upper management.

When women do advance to top management, it is often in areas that are "suitable" for females. The stereotype persists that women are sensitive and understanding, while men are self-reliant, aggressive, and forceful. As a result, positions in human resources, consumer affairs, public relations, and corporate social responsibility are increasingly being offered to women. Such jobs tend to be staff positions, with less power and prospects for advancement than line positions in functional areas such as finance and production.

Women also face other problems. For example, many have heavy family responsibilities, such as child care. Others find that their bosses are not willing to delegate much responsibility to them. Finally, many male executives are more comfortable dealing with other men, and they conduct some of their important business discussions in informal settings such as on the golf course or in the locker room.

What is Being Done?

Many companies are making sincere efforts to improve the status of their female employees. Most are undertaking active hiring programs. In addition, some companies now have supportive programs, such as provision of child care facilities, use of flexible working hours, and financial support for further education and training. Special training programs that help women become more assertive or develop valuable interpersonal networks are also becoming popular. Of course, women are also taking their destinies into their own hands. They are becoming more determined, confident, and politically astute.

ning workbook, *How to Work for a Living and Like It*. It outlines the basic steps and processes for developing a career plan. Regularly scheduled seminars are open to all employees. They deal with such career issues as identifying the experience, education, and skills required for each functional area. The information has been especially helpful for women entering the workforce.[5] (For a discussion of the special problems of women in business, see the box above.)

At AT&T, a number of selection and development procedures are used for career management. An important element of AT&T's approach is to provide employees with challenging first jobs. The approach focuses on identifying competent, demanding superiors who hold high expectations for new employees.

Many other techniques are now being used by companies to manage employees' careers. Tuition reimbursement programs, planned job progression for new employees, career counseling, outside management seminars, and computerized skills inventories are some examples. When interviewing with companies, be sure to ask about their career management practices. See if they fit your interests and needs.

SUMMARY POINTS

1 A career is not simply a job. It is an ongoing sequence of events in which people attempt to control their future rather than simply be controlled. A career is important because it strongly influences a person's quality of life and the amount of recognition and respect he or she receives. It is particularly important that a person entering the workforce do a careful self-analysis of his or her interests, strengths, and weaknesses.

2 To make an intelligent career choice, job seekers need information about jobs in the present and the future. They should think in terms of career clusters, not just specific jobs. Information about employment opportunities can be obtained through college placement services, help-wanted ads, the United States Employment Service, private employment agencies, local organizations, personal contacts, and the College Placement Council.

3 Chances for a successful job search can be increased by starting with a plan. Then job seekers should prepare a thorough resume, showing their qualifications in detail. To accompany the resume, they should prepare a letter of application, which states what job they are seeking, highlights their qualifications, and requests an interview. Along with the resume and letter of application, they should send letters of recommendation. To prepare for the interview, the job seeker should research

the company, prepare questions about the company, anticipate questions that will be asked, and practice answering them. If the interview goes well, the applicant may be asked to visit the company. In deciding which job offer to accept, applicants should consider which one best fits the job characteristics that are most important to them.

4 A career normally passes through five important stages: a preparatory period of early experiences and adjustments in school, the initial work period (part-time jobs), trial work period (first full-time job), stable work period (identification of lifelong career), and retirement.

5 Establishing a successful career is like playing a high-stakes game of chess. Key elements in winning at the success game are to keep your options open, try to become a crucial subordinate to a boss on the move, get noticed, and let the boss know what job you want. If you decide to leave the company, leave on good terms. Consider new careers—don't get into a rut.

6 Some companies aid their employees in achieving their career objectives. There may be a mentor and protege system, in which personal development plans are established. There may also be assessment centers that provide employees with information about their abilities. Some companies provide career planning workbooks and seminars for employees.

REVIEW QUESTIONS

1 Suggest how jobs affect the way society views women and minority members. **1**

2 What is a career cluster? **2**

3 In preparing a resume, what are three topics you should normally *not* cover? **3**

4 What are some factors to consider in analyzing job offers? **3**

5 How can letters of recommendation help you get a job? **3**

6 What are the characteristics of the five career stages? **4**

7 If you decide to leave a company, how should you go about it? Why? **5**

8 How does AT&T attempt to provide employees with challenging first jobs? **6**

KEY TERMS

career cluster 701
resume 703
career objective 705
letter of application 706
success chess 711

DISCUSSION QUESTIONS

1 Do you think organizations should take an active role in managing their employees' careers? Why or why not?

2 What is your own definition of career success?

3 How well do you think your abilities, values, and interests would fit with each of the following jobs: bank teller, personnel manager, salesperson, securities analyst, and purchasing agent?

4 Do you disagree with any of the rules of success chess? Why or why not?

5 What do you think can be done to improve the status of women in business?

EXPERIENTIAL EXERCISES

1 Using Figure 25-8 as an example, type a one-page resume. Do not include references. Although your activities and qualifications may be limited at this point in your life, a thorough, attractive resume is still essential for job hunting success.

2 List your order of preference for the job-related factors suggested below. After you have done this, compare your rank ordering to those of your classmates.

Pleasant work environment
Job security
Travel
Salary
Freedom from supervision
Opportunity for advancement

Fringe benefits
Reasonable working hours
Active social environment (i.e., good mix of males and females)
Good retirement plan

CASES

CASE 25-1
The Economy and Your Career

During the last recession, Daniel Sartorious was an executive at a large, but financially troubled, farm products manufacturing company. He was offered several better-paying and higher-status jobs with other companies. After turning down three such offers, he accepted the fourth one.

Daniel's position in the recession was somewhat unusual. He had been successful, and his skills were in demand among other companies. In deciding whether to take a new job, he looked at the types of jobs that were available during a recession.

The first thing he found was that production managers and financial managers (such as controllers, auditors, and tax experts) are much more likely to get a job in a recession than are marketing and advertising managers. He also found that experience is a real plus. Someone looking for a first job during a recession has a harder time than someone with experience and a successful record. During a recession, employers want people who are cost cutters, action oriented, and profit makers.

He also discovered that people in technical areas are hired at the entry-level (or beginning) positions throughout a recession. In 1991, a recession year, companies stopped hiring entry-level people. When the economy improved, these companies found that they didn't have the personnel they needed to operate. Many companies suffered because of this misjudgment.

Daniel was also impressed by the value of education. One knowledgeable consultant commented that "the woods are full of people looking, but a lot of them aren't properly educated." Daniel was glad that he had spent the extra year in school taking business courses and that he had attended community college courses in finance and management even after he had started his job. These courses were crucial to his getting offers at a time when many co-workers were being laid off, with no prospects of jobs at other companies.

1. Why do you think production managers and financial managers are more in demand in a recession than advertising and marketing managers? Do you think this is wise? Which skills do you think might be most in demand in times of economic expansion?
2. If you were offered a job that offered low pay but a lot of valuable experience, do you think it would be worth the loss in pay in the long run? Why?
3. How did Daniel fit into the career stages model described in this chapter?

CASE 25-2
Job Security vs. Risk

Liz Glazer had been a security analyst for Bear Sterns and Company for the past ten years. She had received her MBA from Emory University in Atlanta, Georgia, and had decided to try to find a job on Wall Street. After a couple of months of pounding the pavement, she had succeeded. At that time, she was one of the few women analysts on "the street." Her career progressed nicely. After five years, she passed all the tests and acquired enough work experience to become a chartered financial analyst (CFA). This designation applies to people who analyze stocks and bonds for a living. Liz specialized in analyzing securities in the health care industry, and she was very proficient at it. Her reports were well received by potential investors. She even appeared as a guest on the television program "Wall Street Week." Her salary was $125,000 a year, and her pay was expected to increase by a few thousand dollars each year.

Her marriage had not been as successful as her professional career. She and her husband had been divorced four years before, and Liz had received custody of all three children. Unfortunately, her husband's career was not nearly as successful as hers, and she had almost total financial responsibility for the children.

At her current salary, that was no problem. However, an exciting opportunity had presented itself, and she was not sure how to handle it. Two former colleagues on Wall Street were about to start a regional brokerage house in Oklahoma City, specializing in trading the securities of companies located in the Southwest. She was invited to become a one-third partner in the proposed firm, which would be called Abelson, Glazer, and Milam.

If she chose to move to Oklahoma City and become a partner, her initial investment would be $150,000 (about 75 percent of her current savings). She would not have to negotiate a salary, because there would be none. All her return would be based on profits and commissions. She knew that in a poor year, there might not be a return—she might even have to put more money in. In a good year, she might make $500,000 or more. Such was the nature of owning a stock brokerage business. Liz had a tough decision to make.

1. Would you recommend that Liz make this career move? What are some key variables for her to consider?
2. Although Liz has achieved a high degree of success in New York City as a recognized stock market analyst, do you think the fact that she is a woman will make it harder for her to be accepted in the Southwest?
3. What do chartered financial analysts (CFAs) do for a living?

Bioplastics, Inc.

In April, 1992, scientists at Michigan State University and James Madison University announced a revolutionary breakthrough. They had genetically engineered a relative of the mustard plant to produce polyhydroxybutyrate (PHB), the biodegradable version of polypropylene, which is used to make plastic containers and wraps.

To Kira Richardson, reading the announcement in *Science* magazine was like a revelation. After seeing the movie "The Graduate" many years earlier, Kira had been convinced that the future was in plastics. Growing up in the 1970s and 1980s, however, she became environmentally conscious, and plastics were the enemy. Also, Kira became fascinated by developments in genetic engineering, which sounded like something out of *The Inquirer* — "Scientists Inject Sheep Genes Into Tomatoes! BLTs Follow Children to School!" Such developments, while a bit scary, began to make plastics seem dull. Now, though, it had all come together in one startling development — the marriage, in a simple plant, of genetic engineering and plastics and environmental consciousness. This, Kira decided, was *really* the future.

So Kira was excited when, just a few months later, she read about a small biotechnology company, Bioplastics, Inc., which had announced its intention to exploit the potential of this new technological development. Better yet, Bioplastics (which had recently changed its name from Biomatics to reflect its new thrust) had emerged as a darling of investors even before this announcement, with its stock more than quadrupling in price since its initial offering less than three years ago. With the announcement of the firm's move into genetically engineered plastics, the stock price shot up again, registering an 80 percent gain within days. If this trend continued, Kira reasoned, Bioplastics would be the IBM of the genetic revolution.

Kira could think of many cases where people had failed to see things which subsequently became obvious: that humans would one day fly (and to the moon), that computers would be as common as typewriters, that concern about the environment would increase. Kira knew that if she made that same kind of mistake when faced with this tremendous investment opportunity, she would regret it for the rest of her life. She decided that she would invest all of her savings, and whatever other funds she could quickly amass, in Bioplastics, Inc. The future, Kira was confident, was green and microwaveable and biodegradable and seemingly limitless. It was all here in one package, and she wanted a part of it.

Questions

1. Do you agree with Kira's conclusions? That is, does this seem like an attractive investment opportunity to you?
2. What are some of the assumptions about Bioplastics, Inc., and about the technological, social, and legal environments facing the firm, that Kira is apparently making in this case? To what extent are these assumptions likely to be valid?
3. What other basic business considerations may be important in this case?
4. What difficulties associated with forecasting does this case illustrate?
5. What threats to critical thinking are evident in this case?

CAREERS APPENDIX

In this appendix, we provide a variety of information to further aid in your career planning. First, we present a listing of qualities bosses say they look for when hiring college graduates. Next, we identify and describe a number of jobs in business, listing number of people employed, growth prospects, and salary information. We then give some suggestions for additional career reading. Finally, we provide the addresses of organizations from which you can request additional career information.

WHAT DO BOSSES WANT?

Executives of over 400 of the nation's largest corporations were asked which qualities they considered most important when hiring college graduates. Seventy qualities were provided for the executives to rank. Fifteen of those considered to be more and less important appear in Table 1. Do any of the rankings surprise you? How do you think you rate on the most important qualities?

JOBS IN BUSINESS

In this section, we identify and describe a number of jobs within several areas of business. To give you an idea of opportunities, we then state the number of people employed, the probable growth rate through the early years of the next century and the latest salary information available for each job.

The figures and job summaries in this section are adapted from the *Occupational Outlook Handbook: 1990–91* edition, prepared by the Bureau of Labor Statistics of the U.S. Department of Labor. Often there are several more-specific job titles in each category. Salaries and duties may vary substantially within each category and may sometimes be outside the range we describe as typical. We suggest you consult the *Occupational Outlook Handbook* for more detailed information.

Jobs in Management

Management careers are ideal for individuals with leadership ability and the desire to work with other people. Typically, they also require some experience.

TABLE A-1   Importance Rankings of 15 Qualities

Quality	Ranking
Ability to Get Things Done	1
Common Sense	2
Honesty/Integrity	3
Dependability	4
Initiative	5
Enthusiasm	9
Intelligence	13
Maturity	22
Writing Skills	26
Personality	28
Academic Major	42
Sense of Humor	43
Grade-Point Average (Overall)	51
Extracurricular Activities	56
Recommendations from Politicians	67

Courtesy of J. Shingleton, Michigan State University.

Managers may find their skills to be useful in many organizations in business, health care, and government. Managerial positions are found at all levels. Since management positions are found in each of the functional areas, we list just a few here.

Supervisors of Blue-Collar Workers. These supervisors direct the activities of workers who perform such tasks as assembling television sets, unloading ships, and servicing autos. They may make work schedules, keep production and employee records, and handle discipline. About 1.8 million blue-collar supervisors were employed in 1988, and slower than average growth is expected through the year 2000. Median annual earnings for blue-collar worker supervisors were about $27,300 in 1988.

Health Service Managers. These managers direct the various functions that make health organizations—from large teaching hospitals to storefront clinics—run smoothly. They have overall responsibility for management decisions, such as preparing budgets, establishing rates, directing, hiring and training, and directing and coordinating the activities of the medical department, nursing department, physical plant, and other departments. Included in this category are health service administrators, who manage and help to manage entire facilities, and health specialists, who are managers in charge of specific clinical departments or services. About 177,000 people worked in some phase of health service management in 1988, and the growth of this field is expected to be much faster than average. Chief executives of small hospitals earned an average of $70,000 in 1988, while chief executives of large hospitals earned an average of $135,000. The median earnings for health service managers in 1988 were $30,524.

Hotel Managers and Assistants. These men and women are responsible for operating lodging establishments profitably. They may determine room rates and credit policy, direct the food service operation, and manage the housekeeping, accounting, maintenance, and security departments. There were about 96,000 wage and salary jobs held by hotel managers and assistant managers in 1988, and growth is expected to be much faster than average through the year 2000. Assistant managers earned an average of $30,000 in 1989, and general managers earned an average of $53,000.

Jobs in Finance, Banking, and Insurance

Careers in finance, banking, and insurance offer exciting opportunities to deal with financial resources. Historically, they have served as excellent routes to the top of an organization.

Actuaries. Actuaries assemble and analyze statistics to calculate the probabilities of death, sickness, injury, disability, unemployment, retirement, and property loss from accident, theft, fire, and other hazards. They use this information to determine the insured loss that can be expected. There were 16,000 actuaries in 1988, and much faster than average growth is expected. To become a member of an actuarial society, a person is required to pass actuarial exams. Passing a certain number of examinations in

a specific exam series leads to an "associate" title, and passing an entire series gives the title "fellow." In 1989, college graduates who had not taken any of these exam averaged $22,000–$26,000. College graduates who had taken the first exam averaged $24,000–$28,000; those who had taken the second exam averaged $26,000–$30,000. Associates averaged between $35,000 and $48,000 a year, while fellows averaged about $47,000–$57,000, and actuary executives averaged $55,000–$100,000.

Financial Managers. This category includes treasurers, controllers, cash managers, and others who prepare financial reports firms need to conduct their operations and satisfy tax and regulatory requirements. In 1988, 673,000 people were employed in the field of financial management, and average growth is expected. The median salary for 1988 was $32,800; the lowest-paid 10 percent earned $17,500, while the top 10 percent earned $52,000.

Bank Tellers. Tellers cash bank customers' checks, process their deposits and withdrawals from checking accounts, and sometimes perform specialized duties such as handling foreign currency. Banks employed 522,000 tellers in 1988, and slower-than-average growth is expected. The median income for bank tellers in 1988 was $12,800. The lowest-paid 10 percent earned $9,200 while the top 10% earned approximately $20,300.

Economists and Market Research Analysts. These men and women devise methods and procedures for obtaining and analyzing data. Economists try to determine the costs and benefits of making, distributing, and using resources in particular ways. They may be concerned with issues such as energy costs, inflation, business cycles, unemployment, tax policy, and farm prices. Economists who work for companies may provide managers with information to use in making pricing, production, or diversification decisions. Market research analysts analyze the buying public and its wants and needs, thus providing the information on which marketing decisions are based. They are concerned with the design, promotion, price, and distribution of a product or service. About 36,000 people were employed as economists and market research analysts in 1988, and faster-than-average growth is expected. The median base salary for full-time economists and market research analysts was about $35,000 in 1988.

Insurance Agents and Brokers. These people sell insurance policies, provide advice about financial planning and insurance needs, prepare reports, maintain records, and help settle policyholders' claims. About 423,000 agents and brokers sold insurance in 1988, and average growth is expected. The median income was $25,000, but 68 percent of agents with more than five years' experience earned considerably more.

Securities and Financial Services Sales Representatives. These are the people who put the "market machinery" into operation when investors want to buy or sell stocks, bonds, shares in mutual funds, or other financial products. They may provide financial counseling, relay orders, or provide price quotations. There were about 200,000 securities sales workers and financial service sales workers in 1988, and growth is expected to be much faster than average. Trainees' salaries averaged about $12,000 to $16,800 in 1988, and the beginning earnings for a security sales representative averaged $28,000. Experienced securities sales representatives who serviced individual investors averaged about $71,000, while those servicing institutional accounts averaged $240,000.

Underwriters. Underwriters appraise and select the risks their insurance companies will insure. They analyze various types of information in deciding whether a risk is acceptable. About 103,000 people worked as underwriters in 1988, and growth is expected to be faster than average. Average annual earnings in 1988 varied widely among the different levels and types of underwriters, ranging from $23,400 to $49,000.

Jobs in Marketing

The many jobs involved in creating time and place utility make marketing a diverse and fascinating field. Marketing jobs often provide great opportunities for creativity, personal accomplishment, and financial reward.

The first four categories listed below are combined in government figures as marketing, advertising, and public relations managers. In 1988 there were 406,000 people employed as marketing, advertising, and public relations managers. The 1988 median salary for these occupations was $36,500, and faster-than-average growth is expected. However, some salaries were substantially higher; figures

between $75,000 and $100,000 were not uncommon. In addition, bonuses often equal 10 percent or more of salaries.

Marketing Managers. These managers develop the firm's detailed marketing strategy. With the help of subordinates, they determine the demand for products and services offered by the firm and its competitors and identify potential customers. Marketing managers develop pricing strategy and work with advertising and sales promotion managers to promote the firm's products and services and attract potential users.

Sales Managers. Sales managers direct the firm's sales program. They assign sales territories and goals and establish training programs for sales representatives. Sales managers advise sales representatives on ways to improve their sales performance. They maintain contact with dealers and distributors and analyze sales statistics gathered by their staffs to determine sales potential and inventory requirements and monitor the preferences of customers.

Advertising Managers. These people oversee the account services, creative services, and media services departments. The account services department is managed by account executives, who assess the need for advertising and (in advertising agencies) maintain the accounts of clients. The creative services department—which develops the subject matter and presentation of advertising—is supervised by a creative director, who oversees the copy chief and art director and their staffs. The media services department is supervised by the media director, who oversees planning groups that decide in which communications media to advertise.

Public Relations Managers. These managers supervise staffs of public relations specialists. They direct publicity programs, designed to gain attention for the firm and its activities from various groups such as consumers, stockholders, and the general public. Public relations managers may confer with labor relations specialists to produce internal company communications—such as news about employee–management relations—and with financial managers to produce company reports. They may also assist company executives in drafting speeches, handling special events such as parties and introduction of new products, and managing other public relations activities.

Wholesale and Retail Buyers. These people purchase goods for their stores. They seek goods that will satisfy customers and generate a profit. About 207,000 buyers worked for retail and wholesale firms in 1988, and slower-than-average growth is expected. The median salary was $24,700 in 1988, and some buyers earned over $45,500.

Manufacturers' and Wholesalers' Sales Representatives. Reps sell manufacturers' and wholesalers' products to other businesses (factories, banks, and retailers) and to other institutions. They visit prospective customers, prepare reports on sales prospects or customers' credit ratings, and handle correspondence. There were 1.8 million manufacturers' and wholesalers' sales workers in 1988, and faster-than-average growth is expected. The median salary was $28,000 for full-time sales representatives, and top salaries were over $51,700.

Retail Sales Workers. These employees sell such things as furniture, clothing, and appliances in retail stores. They may also perform such tasks as making out sales slips, receiving cash payments, and handling returns. In 1988, about 4.57 million sales workers were employed in retail businesses, and growth is expected to be faster than average. Average earnings for full-time sales workers, including bonuses and commissions, were $22,830 for those selling motor vehicles and boats, but only $10,760 for those selling apparel.

Public Relations Specialists. These specialists help businesses maintain a positive public reputation. They inform the public of their organization's policies, activities, and accomplishments and keep management aware of public attitudes. There were 91,000 public relations specialists in 1988, and average growth is expected. The median salary for public relations specialists employed by institutions was $26,100, and the middle 50 percent of salaries were between $19,200 and $40,900.

Real Estate Agents, Brokers and Appraisers. These professionals help people buy, sell and appraise homes and other real estate. They provide information about the housing market and act as a conduit for price negotiations between buyers and sellers. Brokers are independent business people who not only sell real estate owned by others, but also rent and manage properties, make appraisals, and develop new building projects. Agents are generally independent sales workers who contract their services with a licensed broker. There were 422,000 real estate agents, brokers, and appraisers in 1988, and average growth is expected. Full-time agents earned a median of $18,000 a year, and brokers earned $41,000.

Travel Agents. These specialists have the information and know-how to make the best possible travel arrangements for their clients' tastes and budgets. There were about 142,000 travel agents in 1988, and growth is expected to be much faster than average. Most of travel agents' earnings come from commissions from airlines and other carriers, tour operators, and lodging facilities. In 1986, salaried travel agents earned from $12,000 for beginners to over $21,000 for experienced agents.

Jobs in Accounting
Accounting careers are important, challenging, and rewarding. As managers increasingly rely on accounting information to make business decisions, the demand for skilled accounting personnel will continue to grow.

Accountants and Auditors. These professionals prepare and analyze financial reports that provide managers with the up-to-date financial information they need to make decisions. They may work in such areas as taxation, budgeting, costs, and investments. There were 963,000 accountants and auditors in 1988, and faster-than-average growth is expected. Starting salaries for accountants and auditors with a bachelor's degree averaged $25,300, while inexperienced accountants and auditors with master's degrees averaged a starting salary of $28,800.

Bookkeeping, Accounting, and Auditing Clerks. These people maintain systematic and up-to-date records of accounts and business transactions. They also prepare periodic financial statements showing all money received and paid out. Over 2.25 million people worked as bookkeeping, accounting, and auditing clerks in 1988, and little change in this number is expected through the next ten years. The median earnings of bookkeepers and accounting and auditing clerks were $16,000.

Jobs in Operations Management
Individuals pursuing careers in operations management are responsible for the many tasks needed to

keep the modern production and service facilities running properly. Jobs in operations management require considerable mathematical and mechanical skills.

Science Technicians.

These specialists have knowledge of science, mathematics, industrial machinery, and technical processes. They apply technical knowledge to all phases of business—from research and design to manufacturing, sales, and customer service. There were 232,000 persons working as science technicians in 1988, and average growth is expected. The median salary for science technicians was $21,600, and most earnings were between $16,300 and $29,200.

Industrial Engineers.

Industrial engineers determine the most effective ways for an organization to use the basic factors of production—people, machines, and materials. They design data processing systems and control systems, conduct plant location surveys, and apply mathematical concepts to production. There were about 132,000 industrial engineers employed in 1988, and average growth is expected. Starting salaries averaged $28,476, and many industrial engineers earn substantially more.

Production, Planning, and Expediting Clerks.

These men and women coordinate and expedite the flow of work within and among the departments of a firm according to production schedules. This includes reviewing and distributing production schedules and work orders, conferring with department supervisors to determine the progress of work and completion dates, and compiling reports on the progress of work and production problems. There were about 229,000 production, planning, and expediting clerks in 1988, and slower-than-average growth is expected.

Purchasing Agents and Managers.

These managers make sure that the firm has the right materials, supplies, and equipment when they are needed. They obtain goods and services of the quality required at the lowest possible cost. About 458,000 persons worked as purchasing agents and managers in 1988, and average growth is expected. The median salary for purchasing agents and managers was $25,896 in 1988, and most earned between $19,500 and $34,736.

Jobs in Human Resource Management

Individuals with careers in human resource management make sure that organizations get, keep, and develop the best possible employees and use them in productive and satisfying ways. Dealing with people is a challenging task, and considerable training is required for most human resource management positions. Employment and salary figures are not available for all of the specific categories that follow. Personnel, training, and labor relations specialists held a total of about 422,000 jobs in 1988, with about 90 percent of that number employed in the private sector. For these positions as a whole, faster-than-average growth is expected. Median salaries were $34,600 for managers and $26,400 for specialists.

Equal Employment Opportunity (EEO) and Affirmative Action Coordinators.

The work of these employees is to maintain contact with women and minority employees and to investigate and resolve equal employment opportunity grievances. They also examine corporate practices for possible violations and compile and submit EEO reports. The median salary for affirmative action coordinators in 1988 was $33,300.

Compensation Managers.

These managers establish and maintain a firm's pay system. Assisted by staff specialists, they devise ways to ensure fair and equitable pay rates. They may conduct surveys to see how the company's rates compare with others' and to make sure that the firm's pay scale complies with laws and regulations. In addition, compensation managers often oversee their firm's performance evaluation system. The median salary for compensation managers and benefits managers (described below) was $47,300 in 1988.

Employee Benefits Managers.

These specialists handle the company's benefit programs, primarily its health insurance and pension plans. Expertise in designing and administering pension and benefits programs continues to gain in importance as these programs increase in number and complexity. Benefits managers must keep abreast of changing federal and state regulations affecting employee benefits.

Job Analysts.

Sometimes called **position classifiers**, these human resource workers collect and examine information about job duties to prepare job descriptions. Job descriptions explain the duties, training, and skills each job requires. Whenever a large organization introduces a new job or reviews existing ones, it calls upon the expert knowledge of the job analyst.

Labor Relations Specialists. These specialists advise management on all aspects of union–management relations. They help company officials prepare for collective bargaining sessions, participate in contract negotiations, and handle labor relations on a day-to-day basis. The median salary in 1988 was $50,500.

Training Specialists. These men and women develop courses, workshops, and other programs tailored to the training needs of an organization and its employees. Trainers consult with managers and supervisors about specific training needs, prepare manuals and other materials for use in training sessions, and keep employees informed about training opportunities. The median salary in 1988 was $49,400.

Sociologists. Sociologists study human society and social behavior by examining the groups that people form. Industrial sociologists are concerned with many issues relevant to business, such as group decision making, leadership, and power. Several thousand people were employed as sociologists in 1988, many of them in government agencies. The number of people who graduate with advanced degrees in sociology through the year 2000 is likely to exceed the number of job openings. The median annual salary of sociologists and anthropologists combined was $41,200 in business and industry. In general, sociologists with the Ph.D. degree earn substantially more than those without the doctoral degree.

Industrial and Organizational Psychologists. These professionals apply psychological techniques to personnel administration, management, and marketing problems. They are involved in policy planning, applicant screening, training and development, psychological test research, counseling, and organizational development and analysis, among other activities. Psychologists held about 104,000 jobs in 1988, but only a small fraction of those jobs were in business. Faster-than-average growth is expected. The median salary of psychologists with doctorates who worked in business (including self-employed) was $60,100 in 1987.

Jobs in Information Management, Computers, and Statistics

Careers in information management, computers, and statistics offer individuals the chance to deal with the crucial information resources of the organization. They are among the most rapidly growing, dynamic, and exciting career fields.

Computer and Peripheral Equipment Operators. The functions of these people include operating computers and peripheral equipment such as printers, disk drives, and tape readers. About 317,000 persons worked as computer and peripheral equipment operators in 1988, and faster-than-average growth is expected. The median earnings of computer operating personnel were $17,800 in 1988, with most earnings falling between $13,500 and $23,900.

Computer Programmers. Programmers write the detailed instructions, the *programs* or *software*—that list in a logical order the steps the computer must follow to organize data, solve a problem, or do some other work. There were about 519,000 computer programmers in 1988, and growth is expected to be much faster than average. Median earnings in 1988 were $30,600; most programmers earned between $22,100 and $39,900, and the top 10 percent earned over $49,500.

Typists, Word Processors and Data Entry Keyers. These information specialists are vital to the expeditious flow and processing of information. Typists and word processors are concerned mainly with the processing of text; data entry keyers process numerical information. Typists, word processors, and data entry keyers held 1.4 million jobs in 1988, and employment is expected to decline—despite the "information explosion"—because of productivity improvements. Median earnings for typists in metropolitan areas averaged $14,612 in 1988. Word processors averaged $18,148, while data entry keyers averaged $15,002.

Mathematicians. Mathematicians are engaged in a wide variety of activities, ranging from the creation of new theories to the translation of scientific and managerial problems into mathematical terms. Applied mathematicians use mathematics to develop theories, approaches, and techniques to solve practical problems. There were about 16,000 persons working as mathematicians in 1988, and average growth is expected. Starting salaries for mathematicians with bachelor's, master's, and Ph.D. degrees averaged $27,500, $29,600, and $40,700, respectively.

Statisticians.

Statisticians devise, carry out, and interpret the results of surveys and experiments. They may use statistical techniques to predict economic conditions, develop quality control tests, or evaluate the results of new management programs. About 15,000 persons worked as statisticians in 1988, and faster-than-average growth is expected. The average salary for statisticians in the federal government was $41,300. For statisticians with a bachelor's degree but no experience, the average was $15,700 to $19,500.

Computer Systems Analysts.

These specialists plan efficient methods of processing data and handling the results. To develop a new system, they may determine what new data must be collected, the equipment needed for computation, and the steps involved in processing the information. About 403,000 people worked as systems analysts in 1988, and growth is expected to be much faster than average. The median salary of systems analysts was $35,800 in 1988, and most salaries were in the range of $27,100 to $45,400 a year.

Other Jobs in Business

There are many other jobs needed to keep organizations running effectively. A few of them are presented in the following paragraphs.

Lawyers.

Lawyers link the legal system and society. As advocates, lawyers represent opposing parties in criminal and civil trials by presenting arguments in a court of law. As advisers, they counsel their clients as to their legal rights and obligations and suggest courses of action. As we have indicated throughout the text, the legal environment of a firm is becoming increasingly important. About 582,000 men and women worked as lawyers in 1988, and growth is expected to be much faster than average. Beginning salaries in private industry averaged $34,000, and the average salary of the most experienced lawyers in private practice was over $110,000.

Receptionists.

Receptionists greet customers and other visitors, determine their needs, and refer callers to the person who can help them. They also answer questions from the public. About 833,000 persons worked as receptionists in 1988, and growth is expected to be much faster than average. Receptionists earned a median of $13,312 in 1988.

Secretaries.

These men and women perform a variety of administrative and office duties. They schedule appointments, give information to callers, organize and maintain files, fill out forms, and record and transcribe dictation. Over 3.37 million secretaries were employed in 1988, and average growth is expected. The average annual salary for all secretaries was $21,710 in 1988. Salaries vary a great deal, however, reflecting differences in skill, experience, and level of responsibility, ranging from $17,810 to $29,354.

ADDITIONAL READINGS

Billy, C. (ed.). *Business and Management Jobs.* Princeton, N.J.: Peterson's Guides, 1991. (Published annually.)

Block, D. P. *How to Get and Get Ahead on Your First Job.* Lincolnwood, Ill.: National Textbook Company, 1989.

Bolles, R. *What Color Is Your Parachute?* Berkeley, Calif.: Ten Speed Press, 1992.

Fox, M. R. *Put Your Degree to Work: The New Professional's Guide to Career Planning and Job Hunting,* 2nd ed. New York: W. W. Norton, 1988.

Noble, J. *The Job Search Handbook: The Basics of a Professional Job Search.* Holbrook, Mass.: Bob Adams, Inc., 1988.

Steele, J. E., and M. S. Morgan. *Career Planning and Development for College Students and Recent Graduates.* Lincolnwood, Ill.: VGM Career Horizons, 1991.

Yates, M. J. *Resumes That Knock 'Em Dead.* Holbrook, Mass.: Bob Adams, Inc., 1988.

Yales, M. J. *Knock 'Em Dead: Great Answers to Tough Interview Questions,* 4th ed. Holbrook, Mass.: Bob Adams, Inc., 1990.

Yeager, N, and L. Hough. *Power Interviews: Job Winning Tactics from FORTUNE 500 Recruiters.* New York: Wiley, 1990.

ADDITIONAL CAREER INFORMATION

To learn more about opportunities in the various fields of business, we suggest that you write to the following sources. In your letter, indicate that you would like career information.

Small Business Management

Chamber of Commerce of the United States
1615 H Street, N.W.
Washington, DC 20062

National Small Business Administration
1155 15th St., N.W., 7th Floor
Washington, DC 20005

Management

American Management Association, Inc.
135 West 50th Street
New York, NY 10020

Society for Human Resource Management
606 N. Washington St.
Alexandria, VA 22314

Industrial Relations Research Association
7226 Social Science Building
University of Wisconsin
Madison, WI 53706

National Association of Personnel Consultants
3133 Mount Vernon Avenue
Alexandria, VA 22305

Operations Management

National Association of Purchasing Management
2055 E. Centennial Circle
P.O. Box 22160
Tempe, AZ 85285

American Society for Quality Control
310 W. Washington Avenue
Milwaukee, WI 53203

American Production and Inventory Control Society
500 W. Annandale Rd.
Falls Church, VA 22046

Marketing

American Advertising Federation
1400 K St., N.W., Suite 1000
Washington, DC 20005

American Marketing Association
250 S. Wacker Drive, Suite 200
Chicago, IL 60606

Finance

American Bankers Association
1120 Connecticut Avenue, N.W.
Washington, DC 20036

Bank Administration Institute
60 Gould Center
2550 Golf Road
Rolling Meadows, IL 60008

Association for Investment Management and Research
5 Boar's Head Lane
P.O. Box 3668
Charlottesville, VA 22903

New York Stock Exchange
11 Wall Street
New York, NY 10005

Accounting

American Accounting Association
5717 Bessie Drive
Sarasota, FL 34233-2399

American Institute of Certified Public Accountants
1211 Avenue of the Americas
New York, NY 10036

Insurance

American Council of Life Insurance
1001 Pennsylvania Avenue, N.W.
Washington, DC 20004-2599

Data Processing

American Society for Information Science
8720 Georgia Avenue, Suite 501
Silver Springs, MD 20910-3602

Association for Computing Machinery
11 W. 42nd St., 3rd Floor
New York, NY 10036

ENDNOTES

CHAPTER 1

1. "The CEO," *Success,* January/February 1991, p. 9.
2. P. Hofheinz, "The New Russian Revolution," *Fortune,* 19 November 1990, pp. 127–134.
3. "The Richest Man in Hollywood," *Forbes,* 24 December 1990, pp. 94–98.

CHAPTER 2

1. Robert Heilibronner and Lester Thurow, *Five Economic Challenges* (Englewood Cliffs, N.J.: Prentice-Hall, 1981), pp. 3–30.
2. L. Thurow, *The Zero-Sum Society* (New York: Basic Books, 1980), p. 76.
3. K. R. Sheets and S. Peterson, "Texas Takes a Tumble," *U.S. News and World Report,* 21 April 1986, pp. 20–27.
4. I. A. Kaye, "Watch out for Hidden Price Increases," *Consumers' Research,* April 1991, p. 21.
5. Kaye (note 4), p. 22.

CHAPTER 3

1. R. L. Miller and G. A. Jentz, *Fundamentals of Business Law* (St. Paul, Minn.: West Publishing Co., 1990), pp. 13–14.
2. Miller and Jentz (note 1), p. 9.
3. R. A. Anderson, I. Fox, and D. P. Twomey, *Business Law and the Legal Environment,* 14th ed. (Cincinnati, Ohio: South-Western Publishing Co., 1990), pp. 10–16.
4. Miller and Jentz (note 1), p. 178.
5. K. W. Clarkson, R. L. Miller, G. A. Jentz and F. B. Cross, *West's Business Law: Text, Cases, Legal Environment,* 5th ed. (St. Paul, Minn.: West Publishing Co., 1992), pp. 142, 144, 148.
6. Clarkson, Miller, Jentz, and Cross (note 5), p. 840.
7. Anderson, Fox, and Twomey (note 3), pp. 157–159.
8. Clarkson, Miller, Jentz, and Cross (note 5), pp. 403–404.
9. Anderson, Fox, and Twomey (note 3), p. 470.
10. Clarkson, Miller, Jentz, and Cross (note 5), pp. 855–857.
11. H. Gleckman, T. Smart, P. Dwyer, T. Segal, and J. Weber, "Cover Story," *Business Week,* 8 July 1991, pp. 56–57.

CHAPTER 4

1. *Wall Street Journal,* 6 November 1990, p. A1.
2. K. Miller and J. Mitchell, "Car Marketers Test Gray Area of Truth in Advertising," *Wall Street Journal,* 19 November 1990, p. B1; and K. Miller, "Such an Ad Was Almost Certain to Make Somebody Hit the Roof," *Wall Street Journal,* 8 November 1990, p. B1.
3. For instance, see L. P. Cohen, "Milken Pleads Guilty to Six Felony Counts and Issues an Apology," *Wall Street Journal,* 25 April 1990, pp. A1, A12; and L. P. Cohen, "Milken's Stiff 10-Year Sentence Is Filled with Incentives to Cooperate with U.S.," *Wall Street Journal,* 23 November 1990, p. A3.
4. B. Burrough, "How American Express Orchestrated a Smear of Rival Edmond Safra," *Wall Street Journal,* 24 September 1990, pp. A1, A8–A10; and W. Glasgall & J. Meehan, "American Express Slings Mud—and Gets Splattered," *Business Week,* 14 August 1989, pp. 102, 104.
5. For instance, see J. Beaty and S. C. Gwynne, "The Dirtiest Bank of All," *Time,* 29 July 1991, pp. 42–47.
6. A. G. Feliu, "Whistleblowing While You Work," *Business and Society Review,* Winter 1990, pp. 65–67; and "Whistle While You Work," *Personnel Supplement,* June 1990, pp. 4–5.
7. C. H. Deutsch, "Proper Conduct in the Workplace," *New York Times,* 29 July 1990, p. F25.
8. Deutsch (note 7), p. F25.
9. A. L. Otten, "Ethics on the Job: Companies Alert Employees to Potential Dilemmas," *Wall Street Journal,* 14 July 1986. For related discussions, see T. J. Murray, "Ethics Programs: Just a Pretty Face," *Business Month,* September 1987, p. 30; and, "Ethics Codes Spread Despite Skepticism," *Wall Street Journal,* 15 July 1988, p. 13.
10. *Human Resources,* October 1987, pp. 1–2.
11. Otten, *Wall Street Journal,* 14 July 1986. For a discussion of an ethics committee at Boeing, as well as of other corporate efforts to enhance employees' ethical behavior, see J. A. Byrne, "Businesses are Signing Up for Ethics 101," *Business Week,* 15 February 1988, pp. 56–57.
12. Otten (note 11).
13. G. Stricharchuk "Businesses Crack Down on Workers Who Cheat to Help the Company," *Wall Street Journal,* 13 June 1986.
14. For instance, see "Union Carbide Agrees to Settle All Bhopal Litigation for $470 Million in Pact with India's Supreme Court," *Wall Street Journal,* 15 February 1989, p. A3; A. Spaeth, "Court Settlement Stuns Bhopal Survivors," *Wall Street Journal,* 22 February 1989, p. A10; and "The Ghosts of Bhopal," *The Economist,* 18 February 1989, p. 70.
15. M. Chase, "Burroughs Wellcome Reaps Profit, Outrage from Its AZT Drug," *Wall Street Journal,* 15 September 1989, p. A1.
16. A. Nomani, "Lymphomed to Give Indigent Patients Drugs for AIDS," *Wall Street Journal,* 19 October 1988, p. A6.
17. For a discussion of these criticisms, see R. J. Aldag and D. W. Jackson, Jr., "Assessment of Attitudes Toward Social Responsibilities," *Journal of Business Administration,* vol. 8, no. 2, 1977, pp. 65–80.
18. For instance, see S. Toy and L. Driscoll, "Can Perrier Purify Its Reputation?" *Business Week,* 26 February 1990, p. 45.
19. B. Johnson, "Promo Recalls Mean New Sensitivity," *Advertising Age,* 18 June 1990, p. 76.
20. A. R. Karr, "This Corporate Race Belongs to the Safest," *Wall Street Journal,* 5 July 1990, pp. B1, B3.
21. K. B. Noble, "Illness Adds to Mystery of Stealth," *Wisconsin State Journal,* 18 September 1988, p. 3A; and R. L. Rundle, "Lockheed Employees' Health Complaints Prompt Inquiries by 2 Federal Agencies," *Wall Street Journal,* 3 October 1988, p. B12.
22. C. Ansberry and S. J. Adler, "USX Will Settle Bias Case, Is Sued by EPA," *Wall Street Journal,* 27 February 1991, p. B6.
23. S. Wermiel, "Justices Bar 'Fetal Protection' Policies," *Wall Street Journal,* 21 March 1991, p. B1.
24. A. Pastor and J. Davidson, "U.S. Agencies, in Reversal, Told to Bar Bias for Victims of AIDS," *Wall Street Journal,* 7 October 1988, p. B7.
25. Ansberry and Adler, (note 22), p. B6.
26. "Lowly Pencil Involved in Global Controversy," *Wall Street Journal,* 19 October 1990, p. B1.
27. *Wall Street Journal,* 21 June 1984, pp. 1, 20.
28. "The 'Green' Bandwagon Brings Ethical Choices," *Wall Street Journal,* 21 May 1990, p. B2; and J. S. Lublin, "More Charities Reach Out for Corporate Sponsorship," *Wall Street Journal,* 1 October 1990, p. B1.
29. *Wall Street Journal,* 11 July 1984. See also E. D. Lee, "It's All Relative: Mutual Funds Discover 'Socially Responsible' Is in Eye

of Beholder," *Wall Street Journal,* 20 May 1987, p. 35; and C. W. Stevens, "Socially Aware Investing Turns Profitable," *Wall Street Journal,* 29 July 1988, p. 23.

CHAPTER 5

1. S. L. Jacobs, "Partnerships are Easy to Start, But Not Easy to Keep Going," *Wall Street Journal,* 15 April 1985, p. 31.
2. K. W. Clarkson, R. L. Miller, G. A. Jentz, and F. B. Cross, *West's Business Law: Text, Cases, Legal Environment,* 5th ed. (St. Paul, Minn.: West Publishing Co., 1992), p. 774.
3. "One Company's China Debacle" (review of J. Mann, *Beijing Jeep), Fortune,* 6 November 1989, pp. 145–152.
4. A. Ehrbar, "Have Takeovers Gone Too Far?" *Fortune,* 27 May 1985, p. 20.
5. "Let's Make a Deal," *Time,* 23 December 1985, p. 43.

CHAPTER 6

1. U.S. Department of Commerce, Bureau of the Census, *County Business Patterns 1987* (Washington, D.C.: U.S. Government Printing Office, February 1990).
2. D. L. Birch, "The Rise and Fall of Everybody," *Inc.,* December 1987, p. 19.
3. *The Business Failure Record: 1986* (New York: Dun and Bradstreet, Inc., 1988), p. 17.
4. F. Rice, "How to Succeed at Cloning a Small Business," *Fortune,* 28 October 1985, p. 60.
5. P. Larson, "Franchising's Strength Undiminished," *Franchising World,* March–April 1991, p. 6.
6. Rice (note 4), pp. 60–62.
7. S. D. Hunt and J. R. Nevin, "Full Disclosure Laws in Franchising: An Empirical Investigation," *Journal of Marketing,* April 1976, pp. 53–62.

CHAPTER 7

1. M. Weber, *The Theory of Social and Economic Organization,* trans. A. M. Henderson and T. Parsons (New York: Free Press, 1947).
2. This section is based in part on T. E. Deal and A. A. Kennedy, *Corporate Cultures: The Rites and Rituals of Corporate Life* (Reading, Mass.: Addison-Wesley, 1984). The J. C. Penney and PepsiCo examples are from "Corporate Culture," *Business Week,* 27 October 1980, pp. 148–160.
3. R. Levering, M. Moskowitz, and M. Katz, *The 100 Best Companies to Work For in America* (Reading, Mass.: Addison-Wesley, 1984), p. 142.
4. A. L. Wilkins, "The Creation of Company Cultures: The Role of Stories and Human Resource Systems," *Human Resource Management* 23 (1984), p. 43.
5. Deal and Kennedy (note 2), p. 37.
6. W. L. Ulrich, "HRM and Culture: History, Ritual, and Myth," *Human Resources Management* 23 (1984), p. 21.
7. Deal and Kennedy (note 2).
8. T. J. Peters and R. H. Waterman, Jr., *In Search of Excellence* (New York: Harper & Row, 1982), pp. 257–258.
9. A. Q. Nomani, "TWA Readies Plan to Reduce Business Fares," *Wall Street Journal,* 14 October 1991, pp. B1, B4.
10. Henry Mintzberg, "The Manager's Job: Folklore and Fact," *Harvard Business Review,* July/August 1975, pp. 49–61.
11. J. R. P. French and B. Raven, "The Bases of Social Power," in D. Cartwright and A. F. Zander, Eds., *Group Dynamics,* 2nd ed. (Evanston, Ill.: Row, Peterson, 1960). Although it is over 30 years old, this remains the most popular typology of power bases. See also P. M. Podsakoff and C. A. Schriesheim, "Field Studies of French and Raven's Bases of Power: Critique, Re-

analysis, and Suggestions for Future Research," *Psychological Bulletin* 97 (1985), pp. 387–411.
12. For good discussions of political strategies and tactics in organizations, see J. Pfeffer, *Power in Organizations* (Marshfield, Mass.: Pitman, 1981), pp. 137–177; and J. P. Kotter, "Power, Dependence, and Effective Management," *Harvard Business Review,* July–August 1977.
13. This popular categorization of types of change was proposed by H. J. Leavitt, "Applied Organizational Change in Industry: Structural, Technological, and Humanistic Approaches," in J. G. March, Ed., *Handbook of Organizations* (Chicago: Rand-McNally, 1965), p. 1145. For further discussions, see W. L. French and C. H. Bell, Jr., *Organization Development,* 4th ed. (Englewood Cliffs, N.J.: Prentice-Hall, 1990), and E. F. Huse and T. G. Cummings, *Organization Development and Change,* 4th ed. (St. Paul, Minn.: West, 1989).
14. Based on J. P. Kotter and Leonard A. Schlesinger, "Choosing Strategies for Change," *Harvard Business Review,* March–April 1979, pp. 106–114.

CHAPTER 8

1. F. W. Taylor, *The Principles of Scientific Management* (New York: Harper and Bros., 1911).
2. A. H. Maslow, "A Theory of Human Motivation," *Psychological Review,* vol. 50 (1943), pp. 370–396.
3. D. C. McClelland, "Business Drive and National Achievement," *Harvard Business Review,* vol. 40 (1962), pp. 99–112.
4. D. C. McClelland and D. H. Burnham, "Power Is the Great Motivator," *Harvard Business Review,* March–April 1976, pp. 100–110.
5. B. F. Skinner, *Contingencies of Reinforcement* (East Norwalk, Conn.: Appleton-Century-Crofts, 1969).
6. S. Kerr, "On the Folly of Rewarding A, While Hoping for B," *Academy of Management Journal,* vol. 18 (1975), pp. 769–783.
7. L. Silk, "The Great Freedom of Corporate Life: To Question," *Business Month,* April 1989, pp. 11–13.
8. R. Levering, "Paradise, Corporate Style," *Business Month,* July–August 1988, pp. 47–50.
9. D. McGregor, *The Human Side of Enterprise* (New York: McGraw-Hill, 1960).
10. For a discussion of cafeteria-style benefit plans and other innovative approaches, see D. C. Feldman and H. J. Arnold, *Managing Individual and Group Behavior in Organizations* (New York: McGraw-Hill, 1983). See also "Du Pont Joins Move to Offer Employees Flexible Benefits," *Wall Street Journal,* 8 May 1991, p. A16.
11. For discussions of these sorts of behaviors, sometimes called citizenship behaviors, see D. W. Organ, "A Reappraisal and Reinterpretation of the Satisfaction-Causes-Performance Hypothesis," *Academy of Management Review* 2 (1977), pp. 46–53; and T. S. Bateman and D. W. Organ, "Job Satisfaction and the Good Soldier: The Relationship Between Affect and Employee 'Citizenship'," *Academy of Management Journal* 26 (1983), pp. 587–595.
12. R. B. Dunham, *Organizational Behavior: People and Processes in Management* (Homewood, Ill.: Richard D. Irwin, 1984).
13. D. Schwimer, "Managing Stress to Boost Productivity," *Employment Relations Today,* Spring 1991, pp. 23–26.
14. N. Templin, "Johnson & Johnson 'Wellness' Program for Workers Shows Healthy Bottom Line," *Wall Street Journal,* 21 May 1990, pp. B1, B3.
15. T. F. O'Boyle, "Fear and Stress in the Office Take Toll," *Wall Street Journal,* 6 November 1990, pp. B1, B16.
16. For recent discussions of leadership, see W. Bennis, *On Becoming a Leader* (Reading, Mass.: Addison-Wesley, 1989); E. P. Hollander and L. R. Offermann, "Leadership in Organizations: Relationships in Transition," *American Psychologist,* vol.

45 (1990), pp. 179–189; and A. Zaleznik, *The Managerial Mystique: Restoring Leadership in Business* (New York: Harper & Row, 1989).

17. B. M. Bass, "Leadership: Good, Better, Best," *Organizational Dynamics,* Winter 1985, pp. 26–40.

18. M. Weber, *The Theory of Social and Economic Organization,* trans. and ed. A. M. Henderson and T. Parsons (London: Oxford University Press, 1947), p. 348.

19. P. L. Stepankowsky, "Some Swimming Lessons Could Be Best Way to Prepare for This Cruise," *Wall Street Journal,* 17 October 1990, p. B1.

20. S. Netton, "Six Ways to Be 'Family Friendly,'" *Nation's Business,* March 1989, pp. 12–13.

21. G. P. Latham and J. J. Bates, "The 'Practical Significance' of Locke's Theory of Goal Setting," *Journal of Applied Psychology,* vol. 60 (1975), pp. 122–124.

22. J. N. Kondrasuk, "Studies in MBO Effectiveness," *Academy of Management Review,* vol. 6 (1981), pp. 419–430.

23. W. G. Ouchi, *Theory Z* (Reading, Mass.: Addison-Wesley, 1981).

24. This discussion is based largely on "The Payoff from Teamwork," *Business Week,* 10 July 1989, pp. 56–62; "The Cultural Revolution at A. O. Smith," *Business Week,* 29 May 1989, pp. 66, 68; and "Is Teamwork a Management Plot? Mostly Not," *Business Week,* 20 February 1989, p. 70.

CHAPTER 9

1. R. S. Reynolds, Jr., "How to Pick a New Executive," *Fortune,* 1 September 1986, p. 113.

2. See A. Bennett, "Firms Toss Around Big Signing Bonuses to Coax Executives to Change Loyalties," *Wall Street Journal,* 15 June 1990, p. B1.

3. "Big Mac in China," *Wall Street Journal,* 10 September 1990, p. A12.

4. "Only Effervescent Personalities Need Apply," *Business Week,* 10 July 1989, p. 36.

5. R. Koenig, "Toyota Takes Pains, and Time, Filling Jobs at Its Kentucky Plant," *Wall Street Journal,* 1 December 1987, p. 1.

6. D. C. Feldman, *Managing Careers in Organizations* (Glenview, Ill: Scott, Foresman, 1988), pp. 53–55.

7. G. Fuchsberg, "Prominent Psychologists Group Gives Qualified Support to Integrity Tests," *Wall Street Journal,* 7 March 1991, p. B8.

8. G. Fuchsberg, "More Employers Check Credit Histories of Job Seekers to Judge Their Character," *Wall Street Journal,* 30 May 1990, p. B1.

9. William H. Whyte, Jr. *The Organization Man* (New York, N.Y.: Simon & Shuster, © 1956, 1984).

10. For instance, see D. Stipp, "Genetic Testing May Mark Some People As Undesirable to Employers, Insurers," *Wall Street Journal,* 9 July 1990, p. B1.

11. C. H. Deutsch, "Keeping the Talented People," *New York Times,* 12 August 1990, p. F25.

12. G. Fuchsberg, "Well, at Least 'Terminated with Extreme Prejudice' Wasn't Cited," *Wall Street Journal,* 7 December 1990, p. B1.

13. For a discussion of the McJobs program, which McDonald's uses to train handicapped individuals to work in its restaurants, see J. J. Laabs, "The Golden Arches Provide Golden Opportunities," *Personnel Journal,* July 1991, pp. 52–56.

14. H. Shore, "Employee Assistance Programs — Reaping the Benefits," *Sloan Management Review,* Spring 1984, pp. 69–73; D. Reed, "One Approach to Employee Assistance," *Personnel Journal,* August 1983, pp. 648–652.

15. J. J. Koch, "Wells Fargo's and IBM's HIV Policies Help Protect Employees' Rights," *Personnel Journal,* April 1990, pp. 40–48.

16. This section is based on B. Geber, "Simulating Reality," *Training,* April 1990, pp. 41–46.

17. "Bonus Plans for Non-Executives Face Revisions, But They Remain Popular," *Wall Street Journal,* 19 February 1991, p. A1.

18. J. E. Rigdon, "More Firms Try to Reward Good Service, But Incentives May Backfire in Long Run," *Wall Street Journal,* 5 December 1990, p. B1.

19. Ibid.

20. "All Pulling Together, to Get the Carrot," *Wall Street Journal,* 30 April 1990, p. B1.

21. J. Greenwald, "Workers: Risks and Rewards," *Time,* 15 April 1991, pp. 42–43.

22. R. Koenig, "Du Pont Plan Linking Pay to Fibers Profit Unravels," *Wall Street Journal,* 25 October 1991, p. B1.

CHAPTER 10

1. M. Robichaux, "Major League Baseball Players, Owners Reach Accord, But the Damage Remains," *Wall Street Journal,* 20 March 1990, p. A6.

2. M. Cimini, "Collective Bargaining in 1990: Search for Solutions Continues," *Monthly Labor Review,* January 1991, pp. 19–33.

3. C. Hukill, "Labor and the Supreme Court: Significant Issues of 1990–91," *Monthly Labor Review,* January 1991, p. 35.

4. Cimini (note 2), p. 19.

5. Labor Letter, *Wall Street Journal,* 29 January 1991, p. A1.

6. F. Schwadel, "Nordstrom Workers Reject Their Union in Voting at Five Seattle-Area Stores," *Wall Street Journal,* 22 July 1991, p. B3.

7. A. Bauman, "Wages and Compensation: 1990 Negotiated Adjustments," *Monthly Labor Review,* May 1991, pp. 14–22.

8. For a discussion of various sorts of union concessions, see L. A. Bell, "Union Concessions in the 1980s," *FRBNY Quarterly Review,* Summer 1989, pp. 44–58.

9. G. A. Patterson, "GM Gains Accord with Auto Workers for Expanded Work Schedule at Plant," *Wall Street Journal,* 3 July 1991, p. 3.

10. M. K. Hackey, "Injuries and Illnesses In the Workplace," *Monthly Labor Review,* May 1991, pp. 34–35.

11. R. Willis, "Can American Unions Transform Themselves?" *Management Review,* February 1988, p. 18.

12. K. Sheets, "Products Under Fire," *U.S. News & World Report,* 16 April 1990, p. 44.

13. P. Jarley and C. L. Maranto, "Union Corporate Campaigns: An Assessment," *Industrial and Labor Relations Review,* July 1990, pp. 505–525.

14. "Loading of Grain Resumes as Lockout Ends in Vancouver," *Wall Street Journal,* 17 June 1991, p. C8.

15. D. P. Brenskelle, "Employers Win the Right to Hire Temporary Workers After a Lockout," *Employee Relations Law Journal,* Winter 1986/1987, pp. 505–509.

16. A. Bernstein, "Busting Unions Can Backfire on the Bottom Line," *Business Week,* 18 March 1991, p. 108.

17. E. S. Browning, "Japan's Firms Have a Friend: The Unions," *Wall Street Journal,* 28 April 1986, p. 24.

18. A. Bernstein, (note 16), p. 108.

19. R. Laver, "Joining Hands," *Maclean's,* 15 April 1991, pp. 46–47.

20. G. A. Patterson, "Hourly Auto Workers Now on Layoff Have a Sturdy Safety Net," *Wall Street Journal,* 29 January 1991, pp. A1, A6.

21. For instance, see G. Jacobson, "Employee Relations at Xerox: A Model Worth Copying," *Management Review,* February 1988, pp. 22–23, 27.

22. For a discussion of the successful 1989 employee buyout of Lloyd's Lumber Company—now Your Building Centers, Inc.— see S. Burzawa, "Employee Buyout Averts Outside Sale," *Employee Benefit Plan Review,* July 1991, pp. 30–37.

23. C. Farrell, "Suddenly, Blue Chips Are Red-Hot for ESOPs," *Business Week,* 20 March 1989, p. 144.

CHAPTER 11

1. B. Wysocki, Jr., "Meeting Mr. Big Face," *Wall Street Journal,* 14 November 1988, p. B10.

2. T. D. Schellhardt and C. Hymowitz, "U.S. Manufacturers Gird for Competition," *Wall Street Journal,* 2 May 1989, pp. A2, A8. These rather depressing figures notwithstanding, American firms still are world leaders in many areas, from aircraft to flutes to biotechnological drugs to crystal. For instance, see C. Knowlton, "What America Makes Best," *Fortune,* 28 March 1988, pp. 40–53.

3. *Statistical Abstract of the United States,* 109th ed., 1989 (Washington, D.C.: U.S. Department of Commerce, Bureau of the Census), p. 831; and "Productivity: Why It's the No. 1 Underachiever," *Business Week,* 20 April 1987, pp. 54–69. In the non-manufacturing sector, including services, mining, and construction, productivity grew only 0.2 percent annually, and actually declined from 1988 to 1990. On this issue, see R. Henkoff, "Make Your Office More Productive," *Fortune,* 25 February 1991, pp. 72–84.

4. W. Skinner, "The Productivity Paradox," *Harvard Business Review,* July–August 1986, pp. 55–59; and "How the New Productivity Adds Up," *Business Week* 6 June 1988, pp. 103–122.

5. See, for instance, J. B. Dilworth, *Production and Operations Management: Manufacturing and Nonmanufacturing,* 4th ed. (New York: Random House, 1989), p. 6.

6. L. J. Krajewski and L. R. Ritzman, *Operations Management: Strategy and Analysis,* 2nd (Reading, Mass.: Addison-Wesley, 1990), p. 4.

7. S. E. Barndt and D. W. Carvey, *Essentials of Operations Management* (Englewood Cliffs, N.J.: Prentice-Hall, 1982), pp. 45–46. Some of the material in this section is based on R. B. Chase and N. J. Aquilano, *Production and Operations Management: A Life Cycle Approach,* 5th ed. (Homewood, Ill.: Irwin, 1989), p. 359.

8. For a discussion of JIT and related topics, see R. J. Schonberger and E. M. Knod, Jr., *Operations Management: Improving Customer Service,* 4th ed. (Homewood, Il.: Irwin, 1991), pp. 356–420.

9. T. F. O'Boyle, "Firms' Newfound Skill in Managing Inventory May Soften Downturn," *Wall Street Journal,* 19 November 1990, p. A1.

10. See D. Milbank, "Making Honda Parts, U.S. Company Finds, Can Be Road to Ruin," *Wall Street Journal,* 5 October 1990, p. A1.

11. This is based on L. J. Krajewski and L. P. Ritzman, *Operations Management: Strategy and Analysis,* 2nd ed. (Reading, Mass.: Addison-Wesley, 1990), p. 548.

12. D. A. Garvin, "Quality on the Line," *Harvard Business Review,* September–October 1983, pp. 64–75; and M. R. Smith, *Qualitysense: Organizational Approaches to Improving Product Quality and Service* (New York: AMACOM, 1979).

13. See A. Taylor III, "Why Toyota Keeps Getting Better and Better and Better," *Fortune* 19 November 1990, pp. 66–72, 74, 76, 79.

14. G. Fuchsberg, "Gurus of Quality Are Gaining Clout," *Wall Street Journal,* 27 November 1990, p. B1.

15. For a recent review, see E. E. Adams, Jr., "Quality Circle Performance," *Journal of Management,* 1991, pp. 25–39.

16. M. L. Marks, P. H. Mirvis, and J. F. Grady, Jr., "Employee Involvement in a Quality Circle Program: Impact on Quality of Work Life, Productivity, and Absenteeism," *Journal of Applied Psychology,* 1986, pp. 61–69; A. Rafaeli, "Quality Circles and Employee Attitudes," *Personnel Psychology,* 1985, pp. 603–615; and T. L.-P. Tang, P. S. Tollison, and H. D. Whiteside,

"Quality Circle Productivity as Related to Upper-Management Attendance, Circle Initiation, and Collar Color," *Journal of Management,* 1989, pp. 101–113.

17. For instance, see R. W. Griffin, "Consequences of Quality Circles in an Industrial Setting: A Longitudinal Assessment," *Academy of Management Journal,* 1988, pp. 338–358.

18. See S. Maital, "Why Not Software Factories?" *Across the Board,* October 1990, pp. 5–6.

19. O. L. Crocker and S. Miller, "The Effects of Robotics on the Workplace," *Personnel,* September 1988, pp. 26–31, 34, 36.

20. G. L. Miles, "It's a Dirty Job, But Something's Gotta Do It," *Business Week,* 20 August 1990, pp. 92–93, 97.

21. Crocker and Miller, pp. 28–29.

22. *New York Times* (October 14, 1981), p. D1.

23. Unimates were produced by Westinghouse Electric Corp. Unfortunately, this field is another example of American firms' loss of market share. In 1983, Westinghouse, United Technologies Corp., International Business Machine Corp., and Cincinnati Milacron Inc. were actively jumping into the robot market. By late 1990, all these U.S. firms had abandoned the business to the Japanese. See A. K. Naj, "How U.S. Robots Lost the Market to Japan in Factory Automation," *Wall Street Journal,* 6 November 1990, p. A1.

24. See J. A. Mark, "Technological Change and Employment: Some Results from BLS Research," *Monthly Labor Review,* April 1987, pp. 26–29; and L.-A. Lefebvre and E. Lefebvre, "The Impact of Information Technology on Employment and Productivity: A Survey," *National Productivity Review,* Summer 1988, pp. 219–228.

25. See S. Deutsch, "Successful Worker Training Programs Help Ease Impact of Technology," *Monthly Labor Review,* November 1987, pp. 14–20.

26. This discussion is based on O. Port, "The Best-Engineered Part Is No Part at All," *Business Week,* 8 May 1989, p. 150.

27. "Business Bulletin" column, *Wall Street Journal,* 1 September 1988, p. A1.

28. "Smart Factories: America's Turn?" *Business Week,* 8 May 1989, pp. 142–145, 148, 150.

CHAPTER 12

1. R. H. Beeby, "How to Crunch a Bunch of Figures," *Wall Street Journal,* 11 June 1990, p. A10.

2. K. K. Wiegner and J. Schlax, "But Can She Act?" *Forbes,* 10 December 1990, pp. 274–278.

3. *Business Week,* 22 August 1983, p. 98.

4. M. U. Porat, "The Information Economy" (unpublished thesis, Stanford University). As reported in *Wall Street Journal,* 23 February 1981, p. 1.

5. D. R. Vincent, "Information Technology—Should You Curtail Your Investment?" *Financial Executive,* May/June 1990, pp. 50–55.

6. H. Mintzberg, "The Manager's Job: Folklore and Fact," *Harvard Business Review,* July/August 1975, pp. 49–61.

7. T. R. Welter, "Software at the Hands of Executives," *Industry Week,* June 4, 1990, pp. 30–37.

8. D. Freedman, "The Company That Innovation Built," *CIO,* August 1990, pp. 22–33.

9. This section is based on J. G. Burch and G. Grudnitski, *Information Systems: Theory and Practice,* 5th ed. (New York: John Wiley, 1989); R. G. Murdick and J. E. Ross, *Introduction to Management Information Systems* (Englewood Cliffs, N.J., 1977); and J. L. Whitten, L. D. Bentley, and V. M. Barlow, *Systems Analysis and Design Methods,* 2nd ed. (Homewood, Ill.: Irwin, 1989).

10. "Thinking Machines Retakes Title for Fastest Computer," *Wall Street Journal,* 5 June 1991, p. B3; and J. R. Wilke, "Parallel

Processing Computers Attract Crowd of Investors Despite Limited Uses," *Wall Street Journal,* 5 October 1990, p. B1.

11. For instance, see S. E. Arnold, "Storage Technology: A Review of Options and Their Implications for Electronic Publishing," *Online,* July 1991, pp. 39–51; and D. Iles, "CD-ROM Enters Mainstream IS," *Computerworld,* June 5, 1989, pp. 75–79.

12. For a fuller discussion of computer software, see J. O. Hicks, Jr., *Information Systems in Business: An Introduction,* 2nd ed. (St. Paul, Minn.: West, 1990). For a discussion of new software languages that make programming easier, see L. Hooper, "Easy Writer," *Wall Street Journal,* 20 May 1991, pp. R33, R35.

13. For a discussion of application programs, see R. Schultheis and M. Sumner, *Management Information Systems: The Manager's View* (Homewood, Ill.: Irwin, 1989), pp. 160–174.

14. See S. Kolodziej, "The Success of C," *Computerworld,* 2 December 1987, pp. 39–42.

15. *Electronic Market Data Book* (Washington, D.C.: Electronic Industries Association, 1990), p. 51.

16. See E. Schwartz, "Adventures in the On-Line Universe," *Business Week,* 17 June 1991, pp. 112–113.

17. For an interesting discussion of how electronic bulletin boards can be used as informal channels of communication in organizations, see P. B. Carroll, "Computers Indicate Mood at Big Blue Is Practically Indigo," *Wall Street Journal,* 7 August 1991, pp. A1, A4.

18. D. Kneale, "Computer Caution: Linking of Office PCs Is Coming, But Plenty of Obstacles Remain," *Wall Street Journal,* 28 January 1986, pp. 1, 20.

19. For more on computer graphics, see K. K. Wiegner and J. Schlax, "But Can She Act?" *Forbes,* 10 December 1990, pp. 274–278; and R. D. Hof, "Is Silicon Graphics Busting Out of Its Niche?" *Business Week,* 22 April 1991, p. 100.

20. J. Main, "New Ways to Teach Workers What's New," *Fortune,* 1 October 1984, pp. 85–86, 90, 92, 94.

21. M. Fritz, "Chase Lets Computers Do the Teaching," *Computer World,* 15 April 1991, p. 76.

22. J. Main, "Work Won't Be the Same Again," *Fortune,* 28 June 1982, pp. 58–65.

23. Press release, cited in G. B. Davis and M. H. Olson, *Management Information Systems: Conceptual Foundations, Structure, and Development,* 2nd ed. (New York: McGraw-Hill, 1985), pp. 149–150.

24. ARCO's $20 Million Talk Network," *Business Week,* 7 July 1980, p. 81.

25. W. M. Bulkeley, "The Fast Track: Computers Help Firms Decide Whom to Promote," *Wall Street Journal,* 18 September 1985, p. 25.

26. *Electronic Market Data Book,* (Washington, D.C.: Electronics Industries Association, 1990), p. 64.

27. J. Levine, "The Ultimate Sell," *Forbes,* 13 May 1991, pp. 108, 110.

28. For more on computerization of securities markets, see W. E. Sheeline, "Who Needs the Stock Exchange?" *Fortune,* 19 November 1990, pp. 119–124; and, G. Weiss, "After-Hours Trading: A Very Small Step by the Big Board," *Business Week,* 3 June 1991, p. 32.

29. E.I. Schwartz, "Financial Planner of the Masses," *Business Week,* 20 May 1991, p. 141.

30. H. Eglowstein, "Can a Grammar and Style Checker Improve Your Writing?" *Byte,* August 1991, pp. 238–242.

31. D. E. Blumenfeld, L. D. Burns, C. F. Daganzo, M. C. Frick, and R. W. Hall, "Reducing Logistics Costs at General Motors," *Interfaces,* January–February 1987, pp. 26–47.

32. W. J. Broad, "'Smart' Machines Ready to Assume Many NASA Duties," *New York Times,* 9 March 1989, pp. 1, 11.

33. *Business Week,* 9 July 1984, pp. 54–55. See also L. Yamasaki and G. H. Manoochchri, "The Commercial Application of Expert Systems," *SAM Advanced Management Review,* Winter 1991, pp. 42–45, 49.

34. For an interesting example, see F. Rose, "An 'Electronic Clone' of a Skilled Engineer Is Very Hard to Create," *Wall Street Journal,* 12 August 1988, pp. 1, 14.

35. S. Diehl, S. Wszola, B. Kliewer, and L. Stevens, "Rx for Safer Data," *Byte,* August 1991, pp. 218–224, 226, 228.

36. "How Computer Science Was Caught Off Guard by One Young Hacker," *Wall Street Journal,* 7 November 1988, pp. A1, A4. See also D. Stipp and B. Davis, "New Computer Break-Ins Suggest 'Virus' May Have Spurred Hackers," *Wall Street Journal,* 2 December 1988, p. B4.

37. M. Lewyn, "Does Someone Have Your Company's Number?" *Business Week,* 4 February 1991, p. 90.

38. S. Diehl, S. Wszola, B. Kliewer, and L. Stevens, "Rx for Safer Data," *Byte,* August 1991, pp. 218–224, 226, 228.

39. M. Lewyn and E. I. Schwartz, "Why 'The Legion of Doom' Has Little Fear of the Feds," *Business Week,* 15 April 1991, p. 31.

40. "How Personal Computers Can Trip Up Executives," *Business Week,* 24 September 1984, p. 94.

41. P. B. Carroll, "Computer Confusion," *Wall Street Journal,* 4 June 1990, pp. R28–R29.

42. E. Larson, "Crook's Tool: Computers Turn Out to Be Valuable Aid in Employee Crime," *Wall Street Journal,* 14 January 1985, pp. 1, 10.

CHAPTER 13

1. "How British Airways Butters Up the Passengers," *Business Week,* 12 March 1990, p. 94.

2. P. Sellers, "Getting Customers to Love You," *Fortune,* 13 March 1989, p. 39.

3. F. Linden, "Per Capitalism," *Across the Board,* June 1980, p. 67.

4. P. Sellers, "The ABC's of Marketing to Kids," *Fortune,* 8 May 1989, p. 115.

5. *American Demographics,* August 1986.

6. P. Kotler, *Marketing Management, 6th ed. (Englewood Cliffs, N.J.: Prentice-Hall, 1988), pp. 288–289.*

7. D. Farney, "Inside Hallmark's Love Machine," *Wall Street Journal,* 14 February 1990, p. B-1.

8. W. H. Cunningham, I. C. M. Cunningham, and C. M. Swift, *Marketing: A Managerial Approach, 2nd ed. (Cincinnati, Ohio: South-Western Publishing Company, 1987), pp. 67–92.*

9. J. Flint, "The New Number Three," *Forbes,* 11 June 1990, p. 136.

10. F. M. Bass, E. A. Pessemier, and D. R. Lohmann, "An Experimental Study of Relationships Between Attitudes, Brand Preferences and Choice," *Behavioral Science,* November 1972, pp. 532–541.

11. *Report of the Definitions Committee of the American Marketing Association* (Chicago: American Marketing Association, 1961).

12. "King Customer," *Business Week,* 12 March 1990, p. 90.

CHAPTER 14

1. J. Lawrence, "Mobil," *Advertising Age,* 29 January 1991, pp. 12–13.

2. *Statistical Abstract of the United States* (Washington, D.C.: U.S. Department of Commerce, Bureau of the Census, 1990), pp. 12, 45, 521.

3. E. J. McCarthy and W. D. Perreault, *Basic Marketing,* 10th ed. (Homewood, Ill.: Irwin, 1990), pp. 228–233.

4. B. A. Stertz, "Off-Road Vehicles Do Delicate Duty with Quiche Set," *Wall Street Journal,* 5 March 1990, p. A-1.

5. *Wall Street Journal,* 5 March 1990, p. B-3.

6. R. Mitchell, "Masters of Innovation," *Business Week,* 10 April 1989, p. 58.

7. J. H. Davidson, "Why Most New Consumer Brands Fail," *Harvard Business Review,* March/April 1976, pp. 119–120.

8. B. Dumaine, "How Managers Can Succeed Through Speed," *Fortune,* 13 February 1989, pp. 54–56.
9. W. Zellner, "Two Days in Boot Camp—Learning to Love Lexus," *Business Week,* 4 September 1989, pp. 87.
10. Brand-Stretching Can Be Fun—and Dangerous," *The Economist,* 5 May 1990, p. 77.
11. R. F. Hartley, *Marketing Mistakes,* 2nd ed., (Columbus, Ohio: Grid Publishing Co., 1981), pp. 118–119.

CHAPTER 15

1. J. S. Hirsch, "Brash Phar-Mor Chain Has Uneven Selection, But It's Always Cheap," *Wall Street Journal,* 24 June 1991, pp. A1, A7.
2. R. D. Buzzell, "Is Vertical Marketing Profitable?" *Harvard Business Review,* January–February 1983, pp. 92–102.
3. D. J. Bowersox and E. J. McCarthy, "Strategic Development of Planned Vertical Marketing Systems." In L. B. Bucklin (Ed.), *Vertical Marketing Systems* (Glenview, Ill.: Scott, Foresman, 1970), p. 59.
4. U.S. Bureau of the Census, *1987 Statistical Abstract,* pp. 768 and 779, and *1990 Statistical Abstract,* p. 778.
5. D. Machalaha, "Push for Long Trucks Hits Bumpy Road," *Wall Street Journal,* 5 May 1990, p. B-1.

CHAPTER 16

1. D. W. Twedt, "Does the '9 Fixation' in Retail Pricing Really Promote Sales?" *Journal of Marketing,* October 1985, pp. 54–55.
2. J. B. White, "Even Detroit Concedes Sticker Shock," *Wall Street Journal,* 8 August 1991, p. B1.

CHAPTER 17

1. P. Kotler, *Marketing Management,* 7th ed. (Englewood Cliffs, N.J.: Prentice-Hall, 1991), p. 567.
2. D. Kneale, "Zapping TV Ads Appears Pervasive," *Wall Street Journal,* 25 April 1988, p. 3.
3. T. Russell and W. Lane, *Otto Kleppner's Advertising Procedure,* 11th ed. (Englewood CLiffs, N.J.: Prentice-Hall, 1990), pp. 54–58.
4. D. W. Nylen, *Advertising Planning, Implementation and Control* (Cincinnati, Ohio: South-Western Publishing Company, 1986), pp. 47–48.
5. M. J. McCarthy, "MagiCan'ts: How Coca-Cola Stumbled," *Wall Street Journal,* 5 May 1990, p. B1.

CHAPTER 18

1. J. G. Helmkamp, L. F. Indieke, and R. E. Smith, *Principles of Accounting,* 2nd ed. (New York: John Wiley & Sons, 1986). p. 457.
2. Possible sources of industry averages are *Standard and Poor's Industry Surveys* and *Robert Morris and Associates Industry Data.*

CHAPTER 19

1. Actually, the requirement is 3 percent on the first $40 million in deposits and 12 percent on all amounts over $40 million. We assume the banks in this example are in the commonly used 12 percent category.
2. R. D. Block, "The Failure of S&L Deregulation," Rice University manuscript, 1991, p. 4.
3. The Federal Open Market Committee (FOMC) consists of the seven members of the Board of Governors of the Federal Reserve System plus five presidents of Federal Reserve Banks (who rotate).

CHAPTER 20

1. "Private Fiefdom? McGraw-Hill Stockholders Are Getting a Raw Deal," *Barron's,* 5 February 1979, p.5.

CHAPTER 22

1. M. R. Greene, J. S. Trieschmann, and S. G. Gustavson, *Risk & Insurance,* 8th ed. (Cincinnati: South-Western Publishing Co., 1992), p. 4.
2. E. J. Vaughan, *Fundamentals of Risk and Insurance,* 4th ed. (New York: Wiley, 1986), pp. 7–8.
3. *Life Insurance Fact Book* (Washington, D.C.: American Council of Life Insurance, 1990), p. 122.
4. G. E. Rejda, *Principles of Insurance,* 3rd ed. (Glenview, Ill.: Scott Foresman, 1989), pp. 102–103.
5. Greene, Trieschmann, and Gustavson (note 1), p. 334.
6. For additional information, see Greene, Trieschmann, and Gustavson (note 1), pp. 299–332.
7. K. W. Clarkson, R. L. Miller, G. A. Jentz, and F. Cross, *West's Business Law* (St. Paul, Minn.: West Publishing Co., 1992), pp. 458–459.
8. J. R. Marks, *Sharing the Risk* (New York: Insurance Information Institute, 1981), pp 13–14.
9. *Panther Oil & Grease Mfg. Co. v. Segerstrom,* 224 F.2d 216.
10. *White v. Louis Creative Hair Dressers, Inc.,* 10 CCH Neg. 2d 526.
11. Rejda (note 4), p. 509.
12. Marks (note 8), pp. 66–67.
13. Rejda (note 4), pp. 506–507.
14. "The 50 Largest Life Insurance Companies," *Fortune,* 3 June 1991, pp. 272–273.

CHAPTER 23

1. This vignette is based on information from M. Charlier, "U.S. Brewers' Foreign Growth Proves Tricky," *Wall Street Journal,* 9 September 1991, p. B1.
2. D. A. Ball and W. H. McCulloch, Jr., *International Business, Introduction and Essentials,* 4th ed. (Homewood, Ill.: BPI Irwin, 1990), pp. 85, 585.
3. Ibid., pp. 85–86.
4. G. C. Hufbauer, D. T. Berliner, and K. A. Elliott, *Trade Protection in the United States: 31 Case Studies* (London: Institute for International Economics, 1986).
5. M. R. Czinkota and I. A. Ronkainen, *International Marketing,* 2nd ed. (Chicago: Dryden Press, 1990), p. 142.
6. A. C. Shapiro, *Multinational Financial Management,* 3rd ed. (Boston: Allyn and Bacon, 1989), p. 628.
7. Czinkota, and Ronkainen (note 5), pp. 282–284.
8. M. R. Czinkota, P. Rivoli, and I. A. Ronkainen *International Business* (Chicago: Dryden Press, 1989), pp. 276–278.
9. J. K. Galbraith, "The Defense of the Multinational Company," *Harvard Business Review,* March/April 1978, pp. 82–93.
10. Czinkota, Rivoli, and Ronkainen (note 8), p. 348.
11. L. Therrien, "The Rival Japan Respects," *Business Week,* 13 November 1989, p. 109.

CHAPTER 24

1. J. E. Bishop, "Tobacco Plants Become Assembly Lines For Scientists Producing New Chemicals," *Wall Street Journal,* 14 May 1991, pp. B1, B6.

2. D. Stipp, " 'Wind Farms' May Energize the Midwest," *Wall Street Journal,* 6 September 1991, p. B1.

3. C. Forman, "Another Coup Casualty: All Three Moscow Stocks Sink," *Wall Street Journal,* 9 September 1991, p. C1.

4. Laurence Hooper, "IBM Scientists Create a Switch with One Atom," *Wall Street Journal,* 15 August 1991, p. B1.

5. "Angels Dancing on a Pinhead," *The Economist,* 2 February 1991, p. 82. See also Amal K. Naj, "Researchers Isolate Bacteria Protein That Can Store Data in 3 Dimensions," *Wall Street Journal,* 4 September 1991, p. B4.

6. G. Stix, "Golden Screws," *Scientific American,* September 1991, pp. 167–169.

7. G. Fuchsberg, "Many Businesses Responding Too Slowly to Rapid Work Force Shifts, Study Says," *Wall Street Journal,* 20 July 1990, pp. B1, B4.

8. These are drawn from Christopher Cerf and Victor Navasky, *The Experts Speak, The Definitive Compendium of Authoritative Misinformation* (New York: Pantheon Books, 1984).

9. U.S. Bureau of the Census, *Statistical Abstract of the United States: 1991,* 11th ed. (Washington, D.C., 1991); and "Retirees Pose Burden for Economy," *Wall Street Journal,* 16 September 1991; p. A1.

10. "Snapshots of the Nation," *Wall Street Journal,* 9 March 1990, p. R13.

11. F. Linden, "Latin Beat," *Across the Board,* June 1991, pp. 9–10.

12. A. Swasy, "Changing Times: Marketers Scramble to Keep Pace with Demographic Shifts," *Wall Street Journal,* 22 March 1991, p. B6.

13. W. M. Bulkeley, "Lotus Creates Controversy by Extending Benefits to Partners of Gay Employees," *Wall Street Journal,* 25 October 1991, pp. B1, B10.

14. M. Chase, "Technology & Health: New Cases of AIDS in U.S. and Europe to Taper Off in '95, Says Health Group," *Wall Street Journal,* 18 June 1991, p. B4.

15. M. Schroeder, "Low Demand, Flat-Rolled Profits," *Business Week,* 14 January 1991, p. 76.

16. J. M. Snyder, "Introduction," in Nicholai D. Kondratieff, *The Long Wave Cycle,* translated by Guy Daniels (New York: Richardson and Snyder, 1984; originally published in 1926).

17. O. M. Amos, Jr. and Kevin M. Currier, "The Foundations of a Hierarchial Theory of the Long-Wave Phenomenon," *Southern Economic Journal,* July 1989, pp. 142–156.

18. W. M. Bulkeley, "Sophistication, Popularity Gain for Palmtops," *Wall Street Journal,* 16 September 1991, pp. B1, B3.

19. G. P. Zachary, "For People Always on the Run, 'Pen Computers' Come of Age," *Wall Street Journal,* 17 October 1991, pp. B1, B6.

20. "It's a Dirty Job, But Something's Gotta Do It," *Business Week,* 20 August 1990, pp. 92–93, 97.

21. "The Lonely and the Brave," *The Economist,* 26 January 1991, p. 62; and A. Zipser, "Foot in the Door: Robots Are Just Starting to Realize Their Promise," *Barron's,* 8 October 1990, pp. 18, 19, 67.

22. See "Buckyballs: Fullerenes Open New Vistas in Chemistry," *Scientific American,* January 1991, pp. 114–116; David Stipp, "Higher-Temperature Superconducting by Buckyballs Is Indicated in Tests," *Wall Street Journal,* 24 May 1991, p. B2; and "Roll Out the Buckyballs!" *National Geographic,* November 1991, p. 2.

23. *Wall Street Journal,* 19 August 1983, p. 1.

24. J. E. Rigdon, "More Companies Send Staffs on Retreats to Spur Creativity and Jolt Thinking," *Wall Street Journal,* 16 October 1991, pp. B1, B8.

25. T. F. O'Boyle, "From Pyramid to Pancake," *Wall Street Journal,* 4 June 1990, pp. R37–R38.

CHAPTER 25

1. E. Ginzberg, J. W. Ginzberg, S. Axelrod, and J. L. Herma, *Occupational Choice* (New York: Columbia University Press, 1951), pp. 60–72.

2. D. C. Miller and W. H. Form, *Industrial Sociology* (New York: Harper and Row, 1964), pp. 541–545. For a more recent discussion of career stages, see R. J. Aldag and T. M. Stearns, *Management,* 2nd ed. (Cincinnati: South-Western Publishing Co., 1991), pp. 337–345.

3. E. E. Jennings, *Routes to the Executive Suite* (New York: McGraw-Hill, 1971), pp. 304–318.

4. H. Z. Levine, "Career Planning," *Personnel,* vol. 62, no. 3 (March 1985): pp. 67–72.

5. D. B. Mlller, "Career Planning and Management in Organizations," *S.A.M. Advanced Management Journal,* Spring 1978, p. 36.

GLOSSARY

A

ability tests tests measuring whether the applicant has certain skills required to perform the job tasks.

absolute advantage a country's ability to produce a product more cheaply than another country can.

acceptance an expression of willingness to be legally bound by the terms of an offer.

accessories industrial products, including tools or equipment, that have a fairly short life and are used in the production of a firm's products or in its offices.

accidental loss a principle of insurance: only losses that may or may not happen—that are accidental—are insurable.

accounting equation
Assets = Liabilities + Owners' Equity.

accounts payable purchases for which the firm has not yet paid.

accounts receivable the amount owed to the firm as a result of credit sales.

accrual method of accounting the method normally used for financial statements, in which revenues and expenses are recognized when they occur rather than when cash changes hands.

accrued expenses money owed for services, to be paid after their performance.

accumulated depreciation the sum of all depreciation to date.

acid-test or quick ratio a measure of whether a firm can pay its short-term debts from liquid assets, calculated as cash plus marketable securities plus accounts receivable divided by current liabilities.

acquisition the purchase of one company by another.

actuaries people employed by insurance companies to develop statistics from historical data and predict future losses based on those statistics.

administered vertical marketing system a marketing system in which channel coordination is achieved through the leadership of a member firm, not through ownership of the entire channel.

administrative expenses overhead expenses incurred in the administration or general operations of the business.

administrative law rules and regulations issued by governmental boards, commissions, and agencies.

advertising agencies companies that develop advertising strategies and campaigns for other companies.

advertising spiral the three stages of the advertising campaign that are used as the product moves through the product life cycle; the pioneering, competitive, and retentive stages.

advertising any paid, nonpersonal presentation of ideas, goods, or services to the market.

advocacy advertising institutional advertising designed to present a firm's position on a public issue, to influence public opinion or educate the public.

affirmative action programs that give special consideration in hiring and promotion decisions to members of minority groups and, in some cases, women.

agency shop a specialized type of union shop, in which employees are not required to join a union but must pay union dues as a condition of employment.

agents intermediaries who are paid a fee for bringing buyer and seller together and assisting in the sale transaction without taking title to the merchandise.

agreement the basic element of a contract; composed of an offer and an acceptance.

allowance for bad debt a special account set up to reflect the amount of accounts receivable that may not be collectible in the future.

allowances partial refunds to customers for products that they return to the firm.

analytic transformation a production process in which a basic material is broken down into one or more final products.

antitrust law laws intended to regulate businesses or trusts.

appellate courts federal or state courts that hear cases from lower courts.

application blank a selection tool in which a form is completed by job applicants to provide the hiring firm with information about educational background, work experience, and outside interests.

application software programs that perform specific tasks for the computer user, such as balancing a budget or computing statistics.

arbitration a private procedure for dispute resolution, in which both parties agree to argue their case before a neutral third party and to accept this arbitrator's decision (Chapter 3); a process in which an arbitrator listens to the arguments of labor and management, weighs the merits of each argument, and then makes a binding judgment (Chapter 10).

arithmetic/logic unit the part of the CPU that performs the mathematical and logical operations on the data.

articles of partnership a legal agreement which defines the role of each partner in the operation of a business partnership and how much money each partner is expected to invest.

artificial intelligence (AI) computer programs that simulate human reasoning.

assessment center a center employing human resources

experts and a variety of selection procedures to systematically evaluate the qualifications of job candidates.

asset-backed security offering a large volume of accounts receivable sold as a package to the public in the form of a security.

assets property, equipment, supplies, and other resources used by a firm to conduct its regular business activities.

assignment sale of a patent by its holder to another person or organization.

auditor an accountant who verifies the records and transactions of the firm.

authorization card a card signed by a worker, which designates the union as the worker's bargaining agent.

autocratic leaders leaders who make decisions themselves, without inputs from their subordinates.

automatic teller machine (ATM) a machine that allows customers to make cash withdrawals, deposits, and transfers between accounts anytime by using an access card.

automobile insurance insurance that protects against injuries to people and damage to property from auto-

B

balance of trade a measure of the dollar volume of exports relative to the dollar volume of imports over a defined period.

balance sheet a financial "snapshot" of the business showing the balance of the firm's assets, liabilities, and owners' equity at one moment in time.

bankruptcy a condition in which a firm is forced out of business because it is unable to pay its debts.

bar coding patterns of bars and spaces printed on products or other materials to represent information; the bars and spaces are read by computers equipped with special scanning devices.

bargaining unit the group of employees whom the union represents if it receives the majority of votes.

BASIC a computer language that is easy to learn; used frequently by small computers.

basic industries heavy manufacturing industries, such as steel, automobile, airplane, chemical, machinery, rubber, and glass.

batch processing a type of data processing in which data are collected for some period of time and then processed all at the same time.

behavior modeling an off-the-job training approach in which supervisory trainees deal with actual employee problems and are given immediate feedback on their performance; trainees observe the behavior of a model supervisor and then imitate that behavior.

beneficiary person who receives benefits from a life insurance policy.

binary system a system that is composed of two digits, 0 and 1; machine language is based on this system.

biotechnology a field in which new products are developed through recombinant genetics, or gene splicing.

bits the two digits that compose the binary system.

blanket bond insurance that protects the business against losses caused by dishonesty of any of its employees.

board of directors a group of individuals elected by common stockholders to represent their interests, set corporate policy, and assume ultimate responsibility for management of the corporation.

bond a contract between the issuer and the buyer. The purchase price represents a loan to the issuing firm for which the firm pays the buyer interest.

bond indenture the terms of the lending agreement associated with a bond.

bonds payable an obligation on the books of the issuing firm to repay long-term bonds.

boycott a tactic by which union members and other people who agree with the union's goals refuse to purchase or handle a company's goods or services.

brainstorming a creativity enhancement technique in which individuals are encouraged to generate many free-wheeling ideas, building on the ideas of others and avoiding evaluation.

brand any name, symbol, or design that identifies a firm and its products.

brand advertisements *or* **product advertisements** advertising that promotes specific products to final consumers.

breach of contract the violation of one or more provisions of a contract by a party to the contract.

breach of warranty a violation that occurs when the seller's representation of a product's qualities or characteristics does not hold true.

break-even analysis an approach to cost pricing that shows how alternative prices affect the firm's profit on a product.

break-even point the volume of sales at which total revenue exactly equals total cost.

bribe a payment made "up front" to influence a transaction.

budget a detailed financial plan showing estimated revenues and expenses for a specified future period, usually one year.

budget deficit a situation in which total federal spending exceeds total tax receipts.

budget surplus a situation in which total tax receipts exceed total federal spending.

bureaucracy Max Weber's name for his view of an efficient, fair organization (also called the classical or mechanistic design).

burglary forced entry.

burnout a reaction to sustained stress, characterized by physical and emotional exhaustion, feelings of low personal accomplishment, and negative attitudes toward the job, others, and life in general.

business an organization that combines inputs of raw materials, capital, labor, and management skills, to produce useful outputs of goods and services, in order to earn a profit.

business ethics rules about how businesses and their employees ought to behave.

business-income insurance insurance that protects a business from losses incurred from not being able to sell a product because of some extraordinary event.

business plan a document that outlines the firm's future goals and objectives and indicates how they are to be achieved.

business tort any action by a business in which the effect is to improperly interfere with the rights of another business.

buying on margin a speculative practice in which an investor finances part of a stock purchase with borrowed money.

bytes strings of eight bits, which are used to represent characters on the computer keyboard.

C

C a popular computer language, noted for its portability between different computer systems.

cafeteria-style benefit plans benefit plans in which employees can choose from a wide range of alternative benefits, tailoring them to their particular situations.

call an option to buy shares of stock at some specified price during a certain period of time.

canned (packaged) programs computer programs that are already written and available for purchase.

capital the money it takes to start a business and to purchase production equipment and inventory.

capital budget a budget that estimates expenditures related to long-term asset acquisitions, such as machinery and equipment.

capital budgeting the process of managing the long-term asset decisions of the firm.

capital structure a firm's long-term financing mix, showing the breakdown between debt and equity financing.

career cluster a group of related jobs in which a person's skills and knowledge would probably be useful.

career objective a statement describing your area of interest, the type of organization for which you would like to work, and the level of position you want.

cash the most liquid of all business assets; includes checking account balances as well as currency and coin.

cash budget a budget used to forecast cash balances at the end of each month and for the entire year.

cash discount a discount offered when the buyer pays for the product within a certain period of time.

cash flow the actual funds that are moving in and out of the firm.

cash management program bank program for advising firms on managing their cash balances by establishing a system for tracking cash flow.

cash value the savings portion of a life insurance policy.

catalog showrooms large retail stores that feature a wide assortment of sample merchandise on display but make sales from stock stored in a central warehouse.

catastrophic hazard a principle of insurance: insurance companies must spread their risk so that no single disaster forces them to pay all their clients at once.

cease and desist order a ruling by the Federal Trade Commission requiring a company to stop an unfair business practice.

central processing unit (CPU) the part of the computer that processes and stores information.

ceremonies similar to rituals, but more elaborate productions that occur less frequently.

certificates of deposit (CDs) interest-bearing certificates, offered by financial institutions, that have a fixed maturity date and a penalty for early withdrawal.

certified public accountants (CPAs) licensed accountants who make their services available to the public.

channel of distribution the wholesalers and retailers that link the manufacturer with the consumer.

charisma from the Greek word meaning "divinely inspired gift;" charismatic leaders are seen by subordinates as being extraordinary, and they inspire subordinates to believe in a larger mission.

charter a certificate issued by the state, creating a corporation; contains such facts as scope of business, amount of capital, and number of directors.

check written authorization for the bank to withdraw the specified amount of money from the account and give it to the person or company to whom the check is written.

checkoff an automatic deduction of union dues from a worker's paycheck.

civil law law that defines the duties and responsibilities that exist between two or more individuals or between citizens and their governments, excluding criminal cases.

Civil Rights Act an act which prohibits discrimination in hiring, training, and promotion on the basis of race, color, sex, religion, or national origin.

classical *or* **mechanistic organizational design** a view of organizational design characterized by heavy reliance on rules and regulations, job simplification, adherence to the chain of command, and the objective of efficiency.

classical view the view that when businesses produce goods and offer services in the most efficient way possible, they are also unintentionally promoting the social interest.

Clayton Act an act which outlaws tying and exclusive agreements, prohibits companies from purchasing stock in competing companies if the effect would be to reduce competition, and prohibits persons from sitting on boards of directors of two or more competing companies that have sales exceeding $1 million.

closed shops organizations that require a prospective employee to join the union as a condition of employment, an illegal practice.

closed-end fund a type of mutual fund in which the membership (as represented by number of total shares) is restricted.

closing the sale the sales technique of concluding the presentation by asking the customer to purchase the product or service.

COBOL a computer language that processes data in a language something like English.

code of ethics a list of principles of appropriate behavior.

codetermination formal worker participation on the governing bodies of companies.

coercive power power based on one person's ability to affect the punishment that another receives.

coinsurance clause a clause in most fire insurance policies that requires the policyholder to purchase enough insurance to cover a specified percentage of the value of the property in order to obtain full reimbursement for loss in the event of a fire.

cold call a visit by a salesperson to a prospective customer with whom he or she has not previously done business.

collective bargaining the process by which representatives of labor and management negotiate an agreement covering pay scales and terms of work.

commercial paper unsecured short-term promissory notes issued by large corporations.

commercialization the sixth and final stage in the development of new products, in which the product is made available to the market.

commission compensation in proportion to the amount of sales generated.

commission broker the person on the floor of the exchange who walks over to the trading areas and fulfills the instructions of a stockbroker's customer.

common law unwritten law or case law made by judges in reaching decisions on cases brought before their courts.

common stock stock whose owners have last claim to corporate assets but have voting rights.

common stockholders stockholders who have last claim to corporate assets but have the right to elect the board of directors, vote on changes in the corporate charters, and vote on the appointment of an accountant to audit the firm's books.

community shopping center a shopping center that is likely to feature a drugstore or supermarket, a medium-sized department store, and several specialty stores.

comparative advantage a country's ability to produce some products more cheaply than other products.

competitive stage the second stage in the advertising spiral, which stresses the unique features of a product, especially the features most desired by buyers.

compiler a component inside the computer that translates symbolic language into machine language.

components industrial products that are expensive, processed items that become a physical part of the product the firm is producing.

computer a machine that carries out complex and repetitious operations at very high speeds.

computer virus a program that automatically copies itself, "infects" other programs, and then plays a trick or otherwise disrupts computer functioning.

computer-aided design (CAD) the use of computer graphics programs to design new products or processes.

computer-aided manufacturing (CAM) the use of computer programs to control production machinery.

congeneric acquisition a business combination in which one company buys another that is in a different industry but performs a related activity.

conglomerate acquisition a form of business combination in which one company buys another that is in a different industry and performs an unrelated activity.

consideration that which each party to a contract agrees to give up (Chapter 3); leader behaviors that show friendship, trust, respect, and warmth (Chapter 8).

consumer price index (CPI) a statistical system for measuring price changes in a group of goods and services that most consumers buy.

consumer products goods produced for sale to individuals and families for personal consumption.

consumer sovereignty the concept that consumers decide which goods and services are produced when they choose to buy or not to buy specific goods and services.

consumerism a social movement aiming to increase the power of consumers relative to that of sellers.

continuous manufacturing a mechanized manufacturing process that produces a flow of goods at a predetermined rate.

contract administration interpreting and following the union contract on a daily basis.

contract a legally enforce-able agreement between two or more parties that defines the responsibilities of each party in the performance of a specified action.

contractual capacity the ability to enter into a legally binding contract.

contractual vertical marketing system a marketing system in which independent organizations within the channel enter into a formal contract to coordinate their marketing efforts.

control chart a chart used for quality control, showing the average level and the upper and lower control limits of critical production parameters, such as number of defects per unit.

control unit the part of the CPU that directs the internal operations of the computer.

controlling the management function involving activities that ensure that actual performance is in line with intended performance.

convenience goods consumer goods that are purchased frequently, immediately, and with little shopping effort.

convenience stores small supermarkets that offer a limited selection in terms of brands and package sizes.

convertible term life insurance term life insurance that may be changed to a permanent type of life insurance.

Cooling-Off Rule a rule adopted by the Federal Trade Commission that permits anyone buying a product or service valued at $25 or more from a door-to-door salesperson to cancel the purchase within 72 hours and receive a full refund.

cooperative *or* **co-op** a business that is owned by its user members.

cooperative advertising advertising promotions in which costs are shared by the retailer and the manufacturer.

copyright law law which protects authors, artists, photographers, designers, and others from the unauthorized copying, duplication, or publication of their works.

corporate campaign a tactic in which a union attacks a company by pressuring people or organizations important to that company.

corporate vertical marketing system a marketing system in which all or most links in the system (manufacturer, wholesaler, retailers) are owned by one firm.

corporation a business owned by its stockholders; a corporation is a legal entity with many of the rights, duties, and powers of a person, but separate from the people who own and manage it.

corrective action action taken by management to get lagging production jobs back on schedule.

corrective advertising advertising which serves to correct previous misleading advertising and to tell the public the truth about the product.

cost of goods sold the amount of money spent by the seller to produce or buy the merchandise sold.

cost-of-living adjustment (COLA) the adjustment of wages during the life of the labor contract in relation to changes in the consumer price index.

cost pricing a philosophy of pricing in which production or purchase cost is the starting point in making pricing decisions.

coupon a piece of paper entitling its holder to a discount on a particular product.

credit union a member-owned, nonprofit financial institution.

criminal law law that regulates behavior against the state, as defined by local, state, and federal laws.

critical path the sequence of in-series activities requiring the longest time for completion.

culture a set of values, ideas, and attitudes that shape human behavior.

cumulative discounts discounts offered when total purchases over a period of time reach a certain amount.

cumulative preferred preferred stock that carries forward to the next year any dividends not paid in the previous year.

current assets cash and other liquid assets that the firm expects to use, sell, or turn into cash within one year.

current liabilities liabilities that must be paid within one year.

current ratio a measure of whether a firm can pay its short-term debts, calculated as current assets divided by current liabilities.

D

data processing manipulating data into some usable form.

debentures bonds not backed by specific collateral, but rather by the overall strength of the corporation.

debt to net worth ratio a measure of money owed to creditors relative to the equity value of the company, calculated as total liabilities divided by owners' equity (or net worth).

decision support system (DSS) a class of systems that helps managers consider alternatives in making decisions.

decisional roles roles managers perform as part of the company's decision-making system, including entrepreneur, disturbance handler, resource allocator, and negotiator.

decline stage the fourth and final period in the product life cycle, which is characterized by lessening demand for the product and few firms in the market.

decreasing term life insurance term life insurance in which the amount of protection decreases during the term of the contract.

deductible a specified amount that the policyholder must pay toward a loss before the insurance company pays anything.

deflation a general decline in the price level of goods and services.

demand the quantities of a good or service that consumers are willing and able to buy at various prices over a given time period.

demand curve a graph that shows the relationship between price and quantity demanded.

demand deposit a checking account at a commercial bank or other financial institution.

demand pricing a method of pricing in which price is determined by the level of demand for the product.

democratic leaders leaders who allow subordinates to participate in decision making.

demography the social science that studies characteristics of human populations.

demotion a move down in the organizational hierarchy, to a lower title, less responsibility, and lower salary.

department stores large retail stores, divided into a number of specialty units or departments, that sell a wide variety of mostly nonfood merchandise.

departmentalization breaking an organization into smaller units or departments to facilitate management.

Depository Institutions Deregulation and Monetary Control Act of 1980 a law that deregulated the banking industry by phasing out interest rate ceilings and allowing interest to be paid on checking accounts.

depreciation the gradual write-off of the value of a fixed asset over its useful life, rather than writing off the entire cost at time of purchase.

design for manufacturability (DFM) a design concept that uses computer programs to simplify product design and minimize the number of component parts in the product.

developing countries those countries, predominantly in Asia, Africa, and Latin America, whose per capita incomes and standards of living are far below those of other countries, but whose population growth rates are among the highest in the world.

devil's advocate an individual who is given the task of finding faults in a proposed action in order to induce necessary conflict.

differential pricing the practice of pricing products differently to match varying levels of demand in different market segments.

direct mail advertisements sent through the mail.

directing the management function of guiding employee actions toward achievement of the company's goals.

directors and officers (D&O) insurance insurance that protects the directors and officers of a corporation from being personally sued by stockholders who feel that the firm has been mismanaged.

disability-income insurance insurance that pays all or part of a person's salary when that person is unable to work because of illness, disease, or injury.

discount the difference between the list price and the selling price.

discount brokers stockbrokers who offer only a few services to customers but charge considerably lower fees for handling stock transactions than full-service brokers.

discount rate the interest rate charged when commercial banks borrow short-term money from their regional Federal Reserve Bank.

discount store a retail store that offers popular items at low prices by keeping operating costs down.

dispatching the preparing and issuing of work orders.

distribution channel an organized network of people and businesses through which goods and services flow from producers to end users.

diversification buying a variety of stocks or bonds in many different companies in different industries, to reduce risk.

dividends cash payments that the corporation makes to its stockholders, based on corporate earnings.

division of labor the breaking down of complex jobs into simpler, smaller tasks.

documentation the process of providing a permanent record of a computer program.

door-to-door selling retail efforts in which sales are made by visiting prospective customers in their homes.

double-entry bookkeeping a method of financial record keeping based on the accounting equation, showing two entries in the books for each transaction.

dual trading trading in the same security on the New York Stock Exchange and on regional exchanges.

duress a condition in which a person is forced to enter into an agreement.

E

earnings per share a measure of the money a firm makes per share of common stock, calculated as net income, divided by shares of common stock outstanding.

economic analysis the third stage in the development of new products, in which the likely profitability of the product is estimated.

economic communities groups of nations that form alliances to reap economic benefits from mutual cooperation.

Economic Order Quantity (EOQ) the least-cost reorder quantity.

economies of scale the economic principle that as more units of a product are produced, the average cost of producing each unit decreases.

economies of scope an objective of the factory of the future; computerized control allows automated machinery to produce a variety of goods cheaply.

ego drive a special kind of motivation, in which people feel a personal stake in completing each task successfully.

electronic bulletin boards message and information services that microcomputer users can access through a modem.

electronic cottage a home that is linked via telecommunications and computer technologies to large centralized databases and production centers.

electronic funds transfer (EFT) the movement of funds instantaneously between accounts by electronic means.

electronic mail software that enables users to send and receive written messages through their computers.

embargo a complete prohibition on the importation of a product.

empathy the ability to understand someone else's problems.

employee buyout a purchase in which the employees of the firm use their own assets, frequently their pension funds, to purchase a company from its stockholders or the parent company.

employee stock ownership plans (ESOPs) plans in which workers receive company stock as part of the menu of benefits.

entrepreneur a person who starts, organizes, manages, and assumes responsibility for a business or other enterprise.

Equal Employment Act an act which supplements the Civil Rights Act, making it illegal to discriminate in hiring, training, and promotion in local and state governments, as well as the federal government.

equity rights or claims against the assets of the firm; indicates how the assets have been financed.

ethics principles of morality or rules of conduct.

exclusive agreement an agreement in which, as a condition of sale, the seller forbids the buyer from purchasing for resale the products of competing sellers.

exclusive distribution a retailing approach whereby a product is made available through only a few stores in a geographic market.

expectancy theory a theory of motivation stating that employees will be motivated to engage in an act only if they feel they can accomplish the act and that accomplishment of the act will lead to desired outcomes.

expert power power based on one person's perception that another has needed knowledge, skills, or perspectives in a given area.

expert system a computer program that helps solve problems by applying decision rules and information provided by an expert in the field.

export a domestically produced good or service that is sold in another country.

express warranty any fact or promise made by the seller to the buyer concerning a product.

expropriation without reimbursement a takeover of the assets of a foreign firm by the host country's government without offering compensation.

extended coverage insurance that protects a building and its contents against windstorm, hail, explosion, smoke, civil strife, riot resulting from a strike, and damage from aircraft, automobiles, and trucks.

external expansion the process of growing in which a firm purchases or merges with another company.

extinction the disappearance of an unrewarded behavior.

extra-expense insurance insurance that protects against the high cost of keeping a business operating after a major accident has occurred.

extrinsic rewards rewards given to an employee by others, such as pay raises, promotions, and other symbols of recognition.

F

factoring accounts receivable selling accounts receivable to a financial institution.

factory of the future the computer-based integration of design, process, and control functions in the manufacturing environment.

factory outlet a discount store owned by a manufacturer and used to sell merchandise that has been discontinued, did not pass inspection, or is last year's model.

Fair Credit Reporting Act gives consumers the right to be notified of credit bureau reporting activities, to have access to the information in their credit reports, and to correct misleading or false information in their credit reports.

Fair Labor Standards Act an act which established the minimum wage, the 40-hour work week, and regulations affecting child labor.

family brand the same brand name used for most or all the firm's products.

Federal Deposit Insurance Corporation (FDIC) Federal agency that protects depositors against losses up to $100,000 in federally insured accounts at financial institutions.

Federal Reserve System (the Fed) a government agency that acts as the central bank for the U.S. and controls the money supply through reserve requirements, open market operations, and discount rates.

Federal Trade Commission Act an act which established the Federal Trade Commission to enforce the Clayton Act and gave the commission authority to define "unfair methods of competition" and to issue cease and desist orders.

fidelity bonds insurance that protects an employer from losses due to employee dishonesty.

final consumers individuals who purchase products, usually in small amounts, for their own use or for the use of a family member or friend.

financial accounting a type of accounting that is concerned with providing financial information to people outside the firm.

Financial Institutions Reform, Recovery and Enforcement Act of 1989 (FIRREA) the most important legislation passed to help solve the problems of the savings and loan industry.

financial management the acquisition and management of funds for a firm.

financial rewards monetary rewards given to an employee, such as pay and cash bonuses.

finished goods products that are ready for shipment or sale to a buyer.

fire insurance insurance that protects the insured building and its contents against financial loss caused by fire or subsequent smoke and water damage.

first-in, first-out (FIFO) a method that values inventory based on the premise that the first items put into inventory are the first ones sold.

five-year financial plan a plan that lays out a five-year forecast of the firm's earnings and expenses.

fixed assets nonliquid assets that the firm expects to hold for the long term or permanently.

fixed costs costs that do not vary with the level of production or sales.

fixed-position layout a facility design in which the workers, rather than the material or parts, move from one work center or machine to another.

fixed price a price that is not negotiable between the buyer and seller.

fixed-rate loans loans on which the interest rate is specified at the outset and never changes.

flextime a flexible work schedule that allows employees to choose their own work hours, within specified guidelines.

float the use of funds from the time you write a check to the time it clears your account.

FOB-destination pricing a pricing policy in which the seller pays all costs of transporting the goods to the buyer.

FOB-factory pricing a pricing policy in which the buyer pays all costs of shipping the merchandise once it leaves the seller's place of business.

focus groups a method of marketing research in which a small group of people, led by a moderator, are asked to participate in an open-ended discussion of a particular subject regarding buyer behavior.

follow-up the process of keeping track of work completed and any delays that may have occurred.

forecast a prediction of future values of a variable based on known or past values of the variable or of other related variables.

forecasting predicting the future using analytic techniques.

foreign funds mutual funds that specialize in worldwide investments.

form transformation the processing or conversion of materials into finished products.

FORTRAN a computer language used for mathematical and statistical applications.

forward buying in materials purchasing, the buying of more of a good than is immediately needed for production.

4/40 workweek an approach to job redesign in which employees work ten hours a day for four days.

franchisee the person or group that buys a franchise, obtaining the right to use the franchising organization's name and trademark and paying a fee or royalty in return.

franchising the right to use another firm's name and products and market them within a specified territory.

franchisor the business granting a franchise license, along with exclusive territorial distribution, use of its emblem, and other benefits.

fraud a willful misrepresentation of fact.

frequency the number of times a person is exposed to an advertisement.

fringe benefits any benefits received by employees in addition to regular pay.

full-service brokers stockbrokers who buy and sell stocks and also provide research and other services to their customers.

full-service merchant wholesalers wholesalers who take title to and possession of the products they sell and who perform the functions of contacting and transporting, providing market information to their suppliers, and offering credit and managerial services to their customers.

functional or process departmentalization departmentalization on the basis of similar skills.

G

Gantt chart a schedule chart for monitoring flow of work and schedule status of work in process.

General Agreement on Tariffs and Trade (GATT) a 1947 international accord that established rules for settling trade disputes and aimed to stimulate international trade by developing nations.

general partners partners who have responsibility for running the business and are legally liable for all of its debts.

generally accepted accounting principles (GAAP) broad rules adopted by the accounting profession for measuring and reporting the financial activities of a firm.

givebacks in labor-management bargaining, a reduction in wages and benefits, or a delay in receiving increases previously negotiated; typically accepted by the union in exchange for greater job security.

Glass-Steagall Act of 1933 a law that limited the rights of banks to engage in investment activities.

goal assessment an approach to assessing organizational effectiveness that is concerned with whether the organization reaches the growth, sales, profitability, or other goals management has set for it.

goal setting a motivational tool involving the selection of work-related objectives for employees.

goods-producing industries a sector of the economy that creates tangible output, such as automobiles, housing, or agricultural products.

gray market stores retail stores that buy products from other retailers that purchased too much merchandise or must raise cash quickly; the stores then sell the products at a considerable discount.

grievance procedure a set of steps contained in the labor contract, specifying what must be done when disputes over contract provisions arise.

gross national product (GNP) total market value of all final goods and services produced by an economy in a given period of time.

gross profit the difference between net sales and cost of goods sold.

gross sales revenue received from selling the firm's products or services, including cash sales and sales charged or made on account.

group-technology layout a facility design that gathers dissimilar machines into work centers (or cells) to work on products having similar shapes and processing requirements.

growth funds mutual funds that specialize in small companies with strong growth potential.

H

hackers computer buffs who illegally gain access to, and sometimes tamper with, computer files.

hardware the computer and its support equipment.

Hawthorne effect a change in behavior occurring because someone is singled out for attention.

health insurance insurance that covers medical costs resulting from injury or disease.

health maintenance organization (HMO) private group of physicians that provides members with medical and hospital care for a fixed, prepaid fee.

heroes company role models whose deeds, character, and support of the existing organizational culture highlight the values a company wishes to reinforce.

hierarchy of authority ranking of people in an organization according to their authority.

holding costs the expense of storing, or holding, the inventory in the firm's warehouse or on its stock shelves.

homeowners' insurance an insurance policy that provides a broad range of coverage to protect the policyholder's home, other structures, personal property, etc., at a relatively low price.

horizontal acquisition a form of business combination in which one company buys another that is in the same industry and performs the same function.

human change a form of organizational change that involves improving employee attitudes, skills, or knowledge.

human resource planning the process of analyzing an organization's human resource needs and developing a program to satisfy them.

I

idea generation the first stage in the development of new products, in which new product ideas from all sources are collected.

implied warranty the guarantee by the seller that the product sold is at least of average quality and is adequately packaged and labeled.

import quota a specific limit placed on the number of units of a product that may be imported into a country.

import a foreign-made good or service that is purchased domestically.

in-basket an assessment approach in which the job recruit's performance is evaluated in terms of how well and how quickly the recruit organizes a series of tasks and makes decisions concerning them.

income from operations gross profit minus total operating expenses.

income statement a financial statement that shows all the firm's revenues and expenses over an interval and the resulting profit or loss for that period.

income tax payable the estimated amount of money owed to the government on income already earned.

individual brand a different brand name used for each of a firm's products.

individual fidelity bond insurance that protects a business against losses from dishonesty by one or more specified employees.

individual retirement account (IRA) a savings plan in which all contributions are tax deductible and all future returns on the funds are not taxed until retirement.

industrial advertising advertising designed to tell industrial customers how they can use the advertised product to make their businesses more profitable.

industrial products goods and services sold to private businesses or public agencies, to be used in turn to produce other goods and services.

inflation a rise in the general price of goods and services.

information knowledge communicated or received concerning a particular fact or circumstance.

information managers managers responsible for designing and controlling the systems that gather, process, and distribute information.

informational roles roles managers perform when they serve as focal persons for gathering, receiving, and transmitting information that concerns members of the work unit, including monitor, disseminator, and spokesperson.

infrastructure basic communication and transportation facilities.

initiating structure leader behaviors that define and structure the way subordinates do their jobs.

injunction a court order requiring someone to do or stop doing something; management can use an injunction to make striking employees return to work or face a penalty.

input unit the means through which data and programs enter a computer system.

inspection the comparison of products against standards, approving those that meet them and rejecting those that do not.

installations industrial products that are major capital items, such as buildings and expensive pieces of equipment.

institutional advertising advertising designed to build a positive image for a company.

insurable interest a principle of insurance: the only accidents that are insurable are those that would cause the policyholder a real financial loss.

intangible assets assets that are not physical objects, including patents, licenses, and goodwill.

intensive distribution a retailing approach whereby a product is made available through as many stores as possible.

interest rate the price paid for the use of money over a stated period of time.

interest tests tests measuring a person's likes and dislikes for various activities.

intermediaries members of the distribution channel between the manufacturer and the consumer.

intermittent manufacturing a type of mechanized manufacturing process in which a product is processed in lots rather than in a continuous flow.

internal expansion the process of growing by increasing sales and capital investment.

internal process assessment an approach to assessing organizational effectiveness that focuses on organizational health.

International Monetary Fund (IMF) an international bank that helps stabilize the international monetary system by monitoring exchange rates and making short-term loans to members with balance-of-payments problems.

interpersonal roles roles managers perform when they engage in interpersonal relationships, including figurehead, leader, and liaison.

interviews a selection tool in which a representative of the hiring firm asks a job candidate a series of questions to determine how well the candidate's skills and interests match the job requirements.

intrinsic rewards rewards related to the job itself and the pleasure and sense of accomplishment that it gives to the employee.

introduction stage the first stage in the product life cycle, when a product is truly new, a market usually does not as yet exist, and competition is scarce.

inventory management the process of balancing holding costs and stockout costs.

inventory turnover ratio a measure of how many times a year the firm sells its inventory, calculated as cost of goods sold divided by average inventory.

investment bankers companies that help firms raise needed capital in the securities markets by underwriting the sale of new stock or bond issues.

J

job analysis the systematic study of a job to determine its characteristics.

job description a short summary of the basic tasks making up a job.

job enrichment an approach to job redesign that gives employees more responsibility for the overall job.

job evaluation an evaluation performed to determine the relative worth of a job in the firm.

job redesign changes in the nature or schedule of an employee's task-related activities.

job sharing an approach to job redesign that allows two or more people to share a single job.

job shop a type of intermittent manufacturing in which products are manufactured or assembled to a customer's purchase order or specification.

job specification a summary of the qualifications needed in a worker for a specific job.

joint venture an agreement between two or more businesses for the joint production and/or sale of a product or service.

junk bonds low-rated, high-yielding bonds.

just-in-time (JIT) a method of inventory control in which the firm maintains very small inventories and obtains materials for production just in time for use.

K

kaizen the Japanese term for constant improvement of products and processes.

kanban another term for just-in-time inventory control, named for the Japanese word for the control cards used in JIT.

kickback a payment by someone who has won a contract or made a sale through favorable treatment to the party providing the favor.

knowledge base data and decision rules contained in expert systems representing the needed expertise.

L

labor union an organization made up of workers who have united to achieve their job-related goals.

Labor–Management Relations Act (also known as the Taft-Hartley Act) forbids unions from refusing to bargain with an employer if the NLRB has certified a specific union for a firm, from requiring an employer to pay for work not performed, and from engaging in a secondary boycott.

last-in, first-out (LIFO) a method that values inventory based on the premise that the last items put into inventory are the first ones sold.

law the standards of conduct established and enforced by government.

law of adverse selection a principle of insurance: people or organizations that are more likely to need insurance are also more likely to want insurance.

law of demand an economic law stating that consumers are willing to buy more of a product at a lower price than at a higher price.

law of effect a learning theory law: behavior that is rewarded will be repeated, and behavior that is not rewarded will not be repeated.

law of large numbers a principle of insurance: the probability of an event occurring in the future can be predicted from the past rate of occurrence.

law of supply an economic law stating that producers are willing to produce more of a product at a higher price than at a lower price.

lead time the time from order placement to delivery.

leadership the use of influence to direct and coordinate the activities of a group toward goal attainment.

learning theory an approach to motivation, stating that the consequences of an act determine whether the act will be repeated.

legitimate power power that exists when one person believes that another has the right to give orders or otherwise exercise force.

letter of application a letter accompanying a resume that states the position for which you are applying and your most significant qualifications, with the goal of obtaining an interview.

level term life insurance term life insurance in which the amount of protection is the same during each year of the term contract.

leveraged buyout a purchase in which the buyer uses the assets of the firm that is being bought as security for the loan to buy the business.

liabilities debt and obligations owed by a business to its creditors; legal obligations to pay in the future.

liability insurance insurance that protects against losses resulting from harm caused to people or their property.

license the assigning of patent rights for a limited period of time to a particular person or organization.

licensing an approach to selling products in foreign countries in which a firm in one country agrees to allow a firm from another country to use its intellectual property for a fee.

life insurance insurance that pays a cash benefit to a designated person when the insured person dies.

limit order an investor's instruction that requires the commission broker to purchase the stock only at a certain price, or lower, or sell it at a certain price, or higher.

limited liability stockholders' exemption from being sued by the corporation's creditors for payment of claims.

limited life insurance whole life insurance in which the policyholder pays higher premiums, but only until the policy is paid up.

limited partners partners who contribute money or capital to a partnership, play no role in its management, and are not legally responsible for the partnership's debts.

limited-service merchant wholesalers wholesalers who take title to the products they sell but do not perform all the functions of a full-service merchant wholesaler.

line of credit an agreement between a bank and a borrower specifying how much the bank is willing to lend the borrower over a certain period of time, although the bank can lower the amount if conditions warrant.

line position a job in the direct chain of command that begins with the board of directors and ends with production and sales employees; line personnel contribute directly to the company's main business.

list price the publicly stated price for which a firm or store expects to sell a product.

listing a creativity enhancement technique that involves asking a series of questions about a currently available alternative.

load fund a mutual fund that charges a commission.

loading the process of determining how many hours each machine or workstation will operate.

local marketing subsidiary a means of marketing products abroad in which an office is established in the host country, staffed by local residents but managed by executives from the parent company.

lockout a management tactic in which the company prevents union members from working, often by shutting down its operations.

long wave theory a theory of economic growth: that 50-year "waves" alternate between economic prosperity and economic decline; economic growth is theorized to be technologically driven.

long-term liabilities debts that do not have to be paid for at least 12 months.

loss leader a product that is sold at or below cost in order to stimulate the sales of other products.

loss-of-earning-power insurance insurance that protects businesses against lost income caused by some unusual event.

low-load fund a mutual fund that charges a commission lower than that of a full load fund.

M

macromarketing the study of how goods and services are distributed from buyers to sellers.

mail-order houses retail businesses that display their merchandise in catalogs and fill orders through the mail.

management the art of getting things done through people.

Management by Objectives a motivational technique in which the manager and employee jointly set goals, against which the employee is later evaluated.

management games an off-the-job training technique in which trainees are presented with a simulated business situation requiring some type of decision to be made.

Management information system (MIS) a system for gathering information, transforming it into useful forms, and distributing it to decision makers.

management process the flow of the interconnected managerial activities of planning, organizing, staffing, directing, and controlling.

management-rights clause a clause in a labor contract that lists the areas of operation in which management may take actions without having to obtain permission from the union.

management science or operations research the development and application of mathematical models to business problems.

managerial accounting a type of accounting that is concerned with providing management with the financial information necessary to operate the firm.

manifest needs needs that are acquired through the interaction of the individual with his or her environment.

manufacturer-owned wholesaler a wholesale enterprise owned and operated by the product manufacturer.

margin the unit selling price minus the variable costs per unit.

marine insurance insurance that protects ship owners against damage to the ship and/or its cargo; can also be extended to cover property being transported by truck and train.

markdown a discount designed to encourage customers to buy a product that they otherwise would not purchase at that time.

market the sum total of all sales for a given kind of good among all buyers and sellers.

market coverage the extent to which a product is readily available to consumers.

market growth stage the second stage in the product life cycle, which is characterized by rapid sales increase, supply that falls short of demand, and eventually intense competition.

market order an investor's instruction that authorizes the commission broker to buy or sell a stock at the best possible price.

market price the price for a good or service at which the quantity supplied to the market is equal to the quantity demanded.

market segment a limited group of customers whose wants and needs most closely match the product's characteristics.

market segmentation the process of identifying groups of customers with similar characteristics and modifying the product or selling strategies to match the characteristics of each group.

market share the percentage of total industry sales controlled by a firm.

marketable securities company holdings in stocks, bonds, money market accounts, and other securities readily convertible to cash.

marketing the process of planning and executing the conception, pricing, promotion, and distribution of ideas, goods, and services, to create exchanges that satisfy individual and organizational objectives.

marketing concept a philosophy that marketing is a customer-oriented activity and that the overall objective of a firm is to develop products and services that satisfy customer needs.

marketing mix the four key elements in marketing decisions: product, distribution, price, and promotion.

marketing research the systematic gathering, recording, and analyzing of data about problems relating to the marketing of goods and services.

markup the amount added to production or purchase cost to arrive at the selling price.

markup pricing or **cost-plus pricing** the practice of establishing price by adding a predetermined percentage to the cost of manufacturing or purchasing the product.

master budget a budget that ties together the operating budget, the capital budget, and the cash budget, ensuring that there is consistency in their projections and outlook.

materials requirement planning (MRP) an inventory control technique that uses a computer to coordinate information about orders for the finished product, the amount of various materials on hand, and the production sequence, to make sure that the right materials are available at the right time in the production cycle.

materials science a branch of technology that deals with the development of super-materials.

matrix departmentalization a flexible approach to departmentalization, in which the employee reports to both a functional superior and a project superior.

maturity stage the third stage in the product life cycle, which is characterized by peaking sales, declining profits, and few entries into the market.

mediation a process in which an experienced and knowledgeable neutral person helps the union and management reach an agreement.

medium of exchange a function of money; makes exchanging goods and services easier by eliminating the need for a barter system.

memory the part of the computer that stores all information.

merchandise inventory a balance sheet current asset category that includes finished goods, work in process, and raw materials.

merger the joining of two companies to form a single new company.

microcomputer the smallest, slowest, and least expensive computer; often called a personal computer.

microprocessors tiny wafer-shaped chips that can hold millions of pieces of information.

minicomputer an intermediate-sized computer whose speed, capacity, and cost fall between those of the mainframe and the microcomputer.

misrepresentation that which occurs when a consumer relies on false information from a manufacturer, seller, or their agents in making a purchase decision.

modem a device for connecting microcomputers via telephone lines.

money anything that is generally accepted as payment for goods and services.

money market accounts limited checking accounts (three checks per month) that carry interest rates competitive with those offered by brokerage houses for their money market funds.

money market funds funds that invest in short-term, high-yield investments.

monopolistic competition a market structure in which many sellers of similar products are able to achieve some product differentiation, enabling them to carve out market niches.

monopoly a market structure characterized by a complete absence of competition: one producer and many small buyers.

motivation the attempt to satisfy a need.

multinational corporation a corporation that sells its products anywhere in the world where there is a market for them.

municipal bond a bond issued by a city or state on which the interest is exempted from federal taxation.

mutual fund an association of many small investors, who pool their funds and buy securities.

mutual insurance companies nonprofit insurance companies owned by the insurance policyholders.

mutual savings banks financial institutions similar to S&Ls except that they are member-owned.

N

name advertising advertising designed to put the name of the product or the company's trademark in front of as many people as possible.

National Labor Relations Act an act which created the National Labor Relations Board to monitor union elections and to prevent employers from engaging in unfair labor practices.

need something that people require.

need for achievement an acquired need manifested by the desire to do well regardless of the goal pursued.

need for affiliation an acquired need manifested by a desire to establish and maintain friendly and warm relations with other people.

need for power an acquired need manifested by a desire to control other people, to influence their behavior, and to be responsible for them.

need hierarchy Maslow's view that people are motivated by needs, and that needs are arranged in a hierarchy: needs at "lower" levels must be satisfied before needs at "higher" levels become motivating.

negligence failure to use ordinary care in the performance of an action.

negotiated price a price that can be negotiated between the buyer and the seller.

neighborhood shopping center the smallest type of shopping center, consisting of a strip of stores along a main roadway, with the major tenant being a supermarket or drugstore.

net income after taxes the amount of money the firm made during the period; net income before taxes minus federal income taxes.

net income before taxes income from operations plus other income minus other expenses.

net period the length of time for which the seller extends credit to the buyer.

net sales gross sales minus returns and allowances.

networking the linking together of computers to enable users to communicate with each other, share resources, and access tremendous amounts of information.

net worth owners' equity calculated as total assets minus total liabilities.

new product a product that performs a new function for the buyer or represents a significant improvement over existing products.

no-fault insurance automobile insurance under which parties to an accident recover medical and hospital expenses and any losses in income from their own insurance companies, regardless of who was at fault.

no-load fund a mutual fund that does not charge a commission.

noncumulative discounts discounts offered when an individual purchase is larger than a specified amount.

nonfinancial rewards rewards that do not involve money, such as praise, status, and privileges.

nonprofit corporations organizations incorporated like for-profit corporations except that they do not exist to make a profit, they pay no dividends or income taxes, and members are protected against liability.

nonstore retailing methods of selling merchandise to final consumers other than through retail stores.

note receivable a signed note in which one party promises to pay another a certain amount of money over a designated period of time.

notes payable purchases for which the firm has signed a legal document stating when payment is due.

NOW account a bank account that allows unlimited check-writing and pays interest but requires a minimum balance of a few hundred dollars.

O

Occupational Safety and Health Administration (OSHA) an agency which sets and enforces health and safety standards for individual industries.

odd/even pricing giving a product an odd price, rather than an even amount, so as to attract potential buyers.

odd lots stock transactions involving fewer than 100 shares.

offer a proposal to enter into a contractual relationship.

offset agreement a policy in which host governments force foreign suppliers to agree to reciprocal trade arrangements with their customers.

oligopoly a market structure in which a few large producers sell similar but not identical products to many small buyers.

ombudsman an individual employed by a company to check out and resolve employee complaints.

on-line processing instant input and output processing as a result of a direct hook-up of all input and output units to the main computer.

on-the-job training training conducted while an employee performs job-related tasks.

open account an informal credit arrangement by which a buyer makes purchases and pays for them later.

open-end fund a type of mutual fund in which the membership (as represented by number of total shares) is unrestricted.

open market operations the buying and selling of U.S. government securities by the Fed to influence the money supply.

open shops organizations that do not force employees to belong to a union or to pay union dues.

operating budget a budget that allocates dollar amounts to costs and expenses needed to run the business.

operating expenses selling and administrative expenses.

operations any process that accepts inputs and uses resources to change those inputs in useful ways.

operations management the systematic direction of the processes that transform inputs into finished goods and services.

option the right to buy or sell a stock at a given market price for a certain period of time.

order cycle the length of time between the placing of a purchase order and the delivery of the merchandise to the buyer.

ordering costs the expenses involved in placing an order.

ordinary or **straight life insurance** whole life insurance in which the policyholder pays premiums for life.

organic organizational design a view of organizational design characterized by flexibility of structure, so as to ensure maximum adaptability to a changing environment and free communication among all levels of the organization.

organization chart a schematic representation of an organization's hierarchy of authority.

organizational buyer an individual who purchases products in large quantities, to be used in the production of other products.

organizational culture the emotional, intangible part of the organization, consisting of the values, stories, heroes, and rituals and ceremonies that have special meaning for the people who work for a firm.

organizational effectiveness the degree to which the organization achieves its goals, maintains its health, secures resources needed for survival, and satisfies stakeholders.

organizing the management function of arranging and distributing work among members of the firm.

orientation the process whereby new employees are introduced to their jobs and to the company.

other expenses all expenses that cannot be directly associated with the operations of the firm.

other income revenue from sources other than the primary activity of the firm.

outdoor advertising billboards, signs, and posters used to convey advertising messages.

output units units that present the results of computer operations to the user.

outstanding issues securities already sold by the issuing firm, which can now be bought and sold by investors.

over-the-counter (OTC) market trading stocks through a computerized service that transmits information from various locations instead of through a central marketplace.

owner's equity the value of the owner's investment in the firm.

P

parent company or **holding company** a firm that owns a subsidiary corporation.

partnership a business owned by two or more people.

patent law law which protects inventors by prohibiting other people from making, using, or selling patented inventions for a period of 17 years.

penetration pricing the practice of introducing a product at a relatively low price, to sell a large quantity to a price-sensitive market.

perfect competition a market structure in which many small producers sell identical products to many small buyers, and no buyer or seller is big enough to dictate price.

performance appraisal the process of measuring employee performance against established goals and expectations.

performance standards standards used to define the goals to be achieved by a worker over a specified period.

periodic inventory an inventory system in which a physical count of inventory is done at the end of each accounting period.

peripheral equipment the input and output units of a computer.

perpetual inventory an inventory system that keeps a running count of inventory levels.

personal computers (PCs) microcomputers.

personal selling promoting products through oral presentation to prospective customers, either in person or by phone.

personality tests tests measuring the strengths or weaknesses of personality characteristics that are considered important for good performance of the job.

Peter Principle a principle stating that there is a tendency for good workers to be promoted to positions of greater authority until they eventually reach a "level of incompetence" and will not be promoted again.

physical distribution the movement of products from the manufacturer to the final buyer.

picketing a union tactic in which workers march back and forth in front of the entrances to the workplace, carrying signs listing their grievances and demands.

piece-rate system a compensation plan in which total wages are tied directly to output.

pioneering stage the first stage in the advertising spiral, when the product is introduced to the public.

place utility a measure of the degree to which a product is available where buyers want it.

placement the process of fitting people and jobs together after the people have become employees of the firm.

planning the management function of determining in advance what needs to be done to achieve a particular goal.

pledging accounts receivable using accounts receivable as security, or collateral, for a short-term loan.

point-of-purchase displays product advertisements or displays placed in retail stores where the buying decision is made.

point-of-sale terminals computer terminals at retail stores, which immediately transfer funds from customers' bank accounts to the store's to pay for purchases.

poison pill a technique for fending off an unwanted purchaser, in which the target company adds large amounts of new debt to become less attractive to the buying firm.

post trading a system of stock trading in which each stock traded is assigned to a specific "post" or trading area.

power the ability to exert force on others.

precedents past court decisions used to help decide cases in the same legal area.

predatory behavior the wrongful efforts of a company to focus its attention on customers who have already shown an interest in the product or service sold by another firm.

preferred provider organization (PPO) network of health care providers who have agreed to provide medical care to specific groups of people at a reduced cost.

preferred stock stock whose owners have first claim to corporate assets once debts have been paid but who have no voting rights.

preferred stockholders stockholders who have first claim to the corporation's assets once its debts have been paid, but have no voting rights at stockholders' meetings.

prepaid expenses a balance sheet current asset category consisting of expenses paid in advance.

price what the buyer pays for a product or service.

price discrimination the practice of selling the same product to two or more customers at different prices.

price fixing an agreement by which two or more competing firms jointly determine the prices they will charge for their goods and services.

price skimming the policy of pricing a new product artificially high, to earn extra profits before competition drives the price down.

price/earnings ratio the premium investors are willing to pay for a firm's earning potential.

primary boycott a type of boycott in which union members refuse to patronize a business involved in a dispute with labor.

primary demand desire for a general product category.

primary market the use of securities markets by firms to sell new issues of stocks or bonds to investors.

primary storage unit the computer's main memory, where data and program instructions are stored.

prime rate the interest rate that a bank charges its best customers.

principle of indemnity a principle of insurance: the insured person or firm cannot collect more in damage claims than the dollar loss sustained.

private enterprise or **free market system** a system under which business is free to organize and operate for a profit, in a competitive system with limited government intervention.

procedure-oriented language a language in which the programmer gives instructions to the computer that are in turn translated into machine language by a compiler.

process a flow of connected activities moving toward a purpose or goal.

process layout a facility layout that groups work of a similar function in a single department or work center.

producers firms that convert raw materials and other inputs into finished goods.

product demonstration a sales promotion in which a salesperson actually shows the customer how the product works.

product development the fourth stage in the development of new products, in which a prototype of the product is developed.

product evaluation the second stage in the development of new products, in which new product ideas that are not feasible or not consistent with the firm's objectives are eliminated.

product item an individual product (either a good or a service).

product layout a facility layout in which the location of workstations follows the sequence of steps needed to produce the end product.

product liability accountability for a product defect, breach of product warranty, and any danger caused by the use of a product.

product liability insurance insurance that covers losses resulting from product defect, breach of product warranty, and any danger caused by use of a product.

product life cycle a marketing concept that the life of any product passes through the stages of introduction, growth, maturity, and decline before disappearing from the market.

product line a group of related products.

product mix all the product lines that a firm sells.

production management the process of handling and managing all aspects of the production operation.

production possibilities curve a graphic display of the various combinations of goods that can be produced in an economy with the available resources and technology.

production process the process by which inputs are transformed into outputs.

productivity output per worker hour.

professional corporation an organization of professionals who incorporate to obtain liability protection.

profit sales revenues less all production and other costs; the return to the owners for undertaking the risk inherent in operating a business.

profit margin the difference between a product's cost and its selling price.

profit maximization the maximum dollar value of output (sales revenues) for the minimum dollar value of input (costs and expenses).

profit motive the desire to make money.

profit-sharing plans bonus plans that tie employees' bonuses to levels of, or increases in, company profits.

pro forma income statement a statement estimating future sales and expenses, showing how much money the business is likely to make once it begins operations.

program flowchart a diagram showing the sequence of operations to be performed by the computer.

programmed instruction an off-the-job training technique in which subject matter is broken down into organized, logical sequences; when the trainee gives a correct response, he or she is presented with the next segment of material.

Project Evaluation and Review Technique (PERT) chart a planning and control diagram that depicts each activity required to complete a project, the sequence of the activities, and the time allotted for each activity.

promissory note a form of trade credit in which the buyer draws up a note promising to pay a specified amount by a specified date.

promotion a move up in the organizational hierarchy, generally to a new title, more responsibility, and greater financial rewards (Chapter 9); all techniques available to the firm to communicate to its potential customers about its products or services (Chapter 13).

promotion mix the combination of advertising, personal selling, sales promotion, and publicity used by a firm to communicate product or company information to the market.

promotional discounts discounts offered to encourage customers to buy particular products.

property insurance insurance that protects against damage to real estate and other property.

prospecting locating new customers.

prototype a physical model or a custom-made first version of a new product.

proxy a written statement that authorizes someone else to vote on behalf of a stockholder.

psychological pricing a method of pricing in which psychological or non-economic factors are considered in determining price.

public liability insurance insurance that protects against business risk associated with the ownership and maintenance of property and the actions of a firm's employees.

publicity unpaid media coverage about the firm or its products.

puffery innocent exaggerations used to sell a product.

pure risk situations in which the only possible outcomes are loss or no loss; there is no possibility of gain.

purpose departmentalization departmentalization on the basis of similarity of purpose.

purpose *or* task change a form of organizational change in which the goal of the organization is changed.

put an option to sell shares of stock at some specified price during a certain period of time.

Q

quality circles (QCs) committees of workers who analyze and solve problems relating to quality.

quality control the process of setting standards and measuring the quality of products and services against these standards.

quantity discounts discounts offered to encourage large orders.

R

rain insurance insurance that protects against losses resulting from rain.

raw materials industrial products that are inexpensive, unprocessed items that become a physical part of the product the firm is producing; inputs from which the firm makes its products.

reach a measure of how many people actually saw or heard an advertisement in a given medium.

realistic job preview information given to the recruit, describing what the company and the job are actually like, rather than presenting an overly rosy picture.

recession Two or more consecutive quarters of decline in gross national product (after subtracting the price increase effects of inflation)

recruiting all activities involved in finding interested and qualified applicants for a job opening.

references a selection tool in which information is provided by people who have had previous experience with a job applicant, such as former employers, coworkers, teachers, or acquaintances, concerning the applicant's credentials, past performance, and qualifications for the current position.

referent power power derived from one person's feelings of identity with another, or from the desire for that identity.

regional exchanges stock exchanges located outside of New York City.

regional shopping center the largest type of shopping center, featuring three to five anchor stores and more than 100 specialty stores; the center frequently sponsors events to attract the public.

reorder point the point in the inventory order cycle at which an order is placed.

reorder quantity the size of the inventory order.

repatriation sending profits from an international company back to the country of origin rather than leaving them in the country in which they were earned.

replanning the development of new routing, loading, or scheduling plans in response to changing conditions.

reserve requirements the percentage of total deposits that a bank must hold as cash in its vault or as deposits in the regional Federal Reserve bank.

Resolution Trust Corporation (RTC) a government organization established to handle the closing of insolvent savings and loans and to dispose of their assets.

resume a written presentation telling the prospective employer who you are, what you know, what you have done, what you can do, and what kind of job you would like.

retail advertising store advertising designed to encourage people to buy consumer products at the sponsor's retail outlets.

retailers firms that sell products to final consumers for the consumer's' own use.

retained earnings the amount of funds left at year-end after all expenses, interest payments, taxes, and dividends have been paid.

retentive stage the final stage of the advertising spiral, when the ads aim to foster brand loyalty.

retroduction a creativity enhancement technique that uses "What If?" questions to help free people from mental ruts.

return on owners' equity a measure of profitability that tells how effective the firm has been in earning money on owners' invested capital, calculated as net income divided by owners' equity.

return on sales a measure of the profit generated by each dollar of sales, calculated as net income divided by net sales.

returns products that customers return to the firm, for which they receive a full refund.

revolving credit agreement an agreement similar to a line of credit except that the bank is obligated to extend funds up to the credit limit.

reward power power based on one person's ability to administer desired outcomes to another and to remove or decrease outcomes that are not desired.

risk the uncertainty about future outcomes and the potential for future losses.

rituals guides to behavior in daily organizational life, including evaluation and reward procedures, regular staff meetings, and farewell parties.

robbery taking property by force.

robot a machine that can be programmed to do a variety of tasks automatically.

robotics a field of study concerned with the construction, maintenance, and application of automatically controlled mechanisms in production processes.

role playing an approach to employee selection in which job recruits pretend to be actual employees in job situations.

round lots stock traded in lots of 100.

routing the process of determining workflows in production.

S

S-corporation a special type of corporation that is taxed as though it were a partnership.

sales promotions direct inducements to purchase a product, such as free samples, coupons, gifts, and sweepstakes.

samples small portions of a product, given away to encourage potential customers to try the product.

satisfaction the state of need fulfillment.

savings account a low-paying bank account that does not allow checkwriting.

schedule chart a planning and control diagram that shows when each job order is to be performed at each machine, department, or workstation.

scheduling the process of determining when an operation is to be performed at a machine or workstation.

Scientific Management an attempt to find the "one best way" to perform a job; this approach emphasized efficiency and led to simplified jobs.

scoring approach an approach used to select from among alternatives in which each alternative is assigned a score, and the alternative with the best score is chosen.

screening the identification of obviously unqualified applicants for a position before gathering additional selection information on those applicants.

screening approach an approach used to select from among alternatives in which each alternative is identified as either satisfactory or unsatisfactory, and unsatisfactory alternatives are eliminated.

seasonal discount a discount based on the time of year.

secondary boycott a boycott of a firm that does business with a firm that is being struck by a labor union; a type of boycott in which nonunion members, such as suppliers and customers, support the union by refusing to deal with a business involved in a labor dispute.

secondary market the use of securities markets by investors for buying and selling securities with each other.

secondary storage extra memory outside the primary storage unit of the central processing unit.

sector a major division of the economy: producers of physical goods or providers of intangible services.

secured bonds bonds that are backed by the pledge of a specific asset in case the issuer fails to pay.

secured loan a loan that requires the borrower to pledge some form of asset as payment for the loan in case the borrower cannot repay it.

securities stocks and bonds, issued by corporations and government bodies, that can be bought and sold in securities markets.

securities markets a central place where organizations can sell stocks and bonds to raise money for expansion and where investors can buy and sell stocks.

selection the process of evaluating each candidate's qualifications and hiring the one whose skills and interests best match the job requirements.

selective demand desire for a particular product or service.

selective distribution a retailing approach whereby a product is made available through several, but not all, retailers in a market.

selling expenses expenses that result directly from the firm's sales efforts.

selling short a speculative technique that involves selling stock before purchasing it, to try to make money when stock prices are falling.

seniority the number of years spent with the company.

sensitivity training an off-the-job training technique designed to develop participants' sensitivity, self-insight, and awareness of group processes.

service intangible deed or performance.

service businesses businesses that sell a service rather than a product.

service liability insurance insurance that protects against losses resulting from a service that was improperly provided.

service-producing industries a sector that provides intangible benefits, such as financial services, legal advice, medical care, and government assistance.

share-draft accounts interest-bearing checking accounts offered by credit unions.

Sherman Act the first antitrust law, which declares illegal "every contract, combination . . . or conspiracy, in restraint of trade or commerce."

shopping goods consumer goods for which the buyer actively considers price, quality, style, and value before making a purchase decision.

single-premium life insurance whole life insurance in which the insured makes one payment and the insurance is fully paid.

small business a business that is independently owned and operated and is not dominant in its field of operation.

Small Business Administration (SBA) the principal government agency concerned with the financing, operation, and management of small businesses.

social audit a step-by-step examination of all the activities that make up the firm's social programs.

social learning learning that occurs through social channels.

social responsibility the responsibility of businesses to pursue goals that benefit society.

social security required insurance, through which the federal government provides benefits to the elderly and the disabled.

software or programs step-by-step instructions that tell the computer what to do.

sole proprietorship a business owned by one person.

span of control the number of employees that a manager directly supervises.

spatial transformation the process whereby inputs are transformed spatially, such as in the movement of goods from one place to another.

special courts state or federal courts that hear specific types of cases involving matters such as international trade, taxes, or probate problems.

specialty advertising advertising messages that appear on products such as calendars, T-shirts, coffee mugs, caps, and ballpoint pens.

specialty funds mutual funds that have a unique approach to investments, such as investing in a special cause or a given industry.

specialty goods consumer goods for which shoppers are willing to make a special shopping effort; these goods generally command brand loyalty.

specialty stores retail stores that meet the needs of a particular market segment, usually selling only one type of product.

speculative risk situations in which there exists a possibility of loss as well as of gain.

speculators those who are willing to accept greater risk in the securities market if it means a potentially greater profit.

staff position a position that is outside the primary chain of command; staff personnel support line personnel by providing information, giving advice, or providing specialized services.

staffing the management function dealing with the recruitment, selection, and placement of the members of the firm.

stakeholder any party that has an interest or stake in a company, including employees, members of the community where the firm is located, and suppliers of the company.

standard of value a function of money; a standard by which the values of objects can be compared.

standardization strategy the practice of using the same marketing strategy for all of a firm's foreign markets.

statement of cash flows a financial statement that reflects the movement of cash resources in and out of the firm.

statistical quality control a method of monitoring production quality that assumes that flaws in manufacturing systems, not errors by production workers, are the primary cause of quality problems.

statute a law enacted by a legislative body.

statutory law the legal rules and regulations enacted by legislative bodies.

stock certificate a document signifying ownership of shares in the company.

stock dividend dividend paid in additional shares of stock rather than cash.

stockholders *or* **shareholders** the owners of the firm.

stock insurance companies private insurance companies organized to provide insurance for policyholders and profits for stockholders.

stock market indicators indexes of stock market performance, used by investors to evaluate the performance of a particular stock against the market.

stock split distribution of one or more new shares to stockholders for every share they already hold.

stockbroker the person who initiates the buying or selling of a stock by wiring the instructions to a commission broker on the floor of an exchange.

stockholder owner of part of a business and its profits, through ownership of stock.

stockholder wealth maximization maximizing the firm's value for stockholders, which is the overriding goal in managing the firm's financial affairs.

stockout costs the expenses incurred when a firm runs out of inventory.

stop order an investor's instruction that requires the commission broker to buy or sell stock when the price reaches a specified figure, to protect a gain or minimize a loss.

storage media the "machine readable" form on which data and programs are stored for computer processing at a later time.

store of wealth a function of money; a way of saving purchasing power until it is needed to buy something.

stories narratives repeated among employees and usually based on fact; they help pass on a culture by acting as maps of how things are done.

strategic constituencies assessment an approach to assessing organizational effectivenesss that focuses on the extent to which important constituencies are satisfied.

stress a physiological state in which adrenaline courses into the bloodstream and then to muscles and organs, resulting in feelings of strain or pressure.

strict liability a theory claiming that product liability may exist whenever the quality of the product itself is questioned.

strike a temporary work stoppage by employees, aimed at pressuring management to agree to their demands.

strikebreakers workers hired by the company to replace workers on strike.

structural change a form of organizational change involving alteration of the firm's formal authority structure or of job definitions.

subrogation provision a clause in most fire insurance policies that gives the company the right to recover damages from the party who caused a loss.

subsidiary corporation a corporation in which the majority of the firm's common stock is owned by another company.

success chess rules suggested for managing your career successfully.

Super-NOW account a bank account similar to a NOW account, but paying higher interest and requiring a higher minimum balance.

superconductor a special material that conducts electricity without resistance.

supermarkets large retail outlets; the primary sellers of food and other household products in the United States.

superregional bank a bank holding company which crosses state lines in a specific region of the country to gain increased power.

superstores or hypermarkets very large supermarkets that carry a full line of food products, as well as numerous other items often purchased by consumers.

supplies industrial products that are used in the production of a product but do not become part of the product, such as maintenance supplies.

supply the quantities of output that producers are willing and able to make available to the market at various prices over a given time period.

supply curve a graph that shows the relationship between price and quantity supplied.

supreme court the highest court in a state or federal system; state supreme courts have final authority in all cases that have no questions involving federal law or the U.S. Constitution; the federal Supreme Court takes cases appealed from state supreme courts and handles all cases involving ambassadors to the U.S. and disputes involving states.

sweepstakes a contest in which prizes are awarded on the basis of chance.

synthetic transformation a production process in which basic parts, components, or chemicals are combined to form a finished product.

system software set of programs that manages the resources of the computer, such as processing time and storage space, so that they are used efficiently.

systems resource assessment an approach to assessing organizational effectiveness that considers whether the organization is able to acquire the resources it needs to survive and prosper.

T

target-market-share pricing the practice of setting price to obtain a specified share of the market.

target-return-on-investment pricing the practice of setting price to achieve a specified yield on an investment.

tariff a tax on imported products.

taxation a process by which the government acquires rev-

enue through taxes on income, property, sales, and payrolls.

technological change a form of organizational change that occurs when a new means is used to transform resources into a product or service.

teleconferencing two-way audio and video communications among distant locations.

temporal transformation the process whereby inputs are transformed in time, such as the storage of goods.

term life insurance life insurance that pays a death benefit if the insured person dies within a specified period but has no value when the policy expires.

term loans longer bank loans, normally for one to seven years.

terms of trade the conditions the seller gives the buyer when offering short-term credit.

test a systematic and standardized procedure for obtaining information from individuals.

test marketing the fifth stage in the development of new products, in which there is limited introduction of a new product to a few selected geographic markets, for a short time, under controlled conditions.

Theory X a theory that assumes workers are lazy and self-indulgent, require constant supervision, and work only because they get paid.

Theory Y a theory that assumes workers are responsible, like to work, and value intrinsic rewards.

Theory Z a theory developed by William Ouchi, which attempts to combine the best of Japanese and American management practices to solve human resource problems.

time-sharing in data processing, the hook-up of many different terminals to the same main computer.

time utility a measure of the degree to which a product is available when buyers want it.

total quality control a concept based on the premise that everyone from the top to the bottom of the organization is responsible for the quality of goods and services.

trade acceptance a form of trade credit in which the seller draws up a note, which the buyer signs.

trade advertising advertising designed to influence members of the channel of distribution to carry the firm's products.

trade credit financing of a purchase by the supplier, who gives the buyer 30 days or more to pay.

trade deficit a situation in which total imports exceed total exports.

trade libel the spreading of false information about the products of another firm.

trademark a name, term, or symbol used to identify a firm and its products.

trade show a gathering of many producers in the same industry, to display their products to customers.

trade surplus a situation in which total exports exceed total imports.

transaction loan credit extended by the bank for a specific purpose.

transformational leaders leaders with behaviors and qualities that motivate followers to do more than they expected to do by inspiring enthusiasm, faith, loyalty, and pride and trust and encourage them to transcend their self-interests.

traveler's cheques a guaranteed check accepted anywhere in the world and, if lost or stolen, reimbursed at full value by the issuing company.

trial courts state or federal courts that hear civil or criminal cases involving possible violations of state or federal law.

trust management a bank program that manages investments for pension funds, university endowments, and wealthy individuals.

Truth-in-Lending Act an act which authorizes the Federal Reserve Board to specify how interest rates on consumer purchases are to be calculated and reported to the consumer.

tying agreement an agreement in which a seller agrees to sell a product to a buyer on the condition that the buyer also purchases other, often unwanted, merchandise from the seller.

U

uncontrollable environmental factors circumstances beyond the firm's control that affect the way it markets its products, including demographic changes, competition, economics, social trends, and technological changes.

underwriting the agreement by investment bankers to buy new issues of stocks or bonds from the issuing corporation and resell them to the public.

unemployment insurance government insurance that provides cash benefits to involuntarily unemployed individuals and helps unemployed people find jobs.

Uniform Commercial Code (UCC) a comprehensive set of business laws governing commercial transactions.

uniform-delivered pricing a pricing policy in which the seller charges its customers the same delivered price, regardless of where the customers are located or how much it costs to ship the merchandise.

union security clauses clauses in labor contracts that specify whether union membership is required of all employees in the bargaining unit.

union shops organizations that require new employees to join the union after a designated period of employment.

union stewards individuals who represent members of a local union in a plant.

universal life insurance term life insurance with a savings component.

universal product code (UPC) a system developed by government and industry representatives, in which products can be identified or "read" by electronic scanners from a bar code printed on the product's packaging.

unlimited liability in a sole proprietorship or a partnership, the sole proprietor or partners are liable for all obligations of the business.

unscheduled personal property insurance a portion of a homeowners' insurance policy that protects property owned or used by the policyholder anywhere in the world against theft, damage resulting from fire, vandalism, or other perils.

urban migration the movement of people to or from large cities, small cities, or rural areas, as well as shifts between the suburbs and downtown in metropolitan areas.

utility general measure of the extent to which a product or service satisfies customers' needs.

V

validity the degree to which predictions from selection information are supported by evidence.

value added sales value added to the product by the production process, computed as the sales dollar value of output minus the cost of raw materials and semifinished inputs brought from other manufacturers.

values deep-seated, pervasive standards that influence almost every aspect of our lives: our moral judgments, responses to others, and commitments to personal and organizational goals.

variable costs costs that vary with the level of production or sales of the product.

variable life insurance a whole life policy in which the death benefit and cash value fluctuate with the value of the securities purchased with the premiums.

variable-rate loan a loan in which the interest rate changes with market conditions.

vertical acquisition a business combination in which one company buys another that is in the same industry but performs a different production or distribution activity.

vertical marketing system a mechanism that permits members of a distribution channel to cooperate on a long-term basis.

visual display terminal (VDT) computer hardware that includes a keyboard to input data and instructions and a television-like screen for displaying output.

W

warehouse stores discount stores that stack large quantities of merchandise on the shelves and have an interior resembling a warehouse more than a retail outlet.

warranty the representation by the seller that a product has certain qualities or characteristics.

wheel of retailing a theory that most new types of retailers begin as low-cost, low-price operations and evolve to higher-cost, higher-service, more expensive operations.

whistleblower someone who reports illegal activity in the firm to the press, government, or other parties outside the firm.

white knight a second, more acceptable buyer, which the target company locates in order to fend off an unwanted takeover.

whole life insurance life insurance that gives lifetime protection to the insured person.

wholesaler a firm that helps a manufacturer sell its products to other businesses for eventual resale to final consumers; intermediaries between manufacturers and retailers or between manufacturers and industrial buyers.

work in process unfinished products that still need to move through one or more stages in the manufacturing process.

work sample tests tests measuring how well applicants perform selected job tasks.

worker's compensation insurance government insurance that pays benefits to employees who suffer job-related accidents or disease.

World Bank an international bank that makes long-term loans to developing countries to stimulate economic development.

world-class manufacturing a set of manufacturing processes designed to achieve a sustained global advantage through the continuous improvement of manufacturing capability.

Z

zone-delivered pricing a pricing policy in which the seller assigns each customer to a geographic zone and, within each zone, charges the same delivered price for the goods.

SUBJECT INDEX

NAME INDEX

COMPANY INDEX

PHOTO CREDITS